Mathematics

Grade 8

Jennie M. Bennett
Edward B. Burger
David J. Chard
Earlene J. Hall
Paul A. Kennedy
Freddie L. Renfro
Tom W. Roby
Janet K. Scheer
Bert K. Waits

HOLT McDOUGAL

Cover Photo: Colorful slinky
Grayce Pedulla Dillon

Printed in the U.S.A.

ISBN 978-0-547-64719-7

2 3 4 5 6 7 8 9 10 0868 20 19 18 17 16 15 14 13 12 11

4500302891 B C D E F G

Jennie M. Bennett, Ed.D., is a recently retired mathematics teacher at Hartman Middle School in Houston, Texas. She is past president of the Benjamin Banneker Association, the former First Vice-President of NCSM, and a former board member of NCTM.

Edward B. Burger, Ph.D., is Professor of Mathematics and Chair at Williams College and is the author of numerous articles, books, and videos. He has won many prestigious writing and teaching awards offered by the Mathematical Association of America. In 2006, Dr. Burger was named Reader's Digest's "Best Math Teacher" in its "100 Best of America" issue. He has made numerous television and radio appearances and has given countless mathematical presentations around the world.

David J. Chard, Ph.D., is the Leon Simmons Dean of the School of Education and Human Development at Southern Methodist University. He is a Past President of the Division for Research at the Council for Exceptional Children, a member of the International Academy for Research on Learning Disabilities, and has been the Principal Investigator on numerous research projects for the U.S. Department of Education. He is the author of several research articles and books on instructional strategies for students struggling in school.

Earlene J. Hall, Ed.D., is the Middle School Mathematics Supervisor for the Detroit Public Schools district. She teaches graduate courses in Mathematics Leadership at University of Michigan Dearborn. Dr. Hall has traveled extensively throughout Africa and China and has made numerous presentations including topics such as Developing Standards Based Professional Development and Culture Centered Education. She was a member of the NCTM 2009 Yearbook Panel.

Paul A. Kennedy, Ph.D., is a professor in the Department of Mathematics at Colorado State University. Dr. Kennedy is a leader in mathematics education. His research focuses on developing algebraic thinking by using multiple representations and technology. He is the author of numerous publications.

Freddie L. Renfro, MA, has 35 years of experience in Texas education as a classroom teacher and director/coordinator of Mathematics PreK-12 for school districts in the Houston area. She has served as a reviewer and TXTEAM trainer for Texas Math Institutes and has presented at numerous math workshops.

Tom W. Roby, Ph.D., is Associate Professor of Mathematics and Director of the Quantitative Learning Center at the University of Connecticut. He founded and co-directed the Bay Area-based ACCLAIM professional development program. He also chaired the advisory board of the California Mathematics Project and reviewed content for the California Standards Tests.

Janet K. Scheer, Ph.D., Executive Director of Create A Vision™, is a motivational speaker and provides customized K-12 math staff development. She has taught and supervised internationally and nationally at all grade levels.

Bert K. Waits, Ph.D., is a Professor Emeritus of Mathematics at The Ohio State University and cofounder of T³ (Teachers Teaching with Technology), a national professional development program. Dr. Waits is also a former board member of NCTM and an author of the original NCTM Standards.

Program Reviewers

Judy Broughton
Math Teacher
Poplar Street Sixth Grade Center
North Little Rock, AR

Troy Deckebach
Math Teacher
Tredyffrin-Easttown Middle School
Berwyn, PA

Maridith Gebhart
Math Teacher
Ramay Junior High School
Fayetteville, AR

Ruth Harbin-Miles
District Math Coordinator—Retired
Instructional Resource Center
Olathe, KS

Kim Hayden
Math Teacher
Clermont County School District
Milford, OH

Rhoni Herell
Math Teacher
Enid Waller Junior High
Enid, OK

Becky Lowe
Math Teacher
Bartlesville Mid-High
Bartlesville, OK

George Maguschak
Math Teacher/Building Chairperson
Wilkes-Barre Area
Wilkes-Barre, PA

Samantha McGlennen
Math Teacher/Department Coordinator
Summit Middle School
Fort Wayne, IN

Diane McIntire
Math Teacher
Garfield School
Kearny, NJ

Kenneth McIntire
Math Teacher
Lincoln School
Kearny, NJ

Tim Messal
Math Teacher/Math Department Chair
Woodside Middle School
Fort Wayne, IN

Vicki Perryman Petty
Math Teacher
Central Middle School
Murfreesboro, TN

Laronda Raines-Langham
Math Teacher
North Jefferson Middle School
Kimberly, AL

Rene Rush
Math Teacher
Colonial Heights Middle School
Colonial Heights, VA

Jennifer Sawyer
Math Teacher
Shawboro, NC

Shelly Schram
Math Teacher
East Grand Rapids Middle School
East Grand Rapids, MI

Richard Seavey
Math Teacher—Retired
Metcalf Junior High
Eagan, MN

Gail M. Sigmund
Math Teacher—Retired
Charles A. Mooney Preparatory School
Cleveland, OH

Jeffrey Slagel
Math Department Chair
South Eastern Middle School
Fawn Grove, PA

Paul Turney
Math Teacher
Ladue School District
St. Louis, MO

Dave Warren
Math Teacher
Meridian Middle School
Meridian, ID

Marilyn Wheeler
Math Teacher
Cityside Middle School
Zeeland, MI

Field Test Participants

Wendy Black
Southmont Jr. High
Crawfordsville, IN

Barbara Broeckelman
Oakley Middle School
Oakley, KS

Cindy Bush
Riverside Middle School
Greer, SC

Cadian Collman
Cutler Ridge Middle School
Miami, FL

Dora Corcini
Eisenhower Middle School
Oregon, OH

Deborah Drinkwalter
Sedgefield Middle School
Goose Creek, SC

Susan Gomez
Glades Middle School
Miami, FL

LaChandra Hogan
Apollo Middle School
Hollywood, FL

Ty Inlow
Oakley Middle School
Oakley, KS

Leighton Jenkins
Glades Middle School
Miami, FL

Heather King
Clever Middle School
Clever, MO

Dianne Marrett
Pines Middle School
Pembroke Pines, FL

Angela J. McNeal
Audubon Middle School
Los Angeles, CA

Wendy Misner
Lakeland Middle School
LaGrange, IN

Vanessa Nance
Pines Middle School
Pembroke Pines, FL

Teresa Patterson
Damonte Ranch High School
Reno, NV

Traci Peters
Cario Middle School
Mount Pleasant, SC

Ashley Piatt
East Forsyth Middle School
Kernersville, NC

Jeannine Quigley
Wilbur Wright Middle School
Dayton, OH

Shioban Smith-Haye
Apollo Middle School
Hollywood, FL

Jill Snipes
Bunn Middle School
Bunn, NC

Cathy Spencer
Oakridge Junior High
Oakridge, OR

Connie Vaught
K.D. Waldo School
Aurora, IL

Shelley Weeks
Lewis Middle School
Valparaiso, FL

Jennie Woo
Gaithersburg Middle School
Gaithersburg, MD

Reggie Wright
West Hopkins School
Nebo, KY

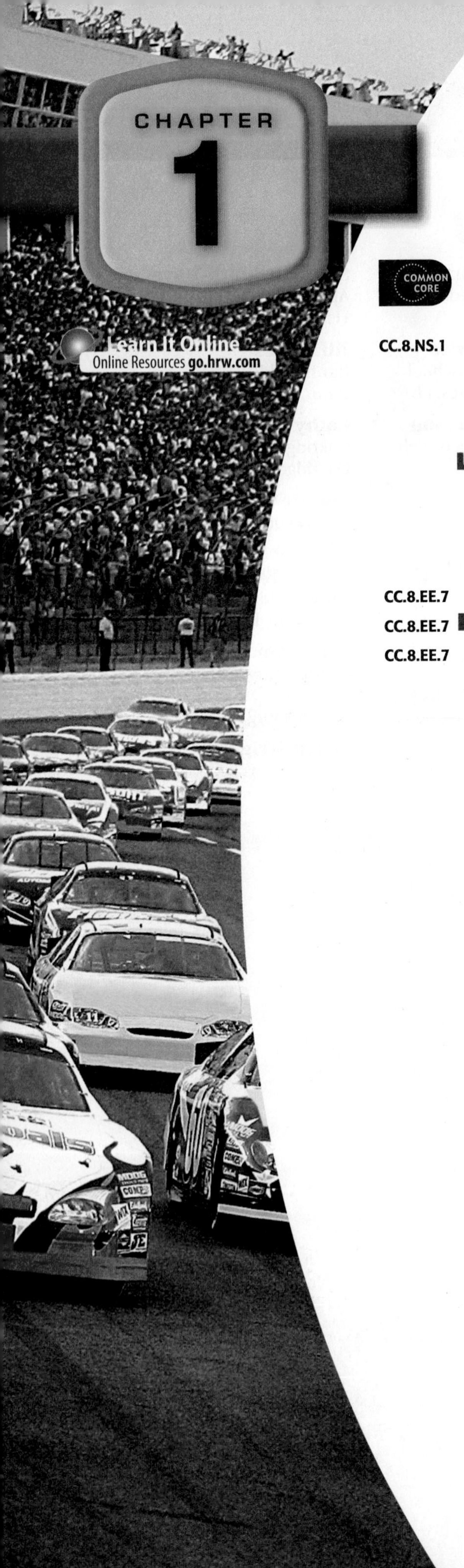

Rational Numbers

COMMON CORE

Graphs and Functions

COMMON CORE

(all) Richard Cooke/Alamy

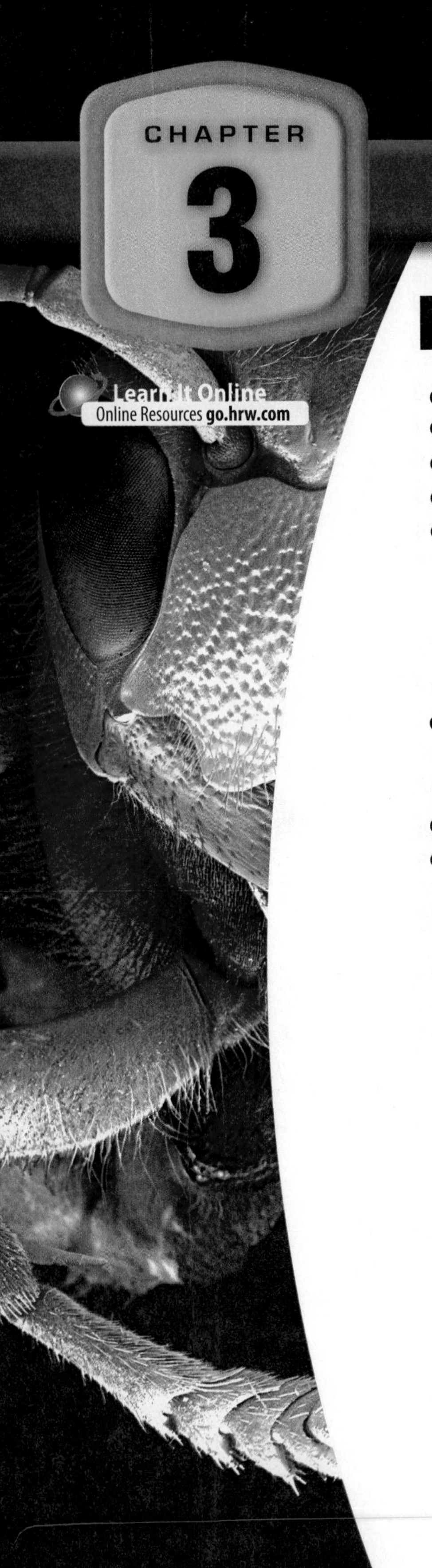

Exponents and Roots

COMMON CORE

Ratios, Proportions, and Similarity

CHAPTER 4

COMMON CORE

(bkgd) First/zefa/Corbis Eduardo; Garcia/Taxi/Getty Images

Geometric Relationships

COMMON CORE

Measurement and Geometry

CHAPTER 6

age fotostock/SuperStock

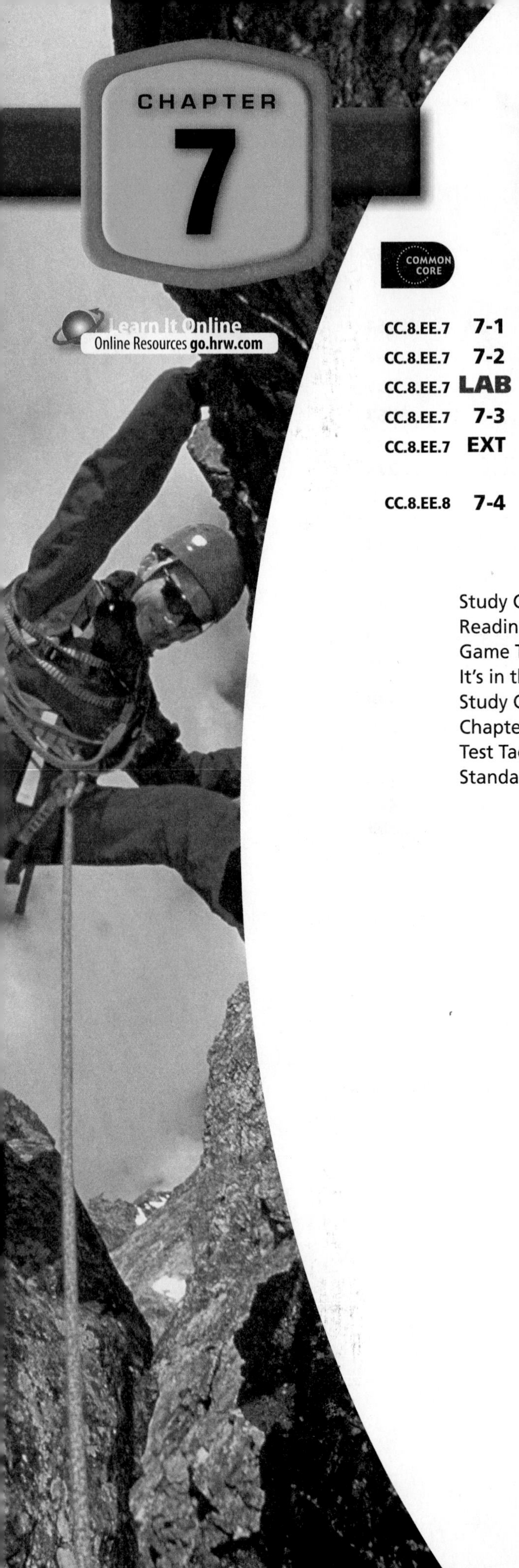

Multi-Step Equations

COMMON CORE

M. Colonel/Photo Researchers, Inc.

Graphing Lines

CHAPTER 8

COMMON CORE

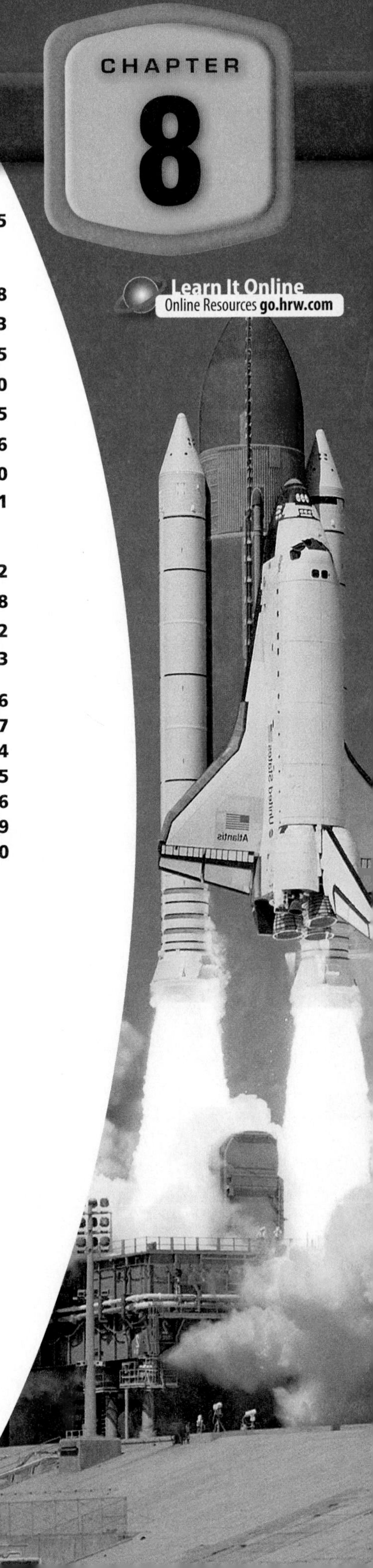

Stocktrek Images/Getty Images

Data, Prediction, and Linear Functions

COMMON CORE

Standards for Mathematical Content
Correlation for Holt McDougal Mathematics Grade 8

Standards	Descriptor	Page Citations
CC.8.NS	**THE NUMBER SYSTEM**	
Know that there are numbers that are not rational, and approximate them by rational numbers		
CC.8.NS.1	Understand informally that every number has a decimal expansion; the rational numbers are those with decimal expansions that terminate in 0s or eventually repeat. Know that other numbers are called irrational	**SE:** 7–8, 40, 43, 123, 125, 128–129, 148
CC.8.NS.2	Use rational approximations of irrational numbers to compare the size of irrational numbers, locate them approximately on a number line diagram, and estimate the value of expressions (e.g., π^2)	**SE:** 116–119, 128–129, 135, 148–149, 210, 403
CC.8.EE	**EXPRESSIONS AND EQUATIONS**	
Work with radicals and integer exponents		
CC.8.EE.1	Know and apply the properties of integer exponents to generate equivalent numerical expressions	**SE:** 96–99, 104, 147, 149, 200, 342
CC.8.EE.2	Use square root and cube root symbols to represent solutions to equations of the form $x^2 = p$ and $x^3 = p$, where p is a positive rational number. Evaluate square roots of small perfect squares and cube roots of small perfect cubes. Know that $\sqrt{2}$ is irrational	**SE:** 112–114, 120–121, 123, 147, 149, 285
CC.8.EE.3	Use numbers expressed in the form of a single digit times an integer power of 10 to estimate very large or very small quantities, and to express how many times as much one is than the other	**SE:** 100–108
CC.8.EE.4	Perform operations with numbers expressed in scientific notation, including problems where both decimal and scientific notation are used. Use scientific notation and choose units of appropriate size for measurements of very large or very small quantities (e.g., use millimeters per year for seafloor spreading). Interpret scientific notation that has been generated by technology	**SE:** 100–111, 115

SE = Student Edition

Standards for Mathematical Content
Correlation for Holt McDougal Mathematics Grade 8

Standards	Descriptor	Page Citations
Understand the connections between proportional relationships, lines, and linear equations		
CC.8.EE.5	Graph proportional relationships, interpreting the unit rate as the slope of the graph. Compare two different proportional relationships represented in different ways	**SE:** 346–349, 362–365, 404–407
CC.8.EE.6	Use similar triangles to explain why the slope m is the same between any two distinct points on a non-vertical line in the coordinate plane; derive the equation $y = mx$ for a line through the origin and the equation $y = mx + b$ for a line intercepting the vertical axis at b	**SE:** 343–344, 346–348, 351–354, 360, 363, 365, 377–379
Analyze and solve linear equations and pairs of simultaneous linear equations		
CC.8.EE.7	Solve linear equations in one variable	**SE:** 26–36, 42–44, 53, 69, 73, 89, 159, 280, 297, 301–305, 308–313, 317, 321, 324, 327, 329, 335
CC.8.EE.7a	Give examples of linear equations in one variable with one solution, infinitely many solutions, or no solutions. Show which of these possibilities is the case by successively transforming the given equation into simpler forms, until an equivalent equation of the form $x = a$, $a = a$, or $a = b$ results (where a and b are different numbers).	**SE:** 308–315
CC.8.EE.7b	Solve linear equations with rational number coefficients, including equations whose solutions require expanding expressions using the distributive property and collecting like terms	**SE:** 26–36, 42–44, 53, 69, 73, 89, 159, 280, 297, 301–303, 308–313, 317, 321, 324, 327, 329, 335
CC.8.EE.8	Analyze and solve pairs of simultaneous linear equations	**SE:** 318–322, 327, 329, 368–372
CC.8.EE.8a	Understand that solutions to a system of two linear equations in two variables correspond to points of intersection of their graphs, because points of intersection satisfy both equations simultaneously	**SE:** 368–372
CC.8.EE.8b	Solve systems of two linear equations in two variables algebraically, and estimate solutions by graphing the equations. Solve simple cases by inspection	**SE:** 318–322, 328–329, 368–372
CC.8.EE.8c	Solve real-world and mathematical problems leading to two linear equations in two variables	**SE:** 318–322, 328–329, 368, 370–372

SE = Student Edition

Standards	Descriptor	Page Citations
CC.8.F	**FUNCTIONS**	
Define, evaluate, and compare functions		
CC.8.F.1	Understand that a function is a rule that assigns to each input exactly one output. The graph of a function is the set of ordered pairs consisting of an input and the corresponding output.[1] [1]Function notation is not required in Grade 8	**SE:** 66–76, 82–83, 104, 173, 360, 362–366, 400–403, 408, 413
CC.8.F.2	Compare properties of two functions each represented in a different way (algebraically, graphically, numerically in tables, or by verbal descriptions).	**SE:** 404–407
CC.8.F.3	Interpret the equation $y = mx + b$ as defining a linear function, whose graph is a straight line; give examples of functions that are not linear	**SE:** 351–354, 360, 400–403, 408, 414–415
Use functions to model relationships between quantities		
CC.8.F.4	Construct a function to model a linear relationship between two quantities. Determine the rate of change and initial value of the function from a description of a relationship or from two (x, y) values, including reading these from a table or from a graph. Interpret the rate of change and initial value of a linear function in terms of the situation it models, and in terms of its graph or a table of values.	**SE:** 70–76, 82–83, 104, 339–342, 351–354, 357–358, 401–407
CC.8.F.5	Describe qualitatively the functional relationship between two quantities by analyzing a graph (e.g., where the function is increasing or decreasing, linear or nonlinear). Sketch a graph that exhibits the qualitative features of a function that has been described verbally	**SE:** 69, 72–73, 338–342, 352–354, 364, 366

Standards	Descriptor	Page Citations
CC.8.G	**GEOMETRY**	
Understand congruence and similarity using physical models, transparencies, or geometry software		
CC.8.G.1	Verify experimentally the properties of rotations, reflections, and translations:	**SE:** 220–221, 226–230, 237
CC.8.G.1a	Lines are taken to lines, and line segments to line segments of the same length	**SE:** 231–234
CC.8.G.1b	Angles are taken to angles of the same measure	**SE:** 231–234
CC.8.G.1c	Parallel lines are taken to parallel lines	**SE:** 231–234
CC.8.G.2	Understand that a two-dimensional figure is congruent to another if the second can be obtained from the first by a sequence of rotations, reflections, and translations; given two congruent figures, describe a sequence that exhibits the congruence between them	**SE:** 220–221, 226–229, 239–244
CC.8.G.3	Describe the effect of dilations, translations, rotations, and reflections on two-dimensional figures using coordinates	**SE:** 174–180, 186–187, 226–229, 231–235, 239–244
CC.8.G.4	Understand that a two-dimensional figure is similar to another if the second can be obtained from the first by a sequence of rotations, reflections, translations, and dilations; given two similar two-dimensional figures, describe a sequence that exhibits the similarity between them	**SE:** 168–180, 190, 231–234, 239–243
CC.8.G.5	Use informal arguments to establish facts about the angle sum and exterior angle of triangles, about the angles created when parallel lines are cut by a transversal, and the angle-angle criterion for similarity of triangles	**SE:** 202–203, 206–210, 212, 218, 231–235, 239–243, 249, 251, 254–255
Understand and apply the Pythagorean Theorem		
CC.8.G.6	Explain a proof of the Pythagorean Theorem and its converse	**SE:** 131, 136–137
CC.8.G.7	Apply the Pythagorean Theorem to determine unknown side lengths in right triangles in real-world and mathematical problems in two and three dimensions	**SE:** 132–135, 142, 148–149
CC.8.G.8	Apply the Pythagorean Theorem to find the distance between two points in a coordinate system	**SE:** 138–142, 148–149
Solve real-world and mathematical problems involving volume of cylinders, cones, and spheres		
CC.8.G.9	Know the formulas for the volumes of cones, cylinders, and spheres and use them to solve real-world and mathematical problems	**SE:** 267–271, 276–280, 282–285, 291–293, 305

SE = Student Edition

Standards	Descriptor	Page Citations
CC.8.SP	**STATISTICS AND PROBABILITY**	
Investigate patterns of association in bivariate data		
CC.8.SP.1	Construct and interpret scatter plots for bivariate measurement data to investigate patterns of association between two quantities. Describe patterns such as clustering, outliers, positive or negative association, linear association, and nonlinear association	**SE:** 386–395
CC.8.SP.2	Know that straight lines are widely used to model relationships between two quantitative variables. For scatter plots that suggest a linear association, informally fit a straight line, and informally assess the model fit by judging the closeness of the data points to the line	**SE:** 387–388, 390–393
CC.8.SP.3	Use the equation of a linear model to solve problems in the context of bivariate measurement data, interpreting the slope and intercept	**SE:** 390–395
CC.8.SP.4	Understand that patterns of association can also be seen in bivariate categorical data by displaying frequencies and relative frequencies in a two-way table. Construct and interpret a two-way table summarizing data on two categorical variables collected from the same subjects. Use relative frequencies calculated for rows or columns to describe possible association between the two variables	**SE:** 396–397

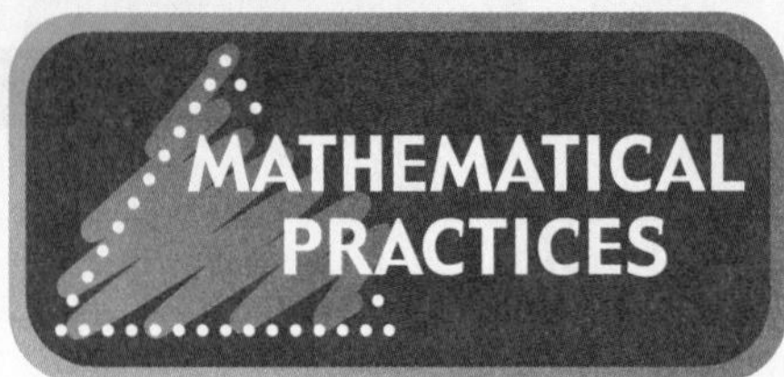

Mastering the Standards

for Mathematical Practice

The topics described in the Standards for Mathematical Content will vary from year to year. However, the *way* in which you learn, study, and think about mathematics will not. The Standards for Mathematical Practice describe skills that you will use in all of your math courses. These pages show some features of your book that will help you gain these skills and use them to master this year's topics.

1 Make sense of problems and persevere in solving them.

Mathematically proficient students start by explaining to themselves the meaning of a problem... They analyze givens, constraints, relationships, and goals. They make conjectures about the form... of the solution and plan a solution pathway...

In your book

Focus on Problem Solving describes a four-step plan for problem solving. The plan is introduced at the beginning of your book, and practice appears throughout.

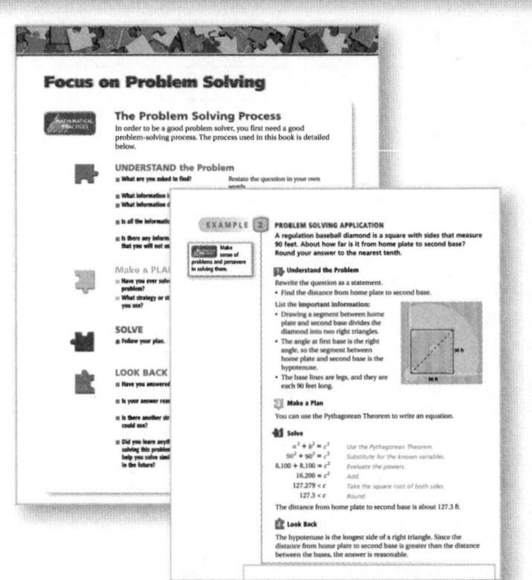

Focus on Problem Solving

MATHEMATICAL PRACTICES

The Problem Solving Process

In order to be a good problem solver, you first need a good problem-solving process. The process used in this book is detailed below.

UNDERSTAND the Problem

- What are you asked to find? — Restate the question in your own words.
- What information i
- What information d
- Is all the informatio
- Is there any inform that you will not us

Make a PLA

- Have you ever solv problem?
- What strategy or st you use?

SOLVE

- Follow your plan.

LOOK BACK

- Have you answered
- Is your answer reas
- Is there another str could use?
- Did you learn anyth solving this problem help you solve simi in the future?

EXAMPLE 2 — Make sense of problems and persevere in solving them.

PROBLEM SOLVING APPLICATION

A regulation baseball diamond is a square with sides that measure 90 feet. About how far is it from home plate to second base? Round your answer to the nearest tenth.

Understand the Problem

Rewrite the question as a statement.

- Find the distance from home plate to second base.

List the **important information:**

- Drawing a segment between home plate and second base divides the diamond into two right triangles.
- The angle at first base is the right angle, so the segment between home plate and second base is the hypotenuse.
- The base lines are legs, and they are each 90 feet long.

Make a Plan

You can use the Pythagorean Theorem to write an equation.

Solve

$a^2 + b^2 = c^2$	*Use the Pythagorean Theorem.*
$90^2 + 90^2 = c^2$	*Substitute for the known variables.*
$8{,}100 + 8{,}100 = c^2$	*Evaluate the powers.*
$16{,}200 = c^2$	*Add.*
$127.279 < c$	*Take the square root of both sides.*
$127.3 < c$	*Round.*

The distance from home plate to second base is about 127.3 ft.

Look Back

The hypotenuse is the longest side of a right triangle. Since the distance from home plate to second base is greater than the distance between the bases, the answer is reasonable.

2 Reason abstractly and quantitatively.
3 Construct viable arguments and critique the reasoning of others.

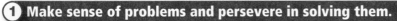

Mathematically proficient students... justify their conclusions, [and]... distinguish correct... reasoning from that which is flawed.

In your book

Think and Discuss asks you to evaluate statements, explain relationships, apply mathematical principles, and justify your reasoning.

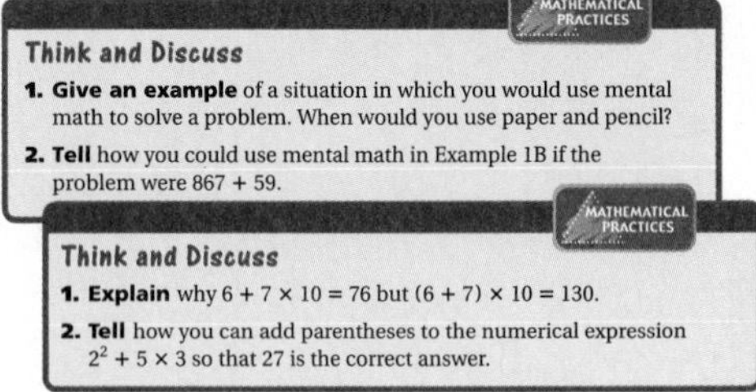

MATHEMATICAL PRACTICES

Think and Discuss

1. **Give an example** of a situation in which you would use mental math to solve a problem. When would you use paper and pencil?
2. **Tell** how you could use mental math in Example 1B if the problem were 867 + 59.

MATHEMATICAL PRACTICES

Think and Discuss

1. **Explain** why $6 + 7 \times 10 = 76$ but $(6 + 7) \times 10 = 130$.
2. **Tell** how you can add parentheses to the numerical expression $2^2 + 5 \times 3$ so that 27 is the correct answer.

4 Model with mathematics.

Mathematically proficient students can apply... mathematics... to... problems... in everyday life, society, and the workplace...

In your book

Application exercises and **Real-World Connections** apply mathematics to other disciplines and in real-world scenarios.

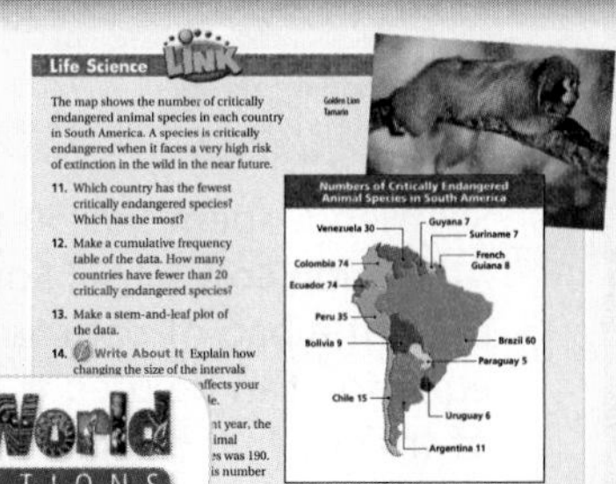

5 Use appropriate tools strategically.

Mathematically proficient students consider the available tools when solving a... problem... [and] are... able to use technological tools to explore and deepen their understanding...

In your book

Hands-on Labs and **Technology Labs** use concrete and technological tools to explore mathematical concepts.

6 Attend to precision.

Mathematically proficient students... communicate precisely... with others and in their own reasoning... [They] give carefully formulated explanations...

In your book

Reading and Writing Math and **Write About It** help you learn and use the language of math to communicate mathematics precisely.

7 Look for and express regularity in repeated reasoning.
8 Look for and make use of structure.

Mathematically proficient students... look both for general methods and for shortcuts...

In your book

Lesson examples group similar types of problems together, and the solutions are carefully stepped out. This allows you to make generalizations about—and notice variations in—the underlying structures.

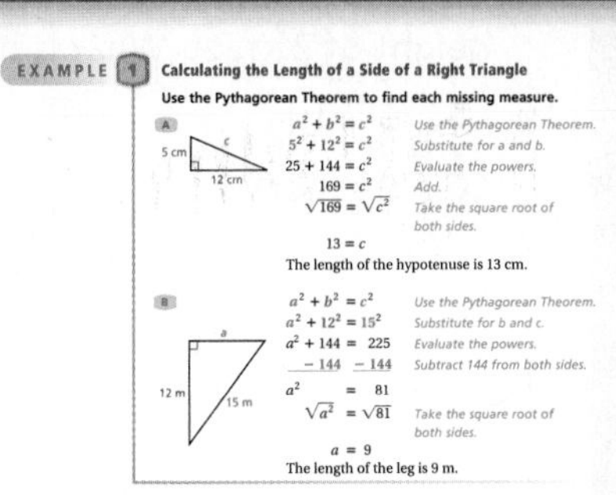

Countdown to Mastery

WEEK 1

DAY 1

Six friends spent \$55.50 at the movies. Admission cost \$7.50. Some of them bought a bag of popcorn for \$3.50. Which equation can be used to find the number of friends that bought popcorn?

Ⓐ $7.5p + 6(3.5) = 55.5$

Ⓑ $3.5p + 6(7.5) = 55.5$

Ⓒ $3.5p + 55.5 = 6(7.5)$

Ⓓ $6p + 3(7.5) = 55.5$

DAY 2

Solve: $10 - 2x = 17$

Ⓕ -13.5

Ⓖ -3.5

Ⓗ 3.5

Ⓙ 9

DAY 3

The graph shows the amount of money Ravi saved during four months. In October, he saved x dollars. If his total savings for June through October is 6 times the amount saved in October, how much did he save in October?

Ⓐ \$26

Ⓑ \$30

Ⓒ \$42

Ⓓ \$54

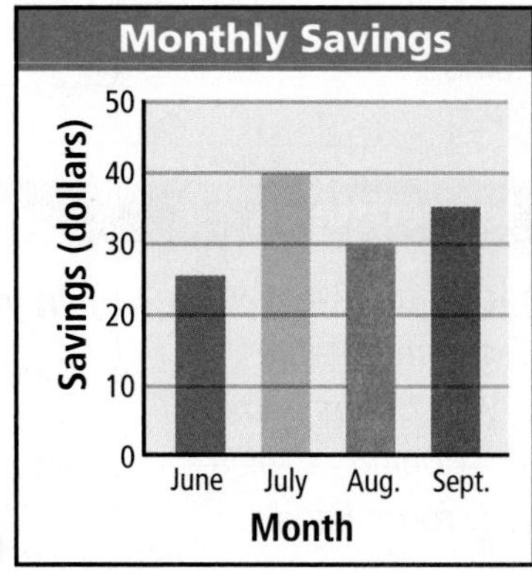

DAY 4

A rectangle has a width of $3\frac{1}{2}$ feet and a height of $2\frac{2}{3}$ feet. What is its area?

Ⓕ $6\frac{1}{2}$ ft²

Ⓖ $8\frac{2}{3}$ feet²

Ⓗ $9\frac{1}{3}$ ft²

Ⓙ $13\frac{1}{3}$ ft²

DAY 5

Shauntay bought a skirt for \$32 and a pair of sandals. The solution of the equation $61 = 32 + x$ gives the price of the sandals. What was the total amount that she paid for the skirt and the sandals?

Ⓐ \$29

Ⓑ \$61

Ⓒ \$93

Ⓓ \$125

Countdown to Mastery

WEEK 2

DAY 1

Tom bought a pack of pencils for $1.99 and 3 notebooks. He spent $6.46. How much did each notebook cost?

Ⓐ $1.19

Ⓑ $1.33

Ⓒ $1.49

Ⓓ $2.15

DAY 2

In the morning, Pablo drives 120 miles. This is one-third of the total distance he needs to drive. What equation can you solve to find the total distance Pablo must drive?

Ⓕ $3d = 120$

Ⓖ $\frac{1}{3}d = 120$

Ⓗ $d = \frac{1}{3} \cdot 120$

Ⓙ $d + \frac{1}{3} = 120$

DAY 3

Greg ate two apples, a peach, and a mango. He consumed a total of 385 calories by eating these fruits. What equation can you solve to find the number of calories in the mango?

Ⓐ $250 + x = 385$

Ⓑ $155 + x = 385$

Ⓒ $385 - x = 150$

Ⓓ $385 - x = 190$

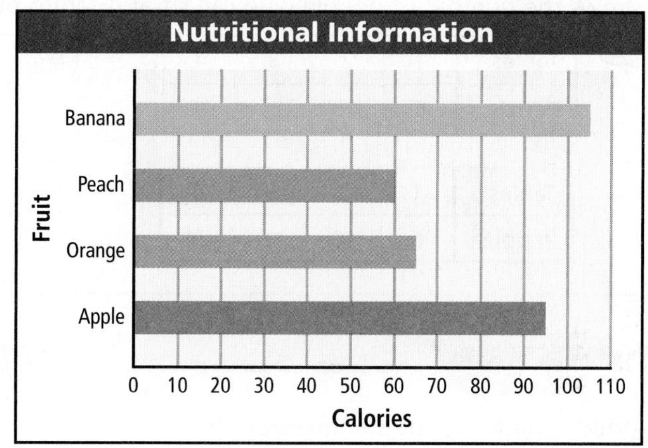

DAY 4

Ivy's Fresh Eggs transports its eggs in crates. How many crates will 8 trucks carry?

Trucks	2	3	4	5
Crates	80	120	160	200

Ⓕ 220

Ⓖ 280

Ⓗ 320

Ⓙ 360

DAY 5

The lowest temperature ever recorded in Alabama was −27°F. The lowest temperature ever recorded in Connecticut was −32°F. The record low for Connecticut is halfway between the record lows of Alabama and Kentucky. What was the lowest temperature ever recorded in Kentucky?

Ⓐ −37°F

Ⓑ −35.5°F

Ⓒ −29.5°F

Ⓓ −22°F

Countdown to Mastery

WEEK 3

DAY 1

Peaches cost p dollars per pound. Zack buys $4\frac{1}{2}$ pounds of peaches and a jar of peanut butter that costs \$2. Altogether, he spends \$11. Which equation represents this situation?

(A) $4\frac{1}{2} + p = 11$

(B) $4\frac{1}{2} + p = 9$

(C) $4\frac{1}{2}p = 11$

(D) $4\frac{1}{2}p = 9$

DAY 2

Vonda jogs the same distance each day. After 8 days, the total distance she has jogged is 33.6 kilometers. Paul jogs 2.7 km less than Vonda each day. How far does Paul jog each day?

(F) 1.5 km

(G) 2.7 km

(H) 6.9 km

(J) 30.9 km

DAY 3

At a restaurant, a rectangular table can seat 1 person on each end and 2 on each side. When 2 tables are pushed together end to end, 10 people can sit. Which table shows the number of people who can sit at 4 tables pushed together?

(A)

Tables	1	2	3	4
People	6	10	14	18

(B)

Tables	1	2	3	4
People	6	10	18	24

(C)

Tables	1	2	3	4
People	6	10	12	16

(D)

Tables	1	2	3	4
People	6	10	24	48

DAY 4

Which point is located in quadrant III?

(F) (–3, 5)

(G) (–7, –1)

(H) (10, 1)

(J) (4, –6)

DAY 5

What function fits the values in the table?

x	1	2	3	4
$f(x)$	4	–1	–6	–11

(A) $f(x) = x + 3$

(B) $f(x) = 5x - 9$

(C) $f(x) = 4x$

(D) $f(x) = -5x + 9$

Countdown to Mastery

WEEK 4

DAY 1

A bucket can hold $2\frac{1}{4}$ gallons of water. Jake has 5 buckets and each is $\frac{1}{3}$ full. How much water is there altogether?

Ⓐ $\frac{3}{4}$ gallon

Ⓑ $1\frac{2}{3}$ gallons

Ⓒ $3\frac{3}{4}$ gallons

Ⓓ $11\frac{1}{4}$ gallons

DAY 2

Sandra uses 3.6 meters of ribbon to weave a small rug and 4.2 meters to weave a large rug. She makes 12 small rugs and some large rugs and uses a total of 60 meters of ribbon. How many large rugs does she make?

Ⓕ 2 Ⓗ 8

Ⓖ 4 Ⓙ 16

DAY 3

The table shows the lengths of some trails in Pennsylvania's Allegheny National Forest. Last summer, the Ramirez family hiked each of these trails as well as the Twin Lakes Trail. They hiked a total of 41.2 miles. What is the length of the Twin Lakes Trail?

Allegheny National Forest Hiking Trails	
Trail Name	**Length (mi)**
Beaver Meadows	7.1
Buzzard Swamp	9.6
Little Drummer	3.1
Mill Creek	5.6

Ⓐ 6.4 mi

Ⓑ 15.8 mi

Ⓒ 25.4 mi

Ⓓ 66.6 mi

DAY 4

Albert orders 6 cases of dog food online. The shipping charge is $5.75 and he spends a total of $32.75 on the order. What does it cost to order 4 cases of dog food, assuming the same shipping charge?

Ⓕ $18 Ⓗ $23.75

Ⓖ $21.83 Ⓙ $27

DAY 5

At the factory, boxes of paper clips are packed into shipping cases. How many boxes come in 5 cases?

Cases	2	3	4	5
Boxes	192	288	384	?

Ⓐ 384 Ⓒ 500

Ⓑ 480 Ⓓ 672

Countdown to Mastery

WEEK 5

DAY 1

Lauren drives 3.2 km farther than Cara, and Cara drives 4.9 km farther than Vance. If Lauren drives a total of 15.3 km, what equation can you use to find the distance d that Vance drives?

Ⓐ $15.3 = d + 8.1$

Ⓑ $15.3 = 3.2d$

Ⓒ $3.2 = 4.9 + d + 15.3$

Ⓓ $8.1 = 15.3 + d$

DAY 2

Sue needed $3\frac{2}{7}$ yards of fringe to trim each drape. If she had 8 drapes to trim, how much fringe did she need?

Ⓕ $4\frac{6}{7}$ yards

Ⓖ $11\frac{2}{7}$ yards

Ⓗ $24\frac{3}{7}$ yards

Ⓙ $26\frac{2}{7}$ yards

DAY 3

The table shows the number of sit-ups Flora does each day. Assuming the pattern continues, predict the number of sit-ups Flora will do on Sunday.

Day	M	T	W	Th	F	S	Su
Number of Sit-ups	7	12	17	22	27		

Ⓐ 32

Ⓑ 37

Ⓒ 42

Ⓓ 47

DAY 4

The table shows how much different numbers of tickets to a hockey game cost. How many dollars would 10 tickets cost?

Tickets	2	3	5	8
Cost ($)	4.80	7.20	12.00	19.20

Ⓕ $21.60

Ⓖ $24.00

Ⓗ $29.20

Ⓙ $32.00

DAY 5

Jason has $5000 in his savings account. Each month he withdraws $15. What equation shows the amount y in his account after x years?

Ⓐ $y = 5000 - 180x$

Ⓑ $y = 5000 + 180x$

Ⓒ $y = 5000x - 15$

Ⓓ $y = 15 - 5000x$

Countdown to Mastery

WEEK 6

DAY 1

The figure is reflected across the *y*-axis. What is the location of point *A* after the reflection?

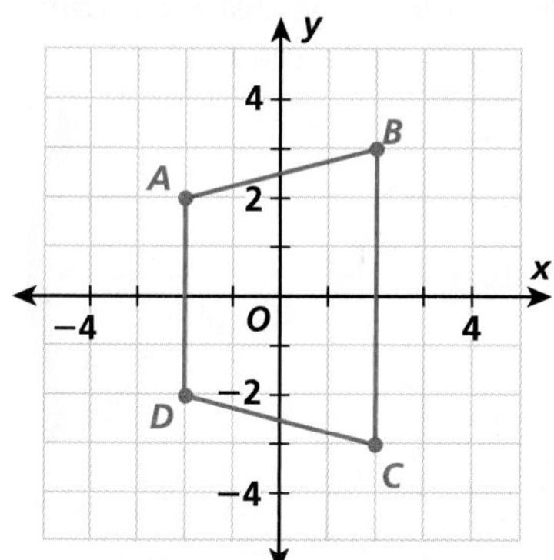

Ⓐ (2, 2) Ⓒ (2, −2)

Ⓑ (−2, 2) Ⓓ (−2, −2)

DAY 2

The figure is translated 2 units down and 3 units left. What is the location of point *H* after the translation?

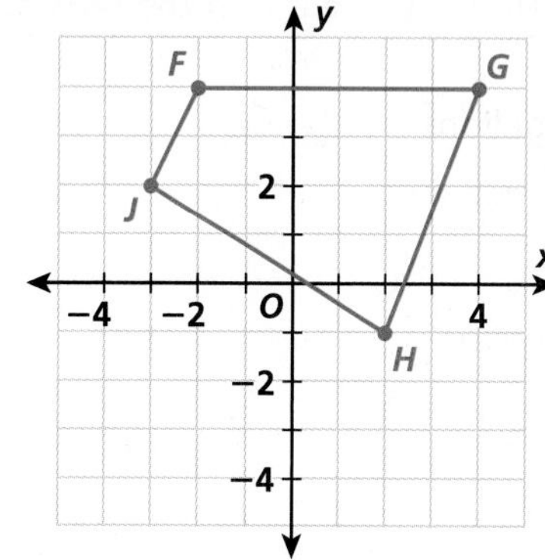

Ⓕ (2, −1) Ⓗ (0, −4)

Ⓖ (−1, −3) Ⓙ (-3, −1)

DAY 3

A rain barrel collects 440 gallons of water for every inch of rainfall. How much did the barrel collect on Thursday?

Ⓐ 110 gallons

Ⓑ 330 gallons

Ⓒ 1,320 gallons

Ⓓ 2,200 gallons

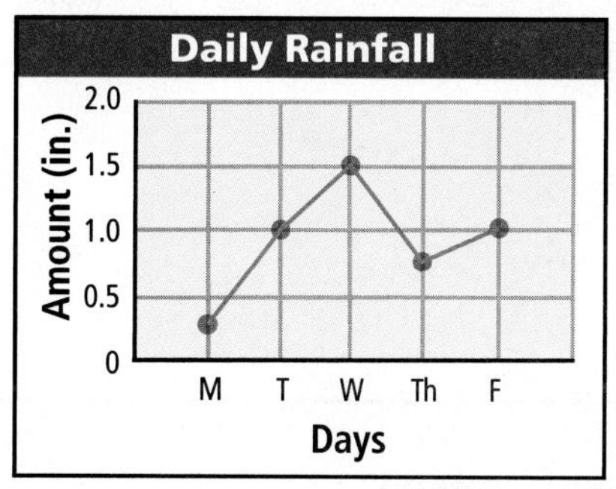

DAY 4

Blake works in a cheese store. The table shows how many cheese tidbits he has made at the end of each hour. If he continues at the same pace, how many tidbits will Blake have made in 6 hours?

Hours	2	3	4
Cheese Tidbits	234	351	468

Ⓕ 585 Ⓗ 819

Ⓖ 702 Ⓙ 1404

DAY 5

Divide. Write the answer in scientific notation.

$(13.2 \times 10^8) \div (4.0 \times 10^4)$

Ⓐ 3.4×10^2 Ⓒ 3.4×10^4

Ⓑ 3.4×10^3 Ⓓ 3.4×10^{12}

Countdown to Mastery

WEEK 7

DAY 1

The gas tank of Tim's car holds $12\frac{1}{2}$ gallons when it is full. Starting with a full tank, Tim uses $\frac{2}{5}$ of a tank. Then he adds $1\frac{1}{2}$ gallons of gas. How much gas is in the tank at this point?

Ⓐ 4 gallons

Ⓑ $6\frac{1}{2}$ gallons

Ⓒ $7\frac{1}{2}$ gallons

Ⓓ 9 gallons

DAY 2

The figure shows the distance from the surface of Saturn to the E ring. The distance to the G ring is 3.08×10^5 km less than this. What is the distance from the surface of Saturn to the G ring?

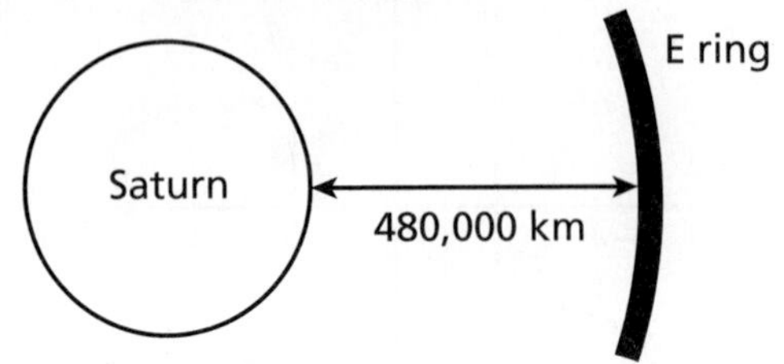

Ⓕ 17,200 km

Ⓖ 172,000 km

Ⓗ 44,920 km

Ⓙ 449,200 km

DAY 3

What equation is represented by the graph?

Ⓐ $y = 2x + 0.5$

Ⓑ $y = 0.5x + 0.5$

Ⓒ $y = 0.5x - 1$

Ⓓ $y = -0.5x + 0.5$

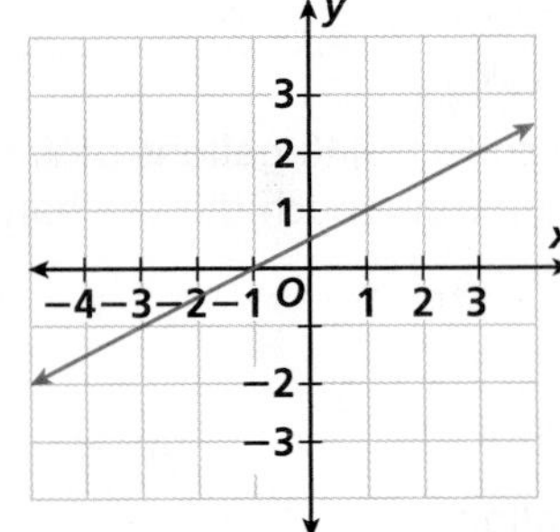

DAY 4

Ricardo plots the points (0, 0), (6, 0), and (0, 8). Then he connects the points to form a right triangle. What is the length of the triangle's hypotenuse?

Ⓕ 5

Ⓖ 10

Ⓗ 14

Ⓙ 100

DAY 5

Every 2 hours, a hive of honeybees can produce 150 grams of honey. How many grams of honey does the hive produce in 5 hours?

Ⓐ 300

Ⓑ 375

Ⓒ 450

Ⓓ 750

Countdown to Mastery

WEEK 8

DAY 1

Ronnie ties his dog to an 8-foot length of rope attached to a pole. About how far does the dog run when he runs once around the pole?

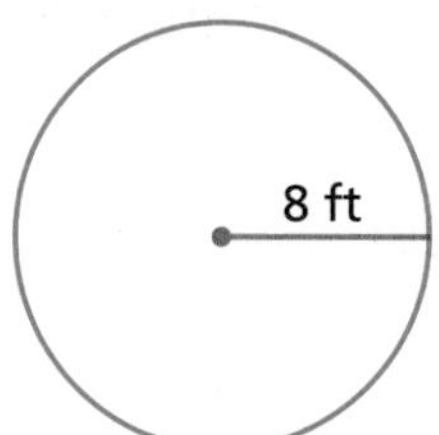

Ⓐ 25 feet
Ⓑ 50 feet
Ⓒ 100 feet
Ⓓ 200 feet

DAY 2

The ordered pair $(-1, 3)$ appears in a table of values for the equation $y = 3x + \blacksquare$. What is the missing number in the equation?

Ⓕ 0
Ⓖ 2
Ⓗ 3
Ⓙ 6

DAY 3

The table gives data on three students' typing speeds. They each type a 1000-word essay. Assuming they type without stopping, which students type the essay in less than 20 minutes?

Ⓐ None of them
Ⓑ All of them
Ⓒ Lee and Brian
Ⓓ Stacey and Brian

Typing Speeds

Name	Number of Words	Minutes
Lee	360	6
Stacey	305	8
Brian	312	5

DAY 4

Peter has a rectangular photograph that is 6 inches long and 4 inches wide. He has it made into a similar poster that is 15 inches long. What is the perimeter of the poster?

Ⓕ 10 in.
Ⓖ 25 in.
Ⓗ 50 in.
Ⓙ 150 in.

DAY 5

Carolyn is building a triangular headboard for her bed. What is its height? Round your answer to the nearest tenth.

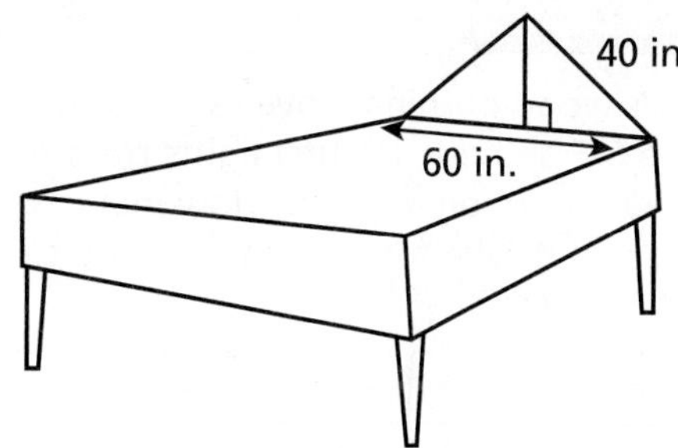

Ⓐ 8.3 inches
Ⓑ 10 inches
Ⓒ 26.5 inches
Ⓓ 100 inches

Countdown to Mastery

WEEK 9

DAY 1

Between what two integers is the number $-\sqrt{50}$?

Ⓐ –51 and –50
Ⓑ –26 and –25
Ⓒ –8 and –7
Ⓓ 7 and 8

DAY 2

The annual Iowa State Fair runs for 11 days. Each day, the fair attracts an average of 9.1×10^4 visitors. About how many people visit the fair each year?

Ⓕ 10,000
Ⓖ 100,000
Ⓗ 1,000,000
Ⓙ 10,000,000

DAY 3

The graph shows the cost of renting inline skates. How much does it cost to rent skates for 4.5 hours?

Ⓐ \$10
Ⓑ \$11
Ⓒ \$12
Ⓓ \$13

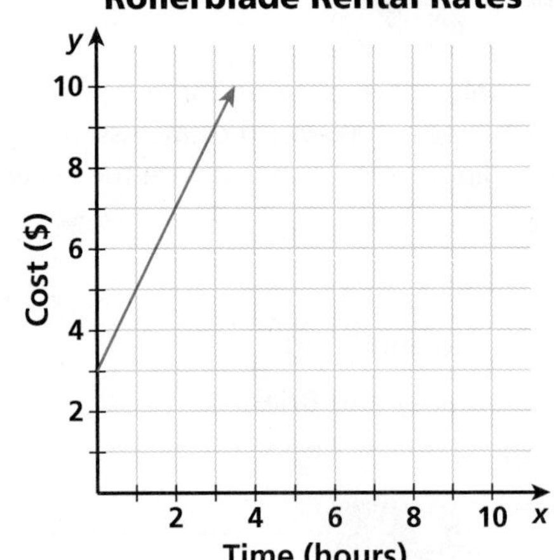

DAY 4

Steve's wood-burning stove can heat his house 6°F an hour. He first lights the stove at 6:00 AM when it is 52°F. How many hours will it take for the temperature to reach 82°F?

Hour	0	1	2	3	4
Temperature (°F)	52	58	64		

Ⓕ 3
Ⓖ 4
Ⓗ 5
Ⓙ 6

DAY 5

Jonathan drives 260 feet in 6 seconds. What is his approximate speed in miles per hour?

Ⓐ 20 mi/h
Ⓑ 30 mi/h
Ⓒ 40 mi/h
Ⓓ 50 mi/h

Countdown to Mastery

WEEK 10

DAY 1

The table shows the rate at which a tank is filling with water. What equation expresses the relationship between the time x and the amount of water y?

Time (min)	3	5	6
Amount of Water in Tank (gal)	25.5	42.5	51

(A) $y = x + 22.5$

(B) $y = 6x + 7.5$

(C) $y = 8.5x$

(D) $y = 22.5 - x$

DAY 2

If figure *ABCD* is dilated by a scale factor of 3, which ordered pair describes the new location of *C*?

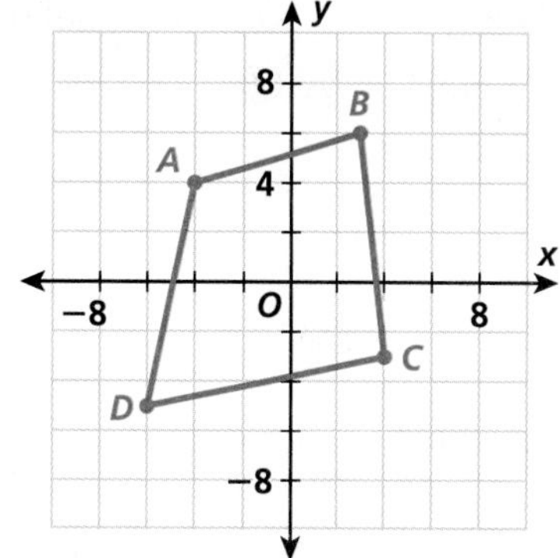

(F) (−12, 9)

(G) (9, 18)

(H) (4, −3)

(J) (12, −9)

DAY 3

A theater has orchestra seats and balcony seats. The ratio of orchestra seats to balcony seats is 3:2. There are 1000 seats altogether in the theater. How many orchestra seats are there?

(A) 200

(B) 300

(C) 400

(D) 600

DAY 4

A chandelier uses three different sizes of bulbs. Each bulb has a diameter that is twice as large as the previous one. What is the diameter of the largest bulb?

C = 6.28 in.

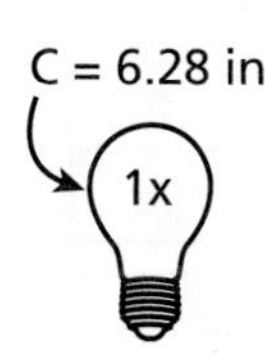

(F) 2 inches

(G) 3.14 inches

(H) 8 inches

(J) 12.56 inches

DAY 5

Mr. Bryce bought a hybrid car that can travel 240 miles on 8 gallons of gas. How far can Mr. Bryce travel on 10 gallons of gas?

(A) 280 miles

(B) 300 miles

(C) 480 miles

(D) 2400 miles

Countdown to Mastery

WEEK 11

DAY 1

Two sides of a right triangle are 10 meters. What is the length of the remaining side to the nearest tenth?

Ⓐ 3.2 meters
Ⓑ 4.5 meters
Ⓒ 10.8 meters
Ⓓ 14.1 meters

DAY 2

Christina wants to paint a circle with a radius of 4 feet on her bedroom wall. If 1 can of paint covers 26 square feet, how many cans of paint will Christina need to buy?

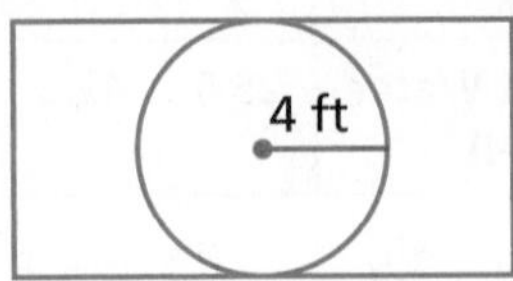

Ⓕ 1
Ⓖ 2
Ⓗ 3
Ⓙ 4

DAY 3

The ratio of dogs to cats in a pet shelter is 7:5. There are 24 dogs and cats. How many more dogs than cats are there?

Ⓐ 2
Ⓑ 4
Ⓒ 10
Ⓓ 14

DAY 4

Ms. Chu orders 15 calculators for her classroom. There is a shipping fee of $8.75 on the order. The total cost of the order is $380. When she gets the calculators, she finds that two do not work. She asks for a refund of the cost of these two calculators. What is the amount of the refund?

Ⓕ $24.75
Ⓖ $25.33
Ⓗ $49.50
Ⓙ $50.66

DAY 5

Justin has three rectangular tiles. The table gives the lengths and widths of the tiles. Which tiles, if any, are similar?

Tile	*A*	*B*	*C*
Length (cm)	12	14	16
Width (cm)	9	8	12

Ⓐ None are similar
Ⓑ All are similar
Ⓒ *A* and *B*
Ⓓ *A* and *C*

Countdown to Mastery

WEEK 12

DAY 1

The Wonder Wheel is a Ferris wheel at the Coney Island amusement park in New York. The ride has stationary cars and swinging cars. The ratio of stationary cars to swinging cars is 1:2. There are 16 swinging cars. How many cars are there altogether?

Ⓐ 16 Ⓒ 24

Ⓑ 20 Ⓓ 32

DAY 2

The measure of $\angle A$ is 143° and $\angle A$ is supplementary to $\angle B$. $\angle C$ is complementary to $\angle B$. What is $m\angle C$?

Ⓕ 37° Ⓗ 74°

Ⓖ 53° Ⓙ 143°

DAY 3

What is the value of *m* in the triangle shown here?

Ⓐ 2 Ⓒ 5

Ⓑ 4 Ⓓ 10

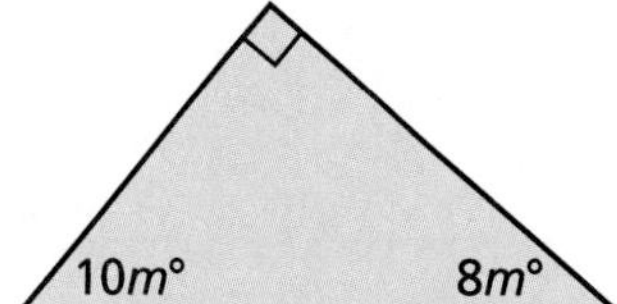

DAY 4

Find *AC* to the nearest tenth.

Ⓕ 8.9 cm

Ⓖ 11.9 cm

Ⓗ 12.1 cm

Ⓙ 16.0 cm

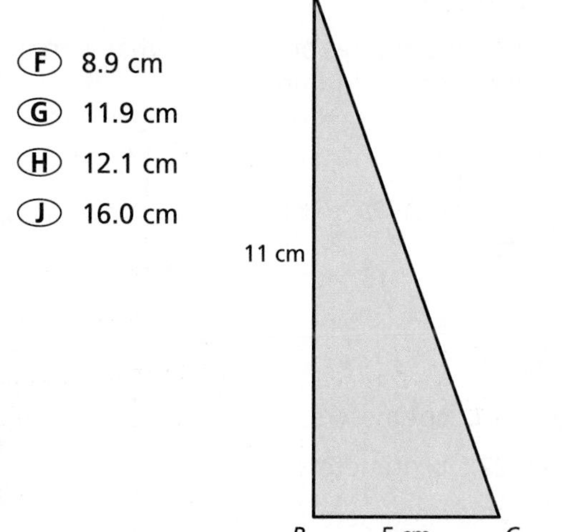

DAY 5

For the linear function shown, what is the value of *x* when $f(x) = 4$?

$$f(x) = 2x - 1$$

Ⓐ 2 Ⓒ 3

Ⓑ 2.5 Ⓓ 7

Countdown to Mastery

WEEK 13

DAY 1

Which of the following correctly shows the length of the Earth's equator?

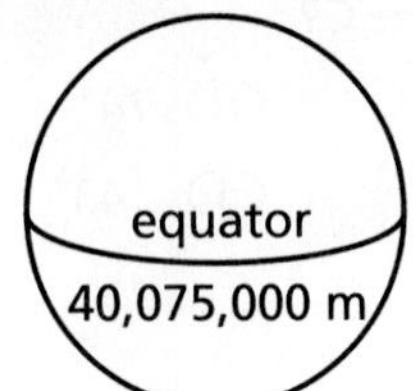

Ⓐ 0.40075×10^7 meters

Ⓑ 4.0075×10^7 meters

Ⓒ 40.075×10^7 meters

Ⓓ $4{,}007.5 \times 10^7$ meters

DAY 2

Figure *ABCD* is dilated by a scale factor of $\frac{3}{2}$. What are the coordinates of *C* after the dilation?

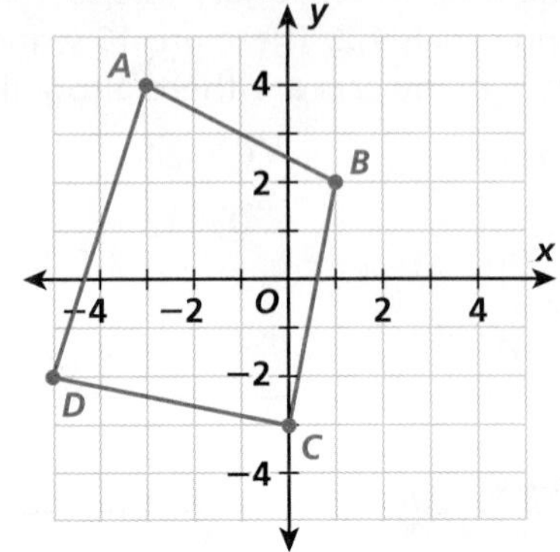

Ⓕ $(2, -4)$

Ⓖ $(0, -4\frac{1}{2})$

Ⓗ $(0, -1\frac{1}{2})$

Ⓙ $(0, -2)$

DAY 3

Which two angles are opposite interior angles?

Ⓐ 1 and 2

Ⓑ 2 and 7

Ⓒ 4 and 5

Ⓓ 3 and 5

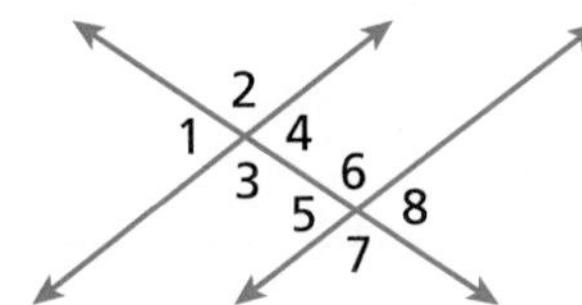

DAY 4

The rectangle is enlarged by a scale factor of 3. What is the perimeter of the enlarged rectangle?

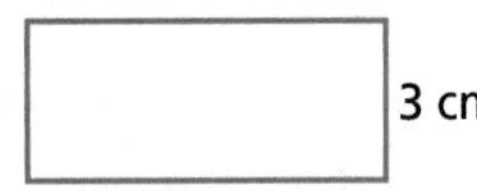

Ⓕ 30 centimeters

Ⓖ 32 centimeters

Ⓗ 60 centimeters

Ⓙ 189 centimeters

DAY 5

If these two figures are similar, what is the missing length of figure B?

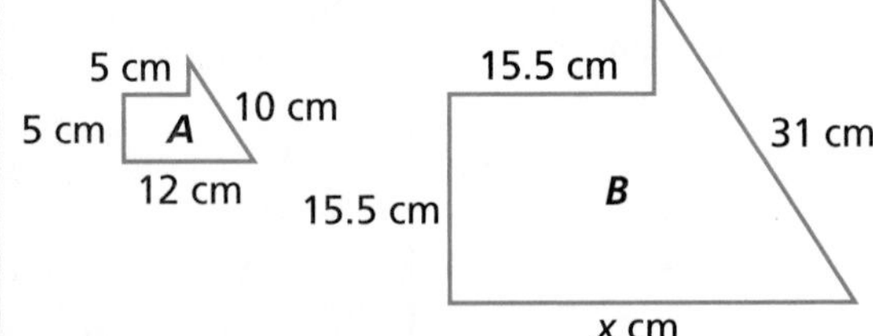

Ⓐ 3.1 centimeters

Ⓑ 22.5 centimeters

Ⓒ 25.2 centimeters

Ⓓ 37.2 centimeters

Countdown to Mastery

WEEK 14

DAY 1

Television screen size is measured on the diagonal. What is the height of this screen? Round your answer to the nearest tenth.

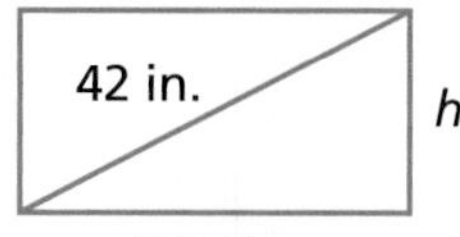

Ⓐ 4.5 inches
Ⓑ 9.0 inches
Ⓒ 18.9 inches
Ⓓ 20.3 inches

DAY 2

The figure is reflected across the *x*-axis. What are the coordinates of point *H* after the reflection?

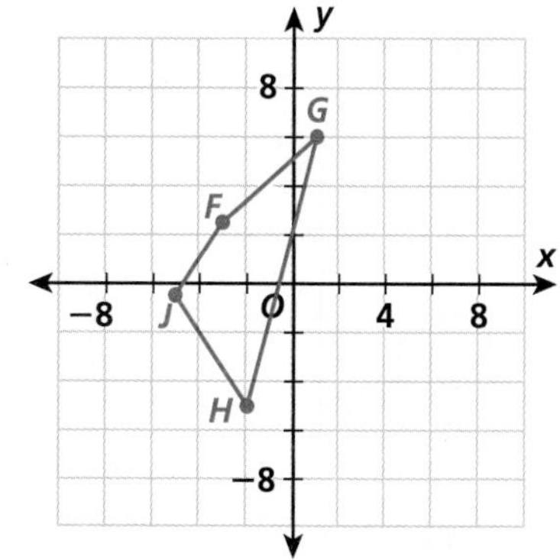

Ⓕ (−2, 5)
Ⓖ (2, −5)
Ⓗ (−1, 2.5)
Ⓙ (1, −2.5)

DAY 3

In $\triangle JKL$, $m\angle K$ is twice as large as $m\angle J$ and $m\angle L$ is three times as large as $m\angle J$. What is $m\angle J$?

Ⓐ 10°
Ⓑ 18°
Ⓒ 30°
Ⓓ 45°

DAY 4

If these two figures are similar, what is the missing measure in figure B?

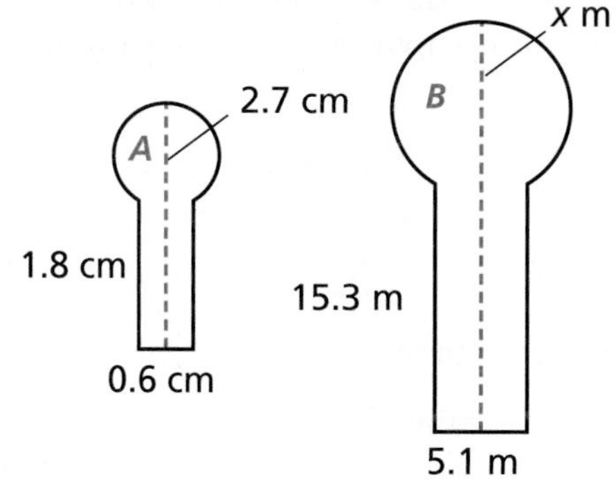

Ⓕ 18 centimeters
Ⓖ 20.4 centimeters
Ⓗ 22.95 centimeters
Ⓙ 30.6 centimeters

DAY 5

Gina is drawing a scale model of a park. If the scale factor is 1 inch = 4 feet, what is the perimeter of the actual park?

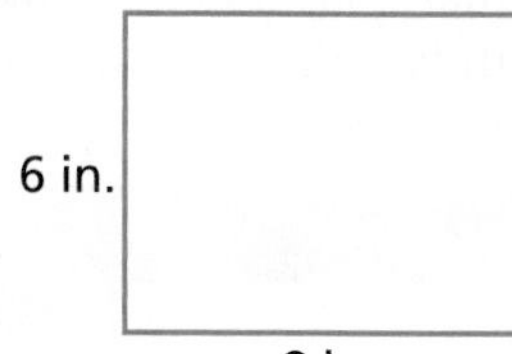

Ⓐ 28 feet
Ⓑ 56 feet
Ⓒ 112 feet
Ⓓ 768 feet

Countdown to Mastery

WEEK 15

DAY 1

If figure *LMNO* is reflected across the *x*-axis, which point(s) will **not** change locations?

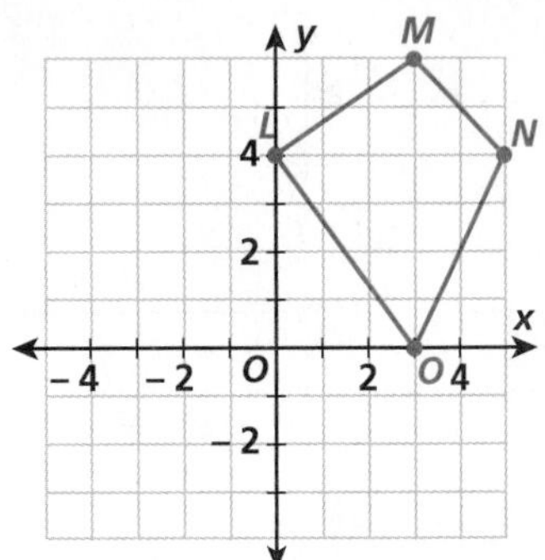

Ⓐ *L* and *O*
Ⓑ *L*
Ⓒ *O*
Ⓓ *L* and *N*

DAY 2

If figure *PQRS* is dilated by a scale factor of $\frac{1}{2}$, which point will be located at $\left(2, -1\frac{1}{2}\right)$?

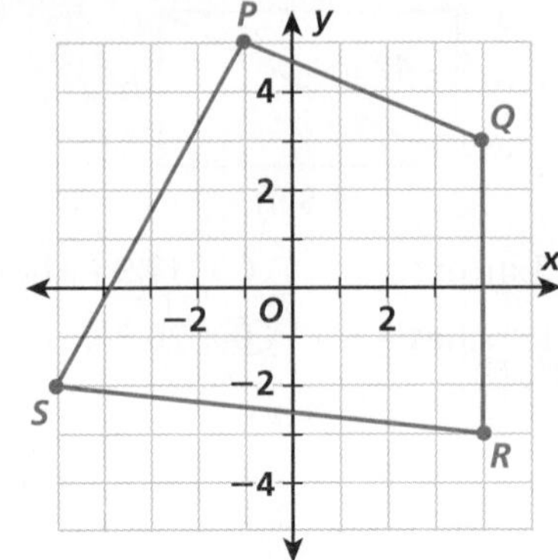

Ⓕ *P*
Ⓖ *Q*
Ⓗ *R*
Ⓙ *S*

DAY 3

An isosceles triangle has a 40 degree angle. If this is the vertex angle, which shows the measures of the angles of the triangle in degrees?

Ⓐ 40-40-100
Ⓑ 40-70-70
Ⓒ 40-60-60
Ⓓ 40-60-80

DAY 4

A box of crackers is a rectangular prism with the dimensions shown below. The box is one-fourth full. What is the volume of the crackers in the box?

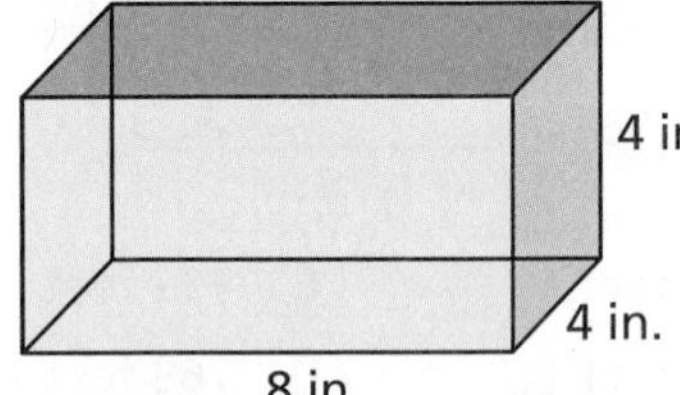

Ⓕ 4 in^3
Ⓖ 16 in^3
Ⓗ 32 in^3
Ⓙ 40 in^3

DAY 5

What is the side length of this square? Round your answer to the nearest tenth.

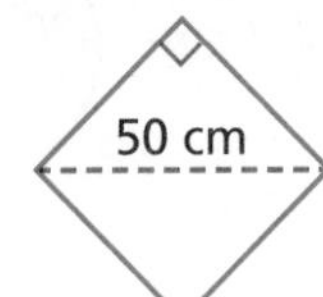

Ⓐ 5.0 centimeters
Ⓑ 11.2 centimeters
Ⓒ 25.0 centimeters
Ⓓ 35.4 centimeters

Countdown to Mastery

WEEK 16

Day 1

Laura does $\frac{2}{5}$ of the gardening in $1\frac{1}{4}$ hours. If she does the entire job 4 times a month, how many hours per month does she spend gardening?

Ⓐ $8\frac{1}{2}$ hours

Ⓑ 10 hours

Ⓒ $12\frac{1}{2}$ hours

Ⓓ 25 hours

Day 2

The Firefighters' Fountain in Kansas City is a circle with a diameter of 80 ft. For a ceremony, candles are placed approximately every 25 ft around the edge of the fountain. How many candles are needed?

Ⓕ 5

Ⓖ 10

Ⓗ 20

Ⓙ 200

Day 3

Figures A and B are similar. If the area of Figure A is 218.75 square centimeters, which expression could you use to determine the area of Figure B?

Figure A

17.5 cm

218.75 cm^2

Figure B

? 3.5 cm

Ⓐ $17.5 \div 3.5$

Ⓑ $218.75 \div 25$

Ⓒ $5 \cdot 218.75$

Ⓓ $3.5 \cdot 17.5$

Day 4

Katie wants to frame this stained-glass window with wood. What length of wood does she need to buy? Round your answer to the nearest tenth.

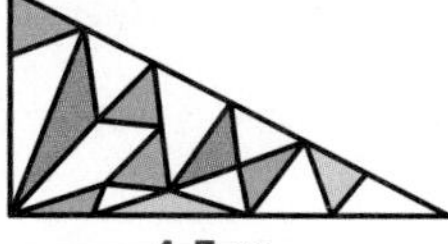

Ⓕ 5 meters

Ⓖ 6.8 meters

Ⓗ 11.8 meters

Ⓙ 13.5 meters

Day 5

What is the area of the figure with vertices (1, 1), (7, 1), (6, 4), and (2, 4)?

Ⓐ 12 units^2

Ⓑ 15 units^2

Ⓒ 18 units^2

Ⓓ 30 units^2

Countdown to Mastery

WEEK 17

DAY 1

A circle has center (3, 3) and the circle passes through the point (3, 1). What is the circumference of the circle?

Ⓐ 2π units

Ⓑ 3π units

Ⓒ 4π units

Ⓓ 8π units

DAY 2

A rectangular prism has a base that is 3 cm by 8 cm. Its height is 6 cm. What is the volume of the prism?

Ⓕ 24 cm^3

Ⓖ 36 cm^3

Ⓗ 48 cm^3

Ⓙ 51 cm^3

DAY 3

Nick buys a new fish tank for his living room. Which is the best estimate of the volume of water Nick needs to fill the tank?

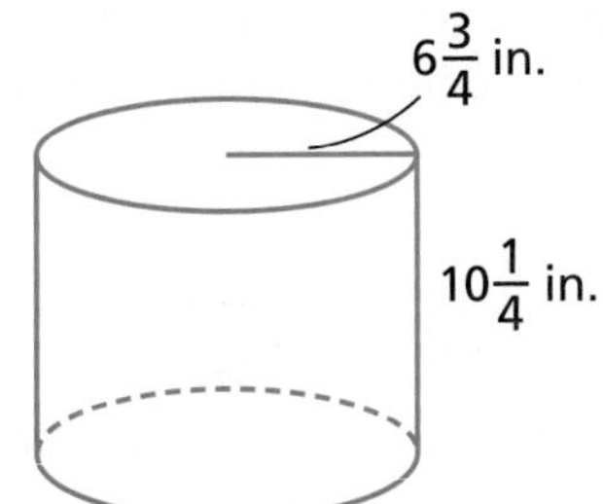

Ⓐ 70 cubic inches

Ⓑ 147 cubic inches

Ⓒ 1080 cubic inches

Ⓓ 1470 cubic inches

DAY 4

If $\triangle ACE$ is similar to $\triangle BCD$, what is the length of AC?

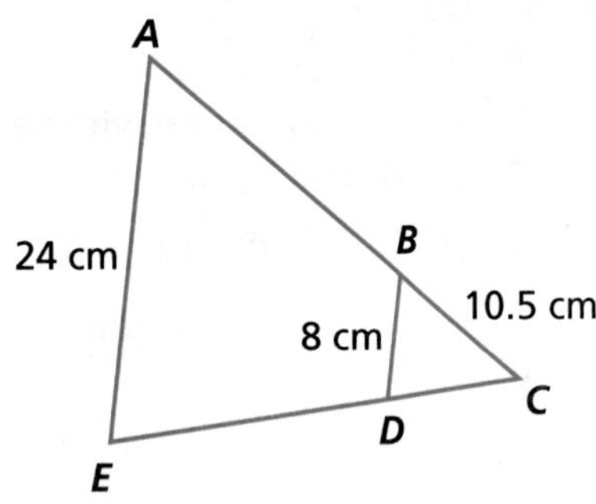

Ⓕ 5.5 centimeters

Ⓖ 13.5 centimeters

Ⓗ 21.5 centimeters

Ⓙ 31.5 centimeters

DAY 5

What is the slope of the linear function?

x	$f(x)$
5	3
3	6
1	9

Ⓐ –3

Ⓑ –1.5

Ⓒ 1.5

Ⓓ 3

Countdown to Mastery

WEEK 18

DAY 1

The table shows the number of wins by the Arizona Cardinals football team in four seasons. Given that the average number of wins for these seasons is 6, how many games did the team win in the 2006 season?

Arizona Cardinals	
Season	**Wins**
2004	6
2005	5
2006	?
2007	8

Ⓐ 4 Ⓒ 6

Ⓑ 5 Ⓓ 8

DAY 2

Two hats and two pairs of gloves cost $15. One hat and three pairs of gloves cost $16.50. How much does a hat cost?

Ⓕ $2.90

Ⓖ $3.00

Ⓗ $3.75

Ⓙ $4.50

DAY 3

Solve: $x - 2y = 3$

$x - y = 1$

Ⓐ (1, –1) Ⓒ (–1, –2)

Ⓑ (3, 2) Ⓓ (–1, 2)

DAY 4

Nina uses equilateral triangles to create the figure shown here. Find the side length x to the nearest tenth.

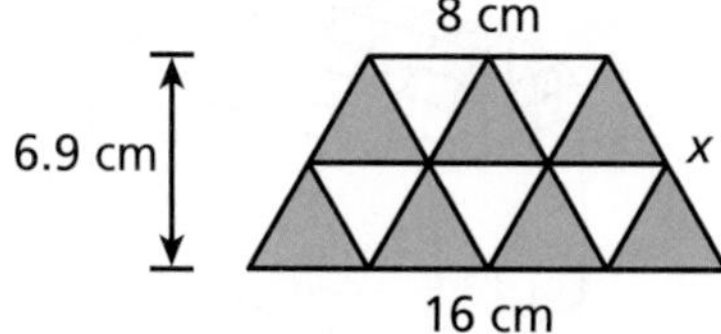

Ⓕ 7.7 cm

Ⓖ 8.0 cm

Ⓗ 9.3 cm

Ⓙ 12.0 cm

DAY 5

What is the scale factor from the smaller to larger rectangle?

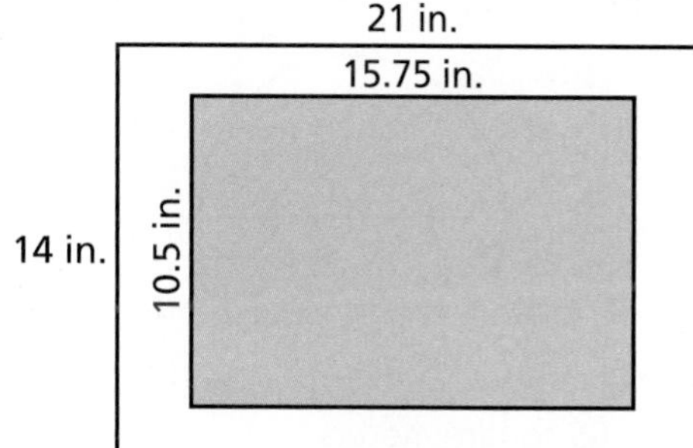

Ⓐ 1.3 Ⓒ 0.75

Ⓑ $\frac{4}{3}$ Ⓓ $\frac{2}{3}$

Countdown to Mastery

WEEK 19

DAY 1

A table tennis ball has a diameter of 40 mm. What is the volume of a table tennis ball in cubic millimeters?

Ⓐ $\frac{3,200\pi}{3}$
Ⓑ $\frac{64,000\pi}{3}$
Ⓒ $\frac{32,000\pi}{3}$
Ⓓ $1,600\pi$

DAY 2

Simplify: $4x - 12y + 2x + y^2$

Ⓕ $6x - 12y + y^2$
Ⓖ $6x - 11y^2$
Ⓗ $6x - 11y^3$
Ⓙ $2x - 12y + y^2$

DAY 3

Mia made this net of a triangular prism. What is the volume of the prism?

Ⓐ 321 cm^3
Ⓑ 337.5 cm^3
Ⓒ 675 cm^3
Ⓓ 915 cm^3

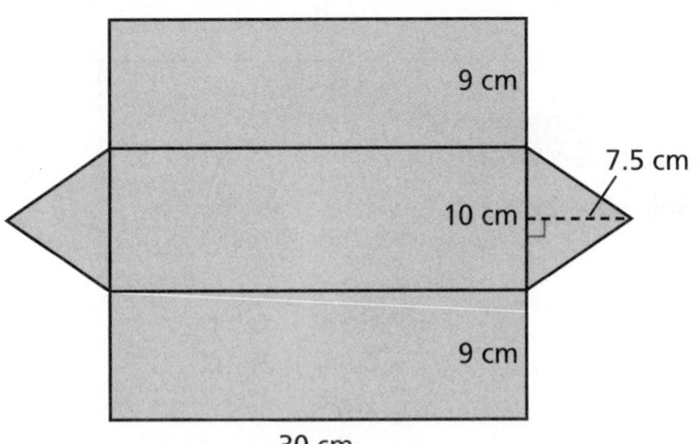

DAY 4

Paola drew a circle with four congruent circles inside it. If the area of the large circle is 167.2 square meters, what is the area of one small circle?

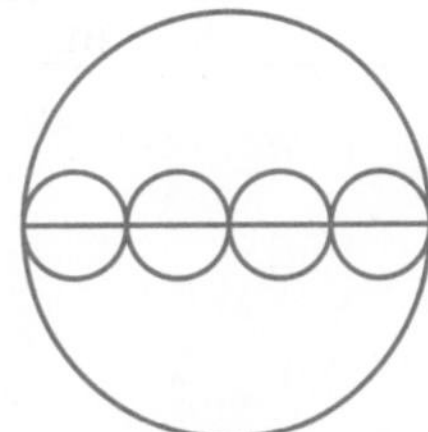

Ⓕ 5.65 square meters
Ⓖ 10.45 square meters
Ⓗ 18.54 square meters
Ⓙ 41.83 square meters

DAY 5

The roof of the greenhouse, which forms half a cylinder, is covered in glass. What is the volume of the glass roof?

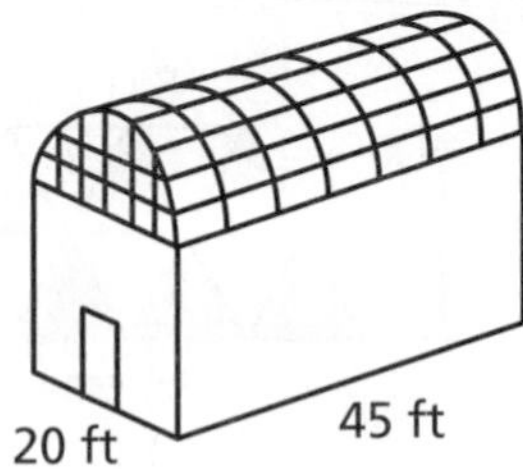

Ⓐ 1,727 ft^3
Ⓑ 12,810 ft^3
Ⓒ 14,130 ft^3
Ⓓ 56,520 ft^3

Countdown to Mastery

WEEK 20

DAY 1

The point (a, b) is reflected over the x-axis. What are the coordinates of the image?

Ⓐ $(a, -b)$

Ⓑ $(-a, b)$

Ⓒ (b, a)

Ⓓ (a, b)

DAY 2

Find the volume of a cone with a radius of 3 inches and a height of 5 inches.

Ⓕ 12π in^3

Ⓖ 15π in^3

Ⓗ 18π in^3

Ⓙ 60π in^3

DAY 3

What is the equation for the graph?

Ⓐ $y = x - 1$

Ⓑ $y = 2x + 2$

Ⓒ $y = 2x - 1$

Ⓓ $y = 0.5x - 1$

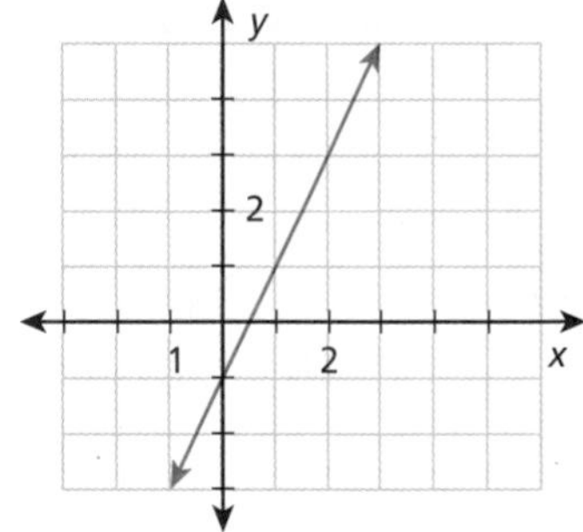

DAY 4

In this figure, each rectangle has $\frac{1}{4}$ less area than the rectangle directly enclosing it. What is the area of the smallest rectangle in this figure?

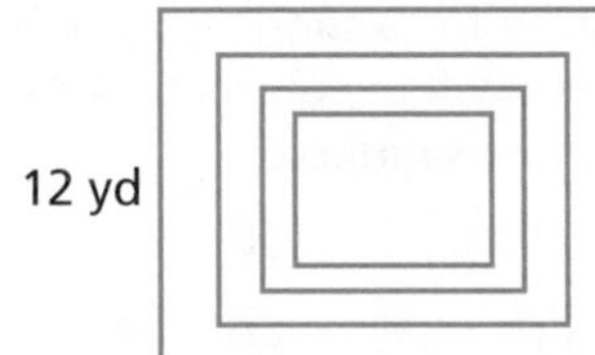

Ⓕ 81 square yards

Ⓖ 108 square yards

Ⓗ 144 square yards

Ⓙ 192 square yards

DAY 5

Kayla drove 512 mi over two days. The first day, she drove for 6 hours. The second day, she drove 188 miles. What was Kayla's average speed the first day?

Ⓐ 45 mi/h

Ⓑ 52 mi/h

Ⓒ 54 mi/h

Ⓓ 65 mi/h

Countdown to Mastery

WEEK 21

DAY 1

Each morning, Keri buys two bagels and a coffee drink. The coffee drink costs $2.50. At the end of a 5-day work week, she has spent a total of $27.50 on the bagels and coffee. What is the price of each bagel?

(A) $0.75
(B) $1.50
(C) $3.00
(D) $3.50

DAY 2

Approximately 6.0×10^5 gallons of water flows over the "horseshoe" section of Niagara Falls every second. How many gallons of water flow over this part of the falls in one minute?

(F) 3.6×10^6
(G) 2.16×10^7
(H) 3.6×10^7
(J) 2.16×10^9

DAY 3

Solve the system: $2x - y = -5$

$3x + y = -5$

(A) (2, 1)
(B) (–2, 1)
(C) (–1, –2)
(D) No solution

DAY 4

What is the y-intercept for the linear function shown in the table?

x	–5	3	7
y	10	12	13

(F) –1
(G) 0
(H) 7
(J) 11

DAY 5

Jimmy buys 44 feet of wood to build a square frame for a sandbox. The height of the sandbox will be 1.5 feet. What is the volume of the sandbox?

(A) 121 ft^3
(B) 154.5 ft^3
(C) 181.5 ft^3
(D) 192 ft^3

Countdown to Mastery

WEEK 22

DAY 1

Which conclusion can you draw about worker productivity based on the scatter plot?

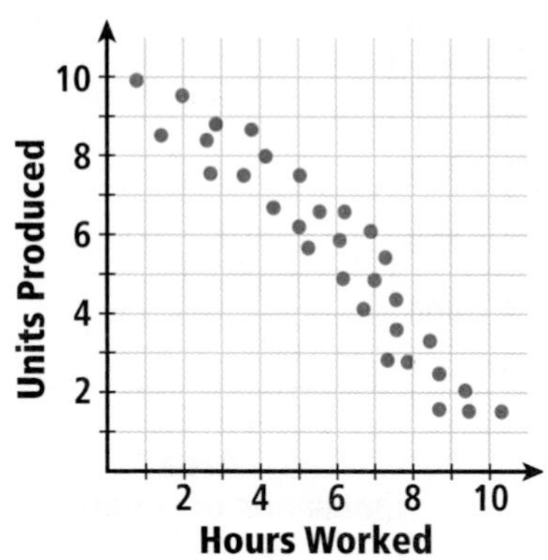

Ⓐ Productivity increases during the work day.

Ⓑ There is no trend for productivity in the scatter plot.

Ⓒ As the work day progresses, productivity declines.

Ⓓ Productivity remains constant during the work day.

DAY 2

The function $f(x)$ is graphed below. How does its slope compare to the slope of $g(x) = -\frac{3}{2}x + 3$?

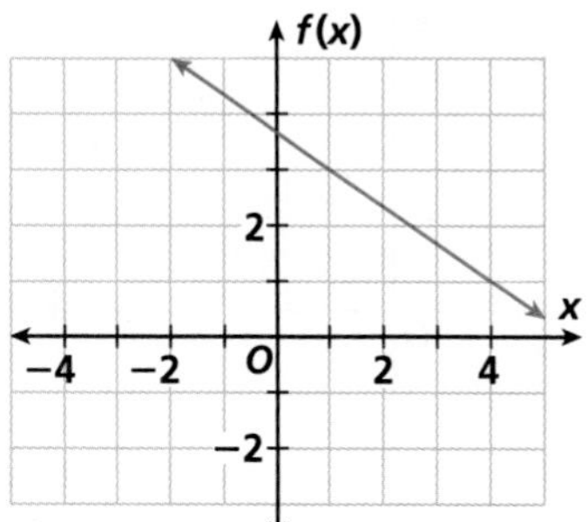

Ⓕ slope of $f <$ slope of g

Ⓖ slope of $f >$ slope of g

Ⓗ slope of $f =$ slope of g

Ⓙ The slopes are negative reciprocals.

DAY 3

An aquarium in the shape of a rectangular prism has a volume of 2160 in^3. It has a length of 15 in. and a width of 12 in. What is the height of the aquarium?

Ⓐ 6 in.

Ⓑ 12 in.

Ⓒ 15 in.

Ⓓ 80 in.

DAY 4

Ben is building a wall. What length of wood does Ben need to buy to create two cross beams for the frame? Round your answer to the nearest tenth.

Ⓕ 4.3 meters

Ⓖ 5.8 meters

Ⓗ 8.5 meters

Ⓙ 11.6 meters

DAY 5

What is the slope of the graph of the equation $2y - 4x = 10$?

Ⓐ -2

Ⓑ $-\frac{1}{2}$

Ⓒ 2

Ⓓ 5

Countdown to Mastery

WEEK 23

DAY 1

Which equation describes the relationship shown in the graph?

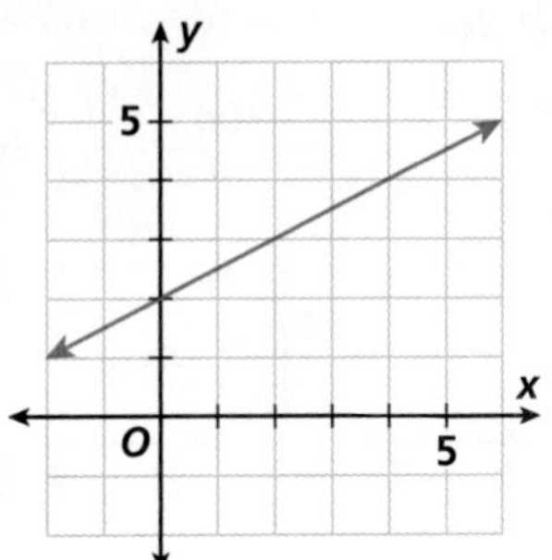

Ⓐ $y = 2x + \frac{1}{2}$

Ⓑ $y = \frac{1}{2}x - 2$

Ⓒ $y = \frac{1}{2}x + 2$

Ⓓ $y = 2x + 2$

DAY 2

Which conclusion can you draw based on the data in this scatter plot?

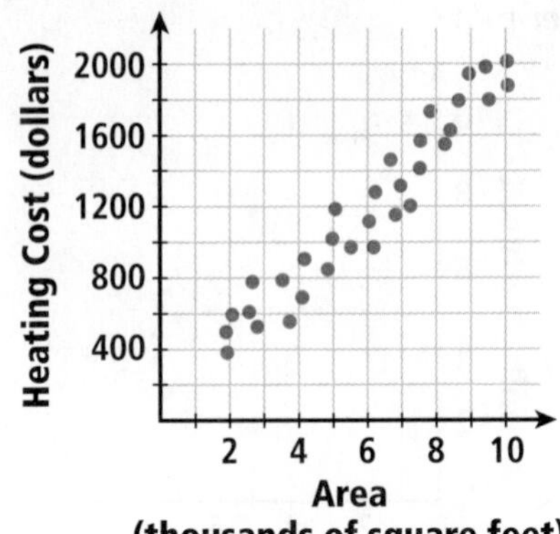

Ⓕ The smaller the area, the more expensive the heating costs.

Ⓖ Heating costs remain constant.

Ⓗ The scatter plot does not show a trend.

Ⓙ The larger the area, the greater the heating costs.

DAY 3

In a right triangle, the ratio of the acute angle measures is 3 to 5. What are the acute angle measures?

Ⓐ 30° and 50°

Ⓑ 33.75° and 56.25°

Ⓒ 33° and 55°

Ⓓ 36° and 60°

DAY 4

If the two rectangles are similar, what is the area of the smaller rectangle?

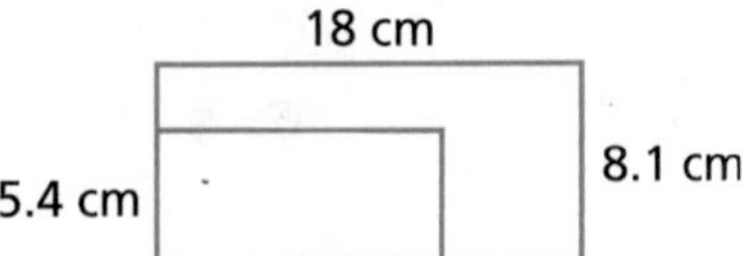

Ⓕ 13.8 cm^2

Ⓖ 34.8 cm^2

Ⓗ 64.8 cm^2

Ⓙ 145.8 cm^2

DAY 5

The temperature inside a freezer is 29°F. The temperature decreases at the rate of 6°F per hour. What equation gives a linear function for the temperature y inside the freezer after x hours?

Ⓐ $y = 29x - 6$

Ⓑ $y = 6x - 29$

Ⓒ $y = 6 - 29x$

Ⓓ $y = 29 - 6x$

Countdown to Mastery

WEEK 24

DAY 1

When it operates at capacity, the Magic Mile chairlift in Mount Hood, Oregon, carries 1,500 passengers in 30 minutes. How many passengers can the chairlift carry in 5 hours?

Ⓐ 3,000
Ⓑ 9,000
Ⓒ 15,000
Ⓓ 45,000

DAY 2

A quadrilateral in the plane has vertices at $A(0, 0)$, $B(1, 6)$, $C(8, 6)$, and $D(7, 0)$. If the figure is translated 3 units to the left, what are the coordinates of the image of point C?

Ⓕ C' (8, 3)
Ⓖ C' (5, 6)
Ⓗ C' (8, –6)
Ⓙ C' (5, 3)

DAY 3

The figure shown is rotated 90° clockwise about the origin. What are the coordinates of the image of point H?

Ⓐ (1, –3)
Ⓑ (3, –1)
Ⓒ (–1, 3)
Ⓓ (–1, –3)

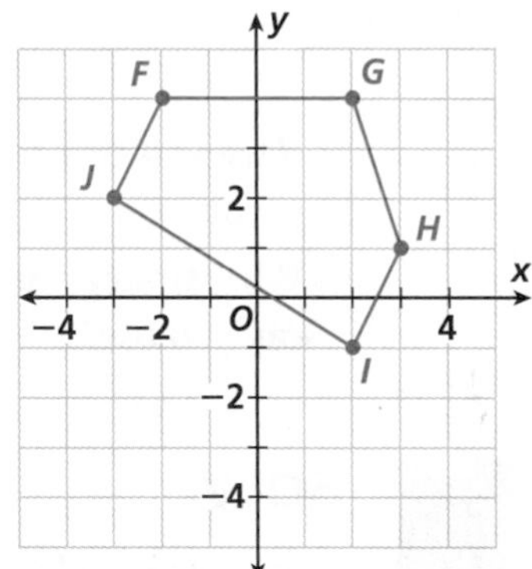

DAY 4

Mrs. Weyland is making 7 cups of juice for her children's friends. If she wants to serve each guest $\frac{3}{4}$ cup of juice, how many children will the juice serve?

Ⓕ 8
Ⓖ 9
Ⓗ 10
Ⓙ 11

DAY 5

The point (1, 4) is reflected over the y-axis, and then rotated 90° clockwise about the origin. What are the coordinates of the image after both transformations?

Ⓐ (4, 1)
Ⓑ (–1, –4)
Ⓒ (4, –1)
Ⓓ (1, –4)

Focus on Problem Solving

The Problem Solving Process

In order to be a good problem solver, you first need a good problem-solving process. A process or strategy will help you to understand the problem, to work through a solution, and to check that your answer makes sense. The process used in this book is detailed below.

UNDERSTAND the Problem

- **What are you asked to find?** Restate the problem in your own words.
- **What information is given?** Identify the important facts in the problem.
- **What information do you need?** Determine which facts are needed to solve the problem.
- **Is all the information given?** Determine whether all the facts are given.

Make a PLAN

- **Have you ever solved a similar problem?** Think about other problems like this that you successfully solved.
- **What strategy or strategies can you use?** Determine a strategy that you can use and how you will use it.

SOLVE

- **Follow your plan.** Show the steps in your solution. Write your answer as a complete sentence.

LOOK BACK

- **Have you answered the question?** Be sure that you answered the question that is being asked.
- **Is your answer reasonable?** Your answer should make sense in the context of the problem.
- **Is there another strategy you could use?** Solving the problem using another strategy is a good way to check your work.
- **Did you learn anything while solving this problem that could help you solve similar problems in the future?** Try to remember the problems you have solved and the strategies you used to solve them.

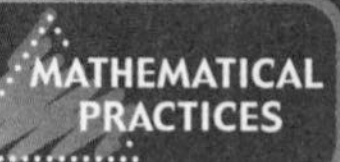

Using the Problem Solving Process

In a game at an amusement park, players throw 3 darts at a target to score points and win prizes. If each dart lands within the target area, how many different total scores are possible?

UNDERSTAND the Problem

Identify the important information.

- A player throws three darts at the target.
- Each dart can score 2 points, 5 points, or 10 points.

The answer will be the number of different scores a player could earn.

Make a PLAN

You can **make an organized list** to determine all possible outcomes and score totals. List the value of each dart and the point total for all three darts.

SOLVE

You can organize your list by the number of darts that land in the center. All three darts could hit the center circle. Or, two darts could hit the center circle and the third could hit a different circle. One dart could hit the center circle, or no darts could hit the center circle.

3 Darts Hit Center	2 Darts Hit Center	1 Dart Hits Center	0 Darts Hit Center
10 + 10 + 10 = 30	10 + 10 + 5 = 25	10 + 5 + 5 = 20	5 + 5 + 5 = 15
	10 + 10 + 2 = 22	10 + 5 + 2 = 17	5 + 5 + 2 = 12
		10 + 2 + 2 = 14	5 + 2 + 2 = 9
			2 + 2 + 2 = 6

Count the different outcomes. There are 10 possible scores.

LOOK BACK

You could have listed outcomes in random order, but because your list is organized, you can be sure that you have not missed any possibilities. Check to be sure that every score is different.

Using Your Book for Success

This book has many features designed to help you learn and study math. Becoming familiar with these features will prepare you for greater success on your exams.

Learn

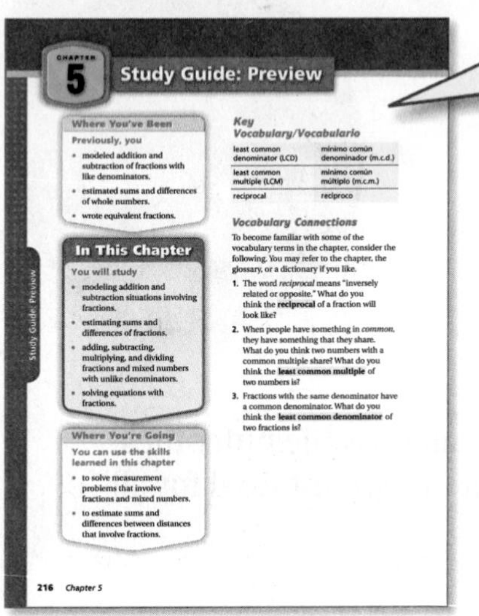

Before starting a chapter, read the **Study Guide: Preview** to help you understand the concepts that are taught in the chapter.

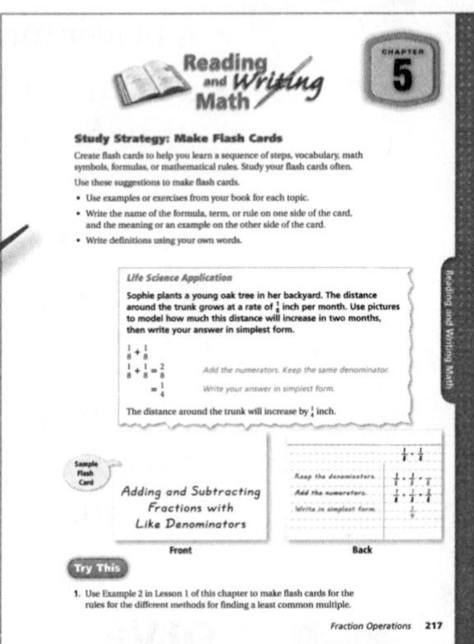

Review the **Reading and Writing Math** to learn about reading, writing, and study strategies.

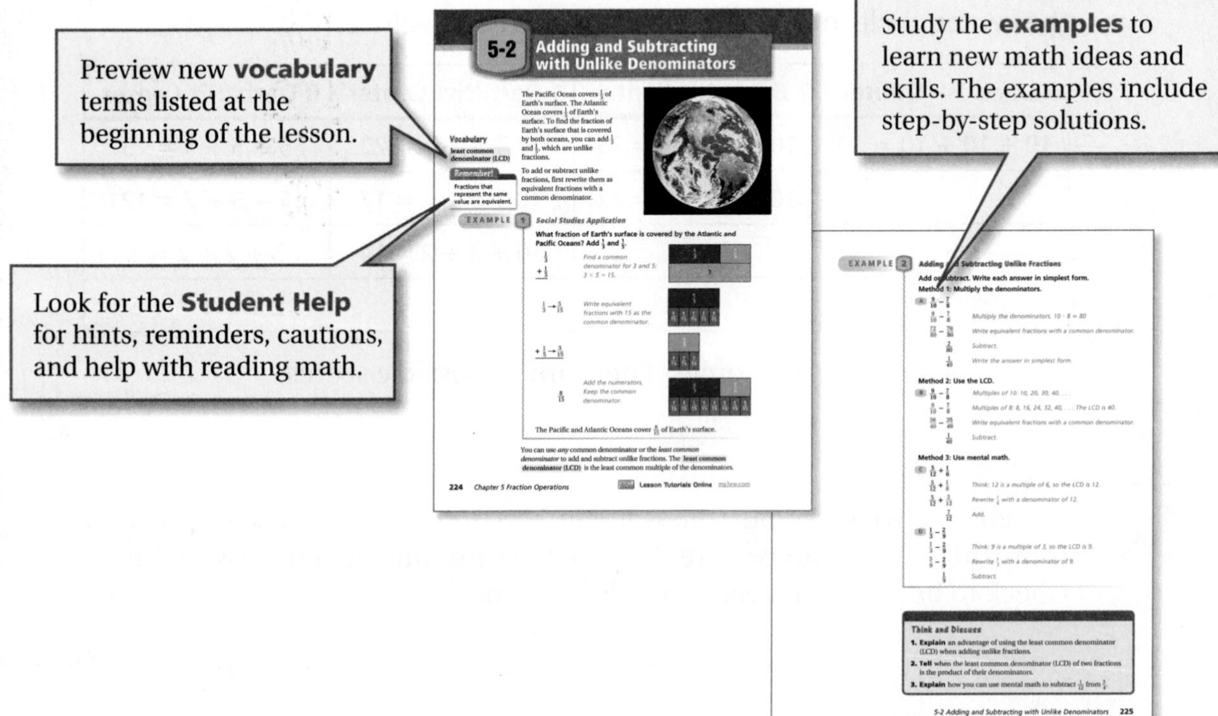

Preview new **vocabulary** terms listed at the beginning of the lesson.
Study the **examples** to learn new math ideas and skills. The examples include step-by-step solutions.
Look for the **Student Help** for hints, reminders, cautions, and help with reading math.

Practice

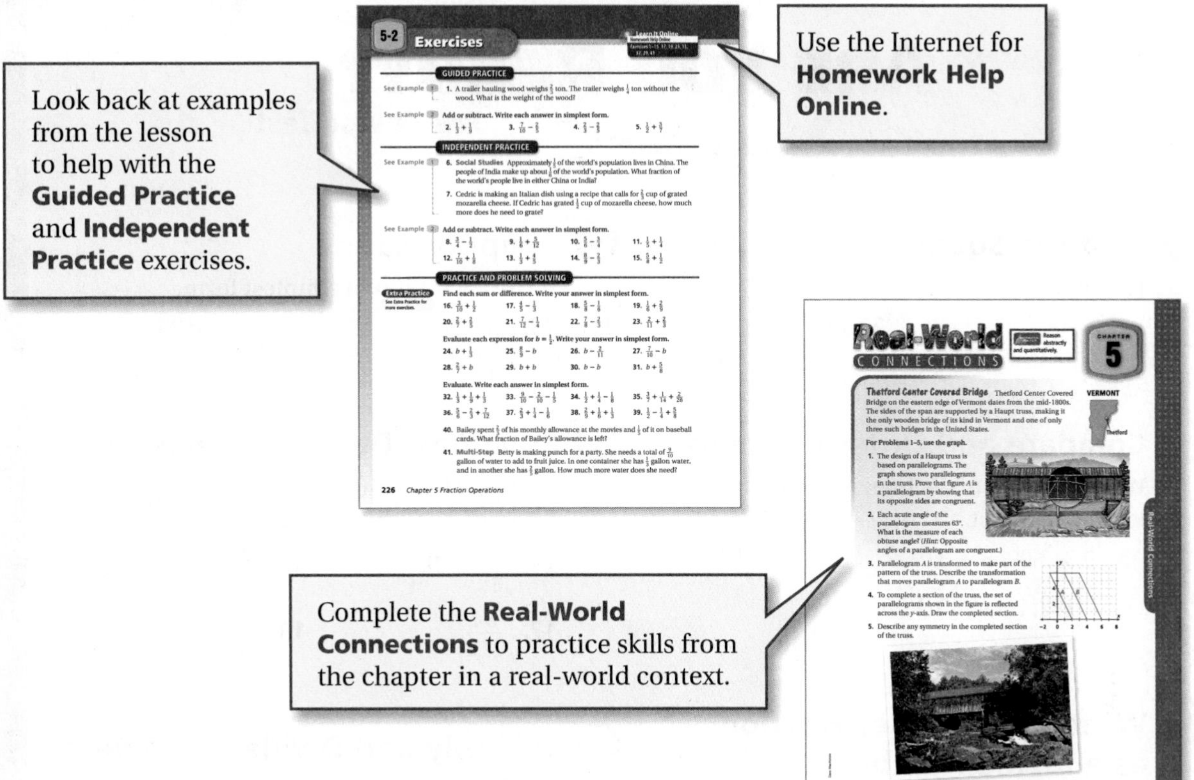

Look back at examples from the lesson to help with the **Guided Practice** and **Independent Practice** exercises.
Use the Internet for **Homework Help Online**.
Complete the **Real-World Connections** to practice skills from the chapter in a real-world context.

Review

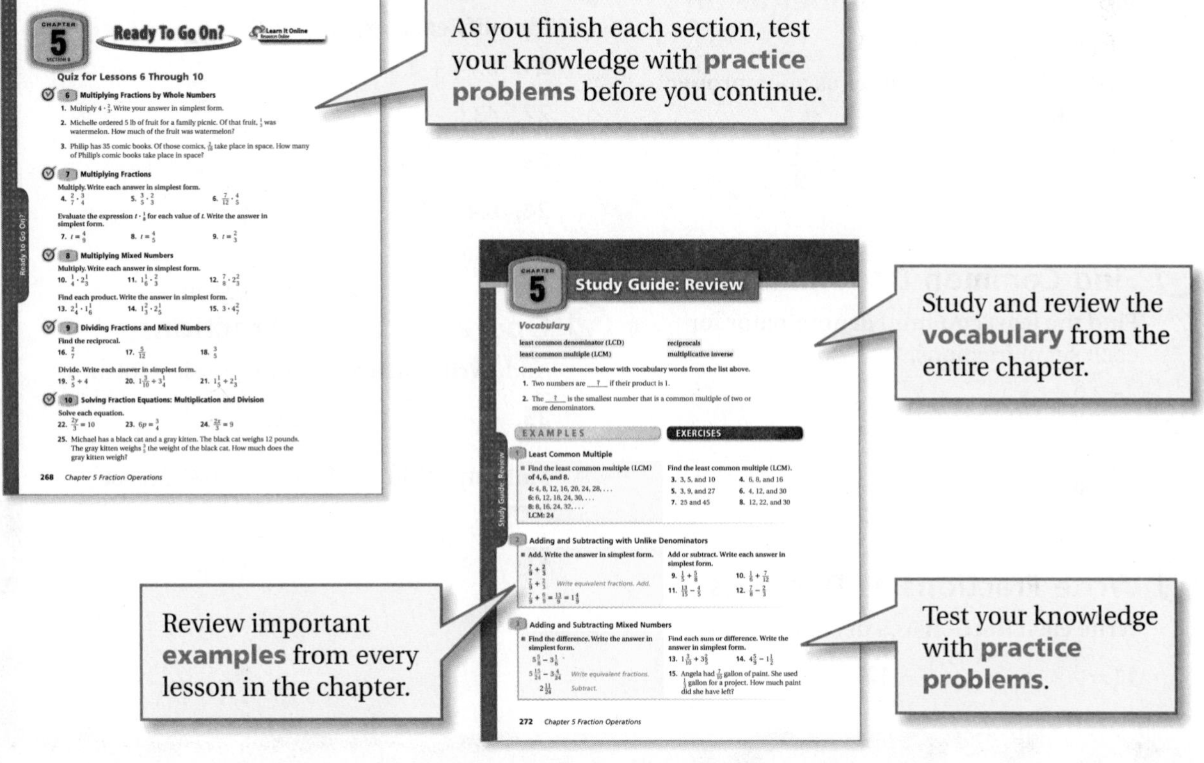

As you finish each section, test your knowledge with **practice problems** before you continue.
Study and review the **vocabulary** from the entire chapter.
Review important **examples** from every lesson in the chapter.
Test your knowledge with **practice problems**.

ARE YOU READY?

Pre-Course Test

Find the Square of a Number

Evaluate.

1. 31^2

2. $(5.6)^2$

Compare and Order Decimals

Write each set of decimals in order from least to greatest.

3. 9.3, 3.09, 3.9, 3.011

4. 2.187, 2.1, 1.85, 1.58

Write an Improper Fraction as a Mixed Number

Write each improper fraction as a mixed number.

5. $\frac{29}{6}$

6. $\frac{131}{15}$

Write a Mixed Number as an Improper Fraction

Write each mixed number as an improper fraction.

7. $8\frac{3}{7}$

8. $19\frac{4}{9}$

Find Common Denominators

Find the least common denominator for each set of fractions.

9. $\frac{3}{8}$ and $\frac{5}{6}$

10. $\frac{1}{8}, \frac{1}{9},$ and $\frac{1}{12}$

Write Fractions as Decimals

Write each fraction as a decimal.

11. $\frac{3}{5}$

12. $\frac{17}{25}$

Simplify Ratios

Write each ratio in simplest form.

13. 38:42

14. 150 to 36

Fractions, Decimals, Percents

Write each fraction as a decimal and a percent.

15. $\frac{7}{8}$

16. $\frac{9}{75}$

17. $\frac{84}{112}$

18. $\frac{120}{75}$

Multiply and Divide by Powers of Ten

Multiply or divide.

19. 863(1000)

20. $\frac{19}{10{,}000}$

Decimal Operations

Simplify each expression.

21. $8.76 + 3.5$

22. $43.8 - 5.9$

23. $16.7 \cdot 5.3$

24. $6.4 \div 2.5$

Operations with Fractions

Add. Write each answer in simplest form.

25. $\frac{3}{8} + \frac{5}{12}$

26. $\frac{2}{3} + \frac{3}{4} + \frac{4}{5}$

Multiply. Write each answer in simplest form.

27. $\frac{3}{4} \cdot \frac{8}{9}$

28. $\frac{5}{7} \cdot \frac{3}{8}$

Multiply with Fractions and Decimals

Multiply. Write each answer to the nearest tenth.

29. $\frac{1}{3}(3.14)(2.3)^2(18)$

30. $\frac{4}{3}(3.14)(3.6)^3$

Integer Operations

Simplify each expression.

31. $38 - (-16)$

32. $21(-34)$

Multiplication Properties (Distributive)

Replace each ■ with a number so that each equation illustrates the Distributive Property.

33. $6 \times (50 + 22) = 6 \times 50 + 6 \times$ ■

34. $25 \times ($■$ - 3) = 25 \times 9 - 25 \times 3$

Order of Operations

Simplify by using the order of operations.

35. $(31 - 9) - 12 \div 2$

36. $36 \div 3 + 72 \div 9$

37. $8(16 - 7)$

38. $100 - 28 \times 2$

Evaluate Expressions

Evaluate each expression for the given value(s) of the variable(s).

39. $5x - 8$ for $x = -18$

40. $-3x + 4$ for $x = 21$

41. $a + (b - 1)c$ for $a = 8, b = 7, c = 3$

42. $a \times b^c$ for $a = 2, b = 3, c = 4$

Solve One-Step Equations

Use mental math to solve each equation.

43. $m + 7 = -25$

44. $p - 8 = -16$

Solve Two-Step Equations

Solve each equation.

45. $16w + 19 = 67$

46. $23x - 98 = 63$

Graph Linear Equations

Use the slope and the *y*-intercept to graph each line.

47. $y = \frac{2}{3}x + 2$

48. $y = -\frac{1}{2}x - 4$

Read a Table

Use the table for problems 49 and 50.

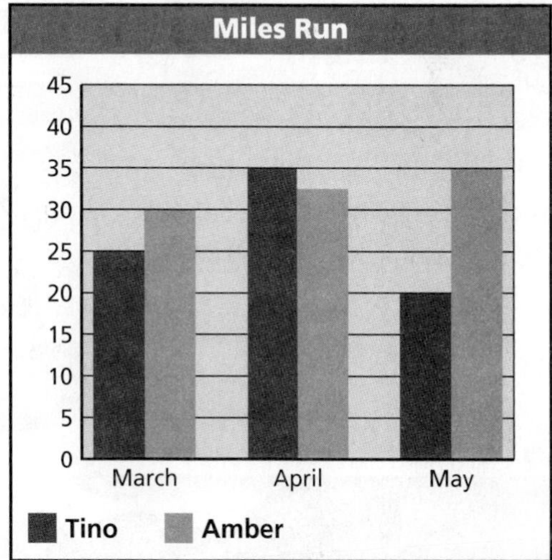

49. How many total miles did Tino run in March, April, and May?

50. For which month did Amber run the least number of miles?

CHAPTER

1 Rational Numbers

Chapter Focus

- Multiply and divide rational numbers.
- Use the arithmetic of rational numbers to solve equations.

Why Learn This?

Auto racing speeds, times, and victory margins can be expressed as rational numbers, such as fractions and decimals.

Learn It Online
Chapter Project Online

Are You Ready?

Vocabulary

Choose the best term from the list to complete each sentence.

1. A number that consists of a whole number and a fraction is called a(n) __?__.
2. A(n) __?__ is a number that represents a part of a whole.
3. A fraction whose absolute value is at least 1 is called a(n) __?__, and a fraction whose absolute value is between 0 and 1 is called a(n) __?__.
4. A(n) __?__ names the same value.

equivalent fraction
fraction
improper fraction
mixed number
proper fraction

Complete these exercises to review skills you will need for this chapter.

Model Fractions

Write a fraction to represent the shaded portion of each diagram.

5.

6.

7.

8.

Write a Fraction as a Mixed Number

Write each improper fraction as a mixed number.

9. $\frac{22}{7}$ **10.** $\frac{18}{5}$ **11.** $\frac{104}{25}$ **12.** $\frac{65}{9}$ **13.** $\frac{37}{3}$

Write a Mixed Number as a Fraction

Write each mixed number as an improper fraction.

14. $7\frac{1}{4}$ **15.** $10\frac{3}{7}$ **16.** $5\frac{3}{8}$ **17.** $11\frac{1}{11}$ **18.** $3\frac{5}{6}$

Write Equivalent Fractions

Supply the missing information.

19. $\frac{3}{8} = \frac{\blacksquare}{24}$ **20.** $\frac{5}{13} = \frac{\blacksquare}{52}$ **21.** $\frac{7}{12} = \frac{\blacksquare}{36}$ **22.** $\frac{8}{15} = \frac{\blacksquare}{45}$ **23.** $\frac{3}{5} = \frac{\blacksquare}{75}$

Study Guide: Preview

Where You've Been

Previously, you

- compared and ordered positive rational numbers.
- added, subtracted, multiplied, and divided integers.
- used models to solve equations.

In This Chapter

You will study

- using appropriate operations to solve problems involving fractions and decimals.
- finding solutions to application problems using equations.
- solving two-step equations.

Where You're Going

You can use the skills learned in this chapter

- to add and manipulate measurements.
- to find the size of a fraction of a group or an item.
- to solve more complicated equations in future math courses.

Key Vocabulary/Vocabulario

rational number	número racional
reciprocal	recíproco
relatively prime	primo relativo

Vocabulary Connections

To become familiar with some of the vocabulary terms in the chapter, consider the following. You may refer to the chapter, the glossary, or a dictionary if you like.

1. The word *rational* has as its root the word *ratio* and sounds somewhat like the word *fraction*. What do you think a **rational number** is in math?
2. The word *relative* means "in relation to each other." What do you think **relatively prime** numbers are?

Writing Strategy: Translate Between Words and Math

When reading a real-world math problem, look for key words to help you translate between the words and the math.

There are several different ways to indicate a mathematical operation in words.

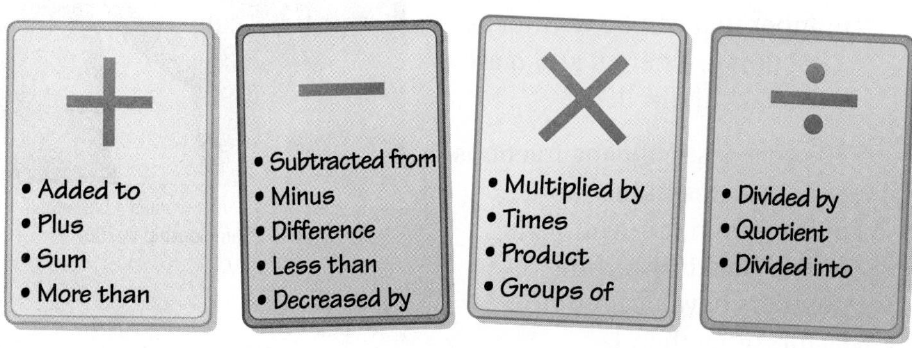

+
• Added to
• Plus
• Sum
• More than
−
• Subtracted from
• Minus
• Difference
• Less than
• Decreased by
×
• Multiplied by
• Times
• Product
• Groups of
÷
• Divided by
• Quotient
• Divided into

In the problem below, use the highlighted terms to translate the words into math.

The Montez family went to the state fair over the weekend. They spent \$52.50 on rides, food, and drinks, in addition to the \$5.50-per-person price of admission. How much did the Montez family spend at the fair?

They spent \$52.50 **in addition to** \$5.50 **per** **person**.

Let p represent the number of people.

\$52.50 + \$5.50 × p $= 52.5 + 5.5p$

Try This

Identify the mathematical operation described by the key terms in each statement. Explain your choice.

1. The male calf weighs 0.55 pounds less than the female calf.
2. Bob has 9 more books than Kerri.
3. The number of treats is divided by the number of students.
4. The rate is \$15 plus two times the cost of the paint.

1-1 Rational Numbers

COMMON CORE

CC.8.NS.1: Understand informally that every number has a decimal expansion; the rational numbers are those with decimal expansions that terminate in 0s or eventually repeat. Know that other numbers are called irrational.

Vocabulary

rational number

relatively prime

In 2007, there were 335 NCAA Division I women's basketball teams. At the end of the season, 64 teams were selected for the women's NCAA basketball tournament. Only $\frac{64}{335}$ of the teams qualified for the tournament.

The Tennessee Lady Vols women's basketball team won its seventh national championship in 2007.

A **rational number** is any number that can be written as a fraction $\frac{n}{d}$, where n and d are integers and $d \neq 0$.

The goal of simplifying fractions is to make the numerator and the denominator *relatively prime.* **Relatively prime** numbers have no common factors other than 1.

You can often simplify fractions by dividing both the numerator and denominator by the same nonzero integer. You can simplify the fraction $\frac{12}{15}$ to $\frac{4}{5}$ by dividing both the numerator and denominator by 3.

12 of the 15 boxes are shaded.

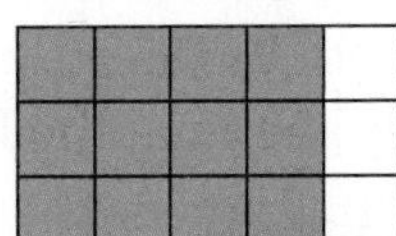

$$\frac{12 \div 3}{15 \div 3} = \frac{4}{5}$$

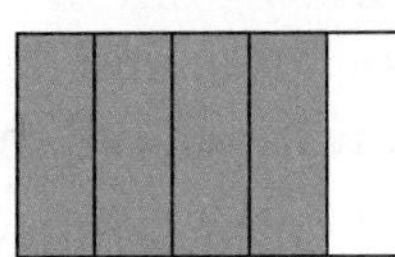

4 of the 5 boxes are shaded.

The same total area is shaded.

EXAMPLE 1 Simplifying Fractions

Remember!

$\frac{0}{a} = 0$ for $a \neq 0$

$\frac{a}{a} = 1$ for $a \neq 0$

$\frac{-7}{8} = \frac{7}{-8} = -\frac{7}{8}$

Simplify.

A $\frac{9}{55}$

$9 = 3 \cdot 3$, $55 = 5 \cdot 11$; there are no common factors.

$\frac{9}{55} = \frac{9}{55}$ *9 and 55 are relatively prime.*

B $\frac{-24}{32}$

$\frac{-24}{32} = \frac{-24 \div 8}{32 \div 8}$ *$24 = (2 \cdot 2 \cdot 2) \cdot 3$, $32 = (2 \cdot 2 \cdot 2) \cdot 2 \cdot 2$; 8 is a common factor.*

$= \frac{-3}{4}$, or $-\frac{3}{4}$ *Divide the numerator and denominator by 8.*

Gregory Shamus/Getty Images

Writing Math

A repeating decimal can be written with a bar over the digits that repeat. So $0.13333\ldots = 0.1\overline{3}$.

Decimals that terminate or repeat are rational numbers.

Rational Number	Description	Written as a Fraction
-3.2	Terminating decimal	$-3\frac{2}{10}$
$0.1\overline{3}$	Repeating decimal	$\frac{2}{15}$

To write a terminating decimal as a fraction, identify the place value of the digit farthest to the right. Then write all of the digits after the decimal point as the numerator with the place value as the denominator.

EXAMPLE 2 Writing Decimals as Fractions

Write each decimal as a fraction in simplest form.

A -5.59

$-5.59 = -5\frac{59}{100}$ *9 is in the hundredths place.*

B 0.5714

$0.5714 = \frac{5714}{10{,}000}$ *4 is in the ten-thousandths place.*

$= \frac{2857}{5000}$ *Simplify by dividing by the common factor 2.*

To write a fraction as a decimal, divide the numerator by the denominator.

EXAMPLE 3 Writing Fractions as Decimals

Write each fraction as a decimal.

A $\frac{5}{4}$

```
    1.25
 4)5.00
  -4
   10
   -8
    20
   -20
     0
```

The remainder is 0. This is a terminating decimal.

The fraction $\frac{5}{4}$ is equivalent to the decimal 1.25.

B $-\frac{1}{6}$

$0.1\overline{6}$

```
    0.16
 6)1.000
  -6
   40
  -36
    40
```

Leave the negative sign off while dividing.

The pattern repeats.

The fraction $-\frac{1}{6}$ is equivalent to the decimal $-0.1\overline{6}$.

MATHEMATICAL PRACTICES

Think and Discuss

1. **Explain** how you can be sure that a fraction is simplified.
2. **Give** the sign of a fraction in which the numerator is negative and the denominator is negative.

1-1 Exercises

Learn It Online
Homework Help Online
Exercises 1-56, 59, 63

GUIDED PRACTICE

See Example 1 **Simplify.**

1. $\frac{11}{22}$
2. $\frac{6}{10}$
3. $-\frac{16}{24}$
4. $\frac{14}{25}$
5. $\frac{17}{51}$
6. $\frac{57}{69}$
7. $-\frac{6}{8}$
8. $\frac{9}{28}$
9. $\frac{49}{112}$
10. $\frac{22}{44}$

See Example 2 **Write each decimal as a fraction in simplest form.**

11. 0.75
12. 1.125
13. 0.4
14. 0.35
15. −2.2
16. 0.625
17. 3.21
18. −0.3878

See Example 3 **Write each fraction as a decimal.**

19. $\frac{5}{8}$
20. $-\frac{3}{5}$
21. $\frac{5}{12}$
22. $\frac{1}{4}$
23. $\frac{1}{9}$
24. $-\frac{18}{9}$
25. $\frac{3}{8}$
26. $-\frac{14}{5}$
27. $\frac{5}{4}$
28. $\frac{2}{3}$

INDEPENDENT PRACTICE

See Example 1 **Simplify.**

29. $\frac{21}{28}$
30. $\frac{25}{65}$
31. $-\frac{17}{34}$
32. $-\frac{17}{21}$
33. $\frac{25}{30}$
34. $\frac{13}{17}$
35. $\frac{22}{35}$
36. $\frac{64}{76}$
37. $-\frac{78}{126}$
38. $\frac{14}{22}$

See Example 2 **Write each decimal as a fraction in simplest form.**

39. 0.6
40. 3.5
41. 0.72
42. −0.183
43. 1.377
44. 1.450
45. −1.4
46. −2.9

See Example 3 **Write each fraction as a decimal.**

47. $-\frac{3}{8}$
48. $\frac{7}{12}$
49. $-\frac{9}{5}$
50. $\frac{13}{20}$
51. $\frac{8}{5}$
52. $\frac{18}{40}$
53. $-\frac{23}{5}$
54. $\frac{28}{25}$
55. $\frac{4}{3}$
56. $-\frac{7}{4}$

PRACTICE AND PROBLEM SOLVING

Extra Practice
See Extra Practice for more exercises.

Mental Math Make up a fraction that cannot be simplified and has the following characteristics.

57. a denominator of 36
58. a denominator of 24
59. **Sports** The thickness of a surfboard is often matched to the weight of the rider. For example, a person weighing 170 pounds might need a surfboard that is 3.375 inches thick. Write 3.375 as a fraction in simplest form.
60. Bondi weighed his mobile phone and found it to be approximately $\frac{7}{25}$ pound. What is the weight of Bondi's phone written as a decimal?

61. **a.** Simplify each fraction.

$\frac{8}{18}$ $\frac{8}{48}$ $\frac{5}{20}$ $\frac{21}{45}$ $\frac{18}{32}$ $\frac{24}{50}$ $\frac{45}{72}$ $\frac{36}{96}$

b. Write the denominator of each simplified fraction as the product of prime factors.

c. Write each simplified fraction as a decimal. Label each as a terminating or repeating decimal.

62. **Measurement** The ruler is marked at every $\frac{1}{16}$ in. Do the labeled measurements convert to terminating or repeating decimals?

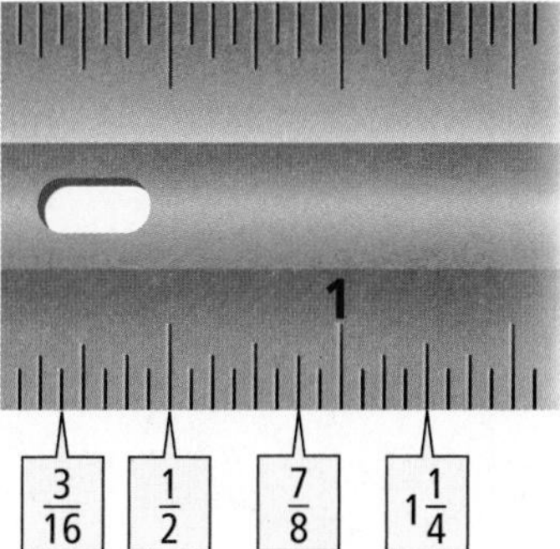

63. **Critical Thinking** The greatest common factor, GCF, is the largest common factor of two or more given numbers. Find and remove the GCF of 42 and 68 from the fraction $\frac{42}{68}$. Can the resulting fraction be further simplified? Explain.

64. **What's the Error?** A student simplified a fraction in this manner: $\frac{-25}{-30} = -\frac{5}{6}$. What error did the student make?

65. **Write About It** Using your answers to Exercise 61, examine the prime factors in the denominators of the simplified fractions that are equivalent to terminating decimals. Then examine the prime factors in the denominators of the simplified fractions that are equivalent to repeating decimals. What pattern do you see?

66. **Challenge** A student simplified a fraction to $-\frac{2}{9}$ by removing the common factors, which were 2 and 9. What was the original fraction?

Test Prep

67. **Multiple Choice** If $y = -\frac{3}{9}$, which is NOT equal to y?

Ⓐ $\frac{-1}{3}$ Ⓑ $-\frac{1}{3}$ Ⓒ $-\left(\frac{-1}{3}\right)$ Ⓓ $-\left(\frac{-1}{-3}\right)$

68. **Multiple Choice** Which shows the decimal 0.68 as a fraction in simplest form?

Ⓕ $\frac{17}{25}$ Ⓖ $\frac{34}{50}$ Ⓗ $\frac{3}{4}$ Ⓙ $\frac{6}{8}$

69. **Gridded Response** What is the decimal equivalent of the fraction $\frac{119}{4}$?

1-2 Multiplying Rational Numbers

Andrew walks his dog each day. His route is $\frac{1}{8}$ mile. What is the total distance that Andrew walks his dog in a 5-day week?

Recall that multiplication is repeated addition.

$$3\left(\frac{1}{4}\right) = \frac{1}{4} + \frac{1}{4} + \frac{1}{4}$$

$$= \frac{1+1+1}{4}$$

$$= \frac{3}{4}$$

Notice that multiplying a fraction by a whole number is the same as multiplying the whole number by just the numerator of the fraction and keeping the same denominator.

RULES FOR MULTIPLYING TWO RATIONAL NUMBERS
If the signs of the factors are the same, the product is positive.
(+) · (+) = (+) **or** (−) · (−) = (+)
If the signs of the factors are different, the product is negative.
(+) · (−) = (−) **or** (−) · (+) = (−)

EXAMPLE 1 Multiplying a Fraction and an Integer

Multiply. Write each answer in simplest form.

A $6\left(\frac{2}{3}\right)$

$6\left(\frac{2}{3}\right)$

$\frac{6 \cdot 2}{3}$

$\frac{12}{3}$ *Multiply.*

4 *Simplify.*

B $-2\left(3\frac{1}{5}\right)$

$-2\left(3\frac{1}{5}\right)$

$-2\left(\frac{16}{5}\right)$ $\quad 3\frac{1}{5} = \frac{3(5)+1}{5} = \frac{16}{5}$

$-\frac{32}{5}$ *Multiply (−) · (+) = (−).*

$-6\frac{2}{5}$ *Simplify.*

Helpful Hint

To write $-\frac{32}{5}$ as a mixed number, divide:

$$-\frac{32}{5} = -6 \text{ R2}$$

$$= -6\frac{2}{5}$$

Sam Dudgeon/HMH

Video Lesson Tutorials Online my.hrw.com

EXAMPLE 2 Multiplying Fractions

Caution!

A fraction is in lowest terms, or simplest form, when the numerator and denominator have no common factors.

Multiply. Write each answer in simplest form.

A $-\frac{3}{5}\left(-\frac{1}{4}\right)$

$-\frac{3}{5}\left(-\frac{1}{4}\right) = \frac{-3}{5}\left(\frac{-1}{4}\right)$

$= \frac{(-3)(-1)}{5(4)}$ *Multiply numerators. Multiply denominators.*

$= \frac{3}{20}$ *Simplify.*

B $\frac{5}{12}\left(-\frac{12}{5}\right)$

$\frac{5}{12}\left(-\frac{12}{5}\right) = \frac{5}{12}\left(-\frac{12}{5}\right)$

$= \frac{{}^{1}\cancel{5}(-\cancel{12})^{-1}}{{}_{1}\cancel{12}(\cancel{5})_{1}}$ *Look for common factors: 12, 5.*

$= \frac{-1}{1} = -1$ *Simplify.*

EXAMPLE 3 Multiplying Decimals

Multiply.

A $-5.2(-5)$

$-5.2 \cdot (-5) = 26.0$ *Product is positive with 1 decimal place.*

$= 26$

You can drop the zero after the decimal point.

B $-0.07(4.6)$

$-0.07 \cdot 4.6 = -0.322$

Product is negative with 3 decimal places.

EXAMPLE 4 *Recreation Application*

Andrew walks his dog $\frac{1}{8}$ mile each day. What is the total distance that Andrew walks his dog in a 5-day week?

$\frac{1}{8}(5) = \frac{1 \cdot 5}{8}$

$= \frac{5}{8}$ *Multiply.*

Andrew walks his dog $\frac{5}{8}$ mile in a 5-day week.

Think and Discuss

1. **Give an example** of a multiplication problem with two factors where the product is **a.** greater than the factors. **b.** between the factors. **c.** less than the factors.
2. **Give an example** of two fractions whose product is an integer due to common factors.

1-2 Exercises

Learn It Online
Homework Help Online
Exercises 1-38, 39, 41, 45, 47, 49, 51, 53

GUIDED PRACTICE

See Example 1 — Multiply. Write each answer in simplest form.

1. $5\left(\frac{1}{2}\right)$ 2. $-7\left(1\frac{3}{4}\right)$ 3. $3\left(\frac{5}{8}\right)$ 4. $-4\left(5\frac{2}{3}\right)$

See Example 2

5. $-\frac{1}{4}\left(-\frac{5}{8}\right)$ 6. $\frac{3}{8}\left(-\frac{7}{10}\right)$ 7. $6\frac{3}{7}\left(\frac{7}{8}\right)$ 8. $-\frac{3}{5}\left(-\frac{5}{9}\right)$

See Example 3 — Multiply.

9. $-2.1(-7)$ 10. $0.03(5.4)$ 11. $-4.8(-2)$ 12. $-0.15(2.8)$

See Example 4

13. Tran jogs $\frac{3}{4}$ mile each day. How far does Tran jog in 6 days?

INDEPENDENT PRACTICE

See Example 1 — Multiply. Write each answer in simplest form.

14. $5\left(\frac{1}{7}\right)$ 15. $-3\left(1\frac{5}{6}\right)$ 16. $9\left(\frac{4}{21}\right)$ 17. $-7\left(1\frac{2}{3}\right)$

18. $9\left(\frac{14}{15}\right)$ 19. $-3\left(6\frac{7}{9}\right)$ 20. $8\left(\frac{3}{4}\right)$ 21. $-7\left(3\frac{1}{5}\right)$

See Example 2

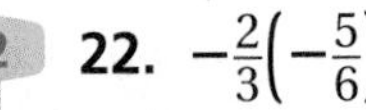

22. $-\frac{2}{3}\left(-\frac{5}{6}\right)$ 23. $\frac{2}{9}\left(-\frac{7}{8}\right)$ 24. $5\frac{7}{8}\left(\frac{5}{11}\right)$ 25. $-\frac{1}{3}\left(-\frac{7}{8}\right)$

26. $\frac{3}{7}\left(-\frac{5}{6}\right)$ 27. $2\frac{1}{7}\left(\frac{7}{10}\right)$ 28. $-\frac{2}{3}\left(-\frac{1}{9}\right)$ 29. $\frac{7}{8}\left(\frac{3}{5}\right)$

See Example 3 — Multiply.

30. $-1.7(-4)$ 31. $-0.05(4.7)$ 32. $-6.2(-7)$ 33. $-0.75(5.5)$

34. $-6.2(-9)$ 35. $-0.08(6.2)$ 36. $-2.4(-9)$ 37. $-0.04(9.2)$

See Example 4

38. There was $\frac{3}{4}$ of a pizza left over from a family gathering. The next day, Tina ate $\frac{1}{2}$ of what was left. How much of the whole pizza did Tina eat?

PRACTICE AND PROBLEM SOLVING

Extra Practice
See Extra Practice for more exercises.

39. **Consumer Economics** At a bookstore, the ticketed price of a book is $\frac{1}{4}$ off the original price. Kayla has a discount coupon for $\frac{1}{2}$ off the ticketed price. What fraction of the original price is the additional discount?

Multiply.

40. $6\left(\frac{3}{7}\right)$ 41. $-5\left(1\frac{8}{11}\right)$ 42. $7\left(\frac{4}{5}\right)$ 43. $5\left(3\frac{1}{9}\right)$

44. $\frac{4}{11}\left(-\frac{4}{7}\right)$ 45. $3\frac{5}{6}\left(\frac{7}{9}\right)$ 46. $-\frac{8}{9}\left(-\frac{3}{5}\right)$ 47. $\frac{5}{12}\left(-\frac{11}{16}\right)$

Estimate each product.

48. $1.499 \cdot 3.998$ 49. $-0.95 \cdot 5.03$ 50. $\left(\frac{8}{15}\right)\left(\frac{12}{25}\right)$ 51. $-4\left(\frac{10}{19}\right)$

52. **Health** The directions for a pain reliever recommend that children 96 pounds and over take 4 tablets every 4 hours as needed, and children who weigh between 60 and 71 pounds take only $2\frac{1}{2}$ tablets every 4 hours as needed. Each tablet is $\frac{4}{25}$ gram.

a. If a 105-pound child takes 4 tablets, how many grams of pain reliever is he or she receiving?

b. How many grams of pain reliever is the recommended dose for a child weighing 65 pounds?

LINK

Animals

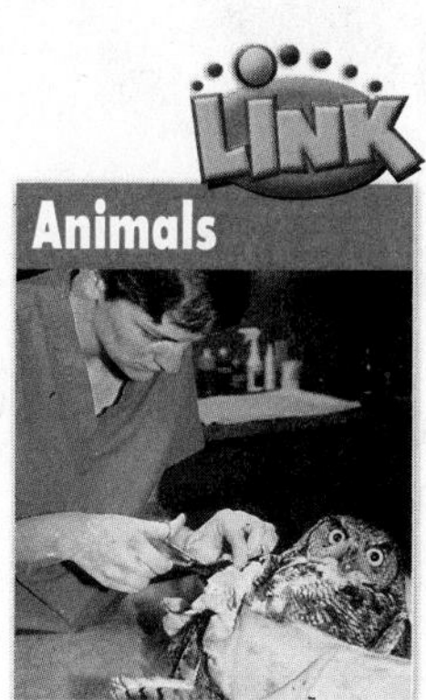

There are fewer than 30 veterinary colleges in the United States.

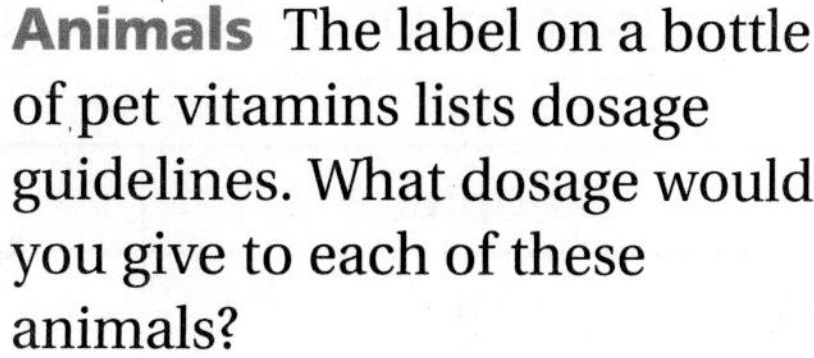

53. **Animals** The label on a bottle of pet vitamins lists dosage guidelines. What dosage would you give to each of these animals?

a. a 50 lb adult dog

b. a 12 lb cat

c. a 40 lb pregnant dog

Do-Good Pet Vitamins

- **Adult dogs:** $\frac{1}{2}$ tsp per 20 lb body weight
- **Puppies, pregnant dogs, or nursing dogs:** $\frac{1}{2}$ tsp per 10 lb body weight
- **Cats:** $\frac{1}{4}$ tsp per 2 lb body weight

54. **What's the Error?** A student multiplied two mixed numbers in the following fashion: $2\frac{4}{7} \cdot 3\frac{1}{4} = 6\frac{1}{7}$. What's the error?

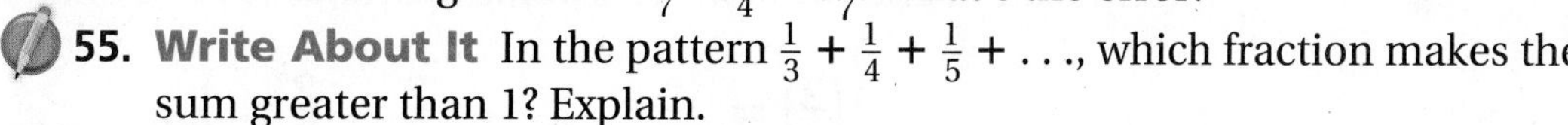

55. **Write About It** In the pattern $\frac{1}{3} + \frac{1}{4} + \frac{1}{5} + \ldots$, which fraction makes the sum greater than 1? Explain.

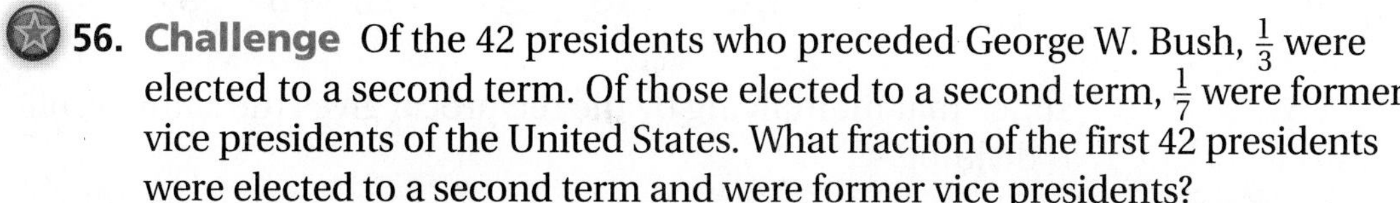

56. **Challenge** Of the 42 presidents who preceded George W. Bush, $\frac{1}{3}$ were elected to a second term. Of those elected to a second term, $\frac{1}{7}$ were former vice presidents of the United States. What fraction of the first 42 presidents were elected to a second term and were former vice presidents?

Test Prep

57. **Multiple Choice** Lindsay walked $\frac{3}{4}$ mile on Monday. She walked $1\frac{5}{8}$ that distance on Tuesday. How far did she walk on Tuesday?

Ⓐ $1\frac{7}{32}$ miles Ⓑ $1\frac{15}{32}$ miles Ⓒ $2\frac{3}{8}$ miles Ⓓ $2\frac{15}{32}$ miles

58. **Multiple Choice** What is the product of $-5\frac{1}{3}$ and $3\frac{3}{4}$?

Ⓕ -20 Ⓖ $-15\frac{1}{4}$ Ⓗ $15\frac{1}{4}$ Ⓙ 20

59. **Multiple Choice** Multiply: -0.98×-8.4.

Ⓐ -82.83 Ⓑ -8.232 Ⓒ 8.232 Ⓓ 82.83

John Giustina/Bruce Coleman, Inc.

1-3 Dividing Rational Numbers

Vocabulary
reciprocal

A number and its **reciprocal** have a product of 1. To find the reciprocal of a fraction, exchange the numerator and the denominator. Remember that an integer can be written as a fraction with a denominator of 1.

Number	Reciprocal	Product
$\frac{3}{4}$	$\frac{4}{3}$	$\frac{3}{4}\left(\frac{4}{3}\right) = 1$
$-\frac{5}{12}$	$-\frac{12}{5}$	$-\frac{5}{12}\left(-\frac{12}{5}\right) = 1$
6	$\frac{1}{6}$	$6\left(\frac{1}{6}\right) = 1$

Multiplication and division are inverse operations. They undo each other.

$$\frac{1}{3}\left(\frac{2}{5}\right) = \frac{2}{15} \longrightarrow \frac{2}{15} \div \frac{2}{5} = \frac{1}{3}$$

Notice that multiplying by the reciprocal gives the same result as dividing.

$$\left(\frac{2}{15}\right)\left(\frac{5}{2}\right) = \frac{2 \cdot 5}{15 \cdot 2} = \frac{10}{30} = \frac{1}{3}$$

DIVIDING RATIONAL NUMBERS IN FRACTION FORM

Words	Numbers	Algebra
To divide by a fraction, multiply by the reciprocal.	$\frac{1}{7} \div \frac{4}{5} = \frac{1}{7} \cdot \frac{5}{4} = \frac{5}{28}$	$\frac{a}{b} \div \frac{c}{d} = \frac{a}{b} \cdot \frac{d}{c} = \frac{ad}{bc}$

EXAMPLE 1

Dividing Fractions

Divide. Write each answer in simplest form.

A $\frac{7}{15} \div \frac{4}{5}$

$\frac{7}{15} \div \frac{4}{5} = \frac{7}{15} \cdot \frac{5}{4}$ *Multiply by the reciprocal.*

$= \frac{7 \cdot \cancel{5}^{1}}{{}_{3}\cancel{15} \cdot 4}$ *Divide out common factors.*

$= \frac{7}{12}$ *Simplest form*

Divide. Write each answer in simplest form.

B $5\frac{1}{3} \div (-7)$

$5\frac{1}{3} \div (-7) = \frac{16}{3} \div \left(-\frac{7}{1}\right)$ — *Write as improper fractions.*

$= \frac{16}{3}\left(-\frac{1}{7}\right)$ — *Multiply by the reciprocal.*

$= \frac{16 \cdot (-1)}{3 \cdot 7}$ — *No common factors*

$= -\frac{16}{21}$ — *Simplest form*

When dividing a decimal by a decimal, multiply both numbers by a power of 10 so you can divide by a whole number. To decide which power of 10 to multiply by, look at the denominator. The number of decimal places is the number of zeros to write after the 1.

$$\frac{1.32}{0.4} = \frac{1.32}{0.4}\left(\frac{10}{10}\right) = \frac{13.2}{4}$$

1 decimal place — *1 zero*

EXAMPLE 2 Dividing Decimals

Find 7.48 ÷ 0.4.

$7.48 \div 0.4 = \frac{7.48}{0.4}\left(\frac{10}{10}\right) = \frac{74.8}{4}$ — *0.4 has 1 decimal place, so use $\frac{10}{10}$.*

$= 18.7$ — *Divide.*

EXAMPLE 3 Evaluating Expressions with Fractions and Decimals

Evaluate each expression for the given value of the variable.

A $\frac{7.2}{n}$ **for** $n = -0.24$

$-\frac{7.2}{0.24} = -\frac{7.2}{0.24}\left(\frac{100}{100}\right)$ — *0.24 has 2 decimal places, so use $\frac{100}{100}$.*

$= -\frac{720}{24}$ — *Divide.*

$= -30$

When $n = -0.24$, $\frac{7.2}{n} = -30$.

B $m \div \frac{5}{24}$ **for** $m = 3\frac{3}{4}$

$3\frac{3}{4} \div \frac{5}{24} = \frac{15}{4} \cdot \frac{24}{5}$ — *Rewrite $3\frac{3}{4}$ as an improper fraction and multiply by the reciprocal.*

$= \frac{\overset{3}{\cancel{15}} \cdot \overset{6}{\cancel{24}}}{\underset{1}{\cancel{4}} \cdot \underset{1}{\cancel{5}}}$ — *Divide out common factors.*

$= \frac{18}{1} = 18$

When $m = 3\frac{3}{4}$, $m \div \frac{5}{24} = 18$.

EXAMPLE 4 PROBLEM SOLVING APPLICATION

MATHEMATICAL PRACTICES Make sense of problems and persevere in solving them.

Ella ate $\frac{2}{3}$ cup of lowfat yogurt. The serving size listed on the container is 6 ounces, or $\frac{3}{4}$ cup. How many servings did Ella eat? How many Calories did Ella eat?

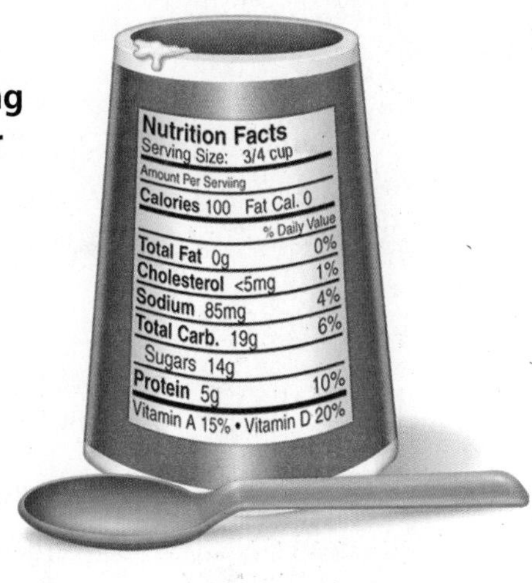

1 Understand the Problem

The number of Calories Ella ate is the number of Calories in the fraction of a serving.

List the **important information:**

- Ella ate $\frac{2}{3}$ cup.
- A full serving is $\frac{3}{4}$ cup.
- There are 100 Calories in one serving.

2 Make a Plan

Set up an equation to find the number of servings Ella ate.

amount Ella ate ÷ serving size = number of servings

Using the number of servings, find the number of Calories Ella ate.

number of servings · Calories per serving = total Calories

3 Solve

Let n = number of servings. Let c = total Calories.

Servings: $\frac{2}{3} \div \frac{3}{4} = n$

$\frac{2}{3} \cdot \frac{4}{3} = n$

$\frac{8}{9} = n$

Calories: $\frac{8}{9} \cdot 100 = c$

$\frac{8 \cdot 100}{9} = c$

$\frac{800}{9} \approx 88.9$

Ella ate $\frac{8}{9}$ of a serving, which is about 88.9 Calories.

4 Look Back

Ella did not eat a full serving, so $\frac{8}{9}$ of a serving is a reasonable answer. Since $\frac{8}{9}$ is less than 1 and 88.9 calories is less than 100, the Calories in a full serving, 88.9 Calories is a reasonable answer.

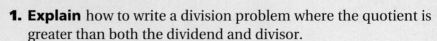

MATHEMATICAL PRACTICES

Think and Discuss

1. **Explain** how to write a division problem where the quotient is greater than both the dividend and divisor.
2. **Model** the product of $\frac{2}{3}$ and $\frac{1}{4}$.

1-3 Exercises

Learn It Online
Homework Help Online
Exercises 1-46, 47, 49

GUIDED PRACTICE

See Example 1 **Divide. Write each answer in simplest form.**

1. $\frac{1}{2} \div \frac{3}{4}$
2. $4\frac{1}{5} \div 5\frac{2}{3}$
3. $-\frac{6}{7} \div 3$
4. $\frac{5}{6} \div \frac{3}{8}$
5. $5\frac{1}{18} \div 4\frac{4}{9}$
6. $-\frac{5}{8} \div 12$
7. $\frac{14}{15} \div \frac{2}{3}$
8. $4\frac{3}{10} \div \frac{3}{5}$

See Example 2 **Find each quotient.**

9. $3.72 \div 0.3$
10. $2.1 \div 0.07$
11. $10.71 \div 0.7$
12. $1.72 \div 0.2$
13. $2.54 \div 0.6$
14. $11.04 \div 0.4$
15. $2.45 \div 0.005$
16. $4.41 \div 0.7$

See Example 3 **Evaluate each expression for the given value of the variable.**

17. $\frac{9.7}{x}$ for $x = -0.5$
18. $\frac{6.2}{x}$ for $x = 0.2$
19. $\frac{40.5}{x}$ for $x = 0.9$
20. $\frac{9.2}{x}$ for $x = 2.3$
21. $\frac{32.4}{x}$ for $x = -1.8$
22. $\frac{14.7}{x}$ for $x = 0.07$

See Example 4

23. You eat $\frac{1}{4}$ ounce of cheddar cheese. One serving of cheddar cheese is $1\frac{1}{2}$ ounces. How much of a serving did you eat?

INDEPENDENT PRACTICE

See Example 1 **Divide. Write each answer in simplest form.**

24. $\frac{1}{6} \div \frac{3}{4}$
25. $4\frac{2}{5} \div 3\frac{1}{2}$
26. $-\frac{5}{12} \div \frac{2}{3}$
27. $\frac{4}{5} \div \frac{1}{2}$
28. $1\frac{2}{3} \div 2\frac{1}{6}$
29. $-\frac{2}{9} \div \frac{7}{12}$
30. $\frac{2}{3} \div \frac{3}{10}$
31. $2\frac{3}{8} \div 1\frac{1}{6}$

See Example 2 **Find each quotient.**

32. $12.11 \div 0.7$
33. $2.49 \div 0.03$
34. $6.64 \div 0.4$
35. $4.85 \div 0.5$
36. $5.49 \div 0.003$
37. $32.44 \div 0.8$
38. $9.36 \div 0.03$
39. $12.24 \div 0.9$

See Example 3 **Evaluate each expression for the given value of the variable.**

40. $\frac{7.2}{x}$ for $x = -0.4$
41. $\frac{9.6}{x}$ for $x = 0.8$
42. $\frac{15}{x}$ for $x = -0.05$
43. $\frac{15.4}{x}$ for $x = -1.4$
44. $\frac{4.24}{x}$ for $x = 0.8$
45. $\frac{22.2}{x}$ for $x = 0.06$

See Example 4

46. The platform on the school stage is $8\frac{3}{4}$ feet wide. Each chair is $1\frac{5}{12}$ feet wide. How many chairs will fit across the platform?

PRACTICE AND PROBLEM SOLVING

Extra Practice
See Extra Practice for more exercises.

47. Maya is drinking her favorite juice. There are $2\frac{3}{4}$ servings remaining in the bottle. Maya pours only $\frac{1}{4}$ of a serving into her glass at a time. How many glasses can Maya have before the bottle is empty?

48. **Estimation** The width of a DVD case is about $\frac{1}{3}$ inch. About how many DVD cases are in a box set if the set is about $1\frac{3}{4}$ inches thick?

49. **Social Studies** Nesting dolls called *matrushkas* are a well-known type of Russian folk art. Use the information in the picture to find the height of the largest doll.

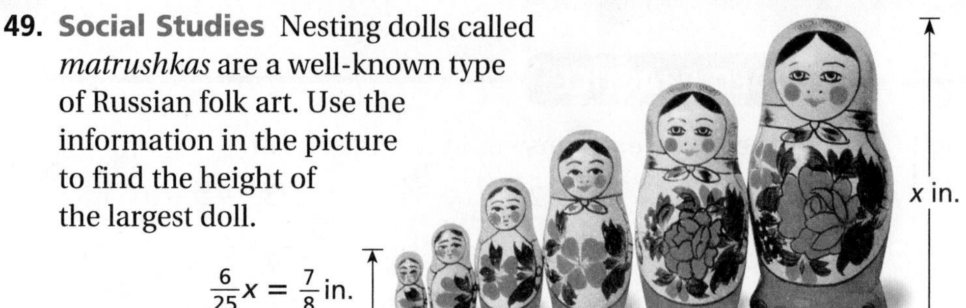

50. **Estimation** A cereal box holds $9\frac{1}{5}$ servings. Leo's bowl holds $1\frac{5}{8}$ servings. Approximately how many times can Leo fill his bowl?

51. **Choose a Strategy** Before 2000, the prices of all stocks traded on the New York Stock Exchange were given in fractions. When a stock is split 2-for-1, the price of the stock is halved and the number of shares doubles. A stock trading at $\$20\frac{1}{4}$ was split 2-for-1. What was the price of the stock after the split?

52. **Write About It** What are the effects of multiplying and dividing a positive rational number by a rational number greater than 1? by a rational number between 0 and 1?

53. **Challenge** In 2006, the U.S. Census Bureau estimated that about $\frac{27}{10,000}$ of the U.S. population resided in Mecklenburg County, North Carolina, which represented $\frac{3}{100}$ of North Carolina residents. What fraction of U.S. residents lived in North Carolina?

Test Prep

54. **Multiple Choice** Evaluate the expression $\frac{7.92}{x}$ for $x = 3.3$.

Ⓐ 2.4 Ⓑ 4.62 Ⓒ 11.22 Ⓓ 26.136

55. **Multiple Choice** A recipe calls for $2\frac{1}{2}$ cups of sugar to make a batch of cookies. To make one-third of a batch, Betty needs to divide the amount of each ingredient in the recipe by 3. How many cups of sugar will she use?

Ⓕ $\frac{3}{4}$ cup Ⓖ $\frac{5}{6}$ cup Ⓗ $1\frac{1}{5}$ cups Ⓙ $7\frac{1}{2}$ cups

56. **Gridded Response** Frank bought 12.6 gallons of gasoline for \$26.96. How much, to the nearest cent, was the cost per gallon of gasoline?

1-4 Adding and Subtracting with Unlike Denominators

Two hikers on the Appalachian Trail are $5\frac{3}{4}$ miles from the trail head. The hikers walk $2\frac{1}{8}$ miles before taking a break. They then hike another $1\frac{1}{2}$ miles before taking a second break. How many more miles do they have to hike before reaching the trail head?

To solve this problem, you must add and subtract rational numbers with unlike denominators. First find a common denominator using one of these methods:

Method 1 Find a common denominator by multiplying one denominator by the other denominator.

Method 2 Find the least common denominator (LCD).

EXAMPLE 1 Adding and Subtracting Fractions with Unlike Denominators

Add or subtract.

A $\frac{4}{5} + \frac{1}{6}$

Method 1: $\frac{4}{5} + \frac{1}{6}$ *Find a common denominator: 5(6) = 30.*

$\frac{4}{5}\left(\frac{6}{6}\right) + \frac{1}{6}\left(\frac{5}{5}\right)$ *Multiply by fractions equal to 1.*

$\frac{24}{30} + \frac{5}{30}$ *Rewrite with a common denominator.*

$\frac{29}{30}$ *Simplify.*

B $2\frac{1}{6} - 2\frac{2}{9}$

Method 2: $2\frac{1}{6} - 2\frac{2}{9}$

$\frac{13}{6} - \frac{20}{9}$ *Write as improper fractions.*

Multiples of 6: 6, 12, (18), . . .
Multiples of 9: 9, (18), 27, . . . *List the multiples of each denominator and find the LCD.*

$\frac{13}{6}\left(\frac{3}{3}\right) - \frac{20}{9}\left(\frac{2}{2}\right)$ *Multiply by fractions equal to 1.*

$\frac{39}{18} - \frac{40}{18}$ *Rewrite with the LCD.*

$-\frac{1}{18}$ *Simplify.*

Helpful Hint

You may also use *prime factorization* to find the LCD. See the Skills Bank.

EXAMPLE 2 Evaluating Expressions with Rational Numbers

Evaluate $n - \frac{11}{16}$ for $n = -\frac{1}{3}$.

$n - \frac{11}{16} = \left(-\frac{1}{3}\right) - \frac{11}{16}$ — *Substitute $-\frac{1}{3}$ for n.*

$= \left(-\frac{1}{3}\right)\left(\frac{16}{16}\right) - \frac{11}{16}\left(\frac{3}{3}\right)$ — *Multiply by fractions equal to 1.*

$= -\frac{16}{48} - \frac{33}{48}$ — *Rewrite with a common denominator: 3(16) = 48.*

$= -\frac{49}{48}$, or $-1\frac{1}{48}$ — *Simplify.*

EXAMPLE 3 *Recreation Application*

Clingman's Dome, on the Tennessee-North Carolina border, is the Appalachian Trail's highest point at 6643 feet.

Two hikers on the Appalachian Trail are $5\frac{3}{4}$ miles from the trail head. The hikers cover $2\frac{1}{8}$ miles before taking a break. They then hike another $1\frac{1}{2}$ miles before taking a second break. How many more miles do the hikers have to go before reaching the trail head?

$2\frac{1}{8} + 1\frac{1}{2}$ — *Add to find the distance hiked.*

$\frac{17}{8} + \frac{3}{2}$ — *Write as improper fractions.*

$\frac{17}{8} + \frac{12}{8}$ — *The LCD is 8.*

$\frac{29}{8}$, or $3\frac{5}{8}$

The hikers have hiked $3\frac{5}{8}$ miles. Now find the number of miles remaining.

$5\frac{3}{4} - 3\frac{5}{8}$ — *Subtract the distance hiked from the total distance.*

$\frac{23}{4} - \frac{29}{8}$ — *Write as improper fractions.*

$\frac{46}{8} - \frac{29}{8}$ — *The LCD is 8.*

$\frac{17}{8}$, or $2\frac{1}{8}$ — *Simplify.*

The hikers have $2\frac{1}{8}$ miles to go before reaching the trail head.

MATHEMATICAL PRACTICES

Think and Discuss

1. **Give an example** of two denominators with no common factors.
2. **Tell** if $-2\frac{1}{5} - \left(-2\frac{3}{16}\right)$ is positive or negative. Explain.
3. **Explain** how to add $2\frac{2}{5} + 9\frac{1}{3}$ without first writing them as improper fractions.

1-4 Exercises

Learn It Online
Homework Help Online
Exercises 1-23, 25, 29, 31

GUIDED PRACTICE

See Example 1 **Add or subtract.**

1. $\frac{4}{7} + \frac{1}{3}$
2. $\frac{1}{2} - \frac{7}{8}$
3. $3\frac{1}{2} + \left(-7\frac{4}{5}\right)$
4. $3\frac{7}{12} + \left(-2\frac{4}{5}\right)$

See Example 2 **Evaluate each expression for the given value of the variable.**

5. $4\frac{3}{8} + x$ for $x = -3\frac{2}{9}$
6. $n - \frac{3}{8}$ for $n = -\frac{4}{5}$
7. $\frac{3}{7} + y$ for $y = \frac{1}{2}$

See Example 3

8. Gavin needs $2\frac{5}{8}$ yards of fabric each to make two shirts. This amount is cut from a bolt containing $9\frac{1}{4}$ yards of fabric. How much fabric remains on the bolt?

INDEPENDENT PRACTICE

See Example 1 **Add or subtract.**

9. $\frac{7}{13} + \frac{2}{7}$
10. $\frac{1}{3} + \frac{4}{7}$
11. $\frac{11}{12} - \frac{4}{5}$
12. $\frac{2}{5} + \frac{14}{15}$
13. $5\frac{4}{5} + \left(-3\frac{2}{7}\right)$
14. $\frac{5}{9} - \frac{11}{14}$
15. $2\frac{1}{4} - 4\frac{3}{7}$
16. $\frac{1}{5} + \frac{8}{9}$

See Example 2 **Evaluate each expression for the given value of the variable.**

17. $2\frac{3}{4} + x$ for $x = -3\frac{2}{3}$
18. $n - \frac{2}{3}$ for $n = \frac{3}{4}$
19. $r - \frac{4}{5}$ for $r = \frac{3}{4}$
20. $3\frac{1}{6} + x$ for $x = -2\frac{5}{7}$
21. $n - \frac{11}{13}$ for $n = \frac{2}{3}$
22. $\frac{12}{17} - n$ for $n = \frac{1}{2}$

See Example 3

23. An oxygen tank contained $212\frac{2}{3}$ liters of oxygen before $27\frac{1}{3}$ liters were used. If the tank can hold $240\frac{3}{8}$ liters, how much space in the tank is unused?

PRACTICE AND PROBLEM SOLVING

Extra Practice
See Extra Practice for more exercises.

24. **Multi-Step** The heights of the starting players for the Davis High School boy's basketball team are $78\frac{1}{8}$ in., 74 in., $71\frac{5}{8}$ in., $70\frac{3}{4}$ in., and $69\frac{1}{2}$ in. Find the average height of the starting players.

25. **Measurement** A water pipe has an outside diameter of $1\frac{1}{4}$ inches and a wall thickness of $\frac{5}{16}$ inch. What is the inside diameter of the pipe?

$1\frac{1}{4}$ in.
$\frac{5}{16}$ in.

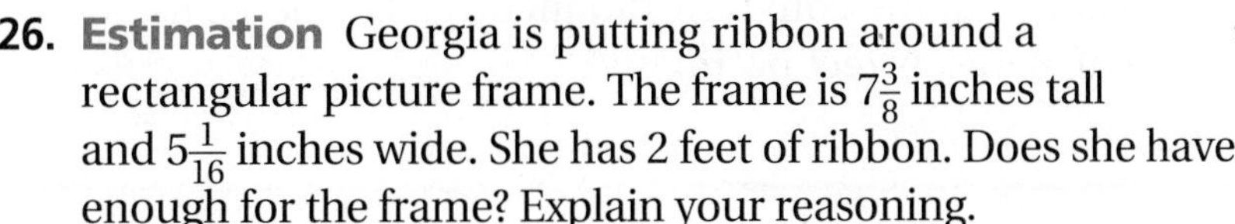

26. **Estimation** Georgia is putting ribbon around a rectangular picture frame. The frame is $7\frac{3}{8}$ inches tall and $5\frac{1}{16}$ inches wide. She has 2 feet of ribbon. Does she have enough for the frame? Explain your reasoning.

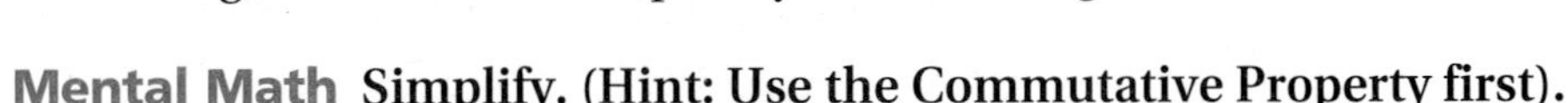

Mental Math **Simplify. (Hint: Use the Commutative Property first).**

27. $\frac{2}{7} + \frac{3}{5} + \frac{5}{7} + \frac{2}{5}$
28. $\frac{5}{9} - \frac{1}{3} - \frac{2}{9}$
29. $4\frac{1}{3} - 2\frac{1}{2} - 1\frac{1}{3}$

Earth Science 

Niagara Falls, on the border of Canada and the United States, has two major falls, Horseshoe Falls on the Canadian side and American Falls on the U.S. side. Surveys of the erosion of the falls began in 1842. From 1842 to 1905, Horseshoe Falls eroded $239\frac{2}{5}$ feet.

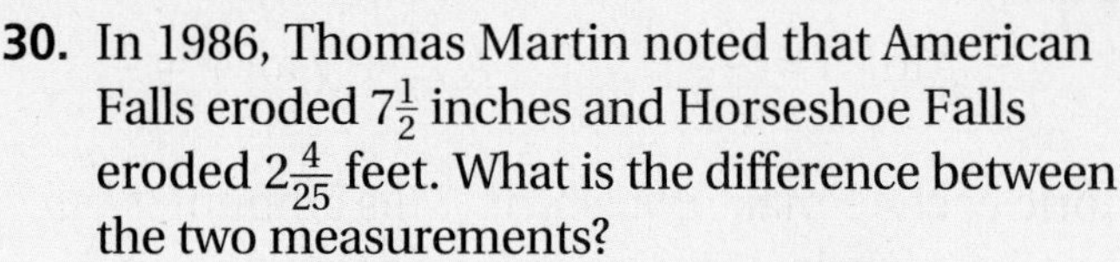

30. In 1986, Thomas Martin noted that American Falls eroded $7\frac{1}{2}$ inches and Horseshoe Falls eroded $2\frac{4}{25}$ feet. What is the difference between the two measurements?

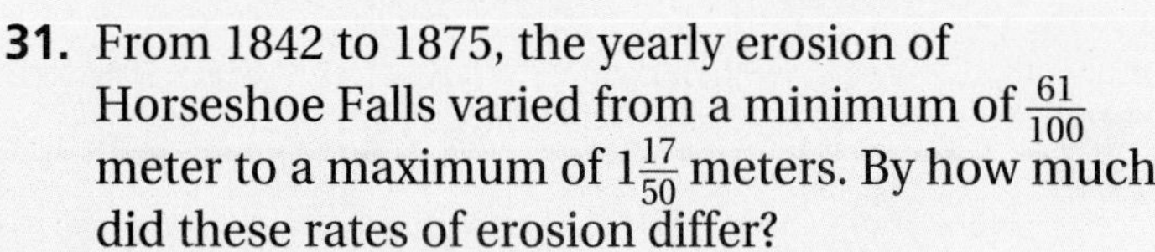

31. From 1842 to 1875, the yearly erosion of Horseshoe Falls varied from a minimum of $\frac{61}{100}$ meter to a maximum of $1\frac{17}{50}$ meters. By how much did these rates of erosion differ?

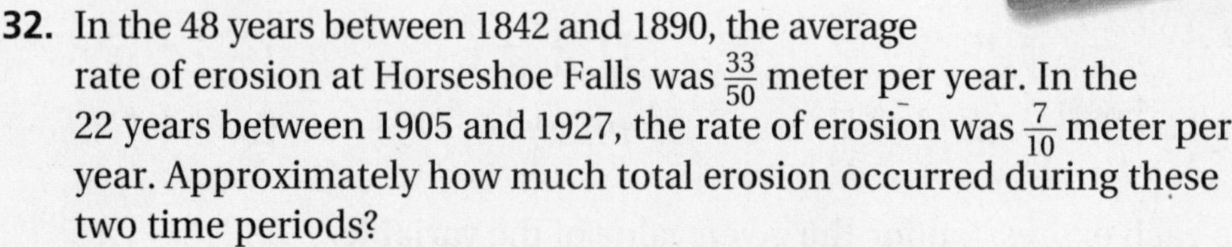

32. In the 48 years between 1842 and 1890, the average rate of erosion at Horseshoe Falls was $\frac{33}{50}$ meter per year. In the 22 years between 1905 and 1927, the rate of erosion was $\frac{7}{10}$ meter per year. Approximately how much total erosion occurred during these two time periods?

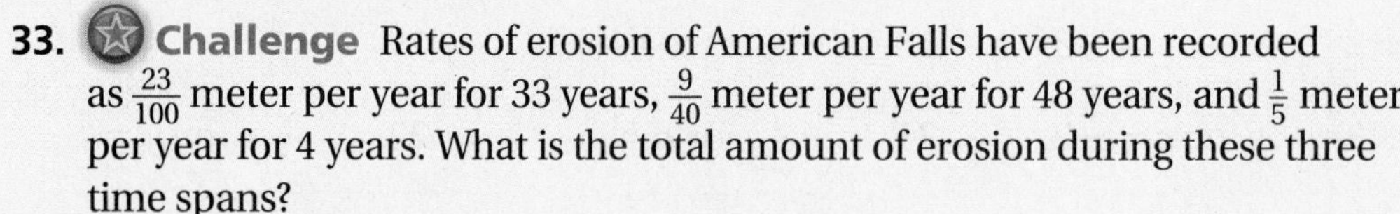

33. **Challenge** Rates of erosion of American Falls have been recorded as $\frac{23}{100}$ meter per year for 33 years, $\frac{9}{40}$ meter per year for 48 years, and $\frac{1}{5}$ meter per year for 4 years. What is the total amount of erosion during these three time spans?

Test Prep

34. Multiple Choice A $4\frac{5}{8}$ ft section of wood was cut from a $7\frac{1}{2}$ ft board. How much of the original board remained?

Ⓐ $3\frac{5}{8}$ ft　Ⓑ $3\frac{9}{16}$ ft　Ⓒ $2\frac{7}{8}$ ft　Ⓓ $2\frac{3}{8}$ ft

35. Extended Response A rectangular swimming pool measured $75\frac{1}{2}$ feet by $25\frac{1}{4}$ feet. Schmidt Pool Supply computed the perimeter of the pool to be $200\frac{1}{3}$ feet. Explain what the company did incorrectly when computing the perimeter. What is the correct perimeter?

Add and Subtract Fractions

Use with Adding and Subtracting with Unlike Denominators

You can add and subtract fractions using your graphing calculator. To display decimals as fractions, use the MATH key.

Use appropriate tools strategically.

Activity

1 Use a graphing calculator to add $\frac{7}{12} + \frac{3}{8}$. Write the sum as a fraction.

Type 7 ÷ 12 and press ENTER. You can see that the decimal equivalent is a repeating decimal, $0.58\overline{3}$.

Type + 3 ÷ 8 ENTER. The decimal form of the sum is displayed.

Press MATH 1:▶Frac ENTER Ans▶Frac ENTER.

The fraction form of the sum, $\frac{23}{24}$, is displayed as 23/24.

2 Use a graphing calculator to subtract $\frac{3}{5} - \frac{2}{3}$. Write the difference as a fraction.

Type 3 ÷ 5 − 2 ÷ 3 MATH 1:▶Frac ENTER Ans▶Frac ENTER.

The answer is $-\frac{1}{15}$.

Think and Discuss

1. Why is the difference in **2** negative?
2. Type 0.33333 . . . (pressing 3 at least twelve times). Press MATH 1:▶Frac ENTER Ans▶Frac ENTER to write $0.\overline{3}$ as a fraction. Now do the same for $0.\overline{9}$. What happens to $0.\overline{9}$? How does the fraction for $0.\overline{3}$ help to explain this result?

Try This

Use a calculator to add or subtract. Write each result as a fraction.

1. $\frac{1}{4} + \frac{2}{7}$ **2.** $\frac{7}{8} - \frac{2}{3}$ **3.** $\frac{7}{15} + \frac{3}{10}$ **4.** $\frac{1}{3} - \frac{5}{7}$

5. $\frac{5}{32} + \frac{2}{11}$ **6.** $\frac{31}{101} - \frac{3}{5}$ **7.** $\frac{4}{15} + \frac{7}{16}$ **8.** $\frac{3}{35} - \frac{3}{37}$

CHAPTER 1 SECTION A

Ready To Go On?

Quiz for Lessons 1 Through 4

1 Rational Numbers

Simplify.

1. $\frac{12}{36}$ 2. $\frac{15}{48}$ 3. $\frac{33}{88}$ 4. $\frac{55}{122}$

Write each fraction as a decimal.

5. $\frac{5}{3}$ 6. $-1\frac{7}{8}$ 7. $7\frac{23}{50}$ 8. $\frac{4}{11}$

2 Multiplying Rational Numbers

Multiply. Write each answer in simplest form.

9. $2\left(4\frac{2}{3}\right)$ 10. $2\frac{2}{5}\left(\frac{7}{36}\right)$ 11. $3.8\,(4)$ 12. $\frac{-1}{7}\left(\frac{-3}{4}\right)$

13. Robert has a piece of twine that is $\frac{3}{4}$ yard long. He needs a piece of twine that is $\frac{2}{3}$ of this length. What length of twine does Robert need?

3 Dividing Rational Numbers

Divide. Write each answer in simplest form.

14. $\frac{3}{5} \div \frac{4}{15}$ 15. $2.7 \div 3$ 16. $-\frac{2}{3} \div 1$ 17. $-4\frac{6}{7} \div 2\frac{5}{6}$

18. A cookie recipe calls for $2\frac{1}{4}$ cups of flour. The yield of the recipe is two dozen cookies. How much flour goes into each cookie?

4 Adding and Subtracting with Unlike Denominators

Add or subtract. Write each answer in simplest form.

19. $\frac{2}{7} + \frac{1}{4}$ 20. $1\frac{2}{3} + 3\frac{5}{9}$ 21. $6\frac{4}{7} - 3\frac{1}{5}$ 22. $3\frac{1}{6} - 1\frac{3}{4}$

23. An office water cooler contains $4\frac{1}{4}$ gallons of water at noon. By 2:30, it contains only $1\frac{2}{5}$ gallons of water. How much water was used in that time?

Make sense of problems and persevere in solving them.

Focus on Problem Solving

Look Back

• **Is your answer reasonable?**

After you solve a word problem, ask yourself if your answer makes sense. You can round the numbers in the problem and estimate to find a reasonable answer. It may also help to write your answer in sentence form.

Read the problems below and tell which answer is most reasonable.

1. Tonia calculates that she needs $47\frac{2}{3}$ pounds of compost to spread on her garden. There are 38.9 pounds of compost in her compost pile. How much compost does Tonia need to purchase?
   (A) about 9 pounds
   (B) about 87 pounds
   (C) about 6 pounds
   (D) about 15 pounds

2. The Qin Dynasty in China began about 2170 years before the People's Republic of China was formed in 1949. When did the Qin Dynasty begin?
   (F) before 200 B.C.E.
   (G) between 200 B.C.E. and 200 C.E.
   (H) between 200 C.E. and 1949 C.E.
   (J) after 1949 C.E.

3. On Mercury, the coldest temperature is about 600 °C below the hottest temperature of 430 °C. What is the coldest temperature on the planet?
   (A) about 1030 °C
   (B) about −1030 °C
   (C) about −170 °C
   (D) about 170 °C

4. Julie is balancing her checkbook. Her beginning balance is \$325.46, her deposits add up to \$285.38, and her withdrawals add up to \$683.27. What is her ending balance?
   (F) about −\$70
   (G) about −\$600
   (H) about \$700
   (J) about \$1300

Dean Conger/Corbis

1-5 Solving Equations with Rational Numbers

COMMON CORE

CC.8.EE.7: Solve linear equations in one variable. ***Also CC.8.EE.7b***

Painting a house can be a difficult task. In order to have a good surface for the new paint, the old paint must be cleaned, and sometimes even scraped off completely.

Sully runs his own house-painting business. When he plans a job, he estimates that he can paint $\frac{2}{5}$ of a house in one work day. You can write and solve an equation to find how long it would take Sully to paint 3 houses.

Interactivities Online ▶

EXAMPLE 1 Solving Equations with Decimals

Solve.

A $y - 17.5 = 11$

$$\begin{aligned} y - 17.5 &= 11 \\ +17.5 & \quad +17.5 \\ y &= 28.5 \end{aligned}$$

Use the Addition Property of Equality: Add 17.5 to both sides.

B $-4.2p = 12.6$

$$-4.2p = 12.6$$

$$\frac{-4.2p}{-4.2} = \frac{12.6}{-4.2}$$

Use the Division Property of Equality: Divide both sides by −4.2.

$$p = -3$$

C $\frac{t}{7.5} = 4$

$$\frac{t}{7.5} = 4$$

$$7.5 \cdot \frac{t}{7.5} = 4 \cdot 7.5$$

Use the Multiplication Property of Equality: Multiply both sides by 7.5.

$$t = 30$$

Remember!

Once you have solved an equation, it is a good idea to check your answer. To check your answer, substitute your answer for the variable in the original equation.

EXAMPLE 2 Solving Equations with Fractions

Solve.

A $x + \frac{1}{9} = -\frac{4}{9}$

$$x + \frac{1}{9} = -\frac{4}{9}$$

$$x + \frac{1}{9} - \frac{1}{9} = -\frac{4}{9} - \frac{1}{9}$$

Subtract $\frac{1}{9}$ from both sides.

$$x = -\frac{5}{9}$$

Video Lesson Tutorials Online my.hrw.com

Solve.

B $x - \frac{1}{8} = \frac{9}{16}$

$$x - \frac{1}{8} = \frac{9}{16}$$

$$x - \frac{1}{8} + \frac{1}{8} = \frac{9}{16} + \frac{1}{8}$$ *Add $\frac{1}{8}$ to both sides.*

$$x = \frac{9}{16} + \frac{2}{16}$$ *Find a common denominator, 16.*

$$x = \frac{11}{16}$$

C $\frac{3}{5}w = \frac{3}{16}$

$$\frac{3}{5}w = \frac{3}{16}$$

$$\frac{3}{5}w \div \frac{3}{5} = \frac{3}{16} \div \frac{3}{5}$$ *Divide both sides by $\frac{3}{5}$.*

$$\frac{\cancel{3}^1}{{}_1\cancel{5}}w \cdot \frac{\cancel{5}^1}{\cancel{3}_1} = \frac{{}^1\cancel{3}}{16} \cdot \frac{5}{\cancel{3}_1}$$ *Multiply by the reciprocal. Simplify.*

$$w = \frac{5}{16}$$

EXAMPLE 3 Solving Word Problems Using Equations

Sully has agreed to paint 3 houses. If he knows that he can paint $\frac{2}{5}$ of a house in one day, how many days will it take him to paint all 3 houses?

Write an equation:

number of days	×	*houses per day*	=	*number of houses*
d	×	$\frac{2}{5}$	=	3

$$d \cdot \frac{2}{5} = 3$$

$$d \cdot \frac{2}{5} \div \frac{2}{5} = 3 \div \frac{2}{5}$$ *Divide both sides by $\frac{2}{5}$.*

$$d \cdot \frac{2}{5} \cdot \frac{5}{2} = 3 \cdot \frac{5}{2}$$ *Multiply by the reciprocal.*

$$d = \frac{15}{2}, \text{ or } 7\frac{1}{2}$$ *Simplify.*

Sully can paint 3 houses in $7\frac{1}{2}$ days.

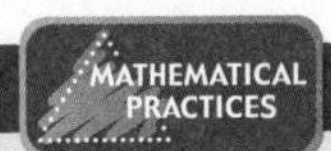

Think and Discuss

1. **Explain** the first step in solving an addition equation with fractions having *like* denominators.
2. **Explain** the first step in solving an addition equation with fractions having *unlike* denominators.

1-5 Exercises

Learn It Online
Homework Help Online
Exercises 1–28, 29, 31, 33, 35, 39, 43

GUIDED PRACTICE

See Example 1 **Solve.**

1. $y + 17.3 = -65$
2. $-5.2f = 36.4$
3. $\frac{m}{3.2} = -6$
4. $r - 15.8 = 24.6$
5. $\frac{s}{15.42} = 6.3$
6. $0.06g = 0.474$

See Example 2

7. $x + \frac{1}{9} = -\frac{4}{9}$
8. $-\frac{3}{8} + k = -\frac{7}{8}$
9. $\frac{5}{6}w = -\frac{7}{18}$
10. $m - \frac{4}{3} = -\frac{4}{3}$
11. $\frac{7}{17}y = -\frac{56}{17}$
12. $t + \frac{4}{13} = \frac{12}{39}$

See Example 3

13. Alonso runs a company called Speedy House Painters. His workers can paint $\frac{3}{4}$ of a house in one day. How many days would it take them to paint 6 houses?

INDEPENDENT PRACTICE

See Example 1 **Solve.**

14. $y + 16.7 = -49$
15. $4.7m = -32.9$
16. $-\frac{h}{7.8} = 2$
17. $k - 3.2 = -6.8$
18. $\frac{z}{11.4} = 6$
19. $c + 5.98 = 9.1$

See Example 2

20. $j + \frac{1}{3} = \frac{3}{4}$
21. $\frac{5}{6}d = \frac{3}{15}$
22. $7h = \frac{14}{33}$
23. $\frac{2}{3} + x = \frac{5}{8}$
24. $x - \frac{1}{16} = \frac{7}{16}$
25. $r + \frac{4}{7} = -\frac{1}{7}$
26. $\frac{5}{6}c = \frac{7}{24}$
27. $\frac{7}{8}d = \frac{11}{12}$

See Example 

28. A professional lawn care service can mow $2\frac{3}{4}$ acres of lawn in one hour. How many hours would it take them to mow a lawn that is $6\frac{7}{8}$ acres?

PRACTICE AND PROBLEM SOLVING

Extra Practice
See Extra Practice for more exercises.

Earth Science The largest of all known diamonds, the Cullinan diamond, weighed 3106 carats before it was cut into 105 gems. The largest cut, Cullinan I, or the Great Star of Africa, weighs $530\frac{1}{3}$ carats. Another cut, Cullinan II, weighs $317\frac{2}{5}$ carats. Cullinan III weighs $94\frac{2}{5}$ carats, and Cullinan IV weighs $63\frac{3}{5}$ carats.

29. How many carats of the original Cullinan diamond were left after the Great Star of Africa and Cullinan II were cut?
30. How much more does Cullinan II weigh than Cullinan IV?
31. Which diamond weighs 223 carats less than Cullinan II?
32. **Nutrition** An entire can of chicken noodle soup has 6.25 grams of total fat. There are 2.5 servings per can. How many grams of total fat are in a single serving of chicken noodle soup?

Solve.

33. $z - \frac{2}{9} = \frac{1}{9}$

34. $-5f = -1.5$

35. $\frac{j}{7.2} = -3$

36. $\frac{2}{5} + x = 0.25$

37. $t - \frac{3}{4} = 6\frac{1}{4}$

38. $\frac{x}{0.5} = \frac{7}{8}$

39. $\frac{6}{7}d = -\frac{3}{7}$

40. $-4.7g = -28.2$

41. $\frac{v}{5.5} = -5.5$

42. $r + \frac{5}{6} = -3\frac{1}{6}$

43. $y + 2.8 = -1.4$

Solve. Justify each step.

44. $-3c = \frac{3}{20}$

45. $y - 57 = -2.8$

46. $\frac{m}{0.8} = -7$

47. **Multi-Step** Jack is tiling along the walls of the rectangular kitchen with the tile shown. The kitchen has a length of $243\frac{3}{4}$ inches and a width of $146\frac{1}{4}$ inches.

a. How many tiles will fit along the length of the room?

b. How many tiles will fit along its width?

c. If Jack needs 48 tiles to tile around all four walls of the kitchen, how many boxes of ten tiles must he buy? (*Hint:* He must buy whole boxes of tile.)

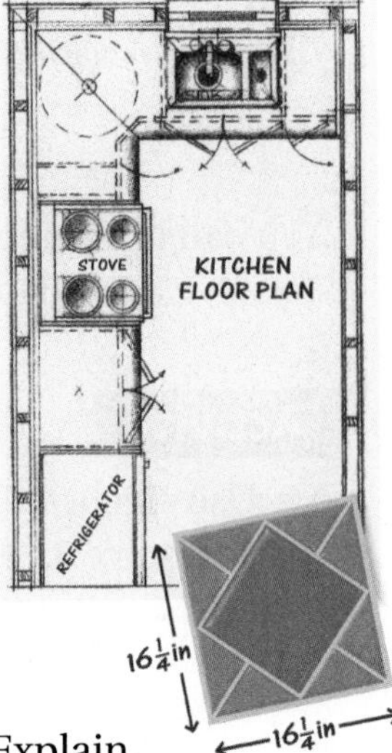

48. **What's the Error?** Janice is thinking about buying a DVD writer that burns 4.8 megabytes of data per second. She figures that it would take 16 minutes to burn 200 megabytes of data. What was her error?

49. **Write About It** If a is $\frac{1}{3}$ of b, is it correct to say $\frac{1}{3}a = b$? Explain.

50. **Challenge** A 200-carat diamond was cut into two equal pieces to form two diamonds. One of the diamonds was cut again, reducing it by $\frac{1}{5}$ its weight. In a final cut, it was reduced by $\frac{1}{4}$ its new weight. How many carats remained?

Test Prep

51. **Multiple Choice** If $\frac{12}{36} = 2w$, what is the value of w?

Ⓐ $\frac{24}{36}$ Ⓑ $\frac{24}{72}$ Ⓒ $\frac{1}{3}$ Ⓓ $\frac{1}{6}$

52. **Short Response** The performance of a musical arrangement lasted $6\frac{1}{4}$ minutes. The song consisted of 3 verses that each lasted the same number of minutes. Write and solve an equation to find the length of each verse.

Model Two-Step Equations

Use with Solving Two-Step Equations

Learn It Online
Lab Resources Online

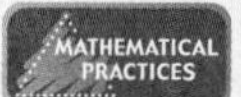

Use appropriate tools strategically.

CC.8.EE.7: Solve linear equations in one variable. ***Also CC.8.EE.7b***

KEY

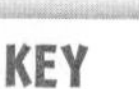 = +1

= −1

= variable

REMEMBER

 = 0

- You can perform the same operation with the same numbers on both sides of an equation without changing the value of the equation.

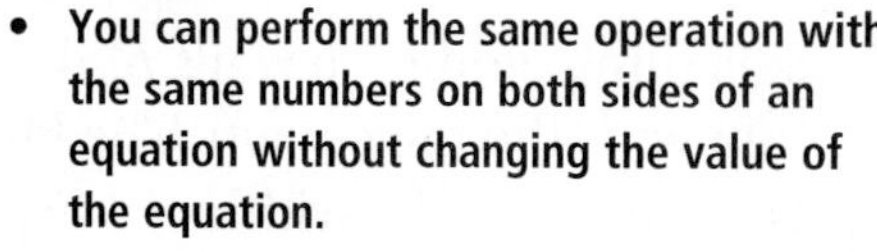

You can use algebra tiles to model and solve two-step equations. To solve a two-step equation, you use two different operations.

Activity

1 Use algebra tiles to model and solve $3s + 4 = 10$.

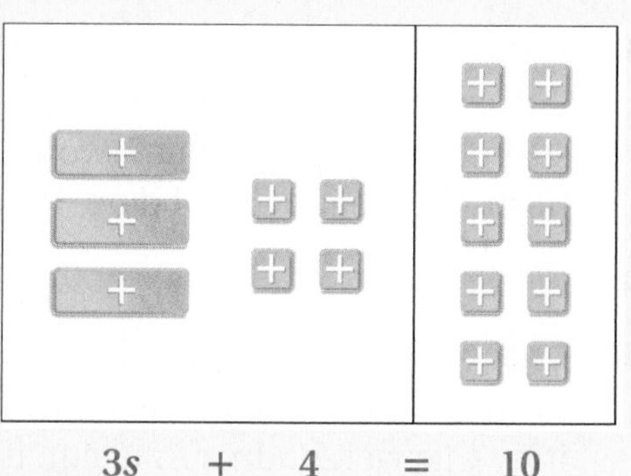

$3s \quad + \quad 4 \quad = \quad 10$

Two steps are needed to solve this equation.

Step 1: Remove 4 yellow tiles from each side.

$3s \quad = \quad 6$

Step 2: Divide each side into 3 equal groups.

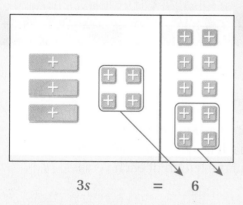

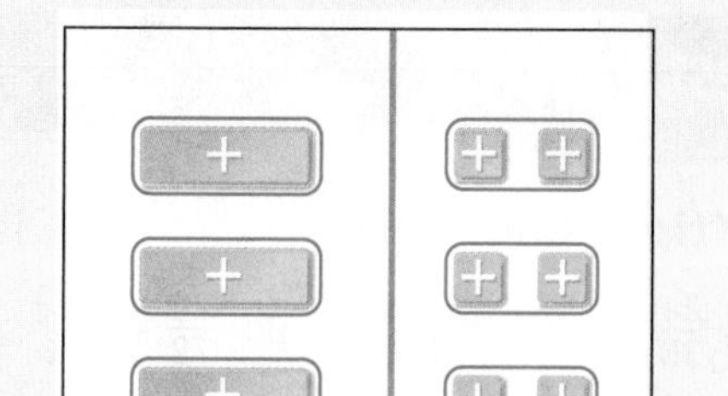

$s \quad = \quad 2$

Substitute to check:

$$3s + 4 = 10$$
$$3(2) + 4 \stackrel{?}{=} 10$$
$$6 + 4 \stackrel{?}{=} 10$$
$$10 \stackrel{?}{=} 10 \checkmark$$

2 Use algebra tiles to model and solve $2r + 4 = -6$.

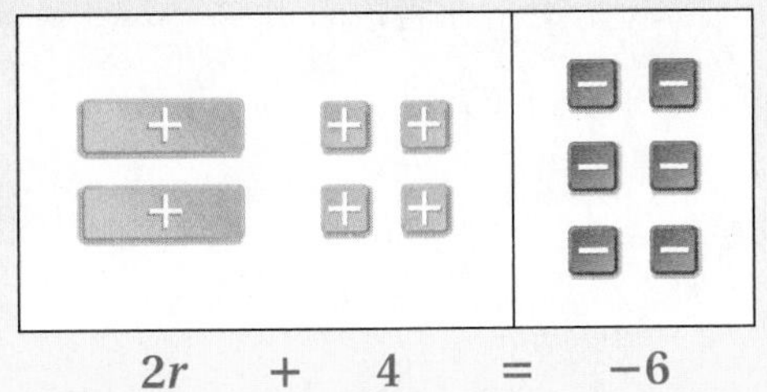

Step 1: Since 4 is being added to $2r$, add 4 red tiles to both sides and remove the zero pairs on the left side.

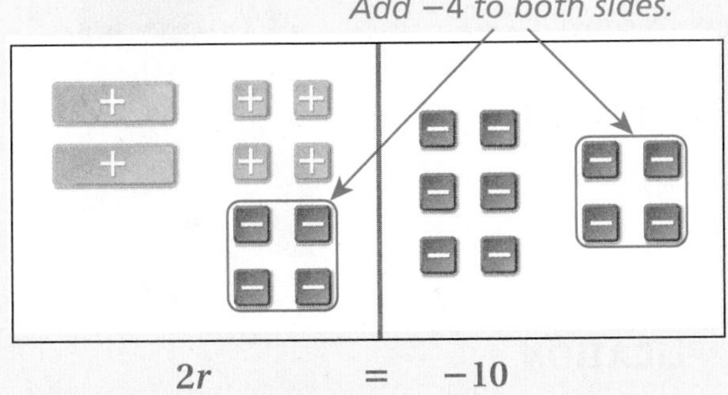

Step 2: Divide each side into 2 equal groups.

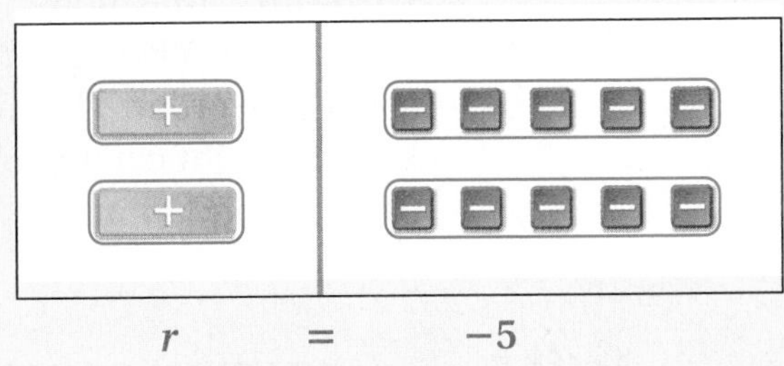

Substitute to check:

$$2r + 4 \stackrel{?}{=} -6$$
$$2(-5) + 4 \stackrel{?}{=} -6$$
$$-10 + 4 \stackrel{?}{=} -6$$
$$-6 \stackrel{?}{=} -6 \checkmark$$

Think and Discuss

1. Why can you add zero pairs to one side of an equation without having to add them to the other side as well?
2. Show how you could have modeled to check your solution for each equation.

Try This

Use algebra tiles to model and solve each of the following equations.

1. $2x + 3 = 5$
2. $4p - 3 = 9$
3. $5r - 6 = -11$
4. $3n + 5 = -4$
5. $6b + 8 = 2$
6. $2a + 2 = 6$
7. $4m + 4 = 4$
8. $7h - 8 = 41$

9. Gerry walked dogs five times a week and got paid the same amount each day. One week his boss added on a $15 bonus. That week Gerry earned $90. What was his daily salary?

1-6 Solving Two-Step Equations

COMMON CORE

CC.8.EE.7: Solve linear equations in one variable. ***Also CC.8.EE.7b***

Sometimes more than one inverse operation is needed to solve an equation. Before solving, ask yourself, "What is being done to the variable and in what order?" One method to solve the equation is to then work backward to undo the operations.

The Kuhr family bought tickets to see a circus. The ticket service charged a service fee for the order. The number of tickets the Kuhrs bought can be found by solving a two-step equation.

EXAMPLE 1 PROBLEM SOLVING APPLICATION

MATHEMATICAL PRACTICES Make sense of problems and persevere in solving them.

The Kuhr family spent $52.00 for circus tickets. This cost included a $3.25 service fee for the order, and the circus tickets cost $9.75 each. How many tickets did the Kuhrs buy? Justify your answer.

1 Understand the Problem

The **answer** is the number of tickets that the Kuhrs bought. List the **important information:** The service fee is $3.25 per order, the tickets cost $9.75 each, and the total cost is $52.

Let t represent the number of tickets bought.

Total cost	=	Tickets	+	Service Fee
52.00	=	$9.75t$	+	3.25

Interactivities Online ▶

2 Make a Plan

Think: First the variable is **multiplied by 9.75**, and then **3.25 is added** to the result. Work backward to solve the equation. Undo the operations in reverse order: First **subtract 3.25** from both sides of the equation, and then **divide** both sides of the new equation **by 9.75.**

3 Solve

$$\begin{aligned} 52.00 &= 9.75t + 3.25 \\ -3.25 &\quad\quad\;\; -3.25 \\ 48.75 &= 9.75t \end{aligned}$$

Step 1: Subtract 3.25 from both sides.

$$\frac{48.75}{9.75} = \frac{9.75t}{9.75}$$

Step 2: Divide both sides by 9.75.

$$5 = t$$

The Kuhrs bought 5 tickets.

Eric Gaillard/Reuters/Corbis

4 Look Back

You can use a table to decide whether your answer is reasonable.

Tickets	Cost of Tickets	Service Charge	Total Cost
1	\$9.75	\$3.25	\$13.00
2	\$19.50	\$3.25	\$22.75
3	\$29.25	\$3.25	\$32.50
4	\$39.00	\$3.25	\$42.25
5	\$48.75	\$3.25	\$52.00

Five tickets is a reasonable answer.

Sometimes, a two-step equation contains a term or an expression with a denominator. In these cases, it is often easier to first multiply both sides of the equation by the denominator in order to remove it, and then work to isolate the variable.

EXAMPLE 2 Solving Two-Step Equations

Solve $\frac{r+7}{4} = 5$.

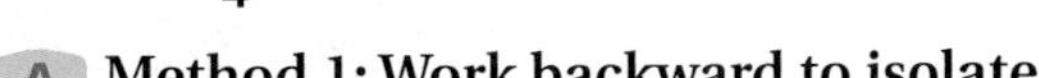

A Method 1: Work backward to isolate the variable.

$\frac{r+7}{4} = 5 \longrightarrow \frac{r}{4} + \frac{7}{4} = 5$ *Rewrite the expression as the sum of two fractions.*

Think: First the variable is **divided by 4**, and then $\frac{7}{4}$ **is added.**

$\frac{r}{4} + \frac{7}{4} = 5$

To isolate the variable, **subtract** $\frac{7}{4}$, and then **multiply by 4.**

$\frac{r}{4} + \frac{7}{4} - \frac{7}{4} = 5 - \frac{7}{4}$ *Subtract $\frac{7}{4}$ from both sides.*

$(4)\frac{r}{4} = \frac{13}{4}(4)$ *Multiply both sides by 4.*

$r = 13$

Remember!

To subtract $\frac{7}{4}$ from 5, write 5 as a fraction with a denominator of 4.

$\frac{20}{4} - \frac{7}{4} = \frac{13}{4}$

B Method 2: Multiply both sides of the equation by the denominator.

$\frac{r+7}{4} = 5$

$(4)\frac{r+7}{4} = 5(4)$ *Multiply both sides by 4.*

$r + 7 = 20$

$\underline{-7 \quad -7}$ *Subtract 7 from both sides.*

$r = 13$

Think and Discuss

1. Describe how you would solve $4(x - 2) = 16$.

2. Explain how to check your solution to an equation.

1-6 Exercises

Learn It Online
Homework Help Online
Exercises 1–18, 19, 23, 31, 33, 35, 39, 41

GUIDED PRACTICE

See Example 1

1. Adele is paid a weekly salary of \$685. She is paid an additional \$23.50 for every hour of overtime she works. This week her total pay, including regular salary and overtime, was \$849.50. How many hours of overtime did Adele work this week?

See Example 2

Solve.

2. $\frac{t-3}{2} = 75$
3. $\frac{t+10}{6} = 11$
4. $\frac{r-12}{7} = 6$
5. $\frac{x+7}{11} = 11$
6. $\frac{b+24}{2} = 13$
7. $\frac{q-11}{5} = 23$
8. $\frac{a-3}{28} = 3$
9. $\frac{y-13}{8} = 14$

INDEPENDENT PRACTICE

See Example 1

10. The cost of a family membership at a health club is \$58 per month plus a one-time \$129 start-up fee. If a family spent \$651, how many months is their membership?

See Example 2

Solve.

11. $\frac{m+6}{-3} = 4$
12. $\frac{c-1}{2} = 12$
13. $\frac{g-2}{2} = -46$
14. $\frac{h+20}{9} = 11$
15. $\frac{h+19}{19} = 2$
16. $\frac{y-3}{4} = -27$
17. $\frac{z-4}{10} = 9$
18. $\frac{n-31}{10} = 22$

PRACTICE AND PROBLEM SOLVING

Extra Practice
See Extra Practice for more exercises.

Solve.

19. $5w + 2.7 = 12.8$
20. $15 - 3x = -6$
21. $\frac{m}{5} + 6 = 9$
22. $\frac{z+9}{4} = 2.1$
23. $2x + \frac{2}{3} = \frac{4}{5}$
24. $9 = -5g - 23$
25. $6z - 3 = 0$
26. $\frac{5}{2}d - \frac{3}{2} = -\frac{1}{2}$
27. $58k + 35 = 615$
28. $8 = 6 + \frac{p}{2}$
29. $40 - 3n = -23$
30. $\frac{17+s}{15} = -4$
31. $9y - 7.2 = 4.5$
32. $\frac{2}{3} - 6h = -\frac{13}{6}$
33. $-1 = \frac{5}{8}b + \frac{3}{8}$

Translate each sentence into an equation. Then solve the equation.

34. The quotient of a number and 2, minus 9, is 14.
35. A number decreased by 7 and then divided by 5 is 13.
36. The sum of 15 and 7 times a number is 99.
37. Show two ways to solve the equation $\frac{m-3}{2} = 37$. Check your answer.
38. **Consumer Math** A long distance phone company charges \$19.95 per month plus \$0.05 per minute for calls. If a family's monthly long distance bill is \$23.74, how many minutes of long distance did they use?

Life Science 

Venom is collected from snakes and injected into horses, which develop antibodies. The horses' blood is sterilized to make antivenom.

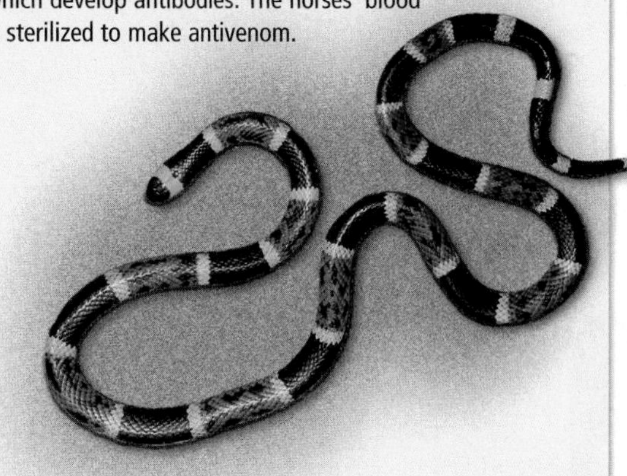

About 20% of the more than 2500 species of snakes are venomous. The United States has 20 native venomous snake species.

39. The inland taipan of central Australia is the world's most toxic venomous snake. Just 1 mg of its venom can kill 1000 mice. One bite contains up to 110 mg of venom. About how many mice could be killed with just one inland taipan bite?

40. A rattlesnake grows a new rattle segment each time it sheds its skin. Rattlesnakes shed their skin an average of three times per year. However, segments often break off. If a rattlesnake had 44 rattle segments break off in its lifetime and it had 10 rattles when it died, approximately how many years did the rattlesnake live?

41. All snakes shed their skin. The shed skin of a snake is an average of 10% longer than the actual snake. If the shed skin of a coral snake is 27.5 inches long, estimate the length of the coral snake.

42. **Challenge** Black mambas feed mainly on small rodents and birds. Suppose that a black mamba is 100 feet away from an animal that is running at 8 mi/h. About how long will it take for the mamba to catch the animal? (*Hint*: 1 mile = 5280 feet)

Records of World's Most Venomous Snakes

Category	Record	Type of Snake
Fastest	12 mi/h	Black mamba
Longest	18 ft 9 in.	King cobra
Heaviest	34 lb	Eastern diamondback rattlesnake
Longest fangs	2 in.	Gaboon viper

Test Prep

43. Multiple Choice A plumber charges $75 for a house call plus $45 per hour. How many hours did the plumber work if he charged $210?

Ⓐ 2 Ⓑ 3 Ⓒ 4 Ⓓ 6

44. Gridded Response What value of y makes the equation $4.4y + 1.75 = 43.99$ true?

Quiz for Lessons 5 Through 6

5 Solving Equations with Rational Numbers

Solve.

1. $p - 1.2 = -5$

2. $-9w = 13.5$

3. $\frac{m}{3.7} = -8$

4. $x + \frac{1}{9} = -\frac{4}{7}$

5. $m - \frac{3}{4} = -\frac{4}{3}$

6. $\frac{7}{33}y = -\frac{56}{3}$

7. $\frac{y}{-2.6} = 3.2$

8. $s + 0.45 = 10.07$

9. $p + 2.7 = 4.5$

10. $\frac{h}{2.5} = 3.8$

11. $y - \frac{7}{8} = -\frac{25}{12}$

12. $\frac{8}{11}k = \frac{29}{44}$

13. The Montegro Flooring Company can replace 200 square feet of carpet with tile in one day. They accept a job replacing carpet with tile in an apartment that measures 977.5 square feet. How many days will it take the Montegro Flooring Company to complete this job?

14. From start to finish, Ellen took $15\frac{2}{3}$ days to write a research paper for her literature class. This was $\frac{9}{10}$ the time it took Rebecca to write her paper. How long did it take Rebecca to write her research paper?

6 Solving Two-Step Equations

Solve.

15. $\frac{x + 7}{6} = -48$

16. $3x + 4.2 = 21$

17. $\frac{1}{4}y - \frac{2}{3} = \frac{5}{6}$

18. $\frac{y}{12} + 6 = -72$

19. $-5p + 10 = 75$

20. $\frac{r - 2}{-7} = 3$

21. $2w + 7.1 = 2.85$

22. $-8.9y - 10.11 = 74.44$

23. $\frac{p + 17}{25} = 4$

24. Marvin sold newspaper subscriptions during summer break. He earned $125.00 per week plus $5.75 for each subscription that he sold. During the last week of the summer, Marvin earned $228.50. How many subscriptions did he sell that week?

25. A cell phone company charges $13.50 per month plus $3\frac{1}{2}$ cents for each minute used. If Angelina's cell phone bill was $17.70 last month, how many minutes did she use?

The Colorado Trail The Colorado Trail makes it possible to hike nearly 500 miles from Denver to Durango. As the trail winds through the Rocky Mountains, hikers are treated to lakes, creeks, and six wilderness areas. With an average elevation of 10,000 feet, the trail also offers stunning views.

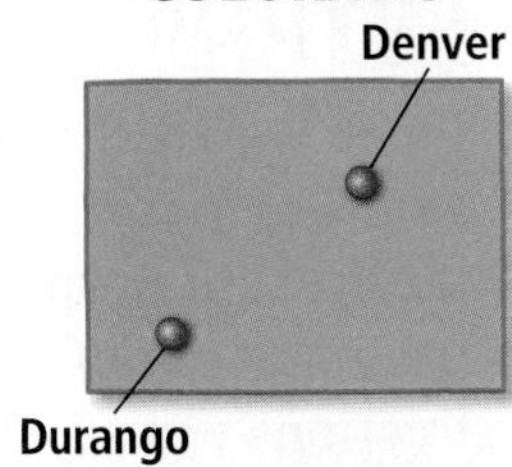

1. The Colorado Trail consists of 28 segments. Segment 18 is $13\frac{4}{5}$ miles long. Segment 19 is 13.7 miles long. Which segment is longer? How much longer?

2. The map gives information on the first five segments of the trail. What is the total length of these five segments?

3. A hiker wants to walk Segment 2 of the trail. She has already covered $\frac{1}{4}$ of the segment.

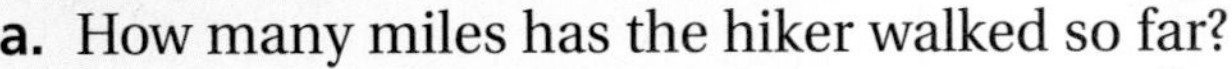

   a. How many miles has the hiker walked so far?

   b. How many more miles must she hike to finish Segment 2?

   c. The hiker walks at a rate of $2\frac{1}{2}$ miles per hour. How long will it take her to hike the entire length of Segment 2?

4. The Colorado Trail Foundation sells guidebooks for the trail. The books cost \$22.95 each, and shipping is \$5.00 per order. A hiking club places an order that totals \$142.70. How many books did the hiking club order?

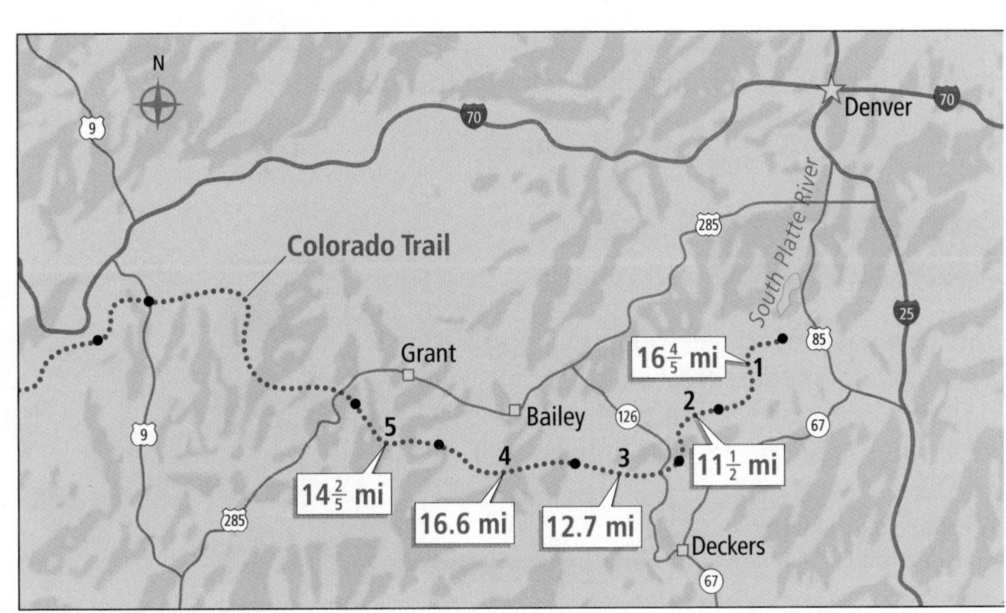

Jack Olson

Real-World Connections

Game Time

Egyptian Fractions

If you were to divide 9 loaves of bread among 10 people, you would give each person $\frac{9}{10}$ of a loaf. The answer was different on the ancient Egyptian Ahmes papyrus, because ancient Egyptians used only *unit fractions,* which have a numerator of 1. All other fractions were written as sums of different unit fractions. So $\frac{5}{6}$ could be written as $\frac{1}{2} + \frac{1}{3}$, but not as $\frac{1}{6} + \frac{1}{6} + \frac{1}{6} + \frac{1}{6} + \frac{1}{6}$.

Method	Example
Suppose you want to write a fraction as a sum of different unit fractions.	$\frac{9}{10}$
Step 1. Choose the largest fraction of the form $\frac{1}{n}$ that is less than the fraction you want.	0, $\frac{1}{5}$ $\frac{1}{4}$ $\frac{1}{3}$, $\frac{1}{2}$, $\frac{9}{10}$ $\frac{1}{1}$
Step 2. Subtract $\frac{1}{n}$ from the fraction you want.	$\frac{9}{10} - \frac{1}{2} = \frac{2}{5}$ remaining
Step 3. Repeat steps 1 and 2 using the difference of the fractions until the result is a unit fraction.	0, $\frac{1}{5}$ $\frac{1}{4}$ $\frac{1}{3}$ $\frac{2}{5}$ $\frac{1}{2}$, $\frac{1}{1}$ $\frac{2}{5} - \frac{1}{3} = \frac{1}{15}$ remaining
Step 4. Write the fraction you want as the sum of the unit fractions.	$\frac{9}{10} = \frac{1}{2} + \frac{1}{3} + \frac{1}{15}$

Write each fraction as a sum of different unit fractions.

1. $\frac{3}{4}$ **2.** $\frac{5}{8}$ **3.** $\frac{11}{12}$ **4.** $\frac{3}{7}$ **5.** $\frac{7}{5}$

Egg Fractions

This game is played with an empty egg carton. Each compartment represents a fraction with a denominator of 12. The goal is to place tokens in compartments with a given sum.

A complete copy of the rules is available online.

Jenny Thomas/HMH

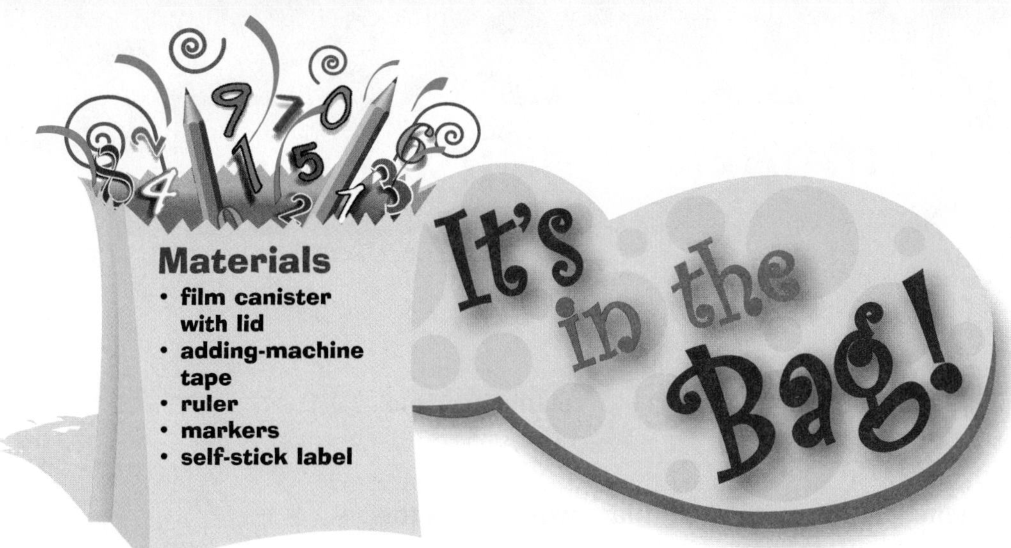

Materials
• film canister with lid
• adding-machine tape
• ruler
• markers
• self-stick label
It's in the Bag!

PROJECT Canister Carry-All

Turn a film canister into a handy carrying case for a number line and notes about rational numbers.

Directions

1. If necessary, cut off a strip along the bottom edge of the adding-machine tape so that the tape will fit into the film canister when it is rolled up. When you're done, the tape should be about $1\frac{3}{4}$ in. wide. **Figure A**

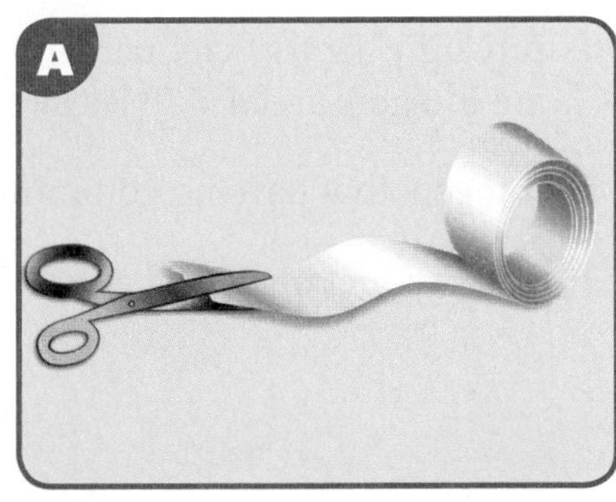

2. Use a ruler to make a long number line on one side of the adding-machine tape. **Figure B**

3. Write the number and title of the chapter on a self-stick label. Then peel the backing off the label and place the label on the outside of the canister.

Taking Note of the Math

Place examples of rational numbers on the number line. Choose examples that will help you remember how to compare and order rational numbers. Then turn the adding-machine tape over, and use the other side to write notes and sample problems from the chapter.

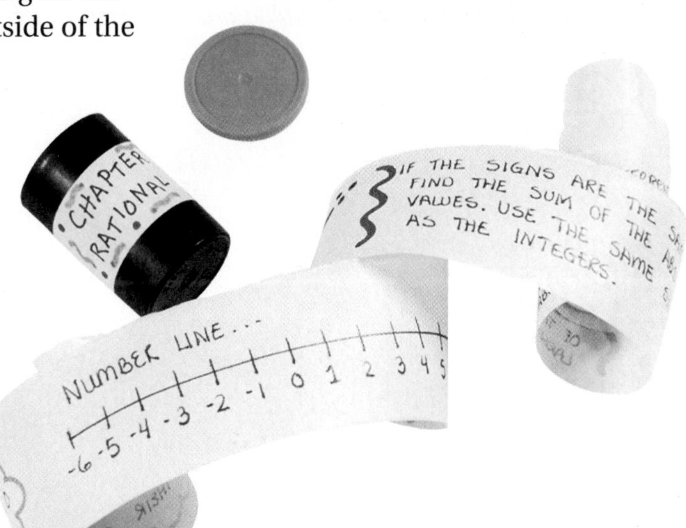

Sam Dudgeon/HMH

Study Guide: Review

Vocabulary

rational number

relatively prime

reciprocal

Complete the sentences below with vocabulary words from the list above.

1. Any number that can be written as a fraction $\frac{n}{d}$ (where n and d are integers and $d \neq 0$) is called a ___?___.

2. Integers that have no common factors other than 1 are ___?___.

3. The product of a number and its ___?___ is 1.

EXAMPLES

EXERCISES

1 Rational Numbers

■ **Write 0.8 as a fraction.**

$0.8 = \frac{8}{10}$ *8 is in the tenths place.*

$= \frac{8 \div 2}{10 \div 2}$ *Divide numerator and denominator by 2.*

$= \frac{4}{5}$

Write each decimal as a fraction.

4. 0.6
5. 0.25
6. 0.525

Write each fraction as a decimal.

7. $\frac{7}{4}$
8. $\frac{4}{15}$
9. $\frac{7}{9}$

Simplify.

10. $\frac{14}{21}$
11. $\frac{22}{33}$
12. $\frac{75}{100}$

Study Guide: Review

EXAMPLES

EXERCISES

2 Multiplying Rational Numbers

■ **Multiply. Write the answer in simplest form.**

$5\left(3\frac{1}{4}\right) = \left(\frac{5}{1}\right)\left(\frac{3(4)+1}{4}\right)$

$= \left(\frac{5}{1}\right)\left(\frac{13}{4}\right)$ *Write as improper fractions.*

$= \frac{65}{4} = 16\frac{1}{4}$ *Multiply and simplify.*

Multiply. Write each answer in simplest form.

13. $3\left(-\frac{2}{5}\right)$

14. $2\left(3\frac{4}{5}\right)$

15. $\frac{-2}{3}\left(\frac{-4}{5}\right)$

16. $\frac{8}{11}\left(\frac{-22}{4}\right)$

17. $5\frac{1}{4}\left(\frac{3}{7}\right)$

18. $2\frac{1}{2}\left(1\frac{3}{10}\right)$

19. $4\frac{7}{8}\left(2\frac{2}{3}\right)$

20. $(-1.75)(-4)$

21. A file transferred $2\frac{3}{4}$ Gb of data each minute for $13\frac{1}{2}$ minutes. How many Gb of data were transferred?

3 Dividing Rational Numbers

■ **Divide. Write the answer in simplest form.**

$\frac{7}{8} \div \frac{3}{4} = \frac{7}{8} \cdot \frac{4}{3}$ *Multiply by the reciprocal.*

$= \frac{7 \cdot 4}{8 \cdot 3}$ *Write as one fraction.*

$\frac{7 \cdot \cancel{4}^{1}}{_{2}\cancel{8} \cdot 3} = \frac{7 \cdot 1}{2 \cdot 3}$ *Remove common factors.*

$\frac{7}{6} = 1\frac{1}{6}$

Divide. Write each answer in simplest form.

22. $3.4 \div 0.2$

23. $-0.1 \div 80$

24. $\frac{3}{4} \div \frac{1}{8}$

25. $\frac{3}{10} \div \frac{4}{5}$

26. $\frac{2}{3} \div 3$

27. $4 \div \frac{-1}{4}$

28. $3\frac{3}{4} \div 3$

29. $1\frac{1}{3} \div \frac{2}{3}$

4 Adding and Subtracting with Unlike Denominators

■ **Add.**

$\frac{3}{4} + \frac{2}{5}$ *Multiply denominators, 4 • 5 = 20.*

$\frac{3 \cdot 5}{4 \cdot 5} = \frac{15}{20}$ $\frac{2 \cdot 4}{5 \cdot 4} = \frac{8}{20}$

$\frac{15}{20} + \frac{8}{20} = \frac{15+8}{20} = \frac{23}{20} = 1\frac{3}{20}$ *Add and simplify.*

Add or subtract.

30. $\frac{5}{6} + \frac{1}{3}$

31. $\frac{5}{6} - \frac{5}{9}$

32. $3\frac{1}{2} + 7\frac{4}{5}$

33. $7\frac{1}{10} - 2\frac{3}{4}$

34. $\frac{19}{20} + \frac{7}{3}$

35. $-1\frac{5}{9} - 7\frac{3}{4}$

EXAMPLES

EXERCISES

5 Solving Equations with Rational Numbers

Solve.

■ $x - 13.7 = -22$

$\underline{+13.7 = +13.7}$ *Add 13.7 to each side.*

$x = -8.3$

■ $\frac{7}{9}x = \frac{2}{5}$

$\frac{9}{7} \cdot \frac{7}{9}x = \frac{9}{7} \cdot \frac{2}{5}$ *Multiply both sides by $\frac{9}{7}$.*

$x = \frac{18}{35}$

Solve.

36. $y + 7.8 = -14$

37. $2.9z = -52.2$

38. $w + \frac{3}{4} = \frac{1}{8}$

39. $\frac{3}{8}p = \frac{3}{4}$

40. $x - \frac{7}{9} = \frac{2}{11}$

41. $7.2x = -14.4$

42. $y - 18.7 = 25.9$

43. $\frac{19}{21}t = -\frac{38}{7}$

44. Freda paid $126 for groceries for her family. This was $1\frac{1}{6}$ as much as she paid the previous time she shopped. How much did Freda pay on her previous shopping trip?

6 Solving Two-Step Equations

Solve.

■ $7x + 12 = 33$

Think: First the variable is multiplied by 7, and then 12 is added. To isolate the variable, subtract 12, and then divide by 7.

$7x + 12 = 33$

$\underline{\quad - 12 \quad - 12}$ *Subtract 12 from both sides.*

$7x = 21$

$\frac{7x}{7} = \frac{21}{7}$ *Divide both sides by 7.*

$x = 3$

■ $\frac{z}{3} - 8 = 5$

Think: First the variable is divided by 3, and then 8 is subtracted. To isolate the variable, add 8, and then multiply by 3.

$\frac{z}{3} - 8 = 5$

$\underline{\quad + 8 \quad +8}$ *Add 8 to both sides.*

$\frac{z}{3} = 13$

$3 \cdot \frac{z}{3} = 3 \cdot 13$ *Multiply both sides by 3.*

$z = 39$

Solve.

45. $3m + 5 = 35$

46. $55 = 7 - 6y$

47. $2c + 1 = -31$

48. $5r + 15 = 0$

49. $\frac{t}{2} + 7 = 15$

50. $\frac{w}{4} - 5 = 11$

51. $-25 = \frac{r}{3} - 11$

52. $\frac{h}{5} - 9 = -19$

53. $\frac{x + 2}{3} = 18$

54. $\frac{d - 3}{4} = -9$

55. $21 = \frac{a - 4}{3}$

56. $14 = \frac{c + 8}{7}$

57. Jake weighed 150.7 pounds with his army boots on, and 144.9 pounds without them. What is the weight of each boot?

58. A music service charges a $2.99 monthly membership fee plus $0.05 for each song purchased. If Naomi's charge for the month was $10.89, how many songs did she purchase?

Chapter Test

Simplify.

1. $\frac{36}{72}$
2. $\frac{21}{35}$
3. $-\frac{16}{88}$
4. $\frac{18}{25}$

Write each decimal as a fraction in simplest form.

5. 0.225
6. 0.04
7. −0.101
8. 0.875

Write each fraction as a decimal.

9. $\frac{7}{8}$
10. $-\frac{13}{25}$
11. $\frac{5}{12}$
12. $\frac{4}{33}$

Add or subtract. Write each answer in simplest form.

13. $2\frac{1}{3} - 1\frac{5}{6}$
14. $7\frac{7}{8} + 2\frac{1}{3}$
15. $8\frac{1}{5} - \frac{2}{3}$
16. Justin worked $2\frac{2}{3}$ hours on Thursday and $6\frac{3}{4}$ hours on Friday. How many hours did he work both days?
17. Kory is making Thai food for several friends. She needs to triple her recipe. The recipe calls for $\frac{3}{4}$ teaspoon of curry. How much curry does she need?

Multiply or divide. Write each answer in simplest form.

18. 9(0.63)
19. $\frac{7}{8} \div \frac{5}{24}$
20. $\frac{2}{3}\left(\frac{-9}{20}\right)$
21. $3\frac{3}{7}\left(1\frac{5}{16}\right)$
22. $34 \div 3.4$
23. $-4\frac{2}{3} \div 1\frac{1}{6}$
24. Lucie drank $\frac{3}{4}$ pint of bottled water. One serving of the water is $\frac{7}{8}$ pint. How much of a serving did Lucie drink?

Solve.

25. $x - \frac{1}{4} = -\frac{3}{8}$
26. $-3.14y = 53.38$
27. $\frac{x+7}{12} = 11$
28. $-2k = \frac{1}{4}$
29. $2h - 3.24 = -1.1$
30. $\frac{4}{7}y + 7 = 31$
31. Rachel walked to a friend's house, then to the store, and then back home. The distance from Rachel's house to her friend's house is $1\frac{5}{6}$ miles. This is twice the distance from Rachel's house to the store. How far does Rachel live from the store?
32. Tickets to an orchestra concert cost $25.50 apiece plus a $2.50 handling fee for each order. If Jamal spent $79, how many tickets did he purchase?

Chapter Test

CHAPTER 1

Cumulative Assessment

Multiple Choice

1. What is the value of the expression $12 - k$ if $k = -3$?

   Ⓐ -15 Ⓒ 9
   Ⓑ -9 Ⓓ 15

2. Which expression is equivalent to $2x - 5$ if $x = -4$?

   Ⓕ -13 Ⓗ 3
   Ⓖ -3 Ⓙ 13

3. Which of the following is equivalent to $\frac{20}{9}$?

   Ⓐ $1\frac{2}{9}$ Ⓒ $\frac{10}{3}$
   Ⓑ 2.3 Ⓓ $2.\overline{2}$

4. Which value of x is the solution of the equation $\frac{x}{3} = -12$?

   Ⓕ $x = -36$ Ⓗ $x = -4$
   Ⓖ $x = -15$ Ⓙ $x = 9$

5. If a pitcher contains $\frac{3}{4}$ gallon of juice and each glass will hold $\frac{1}{8}$ gallon of juice, how many glasses can be filled?

   Ⓐ $\frac{3}{32}$ glass Ⓒ 6 glasses
   Ⓑ $\frac{3}{4}$ glass Ⓓ 8 glasses

6. Skip drove 55.6 miles. Then he drove another $42\frac{1}{5}$ miles. How many miles did he drive in all?

   Ⓕ 97.7 miles Ⓗ 97.8 miles
   Ⓖ 98.5 miles Ⓙ 13.4 miles

7. Which number is greater than $\frac{3}{4}$?

   Ⓐ $\frac{4}{5}$ Ⓒ $\frac{5}{8}$
   Ⓑ 0.75 Ⓓ $0.\overline{6}$

8. Which model correctly represents the number $\frac{1}{4}$?

   Ⓕ 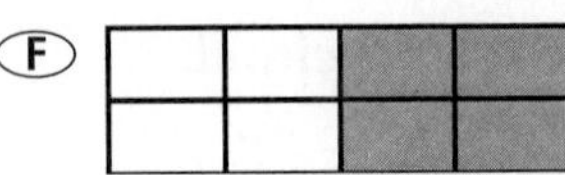

   Ⓖ 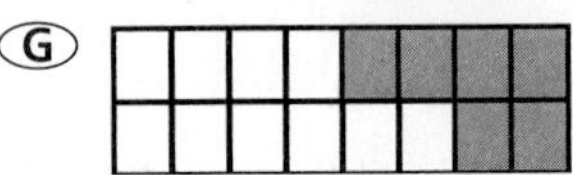

   Ⓗ 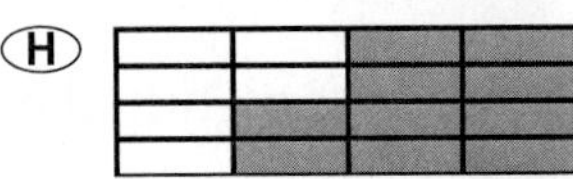

   Ⓙ 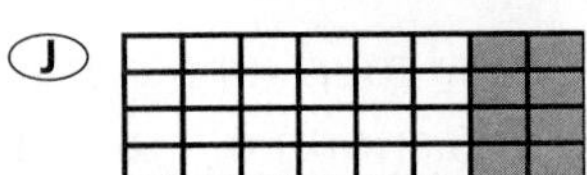

9. According to the graph, what fraction of games resulted in something other than a tie?

   Ⓐ $\frac{9}{10}$ Ⓒ $\frac{6}{15}$
   Ⓑ $\frac{3}{10}$ Ⓓ $\frac{9}{50}$

10. Which value of x makes the equation $\frac{2}{3}x = -\frac{5}{9}$ true?

    Ⓕ $x = -\frac{5}{9}$ Ⓗ $x = -1\frac{1}{4}$
    Ⓖ $x = \frac{1}{6}$ Ⓙ $x = 1\frac{1}{4}$

11. If $\frac{3}{5} = 9s$, what is the value of s?

    Ⓐ 15 Ⓒ $\frac{5}{3}$
    Ⓑ $\frac{27}{5}$ Ⓓ $\frac{1}{15}$

12. Jeremy has started drinking $\frac{1}{4}$ cup of grape juice every Wednesday at lunch. If he has had a total of 5 cups of juice so far, how many Wednesdays has Jeremy had grape juice?

(F) 4 (H) 20

(G) 5 (J) 80

Make sure you look at all the answer choices before making your decision. Try substituting each answer choice into the problem if you are unsure of the answer.

13. Oscar bought a bag of almonds. He ate $\frac{3}{8}$ of the bag on Sunday. On Monday, he ate $\frac{2}{3}$ of the almonds left. What fraction of the entire bag did he eat on Monday?

(A) $\frac{9}{16}$ (C) $\frac{1}{4}$

(B) $\frac{5}{12}$ (D) $\frac{1}{12}$

Gridded Response

14. The diameter of a standard CD is $4\frac{3}{4}$ in. The diameter of the circular hole in the middle is $\frac{1}{2}$ in. Find the distance from the edge of the hole to the outer edge of the CD.

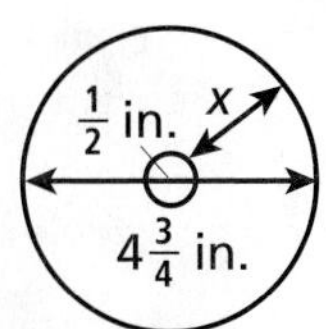

15. Simplify: $7\frac{4}{5} - 3\frac{1}{2} + 6\frac{7}{10}$.

16. Alana has three times as many pairs of shoes as Marie. If Alana has 18 pairs of shoes, how many pairs of shoes does Marie have?

17. Fifteen students earned the National Merit Scholarship out of 600 students in the school. Write this value as a simplified fraction.

Short Response

S1. A health club charges a one-time fee of \$99 and then \$39 per month for membership. Let m represent the number of months, and let C represent the total amount of money spent on the health club membership.

a. Write an equation that relates m and C.

b. If Jillian has spent \$801 on her membership, how many months has she been a member of the club?

S2. The sum of 7 and the absolute value of a number is the same as 12.

a. Write an equation that can be used to solve for the number.

b. Describe the first step of solving the equation.

c. Determine how many numbers make the equation true. Explain your reasoning.

S3. Brigid has a $21\frac{1}{4}$ in. long ribbon. For a project she is cutting it into $\frac{3}{4}$ in. pieces. Into how many $\frac{3}{4}$ in. pieces can she cut the ribbon? Show or explain how you found your answer.

Extended Response

E1. Use a diagram to model the expression $\frac{4}{5} \div \frac{4}{3}$.

a. Draw a diagram to model the fraction $\frac{4}{5}$.

b. What fraction do you multiply by that is equivalent to dividing by $\frac{4}{3}$?

c. Use your answer from part b and shade that fraction of the $\frac{4}{5}$ that is already shaded. What does this shaded area represent?

d. Use your diagram to write the quotient in simplest form.

CHAPTER 2

Graphs and Functions

COMMON CORE

Chapter Focus

- Use functions to represent, analyze, and solve problems.
- Translate among representations of functions.

Why Learn This?

You can often use functions to describe the relationship between two quantities mathematically. For example, you can use a function to show how the altitude of a plane changes over time.

Learn It Online
Chapter Project Online

Are You Ready?

Vocabulary

Choose the best term from the list to complete each sentence.

1. An __?__ states that two expressions have the same value.
2. Any number that can be written as a fraction is a __?__.
3. A __?__ serves as a placeholder for a number.
4. An __?__ can be a whole number or its opposite.

algebraic expression
equation
integer
rational number
variable

Complete these exercises to review skills you will need for this chapter.

Whole Number Operations

Simplify each expression.

5. $5 + 12$ **6.** $18 - 9$ **7.** $25 \cdot 11$ **8.** $56 \div 4$

9. $8 \cdot 40$ **10.** $102 \div 3$ **11.** $250 - 173$ **12.** $107 + 298$

Decimal Operations

Simplify each expression.

13. $1.25 + 3.7$ **14.** $52.7 - 12.9$ **15.** $3.2 \cdot 1.2$ **16.** $5.7 \div 0.3$

17. $2.84 \div 1.3$ **18.** $17.5 \cdot 12.1$ **19.** $17.5 - 12.45$ **20.** $2.75 + 13.254$

Operations with Fractions

Simplify each expression.

21. $\frac{2}{3} - \frac{1}{2}$ **22.** $\frac{13}{18} + \frac{19}{24}$ **23.** $\frac{7}{8}\left(\frac{6}{11}\right)$ **24.** $\frac{9}{10} \div \frac{9}{13}$

25. $\frac{5}{6}\left(\frac{8}{15}\right)$ **26.** $\frac{11}{12} \div \frac{121}{144}$ **27.** $\frac{1}{6} + \frac{5}{8}$ **28.** $\frac{19}{20} - \frac{4}{5}$

Integer Operations

Simplify each expression.

29. $-15 + 7$ **30.** $25 - (-23)$ **31.** $20(-13)$ **32.** $\frac{-108}{9}$

33. $\frac{161}{-7}$ **34.** $-13 + (-28)$ **35.** $-72 - 18$ **36.** $-31(14)$

CHAPTER 2

Study Guide: Preview

Where You've Been

Previously, you

- located and named integers on a number line.
- graphed data to demonstrate familiar relationships.
- interpreted graphs, tables, and equations.

In This Chapter

You will study

- locating ordered pairs of rational numbers on a coordinate plane.
- generating different representations of data using tables, graphs, and equations.
- using functions to describe relationships among data.

Where You're Going

You can use the skills learned in this chapter

- to identify different types of functions.
- to make predictions based on analysis of data.

Key Vocabulary/Vocabulario

coordinate plane	plano cartesiano
domain	dominio
function	función
ordered pair	par ordenado
origin	origen
quadrant	cuadrante
range	recorrido o rango
x-axis	eje de las x
y-axis	eje de las y

Vocabulary Connections

To become familiar with some of the vocabulary terms in the chapter, consider the following. You may refer to the chapter, the glossary, or a dictionary if you like.

1. The word **origin** means "beginning." How do you think this might apply to graphing?
2. The root of the word **quadrant** is *quad*, which means "four." What do you think a quadrant of a graph might be?
3. The word *ordered* means "arranged according to a rule." Do you think it matters which number comes first in an **ordered pair** ? Explain.

Study Guide: Preview

Reading Strategy: Read a Lesson for Understanding

You need to be actively involved as you work through each lesson in your textbook. To begin with, find the lesson's objective, which your teacher will provide to you. As you progress through the lesson, keep the objective in mind while you work through examples and answer questions.

Lesson Features | **Reading Tips**

Rational Numbers

Identify the title of the lesson and look through the lesson to get a feel for the objective of the lesson.

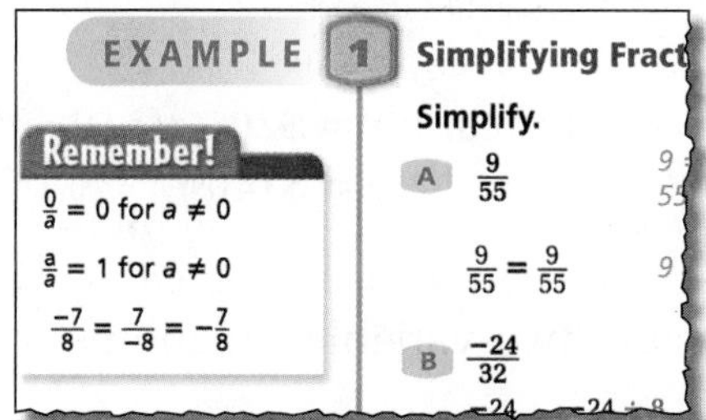

EXAMPLE 1 Simplifying Fract

Remember!
$\frac{0}{a} = 0$ for $a \neq 0$
$\frac{a}{a} = 1$ for $a \neq 0$
$\frac{-7}{8} = \frac{7}{-8} = -\frac{7}{8}$

Simplify.

A $\frac{9}{55}$

$\frac{9}{55} = \frac{9}{55}$

B $\frac{-24}{32}$

Work through each example. The examples help to demonstrate the lesson objectives.

Think and Discuss

1. Explain how you can be su

2. Give the sign of a fraction i the denominator is negative

Check your understanding of the lesson by answering the *Think and Discuss* questions.

Try This

Choose a lesson from this chapter to answer each question.

1. What is the objective of the lesson?
2. What questions or problems did you have when you read the lesson?
3. Write your own example problem similar to Example 2.
4. What skill is being practiced in the first *Think and Discuss* question?

2-1 Ordered Pairs

Vocabulary
ordered pair

The company that makes team uniforms for a soccer league charges a $20 fee for team artwork and $10 for each jersey. Dominic's team has 14 players, and Alyssa's team has 12 players. Find the cost for a set of jerseys for each team.

Let y be the total cost of a set of jerseys and x be the number of jerseys needed.

total cost of jerseys = $20 + $10 · number of jerseys

$$y = \$20 + \$10 \cdot x$$

Dominic's team: $y = \$20 + (\$10 \cdot 14)$
$y = \$160$

Alyssa's team: $y = \$20 + (\$10 \cdot 12)$
$y = \$140$

An **ordered pair** (x, y) is a pair of numbers that can be used to locate a point on a coordinate plane. A solution of a two-variable equation can be written as an ordered pair.

The ordered pair (14, 160) is a solution because $160 = \$20 + (\$10 \cdot 14)$.
The ordered pair (12, 140) is a solution because $140 = \$20 + (\$10 \cdot 12)$.

EXAMPLE 1 **Deciding Whether an Ordered Pair Is a Solution of an Equation**

Determine whether each ordered pair is a solution of $y = 3x + 2$.

Helpful Hint
The order in which a solution is written is important. Always write x first, then y.

A (2, 5)

$y = 3x + 2$
$5 \stackrel{?}{=} 3(2) + 2$ *Substitute 2 for x and 5 for y.*
$5 \neq 8$ ✗ *Simplify.*

(2, 5) is *not* a solution.

B (3, 11)

$y = 3x + 2$
$11 \stackrel{?}{=} 3(3) + 2$ *Substitute 3 for x and 11 for y.*
$11 = 11$ ✓ *Simplify.*

(3, 11) is a solution.

Video Lesson Tutorials Online my.hrw.com

EXAMPLE 2 Creating a Table of Ordered Pair Solutions

Use the given values to make a table of solutions.

Helpful Hint

A table of solutions can be set up vertically or horizontally.

A $y = 8x$ for $x = 1, 2, 3, 4$

x	$8x$	y	(x, y)
1	8(1)	8	(1, 8)
2	8(2)	16	(2, 16)
3	8(3)	24	(3, 24)
4	8(4)	32	(4, 32)

B $n = 4m - 3$ for $m = -4, -3, -2, -1$

m	−4	−3	−2	−1
$4m - 3$	4(−4) − 3	4(−3) − 3	4(−2) − 3	4(−1) − 3
n	−19	−15	−11	−7
(m, n)	(−4, −19)	(−3, −15)	(−2, −11)	(−1, −7)

EXAMPLE 3 *Consumer Math Application*

In most states, the price of each item is not the total cost. Sales tax must be added. If sales tax is 6%, the equation for total cost is $c = 1.06p$, where p is the price before tax.

A **How much will Dominic's $160 set of jerseys cost after sales tax?**

$c = 1.06(160)$ *The price of Dominic's set of jerseys before tax is $160.*

$c = 169.6$ *Multiply.*

After tax, Dominic's $160 set of jerseys will cost $169.60, so (160, 169.60) is a solution of the equation.

B **How much will Alyssa's $140 set of jerseys cost after sales tax?**

$c = 1.06(140)$ *The price of Alyssa's set of jerseys before tax is $140.*

$c = 148.4$ *Multiply.*

After tax, Alyssa's $140 set of jerseys will cost $148.40, so (140, 148.40) is a solution of the equation.

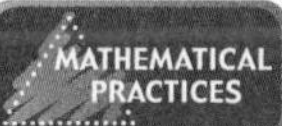

Think and Discuss

1. **Describe** how to find a solution of a two-variable equation.
2. **Explain** why an equation with two variables has an infinite number of solutions.
3. **Give** two equations using x and y that have (1, 2) as a solution.

2-1 Exercises

Learn It Online
Homework Help Online
Exercises 1–16, 17, 19, 21, 23

GUIDED PRACTICE

See Example 1 — **Determine whether each ordered pair is a solution of $y = 2x - 4$.**

1. (3, 2) **2.** (−4, 5) **3.** (6, 8) **4.** (2, 0)

See Example 2 — **Use the given values to make a table of solutions.**

5. $y = 2x$ for $x = 1, 2, 3, 4$

6. $y = 4x - 1$ for $x = -4, -3, -2, -1$

See Example 3

7. The cost of a small frozen yogurt is $2.50 plus $0.15 per topping. The equation that gives the total cost c of a small frozen yogurt is $c = 0.15n + 2.50$, where n is the number of toppings. What is the cost of a small frozen yogurt with 3 toppings?

INDEPENDENT PRACTICE

See Example 1 — **Determine whether each ordered pair is a solution of $y = 4x + 3$.**

8. (2, 9) **9.** (4, 20) **10.** (5, 23) **11.** (6, 28)

See Example 2 — **Use the given values to make a table of solutions.**

12. $y = 2x - 1$ for $x = 1, 2, 3, 4$

13. $y = 3x + 9$ for $x = -4, -3, -2, -1$

14. $y = 4x - 5$ for $x = 2, 4, 6, 8$

15. $y = 3x - 4$ for $x = 2, 4, 6, 8$

See Example 3

16. The fine for speeding in one town is $90 plus $7 for every mile over the speed limit. The equation that gives the total cost c of a speeding ticket is $c = 90 + 7m$, where m is the number of miles over the posted speed limit. Rhonda was issued a ticket for going 63 mi/h in a 50 mi/h zone. What was the total cost of the ticket?

PRACTICE AND PROBLEM SOLVING

Extra Practice
See Extra Practice for more exercises.

Determine whether each ordered pair is a solution of $y = x + 3$.

17. (4, 7) **18.** (−3, 0) **19.** (5, 8) **20.** (2, 6)

Determine whether each ordered pair is a solution of $y = 3x - 5$.

21. (−2, 2) **22.** (4, 8) **23.** (3, 4) **24.** (6, 12)

25. Multi-Step A wireless phone company charges a monthly fee of $39.99 plus $0.49 per minute for usage that exceeds the included minutes. Write an equation for the monthly cost c in terms of the number of exceeded minutes m. Solve the equation to find the cost when the number of exceeded minutes is 29. Write your answer as an ordered pair.

26. Geometry The perimeter P of a square is four times the length of one side s, or $P = 4s$. Is (14, 55) a solution of this equation? If not, find a solution that uses one of the given values.

In 1513, Ponce de León went in search of the legendary Fountain of Youth, which people believed would give them eternal youth. While searching, he discovered Florida, which he named Pascua de Florida.

Use the given values to make a table of solutions.

27. $y = 2x - 2$ for $x = 1, 2, 3, 4$

28. $y = 3x - 1$ for $x = -4, -3, -2, -1$

29. $y = x + 7$ for $x = 1, 2, 3, 4$

30. $y = 3x + 2$ for $x = 2, 4, 6, 8, 10$

31. **History** The life expectancy of Americans has been rising steadily since 1940. An ordered pair can be used to show the relationship between your birth year and life expectancy.

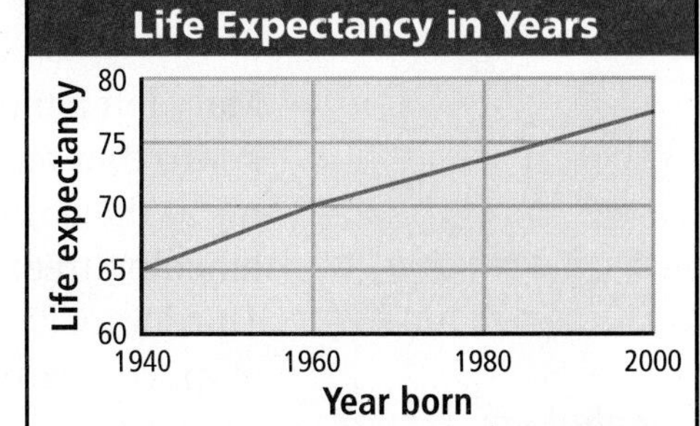

a. Write an ordered pair that shows the approximate life expectancy of an American born in 1980.

b. The data on the chart can be approximated by the equation $L = 0.2n - 323$, where L is the life expectancy and n is the year of birth. Use the equation to find an ordered pair that shows the approximate life expectancy for an American born in 2020.

32. **Critical Thinking** Two solutions of an equation are (6, 5) and (8, 5). What could the equation be? Explain.

33. **What's The Error?** A student thinks that (1, 2) is a solution to $y = 2x - 3$. While checking the solution, the student gets $1 = 2(2) - 3$. What is wrong with this calculation? Explain the error.

34. **Write About It** Write an equation that has (2, 6) as a solution. Explain how you found the equation.

35. **Challenge** In the NBA, a shot made from beyond the arc is worth 3 points. A shot made on or in front of the arc is worth 2 points. If x equals the number of 3-point baskets scored and y equals the number of 2-point baskets scored, find the possible solutions of the equation $36 = 3x + 2y$.

Test Prep

36. **Multiple Choice** Which ordered pair is a solution of $2y - 3x = 8$?

(A) (6, 13) (B) (19, 4) (C) (10, 4) (D) (4, 0)

37. **Multiple Choice** Which ordered pair is NOT a solution of $y = 3x - 2$?

(F) (0, −2) (G) (−2, −8) (H) (2, 4) (J) (2, 0)

2-2 Graphing on a Coordinate Plane

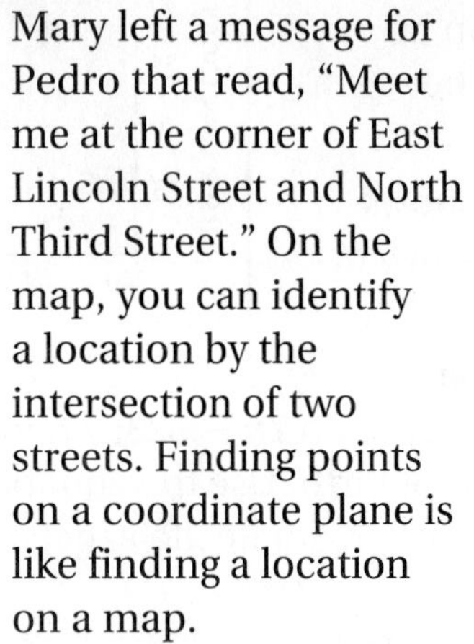

Mary left a message for Pedro that read, "Meet me at the corner of East Lincoln Street and North Third Street." On the map, you can identify a location by the intersection of two streets. Finding points on a coordinate plane is like finding a location on a map.

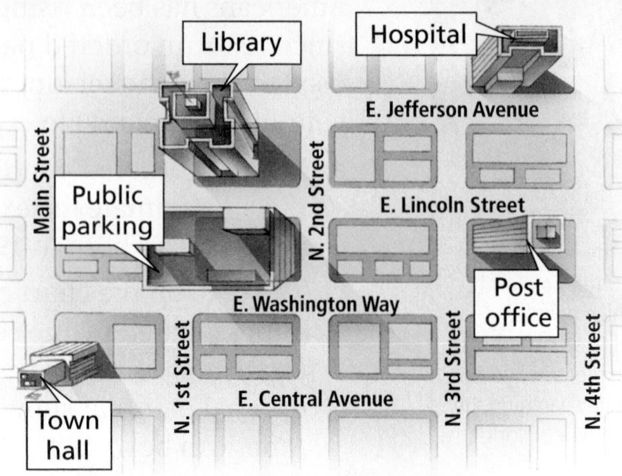

Vocabulary

coordinate plane

x-axis

y-axis

quadrant

x-coordinate

y-coordinate

origin

The **coordinate plane** is formed by two number lines, the ***x*-axis** and the ***y*-axis**. They intersect at right angles and divide the plane into four **quadrants**. The ***x*-coordinate** is the first number in an ordered pair. The ***y*-coordinate** is the second number of an ordered pair.

Helpful Hint

The sign of a number indicates which direction to move.
Positive: up or right
Negative: down or left

Interactivities Online ▶

To plot an ordered pair, begin at the **origin**, the point (0, 0). It is the intersection of the *x*-axis and the *y*-axis. The *x*-coordinate tells how many units to move left or right; the *y*-coordinate tells how many units to move up or down.

move right 2 units

move up 3 units

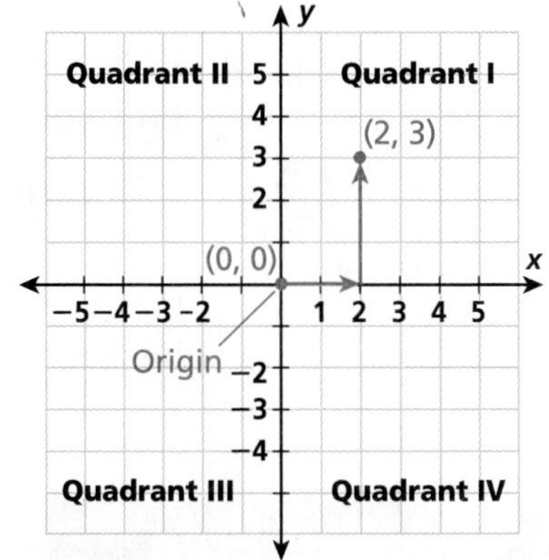

EXAMPLE 1 Finding the Coordinates and Quadrants of Points on a Plane

Give the coordinates and quadrant of each point.

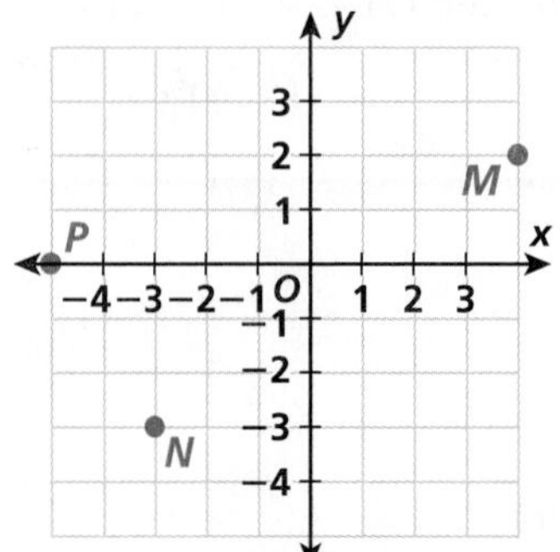

Point *M* is (4, 2); in Quadrant I.

4 units right, 2 units up

Point *N* is (−3, −3); in Quadrant III.

3 units left, 3 units down

Point *P* is (−5, 0); it has no quadrant because *P* is on the *x*-axis.

5 units left, 0 units up

Video Lesson Tutorials Online my.hrw.com

EXAMPLE 2 Graphing Points on a Coordinate Plane

Graph each point on a coordinate plane.

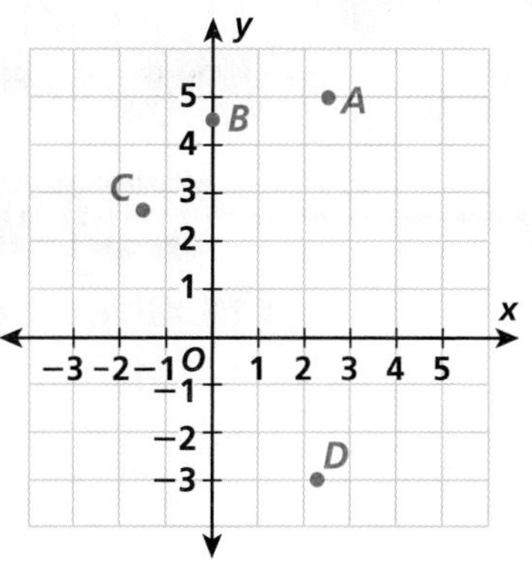

A $A(2.5, 5)$

right 2.5, up 5

B $B\left(0, 4\frac{1}{2}\right)$

right 0, up $4\frac{1}{2}$

C $C\left(-1\frac{1}{2}, 2.7\right)$

left $1\frac{1}{2}$, up 2.7

D $D(2.3, -3)$

right 2.3, down 3

You can find the horizontal or vertical distance between two points on the coordinate plane by subtracting their *x*- or *y*-coordinates. Because distance cannot be negative, find the absolute value of the difference.

DISTANCE BETWEEN POINTS

Given two points (x_1, y_1) and (x_2, y_2):

Horizontal distance $= |x_2 - x_1|$

Vertical distance $= |y_2 - y_1|$

EXAMPLE 3 Finding Horizontal and Vertical Distances

Helpful Hint

The order of the points does not matter when you find the distance between them. For Example 1A:
$|4 - (-6)| = |10| = 10$
$|-6 - 4| = |-10| = 10$

Find the distance between each pair of points.

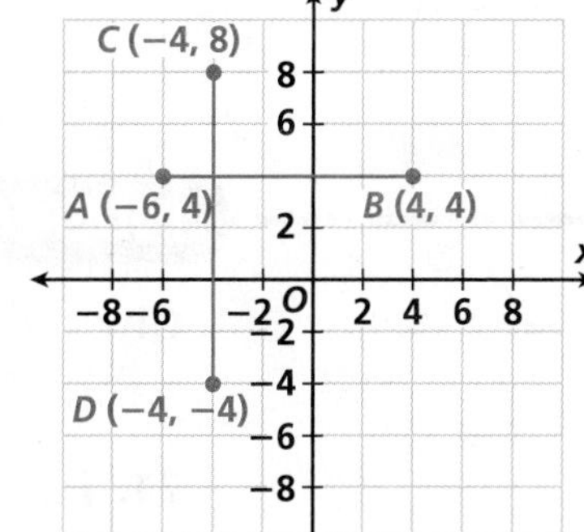

A A and B

Use the x-coordinates.

Distance $= |4 - (-6)|$
$= |10|$
$= 10$

The points are 10 units apart.

B C and D

Use the y-coordinates.

Distance $= |-4 - 8|$
$= |-12|$
$= 12$

The points are 12 units apart.

Think and Discuss

MATHEMATICAL PRACTICES

1. Explain how you could find the distance between the points (5, 7) and (5, −8) on the coordinate plane.

2-2 Exercises

Learn It Online
Homework Help Online
Exercises 1–36, 37, 41, 45

GUIDED PRACTICE

See Example 1 Give the coordinates and quadrant of each point.

1. A
2. B
3. C
4. D
5. E
6. F

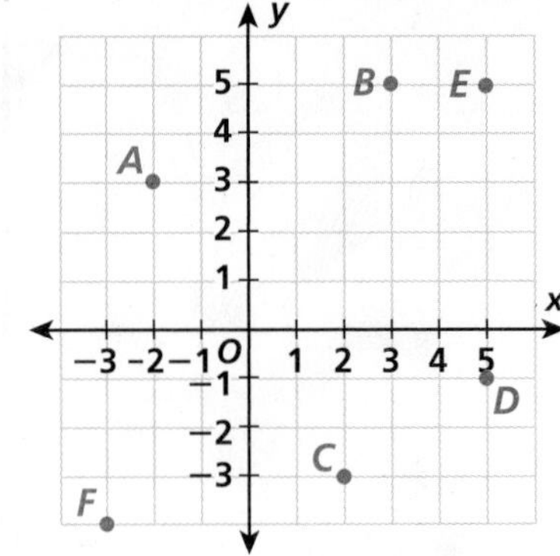

See Example 2 Graph each point on a coordinate plane.

7. $A(3.5, 4)$
8. $B\left(6, 1\frac{1}{3}\right)$
9. $C(-1, 6)$
10. $D\left(2.7, -5\frac{1}{2}\right)$
11. $E(4.5, 7)$
12. $F(6, -2)$
13. $G\left(3, 7\frac{1}{2}\right)$
14. $H(1.5, -4)$

See Example 3 Find the distance between each pair of points.

15. A and B
16. C and D
17. A and E
18. F and D

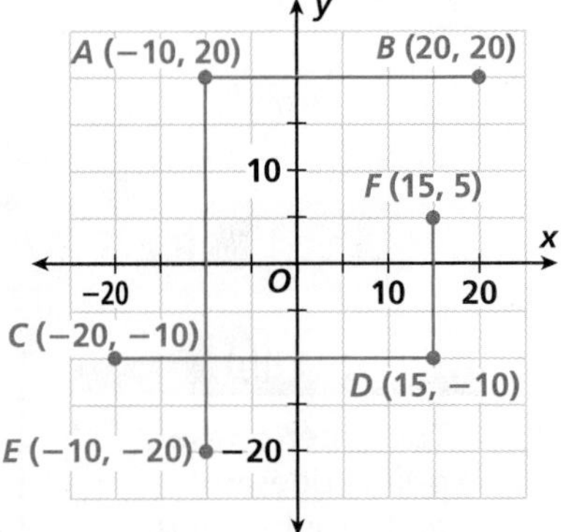

INDEPENDENT PRACTICE

See Example 1 Give the coordinates and quadrant of each point.

19. G
20. H
21. J
22. K
23. L
24. M

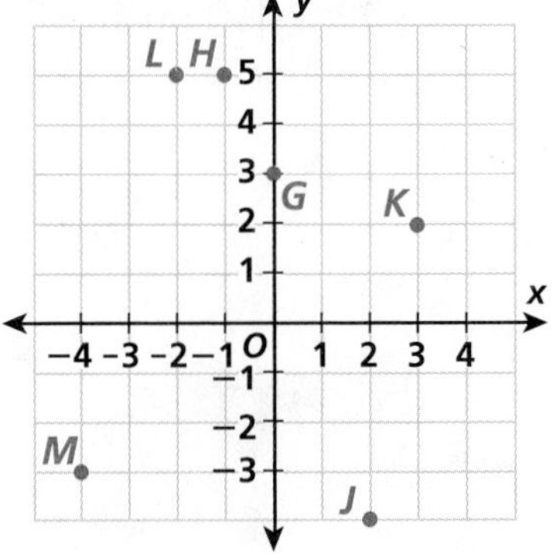

See Example 2 Graph each point on a coordinate plane.

25. $A\left(2\frac{1}{3}, 6.5\right)$
26. $B(0.7, 4.2)$
27. $C(-1, -7)$
28. $D(-2.7, 0)$
29. $E\left(4\frac{1}{3}, 7\right)$
30. $F(-2, 5)$
31. $G(0, 3)$
32. $H(6.5, 3)$

See Example 3

Find the distance between each pair of points.

33. A and B

34. B and C

35. C and D

36. D and E

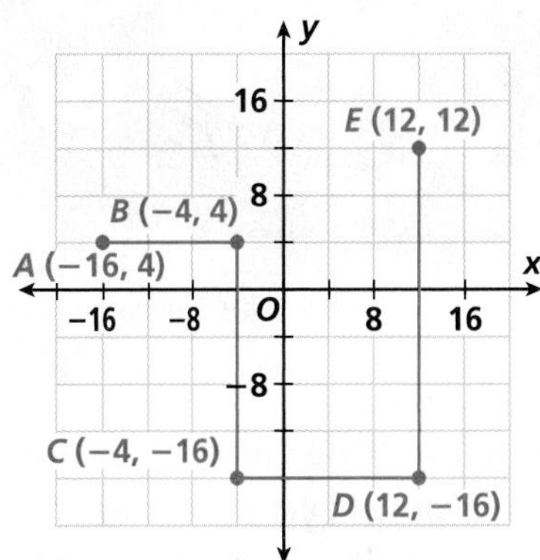

PRACTICE AND PROBLEM SOLVING

Extra Practice

See Extra Practice for more exercises.

Find the distance between each pair of points.

37. (5, −4) and (5, 10)

38. (12, 18) and (30, 18)

39. (−8, −7) and (−22, −7)

40. (−4, −12) and (−4, 15)

41. **Recreation** Monica and Derrick started riding their bikes from the same point. Monica rode 6 kilometers east and 2 kilometers south. Derrick rode 1 kilometer north, 4 kilometers west, and 3 kilometers south.
   a. Show Monica's and Derrick's paths on a coordinate grid. Let the origin represent their starting point.
   b. How far apart are Monica and Derrick at the end of their rides?

42. **Write About It** The point (0, 0) on the coordinate plane is called the origin. Explain why this is.

43. **Challenge** Write a problem whose solution is a geometric shape on the coordinate plane.

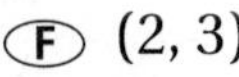

Test Prep

44. **Multiple Choice** What is the distance from point X to point Y?

   Ⓐ 3 units Ⓑ 4 units Ⓒ 6 units Ⓓ 9 units

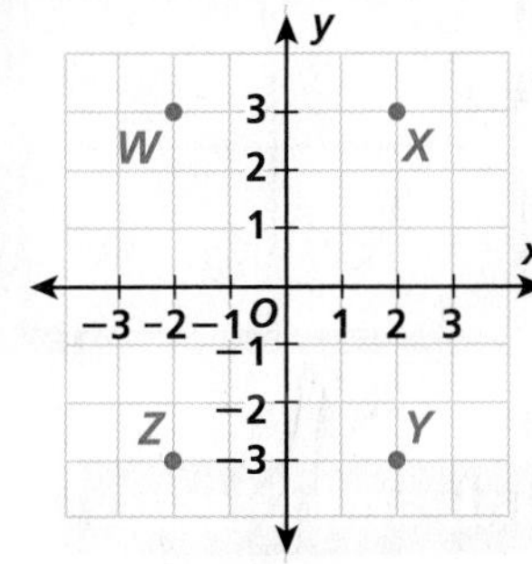

45. **Multiple Choice** Which ordered pair shows the coordinates for point W on the grid?

   Ⓕ (2, 3) Ⓖ (−2, 3) Ⓗ (2, −3) Ⓙ (−2, −3)

Technology LAB

Graph Points

Use with Graphing on a Coordinate Plane

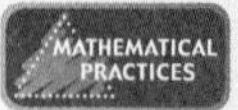

Use appropriate tools strategically.

On a graphing calculator, the WINDOW menu settings determine which points you see and the spacing between those points. In the standard viewing window, the x- and y-values each go from -10 to 10, and the tick marks are one unit apart. The boundaries are set by **Xmin, Xmax, Ymin**, and **Ymax. Xscl** and **Yscl** give the distance between the tick marks.

WINDOW
Xmin=-10
Xmax=10
Xscl=1
Ymin=-10
Ymax=10
Yscl=1
Xres=1

Activity

Plot the points (2, 5), (-2, 3), ($-\frac{3}{2}$, 4), and (1.75, -2) in the standard window. Then change the minimum and maximum x- and y-values of the window to -5 and 5.

Press WINDOW to check that you have the standard window settings.

To plot (2, 5), press  2nd PRGM (DRAW) **POINTS** ENTER.

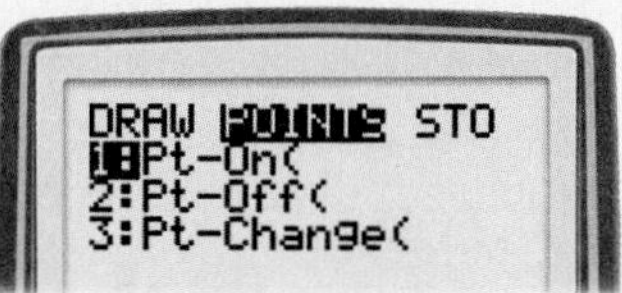

Then press 2 , 5 ENTER. After you see the grid with a point at (2, 5), press 2nd MODE (QUIT) to quit. Repeat the steps above to graph (-2, 3), ($-\frac{3}{2}$, 4), and (1.75, -2).

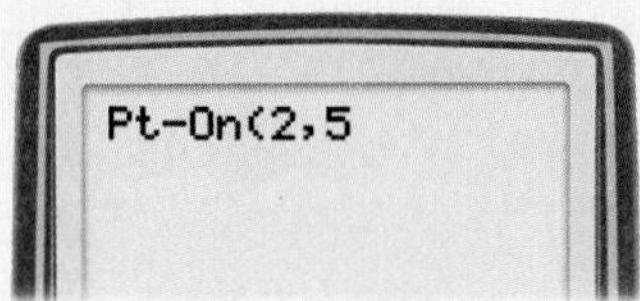

This is the graph in the standard window.

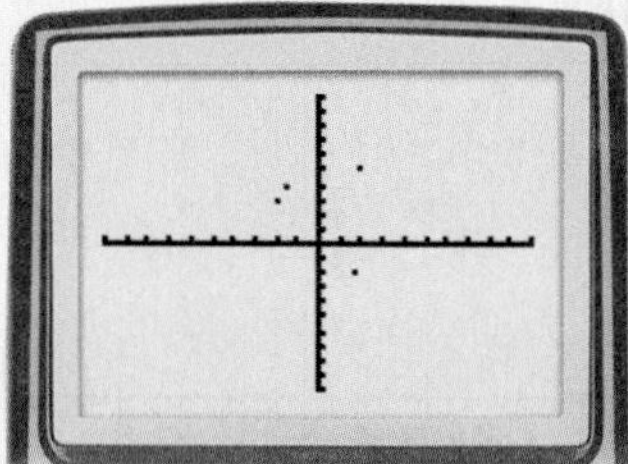

Press WINDOW. Change the **Xmin, Xmax, Ymin,** and **Ymax** values as shown.

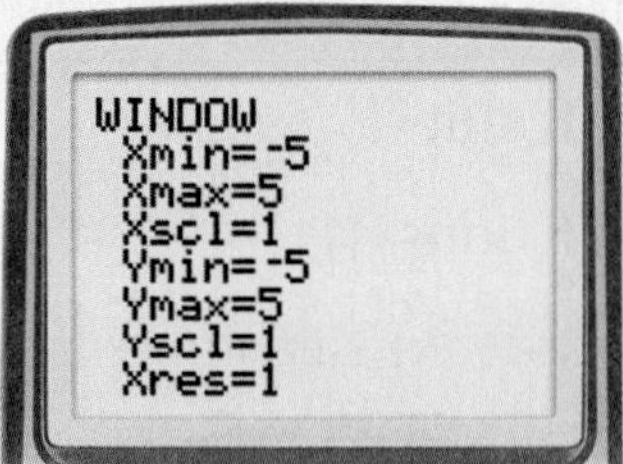

Repeat the steps above to graph the points in the new window.

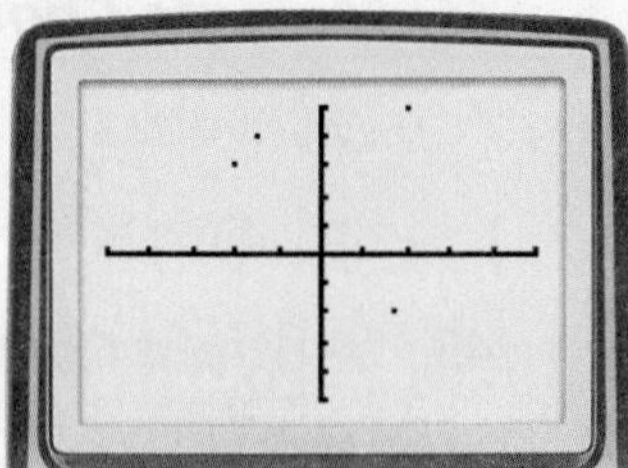

Think and Discuss

1. Compare the two graphs above. Describe and explain any differences you see.

Try This

Graph the points (-3, -8), (2, 3), (3.5, 6), (4, 9), and (-5.5, 11) in each window.

1. standard window

2. **Xmin** = -10; **Xmax** = 10; **Ymin** = -15; **Ymax** = 15; **Yscl** = 3

2-3 Interpreting Graphs

COMMON CORE

CC.8.F.5: Describe qualitatively the functional relationship between two quantities by analyzing a graph. Sketch a graph that exhibits the qualitative features of a function that has been described verbally.

Vocabulary

continuous graph

discrete graph

Graphs can be used to model a variety of situations. For example, a graph can show the relationship between a snowboarder's speed during a race and the time since the race began. Trends in the graph indicate whether the snowboarder's speed is increasing or decreasing.

To relate a graph to a given situation, use key words in the description.

EXAMPLE 1 Matching Situations to Graphs

The graphs show the speeds of three snowboarders during a race. Tell which graph corresponds to each situation.

Graph 1

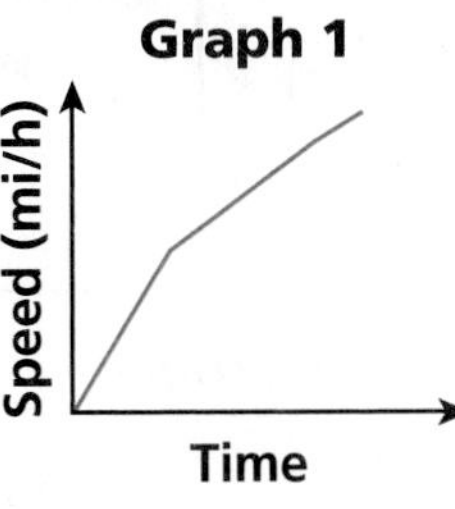

Graph 2

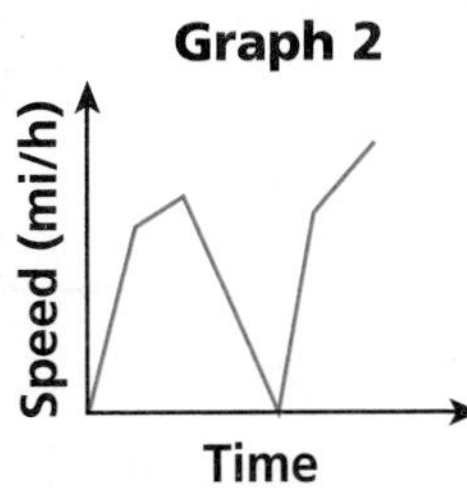

Graph 3

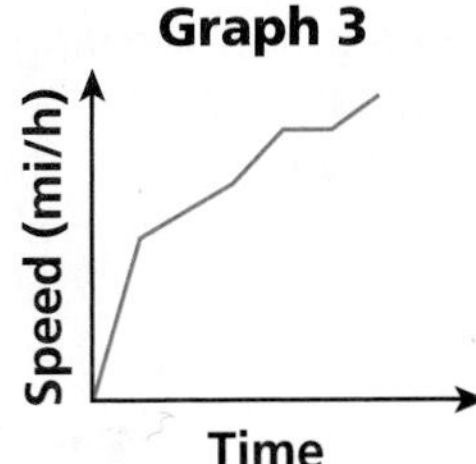

A Jordan gets off to a good start and continues through the course, picking up speed.

Graph 1—The racer's speed increases throughout the race.

B Ethan gets off to a good start and picks up speed. Toward the end of the race, he nearly falls and his speed stops increasing. He rights himself and finishes the race, reaching his greatest speed.

Graph 3—The racer's speed increases for most of the race. Then his speed remains constant for a short period, indicating the point where he nearly fell. The racer then picks up speed to finish the race.

C Xavier gets off to a good start but falls around the middle of the race. He gets up and finishes the race, gaining speed through the finish line.

Graph 2—The racer's speed increases until about halfway through the race, when it drops to 0. A speed of 0 indicates that the racer has stopped or fallen. After this, the racer's speed increases through the finish line.

A **continuous graph** is a graph made up of connected lines or curves. The graphs in Example 1 are continuous graphs.

A **discrete graph** is a graph made up of distinct, or unconnected, points. The graph on photo printing costs is an example of a discrete graph.

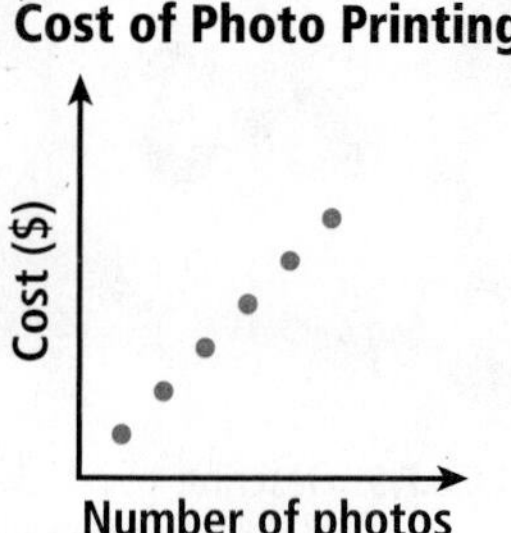

EXAMPLE 2 Creating a Graph of a Situation

Create a graph for each situation. Tell whether the graph is continuous or discrete.

A The table shows the altitude of an airplane over time.

Graph points for the data in the table.

Time (min)	Altitude (ft)
0	0
10	10,000
20	20,000
30	30,000
60	30,000
70	20,000
80	10,000
90	0

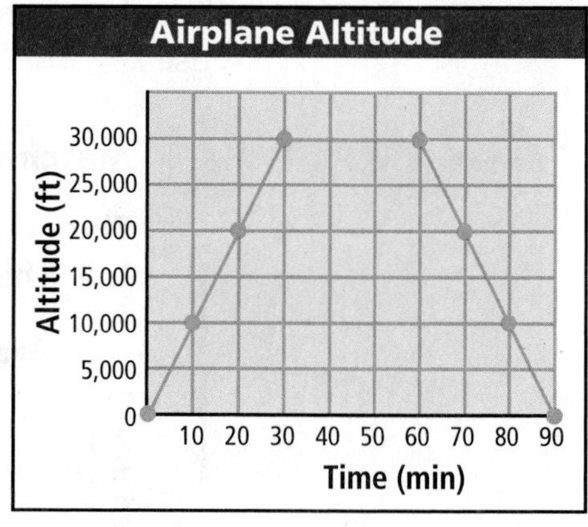

Since every value of time has a corresponding altitude, connect the points.

The graph is continuous.

B Tickets to a concert cost $15 each.

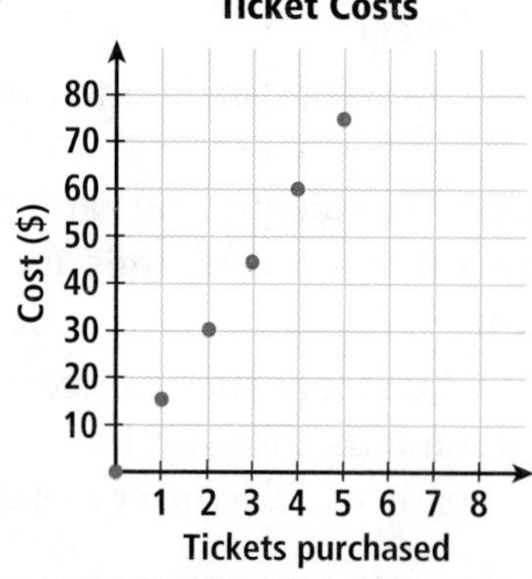

The cost (y-axis) increases by $15 for each ticket purchased (x-axis).

Because each person can only buy whole tickets or none at all, the graph is distinct points.

The graph is discrete.

Helpful Hint

The plane's altitude cannot change from 0 ft to 10,000 ft without the plane traveling through all the altitudes in between. Therefore, the graph showing the altitude is continuous.

Think and Discuss

MATHEMATICAL PRACTICES

1. **Give** a situation that, when graphed, would include a horizontal segment.

2-3 Exercises

Learn It Online
Homework Help Online
Exercises 1–10, 13, 17, 19

GUIDED PRACTICE

See Example 1

The graphs give the speeds in mi/h of three people who are riding snowmobiles. Tell which graph corresponds to each situation.

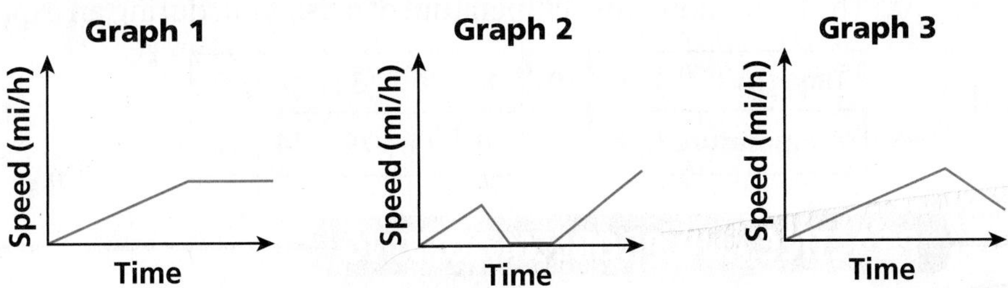

1. David begins his ride slowly but then stops to talk with some friends. After a few minutes, he continues his ride, gradually increasing his speed.
2. Amber steadily increases her speed through most of her ride. Then she slows down as she nears some trees.
3. Kai steadily increases his speed for the first part of his ride. He then keeps a constant speed as he continues his ride.

See Example 2

Create a graph for each situation. Tell whether the graph is continuous or discrete.

4. The table shows the speed of a ride at an amusement park at various times.

Time	3:20	3:21	3:22	3:23	3:24	3:25
Speed (mi/h)	0	14	41	62	8	0

5. A Web site charges \$0.90 for each song a customer downloads. Melanie can download no more than 3 songs.

INDEPENDENT PRACTICE

See Example 1

The graphs give the speeds in mi/h of three dogs during an obstacle course race. Tell which graph corresponds to each situation.

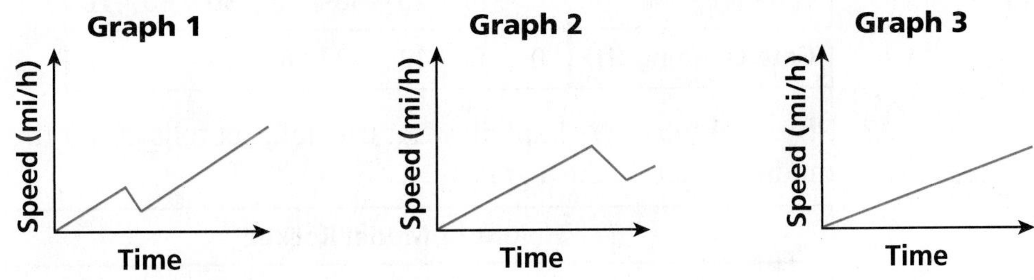

6. Brandy increases her speed throughout the race.
7. Bruno starts well but soon has to slow down to run around cones. After this, he steadily increases his speed.
8. Max gets off to a fast start and picks up speed. He slows down near the end of the race for a tunnel but then increases his speed right afterward.

See Example 2 **Create a graph for each situation. Tell whether the graph is continuous or discrete.**

9. The table shows the relationship between the number of targets a person hits in a game of laser tag and that person's score.

Targets hit	0	1	2	3	4	5	6
Score	0	8	16	24	32	40	48

10. The table shows the temperature of a fish tank during an experiment.

Time (h)	0	1	2	3	4	5
Temperature (°F)	82	80	78	76	74	72

PRACTICE AND PROBLEM SOLVING

Extra Practice
See Extra Practice for more exercises.

Write a possible situation for each graph.

11.

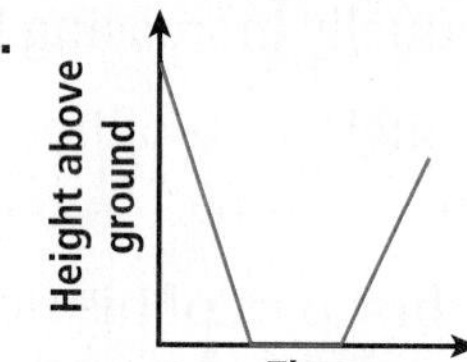

12.

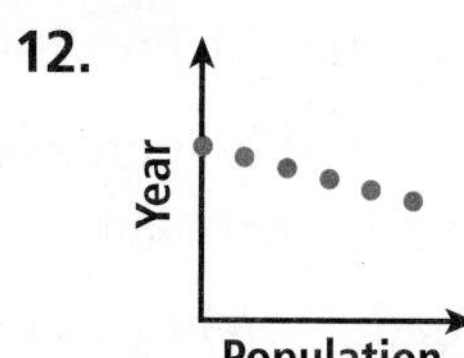

Tell whether each situation would be represented by a continuous graph or a discrete graph.

13. A bookstore has 12 copies of a bestseller. Each copy is on sale for $16.00.

14. The volume of water in a swimming pool steadily decreases by 20 gallons per minute for a period of 3 hours.

15. The table shows the number of passengers on a subway after various stops.

Stop	1	2	3	4	5	6
Passengers	22	30	36	32	32	18

16. Security Create a graph that illustrates the information in the table about the movement of an electronic security gate.

Time (s)	0	10	20	30	40	50	60	70
Gate Opening (ft)	0	6	12	12	6	10	3	0

17. Physical Science Explain what the data set tells about the flight of a model rocket. Make a graph.

Height of Model Rocket								
Time	1:00	1:01	1:02	1:03	1:04	1:05	1:06	1:07
Average Height (ft)	0	147	153	155	152	148	0	0

18. Write About It Give an example of a situation from your own life that could be modeled by a continuous graph.

Earth Science LINK

19. Use the chart to choose the correct geyser name to label each graph.

Yellowstone National Park Geysers			
Geyser Name	Old Faithful	Grand	Riverside
Duration (min)	1.5 to 5	10	20

a. 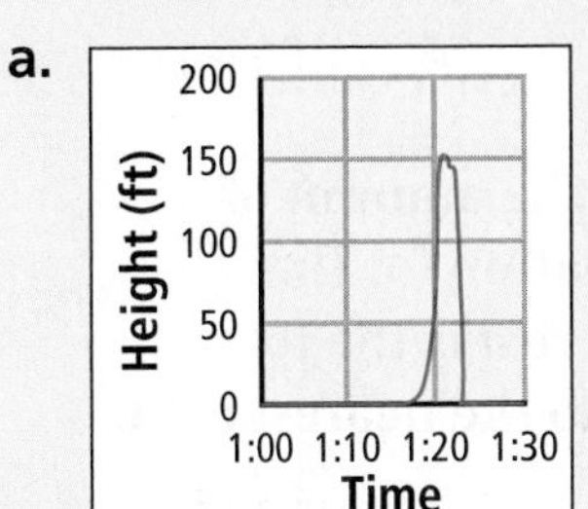

b. 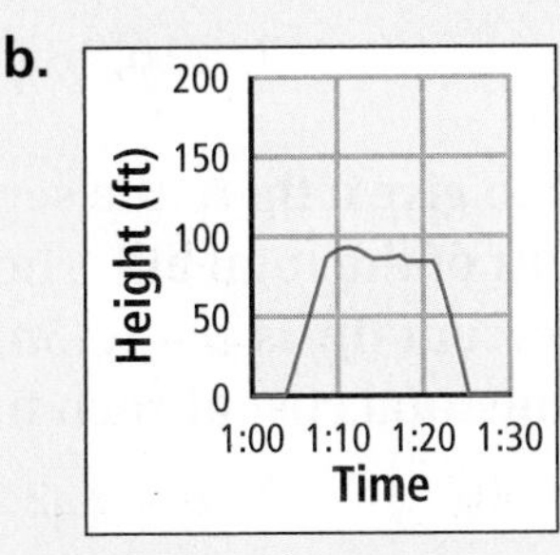

Old Faithful is the most famous geyser at Yellowstone National Park.

Old Faithful Eruption Information	
Duration	**Time Until Next Eruption**
2.5 min	70 min
3 min	72 min
3.5 min	74 min
4 min	82 min
4.5 min	93 min

20. **Challenge** Old Faithful erupts to heights between 105 ft and 184 ft. It erupted at 7:34 A.M. for 4.5 minutes. Later it erupted for 2.5 minutes. It then erupted a third time for 3 minutes. Use the table to determine how many minutes followed each of the three eruptions. Sketch a possible graph of height over time.

Test Prep

21. **Multiple Choice** Which graph most likely represents a car approaching a stop sign?

Ⓐ 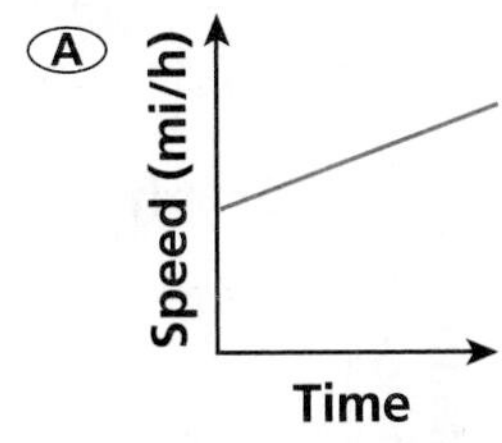

Ⓑ 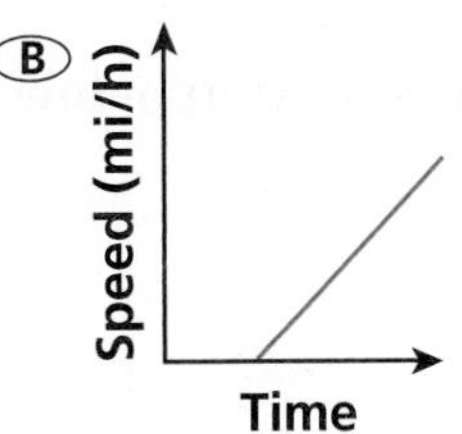

Ⓒ 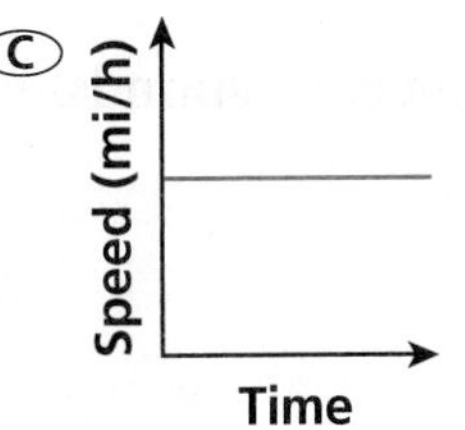

Ⓓ 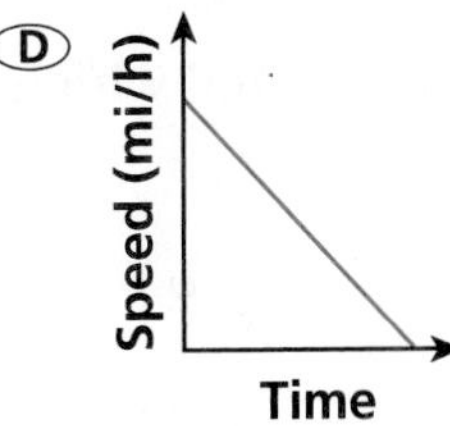

22. **Short Response** Lisa climbed up to the diving board, dove into the water, swam 10 meters, and returned to the surface of the water. Draw a graph to represent her distance from the surface of the water.

CHAPTER 2
SECTION A

Ready To Go On?

Learn It Online
Resources Online

Quiz for Lessons 1 Through 3

1 Ordered Pairs

Determine whether each ordered pair is a solution of $y = 2x - 7$.

1. (14, 21) **2.** (3, 13) **3.** (10, 13) **4.** (1.5, −4)

When dining out, it is customary to give a tip to the server. The amount of the tip is generally 15 to 20 percent of the total bill. The equation for the cost c of a meal, including a 15 percent tip, is $c = 1.15a$, where a is the total amount shown on the bill. Find the total cost of each meal to the nearest cent.

5. a = $35.20 **6.** a = $40.00 **7.** a = $22.35 **8.** a = $15.50

2 Graphing on a Coordinate Plane

Give the coordinates and quadrant of each point.

9. A **10.** B

11. C **12.** D

13. E **14.** F

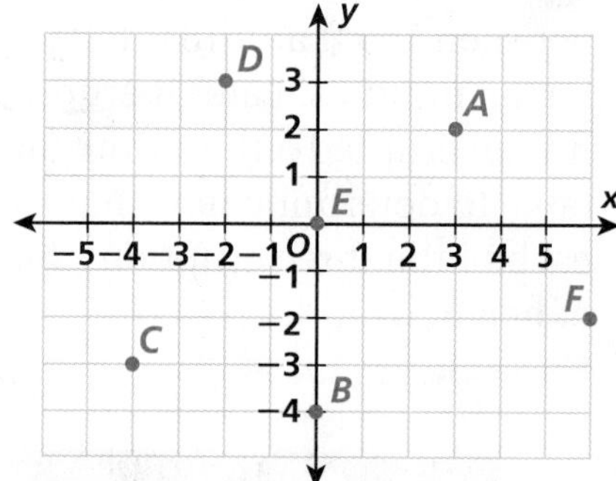

Graph each point on a coordinate plane.

15. $A(-3, -4)$ **16.** $B(4, 0)$ **17.** $C(-2, 2)$ **18.** $D(5, -3)$

3 Interpreting Graphs

Tell which graph corresponds to each situation below.

Graph 1

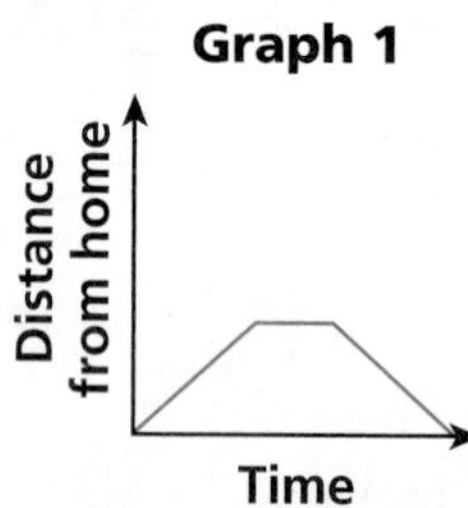

Graph 2

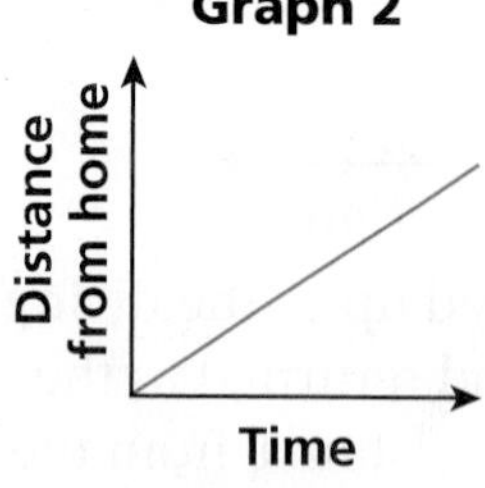

Graph 3

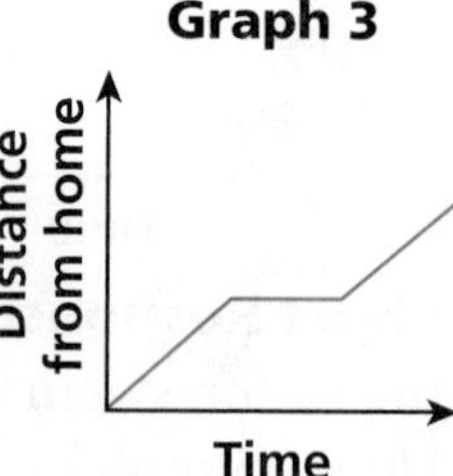

19. Gwendolyn started from home and walked to a friend's house. She stayed with her friend for a while and then walked to another friend's house farther from home.

20. Francisco started from home and walked to the store. After shopping, he walked back home.

21. Celia walks to the library at a steady pace without stopping.

Ready to Go On?

Focus on Problem Solving

MATHEMATICAL PRACTICES Make sense of problems and persevere in solving them.

Make a Plan

- **Prioritize and sequence information**

Some problems contain a lot of information. Read the entire problem carefully to be sure you understand all of the facts. You may need to read it over several times—perhaps aloud so that you can hear yourself say the words.

Then decide which information is most important (prioritize). Is there any information that is absolutely necessary to solve the problem? This information is most important.

Finally, put the information in order (sequence). Use comparison words like *before, after, longer, shorter,* and so on to help you. Write down the sequence before you try to solve the problem.

Read each problem below, and then answer the questions that follow.

1 Five friends are standing in line for the opening of a movie. They are in line according to their arrival. Tiffany arrived 3 minutes after Cedric. Roy took his place in line at 8:01 P.M. He was 1 minute behind Celeste and 7 minutes ahead of Tiffany. The first person arrived at 8:00 P.M. Blanca showed up 6 minutes after the first person. List the time of each person's arrival.

a. Whose arrival information helped you determine each arrival time?

b. Can you determine the order without the time?

c. List the friends' order from the earliest to arrive to the last to arrive.

2 There are four children in the Putman family. Isabelle is half the age of Maxwell. Joe is 2 years older than Isabelle. Maxwell is 14. Hazel is twice Joe's age and 4 years older than Maxwell. What are the ages of the children?

a. Whose age must you figure out first before you can find Joe's age?

b. What are two ways to figure out Hazel's age?

c. List the Putman children from oldest to youngest.

2-4 Functions

COMMON CORE

CC.8.F.1: Understand that a function is a rule that assigns to each input exactly one output. The graph of a function is the set of ordered pairs consisting of an input and the corresponding output. *Also CC.8.EE.7*

Vocabulary

relation

domain

range

function

independent variable

dependent variable

vertical line test

A set of ordered pairs is called a **relation**. The **domain** of a relation is the set of x-values of the ordered pairs. The **range** of a relation is the set of y-values of the ordered pairs.

A **function** is a special type of relation that pairs each *input*, or domain value, with exactly one *output*, or range value.

Function

Each input gives only one output.

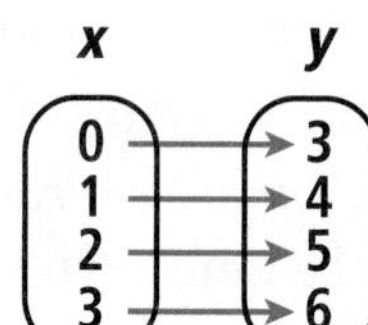

Not a Function

One input gives more than one output.

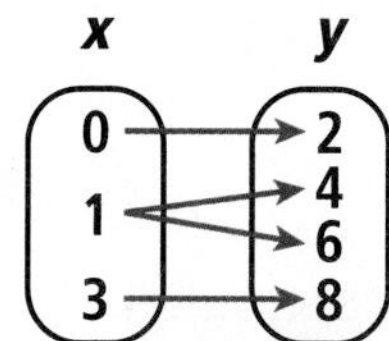

Some functions can be written as equations in two variables. The **independent variable** represents the input of a function. The **dependent variable** represents the output of a function.

Function Rule

$$y = 2x + 9$$

Dependent variable (y) — Independent variable (x)

Functions can also be represented in tables and graphs. If the domain of a function has infinitely many values, it is impossible to represent all of the values in a table, but a table can be used to show some of the values and to help in creating a graph.

EXAMPLE 1 Finding Different Representations of a Function

Interactivities Online ▶

Make a table and a graph of $y = 2x + 1$.

Make a table of inputs and outputs. Use the table to make a graph.

x	$2x + 1$	y
−2	2(−2) + 1	−3
−1	2(−1) + 1	−1
0	2(0) + 1	1
1	2(1) + 1	3
2	2(2) + 1	5

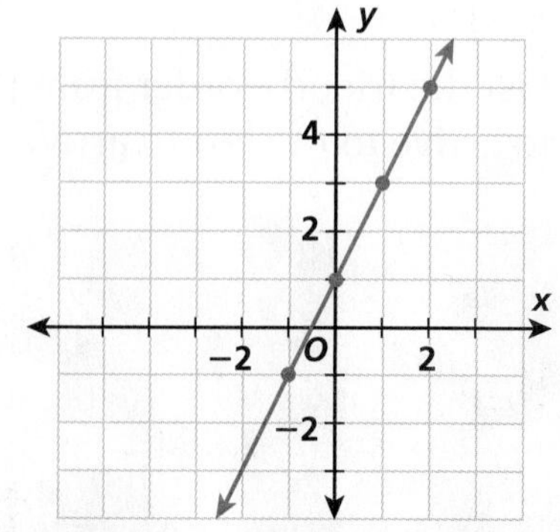

Because a function has exactly one output for each input, you can use the **vertical line test** to test whether a graph is a function. If no vertical line intersects the graph at more than one point, then the relation is a function. If any vertical line intersects the graph at more than one point, then the relation is not a function.

EXAMPLE 2 Identifying Functions

Determine if each relation represents a function.

A

x	y
0	5
1	4
2	3
3	2

Each input x has only one output y. The relation is a function.

B

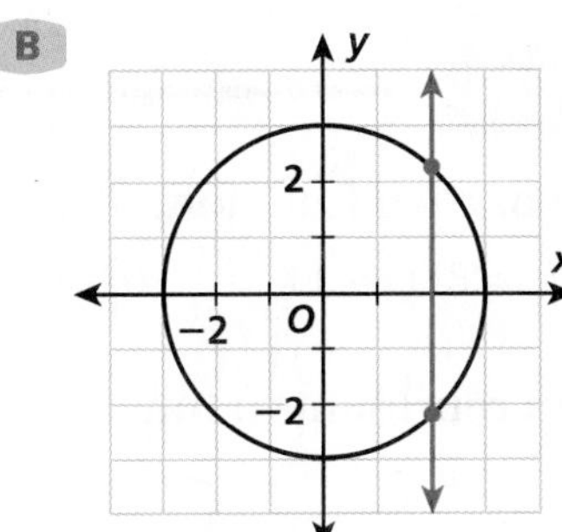

Use the vertical line test. The vertical line shown intersects the graph at two points. The relation is not a function.

C $y = x^2$

Make an input-output table and use it to graph $y = x^2$.

x	y
−2	$(-2)^2 = 4$
−1	$(-1)^2 = 1$
0	$(0)^2 = 0$
1	$(1)^2 = 1$
2	$(2)^2 = 4$

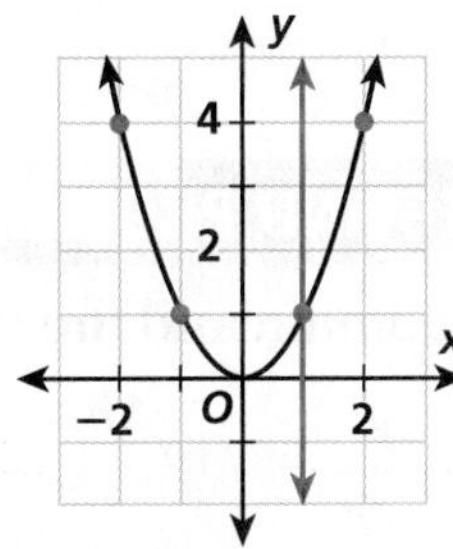

No vertical line will intersect the graph at more than one point. The relation is a function.

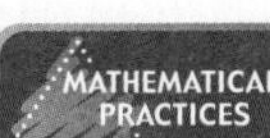

Think and Discuss

1. **Describe** the domain and range for $y = 2$.
2. **Describe** how to tell if a relation is a function.
3. **Identify** the function, the domain, the range, the independent variable, the dependent variable, an input, and the output.

x	$y = 3x - 4$	y
−1	$3(-1) - 4$	−7
0	$3(0) - 4$	−4
1	$3(1) - 4$	−1

2-4 Exercises

Learn It Online
Homework Help Online
Exercises 1–14, 15, 21, 25

GUIDED PRACTICE

See Example 1 **Make a table and a graph of each function.**

1. $y = 2x - 4$ **2.** $y = 3x + 4$ **3.** $y = 4x - 3$ **4.** $y = -x + 1$

See Example 2 **Determine if each relation represents a function.**

5.

x	y
−1	−7
9	1
12	8
15	−7

6.

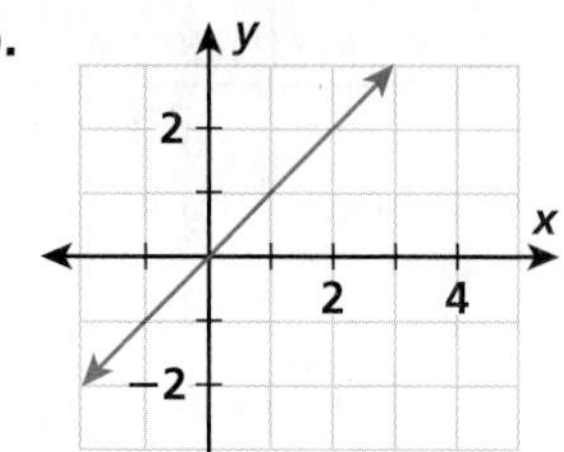

7. $y = 1.5x - 0.5$

INDEPENDENT PRACTICE

See Example 1 **Make a table and a graph of each function.**

8. $y = 2x + 5$ **9.** $y = 3(x + 1)$ **10.** $y = -(3 - x)$ **11.** $y = 2(1 - 2x)$

See Example 2 **Determine if each relation represents a function.**

12.

x	y
2	4
5	5
8	6
2	7

13.

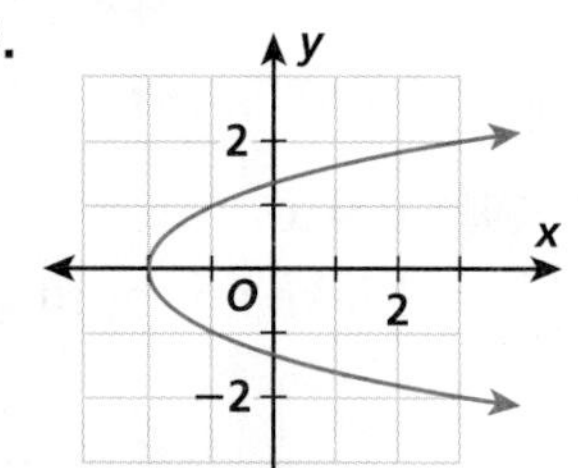

14. $y = -2x + 1$

PRACTICE AND PROBLEM SOLVING

Extra Practice
See Extra Practice for more exercises.

Give the domain and the range of each function.

15.

x	y
1	27
4	39
8	50
14	62

16.

x	y
100	5.4
120	3.5
150	2.7
170	0.2

17.

x	y
30	60
40	50
50	40
60	30

18.

x	y
20	12
25	15
35	21
40	24

19. Sports A distance runner trains by running 750 meters at a time. Her coach records the distance covered by the runner every 20 seconds. The results of one run are presented in the table.

Time x (s)	0	20	40	60	80	100
Distance y (m)	0	150	300	450	600	750

a. Does the relation represent a function?

b. Graph the data to verify your answer for part **a**.

c. Is the graph of the relation discrete or continuous? Explain.

Home Economics

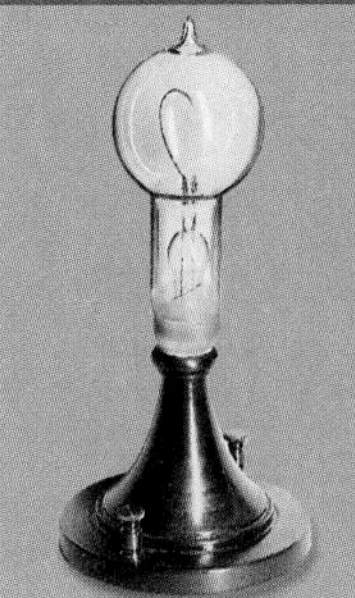

In 1879, Thomas Edison used a carbonized piece of sewing thread to form a light bulb filament that lasted 13.5 hours before burning out.

20. **Business** The function $y = 50x - 750$ gives the daily profit of a company that manufactures x items. Make a table of the function to determine how many items the company must manufacture in order to break even. (*Hint:* When the company breaks even, $y = 0$.)

21. **Home Economics** The cost of using a 60-watt light bulb is given by the function $y = 0.0036x$. The cost is in dollars, and x represents the number of hours the bulb is lit.

    a. How much does it cost to use a 60-watt light bulb 8 hours a day for a week?

    b. What is the domain of the function?

    c. What do the independent and dependent variables of the function represent? How does a change in the independent variable affect the value of the dependent variable?

    d. If the cost of using a 60-watt bulb was \$1.98, for how many hours was it used?

22. **What's the Question?** The following set of points defines a function: $\{(3, 6), (-4, 1), (5, -5), (9, -6), (10, -2), (-2, 10)\}$. If the answer is 6, 1, -5, -6, -2, and 10, what is the question?

23. **Write About It** Can you tell if a relation is a function by just looking at the range? Explain why or why not.

24. **Challenge** Create a table of values for $y = \frac{1}{x}$ using $x = -3, -2, -1, -0.5, -0.25, 0.5, 1, 2$, and 3. Sketch the graph of the function. What happens when $x = 0$?

Test Prep

25. **Multiple Choice** Which relation does NOT represent a function?

    (A) (0, 8), (3, 8), (1, 6)

    (B)

x	4	6	8
y	2	1	9

    (C) $y = 3x + 17$

    (D) (0, 3), (2, 3), (2, 0)

26. **Gridded Response** For the function $y = 1.3x - 5.4$, find y when $x = 9$.

2-5 Equations, Tables, and Graphs

COMMON CORE

CC.8.F.2: Compare properties of two functions each represented in a different way (algebraically, graphically, numerically in tables, or by verbal descriptions). ***Also* CC.8.EE.7, CC.8.F.1, CC.8.F.4, CC.8.F.5**

Many functions can be modeled as equations, tables, or graphs. Each representation shows the same data, but in a different way. For example, you can use an equation, a table, or a graph to show a submersible's depth over time.

EXAMPLE 1

Using Equations to Generate Different Representations of Data

Helpful Hint

The number of minutes m is the independent, or input, variable. The depth d is the dependent, or output, variable.

Make a table and sketch a graph of the path of a submersible diving at 50 ft per minute. The depth of the submersible is represented by the equation $d = -50m$, where d is the depth and m is the number of minutes.

Equation

$d = -50m$

An equation shows how the variables are related.

Table

m	$-50m$	d
0	$-50(0)$	0
1	$-50(1)$	-50
2	$-50(2)$	-100
3	$-50(3)$	-150
4	$-50(4)$	-200

A table identifies values that make the function true.

Graph

A graph is a visual image of the values in the table. In this case, the graph is continuous, so draw a line through the points.

To write an equation from data in a table, you need to look for a pattern in the data. Look for the changes in the input values and the changes in the output values. Then see how the changes are related.

EXAMPLE 2 Using Tables to Generate Different Representations of Data

Use the table to make a graph and to write an equation.

x	0	1	2	3	4
y	0	6	12	18	24

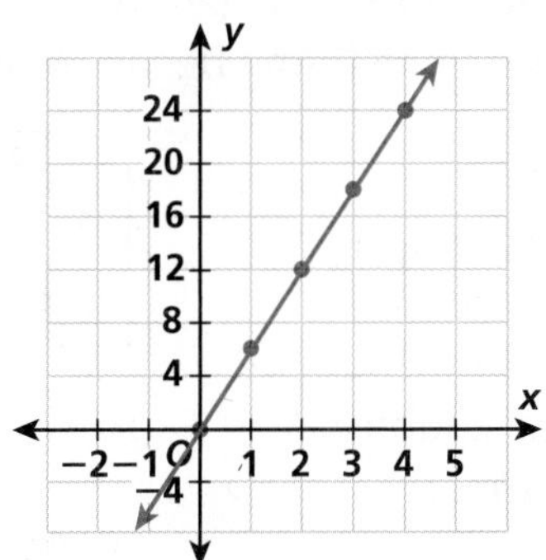

Look for a pattern in the values:

$6 = 6 \cdot 1$ *Each value of y is six times the value of x.*

$12 = 6 \cdot 2$

$18 = 6 \cdot 3$

$y = 6 \cdot x$

To find an equation from a graph, it might be easier to first create a table of values from the graph. Then you can look for a pattern in the values as in Example 2.

EXAMPLE 3 Using Graphs to Generate Different Representations of Data

Use the graph to make a table and to write an equation.

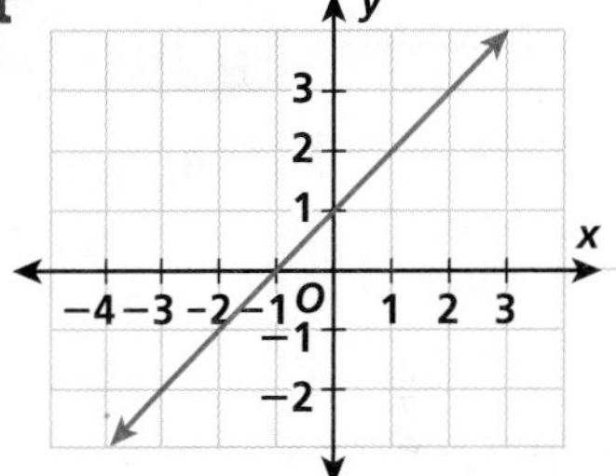

Use the coordinates of several points from the graph.

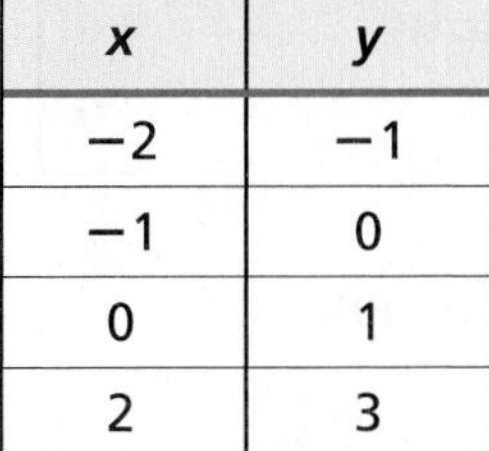

x	*y*
−2	−1
−1	0
0	1
2	3

$-1 = -2 + 1$

$0 = -1 + 1$ *Each value of y is one more than the value of x.*

$1 = 0 + 1$

$3 = 2 + 1$

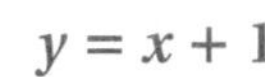

$y = x + 1$

Think and Discuss

1. Which representation of data do you think gives the most accurate information? Justify your answer.

2. Which representation of data do you think shows the relationship most quickly? Justify your answer.

Exercises

Learn It Online
Homework Help Online
Exercises 1–23, 29, 31, 33

GUIDED PRACTICE

See Example 1

1. The amount of water in a pool being filled is represented by the equation $g = 15m$, where g is the number of gallons of water in the pool and m is the number of minutes since filling began. Make a table and sketch a graph of the equation.

See Example 2

2. Use the table to make a graph and to write an equation.

x	0	2	5	9	12
y	3	5	8	12	15

See Example 3

3. Use the graph to make a table and to write an equation.

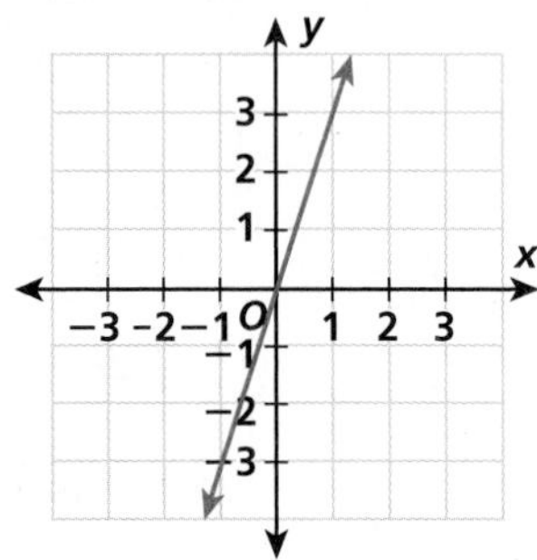

INDEPENDENT PRACTICE

See Example 1

4. The amount of sand in the bottom half of an hourglass is represented by the equation $h = 0.1s$, where h is the height of the sand in centimeters and s is the number of seconds since the top half began draining. Make a table and sketch a graph of the equation.

See Example 2

5. Use the table to make a graph and to write an equation.

x	0	2	4	6	8
y	12	10	8	6	4

See Example 3

6. Use the graph to make a table and to write an equation.

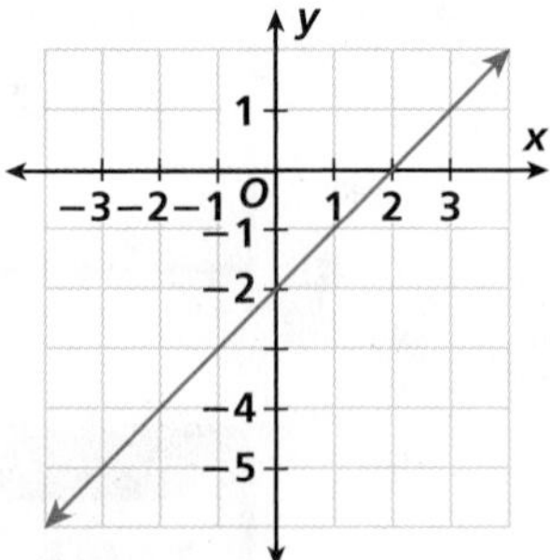

PRACTICE AND PROBLEM SOLVING

Extra Practice
See Extra Practice for more exercises.

7. **Travel** The distance Jackson can drive on a tank of gas is represented by the function $d = 20g$, where d is the distance in miles and g is the number of gallons of gas in the tank. Make a table and sketch a graph of the data.

8. Choose the representation that does not show the same relationship as the other two.

$y = 4x + 1$

x	0	3	6	9	12
y	1	13	25	37	49

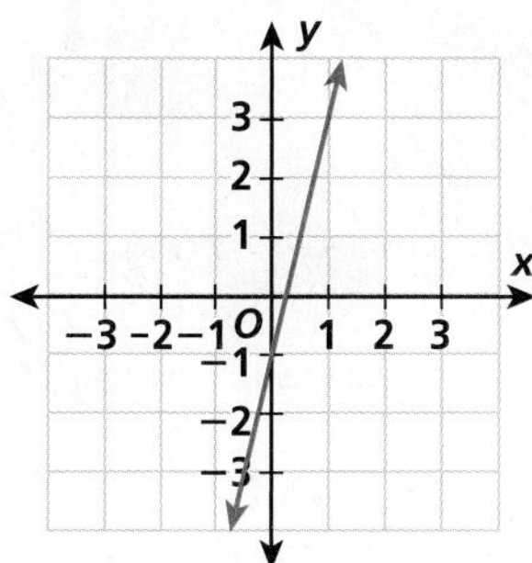

9. **Conservation** A faucet is leaking water at the rate of 2.5 gallons per hour. Let x be the number of hours the faucet leaks and y be the total number of gallons leaked. Write an equation and make a table.

10. **Physical Science** The weight of an object on Saturn's moon Titan is about 0.14 of its weight on Earth.
   a. Write and graph an equation that describes this relationship.
   b. **Estimation** Use your graph to estimate the weight on Titan of a space probe that weighs 703 pounds on Earth.

 11. **Write a Problem** Write a problem that involves the equation $y = 2x + 3$.

 12. **Write About It** Tell how you can use data from a table to write an equation.

 13. **Challenge** Graph the function $y = |x|$. Be sure to include negative values of x. How does the graph differ from the others in this lesson?

Test Prep

14. **Multiple Choice** Jeff began the week with $30.00. He took a city bus to and from school, paying $0.75 for each trip. Let x be the number of trips he took and y be the amount of money he had left at the end of the week. Which equation represents the relationship in the situation?

   Ⓐ $y = 0.75x + 30$
   Ⓑ $y = 30 - 0.75x$
   Ⓒ $x = 3 - 0.75y$
   Ⓓ $y = 0.75x - 30$

15. **Extended Response** The equation $y = 2.5x - 2000$ represents the profit made by a manufacturer that sells a product for $2.50 each, where y is the profit and x is the number of units sold. Construct a table to find the number of units that must be sold for the manufacturer to break even. The break-even point is where profit is equal to 0. Explain the data in the table.

Technology LAB

Use Multiple Representations

Use with Equations, Tables, and Graphs

You can use a graphing calculator to generate a table and a graph from an equation.

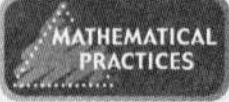

Use appropriate tools strategically.

CCC.8.F.2: Compare properties of two functions each represented in a different way (algebraically, graphically, numerically in tables, or by verbal descriptions). ***Also CC.8.F.1, CC.8.F.4***

Activity 1

Use a graphing calculator to make a table of values for the function $y = 3x + 1$. Then, use the table to find the value of y when $x = 5$.

1. To enter an equation in the calculator, press Y=. Then, enter the function rule. In this case, press 3 X,T,θ,n + 1.

2. Next, adjust the table settings. Press 2nd TBLSE WINDO. The Table Start value (**TblStart**) sets the first value of x to be displayed in the table. The Table Step value (**ΔTbl**) sets the difference between x-values in the table. For this example, set the Table Start value to -3 and the Table Step value to 1.

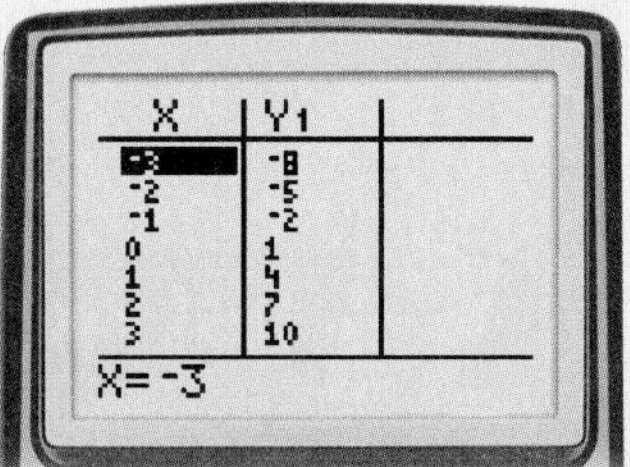

3. Display the table by pressing 2nd TABL GRAPH. Notice that the first x-value in the table is -3 and that the difference between x-values in the table is 1.

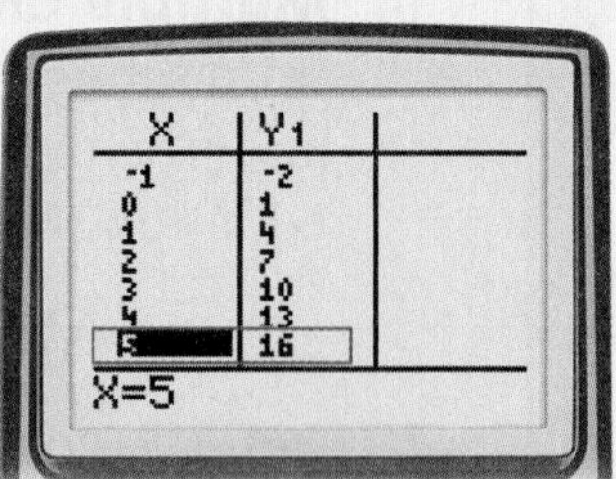

4. Find the value of y when $x = 5$. The greatest value of x in the previous table screen is 3. To see the row for $x = 5$, scroll down by pressing the down arrow key. The table shows that $y = 16$ when $x = 5$.

Think and Discuss

1. Other than using a graphing calculator, how else could you find the value of y when $x = 5$ in Activity 1? Which method is easiest?

2. How could you use the table to find the value of y when $x = -5$?

Try This

Use a graphing calculator to make a table of values for each function. Then, use the table to find the value of the function for the given value of x.

1. $y = 4x + 6$; $x = 6$

2. $y = 3x - 5$; $x = 10$

3. $y = -3x$; $x = 4$

4. $y = -2x - 4$; $x = -2$

Activity 2

Use a graphing calculator to graph the function $y = -x + 3$. Then, use the graph to find the value of y when $x = -4$.

1. Enter the equation in the calculator, as shown in Activity 1. Be sure to use the (–) key instead of the subtraction key to enter the negative sign.

2. Next, select the square window to display the graph. In a square window, the distance between tick marks on the x-axis is the same as the distance between tick marks on the y-axis. Press ZOOM and select **5: ZSquare**. When you press ENTER, the graph of the equation is displayed.

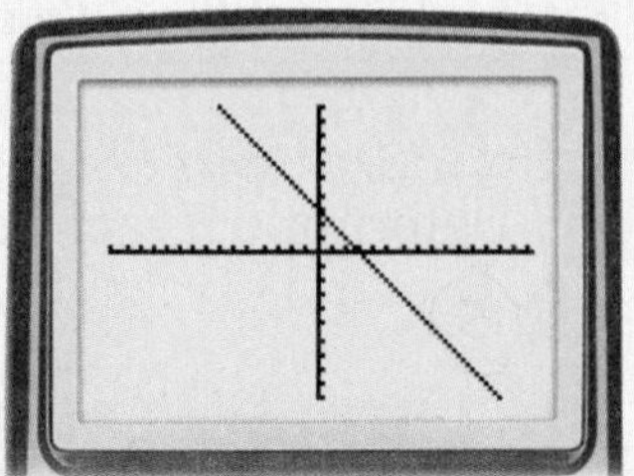

3. Use the Trace feature to find the value of y when $x = -4$. Press TRACE. Enter the value -4 for x, and press ENTER. The calculator shows that $y = 7$ when $x = -4$. It also displays an X at the point $(-4, 7)$.

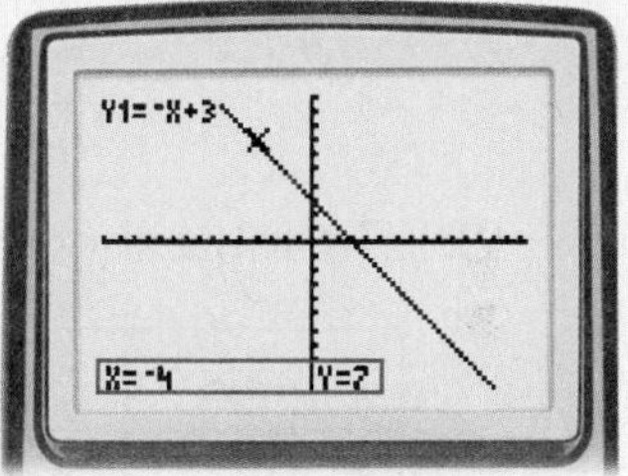

You can also use a graphing calculator to display a table and a graph on the same screen. To do so, press MODE. Use the down arrow key to move the cursor to the last row. Then select **G–T,** which stands for Graph–Table. Press ZOOM and select **5: ZSquare.** The table and the graph of $y = -x + 3$ appear together.

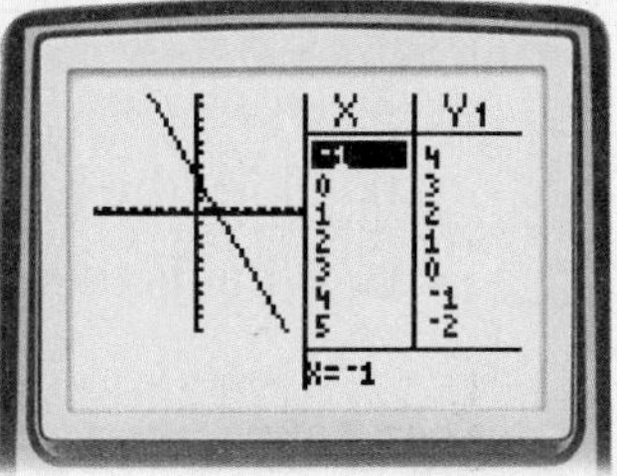

Think and Discuss

1. How could you check whether the calculator graphed the function correctly?
2. **Make a Conjecture** How could you use a graphing calculator to determine whether the graph of a function is a line?

Try This

Use a graphing calculator to graph each function. Then, use the graph to find the value of the function for the given value of x.

1. $y = x - 5$; $x = 3$
2. $y = 2x + 4$; $x = -2$
3. $y = -0.25x$; $x = 2$
4. $y = -x + 3$; $x = -5$
5. Use a graphing calculator to show a table and a graph of $y = x + 6$ on the same screen.

CHAPTER 2
SECTION B

Quiz for Lessons 4 Through 5

4 Functions

Make a table and a graph of each function.

1. $y = x + 7$
2. $y = 4x + 2$
3. $y = \frac{2}{3}x + \frac{1}{3}$
4. $y = 5.2x$

Determine if each relation represents a function.

5.

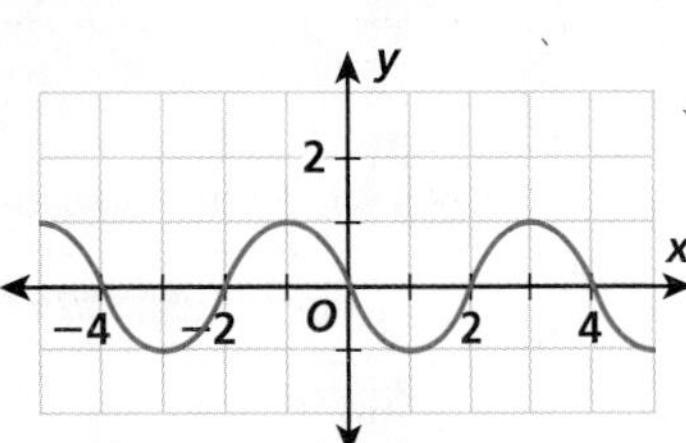

6.

x	y
0	9
1	8
2	7
3	8

7. $y = 4x - 8$
8. $y = x^2$

9. The table shows the costs of various numbers of tickets to an amusement park.

Tickets	1	2	5	10	20
Cost ($)	20	36	85	160	300

a. Graph the data in the table.
b. Does the relation in the table represent a function? Explain how you know.
c. What is the domain of the relation in the table? What is the range?

5 Equations, Tables, and Graphs

Use each table to make a graph and to write an equation.

10.

x	2	4	6	8
y	13	19	25	31

11.

x	3	6	9	12
y	3.5	5	6.5	8

Use each graph to make a table and to write an equation.

12.

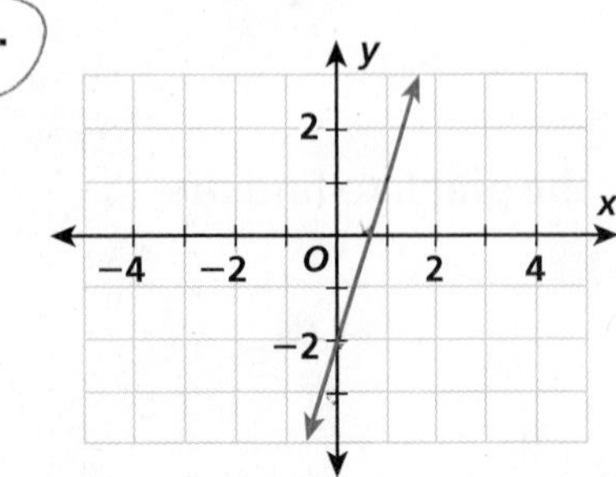

13.

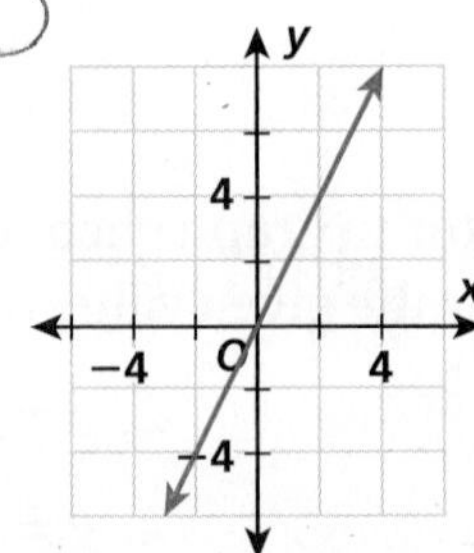

14. The number of tons of plankton that a blue whale eats during the summer is represented by the equation $p = 8d$, where d is the number of days. Make a table and sketch a graph of the equation.

Ready to Go On?

Real-World CONNECTIONS

MATHEMATICAL PRACTICES Reason abstractly and quantitatively.

Loess Hills Scenic Byway Winding its way along the western edge of Iowa, the Loess Hills Scenic Byway gives motorists a view of a remarkable landscape. Highlights along the 220-mile route include unusual landforms such as rippled hills and steep ridges that are found in only two places on Earth: western Iowa and along the Yellow River in China.

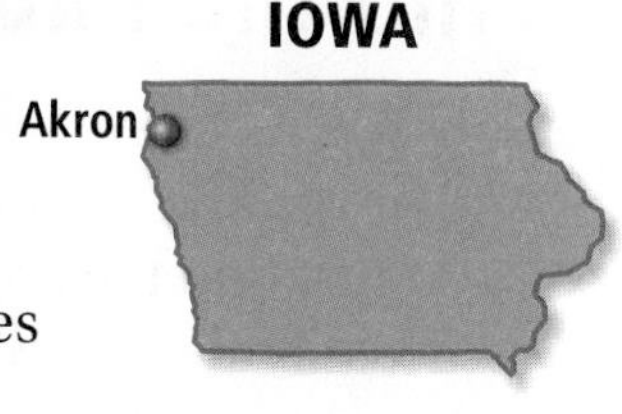

1. Scott starts at the Iowa-Missouri border and drives at an average speed of 40 mi/h to the end of the Loess Hills Scenic Byway in Akron, Iowa. His distance from Akron is given by the equation $y = 220 - 40x$, where y is the distance from Akron in miles and x is the time in hours. Complete the table of data for Scott's drive.

Scott's Driving Data

Time (h)	Distance from Akron (mi)
0	
1	
2	
3	

2. Graph the data from the table on a coordinate plane.

3. How far is Scott from Akron after 5 hours? Explain how you determined your answer.

4. When $y = 0$, the equation becomes $0 = 220 - 40x$. Solve this equation for x. What does the solution represent?

5. Kendra makes the same drive as Scott. The graph shows her data. Describe Kendra's drive in words. What do you think happened after 2 hours?

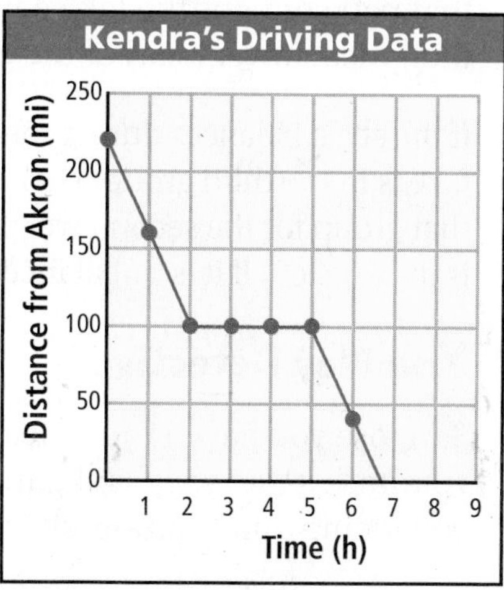

Phil Schermeister/Corbis

Real-World Connections

Game Time

Find the Phony!

Suppose you have nine identical-looking pearls. Eight are real, and one is fake. Using a balance scale that consists of two pans, you must find the bogus pearl. The real pearls weigh the same, and the fake weighs less. The scale can be used only twice. How can you find the phony?

First you must split the pearls into equal groups. Place any three pearls on one side of the scale and any other three on the other side. If one side weighs less than the other, then the fake pearl is on that side. But you are not done yet! You still need to find the imitation, and you can use the scale only once more. Take any of the two pearls from the lighter pan, and weigh them against each other. If one pan is lighter, then that pan contains the fake pearl. If they balance, then the leftover pearl of the group is the fake.

If the scale balances during the first weighing, then you know the fake is in the third group. Then you can choose two pearls from that group for the second weighing. If the scale balances, the fake is the one left. If it is unbalanced, the false pearl is the lighter one.

You Play Detective

Suppose you have 12 identical gold coins in front of you. One is counterfeit and weighs slightly more than the others. How can you identify the counterfeit in three weighings?

Sprouts

You and a partner play against each other to try to make the last move in the game. You start with three dots. Player one draws a path to join two dots or a path that starts and ends at the same dot. A new dot is then placed somewhere on that path. No dot can have more than three paths drawn from it, and no path can cross another.

Learn It Online
Game Time Extra

A complete copy of the rules is available online.

Victoria Smith/HMH

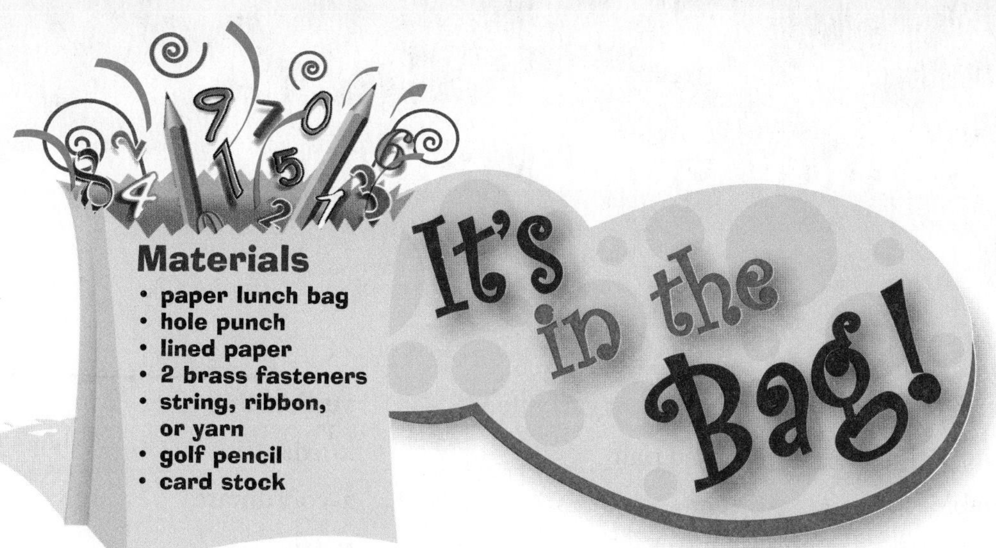

Materials
• paper lunch bag
• hole punch
• lined paper
• 2 brass fasteners
• string, ribbon, or yarn
• golf pencil
• card stock
It's in the Bag!

PROJECT Clipboard Solutions for Graphs and Functions

Make your own clipboard for taking notes on graphs and functions.

Directions

1. Fold the bag flat and hold it with the flap at the top. Punch two holes at the bottom of the flap, about 3 inches apart. The holes should go through only the flap, not the entire bag. **Figure A**

2. Slide about ten sheets of lined paper under the flap and mark where the holes should be punched. Then punch holes through the sheets.

3. Fasten the sheets under the flap using brass fasteners. **Figure B**

4. Punch holes in the upper left and upper right corners of the flap. Tie one end of the string to the left-hand hole. Thread the string through the right-hand hole and tie it there, leaving some slack at the top of the bag. Tie the golf pencil to the end of the string. **Figure C**

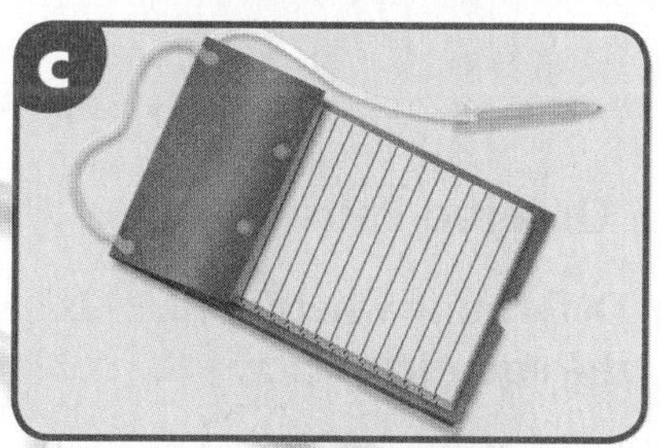

5. Slide a piece of card stock into the bag to make it more sturdy.

Taking Note of the Math

Summarize each lesson of the chapter on a separate page of the clipboard. Use any extra pages to write down sample problems.

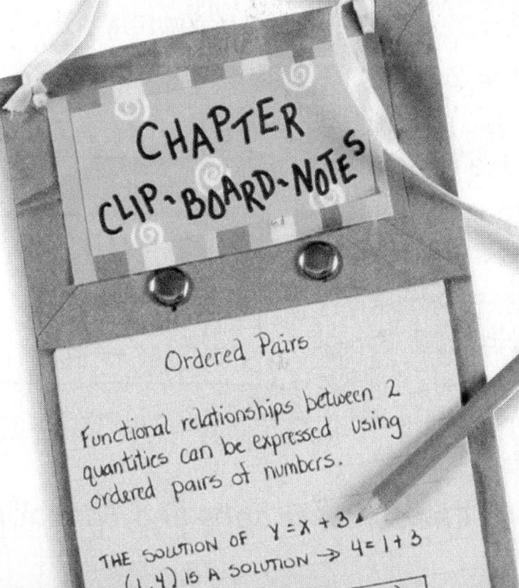

CHAPTER
CLIP-BOARD-NOTES
Ordered Pairs
Functional relationships between 2 quantities can be expressed using ordered pairs of numbers.

CHAPTER 2

Study Guide: Review

Vocabulary

continuous graph	independent variable	vertical line test
coordinate plane	ordered pair	x-axis
dependent variable	origin	x-coordinate
discrete graph	quadrant	y-axis
domain	range	y-coordinate
function	relation	

Complete the sentences below with vocabulary words from the list above.

1. The ___?___ of a relation is the set of y-values of the ordered pairs.
2. A(n) ___?___ is a mathematical relation in which each input corresponds to exactly one output.
3. The ___?___ is the point (0, 0) on a coordinate plane.
4. The ___?___ is a method for testing whether or not a graph represents a function.
5. The coordinate plane is formed by the intersection of two number lines called the ___?___ and the ___?___.

EXAMPLES

1 Ordered Pairs

- **Determine whether (8, 3) is a solution of the equation $y = x - 6$.**

$y = x - 6$

$3 \stackrel{?}{=} 8 - 6$ *Substitute 8 for x and 3 for y.*

$3 \neq 2$ ✗

(8, 3) is not a solution.

- **Use the values to make a table of solutions. $y = 5x - 1$ for $x = 1, 2, 3$**

x	$5x-1$	y	(x, y)
1	$5(1) - 1$	4	(1, 4)
2	$5(2) - 1$	9	(2, 9)
3	$5(3) - 1$	14	(3, 14)

EXERCISES

Determine whether each ordered pair is a solution of the given equation.

6. $(27, 0)$; $y = 81 - 3x$
7. $(4, 5)$; $y = 5x$
8. $(-3, 7)$; $y = 2x + 13$
9. $(2, 4)$; $y = 3x$

Use the values to make a table of solutions.

10. $y = 3x + 2$ for $x = 0, 1, 2, 3, 4$
11. $y = \frac{7}{8}x + 5y$ for $x = 0, 2, 4, 6$
12. $y = 2.2x - 1.7$ for $x = -4, -3, -2, -1$

EXAMPLES

EXERCISES

2 Graphing on a Coordinate Plane

- **Graph $A(3, -1)$, $B(0, 4)$, $C(0, -3)$, and $D(1, 0)$ on a coordinate plane.**

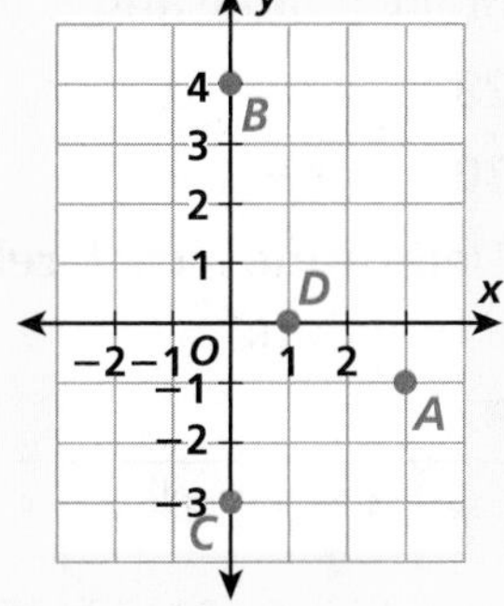

- **Find the distance between points B and C in the graph above.**

Use the y-coordinates to find the vertical distance.

Distance $= |-3 - 4|$

$= |-7| = 7$

The points are 7 units apart.

Graph each point on a coordinate plane.

13. $A(3, 2)$ **14.** $B(-1, 0)$ **15.** $C(0, -5)$

16. $D(1, -3)$ **17.** $E(0, 4)$ **18.** $F(-3, -5)$

19. $G(5, 0)$ **20.** $H(7, 8)$ **21.** $J(0, 0)$

Find the distance between each pair of points.

22. A and B

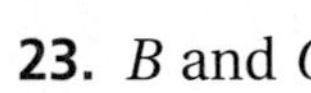

23. B and C

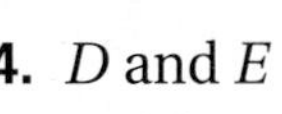

24. D and E

25. F and E

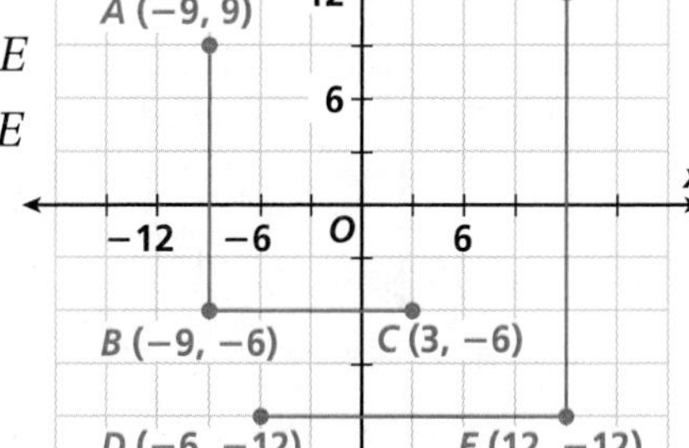

3 Interpreting Graphs

The graphs show the temperature of the liquids in two mugs over time. Tell which graph corresponds to which situation.

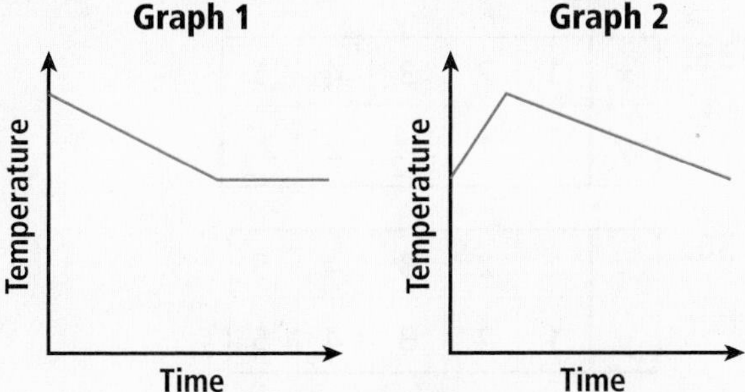

- **Water at room temperature is heated quickly in a microwave. Then the water slowly cools to room temperature.**
  Graph 2—The temperature of the water rises sharply and then gradually decreases.
- **Hot water in a mug slowly cools to room temperature, and then remains at room temperature.**
  Graph 1—The temperature of the water gradually decreases and then remains constant.

The graphs show the height above ground of two elevators over time. Tell which graph corresponds to which situation.

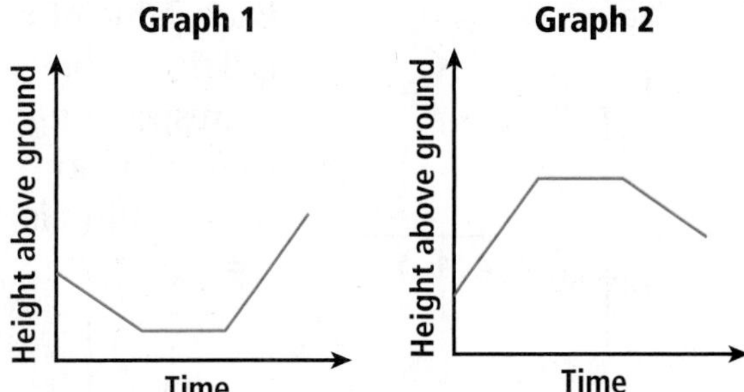

26. An elevator starts at the third floor, then makes a stop at the first floor, and goes up to the fifth floor.

27. An elevator starts at the second floor, then makes a stop at the sixth floor, and goes down to the fourth floor.

EXAMPLES

EXERCISES

4 Functions

■ Make a table and a graph of $y = x - 3$.

x	$x - 3$	y
0	$0 - 3$	-3
1	$1 - 3$	-2
2	$2 - 3$	-1
3	$3 - 3$	0

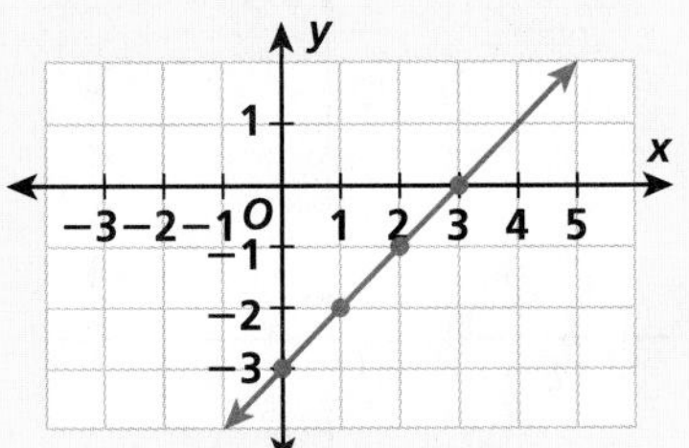

Make a table and a graph of each function.

28. $y = 7x - 4$ **29.** $y = 6x + 1$

30. $y = -2x + 3$ **31.** $y = -3x + 4$

Determine if each relation represents a function.

32.

x	1	2	3	4	5
y	17	19	21	23	25

33.

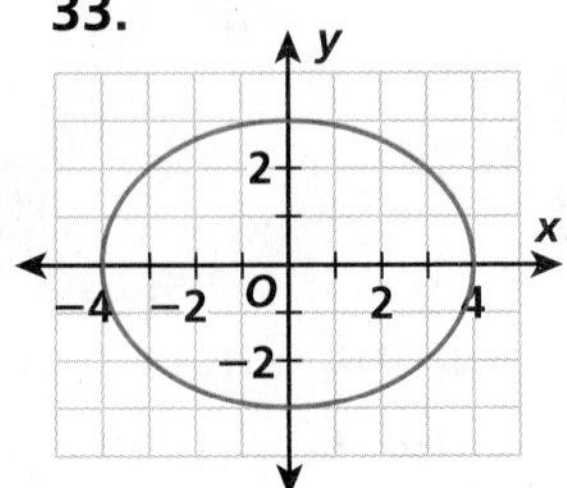

5 Equations, Tables, and Graphs

■ Use the table to make a graph and to write an equation.

x	1	2	3	4	5
y	8	16	24	32	40

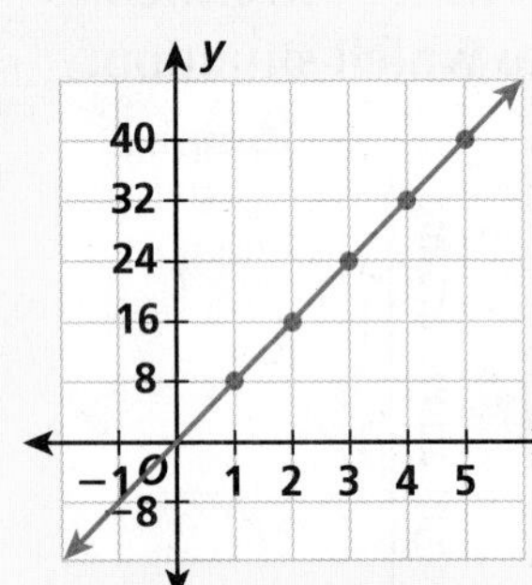

Each value of y is 8 times the corresponding value of x, so the equation is $y = 8x$.

■ Use the graph to make a table and to write an equation.

x	y
-1	-2
0	-1
1	0
2	1

$-2 = -1 - 1$

$-1 = 0 - 1$

$0 = 1 - 1$

$1 = 2 - 1$

Each value of y is one less than the corresponding value of x, so the equation is $y = x - 1$.

Use each table to make a graph and to write an equation.

34.

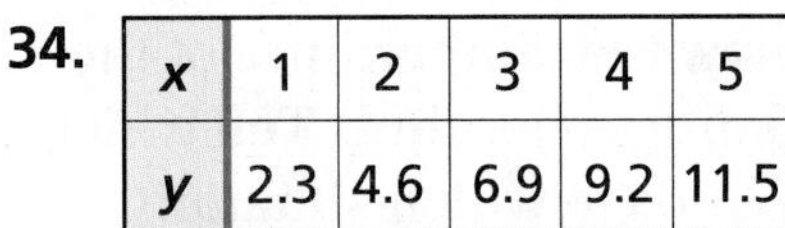

x	1	2	3	4	5
y	2.3	4.6	6.9	9.2	11.5

35.

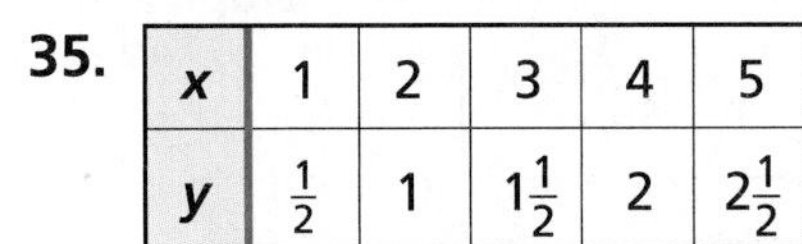

x	1	2	3	4	5
y	$\frac{1}{2}$	1	$1\frac{1}{2}$	2	$2\frac{1}{2}$

36.

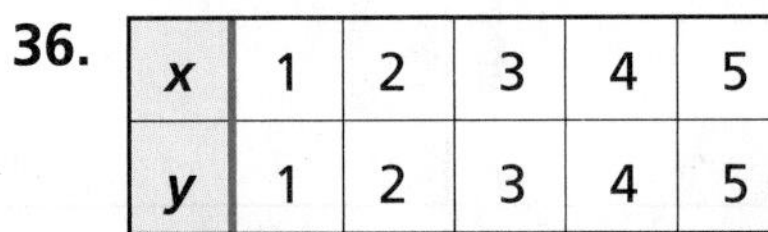

x	1	2	3	4	5
y	1	2	3	4	5

Use each graph to make a table and to write an equation.

37.

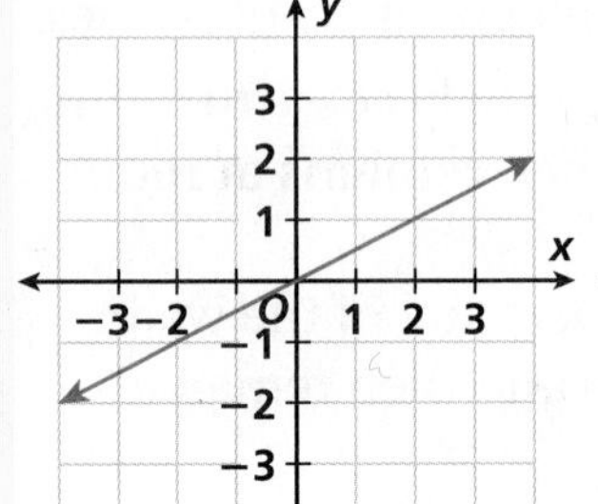

38.

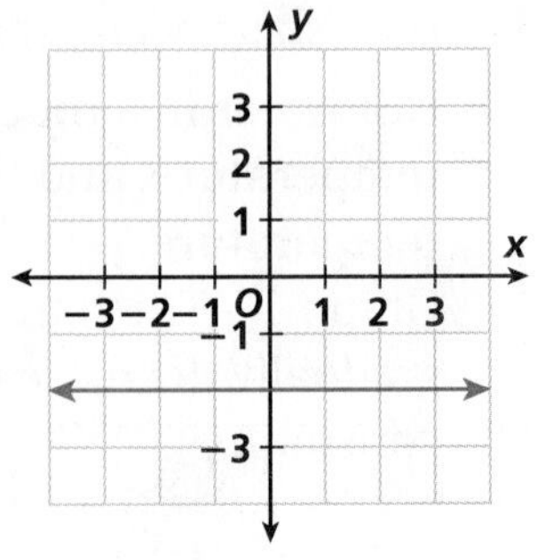

Chapter Test

Determine whether the ordered pair is a solution of the given equation.

1. (6, 5) for $y = 5x - 25$ **2.** (−3, 10) for $y = -3x - 1$ **3.** (2, 4) for $y = 5x - 6$

Give the coordinates for each point.

4. A

5. B

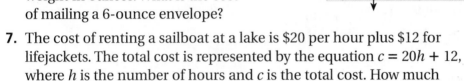

6. The equation that gives the cost c of mailing a large envelope is $c = 0.17w + 0.63$, where w is the weight in ounces. What is the cost of mailing a 6-ounce envelope?

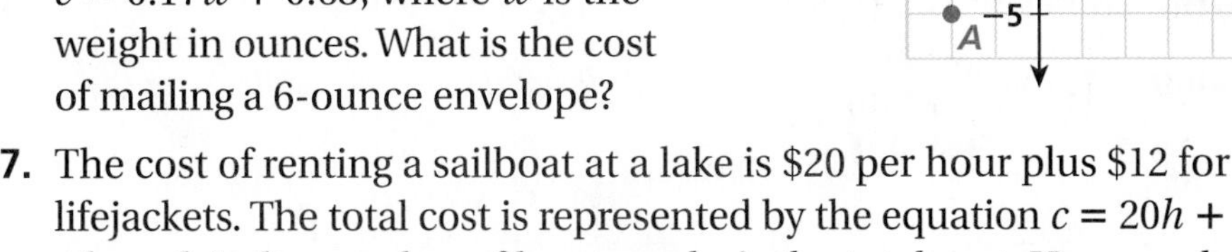

7. The cost of renting a sailboat at a lake is \$20 per hour plus \$12 for lifejackets. The total cost is represented by the equation $c = 20h + 12$, where h is the number of hours and c is the total cost. How much does it cost to rent a sailboat for 3.5 hours?

8. Use the table to graph the speed of the car over time.

Time (s)	0	5	10	15
Speed (mi/h)	0	20	30	35

Tell which graph corresponds to each situation below.

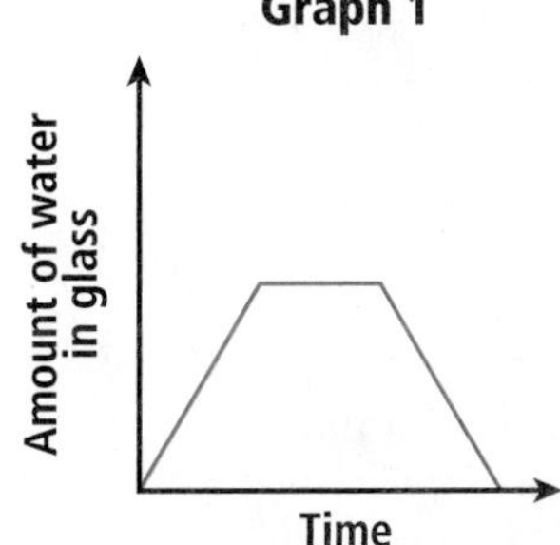

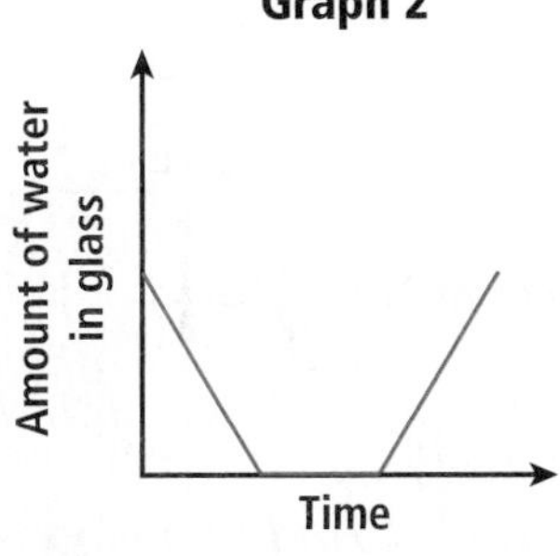

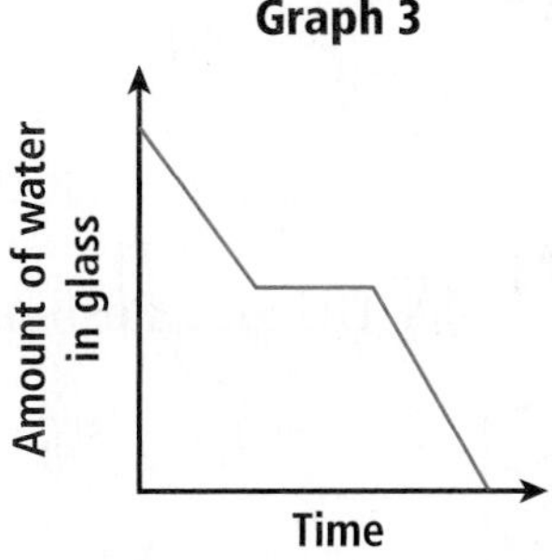

9. Grant drinks half a glass of water, pauses to take a breath, and then drinks the rest of the water in the glass.

10. Marcia fills a glass half full with water, walks outside with it, and then drinks all the water.

Make a table and a graph of each function.

11. $y = 5x - 3$ **12.** $y = 9x + 2$ **13.** $y = -2x - 5$ **14.** $y = \frac{3}{5}x - \frac{2}{3}$

Use each table to make a graph and to write an equation.

15.

x	4	5	6	7
y	12	15	18	21

16.

x	$\frac{1}{2}$	1	$1\frac{1}{2}$	2
y	$3\frac{1}{2}$	7	$10\frac{1}{2}$	14

CHAPTER 2

Test Tackler

STANDARDIZED TEST STRATEGIES

Gridded Response: Write Gridded Responses

When responding to a test item that requires you to place your answer in a grid, you must fill out the grid on your answer sheet correctly, or the item will be marked as incorrect.

EXAMPLE 1

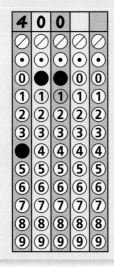

Gridded Response: Divide. 3000 ÷ 7.5

$$3000 \div 7.5 = \frac{3000}{7.5}\left(\frac{10}{10}\right)$$ *7.5 has 1 decimal place, so multiply by $\frac{10}{10}$.*

$$= \frac{30{,}000}{75}$$ *Divide.*

$$= 400$$ *Simplify.*

- Write your answer in the answer boxes at the top of the grid.
- Put only one digit in each box. Do not leave a blank box in the middle of an answer.
- Shade the bubble for each digit in the column beneath it.

EXAMPLE 2

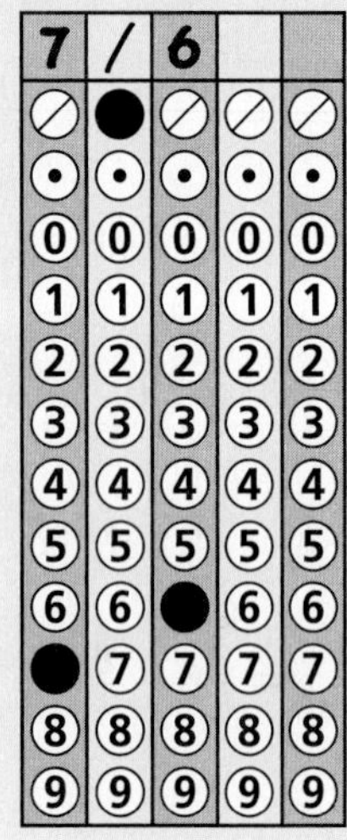

Gridded Response: Solve. $x - \frac{1}{2} = \frac{2}{3}$

$$x - \frac{1}{2} + \frac{1}{2} = \frac{2}{3} + \frac{1}{2}$$ *Add $\frac{1}{2}$ to both sides of the equation.*

$$x = \frac{4}{6} + \frac{3}{6}$$ *Find a common denominator.*

$$x = \frac{7}{6},\ 1\frac{1}{6},\ \text{or } 1.1\overline{6}$$ *Add.*

- Mixed numbers and repeating decimals cannot be gridded, so you must grid the answer as $\frac{7}{6}$.
- Write your answer in the answer boxes at the top of the grid.
- Put only one digit or symbol in each box. On some grids, the fraction bar and the decimal point have a designated box. Do not leave a blank box in the middle of an answer.
- Shade the bubble for each digit or symbol in the column beneath it.

You cannot grid a negative number in a gridded response item because the grid does not include the negative sign. If you get a negative answer to a test item, recalculate the problem because you probably made a math error.

Read each statement and then answer the questions that follow.

Item A

A student correctly evaluated an expression and got $\frac{9}{13}$ as a result. Then the student filled in the grid as shown.

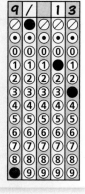

1. What error did the student make when filling in the grid?
2. Explain how to fill in the answer correctly.

Item B

A student added 0.21 and 0.49 and got an answer of 0.7. This answer is displayed in the grid.

3. What errors did the student make when filling in the grid?
4. Explain how to fill in the answer correctly.

Item C

A student found -0.65 as the answer to $-5 \cdot (-0.13)$. Then the student filled in the grid as shown.

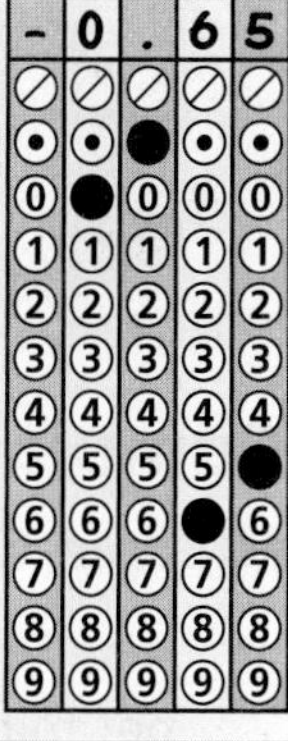

5. What error does the grid show?
6. Another student got an answer of -0.65. Explain why the student knew this answer was wrong.

Item D

A student found that $x = 5\frac{1}{2}$ was the solution to the equation $2x - 3 = 8$. Then the student filled in the grid as shown.

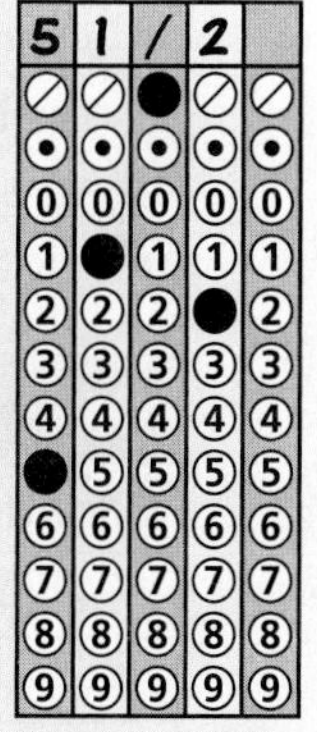

7. What answer does the grid show?
8. Explain why you cannot fill in a mixed number.
9. Write the answer $5\frac{1}{2}$ in two forms that could be entered in the grid correctly.

CHAPTER 2

Standardized Test Prep

Learn It Online
State Test Practice

Cumulative Assessment

Multiple Choice

1. A cell phone company charges $0.21 per minute for phone calls. Which expression represents the cost of a phone call of *m* minutes?

Ⓐ $0.21m$ Ⓒ $0.21 - m$

Ⓑ $0.21 + m$ Ⓓ $0.21 \div m$

2. Laurie had $88 in her bank account on Sunday. The table below shows her account activity for the past 5 days. What is the balance in her account on Friday?

Day	Deposit	Withdraw
Monday	$25	
Tuesday		$58
Wednesday		$45
Thursday	$32	
Friday	$91	

Ⓕ $91 Ⓗ $133

Ⓖ $103 Ⓙ $236

3. Which equation has a solution of $x = -5$?

Ⓐ $2x + 8 = -2$ Ⓒ $\frac{1}{5}x - 6 = -10$

Ⓑ $\frac{1}{5}x + 10 = 5$ Ⓓ $-2x + 10 = -5$

4. You volunteer to bring in 7 gallons of juice for a class party. There are 28 students in the class. You plan to give each student an equal amount of juice. Which equation can you use to determine the amount of juice per student?

Ⓕ $7x = 28$ Ⓗ $28 + x = 7$

Ⓖ $\frac{x}{28} = 7$ Ⓙ $28x = 7$

5. In order to apply for a driver's permit in Ohio, you have to be at least 16 years old. Which graph correctly represents the possible ages of Ohioans who can apply for a driver's permit?

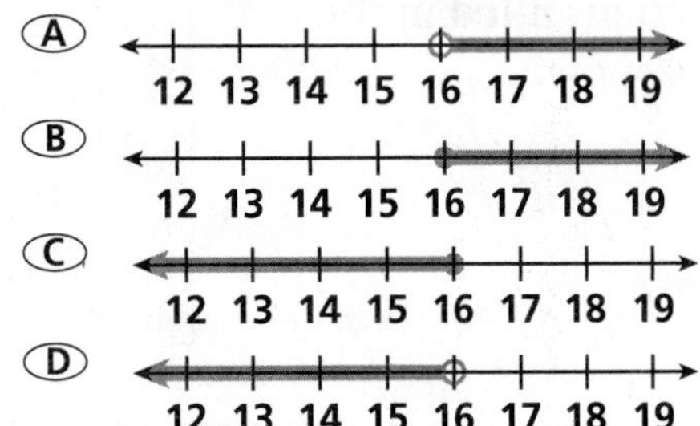

6. Which ordered pair is NOT a solution of $y = 2x - 6$?

Ⓕ (6, 6) Ⓗ (3, 0)

Ⓖ (0, −6) Ⓙ (−3, 0)

7. Which ordered pair is located on the *x*-axis?

Ⓐ (0, −3) Ⓒ (−3, 0)

Ⓑ (3, −3) Ⓓ (1, −3)

8. Which number is closest to 0 on a number line?

Ⓕ $-\frac{7}{8}$ Ⓗ $\frac{9}{16}$

Ⓖ −0.68 Ⓙ 0.54

9. A snack package has 4 ounces of mixed nuts, $1\frac{1}{2}$ ounces of wheat crackers, $5\frac{3}{4}$ ounces of pretzels, and $2\frac{1}{8}$ ounces of popcorn. What is the total weight of the snacks?

Ⓐ $13\frac{3}{8}$ ounces Ⓒ $12\frac{5}{8}$ ounces

Ⓑ $13\frac{1}{8}$ ounces Ⓓ $9\frac{3}{8}$ ounces

10. The graph of the line $y = 2x - 1$ is shown below.

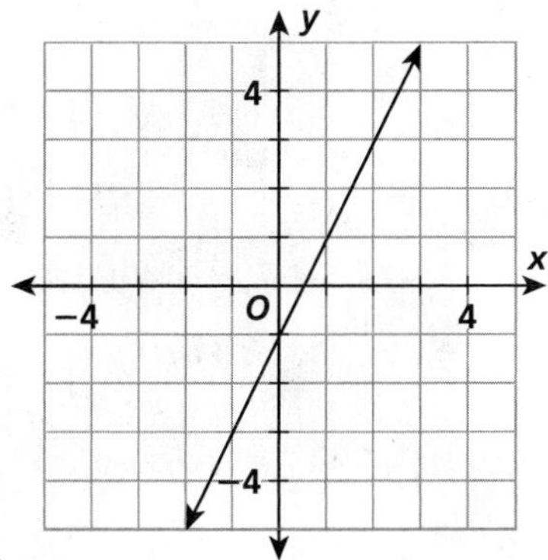

Which list includes only points on this line?

Ⓕ (−1, −2), (0, 0), (1, 2), (2, 4)

Ⓖ (−2, −3), (0, −1), (2, 1), (4, 3)

Ⓗ (−4, 7), (−2, 3), (0, −1), (2, 3)

Ⓙ (0, −1), (1, 1), (2, 3), (3, 5)

Sometimes remembering the rules of integers can help you eliminate one or two of the answer choices.

Gridded Response

11. In 2004, the minimum wage for workers was $5.85 per hour. To find the amount of money someone could make at minimum wage in x hours, use the equation $y = 5.85x$. How much money could a person who worked 5 hours at minimum wage earn?

12. Solve the equation $\frac{4}{9}x = \frac{1}{3}$ for x.

13. The sum of two consecutive integers is 53. What is the smaller of the two numbers?

14. The function $d = -16t^2 + 35$ represents the height of a stone after t seconds when dropped from a bridge 35 feet over a river. What is the height in feet of the stone after 1 second?

Short Response

S1. Consider the set of coordinate points {(−1, 1), (0, 2), (1, 3), (2, 4), (3, 5), (4, 6), (5, 7)}.

a. Determine the domain and the range of the set.

b. Is the set a function? Explain why or why not.

c. Write an equation that will relate x and y.

S2. Pablo leaves for school on his bike at 7:15 and arrives at 7:20. The table shows his rate of speed at one-minute intervals. Represent the information in the table with a line graph.

Time (min)	7:15	7:16	7:17	7:18	7:19	7:20
Speed (mi/h)	0	20	15	3	0	10

S3. A craft club charges $12.95 to join. Members of the club pay $3.50 each month for a craft kit. Find a function that describes the situation, and then find the total charges for a member who buys a year's worth of craft kits. Show your work.

Extended Response

E1. A train travels at a rate of 50 miles per hour from Baton Rouge, Louisiana, to Orlando, Florida. To find the distance y traveled in x hours, use the equation $y = 50x$.

a. Make a table of ordered pairs using the domain $x = 1, 2, 3, 4$, and 5.

b. Graph the solutions from the table of ordered pairs.

c. Maria leaves Baton Rouge at 5:30 A.M. on a train. She needs to be in Orlando by 6:30 P.M. If Baton Rouge is 602 miles from Orlando, will Maria make it on time? Explain.

CHAPTER 3

Exponents and Roots

COMMON CORE

Chapter Focus

- Use exponents and scientific notation to describe numbers.
- Investigate and apply the Pythagorean Theorem.

Why Learn This?

Scientific notation can be used to express a number as small as the weight of a hornet's wing or as large as the number of insects in the world.

Are You Ready?

Vocabulary

Choose the best term from the list to complete each sentence.

1. According to the ___?___, you must multiply or divide before you add or subtract when simplifying a numerical ___?___.
2. An algebraic expression is a mathematical sentence that has at least one ___?___.
3. In a(n) ___?___, an equal sign is used to show that two quantities are the same.
4. You use a(n) ___?___ to show that one quantity is greater than another quantity.

equation
expression
inequality
order of operations
variable

Complete these exercises to review skills you will need for this chapter.

Order of Operations

Simplify by using the order of operations.

5. $12 + 4(2)$	**6.** $12 + 8 \div 4$	**7.** $15(14 - 4)$
8. $(23 - 5) - 36 \div 2$	**9.** $12 \div 2 + 10 \div 5$	**10.** $40 \div 2 \cdot 4$

Equations

Solve.

11. $x + 9 = 21$	**12.** $3z = 42$	**13.** $\frac{w}{4} = 16$
14. $24 + t = 24$	**15.** $p - 7 = 23$	**16.** $12m = 0$

Use Repeated Multiplication

Find the product.

17. $7 \times 7 \times 7 \times 7 \times 7$	**18.** $12 \times 12 \times 12$	**19.** $3 \times 3 \times 3 \times 3$
20. $11 \times 11 \times 11 \times 11$	**21.** $8 \times 8 \times 8 \times 8 \times 8 \times 8$	**22.** $2 \times 2 \times 2$
23. $100 \times 100 \times 100 \times 100$	**24.** $9 \times 9 \times 9 \times 9 \times 9$	**25.** $1 \times 1 \times 1 \times 1$

Multiply and Divide by Powers of Ten

Multiply or divide.

26. $358(10)$	**27.** $358(1000)$	**28.** $358(100{,}000)$
29. $\frac{358}{10}$	**30.** $\frac{358}{1000}$	**31.** $\frac{358}{100{,}000}$

CHAPTER 3

Study Guide: Preview

Where You've Been

Previously, you

- simplified expressions involving order of operations and exponents.
- used models to represent squares and square roots.

In This Chapter

You will study

- operating with numbers in scientific notation.
- approximating the values of irrational numbers.
- modeling the Pythagorean Theorem.
- using the Pythagorean Theorem to solve real-life problems.

Where You're Going

You can use the skills learned in this chapter

- to evaluate expressions containing exponents in future math courses.
- to express the magnitude of interstellar distances.
- to use right triangle geometry in future math courses.

Key Vocabulary/Vocabulario

hypotenuse	hipotenusa
irrational number	número irracional
perfect square	cuadrado perfecto
Pythagorean Theorem	teorema de Pitágoras
real number	número real
scientific notation	notación cientifica

Vocabulary Connections

To become familiar with some of the vocabulary terms in the chapter, consider the following. You may refer to the chapter, the glossary, or a dictionary if you like.

1. The word *irrational* contains the prefix *ir-*, which means "not." Knowing what you do about rational numbers, what do you think is true of **irrational numbers**?
2. The word *real* means "actual" or "genuine." How do you think this applies to math, and how do you think **real numbers** differ from numbers that are not real?

Study Guide: Preview

Study Strategy: Take Effective Notes

Good note taking is an important study strategy. The Cornell system of note taking is an effective way to organize and review main ideas. This method involves dividing your notebook paper into three main sections. You take notes in the note-taking column during the lecture. You write questions and key phrases in the cue column as you review your notes. You write a brief summary of the lecture in the summary area.

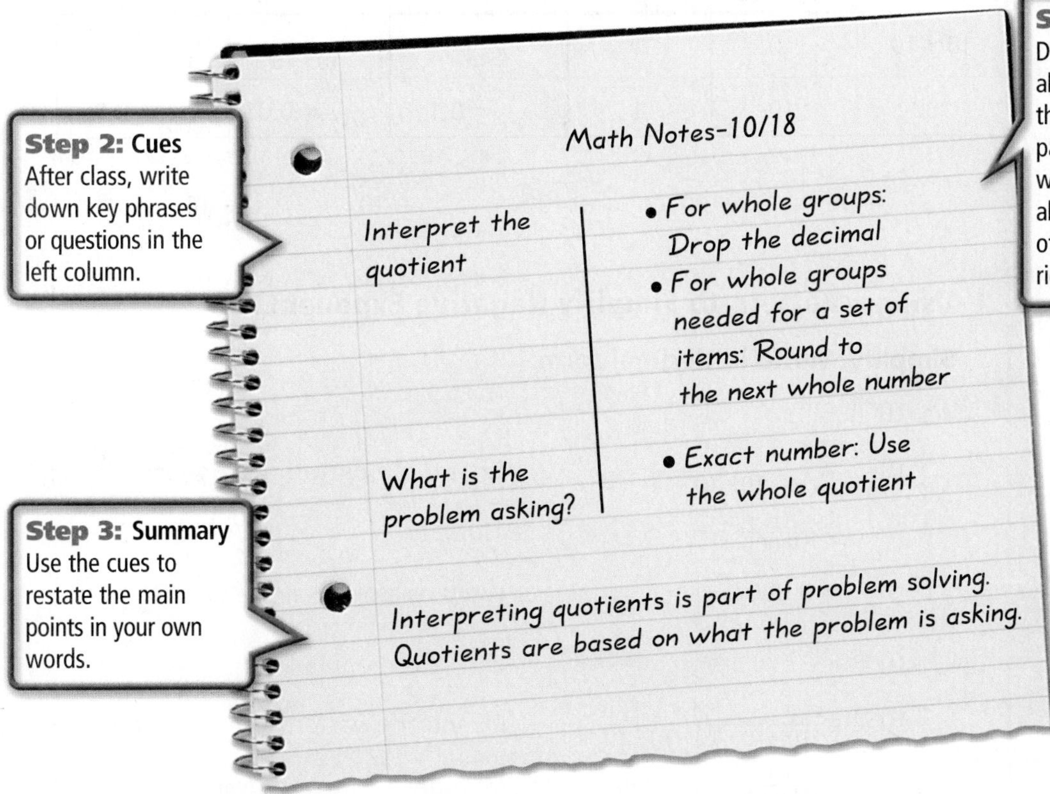

Step 1: Notes
Draw a vertical line about 2.5 inches from the left side of your paper. During class, write your notes about the main points of the lecture in the right column.
Step 2: Cues
After class, write down key phrases or questions in the left column.
Step 3: Summary
Use the cues to restate the main points in your own words.
Math Notes-10/18
Interpret the quotient
• For whole groups: Drop the decimal
• For whole groups needed for a set of items: Round to the next whole number
What is the problem asking?
• Exact number: Use the whole quotient
Interpreting quotients is part of problem solving. Quotients are based on what the problem is asking.

Try This

1. Research and write a paragraph describing the Cornell system of note taking. Describe how you can benefit from using this type of system.
2. In your next class, use the Cornell system of note taking. Compare these notes to your notes from a previous lecture. Do you think your old notes or the notes using the Cornell system would better prepare you for tests and quizzes?

3-1 Integer Exponents

COMMON CORE

CC.8.EE.1: Know and apply the properties of integer exponents to generate equivalent numerical expressions.

This nanoguitar is the smallest playable guitar in the world. It is no larger than a single cell. One string on the nanoguitar is about 10^{-5} meters long.

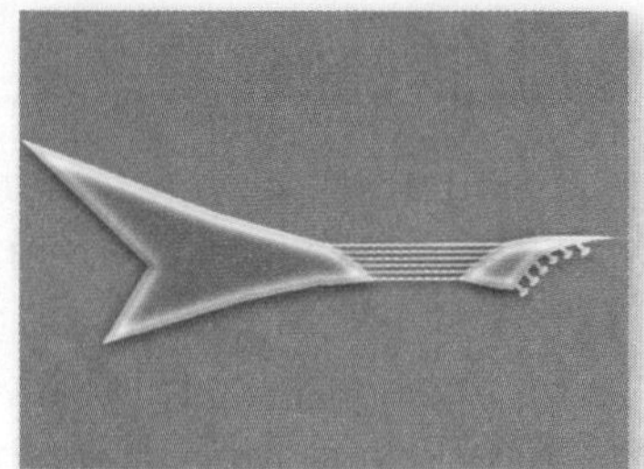

Look for a pattern in the table to extend what you know about exponents to include negative exponents.

Remember!

For a review of multiplying and dividing by powers of 10, see the Skills Bank.

10^2	10^1	10^0	10^{-1}	10^{-2}	10^{-3}
$10 \cdot 10$	10	1	$\frac{1}{10}$	$\frac{1}{10 \cdot 10}$	$\frac{1}{10 \cdot 10 \cdot 10}$
100	10	1	$\frac{1}{10} = 0.1$	$\frac{1}{100} = 0.01$	$\frac{1}{1000} = 0.001$

$\div 10$ $\quad \div 10$ $\quad \div 10$ $\quad \div 10$ $\quad \div 10$

EXAMPLE 1 Using a Pattern to Simplify Negative Exponents

Simplify. Write in decimal form.

A 10^{-4}

$10^{-4} = \frac{1}{10 \cdot 10 \cdot 10 \cdot 10}$ *Extend the pattern from the table.*

$= \frac{1}{10{,}000}$ *Multiply.*

$= 0.0001$ *Write as a decimal.*

B 10^{-5}

$10^{-5} = \frac{1}{10 \cdot 10 \cdot 10 \cdot 10 \cdot 10}$ *Extend the pattern from Example 1A.*

$= \frac{1}{100{,}000} = 0.00001$ *Multiply. Write as a decimal.*

NEGATIVE EXPONENTS

Words	Numbers	Algebra
Any nonzero number raised to a negative power equals 1 divided by that number raised to the opposite (positive) power.	$5^{-3} = \frac{1}{5^3} = \frac{1}{125}$	$b^{-n} = \frac{1}{b^n}$, if $b \neq 0$

EXAMPLE 2 Simplifying Negative Exponents

Simplify.

A $(-2)^{-3}$

$(-2)^{-3}$

$\frac{1}{(-2)^3}$ *Write the power under 1; change the sign of the exponent.*

$\frac{1}{(-2) \cdot (-2) \cdot (-2)}$ *Find the product.*

$-\frac{1}{8}$ *Simplify.*

B 6^{-4}

6^{-4}

$\frac{1}{6^4}$ *Write the power under 1; change the sign of the exponent.*

$\frac{1}{6 \cdot 6 \cdot 6 \cdot 6}$ *Find the product.*

$\frac{1}{1296}$ *Simplify.*

Notice from the table on the previous page that $10^0 = 1$. This is true for any nonzero number to the zero power.

THE ZERO POWER		
Words	**Numbers**	**Algebra**
The zero power of any number except 0 equals 1.	$100^0 = 1$ $(-7)^0 = 1$	$a^0 = 1$, if $a \neq 0$

EXAMPLE 3 Using the Order of Operations

Simplify $2 + (-7)^0 - (4 + 2)^{-2}$.

$2 + (-7)^0 - (4 + 2)^{-2}$

$2 + (-7)^0 - 6^{-2}$ *Add inside the parentheses.*

$2 + 1 - \frac{1}{36}$ *Evaluate the exponents.*

$2\frac{35}{36}$ *Add and subtract from left to right.*

MATHEMATICAL PRACTICES

Think and Discuss

1. Express $\frac{1}{2}$ using a negative exponent.

2. Tell whether an integer raised to a negative exponent can ever be greater than 1. Justify your answer.

3-1 Exercises

Learn It Online
Homework Help Online
Exercises 1–24, 25, 29, 31, 33, 35, 39, 45

GUIDED PRACTICE

See Example 1

Simplify. Write in decimal form.

1. 10^{-2}
2. 10^{-7}
3. 10^{-6}
4. 10^{-10}

See Example 2

Simplify.

5. $(2)^{-6}$
6. $(-3)^{-4}$
7. 3^{-3}
8. $(-2)^{-5}$

See Example 3

9. $4 + 3(4 - 9^0) + 5^{-3}$
10. $7 - 8(2)^{-3} + 13$
11. $(2 + 2)^{-2} + (1 + 1)^{-4}$
12. $2 - (2^{-3})$

INDEPENDENT PRACTICE

See Example 1

Simplify. Write in decimal form.

13. 10^{-1}
14. 10^{-9}
15. 10^{-8}
16. 10^{-12}

See Example 2

Simplify.

17. $(-4)^{-1}$
18. 5^{-2}
19. $(-10)^{-4}$
20. $(-2)^{-6}$

See Example 3

21. $128(2 + 6)^{-3} + (4^0 - 3)$
22. $3 + (-3)^{-2} - (9 + 7)^0$
23. $12 - (-5)^0 + (3^{-3} + 9^{-2})$
24. $5^0 + 49(1 + 6)^{-2}$

PRACTICE AND PROBLEM SOLVING

Extra Practice
See Extra Practice for more exercises.

Simplify.

25. $(18 - 16)^{-5}$
26. $25 + (6 \cdot 10^0)$
27. $(3 \cdot 3)^{-3}$
28. $(1 - 2^{-2})$
29. $3^{-2} \cdot 2^2 \cdot 4^0$
30. $10 + 4^3 \cdot 2^{-2}$
31. $6^2 - 3^2 + 1^{-1}$
32. $16 - [15 - (-2)^{-3}]$

Evaluate each expression for the given value of the variable.

33. $2(x^2 + x)$ for $x = 2.1$
34. $(4n)^{-2} + n$ for $n = 3$
35. $c^2 + c$ for $c = \frac{1}{2}$
36. $m^{-2} \cdot m^0 \cdot m^2$ for $m = 9$

Write each expression as repeated multiplication. Then simplify.

37. 11^{-4}
38. 1^{-10}
39. -6^{-3}
40. $(-6)^{-3}$

41. **Critical Thinking** Show how to represent 5^{-3} as repeated division.

42. **Patterns** Describe the following pattern: $(-1)^1 = \blacksquare$; $(-1)^{-2} = \blacksquare$; $(-1)^{-3} = \blacksquare$; $(-1)^{-4} = \blacksquare$. Determine what $(-1)^{-100}$ would be. Justify your thinking.

43. **Critical Thinking** Evaluate $n^1 \cdot n^{-1}$ for $n = 1, 2,$ and 3. Then make a conjecture what $n^1 \cdot n^{-1}$ is for any integer $n \neq 0$. Explain your reasoning.

Science LINK

44. The sperm whale is the deepest diving whale. It can dive to depths greater than 10^{12} nanometers. Simplify 10^{12}.

45. Blubber makes up 27% of a blue whale's body weight. Davis found the average weight of blue whales and used it to calculate the average weight of their blubber. He wrote the amount as $2^2 \times 3^3 \times 5 \times 71$ pounds. Simplify this product.

46. Most baleen whales migrate an average of $2^5 \times 125$ km each way. The gray whale has the longest known migration of any mammal, a distance of $2^4 \times 3 \times 125$ km farther each way than the average baleen whale migration. How far does the gray whale migrate each way?

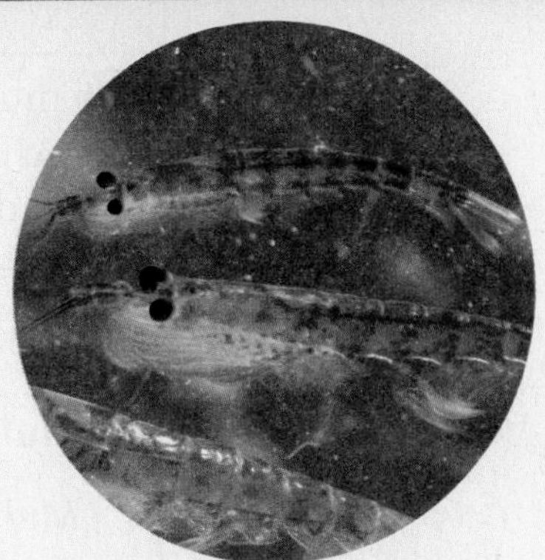

Krill are a food source for different species of baleen whales, such as the humpback whale, pictured above.

47. A blue whale may eat between 6 and 7 tons of krill each day. Krill are approximately $2^{-5} \times 3^{-1} \times 5^{-1}$ of the length of a blue whale. Simplify this product.

48. **Challenge** A cubic centimeter is the same as 1 mL. If a humpback whale has more than 1 kL of blood, how many cubic centimeters of blood does the humpback whale have?

Test Prep

49. **Multiple Choice** Simplify $(-5)^{-2}$.

Ⓐ -25 Ⓑ $-\frac{1}{25}$ Ⓒ $\frac{1}{25}$ Ⓓ 25

50. **Extended Response** Evaluate 8^3, 8^2, 8^1, 8^0, 8^{-1}, and 8^{-2}. Describe the pattern of the values. Use the pattern of the values to predict the value of 8^{-3}.

3-2 Properties of Exponents

COMMON CORE

CC.8.EE.1: Know and apply the properties of integer exponents to generate equivalent numerical expressions.

The factors of a power, such as 7^4, can be grouped in different ways by using the Associative Property. Notice the relationship of the exponents in each product.

$$7 \cdot 7 \cdot 7 \cdot 7 = 7^4$$
$$(7 \cdot 7 \cdot 7) \cdot 7 = 7^3 \cdot 7^1 = 7^4$$
$$(7 \cdot 7) \cdot (7 \cdot 7) = 7^2 \cdot 7^2 = 7^4$$

MULTIPLYING POWERS WITH THE SAME BASE

Words	Numbers	Algebra
To multiply powers with the same base, keep the base and add the exponents.	$3^5 \cdot 3^8 = 3^{5+8} = 3^{13}$	$b^m \cdot b^n = b^{m+n}$

EXAMPLE 1 Multiplying Powers with the Same Base

Multiply. Write the product as one power.

A $5^4 \cdot 5^3$

$5^4 \cdot 5^3$

5^{4+3} *Add exponents.*

5^7

B $a^{12} \cdot a^{12}$

$a^{12} \cdot a^{12}$

a^{12+12} *Add exponents.*

a^{24}

C $16 \cdot 16^{-7}$

$16 \cdot 16^{-7}$

$16^1 \cdot 16^{-7}$ *Think: $16 = 16^1$*

$16^{1+(-7)}$ *Add exponents.*

16^{-6}

D $4^2 \cdot 3^2$

$4^2 \cdot 3^2$ *Cannot combine; the bases are not the same.*

Notice what occurs when you divide powers with the same base.

$$\frac{5^5}{5^3} = \frac{5 \cdot 5 \cdot 5 \cdot 5 \cdot 5}{5 \cdot 5 \cdot 5} = \frac{\cancel{5}^1 \cdot \cancel{5}^1 \cdot \cancel{5}^1 \cdot 5 \cdot 5}{\cancel{5}_1 \cdot \cancel{5}_1 \cdot \cancel{5}_1} = 5 \cdot 5 = 5^2$$

DIVIDING POWERS WITH THE SAME BASE

Words	Numbers	Algebra
To divide powers with the same base, keep the base and subtract the exponents.	$\frac{6^9}{6^4} = 6^{9-4} = 6^5$	$\frac{b^m}{b^n} = b^{m-n}$

EXAMPLE 2 **Dividing Powers with the Same Base**

Divide. Write the quotient as one power.

A $\frac{10^8}{10^5}$

$\frac{10^8}{10^5}$

10^{8-5} *Subtract exponents.*

10^3

B $\frac{x^4}{x^9}$

$\frac{x^4}{x^9}$

x^{4-9}

x^{-5}

To see what happens when you raise a power to a power, use the order of operations.

$(4^3)^2 = (4 \cdot 4 \cdot 4)^2$ *Expand the power inside the parentheses.*

$= (4 \cdot 4 \cdot 4) \cdot (4 \cdot 4 \cdot 4)$ *Apply the power outside the parentheses.*

$= 4^6$ *There are 3 · 2 factors of 4.*

Reading Math

$(9^4)^5$ is read as "nine to the fourth, to the fifth."

RAISING A POWER TO A POWER

Words	Numbers	Algebra
To raise a power to a power, keep the base and multiply the exponents.	$(9^4)^5 = 9^{4 \cdot 5} = 9^{20}$	$(b^m)^n = b^{m \cdot n}$

EXAMPLE 3 **Raising a Power to a Power**

Simplify.

A $(7^5)^3$

$(7^5)^3$ *Multiply exponents.*

$7^{5 \cdot 3}$

7^{15}

B $(8^9)^{11}$

$(8^9)^{11}$ *Multiply exponents.*

$8^{9 \cdot 11}$

8^{99}

C $(2^{-7})^{-2}$

$(2^{-7})^{-2}$

$2^{-7 \cdot (-2)}$ *Multiply exponents.*

2^{14}

D $(x^{10})^{-6}$

$(x^{10})^{-6}$ *Multiply exponents.*

$x^{10 \cdot (-6)}$

x^{-60}

MATHEMATICAL PRACTICES

Think and Discuss

1. Explain why the exponents cannot be added in the product $14^3 \cdot 18^3$.

2. List two ways to express 4^5 as a product of powers.

3-2 Exercises

Learn It Online
Homework Help Online
Exercises 1–24, 25, 27, 33, 37, 39, 41, 43

GUIDED PRACTICE

See Example 1

Multiply. Write the product as one power.

1. $5^6 \cdot 5^9$
2. $12^3 \cdot 12^{-2}$
3. $m \cdot m^3$
4. $5^3 \cdot 7^3$

See Example 2

Divide. Write the quotient as one power.

5. $\frac{6^5}{6^3}$
6. $\frac{a^8}{a^{-1}}$
7. $\frac{12^5}{12^5}$
8. $\frac{5^6}{5^4}$

See Example 3

Simplify.

9. $(3^4)^5$
10. $(2^2)^0$
11. $(4^{-2})^3$
12. $(-y^2)^6$

INDEPENDENT PRACTICE

See Example 1

Multiply. Write the product as one power.

13. $10^{10} \cdot 10^7$
14. $3^4 \cdot 3^4$
15. $r^3 \cdot r^{-2}$
16. $18 \cdot 18^5$

See Example 2

Divide. Write the quotient as one power.

17. $\frac{5^{10}}{5^6}$
18. $\frac{m^{10}}{d^3}$
19. $\frac{t^9}{t^{-4}}$
20. $\frac{3^7}{3^7}$

See Example 3

Simplify.

21. $(5^0)^8$
22. $(6^4)^{-1}$
23. $(3^{-2})^2$
24. $(x^5)^2$

PRACTICE AND PROBLEM SOLVING

Extra Practice
See Extra Practice for more exercises.

Simplify if possible. Write the product or quotient as one power.

25. $\frac{4^7}{4^3}$
26. $3^8 \cdot 3^{-1}$
27. $\frac{a^4}{a^{-3}}$
28. $\frac{10^{18}}{10^9}$
29. $x^3 \cdot x^7$
30. $a^6 \cdot b^9$
31. $(7^4)^3$
32. $2 \cdot 2^4$
33. $\frac{10^4}{5^2}$
34. $\frac{11^7}{11^6}$
35. $\frac{y^8}{y^8}$
36. $y^8 \cdot y^{-8}$

37. There are 26^3 ways to make a 3-letter "word" (from *aaa* to *zzz*) and 26^5 ways to make a 5-letter word. How many times as many ways are there to make a 5-letter word as a 3-letter word?

38. **Astronomy** The mass of the sun is about 10^{27} metric tons, or 10^{30} kilograms. How many kilograms are in one metric ton?

39. **Business** Using the manufacturing terms shown, tell how many dozen are in a great gross. How many gross are in a great gross? Write your answers as quotients of powers and then simplify.

1 dozen	$= 12^1$ items
1 gross	$= 12^2$ items
1 great gross	$= 12^3$ items

40. The distance from Earth to the moon is about 22^4 miles. The distance from Earth to Neptune is about 22^7 miles. Which distance is greater? About how many times as great?

Find the missing exponent.

41. $b^{\blacksquare} \cdot b^4 = b^8$ **42.** $(v^2)^{\blacksquare} = v^{-6}$ **43.** $\frac{w^{\blacksquare}}{w^3} = w^{-3}$ **44.** $(a^4)^{\blacksquare} = a^0$

45. A googol is the number 1 followed by 100 zeros.

a. What is a googol written as a power of 10?

b. What is a googol times a googol written as a power of 10?

46. What's the Error? A student said that $\frac{3^5}{9^5}$ is the same as $\frac{1}{3}$. What mistake has the student made?

47. Write About It Why do you subtract exponents when dividing powers with the same base?

48. Challenge A number to the 11th power divided by the same number to the 8th power equals 64. What is the number?

Test Prep

49. Multiple Choice In computer technology, a kilobyte is 2^{10} bytes in size. A gigabyte is 2^{30} bytes in size. The size of a terabyte is the product of the size of a kilobyte and the size of a gigabyte. What is the size of a terabyte?

Ⓐ 2^{20} bytes Ⓑ 2^{40} bytes Ⓒ 2^{300} bytes Ⓓ 4^{300} bytes

50. Short Response A student claims that $10^3 \cdot 10^{-5}$ is greater than 1. Explain whether the student is correct.

3-3 Scientific Notation

COMMON CORE

CC.8.EE.3: Use numbers expressed in the form of a single digit times an integer power of 10 to estimate very large or very small quantities, and to express how many times as much one is than the other. ***Also CC.8.EE.4***

Vocabulary

scientific notation

Interactivities Online ▶

An ordinary quarter contains about 97,700,000,000,000,000,000,000 atoms. The average size of an atom is about 0.00000003 centimeter across.

The length of these numbers in standard notation makes them awkward to work with. *Scientific notation* is a shorthand way of writing such numbers.

Numbers written in **scientific notation** are written as two factors. One factor is a number greater than or equal to 1 and less than 10. The other factor is a power of 10.

Reading Math

9.77×10^{22} is read as "nine point seven seven times ten to the twenty-second power."

$$9.77 \times 10^{22}$$

Recall from Lesson 4-2 that increasing the exponent in a power of 10 by 1 is the same as multiplying the number by 10. Notice how the decimal point moves in the table below.

$2.345 \times 10^0 = 2.345$	$2.345 \times 10^0 = 2.345$
$2.345 \times 10^1 = 23.45$	$2.345 \times 10^{-1} = 0.2345$
$2.345 \times 10^2 = 234.5$	$2.345 \times 10^{-2} = 0.02345$
$2.345 \times 10^3 = 2345.$	$2.345 \times 10^{-3} = 0.002345$
It moves one place to the right with each increasing power of 10.	*It moves one place to the left with each decreasing power of 10.*

EXAMPLE 1 Translating Scientific Notation to Standard Notation

Write each number in standard notation.

A $\mathbf{3.12 \times 10^9}$

3.12×10^9

$3.12 \times 1{,}000{,}000{,}000$ — *$10^9 = 1{,}000{,}000{,}000$*

$3{,}120{,}000{,}000$ — *Think: Move the decimal right 9 places.*

B $\mathbf{1.35 \times 10^{-4}}$

1.35×10^{-4}

$1.35 \times \frac{1}{10{,}000}$ — *$10^{-4} = \frac{1}{10{,}000}$*

$1.35 \div 10{,}000$ — *Divide by the reciprocal.*

0.000135 — *Think: Move the decimal left 4 places.*

United States Mint image

Writing Math

To write scientific notation for numbers greater than or equal to 1 and less than 10, use a 0 exponent.
$5.63 = 5.63 \times 10^0$

WRITING NUMBERS IN SCIENTIFIC NOTATION

For numbers greater than or equal to 10, use a positive exponent.	For numbers less than 1, use a negative exponent.
$15{,}237 = 1.5237 \times 10^4$ *The decimal moves 4 places.*	$0.00396 = 3.96 \times 10^{-3}$ *The decimal moves 3 places.*

EXAMPLE 2 Translating Standard Notation to Scientific Notation

Write 0.0000003 in scientific notation.

0.0000003

3 *Think: The decimal needs to move 7 places to get a number between 1 and 10.*

$3 \times 10^{\blacksquare}$ *The number is smaller than 1, so the exponent will be negative.*

So 0.0000003 written in scientific notation is 3×10^{-7}.

Check $3 \times 10^{-7} = 3 \times 0.0000001$
$= 0.0000003$ ✔

EXAMPLE 3 *Science Application*

A monarch butterfly has an average mass of 0.5 g. In one roosting colony of Mexico, it was estimated that there were 10 million monarch butterflies. Write the total mass in scientific notation.

10 million = 10,000,000
$0.5 \text{ g} \times 10{,}000{,}000$ *Multiply.*
5,000,000 g *Simplify.*
5×10^6 g *The number is greater than 10, and the decimal moves 6 places.*

In scientific notation, the butterflies have a mass of about 5×10^6 grams.

To compare two numbers written in scientific notation, first compare the powers of ten. The number with the greater power of ten is greater. If the powers of ten are the same, compare the values between one and ten.

$2.7 \times 10^{13} > 2.7 \times 10^9$
$10^{13} > 10^9$

$3.98 \times 10^{22} > 2.52 \times 10^{22}$
$3.98 > 2.52$

EXAMPLE 4 ***Life Science Application***

The major components of human blood are red blood cells, white blood cells, platelets, and plasma. A typical red blood cell has a diameter of approximately 7×10^{-6} meter. A typical platelet has a diameter of approximately 2.33×10^{-6} meter. Which has a greater diameter, a red blood cell or a platelet?

7×10^{-6} ▪ 2.33×10^{-6}

$10^{-6} = 10^{-6}$ *Compare powers of 10.*

$7 > 2.33$ *Compare the values between 1 and 10.*

$7 \times 10^{-6} > 2.33 \times 10^{-6}$

A typical red blood cell has a greater diameter than a typical platelet.

MATHEMATICAL PRACTICES

Think and Discuss

1. **Explain** the benefit of writing numbers in scientific notation.
2. **Describe** how to write 2.977×10^6 in standard notation.
3. **Determine** which measurement would be least likely to be written in scientific notation: size of bacteria, speed of a car, or number of stars in a galaxy.

3-3 Exercises

GUIDED PRACTICE

See Example 1 **Write each number in standard notation.**

1. 4.17×10^3
2. 1.33×10^{-5}
3. 6.2×10^7
4. 3.9×10^{-4}

See Example 2 **Write each number in scientific notation.**

5. 0.000057
6. 0.0004
7. 6,980,000
8. 0.000000025

See Example 3

9. The distance from Earth to the Moon is about 384,000 km. Suppose an astronaut travels this distance a total of 250 times. How many kilometers does the astronaut travel? Write the answer in scientific notation.

See Example 4

10. The maximum length of a particle that can fit through a surgical mask is 1×10^{-4} millimeters. The average length of a dust mite is approximately 1.25×10^{-1} millimeters. Which is longer, the largest particle that can fit through a surgical mask or a dust mite of average length?

INDEPENDENT PRACTICE

See Example 1 **Write each number in standard notation.**

11. 9.2×10^6 **12.** 6.7×10^{-4} **13.** 3.6×10^{-2} **14.** 5.24×10^8

See Example 2 **Write each number in scientific notation.**

15. 0.00007 **16.** 6,500,000 **17.** 100,000,000 **18.** 0.00000003

See Example 3 **19.** Protons and neutrons are the most massive particles in the nucleus of an atom. If a nucleus were the size of an average grape, it would have a mass greater than 9 million metric tons. A metric ton is 1000 kg. What would the mass of a grape-size nucleus be in kilograms? Write your answer in scientific notation.

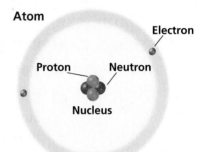

See Example 4 **20.** The orbits of Neptune and Pluto cross each other. Neptune's average distance from the Sun is approximately 4.5×10^9 kilometers. Pluto's average distance from the Sun is approximately 5.87×10^9 kilometers. Which object has the greater average distance from the Sun?

PRACTICE AND PROBLEM SOLVING

Extra Practice

See Extra Practice for more exercises.

Write each number in standard notation.

21. 1.4×10^5 **22.** 3.24×10^{-2} **23.** 7.8×10^1 **24.** 2.1×10^{-6}

25. 5.3×10^{-8} **26.** 8.456×10^{-4} **27.** 5.59×10^5 **28.** 7.1×10^3

29. 7.113×10^6 **30.** 4.5×10^{-1} **31.** 2.9×10^{-4} **32.** 5.6×10^2

LINK

Life Science

This frog is covered with duckweed plants. Duckweed plants can grow both in sunlight and in shade and produce tiny white flowers.

33. **Life Science** Duckweed plants live on the surface of calm ponds and are the smallest flowering plants in the world. They weigh about 0.00015 g.

a. Write this number in scientific notation.

b. If left unchecked, one duckweed plant, which reproduces every 30–36 hours, could produce 1×10^{30} (a nonillion) plants in four months. How much would one nonillion duckweed plants weigh?

34. **Life Science** The diameter of a human red blood cell ranges from approximately 6×10^{-6} to 8×10^{-6} meters. Write this range in standard notation.

35. **Physical Science** The *atomic mass* of an element is the mass, in grams, of one *mole* (mol), or 6.02×10^{23} atoms.

a. How many atoms are there in 2.5 mol of helium?

b. If you know that 2.5 mol of helium weighs 10 grams, what is the atomic mass of helium?

c. Using your answer from part **b,** find the approximate mass of one atom of helium.

36. **Social Studies**

a. Express the population and area of Taiwan in scientific notation.

b. Divide the number of square miles by the population to find the number of square miles per person in Taiwan. Express your answer in scientific notation.

Taiwan

Population: 22,858,872 (July, 2007 estimate)

Area: 14,032 mi^2

Capital: Taipei

Languages: Taiwanese (Min), Mandarin, Hakka dialects

Write each number in scientific notation.

37. 0.00858	38. 0.0000063	39. 5,900,000
40. 7,045,000,000	41. 0.0076	42. 400

43. **Estimation** The distance from Earth to the Sun is about 9.3×10^7 miles. Is this distance closer to 10,000,000 miles or to 100,000,000 miles? Explain.

44. Order the list of numbers below from least to greatest.
1.5×10^{-2}, 1.2×10^6, 5.85×10^{-3}, 2.3×10^{-2}, 5.5×10^6

45. **Write a Problem** An electron has a mass of about 9.11×10^{-31} kg. Use this information to write a problem.

46. **Write About It** Two numbers are written in scientific notation. How can you tell which number is greater?

47. **Challenge** Where on a number line does the value of a positive number in scientific notation with a negative exponent lie?

Test Prep

48. **Short Response** Explain how you can determine the sign of the exponent when 29,600,000,000,000 is written in scientific notation.

49. **Multiple Choice** The distance light can travel in one year is 9.46×10^{12} kilometers. What is this distance in standard form?

Ⓐ 94,600,000,000,000,000 km

Ⓑ 946,000,000,000 km

Ⓒ 9,460,000,000,000 km

Ⓓ 0.000000000946 km

3-4 Operating with Scientific Notation

COMMON CORE

CC.8.EE.4: Perform operations with numbers expressed in scientific notation, including problems where both decimal and scientific notation are used. Use scientific notation and choose units of appropriate size for measurements of very large or very small quantities. Interpret scientific notation that has been generated by technology. ***Also CC.8.EE.3***

Masses of objects in space are so great that astronomers often need to use scientific notation to describe them. The approximate masses of planets in the solar system are given in the table.

NASA

Mass of Planets in the Solar System	
Planet	**Approximate Mass**
Mercury	3.30×10^{23} kg
Venus	4.87×10^{24} kg
Earth	5.97×10^{24} kg
Mars	6.42×10^{23} kg
Jupiter	1.89×10^{27} kg
Saturn	5.69×10^{26} kg
Uranus	8.68×10^{25} kg
Neptune	1.02×10^{26} kg

Source: www.solarsystem.nasa.gov/planets

Use the Mass of Planets table to answer questions in Example 1.

EXAMPLE 1 Division with Scientific Notation

Helpful Hint

You can use the properties of exponents to multiply and divide numbers expressed in scientific notation.

About how many times greater is the mass of Jupiter than the mass of Earth? Write your answer in scientific notation.

Write a unit ratio, or divide, to find how many times.

$\frac{1.89 \times 10^{27} \text{ kg}}{5.97 \times 10^{24} \text{ kg}}$ *Write the ratio of Jupiter's mass to Earth's mass.*

$= \frac{1.89}{5.97} \times \frac{10^{27}}{10^{24}}$ *Divide the coefficients and divide the powers.*

$= 0.3166 \times 10^{3}$ *Subtract exponents.*

$= 3.166 \times 10^{2}$ *Write the result in scientific notation.*

Jupiter's mass is about 3.166×10^{2} times the mass of Earth.

You can also use a calculator to operate with numbers in scientific notation. Recall that on a graphing calculator, 1.89×10^{27} is displayed as 1.89E27.

EXAMPLE 2 Multiplication with Scientific Notation

The mass of the Sun is approximately 3.1 × 10^6 times greater than the mass of Mars. Find the mass of the Sun. Write your answer in scientific notation.

$\frac{\text{mass of Sun}}{6.42 \times 10^{23}\text{ kg}} = 3.1 \times 10^6$ — *The ratio of the Sun's mass to Mars' mass is 3.1 × 10^6.*

mass of Sun

$= (3.1 \times 10^6)(6.42 \times 10^{23}\text{ kg})$ — *Solve for the mass of the Sun.*

$= 3.1 \cdot 6.42 \times 10^{6+23}\text{ kg}$ — *To multiply powers with the same base, add exponents.*

$= 19.902 \times 10^{29}\text{ kg}$

$= 1.9902 \times 10^{30}\text{ kg}$ — *Write the result in scientific notation.*

The mass of the Sun is about 1.99 × 10^{30} kg.

To add or subtract numbers in scientific notation, their powers of 10 must be the same.

EXAMPLE 3 Addition and Subtraction with Scientific Notation

Remember!

A number written in scientific notation has one factor greater than or equal to 1 and less than 10 and the other factor a power of 10.

A **The mass of the Moon is about 7.35 × 10^{22} kg. Find the approximate combined mass of Earth and its moon. Write your answer in scientific notation.**

$$\begin{array}{rcr} 5.97 \times 10^{24}\text{ kg} & \rightarrow & 597 \times 10^{22}\text{ kg} \\ \underline{+7.35 \times 10^{22}\text{ kg}} & \rightarrow & \underline{+7.35 \times 10^{22}\text{ kg}} \\ & & 604.35 \times 10^{22}\text{ kg} \\ & & 6.0435 \times 10^{24}\text{ kg} \end{array}$$

Rewrite so that the powers are the same; then add.

Write the result in scientific notation.

The combined mass of Earth and its moon is about 6.04 × 10^{24} kg.

B **How much greater is the mass of Neptune than the mass of Venus? Write your answer in scientific notation.**

$$\begin{array}{rcr} 1.02 \times 10^{26}\text{ kg} & \rightarrow & 102.00 \times 10^{24}\text{ kg} \\ \underline{-4.87 \times 10^{24}\text{ kg}} & \rightarrow & \underline{-4.87 \times 10^{24}\text{ kg}} \\ & & 97.13 \times 10^{24}\text{ kg} \\ & & 9.713 \times 10^{25}\text{ kg} \end{array}$$

Rewrite so that the powers are the same; then subtract.

Write the result in scientific notation.

Neptune's is about 9.71 × 10^{25} kg greater in mass than Venus.

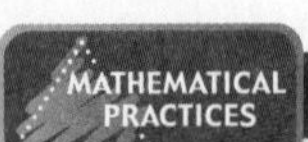

Think and Discuss

1. Explain why numbers written as 604.35 × 10^{22} or 0.317 × 10^3 are *not* written in scientific notation.

3-4 Exercises

GUIDED PRACTICE

Write your answer in scientific notation.

See Example 1

1. A country has a population of 1.35×10^7 people. The country has an area of 5.4×10^4 square miles. Find the population density of the country, in people per square mile.

See Example 2

2. The space shuttle orbits Earth at a speed of approximatately 2.8×10^4 kilometers per hour. The longest shuttle mission was about 4.2×10^2 hours long. Find the approximate distance that shuttle traveled during its mission.

See Example 3

3. In 2007 there were about 7.21×10^7 dogs kept as pets in the United States. In the same year there were about 8.17×10^7 cats kept as pets in the United States. About how many dogs and cats were kept as pets in total?

INDEPENDENT PRACTICE

Write your answer in scientific notation.

See Example 1

4. The diameter of a red blood cell is 8.4×10^{-6}. The diamater of the average cell in the human body is 1×10^{-5}. How many times larger is the diameter of the average cell than the diameter of the red blood cell?

See Example 2

5. The average mass of a grain of sand on a beach is about 1.5×10^{-5} g. There are about 5.1×10^{11} grains of sand in a beach volleyball court. What is the mass of the grains of sand in the beach volleyball court?

See Example 3

6. The 2010 population of India was about 1.16×10^9 people. The 2010 population of the United States was about 3.1×10^8 people. About how many more people lived in India than in the United States in 2010?

PRACTICE AND PROBLEM SOLVING

Extra Practice

See Extra Practice for more exercises.

Perform the indicated operation. Write your answer in scientific notation.

7. $(4.84 \times 10^{11}) \div (8.8 \times 10^4)$

8. $(2.66 \times 10^{13}) \div (9.5 \times 10^5)$

9. $(1.44 \times 10^{13}) \times (3.5 \times 10^2)$

10. $(8.9 \times 10^7) \times (9.8 \times 10^{10})$

11. $(5.01 \times 10^{33}) - (4.1 \times 10^{32})$

12. $(1.2 \times 10^9) + (7.77 \times 10^{12})$

13. $(2.21 \times 10^9) \div (2.6 \times 10^3)$

14. $(2.42 \times 10^{10}) \div (5.5 \times 10^4)$

15. $(6.3 \times 10^{31}) \times (3.5 \times 10^{13})$

16. $(2.2 \times 10^2) \times (4.55 \times 10^{12})$

17. $(3.2 \times 10^{17}) - (2.5 \times 10^{16})$

18. $(6.52 \times 10^{11}) + (8.08 \times 10^{11})$

Write your answer in scientific notation.

19. **Chemistry** There are about 6.022×10^{23} atoms of hydrogen in a mole of hydrogen. How many hydrogen atoms are in 3.5×10^3 moles of hydrogen?

The blue whale is the largest animal that has ever lived on Earth. Weighing up to 50 tons, it's as large as a jet.

Denis Scott/Corbis

Write your answer in scientific notation.

20. **Demographics** New York County in New York had a population of about. 1.54×10^6 people in 2000. Erie County had an population of about 9.5×10^5 people. Find the approximate combined populations of New York and Erie counties in 2000.

21. **Life Science** An adult blue whale can eat 4.0×10^7 krill in 1 day. At that rate, how many krill could an adult blue whale eat in 3.5×10^2 days?

22. **Business** A corporation has 4.8×10^3 employees. The average annual salary for each of its employees is $\$4.5 \times 10^4$. Approximately how much does the corporation pay its employees each year?

23. If there are 8.4×10^3 tiny insects living in each square foot of a field and the field has 6.72×10^2 square feet, how many insects are living in the field?

24. A sample from the Sahara Desert contains 2.173×10^8 grains of sand. A sample from the Chihuahuan Desert has 8.801×10^7 grains of sand. Which sample has more grains of sand? How much more does it have?

25. **Critical Thinking** The average number of stars in a galaxy is about 5×10^{11} and the total number of galaxies is about 5×10^9. If you estimate the total number of stars in the universe to be about 2.5×10^{21}, what assumption are you making?

26. **Write About It** Explain the how multiplication and division of numbers in scientific notation is different than addition and subtraction of them.

27. **What's the Error?** A student found the product of 8×10^6 and 5×10^9 to be 4×10^{15}. Explain the error the student made. What is the correct product?

28. **Challenge** Divide: $(5.95 \times 10^{-3}) \div (1.7 \times 10^{-7})$

Test Prep

29. **Multiple Choice** Jeffrey takes 2.4×10^4 steps during a long-distance run. Each step covers an average distance of 8.1×10^2 mm. What total distance did Jeffrey cover during his run?

    Ⓐ 2.96×10^1 mm

    Ⓑ 1.944×10^7 mm

    Ⓒ 19.44×10^6 mm

    Ⓓ 1.944×10^9 mm

30. **Short Response** The land area of Russia is approximately 1.71×10^7 km^2. The land area of Canada is approximately 9.99×10^6 km^2. How much larger is Russia than Canada?

Multiply and Divide Numbers in Scientific Notation

Use with Operating with Scientific Notation

Learn It Online
Lab Resources Online

MATHEMATICAL PRACTICES Use appropriate tools strategically.

CC.8.EE.4: Perform operations with numbers expressed in scientific notation, including problems where both decimal and scientific notation are used. Use scientific notation and choose units of appropriate size for measurements of very large or very small quantities. Interpret scientific notation that has been generated by technology.

You can use a graphing calculator to perform operations with numbers written in scientific notation. Use the key combination 2nd , (EE) to enter numbers in scientific notation. On a graphing calculator, 9.5×10^{16} is displayed as 9.5E16.

Activity

Use a calculator to find $(4.8 \times 10^{12})(9.4 \times 10^{9})$.

Press 4.8 2nd , (EE) 12 × 9.4 2nd , (EE) 9 ENTER.

The calculator displays the answer 4.512 E22, which is the same as 4.512×10^{22}.

Think and Discuss

1. When you use the associative and commutative properties to multiply 4.8×10^{12} and 9.4×10^{9}, you get $(4.8 \cdot 9.4)(10^{12} \cdot 10^{9}) = 45.12 \times 10^{21}$. Explain why this answer is different from the answer you obtained in the activity.

Try This

Use a graphing calculator to multiply or divide.

1. $(5.76 \times 10^{13})(6.23 \times 10^{-20})$
2. $\frac{9.7 \times 10^{10}}{2.9 \times 10^{7}}$
3. $(1.6 \times 10^{5})(9.65 \times 10^{9})$
4. $\frac{5.25 \times 10^{13}}{6.14 \times 10^{8}}$
5. $(1.1 \times 10^{9})(2.2 \times 10^{3})$
6. $\frac{8.56 \times 10^{97}}{2.34 \times 10^{80}}$
7. $(2.74 \times 10^{11})(3.2 \times 10^{-5})$
8. $\frac{5.82 \times 10^{-11}}{8.96 \times 10^{11}}$
9. $(4.5 \times 10^{12})(3.7 \times 10^{8})$
10. The star Betelgeuse, in the constellation of Orion, is approximately 3.36×10^{15} miles from Earth. This is approximately 1.24×10^{6} times as far as Pluto's minimum distance from Earth. What is Pluto's approximate minimum distance from Earth? Write your answer in scientific notation.
11. If 446 billion telephone calls were placed by 135 million United States telephone subscribers, what was the average number of calls placed per subscriber?

Quiz for Lessons 1 Through 4

1 Integer Exponents

Simplify.

1. 10^{-6} **2.** $(-3)^{-4}$ **3.** -6^{-2} **4.** 4^0

5. $8 + 10^0(-6)$ **6.** $5^{-1} + 3(5)^{-2}$ **7.** $-4^{-3} + 2^0$ **8.** $3^{-2} - (6^0 - 6^{-2})$

2 Properties of Exponents

Simplify. Write the product or quotient as one power.

9. $9^3 \cdot 9^5$ **10.** $\frac{5^{10}}{5^{10}}$ **11.** $q^9 \cdot q^6$ **12.** $3^3 \cdot 3^{-2}$

Simplify.

13. $(3^3)^{-2}$ **14.** $(4^2)^0$ **15.** $(-x^2)^4$ **16.** $(4^{-2})^5$

17. The mass of the known universe is about 10^{23} solar masses, which is 10^{50} metric tons. How many metric tons is one solar mass?

3 Scientific Notation

Write each number in scientific notation.

18. 0.00000015 **19.** 99,980,000 **20.** 0.434 **21.** 100

Write each number in standard notation.

22. 1.38×10^5 **23.** 4×10^6 **24.** 1.2×10^{-3} **25.** 9.37×10^{-5}

26. The population of Georgia is approaching 10 million, and the per capita income is approximately $24,000. Write the estimated total income for Georgia residents in scientific notation.

27. Picoplankton can be as small as 0.00002 centimeter. Microplankton are about 100 times as large as picoplankton. How large is a microplankton that is 100 times the size of the smallest picoplankton? Write your answer in scientific notation.

4 Operating with Scientific Notation

Perform the indicated operation. Write your answer in scientific notation.

28. $(2.05 \times 10^8) \times (3.2 \times 10^{14})$ **29.** $(7.75 \times 10^{-16}) \div (3.1 \times 10^4)$

30. $(9.1 \times 10^{-5}) - (4.9 \times 10^{-4})$ **31.** $(5.3 \times 10^7) + (8 \times 10^5)$

Make sense of problems and persevere in solving them.

Focus on Problem Solving

Solve

• **Choose an operation**

To decide whether to add, subtract, multiply, or divide to solve a problem, you need to determine the action taking place in the problem.

Action	Operation
Combining numbers or putting numbers together	Addition
Taking away or finding out how far apart two numbers are	Subtraction
Combining equal groups	Multiplication
Splitting things into equal groups or finding how many equal groups you can make	Division

Determine the action for each problem. Write the problem using the actions. Then show what operation you used to get the answer.

1. Mary is making a string of beads. If each bead is 7.0×10^{-1} cm wide, how many beads does she need to make a string that is 35 cm long?

2. The total area of the United States is 9.63×10^6 square kilometers. The total area of Canada is 9.98×10^6 square kilometers. What is the total area of both the United States and Canada?

3. Suppose $\frac{1}{3}$ of the fish in a lake are considered game fish. Of these, $\frac{2}{5}$ meet the legal minimum size requirement. What fraction of the fish in the lake are game fish that meet the legal minimum size requirement?

4. Part of a checkbook register is shown below. Find the amount in the account after the transactions shown.

RECORD ALL CHARGES OR CREDITS THAT AFFECT YOUR ACCOUNT

TRANSACTION	DATE	DESCRIPTION	AMOUNT	FEE	DEPOSITS	BALANCE $287.34
Withdrawal	11/16	autodebit for phone bill	$43.16			$43.16
Check 1256	11/18	groceries	$27.56			$27.56
Check 1257	11/23	new clothes	$74.23			$74.23
Withdrawal	11/27	ATM withdrawal	$40.00	$1.25		$41.25

3-5 Squares and Square Roots

COMMON CORE

CC.8.EE.2: Use square root and cube root symbols to represent solutions to equations of the form $x^2 = p$ and $x^3 = p$, where p is a positive rational number. Evaluate square roots of small perfect squares and cube roots of small perfect cubes. Know that $\sqrt{2}$ is irrational.

Vocabulary

square root

principal square root

perfect square

Think about the relationship between the area of a square and the length of one of its sides.

area = 36 square units
side length = 6 units because $6^2 = 36$

A number that when multiplied by itself to form a product is the **square root** of that product. Taking the square root of a nonnegative number is the inverse of squaring the number.

$6^2 = 36 \qquad \sqrt{36} = 6$

Karate matches may be held on a square mat with an area of 64 m^2 or 676 ft^2.

Interactivities Online ▶

Every positive number has two square roots, one positive and one negative. The radical symbol $\sqrt{\ }$ indicates the nonnegative or **principal square root**. The symbol $-\sqrt{\ }$ is used to indicate the negative square root.

$\sqrt{16} = 4 \qquad 4^2 = 16$

$-\sqrt{16} = -4 \qquad (-4)^2 = 16$

Caution!

$\sqrt{-49}$ is not the same as $-\sqrt{49}$. A negative number has no real square roots.

You can use the *plus or minus* symbol, ±, to indicate both square roots.

$\pm\sqrt{16} = \pm 4$

The numbers 16, 36, and 49 are examples of perfect squares. A **perfect square** is a number that has integers as its square roots. Other perfect squares include 1, 4, 9, 25, 64, and 81.

EXAMPLE 1 Finding the Positive and Negative Square Roots of a Number

Find the two square roots of each number.

A 81

$\sqrt{81} = 9$ — *9 is a square root, since $9 \cdot 9 = 81$.*

$-\sqrt{81} = -9$ — *−9 is also a square root, since $-9 \cdot -9 = 81$.*

B 1

$\sqrt{1} = 1$ — *1 is a square root, since $1 \cdot 1 = 1$.*

$-\sqrt{1} = -1$ — *−1 is also a square root, since $-1 \cdot -1 = 1$.*

C 144

$\sqrt{144} = 12$ — *12 is a square root, since $12 \cdot 12 = 144$.*

$-\sqrt{144} = -12$ — *−12 is also a square root, since $-12 \cdot (-12) = 144$.*

Video Lesson Tutorials Online my.hrw.com

EXAMPLE 2 **Computer Application**

Remember!

The area of a square is s^2, where s is the length of a side.

The square computer icon contains 676 pixels. How many pixels tall is the icon?

Write and solve an equation to find the length of a side.

$s^2 = 676$

$s = \pm\sqrt{676}$

$s = \pm 26$ *676 is a perfect square.*

Use the positive square root; a negative length has no meaning. The icon is 26 pixels tall.

The square computer icon contains 676 colored dots that make up the picture. These dots are called *pixels.*

In the order of operations everything under the square root symbol is treated as if it were in parentheses. $\sqrt{5-3} = \sqrt{(5-3)}$

EXAMPLE 3 **Simplify Expressions Involving Square Roots**

Simplify each expression.

A $3\sqrt{25} + 4$

$3\sqrt{25} + 4 = 3(5) + 4$ *Simplify the square root.*

$= 15 + 4$ *Multiply.*

$= 19$ *Add.*

B $\sqrt{\frac{16}{4}} + \frac{1}{2}$

$\sqrt{\frac{16}{4}} + \frac{1}{2} = \sqrt{4} + \frac{1}{2}$ *$\frac{16}{4} = 4$.*

$= 2 + \frac{1}{2}$ *Simplify the square roots.*

$= 2\frac{1}{2}$ *Add.*

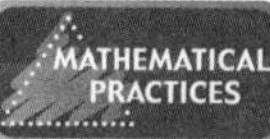

Think and Discuss

1. **Describe** what is meant by a perfect square. Give an example.
2. **Explain** how many square roots a positive number can have. How are these square roots different?
3. **Decide** how many square roots 0 has. Tell what you know about square roots of negative numbers.

3-5 Exercises

Learn It Online
Homework Help Online
Exercises 1–26, 29, 31, 35, 39, 41, 45

GUIDED PRACTICE

See Example 1

Find the two square roots of each number.

1. 4
2. 16
3. 64
4. 121
5. 1
6. 441
7. 9
8. 484

See Example 2

9. A square court for playing the game four square has an area of 256 ft^2. How long is one side of the court?

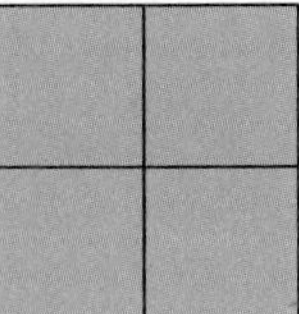

Area = 256 ft^2

See Example 3

Simplify each expression.

10. $\sqrt{5+11}$
11. $\sqrt{\frac{81}{9}}$
12. $3\sqrt{400} - 125$
13. $-(\sqrt{169} - \sqrt{144})$

INDEPENDENT PRACTICE

See Example 1

Find the two square roots of each number.

14. 25
15. 144
16. 81
17. 169
18. 196
19. 400
20. 361
21. 225

See Example 2

22. Elisa found a square digital image of a famous painting on a Web site. The image contained 360,000 pixels. How many pixels tall is the image?

See Example 3

Simplify each expression.

23. $\sqrt{25} - 6$
24. $\sqrt{\frac{64}{4}}$
25. $-(\sqrt{36}\sqrt{9})$
26. $5(\sqrt{225} - 10)$

PRACTICE AND PROBLEM SOLVING

Extra Practice
See Extra Practice for more exercises.

Find the two square roots of each number.

27. 529
28. 289
29. 576
30. 324

Compare. Write <, >, or =.

31. $4 + \sqrt{4}$ ▯ $8 - \sqrt{4}$
32. $16\sqrt{9}$ ▯ $9\sqrt{16}$
33. $-\sqrt{1} + 4$ ▯ $1 - \sqrt{36}$

34. **Language Arts** Zacharias Dase's calculating skills were made famous by *Crelle's Journal* in 1844. Dase produced a table of factors of all numbers between 7,000,000 and 10,000,000. He listed 7,022,500 as a perfect square. What is the square root of 7,022,500?

35. **Sports** A karate match is held on a square mat that has an area of 676 ft^2. What is the length of the mat?

36. **Estimation** Mr. Barada bought a square rug. The area of the rug was about 68.06 ft^2. He estimated that the length of a side was about 7 ft. Is Mr. Barada's estimate reasonable? Explain.

37. **Multi-Step** An office building has a square courtyard with an area of 289 ft^2. What is the distance around the edge of the courtyard?

Find the two square roots of each number.

38. $\frac{1}{9}$ 39. $\frac{1}{121}$ 40. $\frac{16}{9}$ 41. $\frac{81}{16}$

42. $\frac{9}{4}$ 43. $\frac{324}{81}$ 44. $\frac{1000}{100{,}000}$ 45. $\frac{169}{676}$

46. **Games** A chessboard contains 32 black and 32 white squares. How many squares are along each side of the game board?

LINK

Games

In 1997, Deep Blue became the first computer to win a match against a chess grand master when it defeated world champion Garry Kasparov.

47. **Hobbies** A quilter wants to use as many of his 65 small fabric squares as possible to make one large square quilt.
    a. How many small squares can the quilter use? How many small squares would he have left?
    b. How many more small squares would the quilter need to make the next largest possible square quilt?

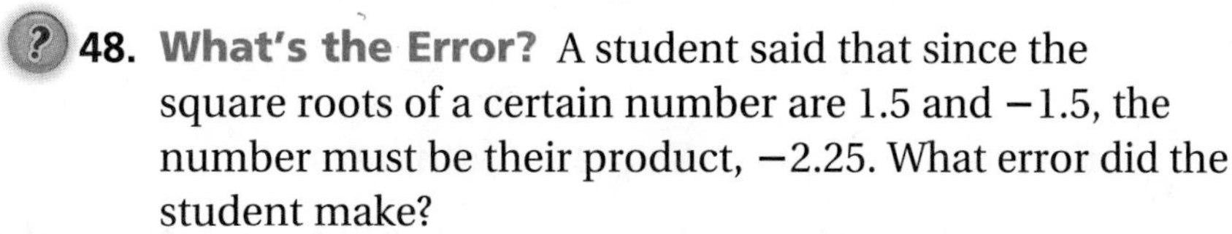

48. **What's the Error?** A student said that since the square roots of a certain number are 1.5 and −1.5, the number must be their product, −2.25. What error did the student make?

49. **Write About It** Explain the steps you would take to simplify the expression $\sqrt{14 + 35} - 20$.

50. **Challenge** The square root of a number is four less than three times seven. What is the number?

Test Prep

51. **Multiple Choice** Which number does NOT have a square root that is an integer?

Ⓐ 81 Ⓑ 196 Ⓒ 288 Ⓓ 400

52. **Short Response** Deanna knows that the floor in her kitchen is a square with an area of 169 square feet. The perimeter of her kitchen floor is found by adding the lengths of all its sides. What is the perimeter of her kitchen floor? Explain your answer.

3-6 Estimating Square Roots

COMMON CORE

CC.8.NS.2: Use rational approximations of irrational numbers to compare the size of irrational numbers, locate them approximately on a number line diagram, and estimate the value of expressions.

A couple wants to install a square stained-glass window with wood trim. You can calculate the length of the trim using your knowledge of squares and square roots.

Recall that a perfect square is a number whose square roots are integers. For example, 25 and 100 are perfect squares.

You can use the square roots of perfect squares to estimate the square roots of other numbers.

EXAMPLE 

Estimating Square Roots of Numbers

The $\sqrt{30}$ is between two consecutive integers. Name the integers. Explain your answer.

$\sqrt{30}$

16, 25, 36, 49	*List perfect squares near 30.*
$25 < 30 < 36$	*Find the perfect squares nearest 30.*
$\sqrt{25} < \sqrt{30} < \sqrt{36}$	*Find the square roots of the perfect squares.*
$5 < \sqrt{30} < 6$	

$\sqrt{30}$ is between 5 and 6 because 30 is between 25 and 36.

EXAMPLE 

Recreation Application

While searching for a lost hiker, a helicopter covers a square area of 150 mi^2. What is the approximate length of each side of the square area? Round your answer to the nearest mile.

121, 144, 169, 196	*List perfect squares near 150.*
$144 < 150 < 169$	*Find the perfect squares nearest 150.*
$\sqrt{144} < \sqrt{150} < \sqrt{169}$	*Find the square roots of the perfect squares.*
$12 < \sqrt{150} < 13$	
$\sqrt{150} \approx 12$	*150 is closer to 144 than 169, so $\sqrt{150}$ is closer to 12 than 13.*

Each side of the area is about 12 miles long.

You can use the square roots of perfect squares to approximate the square root of a value that is not a perfect square.

EXAMPLE 3 Approximating Square Roots to the Nearest Hundredth

Approximate $\sqrt{200}$ to the nearest hundredth.

Step 1: Find the value of the whole number.

$196 < 200 < 225$	*Find the perfect squares nearest 200.*
$\sqrt{196} < \sqrt{200} < \sqrt{225}$	*Find the square roots of the perfect squares.*
$14 < \sqrt{200} < 15$	*The number will be between 14 and 15.*

The whole number part of the answer is 14.

Step 2: Find the value of the decimal.

$200 - 196 = 4$	*Find the difference between the given number, 200, and the lower perfect square.*
$225 - 196 = 29$	*Find the difference between the greater perfect square and the lower perfect square.*
$\frac{4}{29}$	*Write the difference as a ratio.*
$4 \div 29 \approx 0.138$	*Divide to find the approximate decimal value.*

Reading Math 

The symbol ≈ means "is approximately equal to."

Step 3: Find the approximate value.

$14 + 0.138 = 14.138$	*Combine the whole number and decimal.*
$14.138 \approx 14.14$	*Round to the nearest hundredth.*

The approximate value of $\sqrt{200}$ to the nearest hundredth is 14.14.

You can also use a calculator to approximate the square root of a value that is not a perfect square.

EXAMPLE 4 Using a Calculator to Estimate the Value of a Square Root

Use a calculator to find $\sqrt{700}$. Round to the nearest tenth.

$\sqrt{700} \approx 26.45751311$	*Use a calculator.*
$\sqrt{700} \approx 26.5$	*Round to the nearest tenth.*

$\sqrt{700}$ rounded to the nearest tenth is 26.5.

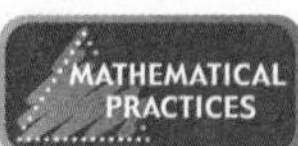

Think and Discuss

1. **Discuss** whether 9.5 is a good first guess for $\sqrt{75}$.
2. **Determine** which square root or roots would have 7.5 as a good first guess.

3-6 Exercises

Learn It Online
Homework Help Online
Exercises 1–32, 33, 37, 41, 49

GUIDED PRACTICE

See Example 1

Each square root is between two consecutive integers. Name the integers. Explain your answer.

1. $\sqrt{40}$
2. $\sqrt{90}$
3. $\sqrt{156}$
4. $\sqrt{306}$
5. $\sqrt{250}$

See Example 2

6. A gallon of water sealant can cover a square deck with an area of 190 square feet. About how long is each side of the deck? Round your answer to the nearest foot.

See Example 3

Approximate each square root to the nearest hundredth.

7. $\sqrt{42}$
8. $\sqrt{73}$
9. $\sqrt{156}$
10. $\sqrt{236}$
11. $\sqrt{275}$

See Example 4

Use a calculator to find each value. Round to the nearest tenth.

12. $\sqrt{74}$
13. $\sqrt{34.1}$
14. $\sqrt{3600}$
15. $\sqrt{190}$
16. $\sqrt{5120}$

INDEPENDENT PRACTICE

See Example 1

Each square root is between two consecutive integers. Name the integers. Explain your answer.

17. $\sqrt{52}$
18. $\sqrt{3}$
19. $\sqrt{600}$
20. $\sqrt{2000}$
21. $\sqrt{410}$

See Example 2

22. The area of a square field is 200 ft^2. What is the approximate length of each side of the field? Round your anwer to the nearest foot.

See Example 3

Approximate each square root to the nearest hundredth.

23. $\sqrt{19}$
24. $\sqrt{84}$
25. $\sqrt{123}$
26. $\sqrt{251}$
27. $\sqrt{290}$

See Example 4

Use a calculator to find each value. Round to the nearest tenth.

28. $\sqrt{58}$
29. $\sqrt{91.5}$
30. $\sqrt{550}$
31. $\sqrt{150}$
32. $\sqrt{330}$

PRACTICE AND PROBLEM SOLVING

Extra Practice

See Extra Practice for more exercises.

Write the letter that identifies the position of each square root.

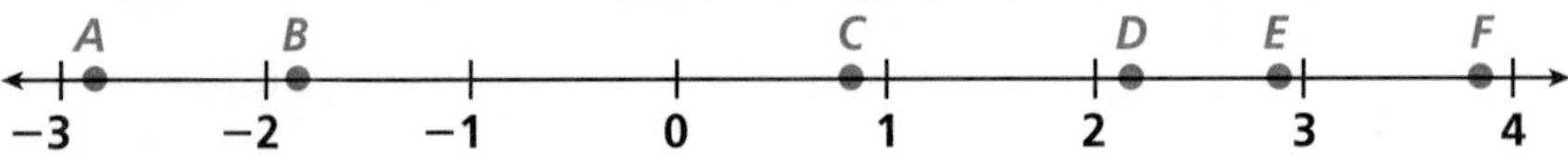

33. $-\sqrt{3}$
34. $\sqrt{5}$
35. $\sqrt{7}$
36. $-\sqrt{8}$
37. $\sqrt{14}$
38. $\sqrt{0.75}$

39. A couple wants to install a square stained-glass window that has an area of 500 square inches. To the nearest tenth of an inch, what length of wood trim is needed to go around the window?

40. Each square on Laura's chessboard is 13 square centimeters. A chessboard has 8 squares on each side. To the nearest hundredth, what is the width of Laura's chessboard?

LINK

Science

Pilots rely on visual information as well as instruments when in flight.

41. **Multi-Step** On a baseball field, the infield area created by the baselines is a square. In a youth baseball league for 9- to 12-year-olds, this area is 3600 ft^2. The distance between each base in a league for 4-year-olds is 20 ft less than it is for 9- to 12-year-olds. What is the distance between each base for 4-year-olds?

Order the numbers from least to greatest.

42. $\sqrt{50}, \frac{15}{2}, 7.7, \frac{\sqrt{160}}{2}$

43. $1.1, \frac{1}{3}\sqrt{9}, \frac{8}{9}, \sqrt{2}$

44. **Multi-Step** Find the perimeter of the square shown.

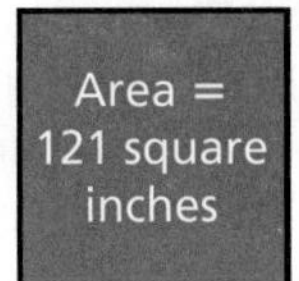

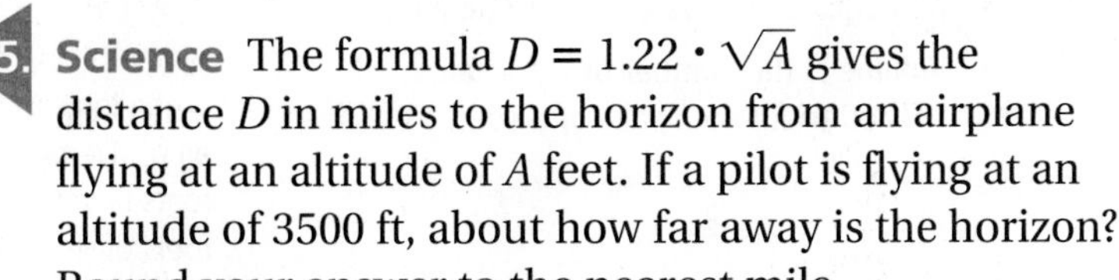

45. **Science** The formula $D = 1.22 \cdot \sqrt{A}$ gives the distance D in miles to the horizon from an airplane flying at an altitude of A feet. If a pilot is flying at an altitude of 3500 ft, about how far away is the horizon? Round your answer to the nearest mile.

46. **Multi-Step** A square poster is made up of 40 rows of 40 photos each. The area of each square photo is 4 cm. How long is each side of the poster?

47. **What's The Error?** To find $\sqrt{5}$, Lane said since $2^2 = 4$ and $3^2 = 9$, the number is between 2 and 3 and so the best estimate is $\frac{2+3}{2} = 2.5$. What was the error?

48. **Write About It** Explain how you know whether $\sqrt{29}$ is closer to 5 or 6 without using a calculator.

49. **Challenge** The speed of a tsunami in miles per hour can be found using $r = \sqrt{14.88d}$, where d is the water depth in feet. Suppose the water depth is 25,000 ft.
   - **a.** How fast is the tsunami moving in miles per hour?
   - **b.** How long would it take a tsunami to travel 3000 miles if the water depth were a consistent 10,000 ft?

Test Prep

50. **Multiple Choice** Which expression has a value between 14 and 15?

Ⓐ $\sqrt{188}$ Ⓑ $\sqrt{200}$ Ⓒ $\sqrt{227}$ Ⓓ $\sqrt{324}$

51. **Gridded Response** Find the product $\sqrt{42} \cdot \sqrt{94}$ to the nearest hundredth.

Alan Novelli/Alamy

Explore Cube Roots

Use with Estimating Square Roots

WHAT YOU NEED:

Smallest base 10 blocks (Rainbow cubes or centimeter cubes will also work.)

REMEMBER

- All edges of a cube are the same length.
- Volume is the number of cubic units needed to fill the space of a solid.

Use appropriate tools strategically.

CC.8.EE.2: Use square root and cube root symbols to represent solutions to equations of the form $x^2 = p$ and $x^3 = p$, where p is a positive rational number. Evaluate square roots of small perfect squares and cube roots of small perfect cubes. Know that $\sqrt{2}$ is irrational.

The number of small unit blocks it takes to construct a cube is equal to the volume of the cube. By building a cube with edge length x and counting the number of unit blocks needed to build the cube, you can find x^3 (x-cubed), the volume.

Activity 1

1 **Find 2^3.**

You need to build a cube with an edge length of 2.

Build 3 edges of length 2.

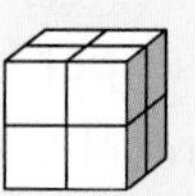

Fill in the rest of the cube.

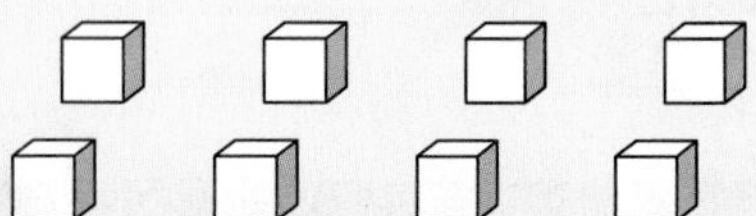

Count the number of unit cubes you needed to build a cube with an edge length of 2.

To make a cube with edge length 2, you need 8 unit blocks. So $2^3 = 8$.

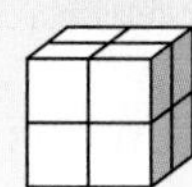

Think and Discuss

1. Why would it be difficult to model 2^4?
2. How can you find the value of a number squared from the model of that number cubed?

Try This

Model the following. How many blocks do you need to model each?

1. 5^3 **2.** 3^3 **3.** 6^3 **4.** 1^3

You can determine whether any number x is a perfect cube by trying to build a cube out of x unit blocks. If you can build a cube with the given number of blocks, then the number is a perfect cube. Its ***cube root*** will be the length of one edge of the cube that is formed.

Activity 2

1 Try to build a cube using 27 unit blocks. Is 27 a perfect cube? If so, what is its cube root?

Start by building a cube with an edge length of 2, since $1^3 = 1$ and $27 > 1$.

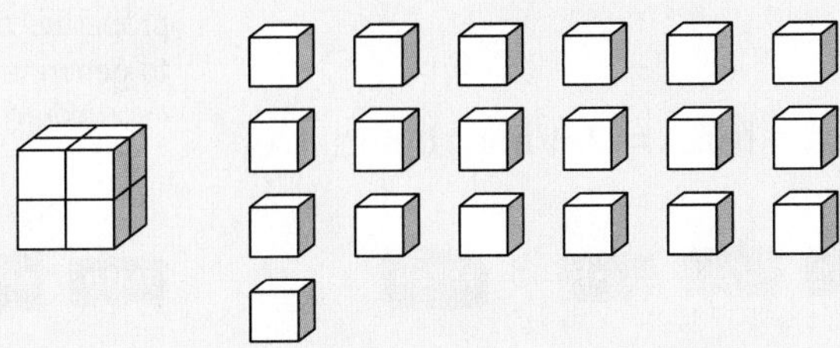

You still have 19 unit blocks left over. So try building a cube with an edge length of 3. Remember that when you add 1 unit cube to any edge you must do the same to all three edges to keep the cube shape.

You can make a cube with edges of length 3 by using 27 small blocks. So 27 is a perfect cube. Its cube root is 3. We write $\sqrt[3]{27} = 3$.

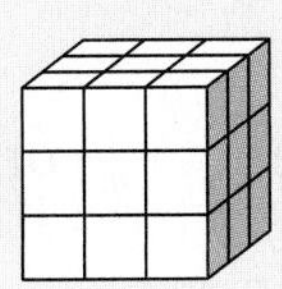

A cube with edges of length 3 can be made with 27 blocks.
length = 3
width = 3
height = 3

Think and Discuss

1. Is 100 a perfect cube? Why or why not?
2. $\sqrt[3]{125} = 5$. Is $\sqrt[3]{2 \cdot 125} = 2 \cdot \sqrt[3]{125} = 10$? Why or why not?
3. Use blocks to model a solid with a length of 3, a height of 2, and a width of 2. How many blocks did you use? Is this a perfect cube?
4. A positive number has two square roots, one positive and one negative. Is this true for cube roots? Justify your answer.

Try This

Model to find whether each number is a perfect cube. If the number is a perfect cube, find its cube root. If not, find the whole numbers that the cube roots are between.

1. 64
2. 75
3. 125
4. 200
5. Make a table with the first ten perfect cubes. Estimate $\sqrt[3]{100}$ using the method you learned in Lesson 4-6 Example 3.

Evaluate Powers and Roots

Use with Estimating Square Roots

Learn It Online
Lab Resources Online

MATHEMATICAL PRACTICES Use appropriate tools strategically.

CC.8.EE.1: Know and apply the properties of integer exponents to generate equivalent numerical expressions.

A graphing calculator can be used to evaluate expressions that have negative exponents and square roots.

Activity

1 Use the STO▸ button to evaluate x^{-3} for $x = 2$. View the answer as a decimal and as a fraction.

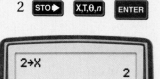

2 STO▸ X,T,θ,n ENTER   X,T,θ,n ^ (−) 3 ENTER   MATH ENTER ENTER

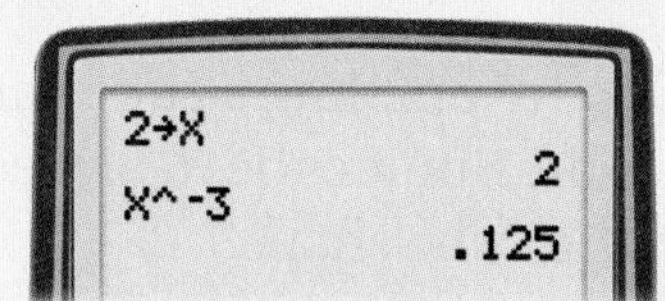

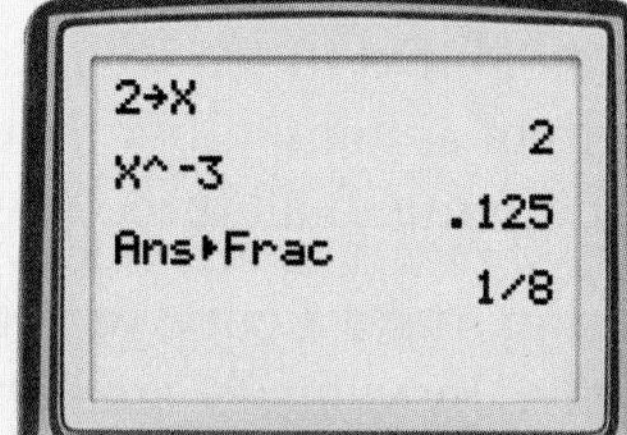

Notice that $2^{-3} = 0.125$, which is equivalent to $\frac{1}{2^3}$, or $\frac{1}{8}$.

2 Use the **TABLE** feature to evaluate $-\sqrt{x}$ for several x-values. Match the settings shown.

Y= (−) 2nd x^2 ($\sqrt{\ }$) X,T,θ,n ENTER   2nd WINDOW (TBLSET)   2nd GRAPH (TABLE)

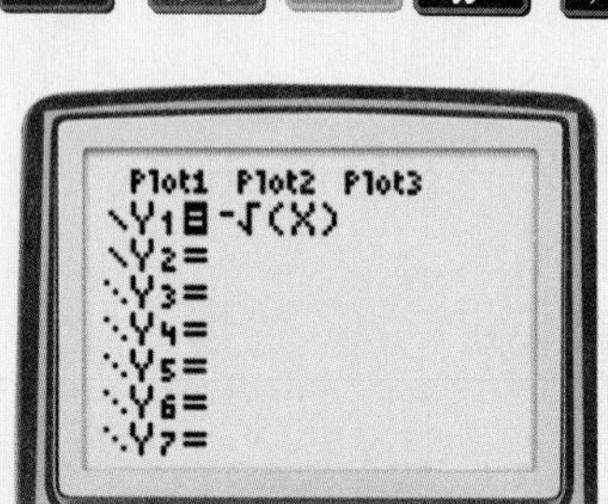

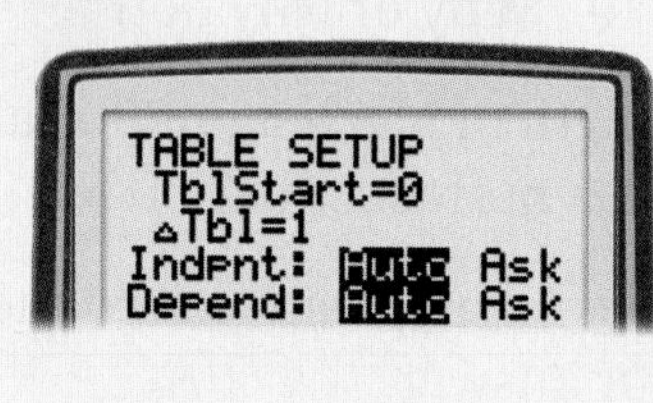

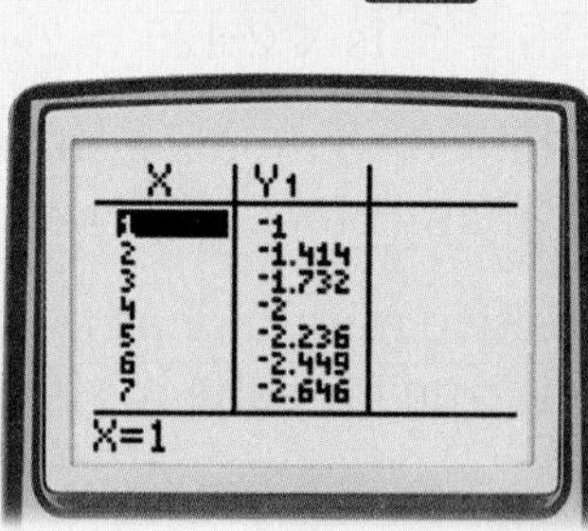

The **Y1** list shows the value of $-\sqrt{x}$ for several x-values.

Think and Discuss

1. When you evaluated 2^{-3} in Activity 1, the result was not a negative number. Is this surprising? Why or why not?

Try This

Evaluate each expression for the given x-value(s). Give your answers as fractions and as decimals rounded to the nearest hundredth.

1. 4^{-x}; $x = 2$

2. $\sqrt{x}$; $x = 1, 2, 3, 4$

3. x^{-2}; $x = 1, 2, 5$

3-7 The Real Numbers

COMMON CORE

CC.8.NS.1: Understand informally that every number has a decimal expansion; the rational numbers are those with decimal expansions that terminate in 0s or eventually repeat. Know that other numbers are called irrational. ***Also CC.8.EE.2***

Vocabulary

irrational number

real number

Density Property

Biologists classify animals based on shared characteristics. The cardinal is an animal, a vertebrate, a bird, and a passerine.

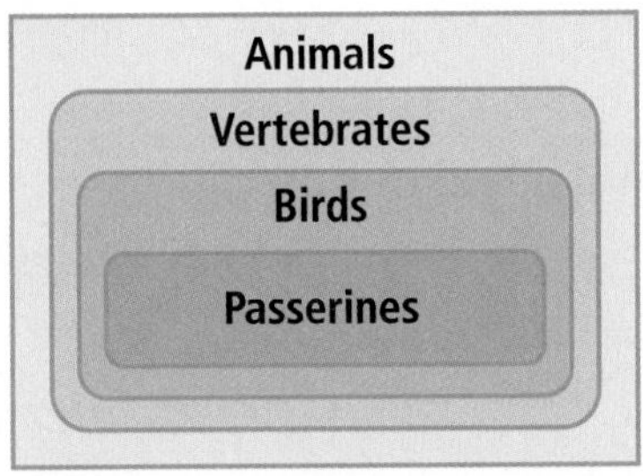

Passerines, such as the cardinal, are also called "perching birds."

Interactivities Online ▶

You already know that some numbers can also be classified as natural numbers, whole numbers, integers, or rational numbers. Recall that rational numbers can be written as fractions and as decimals that either terminate or repeat.

$$3\frac{4}{5} = 3.8 \qquad \frac{2}{3} = 0.\overline{6} \qquad \sqrt{1.44} = 1.2$$

Caution!

A repeating decimal may not appear to repeat on a calculator because calculators show a finite number of digits.

Irrational numbers can only be written as decimals that do *not* terminate or repeat. If a whole number is not a perfect square, then its square root is an irrational number.

$\sqrt{2} = 1.41421356237...$

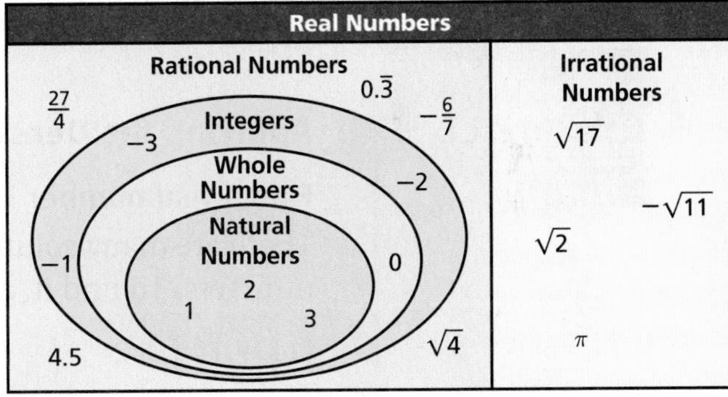

The set of **real numbers** consists of the set of rational numbers and the set of irrational numbers.

EXAMPLE 1 Classifying Real Numbers

Write all names that apply to each number.

A $\sqrt{3}$ — *3 is a whole number that is not a perfect square.*

irrational, real

B -52.28 — *−52.28 is a terminating decimal.*

rational, real

C $\frac{\sqrt{16}}{4}$ — $\frac{\sqrt{16}}{4} = \frac{4}{4} = 1$

natural, whole, integer, rational, real

William Leaman/Alamy

The square root of a negative number is not a real number. A fraction with a denominator of 0 is undefined because you cannot divide by zero. So it is not a number at all.

EXAMPLE 2 Determining the Classification of All Numbers

State if each number is rational, irrational, or not a real number. Justify your answer.

A $\sqrt{15}$

irrational — *15 is a whole number that is not a perfect square.*

B $\frac{3}{0}$

undefined, so not a real number

C $\sqrt{\frac{1}{9}}$

rational — *$\left(\frac{1}{3}\right)\left(\frac{1}{3}\right) = \frac{1}{9}$, $\frac{1}{3}$ is a rational number.*

D $\sqrt{-13}$

not a real number — *square root of a negative number*

Reading Math

Mathematicians have defined numbers, such as $\sqrt{-2}$, that are not within the set of real numbers. You will learn about them in later courses.

Any real number can be shown on a number line. The **Density Property** of real numbers states that between any two real numbers is another real number. This property is not true for whole numbers or integers. For instance, there is no integer between −2 and −3.

EXAMPLE 3 Applying the Density Property of Real Numbers

Find a real number between $1\frac{1}{3}$ and $1\frac{2}{3}$.

There are many solutions. One solution is halfway between the two numbers. To find it, add the numbers and divide by 2.

$\left(1\frac{1}{3} + 1\frac{2}{3}\right) \div 2$

$= \left(2\frac{3}{3}\right) \div 2$

$= 3 \div 2 = 1\frac{1}{2}$

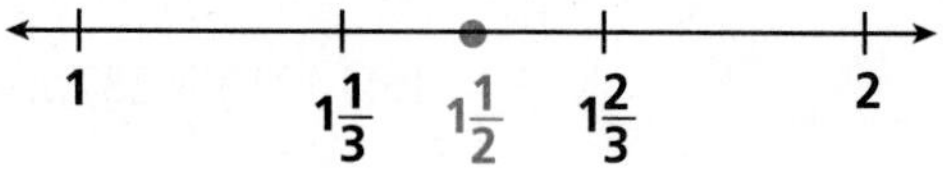

A real number between $1\frac{1}{3}$ and $1\frac{2}{3}$ is $1\frac{1}{2}$.

MATHEMATICAL PRACTICES

Think and Discuss

1. **Explain** how rational numbers are related to integers.
2. **Tell** if a number can be irrational and whole. Explain.
3. **Use** the Density Property to explain why there are infinitely many real numbers between 0 and 1.

3-7 Exercises

Learn It Online
Homework Help Online
Exercises 1–30, 31, 33, 35, 37, 55, 57, 59

GUIDED PRACTICE

See Example 1 — Write all names that apply to each number.

1. $\sqrt{10}$
2. $\sqrt{49}$
3. 0.25
4. $-\frac{\sqrt{16}}{3}$

See Example 2 — State if each number is rational, irrational, or not a real number. Justify your answer.

5. $\sqrt{9}$
6. $\sqrt{\frac{9}{16}}$
7. $\sqrt{72}$
8. $-\sqrt{-3}$
9. $-\sqrt{25}$
10. $\sqrt{-9}$
11. $\sqrt{\frac{25}{-36}}$
12. $\frac{0}{0}$

See Example 3 — Find a real number between each pair of numbers.

13. $3\frac{1}{8}$ and $3\frac{2}{8}$
14. 4.14 and $\frac{29}{7}$
15. $\frac{1}{8}$ and $\frac{1}{4}$

INDEPENDENT PRACTICE

See Example 1 — Write all names that apply to each number.

16. $\sqrt{35}$
17. $\frac{5}{8}$
18. 3
19. $\frac{\sqrt{81}}{-3}$

See Example 2 — State if each number is rational, irrational, or not a real number. Justify your answer.

20. $\frac{\sqrt{-16}}{-4}$
21. $-\sqrt{\frac{0}{4}}$
22. $\sqrt{-8(-2)}$
23. $-\sqrt{3}$
24. $\frac{\sqrt{25}}{8}$
25. $\sqrt{14}$
26. $\sqrt{-\frac{1}{4}}$
27. $-\sqrt{\frac{4}{0}}$

See Example 3 — Find a real number between each pair of numbers.

28. $3\frac{2}{5}$ and $3\frac{3}{5}$
29. $-\frac{1}{10}$ and 0
30. 4 and $\sqrt{9}$

PRACTICE AND PROBLEM SOLVING

Extra Practice
See Extra Practice for more exercises.

Write all names that apply to each number.

31. 6
32. $-\sqrt{36}$
33. $\sqrt{10}$
34. $\frac{1}{3}$
35. $\sqrt{2.56}$
36. $\sqrt{36} + 6$
37. $0.\overline{21}$
38. $\frac{\sqrt{100}}{20}$
39. −4.3134
40. $\sqrt{4.5}$
41. −312
42. $\frac{0}{7}$

43. Explain the difference between $-\sqrt{16}$ and $\sqrt{-16}$.

Give an example of each type of number.

44. an irrational number that is less than −3
45. a rational number that is less than 0.3
46. a real number between $\frac{5}{9}$ and $\frac{6}{9}$
47. a real number between $-3\frac{2}{7}$ and $-3\frac{3}{7}$

48. Find a rational number between $\sqrt{\frac{1}{9}}$ and $\sqrt{1}$.

49. Find a real number between $\sqrt{6}$ and $\sqrt{7}$.

50. Find a real number between $\sqrt{5}$ and $\sqrt{11}$.

51. Find a real number between $\sqrt{50}$ and $\sqrt{55}$.

52. Find a real number between $-\sqrt{20}$ and $-\sqrt{17}$.

53. a. Find a real number between 1 and $\sqrt{3}$.
 b. Find a real number between 1 and your answer to part **a.**
 c. Find a real number between 1 and your answer to part **b.**

For what values of x is the value of each expression a real number?

54. $\sqrt{2x}$

55. $3 - \sqrt{x}$

56. $\sqrt{x + 2}$

Order the values on a number line.

57. $\sqrt{5}, \frac{5}{2}, 2.8, \frac{\sqrt{15}}{2}$

58. $2\sqrt{8}, \sqrt{27}, 5\frac{3}{8}, \frac{\sqrt{225}}{\sqrt{9}}$

59. **What's the Error?** A student said that all integers are whole numbers. What mistake did the student make? Explain.

60. **Write About It** Can you ever use a calculator to determine if a number is rational or irrational? Explain.

61. **Challenge** The circumference of a circle divided by its diameter is an irrational number, represented by the Greek letter π (*pi*). Could a circle with a diameter of 2 have a circumference of 6? Why or why not?

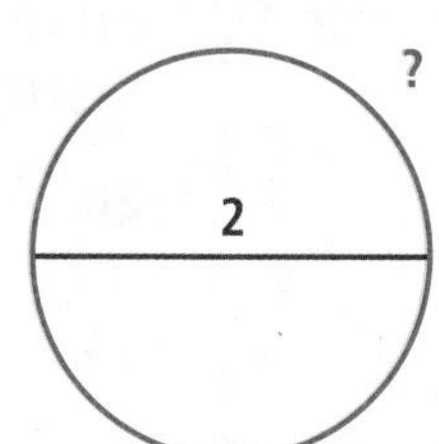

Test Prep

62. **Multiple Choice** Which value is between -10 and -8?

Ⓐ -7.12 Ⓑ $-\sqrt{61}$ Ⓒ $-3 \cdot \pi$ Ⓓ $-\frac{123}{11}$

63. **Multiple Choice** Which value is NOT a rational number?

Ⓕ $0.\overline{7}$ Ⓖ $\frac{11}{13}$ Ⓗ $\sqrt{19}$ Ⓙ $\sqrt{225}$

64. **Multiple Choice** For which values of x is $\sqrt{x - 19}$ a real number?

Ⓐ $x \geq -19$ Ⓑ $x \leq -19$ Ⓒ $x \geq 19$ Ⓓ $x \leq 19$

Mastering the *Standards*

for Mathematical Practice

The topics described in the Standards for Mathematical Content will vary from year to year. However, the *way* in which you learn, study, and think about mathematics will not. The Standards for Mathematical Practice describe skills that you will use in all of your math courses.

Mathematical Practices

1. *Make sense of problems and persevere in solving them.*
2. *Reason abstractly and quantitatively.*
3. *Construct viable arguments and critique the reasoning of others.*
4. *Model with mathematics.*
5. *Use appropriate tools strategically.*
6. *Attend to precision.*
7. *Look for and make use of structure.*
8. *Look for and express regularity in repeated reasoning.*

① Make sense of problems and persevere in solving them.

Mathematically proficient students start by explaining to themselves the meaning of a problem... They analyze givens, constraints, relationships, and goals. They make conjectures about the form... of the solution and plan a solution pathway...

In your book

Focus on Problem Solving describes a four-step plan for problem solving. The plan is introduced at the beginning of your book, and practice with the plan appears throughout the book.

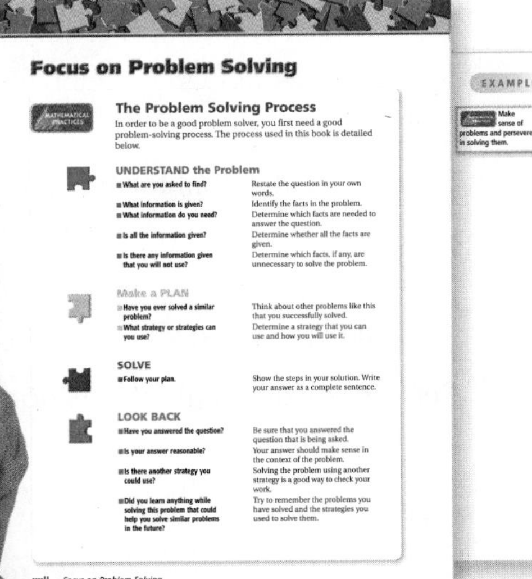

Focus on Problem Solving

MATHEMATICAL PRACTICES

The Problem Solving Process

In order to be a good problem solver, you first need a good problem-solving process. The process used in this book is detailed below.

UNDERSTAND the Problem

What are you asked to find?	Restate the question in your own words.
What information is given?	Identify the facts in the problem.
What information do you need?	Determine which facts are needed to answer the question.
Is all the information given?	Determine whether all the facts are given.
Is there any information given that you will not use?	Determine which facts, if any, are unnecessary to solve the problem.

Make a PLAN

Have you ever solved a similar problem?	Think about other problems like this that you successfully solved.
What strategy or strategies can you use?	Determine a strategy that you can use and how you will use it.

SOLVE

Follow your plan.	Show the steps in your solution. Write your answer as a complete sentence.

LOOK BACK

Have you answered the question?	Be sure that you answered the question that is being asked.
Is your answer reasonable?	Your answer should make sense in the context of the problem.
Is there another strategy you could use?	Solving the problem using another strategy is a good way to check your work.
Did you learn anything while solving this problem that could help you solve similar problems in the future?	Try to remember the problems you have solved and the strategies you used to solve them.

xxii *Focus on Problem Solving*

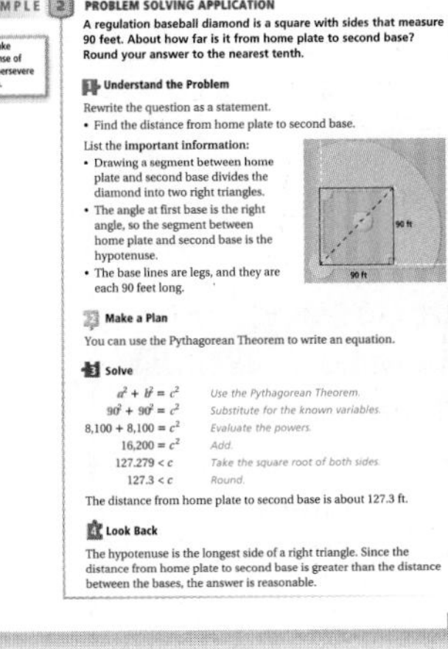

EXAMPLE 2 **PROBLEM SOLVING APPLICATION**

Make sense of problems and persevere in solving them.

A regulation baseball diamond is a square with sides that measure 90 feet. About how far is it from home plate to second base? Round your answer to the nearest tenth.

1 Understand the Problem

Rewrite the question as a statement.

- Find the distance from home plate to second base.

List the **important information:**

- Drawing a segment between home plate and second base divides the diamond into two right triangles.
- The angle at first base is the right angle, so the segment between home plate and second base is the hypotenuse.
- The base lines are legs, and they are each 90 feet long.

2 Make a Plan

You can use the Pythagorean Theorem to write an equation.

3 Solve

$a^2 + b^2 = c^2$	*Use the Pythagorean Theorem.*
$90^2 + 90^2 = c^2$	*Substitute for the known variables.*
$8{,}100 + 8{,}100 = c^2$	*Evaluate the powers.*
$16{,}200 = c^2$	*Add.*
$127.279 < c$	*Take the square root of both sides.*
$127.3 < c$	*Round.*

The distance from home plate to second base is about 127.3 ft.

4 Look Back

The hypotenuse is the longest side of a right triangle. Since the distance from home plate to second base is greater than the distance between the bases, the answer is reasonable.

EXTENSION

Identifying and Graphing Irrational Numbers

COMMON CORE

CC.8.NS.2: Use rational approximations of irrational numbers to compare the size of irrational numbers, locate them approximately on a number line diagram, and estimate the value of expressions.

Vocabulary

irrational numbers

real numbers

Recall that a rational number can be written as a fraction with integers for its numerator and denominator. When rational numbers are written in decimal form, the decimal may be terminating or nonterminating. If a rational number is nonterminating, then it has a repeating pattern.

A decimal that is nonterminating with no repeating pattern is an **irrational number**. For example, $\sqrt{2} = 1.4142135\ldots$, which does not terminate or repeat.

The set of **real numbers** consists of the set of rational numbers and the set of irrational numbers.

Real Numbers

Rational numbers (Integers (Whole numbers))	Irrational numbers

EXAMPLE 1 Identifying Rational and Irrational Numbers

Identify each number as rational or irrational. Justify your answer.

A $\frac{2}{5}$

$\frac{2}{5} = 0.4$ *Write the number in decimal form.*

Because its decimal form is terminating, $\frac{2}{5}$ is rational.

B $\frac{5}{6}$

$\frac{5}{6} = 0.8333\ldots$, or $0.8\overline{3}$ *Write the number in decimal form.*

Because its decimal form is nonterminating and repeating, $\frac{5}{6}$ is rational.

Remember!

By definition, any ratio of integers is a rational number.

C $\sqrt{16}$

$\sqrt{16} = 4$ *Write the number in decimal form.*

Because its decimal form is terminating, $\sqrt{16}$ is rational.

D $\sqrt{7}$

$\sqrt{7} = 2.645751311\ldots$ *Write the number in decimal form.*

There is no pattern in the decimal form of $\sqrt{7}$. It is a nonterminating, nonrepeating decimal. So $\sqrt{7}$ is irrational.

Every point on the number line corresponds to a real number, either a rational number or an irrational number. Between every two real numbers there is always another real number.

EXAMPLE 2

Graphing Rational and Irrational Numbers

Graph the list of numbers on a number line. Then order the numbers from least to greatest.

$1.4, \sqrt{5}, \frac{3}{8}, \pi, -\frac{2}{3}, \sqrt{4}, \sqrt{16}$

Write all the numbers in decimal form, and then graph them.

$1.4, \sqrt{5} \approx 2.236, \frac{3}{8} = 0.375, \pi \approx 3.14, -\frac{2}{3} = -0.\overline{6}, \sqrt{4} = 2.0, \sqrt{16} = 4.0$

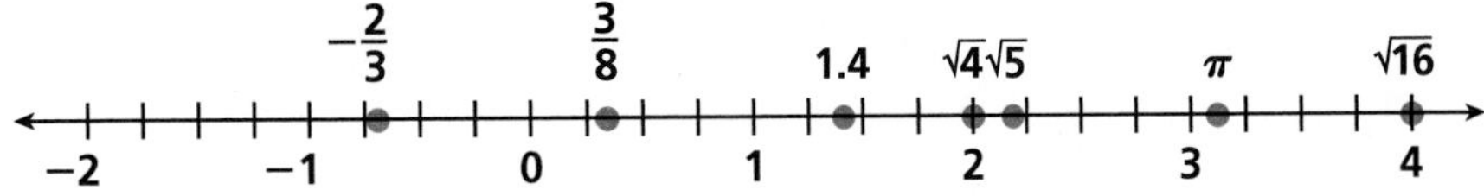

From left to right on the number line, the numbers appear from least to greatest: $-\frac{2}{3} < \frac{3}{8} < 1.4 < \sqrt{4} < \sqrt{5} < \pi < \sqrt{16}.$

EXTENSION

Exercises

Identify each number as rational or irrational. Justify your answer.

1. $\sqrt{8}$ **2.** $\frac{5}{11}$ **3.** $\frac{7}{8}$ **4.** $\sqrt{36}$

5. $\frac{3}{13}$ **6.** $\sqrt{14}$ **7.** 2.800 **8.** $\frac{5}{6}$

9. $\sqrt{5}$ **10.** $\frac{6}{24}$ **11.** $\frac{10}{33}$ **12.** $\sqrt{18}$

Graph each list of numbers on a number line. Then order the numbers from least to greatest.

13. $2.6, 0.5, \sqrt{3}, -\frac{7}{10}, \frac{1}{3}$

14. $\sqrt{12}, \frac{3}{8}, -0.65, \frac{5}{9}, \sqrt{11}$

15. $-1.3, \sqrt{15}, 3.1, -\frac{2}{5}, \sqrt{4}$

16. $-2.1, -\frac{9}{10}, \sqrt{1}, -1.5, \sqrt{9}$

Name the two perfect squares that each square root lies between. Then graph the square root on a number line, and justify its placement.

17. $\sqrt{34}$ **18.** $\sqrt{46}$ **19.** $\sqrt{14}$ **20.** $\sqrt{6}$

21. $\sqrt{99}$ **22.** $\sqrt{63}$ **23.** $\sqrt{71}$ **24.** $\sqrt{13}$

25. What's the Error? A classmate tells you that the square root of any number is irrational. Explain why the classmate is incorrect.

Explore Right Triangles

Use with The Pythagorean Theorem

REMEMBER

Right triangles have 1 right angle and 2 acute angles. The side opposite the right angle is called the *hypotenuse,* and the other two sides are called *legs.*

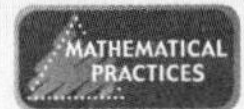

Use appropriate tools strategically.

CC.8.G.6: Explain a proof of the Pythagorean Theorem and its converse.

Activity

1 The Pythagorean Theorem states that if a and b are the lengths of the legs of a right triangle, then c is the length of the hypotenuse, where $a^2 + b^2 = c^2$. Prove the Pythagorean Theorem using the following steps.

a. Draw two squares side by side. Label one with side a and one with side b.

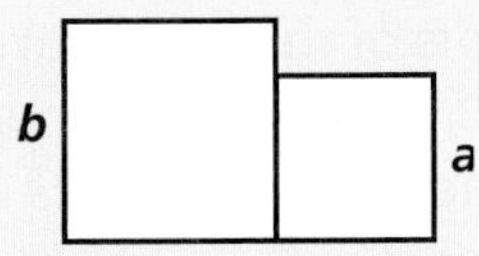

Notice that the area of this composite figure is $a^2 + b^2$.

b. Draw hypotenuses of length c, so that we have right triangles with sides a, b, and c. Use a protractor to make sure that the hypotenuses form a right angle.

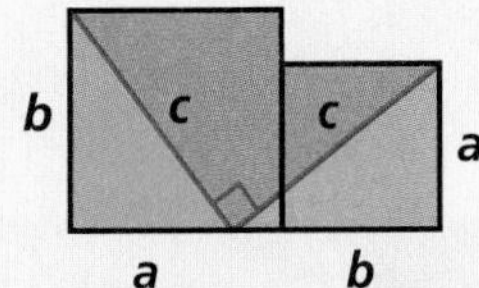

c. Cut out the triangles and the remaining piece.

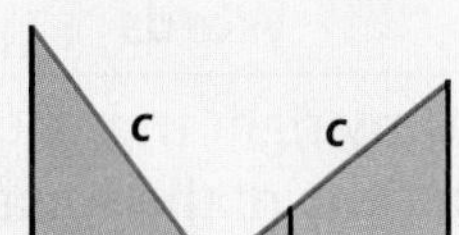

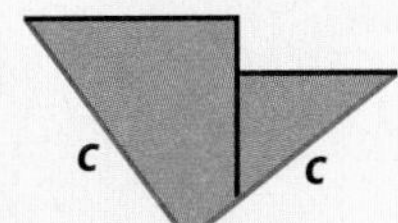

d. Fit the pieces together to make a square with sides c and area c^2. You have shown that the area $a^2 + b^2$ can be cut up and rearranged to form the area c^2, so $a^2 + b^2 = c^2$.

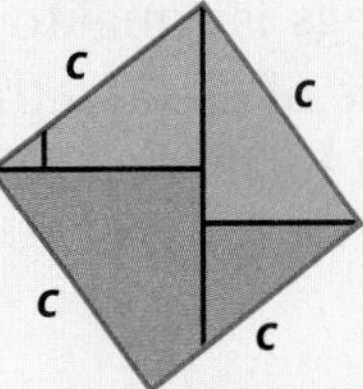

Think and Discuss

1. The diagram shows another way of understanding the Pythagorean Theorem. How are the areas of the squares shown in the diagram related?

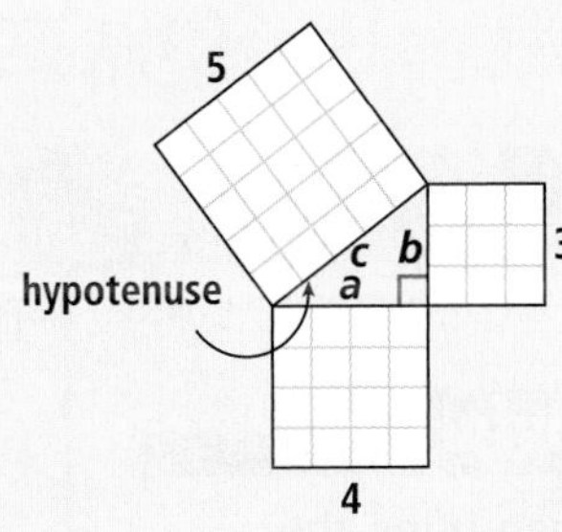

Try This

1. If you know that the lengths of two legs of a right triangle are 8 and 15, can you find the length of the hypotenuse? Show your work.

2. Take a piece of paper and fold the right corner down so that the top edge of the paper matches the side edge. Crease the paper. Without measuring, find the diagonal's length.

3-8 The Pythagorean Theorem

COMMON CORE

CC.8.G.7: Apply the Pythagorean Theorem to determine unknown side lengths in right triangles in real-world and mathematical problems in two and three dimensions. ***Also CC.8.G.6***

Vocabulary

Pythagorean Theorem

leg

hypotenuse

Pythagoras was born on the Aegean island of Samos sometime between 580 B.C.E. and 569 B.C.E. He is best known for the *Pythagorean Theorem,* which relates the side lengths of a right triangle.

A Babylonian tablet known as Plimpton 322 provides evidence that the relationship between the side lengths of right triangles was known as early as 1900 B.C.E. Many people, including U.S. president James Garfield, have written proofs of the Pythagorean Theorem. In 1940, E. S. Loomis presented 370 proofs of the theorem in *The Pythagorean Proposition.*

This statue of Pythagoras is located in the Pythagorion Harbor on the island of Samos.

Paul Doyle/Alamy

Interactivities Online ▶

THE PYTHAGOREAN THEOREM

Words	Numbers	Algebra
In any right triangle, the sum of the squares of the lengths of the two **legs** is equal to the square of the length of the **hypotenuse**.	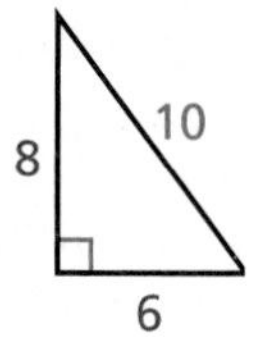 $6^2 + 8^2 = 10^2$ $36 + 64 = 100$	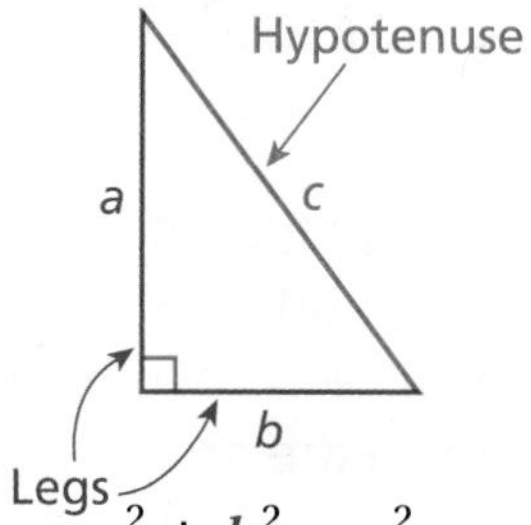 $a^2 + b^2 = c^2$

EXAMPLE 1

Finding the Length of a Hypotenuse

Find the length of each hypotenuse to the nearest hundredth.

Helpful Hint

When using the Pythagorean Theorem to find length, use only the principal square root.

A

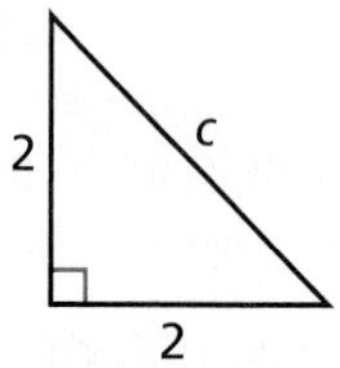

$a^2 + b^2 = c^2$	*Pythagorean Theorem*
$2^2 + 2^2 = c^2$	*Substitute 2 for a and 2 for b.*
$4 + 4 = c^2$	*Simplify powers.*
$8 = c^2$	*Add.*
$\sqrt{8} = c$	*Find the square root.*
$2.83 \approx c$	*Round to the nearest hundredth.*

Video Lesson Tutorials Online my.hrw.com

Find the length of each hypotenuse to the nearest hundredth.

B **triangle with coordinates (3, 1), (0, 5), and (0, 1)**

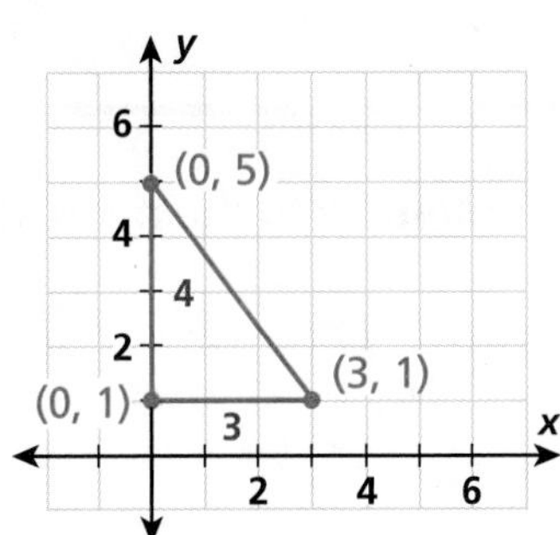

The points form a right triangle with $a = 4$ and $b = 3$.

$a^2 + b^2 = c^2$	*Pythagorean Theorem*
$4^2 + 3^2 = c^2$	*Substitute for a and b.*
$16 + 9 = c^2$	*Simplify powers.*
$25 = c^2$	*Add.*
$\sqrt{25} = c$	*Find the square root.*
$5 = c$	

EXAMPLE 2

Finding the Length of a Leg in a Right Triangle

Helpful Hint

Be sure to substitute the longest side length for *c*.

Solve for the unknown side in the right triangle to the nearest tenth.

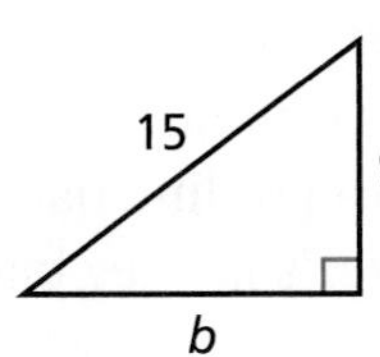

$a^2 + b^2 = c^2$	*Pythagorean Theorem*
$9^2 + b^2 = 15^2$	*Substitute for a and b.*
$81 + b^2 = 225$	*Simplify powers.*
$-81 \quad = -81$	*Subtract 81 from each side.*
$b^2 = 144$	
$b = \sqrt{144} = 12$	*Find the square root.*

EXAMPLE 3

Using the Pythagorean Theorem for Measurement

Mark and Sarah start walking at the same point, but Mark walks 50 feet north while Sarah walks 75 feet east. How far apart are Mark and Sarah when they stop?

Mark and Sarah's distance from each other when they stop walking is equal to the hypotenuse of a right triangle.

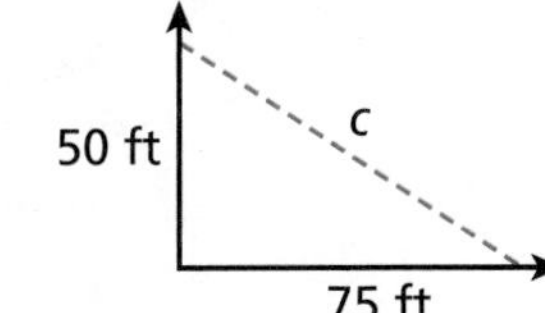

$a^2 + b^2 = c^2$	*Pythagorean Theorem*
$50^2 + 75^2 = c^2$	*Substitute for a and b.*
$2500 + 5625 = c^2$	*Simplify powers.*
$8125 = c^2$	*Add.*
$90.1 \approx c$	*Find the square root.*

Mark and Sarah are approximately 90.1 feet apart.

MATHEMATICAL PRACTICES

Think and Discuss

1. Tell which side of a right triangle is always the longest side.

2. Explain if 2, 3, and 4 cm could be side lengths of a right triangle.

3-8 Exercises

Learn It Online
Homework Help Online
Exercises 1–16, 17, 19, 21, 23

GUIDED PRACTICE

See Example 1 **Find the length of each hypotenuse to the nearest hundredth.**

1. 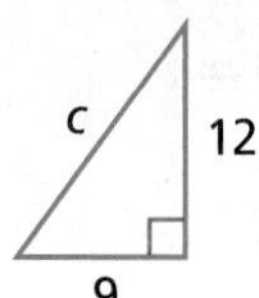

2. 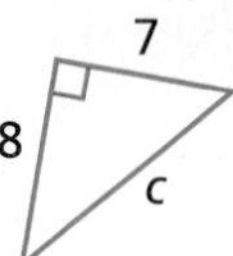

3. 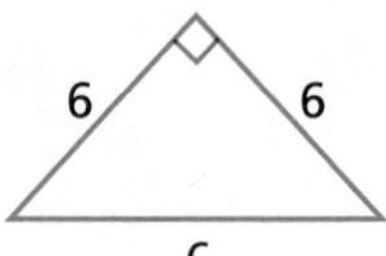

4. triangle with coordinates $(-4, 0)$, $(-4, 5)$, and $(0, 5)$

See Example 2 **Solve for the unknown side in each right triangle to the nearest tenth.**

5. 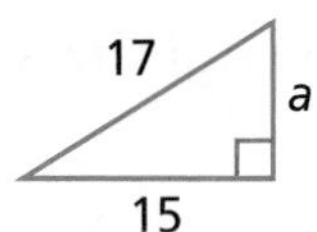

6. 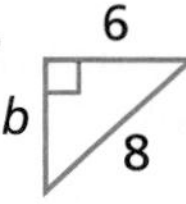

7. 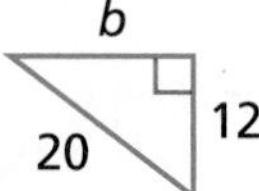

See Example 3

8. A traffic helicopter flies 10 miles due north and then 24 miles due east. Then the helicopter flies in a straight line back to its starting point. What was the distance of the helicopter's last leg back to its starting point?

INDEPENDENT PRACTICE

See Example 1 **Find the length of each hypotenuse to the nearest hundredth.**

9. 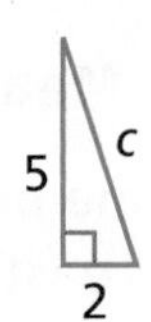

10. 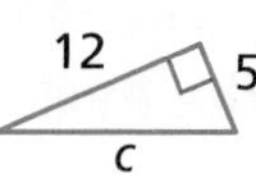

11. 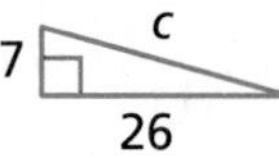

12. triangle with coordinates $(-5, 3)$, $(5, -3)$, and $(-5, -3)$

See Example 2 **Solve for the unknown side in each right triangle to the nearest tenth.**

13. 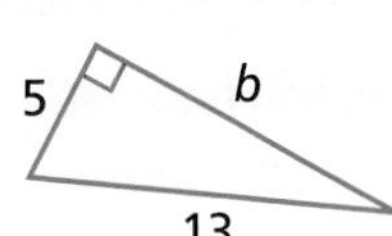

14. 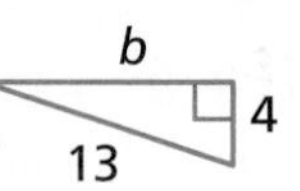

15. 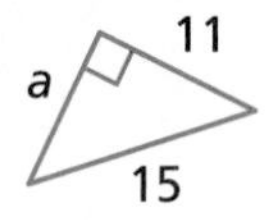

See Example 3

16. Mr. and Mrs. Flores commute to work each morning. Mr. Flores drives 8 miles east to his office. Mrs. Flores drives 15 miles south to her office. How many miles away do Mr. and Mrs. Flores work from each other?

PRACTICE AND PROBLEM SOLVING

Extra Practice
See Extra Practice for more exercises.

Find the missing length for each right triangle to the nearest tenth.

17. $a = 4$, $b = 7$, $c = $ ■
18. $a = $ ■, $b = 40$, $c = 41$
19. $a = 30$, $b = 72$, $c = $ ■
20. $a = 16$, $b = $ ■, $c = 38$
21. $a = $ ■, $b = 47$, $c = 60$
22. $a = 65$, $b = $ ■, $c = 97$

23. For safety reasons, the base of a 24-foot ladder must be placed at least 8 feet from the wall. To the nearest tenth of a foot, how high can a 24-foot ladder safely reach?

24. How far is the sailboat from the lighthouse, to the nearest kilometer?

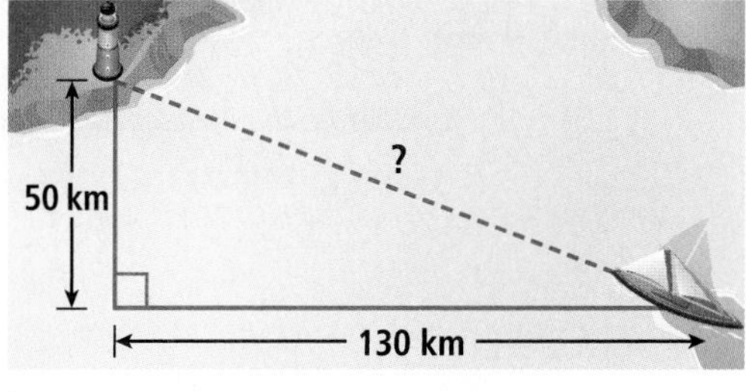

25. **Multi-Step** Two sides of a right triangle are of length 4 inches and 11 inches. The third side may be a leg or may be the hypotenuse. Approximately how much longer would it be if it were the hypotenuse than if it were a leg?

26. **Critical Thinking** A right triangle has leg lengths of 1 foot 6 inches and 2 feet. Find the hypotenuse length and the perimeter in mixed units of feet and inches.

27. **Multi-Step** What was the height of the tree, to the nearest tenth? Explain.

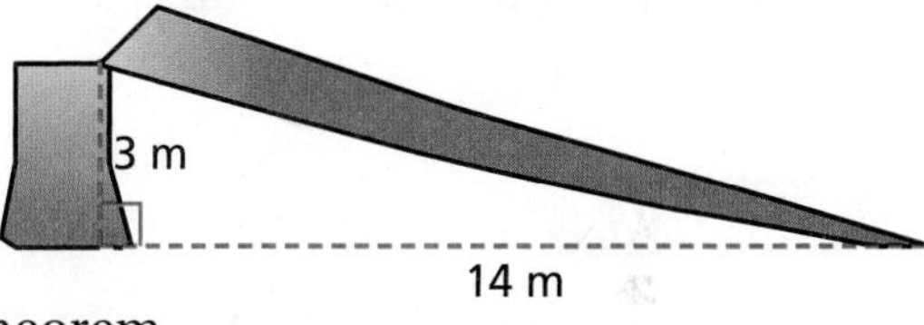

28. **Write a Problem** Use a street map to write and solve a problem that requires the use of the Pythagorean Theorem.

29. **Write About It** Explain how to find the length of the side of any right triangle when you know two of the side lengths.

30. **Challenge** A right triangle has legs of length $3x$ m and $4x$ m and hypotenuse of length 75 m. Find the lengths of the legs of the triangle.

Test Prep

31. **Multiple Choice** A flagpole is 40 feet tall. A rope is tied to the top of the flagpole and secured to the ground 9 feet from the base of the flagpole. What is the length of the rope to the nearest foot?

Ⓐ 19 feet Ⓑ 39 feet Ⓒ 41 feet Ⓓ 1519 feet

32. **Gridded Response** Brad leans his 15-foot ladder against his house. The base of the ladder is placed 4 feet from the base of the house. How far up the house does the ladder reach? Round your answer to the nearest hundredth.

Technology LAB

Explore the Converse of the Pythagorean Theorem

Use before the Pythagorean Theorem

MATHEMATICAL PRACTICES Use appropriate tools strategically.

CC.8.G.6: Explain a proof of the Pythagorean Theorem and its converse.

The Pythagorean theorem states that if a triangle is a right triangle, then its side lengths a, b, and c are related by $a^2 + b^2 = c^2$. In this lab you will investigate the converse of that theorem. That is, if the side lengths a, b, and c of a triangle are related by $a^2 + b^2 = c^2$, then the triangle must be a right triangle.

Activity 1

Complete the table to find triangle side lengths *a*, *b*, and *c* for which $a^2 + b^2 = c^2$.

	$a^2 + b^2 = c^2$	$9 + 16 = 25$	$25 + 144 = 169$	$81 + 144 = 225$
1	$\sqrt{a^2} = a$	$\sqrt{9} = 3$		
2	$\sqrt{b^2} = b$	$\sqrt{16} = 4$		
3	$\sqrt{c^2} = c$	$\sqrt{25} = 5$		
4	**Side Lengths**	3, 4, 5		

5 Using geometry software, create the triangle with side lengths 3, 4, and 5 units. Classify the triangle by its angle measures.

6 Repeat Step 5 for the other two triangles described in the table, and classify the triangles by their angle measures.

Think and Discuss

1. How are the triangles you created in Activity 1 alike? How are they different?

2. **Make a Conjecture** If the side lengths a, b, and c of a triangle satisfy $a^2 + b^2 = c^2$, what type of triangle do you think it must be?

Activity 2

Use geometry software to prove the converse of the Pythagorean Theorem.

1. Create any right triangle *ABC* and label the sides *a*, *b*, and *c*.

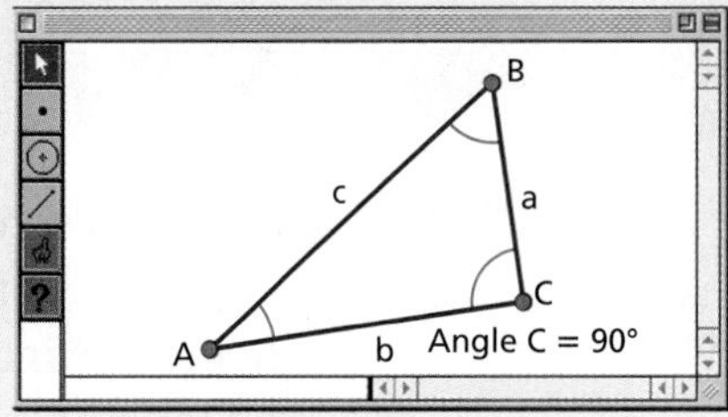

2. Using geometry software, create three segments of same lengths as *a*, *b*, and *c* in your right triangle in Step 1.

Because:
$a = a_2$ $b = b_2$ $c = c_2$

You know that triangle *ABC* from Step 1 is a right triangle, and $a^2 + b^2 = c^2$.

Then, by substitution:
$(a_2)^2 + (b_2)^2 = (c_2)^2$

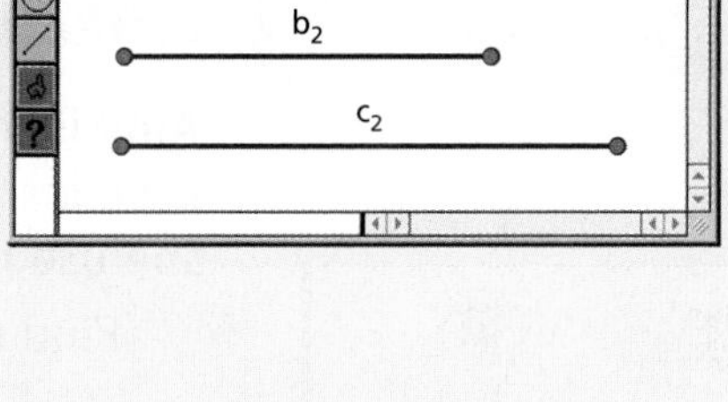

3. Drag the segments around to form a triangle. When you have formed your triangle, use the measuring tool to find out if the triangle is a right triangle.

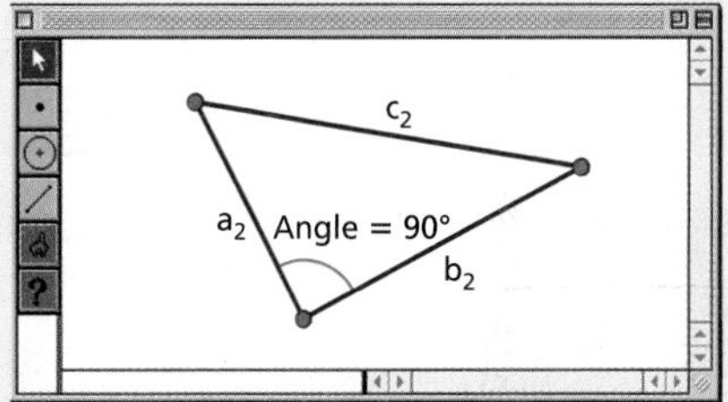

Think and Discuss

1. Do your results from Activity 2 support your conjecture from the Think and Discuss questions after Activity 1? If so, restate your conjecture.

Try This

Use your conjecture from this lab to determine whether a triangle with the given side lengths will be a right triangle.

1. 5, 12, 13

2. 8, 15, 17

3. 2, 4, 7

4. 7, 24, 25

5. 3, 9, 10

6. 12, 13, 25

3-9 Applying the Pythagorean Theorem and Its Converse

COMMON CORE

CC.8.G.8: Apply the Pythagorean Theorem to find the distance between two points in a coordinate system.

Television screens are described by the length of their diagonals. The Pythagorean Theorem can be used to find distances and lengths, such as the diagonal length of an HDTV screen.

EXAMPLE 1 Marketing Application

Amy is making a brochure for the HDTV shown above. The screen is 48 inches wide and 20 inches high. What diagonal length should she use in the brochure?

Find the length of the diagonal of the TV screen.

$20^2 + 48^2 = c^2$ *Use the Pythagorean Theorem.*

$400 + 2304 = c^2$ *Simplify.*

$2704 = c^2$ *Add.*

$\sqrt{2704} = c$

$52 = c$ *Find the square root.*

The diagonal length should be given as 52 inches.

You can use the Pythagorean Theorem to find distance on the coordinate plane. Diagonal distance can be thought of as the hypotenuse of a right triangle. By substituting into the Pythagorean Theorem, you can develop a formula for distance.

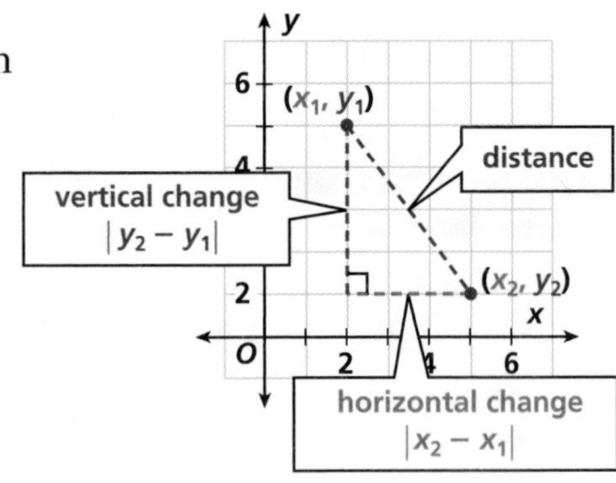

$$c^2 = a^2 + b^2$$

$$\text{distance}^2 = |x_2 - x_1|^2 + |y_2 - y_1|^2$$

$$d = \sqrt{|x_2 - x_1|^2 + |y_2 - y_1|^2}$$

Because the square of the absolute value is always nonnegative, the absolute value symbols are not needed.

THE DISTANCE FORMULA

The distance between two points (x_1, y_1) and (x_2, y_2) on the coordinate plane is

$$d=\sqrt{(x_2 - x_1)^2 + (y_2 - y_1)^2}$$

EXAMPLE 2 Finding Distance on the Coordinate Plane

Find the distances between the points to the nearest tenth.

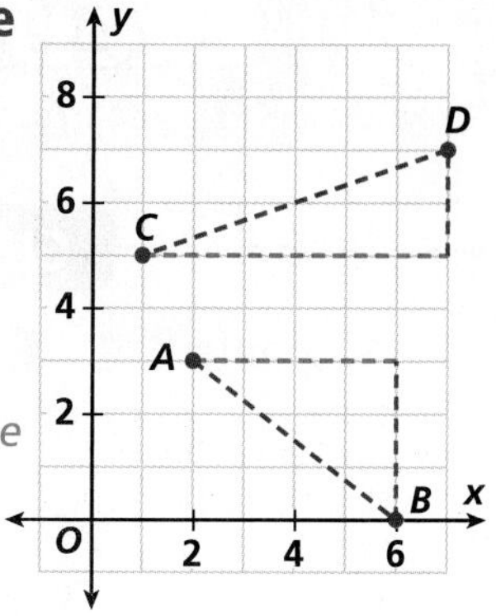

Helpful Hint

You may choose either point A or B as (x_1, y_1).

A *A* and *B*

Let A be (x_2, y_2) and B be (x_1, y_1).

$d = \sqrt{(x_2 - x_1)^2 + (y_2 - y_1)^2}$ *Use the Distance Formula.*

$= \sqrt{(2 - 6)^2 + (3 - 0)^2}$ *Substitute.*

$= \sqrt{(-4)^2 + 3^2}$ *Subtract.*

$= \sqrt{16 + 9}$ *Simplify powers.*

$= \sqrt{25} = 5$ *Take the square root.*

The distance between A and B is 5 units.

B *C* and *D*

Let D be (x_2, y_2) and C be (x_1, y_1).

$d = \sqrt{(x_2 - x_1)^2 + (y_2 - y_1)^2}$ *Use the Distance Formula.*

$= \sqrt{(7 - 1)^2 + (7 - 5)^2}$ *Substitute.*

$= \sqrt{6^2 + 2^2}$ *Subtract.*

$= \sqrt{36 + 4}$ *Simplify powers.*

$= \sqrt{40} \approx 6.3$ *Take the square root.*

The distance to the nearest tenth between C and D is 6.3 units.

The *Converse of the Pythagorean Theorem* states that if a triangle has side lengths a, b, and c and $a^2 + b^2 = c^2$, then the triangle is a right triangle.

EXAMPLE 3 Identifying a Right Triangle

Tell whether the given side lengths form a right triangle.

A 7, 24, 25

$a^2 + b^2 \stackrel{?}{=} c^2$ *Compare $a^2 + b^2$ to c^2.*

$7^2 + 24^2 \stackrel{?}{=} 25^2$ *Substitute.*

$49 + 576 \stackrel{?}{=} 625$ *Simplify.*

$625 = 625$ ✔ *Add.*

The side lengths form a right triangle.

B 5, 8, 12

$a^2 + b^2 \stackrel{?}{=} c^2$

$5^2 + 8^2 \stackrel{?}{=} 12^2$

$25 + 64 \stackrel{?}{=} 144$

$89 \neq 144$ ✘

The side lengths do not form a right triangle.

MATHEMATICAL PRACTICES

Think and Discuss

1. **Make a conjecture** about whether doubling the side lengths of a right triangle makes another right triangle.

3-9 Exercises

Learn It Online
Homework Help Online
Exercises 1–16, 19, 21, 25, 27, 29

GUIDED PRACTICE

See Example 1

1. **Baseball** A regulation baseball diamond is a square with sides that measure 90 feet. About how far is it from home plate to second base? Round your answer to the nearest tenth.

See Example 2

Find the distances between the points to the nearest tenth.

2. A and B 3. B and C 4. A and C

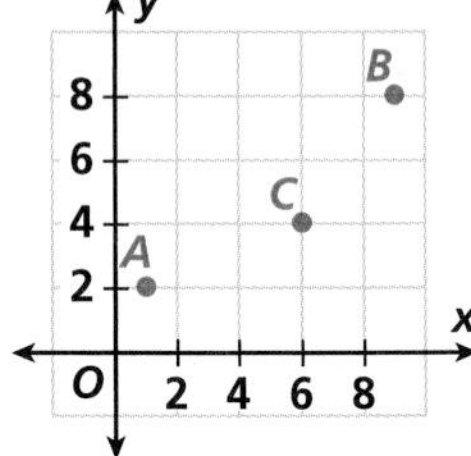

See Example 3

Tell whether the given side lengths form a right triangle.

5. 3, 4, 5
6. 8, 10, 14
7. 0.5, 1.2, 1.3
8. 18, 80, 82

INDEPENDENT PRACTICE

See Example 1

9. **Safety** A ladder must be placed 5 feet from the base of a wall and must reach a height of 11 feet. What length ladder is needed? Round your answer to the nearest tenth.

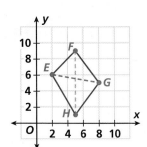

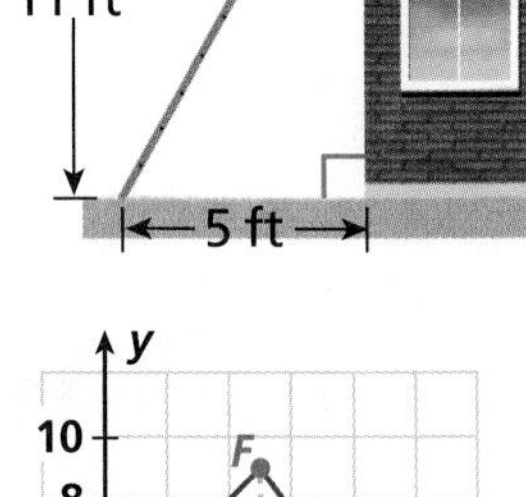

See Example 2

Find the distances between the points to the nearest tenth.

10. G and H 11. E and F 12. E and G

See Example 3

Tell whether the given side lengths form a right triangle.

13. 8, 15, 17
14. 5, 6, 9
15. 2.4, 2.5, 3.6
16. 60, 80, 100

PRACTICE AND PROBLEM SOLVING

Extra Practice
See Extra Practice for more exercises.

Find the distances between the two points to the nearest tenth.

17. (0, 7) and (−5, 3)   18. (−2, −5) and (0, 9)   19. (5, 12) and (−5, −12)

20. **Reasoning** A construction company is pouring a rectangular concrete foundation. The dimensions of the foundation are 24 ft by 48 ft. Describe a procedure to confirm that the sides of the foundation meet at a right angle.

Any three natural numbers that make the equation $a^2 + b^2 = c^2$ true are *Pythagorean triples*. Determine whether each set is a Pythagorean triple.

21. 3, 6, 9
22. 3, 4, 5
23. 5, 12, 13
24. 7, 24, 25
25. 10, 24, 26
26. 8, 14, 16
27. 10, 16, 19
28. 9, 40, 41

29. **Geometry** The *altitude* of a triangle is a perpendicular segment from a vertex to the line containing the opposite side. Find h, the length of the altitude of triangle ABC.

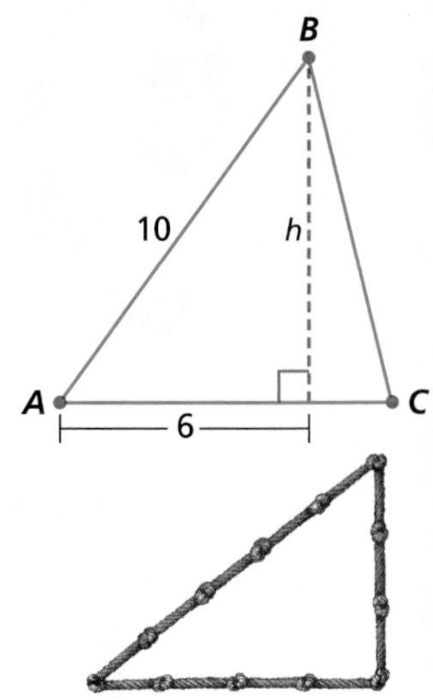

30. **Measurement** Use a standard 8½ in. by 11 in. piece of paper. Measure the diagonal to the nearest 16th of an inch. Does this measurement form a right triangle with the sides? Explain your answer.

31. **History** In ancient Egypt, surveyors made right angles by stretching a rope with evenly spaced knots as shown. Explain why the rope forms a right angle.

32. A *unit square* has a side length of 1 unit. Find the length of the diagonal of a unit square with a side length of 1 inch. Write your answer as a square root and to the nearest hundredth.

33. **What's the Error?** A student said the side lengths 41, 40, and 9 do not form a right triangle, because $9^2 + 41^2 = 1762$ and $40^2 = 1600$, and $1762 \neq 1600$. What error did the student make?

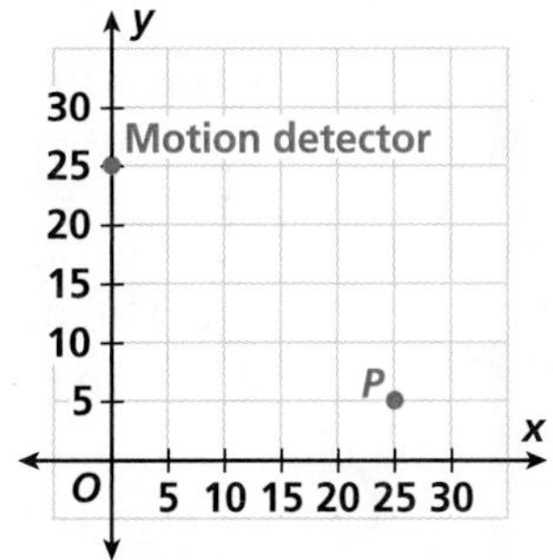

34. **Critical Thinking** The motion detector has a maximum range of 33 feet. Can it spot movement at P? Explain.

35. **Write About It** Explain how to find the distance between two points in the coordinate plane.

36. **Challenge** Find d, the length of the diagonal of the box. Hint: Find the value of c first.

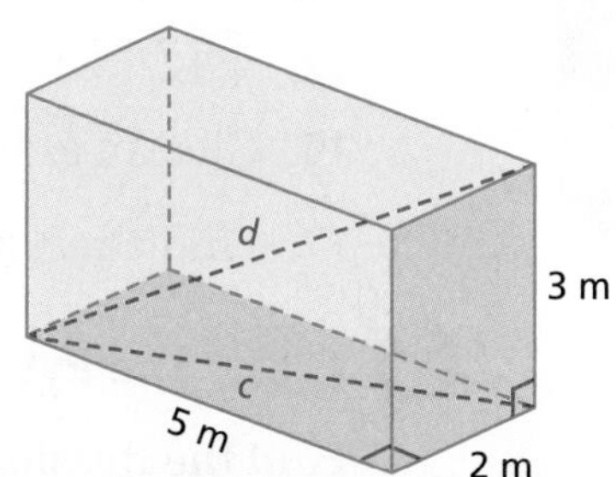

Test Prep

37. **Multiple Choice** Two sides of a right triangle are 9 cm and 15 cm. The third side is not the hypotenuse. How long is the third side?

Ⓐ 3 cm Ⓑ 12 cm Ⓒ 17 cm Ⓓ 21 cm

38. **Gridded Response** Find the distance between $(-6, 8)$ and $(6, -8)$.

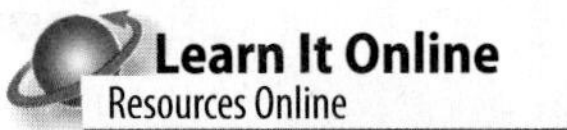

Quiz for Lessons 5 Through 9

5 Squares and Square Roots

Find the two square roots of each number.

1. 16 **2.** 9801 **3.** 10,000 **4.** 529

5. If Jan's living room is 20 ft × 16 ft, will a square rug with an area of 289 ft^2 fit? Explain your answer.

6. How many 2 in. × 2 in. square tiles will fit along the edge of a square mosaic that has an area of 196 square inches?

6 Estimating Square Roots

Each square root is between two consecutive integers. Name the integers. Explain your answer.

7. $-\sqrt{72}$ **8.** $\sqrt{200}$ **9.** $-\sqrt{340}$ **10.** $\sqrt{610}$

11. The area of a chess board is 110 square inches. Find the length of one side of the board to the nearest hundredth.

7 The Real Numbers

Write all names that apply to each number.

12. $\sqrt{12}$ **13.** 0.15 **14.** $\sqrt{1600}$ **15.** $-\frac{\sqrt{144}}{4}$

16. Give an example of an irrational number that is less than -5.

17. Find a real number between 5 and $\sqrt{36}$.

8 The Pythagorean Theorem

Find the missing length for each right triangle. Round your answer to the nearest tenth.

18. $a = 3$, $b = 6$, $c =$ ▇ **19.** $a =$ ▇, $b = 24$, $c = 25$

20. A construction company is pouring a concrete foundation. The measures of two sides that meet in a corner are 33 ft and 56 ft. For the corner to be a right angle, what would the length of the diagonal have to be?

9 Applying the Pythagorean Theorem and Its Converse

Find the distance between the points to the nearest tenth.

21. (3, 2) and (11, 8) **22.** (−1, −1) and (−3, 6)

Tell whether the given side lengths form a right triangle.

23, 7, 9, 11 **24.** 8, 14, 17

Ready to Go On?

Real-World CONNECTIONS

MATHEMATICAL PRACTICES Reason abstractly and quantitatively.

Harvard University's Museums of Natural History

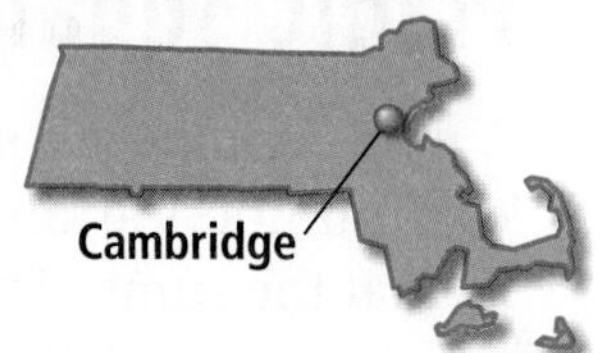

The most visited attraction at Harvard University in Cambridge is the Harvard Museum of Natural History. Each year, more than 150,000 visitors come to explore the museum's collections, which include everything from dinosaur bones to glass flowers to hummingbird eggs.

The table shows the number of some types of specimens at the museum. Use the table for Problems 1–4.

The Collections of the Harvard Museum of Natural History

Category	Number of Specimens
Meteorites	1.5×10^3
Minerals	5.0×10^4
Dried plants	5.0×10^6
Reptile and amphibian skeletons	7.0×10^3
Insects	7.0×10^6

1. Write the number of meteorites in standard notation.

2. Does the museum contain a greater number of minerals or of reptile and amphibian skeletons? Explain how you know.

3. How many more insect specimens than dried plant specimens are there at the museum?

4. The museum contains a total of 2.1×10^7 specimens. Approximately what fraction of the museum's specimens are dried plants? Explain how you determined your answer.

5. The museum features the skeleton of a 42-foot long *Kronosaurus*. The display case is just long enough to house the skeleton. The diagonal length of the rectangular display-case window, from one corner to the opposite corner, is 43 ft. What is the height of the display case, to the nearest tenth of a foot?

Game Time

Magic Squares

A *magic square* is a square with numbers arranged so that the sums of the numbers in each row, column, and diagonal are the same.

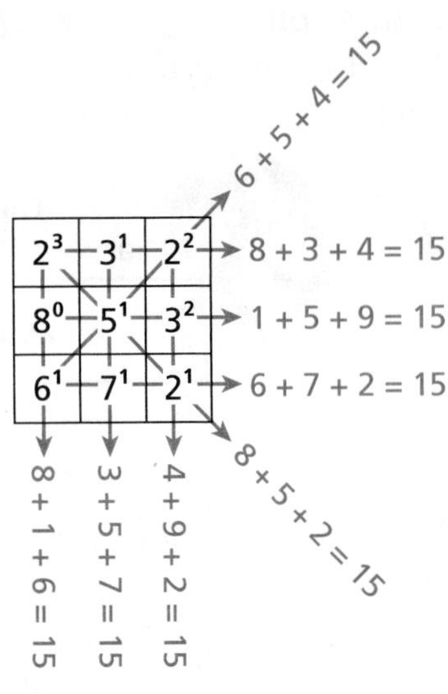

2^3 3^1 2^2
8^0 5^1 3^2
6^1 7^1 2^1
8 + 3 + 4 = 15
1 + 5 + 9 = 15
6 + 7 + 2 = 15
8 + 1 + 6 = 15
3 + 5 + 7 = 15
4 + 9 + 2 = 15
6 + 5 + 4 = 15
8 + 5 + 2 = 15

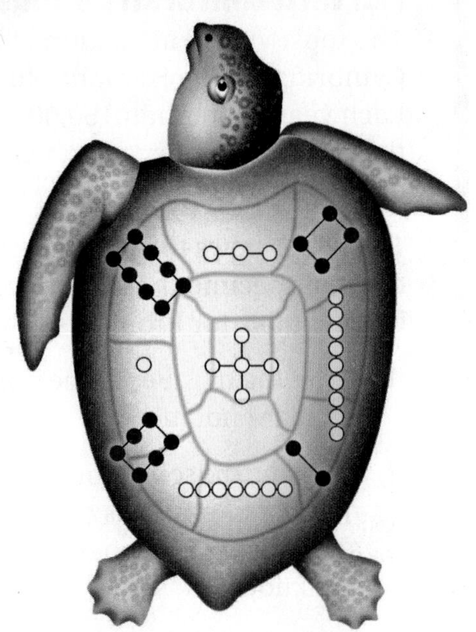

According to an ancient Chinese legend, a tortoise from the Lo river had the pattern of this magic square on its shell.

1 Complete each magic square below.

$\sqrt{36}$		2^2
8^0	$\sqrt{9}$	
	$3^2 - 2$	

	$-(\sqrt{4} + 4)$	$-(9^0)$
$-(\sqrt{16})$		0^3
$-(\sqrt{9})$	$2^0 + 1$	

2 Use the numbers −4, −3, −2, −1, 0, 1, 2, 3, and 4 to make a magic square with row, column, and diagonal sums of 0.

Equation Bingo

Each bingo card has numbers on it. The caller has a collection of equations. The caller reads an equation, and then the players solve the equation for the variable. If players have the solution on their cards, they place a chip on it. The winner is the first player with a row of chips either down, across, or diagonally.

A complete copy of the rules and game boards are available online.

Randall Hyman/HMH Photo

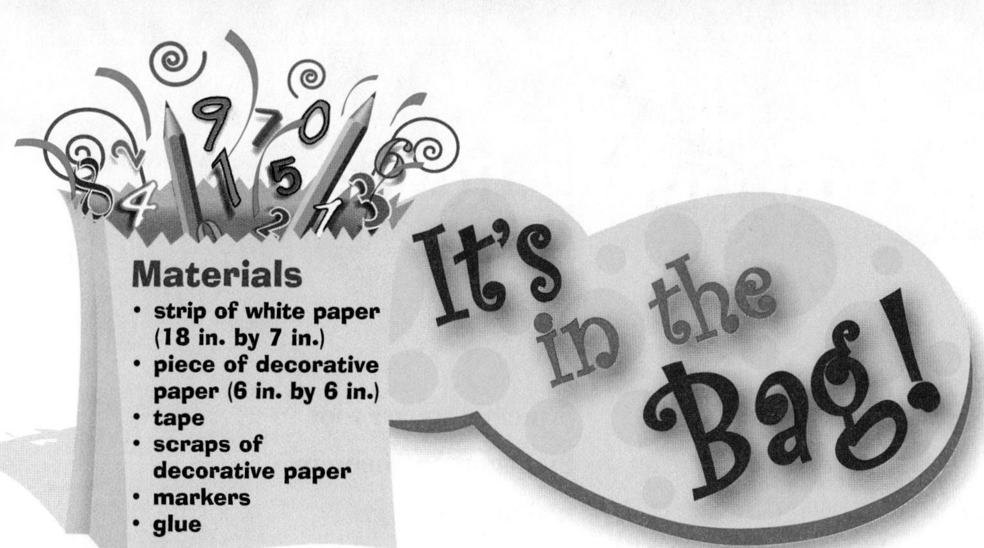

It's in the Bag!
Materials
• strip of white paper (18 in. by 7 in.)
• piece of decorative paper (6 in. by 6 in.)
• tape
• scraps of decorative paper
• markers
• glue

PROJECT It's a Wrap

Design your own energy-bar wrapper to hold your notes on exponents and roots.

Directions

1. Make accordion folds on the strip of white paper so that there are six panels, each about 3 in. wide. **Figure A**

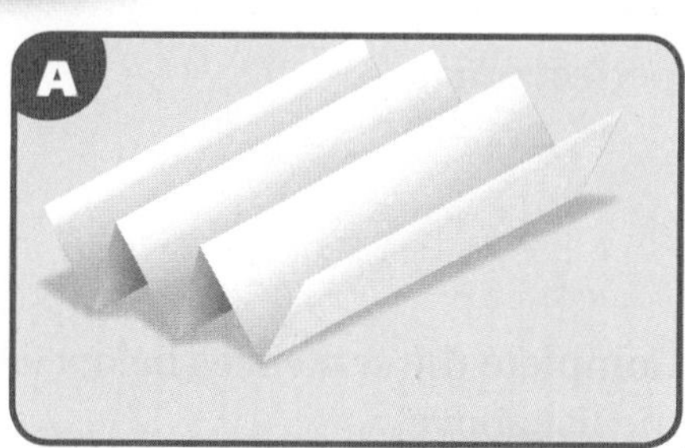

2. Fold up the accordion strip.

3. Wrap the decorative paper around the accordion strip. The accordion strip will stick out on either side. Tape the ends of the decorative paper together to make a wrapper. **Figure B**

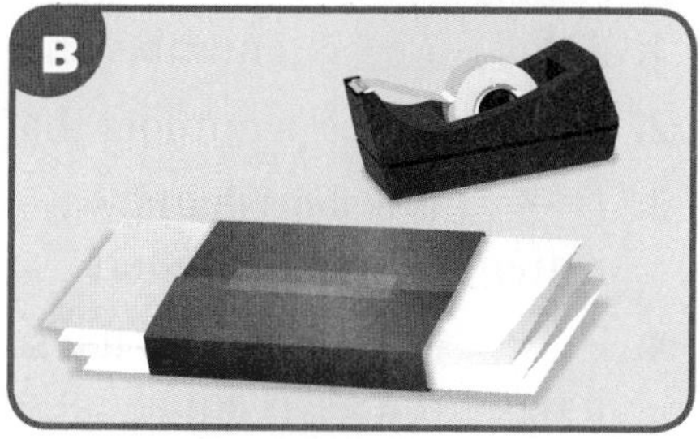

4. Write the number and title of the chapter on scraps of decorative paper, and glue these to the wrapper.

Taking Note of the Math

Use the panels of the accordion strip to take notes on the key concepts in this chapter. Include examples that will help you remember facts about exponents, roots, and the Pythagorean Theorem. Fold up the strip and slide it back into the wrapper.

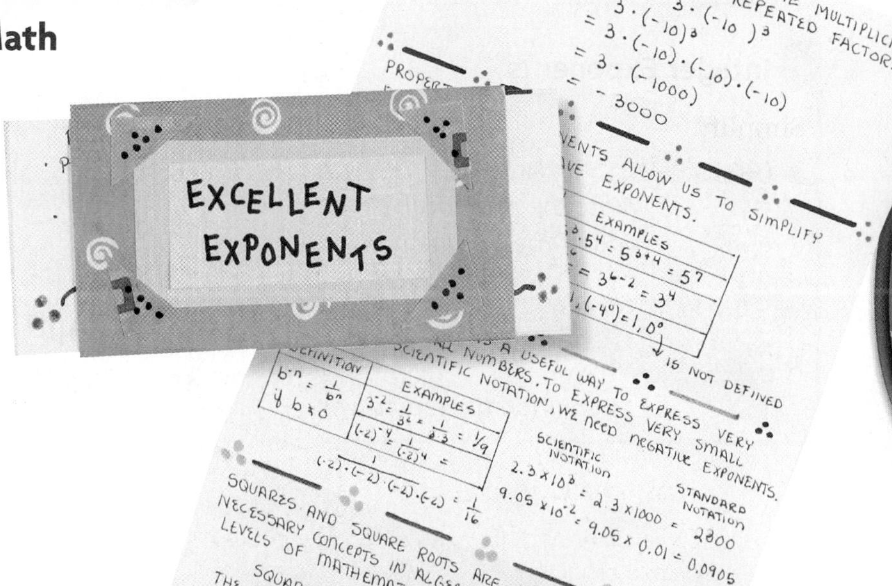

Sam Dudgeon/HMH

Study Guide: Review

Study Guide: Review

Vocabulary

Density Property	principal square root
hypotenuse	Pythagorean Theorem
irrational number	real number
leg	scientific notation
perfect square	square root

Complete the sentences below with vocabulary words from the list above.

1. A(n) ___?___ is a number that has integers as its square roots.
2. A(n) ___?___ is a number that cannot be written as a fraction.
3. ___?___ is a short-hand way of writing extremely large or extremely small numbers.
4. The ___?___ states that the sum of the squares of the ___?___ of a right triangle is equal to the square of the ___?___.
5. The set of ___?___ is the set of all rational and irrational numbers.

EXAMPLES

1 Integer Exponents

Simplify.

■ $(-3)^{-2}$

$\frac{1}{(-3)^2}$ *Write the reciprocal; change the sign of the exponent.*

$\frac{1}{9}$

■ 2^0

1 *Definition of zero power*

EXERCISES

Simplify.

6. 5^{-3}
7. $(-4)^{-3}$
8. 11^{-1}
9. 10^{-4}
10. 100^0
11. -6^{-2}
12. $(9 - 7)^{-3}$
13. $(6 - 9)^{-3}$
14. $(7 - 10)^0$
15. $4^{-1} + (5 - 7)^{-2}$
16. $3^{-2} \cdot 2^{-3} \cdot 9^0$
17. $10 - 9(3^{-2} + 6^0)$

EXAMPLES

EXERCISES

2 Properties of Exponents

Write the product or quotient as one power.

- $2^5 \cdot 2^3$

  2^{5+3} *Add exponents.*

  2^8

- $\frac{10^9}{10^2}$

  10^{9-2} *Subtract exponents.*

  10^7

Write the product or quotient as one power.

18. $4^2 \cdot 4^5$ **19.** $9^2 \cdot 9^4$ **20.** $p \cdot p^3$

21. $15 \cdot 15^2$ **22.** $6^2 \cdot 3^2$ **23.** $x^4 \cdot x^6$

24. $\frac{8^5}{8^2}$ **25.** $\frac{9^3}{9}$ **26.** $\frac{m^7}{m^2}$

27. $\frac{3^5}{3^{-2}}$ **28.** $\frac{4^{-5}}{4^{-5}}$ **29.** $\frac{y^6}{y^{-3}}$

30. $5^0 \cdot 5^3$ **31.** $y^6 \div y$ **32.** $k^4 \div k^4$

3 Scientific Notation

Write in standard notation.

- 3.58×10^4

  $3.58 \times 10{,}000$

  $35{,}800$

- 3.58×10^{-4}

  $3.58 \times \frac{1}{10{,}000}$

  $3.58 \div 10{,}000$

  0.000358

Write in scientific notation.

- $0.000007 = 7 \times 10^{-6}$
- $62{,}500 = 6.25 \times 10^4$

Write in standard notation.

33. 1.62×10^3 **34.** 1.62×10^{-3}

35. 9.1×10^5 **36.** 9.1×10^{-5}

Write in scientific notation.

37. 385 **38.** 0.04

39. 0.000000008 **40.** 73,000,000

41. 0.0000096 **42.** 56,400,000,000

43. A hummingbird weighs about 0.015 pound. Write the weight of 50 hummingbirds in scientific notation.

4 Operating with Scientific Notation

Perform the indicated operation. Write your answer in scientific notation.

- $(3.5 \times 10^{-8}) \times (8.2 \times 10^{12})$

  $(3.5 \times 8.2) \times (10^{-8} \times 10^{12})$

  28.7×10^4

  2.87×10^5 *Write the result in scientific notation.*

Perform the indicated operation. Write your answer in scientific notation.

44. $(5.1 \times 10^8) \times (3.2 \times 10^5)$

45. $(1.6 \times 10^{-5}) \div (3.2 \times 10^{-4})$

46. $(4.8 \times 10^8) - (3.5 \times 10^7)$

47. $(4.72 \times 10^{10}) + (2.9 \times 10^8)$

5 Squares and Square Roots

- **Find the two square roots of 400.**

  $20 \cdot 20 = 400$

  $(-20) \cdot (-20) = 400$

  The square roots are 20 and −20.

Find the two square roots of each number.

48. 16 **49.** 900 **50.** 676

Simplify each expression.

51. $\sqrt{4 + 21}$ **52.** $\frac{\sqrt{100}}{20}$ **53.** $\sqrt{3^4}$

Study Guide: Review

EXAMPLES

EXERCISES

6 Estimating Square Roots

■ **Find the side length of a square with area 359 ft² to one decimal place. Then find the distance around the square to the nearest tenth.**

Side = $\sqrt{359} \approx 18.9$

Distance around $\approx 4(18.9) \approx 75.6$ feet

Find the distance around each square with the area given. Round to the nearest tenth.

54. Area of square *ABCD* is 500 in^2.

55. Area of square *MNOP* is 1750 cm^2.

56. Name the integers $\sqrt{82}$ is between.

7 The Real Numbers

■ **State if the number is rational, irrational, or not a real number.**

$-\sqrt{2}$ irrational *The decimal equivalent does not repeat or end.*

$\sqrt{-4}$ not real *Square root of a negative number*

State if the number is rational, irrational, or not a real number.

57. $\sqrt{81}$ **58.** $\sqrt{122}$ **59.** $\sqrt{-16}$

60. $-\sqrt{5}$ **61.** $\frac{0}{-4}$ **62.** $\frac{7}{0}$

63. Find a real number between $\sqrt{9}$ and $\sqrt{16}$.

8 The Pythagorean Theorem

■ **Find the length of side *b* in the right triangle where $a = 8$ and $c = 17$.**

$8^2 + b^2 = 17^2$ $\quad a^2 + b^2 = c^2$

$64 + b^2 = 289$

$b^2 = 225$

$b = \sqrt{225} = 15$

Find the side length in each right triangle.

64. If $a = 6$ and $b = 8$, find c.

65. If $b = 24$ and $c = 26$, find a.

66. Find the length of the hypotenuse of a right triangle with leg lengths of 10 inches to the nearest tenth.

9 Applying the Pythagorean Theorem and Its Converse

■ **Find the distance between (3, 7) and (−5, 6) to the nearest tenth.**

$\sqrt{(x_2 - x_1)^2 + (y_2 - y_1)^2}$ *Use the Distance Formula.*

$\sqrt{(-5 - 3)^2 + (6 - 7)^2}$ *Substitute.*

$\sqrt{(-8)^2 + (-1)^2}$ *Subtract.*

$\sqrt{64 + 1} = \sqrt{65} \approx 8.1$

Find the distances between the points to the nearest tenth.

67. (1, 4) and (2, 7) **68.** (8, 0) and (0, 8)

69. (−2, 3) and (6, 9)

70. (5, −2) and (−4, 10)

Tell whether the side lengths form a right triangle.

71. 8, 9, 10 **72.** 12, 5, 13 **73.** 9, 12, 15

74. A diagonal piece is added to a 7.5-inch by 10-inch frame to determine if the frame sides meet at a right angle. The piece is 12.5 inches long. Do the sides meet at a right angle? Explain.

Chapter Test

CHAPTER 3

Simplify. Write your answer as one power.

1. $\frac{3^3}{3^6}$
2. $7^9 \cdot 7^2$
3. $(5^{10})^6$
4. $\frac{11^{-7}}{11^7}$
5. $27^3 \cdot 27^{-18}$
6. $(52^{-7})^{-3}$
7. $13^0 \cdot 13^9$
8. $\frac{8^{12}}{8^7}$

Write each number in standard notation.

9. 2.7×10^{12}
10. 3.53×10^{-2}
11. 4.8×10^8
12. 6.09×10^{-3}

Write each number in scientific notation.

13. 19,000,000,000
14. 0.0000039
15. 1,980,000,000
16. 0.00045
17. A sack of cocoa beans weighs about 132 lb. How much would 1000 sacks of cocoa beans weigh? Write the answer in scientific notation.

Perform the indicated operation. Write your answer in scientific notation.

18. $(2.25 \times 10^{-5}) + (5.5 \times 10^{-7})$
19. $(5.8 \times 10^{12}) - (1.8 \times 10^{13})$
20. $(1.5 \times 10^3) \div (7.5 \times 10^{-4})$
21. $(3.2 \times 10^{-4}) \times (5.8 \times 10^{-5})$

Find the two square roots of each number.

22. 196
23. 1
24. 10,000
25. 625

Each square root is between two consecutive integers. Name the integers. Explain your answer.

26. $\sqrt{230}$
27. $\sqrt{125}$
28. $\sqrt{89}$
29. $-\sqrt{60}$
30. A square has an area of 13 ft^2. To the nearest tenth, what is its perimeter?

Write all names that apply to each number.

31. $-\sqrt{121}$
32. $-1.\overline{7}$
33. $\sqrt{-9}$
34. $\frac{\sqrt{225}}{3}$

Find the missing length for each right triangle.

35. $a = 10$, $b = 24$, $c =$ ▒
36. $a =$ ▒, $b = 15$, $c = 17$
37. $a = 12$, $b =$ ▒, $c = 20$
38. Lupe wants to use a fence to divide her square garden in half diagonally. If each side of the garden is 16 ft long, how long will the fence have to be? Round your answer to the nearest hundredth of a foot.

Find the distances between the points to the nearest tenth.

39. (25, 7) and (1, 0)
40. (5, 5) and (−5, −5)
41. (0.5, 3) and (2, −1.5)

Chapter Test

CHAPTER 3

Standardized Test Prep

Learn It Online
State Test Practice

Cumulative Assessment

Multiple Choice

1. Which expression is NOT equivalent to 3 · 3 · 3 · 3 · 3 · 3?

   (A) 3^6
   (B) 9^3
   (C) 18
   (D) 729

2. A number to the 8th power divided by the same number to the 4th power is 16. What is the number?

   (F) 2
   (G) 4
   (H) 6
   (J) 8

3. Which expression is equivalent to 81?

   (A) 2^9
   (B) 3^{-4}
   (C) $\left(\frac{1}{3}\right)^{-4}$
   (D) $\left(\frac{1}{3}\right)^{4}$

4. The airports in the United States screened more than 739,000,000 people in 2005. Which of the following is the same number written in scientific notation?

   (F) 739×10^6
   (G) 7.39×10^{-8}
   (H) 7.39×10^8
   (J) 7.39×10^9

5. For which equation is the ordered pair (−3, 4) a solution?

   (A) $2x - y = -6$
   (B) $x - 2y = 5$
   (C) $\frac{1}{2}x - y = 6$
   (D) $x - \frac{1}{2}y = -5$

6. The population of India is close to 1.14×10^9. Which of the following represents this population written in standard notation?

   (F) 1,140,000,000
   (G) 140,000,000
   (H) 1,140,000
   (J) 114,000

7. Jenny finds that a baby lizard grows about 0.5 inch every week. Which equation best represents the number of weeks it will take for the lizard to grow to 1 foot long if it was 4 inches long when it hatched?

   (A) $0.5w + 4 = 1$
   (B) $0.5w + 4 = 12$
   (C) $\frac{w+4}{12} = 0.5$
   (D) $\frac{w}{0.5+4} = 1$

8. A number *k* is decreased by 8, and the result is multiplied by 8. This product is then divided by 2. What is the final result?

   (F) $8k - 4$
   (G) $4k - 8$
   (H) $4k - 32$
   (J) $8k - 64$

9. Which ordered pair lies on the *x*-axis?

   (A) (−1, 2)
   (B) (1, −2)
   (C) (0, 2)
   (D) (−1, 0)

10. A quilt is made with 10 square pieces of fabric. If the area of each square piece is 169 square inches, what is the length of each square piece?

    (F) 12 inches
    (G) 13 inches
    (H) 14 inches
    (J) 15 inches

11. Which number is NOT between 1.5 and 1.75?

    (A) $1\frac{1}{4}$
    (B) 1.73
    (C) 1.62
    (D) $1\frac{13}{25}$

12. The $\sqrt{18}$ is between which pair of numbers?

    (F) 8 and 9
    (G) 7 and 8
    (H) 4 and 5
    (J) 3 and 4

13. Mrs. Graham ordered five pizzas for her top-performing class. The students ate $\frac{7}{8}$ of the pepperoni pizza, $\frac{3}{4}$ of the cheese pizza, $\frac{4}{5}$ of the veggie pizza, $\frac{2}{3}$ of the Hawaiian pizza, and $\frac{1}{2}$ of the barbecue chicken pizza. How much total pizza was left over?

Ⓕ $3\frac{71}{120}$ Ⓗ $1\frac{49}{120}$

Ⓖ $2\frac{1}{8}$ Ⓙ $1\frac{7}{15}$

Pay attention to the units given in a test question, especially if there are mixed units, such as inches and feet.

Gridded Response

14. What exponent makes the statement $3^? = 27^2$ true?

15. Determine the value of x when $y = 3$ in the graph.

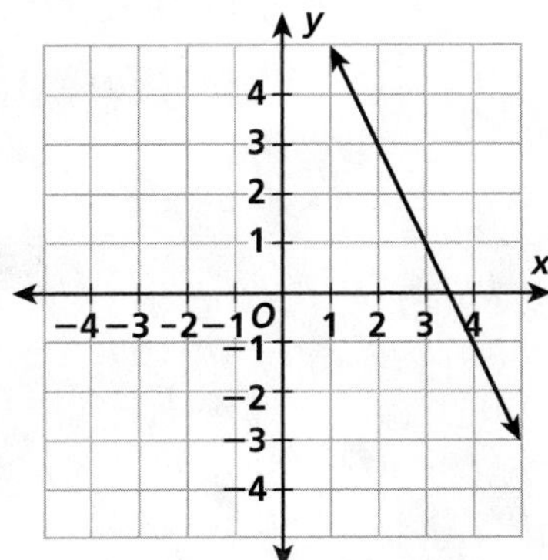

16. Chrissy is 25 years older than her dog. The sum of their ages is 37. How old is Chrissy's dog?

17. Evaluate the expression, $\frac{4}{5} - \left|\frac{1}{2} - x\right|$ for $x = \frac{1}{5}$.

18. The area of a square is 169 square feet. What is the length in feet of a side?

19. From her house, Lea rode her bike 8 miles north and then 15 miles west to a friend's house. How far in miles was she from her house along a straight path?

Short Response

S1. A bag of pinto beans weighs 210 pounds.

a. How much does 10,000 bags of pinto beans weigh? Write your answer in standard form.

b. Write the numbers 210 and 10,000 in scientific notation.

c. Explain how to use rules of exponents to write the weight of 10,000 bags of pinto beans in scientific notation.

S2. Jack works part time with his dad installing carpet. They need to install carpet in a square room that has an area of about 876 square feet. Carpet can only be ordered in whole square yards.

a. About how many feet long is the room?

b. About how many square yards of carpet do Jack and his dad need in order to cover the floor of the room? Explain your reasoning.

Extended Response

E1. Marissa's cat is stuck in a tree. The cat is on a branch 23 feet from the ground. Marissa is 5.5 feet tall, and she owns a 16-foot ladder.

a. Create a table that shows how high up on the tree the top of the ladder will reach if Marissa places the base of the ladder 1 foot, 2 feet, 3 feet, 4 feet, and 5 feet from the tree.

b. How high will Marissa be if she places the base of the ladder the distances from the tree in part **a** and stands on the rung 2.5-feet from the top of the ladder?

c. Do you think Marissa can use this ladder to reach her cat? Explain your reasoning.

CHAPTER 4

Ratios, Proportions, and Similarity

Chapter Focus

- Use ratio and proportionality to solve problems.
- Apply reasoning about similar triangles to solve problems.

Why Learn This?

Some experts say that a ratio of 8 parts dry sand to 1 part water produces the best mixture for sand sculptures. By using ratios and proportions, you can determine the amounts needed to make a mixture, whether you are mixing sand, a particular paint color, or the ingredients of a recipe.

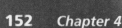

Are You Ready?

Learn It Online
Resources Online

Vocabulary

Choose the best term from the list to complete each sentence.

- common denominator
- corresponding
- inverse operations
- least common denominator
- multiplication equation

1. To solve an equation, you use __?__ to isolate the variable. So to solve the __?__ $3x = 18$, divide both sides by 3.
2. In the fractions $\frac{2}{3}$ and $\frac{1}{6}$, 18 is a(n) __?__, but 6 is the __?__.
3. If two polygons are congruent, all of their __?__ sides and angles are congruent.

Complete these exercises to review skills you will need for this chapter.

Simplify Fractions

Write each fraction in simplest form.

4. $\frac{8}{24}$
5. $\frac{15}{50}$
6. $\frac{18}{72}$
7. $\frac{25}{125}$

Use a Least Common Denominator

Find the least common denominator for each set of fractions.

8. $\frac{2}{3}$ and $\frac{1}{5}$
9. $\frac{3}{4}$ and $\frac{1}{8}$
10. $\frac{5}{7}$, $\frac{3}{7}$, and $\frac{1}{14}$
11. $\frac{1}{2}$, $\frac{2}{3}$, and $\frac{3}{5}$

Order Decimals

Write each set of decimals in order from least to greatest.

12. 4.2, 2.24, 2.4, 0.242
13. 1.1, 0.1, 0.01, 1.11
14. 1.4, 2.53, $1.\overline{3}$, $0.\overline{9}$

Solve Multiplication Equations

Solve.

15. $5x = 60$
16. $0.2y = 14$
17. $\frac{1}{2}t = 10$
18. $\frac{2}{3}z = 9$

Ordered Pairs

Graph each ordered pair on a coordinate plane.

19. $A(0, 4)$
20. $B(2, -3)$
21. $C(-2, 4)$
22. $D(-2, 0)$
23. $E(-1, -1)$
24. $F(5, 3)$
25. $G(-1, 2)$
26. $H(4, -5)$

CHAPTER 4

Study Guide: Preview

Where You've Been

Previously, you

- used division to find ratios.
- used critical attributes to define similarity.
- found solutions to application problems involving proportions.

In This Chapter

You will study

- using unit rates to represent proportional relationships.
- generating similar figures using dilations.
- using proportional relationships in similar figures to find missing measurements.

Where You're Going

You can use the skills learned in this chapter

- to compare prices to find bargains.
- to determine the length of time it will take to travel a given distance at a given rate of speed.
- to determine distance traveled for a given rate of speed over a given period of time.

Key Vocabulary/Vocabulario

cross product	producto cruzado
dilation	dilatación
rate	tasa
scale factor	factor de escala
similar	semejante
unit rate	tasa unitaria

Vocabulary Connections

To become familiar with some of the vocabulary terms in the chapter, consider the following. You may refer to the chapter, the glossary, or a dictionary if you like.

1. The word *cross* can mean "to intersect," forming an "X" shape. Since a *product* is the result of multiplying, what do you suppose you multiply to find the **cross products** of two fractions?
2. Suppose a transformation of a figure produces a figure with the same shape but a different size. You know that a *scale* is the ratio between two sets of measurements. What do you think the **scale factor** of the transformation is?

Study Guide: Preview

Writing Strategy: Write a Convincing Argument

Your ability to write a convincing argument proves that you have a solid understanding of the concept. An effective argument should include the following four parts:

(1) A goal
(2) A response to the goal
(3) Evidence to support the response
(4) A summary statement

50. Write About It
Explain the steps you would take to evaluate the expression $\sqrt{14 + 35} - 20$.

Step 1 **Identify the goal.**

Show how to simplify the given expression. Explain each step of your work.

Step 2 **Provide a response to the goal.**

The order of operations should be used to simplify the expression.

Step 3 **Provide evidence to support your response.**

The expression under the square root symbol must be treated as if it were in parentheses.

$$\sqrt{14 + 35} - 20 = \sqrt{(14 + 35)} - 20$$

Operations in parentheses should be performed first.

$$\sqrt{(14 + 35)} - 20 = \sqrt{49} - 20$$

Next, evaluate the square root.

$$\sqrt{49} - 20 = 7 - 20$$

Finally, perform the subtraction.

$$7 - 20 = -13$$

Simplifying the expression with a scientific calculator gives the same result.

Step 4 **Summarize your argument.**

Based on the order of operations, the expression $\sqrt{14 + 35} - 20$ simplifies to -13.

Try This

Write a convincing argument or explanation.

1. A student said a number raised to a negative power is always negative. What is the student's error?

4-1 Ratios, Rates, and Unit Rates

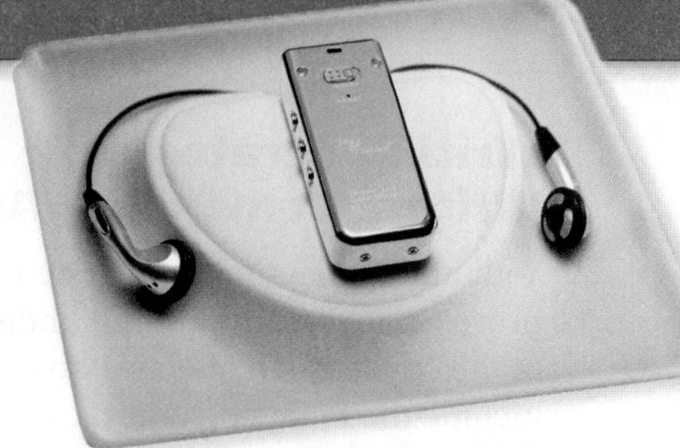

The Excentrique MP-400 MP3 player is made of 24-carat gold.

Density is a ratio that compares mass and volume. Different substances have different densities. For example, gold has a density of $\frac{19{,}300 \text{ kg}}{1 \text{ m}^3}$, or 19,300 kilograms per cubic meter.

Vocabulary

rate

unit rate

unit price

A **rate** is a comparison of two quantities that have different units.

ratio: $\frac{90}{3}$ rate: $\frac{90 \text{ miles}}{3 \text{ hours}}$ ← *Read as "90 miles per 3 hours."*

Unit rates are rates in which the second quantity is 1. The ratio $\frac{90}{3}$ can be simplified by dividing: $\frac{90}{3} = \frac{30}{1}$.

Interactivities Online ▶

unit rate: $\frac{30 \text{ miles}}{1 \text{ hour}}$, or 30 mi/h

EXAMPLE 1

Finding Unit Rates

Miki can type 120 words in 3 minutes. How many words can she type per minute?

$\frac{120 \text{ words}}{3 \text{ minutes}}$ *Write the rate.*

$\frac{120 \text{ words} \div 3}{3 \text{ minutes} \div 3} = \frac{40 \text{ words}}{1 \text{ minute}}$ *Divide to find words per minute.*

Miki can type 40 words in one minute.

Since density is measured in units of mass per unit of volume, it is a unit rate.

EXAMPLE 2

Chemistry Application

Reading Math

Units that result from dividing two different units, such as kg/m^3, are called *derived units.*

A **Four cubic meters of silver has a mass of 41,960 kilograms. What is the density of silver?**

$\frac{41{,}960 \text{ kg}}{4 \text{ m}^3}$ *Write the rate.*

$\frac{41{,}960 \text{ kg} \div 4}{4 \text{ m}^3 \div 4}$ *Divide to find kilograms per 1 m^3.*

$\frac{10{,}490 \text{ kg}}{1 \text{ m}^3}$

Silver has a density of 10,490 kg/m^3.

B **Aluminum weighing 1350 kilograms has a volume of 0.5 cubic meters. What is the density of aluminum?**

$\frac{1350 \text{ kg}}{0.5 \text{ m}^3}$ *Write the rate.*

$\frac{1350 \text{ kg} \cdot 2}{0.5 \text{ m}^3 \cdot 2}$ *Multiply to find kilograms per 1 m^3.*

$\frac{2700 \text{ kg}}{1 \text{ m}^3}$

Aluminum has a density of 2700 kg/m^3.

Courtesy Jens of Sweden

Average rate of speed is the ratio of distance traveled to time. This relationship can be expressed by the formula $r = \frac{d}{t}$, where r is the average rate of speed, d is distance, and t is time.

EXAMPLE 3 Travel Application

A band's tour bus is traveling 525 miles from Charlotte, North Carolina, to Orlando, Florida.

A In the first 5 hours of the trip, the bus travels 260 miles. What is the bus's average speed?

$r = \frac{d}{t}$ *Find the ratio of distance to time.*

$= \frac{260 \text{ mi}}{5 \text{ h}}$ *Substitute 260 miles for d and 5 hours for t.*

$= 52 \text{ mi/h}$ *Divide to find the unit rate.*

The bus's average speed is 52 mi/h.

B The driver estimates that the entire trip will take 8 hours. If the bus keeps traveling at the same average speed, is the driver's estimate reasonable? Explain.

Determine how long the trip will take.

$d = rt$ *Use the formula d = rt.*

$525 = 52t$ *Substitute 525 for d and 52 for r.*

$\frac{525}{52} = \frac{52t}{52}$ *Divide both sides by 52.*

$10.1 \approx t$ *Simplify.*

At an average speed of 52 mi/h, the trip will take about 10 hours. The driver's estimate is not reasonable.

Helpful Hint

The formula $r = \frac{d}{t}$ is equivalent to $d = rt$, as shown below.

$r = \frac{d}{t}$

$r \cdot t = \frac{d}{t} \cdot t$

$rt = d$

Unit price is a unit rate used to compare price per item.

EXAMPLE 4 Finding Unit Prices to Compare Costs

Arnie can buy a 16 oz box of cereal for \$5.49 or a 20 oz box for \$5.99. Which is the better buy?

$\frac{\text{price for box}}{\text{number of ounces}} = \frac{\$5.49}{16 \text{ oz}} \approx \$0.34/\text{oz}$

$\frac{\text{price for box}}{\text{number of ounces}} = \frac{\$5.99}{20 \text{ oz}} \approx \$0.30/\text{oz}$

Divide the price by the number of ounces.

The better buy is the 20 oz box for \$5.99.

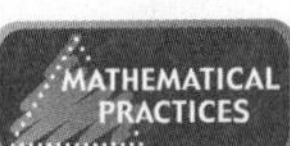

Think and Discuss

1. **Choose** the quantity that has a lower unit price: 6 oz for \$1.29 or 15 oz for \$3.00. Explain your answer.

4-1 Exercises

Learn It Online
Homework Help Online
Exercises 1–9, 11, 13, 15

GUIDED PRACTICE

See Example 1 **1.** Ana Maria's heart beats 225 times in 3 minutes. How many times does her heart beat per minute?

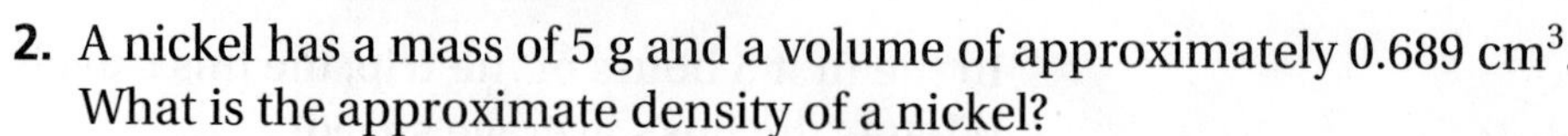
See Example 2 **2.** A nickel has a mass of 5 g and a volume of approximately 0.689 cm^3. What is the approximate density of a nickel?

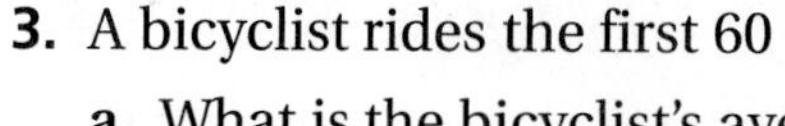
See Example 3 **3.** A bicyclist rides the first 60 kilometers of a 220-kilometer race in 1.5 hours.

a. What is the bicyclist's average speed?

b. A reporter estimates that at this speed the bicyclist will finish the entire race in less than 6 hours. Is the reporter's estimate reasonable? Explain.

See Example 4 **4.** A 16 oz box of crackers costs $3.99 and a 38 oz box of crackers costs $6.99. Which is the better buy?

INDEPENDENT PRACTICE

See Example 1 **5.** Kenji earns $32 in 4 hours. How much does he earn per hour?

See Example 2 **6.** The mass of a diamond is 1.76 g. The volume is 0.5 cm^3. What is the density of the diamond?

See Example 3 **7.** In 1860 and 1861, riders of the Pony Express delivered mail on horseback from St. Joseph, Missouri, to Sacramento, California. The trip of 1966 miles took about 10 days (240 hours).

a. What was the riders' average speed to the nearest tenth of a mile per hour?

b. A student estimates that it would take a Pony Express rider less than 6 hours to travel 75 miles. Is the student's estimate reasonable? Explain.

See Example 4 **8.** One yard of ribbon costs $0.49 and 3 yards of ribbon costs $1.49. Which is the better buy?

9. A 16 oz package of brown rice costs $0.79 and a 32 oz package of brown rice costs $3.49. Which is the better buy?

PRACTICE AND PROBLEM SOLVING

Extra Practice
See Extra Practice for more exercises.

Find each unit rate.

10. travel 804 miles in 16 hours

11. score 84 points in 6 games

12. $7.05 for 3 tacos

13. 64 beats in 4 measures of music

14. Social Studies *Population density* is a unit rate comparing population to area. The nation of Malta has an area of 122 square miles and a population of about 402,000. The U.S. has an area of 3,794,083 square miles and a population of about 301,140,000. What is the approximate population density of Malta? of the U.S.?

Most computer animation runs at 24 frames per second. At this rate, 129,600 frames are needed for a 90-minute animated movie.

Estimation **Estimate each unit rate.**

15. 250 heartbeats in 6 minutes

16. \$107 for 22 magazines

17. 295 words in 6 minutes

18. 17 apples weigh 4 pounds

19. **Multi-Step** Before 1986, a gold bullion in the Federal Reserve Bank was rectangular and had a volume of approximately 727.7 cm^3. The density of gold is 19.3 g/cm^3. A pound is approximately 454 g. Find the weight of one gold bullion to the nearest tenth of a pound.

20. **Entertainment** Tom, Cherise, and Tina work as film animators. The table shows the number of frames each rendered in an 8-hour day.

Frames Rendered	
Name	**Frames**
Tom	203
Cherise	216
Tina	227

a. Find the hourly unit rendering rate for each employee.

b. Who was the most efficient?

c. How many more frames per hour did Cherise render than Tom?

d. How many more frames per hour did Tom and Cherise together render than Tina?

21. **What's the Error?** A clothing store charges \$25 for 4 T-shirts. A student says that the unit price is \$0.16 per T-shirt. What is the error? What is the correct unit price?

22. **Write About It** Explain how to find unit rates. Give an example, and explain how consumers can use unit rates to save money.

23. **Challenge** The size of a television (13 in., 25 in., 32 in., and so on) represents the length of the diagonal of the television screen. An aspect ratio describes a screen by comparing its width to its height. A 25 in. television has an aspect ratio of 4:3. What are the width and height of the screen?

Test Prep

24. **Multiple Choice** A 24 lb bag of dog food sells for \$10.56. What is the unit price per pound?

Ⓐ \$0.44/lb Ⓑ \$0.53/lb Ⓒ \$13.44/lb Ⓓ \$34.56/lb

25. **Extended Response** Flowers can be purchased in bunches of 4 for \$2.48 or 6 for \$3.96. Which is the better buy? Explain.

4-2 Solving Proportions

Vocabulary

cross products

Recall that a proportion is an equation that states that two ratios are equivalent. For example, the proportion $\frac{2}{3} = \frac{4}{6}$ states that the ratios $\frac{2}{3}$ and $\frac{4}{6}$ are equivalent. Ratios that are equivalent are said to be *proportional*, or *in proportion*. You can use a proportion to determine how long it will take a helicopter to reach a fire. (See Example 3.)

In the proportion $\frac{a}{b} = \frac{c}{d}$, the products $a \cdot d$ and $b \cdot c$ are called **cross products**.

$$\frac{a}{b} = \frac{c}{d} \quad \longleftarrow \text{ Proportion}$$

$$a \cdot d = b \cdot c \quad \longleftarrow \text{ Cross products}$$

One way to find whether two ratios are equivalent is to find their cross products.

CROSS PRODUCTS

Cross products in proportions are equal. If the ratios are *not* in proportion, the cross products are not equal.

Proportions		***Not* Proportions**	
$\frac{6}{8} = \frac{9}{12}$	$\frac{5}{2} = \frac{15}{6}$	$\frac{1}{6} \neq \frac{2}{7}$	$\frac{5}{12} \neq \frac{2}{5}$
$8 \cdot 9 = 6 \cdot 12$	$2 \cdot 15 = 5 \cdot 6$	$6 \cdot 2 \neq 1 \cdot 7$	$12 \cdot 2 \neq 5 \cdot 5$
$72 = 72$	$30 = 30$	$12 \neq 7$	$24 \neq 25$

EXAMPLE 1 Using Cross Products to Identify Proportions

A Tell whether the ratios $\frac{5}{6}$ and $\frac{15}{21}$ are proportional.

$$\frac{5}{6} \stackrel{?}{=} \frac{15}{21}$$

$$\frac{5}{6} \stackrel{?}{=} \frac{15}{21} \qquad \textit{Find the cross products.}$$

$$6 \cdot 15 \stackrel{?}{=} 5 \cdot 21$$

$$90 \neq 105$$

Since the cross products are not equal, the ratios are not proportional.

B **A shade of paint is made by mixing 5 parts yellow paint with 7 parts green paint. Will 21 quarts of green paint and 15 quarts of yellow paint make the correct shade? Explain.**

$\frac{\text{5 parts yellow}}{\text{7 parts green}} \stackrel{?}{=} \frac{\text{15 quarts yellow}}{\text{21 quarts green}}$ *Set up two ratios.*

$\frac{5}{7} \stackrel{?}{=} \frac{15}{21}$

$7 \cdot 15 \stackrel{?}{=} 5 \cdot 21$ *Find the cross products.*

$105 = 105$

The cross products are equal. You will get the correct shade of paint.

To solve a proportion that contains a variable, you must find the value that makes the equation true.

EXAMPLE 2 Using Properties of Equality to Solve Proportions

For most people, the ratio of head length to total height is 1:7. If a person is 56 inches tall, what should the length of the person's head be?

$\frac{\text{head length}}{\text{total height}} \rightarrow \frac{1}{7}$ *Write a ratio comparing head length to total height.*

$\frac{1}{7} = \frac{x}{56}$ *Set up the proportion. Let x represent the length of the person's head.*

$(56)\frac{1}{7} = (56)\frac{x}{56}$ *Since x is divided by 56, multiply both sides of the equation by 56.*

$8 = x$

The length of the person's head should be 8 inches.

EXAMPLE 3 Using Cross Products to Solve Proportions

A helicopter used for firefighting travels 25 miles in 20 minutes. At this rate of speed, how long will it take the helicopter to reach a fire that is 60 miles away?

At a constant rate of speed, ratios of distance to time are equivalent.

$\frac{\text{distance 1}}{\text{time 1}} = \frac{\text{distance 2}}{\text{time 2}}$ *Set up a proportion that compares distance to time.*

$\frac{25}{20} = \frac{60}{t}$ *Let t represent the time needed to reach the fire.*

$25 \cdot t = 20 \cdot 60$ *Find the cross products.*

$25t = 1200$ *Multiply.*

$\frac{25t}{25} = \frac{1200}{25}$ *Divide both sides by 25.*

$t = 48$ *Simplify.*

The helicopter will reach the fire in 48 minutes.

EXAMPLE 4 School Application

Helpful Hint

You could also set up a proportion using the number of pages that Lee still needs to read: 374 − 132 = 242.

$\frac{6}{132} = \frac{x}{242}$

Then x represents the number of days it takes to read the rest of the novel.

Lee is reading a 374-page novel for her English class. It takes her 6 days to read the first 132 pages. If she continues to read at the same rate, how many more days will it take her to finish the novel?

Let x represent the number of days it takes Lee to read the entire novel.

$\frac{6}{132} = \frac{x}{374}$	*Set up the proportion.*
$6 \cdot 374 = 132x$	*Find the cross products.*
$\frac{2244}{132} = \frac{132x}{132}$	*Divide both sides by 132.*
$17 = x$	*Simplify.*

It takes Lee 17 days to read the entire novel. Lee has already read for 6 days, so it will take her 17 − 6 = 11 more days to finish the novel.

MATHEMATICAL PRACTICES

Think and Discuss

1. **Explain** what the cross products of two ratios represent.
2. **Tell** what it means if the cross products are not equal.
3. **Describe** how to solve a proportion. Let x represent the missing value.

4-2 Exercises

Learn It Online
Homework Help Online
Exercises 1–20, 25, 29, 31, 33, 39

GUIDED PRACTICE

See Example 1 **Tell whether the ratios are proportional.**

1. $\frac{6}{12} \stackrel{?}{=} \frac{12}{24}$
2. $\frac{2}{9} \stackrel{?}{=} \frac{6}{27}$
3. $\frac{5}{7} \stackrel{?}{=} \frac{10}{15}$
4. $\frac{10}{25} \stackrel{?}{=} \frac{6}{15}$
5. A bubble solution can be made with a ratio of 1 part detergent to 8 parts water. Would a mixture of 56 oz water and 8 oz detergent represent the same ratio? Explain.

See Example 2

6. **Science** The ratio of an object's weight on Earth to its weight on the Moon is 6:1. The first person to walk on the Moon was Neil Armstrong. He weighed 165 pounds on Earth. How much did he weigh on the Moon?

See Example 3

7. A school bus travels 7 miles in 20 minutes. At this rate, how long will it take the school bus to complete its entire 45.5-mile route?

See Example 4

8. Ana is using a photocopier to make 315 copies of a poster. It takes 3 minutes to print the first 63 posters. If the photocopier continues to print at the same rate, how many more minutes will it take to complete the job?

INDEPENDENT PRACTICE

See Example 1

Tell whether the ratios are proportional.

9. $\frac{22}{42} \stackrel{?}{=} \frac{3}{7}$

10. $\frac{17}{51} \stackrel{?}{=} \frac{2}{6}$

11. $\frac{40}{36} \stackrel{?}{=} \frac{20}{16}$

12. $\frac{8}{9} \stackrel{?}{=} \frac{40}{45}$

13. An after-school club had 10 girls and 12 boys. Then 5 more girls and 6 more boys signed up. Did the ratio of girls to boys stay the same? Explain.

See Example 2

14. **School** The ratio of seventh graders to eighth graders participating in a science fair is 4:3. There are 18 eighth graders participating in the science fair. How many seventh graders are there?

See Example 3

15. A dog-sledding team travels 3.5 miles in 15 minutes. At this rate, how far can the team travel in 2 hours (120 minutes)?

See Example 4

16. Jaron is downloading a file. The size of the file is 3200 KB. It takes 3 minutes to download the first 1200 KB of the file. If the file continues downloading at the same rate, how many more minutes will it take to finish downloading?

PRACTICE AND PROBLEM SOLVING

Extra Practice
See Extra Practice for more exercises.

For each set of ratios, find the two that are proportional.

17. $\frac{8}{4}, \frac{24}{12}, \frac{55}{27}$

18. $\frac{1}{4}, \frac{4}{16}, \frac{110}{444}$

19. $\frac{35}{26}, \frac{81}{39}, \frac{27}{13}$

20. $\frac{49}{182}, \frac{7}{26}, \frac{45}{160}$

21. $\frac{0.5}{6}, \frac{0.25}{9}, \frac{1}{12}$

22. $\frac{2}{3}, \frac{8}{9}, \frac{12}{18}$

Solve each proportion.

23. $\frac{\$d}{12 \text{ hours}} = \frac{\$96}{8 \text{ hours}}$

24. $\frac{s \text{ students}}{6 \text{ teachers}} = \frac{209 \text{ students}}{11 \text{ teachers}}$

25. $\frac{m \text{ minutes}}{8 \text{ miles}} = \frac{24 \text{ minutes}}{3 \text{ miles}}$

26. $\frac{\$d}{4 \text{ tickets}} = \frac{\$72 \text{ tickets}}{6 \text{ tickets}}$

27. $\frac{c \text{ computers}}{15 \text{ students}} = \frac{20 \text{ computers}}{25 \text{ students}}$

28. $\frac{m \text{ miles}}{6 \text{ hours}} = \frac{110 \text{ miles}}{2 \text{ hours}}$

29. **Science** One molecule of nitrogen reacting with 3 molecules of hydrogen makes 2 molecules of ammonia. How many molecules of nitrogen must react with 42 molecules of hydrogen to make 28 molecules of ammonia?

30. **Consumer Math** Cat food is on sale at 3 cans for \$1.00. At this rate, how much would 10 cans of cat food cost? Round to the nearest cent.

31. **Multi-Step** Jacob is selling T-shirts at a music festival. Yesterday, he sold 51 shirts and earned \$191.25. How many shirts must Jacob sell today and tomorrow to earn a total of \$536.25 for all three days? Explain how you determined your answer.

Health LINK

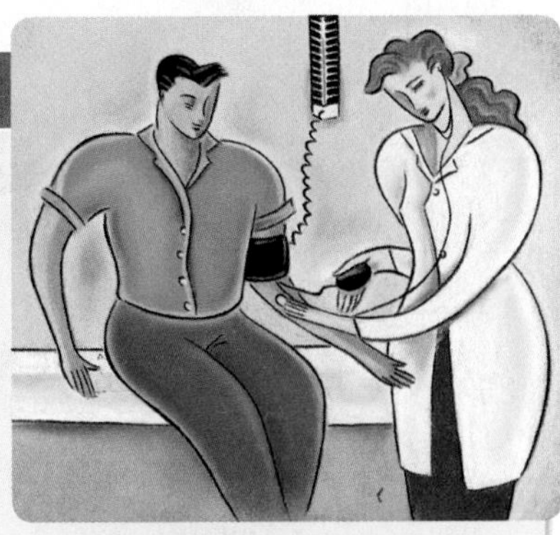

A doctor reports blood pressure in millimeters of mercury (mm Hg) as a ratio of *systolic* blood pressure to *diastolic* blood pressure (such as 140 over 80). Systolic pressure is measured when the heart beats, and diastolic pressure is measured when it rests. Refer to the table of blood pressure ranges for adults for Exercise 32.

Blood Pressure Ranges			
	Normal	Prehypertension	Hypertension (very high)
Systolic	under 120 mm Hg	120–139 mm Hg	140 mm Hg and above
Diastolic	under 80 mm Hg	80–89 mm Hg	90 mm Hg and above

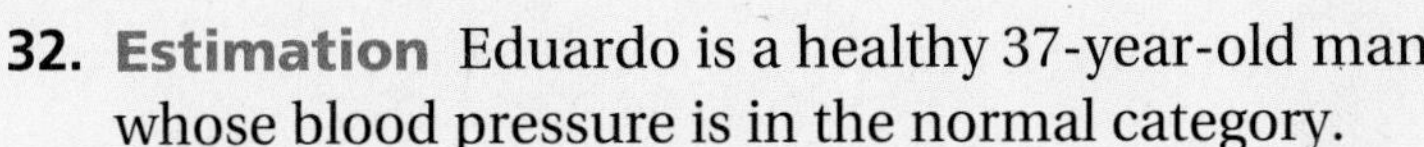

The disc-like shape of red blood cells allows them to pass through tiny capillaries.

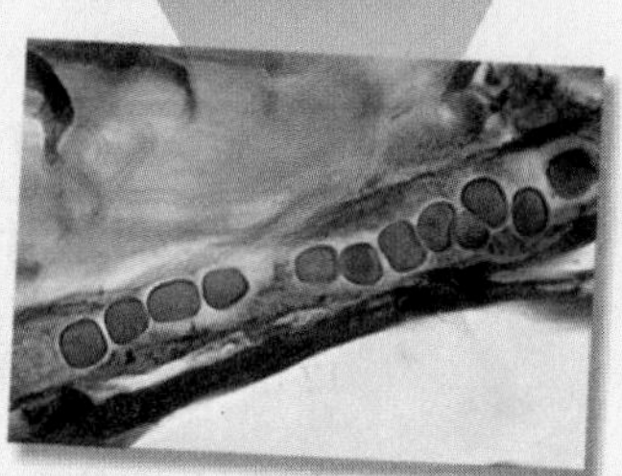

32. **Estimation** Eduardo is a healthy 37-year-old man whose blood pressure is in the normal category.
    a. Calculate an approximate ratio of systolic to diastolic blood pressure in the normal range.
    b. If Eduardo's systolic blood pressure is 102 mm Hg, use the ratio from part **a** to predict his diastolic blood pressure.
33. **Write About It** A ratio related to heart health is LDL cholesterol to HDL cholesterol. The optimal ratio of LDL to HDL is below 3. A patient's total cholesterol is 168 and HDL is 44. Is the patient's ratio optimal? Explain.
34. **Challenge** The sum of Ken's LDL and HDL cholesterol is 210, and his LDL to HDL ratio is 2.75. What are his LDL and HDL?

Test Prep

35. **Multiple Choice** A tree was 3.5 feet tall after 2 years and 8.75 feet tall after 5 years. If the tree grew at a constant rate, how tall was it after 3 years?

    Ⓐ 5 feet Ⓑ 5.25 feet Ⓒ 5.75 feet Ⓓ 6.5 feet

36. **Gridded Response** What value of b makes the proportion $\frac{4}{5} = \frac{b}{20}$ true?

Quiz for Lessons 1 Through 2

1 Ratios, Rates, and Unit Rates

1. The mass of a piece of iron pyrite, or "fools gold," is 57.2 g. The volume is 11 cm^3. What is the density of the piece of iron pyrite?

2. Ricardo is driving from Chicago, Illinois, to Fort Wayne, Indiana.
   a. He drives 28 miles in half an hour. What is his average rate of speed?
   b. Ricardo estimates that he will finish the entire 162-mile trip in about 3 hours. If he keeps driving at the same average speed, is his estimate reasonable? Explain.

Determine the better buy.

3. a long distance phone charge of \$1.40 for 10 min or \$4.50 for 45 min

4. a dozen eggs for \$2.78 or a half dozen for \$1.49

2 Solving Proportions

Solve each proportion.

5. $\frac{\$180}{12 \text{ hours}} = \frac{\$d}{20 \text{ hours}}$

6. $\frac{360 \text{ miles}}{6 \text{ hours}} = \frac{m \text{ miles}}{4 \text{ hours}}$

7. Cody is following a recipe that makes 2 dozen mini corn muffins. Use a proportion to determine how many cups of flour he must use to make 3 dozen mini corn muffins.

Flour (c)	Mini Corn Muffins (dozen)
1.5	2
c	3

8. Tim can input 110 data items in 2.5 minutes. Typing at the same rate, how many data items can he input in 7 minutes?

Ready to Go On?

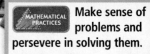

MATHEMATICAL PRACTICES Make sense of problems and persevere in solving them.

Focus on Problem Solving

Solve

- **Choose an operation: multiplication or division**

When you are converting units, think about whether the number in the answer will be greater or less than the number given in the question. This will help you to decide whether to multiply or divide to convert the units.

For example, if you are converting feet to inches, you know that the number of inches will be greater than the number of feet because each foot is 12 inches. So you know that you should multiply by 12 to get a greater number.

In general, if you are converting to smaller units, the number of units will have to be greater to represent the same quantity.

For each problem, determine whether the number in the answer will be greater or less than the number given in the question. Use your answer to decide whether to multiply or divide. Then solve the problem.

1. The speed a boat travels is usually measured in nautical miles per hour, or knots. The Staten Island Ferry in New York, which provides service between Manhattan and Staten Island, can travel at 15.5 knots. Find the speed in miles per hour. (*Hint:* 1 knot = 1.15 miles per hour)

2. When it is finished, the Crazy Horse Memorial in the Black Hills of South Dakota will be the world's largest sculpture. The sculpture's height will be 563 feet. Find the height in meters. (*Hint:* 1 meter ≈ 3.28 feet)

Crazy Horse Memorial

3. The grams of fat per serving of some common foods are given in the table below. Find the number of calories from fat for each serving. (*Hint:* 1 gram of fat = 9 calories)

Food	Fat per Serving (g)
Avocado (1 c, sliced)	22.3
Pretzels (1 oz)	1
Baked Potato (7 oz)	0.4
Plain Bagel (4 oz)	1.8

4. Nearly a quarter of the Texas Gulf Coast is national seashore or state park. At 372 miles long, it is undergoing a seaward advance at the rate of about 0.0095 mile per year. Find the length of the Texas shoreline in kilometers. (*Hint:* 1 mile ≈ 1.61 kilometers)

Explore Similarity

Use with Similar Figures

WHAT YOU NEED:
- Two pieces of graph paper with different-sized boxes, such as 1 cm graph paper and $\frac{1}{4}$ in. graph paper
- Number cube
- Metric ruler
- Protractor

Use appropriate tools strategically.

CC.8.G.4: Understand that a two-dimensional figure is similar to another if the second can be obtained from the first by a sequence of rotations, reflections, translations, and dilations; given two similar two-dimensional figures, describe a sequence that exhibits the similarity between them.

Triangles that have the same shape have some interesting relationships.

Activity

1 Follow the steps below to draw two triangles.

a. On a sheet of graph paper, plot a point below and to the left of the center of the paper. Label the point *A*. On the other sheet of paper, plot a point below and to the left of the center and label this point *D*.

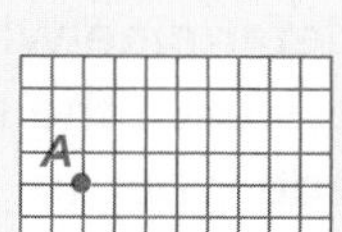

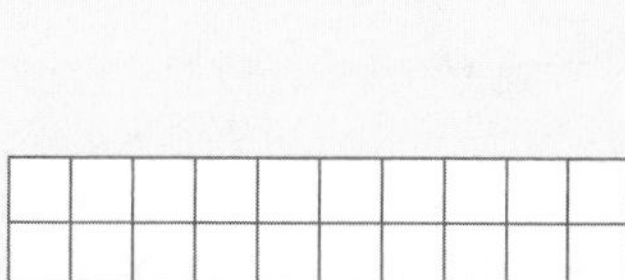

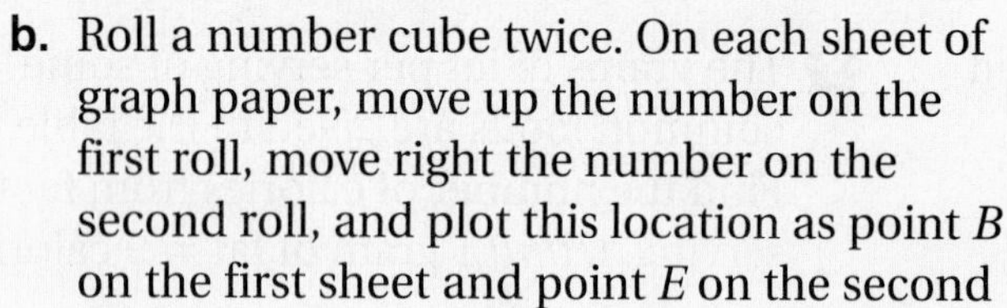

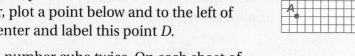

b. Roll a number cube twice. On each sheet of graph paper, move up the number on the first roll, move right the number on the second roll, and plot this location as point *B* on the first sheet and point *E* on the second sheet.

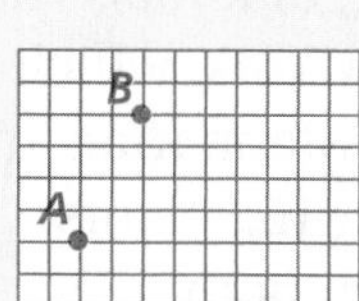

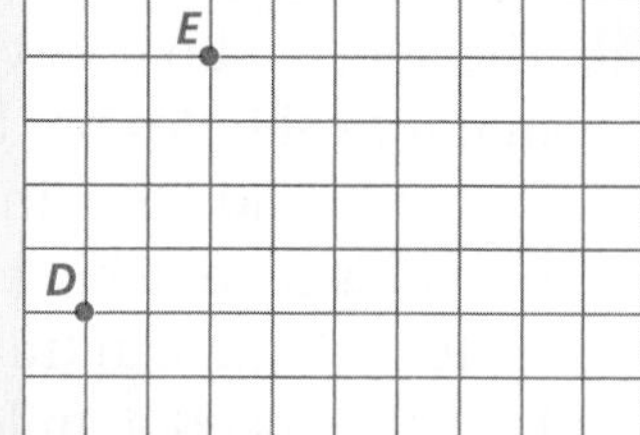

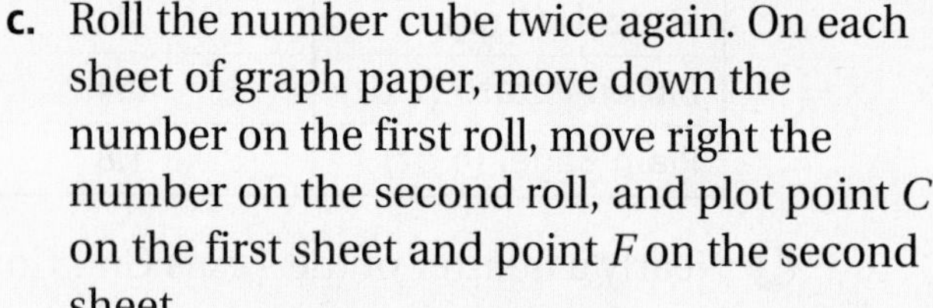

c. Roll the number cube twice again. On each sheet of graph paper, move down the number on the first roll, move right the number on the second roll, and plot point *C* on the first sheet and point *F* on the second sheet.

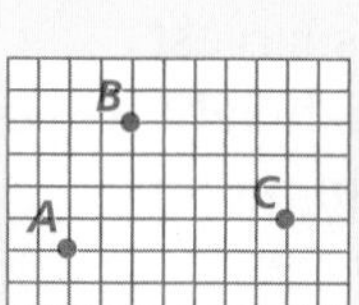

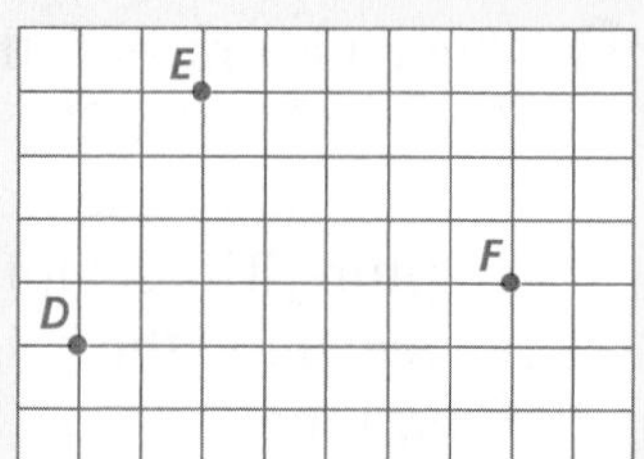

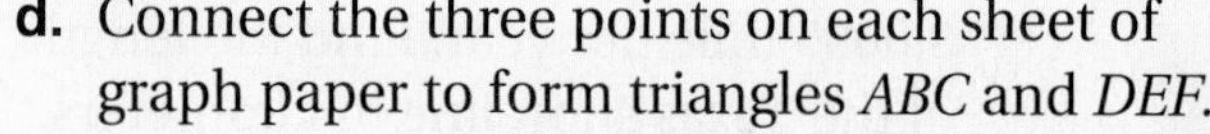

d. Connect the three points on each sheet of graph paper to form triangles *ABC* and *DEF*.

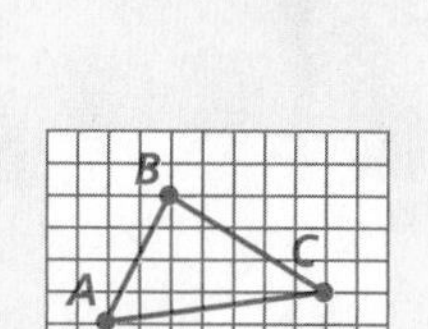

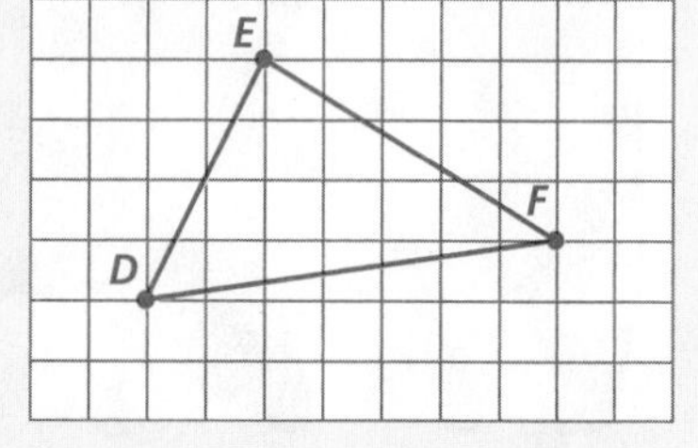

e. Measure the angles of each triangle. Measure the side lengths of each triangle to the nearest millimeter. Find the following:

m∠A	m∠D	m∠B	m∠E	m∠C	m∠F
AB	DE	$\frac{AB}{DE}$	BC	EF	$\frac{BC}{EF}$
AC	DF	$\frac{AC}{DF}$			

2 Follow the steps below to draw two triangles.

a. On one sheet of graph paper, plot a point below and to the left of the center of the paper. Label the point A.

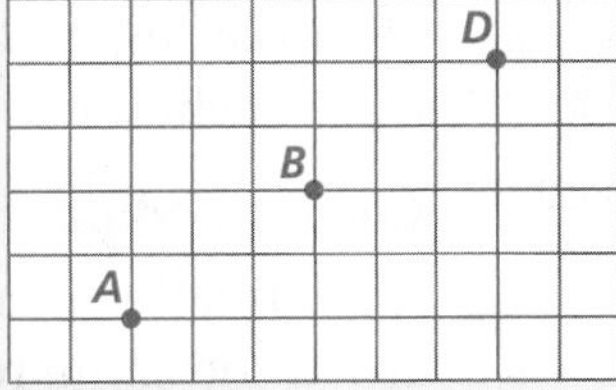

b. Roll a number cube twice. Move up the number on the first roll, move right the number on the second roll, and plot this location as point B. From B, move up the number on the first roll, move right the number on the second roll, and label this point D.

c. Roll a number cube twice. From B, move down the number on the first roll, move right the number on the second roll, and plot this location as point C.

d. From D, move down twice the number on the first roll, move right twice the number on the second roll, and label this point E.

e. Connect points to form triangles ABC and ADE.

f. Measure the angles of each triangle. Measure the side lengths of each triangle to the nearest millimeter.

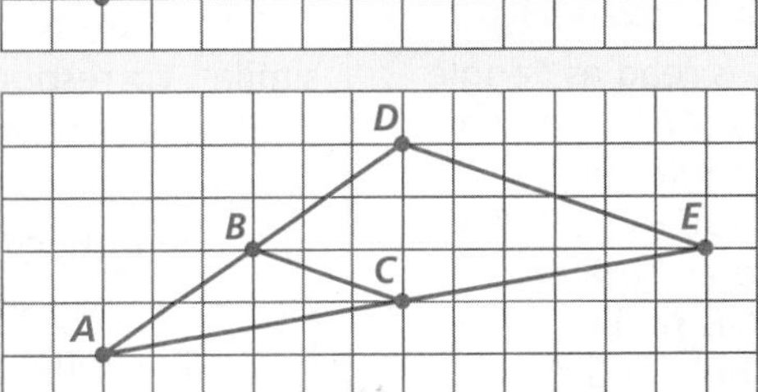

Think and Discuss

1. **Make a Conjecture** How do corresponding angles of triangles with the same shape compare?
2. **Make a Conjecture** How do corresponding side lengths of triangles with the same shape compare?
3. Suppose you enlarge a triangle on a copier machine. What measurements or values would be the same on the enlargement?

Try This

1. Make a small trapezoid on graph paper and triple the length of each side. Compare the angle measures and side lengths of the trapezoids.
2. Make a large polygon on graph paper. Use a copier to reduce the size of the polygon. Compare the angle measures and side lengths of the polygons.

4-3 Similar Figures

COMMON CORE

CC.8.G.4: Understand that a two-dimensional figure is similar to another if the second can be obtained from the first by a sequence of rotations, reflections, translations, and dilations; given two similar two-dimensional figures, describe a sequence that exhibits the similarity between them.

Vocabulary

similar

corresponding sides

corresponding angles

Similar figures have the same shape but not necessarily the same size. You can use properties of similar figures to find how wide a photo will be when it is resized for a Web page.

Corresponding sides of two figures are in the same relative position, and **corresponding angles** are in the same relative position. Two figures are similar if the lengths of corresponding sides are proportional and the corresponding angles have equal measures.

Reading Math

$\angle A$ is read as "angle *A*." $\triangle ABC$ is read as "triangle *ABC*." "$\triangle ABC \sim \triangle EFG$" is read as "triangle *ABC* is similar to triangle *EFG*."

SIMILAR POLYGONS

Words	Diagram	Corresponding Parts
For two polygons to be similar, corresponding angles must have equal measures, and the ratios of the lengths of the corresponding sides must be proportional.	A 53°, 60, 36, 37°, B, 48, C; F 37°, 24, 30, 53° E, G, 18 $\triangle ABC \sim \triangle EFG$	$m\angle A = m\angle E$ $m\angle B = m\angle F$ $m\angle C = m\angle G$ $\frac{AB}{EF} = \frac{BC}{FG} = \frac{AC}{EG} = \frac{2}{1}$

EXAMPLE 1

Identifying Similar Figures

Which triangles are similar?

A

33°
8 in.
13 in.
82°
7 in.
65°

B

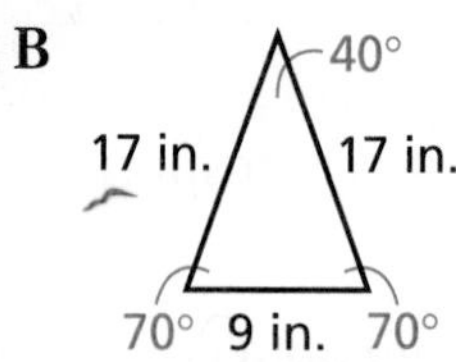

C

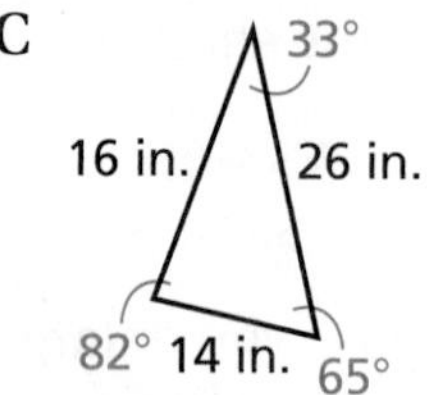

Both triangles *A* and *C* have angle measures of 82°, 33°, and 65°, while triangle *B* has angle measures of 70°, 40°, and 70°, so triangle *B* cannot be similar to triangles *A* or *C*.

Compare the ratios of corresponding sides in triangles *A* and *C* to see if they are proportional.

$\frac{13}{26} = \frac{7}{14} = \frac{8}{16}$ or $\frac{1}{2} = \frac{1}{2} = \frac{1}{2}$

The ratios are equal. So triangle *A* is similar to triangle *C*.

HMH

EXAMPLE 2 Finding Missing Measures in Similar Figures

A picture is 10 inches wide and 8 inches tall. To display the picture on a Web page, the picture must be reduced to 3.5 inches tall. How wide should the picture be on the Web page for the two pictures to be similar?

Set up a proportion. Let w be the width of the picture on the Web page.

width of picture → $\frac{10}{w} = \frac{8}{3.5}$ ← *height of picture*
width of Web page → ← *height of Web page*

$10 \cdot 3.5 = w \cdot 8$ *Find the cross products.*

$35 = 8w$

$\frac{35}{8} = \frac{8w}{8}$ *Divide both sides by 8.*

$4.375 = w$

The picture should be 4.375 in. wide.

EXAMPLE 3 *Architecture Application*

A souvenir model of the pyramid over the entrance of the Louvre in Paris has faces in the shape of a triangle. Two sides are each 4 in. long and the base is 5.1 in. long. On the actual pyramid, each triangular face has two sides that are each 27.8 m long. What is the length of the base of the actual pyramid?

Draw a diagram to help you visualize the problem.

4 in. 4 in.
5.1 in.

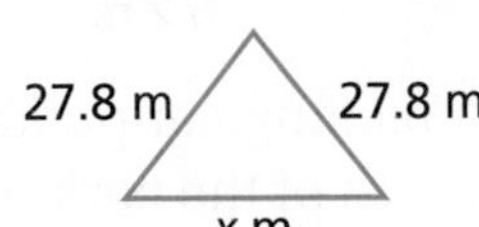

$$\frac{\text{Side of small triangle}}{\text{Side of large triangle}} = \frac{\text{Base of small triangle}}{\text{Base of large triangle}}$$

$\frac{4 \text{ in.}}{27.8 \text{ m}} = \frac{5.1 \text{ in.}}{x \text{ m}}$ *Set up a proportion.*

$4 \cdot x = 27.8 \cdot 5.1$ *Find the cross products.*

$4x = 141.78$ *Multiply.*

$x = \frac{141.78}{4} = 35.445$ *Solve for x.*

The base of the actual pyramid is about 35.4 m long.

Helpful Hint

The proportion can also be set up with ratios that compare the side and base of the small triangle and the side and base of the large triangle:

$\frac{4}{5.1} = \frac{27.8}{x}$

MATHEMATICAL PRACTICES

Think and Discuss

1. Name a pair of real-world items that appear to be similar figures.

4-3 Exercises

Learn It Online
Homework Help Online
Exercises 1–7, 9, 13

GUIDED PRACTICE

See Example 1

1. Which triangles are similar?

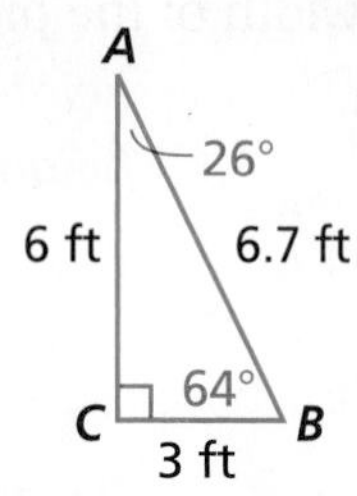

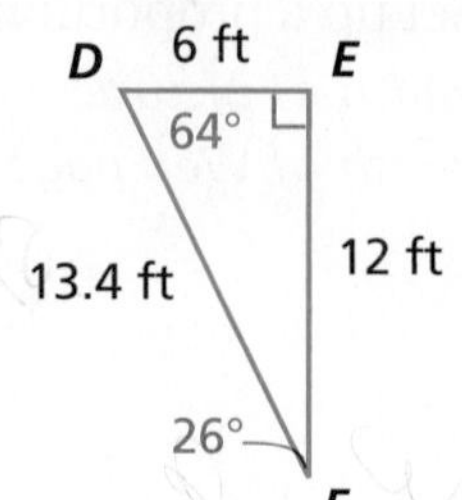

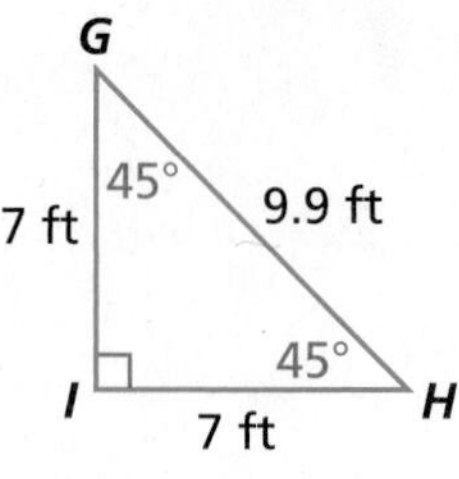

See Example 2

2. Gwen scans a photo that is 4 in. wide by 6 in. tall into her computer. If she scales the height down to 5 in., how wide should the similar photo be?

See Example 3

3. A triangle has sides measuring 11 cm, 16 cm, and 16 cm. A similar triangle has sides measuring x cm, 24 cm, and 24 cm. What is x?

INDEPENDENT PRACTICE

See Example 1

4. Which triangles are similar?

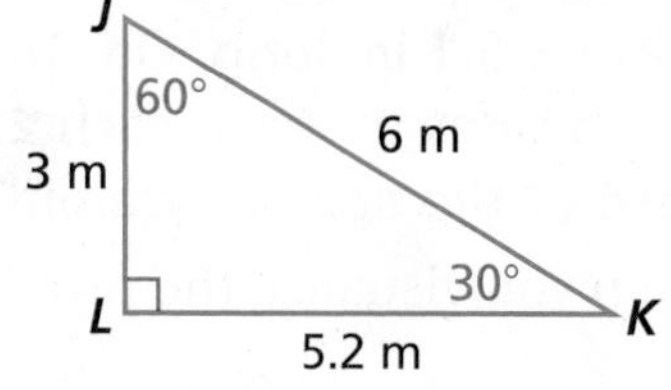

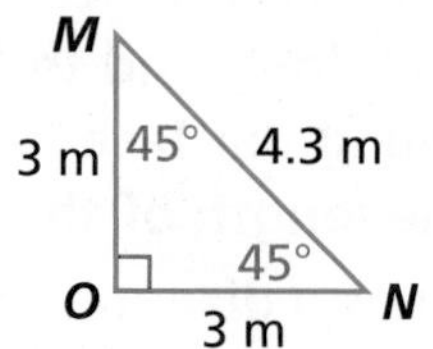

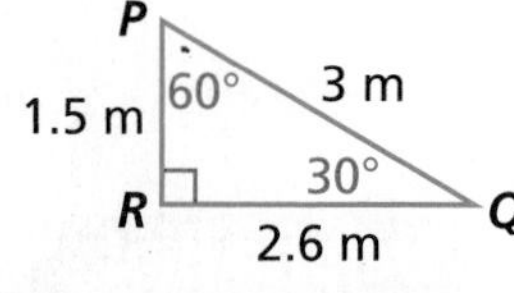

See Example 2

5. A rectangular park measures 6.5 mi wide and 9.1 mi long. On a map, the width of the park is 2.13 in. How long is the park on the map?

See Example 3

6. Vernon drew an 8 in. wide by 5 in. tall picture that will be turned into a 48 ft wide billboard. How tall will the billboard be?

PRACTICE AND PROBLEM SOLVING

Extra Practice
See Extra Practice for more exercises.

Tell whether the figures are similar. If they are not similar, explain.

7.

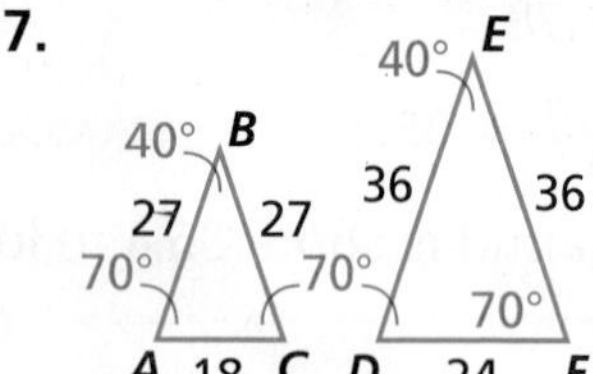

8.

6 in.
4 in.

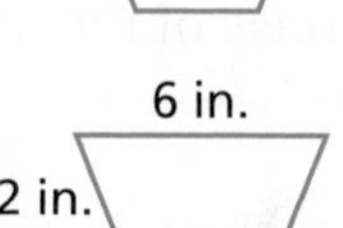

9.

$9\frac{1}{2}$ cm
$2\frac{1}{2}$ cm

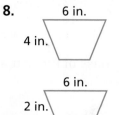

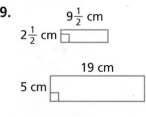

19 cm
5 cm

10. Draw a right triangle with vertices (0, 0), (6, 0), and (6, 4) on a coordinate plane. Draw another triangle with vertices (9, 6), (0, 0) and (9, 0). Could the triangles be similar? Explain.

11. Sari's garden is 12 ft by 16 ft 6 in. Her sketch of the garden is 8 in. by 11 in. Is Sari's sketch similar to the actual garden?

Many reproductions of artwork have been enlarged to fit unusual surfaces.

12. **Multi-Step** The rectangles shown are similar.

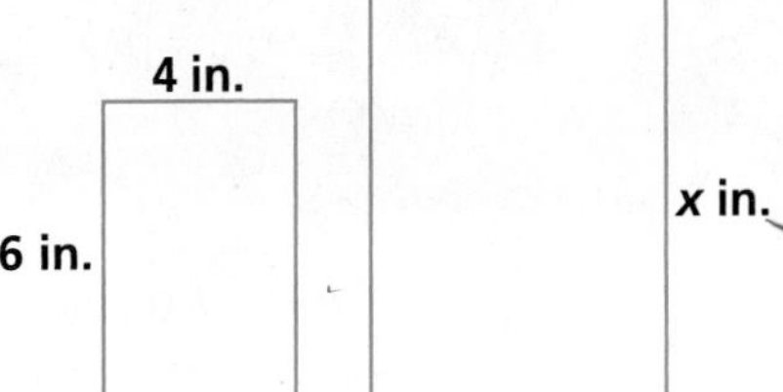

a. Find the length of the larger rectangle.

b. Find the perimeter of each rectangle.

c. Find the ratio of the perimeters and compare it to the ratio of corresponding side lengths.

d. **Make a Conjecture** Make a conjecture about the relationship between the perimeters of similar figures.

13. **Art** Helen is copying a printed reproduction of the Mona Lisa. The print is 24 in. wide and 36 in. tall. If Helen's canvas is 12 in. wide, how tall should her canvas be?

14. A rectangle is 16 cm long and 7 cm wide. A similar rectangle is 3.5 cm wide and x cm long. Find x. Explain how you determined your answer.

15. **Write a Problem** A drawing on a sheet of graph paper shows a rectangle 9 cm wide and 12 cm long. The width of the rectangle is labeled 3 ft. Write and solve a problem about the rectangle.

16. **Write About It** Consider the statement "All similar figures are congruent." Give a counterexample to disprove this conjecture.

17. **Challenge** In right triangle ABC, $\angle B$ is the right angle, $AB = 36$ cm, and $BC = 28$ cm. Right triangle ABC is similar to right triangle DEF. If $DE = 9$ cm, what is the area of triangle DEF?

Test Prep

18. **Multiple Choice** An isosceles triangle has two sides that are each 4.5 centimeters long and a base that is 3 centimeters long. A similar triangle has a base that is 1.5 centimeters long. How long are each of the other two sides of the similar triangle?

Ⓐ 2.25 cm　Ⓑ 3.75 cm　Ⓒ 4.5 cm　Ⓓ 150 cm

19. **Gridded Response** A panoramic photograph is 4 inches wide and 10 inches long. The photograph needs to be enlarged so that its width is 10 inches. What will be the length in inches of the enlarged photograph?

Explore Dilations

Use with Dilations

Learn It Online
Lab Resources Online

Use appropriate tools strategically.

CC.8.G.3: Describe the effect of dilations, translations, rotations, and reflections on two-dimensional figures using coordinates. ***Also CC.8.G.4***

Activity 1

Triangle $A'B'D'$ is a *dilation* of triangle ABD. Point C is called the center of dilation.

1. Use a ruler to measure segments CA' and CA to the nearest millimeter.
2. Calculate the ratio $\frac{CA'}{CA}$.
3. Repeat 1 and 2 for segments CB', CB, CD', and CD. Copy the table below and record your measurements.

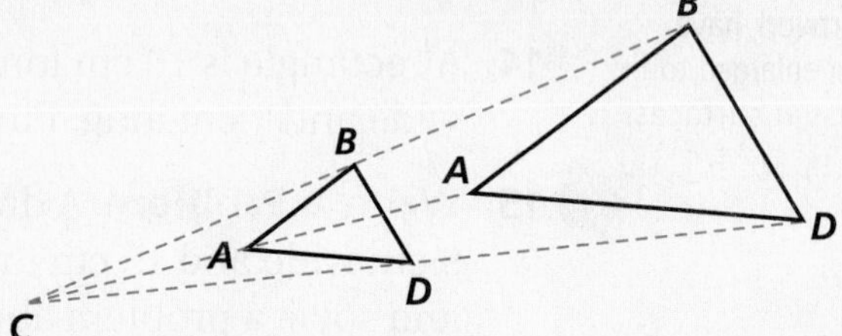

CA'	CA	$\frac{CA'}{CA}$	CB'	CB	$\frac{CB'}{CB}$	CD'	CD	$\frac{CD'}{CD}$

Think and Discuss

1. **Make a Conjecture** What seems to be true about the ratios you calculated? Write a conjecture about the ratios of the segments you measured.
2. Measure segment AD and segment $A'D'$ to the nearest millimeter. What is the ratio of $A'D'$ to AD? How does this compare to the ratios you recorded in the table above?
3. If the corresponding angles of each triangle are congruent, can you conclude that triangles ABD and $A'B'D'$ are similar? Explain.

Try This

Quadrilateral $D'E'F'G'$ is a dilation of quadrilateral $DEFG$.

1. Measure the lengths of the corresponding sides of quadrilaterals $DEFG$ and $D'E'F'G'$. Are the ratios of the corresponding sides in proportion?
2. If the corresponding angles of quadrilaterals $DEFG$ and $D'E'F'G'$ are congruent, can you conclude that the quadrilaterals are similar? Explain.

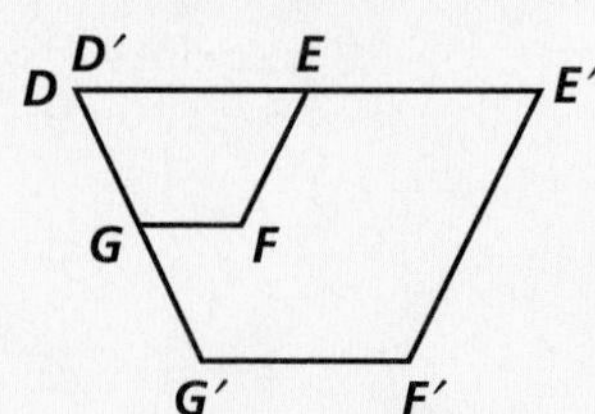

Activity 2

You can also graph dilations in the coordinate plane. Quadrilateral *P′Q′R′S′* is a dilation of *PQRS*. The origin is the center of dilation.

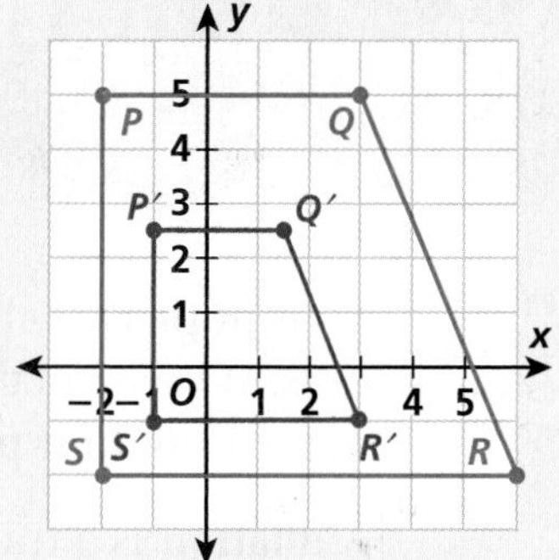

1. For each pair of corresponding vertices, record the *x*- and *y*-coordinates.
2. Calculate the ratio of the coordinates.
3. Copy and complete the table below. The first row of the table has been completed for you.

Vertex	x	y	Vertex	x	y	Ratio of x-coordinates (P′Q′R′S′ ÷ PQRS)	Ratio of y-coordinates (P′Q′R′S′ ÷ PQRS)
P′	−1	2.5	P	−2	5	$\frac{-1}{-2} = 0.5$	$\frac{2.5}{5} = 0.5$
Q′			Q				
R′			R				
S′			S				

Think and Discuss

1. **Make a Conjecture** What seems to be true about the ratios you calculated? Write a conjecture about the ratios of the coordinates of a dilation image to the coordinates of the original.
2. In Activity 1, triangle *A′B′D′* was larger than triangle *ABD*. How is the relationship between quadrilateral *P′Q′R′S′* and quadrilateral *PQRS* different?

Try This

Use triangles *ABC* and *A′B′C′* to complete the following.

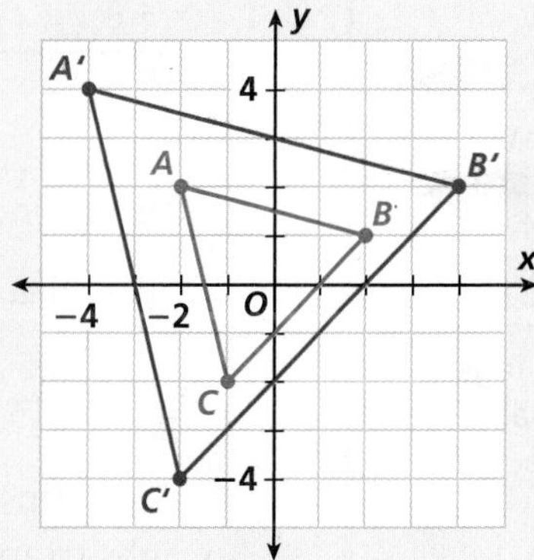

1. For each pair of corresponding vertices, calculate the ratio of the *x*-coordinates and the ratio of the *y*-coordinates.
2. Is triangle *A′B′C′* a dilation of triangle *ABC*? Explain.

4-4 Dilations

COMMON CORE

CC.8.G.3: Describe the effect of dilations, translations, rotations, and reflections on two-dimensional figures using coordinates. ***Also CC.8.G.4***

Your pupils are the black areas in the center of your eyes. When you go to the eye doctor, the doctor may *dilate* your pupils, which makes them larger.

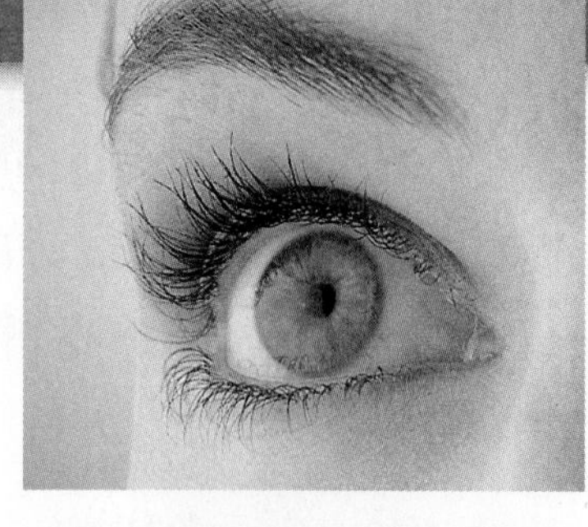

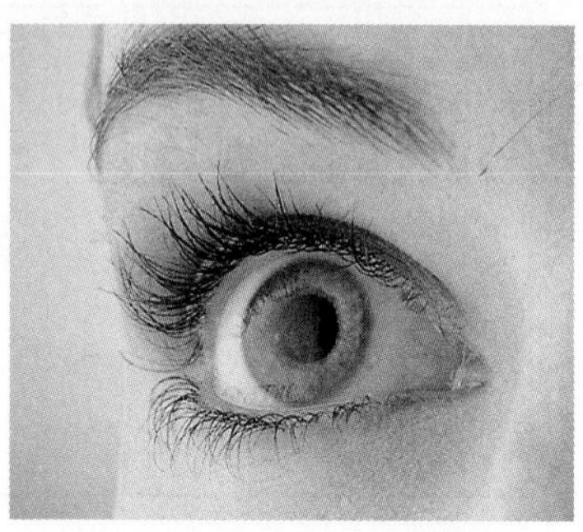

Your pupil works like a camera lens, dilating to let in more or less light.

A **dilation** is a transformation that changes the size, but not the shape, of a figure. After a dilation, the image is similar to the original figure.

Vocabulary

dilation

center of dilation

scale factor

Every dilation has a fixed point that is the *center of dilation.* To find the center of dilation, draw lines that connect each pair of corresponding vertices. The lines intersect at one point. This point is the **center of dilation**.

EXAMPLE 1 Identifying Dilations

Tell whether each transformation is a dilation. Explain.

A

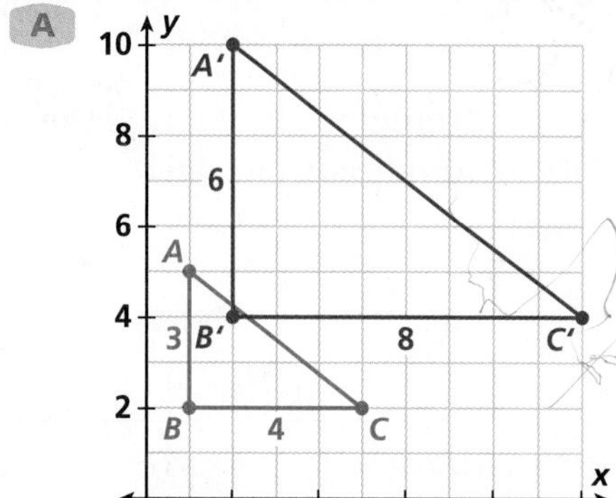

Compare the ratios of corresponding side lengths.

$\frac{A'B'}{AB} = \frac{6}{3} = 2$

$\frac{B'C'}{BC} = \frac{8}{4} = 2$

The ratios are equal, so the right triangles are similar, and triangle $A'B'C'$ is a dilation of triangle ABC.

B

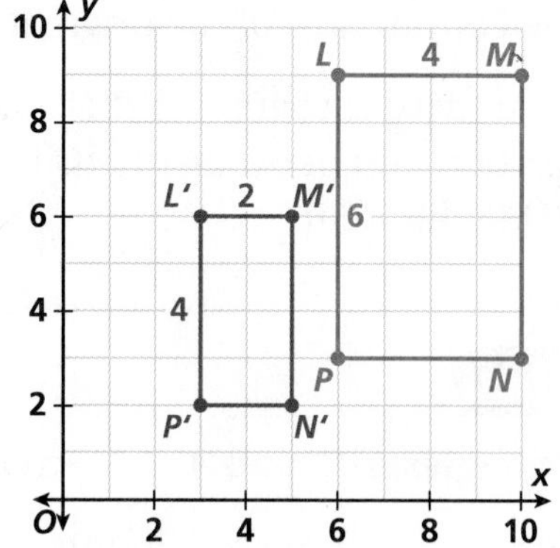

Compare the ratios of corresponding side lengths.

$\frac{L'M'}{LM} = \frac{2}{4} = \frac{1}{2}$

$\frac{L'P'}{LP} = \frac{4}{6} = \frac{2}{3}$

The ratios are not equal, so the rectangles are not similar, and rectangle $L'M'N'P'$ is not a dilation of rectangle $LMNP$.

Helpful Hint

To show that two right triangles are similar, you only need to show that the ratios of their corresponding legs are proportional.

Interactivities Online ▶ A dilation can enlarge or reduce a figure. The **scale factor** describes how much a figure is enlarged or reduced. It represents the ratio of a length on the image to the corresponding length on the original figure.

When a dilation in the coordinate plane has the origin as the center of dilation, you can find points on the image by multiplying the x- and y-coordinates of the original figure by the scale factor.

For scale factor a:

Original point (x, y) Image point $(x', y') = (ax, ay)$

EXAMPLE 2 Using the Origin as the Center of Dilation

Helpful Hint

A scale factor between 0 and 1 reduces a figure. A scale factor greater than 1 enlarges it.

A **Dilate the figure by a scale factor of 2.5. What are the vertices of the image?**

Multiply the coordinates by 2.5 to find the vertices of the image.

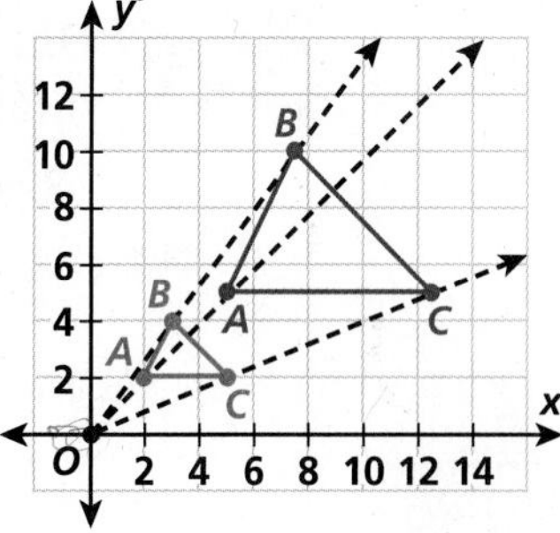

$\triangle ABC$ $\triangle A'B'C'$

$A(2, 2) \rightarrow A'(2.5 \cdot 2, 2.5 \cdot 2) \rightarrow A'(5, 5)$

$B(3, 4) \rightarrow B'(2.5 \cdot 3, 2.5 \cdot 4) \rightarrow B'(7.5, 10)$

$C(5, 2) \rightarrow C'(2.5 \cdot 5, 2.5 \cdot 2) \rightarrow C'(12.5, 5)$

The vertices of the image are $A'(5, 5)$, $B'(7.5, 10)$, and $C'(12.5, 5)$.

B **Dilate the figure by a scale factor of $\frac{2}{3}$. What are the vertices of the image?**

Multiply the coordinates by $\frac{2}{3}$ to find the vertices of the image.

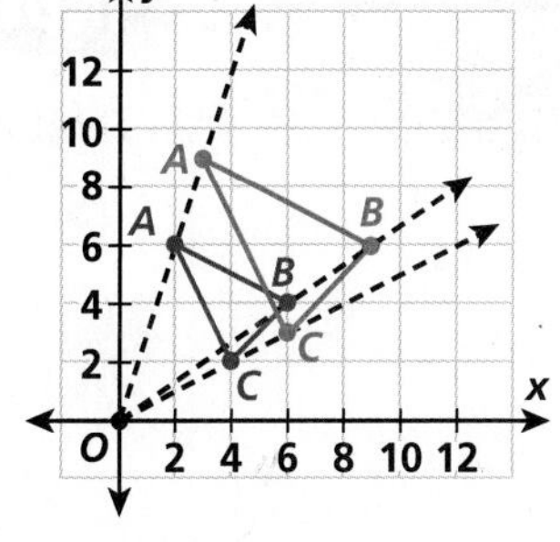

$\triangle ABC$ $\triangle A'B'C'$

$A(3, 9) \rightarrow A'\left(\frac{2}{3} \cdot 3, \frac{2}{3} \cdot 9\right) \rightarrow A'(2, 6)$

$B(9, 6) \rightarrow B'\left(\frac{2}{3} \cdot 9, \frac{2}{3} \cdot 6\right) \rightarrow B'(6, 4)$

$C(6, 3) \rightarrow C'\left(\frac{2}{3} \cdot 6, \frac{2}{3} \cdot 3\right) \rightarrow C'(4, 2)$

The vertices of the image are $A'(2, 6)$, $B'(6, 4)$, and $C'(4, 2)$.

MATHEMATICAL PRACTICES

Think and Discuss

1. **Describe** the image of a dilation with a scale factor of 1.
2. **Describe** the relationship between the corresponding sides of the image and the original figure of a dilation.

4-4 Exercises

Learn It Online
Homework Help Online
Exercises 1–8, 9, 13, 17

GUIDED PRACTICE

See Example 1 Tell whether each transformation is a dilation. Explain.

1.
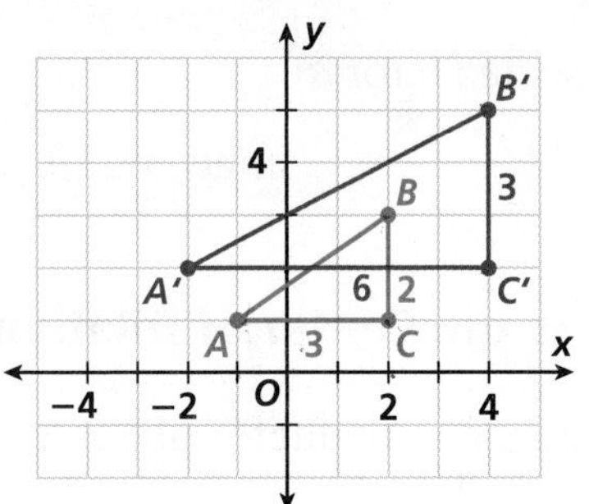

2.
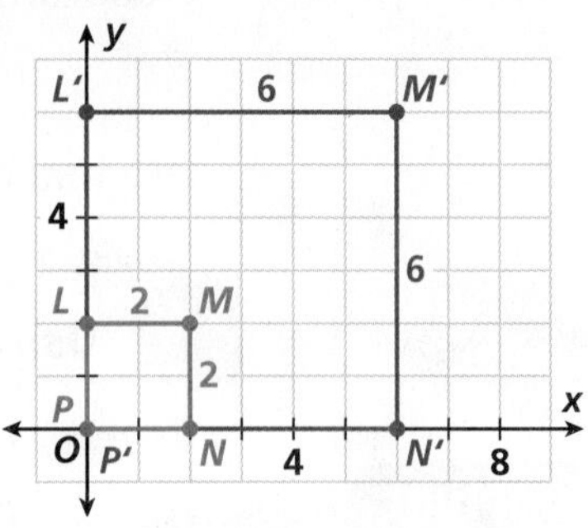

See Example 2 Dilate each figure by the given scale factor with the origin as the center of dilation. What are the vertices of the image?

3.
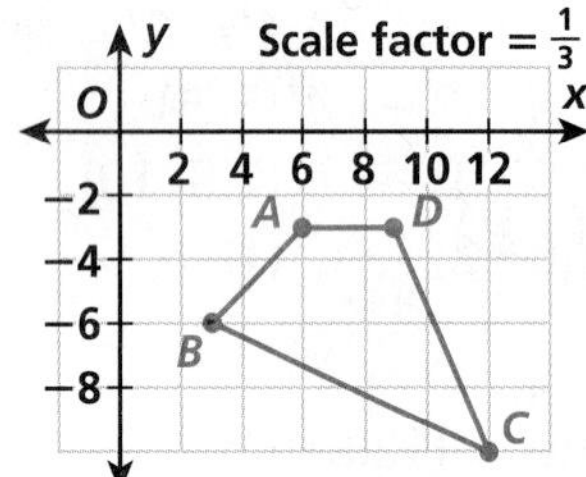

4.
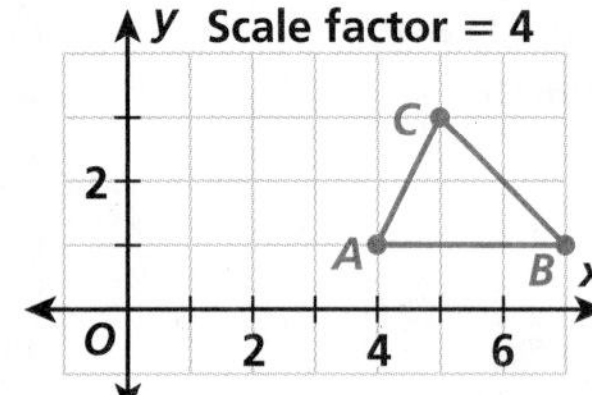

INDEPENDENT PRACTICE

See Example 1 Tell whether each transformation is a dilation. Explain.

5.
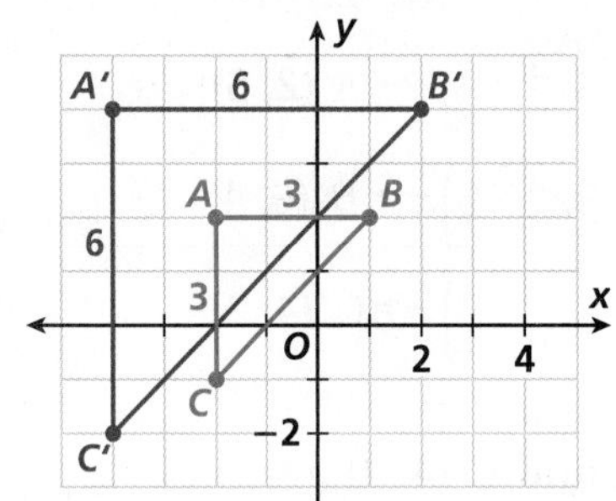

6.
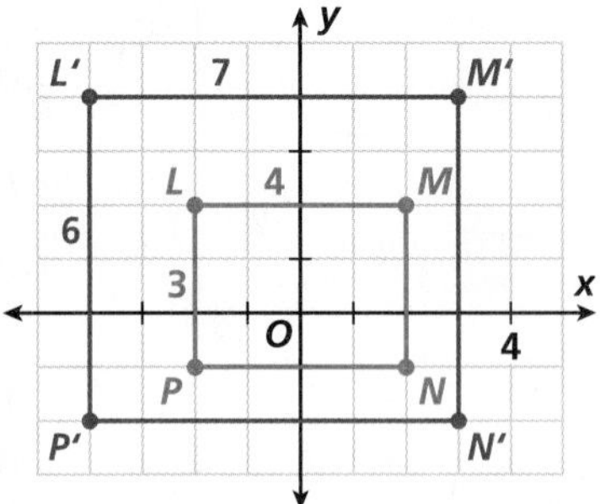

See Example 2 Dilate each figure by the given scale factor with the origin as the center of dilation. What are the vertices of the image?

7.
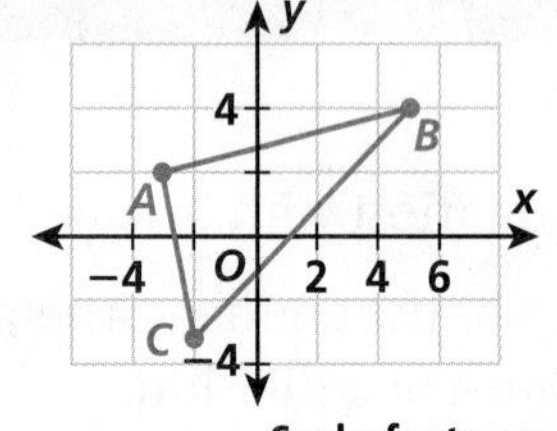

8.
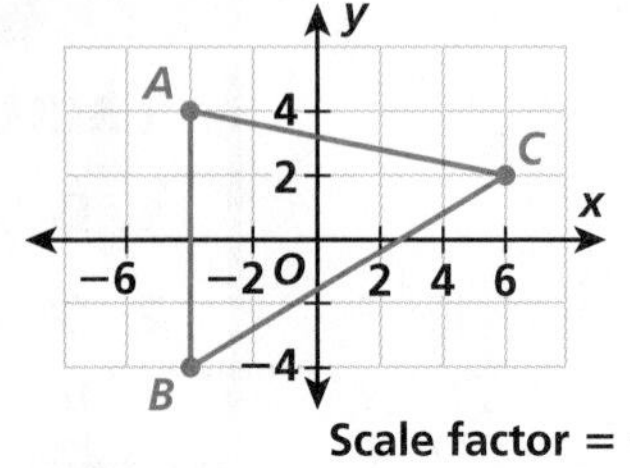

PRACTICE AND PROBLEM SOLVING

Extra Practice
See Extra Practice for more exercises.

9. A rectangle has vertices $A(2, 4)$, $B(7, 4)$, $C(7, 0)$, and $D(2, 0)$. Give the coordinates after dilating from the origin by a scale factor of 1.5.

10. **Choose a Strategy** The perimeter of an equilateral triangle is 36 cm. If the triangle is dilated by a scale factor of 0.75, what is the length of each side of the new triangle?

    (A) 3 cm (B) 4 cm (C) 9 cm (D) 12 cm

LINK Photography

In a camera lens, a larger aperture lets in more light than a smaller one.

11. **Photography** The aperture is the polygonal opening in a camera lens when a picture is taken. The aperture can be small or large. Is an aperture a dilation? Why or why not?

12. **Art** The triangle shown forms part of the design on a set of bedsheets. An artist needs to dilate the design by a scale factor of 1.5 so that it can be used on a matching set of curtains. What are the side lengths of the triangle in the dilated image?

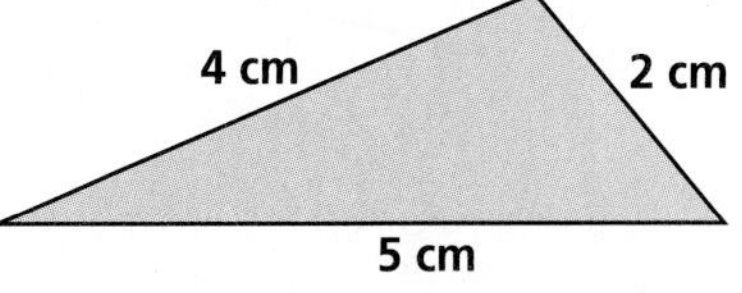

13. **Critical Thinking** A triangle has vertices $R(-5, -4)$, $S(2, 6)$, and $T(4, -3)$. The triangle is dilated so that its image has vertices $R'(-15, -12)$, $S'(6, 18)$, and $T'(12, -9)$. What is the scale factor of the dilation?

14. **Write About It** Explain how you can check the drawing of a dilation for accuracy.

15. **Challenge** What scale factor was used in the dilation of a triangle with vertices $A(4, -8)$, $B(10, 4)$, and $C(-2, 12)$, to the triangle with vertices $A'(-3, 6)$, $B'\left(-7\frac{1}{2}, -3\right)$, and $C'\left(1\frac{1}{2}, -9\right)$?

Test Prep

16. **Multiple Choice** An equilateral triangle has a perimeter of 18 centimeters. If the triangle is dilated by a factor of 0.5, what is the length of each side of the new triangle?

    (A) 36 cm (B) 12 cm (C) 9 cm (D) 3 cm

17. **Short Response** A square has a side length of 4.8 feet. If the square is dilated by a factor of 4, what is the length of a side of the new square? What is its perimeter? What is its area?

Quiz for Lessons 3 Through 4

3 Similar Figures

Tell whether the triangles are similar.

1. $\triangle DEF$ and $\triangle JKL$

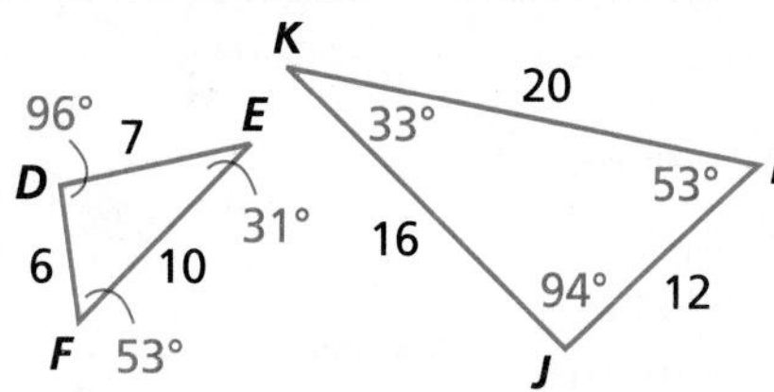

2. $\triangle PQR$ and $\triangle PRS$

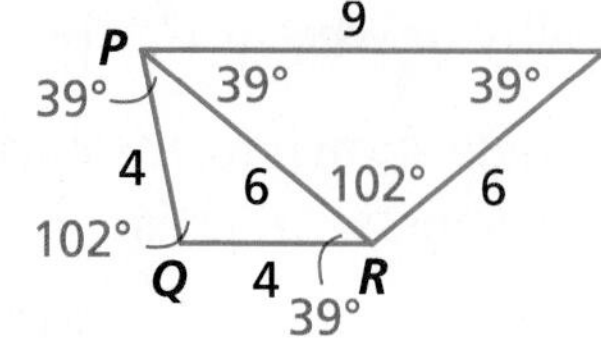

3. $\triangle UVW$ and $\triangle XYZ$

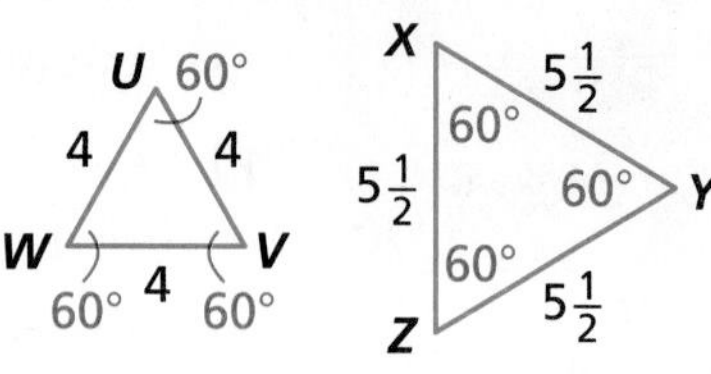

4. A picture 4 in. tall and 9 in. wide is to be scaled to 2.5 in. tall. How wide should the smaller picture be for the two pictures to be similar?

4 Dilations

Tell whether each transformation is a dilation. Explain.

5.

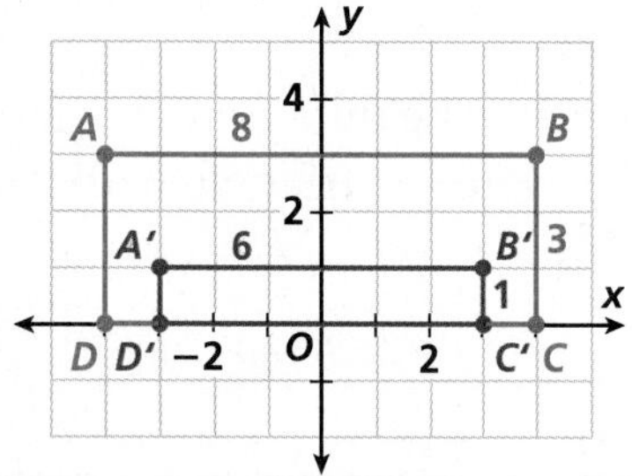

6.

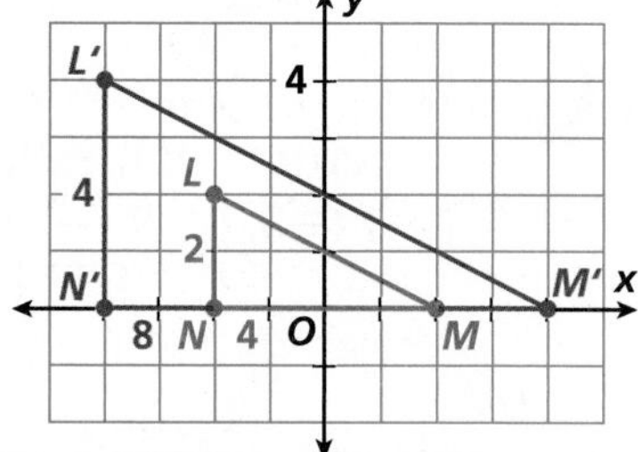

7. A triangle has vertices with coordinates (2, 0), (3, −1), and (−2, −5). If the triangle is dilated by a scale factor of 3 with the origin as the center of dilation, what are the coordinates of the vertices of the image?

Real-World CONNECTIONS

Reason abstractly and quantitatively.

The Stratosphere Tower

Since it opened in 1996, the Stratosphere Tower has been the most prominent feature of the Las Vegas skyline. It is the tallest observation tower in the country and features the Insanity, one of the world's highest thrill rides.

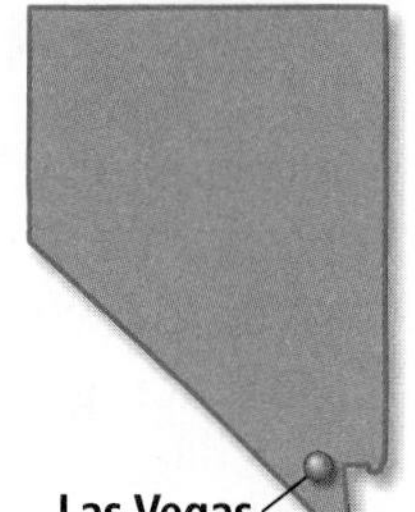

1. On a sunny afternoon, the Stratosphere Tower casts a shadow that is 140 meters long. At the same time, a nearby flagpole that is 10 meters tall casts a shadow that is 4 meters long. Write and solve a proportion to find the height of the Stratosphere Tower.
2. Show how to use dimensional analysis to convert the height of the tower to feet. (*Hint*: 1 m $\approx$ 3.28 ft)
3. An architect's model of the tower uses the scale 1 cm: 5 m. How tall is the model of the tower?

For Problems 4–6, use the table.

Stratosphere Tower Elevators	
Time (s)	**Distance (ft)**
3	120
5	200
8	320

4. The table shows the distance the tower's elevators travel in various amounts of time. What is the elevators' average speed?
5. How far does one of the elevators travel in 20 seconds? Explain how you determined your answer.
6. About long does it take an elevator to go from the ground floor to the observation deck at a height of 869 feet?

(bl) Sam Morris/Las Vegas Sun/Reuters/Corbis; (br) AP Photo/Lennox McLendon

Real-World Connections

Game Time

Copy-Cat

You can use this method to copy a well-known work of art or any drawing. First, draw a grid over the work you want to copy, or draw a grid on tracing paper and tape it over the picture.

Next, on a separate sheet of paper draw a blank grid with the same number of squares. The squares do not have to be the same size. Copy each square from the original exactly onto the blank grid. Do not look at the overall picture as you copy. When you have copied all of the squares, the drawing on your finished grid should look just like the original work.

Suppose you are copying an image from a 12 in. by 18 in. print, and that you use 1-inch squares on the first grid.

1. If you use 3-inch squares on the blank grid, what size will your finished copy be?
2. If you want to make a copy that is 10 inches tall, what size should you make the squares on your blank grid? How wide will the copy be?
3. Choose a painting, drawing, or cartoon, and copy it using the method above.

Tic-Frac-Toe

Draw a large tic-tac-toe board. In each square, draw a blank proportion, $\frac{\blacksquare}{\blacksquare} = \frac{\blacksquare}{\blacksquare}$. Players take turns using a spinner with 12 sections or a 12-sided die. A player's turn consists of placing a number anywhere in one of the proportions. The player who correctly completes the proportion can claim that square. A square may also be blocked by filling in three parts of a proportion that cannot be completed with a number from 1 to 12. The first player to claim three squares in a row wins.

Learn It Online
Game Time Extra

A gameboard is available online.

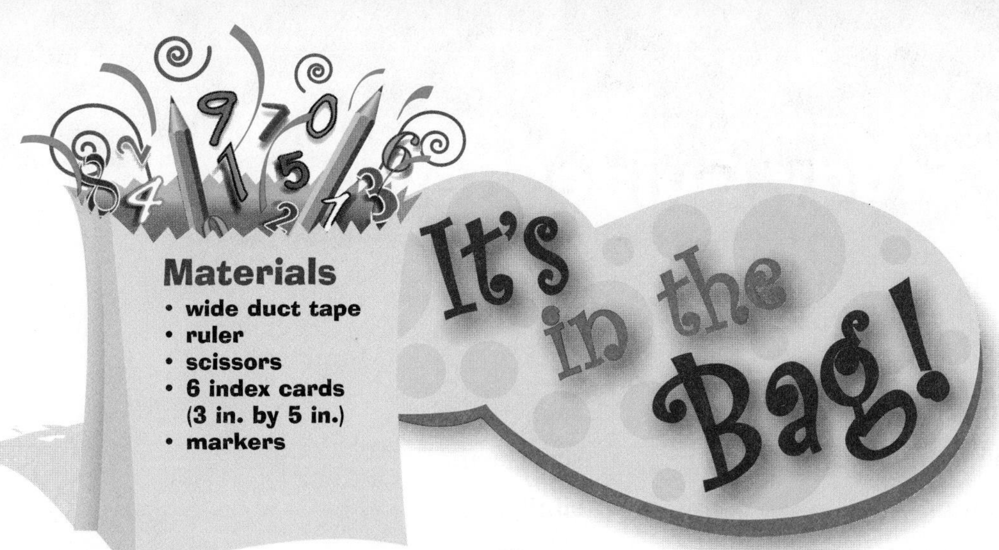

PROJECT A Worthwhile Wallet

Make a duct-tape wallet to carry index cards. The index cards will help you study ratios, proportions, and similarity.

Directions

1. Cut three strips of duct tape at least 9 inches long. Lay the strips next to each other, sticky side up, so that they overlap slightly. The total width should be about $5\frac{1}{2}$ inches. **Figure A**

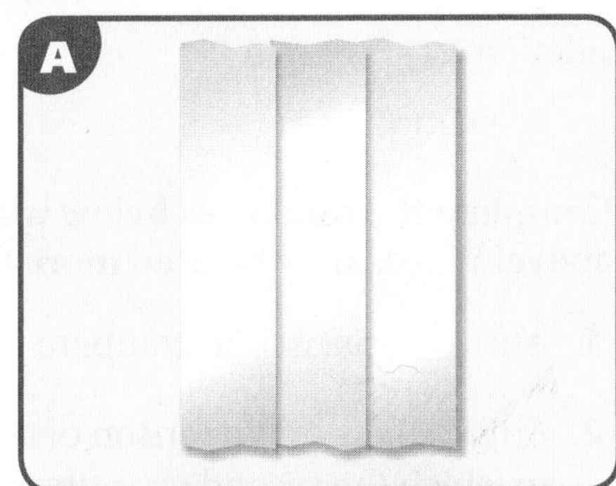

2. Lay three more strips of duct tape on top of the first three, sticky side down. Trim the ends. This will make a sheet of duct-tape "fabric."

3. Fold up the fabric about $3\frac{1}{2}$ inches from the bottom to form a pocket. Use duct tape to seal the sides shut. **Figure B**

4. Fold the top down. Trim the corners of the flap. **Figure C**

Taking Note of the Math

Review the chapter to identify key concepts. Then write vocabulary, examples, and practice problems on the index cards. Store the cards in the duct-tape wallet.

Sam Dudgeon/HMH

Study Guide: Review

Vocabulary

center of dilation	rate
corresponding angles	scale factor
corresponding sides	similar
cross product	unit price
dilation	unit rate

Complete the sentences below with vocabulary words from the list above. Words may be used more than once.

1. A(n) __?__ is used to compare price per item.
2. A(n) __?__ is a comparison of two quantities that have different units. A rate in which the second quantity is 1 is called a(n) __?__.
3. A transformation that changes the size but not the shape of a figure is called a(n) __?__.

EXAMPLES

1 Ratios, Rates, and Unit Rates

■ **Alex can buy a 4 pack of AA batteries for \$2.99 or an 8 pack for \$4.98. Which is the better buy?**

$\frac{\text{price per package}}{\text{number of batteries}} = \frac{\$2.99}{4} \approx \$0.75$ per battery

$\frac{\text{price per package}}{\text{number of batteries}} = \frac{\$4.98}{8} \approx \$0.62$ per battery

The better buy is the 8 pack for \$4.98.

EXERCISES

Determine the better buy.

4. 50 blank CDs for \$14.99 or 75 CDs for \$21.50
5. 6 boxes of 3-inch incense sticks for \$22.50 or 8 boxes for \$30
6. a package of 8 binder dividers for \$23.09 or a 25 pack for \$99.99

EXAMPLES

EXERCISES

2 Solving Proportions

- **Solve the proportion $\frac{18}{12} = \frac{x}{2}$.**

$12x = 18 \cdot 2$ *Find the cross products.*

$\frac{12x}{12} = \frac{36}{12}$ *Divide both sides by 12.*

$x = 3$ *Simplify.*

- **A car travels 145 mi in 2.5 h. At this rate, how far will the car go in 4 h?**

$\frac{145 \text{ mi}}{2.5 \text{ h}} = \frac{x \text{ mi}}{4 \text{ h}}$ *Set up a proportion.*

$580 = 2.5x$ *Find the cross products.*

$232 = x$ *Divide both sides by 2.5.*

The car will travel 232 mi in 4 h.

Solve each proportion.

7. $\frac{3}{5} = \frac{9}{x}$

8. $\frac{24}{h} = \frac{16}{4}$

9. $\frac{w}{6} = \frac{7}{2}$

10. $\frac{3}{8} = \frac{11}{y}$

11. $\frac{16}{20} = \frac{m}{30}$

12. $\frac{11}{16} = \frac{b}{20}$

13. A kayaker traveled 2 miles in 40 minutes. At this rate, how long will it take the kayaker to travel 9 miles?

14. Hiking socks are on sale for 2 pairs for $9.98. At this rate, how much would 5 pairs of socks cost?

3 Similar Figures

- **A stamp 1.2 in. tall and 1.75 in. wide is to be scaled to 4.2 in. tall. How wide should the new stamp be?**

$\frac{1.2}{1.75} = \frac{4.2}{x}$ *Set up a proportion.*

$1.2x = 7.35$ *Find the cross products.*

$x = 6.125$ *Divide both sides by 1.2.*

The larger stamp should be 6.125 in. wide.

15. A picture 3 in. wide by 5 in. tall is to be scaled to 7.5 in. wide to be put on a flyer. How tall should the flyer picture be?

16. A picture 8 in. wide by 10 in. tall is to be scaled to 2.5 in. wide to be put on an invitation. How tall should the invitation picture be?

EXAMPLES

EXERCISES

4 Dilations

■ **Tell whether the transformation is a dilation.**

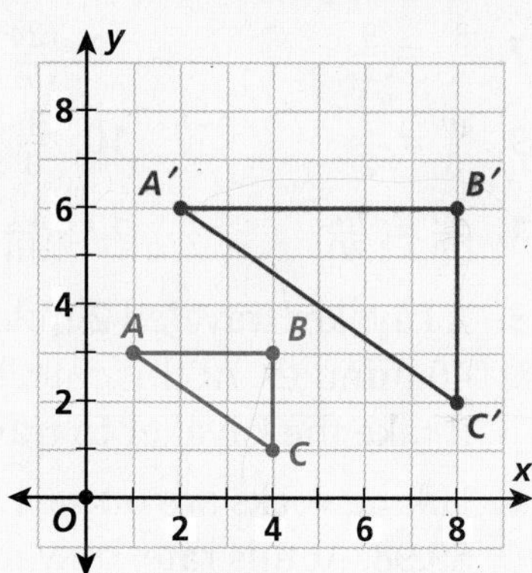

Compare the ratios of corresponding side lengths.

$\frac{A'B'}{AB} = \frac{6}{3} = 2$

$\frac{B'C'}{BC} = \frac{4}{2} = 2$

The ratios are equal, so the right triangles are similar, and triangle $A'B'C'$ is a dilation of triangle ABC.

■ **Dilate triangle ABC by a scale factor of 2 with $O(0, 0)$ as the center of dilation.**

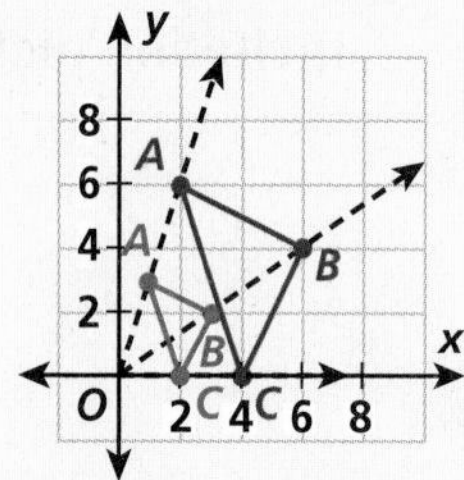

Tell whether each transformation is a dilation.

17.

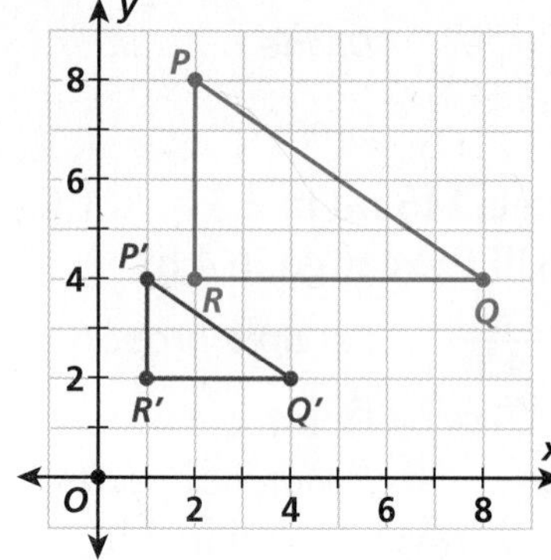

18.

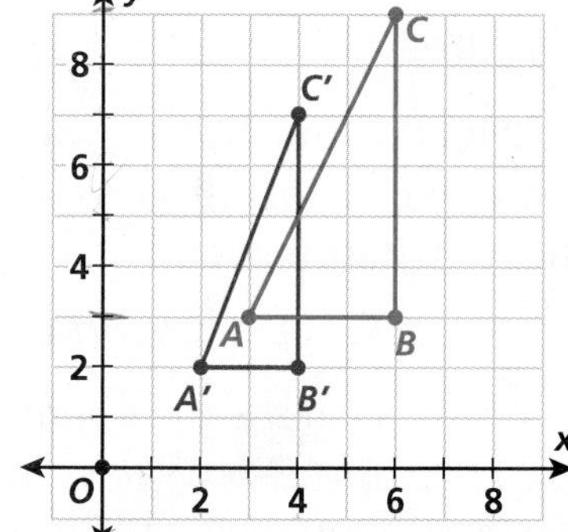

Dilate each triangle ABC by the given scale factor with $O(0, 0)$ as the center of dilation.

19. $A(1, 0)$, $B(1, 2)$, $C(3, 1)$; scale factor = 3

20. $A(4, 6)$, $B(8, 4)$, $C(6, 2)$; scale factor = 0.5

21. $A(2, 2)$, $B(6, 2)$, $C(4, 4)$; scale factor = 1.5

Chapter Test

1. Celeste hiked 1.8 miles in 0.75 hour.
   a. What is her average rate of speed?
   b. Celeste estimates that she will finish her entire 6-mile trip in less than 2 hours. If she keeps hiking at the same average speed, is her estimate reasonable? Explain.
2. You can buy one 10 pack of AAA batteries for $5.49 and get one battery free, or buy two 4 packs for a total of $2.98. Which is the better buy?

Solve each proportion.

3. $\frac{6}{9} = \frac{n}{72}$
4. $\frac{18}{12} = \frac{3}{x}$
5. $\frac{0.7}{1.4} = \frac{z}{28}$
6. $\frac{12}{y} = \frac{32}{16}$
7. Simon bought 5 cans of chili for $10.95. At this rate, how much would 12 cans of chili cost?
8. Fran scans a document that is 8.5 in. wide by 11 in. long into her computer. If she scales the length down to 7 in., how wide should the similar document be?
9. A triangle has sides measuring 8 inches, 8 inches, and 5 inches. A similar triangle has two sides measuring 12 inches each. What is the length of the third side of the similar triangle?

Tell whether each transformation is a dilation. Explain.

10.

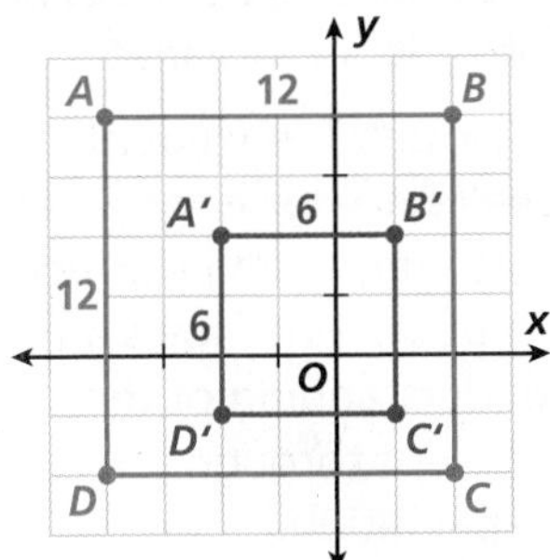

11.

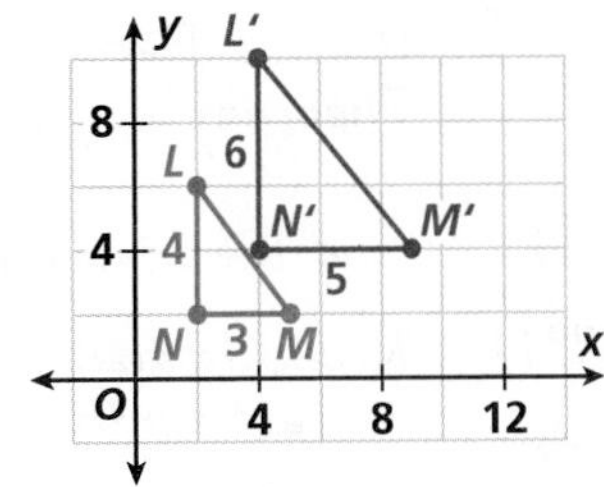

12. A rectangle has vertices $J(3, 3)$, $K(9, 3)$, $L(9, 6)$, and $M(3, 6)$. Give the coordinates after dilating from the origin by a scale factor of $\frac{2}{3}$.

Chapter Test

Short Response: Write Short Responses

To answer a short response test item completely, you must show how you solved the problem and explain your answer. Short response test items are scored using a 2-point scoring rubric. A sample scoring rubric is shown below.

EXAMPLE 1

Short Response A carpenter is pouring a concrete foundation for a garden planter in the shape of a right triangle. The length of one leg of the planter is 18 feet, and the length of the hypotenuse is 22 feet. What is the length of the other leg of the planter? Round your answer to the nearest tenth. Show all of your work.

Here are examples of how different responses were scored using the scoring rubric shown.

Scoring Rubric

2 points: The student demonstrates a thorough understanding of the concept, correctly answers the question, and provides a complete explanation.

1 point: The student correctly answers the question but does not show all work or does not provide an explanation.

1 point: The student makes minor errors, resulting in an incorrect solution, but shows an understanding of the concept through explanation.

0 points: The student gives a response showing no work or giving no explanation, or the student gives no response

2-point response:

Let s = the length of the other leg.

$18^2 + s^2 = 22^2$ *Use the Pythagorean Theorem.*

$s^2 = 160$

$\sqrt{s^2} = \sqrt{160}$ *Find the square root.*

$s \approx 12.64911$ *Round to the nearest tenth.*

$s \approx 12.6$ ft.

The length of the other leg is 12.6 ft.

1-point response:

Let s = the length of the other leg.

$18^2 + s^2 = 22^2$

$324 + s^2 = 484$

$\sqrt{s^2} = \sqrt{160}$

$s = 13$ ft

The length of the other leg is 13 ft.

The student showed all of the work, but there was a minor computation error, which resulted in an incorrect answer.

0-point response:

$s = 12$

The student's answer is not rounded to the nearest tenth, and there is no explanation.

Read short-response test items carefully. If you are allowed to write in the test booklet, underline or circle the parts of the question that tell you what your solution must include. Be sure to use complete sentences in your explanation.

Read each test item, and answer the questions that follow by using the scoring rubric on the previous page.

Item A

Dilate the figure by a scale factor of $\frac{1}{4}$ with the origin as the center of dilation. What are the vertices of the image? Show all of your work.

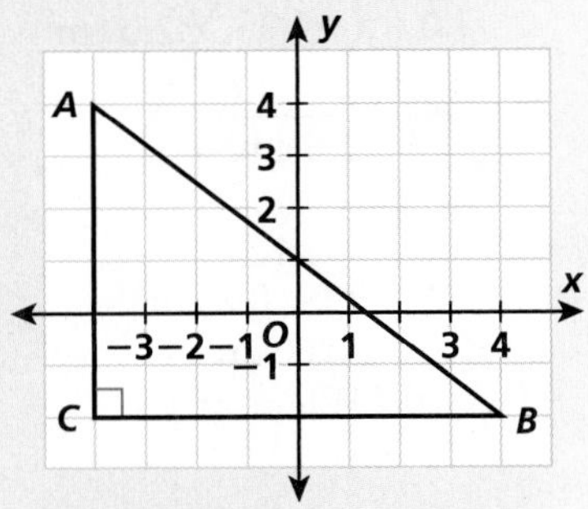

Student's Response

$A'(-1, 1)$, $B'\left(1, -\frac{1}{2}\right)$, $C'\left(-1, -\frac{1}{2}\right)$

1. What score should the student's response receive? Explain your reasoning.
2. What additional information, if any, should the student's answer include in order for the student to receive full credit?

Item B

The ratio of the length of a rectangular garden to its width is 12:5. If the width of the garden is 8 feet, find the area of the garden. Show all of your work.

Student's Response

$\frac{\ell}{w} = \frac{12}{5}$ The ratio of the length to the width is 12:5.

$\frac{12}{5} = \frac{8}{\ell}$; $12\ell = 40$; $\ell = 3.\overline{3}$ The length is 3.3 ft.

$A = \ell w$; $A = 3.3 \times 8 = 26.4$

The area is 26.4 ft².

3. What score should the student's response receive? Explain your reasoning.
4. What additional information, if any, should the student's answer include in order for the student to receive full credit?

Item C

An office supply store charges \$24 for 72 file folders. A student says that the unit price is \$3 per folder. What is the student's error? What is the correct unit price? Show all of your work.

Student's Response

The student divided wrong. The student should have divided 24 by 72, not 72 by 24.

5. What score should the student's response receive? Explain your reasoning.
6. What additional information, if any, should the student's answer include in order for the student to receive full credit?

CHAPTER 4

Standardized Test Prep

Cumulative Assessment

Multiple Choice

1. Which inequality describes the graph?

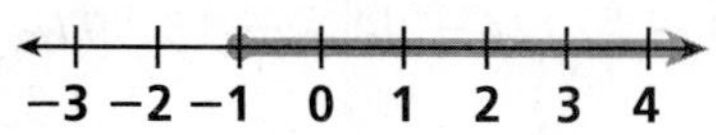

Ⓐ $x < -1$ Ⓒ $x \leq -1$

Ⓑ $x > -1$ Ⓓ $x \geq -1$

2. Which value of x is the solution of the equation $-6x = 48$?

Ⓕ $x = -8$ Ⓗ $x = 42$

Ⓖ $x = -6$ Ⓙ $x = 54$

3. Which two numbers both have an absolute value of 6?

Ⓐ 0 and 6 Ⓒ −3 and 3

Ⓑ −6 and 6 Ⓓ 5 and −1

4. What is the value of the expression $x + 4y - 2$ when $x = 3$ and $y = -1$?

Ⓕ 10 Ⓗ −3

Ⓖ 5 Ⓙ −9

5. If a drinking glass holds $\frac{1}{16}$ gallon of water, how many gallons of water are contained in 8 drinking glasses?

Ⓐ $\frac{1}{8}$ gallon Ⓒ 2 gallons

Ⓑ $\frac{1}{2}$ gallon Ⓓ 64 gallons

6. A turnstile counted 1040 people who entered a zoo in a 4-hour period. Which proportion can be used to find how many people p entered in an 8-hour period at the same hourly rate?

Ⓕ $\frac{4}{1040} = \frac{p}{8}$ Ⓗ $\frac{4}{p} = \frac{8}{1040}$

Ⓖ $\frac{1040}{4} = \frac{p}{8}$ Ⓙ $\frac{4}{1040} = \frac{12}{p}$

7. Which pair of ratios are NOT in proportion?

Ⓐ $\frac{3}{7}$ and $\frac{9}{21}$ Ⓒ $\frac{3}{8}$ and $\frac{4}{9}$

Ⓑ $\frac{9}{4}$ and $\frac{18}{8}$ Ⓓ $\frac{2}{3}$ and $\frac{10}{15}$

8. Which figure is similar to the figure below?

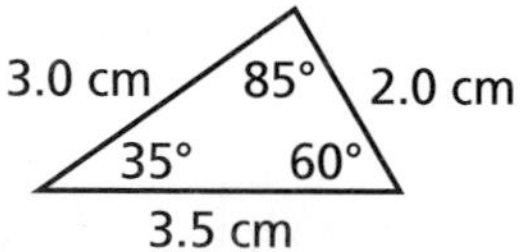

Ⓕ

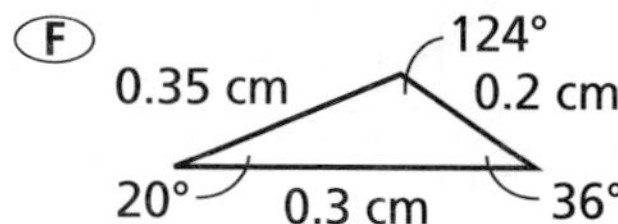

Ⓖ

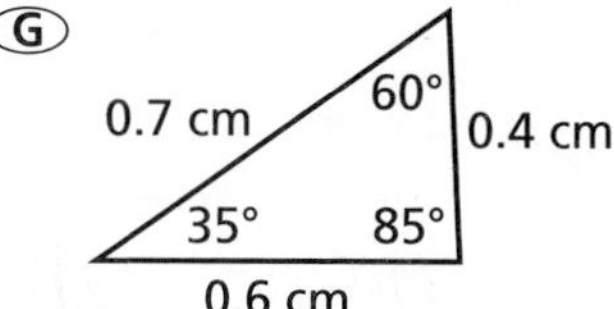

Ⓗ

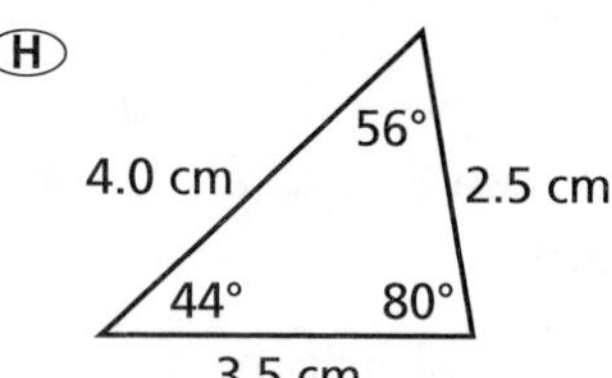

Ⓙ

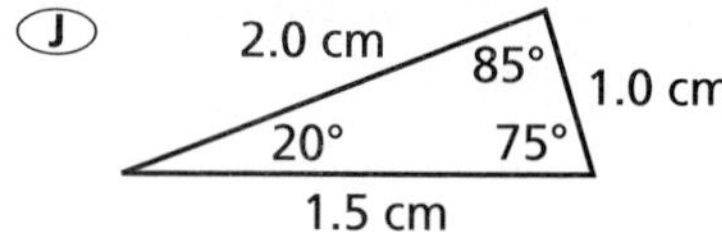

9. Which set of fractions are in order from least to greatest?

Ⓐ $\frac{3}{8}, \frac{1}{4}, \frac{2}{5}, \frac{1}{3}$ Ⓒ $\frac{1}{4}, \frac{1}{3}, \frac{2}{5}, \frac{3}{8}$

Ⓑ $\frac{1}{3}, \frac{1}{4}, \frac{2}{5}, \frac{3}{8}$ Ⓓ $\frac{1}{4}, \frac{1}{3}, \frac{3}{8}, \frac{2}{5}$

It is helpful to draw or redraw a figure. Answers to geometry problems may become clearer as you redraw the figure.

10. The area of a square is 85 square feet. Which measurement best approximates a side length?

(F) 8.8 ft (H) 9.2 ft

(G) 9 ft (J) 9.9 ft

Gridded Response

11. A football team earns a first down when the team has moved the ball 10 yards forward. If a team has moved the ball forward 15 feet, what is the least number of yards the team needs to earn a first down?

12. A ballet class has a rule that all productions must have a ratio of 4 boys for every 5 girls. If there are 12 boys in a production, how many girls can be in the same production?

13. What is the length, in feet, of the base of the sail, x?

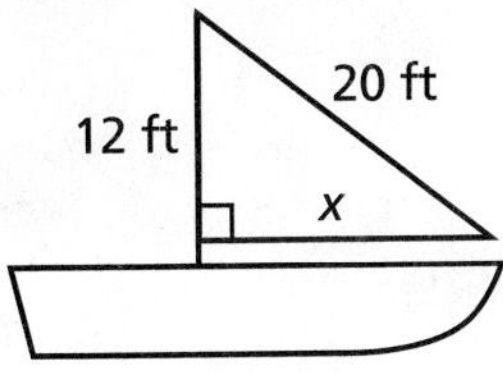

14. A recipe for chili calls for $2\frac{1}{2}$ cups of kidney beans. If a chef makes $4\frac{1}{2}$ batches of the chili recipe, how many cups of kidney beans will she need?

15. If a snail moves 5 centimeters in 10 seconds, how fast in meters per minute can a snail move?

16. Three friends split the cost of a birthday present and a meal for another friend. The present cost $56.75, and the meal cost $23.65. Find the amount that each friend paid.

Short Response

S1. At the student store, the ratio of notebooks sold to three-ring binders sold is 5 to 7.

a. At this rate, how many notebooks can you predict will be sold if 210 three-ring binders are sold? Show your work.

b. At the same rate, predict how many total notebooks and three-ring binders will be sold. Explain your reasoning.

S2. While shopping for school supplies Sara finds boxes of pencils in two sizes. One box has 8 pencils for $0.89, and the other box has 12 pencils for $1.25.

a. Which box is the better bargain? Why? Round your answer to the nearest cent.

b. How much would you save by buying 48 pencils at the better rate? Show your work.

Extended Response

E1. In a scale model of the solar system, the diameter for the model of the Sun is 1 inch. All other distances and sizes in the model can be calculated using the table below.

a. What is the diameter of Pluto in the model?

b. What is Pluto's distance from the Sun in the model?

c. What would Pluto's distance from the Sun be in the model if the Sun's diameter were changed to 2 ft?

	Sun	Mars	Jupiter	Pluto
Diameter (mi)	864,000	4200	88,640	1410
Distance from Sun (million mi)		141	483	3670

CHAPTER 5

Geometric Relationships

COMMON CORE

Chapter Focus

- Describe two-dimensional figures.
- Analyze angles created when a transversal cuts parallel lines.
- Find unknown angle measures.

Why Learn This?

In the art of origami, a single sheet of paper is folded multiple times to make a particular design, such as a crane or dragon. Origami artists must understand the relationships among lines, angles, and polygons to create their works of art.

Learn It Online
Chapter Project Online

Are You Ready?

Vocabulary

Choose the best term from the list to complete each sentence.

1. In the __?__ (4, −3), 4 is the __?__, and −3 is the __?__.

2. The __?__ divide the __?__ into four sections.

3. The point (0, 0) is called the __?__.

4. The point (0, −3) lies on the __?__, while the point (−2, 0) lies on the __?__.

coordinate axes
coordinate plane
ordered pair
origin
***x*-axis**
***x*-coordinate**
***y*-axis**
***y*-coordinate**

Complete these exercises to review skills you will need for this chapter.

Ordered Pairs

Write the coordinates of the indicated points.

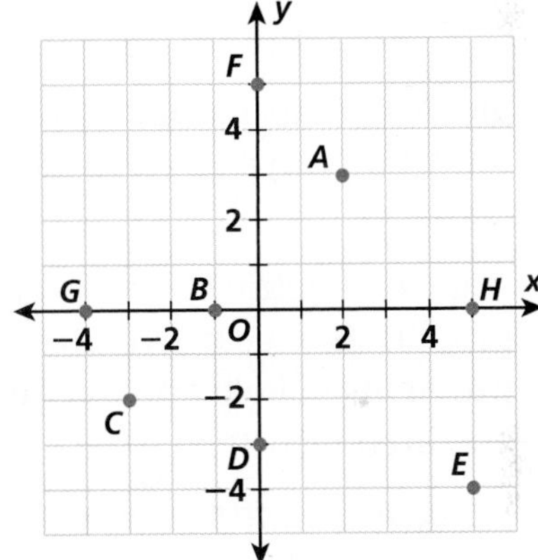

5. point A **6.** point B

7. point C **8.** point D

9. point E **10.** point F

11. point G **12.** point H

Similar Figures

Tell whether the figures in each pair appear to be similar.

13.

14.

Equations

Solve each equation.

15. $2p = 18$ **16.** $7 + h = 21$ **17.** $\frac{x}{3} = 9$ **18.** $y - 6 = 16$

19. $4d + 1 = 13$ **20.** $-2q - 3 = 3$ **21.** $4z - 4 = 16$ **22.** $5x + 3 = 23$

Determine whether the given values are solutions of the given equations.

23. $\frac{2}{3}x + 1 = 7 \quad x = 9$ **24.** $2x - 4 = 6 \quad x = -1$

25. $8 - 2x = -4 \quad x = 5$ **26.** $\frac{1}{2}x + 5 = -2 \quad x = -14$

CHAPTER 5

Study Guide: Preview

Where You've Been

Previously, you

- located and named points on a coordinate plane.
- recognized geometric concepts and properties in fields such as art and architecture.
- used critical attributes to define similarity.

In This Chapter

You will study

- graphing translations and reflections on a coordinate plane.
- using geometric concepts and properties of geometry to solve problems in fields such as art and architecture.
- using critical attributes to define congruency.

Where You're Going

You can use the skills learned in this chapter

- to find angle measures by using relationships within figures.
- to recognize geometric relationships in works of art.

Key Vocabulary/Vocabulario

equilateral triangle	triángulo equilátero
parallel lines	líneas paralelas
perpendicular lines	rectas perpendiculares
reflection	reflexión
transformation	transformación
translation	traslación
transversal	transversal

Vocabulary Connections

To become familiar with some of the vocabulary terms in the chapter, consider the following. You may refer to the chapter, the glossary, or a dictionary if you like.

1. The word *equilateral* contains the roots *equi,* which means "equal," and *lateral,* which means "of the side." What do you suppose an **equilateral triangle** is?
2. The word *transform* can mean "to change in form, appearance, or structure." How do you think a **transformation** might affect a geometric figure?
3. How does an object look different when it is *reflected* in a mirror? How do you think a geometric figure differs from its mathematical **reflection**?

Study Guide: Preview

Writing Strategy: Keep a Math Journal

By keeping a math journal, you can improve your writing and thinking skills. Use your journal to summarize key ideas and vocabulary from each lesson and to analyze any questions you may have about a concept or your homework.

Journal Entry: Read the entry a student made in her journal.

January 27

I'm having trouble with a lesson. I can find what percent one number is of another number, but I get confused about finding percent increase and decrease. My teacher helped me think it through:

Find the percent increase or decrease from 20 to 25.

- First figure out if it is a percent increase or decrease. It goes from a smaller to a larger number, so it is a percent increase because the number is getting larger, or increasing.
- Then find the amount of increase, or the difference, between the two numbers. $25 - 20 = 5$
- Now find what percent the amount of increase, or difference, is of the original number.

$$\frac{\text{amount of increase}}{\text{original number}} \rightarrow \frac{5}{20} = 0.25 = 25\%$$

So it is a 25% increase.

Try This

Begin a math journal. Write in it each day this week, using these ideas as starters. Be sure to date and number each page.

- In this lesson, I already know . . .
- In this lesson, I am unsure about . . .
- The skills I need to complete this lesson are . . .
- The challenges I encountered were . . .
- I handled these challenges by . . .
- In this lesson, I enjoyed/did not enjoy . . .

5-1 Angle Relationships

An **angle** (∠) is formed by two rays, or sides, with a common endpoint called the *vertex*. You can name an angle several ways: by its vertex, by its vertex and a point on each ray, or by a number. When three points are used, the middle point must be the vertex.

Angles are usually measured in degrees (°). Since there are 360° in a circle, one degree is $\frac{1}{360}$ of a circle.

∠*Y*, ∠*XYZ*, ∠*ZYX*, or ∠1

Vocabulary

- angle
- right angle
- acute angle
- obtuse angle
- straight angle
- complementary angles
- supplementary angles
- adjacent angles
- vertical angles
- congruent angles

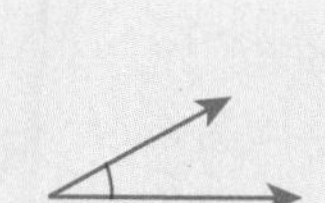

The measure of an **acute angle** is greater than 0° and less than 90°.

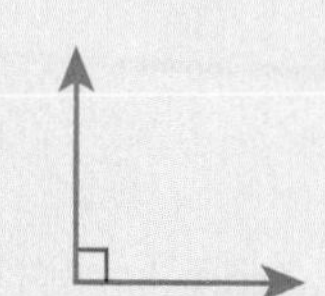

The measure of a **right angle** is 90°.

The measure of an **obtuse angle** is greater than 90° and less than 180°.

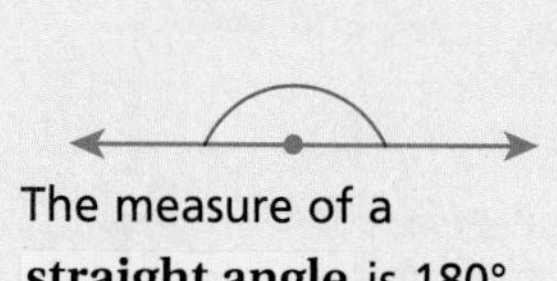

The measure of a **straight angle** is 180°.

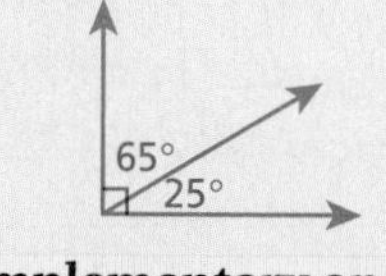

Complementary angles are two angles whose measures add to 90°.

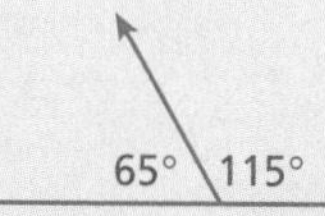

Supplementary angles are two angles whose measures add to 180°.

EXAMPLE 1 Classifying Angles

Reading Math

m∠*AEC* is read as "the measure of angle *AEC*."

Use the diagram to name each figure.

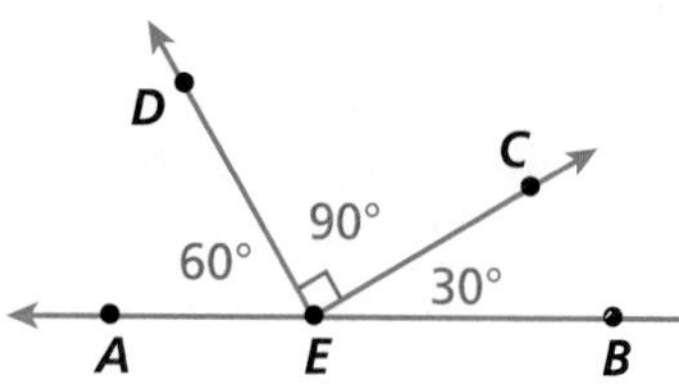

A two acute angles

∠*AED*, ∠*CEB* *m∠AED = 60°; m∠CEB = 30°*

B two obtuse angles

∠*AEC*, ∠*DEB* *m∠AEC = 150°; m∠DEB = 120°*

C a pair of complementary angles

∠*AED*, ∠*CEB* *m∠AED + m∠CEB = 60° + 30° = 90°*

D two pairs of supplementary angles

∠*AED*, ∠*DEB* *m∠AED + m∠DEB = 60° + 120° = 180°*

∠*AEC*, ∠*CEB* *m∠AEC + m∠CEB = 150° + 30° = 180°*

You can use what you know about complementary and supplementary angles to find missing angle measurements.

EXAMPLE 2 Finding Angle Measures

Use the diagram to find each angle measure.

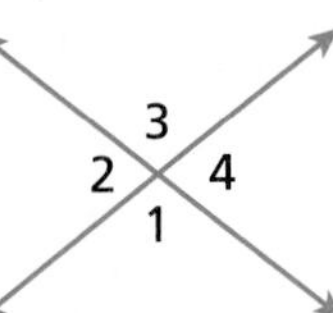

A **If m∠2 = 75°, find m∠3.**

$m\angle 2 + m\angle 3 = 180°$ — *∠2 and ∠3 are supplementary.*

$75° + m\angle 3 = 180°$ — *Substitute 75° for m∠2.*

$\underline{-75°} \qquad \underline{-75°}$ — *Subtract 75° from both sides.*

$m\angle 3 = 105°$

B **Find m∠4.**

$m\angle 3 + m\angle 4 = 180°$ — *∠3 and ∠4 are supplementary.*

$105° + m\angle 4 = 180°$ — *Substitute 105° for m∠3.*

$\underline{-105°} \qquad \underline{-105°}$ — *Subtract 75° from both sides.*

$m\angle 4 = 75°$

Check

Use a protractor to measure ∠3 and ∠4.

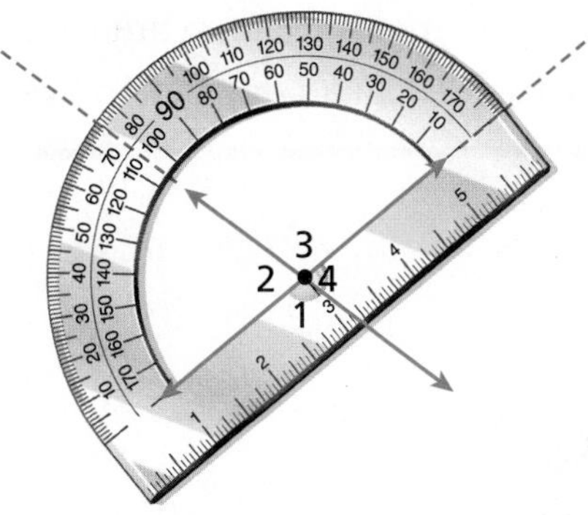

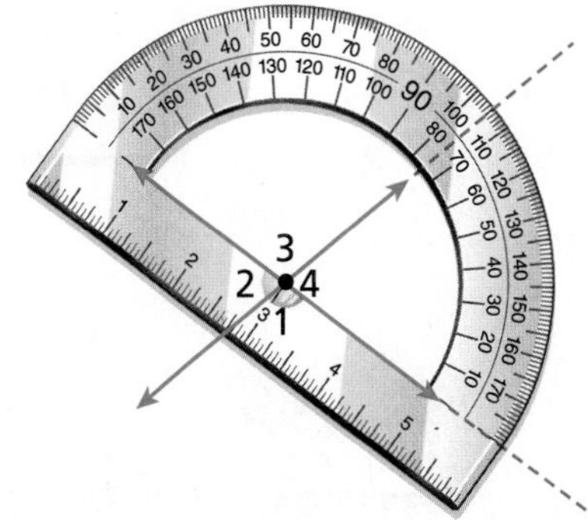

The measurements from the protractors provide support that m∠3 = 105° and m∠4 = 75°.

Caution!

Diagrams are not always drawn to scale. When solving problems about angles, it is best to find your answers mathematically rather than by measuring.

The angles in Example 2 are examples of *adjacent angles* and *vertical angles.* These angles have special relationships because of their positions.

- **Adjacent angles** have a common vertex and a common side, but no common interior points. Angles 1 and 2 in the diagram above are adjacent angles.
- **Congruent angles** have the same measure. In Example 2, you found that ∠2 ≅ ∠4 since both angles measure 75°.
- **Vertical angles** are the *nonadjacent* angles formed by two intersecting lines. Angles 2 and 4 are vertical angles. Vertical angles are congruent.

Writing Math

The symbol for congruence is ≅, which is read as "is congruent to."

EXAMPLE 3 Art Application

An artist is designing a section of a stained glass window. Based on the diagram, what should be the measure of $\angle ECF$?

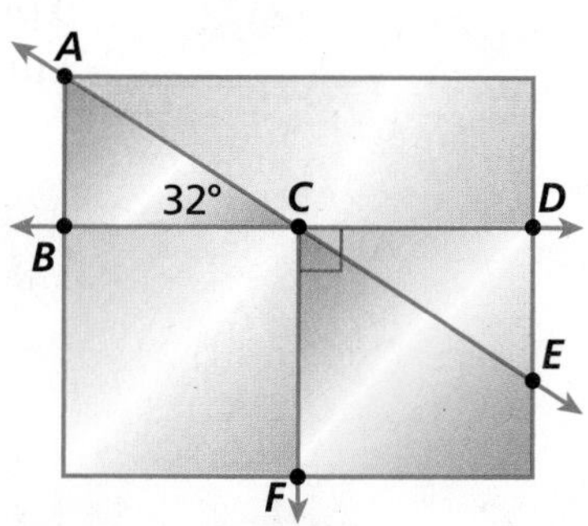

Step 1: Find $m\angle DCE$.

$\angle DCE \cong \angle ACB$ — *Vertical angles are congruent.*

$m\angle DCE = m\angle ACB$ — *Congruent angles have the same measure.*

$m\angle DCE = 32°$ — *Substitute 32° for m∠ACB.*

Step 2: Find $m\angle ECF$.

$m\angle DCE + m\angle ECF = 90°$ — *The angles are complementary.*

$32° + m\angle ECF = 90°$ — *Substitute 32° for m∠DCE.*

$m\angle ECF = 58°$ — *Subtract 32° from both sides.*

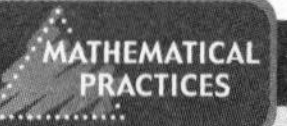

Think and Discuss

1. **Draw** a pair of angles that are adjacent but not supplementary.
2. **Explain** why vertical angles must always be congruent.

5-1 Exercises

Learn It Online
Homework Help Online
Exercises 1–16, 17, 25, 27

GUIDED PRACTICE

See Example 1

Use the diagram to name each figure.

1. a right angle
2. two acute angles
3. an obtuse angle
4. a pair of complementary angles
5. two pairs of supplementary angles

See Example 2

Use the diagram to find each angle measure.

6. If $m\angle 3 = 114°$, find $m\angle 2$.
7. Find $m\angle 1$.

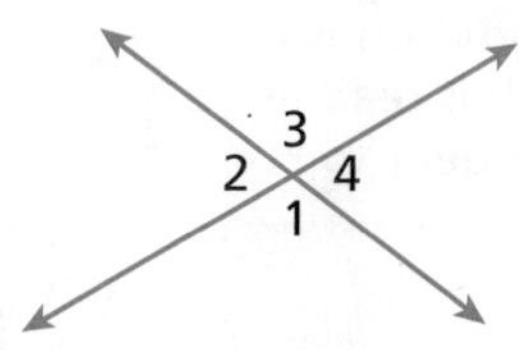

See Example 3

8. **Engineering** The diagram shows the intersection of three metal supports on an amusement park ride. Based on the diagram, what should be the measure of $\angle CBD$?

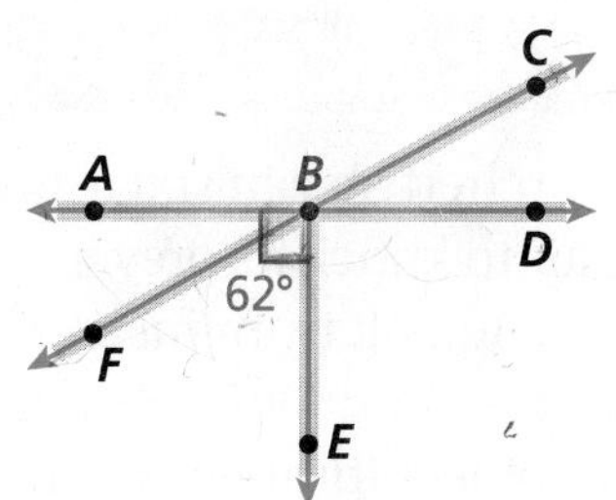

INDEPENDENT PRACTICE

See Example 1

Use the diagram to name each figure.

9. a right angle
10. two acute angles
11. two obtuse angles
12. a pair of complementary angles
13. two pairs of supplementary angles

See Example 2

Use the diagram to find each angle measure.

14. If $m\angle 2 = 126°$, find $m\angle 3$.
15. Find $m\angle 4$.

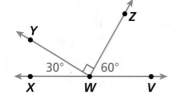

See Example 3

16. **Sewing** The diagram shows the intersection of three seams on a quilt. Based on the diagram, what should be the measure of $\angle ABC$?

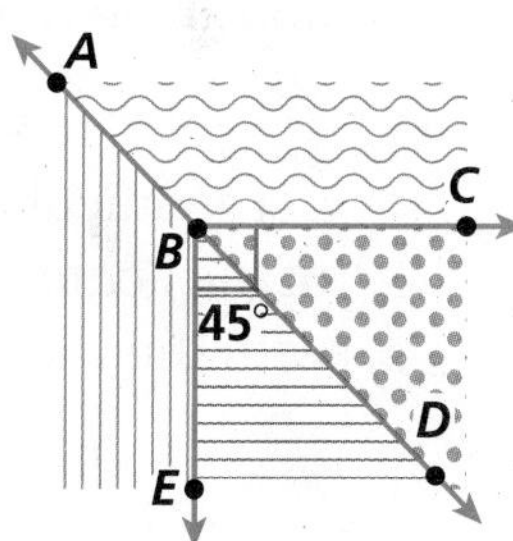

PRACTICE AND PROBLEM SOLVING

Extra Practice

See Extra Practice for more exercises.

Use the figure for Exercises 17–23. Write *true* or *false*. If a statement is false, rewrite it so it is true.

17. $\angle QUR$ is an obtuse angle.
18. $\angle 4$ and $\angle 2$ are supplementary.
19. $\angle 1$ and $\angle 6$ are supplementary.
20. $\angle 3$ and $\angle 1$ are complementary.
21. If $m\angle 1 = 35°$, then $m\angle 6 = 40°$.
22. If $m\angle SUN = 150°$, then $m\angle SUR = 150°$.
23. If $m\angle 1 = x°$, then $m\angle PUQ = 180° - x°$.

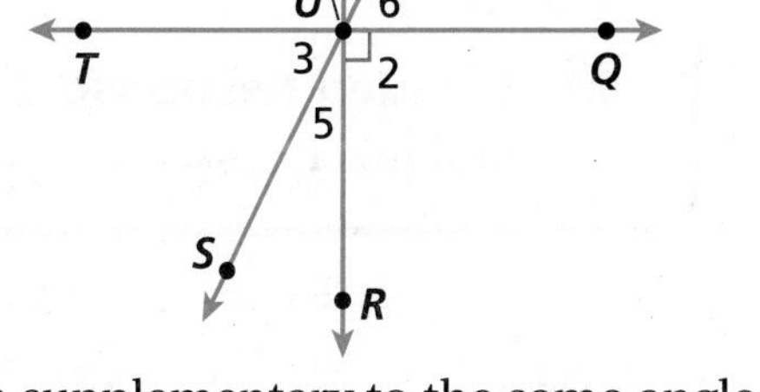

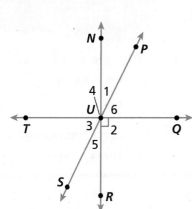

24. **Make a Conjecture** $\angle A$ and $\angle B$ are both supplementary to the same angle. Describe the relationship between $\angle A$ and $\angle B$. Explain your reasoning.
25. **Critical Thinking** The measures of two complementary angles have a ratio of 1:2. What is the measure of each angle?

Physical Science LINK

The archerfish can spit a stream of water up to 3 meters in the air to knock its prey into the water. This job is made more difficult by *refraction,* the bending of light waves as they pass from one substance to another. When you look at an object through water, the light between you and the object is refracted. Refraction makes the object appear to be in a different location. Despite refraction, the archerfish still catches its prey.

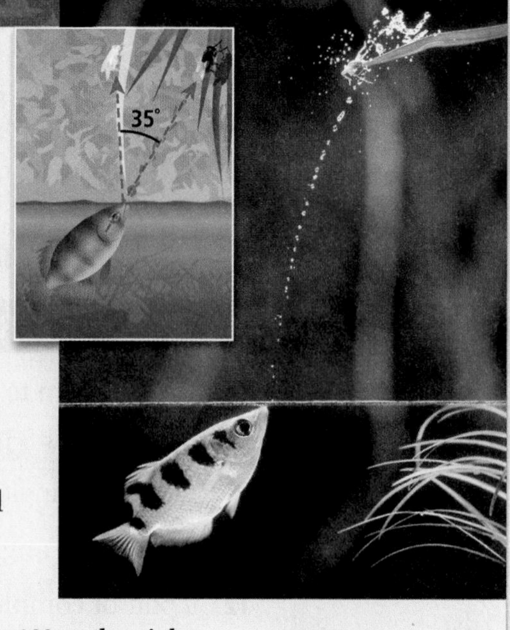

26. Suppose that the measure of the angle between the bug's actual location and the bug's apparent location is 35°.

a. Refer to the diagram. Along the fish's line of vision, what is the measure of the angle between the fish and the bug's apparent location?

b. What is the relationship of the angles in the diagram?

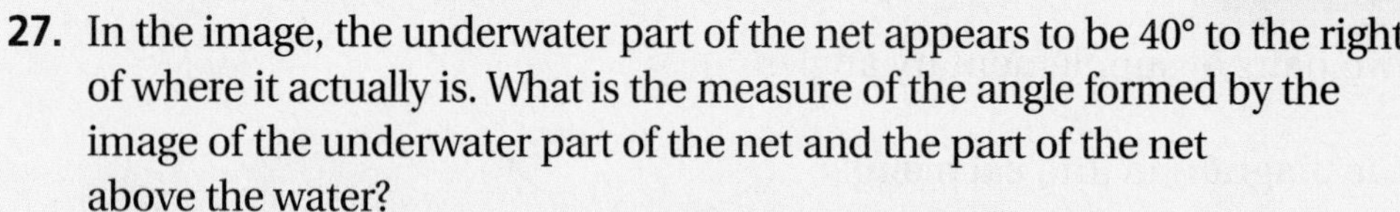

27. In the image, the underwater part of the net appears to be 40° to the right of where it actually is. What is the measure of the angle formed by the image of the underwater part of the net and the part of the net above the water?

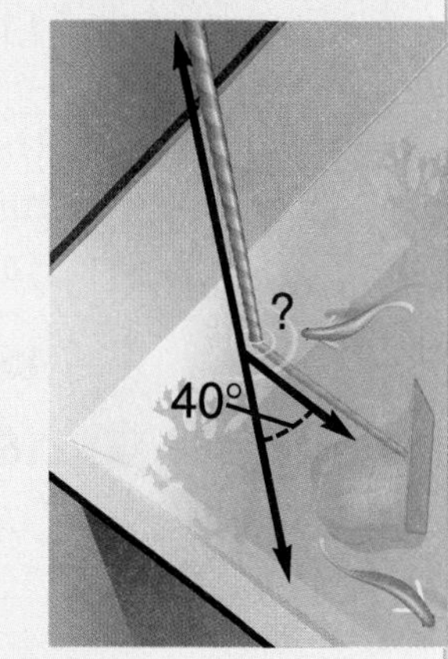

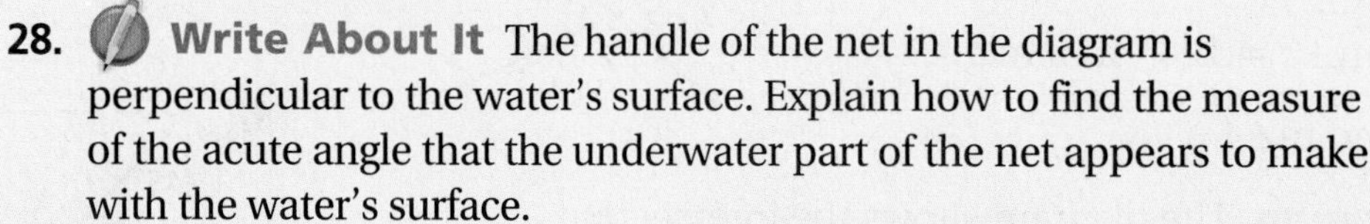

28. **Write About It** The handle of the net in the diagram is perpendicular to the water's surface. Explain how to find the measure of the acute angle that the underwater part of the net appears to make with the water's surface.

29. **Challenge** $\angle 1$ is supplementary to $\angle 2$, and $\angle 2$ is complementary to $\angle 3$. Classify each angle as acute, right, or obtuse, and explain your reasoning.

Test Prep

30. **Multiple Choice** When two angles are complementary, what is the sum of their measures?

Ⓐ 90° Ⓑ 180° Ⓒ 270° Ⓓ 360°

31. **Gridded Response** $\angle 1$ and $\angle 3$ are supplementary angles. If $m\angle 1 = 63°$, find $m\angle 3$.

Bisect Figures

Use with Angle Relationships

When you *bisect* a figure, you divide it into two congruent parts.

Use appropriate tools strategically.

Activity

1 Follow the steps below to bisect a segment.

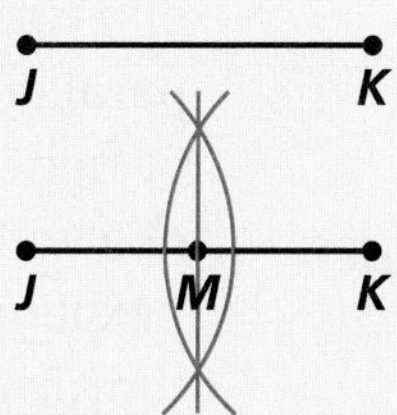

a. Draw $\overline{JK}$ on your paper. Place your compass point on J and draw an arc. Without changing your compass opening, place your compass point on K and draw an arc.

b. Connect the intersections of the arcs with a line. Measure $\overline{JM}$ and $\overline{KM}$. What do you notice?

The bisector of $\overline{JK}$ is a *perpendicular bisector* because it forms right angles with $\overline{JK}$.

2 Follow the steps below to bisect an angle.

a. Draw acute $\angle H$ on your paper.

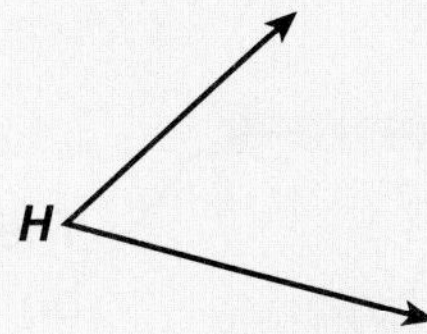

b. Place your compass point on H and draw an arc through both sides of the angle.

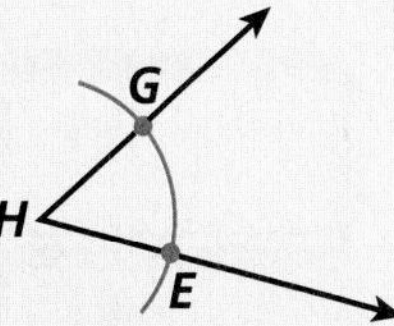

c. Without changing your compass opening, draw intersecting arcs from G and E. Label the intersection D.

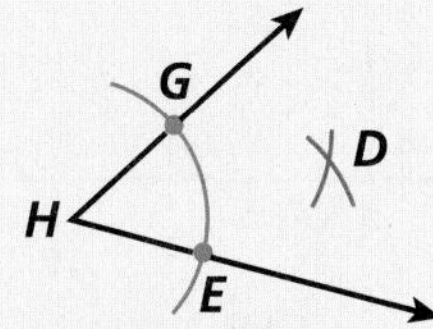

d. Draw $\overrightarrow{HD}$. Measure $\angle GHD$ and $\angle DHE$. What do you notice?

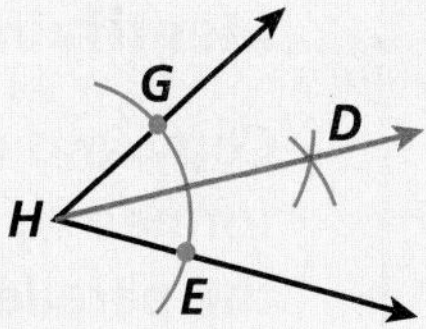

Think and Discuss

1. Explain how to use a compass and a straightedge to divide a segment into four congruent segments. Prove that the segments are congruent.

Try This

Draw each figure, and then use a compass and a straightedge to bisect it. Verify by measuring.

1. a 2-in. segment
2. a 6-in. segment
3. a 48° angle
4. a 110° angle

5-2 Parallel and Perpendicular Lines

COMMON CORE

CC.8.G.5: Use informal arguments to establish facts about the angle sum and exterior angle of triangles, about the angles created when parallel lines are cut by a transversal, and the angle-angle criterion for similarity of triangles.

Vocabulary

parallel lines

perpendicular lines

transversal

Parallel lines are lines in a plane that never meet, such as the lines that mark the lanes in a sprinting race.

The top and bottom sides of a window are also parallel. However, the left or right side and the bottom of a window are like **perpendicular lines**; that is, they intersect at 90° angles.

A **transversal** is a line that intersects two or more lines that lie in the same plane. Transversals to parallel lines form angles with special properties.

The sides of the windows are transversals to the top and bottom.
The top and bottom of the windows are parallel.

EXAMPLE 1 Identifying Congruent Angles Formed by a Transversal

Caution!

You cannot tell if angles are congruent by measuring because measurement is not exact.

Copy and measure the angles formed by the transversal and the parallel lines. Which angles seem to be congruent?

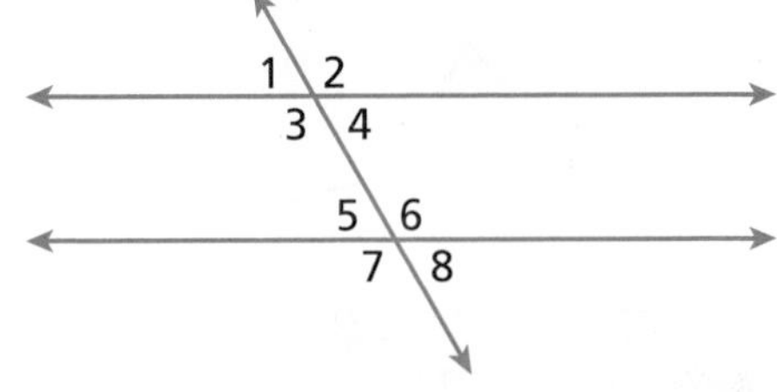

$\angle 1$, $\angle 4$, $\angle 5$, and $\angle 8$ all measure 60°.
$\angle 2$, $\angle 3$, $\angle 6$, and $\angle 7$ all measure 120°.

Angles marked in blue appear congruent to each other, and angles marked in red appear congruent to each other.

$\angle 1 \cong \angle 4 \cong \angle 5 \cong \angle 8$

$\angle 2 \cong \angle 3 \cong \angle 6 \cong \angle 7$

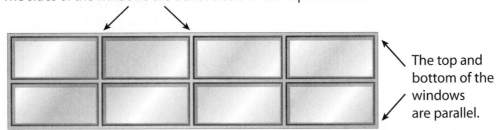

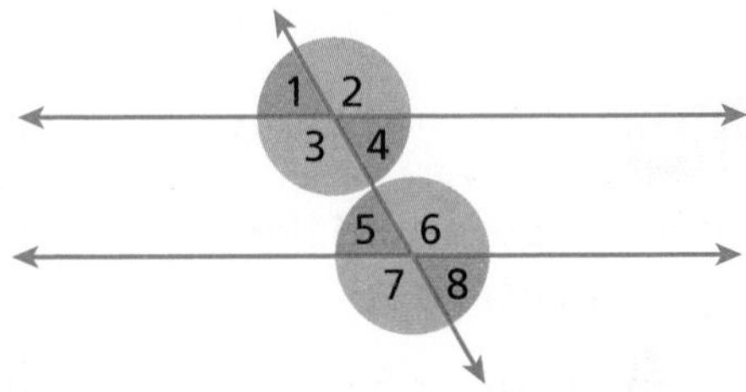

kolvenbach/Alamy

Some pairs of the eight angles formed by two parallel lines and a transversal have special names.

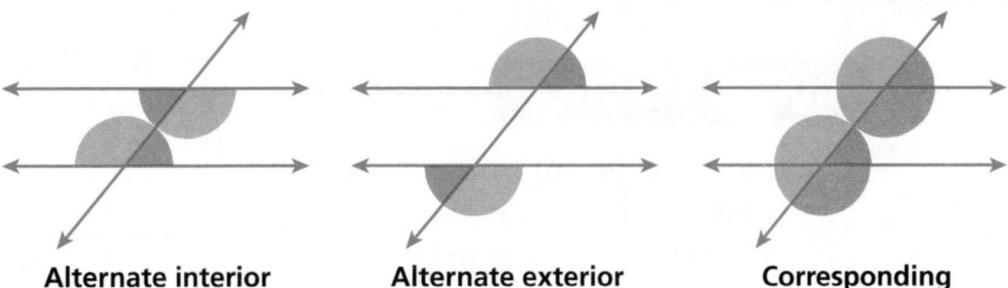

PROPERTIES OF TRANSVERSALS TO PARALLEL LINES

If two parallel lines are intersected by a transversal,

- corresponding angles are congruent,
- alternate interior angles are congruent,
- and alternate exterior angles are congruent.

If the transversal is perpendicular to the parallel lines, all of the angles formed are congruent 90° angles.

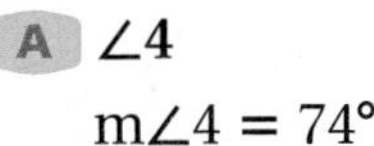

Finding Measures of Angles Formed by Transversals

In the figure, line *a* || line *b*. Find the measure of each angle. Justify your answer.

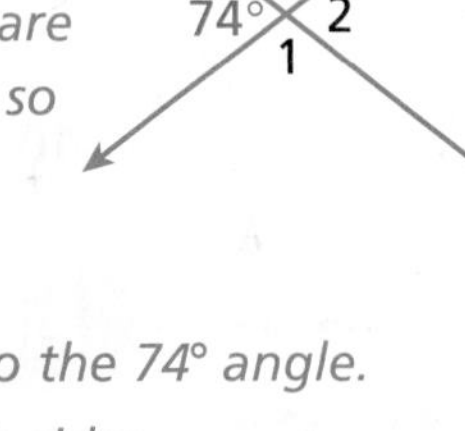

Writing Math

The symbol for parallel is ||. The symbol for perpendicular is ⊥.

A $\angle 4$

$m\angle 4 = 74°$ *The 74° angle and ∠4 are corresponding angles, so they are congruent.*

B $\angle 3$

$m\angle 3 + 74° = 180°$ *∠3 is supplementary to the 74° angle.*

$\quad - 74° \quad - 74°$ *Subtract 74° from both sides.*

$m\angle 3 = 106°$ *Simplify.*

C $\angle 5$

$m\angle 5 = 106°$ *∠3 and ∠5 are alternate interior angles, so they are congruent.*

MATHEMATICAL PRACTICES

Think and Discuss

1. **Tell** how many different angles would be formed by a transversal intersecting three parallel lines. How many different angle measures would there be?
2. **Explain** how a transversal could intersect two other lines so that corresponding angles are *not* congruent.

5-2 Exercises

Learn It Online
Homework Help Online
Exercises 1–10, 11, 15, 17

GUIDED PRACTICE

See Example 1

1. Measure the angles formed by the transversal and the parallel lines. Which angles seem to be congruent?

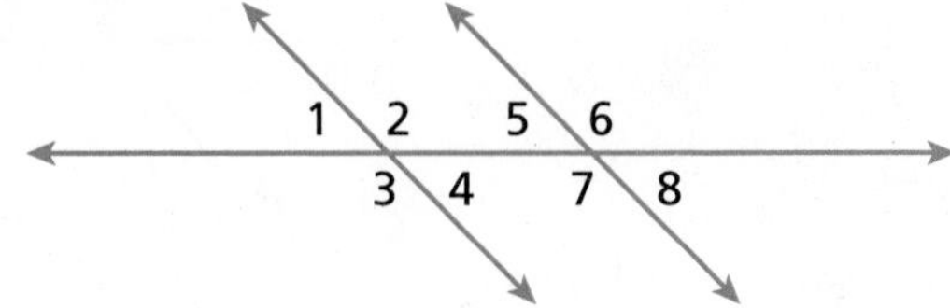

See Example 2

In the figure, line $m \parallel$ line n. Find the measure of each angle. Justify your answer.

2. $\angle 1$
3. $\angle 4$
4. $\angle 6$
5. $\angle 7$

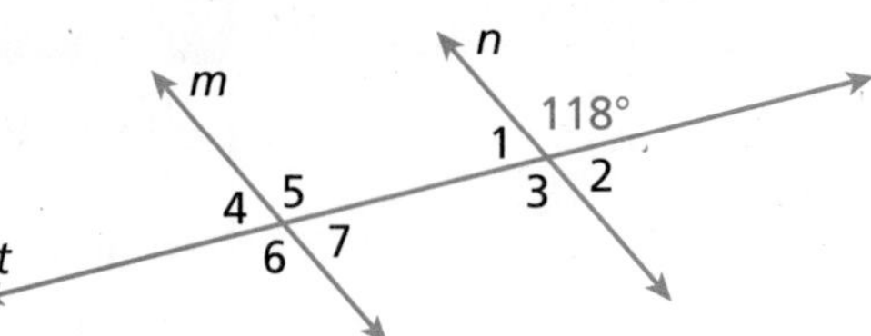

INDEPENDENT PRACTICE

See Example 1

6. Measure the angles formed by the transversal and the parallel lines. Which angles seem to be congruent?

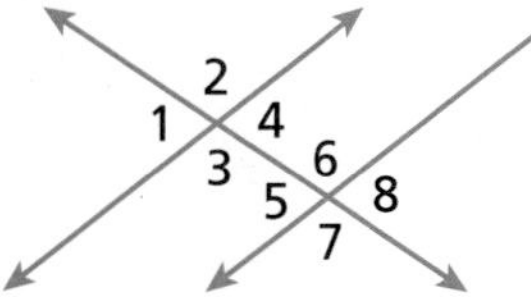

See Example 2

In the figure, line $p \parallel$ line q. Find the measure of each angle. Justify your answer.

7. $\angle 1$
8. $\angle 4$
9. $\angle 6$
10. $\angle 7$

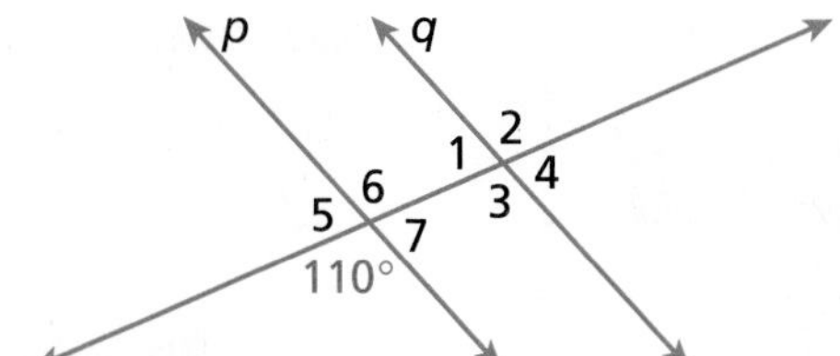

PRACTICE AND PROBLEM SOLVING

Extra Practice
See Extra Practice for more exercises.

In the figure, line $t \parallel$ line s.

11. Name all angles congruent to $\angle 1$.
12. Name all angles congruent to $\angle 2$.
13. Name three pairs of supplementary angles.
14. Which line is the transversal?
15. If m$\angle 4$ is 51°, what is m$\angle 2$?
16. If m$\angle 7$ is 116°, what is m$\angle 3$?
17. If m$\angle 5$ is 91°, what is m$\angle 2$?
18. **Art** The picture shows a painting by Theo van Doesburg titled *Counter-Composition XIII*. Line b is parallel to line a and perpendicular to line c. Find the measures of $\angle 1$, $\angle 2$, and $\angle 3$.

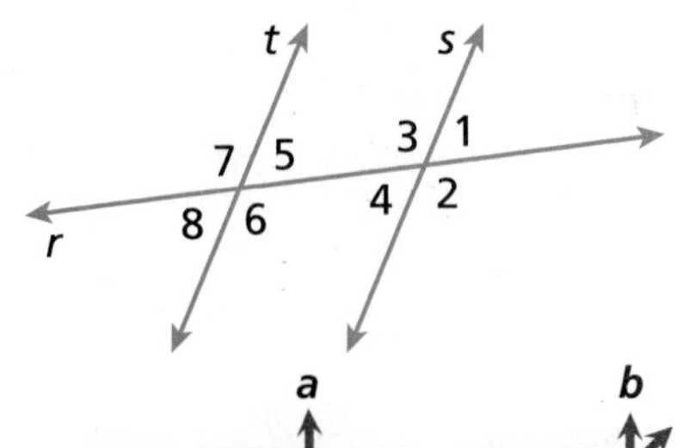

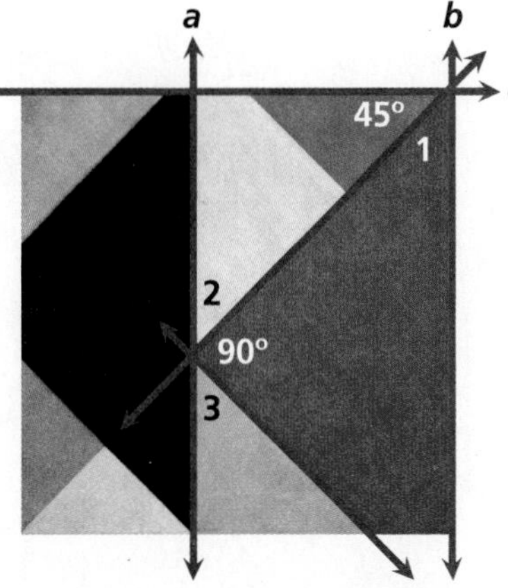

akg-images

LINK **Physical Science**

This hat from the 1937 British Industries Fair is equipped with a pair of parallel mirrors to enable the wearer to see above crowds.

Draw a diagram to illustrate each of the following.

19. line $m \parallel$ line n and transversal h with congruent angles $\angle 1$ and $\angle 3$

20. line $h \parallel$ line j and transversal k with eight congruent angles

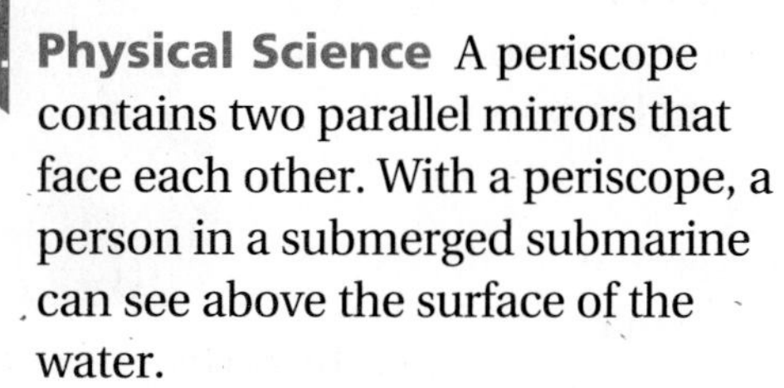

21. Make a Conjecture Two parallel lines are cut by a transversal. Can you determine the measures of all the angles formed if given only one angle measure? Explain.

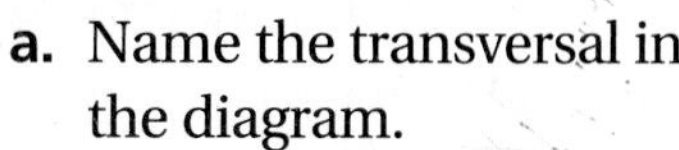

22. Physical Science A periscope contains two parallel mirrors that face each other. With a periscope, a person in a submerged submarine can see above the surface of the water.

a. Name the transversal in the diagram.

b. If $m\angle 1 = 45°$, find $m\angle 2$, $m\angle 3$, and $m\angle 4$.

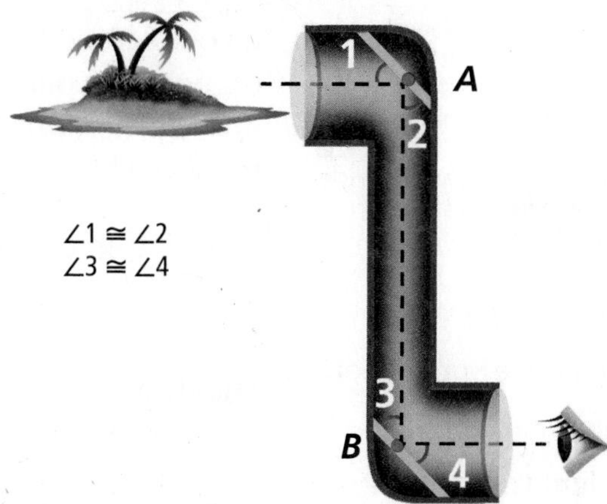

23. Write About It Choose an example of abstract art or architecture with parallel lines. Explain how parallel lines, transversals, or perpendicular lines are used in the composition.

24. Challenge In the figure, $\angle 1$, $\angle 4$, $\angle 6$, and $\angle 7$ are all congruent, and $\angle 2$, $\angle 3$, $\angle 5$, and $\angle 8$ are all congruent. Does this mean that line s is parallel to line t? Explain.

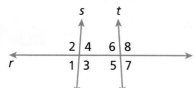

Test Prep

25. Multiple Choice Two parallel lines are intersected by a transversal. The measures of two corresponding angles that are formed are each 54°. What are the measures of each of the angles supplementary to the corresponding angles?

Ⓐ 36° Ⓑ 72° Ⓒ 108° Ⓓ 126°

26. Extended Response Suppose a transversal intersects two parallel lines. One angle that is formed is a right angle. What are the measures of the remaining angles? What is the relationship between the transversal and the parallel lines?

5-3 Triangles

COMMON CORE

CC.8.G.5: Use informal arguments to establish facts about the angle sum and exterior angle of triangles, about the angles created when parallel lines are cut by a transversal, and the angle-angle criterion for similarity of triangles.

Vocabulary

Triangle Sum Theorem

acute triangle

right triangle

obtuse triangle

equilateral triangle

isosceles triangle

scalene triangle

Triangle Inequality Theorem

If you tear off two corners of a triangle and place them next to the third corner, the three angles seem to form a straight angle.

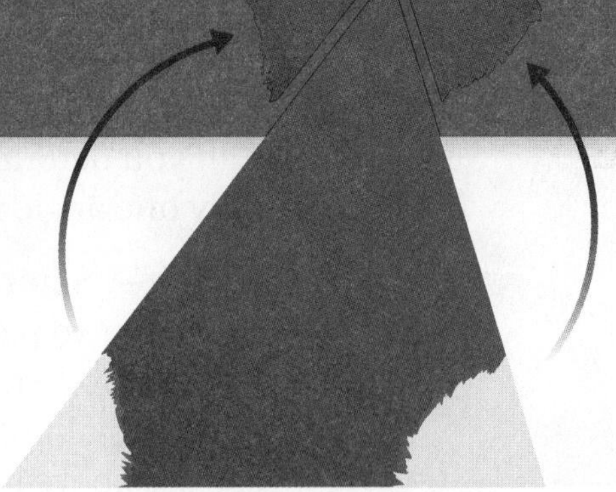

This torn triangle demonstrates an important geometry theorem called the Triangle Sum Theorem.

Draw a triangle and extend one side. Then draw a line parallel to the extended side, as shown.

The three angles in the triangle can be arranged to form a straight angle, or 180°.

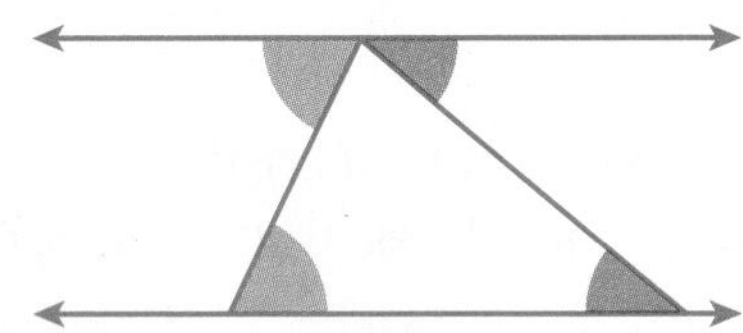

The sides of the triangle are transversals to the parallel lines. The alternate interior angles are congruent.

TRIANGLE SUM THEOREM		
Words	**Numbers**	**Algebra**
The angle measures of a triangle add to 180°.	58°, 43°, 79° $43° + 58° + 79° = 180°$	$r°$, $t°$, $s°$ $r° + s° + t° = 180°$

Interactivities Online ▶

An **acute triangle** has 3 acute angles. A **right triangle** has 1 right angle. An **obtuse triangle** has 1 obtuse angle.

EXAMPLE  1 Finding Angles in Acute, Right, or Obtuse Triangles

A **Find $x°$ in the acute triangle.**

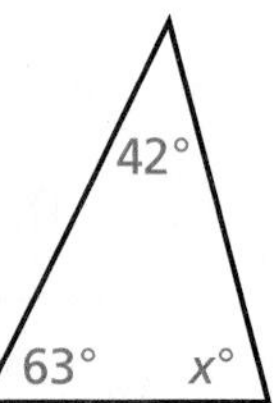

$$63° + 42° + x° = 180° \quad \textit{Triangle Sum Theorem}$$
$$105° + x° = 180°$$
$$\underline{-105°} \quad \underline{-105°} \quad \textit{Subtract 105° from both sides.}$$
$$x° = 75°$$

B **Find $y°$ in the right triangle.**

$$37° + 90° + y° = 180° \quad \textit{Triangle Sum Theorem}$$
$$127° + y° = 180°$$
$$\underline{-127°} \quad \underline{-127°} \quad \textit{Subtract 127° from both sides.}$$
$$y° = 53°$$

An **equilateral triangle** has 3 congruent sides and 3 congruent angles. An **isosceles triangle** has at least 2 congruent sides and 2 congruent angles. A **scalene triangle** has no congruent sides and no congruent angles.

EXAMPLE 2 Finding Angles in Equilateral, Isosceles, or Scalene Triangles

A **Find the angle measures in the equilateral triangle.**

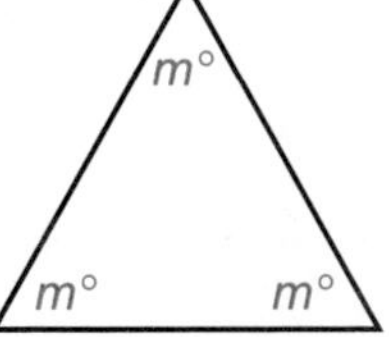

$3m° = 180°$ *Triangle Sum Theorem*

$\frac{3m°}{3} = \frac{180°}{3}$ *Divide both sides by 3.*

$m° = 60°$

All three angles measure 60°.

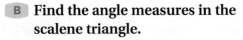

B **Find the angle measures in the scalene triangle.**

$2p° + 3p° + 4p° = 180°$

$9p° = 180°$ *Simplify.*

$\frac{9p°}{9} = \frac{180°}{9}$ *Divide both sides by 9.*

$p° = 20°$

The angle labeled $2p°$ measures $2(20°) = 40°$, the angle labeled $3p°$ measures $3(20°) = 60°$, and the angle labeled $4p°$ measures $4(20°) = 80°$.

EXAMPLE 3 Finding Angles in a Triangle That Meets Given Conditions

The second angle in a triangle is twice as large as the first. The third angle is half as large as the second. Find the angle measures and draw a possible figure.

Let $x°$ = first angle measure. Then $2x°$ = second angle measure, and $\frac{1}{2}(2x)° = x°$ = third angle measure.

$x° + 2x° + x° = 180°$ *Triangle Sum Theorem*

$\frac{4x°}{4} = \frac{180°}{4}$ *Simplify, then divide both sides by 4.*

$x° = 45°$

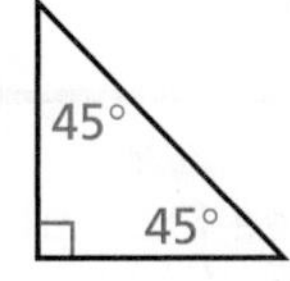

Two angles measure 45° and one angle measures 90°. The triangle has two congruent angles. The triangle is an isosceles right triangle.

The **Triangle Inequality Theorem** states that the sum of the lengths of any two sides of a triangle is greater than the length of the third side.

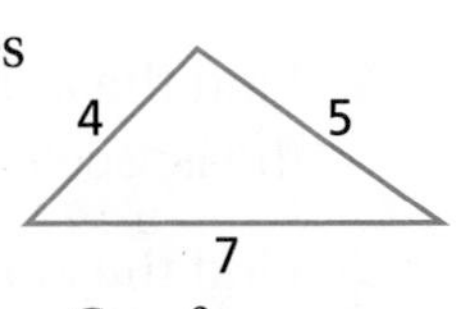

Can form a triangle

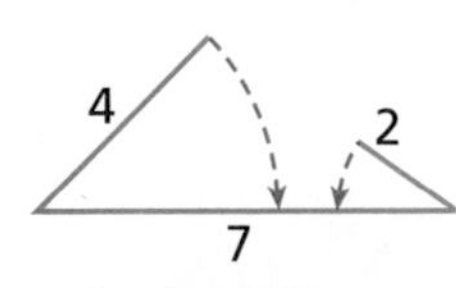

Cannot form a triangle

EXAMPLE 4 Using the Triangle Inequality Theorem

Tell whether a triangle can have sides with the given lengths. Explain.

A **9 cm, 4 cm, 11 cm**

Find the sum of the lengths of each pair of sides and compare it to the third side.

$9 + 4 \overset{?}{>} 11$ $\quad$ $4 + 11 \overset{?}{>} 9$ $\quad$ $9 + 11 \overset{?}{>} 4$

$13 > 11$ ✓ $\quad$ $15 > 9$ ✓ $\quad$ $20 > 4$ ✓

A triangle can have these side lengths. The sum of the lengths of any two sides is greater than the length of the third side.

B **6 ft, 3 ft, 10 ft**

$6 + 3 \overset{?}{>} 10$

$9 \not> 10$ ✗

A triangle cannot have these side lengths. The sum of the lengths of two sides is not greater than the length of the third side.

Think and Discuss

1. **Explain** whether a right triangle can be equilateral. Can it be isosceles? scalene?
2. **Explain** whether a triangle can have 2 right angles. Can it have 2 obtuse angles?

5-3 Exercises

GUIDED PRACTICE

See Example 1

1. Find $q°$ in the acute triangle.
2. Find $r°$ in the right triangle.

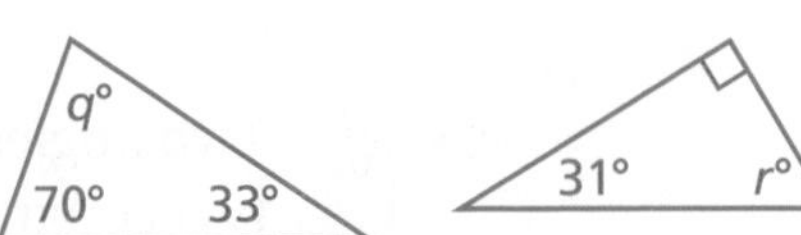

See Example 2

3. Find the angle measures in the equilateral triangle.
4. Find the angle measures in the isosceles triangle.
5. Find the angle measures in the scalene triangle.

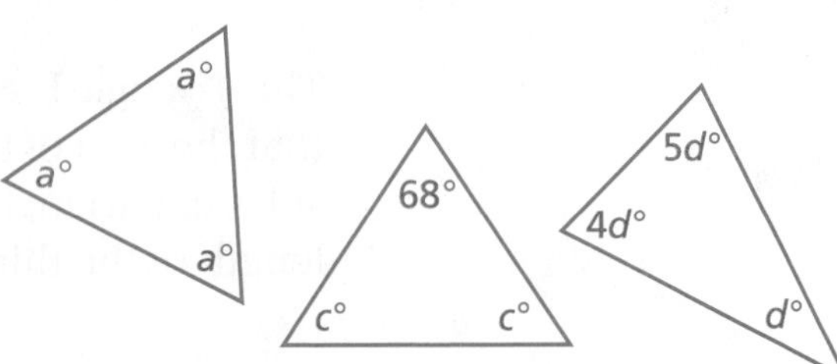

See Example  6. The second angle in a triangle is half as large as the first. The third angle is three times as large as the second. Find the angle measures and draw a possible figure.

See Example 4 **Tell whether a triangle can have sides with the given lengths. Explain.**

7. 4 ft, 7 ft, 14 ft
8. 9 m, 6 m, 10 m
9. 10 in., 15 in., 20 in.

INDEPENDENT PRACTICE

See Example 1

10. Find $s°$ in the right triangle.
11. Find $t°$ in the obtuse triangle.

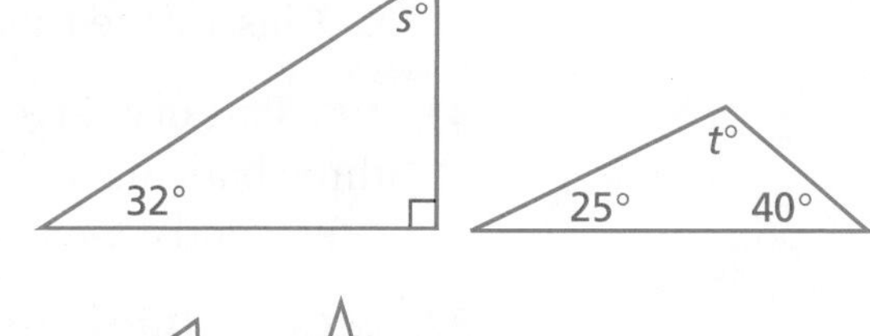

See Example 2

12. Find the angle measures in the equilateral triangle.
13. Find the angle measures in the isosceles triangle.
14. Find the angle measures in the scalene triangle.

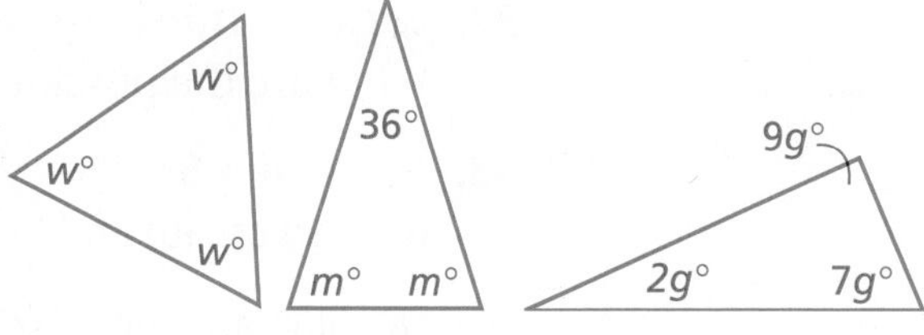

See Example  15. The second angle in a triangle is five times as large as the first. The third angle is two-thirds as large as the first. Find the angle measures and draw a possible figure.

See Example 4 **Tell whether a triangle can have sides with the given lengths. Explain.**

16. 3 yd, 3 yd, 3 yd
17. 1 cm, 4 cm, 5 cm
18. 7 mm, 10 mm, 19 mm

PRACTICE AND PROBLEM SOLVING

Extra Practice

See Extra Practice for more exercises.

Find the value of each variable.

19.

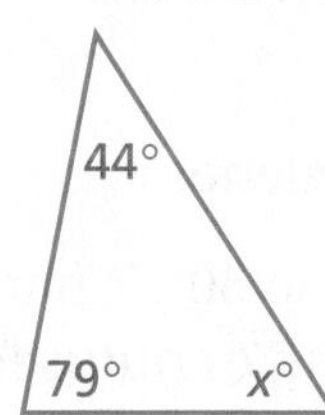

20.

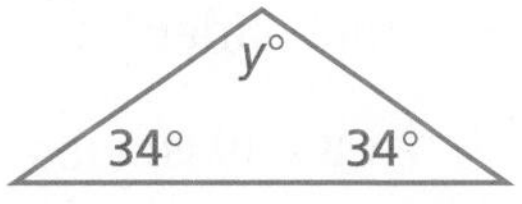

21.

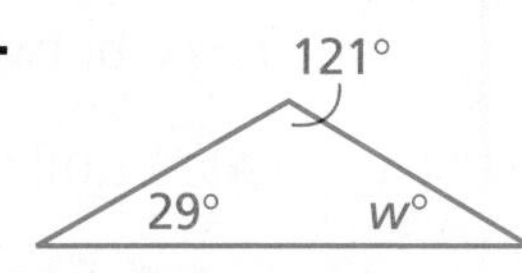

Sketch a triangle to fit each description. If no triangle can be drawn, write *not possible.*

22. acute scalene
23. obtuse equilateral
24. right scalene
25. right equilateral
26. obtuse scalene
27. acute isosceles

28. **Make a Conjecture** Can an acute isosceles triangle have two angles that measure 40°? Explain.

29. **Critical Thinking** Triangle *LMN* is an obtuse triangle and $m\angle L = 25°$. $\angle M$ is the obtuse angle, and its measure in degrees is a whole number. What is the largest $m\angle N$ can be to the nearest whole degree?

30. **Social Studies** American Samoa is a territory of the United States made up of a group of islands in the Pacific Ocean, about halfway between Hawaii and New Zealand. The flag of American Samoa is shown.

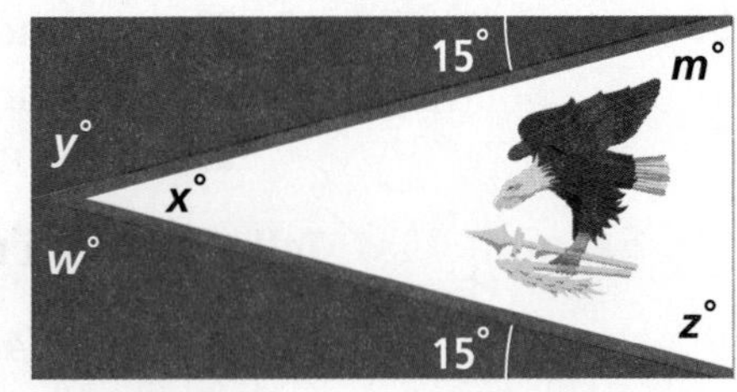

a. Find the measure of each angle in the blue triangles.

b. Use your answers to part **a** to find the angle measures in the white triangle.

c. Classify the triangles in the flag by their sides and angles.

31. **Art** Part of a large metal sculpture will be a triangle formed by welding three bars together. The artist has four bars that measure 10 feet, 6 feet, 4 feet, and 3 feet. Which three of the bars could be used to form a triangle?

32. **Critical Thinking** Two sides of a triangle measure 9 units and 12 units. What are the possible whole-number values of the length of the third side?

33. **Choose a Strategy** Which of the following sets of angle measures can be used to create an isosceles triangle?

Ⓐ 45°, 45°, 95° Ⓑ 49°, 51°, 80° Ⓒ 27°, 27°, 126° Ⓓ 35°, 55°, 100°

34. **Write About It** Explain how to cut a square or an equilateral triangle in half to form two identical triangles. What are the angle measures in the resulting triangles in each case?

35. **Challenge** Construct an equilateral triangle using only a straightedge and a compass. Describe the steps you used. (*Hint*: Review Hands-On Lab *Bisect Figures.*)

Test Prep

36. **Multiple Choice** Which type of triangle can be constructed with a 50° angle between two 8-inch sides?

Ⓐ Equilateral Ⓑ Isosceles Ⓒ Scalene Ⓓ Obtuse

37. **Short Response** Two angles of a triangle are 45° and 30°. What is the measure of the third angle? Is the triangle acute, right, or obtuse?

Technology LAB

Exterior Angles of a Polygon

Use with Triangles

Use appropriate tools strategically.

CC.8.G.5: Use informal arguments to establish facts about the angle sum and exterior angle of triangles . . .

The *exterior angles* of a polygon are formed by extending the polygon's sides. Every exterior angle is supplementary to the angle next to it inside the polygon.

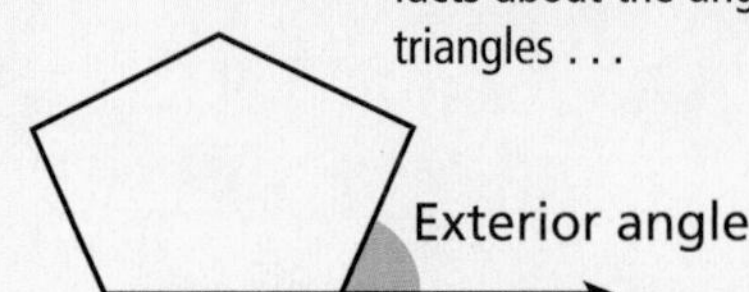

Activity

1 Follow the steps to find the sum of the exterior angle measures for a polygon.

a. Use geometry software to make a pentagon. Label the vertices *A* through *E*.

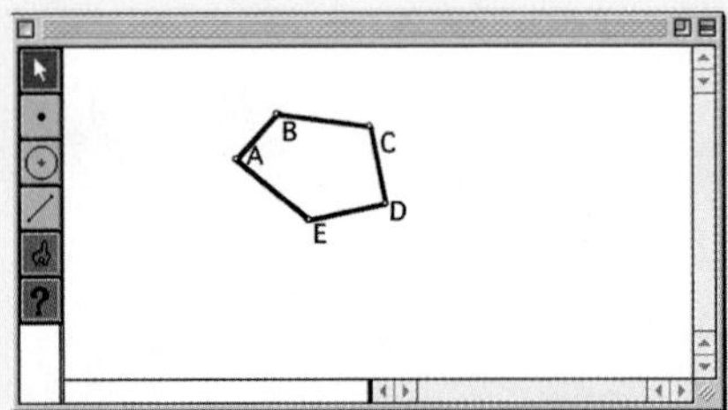

b. Use the **LINE-RAY** tool to extend the sides of the pentagon. Add points *F* through *J* as shown.

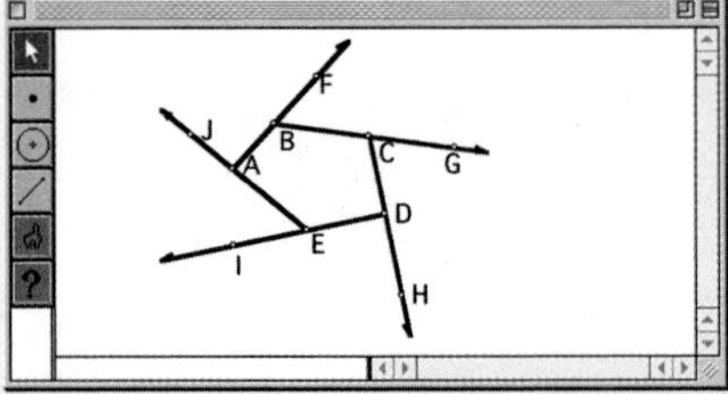

c. Use the **ANGLE MEASURE** tool to measure each exterior angle and the **CALCULATOR** tool to add the measures. Notice the sum.

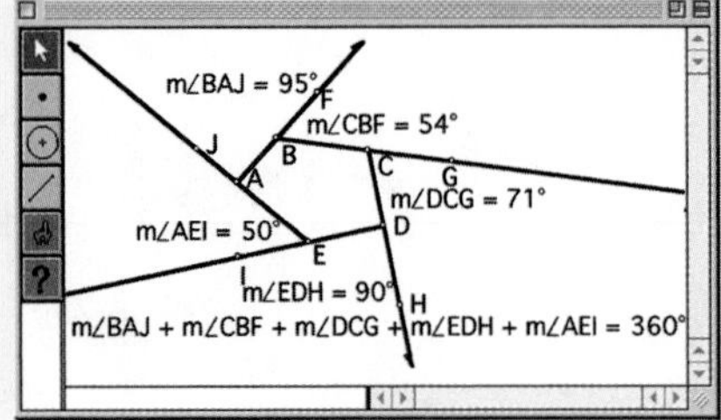

d. Drag vertices *A* through *E* and watch the sum. Notice that the sum of the angle measures is *always* 360°.

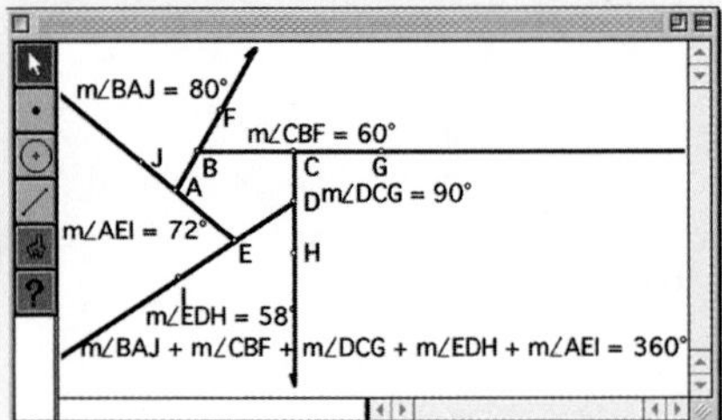

Think and Discuss

1. An exterior angle of a triangle measures 105°. Explain how to find the measure of the adjacent interior angle of the triangle.

Try This

1. Use geometry software to draw any polygon. Find the sum of its exterior angle measures. Drag its vertices to check that the sum is always the same.

5-4 Coordinate Geometry

In computer graphics, a coordinate system is used to create images, from simple geometric figures to realistic figures used in movies.

Properties of the coordinate plane can be used to find information about figures in the plane, such as whether opposite sides are congruent.

Vocabulary
midpoint

EXAMPLE 1 Using Coordinates to Classify Polygons

Graph the polygons with the given vertices. Give the most specific name for each polygon.

A $A(-1, 2), B(-1, -2), C(3, -2)$

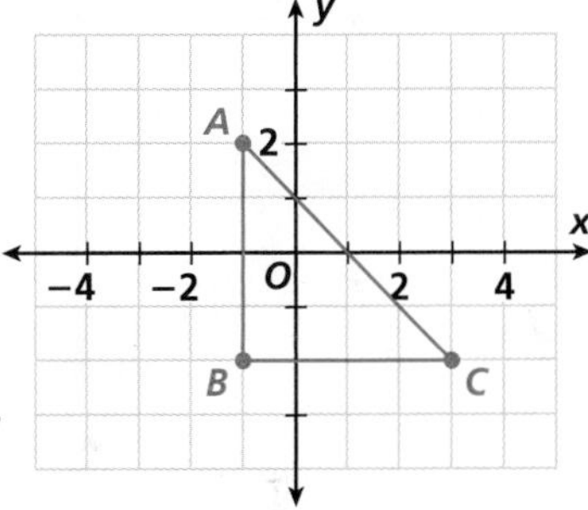

Step 1: Classify the triangle by its angles.

$\angle B$ is a right angle, so $\triangle ABC$ is a right triangle.

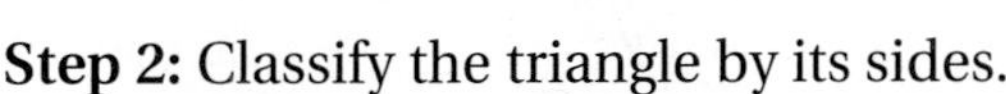

Step 2: Classify the triangle by its sides.

Find the length of each side.

$AB = |-2 - 2| = |-4| = 4$ *Use the y-coordinates.*

$BC = |3 - (-1)| = |4| = 4$ *Use the x-coordinates.*

$AC = \sqrt{[3 - (-1)]^2 + (-2 - 2)^2}$ *Use the Distance Formula.*

$= \sqrt{32} \approx 5.7$

The triangle has two congruent sides, so it is isosceles.

$\triangle ABC$ is a right isosceles triangle.

B $L(-1, 3), M(2, 1), N(2, -3), P(-1, -3)$

Examine the sides of the quadrilateral.

$\overline{LP}$ and $\overline{MN}$ are parallel.

Both sides are vertical.

$\overline{LM}$ and $\overline{PN}$ are *not* parallel.

One side is horizontal, and the other is not.

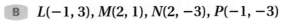

The quadrilateral is a trapezoid because it has only one pair of parallel sides.

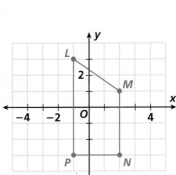

Recall that if a quadrilateral has two pairs of parallel sides, then it is a parallelogram. You can also classify a quadrilateral as a parallelogram by showing that both pairs of opposite sides are congruent. You can use these and other properties of geometric figures to determine the coordinates of a missing vertex.

EXAMPLE 2 Finding the Coordinates of a Missing Vertex

Find the coordinates of each missing vertex.

> **Helpful Hint**
>
> You could also count 4 units down from B to find possible coordinates of A. The other possible location of A is (2, −3). So there are two correct answers!

A **$\triangle ABC$ has a right angle at B and $AB = 4$. Find one set of possible coordinates for A.**

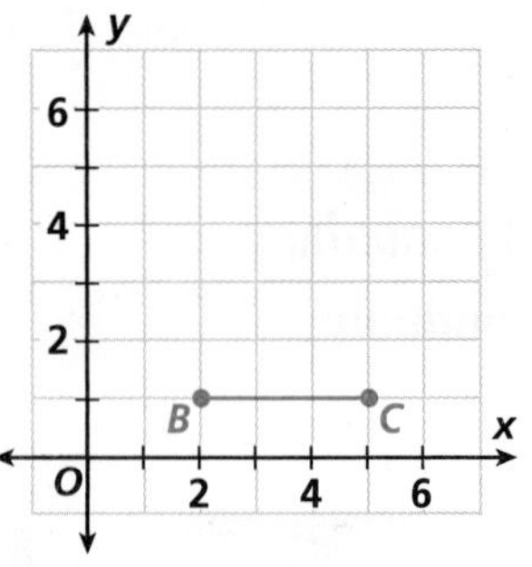

Since $\overline{BC}$ is horizontal, $\overline{AB}$ must be vertical for the triangle to have a right angle at B.

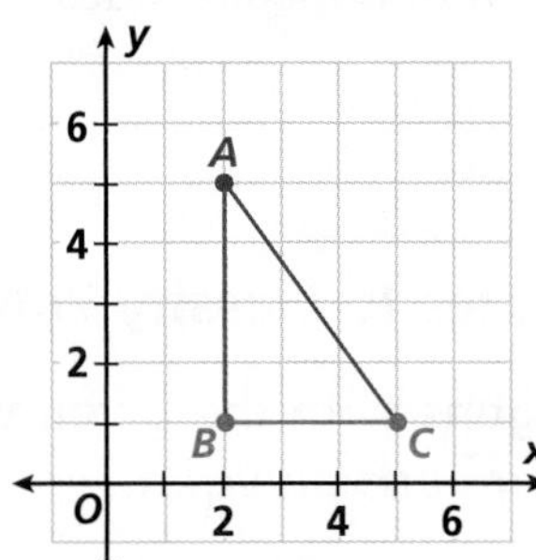

Counting 4 units up from B places A at (2, 5). *1 + 4 = 5, so the y-coordinate of A is 5.*

B **Quadrilateral $LMNP$ is a parallelogram. Find the coordinates of M.**

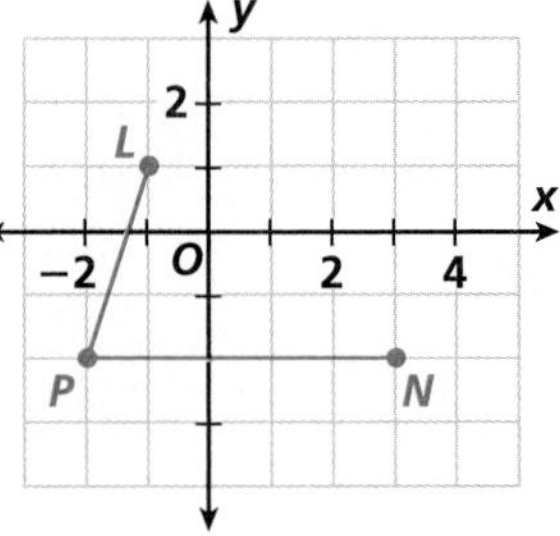

$\overline{LM}$ is horizontal. *$\overline{LM}$ and $\overline{PN}$ must be parallel.*

$LM = 5$ *$\overline{LM}$ and $\overline{PN}$ must be congruent, and $PN = 5$.*

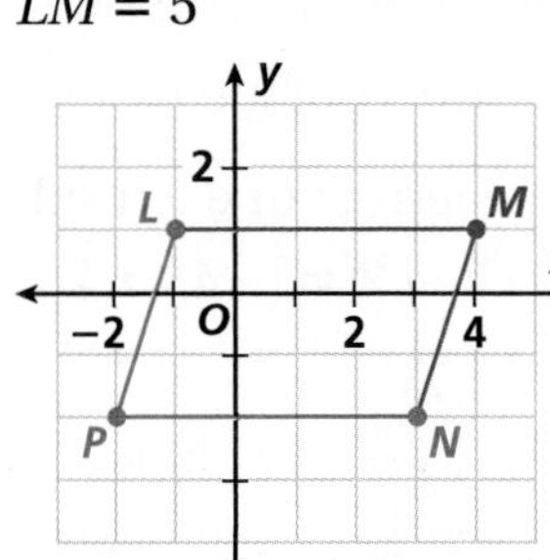

Counting 5 units right from L places M at (4, 1). *−1 + 5 = 4, so the x-coordinate of M is 4.*

The **midpoint** of a segment is the point that divides the segment into two congruent segments.

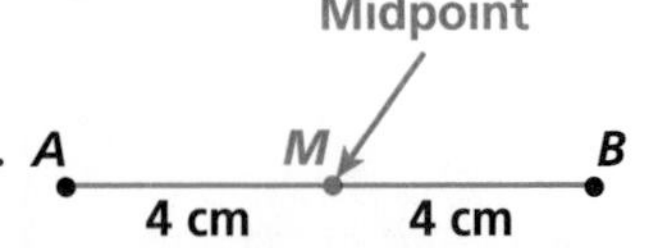

MIDPOINT FORMULA

Words	Numbers	Algebra
The coordinates of the midpoint of a segment can be found by averaging the x-coordinates and the y-coordinates of the segment's endpoints.	Endpoints: (1, 3) and (3, 5) Midpoint: $\left(\frac{1+3}{2}, \frac{3+5}{2}\right) = (2, 4)$	Endpoints: (x_1, y_1) and (x_2, y_2) Midpoint: $\left(\frac{x_1+x_2}{2}, \frac{y_1+y_2}{2}\right)$

EXAMPLE 3 **Finding the Coordinates of a Midpoint**

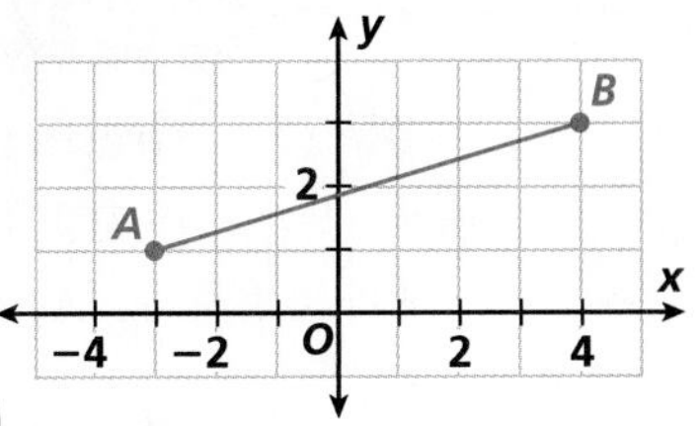

Find the coordinates of the midpoint of $\overline{AB}$.

$\left(\frac{x_1 + x_2}{2}, \frac{y_1 + y_2}{2}\right)$ *Use the formula.*

$\left(\frac{-3 + 4}{2}, \frac{1 + 3}{2}\right)$ *The endpoints are A(−3, 1) and B(4, 3).*

$\left(\frac{1}{2}, \frac{4}{2}\right) = \left(\frac{1}{2}, 2\right)$ *Simplify.*

The coordinates of the midpoint M are $\left(\frac{1}{2}, 2\right)$.

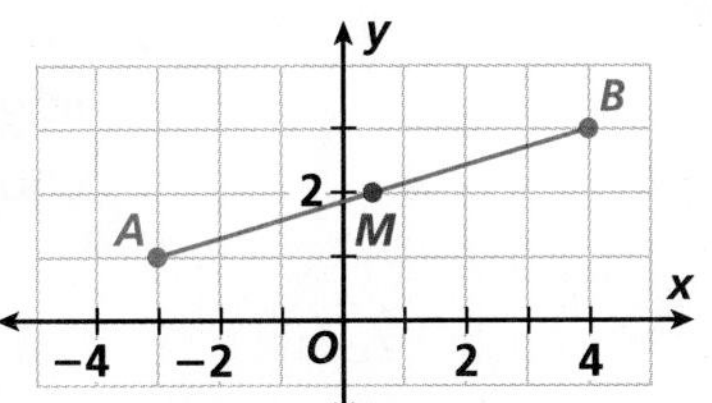

Think and Discuss

1. **Explain** how you can determine whether a triangle on the coordinate plane is isosceles.

5-4 Exercises

GUIDED PRACTICE

See Example 1 **Graph the polygons with the given vertices. Give the most specific name for each polygon.**

1. $A(-1, -2)$, $B(0, 3)$, $C(1, -2)$
2. $D(-3, -2)$, $E(-3, 3)$, $F(2, 3)$, $G(2, -2)$

See Example 2 **Find the coordinates of each missing vertex.**

3. $\triangle RST$ has a right angle at S and $ST = 3$. Find a set of possible coordinates for T.

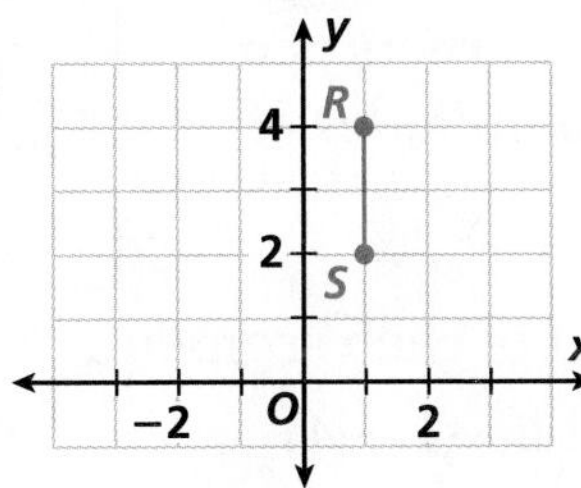

4. Quadrilateral $JKLM$ is a square. Find the coordinates of M.

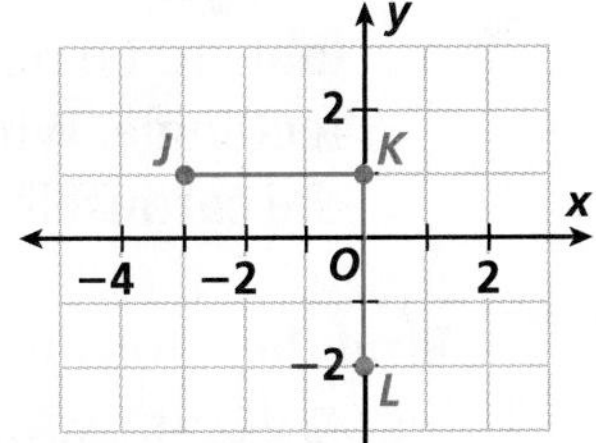

See Example 3 **Find the coordinates of the midpoint of each segment.**

5. $\overline{AB}$
6. $\overline{CD}$

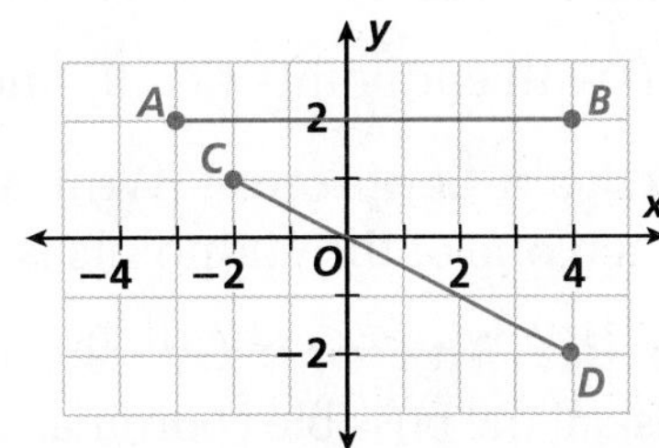

INDEPENDENT PRACTICE

See Example 1

Graph the polygons with the given vertices. Give the most specific name for each polygon.

7. $A(-3, 3)$, $B(2, 1)$, $C(-2, 1)$

8. $D(-4, 3)$, $E(4, 3)$, $F(4, -3)$, $G(-4, -3)$

See Example 2

Find the coordinates of each missing vertex.

9. Trapezoid $ABCD$ has a right angle at D. Find a set of possible coordinates for D.

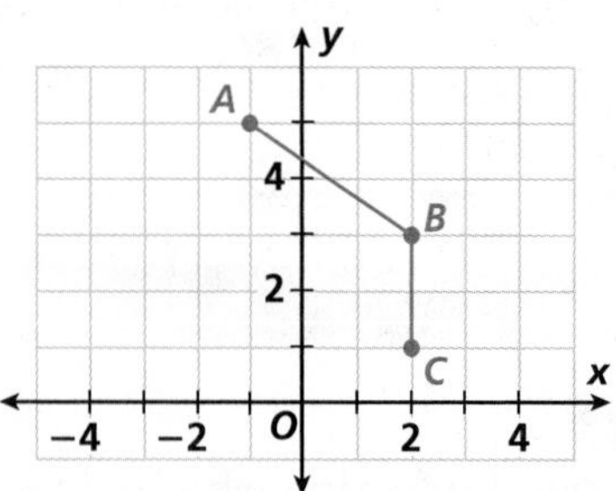

10. Quadrilateral $JKLM$ is a rectangle. Find the coordinates of L.

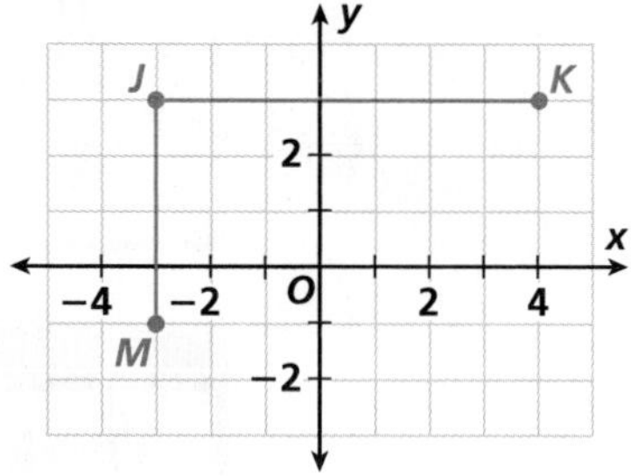

See Example 3

Find the coordinates of the midpoint of each segment.

11. $\overline{AB}$

12. $\overline{CD}$

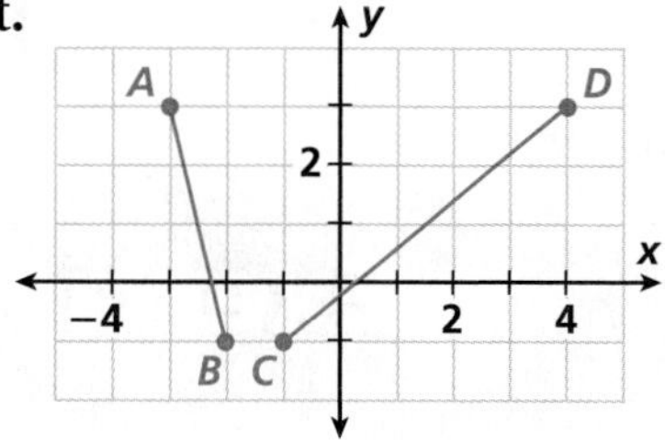

PRACTICE AND PROBLEM SOLVING

Extra Practice

See Extra Practice for more exercises.

Find possible coordinates of the missing vertex.

13. parallelogram $ABCD$ with $A(-3, -1)$, $C(-1, -4)$, and $D(-4, -4)$

14. isosceles $\triangle JKL$ with $J(2, -1)$, $K(5, -4)$, and a right angle at L

15. **Recreation** In a computer game, players get to design an amusement park. The location of each ride is marked on a coordinate grid. Jocelyn wants the four rides shown in the table to be positioned at the four corners of a rectangle. What should be the coordinates of the carousel?

Amusement Park	
Ride	**Location**
Roller coaster	(2, 6)
Fun house	(10, 1)
Bumper cars	(2, 1)
Carousel	?

Find the coordinates of the midpoint of each segment.

16. $\overline{AB}$ with endpoints $A(-5, 8)$ and $B(-1, -4)$

17. $\overline{CD}$ with endpoints $C(7, 0)$ and $D(-5, 10)$

18. **Make a Conjecture** Write a formula for finding a midpoint of a segment when one of the endpoints is the origin. Justify your answer.

19. **Critical Thinking** One side of a square has vertices at $(1, 2)$ and $(1, -2)$. List all the possible coordinates of the other two vertices.

20. **Multi-Step** The map shows several locations in a park. With the help of a GPS device, Nick hides a small box exactly halfway between Tower Rock and Twisted Tree.

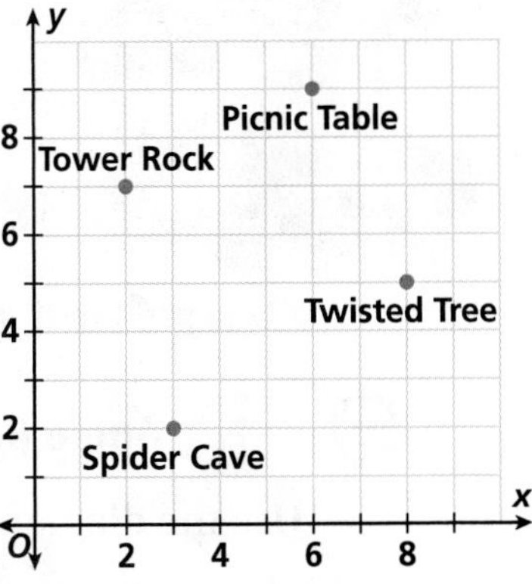

a. What are the map coordinates of the point where Nick hid the box?

b. Each unit on the map represents 100 meters. If Yanisha starts from Tower Rock, how far will she have to walk to reach the hidden box? Round to the nearest meter.

21. **Critical Thinking** One side of a square lies on the x-axis, and one side lies on the y-axis. One vertex of the square is at (3, 3). What are the coordinates of the other 3 vertices?

22. **What's the Question?** Points $P(3, 7)$, $Q(5, 7)$, $R(4, 5)$, and $S(2, 5)$ form the vertices of a polygon. The answer is no, because the segments are not perpendicular. What is the question?

23. **Write About It** Explain how the Distance Formula can help you determine whether a quadrilateral on the coordinate plane is a parallelogram.

24. **Challenge** The points (1, 3), (2, 6), and (3, 4) form three vertices of a parallelogram. List all of the possible coordinates of the fourth vertex of the parallelogram.

Test Prep

25. **Multiple Choice** What type of triangle has vertices at (1, 1), (1, −3), and (3, −3)?

Ⓐ acute   Ⓑ obtuse   Ⓒ isosceles   Ⓓ scalene

26. **Multiple Choice** A parallelogram has vertices at (−6, −2), (−3, −2), and (−1, −4). Which could be the coordinates of the fourth vertex of the parallelogram?

Ⓕ (−3, −5)   Ⓖ (−4, −3)   Ⓗ (−4, −4)   Ⓙ (−8, −4)

27. **Gridded Response** What is the x-coordinate of the midpoint of $\overline{AB}$ with endpoints $A(5, 8)$ and $B(-3, -4)$?

CHAPTER 5

SECTION A

Quiz for Lessons 1 Through 4

1 Angle Relationships

Use the diagram to name each figure.

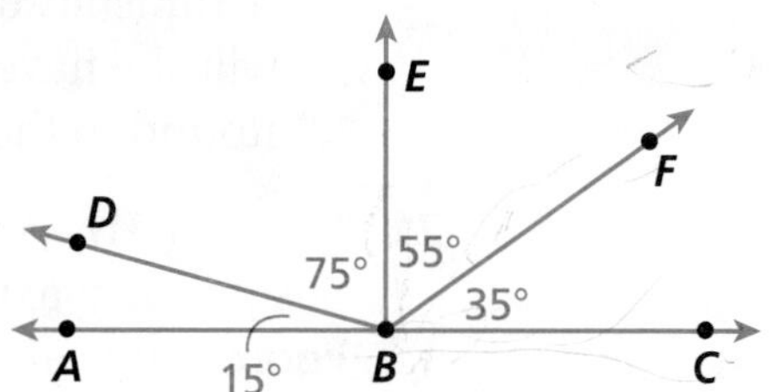

1. two pairs of complementary angles
2. three pairs of supplementary angles
3. two right angles

2 Parallel and Perpendicular Lines

In the figure, line $m \parallel$ line n. Find the measure of each angle. Justify your answer.

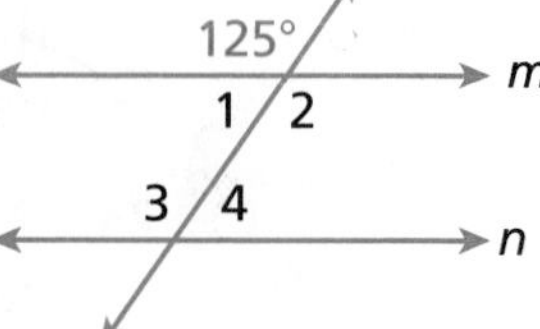

4. $\angle 1$
5. $\angle 2$
6. $\angle 3$

3 Triangles

Find $x°$ in each triangle.

7. 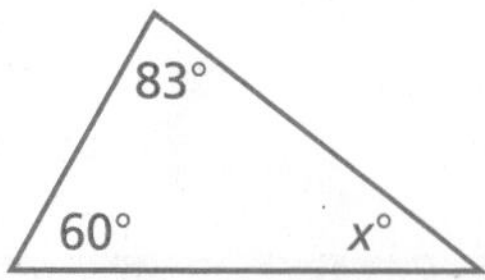

8. 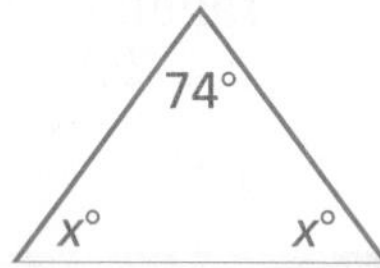

9. Can a triangle have sides with lengths of 9 m, 18 m, and 25 m? Explain.

4 Coordinate Geometry

Graph the polygons with the given vertices. Give the most specific name for each polygon.

10. $A(-2, 1)$, $B(-1, -1)$, $C(-3, -1)$
11. $P(-3, 4)$, $Q(2, 4)$, $R(2, -1)$, $S(-3, -1)$
12. Square $ABCD$ has vertices $A(-1, 1)$, $B(2, 1)$, and $C(2, -2)$. Find the coordinates of D.

Ready to Go On?

Make sense of problems and persevere in solving them.

Focus on Problem Solving

Understand the Problem

- **Restate the problem in your own words**

If you write a problem in your own words, you may understand it better. Before writing a problem in your own words, you may need to read it over several times—perhaps aloud, so you can hear yourself say the words.

Once you have written the problem in your own words, you may want to make sure you included all of the necessary information to solve the problem.

Write each problem in your own words. Check to make sure you have included all of the information needed to solve the problem.

1. In the figure, $\angle 1$ and $\angle 2$ are complementary, and $\angle 1$ and $\angle 5$ are supplementary. If $m\angle 1 = 60°$, find $m\angle 3 + m\angle 4$.

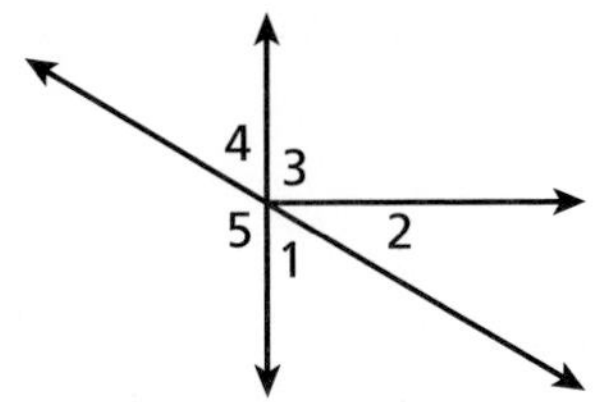

2. In triangle ABC, $m\angle A = 35°$ and $m\angle B = 55°$. Use the Triangle Sum Theorem to determine whether triangle ABC is a right triangle.

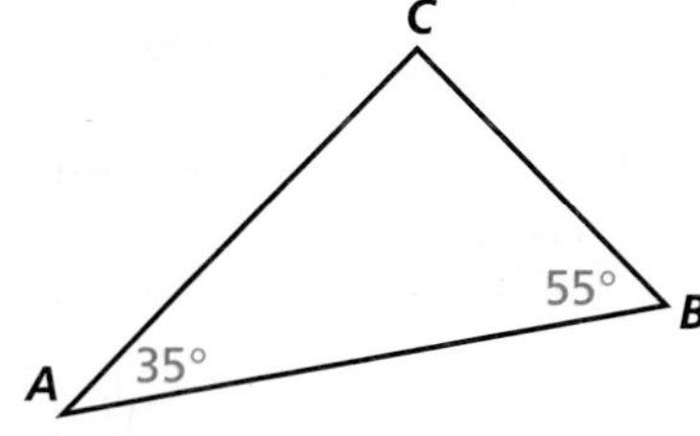

3. The second angle in a quadrilateral is eight times as large as the first angle. The third angle is half as large as the second. The fourth angle is as large as the first angle and the second angle combined. Find the angle measures in the quadrilateral.

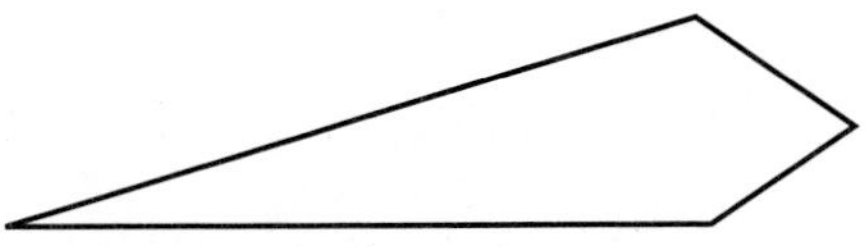

4. Parallel lines m and n are intersected by a transversal, line p. The acute angles formed by line m and line p measure 45°. Find the measure of the obtuse angles formed by the intersection of line n and line p.

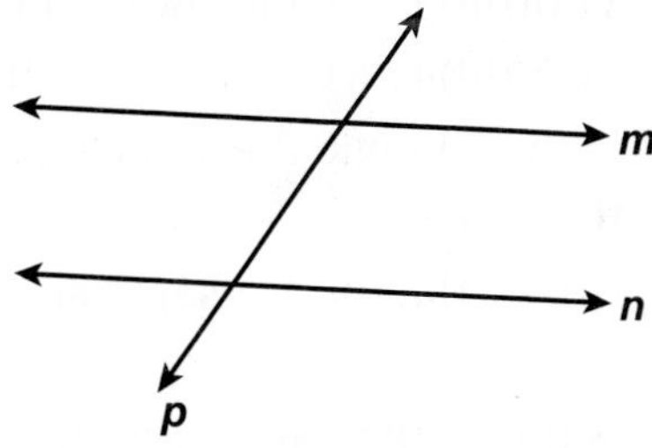

Explore Congruence

Use before Congruence

Learn It Online
Lab Resources Online

MATHEMATICAL PRACTICES Use appropriate tools strategically.

CC.8.G.1: Verify experimentally the properties of rotations, reflections, and translations. ***Also CC.8.G.2***

In this lab you will change, or *transform*, a figure in the coordinate plane, and examine what effect the change, or *transformation*, has on the figure.

Activity 1

1. Draw a triangle with vertices $A(2, 1)$, $B(5, 3)$, and $C(5, 1)$ on a coordinate plane.
2. Trace this triangle and cut it out. Place the triangle cutout on top of the original triangle on the coordinate plane.
3. a. *Slide* the cutout triangle down 5 units. What are the new coordinates of the cutout triangle?
   b. Is the triangle the same shape as it was before the *slide*?
   c. Is the triangle the same size as it was before the *slide*?
   d. Is the triangle in the same position as it was before the *slide*?

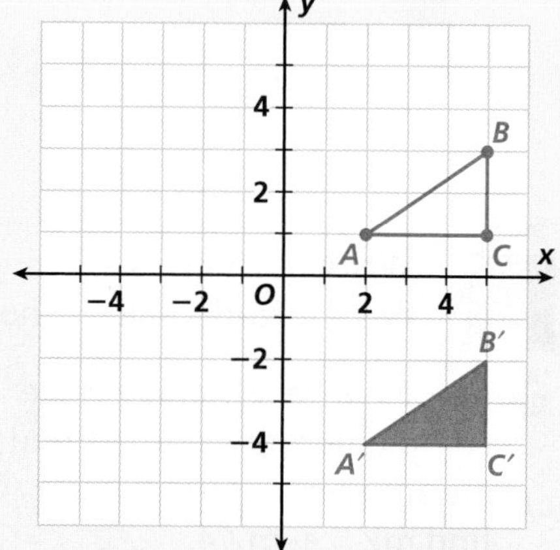

Activity 2

1. Place the triangle cutout back on top of the original triangle on the coordinate plane.
2. a. *Turn* the cutout triangle in the plane so that it moves 90° clockwise around the origin. (See the coordinate plane shown.) What are the new coordinates of the cutout triangle?
   b. Is the triangle the same shape as it was before the *turn*?
   c. Is the triangle the same size as it was before the *turn*?
   d. Is the triangle in the same position as it was before the *turn*?

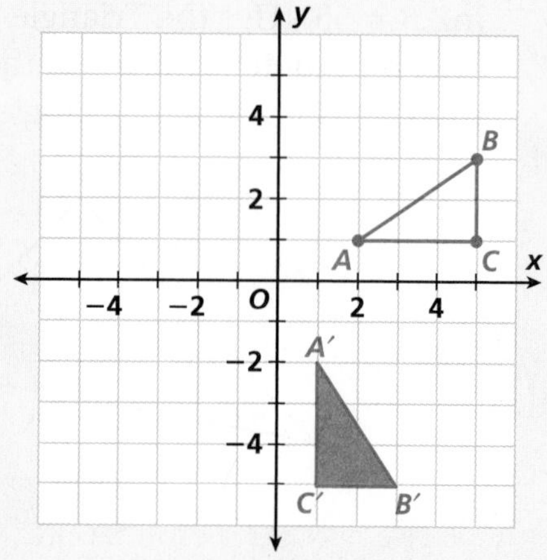

Activity 3

1. Place the triangle cutout back on top of the original triangle on the coordinate plane.

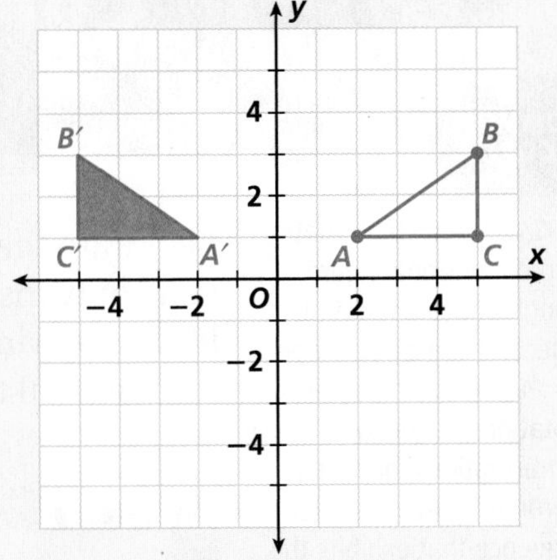

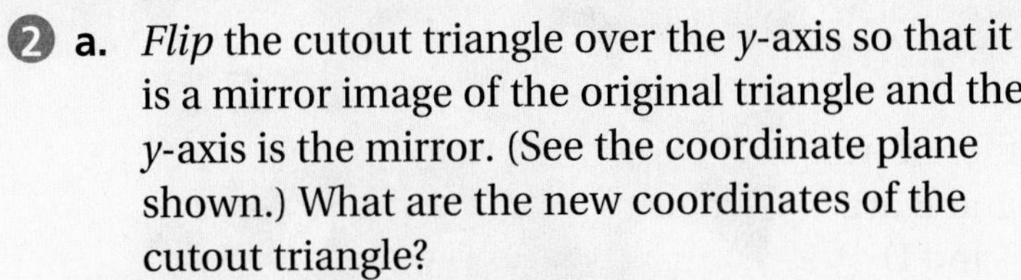

2. **a.** *Flip* the cutout triangle over the y-axis so that it is a mirror image of the original triangle and the y-axis is the mirror. (See the coordinate plane shown.) What are the new coordinates of the cutout triangle?

   b. Is the triangle the same shape as it was before the *flip*?

   c. Is the triangle the same size as it was before the *flip*?

   d. Is the triangle in the same position as it was before the *flip*?

Think and Discuss

1. When you slide, turn, or flip a figure in the plane, does it change shape?
2. When you slide, turn, or flip a figure in the plane, does it change size?
3. When you slide, turn, or flip a figure in the plane, does it change position?

When two figures are the same size and the same shape, they are called *congruent* figures.

4. When you slide, turn, or flip a figure in the plane, does it result in a *congruent* figure?
5. Do you think changing the position of a figure in the plane results in a *congruent* figure?

Try This

Draw a rectangle with vertices $A(-5, 1)$, $B(-5, 5)$, $C(-3, 5)$, and $D(-3, 1)$ on a coordinate plane.

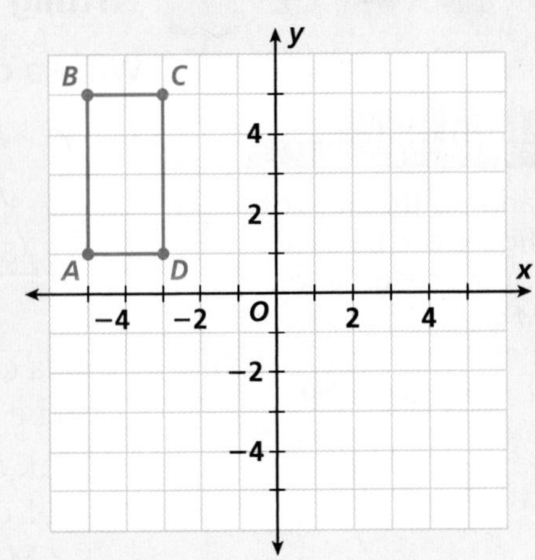

1. *Flip* the rectangle across the x-axis, and give the coordinates of the rectangle after the *flip*? Are the rectangles *congruent*?
2. *Slide* the rectangle 6 units to the right and 1 unit up. Give the coordinates of the rectangle after the *slide*. Are the rectangles *congruent*?
3. *Turn* the rectangle 180° around the origin. Give the coordinates of the rectangle after the *turn*. Are the rectangles *congruent*?

5-5 Congruence

COMMON CORE

CC.8.G.2: Understand that a two-dimensional figure is congruent to another if the second can be obtained from the first by a sequence of rotations, reflections, and translations; given two congruent figures, describe a sequence that exhibits the congruence between them.

Vocabulary

correspondence

congruent figures

Below are the DNA profiles of two pairs of twins. Twins A and B are identical twins. Twins C and D are fraternal twins.

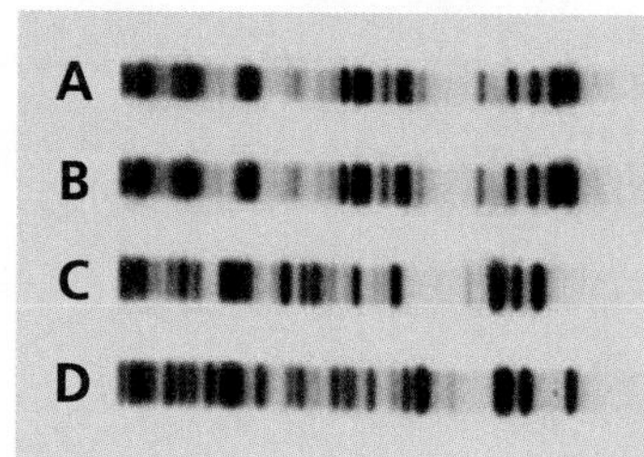

A **correspondence** is a way of matching up two sets of objects. The bands of DNA that are next to each other in each pair match up, or *correspond.* In the DNA of the identical twins, the corresponding bands are the same.

Congruent figures have the same size and shape. If two polygons are congruent, all of their corresponding sides and angles are congruent.

CONGRUENT TRIANGLES

Diagram	Statement	Corresponding Angles	Corresponding Sides
Triangles ABC and DEF	$\triangle ABC \cong \triangle DEF$	$\angle A \cong \angle D$ $\angle B \cong \angle E$ $\angle C \cong \angle F$	$\overline{AB} \cong \overline{DE}$ $\overline{BC} \cong \overline{EF}$ $\overline{AC} \cong \overline{DF}$

EXAMPLE 1 Writing Congruence Statements

Write a congruence statement for each pair of congruent polygons.

> **Helpful Hint**
>
> Marks on the sides of a figure can be used to show congruence.
> $\overline{KM} \cong \overline{RS}$ (1 mark)
> $\overline{KL} \cong \overline{RQ}$ (2 marks)
> $\overline{ML} \cong \overline{SQ}$ (3 marks)

A

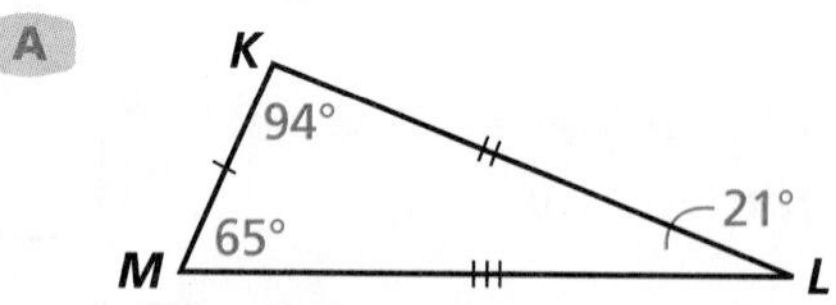

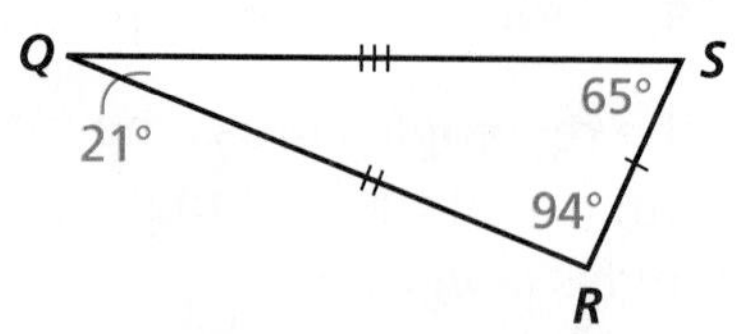

In a congruence statement, the vertices in the second triangle have to be written in order of correspondence with the first triangle.

$\angle K$ corresponds to $\angle R$. $\angle K \cong \angle R$

$\angle L$ corresponds to $\angle Q$. $\angle L \cong \angle Q$

$\angle M$ corresponds to $\angle S$. $\angle M \cong \angle S$

The congruence statement is triangle $KLM \cong$ triangle RQS.

Write a congruence statement for each pair of congruent polygons.

B

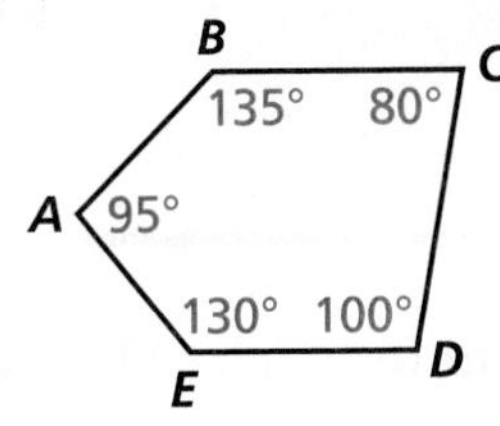

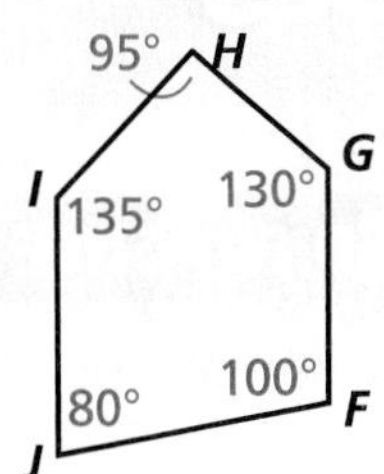

The vertices in the first pentagon are written in order around the pentagon starting at any vertex.

$\angle A$ corresponds to $\angle H$. *$\angle A \cong \angle H$*
$\angle B$ corresponds to $\angle I$. *$\angle B \cong \angle I$*
$\angle C$ corresponds to $\angle J$. *$\angle C \cong \angle J$*
$\angle D$ corresponds to $\angle F$. *$\angle D \cong \angle F$*
$\angle E$ corresponds to $\angle G$. *$\angle E \cong \angle G$*

The congruence statement is pentagon $ABCDE \cong$ pentagon $HIJFG$.

EXAMPLE  2 Using Congruence Relationships to Find Unknown Values

In the figure, quadrilateral *PQSR* ≅ quadrilateral *WTUV*.

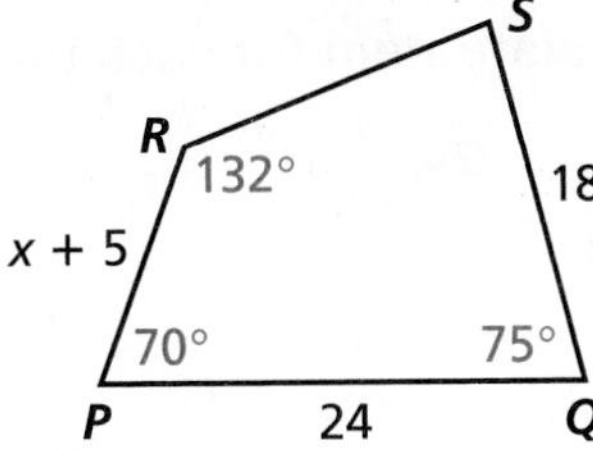

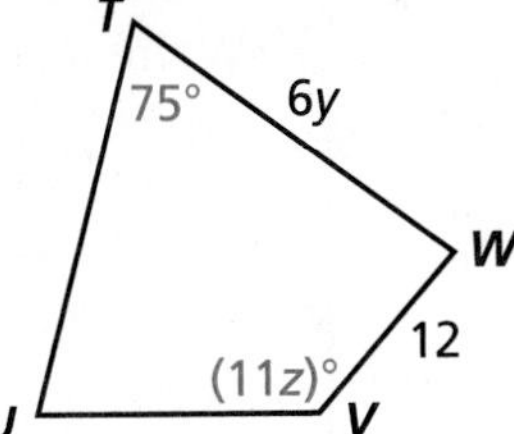

A **Find *x*.**

$x + 5 = 12$ *$\overline{PR} \cong \overline{WV}$*
$-5 = -5$ *Subtract 5 from both sides.*
$x = 7$

B **Find *y*.**

$6y = 24$ *$\overline{WT} \cong \overline{PQ}$*
$\frac{6y}{6} = \frac{24}{6}$ *Divide both sides by 6.*
$y = 4$

C **Find *z*.**

$132 = 11z$ *$\angle R \cong \angle V$*
$\frac{132}{11} = \frac{11z}{11}$ *Divide both sides by 11.*
$12 = z$

Think and Discuss

1. Explain the difference between congruent and similar polygons.

2. Tell how to write a congruence statement for two polygons.

5-5 Exercises

Learn It Online
Homework Help Online
Exercises 1–10, 11, 13, 19

GUIDED PRACTICE

See Example 1

Write a congruence statement for each pair of congruent polygons.

1. 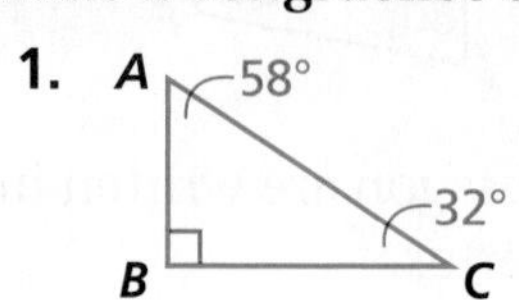

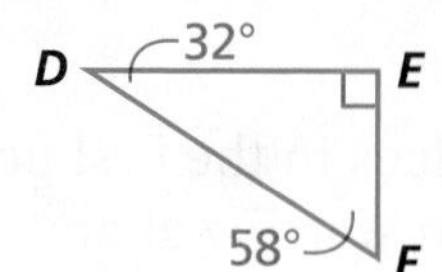

2. 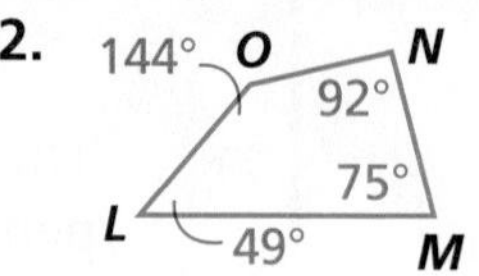

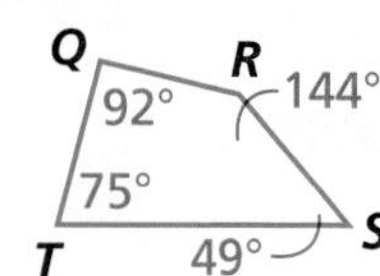

See Example 2

In the figure, triangle *ABC* ≅ triangle *LMN*.

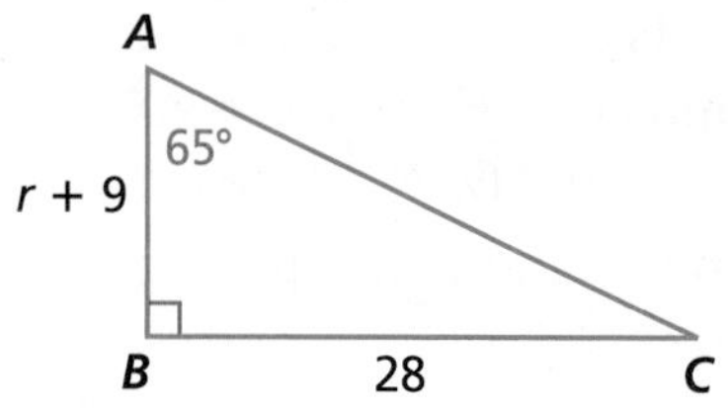

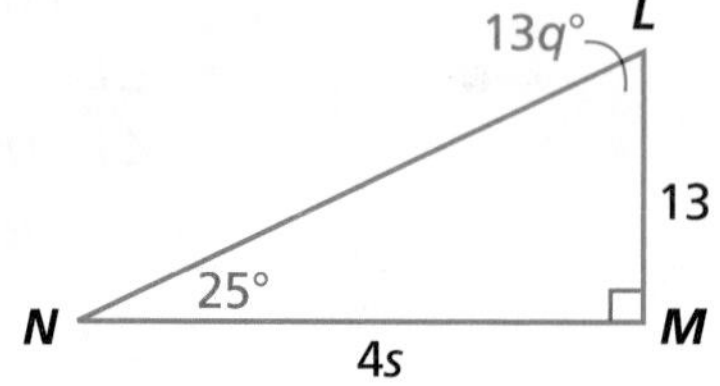

3. Find q.
4. Find r.
5. Find s.

INDEPENDENT PRACTICE

See Example 1

Write a congruence statement for each pair of congruent polygons.

6. 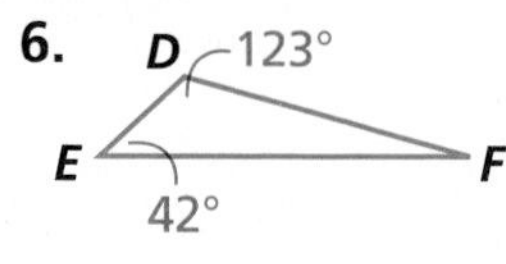

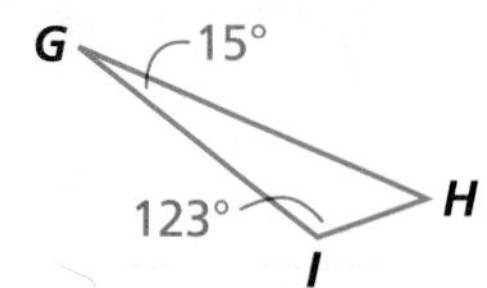

7. 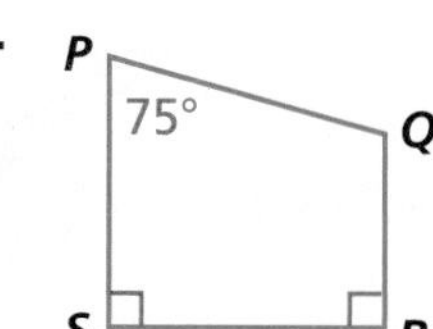

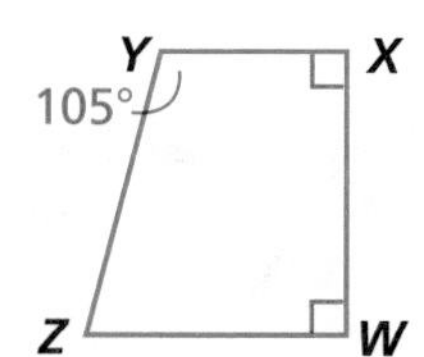

See Example 2

In the figure, quadrilateral *ABCD* ≅ quadrilateral *LMNO*.

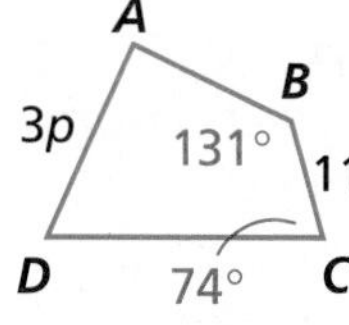

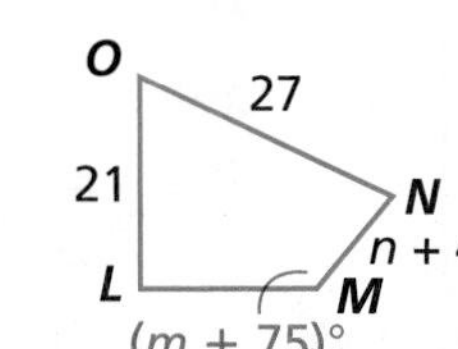

8. Find m.
9. Find n.
10. Find p.

PRACTICE AND PROBLEM SOLVING

Extra Practice
See Extra Practice for more exercises.

Find the value of each variable.

11. pentagon *ABCDE* ≅ pentagon *PQRST*

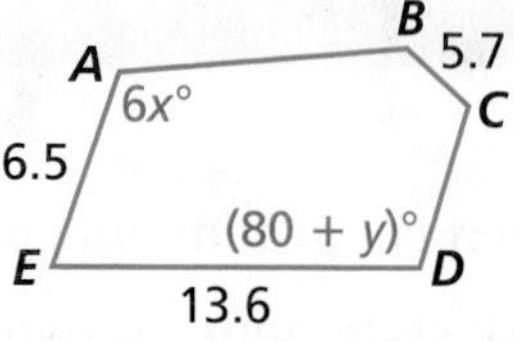

12. hexagon *ABCDEF* ≅ hexagon *LMNOPQ*

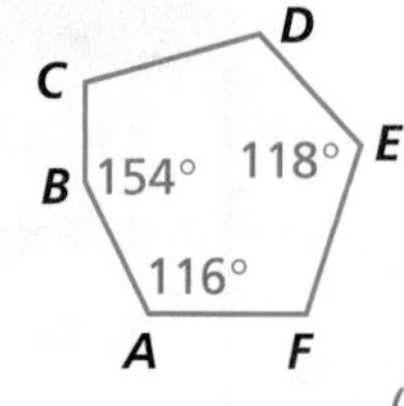

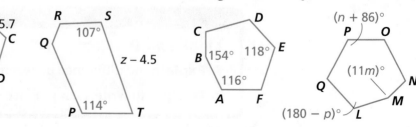

Find the value of each variable.

13. quadrilateral $ABCD \cong$ quadrilateral $EFGH$

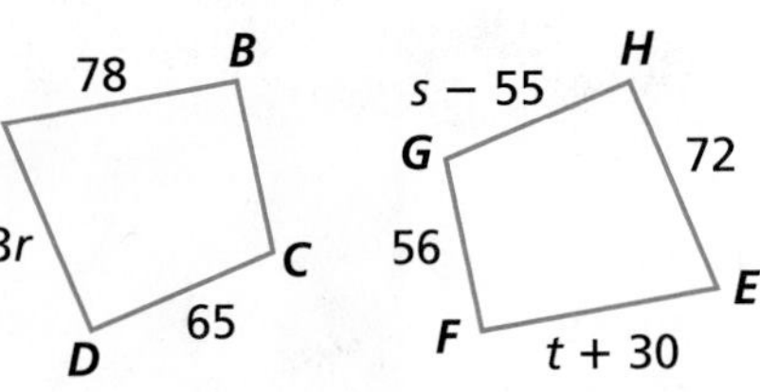

14. heptagon $ABCDEFG \cong$ heptagon $JKLMNOP$

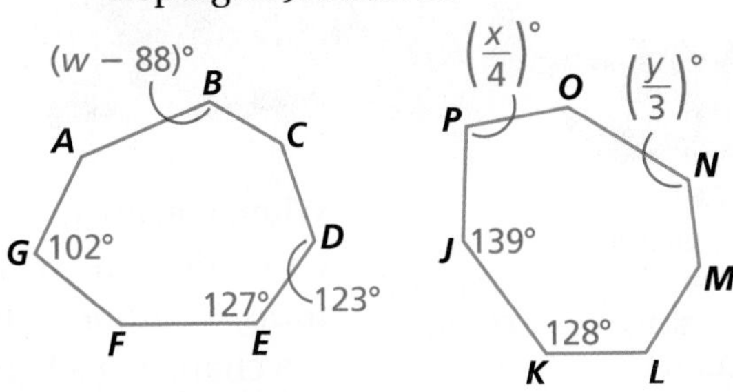

15. **Make a Conjecture** Does a diagonal of a rectangle divide the rectangle into two congruent triangles? Justify your answer.

16. **What's the Error?** Triangle ABC is congruent to triangle FDE. A student claims that $m\angle E = 65°$. What error did the student make? What is the actual measure of $\angle E$?

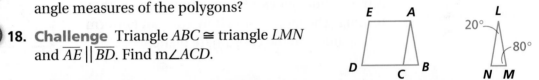

17. **Write About It** How can knowing two polygons are congruent help you find angle measures of the polygons?

18. **Challenge** Triangle $ABC \cong$ triangle LMN and $\overline{AE} \parallel \overline{BD}$. Find $m\angle ACD$.

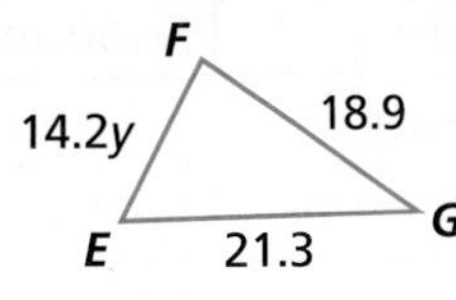

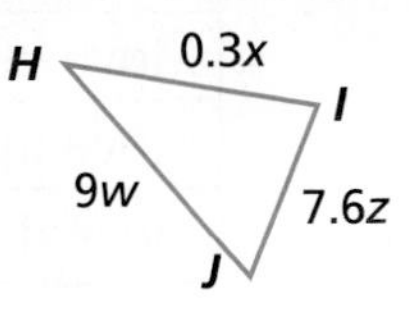

Test Prep

19. **Multiple Choice** Triangle $EFG \cong$ triangle JIH. Find the value of x.

F, 14.2y, 18.9, E, 21.3, G; H, 0.3x, I, 9w, 7.6z, J

Ⓐ 5.67 Ⓑ 30 Ⓒ 63 Ⓓ 71

20. **Multiple Choice** Triangle $ABC \cong$ triangle JKL. $m\angle A = 30°$ and $m\angle B = 50°$. Find $m\angle K$.

Ⓕ 30° Ⓖ 50° Ⓗ 80° Ⓙ 100°

21. **Gridded Response** Quadrilateral $ABCD \cong$ quadrilateral $WXYZ$. The length of $\overline{AB} = 21$ and the length of $\overline{WX} = 7m$. Find m.

5-6 Transformations

COMMON CORE

CC.8.G.1: Verify experimentally the properties of rotations, reflections, and translations. ***Also CC.8.G.2, CC.8.G.3***

Vocabulary

transformation

image

translation

reflection

rotation

center of rotation

When you are on an amusement park ride, you are undergoing a *transformation.* A **transformation** is a change in a figure's position or size. Ferris wheels and merry-go-rounds are *rotations.* Free-fall rides and water slides are *translations.*

Translations, rotations, and reflections are types of transformations. The resulting figure, or **image**, of a translation, rotation, or reflection is congruent to the original figure.

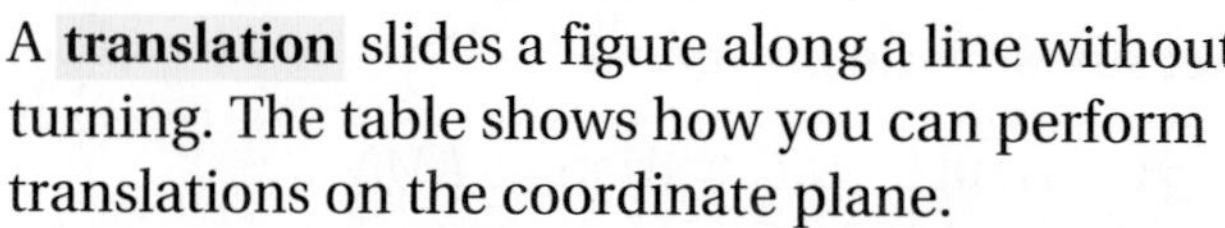

A **translation** slides a figure along a line without turning. The table shows how you can perform translations on the coordinate plane.

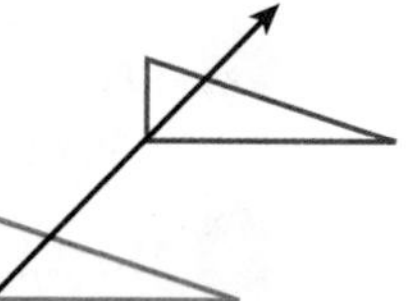

TRANSLATIONS

Type	Rule
Move right a units	Add a to each x-coordinate: $(x, y) \rightarrow (x + a, y)$
Move left a units	Subtract a from each x-coordinate: $(x, y) \rightarrow (x - a, y)$
Move up b units	Add b to each y-coordinate: $(x, y) \rightarrow (x, y + b)$
Move down b units	Subtract b from each y-coordinate: $(x, y) \rightarrow (x, y - b)$

EXAMPLE 1

Graphing Translations on a Coordinate Plane

Graph the translation of $\triangle ABC$ 3 units left and 4 units up.

Subtract 3 from the x-coordinate of each vertex, and **add 4** to the y-coordinate of each vertex.

Rule	Image
$A(1, -1) \rightarrow A'(1 - 3, -1 + 4)$	$A'(-2, 3)$
$B(1, -3) \rightarrow B'(1 - 3, -3 + 4)$	$B'(-2, 1)$
$C(4, -3) \rightarrow C'(4 - 3, -3 + 4)$	$C'(1, 1)$

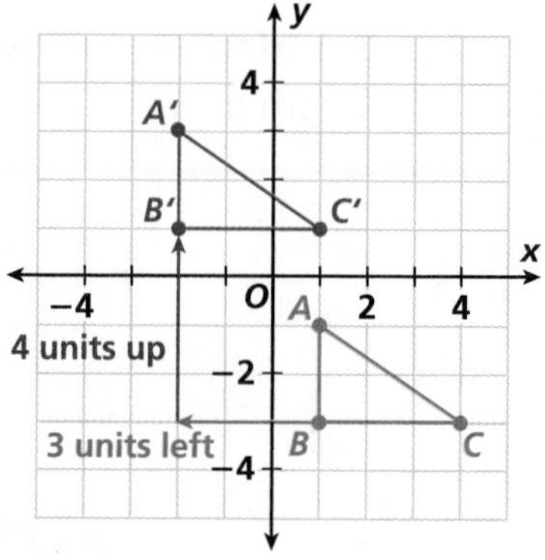

Reading Math

A' is read "A prime." The point A' is the image of point A. Arrow notation describes a transformation. $A \rightarrow A'$ is read "point A goes to point A prime."

Getty Images/PhotoDisc

Video Lesson Tutorials Online my.hrw.com

A **reflection** flips a figure across a line to create a mirror image.

In the example shown, the triangle is reflected across the y-axis. Notice that the x-coordinates of corresponding vertices are opposites and that the y-coordinates stay the same. This suggests a rule that can be used to reflect figures across either axis.

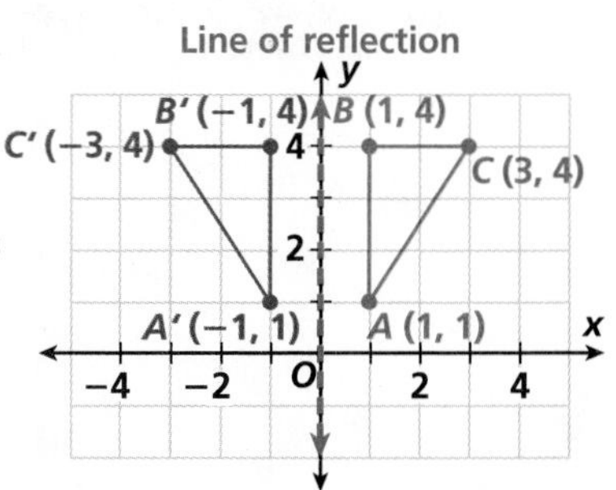

Helpful Hint

In a reflection across the y-axis, only the x-coordinates change. In a reflection across the x-axis, only the y-coordinates change.

REFLECTIONS	
Type	**Rule**
Across the y-axis	Multiply each x-coordinate by -1: $(x, y) \rightarrow (-x, y)$
Across the x-axis	Multiply each y-coordinate by -1: $(x, y) \rightarrow (x, -y)$

EXAMPLE 2 Graphing Reflections on a Coordinate Plane

Graph the reflection of quadrilateral *ABCD* across the *x*-axis.

Multiply the y-coordinate of each vertex by -1.

Rule	Image
$A(2, 4) \rightarrow A'(2, -1 \cdot 4)$	$A'(2, -4)$
$B(4, 4) \rightarrow B'(4, -1 \cdot 4)$	$B'(4, -4)$
$C(4, 1) \rightarrow C'(4, -1 \cdot 1)$	$C'(4, -1)$
$D(1, 1) \rightarrow D'(1, -1 \cdot 1)$	$D'(1, -1)$

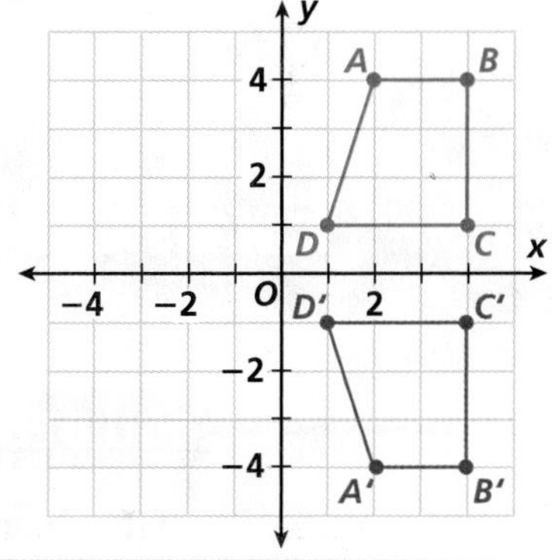

A **rotation** turns a figure around a point, called the **center of rotation**.

In the example shown, the triangle is rotated 180° around the origin. Notice that both the x- and y-coordinates of corresponding vertices are opposites. This suggests a rule that can be used to rotate figures 180° around the origin.

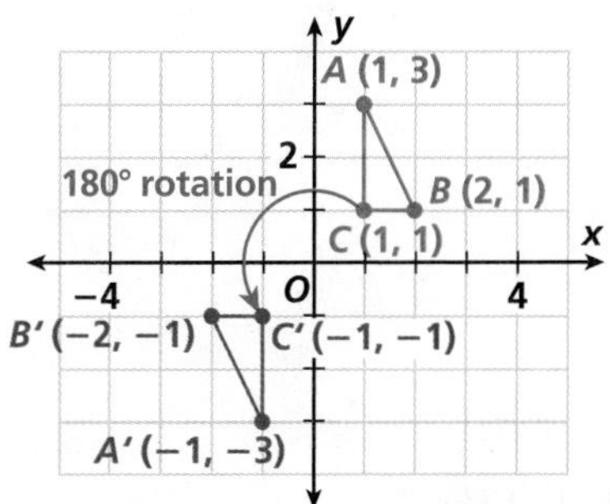

ROTATIONS AROUND THE ORIGIN	
Type	**Rule**
180°	Multiply both coordinates by -1: $(x, y) \rightarrow (-x, -y)$
90° clockwise	Multiply each x-coordinate by -1; then switch the x- and y-coordinates: $(x, y) \rightarrow (y, -x)$
90° counter-clockwise	Multiply each y-coordinate by -1; then switch the x- and y-coordinates: $(x, y) \rightarrow (-y, x)$

EXAMPLE 3

Graphing Rotations on a Coordinate Plane

Graph the rotation of $\triangle ABC$ 90° clockwise around the origin.

Multiply the x-coordinate of each vertex by -1, and then switch the x- and y-coordinates.

Rule	Image
$A(-4, 3) \rightarrow A'(3, -1 \cdot (-4))$	$A'(3, 4)$
$B(-1, 1) \rightarrow B'(1, -1 \cdot (-1))$	$B'(1, 1)$
$C(-4, 1) \rightarrow C'(1, -1 \cdot (-4))$	$C'(1, 4)$

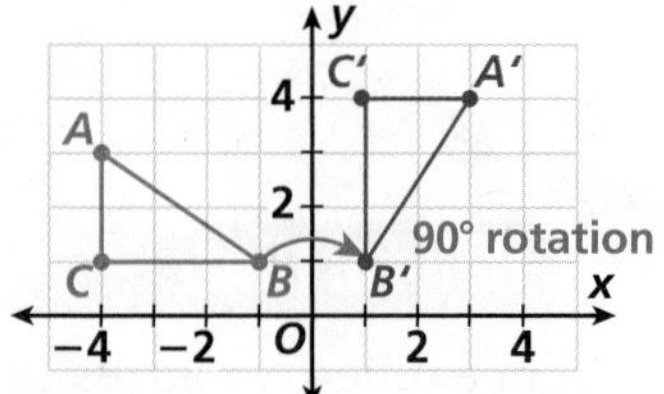

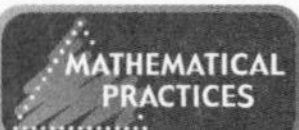

Think and Discuss

1. **Tell** whether the image of a vertical line is sometimes, always, or never vertical after a translation, a reflection, or a rotation.
2. **Describe** what happens to the x-coordinate and the y-coordinate after a point is reflected across the x-axis.

5-6 Exercises

GUIDED PRACTICE

See Example 1 **Graph each translation.**

1. 2 units right and 3 units up

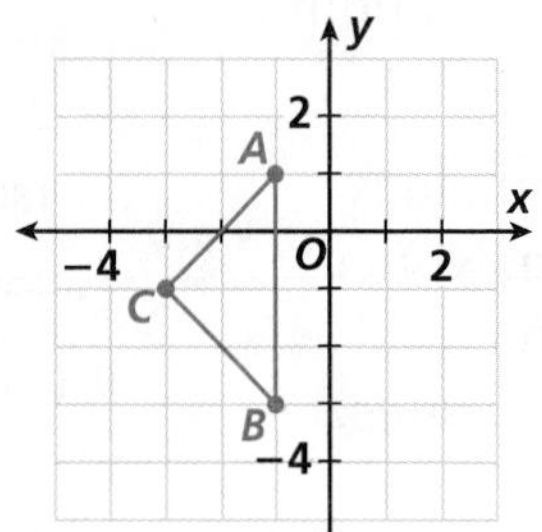

2. 4 units right and 1 unit down

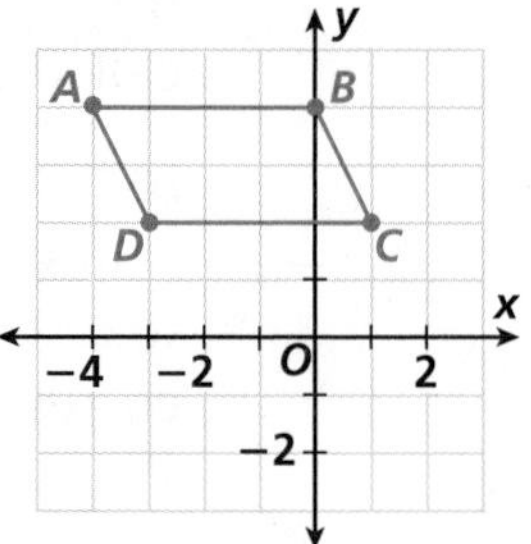

See Example 2 **Graph each reflection.**

3. across the x-axis

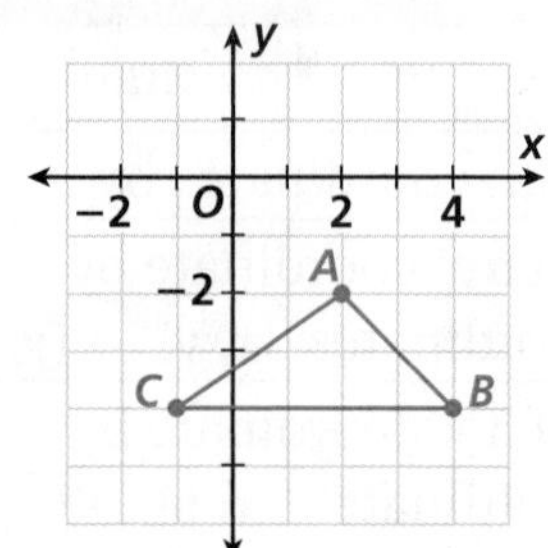

4. across the y-axis

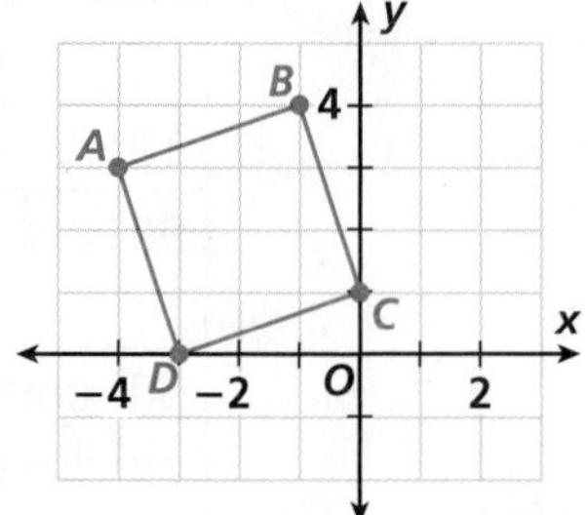

See Example 3

Graph each rotation around the origin.

5. 180°

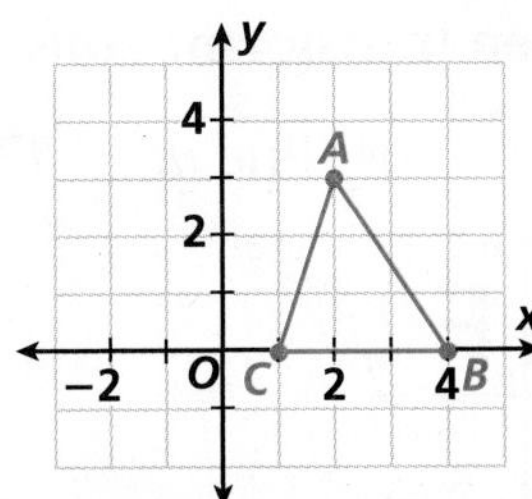

6. 90° clockwise

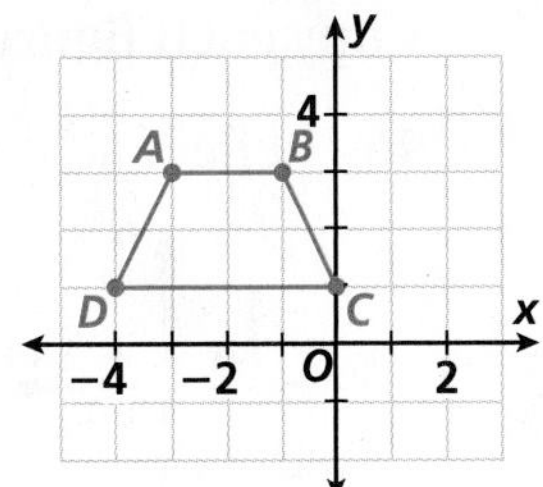

INDEPENDENT PRACTICE

See Example 1

Graph each translation.

7. 4 units left and 2 units up

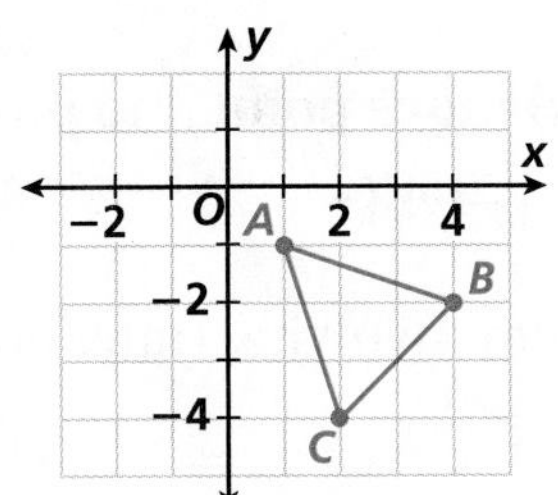

8. 3 units right and 4 units down

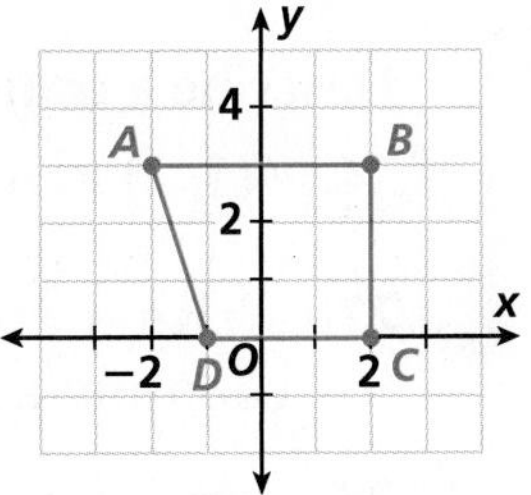

See Example 2

Graph each reflection.

9. across the y-axis

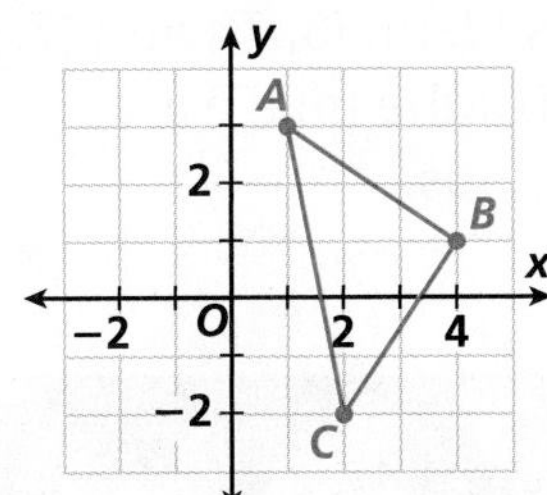

10. across the x-axis

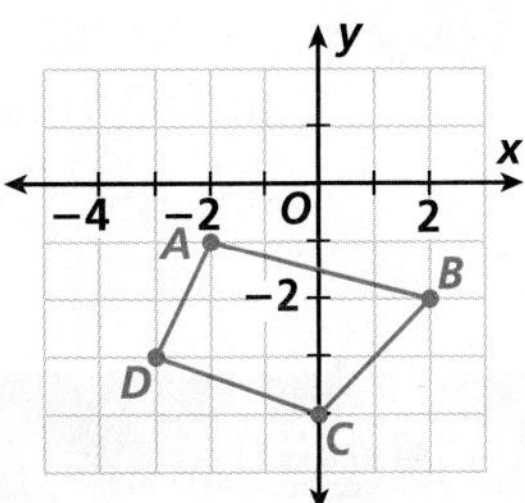

See Example 3

Graph each rotation around the origin.

11. 90° counterclockwise

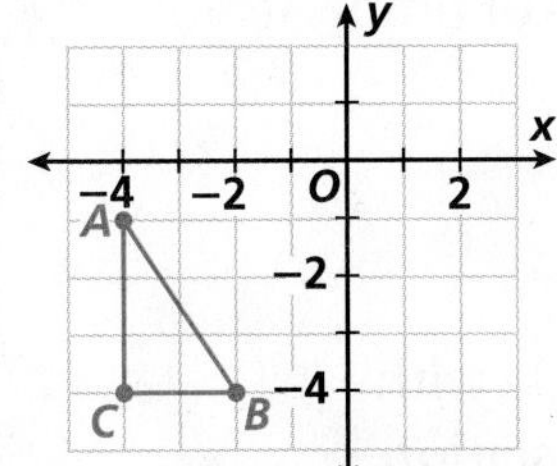

12. 180°

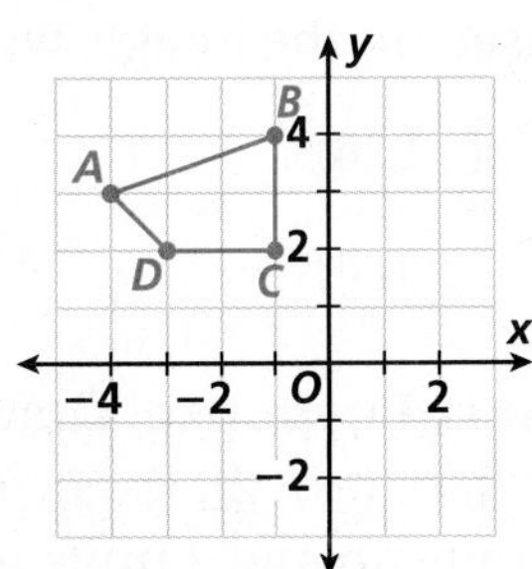

PRACTICE AND PROBLEM SOLVING

Extra Practice

See Extra Practice for more exercises.

13. Art An animator draws the triangle shown, which will form part of a dragon's tail. She then reflects the triangle across the y-axis.

a. What are the new coordinates of the triangle?

b. Describe another way the animator could have moved the triangle to the same position.

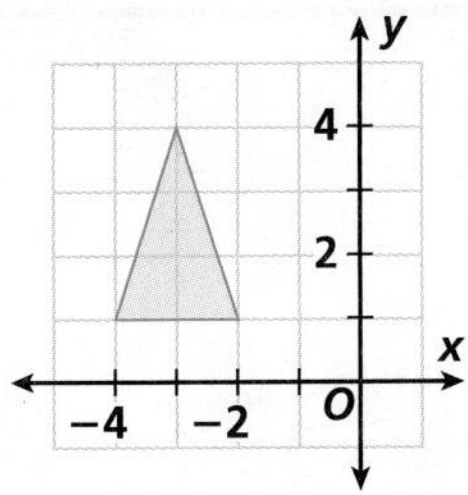

14. **Language Arts** The word CHOICE reflected across a horizontal line still reads CHOICE. Find another example of a word that reads the same after a reflection.

Copy each figure and perform the given transformations.

15. Reflect across line m.

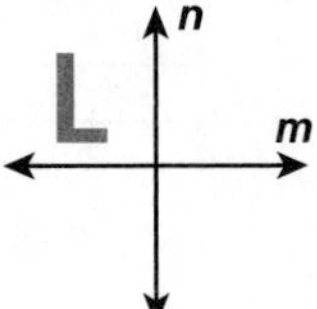

16. Reflect across line n.

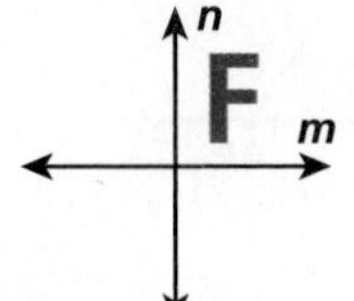

17. Rotate clockwise 90°.

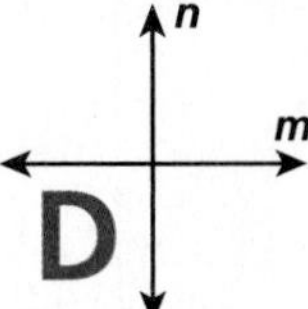

Give the coordinates of each point after a reflection across the given axis.

18. (1, 4); x-axis
19. (−3, 2); x-axis
20. (m, n); x-axis
21. (5, −2); y-axis
22. (−2, 4); y-axis
23. (m, n); y-axis

Describe a transformation that would move point A to point A'.

24. $A(1, 2) \rightarrow A'(4, 2)$
25. $A(1, 2) \rightarrow A'(-1, 2)$
26. $A(1, 2) \rightarrow A'(-1, -2)$

27. **Write a Problem** Write a problem involving transformations on a coordinate grid that result in a pattern.

28. **Write About It** Explain how each type of transformation performed on the arrow would affect the direction the arrow is pointing.

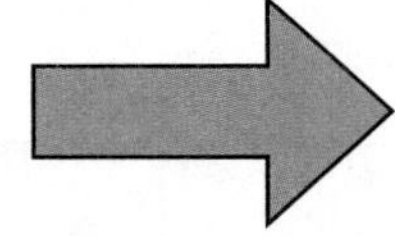

29. **Challenge** A triangle has vertices (2, 5), (3, 7), and (7, 5). After a reflection and a translation, the coordinates of the image are (7, −2), (8, −4), and (12, −2). Describe the transformations.

Test Prep

30. **Multiple Choice** Rectangle $ABCD$ was translated 4 units right and 3 units down to produce the image shown. Based on the image, what are the coordinates of point A?

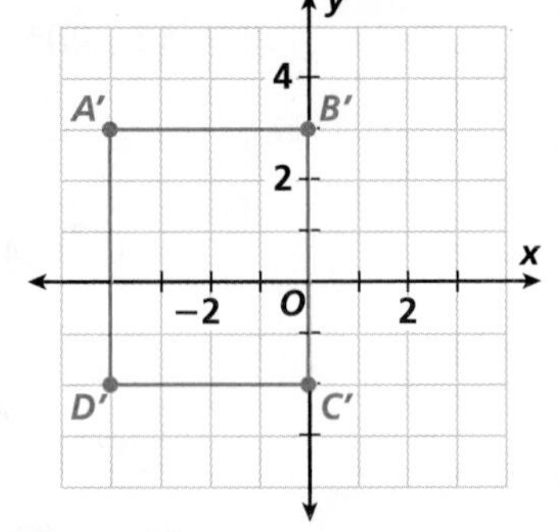

Ⓐ (−8, 6)
Ⓑ (−4, 3)
Ⓒ (−1, −1)
Ⓓ (0, 0)

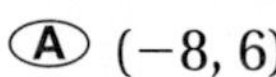

31. **Short Response** Draw the image of a triangle with vertices (−1, 2), (3, 3), and (1, −3) after a translation 2 units up and 2 units to the right.

5-7 Similarity and Congruence Transformations

COMMON CORE

CC.8.G.3: Describe the effect of dilations, translations, rotations, and reflections on two-dimensional figures using coordinates. ***Also CC.8.G.1a, CC.8.G.1b, CC.8.G.1c, CC.8.G.1d***

Vocabulary

similarity transformations

congruence transformations

Artists and graphic designers often use repeated geometric shapes to create a work of art, a company logo, or a pattern for wallpaper or fabric. They use transformations to vary the shape, size, and position of the figures, making a pleasing design.

Transformations that result in an image that is the same shape as the original, but a different size are **similarity transformations**.

EXAMPLE 1 Identifying Similarity Transformations

Identify the transformation from the original to the image, and tell whether the two figures are similar or congruent.

Remember!

A dilation produces an image that is similar to the original.

Original $\triangle ABC$

Image $\triangle A'B'C'$

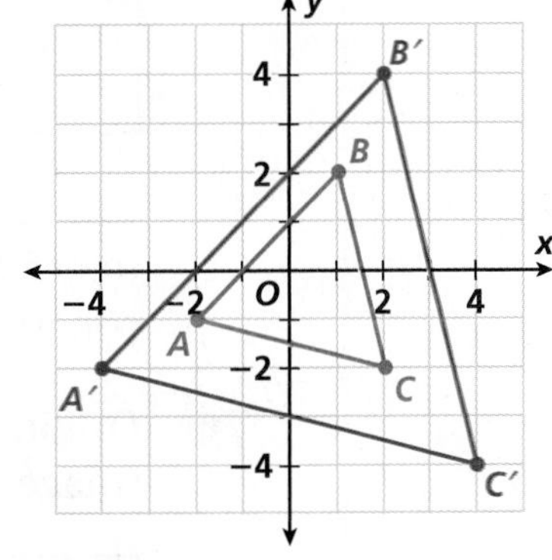

Original vertex	Image vertex
A (−2, −1)	A' 2(−2, −1) = (−4, −2)
B (1, 2)	B' 2(1, 2) = (2, 4)
C (2, −2)	C' 2(2, −2) = (4, −4)

The coordinates of A', B', and C' are double the original coordinates A, B, and C. So the transformation is a dilation and the triangles are similar.

Check

The triangles are similar because corresponding side lengths and corresponding angle measures are equal.

Original	Image
$m\angle A \approx 62°$	$m\angle A' \approx 62°$
$m\angle B \approx 59°$	$m\angle B' \approx 59°$
$m\angle C \approx 59°$	$m\angle C' \approx 59°$

Original lengths	Image lengths
$AB = \sqrt{18} \approx 4.243$	$A'B' = \sqrt{72} \approx 8.485$
$BC = \sqrt{17} \approx 4.123$	$B'C' = \sqrt{68} \approx 8.246$
$CA = \sqrt{17} \approx 4.123$	$C'A' = \sqrt{68} \approx 8.246$

Transformations that result in an image that is the same shape *and* the same size as the original are **congruence transformations**.

EXAMPLE 2 **Identifying Congruence Transformations**

Helpful Hint

Rotations, translations, and reflections do not change the size or shape of a figure.

Identify each transformation from the original to the image, and tell whether the two figures are similar or congruent.

A **Original pentagon *ABCDE***
Image pentagon *A′B′C′D′E′*

Original	Image
A (2, 0)	A′ (−2, 0)
B (3, 2)	B′ (−3, −2)
C (4, 1)	C′ (−4, −1)
D (4, −3)	D′ (−4, 3)
E (2, −3)	E′ (−2, 3)

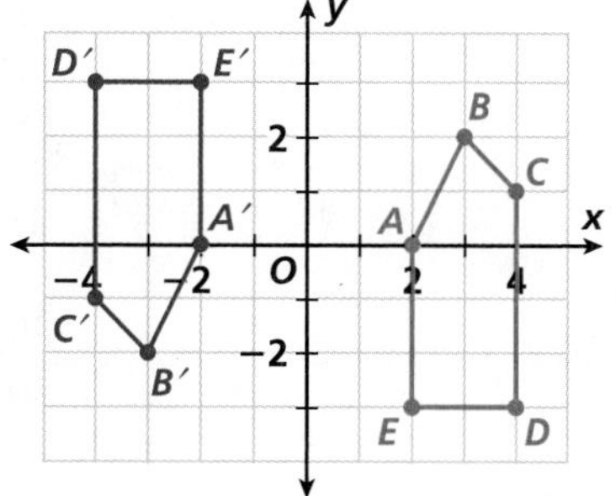

The original and image coordinates are opposites, so the transformation is a rotation of 180°. The pentagons are congruent.

B **Original *ABCD***
Image *A′B′C′D′*

Original	Image
A (1, −3)	A′ (4, 1)
B (1, 1)	B′ (4, 5)
C (3, 1)	C′ (6, 5)
D (3, −3)	D′ (6, 1)

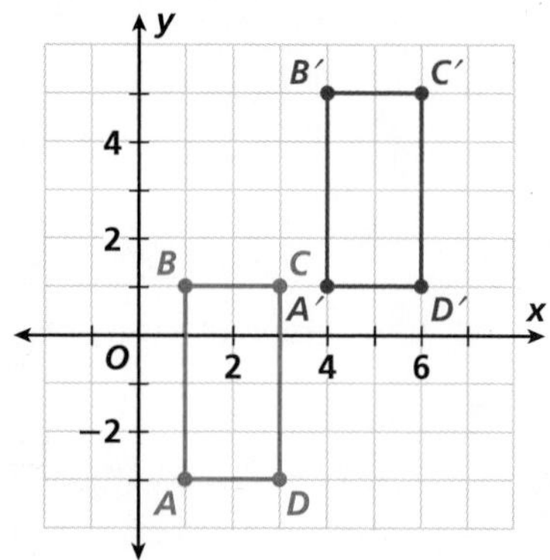

The image is a translation.
$(x, y) \rightarrow (x + 3, y + 4)$
So the quadrilaterals are congruent.

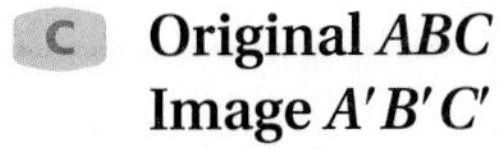

C **Original** *ABC*
Image *A′B′C′*

Original	Image
A (1, 2)	*A′* (1, −2)
B (2, 4)	*B′* (2, −4)
C (4, 1)	*C′* (4, −1)

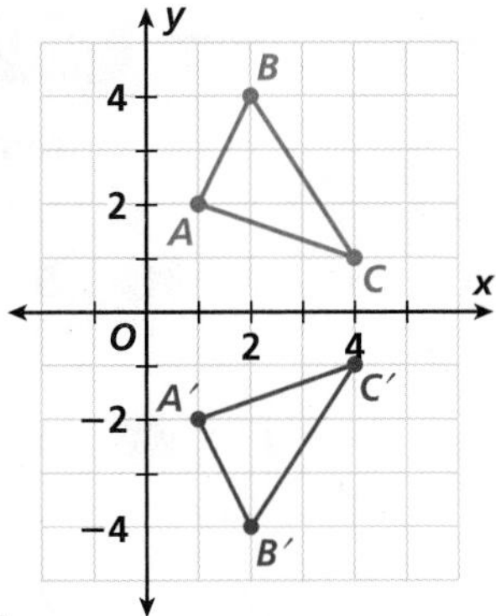

The image is a reflection across the x-axis.

$(x, y) \rightarrow (x, -y)$

So the triangles are congruent.

MATHEMATICAL PRACTICES

Think and Discuss

1. **Explain** how a dilation could possibly be a congruence transformation.
2. **Find** some objects in the room that show a similarity transformation and some objects that show a congruence transformation. Name which transformation is shown by each example you find.

5-7 Exercises

GUIDED PRACTICE

Identify each transformation from the original to the image, and tell whether the two figures are similar or congruent.

See Example 1

1. Original: $A(-3, 3)$, $B(3, 3)$, $C(3, -3)$, $D(-6, -3)$
   Image: $A'(-1, 1)$, $B'(1, 1)$, $C'(1, -1)$, $D'(-2, -1)$

See Example 2

2. Original: $A(-4, 1)$, $B(-4, 6)$, $C(-2, 4)$, $D(-2, 2)$
   Image: $A'(4, 1)$, $B'(4, 6)$, $C'(2, 4)$ $D'(2, 2)$
3. Original: $A(-2, 1)$, $B(2, -3)$, $C(-2, -3)$
   Image: $A'(-1, -2)$, $B'(3, 2)$, and $C'(3, -2)$
4. Original: $A(-3, -2)$, $B(-2, 2)$, and $C(0, -2)$
   Image: $A'(2, 1)$, $B'(3, 5)$, and $C'(5, 1)$

INDEPENDENT PRACTICE

Identify each transformation and tell whether the two figures are similar or congruent.

See Example 1

5. Original: $A(-3, -1)$, $B(1, 2)$, $C(1, -1)$
   Image: $A'(-6, -2)$, $B'(2, 4)$, $C'(2, -2)$

See Example 2

6. Original: $A(-1, -2)$, $B(0, 0)$, $C(2, 0)$, $D(1, -2)$
   Image: $A'(-3, 2)$, $B'(-2, 4)$, $C'(0, 4)$, $D'(-1, 2)$
7. Original: $A(2, 1)$, $B(1, 4)$, $C(4, 3)$
   Image: $A'(2, -1)$, $B'(1, -4)$, $C'(4, -3)$
8. Original: $A(-4, 0)$, $B(-4, 5)$, $C(-2, 5)$, $D(-2, 2)$
   Image: $A'(0, 4)$, $B'(5, 4)$, $C'(5, 2)$, $D'(2, 2)$

PRACTICE AND PROBLEM SOLVING

Extra Practice
See Extra Practice for more exercises.

9. Quadrilateral $A'B'C'D'$ is the image of quadrilateral $ABCD$ after a dilation with a scale factor of 3. Using the origin as the center of the dilation, draw $A'B'C'D'$ and label its vertices with their coordinates. Then state whether $ABCD$ and $A'B'C'D'$ are congruent or similar.

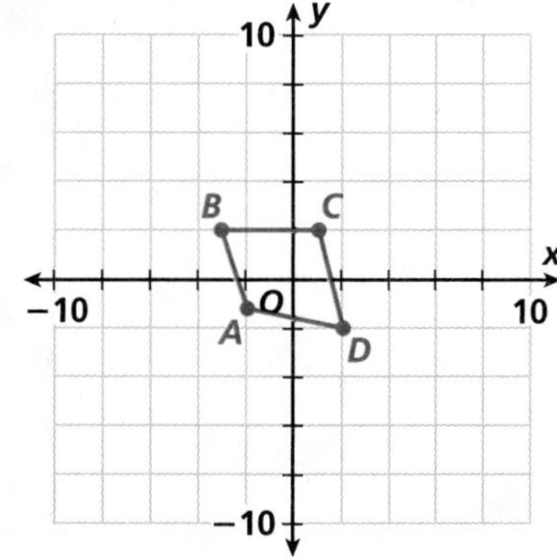

Identify each transformation and tell whether the two figures are similar or congruent.

10. Original: $A(2, -1)$, $B(2, 1)$, $C(3, 2)$, $D(4, 1)$, $E(4, -1)$
    Image: $A'(-2, -1)$, $B'(-2, 1)$, $C'(-3, 2)$, $D'(-4, 1)$, $E'(-4, -1)$
11. Original: $A(-4, -4)$, $B(-4, -2)$, $C(-1, -2)$, $D(-1, -4)$
    Image: $A'(-1, 1)$, $B'(-1, 3)$, $C'(2, 3)$, $D'(2, 1)$
12. Original: $A(-2, -2)$, $B(0, 2)$, $C(2, 0)$
    Image: $A'(-3, -3)$, $B'(0, 3)$, $C'(3, 0)$
13. Original: $A(-3, 0)$, $B(-3, 4)$, $C(-1, 5)$, $D(-1, 3)$
    Image: $A'(3, 0)$, $B'(3, -4)$, $C'(1, -5)$, $D'(1, -3)$
14. Original: $A(-2, -4)$, $B(-2, 2)$, $C(4, 2)$, $D(4, -4)$
    Image: $A'(-1, -2)$, $B'(-1, 1)$, $C'(2, 1)$, $D'(2, -2)$

Identify each transformation, and state whether it is a congruence or similarity transformation.

15. $(x, y) \rightarrow (-x, y)$
16. $(x, y) \rightarrow (x, -y)$
17. $(x, y) \rightarrow (x - 3, y - 2)$
18. $(x, y) \rightarrow (-x, -y)$
19. $(x, y) \rightarrow (0.2x, 0.2y)$
20. $(x, y) \rightarrow (y, -x)$

Hobbies **A quilt uses the design shown. Identify the indicated transformation.**

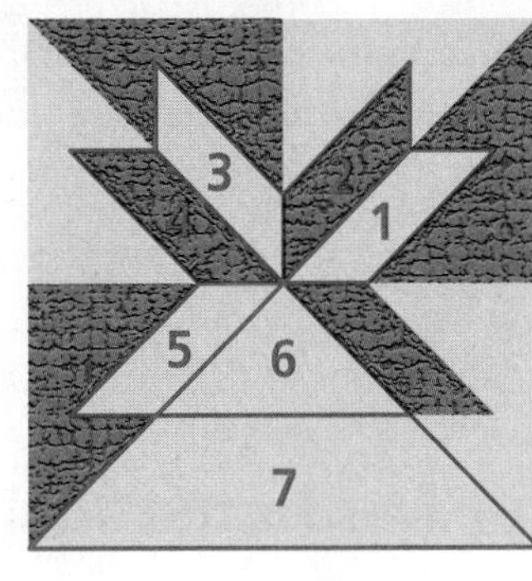

21. from figure 1 to figure 2
22. from figure 2 to figure 4
23. from figure 5 to figure 1
24. from figure 6 to figure 7 (large triangle)

25. **What's the Error?** A student drew the transformation of a triangle at right. The student said that it is a dilation from $\triangle ABC$ to $\triangle A'B'C'$. Explain the error the student made. Explain how to fix the error.

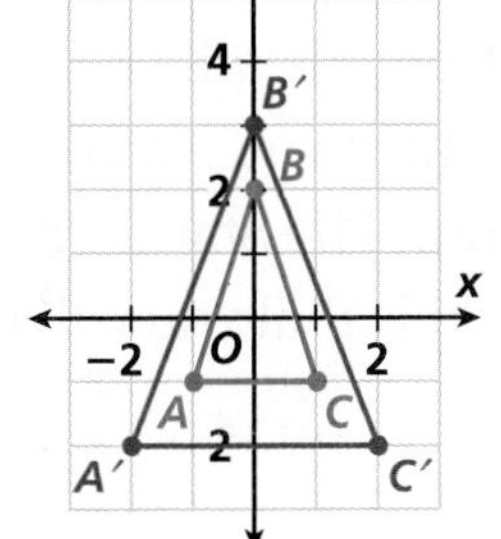

26. **Write About It** How are similarity and congruence transformations alike and how are they different?

27. **Critical Thinking** Was the rectangle below transformed by a rotation or by a reflection? Justify your response.

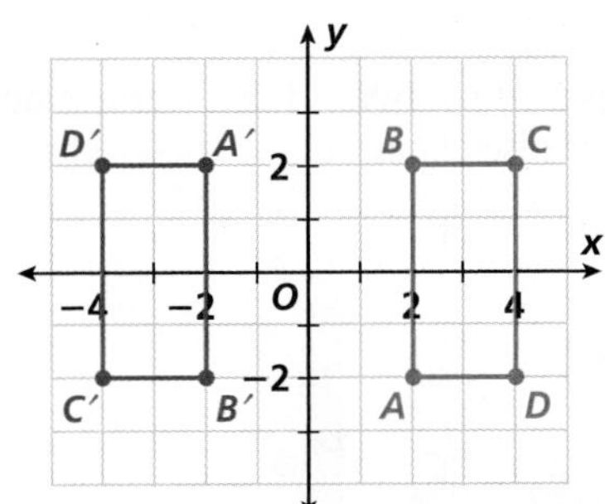

28. **Challenge** The points of an original figure are $A(-3, 3)$, $B(-3, -2)$, $C(1, -2)$ and $D(1, 2)$. What are the corresponding points of its image if the original figure is dilated by a scale factor of 8?

Test Prep

29. **Multiple Choice** Which single transformation can result in an image that is similar, but not congruent, to the original figure?

Ⓐ dilation　Ⓑ reflection　Ⓒ rotation　Ⓓ translation

30. **Short Response** Triangle ABC was transformed to triangle $A'B'C'$ by a rotation of 90°. What is the relationship between the two triangles?

Mastering the Standards

for Mathematical Practice

The topics described in the Standards for Mathematical Content will vary from year to year. However, the *way* in which you learn, study, and think about mathematics will not. The Standards for Mathematical Practice describe skills that you will use in all of your math courses.

Mathematical Practices

1. *Make sense of problems and persevere in solving them.*
2. *Reason abstractly and quantitatively.*
3. *Construct viable arguments and critique the reasoning of others.*
4. *Model with mathematics.*
5. *Use appropriate tools strategically.*
6. *Attend to precision.*
7. *Look for and make use of structure.*
8. *Look for and express regularity in repeated reasoning.*

4 Model with mathematics.

Mathematically proficient students can apply... mathematics... to... problems... in everyday life, society, and the workplace...

In your book

Application exercises and **Real-World Connections** apply mathematics to other disciplines and in real-world scenarios.

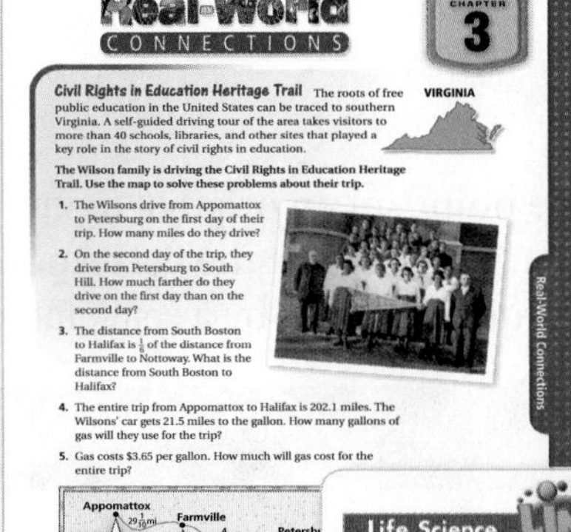

Real-World CONNECTIONS

CHAPTER 3

Civil Rights in Education Heritage Trail The roots of free public education in the United States can be traced to southern Virginia. A self-guided driving tour of the area takes visitors to more than 40 schools, libraries, and other sites that played a key role in the story of civil rights in education.

VIRGINIA

The Wilson family is driving the Civil Rights in Education Heritage Trail. Use the map to solve these problems about their trip.

1. The Wilsons drive from Appomattox to Petersburg on the first day of their trip. How many miles do they drive?
2. On the second day of the trip, they drive from Petersburg to South Hill. How much farther do they drive on the first day than on the second day?
3. The distance from South Boston to Halifax is $\frac{1}{6}$ of the distance from Farmville to Nottoway. What is the distance from South Boston to Halifax?
4. The entire trip from Appomattox to Halifax is 202.1 miles. The Wilsons' car gets 21.5 miles to the gallon. How many gallons of gas will they use for the trip?
5. Gas costs $3.65 per gallon. How much will gas cost for the entire trip?

Real-World Connections

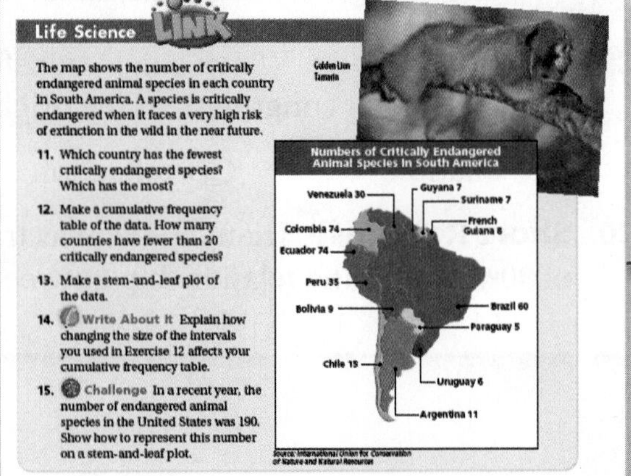

Life Science LINK

The map shows the number of critically endangered animal species in each country in South America. A species is critically endangered when it faces a very high risk of extinction in the wild in the near future.

11. Which country has the fewest critically endangered species? Which has the most?
12. Make a cumulative frequency table of the data. How many countries have fewer than 20 critically endangered species?
13. Make a stem-and-leaf plot of the data.
14. **Write About It** Explain how changing the size of the intervals you used in Exercise 12 affects your cumulative frequency table.
15. **Challenge** In a recent year, the number of endangered animal species in the United States was 190. Show how to represent this number on a stem-and-leaf plot.

PhotoDisc/Getty Images

Combine Transformations

Use with Transformations

Learn It Online
Lab Resources Online

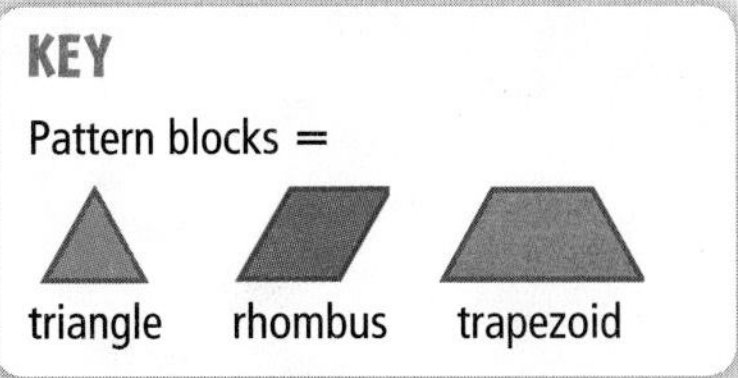

Use appropriate tools strategically.

CC.8.G.2: Understand that a two-dimensional figure is congruent to another if the second can be obtained from the first by a sequence of rotations, reflections, and translations; given two congruent figures, describe a sequence that exhibits the congruence between them. ***Also CC.8.G.1, CC.8.G.3***

You can use a coordinate plane when transforming a geometric figure.

Activity

1 Follow the steps below to transform a figure.

a. Place a rhombus on a coordinate plane. Trace the rhombus, and label the vertices.

b. Rotate the figure 90° clockwise about the origin.

c. Reflect the resulting figure across the x-axis. Draw the image and label the vertices.

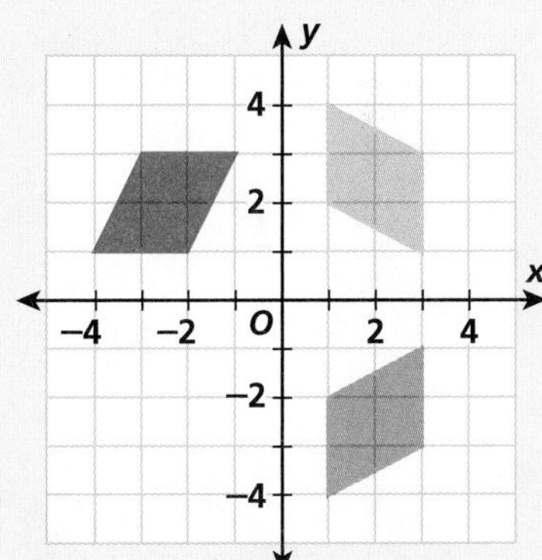

d. Now place a rhombus in the same position as the original figure. Reflect the figure across the line $y = x$.

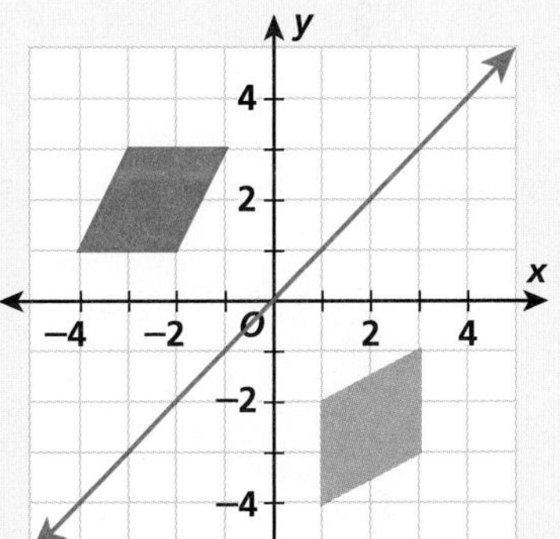

Think and Discuss

1. What do you notice about the images that result from the two transformations in parts **b** and **c** above and the image that results from the single transformation in part **d** above?
2. When you perform two or more transformations on a figure, does it matter in which order the transformations are performed? Explain.

Try This

1. Place a pattern block on a coordinate plane. Trace the block and label the vertices. Perform two different transformations on the figure. Draw the image and label the vertices. Then describe a different way of transforming the original figure to produce the same image.

5-8 Identifying Combined Transformations

COMMON CORE

CC.8.G.3: Describe the effect of dilations, translations, rotations, and reflections on two-dimensional figures using coordinates. ***Also CC.8.G.2, CC.8.G.4***

Many famous geometric designs are created by combining transformations of various geometric figures.

The mysterious crop circles shown here appear to be composed of combined rotations and dilations. If you consider the one piece that is rotated to create the design, you can see that it is similar to each of its rotations.

EXAMPLE 1 Transformation Sequences and Congruence

Identify the combined transformations from the original to the final image, and tell whether the two figures are similar or congruent.

Original $\triangle ABC$

First image $\triangle A'B'C'$

Final image $\triangle A''B''C''$

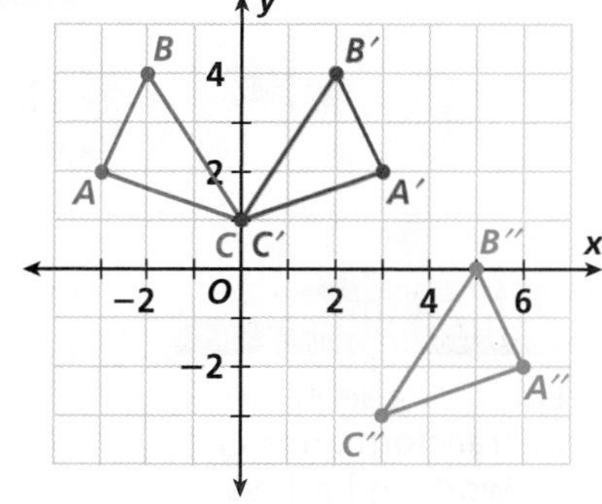

Identify each transformation.

$\Delta ABC \to \Delta A'B'C'$
$A(-3, 2) \to A'(3, 2)$
$B(-2, 4) \to B'(2, 4)$
$C(0, 1) \to C'(0, 1)$

The x-coordinates are opposites.

$(x, y) \to (-x, y)$

This is a reflection across the y-axis.

$\Delta A'B'C' \to \Delta A''B''C''$
$A'(3, 2) \to A''(6, -2)$
$B'(2, 4) \to B''(5, 0)$
$C'(0, 1) \to C''(3, -3)$

The x-coordinates are increased by 3.
The y-coordinates are decreased by 4.

$(x, y) \to (x + 3, y - 4)$

This is a translation.

Each transformation is a congruence transformation. Therefore, the original and final images are congruent.

EXAMPLE 2

Transformation Sequences and Similarity

Identify the combined transformations from the original to the final image, and tell whether the two figures are similar or congruent.

Identify each transformation.

$ABCD \rightarrow \Delta A'B'C'D'$
$A(-3, -2) \rightarrow A'(-2, 3)$
$B(-3, 1) \rightarrow B'(1, 3)$
$C(-2, 1) \rightarrow C'(1, 2)$
$D(-2, -2) \rightarrow D'(-2, 2)$

The x-coordinate is multiplied by −1 and the x- and y-coordinates are switched.

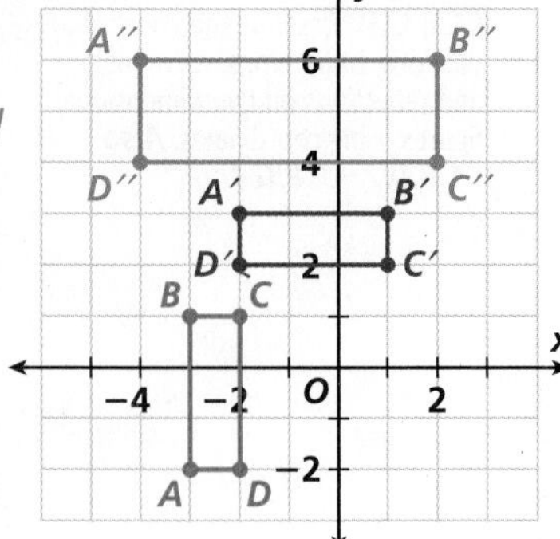

$(x, y) \rightarrow (y, -x)$: a 90° clockwise rotation around the origin.

$A'B'C'D' \rightarrow A''B''C''D''$
$A'(-2, 3) \rightarrow A''(-4, 6)$
$B'(1, 3) \rightarrow B''(2, 6)$
$C'(1, 2) \rightarrow C''(2, 4)$
$D'(-2, 2) \rightarrow D''(-4, 4)$

Both coordinates are multiplied by 2.

$(x, y) \rightarrow (2x, 2y)$: a dilation by a factor of 2 with the origin as the center of dilation. The original and final images are similar.

EXAMPLE 3

Finding Sequences of Transformations

Helpful Hint

Look for a sequence of transformations by working backward from the final image.

Find a sequence of at least two combined transformations from the original to the final image.

$AB = A''B''$ $BC = B''C''$ $AC = A''C''$

The original and final image are congruent, so the sequence has only congruence transformations.

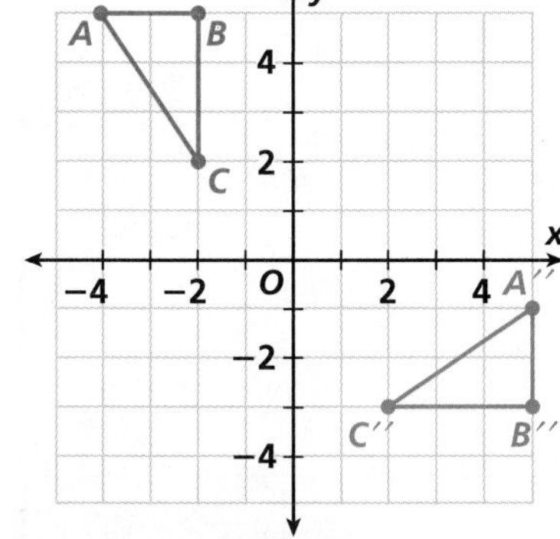

A rotation 90° clockwise:
$(x, y) \rightarrow (y, -x)$
$A(-4, 5) \rightarrow A'(5, 4)$
$B(-2, 5) \rightarrow B'(5, 2)$
$C(-2, 2) \rightarrow C'(2, 2)$

A translation 5 units down:
$(x, y) \rightarrow (x, y - 5)$
$A'(5, 4) \rightarrow A''(5, -1)$
$B'(5, 2) \rightarrow B''(5, -3)$
$C'(2, 2) \rightarrow C''(2, -3)$

Think and Discuss

1. Discuss other possible sequences of transformations that could transform the original figure to the final image in each example.

5-8 Exercises

GUIDED PRACTICE

See Examples 1&2 **Identify the combined transformations from the original to the final image, and tell whether the two figures are similar or congruent.**

1.

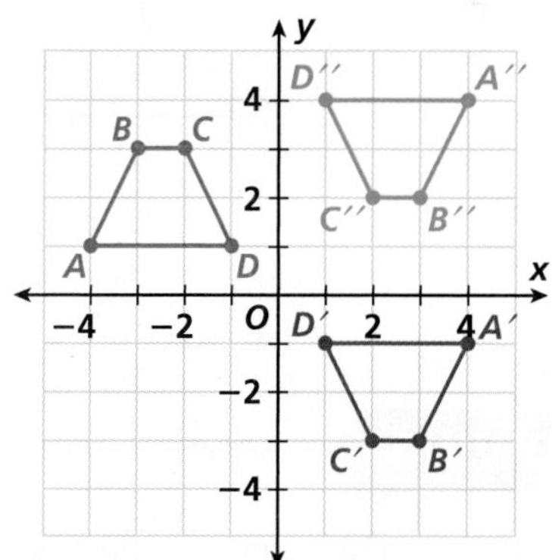

2.

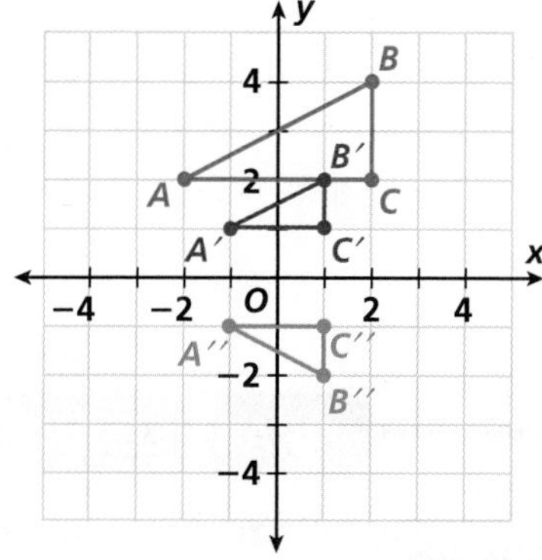

See Example 3 **Find a sequence of at least two combined transformations for transforming the original to the final image.**

3.

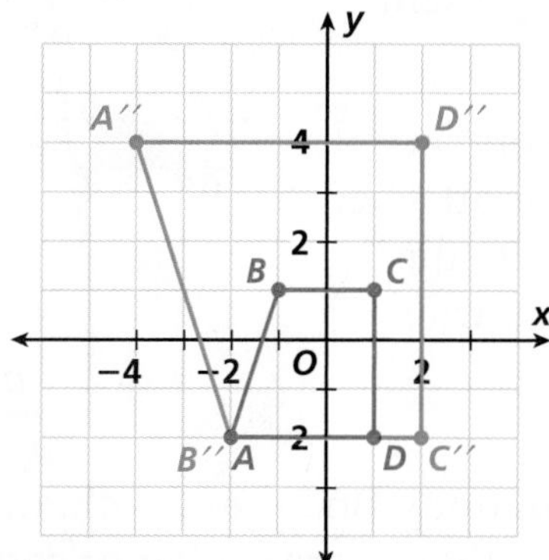

4.

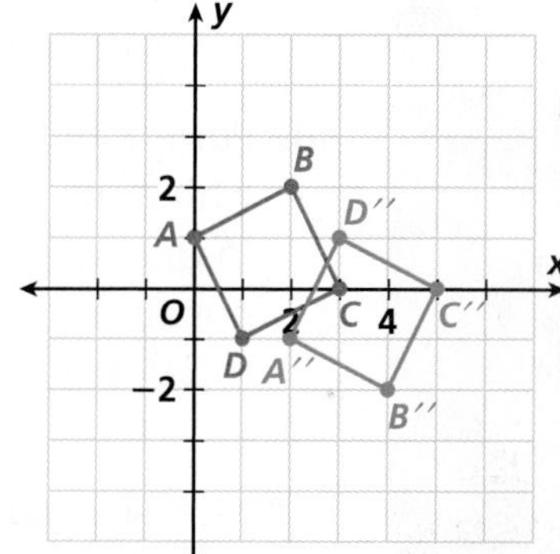

INDEPENDENT PRACTICE

See Examples 1&2 **Identify the combined transformations from the original to the final image, and tell whether the two figures are similar or congruent.**

5.

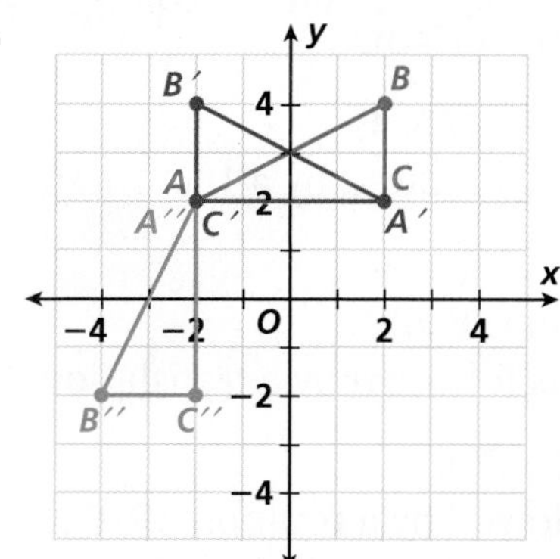

6.

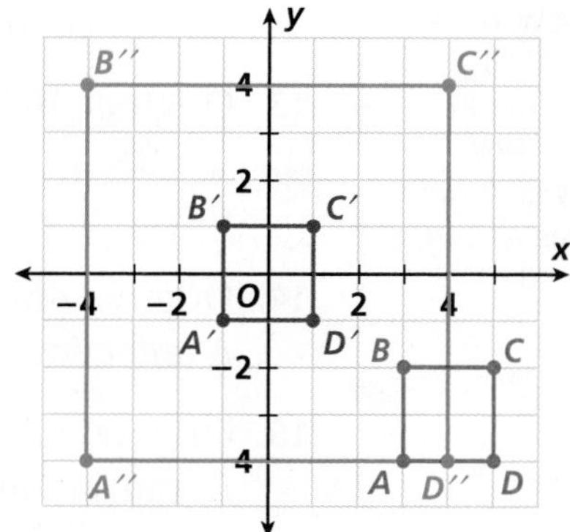

See Example 3

Find a sequence of at least two combined transformations for transforming the original to the final image.

7.

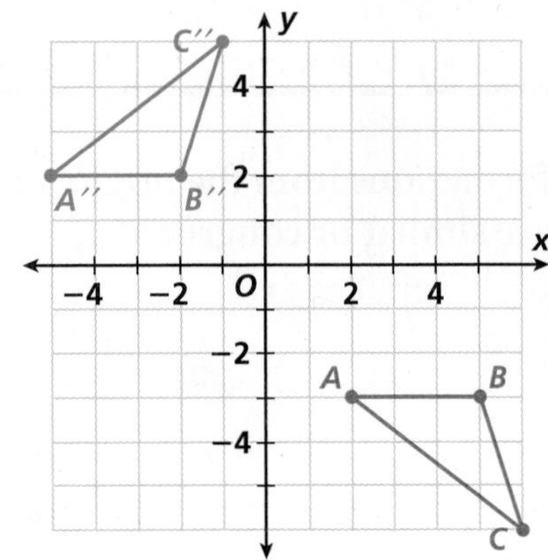

8.

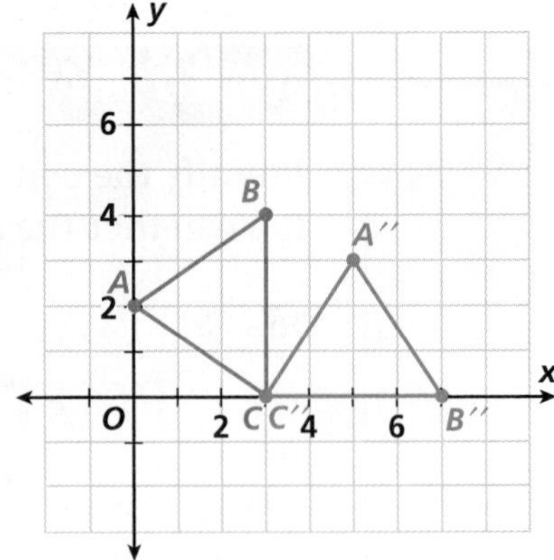

PRACTICE AND PROBLEM SOLVING

Extra Practice

See Extra Practice for more exercises.

Entertainment In the graph shown, the cart of a Ferris wheel is represented by trapezoid *ABCD*.

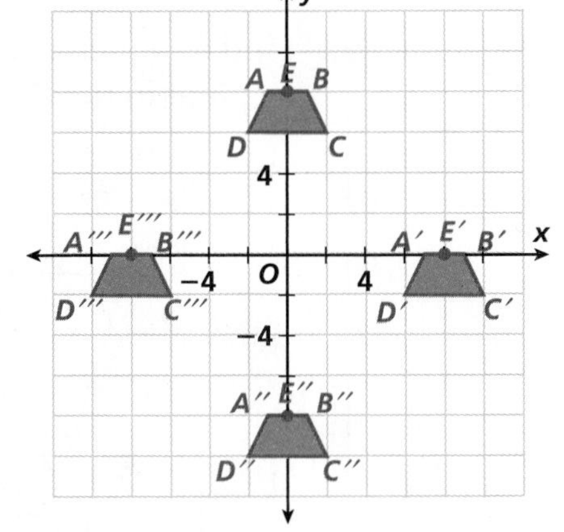

9. The cart is shown in four different positions in the coordinate plane. Do the positions of *ABCD* represent true rotations? Explain.

10. Point *E* in the graph is the point at which the Ferris wheel cart is attached to the "spoke" of the wheel. Do the positions of point *E* represent true rotations? Explain.

LINK Entertainment

The Ferris wheel shown here is located in Vienna, Austria. The first Ferris wheel was designed by George W. Ferris, for the 1893 World's Fair, in Chicago. Now Ferris wheels are common all over the world.

For each sequence of transformations, find the coordinates of the final image and state whether the two figures are similar or congruent.

11. Original *ABC*: $A(-1, -2)$, $B(0, 2)$, $C(1, -1)$
A dilation by a scale factor of 3 with the origin as the center of dilation, followed by a 90° clockwise rotation around the origin.

12. Original *ABCD*: $A(2, -2)$, $B(4, 1)$, $C(6, 1)$, $D(4, -2)$
A translation of 1 unit to the right and 3 units up, followed by a 90° clockwise rotation around the origin.

13. Original *ABC*: $A(4, -2)$, $B(3, 2)$, $C(5, 4)$
A reflection across the *y*-axis, followed by a 180° rotation around the origin.

14. Original *ABC*: $A(3, 3)$, $B(8, 3)$, $C(8, 5)$
A reflection across the *y*-axis followed by a translation 2 units down.

15. Original *ABC*: $A(0, 3)$, $B(4, 3)$, $C(0, 7)$
A translation 2 units up followed by a rotation of 180°.

Identify the combined transformations from the original to the final image, and tell whether the two figures are similar or congruent.

16. Original: ABC, with $A(3, -5)$, $B(3, -2)$, $C(5, -5)$
Final image: $A''B''C''$ with $A''(-2, 2)$, $B''(-2, -1)$, $C''(-4, 2)$

17. Original $ABCDE$ with $A(2, 1)$, $B(2, 3)$, $C(3, 4)$, $D(4, 3)$, $E(4, 1)$
Final image: $A''B''C''D''E''$ with $A''(0, -3)$, $B''(0, -5)$, $C''(1, -6)$, $D''(2, -5)$, $E''(2, -3)$

18. Original: ABC, with $A(1, 5)$, $B(1, 2)$, $C(5, 2)$
Final image: $A''B''C''$ with $A''(2, -10)$, $B''(2, -4)$, $C''(10, -4)$

19. **Critical Thinking** Describe of a sequence of transformations that includes one or more similarity transformations and results in a final image that is congruent to the original.

20. **Write About It** What single transformation can replace the combination of a reflection across the x-axis followed by a reflection across the y-axis? Explain in your own words why these transformations are equivalent.

21. **Challenge** $\triangle ABC$ has vertices $A(-1, -2)$, $B(-2, 2)$, and $C(3, -1)$. Find the coordinates of the images of $\triangle ABC$ after each of the the following transformations:

a. reflection across the x-axis,

b. rotation of 90° clockwise around the origin,

c. reflection across the y-axis,

d. rotation of 90° clockwise around the origin,

e. reflection across the x-axis

Test Prep

22. **Multiple Choice** What are the coordinates of the image of the point $(-4, 3)$ after a rotation of 90° counterclockwise around the origin followed by a translation of 1 unit down and 1 unit left?

Ⓐ $(2, 3)$ Ⓑ $(-3, 4)$ Ⓒ $(-3, -4)$ Ⓓ $(-4, -5)$

23. **Gridded Response** A triangle with vertices $A(2, -2)$, $B(-1, -1)$, and $C(0, 2)$ is reflected across the y-axis and then dilated by a factor of 3 with the origin as the center of dilation. What is the x-coordinate of the image of vertex A?

Quiz for Lessons 5 Through 8

Congruence

In the figure, triangle $ABC \cong$ triangle LMN.

1. Find q.
2. Find r.
3. Find s.

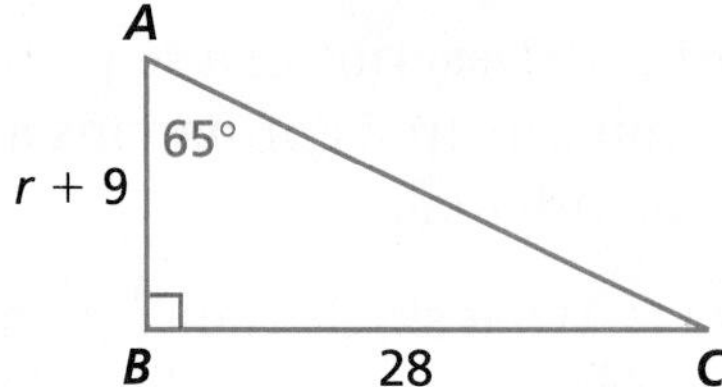

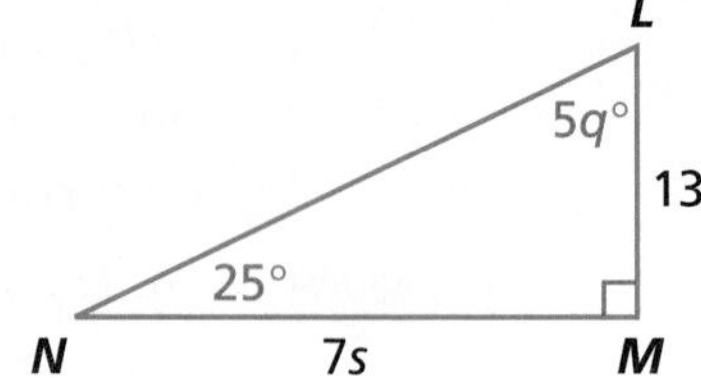

6 Transformations

Graph each transformation.

4. reflection across the x-axis

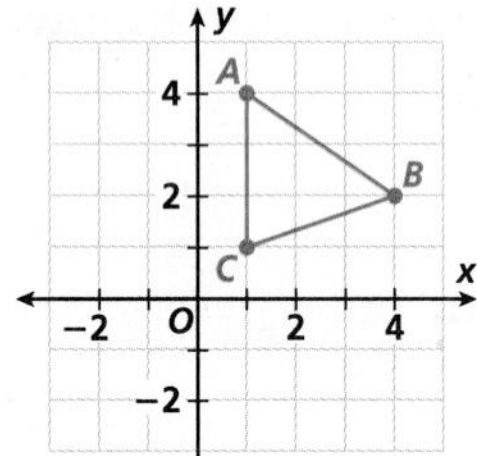

5. 180° rotation about the origin

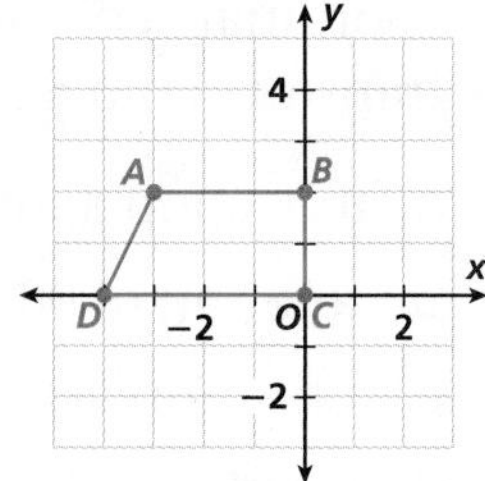

7 Similarity and Congruence Transformations

Identify each transformation and tell whether the two figures are similar or congruent.

6.

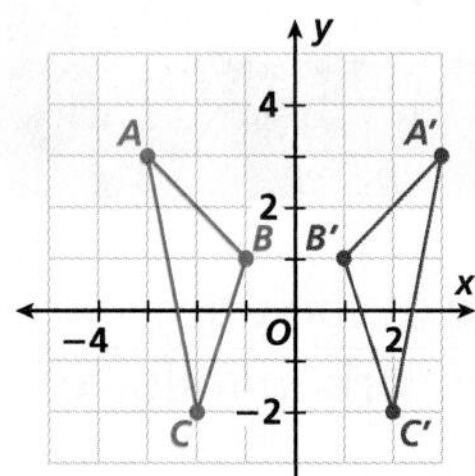

7.

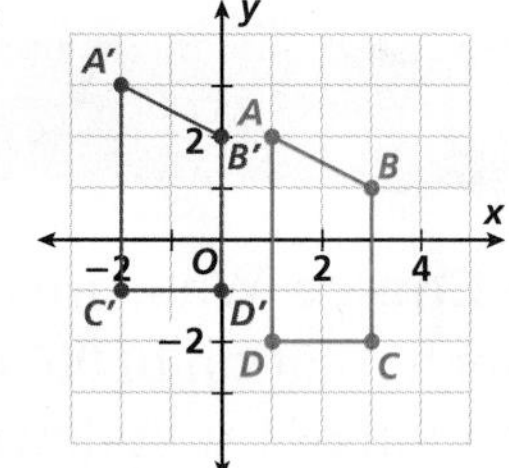

8 Identifying Transformations

8. Identify the combined transformations from the original to the final image, and tell whether the two figures are similar or congruent.

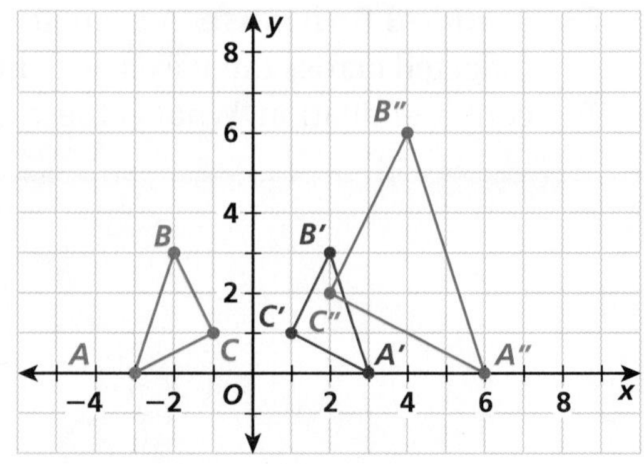

Real-World CONNECTIONS

MATHEMATICAL PRACTICES Reason abstractly and quantitatively.

Thetford Center Covered Bridge

Thetford Center Covered Bridge on the eastern edge of Vermont dates from the mid-1800s. The sides of the span are supported by a Haupt truss, making it the only wooden bridge of its kind in Vermont and one of only three such bridges in the United States.

VERMONT

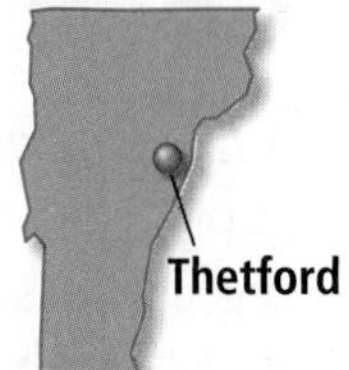

For Problems 1–5, use the graph.

1. The design of a Haupt truss is based on parallelograms. The graph shows two parallelograms in the truss. Prove that figure *A* is a parallelogram by showing that its opposite sides are congruent.
2. Each acute angle of the parallelogram measures 63°. What is the measure of each obtuse angle? (*Hint*: Opposite angles of a parallelogram are congruent.)
3. Parallelogram *A* is transformed to make part of the pattern of the truss. Describe the transformation that moves parallelogram *A* to parallelogram *B*.
4. To complete a section of the truss, the set of parallelograms shown in the figure is reflected across the *y*-axis. Draw the completed section.
5. Describe any symmetry in the completed section of the truss.

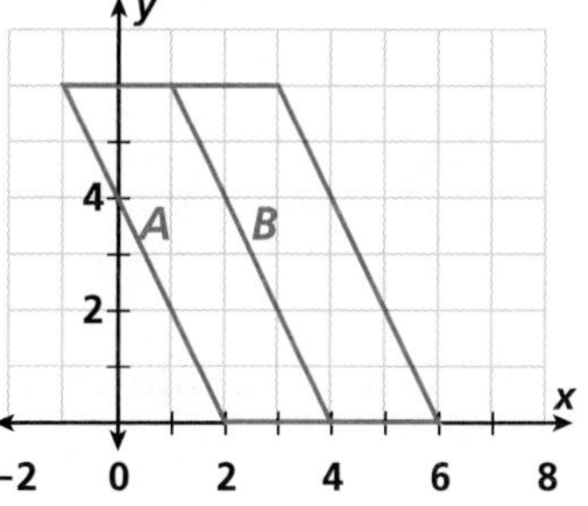

Dave MacKenzie

Real-World Connections

Game Time

Coloring Tessellations

A *tessellation* is a repeating pattern of figures that completely covers a plane with no gaps or overlaps. A regular tessellation consists of regular polygons. Two of the three regular tessellations—triangles and squares—can be colored with two colors so that no two polygons that share an edge are the same color. The third—hexagons—requires three colors.

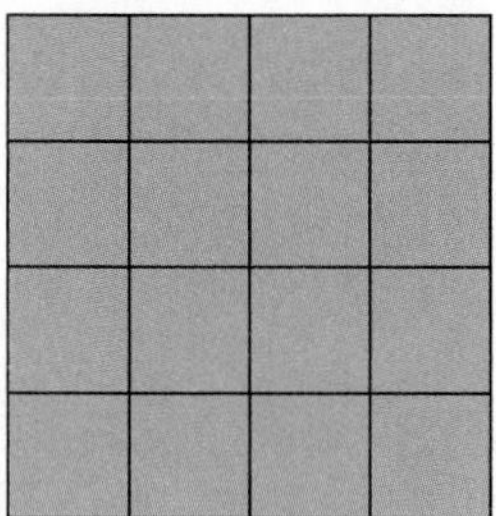
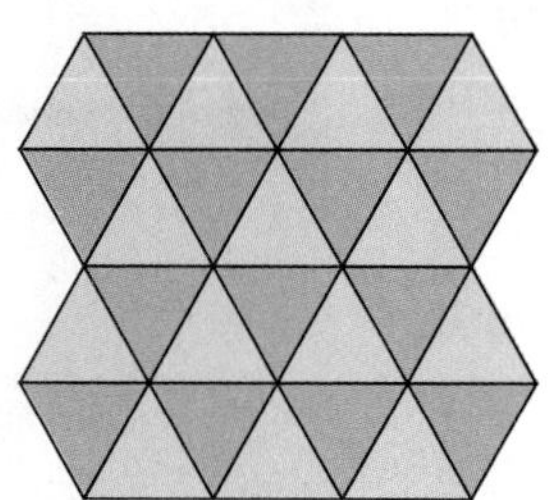
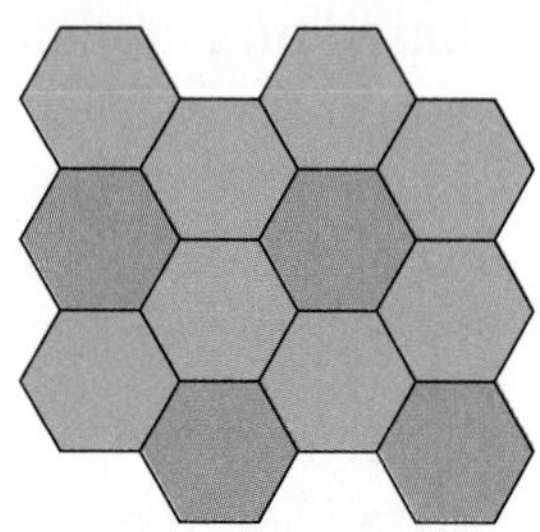

1. Determine if each tessellation can be colored with two colors. If not, tell the minimum number of colors needed.

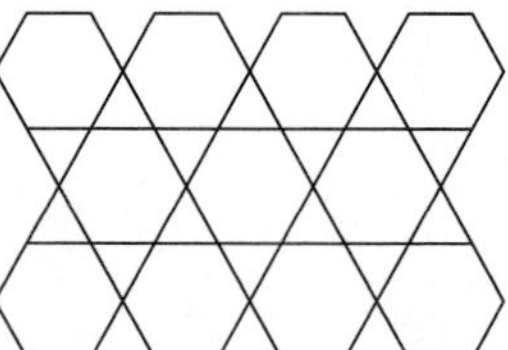
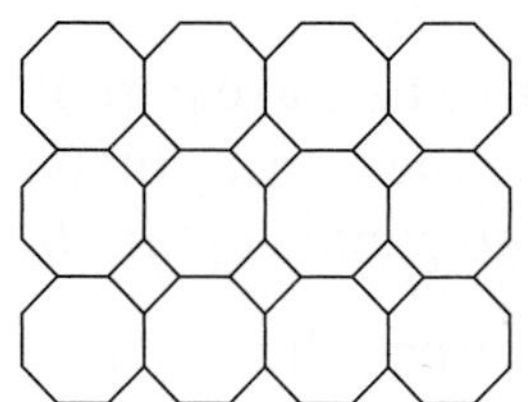
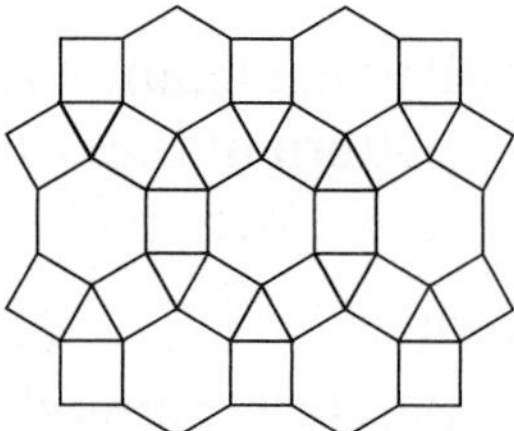

2. Try to write a rule about which tessellations can be colored with two colors.

Polygon Rummy

Jenny Thomas/HMH

The object of this game is to create geometric figures. Each card in the deck shows a property of a geometric figure. To create a figure, you must draw a polygon that matches at least three cards in your hand. For example, if you have the cards "quadrilateral," "a pair of parallel sides," and "a right angle," you could draw a rectangle.

A complete set of rules and playing cards is available online.

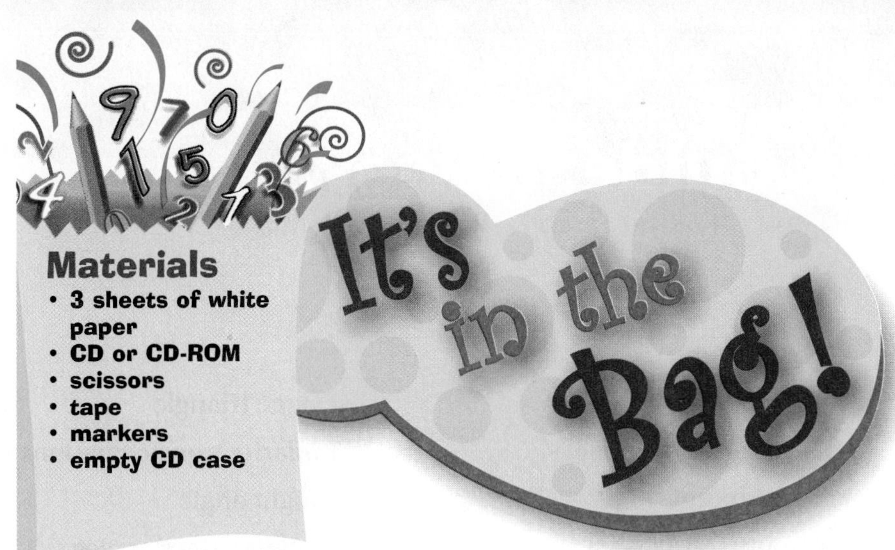

It's in the Bag!
Materials
• 3 sheets of white paper
• CD or CD-ROM
• scissors
• tape
• markers
• empty CD case

PROJECT Project CD Geometry

Make your own CD to record important facts about plane geometry.

1. Fold a sheet of paper in half. Place a CD on top of the paper so that it touches the folded edge. Trace around the CD. **Figure A**

2. Cut out the CD shape, being careful to leave the folded edge attached. This will create two paper CDs that are joined together. Cut a hole in the center of each paper CD. **Figure B**

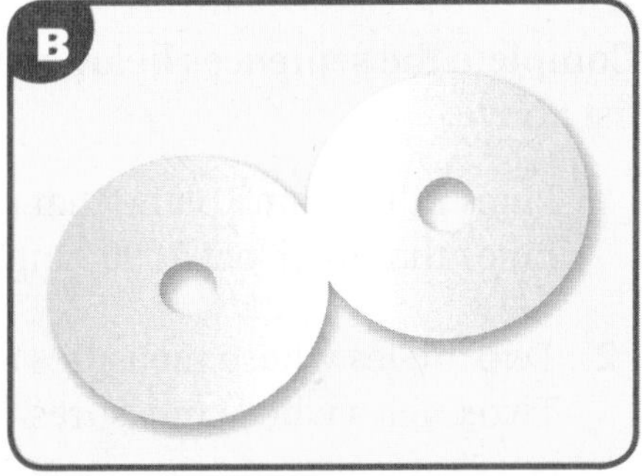

3. Repeat steps 1 and 2 with the other two sheets of paper.

4. Tape the ends of the paper CDs together to make a string of six CDs. **Figure C**

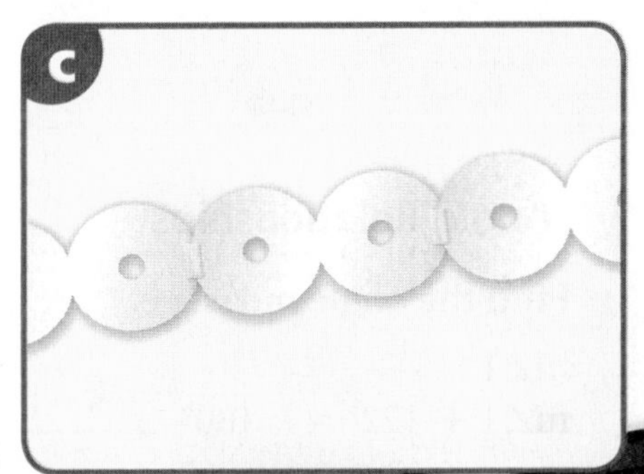

5. Accordion fold the CDs to make a booklet. Write the number and name of the chapter on the top CD. Store the CD booklet in an empty CD case.

Taking Note of the Math

Use the blank pages in the CD booklet to take notes on the chapter. Be sure to include definitions and sample problems that will help you review essential concepts about plane geometry.

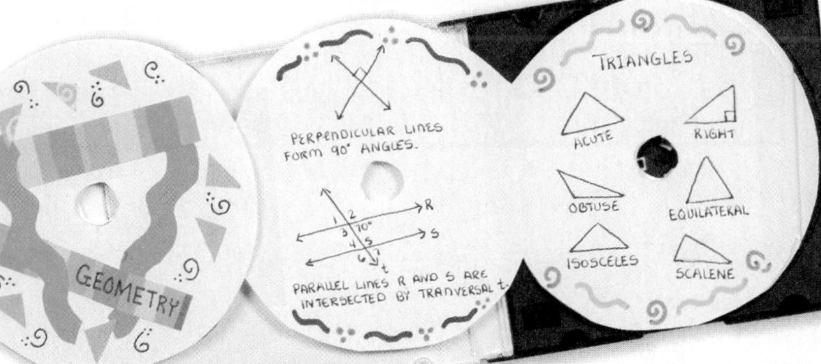

Study Guide: Review

Vocabulary

acute angle
acute triangle
adjacent angles
angle
center of rotation
complementary angles
congruence transformations
congruent angles
congruent figures
correspondence
equilateral triangle
image
isosceles triangle
midpoint
obtuse angle
obtuse triangle
parallel lines
perpendicular lines
reflection
right angle
right triangle
rotation
scalene triangle
similarity transformations
straight angle
supplementary angles
transformation
translation
transversal
Triangle Inequality Theorem
Triangle Sum Theorem
vertical angles

Complete the sentences below with vocabulary words from the list above.

1. Lines in the same plane that never meet are called __?__.
Lines that intersect at 90° angles are called __?__.

2. Two angles whose measures add to 90° are called __?__.
Two angles whose measures add to 180° are called __?__.

EXAMPLES

1 Angle Relationships

■ **Find the angle measure.**

$m\angle 1$

$$\begin{aligned} m\angle 1 + 122^\circ &= 180^\circ \\ -122^\circ \quad & \quad -122^\circ \\ \hline m\angle 1 &= 58^\circ \end{aligned}$$

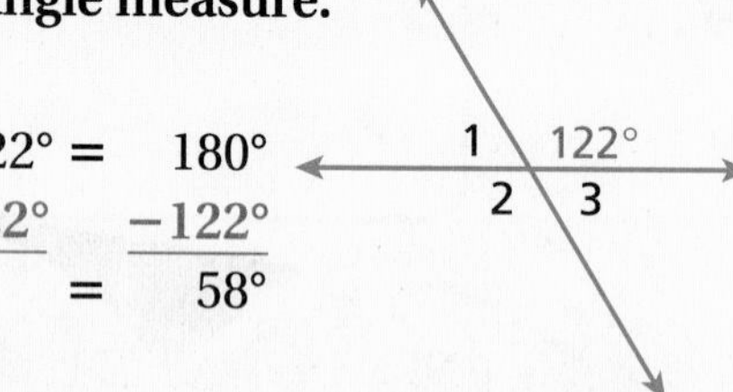

EXERCISES

Find each angle measure.

3. $m\angle 1$

4. $m\angle 2$

5. $m\angle 3$

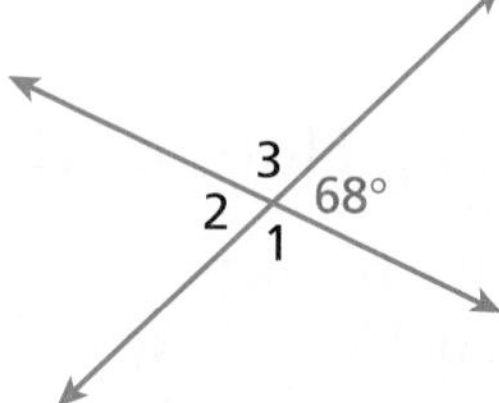

EXAMPLES

EXERCISES

2 Parallel and Perpendicular Lines

Line $j \parallel$ line k. Find each angle measure.

- $m\angle 1$

  $m\angle 1 = 143°$

- $m\angle 2$

$$\begin{aligned} m\angle 2 + 143° &= 180° \\ -143° &\quad -143° \\ m\angle 2 &= 37° \end{aligned}$$

Line $p \parallel$ line q. Find each angle measure.

6. $m\angle 1$
7. $m\angle 2$
8. $m\angle 3$
9. $m\angle 4$
10. $m\angle 5$

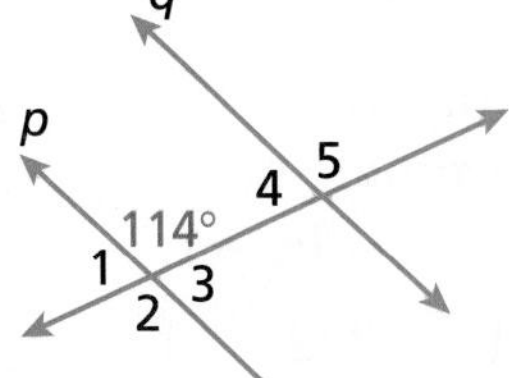

3 Triangles

- **Find $n°$.**

$$\begin{aligned} n° + 50° + 90° &= 180° \\ n° + 140° &= 180° \\ -140° &\quad -140° \\ n° &= 40° \end{aligned}$$

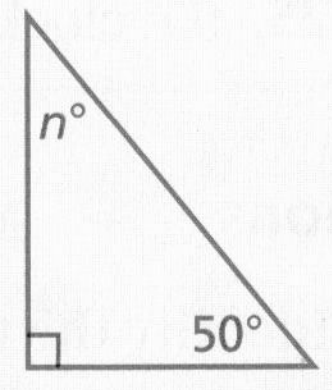

- **Tell whether a triangle can have sides that measure 9 ft, 20 ft, and 30 ft.**

  $9 + 20 \not> 30$ *Triangle Inequality Theorem*

  A triangle cannot have these side lengths.

11. Find $m°$.
12. Find $p°$.

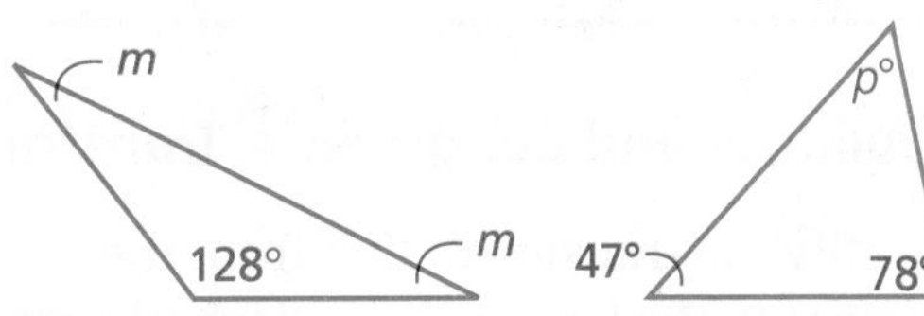

Tell whether a triangle can have sides with the given lengths.

13. 20 m, 41 m, 52 m
14. 16 ft, 20 ft, 38 ft

4 Coordinate Geometry

- **Graph the polygon with the given vertices. Give the most specific name.**

  $D(-2, 3)$, $E(2, 3)$, $F(1, 1)$, $G(-3, 1)$

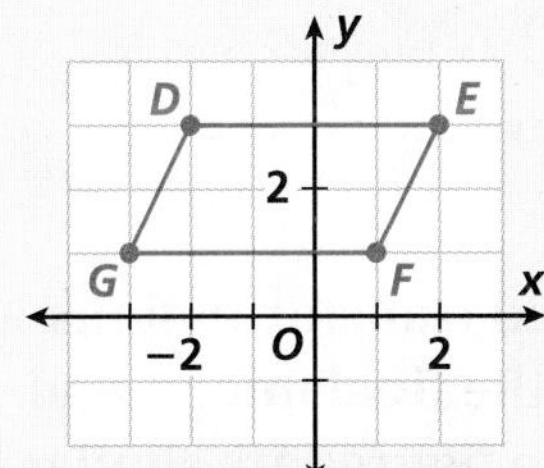

$DE = GF = 4$

$DG = EF = \sqrt{5}$

parallelogram

Graph the polygons with the given vertices. Give the most specific name for each polygon.

15. $A(-2, 0)$, $B(3, -3)$, $C(0, -3)$
16. $Q(2, 3)$, $R(4, 4)$, $S(4, -3)$, $T(2, 0)$
17. $K(2, 3)$, $L(3, 0)$, $M(2, -3)$, $N(1, 0)$
18. $W(2, 2)$, $X(2, -2)$, $Y(-1, -3)$, $Z(-1, 1)$

5 Congruence

- **Triangle $ABC \cong$ triangle FDE. Find x.**

$$\begin{aligned} x - 4 &= 4 \\ +4 &\quad +4 \\ x &= 8 \end{aligned}$$

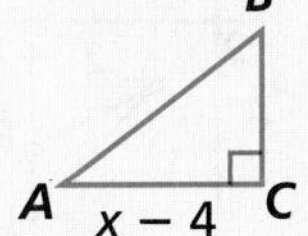

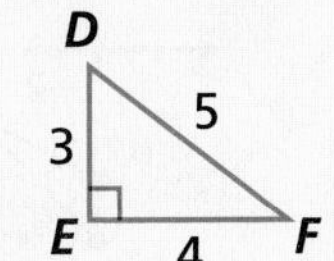

Triangle $JQZ \cong$ triangle ZTV.

19. Find x.
20. Find t.
21. Find q.

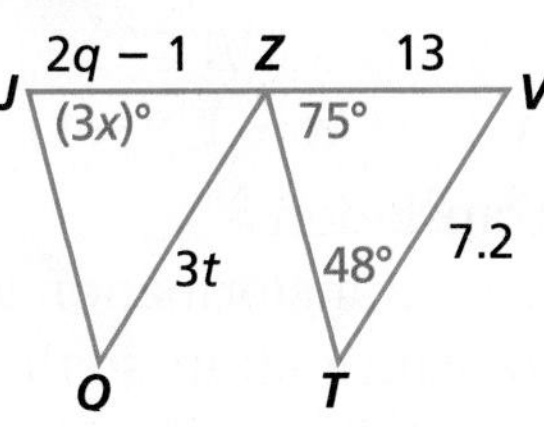

Study Guide: Review

EXAMPLES

EXERCISES

6 Transformations

■ **Graph the reflection of triangle *ABC* across the *x*-axis.**

Multiply the *y*-coordinate of each vertex by −1.

$A(2, 4) \rightarrow A'(2, -4)$
$B(4, 4) \rightarrow B'(4, -4)$
$C(2, 1) \rightarrow C'(2, -1)$

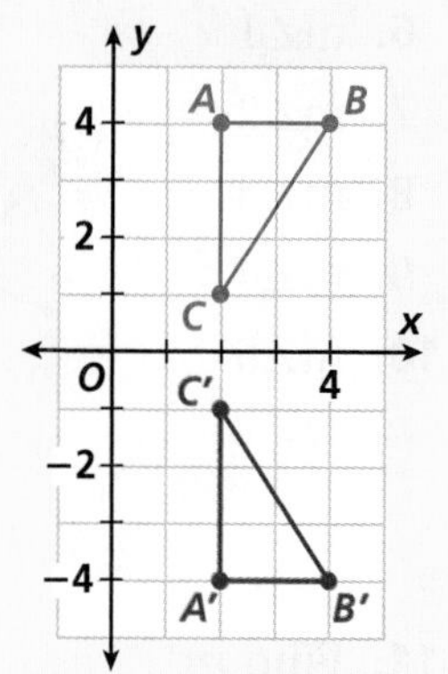

Graph each transformation of triangle *DEF*.

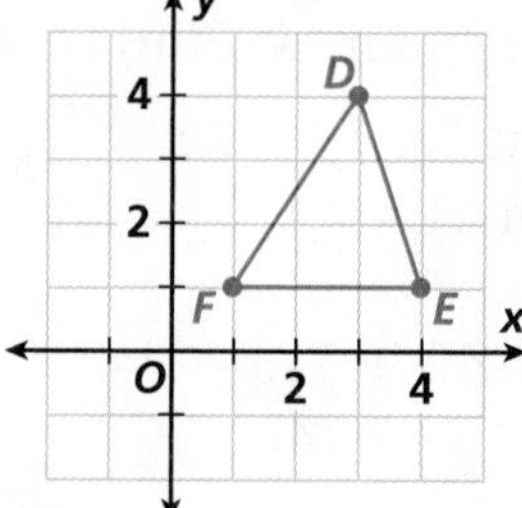

22. reflection across the *y*-axis

23. translation 1 unit left and 3 units up

24. 180° rotation around (0, 0)

25. 90° clockwise rotation around (0, 0)

7 Similarity and Congruence Transformations

■ **Identify the transformation from the original to the image, and tell whether the two figures are similar or congruent.**

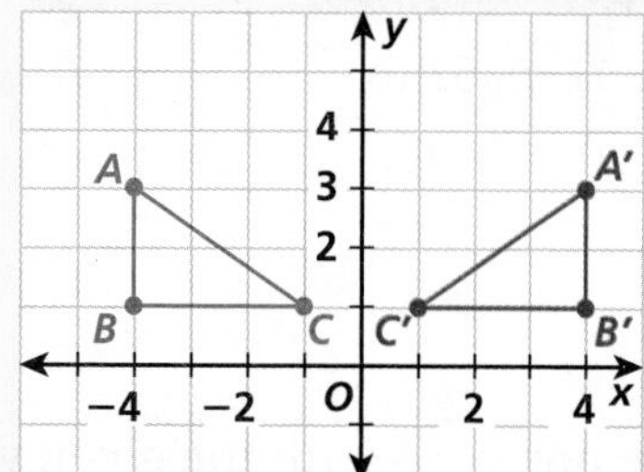

Because $(x, y) \rightarrow (-x, y)$, the image is a reflection across the *x*-axis, and the triangles are congruent.

Identify the transformation from the original to the image, and tell whether the two figures are similar or congruent.

26.

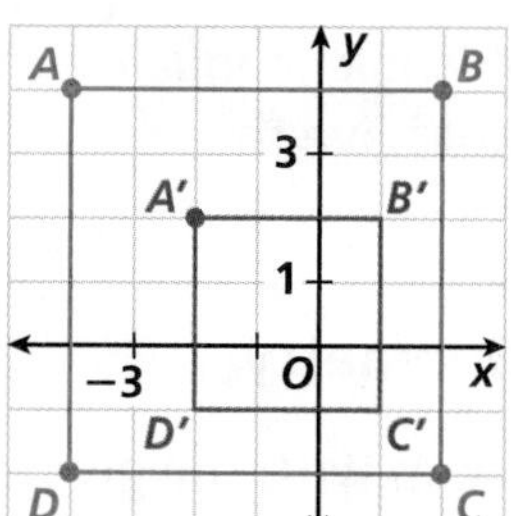

8 Identifying Combined Transformations

■ **Identify the combined transformations from the original to the final image, and state whether the two figures are similar or congruent.**

$ABC \rightarrow A'B'C'$:
$(x, y) \rightarrow (-x, y)$
Reflection
$A'B'C' \rightarrow A''B''C''$:
$(x, y) \rightarrow (x - 1, y - 1)$
Translation
Each transformation is a congruence transformation, so the original and final images are congruent.

Identify the combined transformations from the original to the final image, and state whether the two figures are similar or congruent.

27.

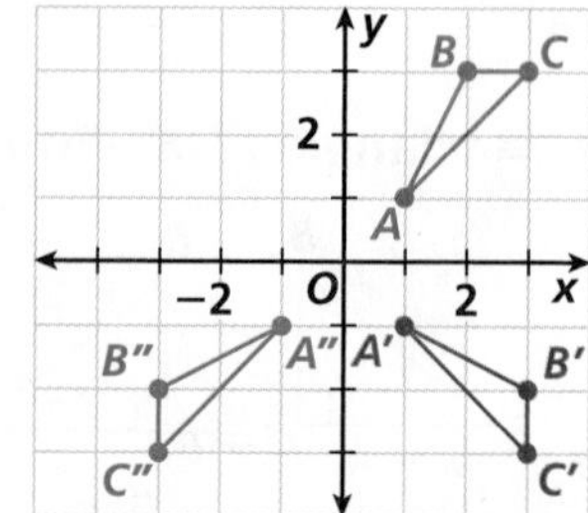

Study Guide: Review

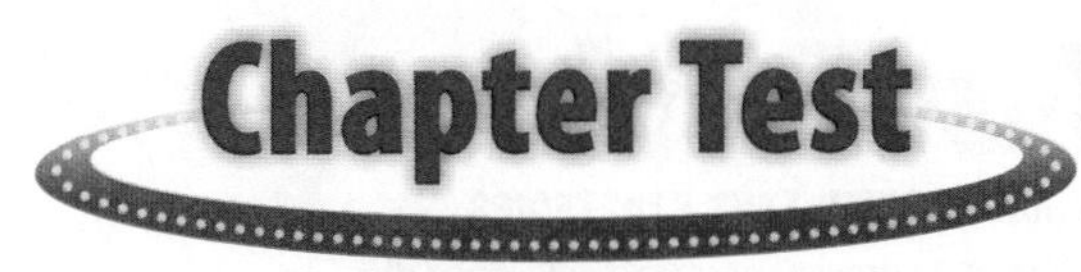

In the figure, line $m \parallel$ line n.

1. Name two pairs of supplementary angles.
2. Find m∠1.
3. Find m∠2.
4. Find m∠3.
5. Find m∠4.
6. Two angles in a triangle have measures of 44° and 57°. What is the measure of the third angle?
7. Can Julia cut a triangular patch for a quilt that has side lengths of $1\frac{1}{2}$ inches, 2 inches, and 4 inches? Explain.

Graph the polygons with the given vertices. Give the most specific name for each polygon.

8. $A(3,4)$, $B(8,4)$, $C(5,0)$, $D(0,0)$
9. $K(-4,0)$, $L(-2,5)$, $M(2,5)$, $N(4,0)$

In the figure, quadrilateral $ABCD \cong$ quadrilateral $LMNO$.

10. Find m.
11. Find n.
12. Find p.

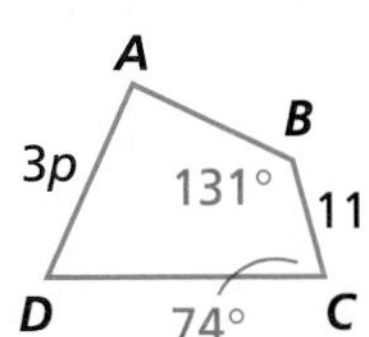

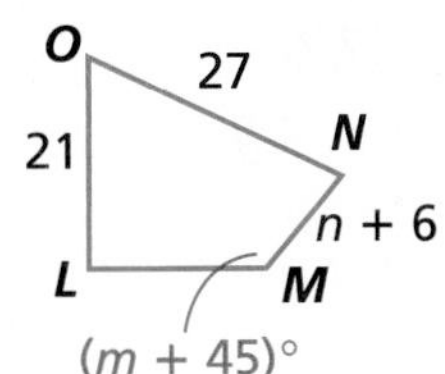

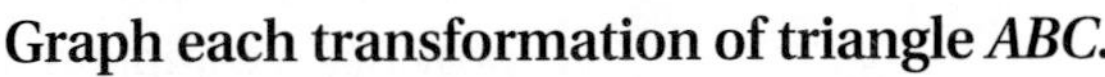

Graph each transformation of triangle ABC.

13. translation 6 units right
14. reflection across the y-axis
15. Identify the transformation from the original to the image, and tell whether the two figures are similar or congruent.

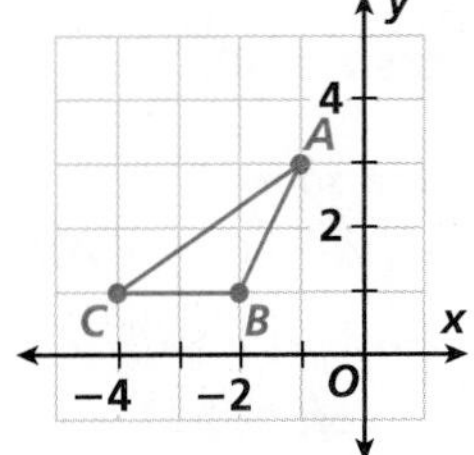

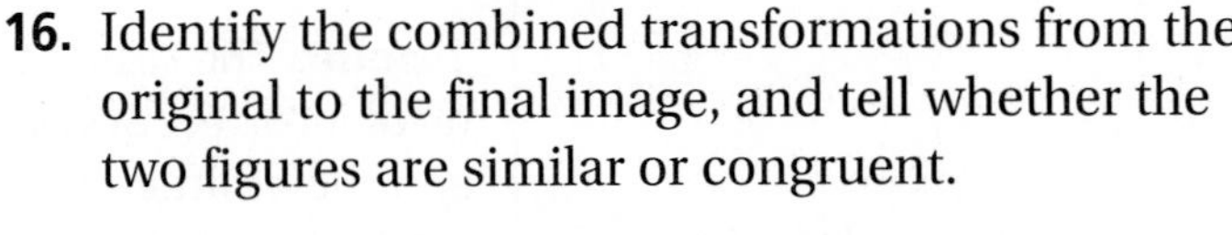

16. Identify the combined transformations from the original to the final image, and tell whether the two figures are similar or congruent.

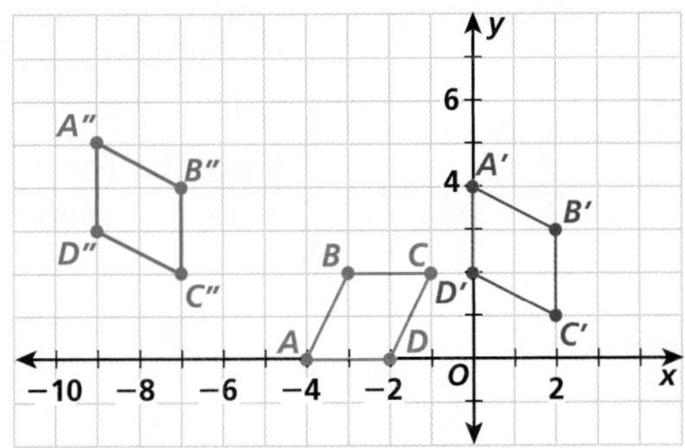

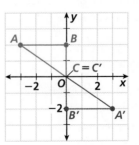

Extended Response: Write Extended Responses

Extended response test items often consist of multi-step problems to evaluate your understanding of a math concept. Extended response questions are scored using a 4-point scoring rubric.

EXAMPLE 1

Extended Response Julianna bought a shirt marked down 20%. She had a coupon for an additional 20% off the sale price. Is this the same as getting 40% off the regular price? Explain your reasoning.

4-point response:

No, the prices are not the same. Suppose the shirt originally cost $40.

20% off a 20% markdown: $40 × 20% = $8; $40 − $8 = $32;
$32 × 20% = $6.40; $32 − $6.40 = $25.60

40% off: $40 × 40% = $16; $40 − $16 = $24

The student answers the question correctly and shows all work.

3-point response:

Yes, it is the same. If the shirt originally cost $25, it would cost $15 after taking 20% off of a 20% discount. A 40% discount off $20 is $15.

Shirt original price = $25	
Shirt at 20% off = $20	$25 × 20% = $5; $25 − $5 = $20
Shirt at 20% off sales price = $15	$20 × 20% = $4; $20 − $4 = $15
Shirt at 40% off = $15	$25 × 40% = $10; $25 − $10 = $15

The student makes a minor computation error that results in an incorrect answer.

2-point response:

No, it is not the same. A $30 shirt with 20% off and then an additional 20% off is $6. A $30 shirt at 40% off is $12.

The student makes major computation errors and does not show all work.

1-point response:

It is the same.

The student shows no work and has the wrong answer.

Scoring Rubric

4 points: The student answers all parts of the question correctly, shows all work, and provides a complete and correct explanation.

3 points: The student answers all parts of the question, shows all work, and provides a complete explanation that demonstrates understanding, but the student makes minor errors in computation.

2 points: The student does not answer all parts of the question but shows all work and provides a complete and correct explanation for the parts answered, or the student correctly answers all parts of the question but does not show all work or does not provide an explanation.

1 point: The student gives incorrect answers and shows little or no work or explanation, or the student does not follow directions.

0 points: The student gives no response.

To receive full credit, make sure all parts of the problem are answered. Be sure to show all of your work and to write a neat and clear explanation.

Read each test item and answer the questions that follow.

Item A
Janell has two job offers. Job A pays $500 per week. Job B pays $200 per week plus 15% commission on her sales. She expects to make $7500 in sales every 4 weeks. Which job pays better? Explain your reasoning.

1. A student wrote this response:

   Job A pays better.

   What score should the student's response receive? Explain your reasoning.

2. What additional information, if any, should the student's response include in order to receive full credit?

3. Add to the response so that it receives a score of 4 points.

4. How much would Janell have to make in sales every 4 weeks for job A and job B to pay the same amount?

Item B
A new MP3 player normally costs $97.99. This week, it is on sale for 15% off its regular price. In addition to this, Jasmine receives an employee discount of 20% off the sale price. Excluding sales tax, what percent of the original price will Jasmine pay for the MP3 player?

5. What information needs to be included in a response to receive full credit?

6. Write a response that would receive full credit.

Item C
Three houses were originally purchased for $125,000. After each year, the value of each house either increased or decreased. Which house had the least value after the third year? What was the value of that house? Explain your reasoning.

		Percent Change in Value		
House	**Original Cost ($)**	**Year 1**	**Year 2**	**Year 3**
A	125,000	1%	1%	1%
B	125,000	4%	−2%	−1%
C	125,000	3%	−2%	2%

7. A student wrote this response:

   House A increased 3% over three years. House B increased 1% over three years. House C increased 3% over three years. So, House B had the least value after the third year. Its value increased 1% of $125,000, or $1250, for a total value of $126,250.

   What score should the student's response receive? Explain your reasoning.

8. What additional information, if any, should the student's response include in order to receive full credit?

Item D
Kara is trying to save $4500 to buy a used car. She has $3000 in an account that earns a yearly simple interest of 5%. Will she have enough money in her account after 3 years to buy a car? If not, how much more money will she need? Explain your reasoning.

9. What information needs to be included in a response to receive full credit?

10. Write a response that would receive full credit.

Test Tackler

CHAPTER 5

Standardized Test Prep

Learn It Online
State Test Practice

Cumulative Assessment

Multiple Choice

1. Which angle is a right angle?

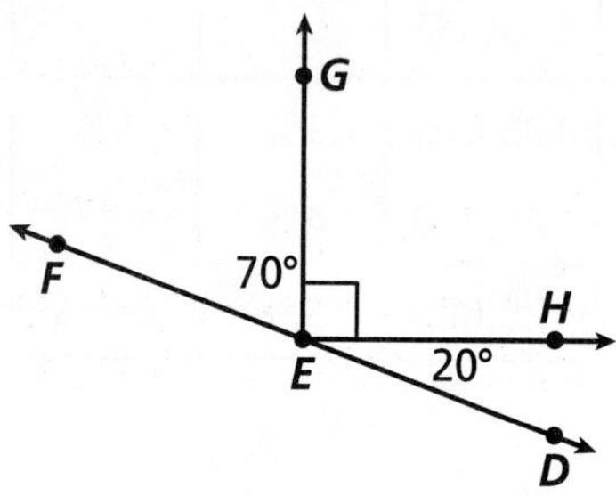

Ⓐ ∠FED Ⓒ ∠GEH

Ⓑ ∠FEG Ⓓ ∠GED

2. A jeweler buys a diamond for $68 and resells it for $298. What is the percent increase to the nearest percent?

Ⓕ 3% Ⓗ 138%

Ⓖ 33% Ⓙ 338%

3. A grocery store sells one dozen ears of white corn for $2.40. What is the unit price for one ear of corn?

Ⓐ $0.05/ear of corn

Ⓑ $0.20/ear of corn

Ⓒ $1.30/ear of corn

Ⓓ $2.40/ear of corn

4. The people of Ireland drink the most milk in the world. All together, they drink more than 602,000,000 quarts each year. What is this number written in scientific notation?

Ⓕ 60.2×10^5

Ⓖ 602×10^6

Ⓗ 6.02×10^8

Ⓙ 6.02×10^9

5. Cara is making a model of a car that is 14 feet long. What other information is needed to find the length of the model?

Ⓐ Car's width Ⓒ Scale factor

Ⓑ Car's speed Ⓓ Car's height

6. For which equation is the point a solution to the equation?

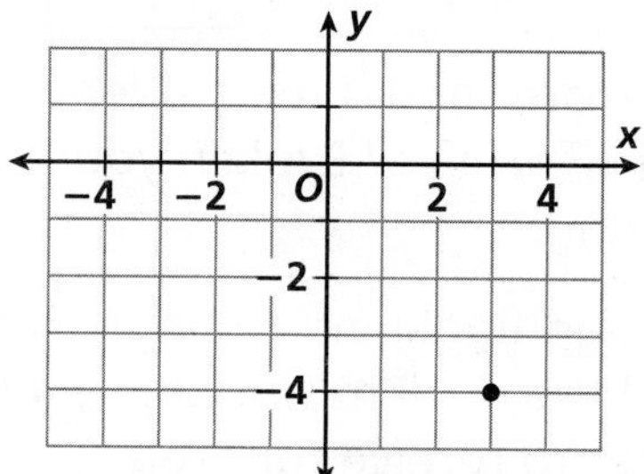

Ⓕ $y = 2x + 1$ Ⓗ $y = -x + 1$

Ⓖ $y = 2x - 2$ Ⓙ $y = -2x + 2$

7. What is q in the acute triangle?

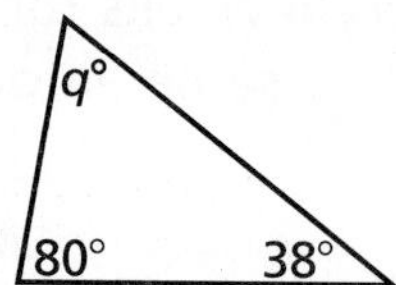

Ⓐ 62 Ⓒ 118

Ⓑ 72 Ⓓ 128

8. Which expression represents "twice the difference of a number and 5"?

Ⓕ $2(x + 5)$ Ⓗ $2(x - 5)$

Ⓖ $2x - 5$ Ⓙ $2x + 5$

9. For which equation is $x = -1$ the solution?

Ⓐ $3x + 8 = 11$ Ⓒ $-3x + 8 = 5$

Ⓑ $8 - x = 9$ Ⓓ $8 + x = 9$

10. Marcus bought a shirt that was on sale for 20% off its regular price. If Marcus paid $20 for the shirt, what is its regular price?

(F) $25 (H) $16

(G) $40 (J) $30

Use logic to eliminate answer choices that are incorrect. This will help you to make an educated guess if you are having trouble with the question.

Gridded Response

Use the following figure for items 11 and 12. Line p is parallel to line q.

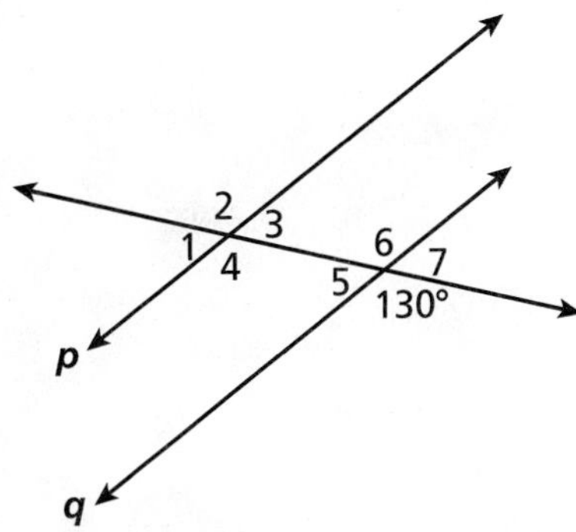

11. What is the measure of $\angle 4$, in degrees?

12. What is the sum of the measures of $\angle 2$ and $\angle 6$, in degrees?

13. Maryann bought a purse on sale for 25% off. She paid $36 for the purse before tax. How much did the purse cost originally?

14. What is the value of the expression $-2xy + y^2$, when $x = -1$ and $y = 4$?

15. A parallelogram has vertices at $A(-2, 4)$, $B(-1, -1)$, $C(1, 0)$, and $D(0, 5)$. What is the x-coordinate of B after the parallelogram is reflected over the y-axis?

16. Guillermo invests $180 at a 4% simple interest rate for 6 months. How much money will Guillermo earn in interest?

Short Response

S1. Triangle ABC, with vertices $A(2, 3)$, $B(4, -5)$, $C(6, 8)$, is reflected across the x-axis to form triangle $A'B'C'$.

a. On a coordinate grid, draw and label triangle ABC and triangle $A'B'C'$.

b. Give the new coordinates for triangle $A'B'C'$.

S2. Complete the table to show the number of diagonals for the polygons with the numbers of sides listed.

Number of Sides	Number of Diagonals
3	0
4	■
5	■
6	■
7	■
n	■

Extended Response

E1. Four people are introduced to each other at a party, and they all shake hands.

a. Explain in words how the diagram can be used to determine the number of handshakes exchanged at the party.

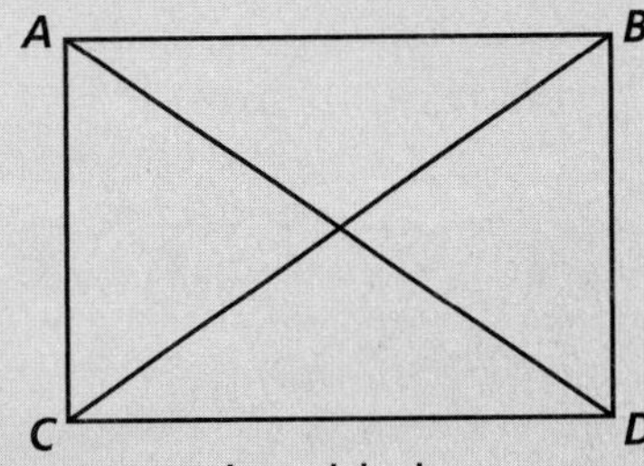

b. How many handshakes are exchanged?

c. Suppose that six people were introduced to each other at a party. Draw a diagram similar to the one shown that could be used to determine the number of handshakes exchanged.

CHAPTER 6

Measurement and Geometry

Chapter Focus

- Analyze figures in two and three dimensions.
- Use fundamental geometric facts to solve problems.

Why Learn This?

Calculating perimeter, area, and volume is important to architects like Frank Lloyd Wright, who designed *Fallingwater*, the home shown here.

Are You Ready?

Vocabulary

Choose the best term from the list to complete each sentence.

1. A(n) __?__ is a number that represents a part of a whole.
2. A(n) __?__ is another way of writing a fraction.
3. To multiply 7 by the fraction $\frac{2}{3}$, multiply 7 by the __?__ of the fraction and then divide the result by the __?__ of the fraction.
4. To round 7.836 to the nearest tenth, look at the digit in the __?__ place.

decimal
denominator
fraction
tenths
hundredths
numerator

Complete these exercises to review skills you will need for this chapter.

Square and Cube Numbers

Evaluate.

5. 16^2 **6.** 9^3 **7.** $(4.1)^2$ **8.** $(0.5)^3$

9. $\left(\frac{1}{4}\right)^2$ **10.** $\left(\frac{2}{5}\right)^2$ **11.** $\left(\frac{1}{2}\right)^3$ **12.** $\left(\frac{2}{3}\right)^3$

Multiply with Fractions

Multiply.

13. $\frac{1}{2}(8)(10)$ **14.** $\frac{1}{2}(3)(5)$ **15.** $\frac{1}{3}(9)(12)$ **16.** $\frac{1}{3}(4)(11)$

17. $\frac{1}{2}(8^2)16$ **18.** $\frac{1}{2}(5^2)24$ **19.** $\frac{1}{2}(6)(3 + 9)$ **20.** $\frac{1}{2}(5)(7 + 4)$

Multiply with Decimals

Multiply. Write each answer to the nearest tenth.

21. $2(3.14)(12)$ **22.** $3.14(5^2)$ **23.** $3.14(4^2)(7)$ **24.** $3.14(2.3^2)(5)$

Multiply with Fractions and Decimals

Multiply. Write each answer to the nearest tenth.

25. $\frac{1}{3}(3.14)(5^2)(7)$ **26.** $\frac{1}{3}(3.14)(5^3)$

27. $\frac{1}{3}(3.14)(3.2)^2(2)$ **28.** $\frac{4}{3}(3.14)(2.7)^3$

29. $\frac{1}{5}\left(\frac{22}{7}\right)(4^2)(5)$ **30.** $\frac{4}{11}\left(\frac{22}{7}\right)(3.2^3)$

31. $\frac{1}{2}\left(\frac{22}{7}\right)(1.7)^2(4)$ **32.** $\frac{7}{11}\left(\frac{22}{7}\right)(9.5)^3$

CHAPTER 6

Study Guide: Preview

Where You've Been

Previously, you

- found the perimeter and area of polygons.
- found the volume of prisms and cylinders.

In This Chapter

You will study

- describing the effect on volume when the dimensions of a solid change proportionally.
- finding the volume of various solids, and the surface area of spheres.

Where You're Going

You can use the skills learned in this chapter

- to determine the distance traveled along a circular route.
- to compare the volumes of containers with different shapes.

Key Vocabulary/Vocabulario

circle	círculo
circumference	circunferincia
diameter	diámetro
sphere	esfera

Vocabulary Connections

To become familiar with some of the vocabulary terms in the chapter, consider the following. You may refer to the chapter, the glossary, or a dictionary if you like.

1. The word **circumference** contains the prefix *circum-*, which means "around." What do you suppose the circumference of a circle is?
2. The Greek prefix *dia-* means "across." What do you suppose the **diameter** of a circle is?

Study Strategy: Concept Map

Concept maps are visual tools for organizing information. A concept map shows how key concepts are related and can help you summarize and analyze information in lessons or chapters.

Create a Concept Map

1. Give your concept map a title.
2. Identify the main idea of your concept map.
3. List the key concepts you learned.
4. Link the concepts to show the relationships between the concepts and the main idea.

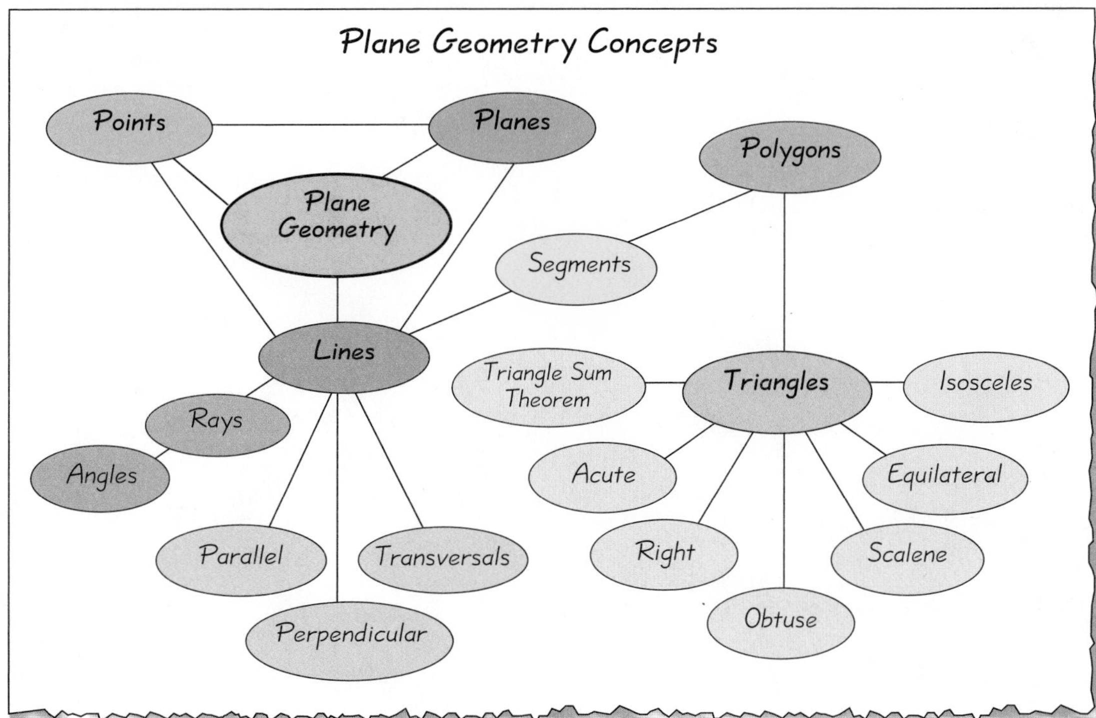

Try This

1. Add more links to the "Polygon" idea in the concept map above.
2. Create your own concept map for another topic you learned about in this course.

Approximate *Pi* by Measuring

Use with Circles

Learn It Online
Lab Resources Online

You can use a ruler and string to measure circles.

MATHEMATICAL PRACTICES **Use appropriate tools strategically.**

Activity

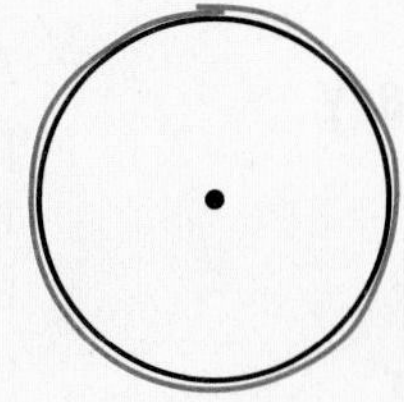

a. Find the distance around three different circular objects by wrapping a piece of string around each of them and using a marker to mark the string where it meets. Be sure that your mark shows on both overlapping parts of the string. Lay the string out straight and use a ruler to measure between the marks. Record the measurements for each object.

b. Measure the distance across each object. Be sure that you measure each circle at its widest point. Record the measurements for each object.

Object	Distance Around	Distance Across	$\frac{\text{Distance Around}}{\text{Distance Across}}$

c. Divide the distance around by the distance across for each object. Round each answer to the nearest hundredth and record it.

Think and Discuss

1. What do you notice about the ratios of the distance around each object to the distance across each object?

2. How could you estimate the distance around a circular object without measuring it if you know the distance across?

Try This

1. Choose three circular objects different from the objects you used in the activity.

a. Measure the distance across each object.

b. Estimate the distance around each object without measuring.

c. Measure the distance around each object and compare each measurement with the estimate from **b**.

6-1 Circles

Many amusement park rides speed the rider along a circular path. Each time around the circle completes one *circumference* of the circle.

Vocabulary

circle

radius

diameter

circumference

A **circle** is the set of points in a plane that are a fixed distance from a given point, called the *center*. A **radius** connects the center to any point on the circle, and a **diameter** connects two points on the circle and passes through the center.

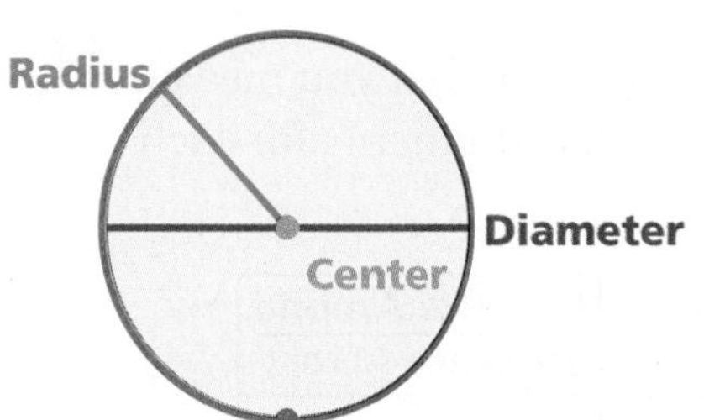

The diameter d is twice the radius r.

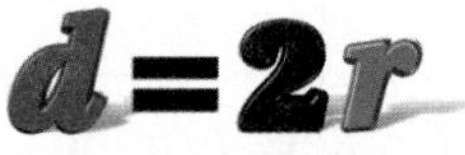

Circumference

The **circumference** of a circle is the distance around the circle. The ratio of the circumference to the diameter $\frac{C}{d}$ of any circle is the same for all circles. This ratio is called pi, or π. You can use this relationship to find a formula for circumference.

Remember!

Pi (π) is an irrational number that is often approximated by the rational numbers 3.14 and $\frac{22}{7}$.

CIRCUMFERENCE OF A CIRCLE		
Words	**Numbers**	**Formula**
The circumference C of a circle is π times the diameter d, or 2π times the radius r.	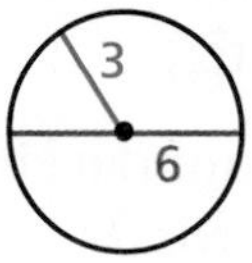 (circle with radius 3, diameter 6) $C = \pi(6)$ $= 2\pi(3)$ ≈ 18.8 units	$C = \pi d$ or $C = 2\pi r$

EXAMPLE 1

Finding the Circumference of a Circle

Find the circumference of each circle, both in terms of π and to the nearest tenth. Use 3.14 for π.

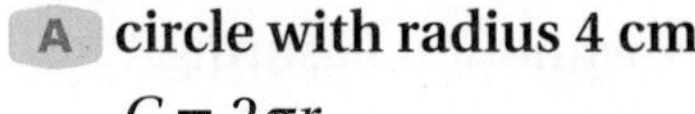

A circle with radius 4 cm

$C = 2\pi r$

$= 2\pi(4)$

$= 8\pi \text{ cm} \approx 25.1 \text{ cm}$

B circle with diameter 4.5 in.

$C = \pi d$

$= \pi(4.5)$

$= 4.5\pi \text{ in.} \approx 14.1 \text{ in.}$

Steve Hamblin/Alamy

Video Lesson Tutorials Online my.hrw.com

AREA OF A CIRCLE		
Words	**Numbers**	**Formula**
The area A of a circle is π times the square of the radius r.	3 $A = \pi(3^2)$ $= 9\pi$ $\approx 28.3 \text{ units}^2$	$A = \pi r^2$

EXAMPLE 2 Finding the Area of a Circle

Find the area of each circle, both in terms of π and to the nearest tenth. Use 3.14 for π.

A circle with radius 5 cm

$A = \pi r^2 = \pi(5^2)$

$= 25\pi \text{ cm}^2 \approx 78.5 \text{ cm}^2$

B circle with diameter 5.6 in.

$A = \pi r^2 = \pi(2.8^2)$ *$\frac{d}{2} = 2.8$*

$= 7.84\pi \text{ in}^2 \approx 24.6 \text{ in}^2$

EXAMPLE 3 Finding Area and Circumference on a Coordinate Plane

Graph the circle with center (2, −2) that passes through (0, −2). Find the area and circumference, both in terms of π and to the nearest tenth. Use 3.14 for π.

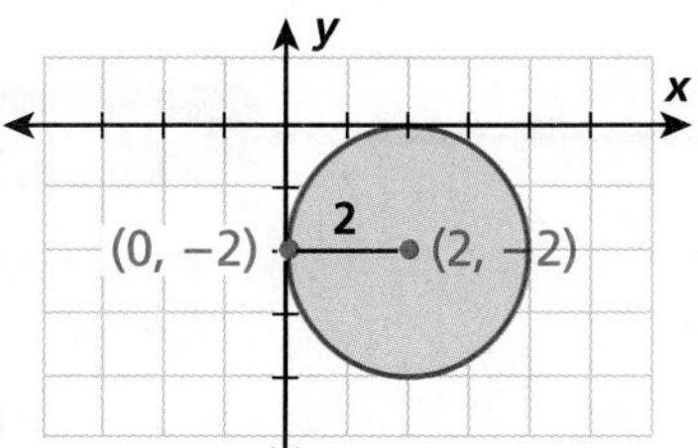

$A = \pi r^2$
$= \pi(2^2)$
$= 4\pi \text{ units}^2$
$\approx 12.6 \text{ units}^2$

$C = \pi d$
$= \pi(4)$
$= 4\pi \text{ units}$
$\approx 12.6 \text{ units}$

EXAMPLE 4 *Physical Science Application*

The radius of a circular swing ride is 29 ft. If a person is on the ride for 18 complete revolutions, how far does the person travel? Use $\frac{22}{7}$ for π.

$C = 2\pi r = 2\pi(29) = \pi 58$ *Find the circumference.*

$\approx 58\left(\frac{22}{7}\right) \approx \frac{1276}{7}$

The distance traveled is the circumference of the ride times the number of revolutions, or about $\frac{1276}{7} \cdot 18 = \frac{22{,}968}{7} \approx 3281.1$ ft.

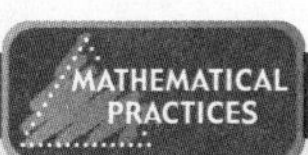

Think and Discuss

1. Give the formula for the area of a circle in terms of the diameter d.

6-1 Exercises

Learn It Online
Homework Help Online
Exercises 1–12, 13, 15, 17, 19, 21, 23, 25

GUIDED PRACTICE

See Example 1
Find the circumference of each circle, both in terms of π and to the nearest tenth. Use 3.14 for π.

1. circle with diameter 6 cm
2. circle with radius 3.2 in.

See Example 2
Find the area of each circle, both in terms of π and to the nearest tenth. Use 3.14 for π.

3. circle with radius 4.1 ft
4. circle with diameter 15 cm

See Example 3
5. Graph a circle with center $(-2, 1)$ that passes through $(-4, 1)$. Find the area and circumference, both in terms of π and to the nearest tenth. Use 3.14 for π.

See Example 4
6. A wheel has a diameter of 3.5 ft. Approximately how far does it travel if it makes 20 complete revolutions? Use $\frac{22}{7}$ for π.

INDEPENDENT PRACTICE

See Example 1
Find the circumference of each circle, both in terms of π and to the nearest tenth. Use 3.14 for π.

7. circle with radius 9 in.
8. circle with diameter 6.3 m

See Example 2
Find the area of each circle, both in terms of π and to the nearest tenth. Use 3.14 for π.

9. circle with diameter 32 cm
10. circle with radius 2.5 yd

See Example 3
11. Graph a circle with center $(1, 0)$ that passes through $(-3, 0)$. Find the area and circumference, both in terms of π and to the nearest tenth. Use 3.14 for π.

See Example 4
12. If the diameter of a wheel is 5 ft, about how many miles does the wheel travel if it makes 134 revolutions? Use $\frac{22}{7}$ for π. (*Hint:* 1 mi = 5280 ft.)

PRACTICE AND PROBLEM SOLVING

Extra Practice
See Extra Practice for more exercises.

Find the circumference and area of each circle to the nearest tenth. Use 3.14 for π.

13.
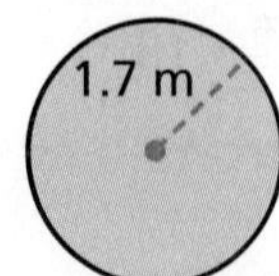

14.
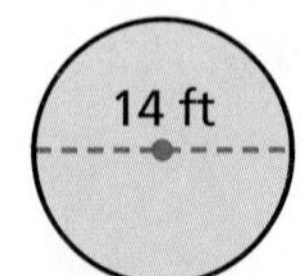

15.
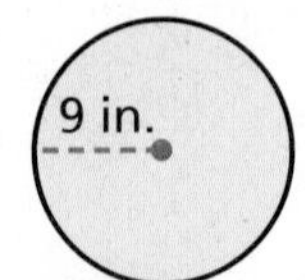

Find the radius of each circle with the given measurement.

16. $C = 26\pi$ in.
17. $C = 12.8\pi$ cm
18. $C = 15\pi$ ft
19. $A = 36\pi\ \text{cm}^2$
20. $A = 289\pi\ \text{in}^2$
21. $A = 136.89\pi\ \text{m}^2$

The London Eye takes its passengers on a 30-minute flight that reaches a height of 450 feet above the River Thames.

Find the shaded area to the nearest tenth. Use 3.14 for π.

22.

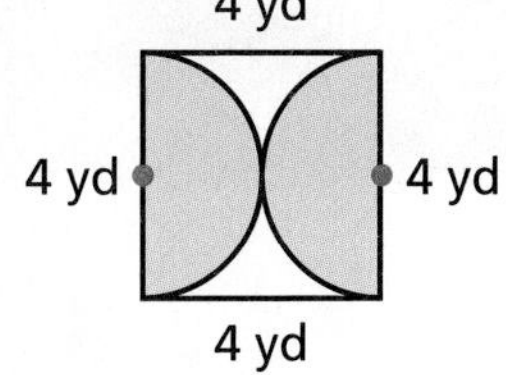

23.

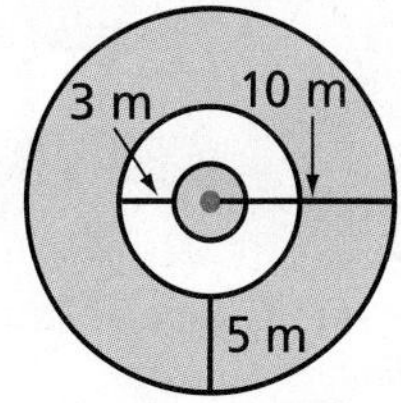

24. Entertainment The London Eye is an observation wheel with a diameter greater than 135 meters and less than 140 meters. Describe the range of the possible circumferences of the wheel to the nearest meter.

25. Sports The radius of a face-off circle on an NHL hockey rink is 15 ft. What are its circumference and area to the nearest tenth? Use 3.14 for π.

26. Food A pancake restaurant serves small silver dollar pancakes and regular-size pancakes.

a. What is the area of a silver dollar pancake to the nearest tenth?

b. What is the area of a regular pancake to the nearest tenth?

c. If 6 silver dollar pancakes are the same price as 3 regular pancakes, which is a better deal?

27. What's the Error? Meryl said that if the diameter of a circle is a whole number, then the circumference is always a rational number. What's the error?

28. Write About It Explain how you would find the area of the composite figure shown. Then find the area.

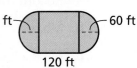

60 ft 60 ft 120 ft

29. Challenge Graph the circle with center (1, 2) that passes through the point (4, 6). Find its area and circumference, both in terms of π and to the nearest tenth.

Test Prep

30. Multiple Choice A circular flower bed has radius 22 inches. What is the circumference of the bed to the nearest tenth of an inch?

Ⓐ 69.1 inches Ⓑ 103.7 inches Ⓒ 138.2 inches Ⓓ 1519.8 inches

31. Gridded Response The first Ferris wheel was constructed for the 1893 World's Fair. It had a diameter of 250 feet. Find the circumference, to the nearest foot, of the Ferris wheel. Use 3.14 for π.

Find Volume of Prisms and Cylinders

Use with Volume of Prisms and Cylinders

Learn It Online
Lab Resources Online

MATHEMATICAL PRACTICES **Use appropriate tools strategically.**

CC.8.G.9: Know the formulas for the volumes of cones, cylinders, and spheres and use them to solve real-world and mathematical problems.

You can use models to explore the volume of rectangular prisms and cylinders.

Activity

1 Use five different-sized rectangular prisms, such as empty cartons.

a. Cover the bottom of each prism with cubes to find the area of the prism's base. Record the information in a table.

b. Fill the prism with cubes. Find the height. Then count the cubes to find the prism's volume. Record the information in a table.

Object	
Area of Base	
Height	
Volume	

2 Use five different-sized cylinders, such as empty cans.

a. Measure the radius of each circular base and calculate its area. Record the information in a table.

b. Measure the height of each cylinder. Record the information in a table.

c. Fill each cylinder with popcorn kernels.

d. Use a measuring cup to find how much popcorn filled the cylinder.

e. Find the approximate volume of each cylinder. 1 cup = 14.4 in^3. Record the information in a table.

Think and Discuss

1. What do you notice about the relationship between the base, the height, and the volume of the rectangular prisms? of the cylinders?

2. Make a conjecture about how to find the volume of any rectangular prism or cylinder.

Try This

1. Use your conjecture to find the volume of a new rectangular prism. Check your conjecture by following the steps in Activity 1. Revise your conjecture as needed.

2. Use your conjecture to find the volume of a new cylinder. Check your conjecture by following the steps in Activity 2. Revise your conjecture as needed.

6-2 Volume of Prisms and Cylinders

COMMON CORE

CC.8.G.9: Know the formulas for the volumes of cones, cylinders, and spheres and use them to solve real-world and mathematical problems.

The largest drum ever built measures 4.8 meters in diameter and is 4.95 meters deep. It was built by Asano Taiko Company in Japan. You can use these measurements to find the approximate volume of the drum, which is roughly a cylinder.

The circumference of the Taiko drum pictured is about half that of the largest drum ever made.

Recall that a cylinder is a three-dimensional figure that has two congruent circular bases, and a prism is a three-dimensional figure named for the shape of its bases. The two bases are congruent polygons. All of the other faces are parallelograms.

Triangular prism

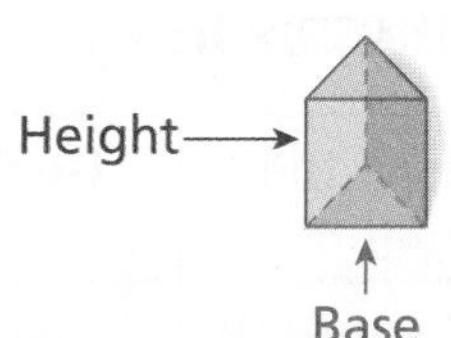

Rectangular prism

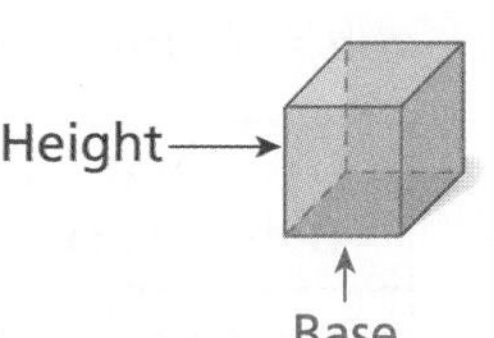

Cylinder

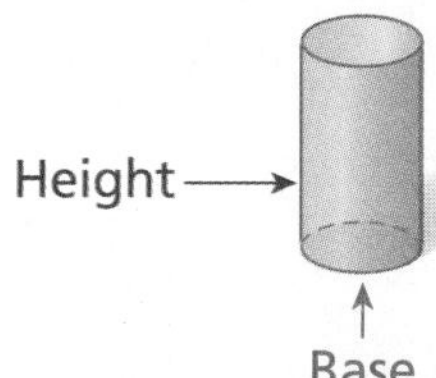

Interactivities Online ▶

VOLUME OF PRISMS AND CYLINDERS

Words	Numbers	Formula
Prism: The volume V of a prism is the area of the base B times the height h.	3, 5, 2 $B = 2(5)$ $= 10 \text{ units}^2$ $V = (10)(3)$ $= 30 \text{ units}^3$	$V = Bh$
Cylinder: The volume of a cylinder is the area of the base B times the height h.	6, 2 $B = \pi(2^2)$ $= 4\pi \text{ units}^2$ $V = (4\pi)(6) = 24\pi$ $\approx 75.4 \text{ units}^3$	$V = Bh$ $= (\pi r^2)h$

EXAMPLE 1 Finding the Volume of Prisms and Cylinders

Remember!

Area is measured in *square units.* Volume is measured in *cubic units.*

Find the volume of each figure to the nearest tenth. Use 3.14 for π.

A **A rectangular prism with base 2 m by 5 m and height 7 m.**

$B = 2 \cdot 5 = 10 \text{ m}^2$ *Area of base*

$V = Bh$ *Volume of prism*

$= 10 \cdot 7 = 70 \text{ m}^3$

Kenneth Hamm/Photo Japan

Find the volume of each figure to the nearest tenth. Use 3.14 for π.

B

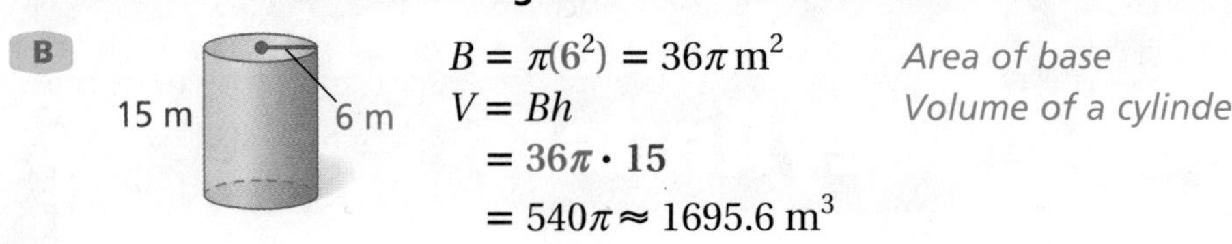

$B = \pi(6^2) = 36\pi \text{ m}^2$ *Area of base*

$V = Bh$ *Volume of a cylinder*

$= 36\pi \cdot 15$

$= 540\pi \approx 1695.6 \text{ m}^3$

C

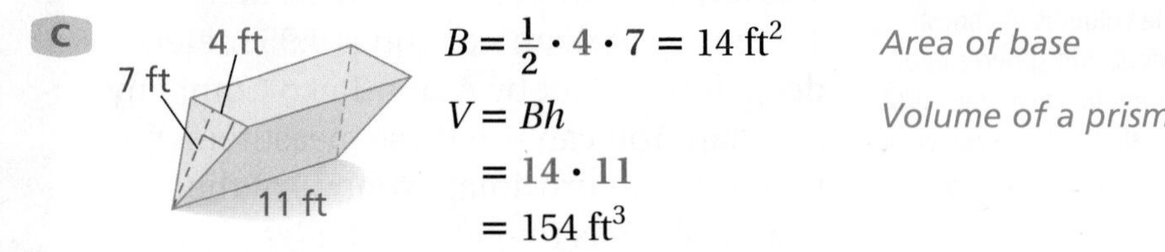

$B = \frac{1}{2} \cdot 4 \cdot 7 = 14 \text{ ft}^2$ *Area of base*

$V = Bh$ *Volume of a prism*

$= 14 \cdot 11$

$= 154 \text{ ft}^3$

The formula for volume of a rectangular prism can be written as $V = \ell wh$, where ℓ is the length, w is the width, and h is the height.

EXAMPLE 2 Exploring the Effects of Changing Dimensions

A **A cereal box measures 6 in. by 2 in. by 9 in. Explain whether doubling the length, width, or height of the box would double the amount of cereal the box holds.**

Original Dimensions	Double the Length	Double the Width	Double the Height
$V = \ell wh$ $= 6 \cdot 2 \cdot 9$ $= 108 \text{ in}^3$	$V = (2\ell)wh$ $= 12 \cdot 2 \cdot 9$ $= 216 \text{ in}^3$	$V = \ell(2w)h$ $= 6 \cdot 4 \cdot 9$ $= 216 \text{ in}^3$	$V = \ell w(2h)$ $= 6 \cdot 2 \cdot 18$ $= 216 \text{ in}^3$

The original box has a volume of 108 in^3. You could double the volume to 216 in^3 by doubling any one of the dimensions. So doubling the length, width, or height would double the amount of cereal the box holds.

B **A can of corn has a radius of 2.5 in. and a height of 4 in. Explain whether doubling the height of the can would have the same effect on the volume as doubling the radius.**

Original Dimensions	Double the Height	Double the Radius
$V = \pi r^2 h$ $= 2.5^2\pi \cdot 4$ $= 25\pi \text{ in}^3$	$V = \pi r^2(2h)$ $= 2.5^2\pi \cdot 8$ $= 50\pi \text{ in}^3$	$V = \pi(2r)^2 h$ $= 5^2\pi \cdot 4$ $= 100\pi \text{ in}^3$

By doubling the height, you would double the volume. By doubling the radius, you would increase the volume four times the original.

EXAMPLE 3 *Music Application*

The Asano Taiko Company of Japan built the world's largest drum in 2000. The drum's diameter is 4.8 meters, and its height is 4.95 meters. Estimate the volume of the drum.

$d = 4.8 \approx 5$

$h = 4.95 \approx 5$

$r = \frac{d}{2} = \frac{5}{2} = 2.5$

$V = (\pi r^2)h$ — *Volume of a cylinder.*

$= (3)(2.5)^2 \cdot 5$ — *Use 3 for π.*

$= (3)(6.25)(5)$

$= 18.75 \cdot 5$

$= 93.75$

≈ 94

The volume of the drum is approximately 94 m^3.

To find the volume of a composite three-dimensional figure, find the volume of each part and add the volumes together.

EXAMPLE  **Finding the Volume of Composite Figures**

Find the volume of the figure.

Volume of figure	=	Volume of rectangular prism	+	Volume of triangular prism
V	=	(6)(9)(5)	+	$\frac{1}{2}$ (6)(3)(9)
	=	270	+	81
	=	351 cm^3		

The volume is 351 cm^3.

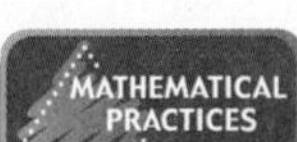

Think and Discuss

1. **Use models** to show that two rectangular prisms can have different heights but the same volume.
2. **Apply** your results from Example 2 to make a conjecture about changing dimensions in a triangular prism.
3. **Use a model** to describe what happens to the volume of a cylinder when the diameter of the base is tripled.

6-2 Exercises

Learn It Online
Homework Help Online
Exercises 1–12, 15, 21

GUIDED PRACTICE

See Example 1

Find the volume of each figure to the nearest tenth. Use 3.14 for π.

1. 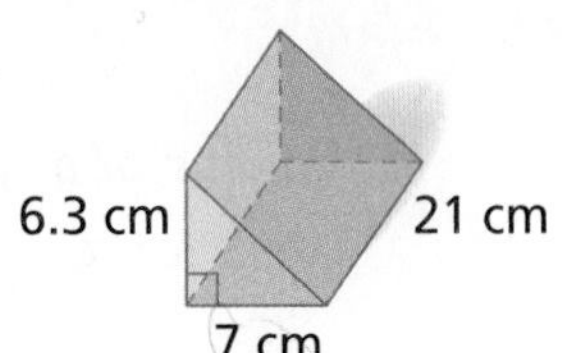

2. 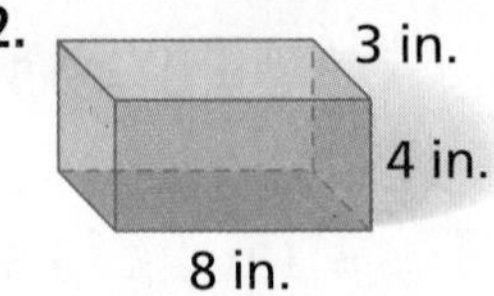

3. 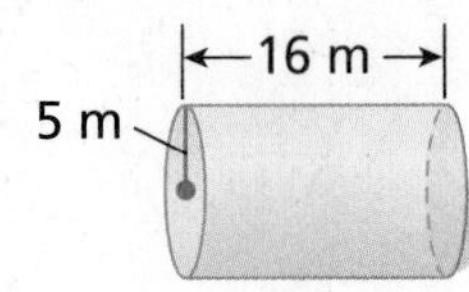

See Example 2

4. A can of juice has a radius 3 in. and a height 6 in. Explain whether tripling the radius would triple the volume of the can.

See Example 3

5. Grain is stored in cylindrical structures called *silos.* Estimate the volume of a silo with diameter 11.1 feet and height 20 feet.

See Example 4

6. Find the volume of the barn.

INDEPENDENT PRACTICE

See Example 1

Find the volume of each figure to the nearest tenth. Use 3.14 for π.

7. 2 in. 5 in. 10 in.

8. 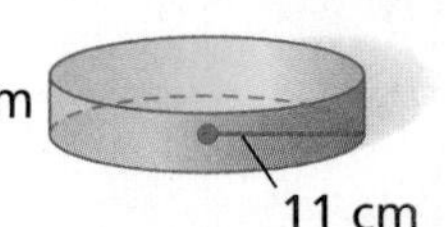

9. 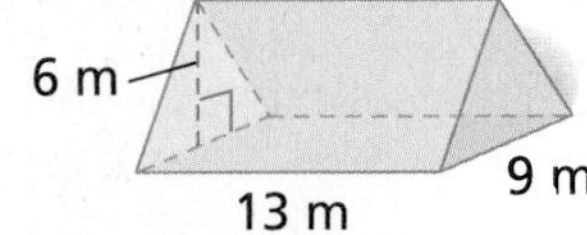

See Example 2

10. A jewelry box measures 7 in. by 5 in. by 8 in. Explain whether increasing the height 4 times, from 8 in. to 32 in., would increase the volume 4 times.

See Example 3

11. A toy box is 5.1 cm by 3.2 cm by 4.2 cm. Estimate the volume of the toy box.

See Example 4

12. Find the volume of the treehouse.

PRACTICE AND PROBLEM SOLVING

Extra Practice
See Extra Practice for more exercises.

13. While Karim was at camp, his father sent him a care package. The box measured 10.2 in. by 19.9 in. by 4.2 in.
    a. Estimate the volume of the box.
    b. What might be the measurements of a box with twice its volume?

Through the 52 large windows of the Giant Ocean Tank, visitors can see 3000 corals and sponges as well as large sharks, sea turtles, barracudas, moray eels, and hundreds of tropical fishes.

14. **Social Studies** The tablet held by the Statue of Liberty is approximately a rectangular prism with volume 1,107,096 in^3. Estimate the thickness of the tablet.

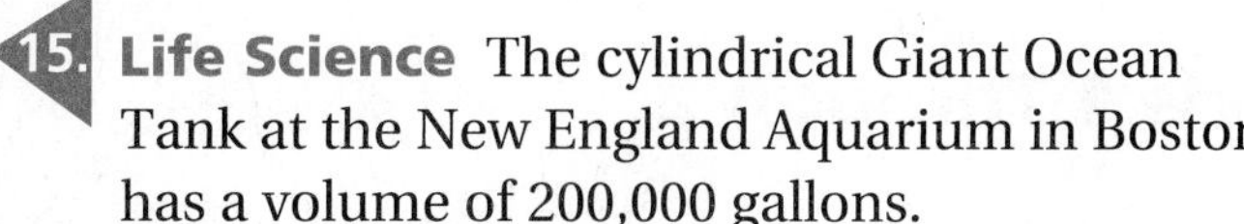

15. **Life Science** The cylindrical Giant Ocean Tank at the New England Aquarium in Boston has a volume of 200,000 gallons.
    a. One gallon of water equals 231 cubic inches. How many cubic inches of water are in the Giant Ocean Tank?
    b. Use your answer from part **a** as the volume. The tank is 24 ft deep. Find the radius in feet of the Giant Ocean Tank.

16. **Life Science** As many as 60,000 bees can live in 3 cubic feet of space. There are about 360,000 bees in a rectangular observation beehive that is 2 ft long by 3 ft high. What is the minimum possible width of the observation hive?

17. **What's the Error?** A student read this statement in a book: "The volume of a triangular prism with height 15 in. and base area 20 in. is 300 in^3." Correct the error in the statement.

18. **Write About It** Explain why 1 cubic yard equals 27 cubic feet.

19. **Challenge** A 5-inch section of a hollow brick measures 12 inches tall and 8 inches wide on the outside. The brick is 1 inch thick. Find the volume of the brick, not the hollow interior.

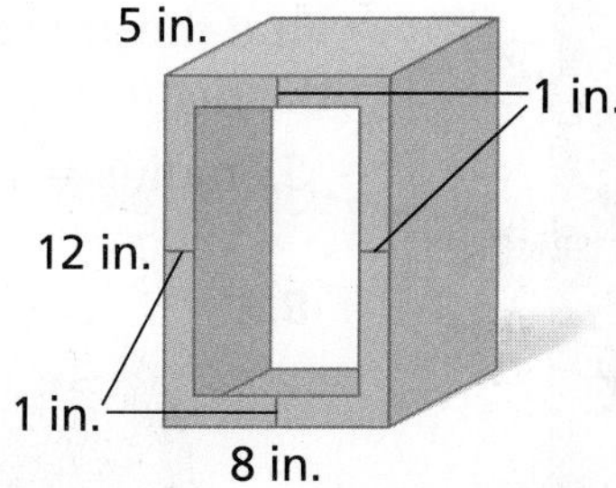

Test Prep

20. **Multiple Choice** Cylinder A has radius 6 centimeters and height 14 centimeters. Cylinder B has radius half as long as cylinder A. What is the volume of cylinder B? Use 3.14 for π and round to the nearest tenth.

    Ⓐ 393.5 cm^3 Ⓑ 395.6 cm^3 Ⓒ 422.3 cm^3 Ⓓ 791.3 cm^3

21. **Multiple Choice** A tractor trailer has dimensions of 13 feet by 53 feet by 8 feet. What is the volume of the trailer?

    Ⓕ 424 ft^3 Ⓖ 689 ft^3 Ⓗ 2756 ft^3 Ⓙ 5512 ft^3

(tr) Dallas and John Heaton/Corbis; (l) Tim Laman/National Geographic/Getty Images/Punchstock

CHAPTER 6 SECTION A

Quiz for Lessons 1 Through 2

1 Volume of Prisms and Cylinders

Find the volume of each figure to the nearest tenth. Use 3.14 for π.

1.

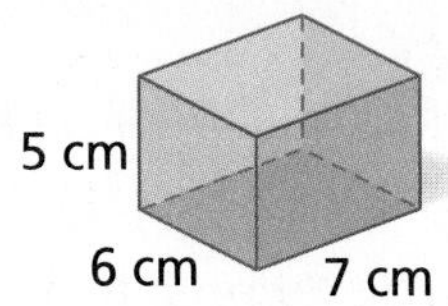

2.

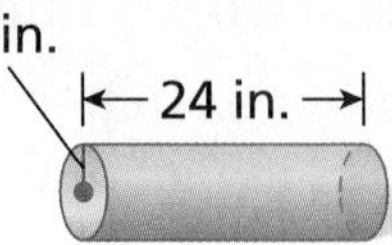

3.

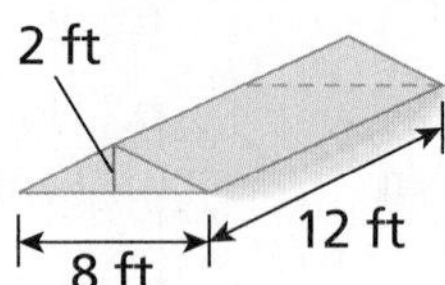

4. An ice cube tray has 12 sections. Each section has the shape of a 3-cm cube. What is the volume of water used to fill the tray?

2 Circles

Find the area and circumference of each circle, both in terms of π and to the nearest tenth. Use 3.14 for π.

5. radius = 19 cm

6. diameter = 4.3 ft

7. radius = $7\frac{1}{2}$ ft

8.

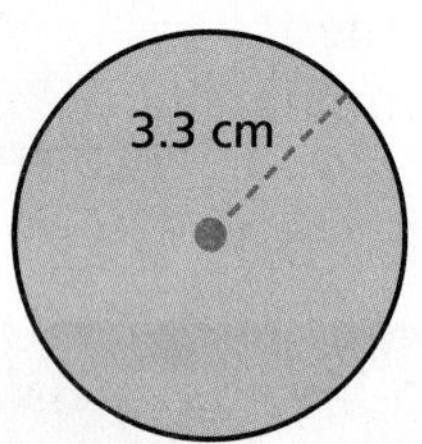

9.

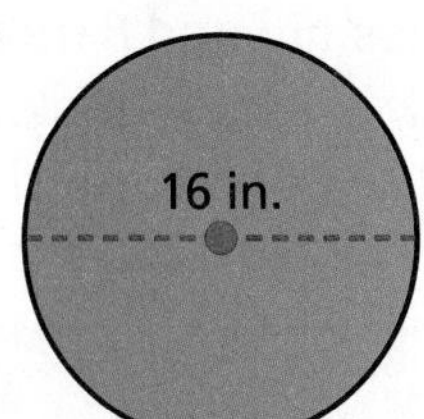

10.

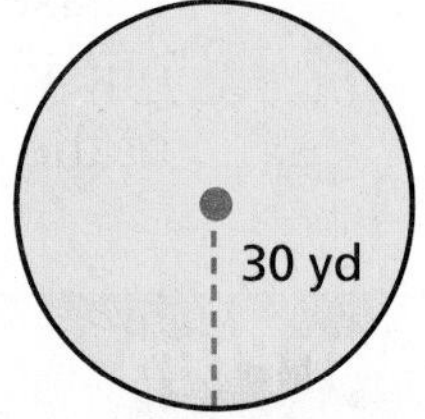

11. Graph a circle with center $(-3, 1)$ that passes through $(1, 1)$. Find the area and circumference, both in terms of π and to the nearest tenth. Use 3.14 for π.

Ready to Go On?

MATHEMATICAL PRACTICES Make sense of problems and persevere in solving them.

Focus on Problem Solving

Look Back

- **Does your solution answer the question?**

When you think you have solved a problem, think again. Your answer may not really be the solution to the problem. For example, you may solve an equation to find the value of a variable, but to find the answer the problem is asking for, the value of the variable may need to be substituted into an expression.

Write and solve an equation for each problem. Check to see whether the value of the variable is the answer to the question. If not, give the answer to the question.

1. Triangle *ABC* is an isosceles triangle. Find its perimeter.

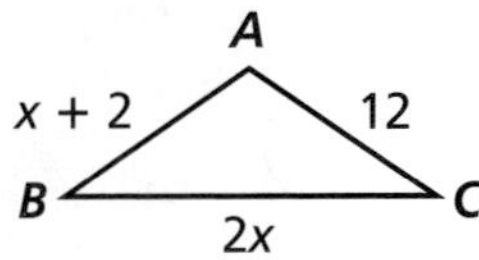

2. Find the measure of the smallest angle in triangle *DEF*.

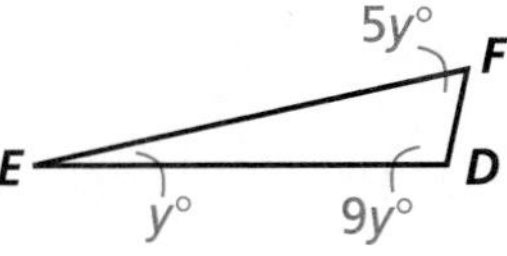

3. Find the measure of the largest angle in triangle *DEF*.

4. Find the area of right triangle *GHI*.

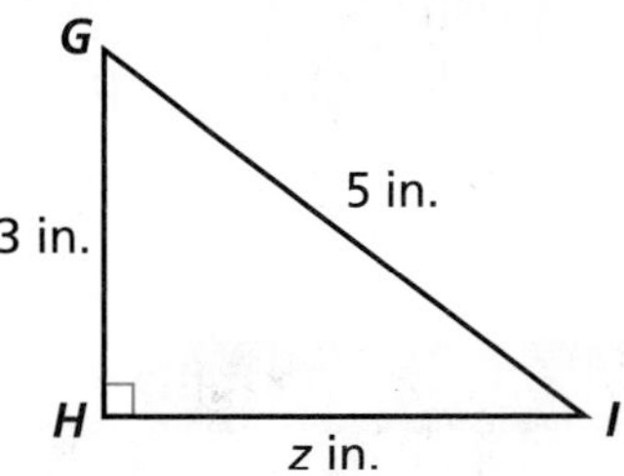

5. A *pediment* is a triangular space filled with statuary on the front of a building. The approximate measurements of an isosceles triangular pediment are shown below. Find the area of the pediment.

50 ft
h
96 ft

Dave G. Houser/Houserstock

Find Volume of Pyramids and Cones

Use with Volume of Pyramids and Cones

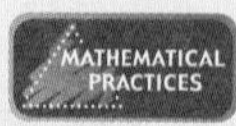

Use appropriate tools strategically.

CC.8.G.9: Know the formulas for the volumes of cones, cylinders . . .

You can use containers to explore the relationship between the volumes of pyramids and prisms and the relationship between the volumes of cones and cylinders.

Activity 1

Find or make a hollow prism and a hollow pyramid that have congruent bases and heights.

a. Fill the pyramid with popcorn kernels. Make sure that the popcorn kernels are level with the opening of the pyramid, and then pour the kernels into the prism.

b. Repeat step **a** until the prism is full and the popcorn kernels are level with the top of the prism. Keep track of the number of full pyramids it takes to fill the prism.

Think and Discuss

1. How many full pyramids did it take to fill a prism with a congruent base and height?
2. Use a fraction to express the relationship between the volume of a pyramid and the volume of a prism with a congruent base and height.
3. If the volume of a prism is Bh, write a rule for the volume of a pyramid.

Try This

1. Use your rule from Think and Discuss 3 to find the volume of another pyramid with the same base area. Check your rule by following the steps in Activity 1. Revise your rule as needed.
2. The volume of a pyramid is 31 in^3. What is the volume of a prism with the same base area and height? Explain your reasoning.
3. The volume of a prism is 27 cm^3. What is the volume of a pyramid with the same base area and height? Explain your reasoning.
4. A glass lantern filled with oil is shaped like a square pyramid. Each side of the base is 5 centimeters long, and the lantern is 11 centimeters tall. What is the volume of the lantern?

Activity 2

Find or make a hollow cylinder and a hollow cone that have congruent bases and heights.

a. Fill the cone with popcorn kernels. Make sure that the popcorn kernels are level with the opening of the cone, and then pour the kernels into the cylinder.

b. Repeat step **a** until the cylinder is full and the popcorn kernels are level with the top of the cylinder. Keep track of the number of full cones it takes.

Think and Discuss

1. How many full cones did it take to fill a cylinder with a congruent base and height?
2. Use a fraction to express the relationship between the volume of a cone and the volume of a cylinder with a congruent base and height.
3. If the volume of a cylinder is Bh or $\pi r^2 h$, write a rule for the volume of a cone.

Try This

1. Use your rule from Think and Discuss 3 to find the volume of another cone. Check your rule by following the steps in Activity 2. Revise your rule as needed.
2. The volume of a cone is 3.7 m^3. What is the volume of a cylinder with the same base and height? Explain your reasoning.
3. The volume of a cylinder is 228 ft^3. What is the volume of a cone with the same base and height? Explain your reasoning.
4. Evan is using a plastic cone to build a sand castle. The cone has a diameter of 10 inches and is 18 inches tall. What is the volume of the cone?
5. Aneesha has two paper cones. The first cone has a radius of 2 inches and a height of 3 inches. The second cone has the same base but is twice the height. Aneesha says that the second cone has twice the volume of the first cone. Is she correct? Explain your reasoning.

6-3 Volume of Pyramids and Cones

COMMON CORE

CC.8.G.9: Know the formulas for the volumes of cones, cylinders, and spheres and use them to solve real-world and mathematical problems. ***Also CC.8.EE.7***

Part of the Rock and Roll Hall of Fame building in Cleveland, Ohio, is a glass pyramid. The entire building was designed by architect I. M. Pei and has approximately 150,000 ft^2 of floor space.

Paul Spinelli/Getty Images Sport

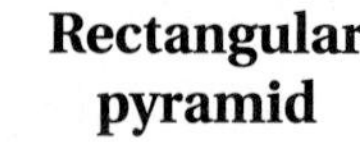

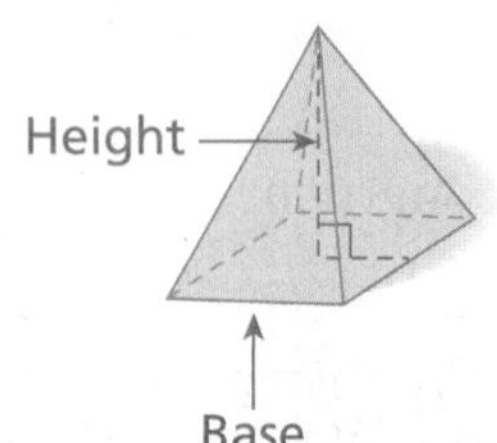

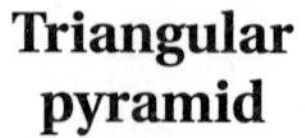

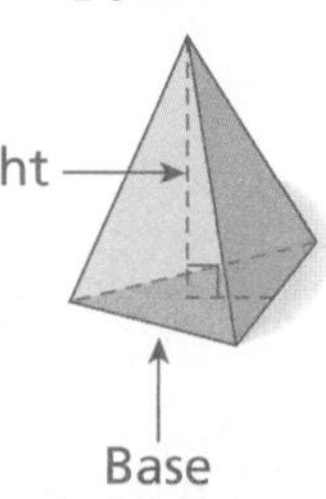

Cone

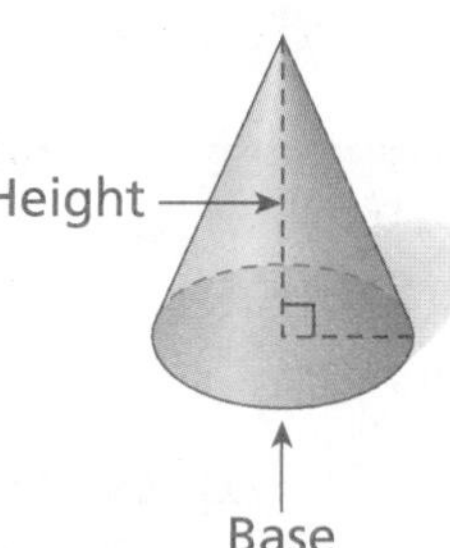

VOLUME OF PYRAMIDS AND CONES

Words	Numbers	Formula
Pyramid: The volume V of a pyramid is one-third of the area of the base B times the height h.	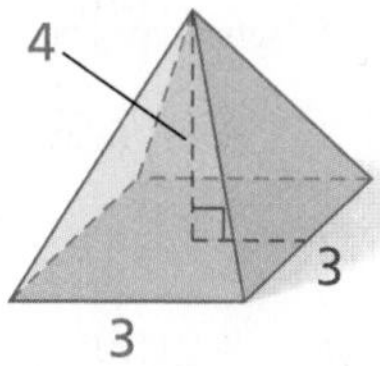 (figure: 4, 3, 3) $B = 3(3)$ $= 9$ units^2; $V = \frac{1}{3}(9)(4)$ $= 12$ units^3	$V = \frac{1}{3}Bh$
Cone: The volume of a cone is one-third of the area of the circular base B times the height h.	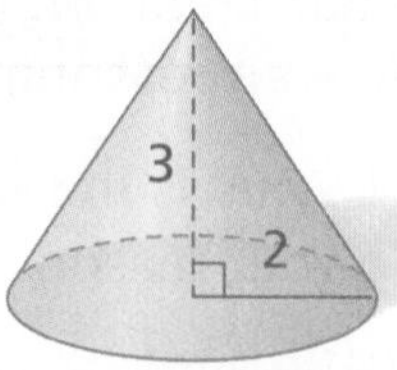 (figure: 3, 2) $B = \pi(2^2)$ $= 4\pi$ units^2; $V = \frac{1}{3}(4\pi)(3)$ $= 4\pi$ ≈ 12.6 units^3	$V = \frac{1}{3}Bh$ or $V = \frac{1}{3}\pi r^2 h$

EXAMPLE 

Finding the Volume of Pyramids and Cones

Find the volume of each figure. Use 3.14 for π.

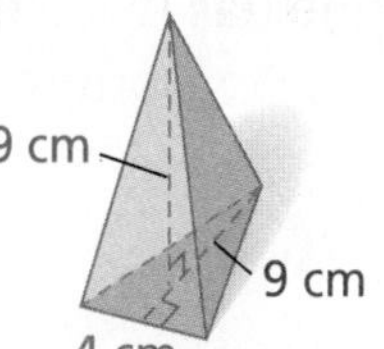

$B = \frac{1}{2}(4 \cdot 9) = 18\text{ cm}^2$

$V = \frac{1}{3} \cdot 18 \cdot 9$ $V = \frac{1}{3}Bh$

$V = 54\text{ cm}^3$

Find the volume of each figure. Use 3.14 for π.

B

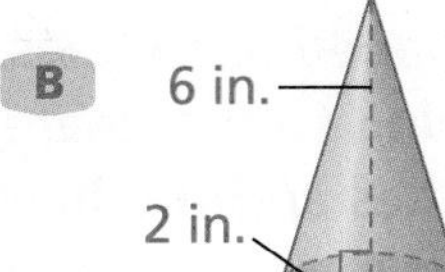

$B = \pi(2^2) = 4\pi \text{ in}^2$

$V = \frac{1}{3} \cdot 4\pi \cdot 6$ *$V = \frac{1}{3}Bh$*

$V = 8\pi \approx 25.1 \text{ in}^3$ *Use 3.14 for π.*

C

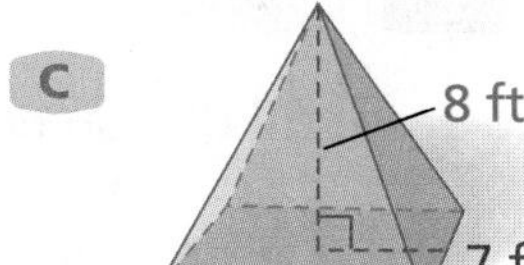

$B = 9 \cdot 7 = 63 \text{ ft}^2$

$V = \frac{1}{3} \cdot 63 \cdot 8$ *$V = \frac{1}{3}Bh$*

$V = 168 \text{ ft}^3$

D

7 mm

8 mm

$B = \pi(7^2) = 49\pi \text{ mm}^2$

$V = \frac{1}{3} \cdot 49\pi \cdot 8$ *$V = \frac{1}{3}Bh$*

$V = \frac{392}{3}\pi \approx 410.3 \text{ mm}^2$ *Use 3.14 for π.*

EXAMPLE 2 Exploring the Effects of Changing Dimensions

A cone has radius 3 m and height 10 m. Explain whether doubling the height would have the same effect on the volume of the cone as doubling the radius.

Original Dimensions	Double the Height	Double the Radius
$V = \frac{1}{3}\pi r^2 h$	$V = \frac{1}{3}\pi r^2 (2h)$	$V = \frac{1}{3}\pi (2r)^2 h$
$= \frac{1}{3}\pi (3^2)(10)$	$= \frac{1}{3}\pi (3^2)(2 \cdot 10)$	$= \frac{1}{3}\pi (2 \cdot 3)^2 (10)$
$\approx 94.2 \text{ m}^3$	$\approx 188.4 \text{ m}^3$	$\approx 376.8 \text{ m}^3$

When the height of the cone is doubled, the volume is doubled. When the radius is doubled, the volume becomes 4 times the original volume.

EXAMPLE 3 *Social Studies Application*

Caution!

A lowercase b is used to represent the length of the base of a two-dimensional figure. A capital B is used to represent the area of the base of a solid figure.

The Great Pyramid of Giza in Egypt is a square pyramid. Its height is 481 ft, and its base has 756 ft sides. Find the volume of the pyramid.

Will & Deni McIntyre/Photo Researchers, Inc.

$B = 756^2 = 571{,}536 \text{ ft}^2$ *$A = bh$*

$V = \frac{1}{3}(571{,}536)(481)$ *$V = \frac{1}{3}Bh$*

$V = 91{,}636{,}272 \text{ ft}^3$

EXAMPLE 4

Using a Calculator to Find Volume

Some traffic pylons are shaped like cones. Use a calculator to find the volume of a traffic pylon to the nearest hundredth if the radius of the base is 5 inches and the height is 24 inches.

Use the *pi* button on your calculator to find the area of the base.

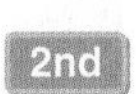 π   5  ENTER $B = \pi r^2$

Next, with the area of the base still displayed, find the volume of the cone.

 24 ×  1  3)  $V = \frac{1}{3}Bh$

The volume of the traffic pylon is approximately 628.32 in^3.

Think and Discuss

1. **Describe** two or more ways that you can change the dimensions of a rectangular pyramid to double its volume.
2. **Use a model** to compare the volume of a cube with 1 in. sides with a pyramid that is 1 in. high and has a 1 in. square base.

6-3 Exercises

Learn It Online
Homework Help Online
Exercises 1–14, 19, 21, 23, 25

GUIDED PRACTICE

See Example 1 **Find the volume of each figure to the nearest tenth. Use 3.14 for π.**

1. 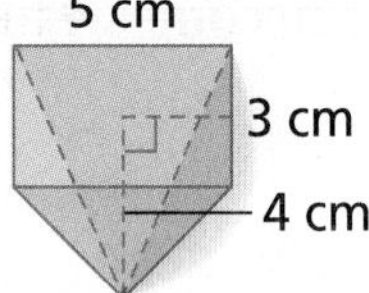

2. 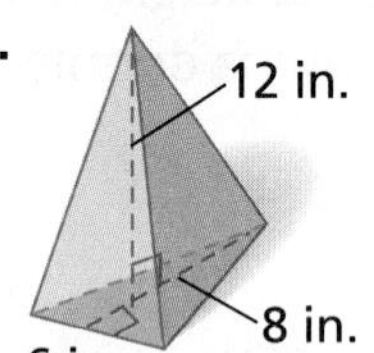

3. 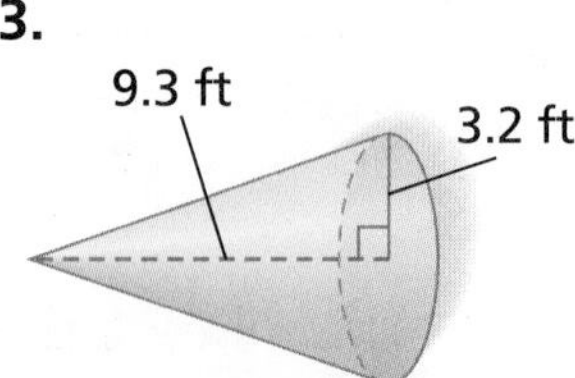

4. 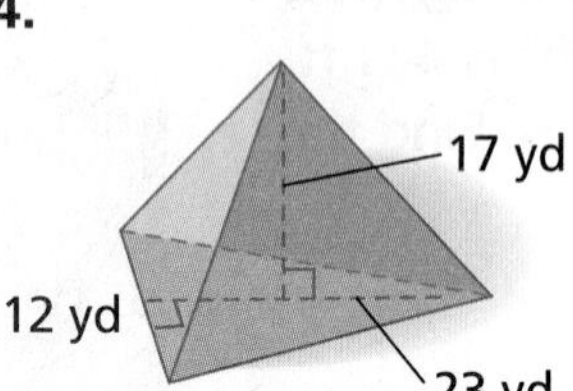

5. 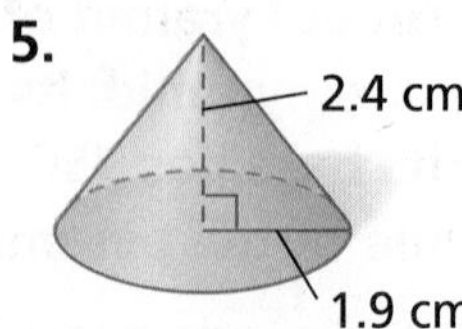

6. 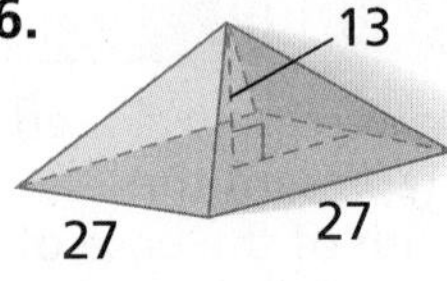

See Example 2 7. A square pyramid has height 6 m and a base that measures 2 m on each side. Explain whether doubling the height would double the volume of the pyramid.

See Example 3

8. The Transamerica Pyramid in San Francisco has a base area of 22,000 ft^2 and a height of 853 ft. What is the volume of the building?

See Example 4

9. Gretchen made a paper cone to hold a gift for a friend. The paper cone was 17 inches high and had a diameter of 6 inches. Use a calculator to find the volume of the paper cone to the nearest hundredth.

INDEPENDENT PRACTICE

See Example 1

Find the volume of each figure to the nearest tenth. Use 3.14 for π.

10.

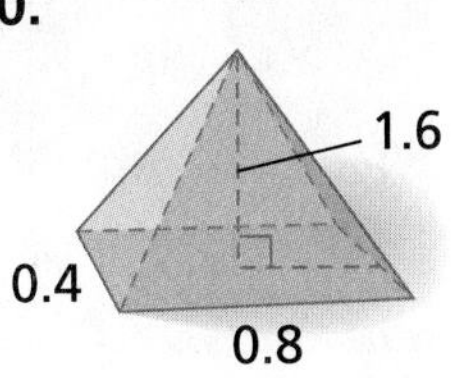

11.

5.5 m
4.9 m
7.8 m

12.

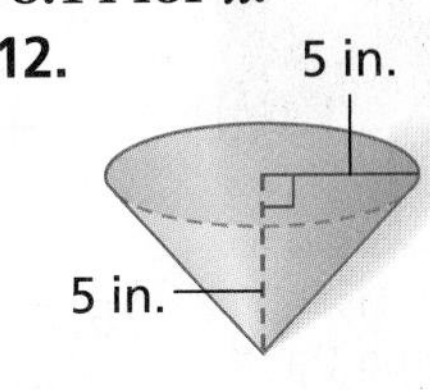

13.

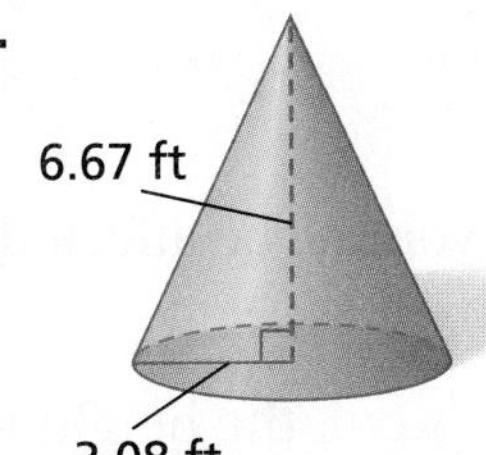

14.

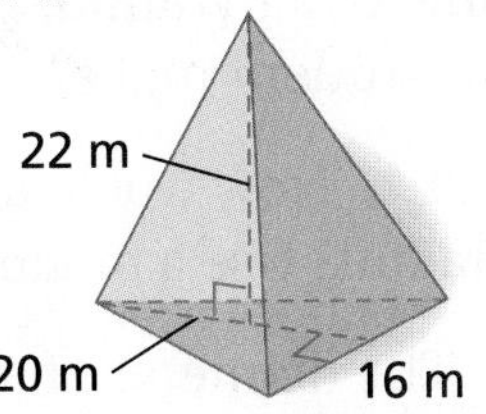

15.

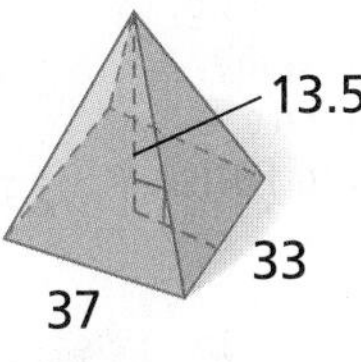

See Example 2

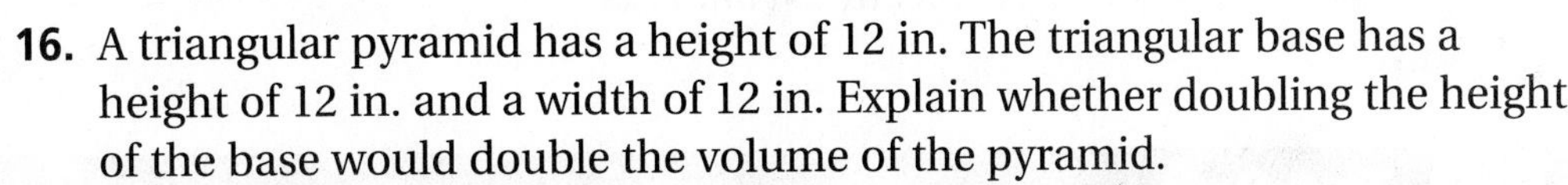

16. A triangular pyramid has a height of 12 in. The triangular base has a height of 12 in. and a width of 12 in. Explain whether doubling the height of the base would double the volume of the pyramid.

See Example 3

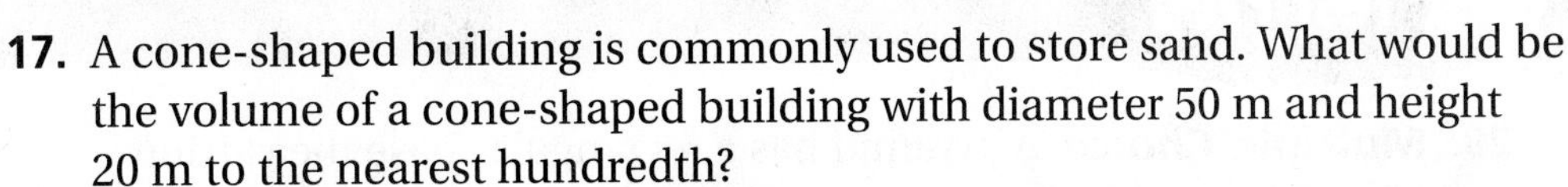

17. A cone-shaped building is commonly used to store sand. What would be the volume of a cone-shaped building with diameter 50 m and height 20 m to the nearest hundredth?

See Example 4

18. Antonio made mini waffle cones for a birthday party. Each waffle cone was 3 inches high and had a radius of $\frac{3}{4}$ inch. Use a calculator to find the volume of the waffle cone to the nearest hundredth.

PRACTICE AND PROBLEM SOLVING

Extra Practice

See Extra Practice for more exercises.

Find the missing measure to the nearest tenth. Use 3.14 for π.

19. cone:
radius = 4 in.
height = ▇
volume = 100.5 in^3

20. cylinder:
radius = ▇
height = 2.5 m
volume = 70.65 m^3

21. triangular pyramid:
base height = ▇
base width = 8 ft
height = 6 ft
volume = 88 ft^3

22. rectangular pyramid:
base length = 3 ft
base width = ▇
height = 7 ft
volume = 42 ft^3

23. **Estimation** Orange traffic cones come in a variety of sizes. Approximate the volume in cubic inches of a traffic cone with height 2 feet and diameter 10 inches by using 3 in place of π.

Architecture

The Mona Lisa by Leonardo Da Vinci is perhaps the world's most famous painting. It is on display at the Louvre museum in Paris, France.

24. **Architecture** The Pyramid of the Sun, in Teotihuacán, Mexico, is about 65 m tall and has a square base with side length 225 m.
    a. What is the volume in cubic meters of the pyramid?
    b. How many cubic meters are in a cubic kilometer?
    c. What is the volume in cubic kilometers of the pyramid to the nearest thousandth?

25. **Architecture** The pyramid at the entrance to the Louvre in Paris has a height of 72 feet and a square base that is 112 feet long on each side. What is the volume of this pyramid?

26. **What's the Error?** A student says that the formula for the volume of a cylinder is the same as the formula for the volume of a pyramid, $\frac{1}{3}Bh$. What error did this student make?

27. **Write About It** How would a cone's volume be affected if you doubled the height? the radius? Use a model to help explain.

28. **Challenge** The diameter of a cone is x cm, the height is 18 cm, and the volume is 96π cm^3. What is x?

Test Prep

29. **Multiple Choice** A pyramid has a rectangular base measuring 12 centimeters by 9 centimeters. Its height is 15 centimeters. What is the volume of the pyramid?

    Ⓐ 540 cm^3 Ⓑ 405 cm^3 Ⓒ 315 cm^3 Ⓓ 270 cm^3

30. **Multiple Choice** A cone has diameter 12 centimeters and height 9 centimeters. Using 3.14 for π, find the volume of the cone to the nearest tenth.

    Ⓕ 1,356.5 cm^3 Ⓖ 339.1 cm^3 Ⓗ 118.3 cm^3 Ⓙ 56.5 cm^3

31. **Gridded Response** Suppose a cone has a volume of 104.7 cubic centimeters and a radius of 5 centimeters. Find the height of the cone to the nearest whole centimeter. Use 3.14 for π.

Mastering the *Standards*

for Mathematical Practice

The topics described in the Standards for Mathematical Content will vary from year to year. However, the *way* in which you learn, study, and think about mathematics will not. The Standards for Mathematical Practice describe skills that you will use in all of your math courses.

Mathematical Practices

1. *Make sense of problems and persevere in solving them.*
2. *Reason abstractly and quantitatively.*
3. *Construct viable arguments and critique the reasoning of others.*
4. *Model with mathematics.*
5. *Use appropriate tools strategically.*
6. *Attend to precision.*
7. *Look for and make use of structure.*
8. *Look for and express regularity in repeated reasoning.*

Use appropriate tools strategically.

Mathematically proficient students consider the available tools when solving a... problem... [and] are... able to use technological tools to explore and deepen their understanding...

In your book

Hands-on Labs and **Technology Labs** use concrete and technological tools to explore mathematical concepts.

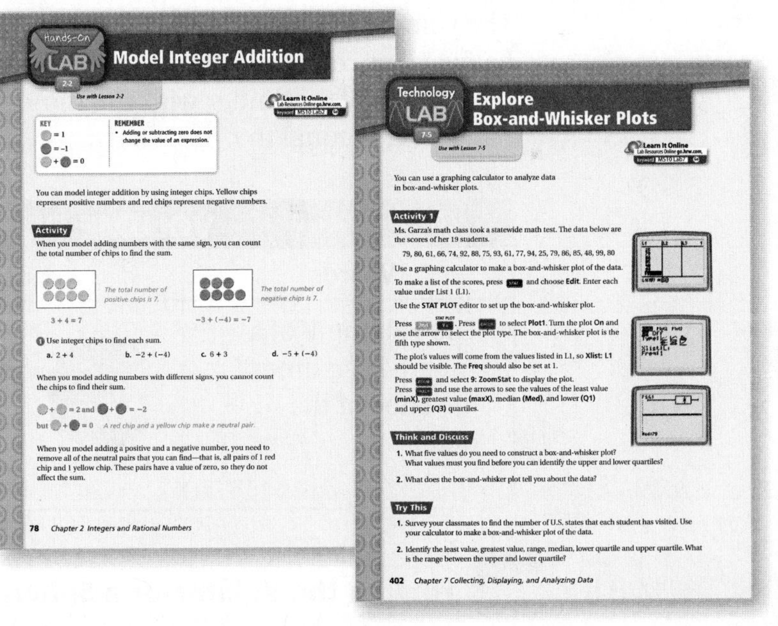

Hands-on LAB 2-2

Model Integer Addition

Use with Lesson 2-2

Learn It Online
Lab Resources Online go.hrw.com,
keyword MS10 Lab2

KEY
= 1
= −1
+ = 0

REMEMBER
- Adding or subtracting zero does not change the value of an expression.

You can model integer addition by using integer chips. Yellow chips represent positive numbers and red chips represent negative numbers.

Activity

When you model adding numbers with the same sign, you can count the total number of chips to find the sum.

The total number of positive chips is 7. $3 + 4 = 7$

The total number of negative chips is 7. $-3 + (-4) = -7$

1. Use integer chips to find each sum.
   a. $2 + 4$ b. $-2 + (-4)$ c. $6 + 3$ d. $-5 + (-4)$

When you model adding numbers with different signs, you cannot count the chips to find their sum.

+ = 2 and + = −2

but + = 0 *A red chip and a yellow chip make a neutral pair.*

When you model adding a positive and a negative number, you need to remove all of the neutral pairs that you can find—that is, all pairs of 1 red chip and 1 yellow chip. These pairs have a value of zero, so they do not affect the sum.

78 *Chapter 2 Integers and Rational Numbers*

Technology LAB 7-5

Explore Box-and-Whisker Plots

Use with Lesson 7-5

Learn It Online
Lab Resources Online go.hrw.com,
keyword MS10 Lab7

You can use a graphing calculator to analyze data in box-and-whisker plots.

Activity 1

Ms. Garza's math class took a statewide math test. The data below are the scores of her 19 students.

79, 80, 61, 66, 74, 92, 88, 75, 93, 61, 77, 94, 25, 79, 86, 85, 48, 99, 80

Use a graphing calculator to make a box-and-whisker plot of the data.

To make a list of the scores, press STAT and choose **Edit**. Enter each value under List 1 (L1).

Use the **STAT PLOT** editor to set up the box-and-whisker plot.

Press 2nd Y=. Press ENTER to select **Plot1**. Turn the plot **On** and use the arrow to select the plot type. The box-and-whisker plot is the fifth type shown.

The plot's values will come from the values listed in L1, so **Xlist: L1** should be visible. The **Freq** should also be set at 1.

Press ZOOM and select **9: ZoomStat** to display the plot.
Press TRACE and use the arrows to see the values of the least value **(minX)**, greatest value **(maxX)**, median **(Med)**, and lower **(Q1)** and upper **(Q3)** quartiles.

Think and Discuss

1. What five values do you need to construct a box-and-whisker plot? What values must you find before you can identify the upper and lower quartiles?
2. What does the box-and-whisker plot tell you about the data?

Try This

1. Survey your classmates to find the number of U.S. states that each student has visited. Use your calculator to make a box-and-whisker plot of the data.
2. Identify the least value, greatest value, range, median, lower quartile and upper quartile. What is the range between the upper and lower quartile?

402 *Chapter 7 Collecting, Displaying, and Analyzing Data*

6-4 Spheres

COMMON CORE

CC.8.G.9: Know the formulas for the volumes of cones, cylinders, and spheres and use them to solve real-world and mathematical problems. ***Also CC.8.EE.2***

Earth is not a perfect *sphere,* but it has been molded by gravitational forces into a spherical shape. Earth has a diameter of about 7926 miles and a surface area of about 197 million square miles.

Vocabulary

sphere

hemisphere

great circle

A **sphere** is the set of points in three dimensions that are a fixed distance from a given point, the center. A plane that intersects a sphere through its center divides the sphere into two halves, or **hemispheres**. The edge of a hemisphere is a **great circle**.

Sphere — Radius, Center

Hemisphere — Great circle

The volume of a hemisphere is exactly halfway between the volume of a cone and the volume of a cylinder with the same radius r and height equal to r.

VOLUME OF A SPHERE		
Words	**Numbers**	**Formula**
The volume V of a sphere is $\frac{4}{3}\pi$ times the cube of the radius r.	3 $V = \frac{4}{3}\pi(3^3)$ $= \frac{108}{3}\pi$ $= 36\pi$ ≈ 113.1 units^3	$V = \frac{4}{3}\pi r^3$

EXAMPLE 1 **Finding the Volume of a Sphere**

Find the volume of a sphere with radius 9 ft, both in terms of π and to the nearest tenth. Use 3.14 for π.

$V = \frac{4}{3}\pi r^3$ *Volume of a sphere*

$= \frac{4}{3}\pi(9)^3$ *Substitute 9 for r.*

$= 972\pi \text{ ft}^3 \approx 3052.1 \text{ ft}^3$

The surface area of a sphere is four times the area of a great circle.

SURFACE AREA OF A SPHERE		
Words	**Numbers**	**Formula**
The surface area S of a sphere is 4π times the square of the radius r.	2 $S = 4\pi(2^2)$ $= 16\pi$ ≈ 50.3 units^2	$S = 4\pi r^2$

EXAMPLE 2

Finding Surface Area of a Sphere

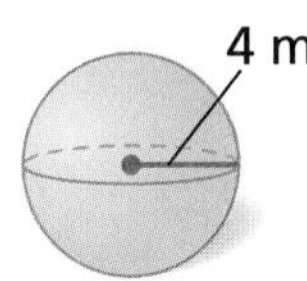

Find the surface area, both in terms of π and to the nearest tenth. Use 3.14 for π.

$S = 4\pi r^2$ *Surface area of a sphere*

$= 4\pi(4^2)$ *Substitute 4 for r.*

$= 64\pi \text{ mm}^2 \approx 201.1 \text{ mm}^2$

EXAMPLE 3

Comparing Volumes and Surface Areas

Compare the volume and surface area of a sphere with radius 42 cm with that of a rectangular prism measuring 56 × 63 × 88 cm.

Sphere:

$V = \frac{4}{3}\pi r^3 = \frac{4}{3}\pi(42)^3$

$\approx \left(\frac{4}{3}\right)\left(\frac{22}{7}\right)(74{,}088)$ *Use $\frac{22}{7}$ for π*

$\approx 310{,}464 \text{ cm}^3$

$S = 4\pi r^2 = 4\pi(42)^2$

$= 7056\pi$

$\approx 7056\left(\frac{22}{7}\right) \approx 22{,}176 \text{ cm}^2$

Rectangular prism:

$V = \ell wh$

$= (56)(63)(88)$

$= 310{,}464 \text{ cm}^3$

$S = 2B + Ph$

$= 2(56)(63) + 2(56 + 63)(88)$

$= 28{,}000 \text{ cm}^2$

The sphere and the prism have approximately the same volume, but the prism has a larger surface area.

MATHEMATICAL PRACTICES

Think and Discuss

1. **Compare** the area of a great circle with the surface area of a sphere.
2. **Explain** which would hold the most water: a bowl in the shape of a hemisphere with radius r, a cylindrical glass with radius r and height r, or a conical drinking cup with radius r and height r.

Exercises

Learn It Online
Homework Help Online
Exercises 1–18,19,21

GUIDED PRACTICE

See Example 1

Find the volume of each sphere, both in terms of π and to the nearest tenth. Use 3.14 for π.

1. $r = 3$ cm **2.** $r = 12$ ft **3.** $d = 3.4$ m **4.** $d = 10$ mi

See Example 2

Find the surface area of each sphere, both in terms of π and to the nearest tenth. Use 3.14 for π.

5.
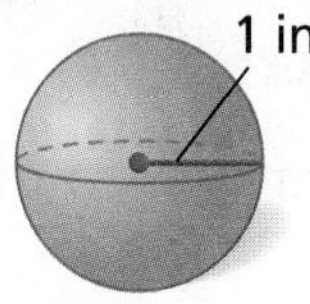

6.
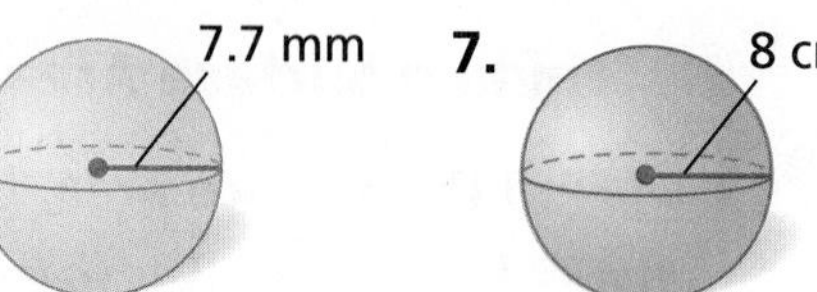

8.
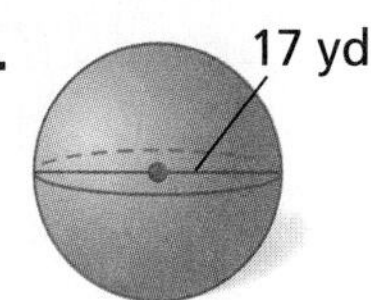

See Example 3

9. Compare the volume and surface area of a sphere with radius 4 in. with that of a cube with sides measuring 6.45 in.

INDEPENDENT PRACTICE

See Example 1

Find the volume of each sphere, both in terms of π and to the nearest tenth. Use 3.14 for π.

10. $r = 14$ ft **11.** $r = 5.7$ cm **12.** $d = 26$ mm **13.** $d = 2$ in.

See Example 2

Find the surface area of each sphere, both in terms of π and to the nearest tenth. Use 3.14 for π.

14.
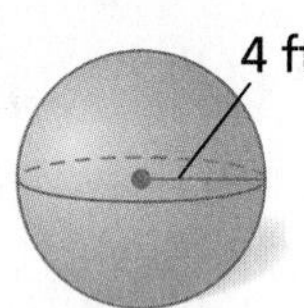

15.
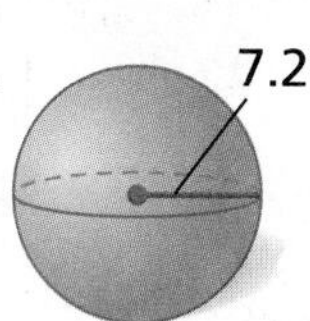

16.
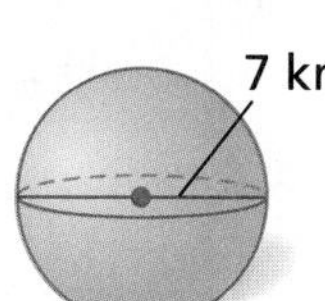

17.
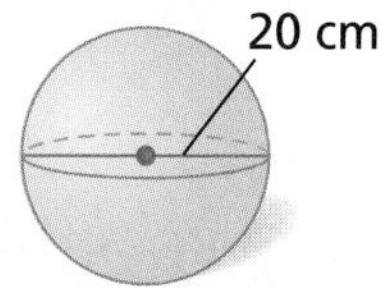

See Example 3

18. Compare the volume and surface area of a sphere with diameter 5 ft with that of a cylinder with height 2 ft and a base with radius 3 ft.

PRACTICE AND PROBLEM SOLVING

Extra Practice
See Extra Practice for more exercises.

Find the missing measurements of each sphere, both in terms of π and to the nearest hundredth. Use 3.14 for π.

19. radius = 6.5 in.
volume = ▢
surface area = 169π in^2

20. radius = 11.2 m
volume = 1873.24π m^3
surface area = ▢

21. diameter = 6.8 yd
volume = ▢
surface area = ▢

22. radius = ▢
diameter = 22 in.
surface area = ▢

23. Use models of a sphere, cylinder, and two cones. The sphere and cylinder have the same diameter and height. The cones have the same diameter and half the height of the sphere. Describe the relationship between the volumes of these shapes.

Life Science 

Eggs come in many different shapes. The eggs of birds that live on cliffs are often extremely pointed to keep the eggs from rolling. Other birds, such as great horned owls, have eggs that are nearly spherical. Turtles and crocodiles also have nearly spherical eggs, and the eggs of many dinosaurs were spherical.

24. To lay their eggs, green turtles travel hundreds of miles to the beach where they were born. The eggs are buried on the beach in a hole about 40 cm deep. The eggs are approximately spherical, with an average diameter of 4.5 cm, and each turtle lays an average of 113 eggs at a time. Estimate the total volume of eggs laid by a green turtle at one time.

Green turtle eggs

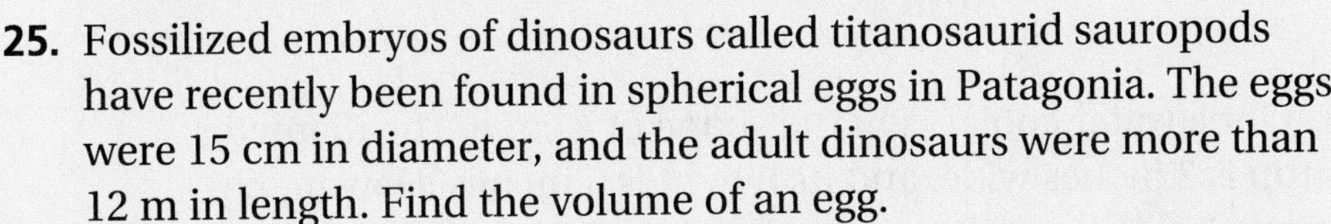

25. Fossilized embryos of dinosaurs called titanosaurid sauropods have recently been found in spherical eggs in Patagonia. The eggs were 15 cm in diameter, and the adult dinosaurs were more than 12 m in length. Find the volume of an egg.

Titanosaurid eggs

26. Hummingbirds lay eggs that are nearly spherical and about 1 cm in diameter. Find the surface area of an egg.

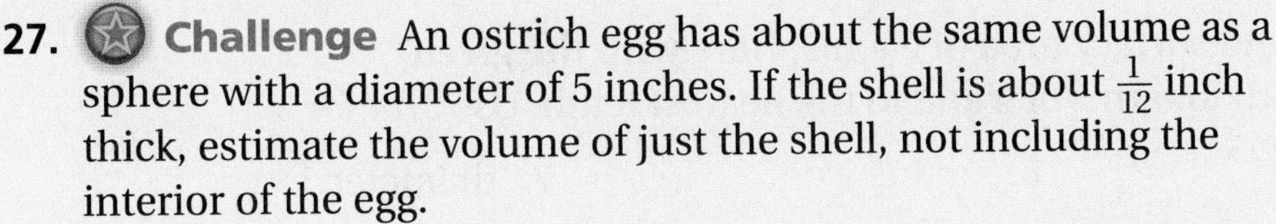

27. **Challenge** An ostrich egg has about the same volume as a sphere with a diameter of 5 inches. If the shell is about $\frac{1}{12}$ inch thick, estimate the volume of just the shell, not including the interior of the egg.

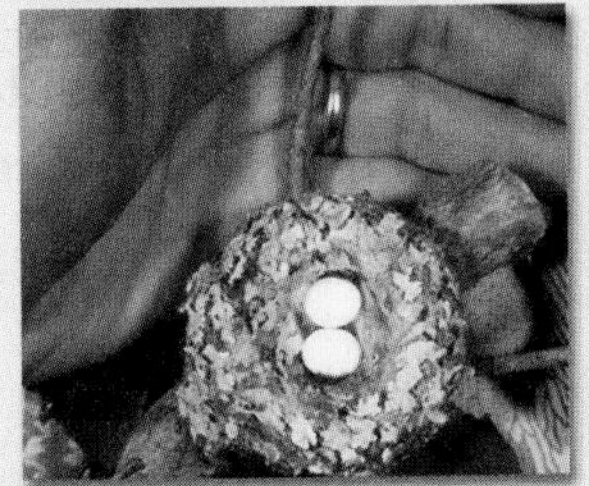
Hummingbird eggs

Test Prep

28. Multiple Choice The surface area of a sphere is 50.24 square centimeters. What is its diameter? Use 3.14 for π.

Ⓐ 1 cm   Ⓑ 2 cm   Ⓒ 2.5 cm   Ⓓ 4 cm

29. Gridded Response Find the surface area, in square feet, of a sphere with radius 3 feet. Use 3.14 for π.

(t) Tom Brakefield/Stockbyte/Getty Images; (br) Ron Austing Frank Lane Picture Agency/Corbis; (fossil eggs) Sinclair Stammers/Science Photo Library/Photo Researchers, Inc.; (turtle eggs) M. Watson/ardea.com

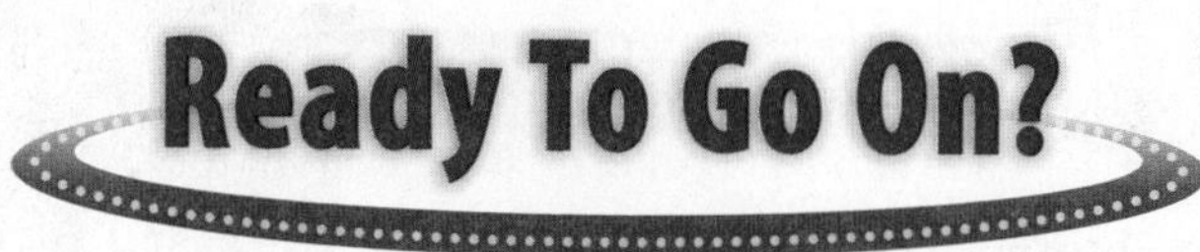

Quiz for Lessons 3 Through 4

3 Volume of Pyramids and Cones

Find the volume of each figure to the nearest tenth. Use 3.14 for π.

1. 7 cm, 5 cm, 6 cm

2. 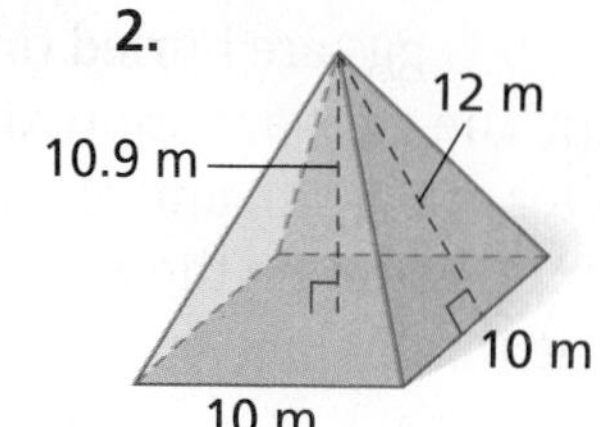

3. 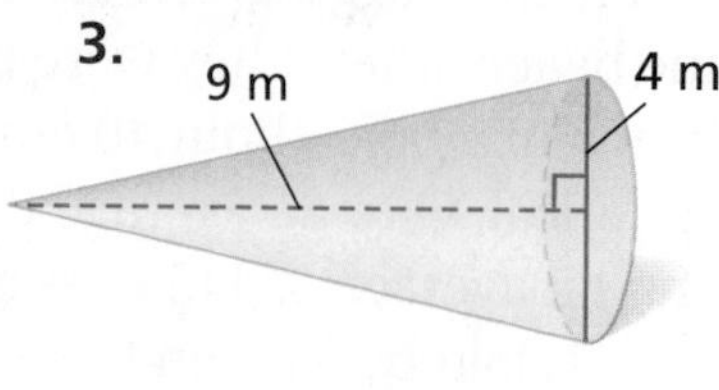

4. A drinking cup for a water cooler is in the shape of a cone. The diameter of the circular top is 2 inches wide, and its height is 3 inches. How much water does the cup hold?

4 Spheres

Find the volume and surface area of each sphere with the given measurements, both in terms of π and to the nearest tenth. Use 3.14 for π.

5. radius 6.6 mm
6. radius 9 cm
7. diameter 15 yd

8. 4.1 cm

9. 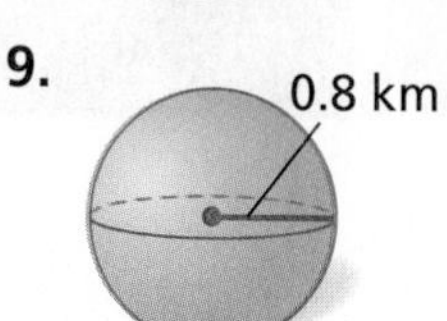

10. 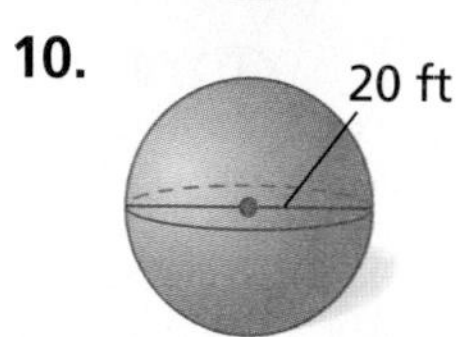

Ready to Go On?

Real-World CONNECTIONS

MATHEMATICAL PRACTICES Reason abstractly and quantitatively.

The Walters Art Museum A visit to the Walters Art Museum in Baltimore is like a trip around the world. The museum houses everything from ancient Roman coffins to Mexican sculptures to European paintings. With more than 28,000 works of art, the museum's collection fills three separate buildings.

A group of students are making copies of some of the artwork at the museum. Use the table for Problems 1–4.

1. Keisha is making a copy of *The Story of a Battle*. She wants to make a frame for the painting from a long strip of wood. How long should the strip of wood be?

2. Marc is making a copy of the mirror. He uses a thin sheet of metal to make the disk. To the nearest square inch, what is the area of metal that he needs?

3. Kate is using cardboard to make a copy of the ivory cabinet.
   a. She decorates all six outer surfaces of the cabinet. What is the area that Kate decorates?
   b. What is the volume of the cabinet?

Chamber of Wonders, The Walters Art Museum, Baltimore

4. Emilio is making a copy of the brush holder.
   a. He paints only the lateral area of the brush holder. Find the area that Emilio paints to the nearest square inch.
   b. To estimate the volume of the brush holder, Emilio uses the expression $3 \times 7^2 \times 2$. Explain the mistake that Emilio made.

Artwork at the Walters Art Museum		
Artwork	**Description**	**Dimensions**
The Story of a Battle	Rectangular painting	Length: $55\frac{1}{8}$ in.; width: $41\frac{1}{8}$ in.
Mirror with lions among grapevines	Bronze disk	Diameter: $9\frac{1}{4}$ in.
Ivory cabinet	Rectangular prism	Length: 9 in.; width: $5\frac{1}{2}$ in.; height: 6 in.
Brush holder	Glass cylinder	Height: $7\frac{3}{8}$ in.; radius: $1\frac{3}{4}$ in.

Game Time

Planes in Space

Some three-dimensional figures can be generated by plane figures.

Experiment with a circle first. Move the circle around. See if you recognize any three-dimensional shapes.

If you rotate a circle around a diameter, you get a sphere.

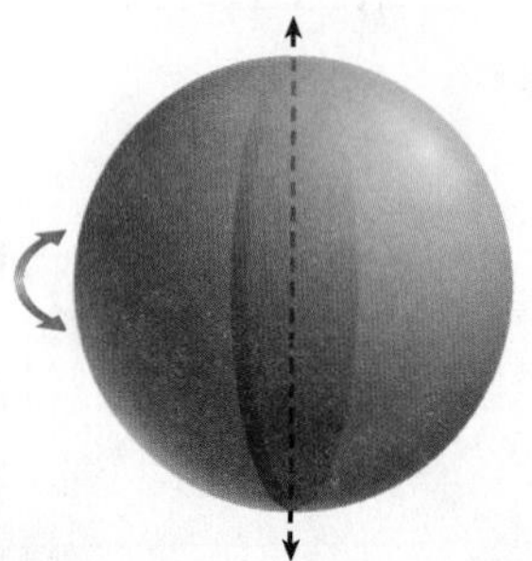

If you translate a circle up along a line perpendicular to the plane that the circle is in, you get a cylinder.

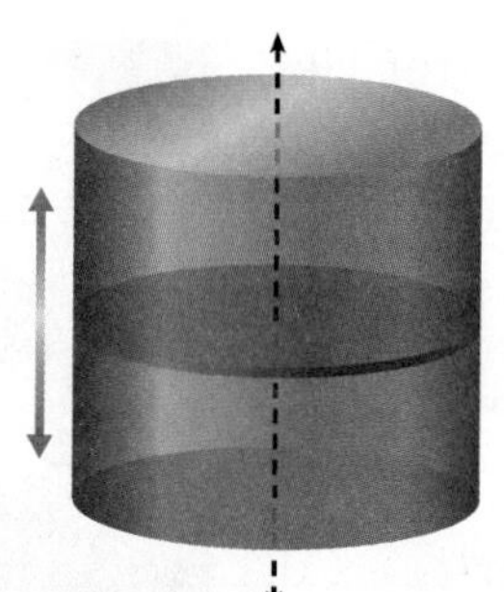

If you rotate a circle around a line outside the circle but in the same plane as the circle, you get a donut shape called a *torus*.

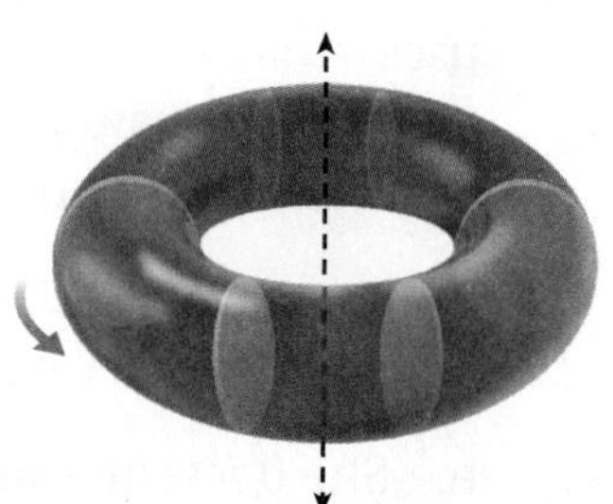

Draw or describe the three-dimensional figure generated by each plane figure.

1. a square translated along a line perpendicular to the plane it is in
2. a rectangle rotated around one of its edges
3. a right triangle rotated around one of its legs

Triple Concentration

The goal of this game is to form *Pythagorean triples,* which are sets of three whole numbers *a*, *b*, and *c* such that $a^2 + b^2 = c^2$. A set of cards with numbers on them are arranged face down. A turn consists of drawing 3 cards to try to form a Pythagorean triple. If the cards do not form a Pythagorean triple, they are replaced in their original positions.

A complete set of rules and cards are available online.

Learn It Online
Game Time Extra

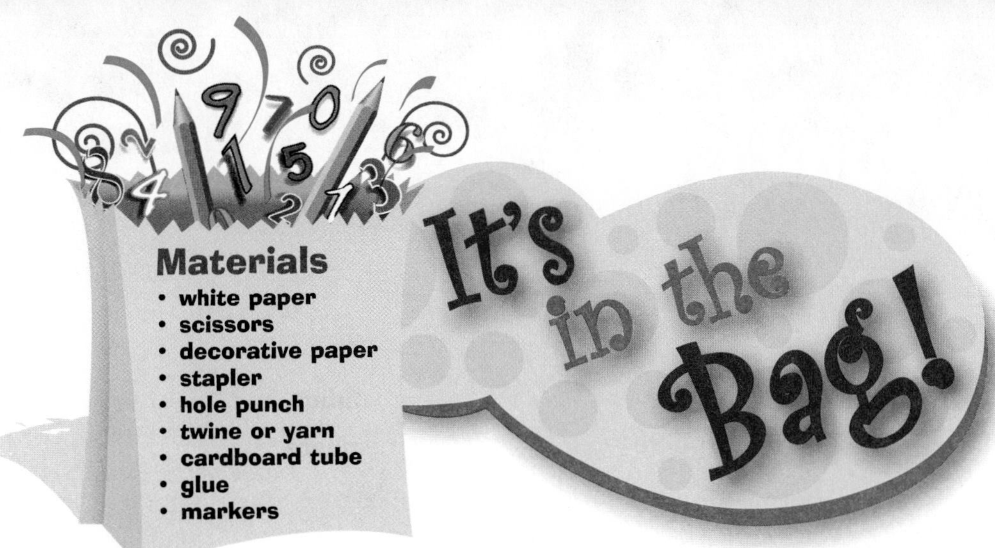

Materials
• white paper
• scissors
• decorative paper
• stapler
• hole punch
• twine or yarn
• cardboard tube
• glue
• markers
It's in the Bag!

PROJECT The Tube Journal

Use this journal to take notes on perimeter, area, and volume. Then roll up the journal and store it in a tube for safekeeping!

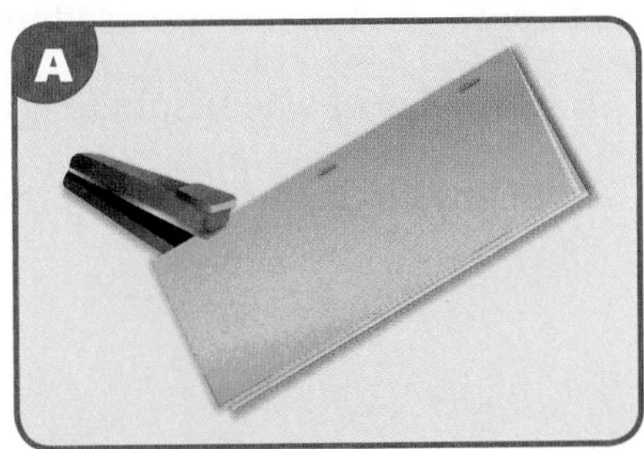

Directions

1. Start with several sheets of paper that measure $8\frac{1}{2}$ inches by 11 inches. Cut an inch off the end of each sheet so they measure $8\frac{1}{2}$ inches by 10 inches.
2. Stack the sheets and fold them in half lengthwise to form a journal that is approximately $4\frac{1}{4}$ inches by 10 inches. Cover the outside of the journal with decorative paper, trim it as needed, and staple everything together along the edge. **Figure A**
3. Punch a hole through the journal in the top left corner. Tie a 6-inch piece of twine or yarn through the hole. **Figure B**
4. Use glue to cover a cardboard tube with decorative paper. Then write the name and number of the chapter on the tube.

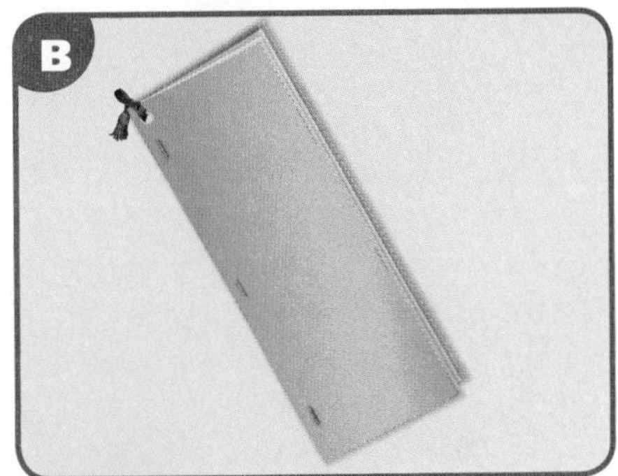

Taking Note of the Math

Use your journal to take notes from this chapter. Then roll up the journal and store it in the cardboard tube. Be sure the twine hangs out of the tube so that the journal can be pulled out easily.

Study Guide: Review

Vocabulary

circle

circumference

diameter

great circle

hemisphere

radius

sphere

Complete the sentences below with vocabulary words from the list above. Words may be used more than once.

1. The edge of a hemisphere is a(n) __?___.
2. In any circle, the length of the ___?___ is twice the length of the radius.

EXAMPLES

EXERCISES

1 Circles

- **Find the area and circumference of a circle with radius 3.1 cm. Use 3.14 for π.**

$A = \pi r^2$ $\quad$ $C = 2\pi r$

$= \pi(3.1)^2$ $\quad$ $= 2\pi(3.1)$

$= 9.61\pi \approx 30.2 \text{ cm}^2$ $\quad$ $= 6.2\pi \approx 19.5 \text{ cm}$

Find the area and circumference of each circle, both in terms of π and to the nearest tenth. Use 3.14 for π.

3. $r = 12$ in.

4. $r = 4.2$ cm

5. $d = 6$ m

6. $d = 1.2$ ft

7.

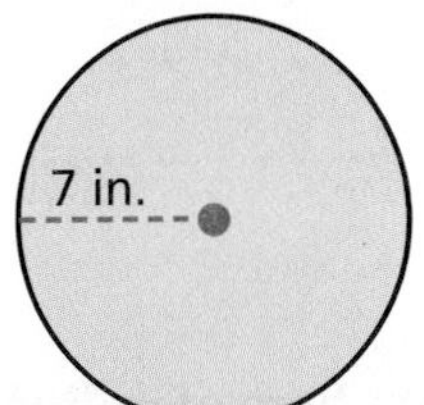

8.

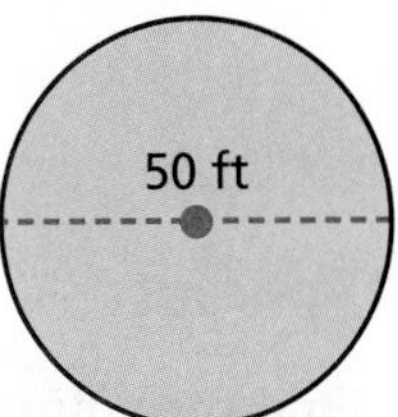

9. Will measures the distance around a tree using a tape measure as 48 inches. Use this measure to find the diameter of a cross section of the tree. Use 3.14 for π and round to the nearest tenth.

2 Volume of Prisms and Cylinders

- **Find the volume to the nearest tenth.**

$V = Bh = (\pi r^2)h$

$= \pi(3^2)(4)$

$= (9\pi)(4) = 36\pi \text{ cm}^3$

$\approx 113.0 \text{ cm}^3$

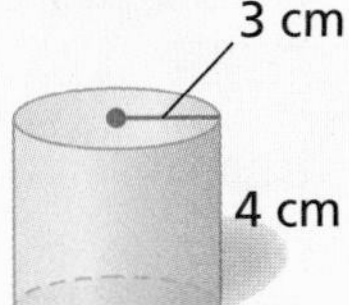

Find the volume to the nearest tenth.

10.

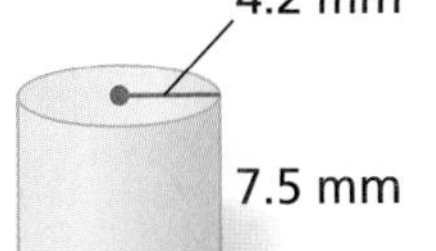

11.

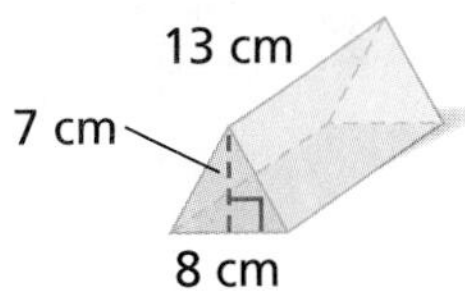

12. A shipping company has a special rate for certain packages. One of the restrictions is that the package cannot exceed a volume of 2,500 cm³. Does the box shown pass this restriction? Explain.

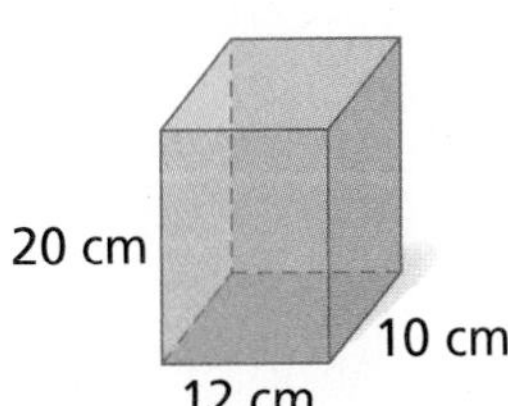

EXAMPLES | EXERCISES

3 Volume of Pyramids and Cones

■ **Find the volume.**

$V = \frac{1}{3}Bh = \frac{1}{3}(5)(6)(7)$

$= 70 \text{ m}^3$

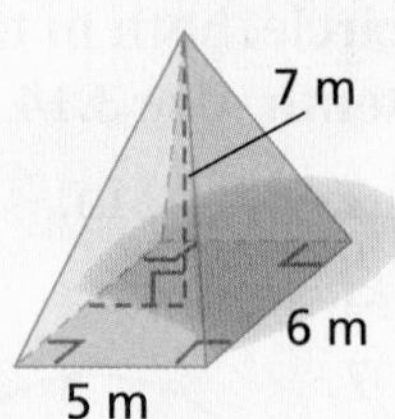

Find the volume of each figure. Use 3.14 for π.

13.

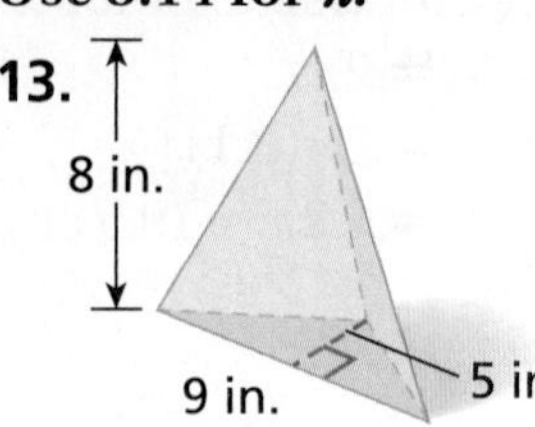

14.

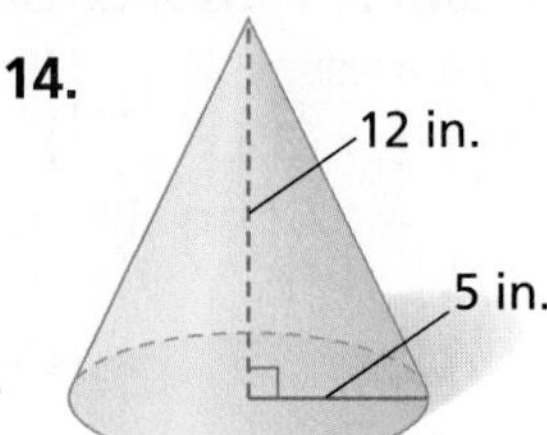

4 Spheres

■ **Find the volume of a sphere of radius 12 cm.**

$V = \frac{4}{3}\pi r^3 = \frac{4}{3}\pi(12^3)$

$= 2304\pi \text{ cm}^3 \approx 7234.6 \text{ cm}^3$

Find the volume of each sphere, both in terms of π and to the nearest tenth. Use 3.14 for π.

15. $r = 6$ in.

16. $d = 36$ m

17.

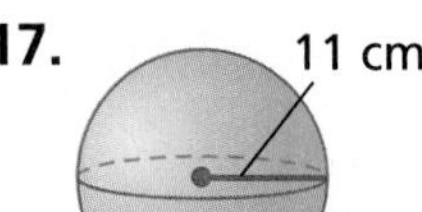

18.

19. Compare the volume and surface area of a sphere with a diameter of 1 foot to a cube with a side length of 1 foot.

Study Guide: Review

Chapter Test

Find the area and circumference of each circle, both in terms of π and to the nearest tenth. Use 3.14 for π.

1. radius = 15 cm
2. diameter = 6.5 ft
3. radius = 2.2 m
4. 3 yd
5. 11 m
6. 7.5 ft

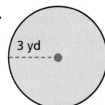

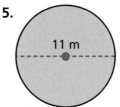

Find the volume of each figure to the nearest tenth. Use 3.14 for π.

7. a cube of side length 8 ft
8. a cylinder of height 5 cm and radius 2 cm
9. a cone of diameter 12 in. and height 18 in.
10. a sphere of radius 9 cm
11. a rectangular prism with base 5 m by 3 m and height 6 m
12. a pyramid with a 3 ft by 3 ft square base and height 4 ft

13.

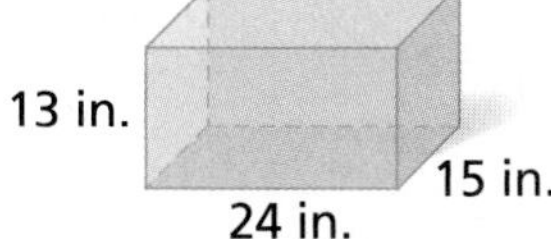

14.

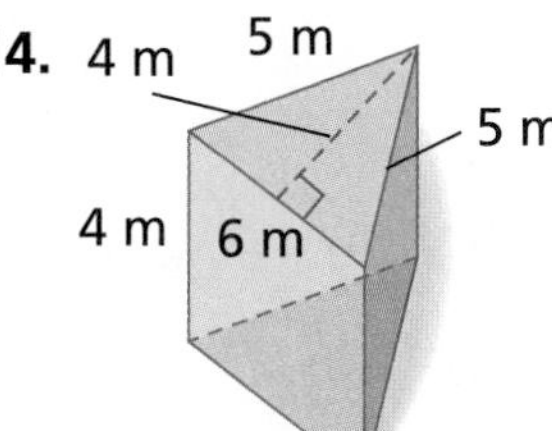

15.

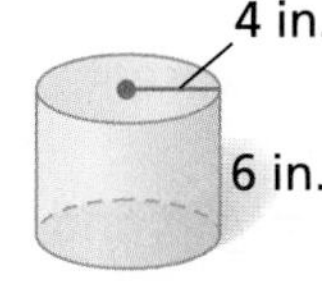

16.

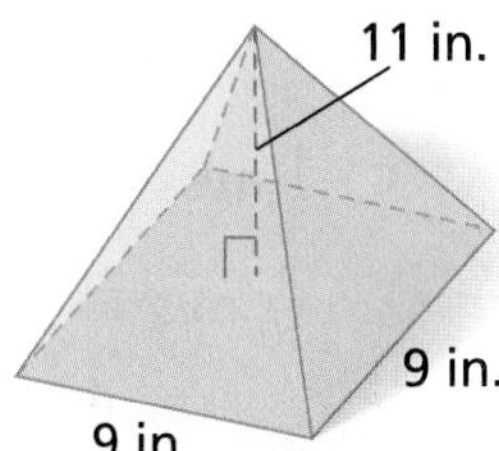

17.

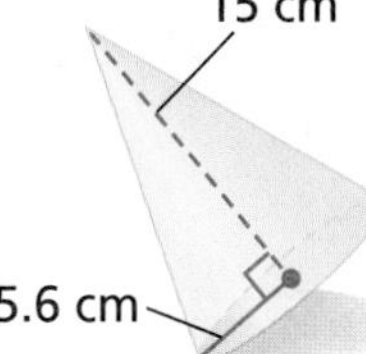

18.

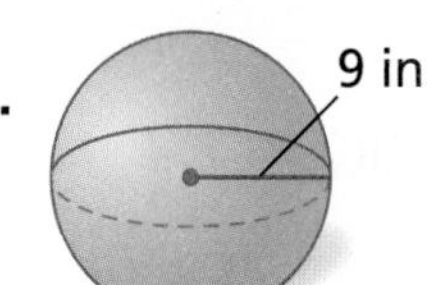

CHAPTER 6

Cumulative Assessment

Multiple Choice

1. Tony uses $\frac{1}{8}$ cup mozzarella cheese for every 16 square inches of pizza. How much mozzarella will he use for a circular pizza with a diameter of 20 inches?

Ⓐ about 2.5 cups Ⓒ about 5 cups

Ⓑ about 4 cups Ⓓ about 6.5 cups

2. Simplify: $\frac{4.5 \times 10^7}{3 \times 10^3}$

Ⓕ 15×10^4

Ⓖ 1.5×10^4

Ⓗ 1.5×10^{-4}

Ⓙ 1.5×10^{10}

3. If $\frac{g^x}{g^5} = g^{-8}$ and $g^{-3} \cdot g^y = g^{12}$, what is the value of $x + y$?

Ⓐ −9 Ⓒ 12

Ⓑ −3 Ⓓ 15

4. Solve: $\frac{4}{x} = \frac{2}{3}$

Ⓕ $x = 5$ Ⓗ $x = 6$

Ⓖ $x = 9$ Ⓙ $x = 12$

5. A triangle has angle measures of 78°, m°, and m°. What is the value of m?

Ⓐ 12 Ⓒ 102

Ⓑ 51 Ⓓ 141

6. Which word does NOT describe the number $\sqrt{16}$?

Ⓕ rational Ⓗ whole

Ⓖ integer Ⓙ irrational

7. For which positive radius, r, are the numerical values of the circumference and area the same?

Ⓐ $r = 1$ Ⓒ $r = 3$

Ⓑ $r = 2$ Ⓓ $r = 4$

8. Which equation describes the graph?

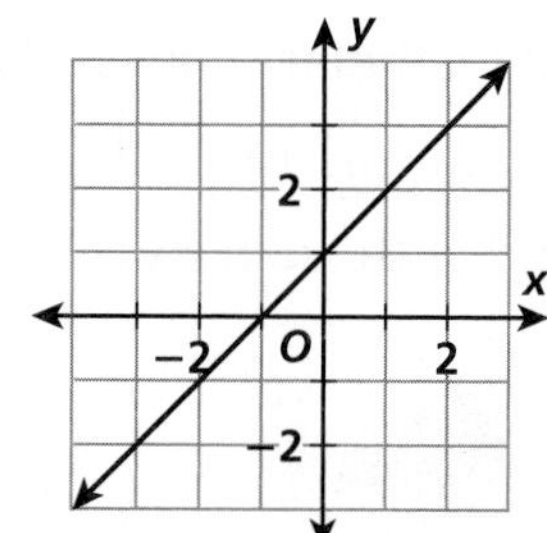

Ⓕ $y = x - 1$ Ⓗ $y = 2x + 1$

Ⓖ $y = x + 1$ Ⓙ $y = x + 2$

9. Armen rollerblades at a rate of 12 km/h. What is Armen's rate in meters per second?

Ⓐ 200 m/s Ⓒ $\frac{1}{3}$ m/s

Ⓑ $3\frac{1}{3}$ m/s Ⓓ $\frac{3}{10}$ m/s

10. What is the solution to the equation $\frac{2}{3}x + \frac{1}{6} = 1$?

Ⓕ $x = \frac{5}{9}$ Ⓗ $x = 1\frac{1}{4}$

Ⓖ $x = \frac{4}{5}$ Ⓙ $x = 3\frac{2}{3}$

11. A plot is similar in shape to the one shown below. If the similar plot has a longest side of 85 m, what is the length of its shortest side?

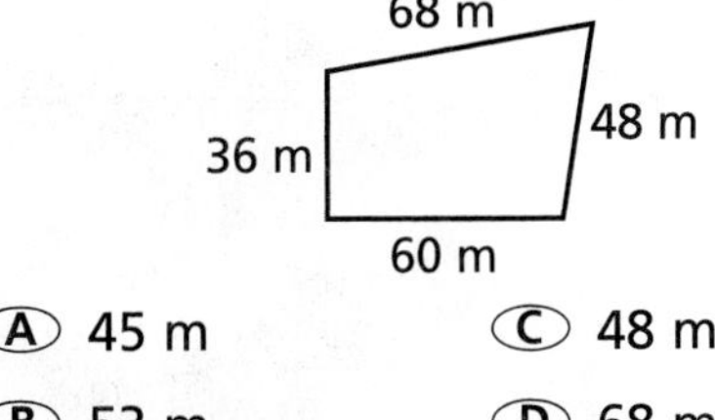

Ⓐ 45 m Ⓒ 48 m
Ⓑ 53 m Ⓓ 68 m

When a variable is used more than one time in an expression or an equation, it always has the same value.

12. The Cougars, the Wildcats, and the Broncos won a total of 18 games during the football season. The Cougars won 2 more games than the Wildcats. The Broncos won $\frac{2}{3}$ as many games as the Wildcats. How many games did the Wildcats win?

Ⓕ 2 Ⓗ 6
Ⓖ 4 Ⓙ 8

Gridded Response

13. A cone-shaped cup has a height of 3 in. and a volume of 9 in^3. What is the length in inches of the diameter of the cone? Round your answer to the nearest hundredth.

14. Shaunda measures the diameter of a ball as 12 in. How many cubic inches of air does this ball hold? Round your answer to the nearest tenth.

15. What is the y-coordinate of the point $(-3, 6)$ that has been translated down 4 units?

16. Given the obtuse triangle, what is the measure of angle x, in degrees?

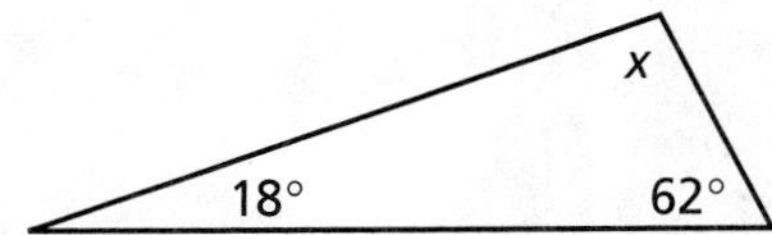

Short Response

S1. A square pyramid has a volume of 360 cubic cm. Its base has a side length of 6 cm. What is the height of the pyramid? Show your work or explain in words how you determined your answers.

S2. A cylinder with a height of 6 in. and a diameter of 4 in. is filled with water. A cone with height 6 in. and diameter 2 in. is placed in the cylinder, point down, with its base even with the top of the cylinder. Draw a diagram to illustrate the situation described, and then determine how much water is left in the cylinder. Show your work.

S3. An airplane propeller is 37 inches from its tip to the center axis of its rotation. Suppose the propeller spins at a rate of 2500 revolutions per minute. How far will a point on the tip of the propeller travel in one minute? How far will the point on the tip travel in one hour? Show your work or explain in words how you determined your answers.

Extended Response

E1. A *geodesic dome* is constructed of triangles. The surface is approximately spherical.

a. A pattern for a geodesic dome that approximates a hemisphere uses 30 triangles with base 8 ft and height 5.63 ft and 75 triangles with base 8 ft and height 7.13 ft. Find the surface area of the dome.

b. The base of the dome is approximately a circle with diameter 41 ft. Use a hemisphere with this diameter to estimate the surface area of the dome.

c. Compare your answer from part **a** with your estimate from part **b**. Explain the difference.

CHAPTER 7

Multi-Step Equations

Chapter Focus

- Use equations to analyze and solve problems.
- Solve systems of two linear equations in two variables.

Why Learn This?

Rock climbers use ropes and other safety equipment to climb cliffs and boulders. You can write and solve an equation to determine the amount of weight a climbing rope can safely hold.

Are You Ready?

Vocabulary

Choose the best term from the list to complete each sentence.

algebraic expression
constant
Distributive Property
equation
variable

1. A letter that represents a value that can change is called a(n) __?__.

2. A(n) __?__ has one or more variables.

3. A(n) __?__ is a mathematical sentence that uses an equal sign to show that two expressions have the same value.

4. When you individually multiply the numbers inside the parentheses by the factor outside the parentheses, you are applying the __?__.

Complete these exercises to review skills you will need for this chapter.

Distribute Multiplication

Replace each ■ with a number so that each equation illustrates the Distributive Property.

5. $6 \cdot (11 + 8) = 6 \cdot 11 + 6 \cdot$ ■

6. $7 \cdot (14 + 12) =$ ■ $\cdot\ 14 +$ ■ $\cdot\ 12$

7. $9 \cdot (6 -$ ■$) = 9 \cdot 6 - 9 \cdot 2$

8. $14 \cdot ($■ $- 7) = 14 \cdot 20 - 14 \cdot 7$

Solve One-Step Equations

Use mental math to solve each equation.

9. $x - 7 = -21$

10. $p + 3 = 22$

11. $14 + v = 30$

12. $b - 5 = 6$

13. $t + 33 = -14$

14. $w + 7 = -7$

Connect Words and Equations

Write an equation to represent each situation.

15. The perimeter P of a rectangle is the sum of twice the length ℓ and twice the width w.

16. The volume V of a rectangular prism is the product of its three dimensions: length ℓ, width w, and height h.

17. The surface area S of a sphere is the product of 4π and the square of the radius r.

18. The cost c of a telegram of 18 words is the cost f of the first 10 words plus the cost a of each additional word.

CHAPTER 7

Study Guide: Preview

Where You've Been

Previously, you

- used models to solve equations.
- solved one- and two-step equations.
- determined if an ordered pair is a solution to an equation.

In This Chapter

You will study

- finding solutions to application problems using algebraic equations.
- solving multi-step equations.
- determining if an ordered pair is a solution to a system of equations.
- solving a system of equations.

Where You're Going

You can use the skills learned in this chapter

- to calculate profits or losses generated by the number of items a business produces.
- to solve complex application problems involving systems of equations in higher-level math courses.

Key Vocabulary/Vocabulario

equivalent expression	expresión equivalente
like term	términos semejantes
simplify	simplificar
solution of a system of equations	solución de un sistema de ecuaciones
system of equations	sistema de ecuaciones
term	término

Vocabulary Connections

To become familiar with some of the vocabulary terms in the chapter, consider the following. You may refer to the chapter, the glossary, or a dictionary if you like.

1. The word *equivalent* contains the same root as the word *equal*. What do you think **equivalent expressions** are?
2. The word *simplify* means "make less complicated." What do you think it means to **simplify** an expression?
3. The adjective *like* means "alike." What do you suppose **like terms** are?
4. A *system* is a group of related objects. What do you think a **system of equations** is?

Study Guide: Preview

Writing Strategy: Write to Justify

The icon appears throughout the book. This icon identifies questions that require you to write a problem or an explanation. Being able to justify your answer is proof that you have an understanding of the concept. You can use a four-step method to write a justification for your solution.

8. Suppose you are playing a game in which two fair dice are rolled. To make the first move, you need to roll doubles or a sum of 3 or 11. What is the probability that you will be able to make the first move?

Step 1 **Rewrite the problem statement in your own words.**

Find the probability of rolling a double or a sum of 3 or 11.

Step 2 **Make a table or other graphic to help explain your thinking.**

1, 1	1, 2	1, 3	1 ,4	1, 5	1, 6
2, 1	2, 2	2, 3	2, 4	2, 5	2, 6
3, 1	3, 2	3, 3	3, 4	3, 5	3, 6
4, 1	4, 2	4, 3	4, 4	4, 5	4, 6
5, 1	5, 2	5, 3	5, 4	5, 5	5, 6
6, 1	6, 2	6, 3	6, 4	6, 5	6, 6

Highlight the number of ways you can roll a double or a sum of 11 or 3.

Step 3 **Give evidence that you have answered the question.**

The probability of rolling a double is $\frac{6}{36}$.

The probability of rolling a sum of 3 is $\frac{2}{36}$.

The probability of rolling a sum of 11 is $\frac{2}{36}$.

Step 4 **Write a complete response.**

The events are mutually exclusive, so you add the probabilities. The probability that you will roll a double or a sum of 11 or 3 is $\frac{6}{36} + \frac{2}{36} + \frac{2}{36} = \frac{10}{36} = \frac{5}{18}$ or approximately 28%.

Try This

Describe a situation using two fair number cubes where the probability that two independent events will occur is $\frac{1}{4}$. Justify your answer.

7-1 Simplifying Algebraic Expressions

COMMON CORE

CC.8.EE.7: Solve linear equations in one variable.

A group of friends order 2 beef tacos, 4 burritos, and 3 chicken tacos. They have a coupon for $1.00 off their purchase.

Vocabulary

terms

like terms

equivalent expressions

simplify

Terms in an expression are separated by plus or minus signs. You can write an expression with 4 terms for the total cost of the order. Let t represent the cost of a taco and b represent the cost of a burrito.

$$2t + 4b + 3t - 1$$

Helpful Hint

Constants such as 4, 0.75, and 11 are like terms because none of them have a variable.

Like terms, such as $2t$ and $3t$, have the same variables raised to the same exponents. Often, like terms have different coefficients.

You can use the Distributive Property to combine like terms.

$2t + 3t = (2 + 3)t$ *Distributive Property*

$= 5t$ *Add within the parentheses.*

When you combine like terms, you change the way an expression looks but not the value of the expression. **Equivalent expressions** have the same value for all values of the variables.

To **simplify** an expression, perform all possible operations, including combining like terms.

EXAMPLE 1 Combining Like Terms to Simplify

Combine like terms.

 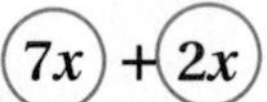 *Identify like terms.*

$(7 + 2)x$ *Distributive Property*

$9x$ *Add within the parentheses.*

B $5m^2 - 2m + 8 - 3m^2 + 6$ *Identify like terms.*

$5m^2 - 3m^2 - 2m + 8 + 6$ *Commutative Property*

$(5m^2 - 3m^2) - 2m + (8 + 6)$ *Associative Property*

$2m^2 - 2m + 14$ *Combine like terms.*

EXAMPLE 2

Combining Like Terms in Two-Variable Expressions

Combine like terms.

A $k + 3n^2 - 2n^2 + 4k$

$1k + 3n^2 - 2n^2 + 4k$ *Identify like terms; the coefficient of k is 1 because 1k = k.*

$5k + n^2$ *Combine coefficients.*

B $3f - 9g^2 + 15$

$3f - 9g^2 + 15$ *No like terms*

EXAMPLE 3

Using the Distributive Property to Simplify

Simplify $6(y + 8) - 5y$.

$6(y + 8) - 5y$

$6(y) + 6(8) - 5y$ *Distributive Property*

$6y + 48 - 5y$ *Multiply.*

$1y + 48$ *Combine coefficients: $6 - 5 = 1$.*

$y + 48$ *$1y = y$*

Remember!

The Distributive Property states that $a(b + c) = ab + ac$ for all real numbers *a*, *b*, and *c*. For example, $2(3 + 5) = 2(3) + 2(5)$.

EXAMPLE 4

Combining Like Terms to Solve Algebraic Equations

Solve $9x - x = 136$.

$9x - x = 136$ *Identify like terms. The coefficient of x is 1.*

$8x = 136$ *Combine coefficients: $9 - 1 = 8$.*

$\frac{8x}{8} = \frac{136}{8}$ *Divide both sides by 8.*

$x = 17$ *Simplify.*

MATHEMATICAL PRACTICES

Think and Discuss

1. Describe the first step in simplifying the expression $2 + 8(3y + 5) - y$.

2. Tell how many sets of like terms are in the expression in Example 1B. What are they?

7-1 Exercises

Learn It Online
Homework Help Online
Exercises 1–45, 47, 49, 51

GUIDED PRACTICE

Combine like terms.

See Example 1
1. $9x - 4x$
2. $2z + 5 + 3z$
3. $6f^2 + 3 - 4f + 5 + 10f^2$
4. $9g + 8g$
5. $7p - 9 - p$
6. $3x^3 + 5 - x^3 + 3 + 4x$

See Example 2
7. $6x + 4y - x + 4y$
8. $4x + 5y - y + 3x$
9. $5x^2 + 3y + 4x^2 - 2y$
10. $6p + 3p + 7z - 3z$
11. $7g + 5h - 12$
12. $3h + 4m^2 + 7h - 4m^2$

See Example 3
Simplify.
13. $4(r + 3) - 3r$
14. $7(3 + x) + 2x$
15. $7(t + 8) - 5t$

See Example 4
Solve.
16. $6n - 4n = 68$
17. $y + 5y = 90$
18. $5p - 2p = 51$

INDEPENDENT PRACTICE

Combine like terms.

See Example 1
19. $7y + 6y$
20. $4z - 5 - 2z$
21. $3a^2 + 6 - 2a^2 + 9 + 5a$
22. $5z - z$
23. $9x + 3 - 4x$
24. $9b^3 + 6 - 3b - 3 - b$
25. $14p - 5p$
26. $7a + 8 - 3a$
27. $3x^2 + 9 + 3x^2 - 4 + 7x^2$

See Example 2
28. $3z + 4z + b - 5$
29. $5a + a + 4z - 3z$
30. $9x^2 + 8y + 2x^2 - 8 - 4y$
31. $6x + 2 + 3x + 6q$
32. $7d - d + 3e + 12$
33. $16a + 7c^2 + 5 - 7a + c$

See Example 3
Simplify.
34. $5(y + 2) - y$
35. $2(3y - 7) + 6y$
36. $3(x + 6) + 8x$
37. $3(4y + 5) + 8$
38. $6(2x - 8) - 9x$
39. $4(4x - 4) + 3x$

See Example 4
Solve.
40. $7x - x = 72$
41. $9p - 4p = 30$
42. $p + 3p = 16$
43. $3y + 5y = 64$
44. $a + 6a = 98$
45. $8x - 3x = 60$

PRACTICE AND PROBLEM SOLVING

Extra Practice
See Extra Practice for more exercises.

46. **Hobbies** Charlie has x state quarters. Ty has 3 more quarters than Charlie has. Vinnie has 2 times as many quarters as Ty has. Write and simplify an expression to show how many state quarters they have in all.

47. **Geometry** A rectangle has length $5x$ and width x. Write and simplify an expression for the perimeter of the rectangle.

Simplify.

48. $6(4\ell + 7k) - 16\ell + 14$
49. $5d + 7 + 4d - 2d - 6$

Solve.

50. $9g + 4g = 52$

51. $12x - 6x = 90$

Write and simplify an expression for each situation.

52. Business A promoter charges \$7 for each adult ticket, plus an additional \$2 per ticket for tax and handling. What is the total cost of x tickets?

53. Sports The number of medals won by each of four countries in the 2006 Winter Olympics is shown below. Suppose a gold medal is worth g points, a silver medal is worth s points, and a bronze medal is worth b points. Write an expression for the total point value of all the medals won by the four countries.

United States	Great Britain	Austria	Sweden
9 Gold	0 Gold	9 Gold	7 Gold
9 Silver	1 Silver	7 Silver	2 Silver
7 Bronze	0 Bronze	7 Bronze	5 Bronze

54. Business A homeowner ordered 14 square yards of carpet for part of the first floor of a new house and 12 square yards of carpet for the basement. The total cost of the order was \$832 before taxes. Write and solve an equation to find the price of each square yard of carpet before taxes.

55. What's the Error? A student said that $3x + 4y$ can be simplified to $7xy$ by combining like terms. What error did the student make?

56. Write About It Write an expression that can be simplified by combining like terms. Then write an expression that cannot be simplified, and explain why it is already in simplest form.

57. Challenge Simplify and solve $3(5x + 4 - 2x) + 5(3x - 3) = 45$.

Test Prep

58. Multiple Choice Terrance bought 3 markers. His sister bought 5 markers. Terrance and his sister spent a total of \$16 on the markers. What was the price of each marker?

Ⓐ \$16 Ⓑ \$8 Ⓒ \$4 Ⓓ \$2

59. Gridded Response Simplify $3(2x + 7) + 10x$. What is the coefficient of x?

7-2 Solving Multi-Step Equations

COMMON CORE

CC.8.EE.7: Solve linear equations in one variable. ***Also CC.8.EE.7b***

To solve a multi-step equation, you may have to simplify the equation first by combining like terms or by using the Distributive Property. Once the equation has been simplified, you can solve it using the properties of equality.

EXAMPLE 1 Simplifying Before Solving Equations

Solve.

A $3x + 5 + 6x - 7 = 25$

$3x + 5 + 6x - 7 = 25$	*Identify like terms.*
$9x - 2 = 25$	*Combine like terms.*
$\underline{\quad + 2 \quad + 2}$	*Add 2 to both sides.*
$9x = 27$	
$\frac{9x}{9} = \frac{27}{9}$	*Divide both sides by 9.*
$x = 3$	

Check

$3x + 5 + 6x - 7 = 25$	
$3(3) + 5 + 6(3) - 7 \stackrel{?}{=} 25$	*Substitute 3 for x.*
$9 + 5 + 18 - 7 \stackrel{?}{=} 25$	*Multiply.*
$25 = 25$ ✔	

B $3(x + 10) + 6 = 12$

$3(x + 10) + 6 = 12$	*Distributive Property*
$3(x) + 3(10) + 6 = 12$	
$3x + 30 + 6 = 12$	*Simplify by multiplying: 3(x) = 3x and 3(10) = 30.*
$3x + 36 = 12$	*Simplify by adding: 30 + 6 = 36.*
$\underline{\quad - 36 \quad -36}$	*Subtract 36 from both sides.*
$3x = -24$	
$\frac{3x}{3} = \frac{-24}{3}$	*Divide both sides by 3.*
$x = -8$	

If an equation contains fractions, it may help to multiply both sides of the equation by the least common denominator (LCD) of the fractions. This step results in an equation without fractions, which may be easier to solve.

EXAMPLE 2 Solving Equations That Contain Fractions

Remember!

The least common denominator (LCD) is the smallest number that each of the denominators will divide into evenly.

Solve $\frac{4p}{9} + \frac{p}{3} - \frac{1}{2} = \frac{11}{6}$.

The LCD is 18.

$$18\left(\frac{4p}{9} + \frac{p}{3} - \frac{1}{2}\right) = 18\left(\frac{11}{6}\right) \quad \textit{Multiply both sides by 18.}$$

$$\overset{2}{\cancel{18}}\left(\frac{4p}{\cancel{9}_1}\right) + \overset{6}{\cancel{18}}\left(\frac{p}{\cancel{3}_1}\right) - \overset{9}{\cancel{18}}\left(\frac{1}{\cancel{2}_1}\right) = \overset{3}{\cancel{18}}\left(\frac{11}{\cancel{6}_1}\right) \quad \textit{Distributive Property}$$

$$8p + 6p - 9 = 33$$

$$14p - 9 = 33 \quad \textit{Combine like terms.}$$

$$\underline{\quad + 9 \quad + 9} \quad \textit{Add 9 to both sides.}$$

$$14p = 42$$

$$\frac{14p}{14} = \frac{42}{14} \quad \textit{Divide both sides by 14.}$$

$$p = 3$$

EXAMPLE  Travel Application

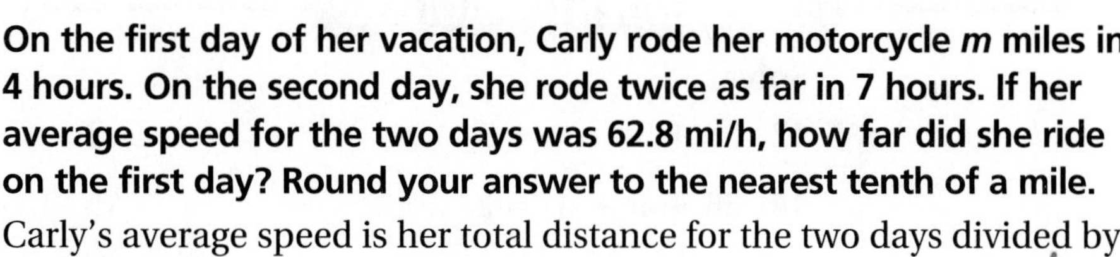

On the first day of her vacation, Carly rode her motorcycle *m* miles in 4 hours. On the second day, she rode twice as far in 7 hours. If her average speed for the two days was 62.8 mi/h, how far did she ride on the first day? Round your answer to the nearest tenth of a mile.

Carly's average speed is her total distance for the two days divided by the total time.

$$\frac{\text{total distance}}{\text{total time}} = \text{average speed}$$

$$\frac{m + 2m}{4 + 7} = 62.8 \quad \textit{Substitute } m + 2m \textit{ for total distance and } 4 + 7 \textit{ for total time.}$$

$$\frac{3m}{11} = 62.8 \quad \textit{Simplify.}$$

$$11\left(\frac{3m}{11}\right) = 11(62.8) \quad \textit{Multiply both sides by 11.}$$

$$3m = 690.8$$

$$\frac{3m}{3} = \frac{690.8}{3} \quad \textit{Divide both sides by 3.}$$

$$m \approx 230.27$$

Carly rode approximately 230.3 miles on the first day.

MATHEMATICAL PRACTICES

Think and Discuss

1. List the steps required to solve $3x - 4 + 2x = 7$.

2. Tell how you would clear the fractions in $\frac{3x}{4} - \frac{2x}{3} + \frac{5}{8} = 1$.

7-2 Exercises

Learn It Online
Homework Help Online
Exercises 1–24, 25, 27, 29, 35

GUIDED PRACTICE

Solve.

See Example 1

1. $7d - 12 + 2d + 3 = 18$

2. $3y + 4y + 6 = 20$

3. $10e - 2e - 9 = 39$

4. $4c - 5 + 14c = 67$

5. $10(h + 1) - 4 = 76$

6. $5(x + 2) - 7 = -32$

See Example 2

7. $\frac{4x}{13} + \frac{3}{13} = -\frac{1}{13}$

8. $\frac{y}{2} - \frac{5y}{6} + \frac{1}{3} = \frac{1}{2}$

9. $\frac{4}{5} - \frac{2p}{5} = \frac{6}{5}$

10. $\frac{15}{8}z + \frac{1}{4} = 4$

See Example 3

11. **Travel** Barry's family drove 843 mi to see his grandparents. On the first day, they drove 483 mi. On the second day, how long did it take to reach Barry's grandparents' house if they averaged 60 mi/h?

INDEPENDENT PRACTICE

Solve.

See Example 1

12. $5n + 3n - n + 5 = 26$

13. $-81 = 7k + 19 + 3k$

14. $36 - 4c - 3c = 22$

15. $12 + 5w - 4w = 15$

16. $9(a - 2) + 15 = 33$

17. $7(y - 4) - 7 = 0$

See Example 2

18. $\frac{3}{8} + \frac{p}{8} = 3\frac{1}{8}$

19. $\frac{7h}{12} - \frac{4h}{12} = \frac{18}{12}$

20. $\frac{4g}{16} - \frac{3}{8} - \frac{g}{16} = \frac{3}{16}$

21. $\frac{7}{12} = \frac{3m}{6} - \frac{m}{3} + \frac{1}{4}$

22. $\frac{4}{13} = -\frac{2b}{13} + \frac{6b}{26}$

23. $\frac{3x}{4} - \frac{21x}{32} = -1\frac{1}{8}$

See Example 3

24. **Recreation** Lydia rode 243 miles in a three-day bike trip. On the first day, Lydia rode 67 miles. On the second day, she rode 92 miles. How many miles per hour did she average on the third day if she rode for 7 hours?

PRACTICE AND PROBLEM SOLVING

Extra Practice
See Extra Practice for more exercises.

Solve and check.

25. $\frac{5n}{8} - \frac{1}{2} = \frac{3}{4}$

26. $4n + 11 - 7n = -13$

27. $7b - 2 - 12b = 63$

28. $\frac{x}{2} + \frac{2}{3} = \frac{5}{6}$

29. $-2x - 7 + 3x = 10$

30. $4(r + 2) + 5r = 26$

31. **Finance** Alessia is paid 1.4 times her normal hourly rate for each hour she works over 30 hours in a week. Last week she worked 35 hours and earned \$436.60. Write and solve an equation to find Alessia's normal hourly rate. Explain how you know that your answer is reasonable.

Sports

You can estimate the weight in pounds of a fish that is L inches long and G inches around at the thickest part by using the formula $W \approx \frac{LG^2}{800}$.

32. **Geometry** One angle of a triangle measures 120°. The other two angles are congruent. Write and solve an equation to find the measure of the congruent angles.

33. **Critical Thinking** The sum of two consecutive numbers is 63. What are the two numbers? Explain your solution.

34. **Sports** The average weight of the top 5 fish at a fishing tournament was 12.3 pounds. The weights of the second-, third-, fourth-, and fifth-place fish are shown in the table. What was the weight of the heaviest fish?

Winning Entries

Caught by	Weight (lb)
Wayne S.	
Carla P.	12.8
Deb N.	12.6
Virgil W.	11.8
Brian B.	9.7

35. **Physical Science** The formula $K = \frac{F - 32}{1.8} + 273$ is used to convert a temperature from degrees Fahrenheit to kelvins. Water boils at 373 kelvins. Use the formula to find the boiling point of water in degrees Fahrenheit.

36. **What's the Error?** A student's work in solving an equation is shown. What error has the student made, and what is the correct answer?

$$\frac{1}{5}x + 5x = 13$$
$$x + 5x = 65$$
$$6x = 65$$
$$x = \frac{65}{6}$$

37. **Write About It** Compare the steps used to solve the following.

$$4x - 8 = 16 \qquad\qquad 4(x - 2) = 16$$

38. **Challenge** List the steps you would use to solve the following equation.

$$\frac{4\left(\frac{1}{3}x - \frac{1}{4}\right) + \frac{4}{3}x}{3} + 1 = 6$$

Test Prep

39. **Multiple Choice** **Solve $4k - 7 + 3 + 5k = 59$.**

Ⓐ $k = 6$　　Ⓑ $k = 6.6$　　Ⓒ $k = 7$　　Ⓓ $k = 11.8$

40. **Gridded Response** Antonio's first four test grades were 85, 92, 91, and 80. What must he score on the next test to have an 88 test average?

(tl) Buddy Mays/Corbis; (tr) Peter Van Steen/HMH

Hands-on
LAB

Model Equations with Variables on Both Sides

Use with Solving Equations with Variables on Both Sides

Learn It Online
Lab Resources Online

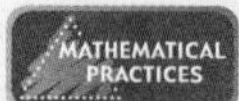
MATHEMATICAL PRACTICES

Use appropriate tools strategically.

CC.8.EE.7: Solve linear equations in one variable. ***Also CC.8.EE.7a, CC.8.EE.7b***

KEY

Algebra tiles

[tile] $= x$ [tile] $= -x$

[tile] $= 1$ [tile] $= -1$

REMEMBER

It will not change the value of an expression if you add or remove zero.

[tile] + [tile] = 0 [tile] + [tile] = 0

To solve an equation with the same variable on both sides of the equal sign, you must first add or subtract to eliminate the variable term from one side of the equation.

Activity

1 **Model and solve the equation $-x + 2 = 2x - 4$.**

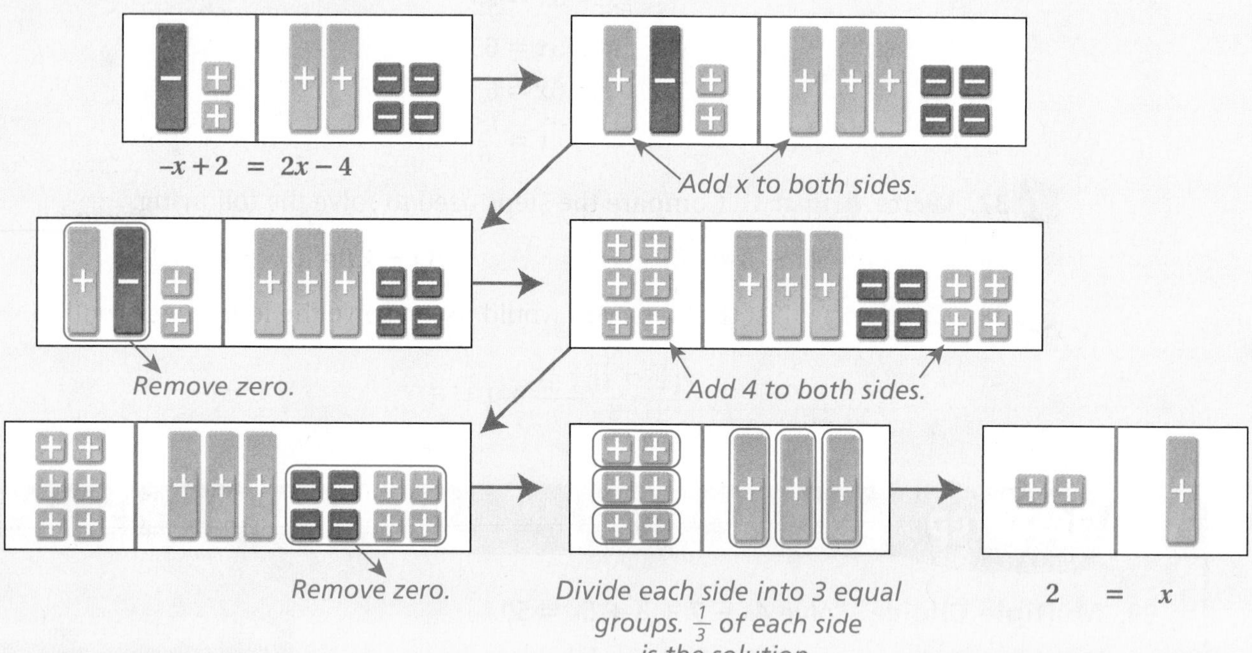
$-x + 2 = 2x - 4$
Add x to both sides.
Remove zero.
Add 4 to both sides.
Remove zero.
Divide each side into 3 equal groups. $\frac{1}{3}$ of each side is the solution.
$2 = x$

Think and Discuss

1. How would you check the solution to $-x + 2 = 2x - 4$ using algebra tiles?
2. Why must you isolate the variable terms by having them on only one side of the equation?

Try This

Model and solve each equation.

1. $x + 3 = -x - 3$
2. $3x = -3x + 18$
3. $6 - 3x = -4x + 8$
4. $3x + 3x + 2 = x + 17$

7-3 Solving Equations with Variables on Both Sides

COMMON CORE

CC.8.EE.7: Solve linear equations in one variable. ***Also CC.8.EE.7a, CC.8.EE.7b***

Vocabulary

literal equation

Some problems produce equations that have variables on both sides of the equal sign. For example, write an equation to find the number of hours for which the cost will be the same for both dog-sitting services.

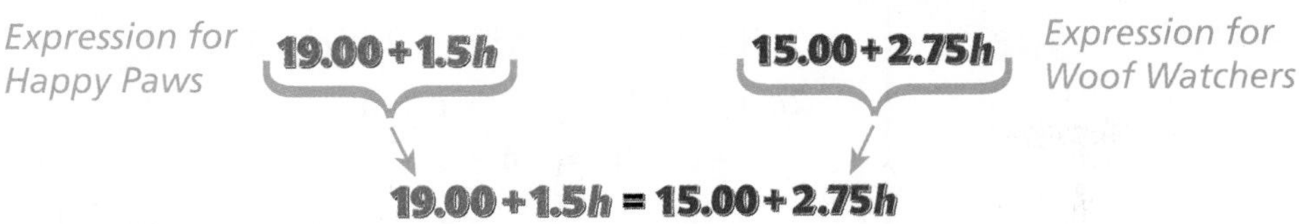

The variable h in these expressions represents the number of hours. The two expressions are equal when the cost is the same.

Solving an equation with variables on both sides is similar to solving an equation with a variable on only one side. You can add or subtract a term containing a variable on both sides of an equation.

Interactivities Online ▶

EXAMPLE 1 Solving Equations with Variables on Both Sides

Helpful Hint

You can always check your solution by substituting the value back into the original equation.

Solve.

A $2a + 3 = 3a$

$$\begin{aligned} 2a + 3 &= 3a \\ \underline{-2a} & \quad \underline{-2a} \\ 3 &= a \end{aligned}$$

Subtract 2a from both sides.

B $3v - 8 = 7 + 8v$

$$\begin{aligned} 3v - 8 &= 7 + 8v \\ \underline{-3v} & \quad \underline{-3v} \\ -8 &= 7 + 5v \\ \underline{-7} & \quad \underline{-7} \\ -15 &= 5v \\ \frac{-15}{5} &= \frac{5v}{5} \\ -3 &= v \end{aligned}$$

Subtract 3v from both sides.

Subtract 7 from both sides.

Divide both sides by 5.

Helpful Hint

If the variables in an equation are eliminated and the resulting statement is false, the equation has no solution.

Solve.

C $g + 7 = g - 3$

$$\begin{aligned} g + 7 &= \quad g - 3 \\ \underline{-g} \quad & \quad \underline{-g} \\ 7 &\neq \quad -3 \end{aligned}$$ *Subtract g from both sides.*

There is no solution. There is no number that can be substituted for the variable g to make the equation true.

To solve multi-step equations with variables on both sides, first combine like terms and clear fractions. Then add or subtract variable terms to both sides so that the variable occurs on only one side of the equation. Then use properties of equality to isolate the variable.

EXAMPLE 2 Solving Multi-Step Equations with Variables on Both Sides

Solve $2c + 4 - 3c = -9 + c + 5$.

$2c + 4 - 3c = -9 + c + 5$

$-c + 4 = -4 + c$ *Combine like terms.*

$\underline{+c} \quad \underline{+c}$ *Add c to both sides.*

$4 = -4 + 2c$

$\underline{+4} \quad \underline{+4}$ *Add 4 to both sides.*

$8 = 2c$

$\frac{8}{2} = \frac{2c}{2}$ *Divide both sides by 2.*

$4 = c$

EXAMPLE 3 *Business Application*

Happy Paws charges a flat fee of \$19.00 plus \$1.50 per hour to keep a dog during the day. A rival service, Woof Watchers, charges a flat fee of \$15.00 plus \$2.75 per hour. Find the number of hours for which you would pay the same total fee to both services.

$19.00 + 1.5h = 15.00 + 2.75h$ *Let h represent the number of hours.*

$\underline{-1.5h} \quad \underline{-1.5h}$ *Subtract 1.5h from both sides.*

$19.00 = 15.00 + 1.25h$

$\underline{-15.00} \quad \underline{-15.00}$ *Subtract 15.00 from both sides.*

$4.00 = 1.25h$

$\frac{4.00}{1.25} = \frac{1.25h}{1.25}$ *Divide both sides by 1.25.*

$3.2 = h$

The two services cost the same when used for 3.2 hours.

EXAMPLE 4 **Fitness Application**

Elaine runs the same distance every day. On Mondays, Fridays, and Saturdays, she runs 3 laps on a running trail and then runs 5 more miles. On Tuesdays and Thursdays, she runs 4 laps on the trail and then runs 2.5 more miles. On Wednesdays, she just runs laps. How many laps does she run on Wednesdays?

First solve for the distance of one lap on the trail.

$3x + 5 = 4x + 2.5$	*Let x represent the distance of one lap.*
$-3x \quad = -3x$	*Subtract 3x from both sides.*
$5 = x + 2.5$	
$-2.5 \quad\quad -2.5$	*Subtract 2.5 from both sides.*
$2.5 = x$	*One lap on the trail is 2.5 miles.*

Caution!

The value of the variable is not necessarily the answer to the question.

Now find the total distance Elaine runs each day.

$3x + 5$	*Choose one of the original expressions.*
$3(2.5) + 5 = 12.5$	*Elaine runs 12.5 miles each day.*

Find the number of laps Elaine runs on Wednesdays.

$2.5n = 12.5$	*Let n represent the number of 2.5-mile laps.*
$\frac{2.5n}{2.5} = \frac{12.5}{2.5}$	*Divide both sides by 2.5.*
$n = 5$	

Elaine runs 5 laps on Wednesdays.

A **literal equation** is an equation with two or more variables. A formula is one type of literal equation. You can solve for one of the variables in a literal equation by using inverse operations.

EXAMPLE 5 **Solving Literal Equations for a Variable**

The equation $P = 2\ell + 2w$ gives the perimeter P of a rectangle with length ℓ and width w. Solve this equation for w.

$P = 2\ell + 2w$	*Locate w in the equation.*
$P = 2\ell + 2w$ $-2\ell \quad -2\ell$	*Since 2ℓ is added to 2w, subtract 2ℓ from both sides to undo the addition.*
$P - 2\ell = 2w$	
$\frac{P - 2\ell}{2} = \frac{2w}{2}$	*Since w is multiplied by 2, divide both sides by 2 to undo the multiplication.*
$\frac{P - 2\ell}{2} = w$	

MATHEMATICAL PRACTICES

Think and Discuss

1. **Explain** how you would solve the equation $3x + 4 - 2x = 6x + 2 - 5x + 2$. What do you think the solution means?

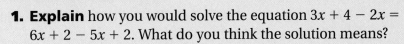

7-3 Exercises

Learn It Online
Homework Help Online
Exercises 1–18, 19, 21, 23, 25

GUIDED PRACTICE

Solve.

See Example 1

1. $6x + 3 = x + 8$
2. $5a - 5 = 7 + 2a$
3. $13x + 15 = 11x - 25$
4. $5t - 5 = 5t + 7$

See Example 2

5. $5x - 2 + 3x = 17 + 12x - 23$
6. $4(x - 5) + 2 = x + 3$

See Example 3

7. A long-distance phone company charges $0.027 per minute and a $2 monthly fee. Another long-distance phone company charges $0.035 per minute with no monthly fee. Find the number of minutes for which the charges for both companies would be the same.

See Example 4

8. June has a set of folding chairs. If she arranges the chairs in 5 rows of the same length, she has 2 chairs left over. If she arranges them in 3 rows of the same length, she has 14 left over. How many chairs does she have?

See Example 5

9. The equation $A = \frac{1}{2}bh$ gives the area A of a triangle, where b is the length of the base and h is the height. Solve this equation for h.

INDEPENDENT PRACTICE

Solve.

See Example 1

10. $3n + 16 = 7n$
11. $8x - 3 = 11 - 6x$
12. $5n + 3 = 14 - 6n$
13. $3(2x + 11) = 6x + 33$

See Example 2

14. $4(x - 5) - 5 = 6x + 7.4 - 4x$
15. $\frac{1}{2}(2n + 6) = 5n - 12 - n$

See Example 3

16. Al's Rentals charges $25 per hour to rent a sailboard and a wet suit. Wendy's Rentals charges $20 per hour plus $15 extra for a wet suit. Find the number of hours for which the total charges for both companies would be the same.

See Example 4

17. Sean and Laura have the same number of action figures in their collections. Sean has 6 complete sets plus 2 individual figures, and Laura has 3 complete sets plus 20 individual figures. How many figures are in a complete set?

See Example 5

18. The equation $A = r\left(\frac{C}{2}\right)$ gives the area A of a circle, where r is the radius and C is the circumference. Solve this equation for C.

PRACTICE AND PROBLEM SOLVING

Extra Practice
See Extra Practice for more exercises.

Solve and check.

19. $3y - 1 = 13 - 4y$
20. $4n + 8 = 9n - 7$
21. $5n + 20n = 5(n + 20)$
22. $3(4x - 2) = 12x$
23. $100(x - 3) = 450 - 50x$
24. $2p - 12 = 12 - 2p$

Sodium and chlorine bond together to form sodium chloride, or salt. The atomic structure of sodium chloride causes it to form cubes.

Both figures have the same perimeter. Find each perimeter.

25.

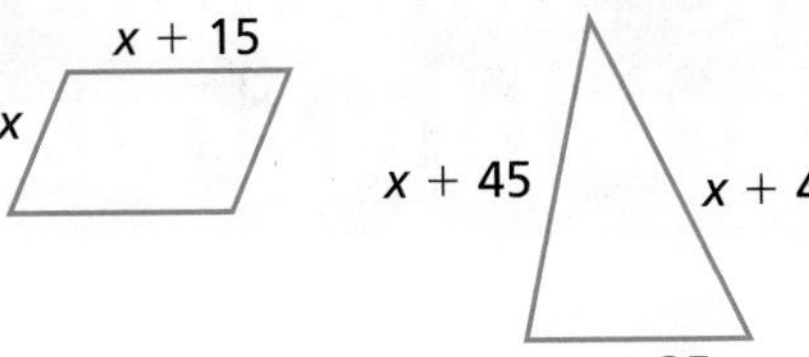

26.

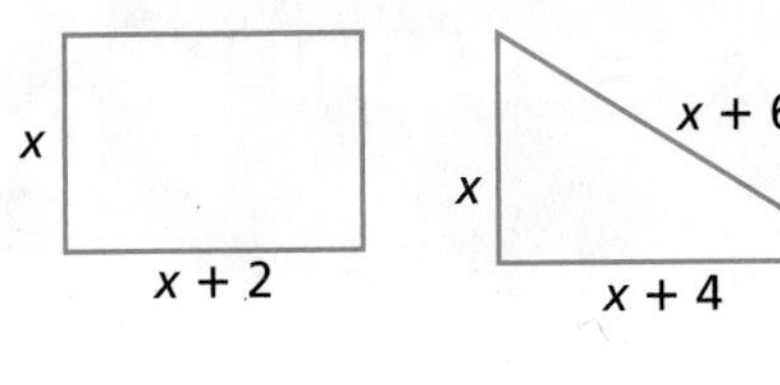

27. The equation $A = P + Prt$ gives the amount A in an account earning simple interest, where P is the principal, r is the annual interest rate, and t is the time in years. Solve this equation for t.

28. **Physical Science** An atom of chlorine (Cl) has 6 more protons than an atom of sodium (Na). The atomic number of chlorine is 5 less than twice the atomic number of sodium. The atomic number of an element is equal to the number of protons per atom.

a. How many protons are in an atom of chlorine?

b. What is the atomic number of sodium?

29. **Business** George and Aaron work for different car dealerships. George earns a monthly salary of \$2500 plus a 5% commission on his sales. Aaron earns a monthly salary of \$3000 plus a 3% commission on his sales. How much must both sell to earn the same amount in a month?

30. **Choose a Strategy** Solve the following equation for t. How can you determine the solution once you have combined like terms?

$3(t - 24) = 7t - 4(t + 18)$

31. **Write About It** Two cars are traveling in the same direction. The first car is going 45 mi/h, and the second car is going 60 mi/h. The first car left 2 hours before the second car. Explain how you could solve an equation to find how long it will take the second car to catch up to the first car.

32. **Challenge** Solve the equation $\frac{x + 2}{8} = \frac{6}{7} + \frac{x - 1}{2}$.

Test Prep

33. **Multiple Choice** Find three consecutive integers so that the sum of the first two integers is 10 more than the third integer.

Ⓐ −7, −6, −5 Ⓑ 4, 5, 6 Ⓒ 11, 12, 13 Ⓓ 35, 36, 37

34. **Multiple Choice** Solve $6w - 15 = 9w$.

Ⓕ $w = 3$ Ⓖ $w = 0$ Ⓗ $w = -1$ Ⓙ $w = -5$

EXTENSION

Possible Solutions of One-Variable Equations

COMMON CORE

CC.8.EE.7: Solve linear equations in one variable. ***Also CC.8.EE.7a***

Until now, when you have solved equations, there has been only one solution. It is also possible for a one-variable equation to have no solutions or infinitely many solutions.

EXAMPLE 1 One-Variable Equations with No Solutions

Solve the equation, and interpret the result.

$2x - 4 = 2(x - 1) + 2$

$2x - 4 = 2(x - 1) + 2$		
$2x - 4 = 2x$		*$2x - 2 + 2$ is $2x$.*
$\underline{\quad +4} \quad \underline{\quad +4}$		*Add 4 to both sides.*
$2x = 2x + 4$		
$\underline{-2x} = \underline{-2x}$		*Subtract 2x from both sides.*
$0 = 4$		*This is a false statement.*

Because $0 = 4$ is never a true statement, the equation can never be true for *any value* of x. There is no solution.

EXAMPLE 2 One-Variable Equations with Infinitely Many Solutions

Solve the equation, and interpret the result.

$-4x + 3(x - 1) = -(x + 3)$

$-4x + 3(x - 1) = -(x + 3)$	
$-4x + 3x - 3 = -x - 3$	*Apply the Distributive Property.*
$-x - 3 = -x - 3$	*Simplify.*
$\underline{\quad +3} = \underline{\quad +3}$	*Add 3 to both sides.*
$-x = -x$	
$\underline{+x} = \underline{+x}$	*Add x to both sides.*
$0 = 0$	*This is a true statement.*

Because $0 = 0$ is always a true statement, the equation is always true for *any value* of x. There are *infinitely many* solutions.

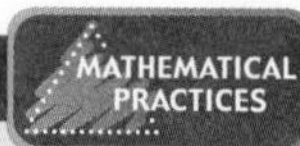

Think and Discuss

1. **Write** an equation that has no solution and an equation that has infinitely many solutions.

EXTENSION

Exercises

Solve the equation, and interpret the result.

1. $-2x - (x - 2) = 5x + 3(x + 1)$
2. $-(2x + 2) - 1 = -x - (x + 3)$
3. $7x + 2(x - 2) = 3(3x + 4)$
4. $-(3x + 2) - (x - 1) = -(2x - 2) - (2x + 4)$
5. $-(x + 2) + (2x - 1) = -(x + 1) + 2(x - 1)$
6. $(4x - 1) - 2(x + 1) = 3x - (4x + 2)$
7. $3(x - 1) - 2x = -2x + 3(x - 1)$
8. $-5(x - 1) + x = 6x - 11$
9. $-(x - 8) + 4x = 2(x + 4) + x$
10. $-(2x - 4) + 3(x - 1) = 2(x - 1) - (x - 3)$
11. $4(x - 2) - 2x = 3x - (x - 2)$
12. $4x - 2(x - 1) = -(x - 1) + 3x$
13. $-2(x + 3) - x = -x - 4(x + 2)$
14. $x - 2(x + 3) = 2x - 3(x + 2)$

Solve the equation, interpret the result, and graph the solution.

15. $-x + 3(x - 1) = 2(x - 1) - 3$
16. $2(x - 4) + 3x = x + 4(x - 2)$
17. $5x - (x - 2) = 2x - (x + 1)$

Write the equation, solve for the unknown, and interpret the result.

18. Four less than three times a number is two less than two times the same number. What is the number?
19. One less than twice a number is two times a number minus two. What is the number?
20. Three times a number minus one is three less than three times the number. What is the number?
21. Four times a number is four less than the number. What is the number?
22. **Challenge** Create an equation with one variable for each of the three solution types (one solution, no solution, infinitely many solutions).

Focus on Problem Solving

MATHEMATICAL PRACTICES Make sense of problems and persevere in solving them.

Make a Plan

- **Write an equation**

Several steps may be needed to solve a problem. It often helps to write an equation that represents the steps.

Example:

Juan's first 3 exam scores are 85, 93, and 87. What does he need to score on his next exam to average 90 for the 4 exams?

Let x be the score on his next exam. The average of the exam scores is the sum of the 4 scores, divided by 4. This amount must equal 90.

Average of exam scores = 90

$$\frac{85 + 93 + 87 + x}{4} = 90$$

$$\frac{265 + x}{4} = 90$$

$$4\left(\frac{265 + x}{4}\right) = 4(90)$$

$$265 + x = 360$$

$$\underline{-265} \quad \underline{-265}$$

$$x = 95$$

Juan needs a 95 on his next exam.

Read each problem and write an equation that could be used to solve it.

1. The average of two numbers is 34. The first number is three times the second number. What are the two numbers?

2. Nancy spends $\frac{1}{3}$ of her monthly salary on rent, 0.1 on her car payment, $\frac{1}{12}$ on food, and 20% on other bills. She has $680 left for other expenses. What is Nancy's monthly salary?

3. A vendor at a concert sells new and used CDs. The new CDs cost 2.5 times as much as the old CDs. If 4 used CDs and 9 new CDs cost $159, what is the price of each item?

4. Amanda and Rick have the same amount to spend on carnival tickets. Amanda buys 4 tickets and has $8.60 left. Rick buys 7 tickets and has $7.55 left. How much does each ticket cost?

Amy Eckert/Photonica/Getty Images

7-4 Systems of Equations

COMMON CORE

CC.8.EE.8: Analyze and solve pairs of simultaneous linear equations. ***Also CC.8.EE.7, CC.8.EE.8b, CC.8.EE.8c***

Tickets for a high school football game were \$8 for adults and \$5 for students. A total of 1970 tickets were sold. The total ticket sales were \$12,220. How many adult tickets were sold, and how many student tickets were sold? You can solve this problem using two equations. (See Exercise 36.)

Vocabulary

system of equations

solution of a system of equations

A **system of equations** is a set of two or more equations that contain two or more variables.

A **solution of a system of equations** is

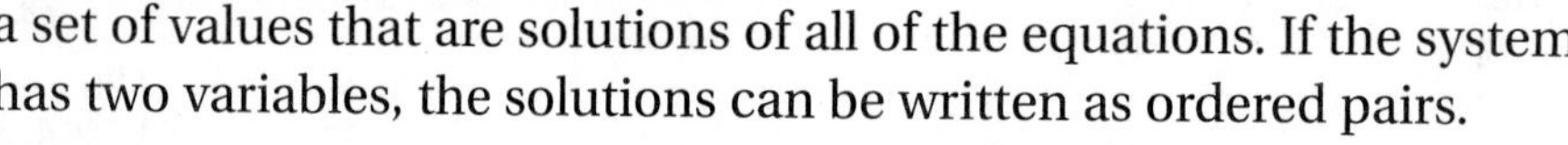

a set of values that are solutions of all of the equations. If the system has two variables, the solutions can be written as ordered pairs.

Interactivities Online ▶

EXAMPLE 1 **Solving Systems of Equations**

Solve each system of equations.

A $y = x + 3$

$y = 2x + 5$

The expressions $x + 3$ and $2x + 5$ both equal y. So by the Transitive Property they are equal to each other.

$y = x + 3$ → $x + 3 = 2x + 5$ ← $y = 2x + 5$

Solve the equation to find x.

$$x + 3 = 2x + 5$$
$$\underline{-x} \quad \underline{-x}$$ *Subtract x from both sides.*
$$3 = x + 5$$
$$\underline{-5} \quad \underline{-5}$$ *Subtract 5 from both sides.*
$$-2 = x$$

To find y, substitute -2 for x in one of the original equations.

$y = x + 3 = -2 + 3 = 1$

The solution is $(-2, 1)$.

Caution!

When solving systems of equations, remember to find values for all of the variables.

B $y = 3x + 8$

$y = -7 + 3x$

$$3x + 8 = -7 + 3x$$ *Transitive Property*
$$\underline{-3x} \quad \underline{-3x}$$ *Subtract 3x from both sides.*
$$8 \neq -7$$

The system of equations has no solution.

Bruce Leighty/Index Stock/Photolibrary

Video Lesson Tutorials Online

To solve a general system of two equations with two variables, you can solve both equations for x or both for y.

EXAMPLE 2 Solving Systems of Equations by Solving for a Variable

Solve each system of equations.

A $x - y = 3$
$x + 5y = 39$

$$\begin{aligned} x - y &= 3 \\ +y \quad &\quad +y \\ x &= 3 + y \end{aligned}$$

Solve both equations for x.

$$\begin{aligned} x + 5y &= 39 \\ -5y \quad &\quad -5y \\ x &= 39 - 5y \end{aligned}$$

$$\begin{aligned} 3 + y &= 39 - 5y \\ +5y \quad &\quad +5y \\ 3 + 6y &= 39 \\ -3 \quad &\quad -3 \\ 6y &= 36 \\ \frac{6y}{6} &= \frac{36}{6} \\ y &= 6 \end{aligned}$$

Add 5y to both sides.

Subtract 3 from both sides.

Divide both sides by 6.

$x = 3 + y$
$= 3 + 6 = 9$ *Substitute 6 for y.*

The solution is (9, 6).

B $3x + y = 8$
$6x + 2y = 16$

$$\begin{aligned} 3x + y &= 8 \\ -3x \quad &\quad -3x \\ y &= 8 - 3x \end{aligned}$$

Solve both equations for y.

$$\begin{aligned} 6x + 2y &= 16 \\ -6x \quad &\quad -6x \\ 2y &= 16 - 6x \\ \frac{2y}{2} &= \frac{16}{2} - \frac{6x}{2} \\ y &= 8 - 3x \end{aligned}$$

$$\begin{aligned} 8 - 3x &= 8 - 3x \\ +3x \quad &\quad +3x \\ 8 &= 8 \end{aligned}$$

Add 3x to both sides.

Since $8 = 8$ is always true, the system of equations has an infinite number of solutions.

Helpful Hint

You can solve for either variable. It is usually easiest to solve for a variable that has a coefficient of 1.

MATHEMATICAL PRACTICES

Think and Discuss

1. Compare an equation to a system of equations.

2. Describe how you would know whether $(-1, 0)$ is a solution of the system of equations below.

$$\begin{aligned} x + 2y &= -1 \\ -3x + 4y &= 3 \end{aligned}$$

7-4 Exercises

Learn It Online
Homework Help Online
Exercises 1–24, 25, 27, 29, 31, 33, 35, 37

GUIDED PRACTICE

Solve each system of equations.

See Example 1

1. $y = x + 1$
   $y = 2x - 1$
2. $y = -2x + 3$
   $y = 5x - 4$
3. $y = 3x - 5$
   $y = 6x + 7$
4. $y = 6x - 12$
   $y = -9x + 3$
5. $y = 5x + 7$
   $y = -3x + 7$
6. $y = 3x + 5$
   $y = 3x - 10$

See Example 2

7. $2x + 2y = 16$
   $2x + 6y = 28$
8. $x + y = 20$
   $x = y - 4$
9. $x + 2y = 21$
   $-x + 3y = 29$
10. $x - y = 2$
    $x + 4y = -8$
11. $x = -3y$
    $x + y = -6$
12. $2x + 4y = 8$
    $x = 3y - 11$

INDEPENDENT PRACTICE

Solve each system of equations.

See Example 1

13. $y = -2x - 1$
    $y = 2x + 3$
14. $y = 3x + 6$
    $y = x + 2$
15. $y = 5x - 3$
    $y = -3x + 13$
16. $y = x + 6$
    $y = -2x - 12$
17. $y = 3x - 1$
    $y = -2x + 9$
18. $y = -2x - 6$
    $y = 3x + 29$

See Example 2

19. $3x + 3y = 15$
    $3x - 6y = -12$
20. $2x + y = 11$
    $y = x - 1$
21. $y = 5x - 2$
    $6x + 3y = 15$
22. $x + y = 5$
    $x - y = 3$
23. $x = -2y + 1$
    $x + 3y = -2$
24. $4x + y = -17$
    $-3x + y = 4$

PRACTICE AND PROBLEM SOLVING

Extra Practice
See Extra Practice for more exercises.

25. **Crafts** Robin cross-stitches bookmarks and wall hangings. A bookmark takes her $1\frac{1}{2}$ days, and a wall hanging takes her 4 days. Robin recently spent 18 days cross-stitching 7 items. Solve the system of equations to find the number of bookmarks b and the number of wall hangings w that Robin cross-stitched.

$$1\tfrac{1}{2}b + 4w = 18$$
$$b + w = 7$$

Solve each system of equations.

26. $y = 3x - 2$
    $y = x + 2$
27. $y = -11x + 5$
    $y = 10x - 37$
28. $5x + 5y = -5$
    $5x - 5y = 25$
29. $3x - y = 5$
    $x - 4y = -2$
30. $2x + 6y = 1$
    $4x - 3y = 0$
31. $x + 1.5y = 7.4$
    $3x - 0.5y = -6.8$
32. $\frac{1}{5}x + \frac{3}{8}y = \frac{1}{2}$
    $2x + 3.75y = 5$
33. $0.25x + 0.6y = 2.5$
    $\frac{1}{4}x + \frac{3}{5}y = 3\frac{3}{7}$
34. $3x + 2y = -44$
    $-3x + 4y = 2$

35. Gustav has 35 dimes and quarters that total \$5.00. Solve the system of equations to find how many dimes and how many quarters he has.

$$d + q = 35$$
$$0.1d + 0.25q = 5$$

LINK

Sports

The original cost of a ticket to the 2007 Super Bowl was about \$600 to \$700. However, many tickets were resold online, often for several thousand dollars apiece.

36. **Sports** Tickets for a high school football game were \$8 for adults and \$5 for students. A total of 1970 tickets were sold. The total ticket sales were \$12,220. Let a represent the number of adult tickets sold and s represent the number of student tickets sold.

   a. Write an equation about the total number of tickets sold.

   b. Write an equation about the total ticket sales.

   c. Solve the system of equations. What does the solution mean?

37. **Geometry** The perimeter of the rectangle is 114 units. The perimeter of the triangle is 63 units. Find x and y.

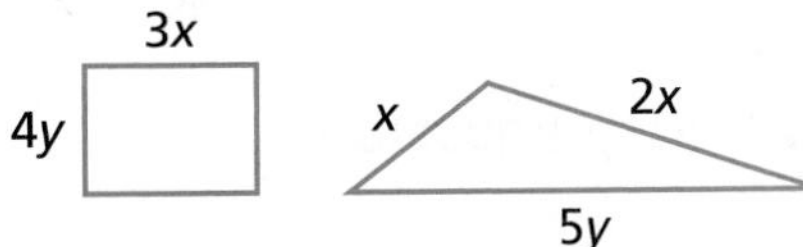

38. **Write a Problem** Write a word problem that requires using a system of equations to solve. Solve the problem.

39. **Write About It** List the steps you would use to solve the system of equations. Explain which variable you would solve for and why.

$$x + 2y = 7$$
$$2x + y = 8$$

40. **Challenge** Solve the system of equations.
$$5x - y - 12z = 61$$
$$-2x + 11y + 8z = 4$$
$$-12x - 8y + 12z = -24$$

Test Prep

41. **Multiple Choice** Carlos has \$3.35 in dimes and quarters. If he has a total of 23 coins, how many dimes does he have?

   (A) 9 (B) 11 (C) 16 (D) 18

42. **Gridded Response** Solve the system of equations. What is the y-value?

$$2x + 3y = 10$$
$$x + 5y = 26$$

CHAPTER 7

SECTION 7A

Ready To Go On?

Learn It Online
Resources Online

Quiz for Lessons 1 Through 4

1 Simplifying Algebraic Expressions

Simplify.

1. $5x + 3x$

2. $6p - 6 - p$

3. $2t^2 + 3 - t + 4 + 5t^2$

4. $3x + 4y - x + 2y$

5. $4n + 2m^3 + 8n - 2m^3$

Solve.

6. $9y - 5y = 8$

7. $7x + 2x = 45$

2 Solving Multi-Step Equations

Solve.

8. $2c + 6c + 8 = 32$

9. $\frac{3x}{7} - \frac{2}{7} = \frac{10}{7}$

10. $\frac{t}{4} + \frac{t}{3} = \frac{7}{12}$

11. $\frac{4m}{3} - \frac{m}{6} = \frac{7}{2}$

12. $\frac{3}{4}b - \frac{1}{5}b = 11$

3 Solving Equations with Variables on Both Sides

Solve.

13. $4x + 11 = x + 2$

14. $q + 5 = 2q + 7$

15. $6n + 21 = 4n + 57$

16. $2m + 6 = 2m - 1$

17. $9w - 2w + 8 = 4w + 38$

18. $-4a - 2a + 11 = 6a - 13$

19. $\frac{7}{12}y - \frac{1}{4} = 2y - \frac{5}{3}$

4 Systems of Equations

Solve each system of equations.

20. $y = -3x + 2$
$y = 4x - 5$

21. $y = 5x - 3$
$y = 2x + 6$

22. $y = -2x + 6$
$y = 3x - 9$

23. $x + y = 8$
$x + 3y = 14$

24. $2x + y = 12$
$3x - y = 13$

25. $4x - 3y = 33$
$x = -4y - 25$

26. The sum of two numbers is 18. Their difference is 8.

a. If the numbers are x and y, write a system of equations to describe their sum and their difference.

b. Solve the system to find the numbers.

Real-World CONNECTIONS

MATHEMATICAL PRACTICES Reason abstractly and quantitatively.

Boot Hill Museum Dodge City was one of the final stopping points of the western cattle drives of the late 1800s. The Boot Hill Museum in Dodge City helps to preserve this historic legacy. The museum includes some 20,000 relics from the town's frontier days in the Wild West. It also features an entire street of reconstructed buildings showing how Dodge City appeared in 1876.

KANSAS

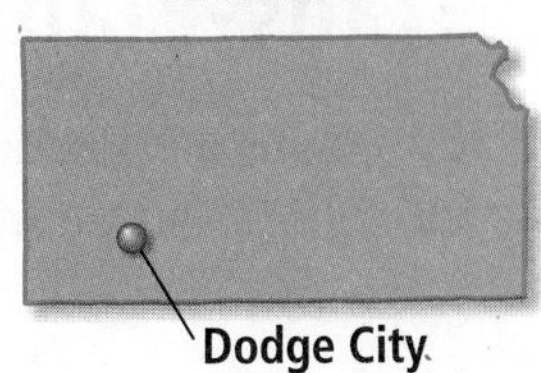

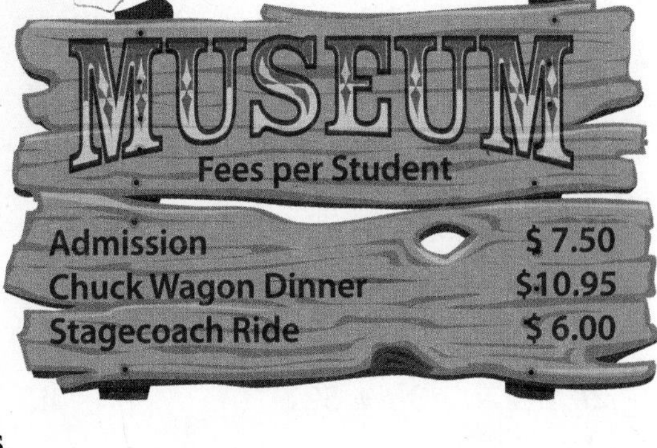

MUSEUM
Fees per Student
Admission $ 7.50
Chuck Wagon Dinner $10.95
Stagecoach Ride $ 6.00

1. The students in a history club plan to visit the museum. Each student will have to pay an admission fee and fees for a chuck wagon dinner and a stagecoach ride.
   a. Write and simplify an expression for the total fees for s students.
   b. There are 15 students in the club. Use the expression to find the total fees.

2. The students plan to raise money for their trip to the museum by selling T-shirts. Each T-shirt costs them \$3.99. Write an expression that gives the students' total expenses for selling t T-shirts.

3. The students sell the T-shirts for \$8.88 each. Write an expression that gives the students' profit for selling t T-shirts. (*Hint*: Their profit is the total amount of income from selling the T-shirts minus their total expenses.)

4. Write and solve an equation to find out how many T-shirts the students must sell to have enough money to pay the museum fees for all 15 students.

5. The students manage to sell only 62 T-shirts. Write and solve an inequality to find the greatest number of students the club can afford to send with the profit from these T-shirts.

Andre Jenny/Alamy

Real-World Connections

Game Time

Trans-Plants

Solve each equation below. Then use the values of the variables to decode the answer to the question.

$3a + 17 = -25$

$2b - 25 + 5b = 7 - 32$

$2.7c - 4.5 = 3.6c - 9$

$\frac{5}{12}d + \frac{1}{6}d + \frac{1}{3}d + \frac{1}{12}d = 6$

$4e - 6e - 5 = 15$

$420 = 29f - 73$

$2(g + 6) = -20$

$2h + 7 = -3h + 52$

$96i + 245 = 53$

$3j + 7 = 46$

$\frac{1}{2}k = \frac{3}{4}k - \frac{1}{2}$

$30l + 240 = 50l - 160$

$4m + \frac{3}{8} = \frac{67}{8}$

$24 - 6n = 54$

$8.4o - 6.8 = 14.2 + 6.3o$

$4p - p + 8 = 2p + 5$

$16 - 3q = 3q + 40$

$4 + \frac{1}{3}r = r - 8$

$\frac{2}{3}s - \frac{5}{6}s + \frac{1}{2} = -\frac{3}{2}$

$4 - 15 = 4t + 17$

$45 + 36u = 66 + 23u + 31$

$6v + 8 = -4 - 6v$

$4w + 3w - 6w = w + 15 + 2w - 3w$

$x + 2x + 3x + 4x + 5 = 75$

$\frac{4 - y}{5} = \frac{2 - 2y}{8}$

$-11 = 25 - 4.5z$

What happens to plants that live in a math classroom?

−7, 9, −10, −11   −16, 18, 10, 15   12, −4, 4, −14, 18, −10   18, 10, 10, −7, 12

24 Points

Jenny Thomas/HMH

This traditional Chinese game is played using a deck of 52 cards numbered 1–13, with four of each number. The cards are shuffled, and four cards are placed face up in the center. The winner is the first player who comes up with an expression that equals 24, using each of the numbers on the four cards once.

Complete rules and a set of game cards are available online.

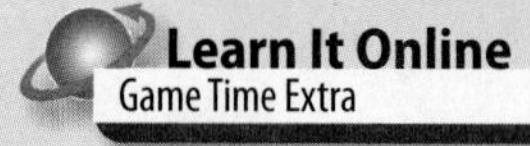

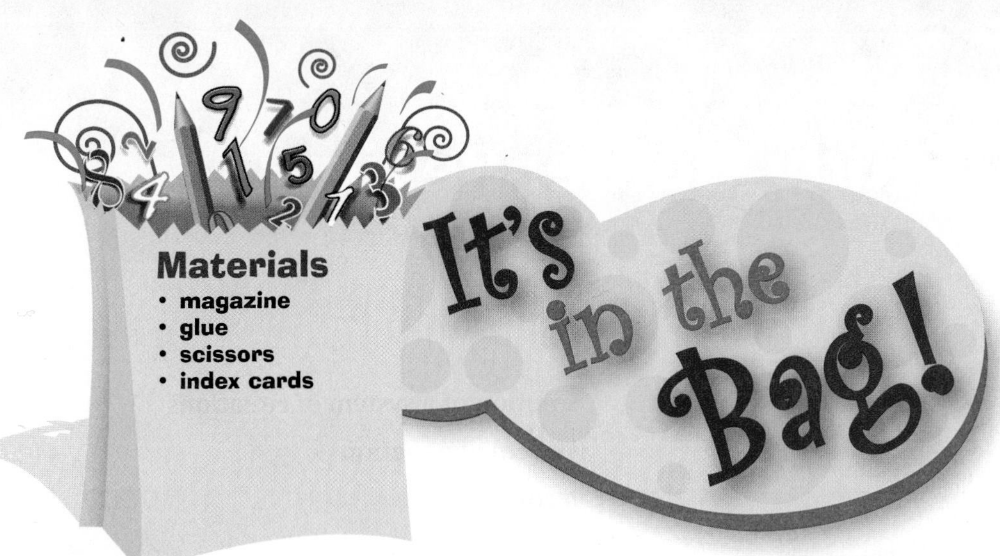

PROJECT Picture Envelopes

Make these picture-perfect envelopes in which to store your notes on the lessons of this chapter.

Directions

1. Flip through a magazine and carefully tear out six pages with full-page pictures that you like.
2. Lay one of the pages in front of you with the picture face down. Fold the page into thirds as shown, and then unfold the page. **Figure A**
3. Fold the sides in, about 1 inch, and then unfold. Cut away the four rectangles at the corners of the page. **Figure B**
4. Fold in the two middle flaps. Then fold up the bottom and glue it onto the flaps. **Figure C**
5. Cut the corners of the top section at an angle to make a flap. **Figure D**
6. Repeat the steps to make five more envelopes. Label them so that there is one for each lesson of the chapter.

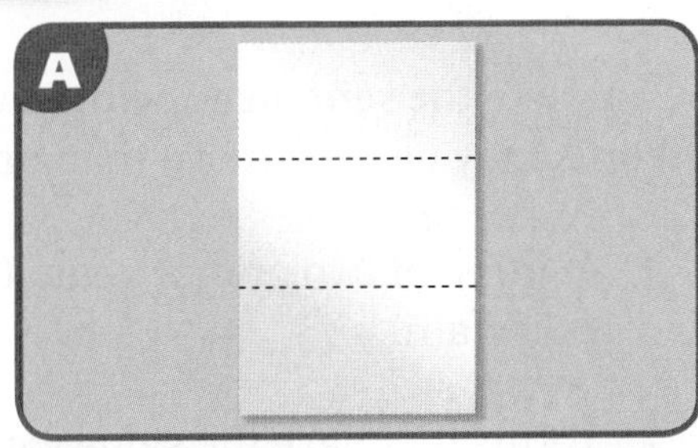

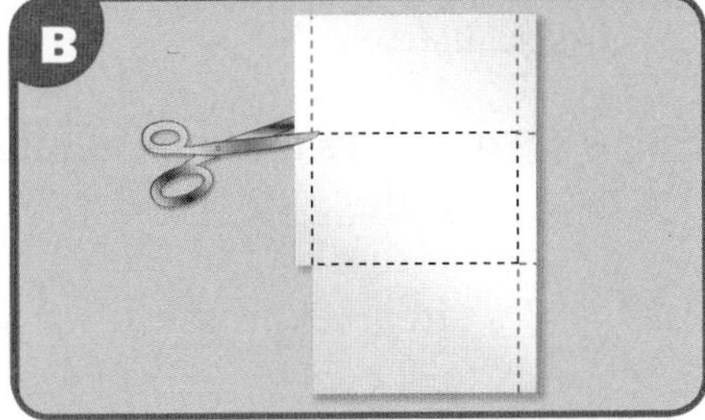

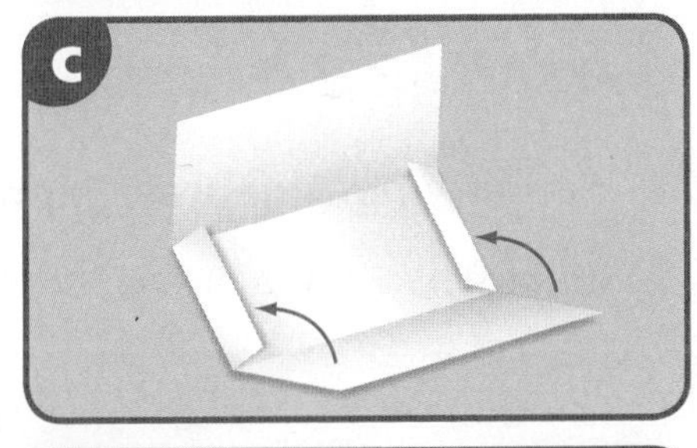

Taking Note of the Math

Use index cards to take notes on the lessons of the chapter. Store the cards in the appropriate envelopes.

CHAPTER 7

Study Guide: Review

Vocabulary

equivalent expression

like terms

literal equation

simplify

solution of a system of equations

system of equations

term

Complete the sentences below with vocabulary words from the list above. Words may be used more than once.

1. A group of two or more equations that contain two or more variables is called a(n) __?__.
2. Terms that have the same variable raised to the same power are __?__.
3. A set of values that are solutions of all the equations of a system is the __?__.
4. __?__ in an expression are set apart by plus or minus signs.

EXAMPLES

1 Simplifying Algebraic Expressions

- **Simplify.**

$3(z - 6) + 2z$

$3z - 3(6) + 2z$ — *Distributive Property*

$3z - 18 + 2z$ — *3z and 2z are like terms.*

$5z - 18$ — *Combine coefficients.*

- **Solve.**

$14p - 8p = 54$

$6p = 54$ — *Combine like terms.*

$\frac{6p}{6} = \frac{54}{6}$ — *Divide both sides by 6.*

$p = 9$

EXERCISES

Simplify.

5. $5(3m - 2) + 4m$
6. $12w + 2(w + 3)$
7. $4x + 3y - 2x$
8. $2t^2 - 4t + 3t^3$

Solve.

9. $7y + y = 48$
10. $8z - 2z = 42$
11. $6y + y = 35$
12. $9z - 3z = 48$
13. The width of a soccer field should be 60% of its length. Write and simplify an expression for the perimeter of a soccer field with a length of x feet.

EXAMPLES

EXERCISES

2 Solving Multi-Step Equations

■ **Solve.**

$\frac{5x}{9} - \frac{x}{6} + \frac{1}{3} = \frac{3}{2}$

$18\left(\frac{5x}{9} - \frac{x}{6} + \frac{1}{3}\right) = 18\left(\frac{3}{2}\right)$ *Multiply both sides by 18.*

$18\left(\frac{5x}{9}\right) - 18\left(\frac{x}{6}\right) + 18\left(\frac{1}{3}\right) = 18\left(\frac{3}{2}\right)$ *Distributive Property*

$10x - 3x + 6 = 27$ *Simplify.*

$7x + 6 = 27$ *Combine like terms.*

$\underline{\quad -6 \quad -6}$ *Subtract 6 from both sides.*

$7x = 21$

$\frac{7x}{7} = \frac{21}{7}$ *Divide both sides by 7.*

$x = 3$

Solve.

14. $3y + 6 + 4y - 7 = -8$

15. $5h - 6 - h + 10 = 12$

16. $\frac{2t}{3} + \frac{1}{3} = -\frac{1}{3}$

17. $\frac{2r}{5} - \frac{4}{5} = \frac{2}{5}$

18. $\frac{z}{3} - \frac{3z}{4} + \frac{1}{2} = -\frac{1}{3}$

19. $\frac{3a}{8} - \frac{a}{12} + \frac{7}{2} = 7$

20. Lianne charges twice as much to walk a large dog as she does to walk a small dog. This week she has time to walk 10 small dogs and 5 large dogs, and she wants to make \$100. How much should she charge per small dog? per large dog?

3 Solving Equations with Variables on Both Sides

■ **Solve.**

$3x + 5 - 5x = -12 + x + 2$

$-2x + 5 = -10 + x$ *Combine like terms.*

$\underline{+2x \qquad\quad +2x}$ *Add 2x to both sides.*

$5 = -10 + 3x$

$\underline{+10 \quad +10}$ *Add 10 to both sides.*

$15 = 3x$

$\frac{15}{3} = \frac{3x}{3}$ *Divide both sides by 3.*

$5 = x$

Solve.

21. $12s = 8 + 2(5s + 3)$

22. $15c - 8c = 5c + 48$

23. $4 - 5x = 3 + x$

24. $4 - 2y = 4y$

25. $2n + 8 = 2n - 5$

26. $4z - 9 = 9z - 34$

27. $6(2x - 10) = 4x + 4$

Study Guide: Review

EXAMPLES

EXERCISES

4 Systems of Equations

■ **Solve the system of equations.**

$$4x + y = 3$$
$$x + y = 12$$

Solve both equations for *y*.

$$\begin{array}{rlrl} 4x + y = & 3 & x + y = & 12 \\ -4x & -4x & -x & -x \\ y = & -4x + 3 & y = & -x + 12 \end{array}$$

$$\begin{array}{rcll} -4x + 3 &=& -x + 12 & \\ +4x & & +4x & \textit{Add 4x to both sides.} \\ 3 &=& 3x + 12 & \\ -12 & & -12 & \textit{Subtract 12 from both sides.} \\ -9 &=& 3x & \\ \frac{-9}{3} &=& \frac{3x}{3} & \textit{Divide both sides by 3.} \\ -3 &=& x & \end{array}$$

$$\begin{aligned} y &= -4x + 3 \\ &= -4(-3) + 3 \quad \textit{Substitute } -3 \textit{ for } x. \\ &= 12 + 3 \\ &= 15 \end{aligned}$$

The solution is (−3, 15).

Solve each system of equations.

28. $y = x + 3$
$y = 2x + 5$

29. $2x - y = -2$
$x + y = 8$

30. $4x + 3y = 27$
$2x - y = 1$

31. $4x + y = 10$
$x - 2y = 7$

32. $y = x - 2$
$-x + y = 2$

33. $y = 3x + 1$
$3x - y = -1$

34. The sum of two numbers is 32. Twice the first number is equal to six times the second number. Find each number.

a. Use a different variable to represent each number and write an equation for each of the first two sentences.

b. Solve the system of equations.

c. Check your answer.

Study Guide: Review

Chapter Test

CHAPTER 7

Simplify.

1. $7x + 5x$
2. $m + 3m - 3$
3. $6n^2 + 1 - n + 5n^2$
4. $2y + 2z + 2$
5. $3(s + 2) - s$
6. $10b + 8(b - 1)$

Solve.

7. $10x - 2x = 16$
8. $\frac{3y + 5y}{3} = 8$
9. $6t + 4t = 120$
10. $4c + 6 + 2c = 24$
11. $\frac{2x}{5} - \frac{3}{5} = \frac{11}{5}$
12. $\frac{2}{5}b - \frac{1}{4}b = 3$
13. $15 - 6g + 8 = 19$
14. $93 + 24k + 26k = 218$
15. $\frac{w}{4} - \frac{w}{5} - \frac{1}{3} = \frac{16}{15}$
16. On her last three quizzes, Elise scored 84, 96, and 88. What grade must she get on her next quiz to have an average of 90 for all four quizzes?
17. Marlene drove 540 miles to visit a friend. She drove 3 hours and stopped for gas. She then drove 4 hours and stopped for lunch. How many more hours did she drive if her average speed for the trip was 60 miles per hour?

Solve.

18. $3x + 13 = x + 1$
19. $q + 7 = 2q + 5$
20. $8n + 24 = 3n + 59$
21. $m + 5 = m - 3$
22. $-3a + 9 = 3a - 9$
23. $9z - 34 = 4z - 9$
24. The rectangle and the triangle have the same perimeter. Find the perimeter of each figure.

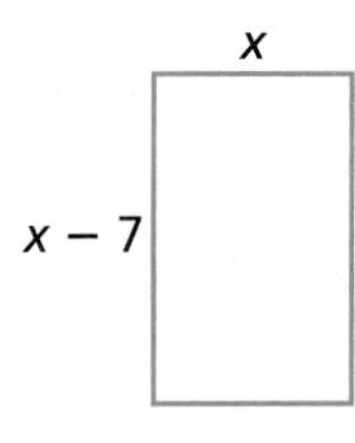

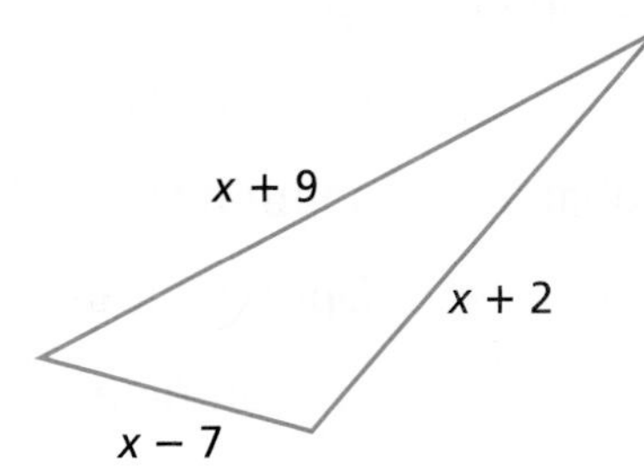

Solve each system of equations.

25. $x - 2y = 16$
$x - y = 8$
26. $y = 2x + 6$
$y = 2x - 3$
27. $x + 5y = 11$
$x + y = 3$
28. $2y + x = 6$
$x - y = -6$
29. $y = 5x + 10$
$y = x - 2$
30. $x - 5y = 4$
$-2x + 10y = -8$

CHAPTER 7

Test Tackler

STANDARDIZED TEST STRATEGIES

Multiple Choice: Answering Context-Based Test Items

For some test items, you cannot answer just by reading the problem statement. You will need to read each option carefully to determine the correct response. Review each option and eliminate those that are false.

EXAMPLE 1

Multiple Choice

Which statement is true for the given spinner?

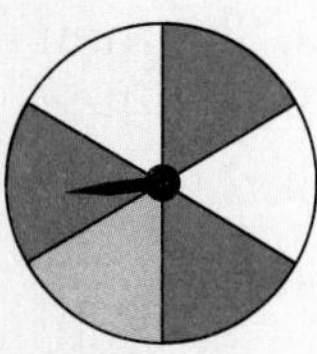

Ⓐ The probability of spinning green is $\frac{1}{3}$.

Ⓑ The probability of spinning blue is $\frac{1}{6}$.

Ⓒ The probability of spinning white is the same as the probability of spinning green.

Ⓓ The probability of spinning green is the same as the probability of spinning yellow or white.

Read each option carefully. Eliminate options that are false.

Option A: Find the probability of spinning green.

$P(\text{green}) = \frac{3}{6}$, or $\frac{1}{2}$ Option A is false.

Option B: Find the probability of spinning blue.

$P(\text{blue}) = \frac{0}{6}$, or 0 Option B is false.

Option C: Find the probabilities and compare.

$P(\text{white}) = \frac{2}{6}$, or $\frac{1}{3}$ $P(\text{green}) = \frac{3}{6}$, or $\frac{1}{2}$

$\frac{1}{3} \neq \frac{1}{2}$, so $P(\text{white}) \neq P(\text{green})$

Option C is false.

Option D: Find the probabilities and compare.

$P(\text{green}) = \frac{3}{6}$, or $\frac{1}{2}$ $P(\text{white or yellow}) = \frac{2}{6} + \frac{1}{6} = \frac{3}{6}$, or $\frac{1}{2}$

$\frac{1}{2} = \frac{1}{2}$, so $P(\text{green}) = P(\text{white or yellow})$

Option D is true. It is the correct response.

Be sure to review all of the answer options carefully before you make your choice.

Read each test item and answer the questions that follow.

Item A
Which equation has a solution of $x = 3$?

(A) $2x - 6 = 3(x - 1)$

(B) $-2x - 6 = \frac{3}{2}(-2x - 2)$

(C) $2(x - 6) = 3x - 1$

(D) $-2(x - 6) = x - 3$

1. What property do you have to use to solve each equation?

2. What two methods could you use to determine if $x = 3$ is a solution of one of the equations?

3. Which is the correct option? Explain.

Item B
An experiment consists of rolling a fair number cube labeled 1 to 6. Which statement is true?

(F) $P(\text{odd}) = P(\text{even})$

(G) $P(\text{multiple of 3}) > P(\text{multiple of 2})$

(H) $P(7) = 1$

(J) $P(\text{less than 4}) = P(\text{greater than 5})$

4. What does *multiple* mean? What are multiples of 3? What are multiples of 2?

5. How many numbers are less than 4 on the number cube? How many numbers are greater than 5?

6. Which is the correct option? Explain.

Item C
Which inequality has 0 as a part of its solution set?

(A) $-3y < -6$

(B) $8a + 3 > 7$

(C) $4 - 9y < 13$

(D) $-\frac{5t}{6} > 5$

7. What must you remember to do if you multiply or divide both sides of an inequality by a negative number?

8. Which is the correct option? Explain.

Item D
A poll was taken at Jefferson Middle School. Which statement is true for the given data?

Favorite Type of Movie	Number of Students
Drama	25
Comedy	40
Science fiction	28
Action	32

(F) The probability that a student at Jefferson Middle School does *not* like dramas best is $\frac{4}{5}$.

(G) The probability that a student likes comedies best is $\frac{17}{25}$.

(H) Out of a population of 1200 students, you can predict that 280 students will like science fiction movies best.

(J) The probability that a student likes action movies best is $\frac{8}{31}$.

9. How can you find the probability of an event not occurring?

10. How can you use probability to make a prediction?

11. Which is the correct option? Explain.

Test Tackler

CHAPTER 7

Standardized Test Prep

Learn It Online
State Test Practice

Cumulative Assessment

Multiple Choice

1. Clarissa has 6 red socks, 4 black socks, 10 white socks, and 2 blue socks in a drawer. If Clarissa chooses one sock at a time, what is the probability that she will choose 2 black socks?

   (A) $\frac{2}{77}$
   (B) $\frac{2}{11}$
   (C) $\frac{3}{121}$
   (D) $\frac{7}{22}$

2. Which situation best describes the graph?

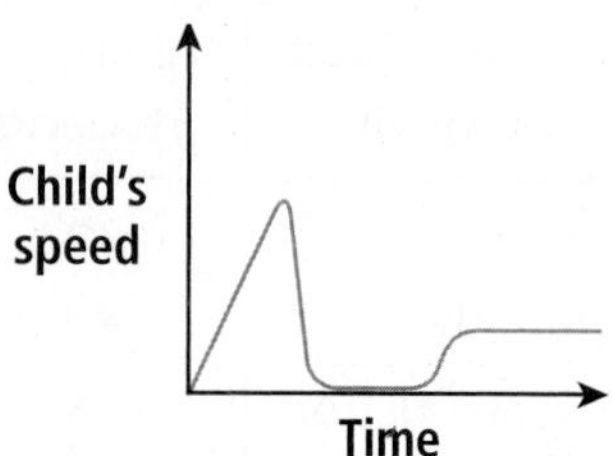

   (F) Linda sits on her bike. She runs to see the neighbor's dog. She sits and pets the dog.
   (G) Jim climbs on the jungle gym. He slides down the pole. He lies in the sand and rests.
   (H) Carlos runs to answer the phone. He sits and talks on the phone. He walks into another room.
   (J) Juan walks to his friend's house. He knocks on the door. He leaves his friend's house.

3. Which ordered pair is the solution of the following system of equations?

$$y = 2x + 6$$
$$x + y = 27$$

   (A) (3, 12)
   (B) (10, 26)
   (C) (7, 20)
   (D) (20, 7)

4. At lunch, each student writes his or her name on a piece of paper and puts the paper in a barrel. The principal draws five names for a free lunch. What type of sampling method is this?

   (F) convenience
   (G) systematic
   (H) random
   (J) biased

5. A trapezoid has two bases b_1 and b_2 and height h. For which values of b_1, b_2, and h is the area of a trapezoid equal to 32 in^2?

   (A) $b_1 = 9$ in., $b_2 = 7$ in., $h = 2$ in.
   (B) $b_1 = 5$ in., $b_2 = 3$ in., $h = 4$ in.
   (C) $b_1 = 2$ in., $b_2 = 8$ in., $h = 4$ in.
   (D) $b_1 = 9$ in., $b_2 = 7$ in., $h = 4$ in.

6. Between which two integers does $-\sqrt{67}$ lie?

   (F) −7 and −6
   (G) −9 and −8
   (H) −11 and −10
   (J) −8 and −7

7. What is the sum of the angle measures of this polygon?

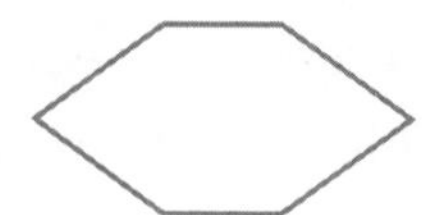

   (A) 180°
   (B) 360°
   (C) 720°
   (D) 1080°

8. If Serena buys a $96 bracelet for 20% off, how much money does Serena save?

   (F) $1.92
   (G) $9.60
   (H) $19.20
   (J) $76.80

9. Which value of x is the solution of the equation $\frac{3x}{8} - \frac{3}{4} = \frac{1}{6}$?

Ⓐ $x = \frac{9}{22}$

Ⓑ $x = \frac{5}{9}$

Ⓒ $x = 1\frac{5}{9}$

Ⓓ $x = 2\frac{4}{9}$

When finding the solution to an equation on a multiple-choice test, work backward by substituting the answer choices provided into the equation.

Gridded Response

10. To prepare for her final exam, Sheyla studied 4 hours on Monday, 3 hours on Tuesday, 1 hour on Wednesday, and 3 hours on Thursday. What is the difference between the median and the mean of the number of hours Sheyla studied?

11. Zina has 10 coins consisting of nickels and dimes in her pocket. She calculates that she has $0.70 altogether. If Zina has two more nickels than dimes, how many nickels does she have?

12. In a school of 1575 students, there are 870 females. What is the ratio of females to males in simplest form?

13. An $8\frac{1}{2}$ in. × 11 in. photograph is being cropped to fit into a special frame. One-fourth of an inch will be cropped from all sides of the photo. What is the area, in square inches, of the photograph that will be seen in the frame?

14. The perimeters of the two figures have the same measure. What is the perimeter of either figure?

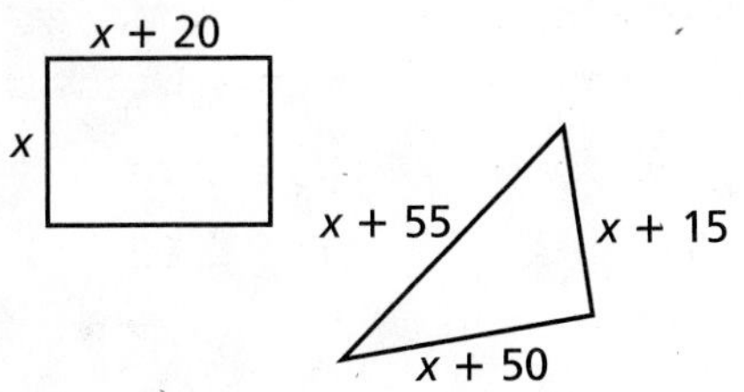

Short Response

S1. Two numbers have a sum of 58. Twice the first number is 8 more than the second number.

a. Write a system of equations that can be used to find the two numbers.

b. What are the two numbers? Show your work.

S2. Alfred and Eugene each spent $62 on campsite and gasoline expenses during their camping trip. Each campsite they used had the same per-night charge. Alfred paid for 4 nights of campsites and $30 of gasoline. Eugene paid for 2 nights of campsites and $46 of gasoline. Write an equation that could be used to determine the cost of one night's stay at a campsite. What was the cost of one night's stay at a campsite?

Extended Response

E1. You are designing a house to fit on a rectangular lot that has 90 feet of lake frontage and is 162 feet deep. The building codes require that the house not be built closer than 10 feet to the lot boundary lines.

a. Write an inequality and solve it to find how long the front of the house facing the lake can be.

b. If you want the house to cover no more than 20% of the lot, what would be the maximum square footage of the house?

c. If you want to spend a maximum of $100,000 building the house, to the nearest whole dollar, what would be the maximum you could spend per square foot for a 1988-square-foot house?

CHAPTER

8 Graphing Lines

Why Learn This?

Graphs of linear equations can be used to display speeds, distances, and other aspects of space shuttle travel.

Learn It Online
Chapter Project Online

Chapter Focus

- Understand that the slope of a line is a constant rate of change.
- Describe aspects of linear equations in different representations.

Stocktrek Images/Getty Images

Are You Ready?

Vocabulary

Choose the best term from the list to complete each sentence.

1. The expression $4 - 3$ is an example of a(n) __?__ expression.
2. When you divide both sides of the equation $2x = 20$ by 2, you are __?__.
3. The expression $7 - 6$ can be rewritten as the __?__ expression $7 + (-6)$.

addition

equation

solving for the variable

subtraction

Complete these exercises to review skills you will need for this chapter.

Operations with Integers

Simplify.

4. $\frac{7-5}{-2}$ **5.** $\frac{-3-5}{-2-3}$ **6.** $\frac{-8+2}{-2+8}$ **7.** $\frac{-16}{-2}$ **8.** $\frac{-22}{2}$ **9.** $-12 + 9$

Evaluate Expressions

Evaluate each expression for the given value of the variable.

10. $3x - 2$ for $x = -2$

11. $4y - 8 + \frac{1}{2}y$ for $y = 2$

12. $3(x + 1)$ for $x = -2$

13. $-3(y + 2) - y$ for $y = -1$

Equations

Solve.

14. $3p - 4 = 8$ **15.** $2(a + 3) = 4$ **16.** $9 = -2k + 27$

17. $3s - 4 = 1 - 3s$ **18.** $7x + 1 = x$ **19.** $4m - 5(m + 2) = 1$

Determine whether each ordered pair is a solution to $-\frac{1}{2}x + 3 = y$.

20. $(4, 1)$ **21.** $\left(-\frac{8}{2}, 2\right)$ **22.** $(0, 5)$ **23.** $(-4, 5)$

24. $(8, 1)$ **25.** $(2, 2)$ **26.** $(-2, 4)$ **27.** $(0, 1)$

CHAPTER 8

Study Guide: Preview

Where You've Been

Previously, you

- located and named points on a coordinate plane using ordered pairs of integers.
- graphed data to demonstrate relationships between sets of data.

In This Chapter

You will study

- locating and naming points on a coordinate plane using ordered pairs of rational numbers.
- generating different representations of data using tables, graphs, and equations.
- graphing linear equations using slope and y-intercept.

Where You're Going

You can use the skills learned in this chapter

- to predict the distance a car needs to come to a complete stop, given its speed.
- to estimate the maximum distance a robotic vehicle can travel during a given period of time.

Key Vocabulary/Vocabulario

constant of variation	constante de variación
direct variation	variación directa
linear equation	ecuación lineal
slope	pendiente
slope-intercept form	forma de pendiente-intersección
x-intercept	intersección con el eje x
y-intercept	intersección con el eje y

Vocabulary Connections

To become familiar with some of the vocabulary terms in the chapter, consider the following. You may refer to the chapter, the glossary, or a dictionary if you like.

1. The word *linear* means "relating to a line." What do you think the graph of a **linear equation** looks like?
2. The word *intercept* can mean "to interrupt a course or path." Where on a graph do you think you should look to find the ***y*-intercept** of a line?
3. The adjective *direct* can mean "passing in a straight line." What do you suppose the graph of an equation with **direct variation** looks like?

Study Guide: Preview

Writing Strategy: Use Your Own Words

Explaining a concept in your own words will help you better understand it. For example, learning to solve two-step inequalities might seem difficult if the textbook does not use the same words that you would use.

As you work through each lesson, do the following:

- Identify the important concepts.
- Use your own words to explain the concepts.
- Use examples to help clarify your thoughts.

What Miguel Reads

Solving a two-step inequality uses the same inverse operations as solving a two-step equation.

Multiplying or dividing an inequality by a negative number reverses the inequality symbol.

What Miguel Writes

Solve a two-step inequality like a two-step equation. Use operations that undo each other.

When you multiply or divide by a negative number, switch the inequality symbol so that it faces the opposite direction.

$-4y > 8$ *Divide by −4 and*
$y < -2$ *switch the symbol.*

Try This

Rewrite each statement in your own words.

1. Like terms can be grouped together because they have the same variable raised to the same power.
2. If an equation contains fractions, consider multiplying both sides of the equation by the least common denominator (LCD) to clear the fractions before you isolate the variable.
3. To solve multi-step equations with variables on both sides, first combine like terms and then clear fractions. Then add or subtract variable terms on both sides so that the variable occurs on only one side of the equation. Then use properties of equality to isolate the variable.

8-1 Graphing Linear Equations

COMMON CORE

CC.8.F.5: Describe qualitatively the functional relationship between two quantities by analyzing a graph. Sketch a graph that exhibits the qualitative features of a function that has been described verbally. ***Also CC.8.F.4***

Vocabulary

linear equation

rate of change

Light travels faster than sound. That's why you see lightning before you hear thunder. The *linear equation* $d = 0.2s$ expresses the approximate distance, d, in miles of a thunderstorm for a given number of seconds, s, between the lightning flash and the thunder rumble.

A **linear equation** is an equation whose solutions fall on a line on the coordinate plane. All solutions of a particular linear equation fall on the line, and all the points on the line are solutions of the equation.

If an equation is linear, a constant change in the x-value corresponds to a constant change in the y-value. The graph shows an example where each time the x-value increases by 3, the y-value increases by 2.

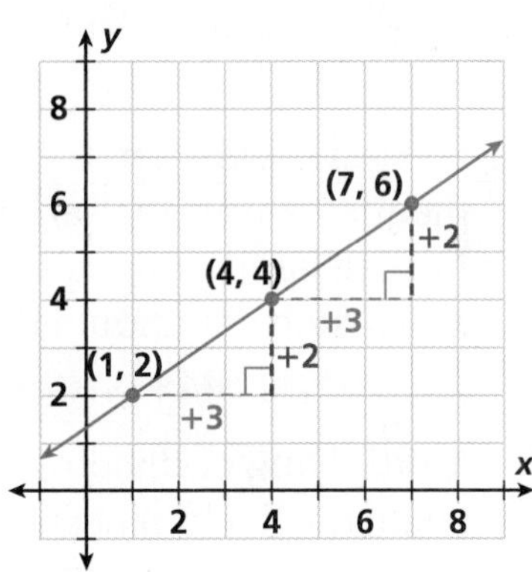

EXAMPLE 1 Graphing Equations

Graph each equation and tell whether it is linear.

A $y = 3x - 4$

Make a table of ordered pairs. Find the differences between consecutive data points.

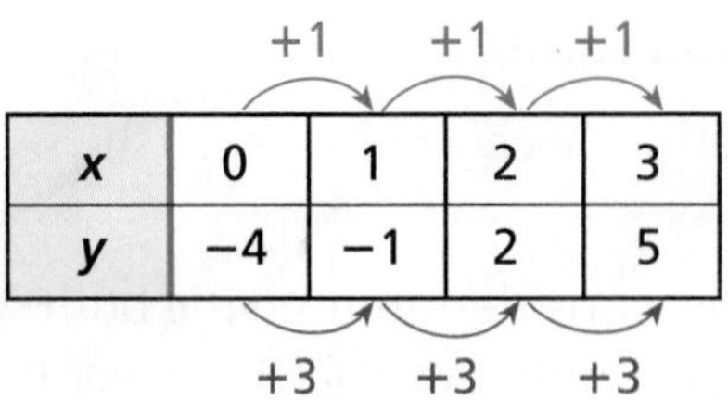

+1 +1 +1

x	0	1	2	3
y	−4	−1	2	5

+3 +3 +3

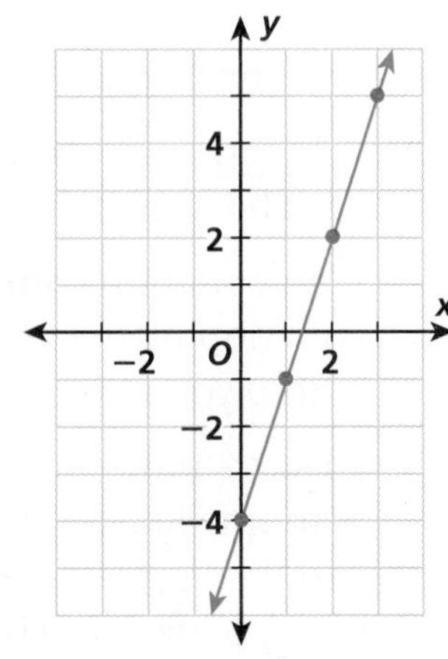

The equation $y = 3x - 4$ is a linear equation because it is the graph of a straight line, and each time x increases by 1 unit, y increases by 3 units.

Caution!

Be careful when graphing each ordered pair. Double check each point you plot.

Graph each equation and tell whether it is linear.

B $y = -x^2$

Make a table of ordered pairs. Find the differences between consecutive data points.

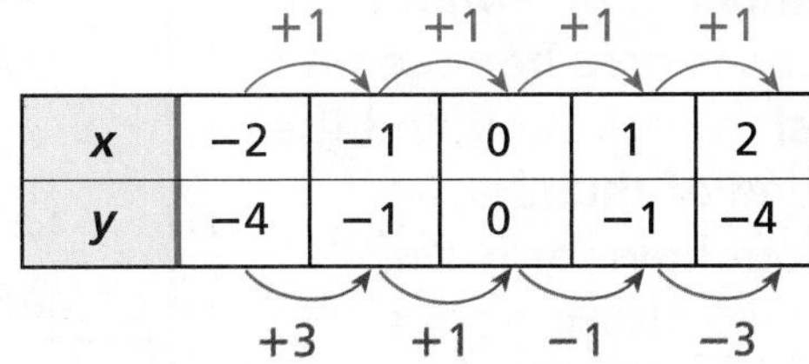

+1 +1 +1 +1

x	−2	−1	0	1	2
y	−4	−1	0	−1	−4

+3 +1 −1 −3

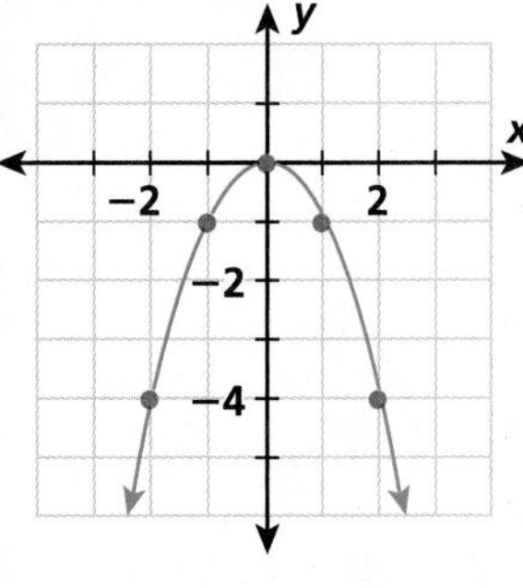

The equation $y = -x^2$ is not a linear equation because its graph is not a straight line. Also notice that as x increases by a constant of 1, the change in y is not constant.

A **rate of change** is a ratio that compares the amount of change in a dependent variable to the amount of change in an independent variable.

$$\text{rate of change} = \frac{\text{change in dependent variable}}{\text{change in independent variable}}$$

The rates of change for a set of data may vary, or they may be constant.

EXAMPLE 2 Identifying Constant and Variable Rates of Change in Data

Determine whether the rates of change are constant or variable.

A

+1 +2 +3 +2

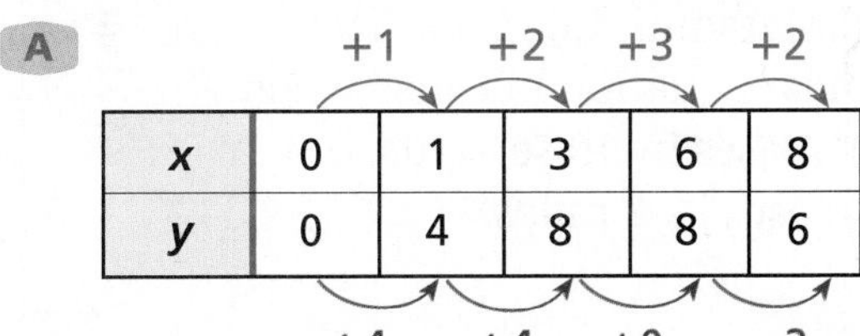

x	0	1	3	6	8
y	0	4	8	8	6

+4 +4 +0 −2

Find the differences between consecutive data points.

$\frac{4}{1} = 4$ $\frac{4}{2} = 2$ $\frac{0}{3} = 0$ $\frac{-2}{2} = -1$

Find each ratio of change in y to change in x.

The table shows nonlinear data. The rates of change are variable.

B

+1 +3 +2 +1

x	0	1	4	6	7
y	1	2	5	7	8

+1 +3 +2 +1

Find the differences between consecutive data points.

$\frac{1}{1} = 1$ $\frac{3}{3} = 1$ $\frac{2}{2} = 1$ $\frac{1}{1} = 1$

Find each ratio of change in y to change in x.

The table shows linear data. The rates of change are constant.

EXAMPLE 3 Physical Science Application

The equation $d = 0.2s$ represents the approximate distance, d, in miles of a thunderstorm when s seconds pass between a flash of lightning and the sound of thunder. About how far is the thunderstorm from each student listed in the table? Graph the relationship between the time between lightning and thunder and the distance of the storm from the student. Is the equation linear?

Student	Time Between Flash and Thunder (s)
Sandy	5
Diego	9
Ted	4
Cecilia	11
Massoud	8

s	$d = 0.2s$	d	(s, d)
5	$d = 0.2(5)$	1.0	(5, 1)
9	$d = 0.2(9)$	1.8	(9, 1.8)
4	$d = 0.2(4)$	0.8	(4, 0.8)
11	$d = 0.2(11)$	2.2	(11, 2.2)
8	$d = 0.2(8)$	1.6	(8, 1.6)

The approximate distances are Sandy, 1 mile; Diego, 1.8 miles; Ted, 0.8 mile; Cecilia, 2.2 miles; and Massoud, 1.6 miles. This is a linear equation because when s increases by 10 seconds, d increases by 2 miles.

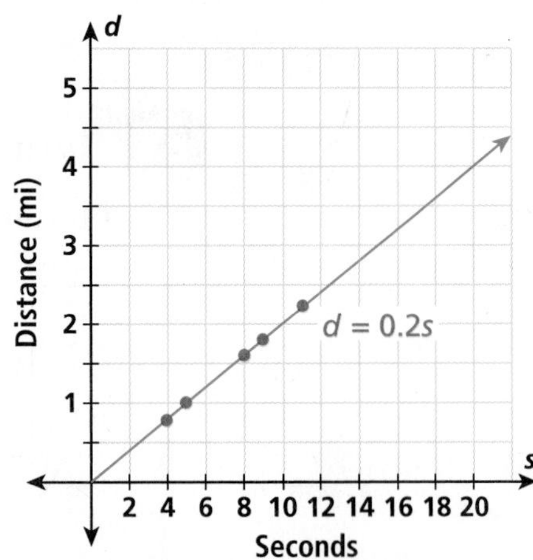

Helpful Hint

The rate of change is constant, 0.2 mi/s.

MATHEMATICAL PRACTICES

Think and Discuss

1. **Explain** whether an equation is linear if three ordered-pair solutions lie on a straight line but a fourth does not.
2. **Compare** the equations $y = 3x + 2$ and $y = 3x^2$. Without graphing, explain why one of the equations is not linear.
3. **Describe** why neither number in the ordered pair can be negative in Example 3.

8-1 Exercises

Learn It Online
Homework Help Online
Exercises 1–15, 17, 19, 21, 23, 25, 27

GUIDED PRACTICE

See Example 1

Graph each equation and tell whether it is linear.

1. $y = x + 1$
2. $y = -3x$
3. $y = x^3$

See Example 2

Determine whether the rates of change are constant or variable.

4.

x	0	1	3	7	8
y	1	3	7	15	17

5.

x	2	4	5	6	7
y	2	6	7	13	14

See Example 3

6. **Life Science** The equation $w = 4d + 5110$ represents the daily weight in pounds of a *Tyrannosaurus Rex* d days after its 14th birthday. How much would it weigh 2 days after its 14th birthday? 3.5 days after? 5 days after? Graph the equation and tell whether it is linear.

INDEPENDENT PRACTICE

See Example 1

Graph each equation and tell whether it is linear.

7. $y = \frac{1}{4}x - 1$
8. $y = -5$
9. $y = \frac{1}{3}x^2$
10. $x = 4$
11. $y = x^2 - 12$
12. $y = 3x + 2$

See Example 2

Determine whether the rates of change are constant or variable.

13.

x	−1	0	3	5	9
y	1	3	6	10	4

14.

x	2	4	6	7	8
y	8	4	0	−2	−4

See Example 3

15. **Business** A charter bus service charges $125 plus $8.50 for each passenger p, represented by the equation $C = 8.5p + 125$. What is the charge for the following numbers of passengers: 50, 100, 150, 200, and 250? Graph the equation and tell whether it is linear.

PRACTICE AND PROBLEM SOLVING

Extra Practice
See Extra Practice for more exercises.

16. The minute hand of a clock moves $\frac{1}{10}$ degree every second. If you look at the clock when the minute hand is 10 degrees past the 12, you can use the equation $y = \frac{1}{10}x + 10$ to find how many degrees past the 12 the minute hand is after x seconds. Graph the equation and tell whether it is linear.

17. **Physical Science** The force exerted on an object by Earth's gravity is given by the formula $F = 9.8m$, where F is the force in newtons and m is the mass of the object in kilograms. How many newtons of gravitational force are exerted on a student with mass 52 kg?

18. **Consumer Math** At a rate of \$0.08 per kilowatt-hour, the equation $C = 0.08t$ gives the cost of a customer's electric bill for using t kilowatt-hours of energy. Complete the table of values, find the rate of change and graph the energy cost equation for t ranging from 0 to 1000.

Kilowatt-hours (t)	540	580	620	660	700	740
Cost in Dollars (C)	■	■	■	■	■	■

Evaluate each equation for $x = -1, 0,$ and 1. Then graph the equation.

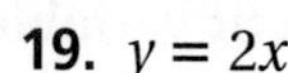

19. $y = 2x$
20. $y = 3x + 4$
21. $y = 5x - 1$
22. $y = x - 8$
23. $y = 2x - 3$
24. $y = 2x + 4$
25. $y = 2x - 4$
26. $y = x + 6$
27. $y = 2x + 3.5$

Transportation

France's *Train à Grande Vitesse* has served over 1,000,000,000 passengers since it began service in 1981.

28. **Transportation** France's high-speed train, *Train à Grande Vitesse* (TGV), has a best-average speed of 254 kilometers per hour. Write an equation that gives the distance the train travels in h hours. Is this a linear equation? Explain.

29. **Entertainment** A driving range charges \$3 to rent a golf club plus \$2.25 for every bucket of golf balls you drive. Write an equation that shows the total cost of driving b buckets of golf balls. Graph the equation. Is it linear?

30. **Critical Thinking** A movie theater charges \$6.50 per ticket. For groups of 20 or more, tickets are reduced to \$4.50 each. Graph the total cost for groups consisting of between 5 and 30 people. Is the relationship linear? Explain your reasoning.

31. **What's the Question?** The equation $C = 7.5n + 1275$ gives the total cost of producing n engines. If the answer is \$16,275, what is the question?

32. **Write About It** Explain how you could show that $y = 6x + 2$ is a linear equation.

33. **Challenge** Three solutions of an equation are (2, 2), (4, 4), and (6, 6). Draw a graph that would show that the equation is not linear.

Test Prep

34. **Multiple Choice** A landscaping company charges \$35 for a consultation fee, plus \$50 per hour. How much would it cost to hire the company for 3 hours?

Ⓐ \$225 Ⓑ \$185 Ⓒ \$150 Ⓓ \$135

35. **Short Response** Evaluate the equation $y = 3x - 5$ for $x = -1, 0, 1$. Then use a graph to tell whether the equation is linear.

AP Photo

Explore Slope

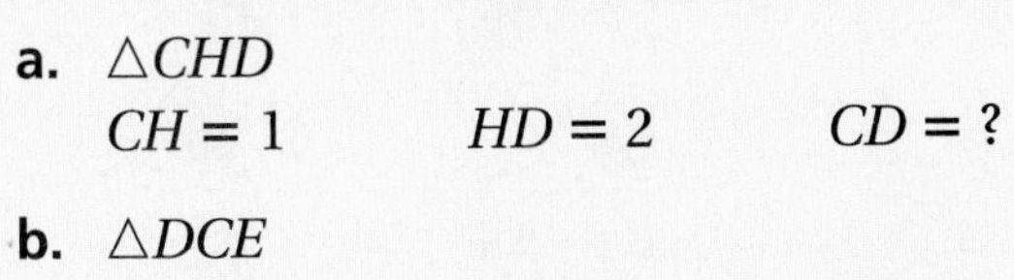

Learn It Online
Lab Resources Online

You can create many right triangles using two points on the graph of a line. In this lab you will investigate properties of those triangles.

MATHEMATICAL PRACTICES Use appropriate tools strategically.

CC.8.EE.6: Use similar triangles to explain why the slope m is the same between any two distinct points on a non-vertical line in the coordinate plane; derive the equation $y = mx$ for a line through the origin and the equation $y = mx + b$ for a line intercepting the vertical axis at b.

Activity 1

1 The lengths of the legs of each triangle are given. Use the Pythagorean theorem to find the length of the hypotenuse in each triangle.

a. $\triangle CHD$
$CH = 1$ $HD = 2$ $CD = ?$

b. $\triangle DCE$
$DG = 1$ $GE = 2$ $DE = ?$

c. $\triangle BJE$
$BJ = 3$ $JE = 6$ $BE = ?$

d. $\triangle BKF$
$BK = 4$ $KF = 8$ $BF = ?$

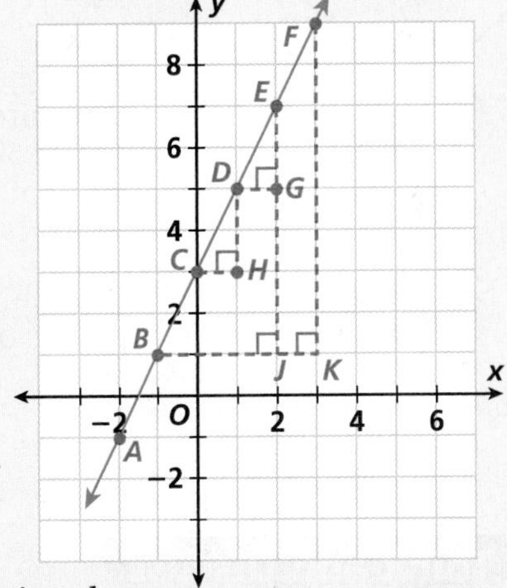

2 Use the side lengths of the triangles to determine whether the triangles formed with the line are similar.

a. Are $\triangle CHD$ and $\triangle BJE$ similar? Justify your response.

b. Are $\triangle BJE$ and $\triangle BKF$ similar? Justify your response.

c. Are $\triangle CHD$ and $\triangle BKF$ similar? Justify your response.

Think and Discuss

1. How are all the triangles in Activity 1 related to the line?
2. Is it possible to create more right triangles from the line? If so, how many triangles can be formed from a graph of this line?

Try This

1. Repeat Activity 1 with a different line and different points on the line. Show that the ratios formed by corresponding leg lengths are proportional.

Activity 2

1. Three right triangles are formed by using the two points on the line to mark off endpoints of the hypotenuse. Name the three right triangles.

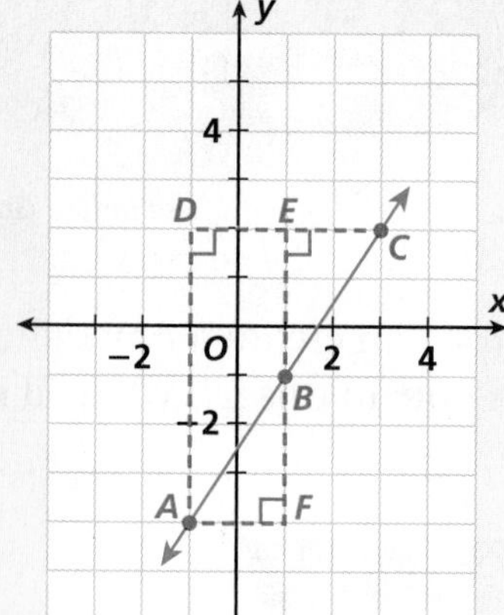

2. Find the ratios of corresponding legs between all three triangles.

$\frac{\text{vertical leg}}{\text{horizontal leg}} \quad \frac{AD}{DC} =$

$\frac{\text{vertical leg}}{\text{horizontal leg}} \quad \frac{BE}{EC} =$

$\frac{\text{vertical leg}}{\text{horizontal leg}} \quad \frac{FB}{AF} =$

3. How do the ratios compare?

4. Make a conjecture, or generalization that might be true about the triangles formed by any two points on a line.

Think and Discuss

1. Discuss how your generalization might help you graph a line more easily.

Try This

1. Find the common ratio of vertical leg length to horizontal leg length for the triangles formed by any two points on the line graphed in the coordinate plane.

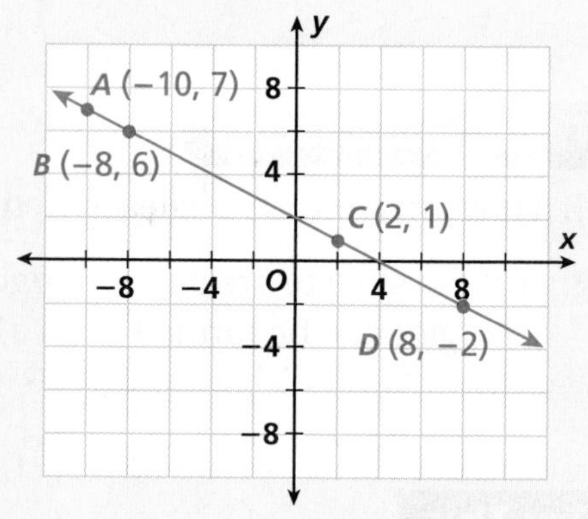

8-2 Slope of a Line

COMMON CORE

CC.8.EE.5: Graph proportional relationships, interpreting the unit rate as the slope of the graph. Compare two different proportional relationships represented in different ways. ***Also CC.8.EE.6***

Vocabulary

rise

run

slope

In skiing, *slope* refers to a slanted mountainside. The steeper a slope is, the higher its difficulty rating will be. In math, slope defines the "slant" of a line. The larger the absolute value of the slope is, the "steeper," or more vertical, the line will be.

The constant rate of change of a line is called the *slope* of the line.

SLOPE OF A LINE

The **rise** is the difference of the y-values of two points on a line.

The **run** is the difference in the x-values of two points on a line.

The **slope** of a line is the ratio of rise to run for any two points on the line.

$$\text{slope} = \frac{\text{rise}}{\text{run}} = \frac{\text{change in } y}{\text{change in } x}$$

(Remember that y is the **dependent variable** and x is the **independent variable**.)

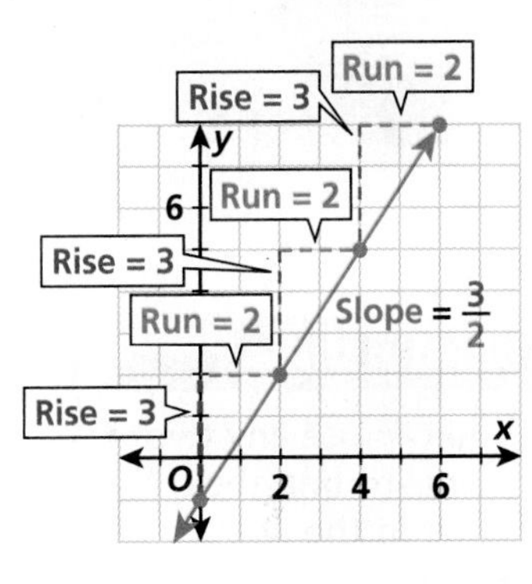

EXAMPLE 1 Finding the Slope of a Line

Find the slope of the line.

Helpful Hint

Notice that it does not matter which point you start with. The slope is the same.

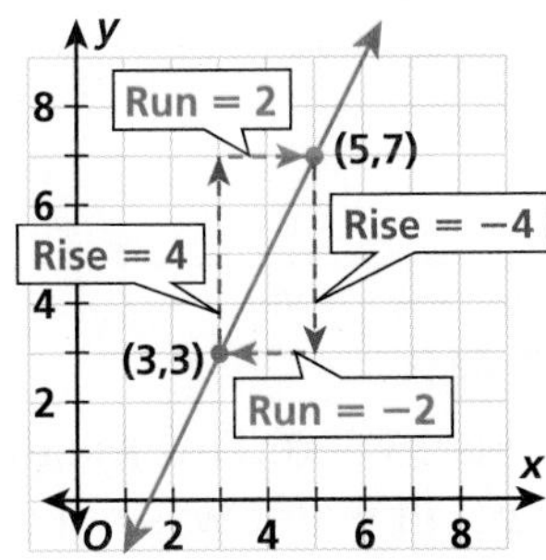

Begin at one point and count vertically to find the rise.

Then count horizontally to the second point to find the run.

$\text{slope} = \frac{4}{2} = 2$

$\text{slope} = \frac{-4}{-2} = 2$

The slope of the line is 2.

Diaphor Agency/Index Stock Imagery

If you know any two points on a line, or two solutions of a linear equation, you can find the slope of the line without graphing. The slope m of a line through the points (x_1, y_1) and (x_2, y_2) is as follows:

$$m = \frac{y_2 - y_1}{x_2 - x_1}$$

It does not matter which point you choose for (x_1, y_1) and which you choose for (x_2, y_2).

EXAMPLE 2 **Finding Slope, Given Two Points**

Find the slope of the line that passes through (1, 7) and (9, 1).

Let (x_1, y_1) be (1, 7) and (x_2, y_2) be (9, 1).

$\frac{y_2 - y_1}{x_2 - x_1} = \frac{1 - 7}{9 - 1}$ *Substitute 1 for y_2, 7 for y_1, 9 for x_2, and 1 for x_1.*

$= \frac{-6}{8} = -\frac{3}{4}$

The slope of the line that passes through (1, 7) and (9, 1) is $-\frac{3}{4}$.

EXAMPLE 3 ***Physical Science Application***

Helpful Hint

You can use any two points to find the slope of the line.

The table shows the volume of water released by Hoover Dam over a certain period of time. Use the data to make a graph. Find the slope of the line and explain what it shows.

Water Released from Hoover Dam	
Time (s)	Volume of Water (m^3)
5	75,000
10	150,000
15	225,000
20	300,000

Graph the data.

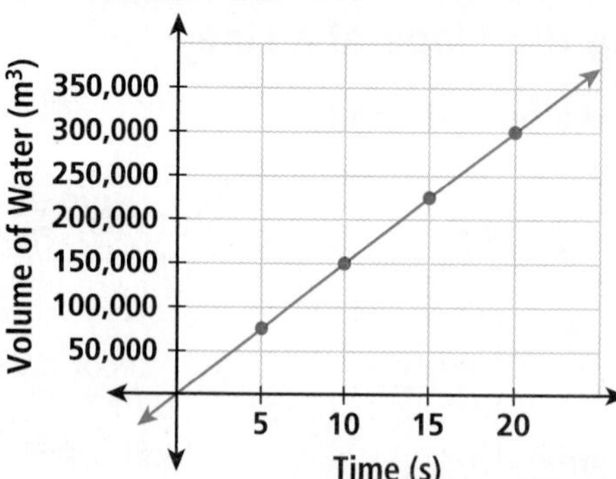

Find the slope of the line.

$\frac{y_2 - y_1}{x_2 - x_1} = \frac{150{,}000 - 75{,}000}{10 - 5}$

$= \frac{75{,}000}{5} = 15{,}000$

The slope of the line is 15,000. This means that for every second that passed, 15,000 m^3 of water was released from Hoover Dam.

The slope of a line may be positive, negative, zero, or undefined. You can tell which of these is the case by looking at the graph of a line—you do not need to calculate the slope.

POSITIVE SLOPE	NEGATIVE SLOPE	ZERO SLOPE	UNDEFINED SLOPE

MATHEMATICAL PRACTICES

Think and Discuss

1. **Explain** why it does not matter which point you choose as (x_1, y_1) and which point you choose as (x_2, y_2) when finding slope.
2. **Give an example** of two pairs of points from each of two parallel lines.

8-2 Exercises

Learn It Online
Homework Help Online
Exercises 1–15, 21, 23

GUIDED PRACTICE

See Example 1 **Find the slope of each line.**

1.

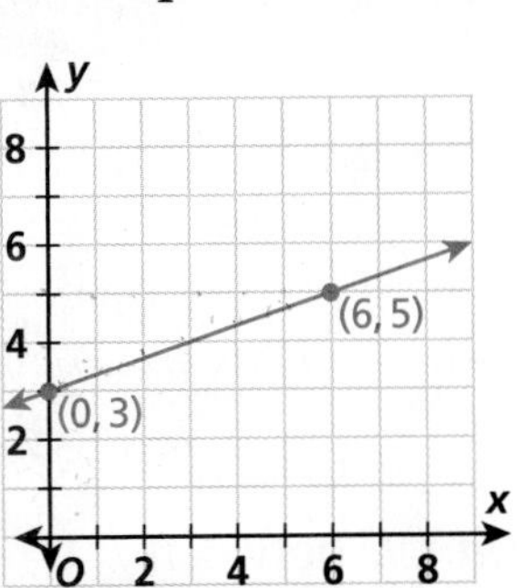

2.

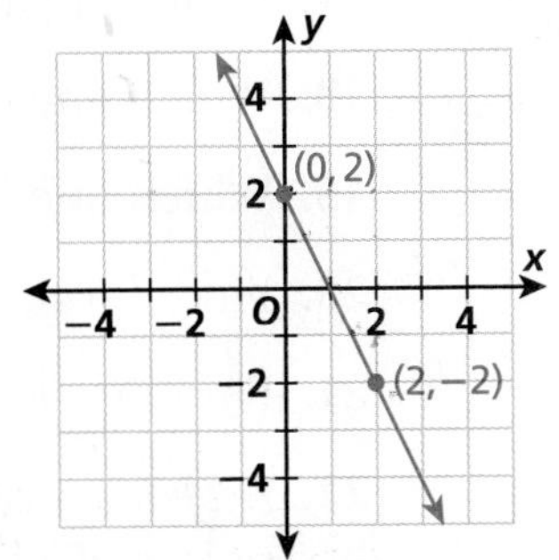

See Example 2 **Find the slope of the line that passes through each pair of points.**

3. (2, 5) and (3, 6)
4. (2, 6) and (0, 2)
5. (−2, 4) and (6, 6)

See Example 3

6. The table shows how much money Marvin earned while helping his mother with yard work one weekend. Use the data to make a graph. Find the slope of the line and explain what it shows.

Time (h)	Money Earned
3	$15
5	$25
7	$35
9	$45

INDEPENDENT PRACTICE

See Example 1

Find the slope of each line.

7.

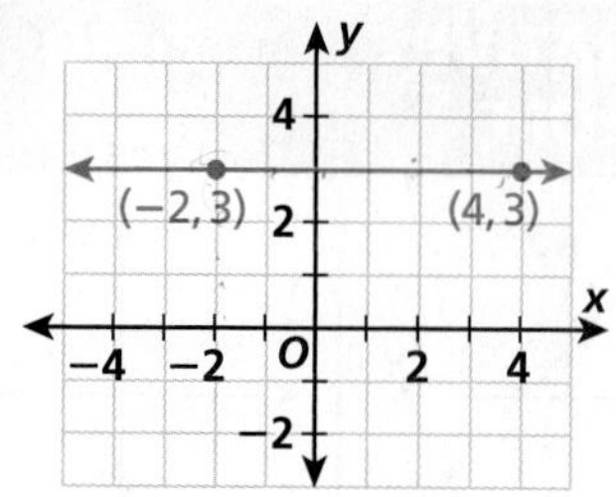

8.

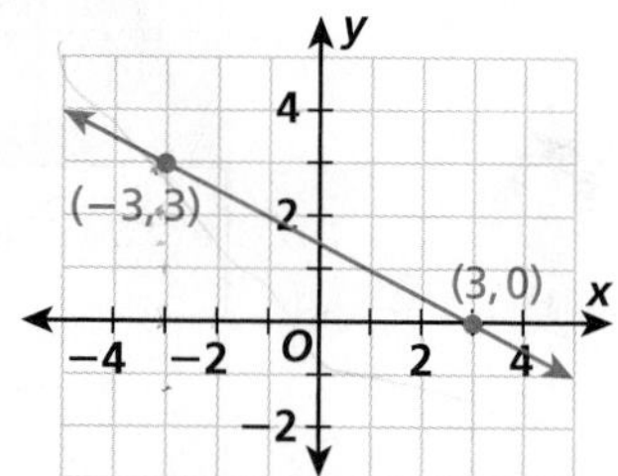

See Example 2

Find the slope of the line that passes through each pair of points.

9. (−2, −2) and (−4, 1) **10.** (0, 0) and (4, −2) **11.** (3, −6) and (2, −1)

12. (4, 2) and (0, 5) **13.** (−2, −3) and (2, 4) **14.** (0, −4) and (−7, 2)

See Example 3

15. The table shows how much water was in a swimming pool as it was being filled. Use the data to make a graph. Find the slope of the line and explain what it shows.

Time (min)	Amount of Water (gal)
10	40
13	52
16	64
19	76

PRACTICE AND PROBLEM SOLVING

Extra Practice

See Extra Practice for more exercises.

For Exercises 16–21, use the graph.

16. Which line has positive slope?

17. Which line has negative slope?

18. Which line has undefined slope?

19. Which line has a slope of 0?

20. Find the slope of line *a*.

21. Find the slope of line *c*.

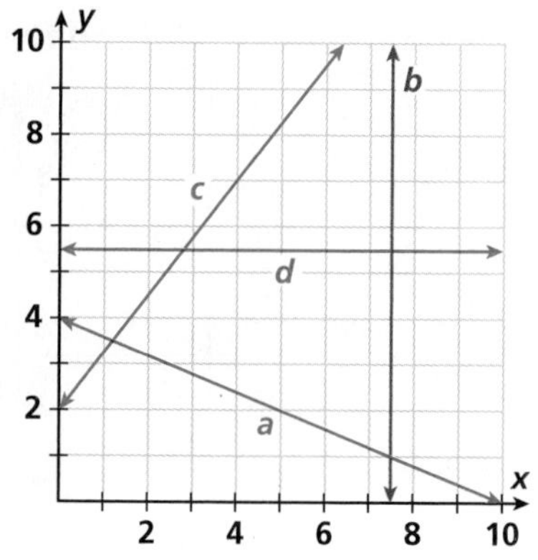

22. Make a Conjecture A *slope triangle* between points of a linear function is formed by the rise, run, and the segment of the linear function between the points.

a. Find the side lengths of the slope triangles formed by $\overline{AB}$, $\overline{BC}$, and $\overline{AC}$.

b. Make a conjecture about the slope triangles formed by the graph of a linear function.

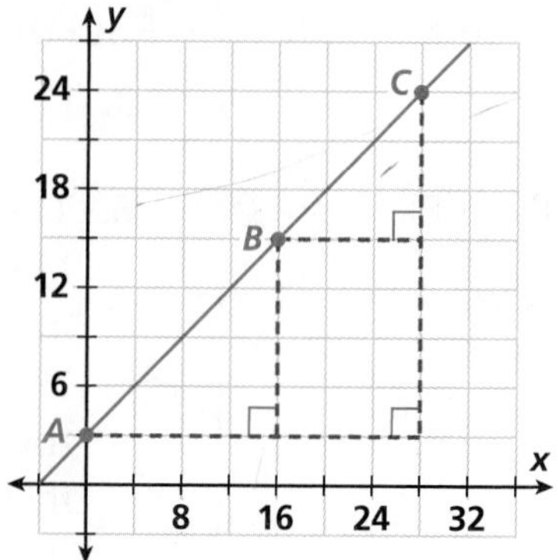

LINK

Construction

Pagodas have multitiered roofs and typically have an odd number of floors.

23. **Architecture** The Luxor Hotel in Las Vegas, Nevada, has a 350-foot-tall glass pyramid. The elevator of the pyramid moves at an incline such that its rate of change is −4 feet in the vertical direction for every 5 feet in the horizontal direction. Graph the line that describes the path it travels. (*Hint:* The point (0, 350) is the top of the pyramid.)

24. **Safety** A wheelchair ramp rises 1.5 feet for every 18 feet of horizontal distance it covers. Find the rate of change of the ramp.

25. **Construction** The angle, or pitch, of a roof is the number of inches it rises vertically for every 12 inches it extends horizontally. Morgan's roof has a pitch of 0. What does this mean?

26. A large container holds 5 gallons of water. It begins leaking at a constant rate. After 10 minutes, the container has 3 gallons of water left. At what rate is the water leaking? After how many minutes will the container be empty?

27. **Manufacturing** A factory produces widgets at a constant rate. After 3 hours, 2520 widgets have been produced. After 8 hours, 6720 widgets have been produced. At what rate are the widgets being produced? How long will it take to produce 10,080 widgets?

28. **What's the Error?** The slope of the line through the points (2, 5) and (−2, −5) is $\frac{2-(-2)}{5-(-5)} = \frac{2}{5}$. What is the error in this statement?

29. **Write About It** The equation of a vertical line is $x = a$, where a is any number. Explain why the slope of a vertical line is undefined, using a specific vertical line.

30. **Challenge** Graph the equations $y = 3x - 4$, $y = -\frac{1}{3}x$, and $y = 3x + 2$ on one coordinate plane. Identify the rate of change of each line. Explain how to tell whether a graph has a constant or variable rate of change.

Test Prep

31. **Multiple Choice** Which best describes the slope of the line that passes through points (4, −4) and (9, −4)?

Ⓐ positive Ⓑ negative Ⓒ zero Ⓓ undefined

32. **Gridded Response** What is the slope of the line that passes through points (−5, 4) and (−7, −2)?

8-3 Using Slopes and Intercepts

COMMON CORE

CC.8.F.4: Construct a function to model a linear relationship between two quantities. Determine the rate of change and initial value of the function from a description of a relationship or from two (x, y) values, including reading these from a table or from a graph. Interpret the rate of change and initial value of a linear function in terms of the situation it models, and in terms of its graph or a table of values. ***Also CC.8.EE.6, CC.8.F.3, CC.8.F.5***

Vocabulary

x-intercept

y-intercept

slope-intercept form

Amy has a gift card for a coffee shop. She can use a linear equation to find the value on the card after a number of purchases.

You can graph a linear equation easily by finding the *x-intercept* and the *y-intercept*. The **x-intercept** of a line is the value of x where the line crosses the x-axis (where $y = 0$). The **y-intercept** of a line is the value of y where the line crosses the y-axis (where $x = 0$).

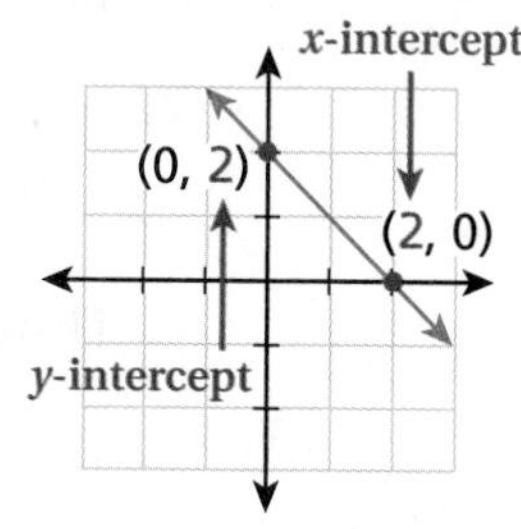

The form $Ax + By = C$, where A, B, and C are real numbers, is called the *standard form of a linear equation.*

Standard form is useful for finding intercepts.

EXAMPLE 1 Finding x-intercepts and y-intercepts to Graph Linear Equations

Find the x-intercept and y-intercept of the line $3x + 4y = 12$. Use the intercepts to graph the equation.

Find the x-intercept ($y = 0$).

$$3x + 4y = 12$$
$$3x + 4(0) = 12$$
$$3x = 12$$
$$\frac{3x}{3} = \frac{12}{3}$$
$$x = 4$$

The x-intercept is 4.

Find the y-intercept ($x = 0$).

$$3x + 4y = 12$$
$$3(0) + 4y = 12$$
$$4y = 12$$
$$\frac{4y}{4} = \frac{12}{4}$$
$$y = 3$$

The y-intercept is 3.

The graph of $3x + 4y = 12$ is the line that crosses the x-axis at the point (4, 0) and the y-axis at the point (0, 3).

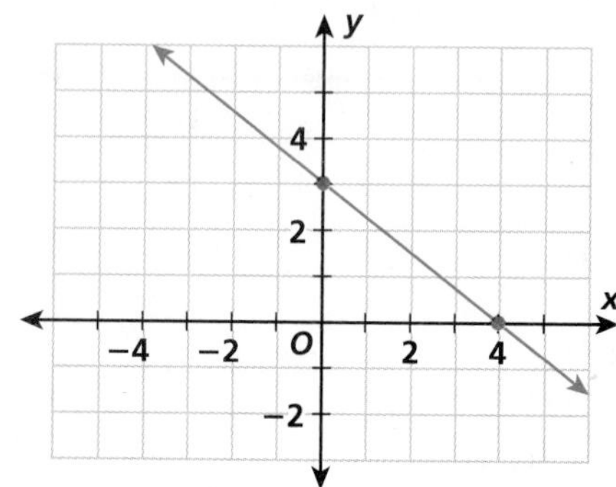

Interactivities Online ▶ In an equation written in **slope-intercept form**, $y = mx + b$, m is the slope and b is the y-intercept.

EXAMPLE 2 **Using Slope-Intercept Form to Find Slopes and *y*-intercepts**

Write each equation in slope-intercept form, and then find the slope and *y*-intercept.

Helpful Hint

For an equation such as $y = x - 6$, write it as $y = x + (-6)$ to read the y-intercept, -6.

A $y = x - 6$

$y = x - 6$

$y = 1x + -6$ *Rewrite the equation to show each part.*

$m = 1$ $b = -6$

The slope of the line $y = x - 6$ is 1, and the y-intercept is -6.

B $8x = 5y$

$8x = 5y$

$5y = 8x$ *Rewrite so y is on the left side.*

$\frac{5y}{5} = \frac{8x}{5}$ *Divide both sides by 5.*

$y = \frac{8}{5}x + 0$ *The equation is in slope-intercept form.*

$m = \frac{8}{5}$ $b = 0$

The slope of the line $8x = 5y$ is $\frac{8}{5}$, and the y-intercept is 0.

C $3x + 7y = 9$

$3x + 7y = 9$

$\underline{-3x} \quad \underline{-3x}$ *Subtract 3x from both sides.*

$7y = 9 - 3x$

$7y = -3x + 9$ *Use the Commutative Property to reorder terms.*

$\frac{7y}{7} = \frac{-3x}{7} + \frac{9}{7}$ *Divide both sides by 7.*

$y = -\frac{3}{7}x + \frac{9}{7}$ *The equation is in slope-intercept form.*

$m = -\frac{3}{7}$ $b = \frac{9}{7}$

The slope of the line $3x + 7y = 9$ is $-\frac{3}{7}$, and the y-intercept is $\frac{9}{7}$.

EXAMPLE 3 Consumer Application

The cash register deducts $2.50 from a $25 Java Cafe gift card for every medium coffee the customer buys. The linear equation $y = -2.50x + 25$ represents the number of dollars y on the card after x medium coffees have been purchased. Graph the equation, and explain the meaning of the slope and y-intercept.

$y = -2.50x + 25$ *The equation is in slope-intercept form.*

$m = -2.50 \quad b = 25$

The line crosses the y-axis at (0, 25) and moves down 2.5 units for every 1 unit it moves right.

The slope represents the rate of change (−$2.50 per medium coffee).

The y-intercept represents the initial amount on the card ($25).

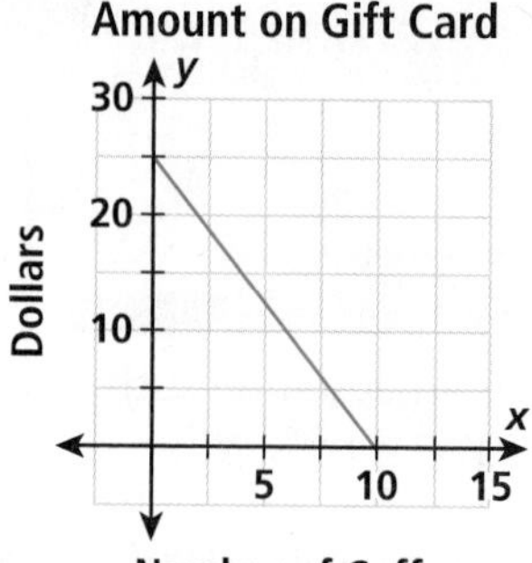

EXAMPLE 4 Writing Slope-Intercept Form

Write the equation of the line that passes through (−3, 1) and (2, −1) in slope-intercept form.

Find the slope.

$$\frac{y_2 - y_1}{x_2 - x_1} = \frac{-1 - 1}{2 - (-3)}$$

$$= \frac{-2}{5} = -\frac{2}{5}$$ *The slope is $-\frac{2}{5}$.*

Substitute either point and the slope into the slope-intercept form and solve for b.

$y = mx + b$

$-1 = -\frac{2}{5}(2) + b$ *Substitute 2 for x, −1 for y, and $-\frac{2}{5}$ for m.*

$-1 = -\frac{4}{5} + b$ *Simplify.*

$+\frac{4}{5} \quad +\frac{4}{5}$ *Add $\frac{4}{5}$ to both sides.*

$-\frac{1}{5} = b$

Write the equation of the line, using $-\frac{2}{5}$ for m and $-\frac{1}{5}$ for b.

$y = -\frac{2}{5}x + \left(-\frac{1}{5}\right)$, or $y = -\frac{2}{5}x - \frac{1}{5}$

Think and Discuss

1. **Describe** the line represented by the equation $y = -5x + 3$.
2. **Give** a real-life example with a graph that has a slope of 5 and a y-intercept of 30.

8-3 Exercises

Learn It Online
Homework Help Online
Exercises 1–24, 33

GUIDED PRACTICE

See Example 1 **Find the x-intercept and y-intercept of each line. Use the intercepts to graph the equation.**

1. $x - y = 4$
2. $3x + 5y = 15$
3. $2x + 3y = -12$
4. $-5x + 2y = 10$

See Example 2 **Write each equation in slope-intercept form, and then find the slope and y-intercept.**

5. $3x = 9y$
6. $3x - y = 14$
7. $2x - 8y = 32$
8. $x + 4y = 12$

See Example 3

9. A freight company charges \$25 plus \$4.50 per pound to ship an item that weighs n pounds. The total shipping charges are given by the equation $C = 4.5n + 25$. Graph the equation for n between 0 and 50 pounds, and explain the meaning of the slope and y-intercept.

See Example 4 **Write the equation of the line that passes through each pair of points in slope-intercept form.**

10. $(-2, -7)$ and $(3, 8)$
11. $(0, 3)$ and $(2, -5)$
12. $(3, 5)$ and $(6, 6)$

INDEPENDENT PRACTICE

See Example 1 **Find the x-intercept and y-intercept of each line. Use the intercepts to graph the equation.**

13. $4y = 24 - 12x$
14. $5x = 15 + 3y$
15. $-y = 12 - 4x$
16. $2x + y = 7$

See Example 2 **Write each equation in slope-intercept form, and then find the slope and y-intercept.**

17. $-y = 3x$
18. $5y + 3x = 10$
19. $-4y - 8x = 8$
20. $3y + 6x = -15$

See Example 3

21. A salesperson receives a weekly salary of \$250 plus a commission of \$12 for each computer sold, n. Weekly pay is given by the equation $P = 12n + 250$. Graph the equation for n between 0 and 50 computers, and explain the meaning of the slope and y-intercept.

See Example 4 **Write the equation of the line that passes through each pair of points in slope-intercept form.**

22. $(0, -6)$ and $(3, 15)$
23. $(-1, 1)$ and $(3, -3)$
24. $(-5, -4)$ and $(15, 0)$

PRACTICE AND PROBLEM SOLVING

Extra Practice
See Extra Practice for more exercises.

Write each equation in standard form. Then use the x-intercept and y-intercept to graph the equation.

25. $y = 2x - 10$
26. $y = \frac{1}{2}x + 3$
27. $y = 5x - 1.5$
28. $y = -\frac{3}{4}x + 10$

29. Write an equation that has the same y-intercept as $y = 2x + 4$.

Life Science LINK

Acute Mountain Sickness (AMS) occurs if you ascend in altitude too quickly without giving your body time to adjust. It usually occurs at altitudes over 10,000 feet above sea level. To prevent AMS you should not ascend more than 1,000 feet per day. And every time you climb a total of 3,000 feet, your body needs two nights to adjust.

Often people will get sick at high altitudes because there is less oxygen and lower atmospheric pressure.

30. The map shows a team's plan for climbing Long's Peak in Rocky Mountain National Park.

a. Make a graph of the team's plan of ascent and find the slope of the line. (Day number should be your x-value, and altitude should be your y-value.)

b. Find the y-intercept and explain what it means.

c. Write the equation of the line in slope-intercept form.

d. Does the team run a high risk of getting AMS?

31. The equation that describes a mountain climber's ascent up Mount McKinley in Alaska is $y = 955x + 16{,}500$, where x is the day number and y is the altitude at the end of the day. What are the slope and y-intercept? What do they mean in terms of the climb?

32. **Challenge** Make a graph of the ascent of a team that follows the rules to avoid AMS exactly and spends the minimum number of days climbing from base camp (17,600 ft) to the summit of Mount Everest (29,035 ft). Can you write a linear equation describing this trip? Explain your answer.

Test Prep

33. Multiple Choice What is the equation in slope-intercept form of the line that passes through points (1, 6) and (−1, −2)?

Ⓐ $y = 2x + 4$ Ⓑ $y = -3x + 6$ Ⓒ $y = 4x - 2$ Ⓓ $y = 4x + 2$

34. Extended Response Write the equation $9x + 7y = 63$ in slope-intercept form. Then identify m and b. Graph the line.

Graph Equations in Slope-Intercept Form

Use with Using Slopes and Intercepts

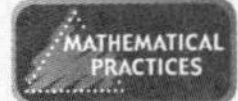 Use appropriate tools strategically.

CC.8.F.3: Interpret the equation $y = mx + b$ as defining a linear function, whose graph is a straight line; give examples of functions that are not linear.

To graph $y = x + 1$, a linear equation in slope-intercept form, in the standard graphing calculator window, press Y= ; enter the right side of the equation, X,T,θ,n + 1; and press ZOOM **6:ZStandard.**

From the slope-intercept equation, you know that the slope of the line is 1. Notice that the standard window distorts the screen, and the line does not appear to have a great enough slope.

Press ZOOM **5:ZSquare**. This changes the scale for x from -10 to 10 to -15.16 to 15.16. The graph is shown at right. Or press ZOOM **8:ZInteger** ENTER. This changes the scale for x to -47 to 47 and the scale for y to -31 to 31.

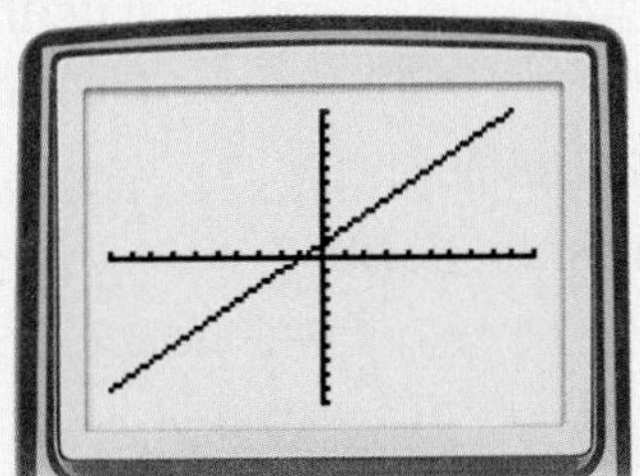

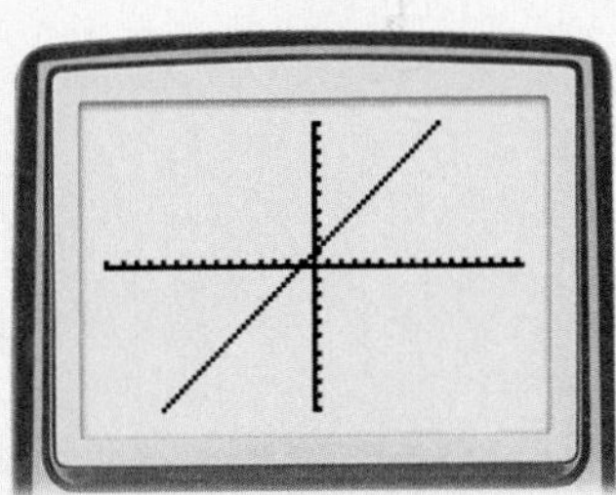

Activity

1 Graph $2x + 3y = 36$ in the integer window. Find the x- and y-intercepts of the graph.

First solve $3y = -2x + 36$ for y.

$y = \frac{-2x + 36}{3}$, so $y = -\frac{2}{3}x + 12$.

Press Y= ; enter the right side of the equation, ((−) 2 ÷ 3) X,T,θ,n + 12; and press ZOOM **8:ZInteger** ENTER.

Press TRACE to see the equation of the line and the y-intercept. The graph in the **ZInteger** window is shown.

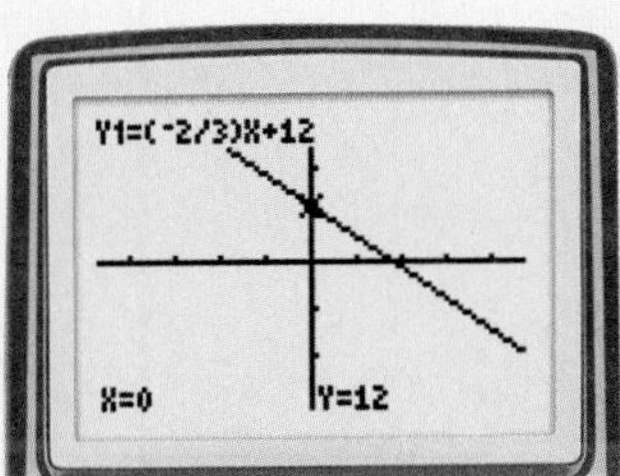

Think and Discuss

1. How do the ratios of the range of y to the range of x in the **ZSquare** and **ZInteger** windows compare?

Try This

Graph each equation in a square window.

1. $y = 3x$ **2.** $3y = x$ **3.** $3y - 6x = 15$ **4.** $2x + 5y = 40$

8-4 Point-Slope Form

COMMON CORE

CC.8.F.4: Construct a function to model a linear relationship between two quantities. Determine the rate of change and initial value of the function from a description of a relationship or from two (*x*, *y*) values, including reading these from a table or from a graph. Interpret the rate of change and initial value of a linear function in terms of the situation it models, and in terms of its graph or a table of values.

Vocabulary

point-slope form

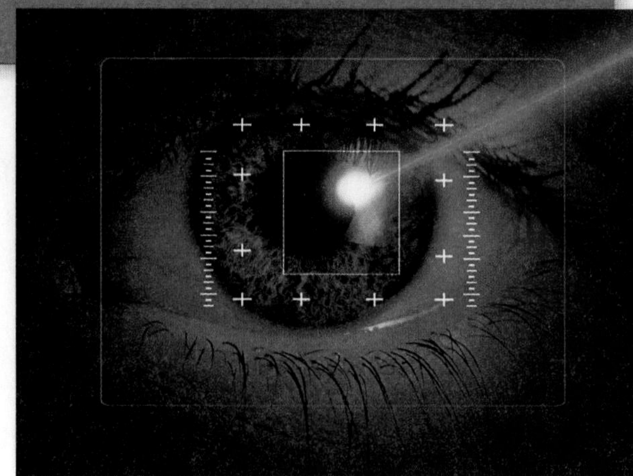

Lasers aim light along a straight path. If you know the destination of the light beam (a point on the line) and the slant of the beam (the slope), you can write an equation in *point-slope form* to calculate the height at which the laser is positioned.

The **point-slope form** of an equation of a line with slope m passing through (x_1, y_1) is $y - y_1 = m(x - x_1)$.

Point on the line	Point-slope form
(x_1, y_1)	$y - y_1 = m(x - x_1)$ (Slope → m)

EXAMPLE 1

Using Point-Slope Form to Identify Information About a Line

Use the point-slope form of each equation to identify a point the line passes through and the slope of the line.

A $y - 9 = -\frac{2}{3}(x - 21)$

$y - y_1 = m(x - x_1)$

$y - 9 = -\frac{2}{3}(x - 21)$ *The equation is in point-slope form.*

$m = -\frac{2}{3}$ *Read the value of m from the equation.*

$(x_1, y_1) = (21, 9)$ *Read the point from the equation.*

The line defined by $y - 9 = -\frac{2}{3}(x - 21)$ has slope $-\frac{2}{3}$, and passes through the point (21, 9).

B $y - 2 = 3(x + 8)$

$y - y_1 = m(x - x_1)$

$y - 2 = 3(x + 8)$

$y - 2 = 3[x - (-8)]$ *Rewrite using subtraction instead of addition.*

$m = 3$

$(x_1, y_1) = (-8, 2)$

The line defined by $y - 2 = 3(x + 8)$ has slope 3, and passes through the point (−8, 2).

EXAMPLE 2 Writing the Point-Slope Form of an Equation

Write the point-slope form of the equation with the given slope that passes through the indicated point.

A **the line with slope –2 passing through (4, 1)**

$y - y_1 = m(x - x_1)$

$y - 1 = -2(x - 4)$ *Substitute 4 for x_1, 1 for y_1, and −2 for m.*

The equation of the line with slope −2 that passes through (4, 1) in point-slope form is $y - 1 = -2(x - 4)$.

B **the line with slope 5 passing through (−2, 4)**

$y - y_1 = m(x - x_1)$

$y - 4 = 5[x - (-2)]$ *Substitute −2 for x_1, 4 for y_1, and 5 for m.*

$y - 4 = 5(x + 2)$

The equation of the line with slope 5 that passes through (−2, 4) in point-slope form is $y - 4 = 5(x + 2)$.

EXAMPLE 3 *Medical Application*

Suppose that laser eye surgery is modeled on a coordinate grid. The laser is positioned at the *y*-intercept so that the light shifts down 1 mm for each 40 mm it shifts to the right. The light reaches the center of the cornea of the eye at (125, 0). Write the equation of the light beam in point-slope form, and find the height of the laser.

As x increases by 40, y decreases by 1, so the slope of the line is $-\frac{1}{40}$. The line must pass through the point (125, 0).

$y - y_1 = m(x - x_1)$

$y - 0 = -\frac{1}{40}(x - 125)$ *Substitute 125 for x_1, 0 for y_1, and $-\frac{1}{40}$ for m.*

The equation of the line the laser beam travels along, in point-slope form, is $y = -\frac{1}{40}(x - 125)$. Substitute 0 for x to find the y-intercept.

$y = -\frac{1}{40}(0 - 125)$

$y = -\frac{1}{40}(-125)$

$y = 3.125$

The y-intercept is 3.125, so the laser is at a height of 3.125 mm.

MATHEMATICAL PRACTICES

Think and Discuss

1. **Describe** the line, using the point-slope equation, that has a slope of 2 and passes through (−3, 4).
2. **Tell** how you find the point-slope form of the line when you know the coordinates of two points.

8-4 Exercises

Learn It Online
Homework Help Online
Exercises 1-18, 19, 21

GUIDED PRACTICE

See Example 1

Use the point-slope form of each equation to identify a point the line passes through and the slope of the line.

1. $y - 2 = -3(x + 6)$
2. $y - 8 = 7(x - 14)$
3. $y + 3.7 = 3.2(x - 1.7)$
4. $y + 1 = 11(x - 1)$
5. $y + 6 = -4(x - 8)$
6. $y - 7 = 4(x + 3)$

See Example 2

Write the point-slope form of the equation with the given slope that passes through the indicated point.

7. the line with slope 5 passing through (0, 6)
8. the line with slope −8 passing through (−11, 7)

See Example 3

9. A basement filled with water from a rainstorm is drained at a rate of 10.5 liters per minute. After 40 minutes, there are 840 liters of water remaining. Write the equation of a line in point-slope form that models the situation. How long does it take to drain the basement?

INDEPENDENT PRACTICE

See Example 1

Use the point-slope form of each equation to identify a point the line passes through and the slope of the line.

10. $y - 2 = \frac{3}{4}(x + 9)$
11. $y + 9 = 4(x + 5)$
12. $y - 2 = -\frac{1}{6}(x - 11)$
13. $y - 13 = 16(x - 4)$
14. $y - 5 = -1.4(x - 6.7)$
15. $y + 9 = 1(x - 3)$

See Example 2

Write the point-slope form of the equation with the given slope that passes through the indicated point.

16. the line with slope −5 passing through (−3, −5)
17. the line with slope 6 passing through (−3, 0)

See Example 3

18. A stretch of highway has a 5% grade, so the road rises 1 ft for each 20 ft of horizontal distance. The beginning of the highway ($x = 0$) has an elevation of 2344 ft. Write an equation in point-slope form, and find the highway's elevation 7500 ft from the beginning.

PRACTICE AND PROBLEM SOLVING

Extra Practice
See Extra Practice for more exercises.

Write the point-slope form and slope-intercept form of each line described below.

19. the line with slope 4 that passes through (−2, 3)
20. the line with slope $\frac{1}{3}$ that passes through (8, −2)
21. the line with slope −1 that passes through (−5, −7)
22. the line with slope −10 that passes through (−3, 0)
23. **Critical Thinking** Compare finding the equation of a line using two known points to finding it using one known point and the slope of the line.

Mount Etna, a volcano in Sicily, Italy, has been erupting for over half a million years. It is one of the world's most active volcanoes. When it erupted in 1669 it almost completely destroyed the city of Catania.

24. **Life Science** An elephant's tusks grow throughout its life. Each month, an elephant tusk grows about 1 cm. Suppose you started observing an elephant when its tusks were 12 cm long. Write an equation in point-slope form that describes the length of the elephant's tusks after m months of observation.

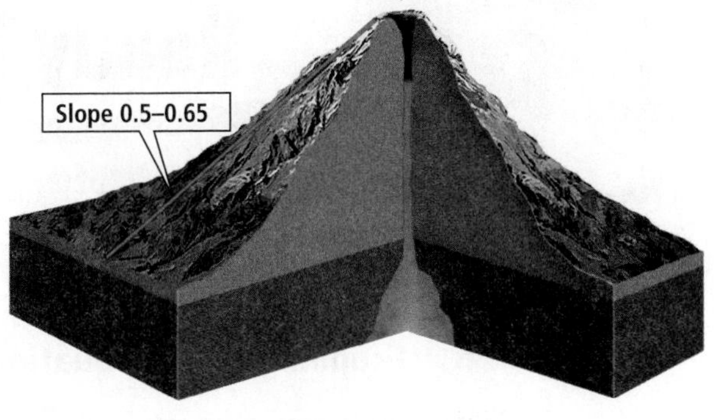

25. **Earth Science** Jorullo is a cinder cone volcano in Mexico. Suppose Jorullo is 315 m tall, 50 m from the center of its base. Use the average slope of a cinder cone shown in the diagram to write an equation in point-slope form that approximately models the height of the volcano, x meters from the center of its base.

26. **Write a Problem** Write a problem about the point-slope form of an equation using the data on a car's fuel economy.

Fuel Economy		
Gas Tank Capacity	City Efficiency	Highway Efficiency
14 gal	26 mi/gal	34 mi/gal

27. **Write About It** Explain how you could convert an equation in point-slope form to slope-intercept form.

28. **Challenge** The value of one line's x-intercept is the opposite of the value of its y-intercept. The line contains the point $(9, -3)$. Find the point-slope form of the equation.

Test Prep

29. **Multiple Choice** What is the point-slope form of a line with slope $\frac{3}{4}x$ that passes through the point $(-16, 5)$?

Ⓐ $y - 5 = \frac{3}{4}(x - 16)$

Ⓑ $y - 5 = -\frac{4}{3}(x + 16)$

Ⓒ $y - 5 = \frac{3}{4}(x + 16)$

Ⓓ $y - 5 = -\frac{4}{3}(x - 16)$

30. **Gridded Response** Use the point-slope form of the equation $y - 6 = 8(x + 1)$. What is the y-value of the y-intercept?

CHAPTER 8

SECTION A

Learn It Online
Resources Online

Quiz for Lessons 1 Through 4

1 Graphing Linear Equations

Graph each equation and tell whether it is linear.

1. $y = 2 - 4x$ **2.** $x = 2$ **3.** $y = 3x^2$

4. At Maggi's Music, the equation $u = \frac{3}{4}n + 1$ represents the price for a used CD u with a selling price n when the CD was new. How much will a used CD cost for each of the listed new prices? Graph the equation and tell whether it is linear.

New Price	Used Price
$8	▪
$12	▪
$14	▪
$20	▪

2 Slope of a Line

Find the slope of the line that passes through each pair of points.

5. (6, 3) and (2, 4) **6.** (1, 4) and (−1, −3) **7.** (0, −3) and (−4, 0)

Find the slope of each line.

8.

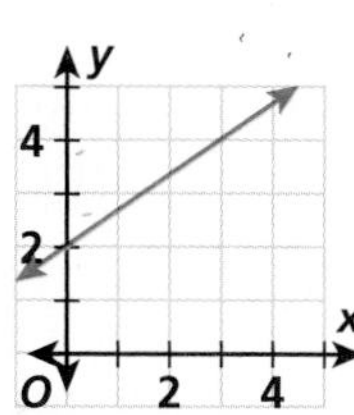

9.

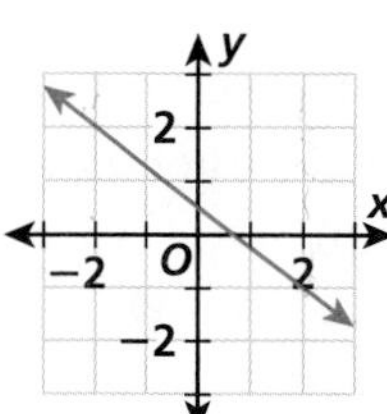

10.

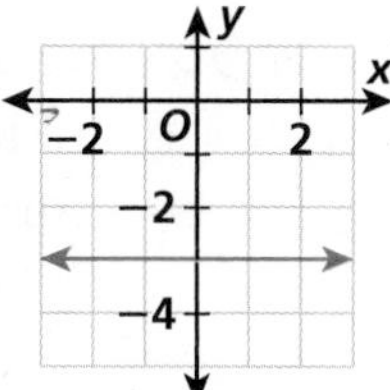

3 Using Slopes and Intercepts

11. A camp charges families $625 per month for one child and then $225 per month for each additional child. The linear equation $y = 225x + 625$ represents the amount a family with x additional children would pay. Identify the slope and y-intercept, and use them to graph the equation.

Write the equation of the line that passes through each pair of points in slope-intercept form.

12. (−4, 3) and (−2, 1) **13.** (2, 7) and (5, 2) **14.** (4, 2) and (2, −5)

4 Point-Slope Form

Use the point-slope form of each equation to identify a point the line passes through and the slope of the line.

15. $y + 5 = -3(x - 2)$ **16.** $y = -(x + 3)$ **17.** $y - 7 = -3x$

Write the point-slope form of the equation with the given slope that passes through the indicated point.

18. slope −3, passing through (7, 2) **19.** slope 2, passing through (−5, 3)

Focus on Problem Solving

Understand the Problem

- **Identify important details in the problem**

When you are solving word problems, you need to find the information that is important to the problem.

You can write the equation of a line if you know the slope and one point on the line or if you know two points on the line.

Example:

A school bus carrying 40 students is traveling toward the school at **30 mi/hr**. After **15 minutes**, it has **20 miles to go**. How far away from the school was the bus when it started?

You can write the equation of the line in point-slope form.

$$y - y_1 = m(x - x_1)$$

$$y - (-20) = 30(x - 0.25)$$ *The slope is the rate of change, or 30.*

$$y + 20 = 30x - 7.5$$ *15 minutes = 0.25 hours*

$$\underline{-20} \qquad \underline{-20}$$ *(0.25, −20) is a point on the line.*

$$y = 30x - 27.5$$

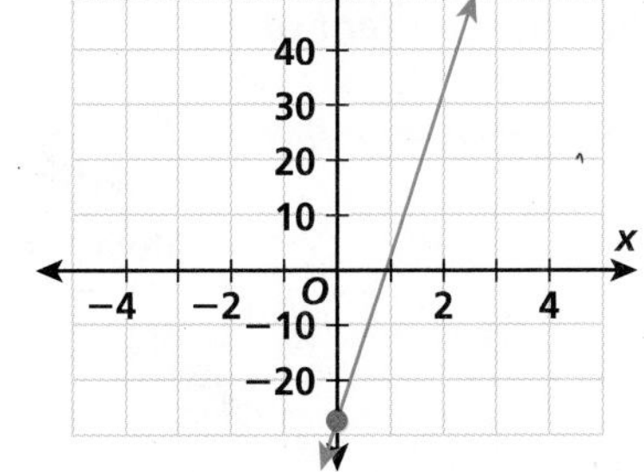

The y-intercept of the line is −27.5. At 0 minutes, the bus had 27.5 miles to go.

Read each problem, and identify the information needed to write the equation of a line. Give the slope and one point on the line, or give two points on the line.

1. At sea level, water boils at 100 °C. At an altitude of 600 m, water boils at 95 °C. If the relationship is linear, estimate the temperature that water would boil at an altitude of 1800 m.

2. Omar earns a weekly salary of $560, plus a commission of 8% of his total sales. How many dollars in merchandise does he have to sell to make $600 in one week?

3. A community activities group has a goal of passing out 5000 fliers advertising a charity run. On Saturday, the group passed out 2000 fliers. If the group can pass out 600 fliers per week, how long will it take them to pass out the remaining fliers to the community?

4. Kayla rents a booth at a craft fair. If she sells 50 bracelets, her profit is $25. If she sells 80 bracelets, her profit is $85. What would her profit be if she sold 100 bracelets?

8-5 Direct Variation

COMMON CORE

CC.8.F.5: Describe qualitatively the functional relationship between two quantities by analyzing a graph. Sketch a graph that exhibits the qualitative features of a function that has been described verbally. ***Also*** ***CC.8.F.1, CC.8.EE.5, CC.8.EE.6***

Vocabulary

direct variation

constant of variation

An amplifier generates intensity of sound from watts of power in a constant ratio. Sound output *varies directly* with the power input.

A **direct variation** is a linear function that can be written as $y = kx$, where k is a nonzero constant called the **constant of variation**.

Solve $y = kx$ for k.

$$y = kx$$

$$\frac{y}{x} = \frac{kx}{x} \qquad \textit{Divide both sides by x.}$$

$$\frac{y}{x} = k$$

Reading Math

The constant of variation is also called the *constant of proportionality*.

The value of k is the ratio of y to x. This ratio is the same for all ordered pairs that are solutions of a direct variation.

Since the rate of change k is constant for any direct variation, the graph of a direct variation is always linear. The graph of any direct variation always contains the point (0, 0) because for any value of k, $0 = k \cdot 0$.

EXAMPLE 1 Determining Whether a Data Set Varies Directly

Determine whether the data sets show direct variation.

A

Shoe Sizes					
U.S. Size	7	8	9	10	11
European Size	39	41	43	44	45

Method 1 Make a graph.

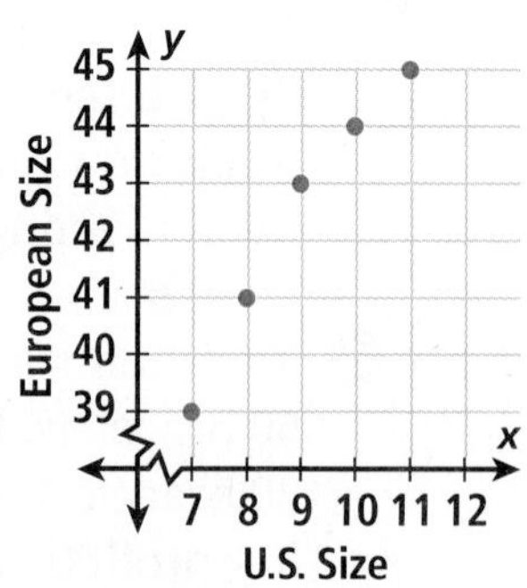

The graph is not linear.

Method 2 Compare ratios.

$\frac{39}{7} \times \frac{45}{11}$ → 315, 429

315 ≠ 429
The ratios are not proportional.

Both methods show the relationship is not a direct variation.

Video Lesson Tutorials Online my.hrw.com

Determine whether the data sets show direct variation.

B

Sound Intensity					
Input Signal Power (W)	6	8	12	20	28
Output Sound Intensity $\left(\frac{W}{m^2}\right)$	4.5	6	9	15	21

Method 1 Make a graph.

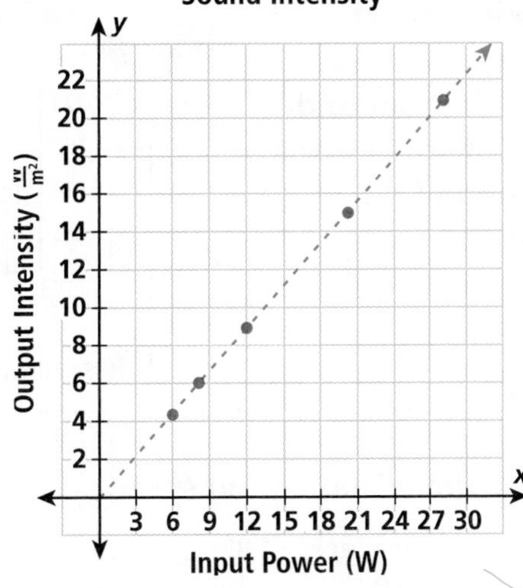

The points lie in a straight line.

(0, 0) is on the line.

Method 2 Compare ratios.

$\frac{6}{4.5} = \frac{8}{6} = \frac{12}{9} = \frac{20}{15} = \frac{28}{21}$ *The ratio is constant.*

Both methods show the relationship is a direct variation.

EXAMPLE 2 Finding Equations of Direct Variation

Find each equation of direct variation, given that y varies directly with x.

A **y is 48 when x is 3**

$y = kx$	*y varies directly with x.*
$48 = k \cdot 3$	*Substitute for x and y.*
$16 = k$	*Solve for k.*
$y = 16x$	*Substitute 16 for k in the original equation.*

B **y is 15 when x is 10**

$y = kx$	*y varies directly with x.*
$15 = k \cdot 10$	*Substitute for x and y.*
$\frac{3}{2} = k$	*Solve for k.*
$y = \frac{3}{2}x$	*Substitute $\frac{3}{2}$ for k in the original equation.*

EXAMPLE 3 Physical Science Application

When a driver applies the brakes, a car's total stopping distance is the sum of the reaction distance and the braking distance. The reaction distance is the distance the car travels before the driver presses the brake pedal. The braking distance is the distance the car travels after the brakes have been applied.

Determine whether there is a direct variation between either data set and speed. If so, find the equation of direct variation.

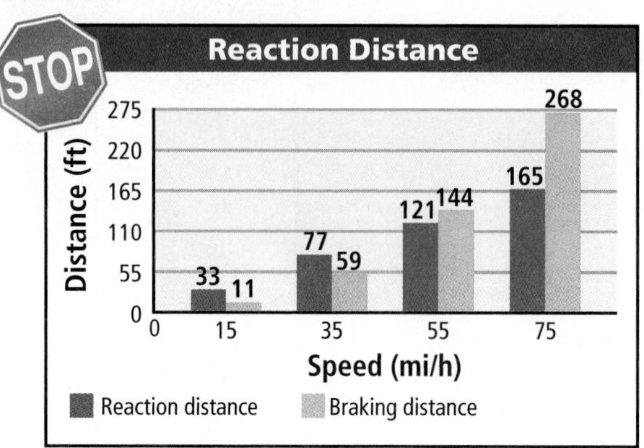

A reaction distance and speed

$$\frac{\text{reaction distance}}{\text{speed}} = \frac{33}{15} = 2.2 \qquad \frac{\text{reaction distance}}{\text{speed}} = \frac{77}{35} = 2.2$$

The first two pairs of data result in a common ratio. In fact, all of the reaction distance to speed ratios are equivalent to 2.2.

$$\frac{\text{reaction distance}}{\text{speed}} = \frac{33}{15} = \frac{77}{35} = \frac{121}{55} = \frac{165}{75} = 2.2$$

The variables are related by a constant ratio of 2.2 to 1, and (0, 0) is included. The equation of direct variation is $y = 2.2x$, where x is the speed, y is the reaction distance, and 2.2 is the constant of proportionality.

B braking distance and speed

$$\frac{\text{braking distance}}{\text{speed}} = \frac{11}{15} = 0.7\overline{3} \qquad \frac{\text{braking distance}}{\text{speed}} = \frac{59}{35} \approx 1.69$$

$0.7\overline{3} \neq 1.69$

If any of the ratios are not equal, then there is no direct variation. It is not necessary to compute additional ratios.

MATHEMATICAL PRACTICES

Think and Discuss

1. **Describe** the slope and the y-intercept of a direct variation equation.
2. **Compare** and contrast proportional and non-proportional linear relationships.

8-5 Exercises

Learn It Online
Homework Help Online
Exercises 1–17, 19

GUIDED PRACTICE

See Example 1

Determine whether the data set shows direct variation.

1. The table shows an employee's pay per number of hours worked.

Hours Worked	0	1	2	3	4	5	6
Pay ($)	0	9.50	19.00	28.50	38.00	47.50	57.00

See Example 2

Find each equation of direct variation, given that y varies directly with x.

2. y is 12 when x is 3
3. y is 18 when x is 6
4. y is 10 when x is 12
5. y is 5 when x is 10
6. y is 360 when x is 3
7. y is 4 when x is 36

See Example 3

8. The table shows how many hours it takes to travel 600 miles, depending on your speed in miles per hour. Determine whether there is direct variation between the two data sets. If so, find the equation of direct variation.

Speed (mi/h)	5	6	7.5	10	15	30	60
Time (h)	120	100	80	60	40	20	10

INDEPENDENT PRACTICE

See Example 1

Determine whether the data set shows direct variation.

9. The table shows the amount of current flowing through a 12-volt circuit with various resistances.

Resistance (ohms)	48	24	12	6	4	3	2
Current (amps)	0.25	0.5	1	2	3	4	6

See Example 2

Find each equation of direct variation, given that y varies with x.

10. y is 3.5 when x is 3.5
11. y is 3 when x is 9
12. y is 96 when x is 4
13. y is 4 when x is 26
14. y is 48 when x is 3
15. y is 5 when x is 50

See Example 3

16. The table shows how many hours it takes to drive certain distances at a speed of 30 miles per hour. Determine whether there is direct variation between the two data sets. If so, find the equation of direct variation.

Distance (mi)	15	30	60	90	120	150	180
Time (h)	0.5	1	2	3	4	5	6

PRACTICE AND PROBLEM SOLVING

Extra Practice

See Extra Practice for more exercises.

Tell whether each equation represents direct variation between x and y.

17. $y = 217x$ **18.** $y = -3x^2$ **19.** $y = \frac{k}{x}$ **20.** $y = 4\pi x$

21. Critical Thinking Is every linear relationship a direct variation? Is every direct variation a linear relation? Explain.

LINK

Life Science

Although snakes shed their skins all in one piece, most reptiles shed their skins in much smaller pieces.

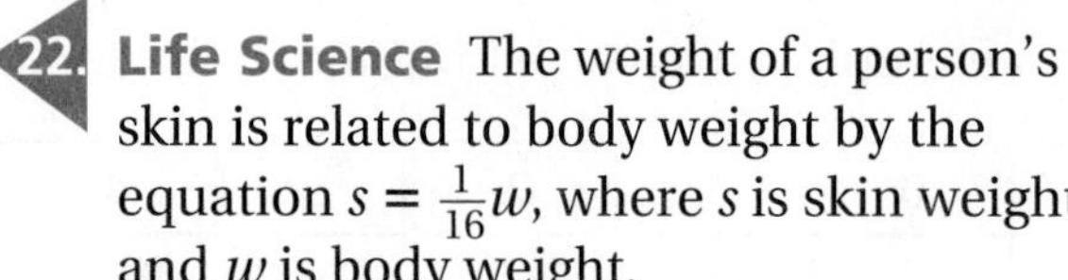

22. Life Science The weight of a person's skin is related to body weight by the equation $s = \frac{1}{16}w$, where s is skin weight and w is body weight.

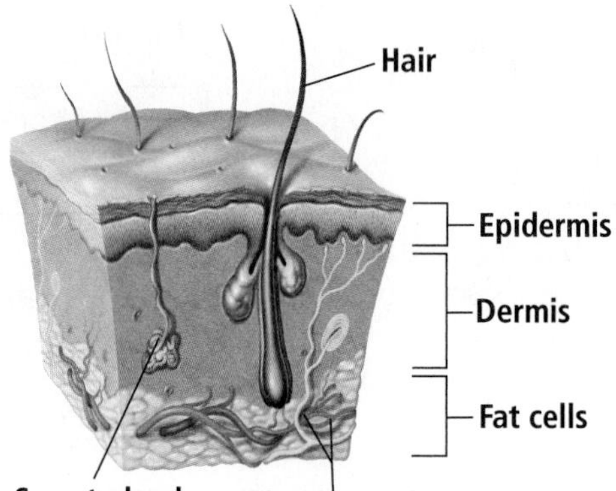

a. Does this equation show direction variation between body weight and skin weight?

b. If a person calculates skin weight as $9\frac{3}{4}$ lb, what is the person's body weight?

23. Write a Problem The perimeter P of a square varies directly with the length l of a side. Write a direct variation problem about the perimeter of a square.

24. Write About It Describe how the constant of proportionality k affects the appearance of the graph of a direct variation equation.

25. Challenge Watermelons are being sold at 79¢ a pound. What condition would have to exist for the price paid and the number of watermelons sold to represent a direct variation?

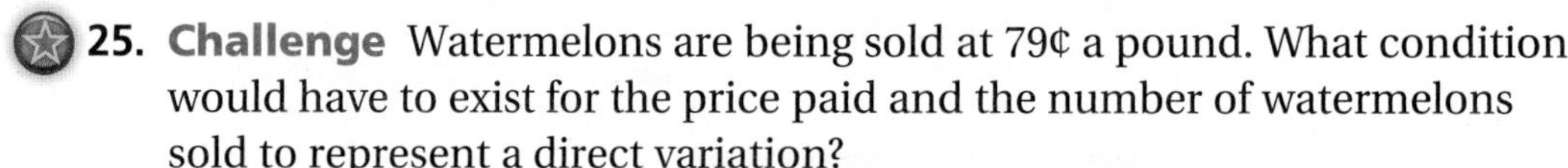

Test Prep

26. Multiple Choice Given that y varies directly with x, what is the equation of direct variation if y is 16 when x is 20?

Ⓐ $y = 1\frac{1}{5}x$ Ⓑ $y = \frac{5}{4}x$ Ⓒ $y = \frac{4}{5}x$ Ⓓ $y = 0.6x$

27. Gridded Response If y varies directly with x, what is the value of x when $y = 14$ and $k = \frac{1}{2}$?

8-6 Solving Systems of Linear Equations by Graphing

COMMON CORE

CC.8.EE.8: Analyze and solve pairs of simultaneous linear equations. ***Also CC.8.EE.8a, CC.8.EE.8b, CC.8.EE.8c***

When two airplanes leave an airport at different times and fly at different rates to the same destination, a system of linear equations can be used to determine if and where one plane will overtake the other.

You can verify the coordinates of the intersections algebraically. When you graph a system of linear equations in the coordinate plane, any solution of the system is where the lines intersect.

EXAMPLE 1 Graphing a System of Linear Equations to Solve a Problem

A plane left Miami traveling 300 mi/h. After the plane had traveled 1200 miles, a jet started along the same route flying 500 mi/h. Graph the system of linear equations. How long after the jet takes off will it catch the plane? What distance will the jet have traveled?

Let t = time in hours the jet flies.
Let d = distance in miles the jet flies.

Plane distance: $d = 300t + 1200$
Jet distance: $d = 500t$

Graph each equation. The point of intersection appears to be (6, 3000).

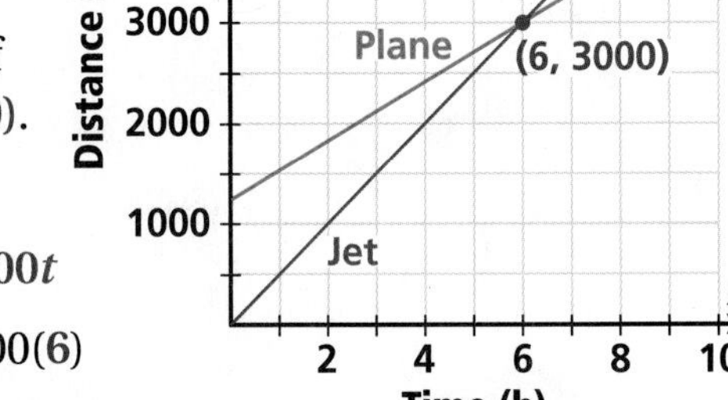

Check

$d = 300t + 1200$	$d = 500t$
$3000 \stackrel{?}{=} 300(6) + 1200$	$3000 \stackrel{?}{=} 500(6)$
$3000 = 3000$ ✔	$3000 = 3000$ ✔

Plane 2 will catch up after 6 hours in flight, 3000 miles from Miami.

Caution!

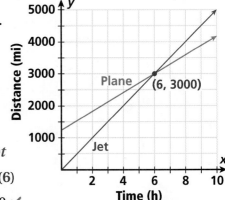

When you solve a system of linear equations by graphing, be sure to check your solution algebraically. This is especially important when the solution is not an integer value.

Not all systems of linear equations have graphs that intersect in one point. There are three possibilities for the graph of a system of two linear equations, and each represents a different solution set.

Intersecting Lines
different slopes and intercepts

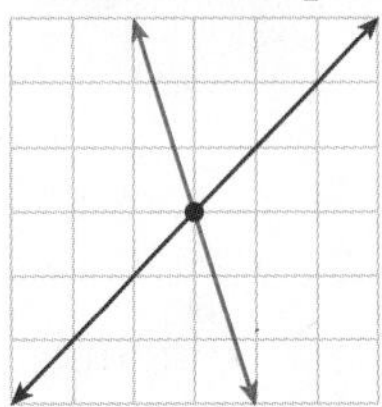

one solution

Parallel Lines
same slope, different intercepts

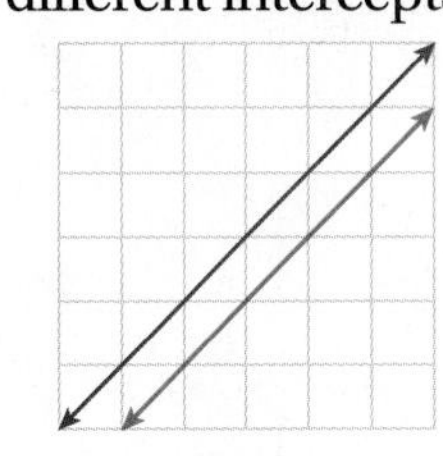

no solution

Same Line
same slope, same intercept

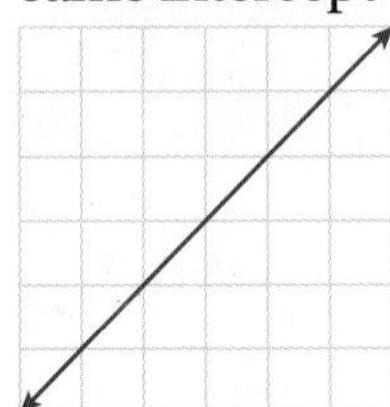

infinitely many solutions

Reading Math

When the graphs of two equations are the same line, the lines are *coinciding lines.*

EXAMPLE 2 Solving Systems of Linear Equations by Graphing

Solve each linear system by graphing. Check your answer.

A $-x = -1 + y$
$x + y = 4$

Step 1: Solve both equations for y.

$$\begin{aligned} -x &= -1 + y \\ +1 &\quad +1 \\ -x + 1 &= y \\ y &= -x + 1 \end{aligned} \qquad \begin{aligned} x + y &= 4 \\ -x &\quad -x \\ y &= -x + 4 \end{aligned}$$

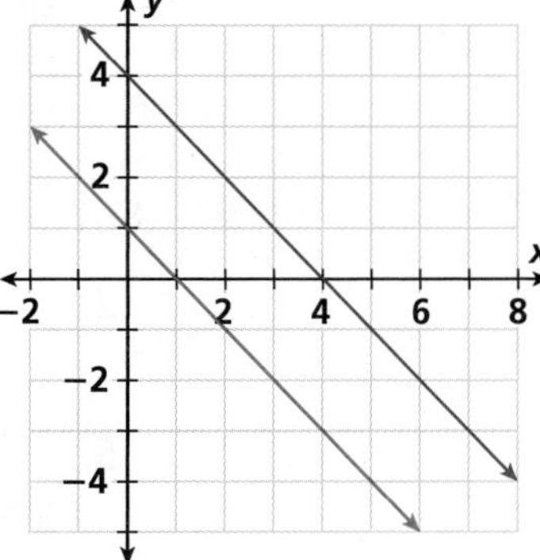

Step 2: Graph.

The lines are parallel, so the system has no solution.

Check

$$y \stackrel{?}{=} y$$ *Both expressions equal y.*

$$-x + 1 \stackrel{?}{=} -x + 4$$ *Add x to both sides.*

$$+x \qquad +x$$

$$1 \neq 4 \text{ ✗}$$ *1 = 4 is never true.*

> **Remember!**
> The transitive property lets you set two expressions that equal *y* equal to each other.

B $-x + y = 8$
$y - 8 = x$

Step 1: Solve both equations for y.

$$\begin{aligned} -x + y &= 8 \\ +x &\quad +x \\ y &= x + 8 \end{aligned} \qquad \begin{aligned} y - 8 &= x \\ +8 &\quad +8 \\ y &= x + 8 \end{aligned}$$

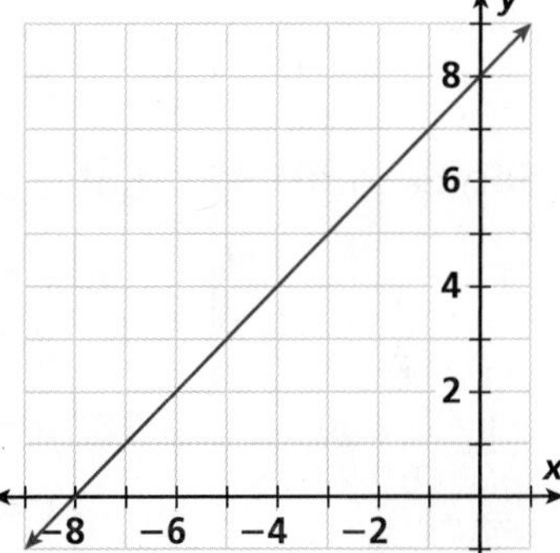

Step 2: Graph.

The lines are the same, so the system has infinitely many solutions.

Check

$$y \stackrel{?}{=} y$$

$$x + 8 \stackrel{?}{=} x + 8$$ *Both expressions equal y.*

$$-x \qquad -x$$ *Subtract x from both sides.*

$$8 = 8 \text{ ✓}$$ *8 = 8 is always true.*

Think and Discuss

1. **Explain** why finding the exact solution of a linear system of equations by graphing may present a challenge.
2. **Describe** the solution of a system of linear equations, where the lines have the same slope but different *y*-intercepts.

8-6 Exercises

Learn It Online
Homework Help Online
Exercises 1–14, 15, 17

GUIDED PRACTICE

See Example 1

1. Two bicyclists are racing toward the finish line of a race. The first bicyclist has a 105-meter lead and is pedaling 12 meters per second. The second bicyclist is pedaling 15 meters per second. Graph the system of linear equations. How long will it take for the second bicyclist to pass the first? What distance does the second bicyclist travel?

See Example 2

Solve each system of linear equations by graphing. Check your answer.

2. $y = 3x - 4$
$y = x + 2$

3. $y = 3x + 2$
$4x = y$

4. $2x + y = 1$
$-3x + y = -9$

5. $y = 2x$
$y = 3x - 3$

6. $y = -3x + 2$
$-3x - y = -2$

7. $y - x = -3$
$x - 3y = 9$

INDEPENDENT PRACTICE

See Example 1

8. Melissa has a choice of two phone plans. The first plan has a monthly fee of $40 and charges $0.50 per additional peak minute over included minutes. The second plan has a monthly fee of $50 and charges $0.25 per additional peak minute over an equal number of included minutes. Graph the system of linear equations. Find the number of additional peak minutes for which the second plan will be as cheap as the first, and tell how much Melissa would pay for that month.

See Example 2

Solve each system of linear equations by graphing. Check your answer.

9. $y = -x - 1$
$y = 2x + 14$

10. $-2y = 6x + 12$
$y = -3x - 6$

11. $3y - 7 = 2x$
$y + 2x = 5$

12. $y = 2x - 1$
$y = -4x + 11$

13. $y = -x - 4$
$x + y = 0$

14. $y = 2x + 2$
$\frac{1}{2}y - 1 = x$

PRACTICE AND PROBLEM SOLVING

Extra Practice
See Extra Practice for more exercises.

Graph the line containing the points in each set of linear data. Find the intersection of each graph.

15.

x	y
−2	2
0	8
2	14
4	20

x	y
−2	−3
0	−7
2	−11
4	−15

16.

x	y
−2	7
0	5
2	3
4	1

x	y
−2	4
0	2
2	0
4	−2

17. Band members bought a large number of T-shirts for $100. Each T-shirt cost $8 to print and will sell for $12. Graph a system of equations to find the number of T-shirts the band members need to print and sell in order to break even. What will the band's costs and revenue be?

The longest escalators are over 400 ft long and take about three minutes to ride.

18. Use the graph to estimate the solution of the system of equations.

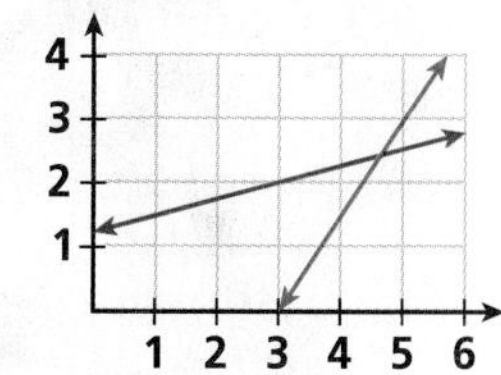
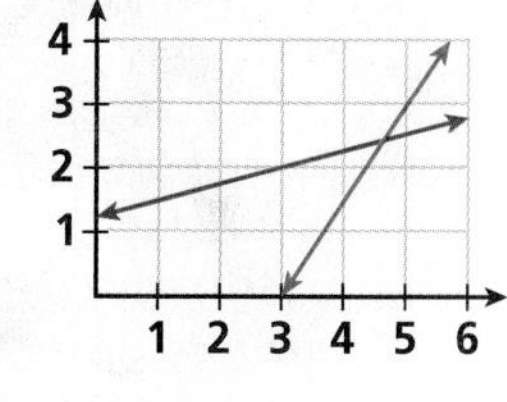

19. **Critical Thinking** Can a system of two direct variation equations have no solution? Explain.

20. **Architecture** An escalator has a height given by $h = \frac{1}{2}d$, where d is the horizontal distance as the escalator rises and h is the vertical height in feet from the ground. The escalator coming down from the floor above has a height given by $h = 20 - \frac{1}{2}d$ over that same distance.

a. Graph the linear system representing the equations.

b. At what vertical height do the escalators cross?

c. What straight line distance would a person on the first escalator travel to reach the point where the escalators cross?

21. **What's the Error?** Rico says there is one solution to the system of linear equations shown. Brynne says there is no solution. Who is correct? Explain.

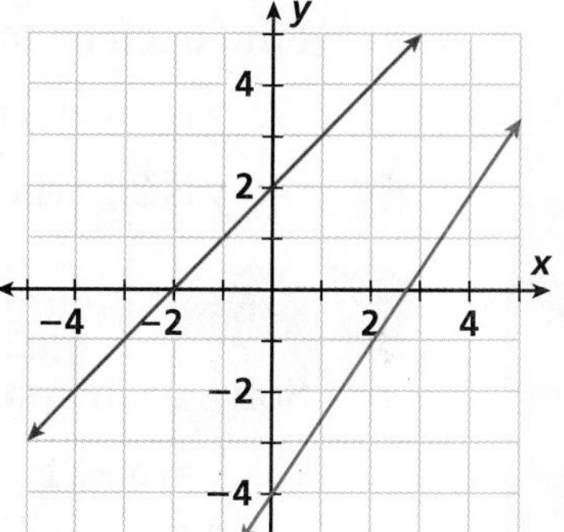

22. **Write About It** The points (2, −2) and (4, −4) are solutions of a system of linear equations. Make a conjecture about the equations and the graph.

23. **Challenge** Graph the system of inequalities $y \leq 3x + 1$ and $y > x + 2$. Test a point in each regions formed in both inequalities. Shade the solution region.

Test Prep

24. **Multiple Choice** Which statement describes the solution of a system of linear equations for two lines with the same slope and different y-intercepts?

Ⓐ one nonzero solution Ⓒ infinitely many solutions

Ⓑ no solution Ⓓ solution of 0

25. **Gridded Response** What is the x-value of the solution to the system of equations?

$y = 4x - 4$
$6x + y = 1$

CHAPTER 8 SECTION B

Ready To Go On?

Learn It Online
Resources Online

Quiz for Lessons 5 and 6

5 Direct Variation

1. The table shows an employee's pay per number of hours worked. Make a graph to determine whether the data sets show direct variation.

Hours Worked	0	1	2	3	4	5	6
Pay ($)	0	8.50	17.00	25.50	34.00	42.50	51.00

Find each equation of direct variation, given that *y* varies directly with *x*.

2. y is 10 when x is 2
3. y is 16 when x is 4
4. y is 2.5 when x is 2.5
5. y is 2 when x is 8

6 Solving Systems of Linear Equations by Graphing

Solve each system of linear equations by graphing. Check your answer.

6. $y = x - 1$
   $y = 2x - 3$
7. $y = 3x + 2$
   $y = 3x - 2$
8. $3x + y = 7$
   $2x - 5y = -1$
9. $y - 1 = 2x$
   $-y = -2x - 1$
10. $2y = 8$
    $3y = 2x + 6$
11. $2y - 4x = -6$
    $y = 2x$

12. A balloon begins rising from the ground at the rate of 4 meters per second at the same time a parachutist's chute opens at a height of 200 meters. The parachutist descends at 6 meters per second. Graph to find the time it will take for them to be at the same height and find that height.

13. A system of linear equations is graphed at right. What is the solution of the system?

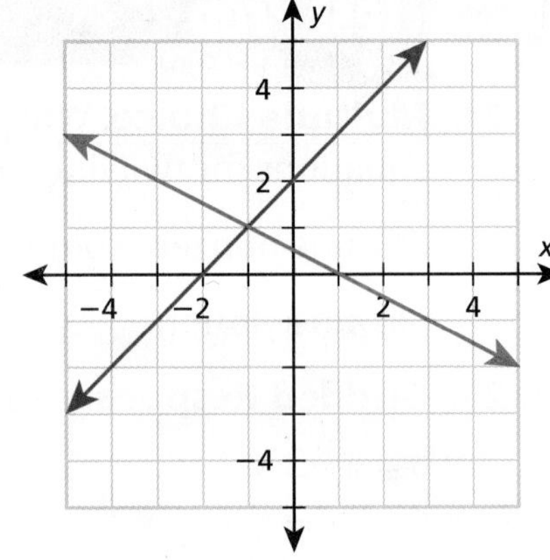

Ready to Go On?

Real-World CONNECTIONS

MATHEMATICAL PRACTICES Reason abstractly and quantitatively.

Beckley Exhibition Coal Mine Coal mining has played an important role in the history of West Virginia, and there is no better place to learn about it than the Beckley Exhibition Coal Mine. A working mine until 1910, the site now features a tour that takes visitors 1500 feet below ground in authentic mine cars.

WEST VIRGINIA

Beckley

Miners were paid by the amount of coal they produced. Use the table about typical miner wages for Problems 1–3.

1. Do the data in the table show direct variation? Explain.
2. Write an equation that gives the wages y for a miner who produced x tons of coal.
3. Graph the equation and tell whether it is linear.

Typical Coal Miner Wages in 1910		
Miner	Weight of Coal (Tons)	Wages
A	3	\$1.35
B	5	\$2.25
C	2	\$0.90
D	4	\$1.80

4. A historian collects data on typical monthly wages for coal miners in 1910. Then she makes a graph of the data, with the number of months on the x-axis and the wages on the y-axis. The line passes through the points (3, 183) and (5, 305).

   a. What is the slope of the line? What does the slope represent?

   b. What is the equation of the line?

   c. What is the y-intercept of the line? What does the y-intercept represent?

   d. Use the equation to find the wages of a miner who worked for 9 months.

Visitors take a tour of the coal mine.

Real-World Connections

Game Time

Graphing in Space

You can graph a point in two dimensions using a coordinate plane with an x- and a y-axis. Each point is located using an ordered pair (x, y). In three dimensions, you need three coordinate axes, and each point is located using an ordered triple (x, y, z).

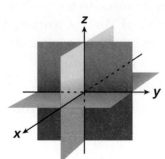

To graph a point, move along the x-axis the number of units of the x-coordinate. Then move left or right the number of units of the y-coordinate. Then move up or down the number of units of the z-coordinate.

Plot each point in three dimensions.

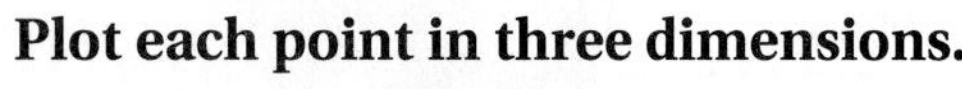

1. $(1, 2, 5)$
2. $(-2, 3, -2)$
3. $(4, 0, 2)$

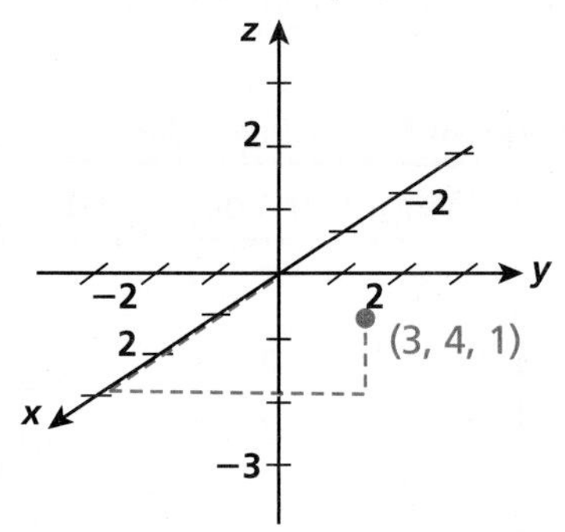

The graph of the equation $y = 2$ in three dimensions is a plane that is perpendicular to the y-axis and is two units to the right of the origin.

Describe the graph of each plane in three dimensions.

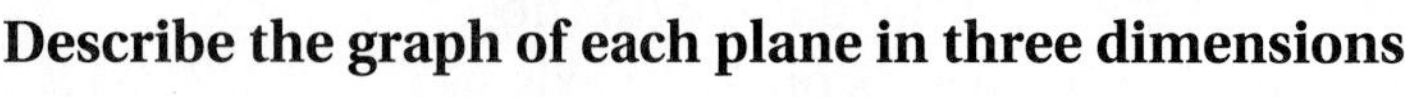

4. $x = 3$
5. $z = 1$
6. $y = -1$

Line Solitaire

Roll a red and a blue number cube to generate the coordinates of points on a coordinate plane. The x-coordinate of each point is the number on the red cube, and the y-coordinate is the number on the blue cube. Generate seven ordered pairs and plot the points on the coordinate plane. Then try to write the equations of three lines that divide the plane into seven regions so that each point is in a different region.

Jenny Thomas/HMH

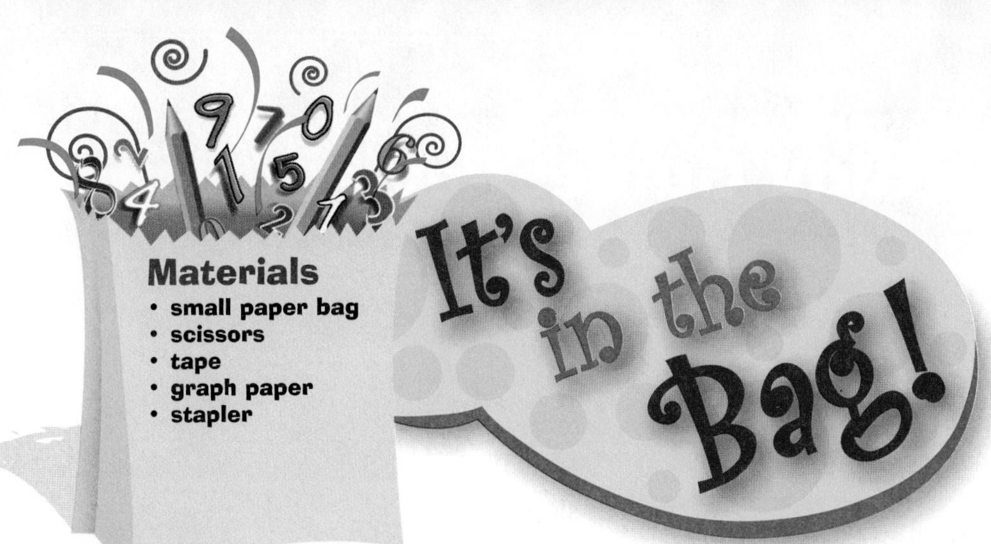

PROJECT Graphing Tri-Fold

Use this organizer to hold notes, vocabulary, and practice problems related to graphing.

Directions

1. Hold the bag flat with the flap facing you at the bottom. Fold up the flap. Cut off the part of the bag above the flap. **Figure A**

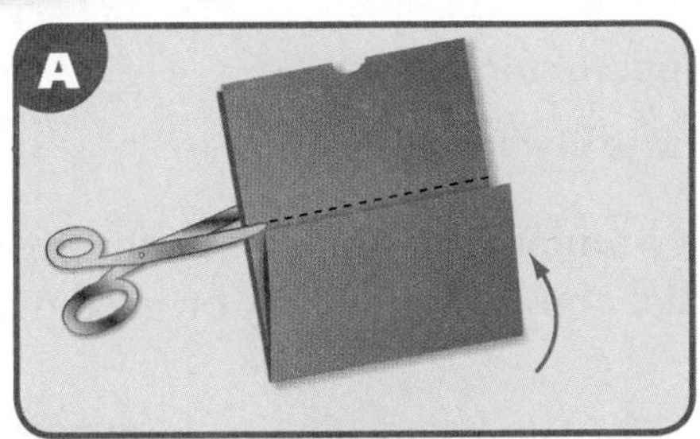

2. Unfold the bag. Cut down the middle of the top layer of the bag until you get to the flap. Then cut across the bag just above the flap, again cutting only the top layer of the bag. **Figure B**

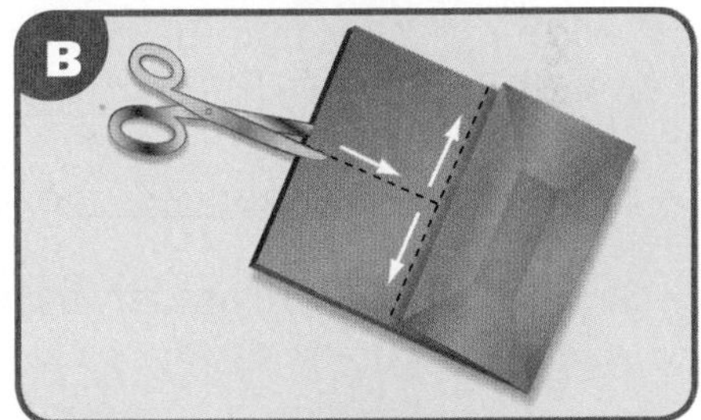

3. Open the bag. Cut away the sides at the bottom of the bag. These sections are shaded in the figure. **Figure C**

4. Unfold the bag. There will be three equal sections at the bottom of the bag. Fold up the bottom section and tape the sides to create a pocket. **Figure D**

5. Trim several pieces of graph paper to fit in the middle section of the bag. Staple them to the bag to make a booklet.

Taking Note of the Math

Write definitions of vocabulary words behind the "doors" at the top of your organizer. Graph sample linear equations on the graph paper. Use the pocket at the bottom of the organizer to store notes on the chapter.

Study Guide: Review

Vocabulary

constant of variation	rise
direct variation	run
linear equation	slope
linear inequality	slope-intercept form
point-slope form	x-intercept
rate of change	y-intercept

Complete the sentences below with vocabulary words from the list above. Words may be used more than once.

1. The x-coordinate of the point where a line crosses the x-axis is its __?__, and the y-coordinate of the point where the line crosses the y-axis is its __?__.
2. $y = mx + b$ is the __?__ of a line, and $y - y_1 = m(x - x_1)$ is the __?__.
3. Two variables related by a constant ratio are in __?__.

EXAMPLES

1 Graphing Linear Equations

■ **Graph $y = x - 2$. Tell whether it is linear.**

x	$x - 2$	y	(x, y)
−1	−1 − 2	−3	(−1, −3)
0	0 − 2	−2	(0, −2)
1	1 − 2	−1	(1, −1)
2	2 − 2	0	(2, 0)

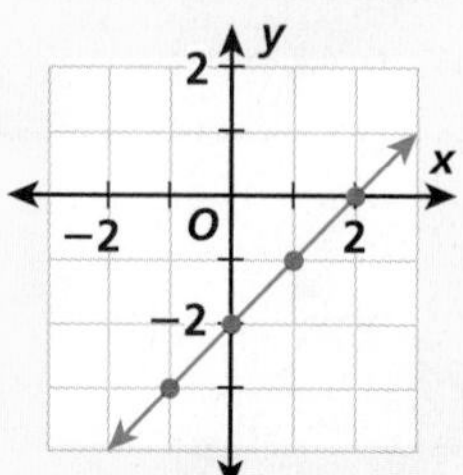

$y = x - 2$ is linear; its graph is a line.

EXERCISES

Graph each equation and tell whether it is linear.

4. $y = 4x - 2$
5. $y = 2 - 3x$
6. $y = -2x^2$
7. $y = 2x^3$
8. $y = -x^3$
9. $y = 2x$
10. $y = \frac{12}{x}$ for $x \neq 0$
11. $y = -\frac{10}{x}$ for $x \neq 0$

EXAMPLES

EXERCISES

2 Slope of a Line

■ **Find the slope of the line that passes through (−1, 2) and (1, 3).**

Let (x_1, y_1) be (−1, 2) and (x_2, y_2) be (1, 3).

$$\frac{y_2 - y_1}{x_2 - x_1} = \frac{3-2}{1-(-1)}$$
$$= \frac{1}{2}$$

The slope of the line that passes through (−1, 2) and (1, 3) is $\frac{1}{2}$.

Find the slope of the line that passes through each pair of points.

12. (4, 2) and (8, 5)

13. (4, 3) and (5, −1)

14. (3, 3) and (−2, −3)

15. (−1, 2) and (5, −4)

16. (−3, −3) and (−4, −2)

17. (−2, −3) and (0, 0)

18. (−5, 7) and (−1, −2)

19. The equation $v = -1.75n + 50$ represents the value remaining on a debit card after n smoothies have been purchased. Graph the equation and explain the meaning of the slope and y-intercept in the problem.

3 Using Slopes and Intercepts

■ **Write $3x + 4y = 12$ in slope-intercept form. Identify the slope and y-intercept.**

$3x + 4y = 12$

$4y = -3x + 12$ *Subtract 3x from both sides.*

$\frac{4y}{4} = \frac{-3x}{4} + \frac{12}{4}$ *Divide both sides by 4.*

$y = -\frac{3}{4} + 3$ *slope-intercept form*

$m = -\frac{3}{4}$ and $b = 3$

Write each equation in slope-intercept form. Identify the slope and y-intercept.

20. $3y = 4x + 15$

21. $5y = 6x - 10$

22. $2x + 3y = 12$

23. $4y - 7x = 12$

Write the equation of the line that passes through each pair of points in slope-intercept form.

24. (0, 4) and (−1, 1)

25. (−1, 5) and (2, −4)

26. (6, 5) and (−3, 8)

27. (3, −1) and (−1, −3)

4 Point-Slope Form

■ **Write the point-slope form of the line with slope −4 that passes through (3, −2).**

$y - y_1 = m(x - x_1)$

$y - (-2) = -4(x - 3)$ *Substitute 3 for x_1,*

$y + 2 = -4(x - 3)$ *−2 for y_1, −4 for m.*

In point-slope form, the equation of the line with slope −4 that passes through (3, −2) is $y + 2 = -4(x - 3)$.

Write the point-slope form of each line with the given conditions.

28. slope 2, passes through (3, 4)

29. slope −4, passes through (−2, 3)

30. slope $-\frac{5}{6}$, passes through (0, −3)

31. slope $\frac{2}{7}$, passes through (0, 0)

Study Guide: Review

EXAMPLES

EXERCISES

5 Direct Variation

■ **y varies directly with x, and y is 32 when x is 4. Write the equation of direct variation.**

$y = kx$	*y varies directly with x.*
$32 = k \cdot 4$	*Substitute 4 for x and 32 for y.*
$8 = k$	*Solve for k.*
$y = 8x$	*Substitute 8 for k in the original equation.*

y varies directly with x. Write the equation of direct variation for each set of conditions.

32. y is 42 when x is 7

33. y is 78 when x is 6

34. y is 8 when x is 56

6 Solving Systems of Linear Equations by Graphing

■ **Solve the linear system by graphing. Check your answer.**

$4y - 12 = x$

$4y = 3x + 1$

Solve both equations for y.

$4y - 12 = x$ $4y = 3x + 4$

$4y = x + 12$ $\frac{4y}{4} = \frac{3x}{4} + \frac{4}{4}$

$\frac{4y}{4} = \frac{x}{4} + \frac{12}{4}$ $y = \frac{3x}{4} + 1$

$y = \frac{x}{4} + 3$

The solution appears to be (4, 4).

Check.

$\frac{x}{4} + 3 \stackrel{?}{=} \frac{3x}{4} + 1$

$\frac{4}{4} + 3 \stackrel{?}{=} \frac{3(4)}{4} + 1$

$1 + 3 \stackrel{?}{=} 3 + 1$

$4 = 4$ ✓

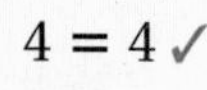

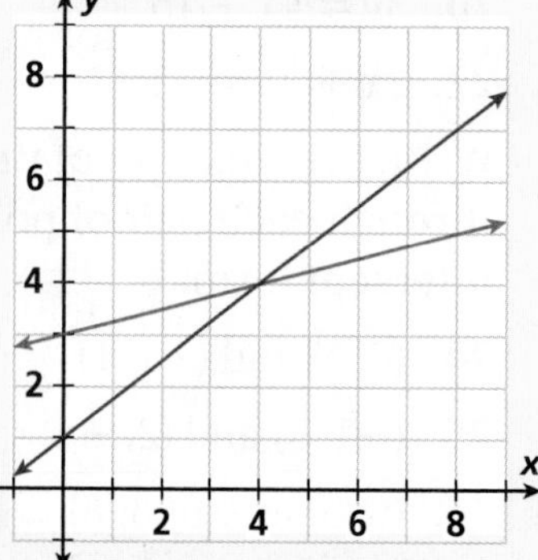

Solve the linear system by graphing. Check your answer.

35. $x = y + 2$
$y = 2x$

36. $3 - 2x = y$
$y = 3x - 2$

37. $2y + 2x = 6$
$y = -x$

38. $x = -y + 4$
$y - 4 = -x$

Graph each equation and tell whether it is linear.

1. $y = x + 2$
2. $y = -2x$
3. $y = -2x^2$
4. $y = 0.5x + 1$

Find the slope of the line that passes through each pair of points.

5. $(0, -8)$ and $(-1, -10)$
6. $(0, -2)$ and $(-5, 0)$
7. $(3, 1)$ and $(0, 3)$
8. Determine whether the graph shows a constant or variable rate of change.

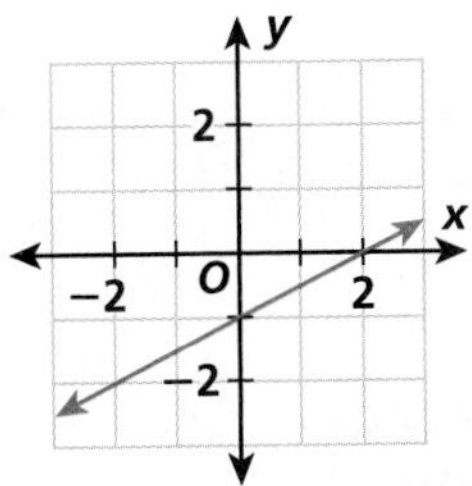

Write the equation of the line that passes through each pair of points in slope-intercept form.

9. $(-1, -6)$ and $(2, 6)$
10. $(0, 5)$ and $(3, -1)$
11. $(-6, -3)$ and $(12, 0)$

Use the point-slope form of each equation to identify a point the line passes through and the slope of the line.

12. $y - 4 = -2(x + 7)$
13. $y + 2.4 = 2.1(x - 1.8)$
14. $y + 8 = -6(x - 9)$

Write the point-slope form of the equation with the given slope that passes through the indicated point.

15. slope -2, passing through $(-4, 1)$
16. slope 3, passing through $(2, 0)$

Find each equation of direct variation, given that *y* varies directly with *x*.

17. y is 225 when x is 25
18. y is 0.1875 when x is 0.25
19. x is 13 when y is 91
20. **a.** A dragonfly can beat its wings 30 times per second. Write and graph an equation showing the relationship between flying time and the number of times the dragonfly beats its wings.
    b. Do the equation and graph represent a direct variation? Explain.

Solve each system of linear equations by graphing. Check your answer.

21. $y = x + 1$
    $x = y + 1$
22. $y = 2x$
    $y = x - 2$
23. $3x + 2y = 12$
    $y = 6 - \frac{3}{2}x$

Chapter Test

Cumulative Assessment

Multiple Choice

1.

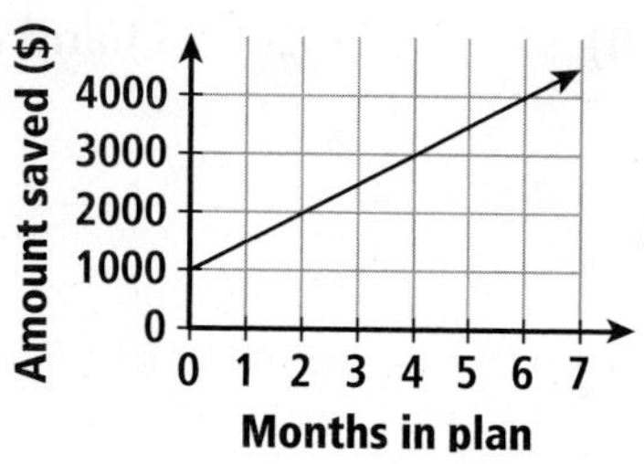

The line graph shows the activity of a savings account. What does the y-intercept represent?

Ⓐ Every month $1000 is deposited.

Ⓑ The initial deposit is $1000.

Ⓒ There is no initial deposit.

Ⓓ After the second month, there is $2000 in the savings account.

2. Which of the following is NOT a rational number?

Ⓕ $-\sqrt{196}$ Ⓗ $-\sqrt{10}$

Ⓖ $-5.8\overline{3}$ Ⓙ $-\frac{2}{3}$

3. What is the volume of a sphere whose surface area is 200.96 cm^2? Use 3.14 for π.

Ⓐ 50.24 cm^3 Ⓒ 267.95 cm^3

Ⓑ 133.98 cm^3 Ⓓ 803.84 cm^3

4. What is the slope of the line?
$6x + 2y = -7$

Ⓕ -7 Ⓗ 2

Ⓖ -3 Ⓙ 6

5. Between which two consecutive integers does the square root of 50 lie?

Ⓐ 6 and 7 Ⓒ 8 and 9

Ⓑ 7 and 8 Ⓓ 49 and 51

6. The graph of a line passes through the points (0, 4) and (−7, 0). What is the x-intercept of the graph?

Ⓕ -7 Ⓗ 0

Ⓖ -3 Ⓙ 4

7. Solve the system:
$x + y = 4$
$2x - y = -7$

Ⓐ (2, 2) Ⓒ (−3, 1)

Ⓑ (4, 1) Ⓓ (−1, 5)

8. What is the product written in scientific notation?
$(8.5 \times 10^{12})(9 \times 10^{12})$

Ⓕ 76.5×10^{24}

Ⓖ 7.65×10^{12}

Ⓗ 7.65×10^{25}

Ⓙ 76.5×10^{12}

9. A pyramid has a square base with side 10 m. The height of the pyramid is 9 m. What is the volume of the pyramid?

Ⓐ 300 m^3 Ⓒ 450 m^3

Ⓑ 325 m^3 Ⓓ 900 m^3

Remember that you can write both fractions and terminating decimals as answers for gridded-response test questions.

Gridded Response

10. What is the value of x so that the slope of the line passing through the points $(-1, 4)$ and $(x, 1)$ is $-\frac{3}{4}$?

11. If $\triangle JKL$ and $\triangle MNP$ are similar, what is the perimeter of $\triangle JKL$?

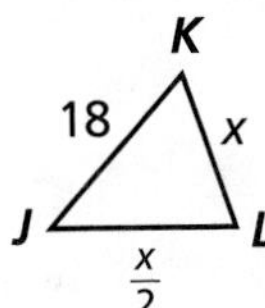

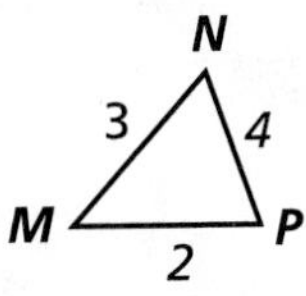

12. What is the slope of a line perpendicular to the line $y - 6 = -4(x + 8)$?

13. What is $f(-2)$ for the function $f(x) = -\frac{2}{3}x - \frac{7}{8}$?

14. For the linear function $y = 2x - 9$, find the value of x when $y = 3$.

15. A right triangle has legs that measure 1.5 cm and 2 cm. What is the length of the hypotenuse in cm?

Short Response

S1. Scientists have found that a linear equation can be used to model the relation between the outdoor temperature and the number of chirps per minute crickets make. If a snowy tree cricket makes 100 chirps/min at 63°F and 178 chirps/min at 77°F, at what approximate temperature does the cricket make 126 chirps/min? Show your work.

S2. Plot the points $A(-5, -4)$, $B(1, -2)$, $C(2, 3)$, and $D(-4, 1)$. Use straight segments to connect the four points in order. Then find the slope of each line segment. What special kind of quadrilateral is $ABCD$? Explain.

S3. Write an equation in slope-intercept form that has the same slope as $-6x - 3y = 3$ and the same y-intercept as $-3y + 5 = 9x + 5$. Tell whether your equation is a direct variation. Explain.

Extended Response

E1. Paul Revere had to travel 3.5 miles to Charlestown from Boston by boat. Assume that from Charlestown to Lexington, he was able to ride a horse that traveled at a rate of $\frac{1}{8}$ mile per minute. His total distance traveled y is the sum of the distance to Charlestown and the distance from Charlestown to Lexington.

a. Write a linear equation that could be used to find the distance y Paul Revere traveled in x minutes.

b. What does the slope of the line represent?

c. What does the y-intercept of the line represent?

d. Graph your equation from part **a** on a coordinate plane.

CHAPTER 9

Data, Prediction, and Linear Functions

		COMMON CORE
9A	**Data and Prediction**	
9-1	Scatter Plots	CC.8.SP.1
9-2	Linear Best Fit Models	CC.8.SP.3
LAB	Create a Scatter Plot	CC.8.SP.2
EXT	Patterns in Two-Way Tables	CC.8.SP.4
9B	**Linear Functions**	
9-3	Linear Functions	CC.8.F.1
9-4	Comparing Multiple Representations	CC.8.F.2

Chapter Focus

- Use models for data to make predictions.
- Identify, write, and use linear functions.

Why Learn This?

The winning times for races, such as the long hurdles, generally improve over time. You can use the data over several years to make a model that can help predict future winning times.

Learn It Online
Chapter Project Online

Are You Ready?

Vocabulary

Choose the best term from the list to complete each sentence.

1. An equation whose solutions fall on a line on a coordinate plane is called a(n) __?__.
2. When the equation of a line is written in the form $y = mx + b$, m represents the __?__ and b represents the __?__.
3. To write an equation of the line that passes through (1, 3) and has slope 2, you might use the __?__ of the equation of a line.

linear equation
point-slope form
slope
***x*-intercept**
***y*-intercept**

Complete these exercises to review skills you will need for this chapter.

Ordered Pairs

Give the coordinates and quadrant of each point.

4. A
5. B
6. C
7. D
8. E
9. F

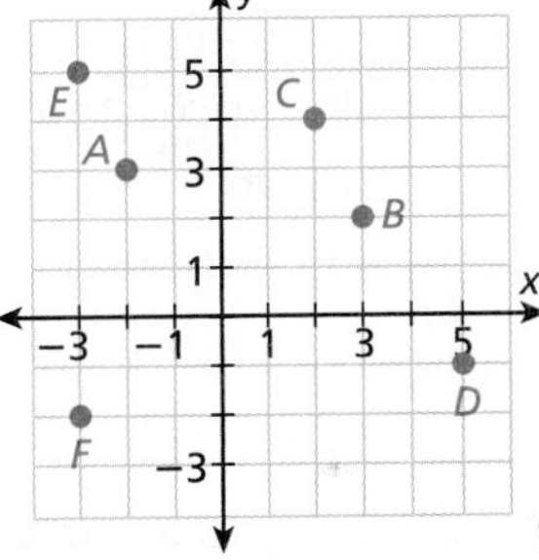

Evaluate Expressions

Evaluate each expression for the given values of the variables.

10. $a + (b - 1)c$ for $a = 6, b = 3, c = -4$
11. $a \cdot b^c$ for $a = -2, b = 4, c = 2$
12. $(ab)^c$ for $a = 3, b = -2, c = 2$
13. $-(a + b) + c$ for $a = -1, b = -4, c = -10$

Graph Linear Equations

Use the slope and the *y*-intercept to graph each line.

14. $y = \frac{2}{3}x + 4$
15. $y = -\frac{1}{2}x - 2$
16. $y = 3x + 1$
17. $2y = 3x - 8$
18. $3y + 2x = 6$
19. $x - 5y = 5$

CHAPTER 9

Study Guide: Preview

Where You've Been

Previously, you

- determined whether a relation is a function.
- wrote linear equations in different forms.
- graphed data to demonstrate relationships in familiar concepts.

In This Chapter

You will study

- finding and evaluating an algebraic expression to determine any term in an arithmetic sequence.
- using function rules to describe patterns in sequences.
- determining if a sequence can be arithmetic, geometric, or neither.
- identifying and graphing different types of functions.

Where You're Going

You can use the skills learned in this chapter

- to use compound interest rates to predict the interest earned on money invested in a savings account.
- to understand and explore topics in physics, such as waves, cycles, and frequencies.

Key Vocabulary/Vocabulario

clustering	arracimando
correlation	correlación
linear function	función lineal
line of best fit	línea de mejor ajuste
scatter plot	diagrama de dispersión

Vocabulary Connections

To become familiar with some of the vocabulary terms in the chapter, consider the following. You may refer to the chapter, the glossary, or a dictionary if you like.

1. *Cluster* can mean a group of things or people together. What do you think **clustering** of data points on a graph might be?
2. *Linear* means pertaining to or represented by lines. What do you think the graph of a **linear function** would look like?

Study Strategy: Use Multiple Representations

By using multiple representations to introduce a math concept, you can understand the concept more clearly. As you study, take note of the use of the tables, lists, graphs, diagrams, symbols, and words to help clarify concepts.

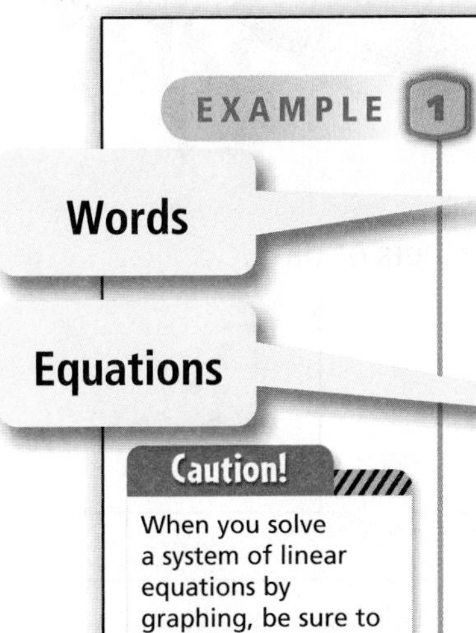

Caution!

When you solve a system of linear equations by graphing, be sure to check your solution algebraically. This is especially important when the solution is not an integer value.

EXAMPLE 1 Graphing a System of Linear Equations to Solve a Problem

A plane left Miami traveling 300 mi/h. After the plane had traveled 1200 miles, a jet started along the same route flying 500 mi/h. Graph the system of linear equations. How long after the jet takes off will it catch the plane? What distance will the jet have traveled?

Let t = time in hours the jet flies.
Let d = distance in miles the jet flies.
Plane distance: $d = 300t + 1200$
Jet distance: $d = 500t$

Graph each equation. The point of intersection appears to be (6, 3000).

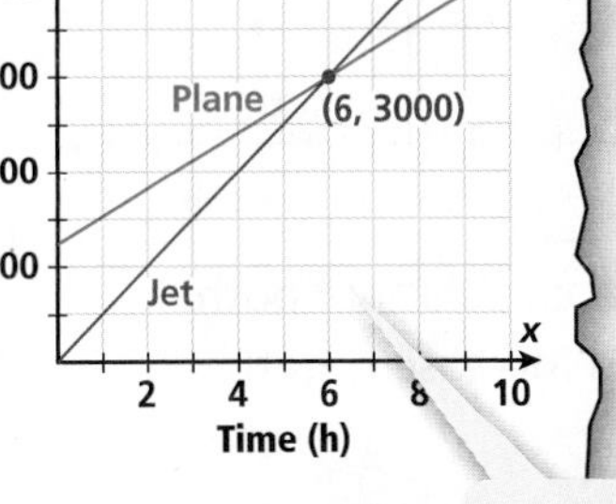

Check

$d = 300t + 1200$	$d = 500t$
$3000 \stackrel{?}{=} 300(6) + 1200$	$3000 \stackrel{?}{=} 500(6)$
$3000 = 3000$ ✔	$3000 = 3000$ ✔

Plane 2 will catch up after 6 hours in flight, 3000 miles from Miami.

Try This

Find a different representation for each relationship.

1. The area A of a certain rectangle is 48 cm^2. The base is 3 times longer than the height. What are the dimensions of the rectangle?

2.

x	−2	−1	0
y	0	1	2

3. $x = -2$

9-1 Scatter Plots

COMMON CORE

CC.8.SP.1: Construct and interpret scatter plots for bivariate measurement data to investigate patterns of association between two quantities. Describe patterns ... ***Also CC.8.SP.2***

Vocabulary

scatter plot

correlation

line of best fit

In many Olympic sports, athletes keep improving and setting new records. One way to show how the winning times have changed over time is by using a *scatter plot.*

A **scatter plot** is a graph with points plotted to show a relationship between two sets of data. You can use a scatter plot to investigate the relationship between the year in which an Olympic event is held and the winning time.

Correlation describes the relationship between two sets of data.

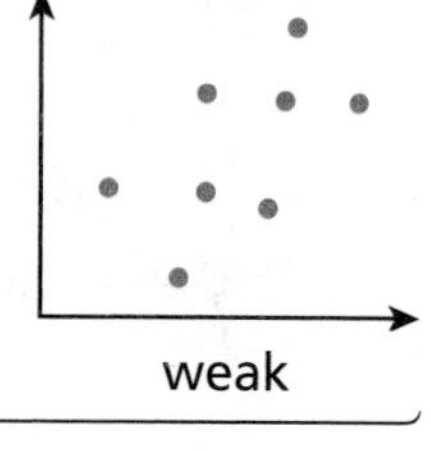

Positive correlation: both data sets increase together.

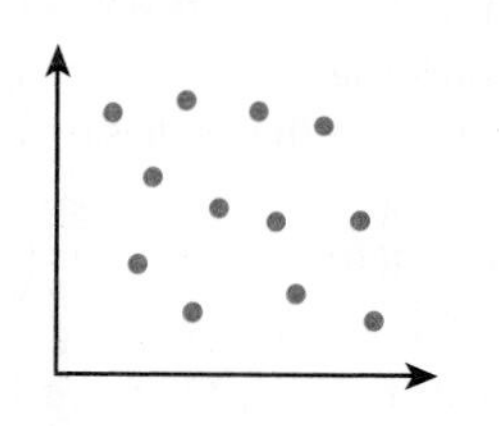

No correlation: changes in one data set do not affect the other data set.

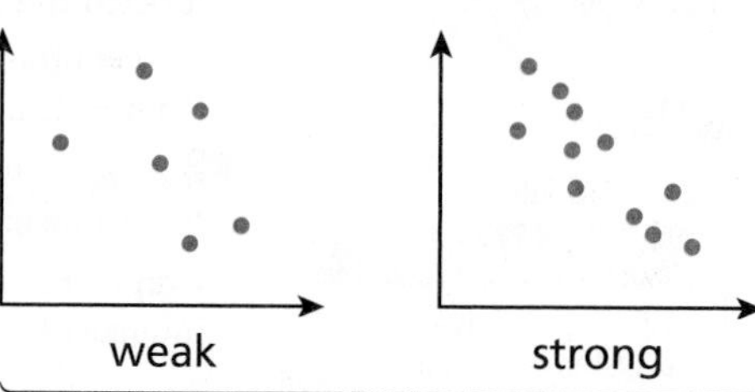

Negative correlation: as one data set increases, the other decreases.

EXAMPLE 1 Describing Correlation from Scatter Plots

The table shows the winning times for the Olympic women's 3000-meter speed skating race. Use the given data to make a scatter plot, and describe the correlation.

Years since 1976	4	8	12	16	18	22	26	30
Winning time (min)	4.54	4.41	4.20	4.33	4.29	4.12	3.96	4.04

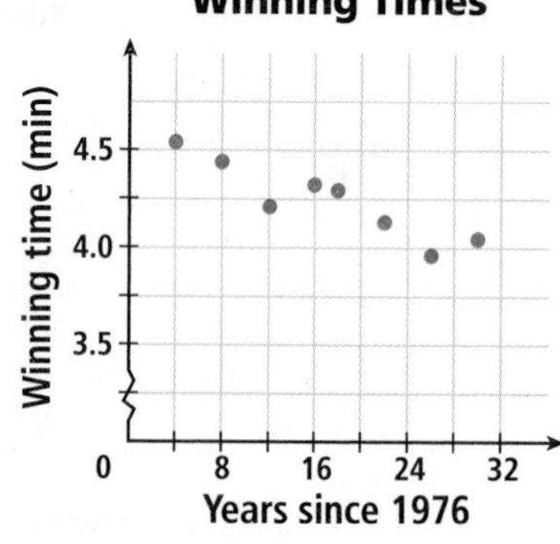

Use the table to make ordered pairs for the scatter plot.

The x-value represents the number of years since 1976, and the y-value represents the winning time.

Plot the ordered pairs.

As the number of years increases, the winning times tend to decrease. There is a negative correlation between the two data sets.

Helpful Hint

A strong correlation does not mean there is a cause-and-effect relationship. For example, your age and the price of a regular movie ticket are both increasing, so they are positively correlated.

Bob Thomas/Getty Images

A **line of best fit** is a straight line that comes closest to the points on a scatter plot. You can use a line of best fit to help you make predictions.

EXAMPLE 2 Using a Scatter Plot to Make Predictions

Make a scatter plot of the data, and draw a line of best fit. Then use the data to predict the exam grade of a student who studies 4 hours per week.

Hours studied	5	9	3	12	1	2	6	7
Exam grade	80	95	75	98	70	95	82	88

Step 1: Make a scatter plot.

Let hours studied represent the independent variable x and exam grade represent the dependent variable y.

A student's exam grade may be dependent on the number of hours studied.

Step 2: Draw a line of best fit.

Draw a line that has about the same number of points above and below it. Ignore any outliers when drawing a line of best fit.

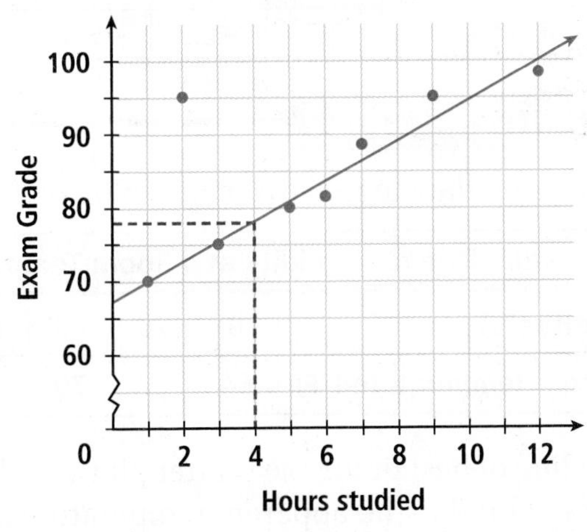

The data point (2, 95) is an outlier because it lies far away from the other data points.

Step 3: Make a prediction.

According to the graph, a student who studies 4 hours per week should earn a score of about 78.

Find the point on the line whose x-value is 4. The corresponding y-value is about 78.

Reading Math

A *trend line* is a line on a scatter plot that helps show the correlation between data sets more clearly. A line of best fit is a trend line.

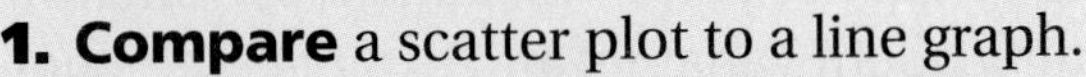

MATHEMATICAL PRACTICES

Think and Discuss

1. **Compare** a scatter plot to a line graph.
2. **Tell** how you can tell which variable to use as the independent variable and which variable to use as the dependent variable when making a scatter plot.

9-1 Exercises

Learn It Online
Homework Help Online
Exercises 1–4, 5, 9, 11

GUIDED PRACTICE

See Example 1

1. Use the given data to make a scatter plot, and describe the correlation.

Country	Area (mi^2)	Population
Guatemala	42,467	12,728,111
Honduras	43,715	7,483,763
El Salvador	8,206	6,948,073
Nicaragua	50,503	5,675,356
Costa Rica	19,929	4,133,884
Panama	30,498	3,242,173

See Example 2

2. Make a scatter plot of the data, and draw a line of best fit. Then use the data to predict the wind chill at 35 mi/h.

Apparent Temperature Due to Wind at 15 °F						
Wind speed (mi/h)	10	20	30	40	50	60
Wind chill (°F)	2.7	−2.3	−5.5	−7.9	−9.8	−11.4

INDEPENDENT PRACTICE

See Example 1

3. Use the given data to make a scatter plot, and describe the correlation.

Temperature Due to Humidity at a Room Temperature of 72 °F						
Humidity (%)	0	20	40	60	80	100
Apparent temperature (°F)	64	67	70	72	74	76

See Example 2

4. Draw a line of best fit for the scatter plot you drew in Exercise 3. Then use the data to predict the apparent temperature at 70% humidity.

PRACTICE AND PROBLEM SOLVING

Extra Practice
See Extra Practice for more exercises.

5. **Recreation** Use the data in the table.

High Temperatures and Swimming Pool Visitors							
High temperature (°F)	95	92	85	90	98	88	94
Pool visitors	312	305	256	124	352	270	320

a. Make a scatter plot of the data. Tell which variable you used for the independent variable, and explain your choice.

b. Which data point represents an outlier? Explain.

c. Predict the number of visitors to the swimming pool on a day when the high temperature is 100 °F. Explain how you determined your answer.

Life Science LINK

About 50 million Americans suffer from allergies. Airborne pollen generated by trees, grasses, plants, and weeds is a major cause of illness and disability. Because pollen grains are small and light, they can travel through the air for hundreds of miles. Pollen levels are measured in grains per cubic meter.

Some common substances that cause allergies include pollens, dust mites, and mold spores.

6. Use the given data to make a scatter plot. Describe the correlation.

Pollen Levels

Day	Weed Pollen	Grass Pollen
1	350	16
2	51	1
3	49	9
4	309	3
5	488	29
6	30	3
7	65	12

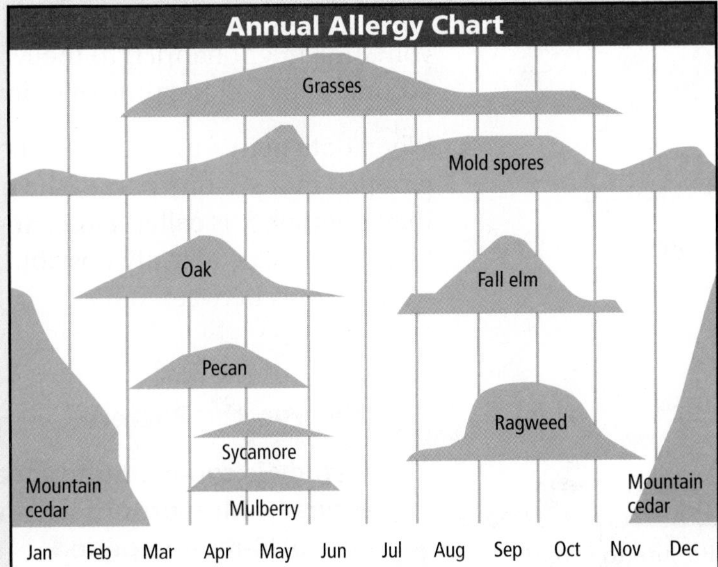

Source: Central Texas Allergy and Asthma Center

7. Explain how the pollens are compared in the chart at right.

Use the chart at right to determine if the pollens have a positive, a negative, or no correlation.

8. mountain cedar, grass

9. fall elm, ragweed

10. **Challenge** Use the allergy chart to explain the difference between correlation and a cause-and-effect relationship.

Test Prep

11. Multiple Choice Does the size of a box of cereal and the price of the cereal have a positive, negative, or no correlation?

Ⓐ Positive Ⓑ Negative Ⓒ Scatter plot Ⓓ No correlation

12. Short Response What type of correlation exists between a person's birthday and his or her height? Explain.

9-2 Linear Best Fit Models

COMMON CORE

CC.8.SP.3: Use the equation of a linear model to solve problems in the context of bivariate measurement data, interpreting the slope and intercept. ***Also CC.8.SP.1, CC.8.SP.2***

Have you ever noticed how some people can type really well without even looking at the keys? What do you think might happen to their accuracy after a long time of typing?

Vocabulary

clustering

When data points in a scatter plot are grouped more in one part of the graph than another, it is called **clustering**. Clustering helps identify possible relationships between data.

EXAMPLE 1 Observe the Pattern

Helpful Hint

Be sure to consider outliers when making predictions or drawing conclusions from data. One outlier can greatly change some statistical measures.

A study is conducted to measure the effect of fatigue on typing accuracy. Measures of accuracy are recorded every five minutes over a 40-minute period.

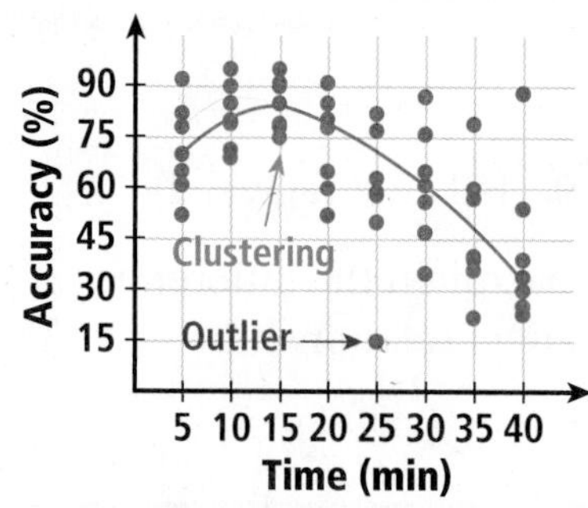

A Describe the pattern.
The scatter plot appears to have a non-linear pattern of association, which means that the points do *not* appear follow a linear pattern. In fact, the points appear to follow a curved pattern.

B Identify any clustering.
There appears to be clustering of the data points at 10 and 15 minutes. After 15 minutes, the results become less clustered.

C Identify any possible outliers.
There appears to be an outlier data point at 25 minutes. Another possible outlier is at 40 minutes.

For data that appear to have a linear pattern of association, you can use a line of best fit to make predictions. The predictions, however, are only good if the model is a good fit. In Example 2, you learn to assess a line of best fit.

EXAMPLE 2 Assessing the Line of Best Fit

Compare the given scatter plots of data and their lines of best fit. Tell which model better fits the data. Explain your answer.

Graph A

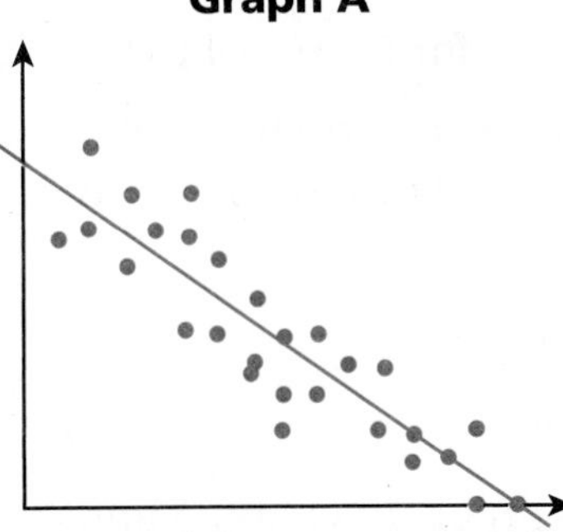

Graph B

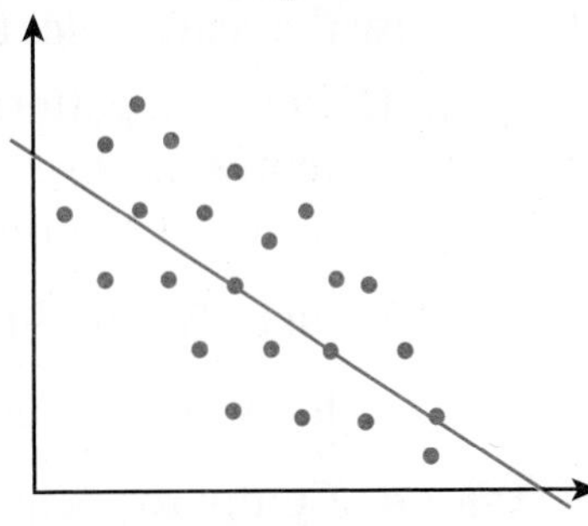

Both scatter plots show data sets that have a negative correlation.

The points in Graph A are closer to the line of best fit than in Graph B. So the linear model in Graph A fits the data better than the linear model in Graph B.

EXAMPLE 3 *Economics Application*

Estimate an equation for the line of best fit, and tell what the slope and *y*-intercept represent in terms of the data it models.

Draw an estimated line of best fit through the points and write its equation.

$$y = 8.7x + 8$$

A slope of 8.7 indicates that salary would increase by $8,700 for each additional year of post high school education that one receives.

A *y*-intercept of 8 indicates that with no post high school education, an annual salary would begin at about $8,000.

Post High School Education and Salary

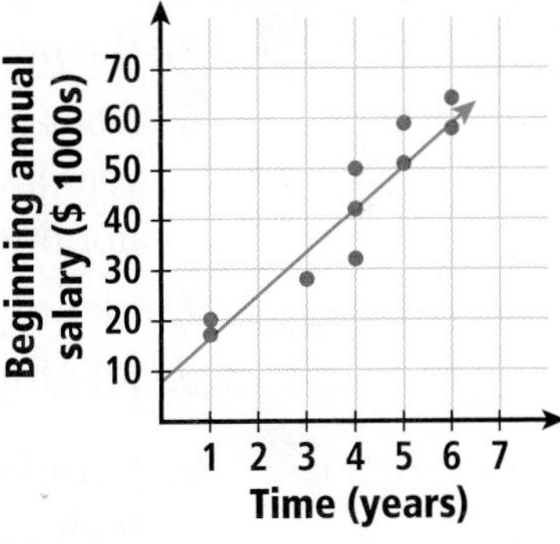

MATHEMATICAL PRACTICES

Think and Discuss

1. Explain the difference between a line of best fit that indicates a positive correlation between data and one that indicates a negative correlation between data in a scatterplot.

9-2 Exercises

GUIDED PRACTICE

See Example 1

Use the scatter plot at right for Exercises 1–3.

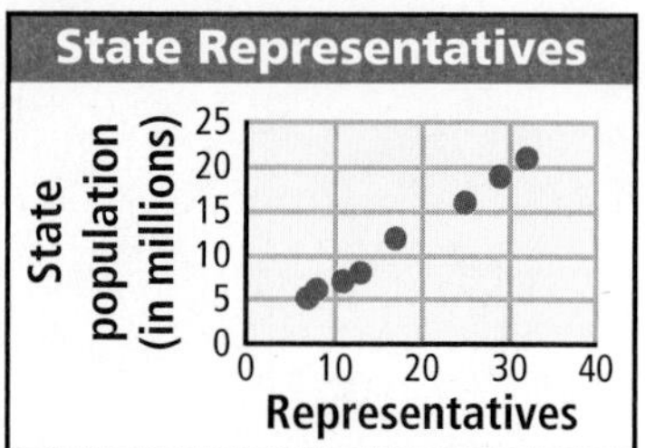

1. Does the pattern of association between representatives and population appear to be linear or nonlinear?
2. Identify any clustering.
3. Identify any possible outliers.

See Example 2

4. Compare the scatter plots in Graph A and Graph B and their lines of best fit. Tell which model better fits the data. Explain your answer.

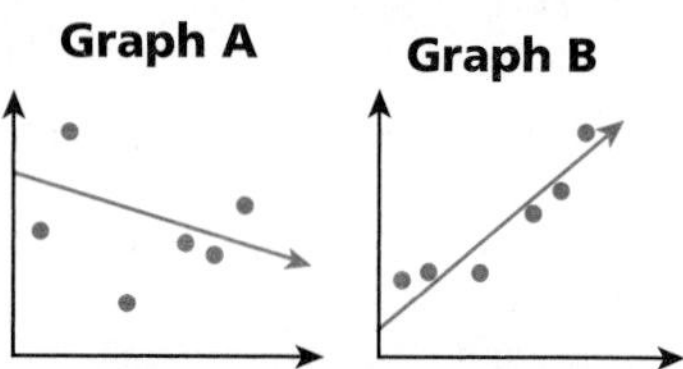

See Example 3

5. Find an equation for the line of best fit, and tell what the slope and y-intercept represent in terms of the data it models.

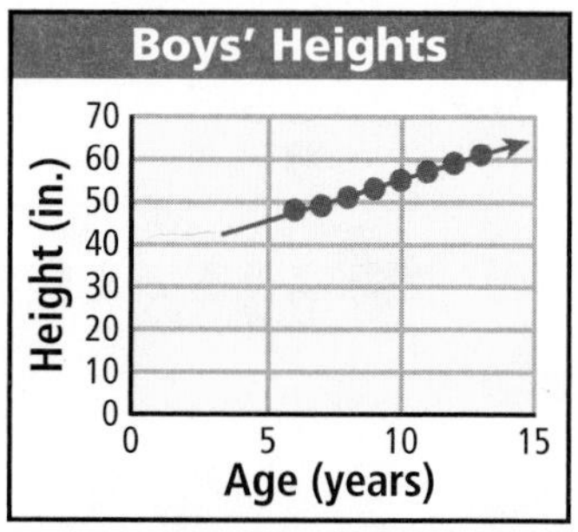

INDEPENDENT PRACTICE

See Example 1

Use the population scatter plot for Exercises 6–8.

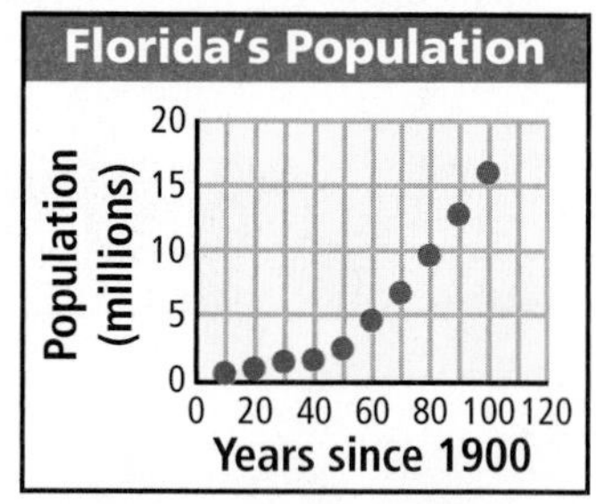

6. Does the pattern of association between year and population appear to be linear or nonlinear?
7. Identify any clustering.
8. Identify any possible outliers.

See Example 2

9. Compare the given scatter plots of data and their lines of best fit. Tell which model better fits the data. Explain your answer.

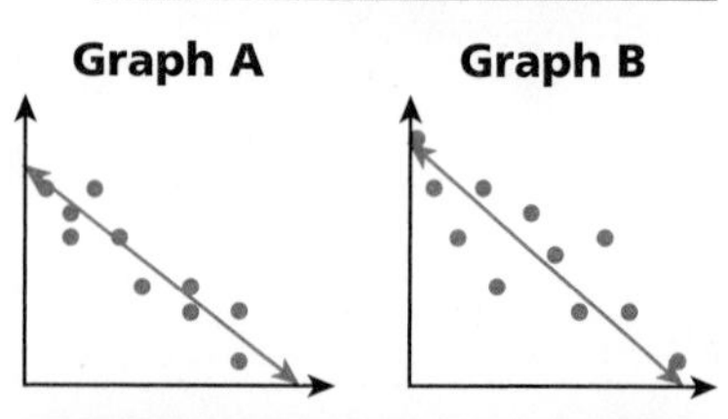

See Example 3

10. Find an equation for the line of best fit, and tell what the slope and y-intercept represent in terms of the data it models.

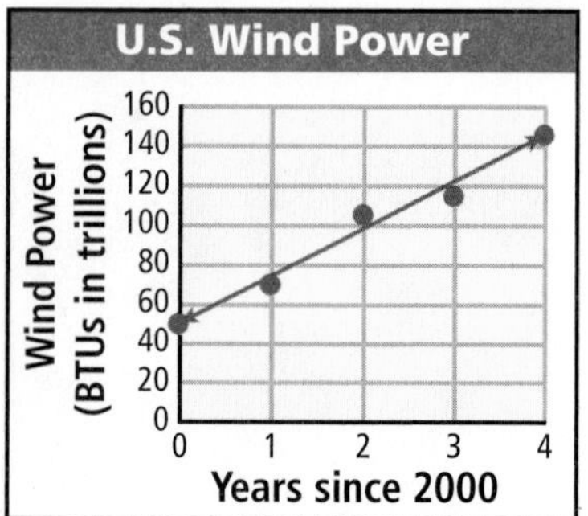

PRACTICE AND PROBLEM SOLVING

Extra Practice

See Extra Practice for more exercises.

Entertainment

People buy small toys, like the plastic whistles shown, by the thousands so they can pay a very low price for the toys. Then they sell the toys in smaller quantities for a much greater price.

Entertainment The scatter plot shows data for the number of small toys sold x and price y per toy.

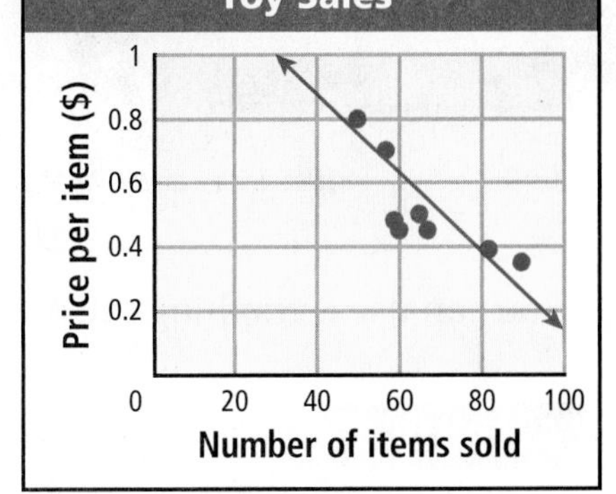

11. Identify any clustering.

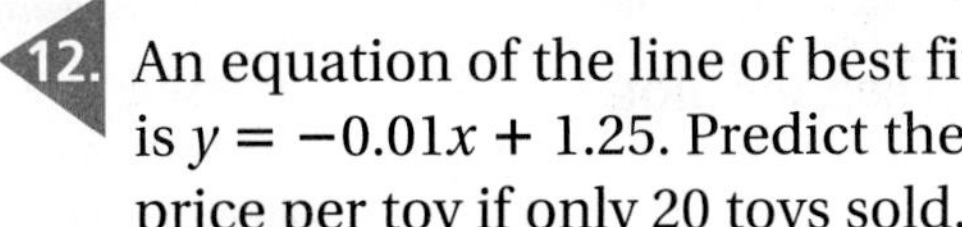

12. An equation of the line of best fit is $y = -0.01x + 1.25$. Predict the price per toy if only 20 toys sold.

Use the scatter plot for Exercises 13–16.

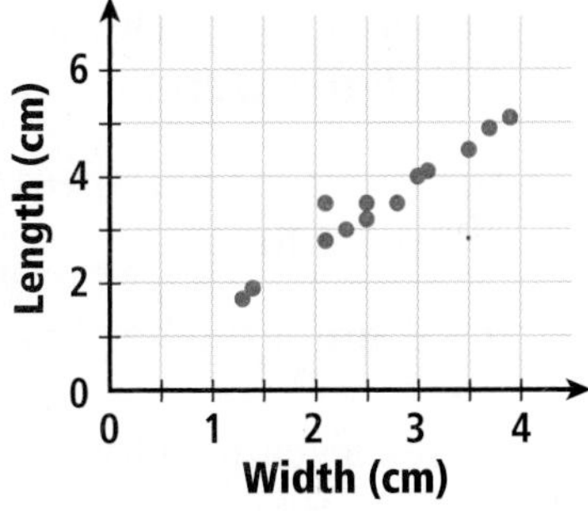

13. Identify any possible outliers.

14. Identify any clustering.

15. Is the correlation positive or negative?

16. Predict the length for a 3-cm width.

17. **Write About It** Describe a situation in which there is a linear relationship and a situation in which the variables would have a nonlinear relationship.

18. **Challenge** Describe a situation in which there is a linear relationship modeled with a line of best fit having a slope of about -2.

Test Prep

19. **Multiple Choice** Which equation best represents a line of best fit for the following scatter plot of data?

Ⓐ $y = -20x + 60$ Ⓒ $y = 2x + 60$

Ⓑ $y = -2x + 60$ Ⓓ $y = 20x + 60$

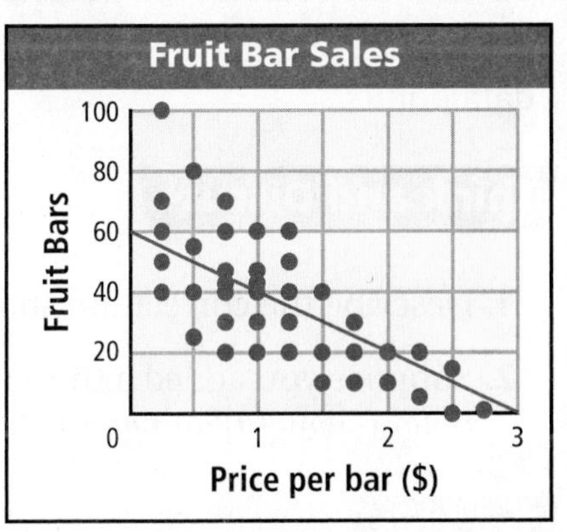

20. **Short Answer** Interpret the meaning of the rate of change and y-intercept of the line of best fit in terms of the situation in models in Exercise 19.

Technology LAB Create a Scatter Plot

Use with Scatter Plots

Use appropriate tools strategically.

You can use a graphing calculator to make a scatter plot.

CC.8.SP.2: ... For scatter plots that suggest a linear association, informally fit a straight line, and informally assess the model fit by judging the closeness of the data points to the line. ***Also CC.8.SP.1***

Activity 1

The table shows heights and weights of students in Mr. Devany's class. Use a graphing calculator to create a scatter plot of the data.

Height (in.)	Weight (lb)
41	92
43	111
46	105
50	120
51	110
55	107
60	125
62	125
62	125
66	152
69	175
70	210

To enter the data, press STAT and select **1:Edit.**

In L1, enter the heights. In L2, enter the weights.

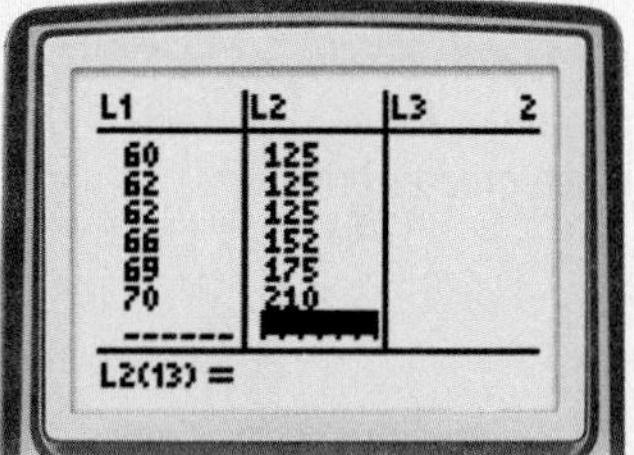

To see a scatter plot of the data,

press 2nd [STAT PLOT] Y= ENTER to select "STAT PLOTS 1:"

Scroll and press ENTER to select "On" and the scatter plot icon. Scroll to "Xlist=" and

press 2nd [L1] 1 to select List 1.

Scroll to "Ylist=" and press 2nd [L2] 2 to select List 2. Finally, scroll to "Mark:" and choose the box.

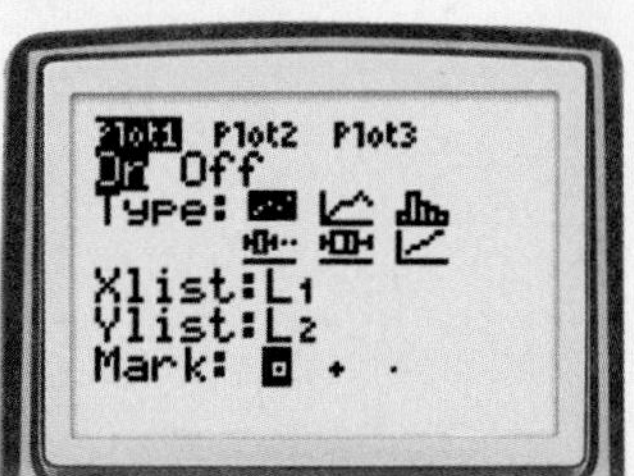

To view the scatter plot, press ZOOM and select **9: Zoom Stat.**
Press TRACE and the arrow keys to read the coordinates of the data points.

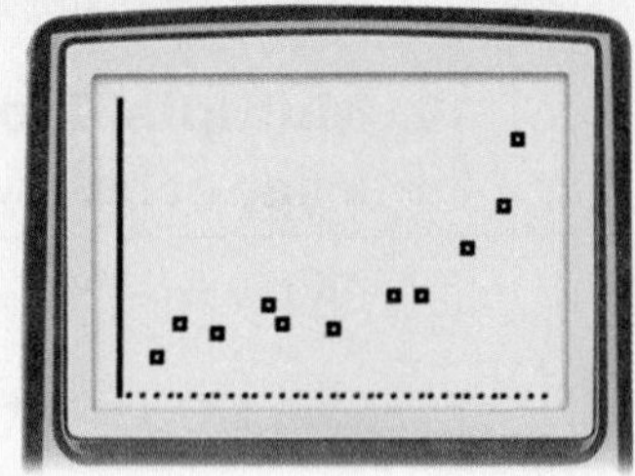

Think and Discuss

1. Describe the correlation shown in the scatter plot.
2. Suppose you added a third category: boy or girl. How could the height, weight, and gender data be displayed?

Try This

Use a graphing calculator to create a scatter plot of the data.

1.

x	52	36	13	41	39	52	18	50	44	30	51
y	10	15	27	15	12	9	27	10	11	21	4

Activity 2

You can use a graphing calculator to find a line of best fit on a scatter plot.

x	y
2	26.1
4	21.5
6	17.4
8	13.2
10	11.7
12	8.5
14	4.2
16	1.9

Create a scatter plot of the data shown. Use a line of best fit to predict the value of y when $x = 11$.

Follow the steps in Activity 1 to make a scatter plot of the data.

To find a line of best fit, press STAT and move the cursor to the Calculate **(CALC)** menu. Select **4:LinReg(ax+b)** and press ENTER. The calculator displays the equation of a line of best fit.

To graph the line of best fit, press Y=. Then press VARS and select **5:Statistics.** Move the cursor to the **EQ** menu and select **1:RegEQ** to choose the equation of the line of best fit. To see the scatter plot and the graph of the line, press ZOOM and select **9:ZoomStat.**

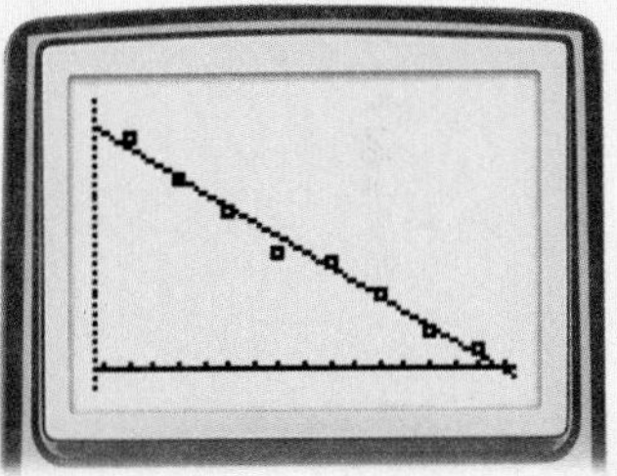

Use the Calculate menu to find the value of y when $x = 11$. Press 2nd CALC TRACE. Select **1: value.** Enter the value 11 for x, and press ENTER. The screen shows that $y \approx 9.68$ when $x = 11$.

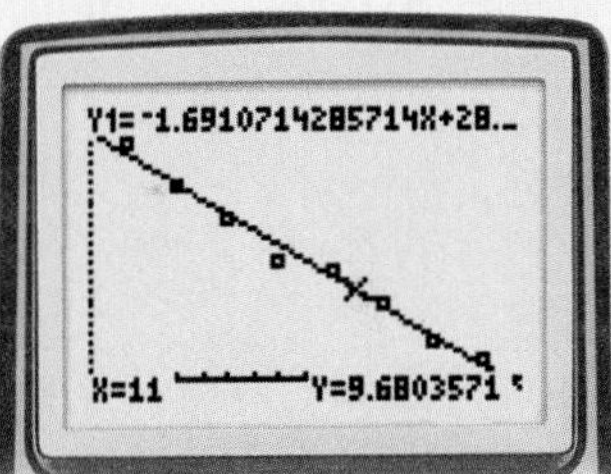

Think and Discuss

1. What uses might a line of best fit have in the real world?
2. What type of correlation does the data have in Activity 2? How do you know?

Try This

1. Use a graphing calculator to create a scatter plot of the data shown. Use a line of best fit to predict the value of y when $x = 8$.

x	0	5	10	15	20	25
y	0.8	15.2	32.4	46.3	60.1	74.4

2. Complete a table relating shoe size and shoe length in centimeters. Since female and male shoes are sized differently, collect data from female students only or from male students only. Create a scatter plot of your data. Then use a line of best fit to predict the length of a typical size 8 shoe.

EXTENSION Patterns in Two-Way Tables

COMMON CORE

CC.8.SP.4: Understand that patterns of association can also be seen in bivariate categorical data by displaying frequencies and relative frequencies in a two-way table. Construct and interpret a two-way table … Use relative frequencies calculated for rows or columns …

You have seen how to use scatter plots to examine two-variable data. You can also examine two-variable data in a *two-way table.* A **two-way table** displays two-variable data by organizing it into rows and columns.

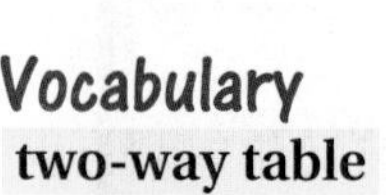

Vocabulary
two-way table

EXAMPLE 1

Constructing a Two-Way Table

Marisa took a survey of 100 pet owners to find out whether cats and dogs preferred being inside or outside during the day.

Construct a two-way table for the results.

- **35 out of 50 cats prefer being inside.**
- **20 out of 50 dogs prefer being inside.**

Identify the two variables, and create the rows and columns for them. Then use the information given to complete the table.

Pet		Preference: Inside	Preference: Outside	*Total*
Pet	Cats	35	15	50
Pet	Dogs	20	30	50
	Total	55	45	100

The variables are pets and preference.
There are 50 cats.
There are 50 dogs.

Notice that the totals, or cumulative frequencies, allow you to see that the sample of the survey was evenly distributed among the pet variables (dogs and cats).

Finally, include the relative frequencies with each of the results in the two-way table.

Pet		Preference: Inside	Preference: Outside	*Total*
Pet	Cats	$35\left(\frac{35}{50} = 70\%\right)$	$15\left(\frac{15}{50} = 30\%\right)$	$50\left(\frac{50}{100} = 50\%\right)$
Pet	Dogs	$20\left(\frac{20}{50} = 40\%\right)$	$30\left(\frac{30}{50} = 60\%\right)$	$50\left(\frac{50}{100} = 50\%\right)$
	Total	$55\left(\frac{55}{100} = 55\%\right)$	$45\left(\frac{45}{100} = 45\%\right)$	100%

EXAMPLE 2 **Interpreting a Two-Way Table**

Use the two-way table from Example 1 to describe relationships that you can see in the data.

Preference

Pet	Inside	Outside	*Total*
Cats	35 $\left(\frac{35}{50} = 70\%\right)$	15 $\left(\frac{15}{50} = 30\%\right)$	50 $\left(\frac{50}{100} = 50\%\right)$
Dogs	20 $\left(\frac{20}{50} = 40\%\right)$	30 $\left(\frac{30}{50} = 60\%\right)$	50 $\left(\frac{50}{100} = 50\%\right)$
Total	55 $\left(\frac{55}{100} = 55\%\right)$	45 $\left(\frac{45}{100} = 45\%\right)$	100%

Since an equal number of cat and dog owners were suveyed, the percentages can be compared. Cats seem to prefer being inside (70% to 30%) and dogs prefer being outside (60% to 40%).

Think and Discuss

1. Compare the preference cats have of being inside to the preference dogs have of being outside, according to the two-way table from Example 1. Are the preferences equally strong?

Exercises

The two-way table shows the results from a survey of dog and cat owners about whether their pet prefers dry food or wet food.

1. Complete the two-way table by finding the cumulative frequencies and the percentages.
2. Does the two-way table show any difference in preferences between dogs and cats? Explain.

Food Preference

Pet	Dry	Wet	*Total*
Cats	10	30	
Dogs	20	20	
Total			

The data from a survey of 7th and 8th graders about their sports preferences is shown.

3. Complete the two-way table with cumulative frequencies and percentages. Then describe any relationship you see in the data.

Sports Preference

Class	Soccer	Basketball	*Total*
7th	15	15	
8th	45	45	
Total			

Quiz for Lessons 1 and 2

1 Scatter Plots

1. Use the given data of the estimated U.S. population to make a scatter plot, and describe the correlation.

Year	1998	1999	2000	2001	2002	2003	2004
Population (in millions)	270.2	272.7	282.2	285.1	287.9	290.8	293.7

2 Linear Best Fit Models

The scatter plot shows Jen's table tennis rating over time.

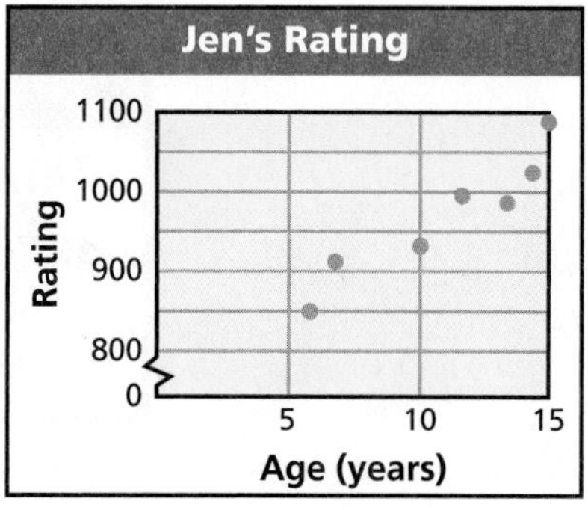

2. Find an equation for the line of best fit. What does the slope represent in terms of the data it models?
3. Use the line of best fit to predict Jen's table tennis rating at age 20.

Use the scatter plot at right for Exercises 4 and 5.

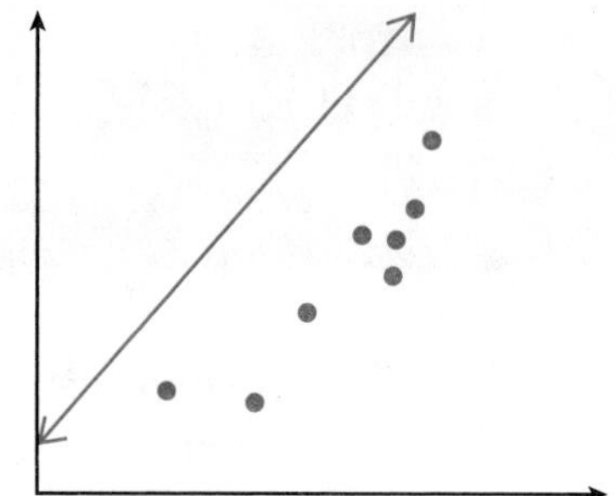

4. Describe the pattern of the data.
5. Is the line shown on the scatter plot a correct line of best fit? Explain.

Ready to Go On?

Make sense of problems and persevere in solving them.

Focus on Problem Solving

Make a Plan

- **Choose a method of computation**

When solving problems, you must decide which calculation method is best: paper and pencil, calculator, or mental math. Your decision will be based on many factors, such as the problem context, the numbers involved, and your own number sense. Use the following table as a guideline.

Paper and Pencil	Calculator	Mental Math
Use when solving multi-step problems so you can see how the steps relate.	Use when working complex operations.	Use when performing basic operations or generating simple estimates.

For each problem, tell whether you would use a calculator, mental math, or pencil and paper. Justify your choice, and then solve the problem.

1. The local high school radio station has 500 CDs. Each week, the music manager gets 25 new CDs. How many CDs will the station have in 8 weeks?

2. There are 360 deer in a forest. The population each year is 10% more than the previous year. How many deer will there be after 3 years?

3. Heidi works 8-hour shifts frosting cakes. She has frosted 12 cakes so far, and she thinks she can frost 4 cakes an hour during the rest of her shift. How many more hours will it take for her to frost a total of 32 cakes?

4. Kai has $170 in a savings account that earns 3% simple interest each year. How much interest will he have earned in 14 years?

5. A company's logo is in the shape of an isosceles triangle. When appearing on the company's stationery, the logo has a base of 5.1 cm and legs measuring 6.9 cm each. When appearing on a company poster, the similar logo has a base of 14.79 cm. Estimate the length of each leg of the logo on the poster.

6. Margo and her friends decided to hike the Wildcat Rock trail. After hiking $\frac{1}{4}$ of the way, they turned back because it began to rain. How far did they hike in all?

Trail	Distance (mi)
Meadowlark	$5\frac{3}{8}$
Key Lake	$4\frac{1}{2}$
Wildcat Rock	$6\frac{1}{4}$
Eagle Lookout	8

9-3 Linear Functions

COMMON CORE

CC.8.F.1: Understand that a function is a rule that assigns to each input exactly one output. The graph of a function is the set of ordered pairs consisting of an input and the corresponding output. ***Also CC.8.F.3, CC.8.F.4***

Vocabulary

linear function

function notation

The *Queen Elizabeth 2*, or *QE2*, is one of the largest passenger ships in the world. The amount of fuel carried by the *QE2* decreases over time during a voyage. This relationship can be approximated by a *linear function*. A **linear function** is a function that can be described by a linear equation.

One way to write a linear function is by using *function notation*. If x represents the input value of a function and y represents the output value, then the **function notation** for y is $f(x)$, where f names the function.

For the function $y = x + 4$, the function notation is $f(x) = x + 4$.

Helpful Hint

Sometime you will see functions written using y, and sometimes you will see functions written using $f(x)$.

Output value — Input value

$$f(x) = x + 4$$

f of x equals x plus 4.

Output value — Input value

$$f(1) = 1 + 4 = 5$$

f of 1 equals 1 plus 4, or 5.

Any linear function can be written in slope-intercept form $f(x) = mx + b$, where m is the slope of the function's graph and b is the y-intercept. Notice that in this form, x has an exponent of 1, and x does not appear in denominators or exponents.

EXAMPLE 1 Identifying Linear Functions

Determine whether each function is linear. If so, give the slope and y-intercept of the function's graph.

A $f(x) = 5(x + 2)$

$f(x) = 5(x + 2)$	*Write the equation in slope-intercept form.*
$f(x) = 5(x) + 5(2)$	*Use the Distributive Property.*
$f(x) = 5x + 10$	*Simplify.*

The function is linear because it can be written in the form $f(x) = mx + b$. The slope m is 5, and the y-intercept b is 10.

B $f(x) = x^2 + 1$

This function is not linear because x has an exponent other than 1. The function cannot be written in the form $f(x) = mx + b$.

Colin Prior/Stone/Getty Images

EXAMPLE 2 **Writing the Equation for a Linear Function**

Write a rule for each linear function.

A

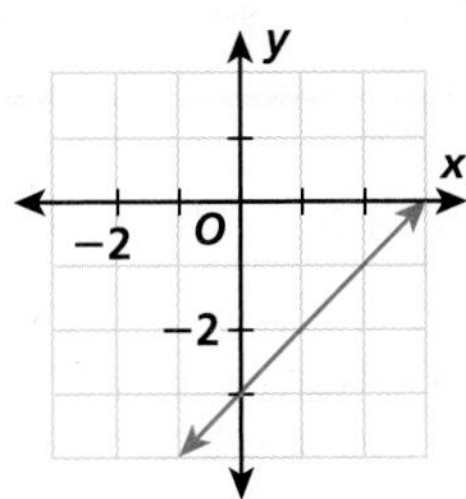

Step 1: Identify the y-intercept b from the graph.

$b = -3$

Step 2: Locate another point (x, y).

$(1, -2)$

Step 3: Substitute the x- and y-values into the equation $y = mx + b$, and solve for m.

$-2 = m(1) + -3$

$1 = m$

In function notation, the rule is $f(x) = 1x + (-3)$ or $f(x) = x - 3$.

B

x	y
−2	−16
−1	−13
1	−7
2	−4

Step 1: Locate two points.

$(1, -7)$ and $(2, -4)$

Step 2: Find the slope m.

$m = \frac{y_2 - y_1}{x_2 - x_1} = \frac{-4 - (-7)}{2 - 1} = 3$

Step 3: Substitute the slope and the x- and y-values into the equation $y = mx + b$, and solve for b.

$-7 = 3(1) + b$

$-10 = b$

In function notation, the rule is $f(x) = 3x + (-10)$ or $f(x) = 3x - 10$.

EXAMPLE 3 ***Physical Science Application***

At the beginning of a voyage, the *Queen Elizabeth 2*'s fuel tanks contain about 1,000,000 gallons of fuel. At cruising speed, this fuel is used at a rate of about 3500 gallons per hour. Find a rule for the linear function that describes the amount of fuel remaining in the ship's tanks. Use it to estimate how much fuel is left after 10 days.

To write the rule, determine the slope and y-intercept.

$m = -3500$ — *The rate of change in fuel is −3500 gal/h.*

$b = 1{,}000{,}000$ — *The initial amount of fuel is 1,000,000 gal.*

$f(x) = -3500x + 1{,}000{,}000$ — *f(x) is the amount of fuel in gallons, and x is the time in hours.*

$f(240) = -3500(240) + 1{,}000{,}000$ — *10 days = 240 hours, so evaluate the function for x = 240.*

$= 160{,}000$

After 10 days, there are 160,000 gallons of fuel remaining.

Helpful Hint

The slope in Example 3 is negative because the amount of fuel is decreasing over time. A decrease indicates a negative rate of change.

MATHEMATICAL PRACTICES

Think and Discuss

1. **Describe** how to use a graph to find the equation of a linear function.

9-3 Exercises

Learn It Online
Homework Help Online
Exercises 1–12, 13, 15, 21

GUIDED PRACTICE

See Example 1

Determine whether each function is linear. If so, give the slope and *y*-intercept of the function's graph.

1. $f(x) = 4x - 3x + 3$
2. $f(x) = x^3 + 1$
3. $f(x) = 3(2x - 1)$

See Example 2

Write a rule for each linear function.

4.

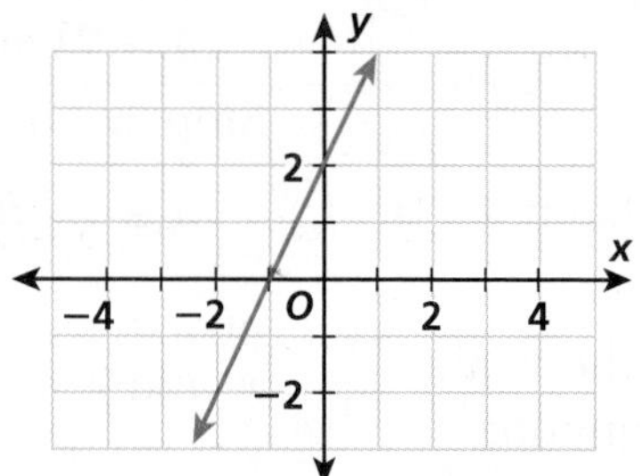

5.

x	y
−1	6
0	4
1	2
2	0

See Example 3

6. Liza earns $480 per week for 40 hours of work. If she works overtime, she makes $18 per overtime hour. Find a rule for the linear function that describes her weekly salary if she works *x* hours of overtime. Use it to find how much Liza earns if she works 6 hours of overtime.

INDEPENDENT PRACTICE

See Example 1

Determine whether each function is linear. If so, give the slope and *y*-intercept of the function's graph.

7. $f(x) = -4(x - 2)$
8. $f(x) = 2x + 5x$
9. $f(x) = \frac{7}{x}$

See Example 2

Write a rule for each linear function.

10.

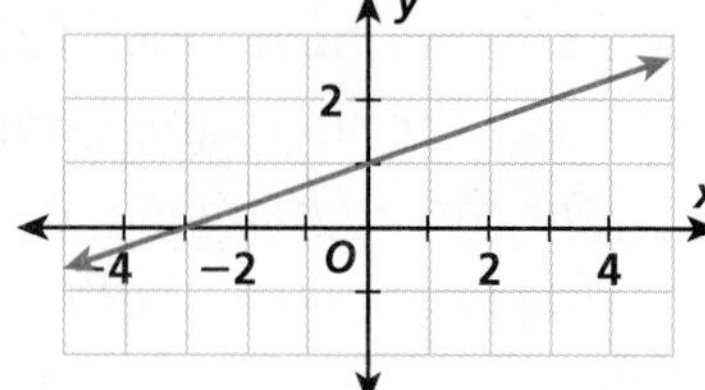

11.

x	y
−1	−11
0	−5
1	1
2	7

See Example 3

12. A swimming pool contains 1500 gallons of water. The pool is being drained for the season at a rate of 35 gallons per minute. Find a rule for the linear function that describes the amount of water in the tank. Use it to determine how much will be in the tank after 25 minutes.

PRACTICE AND PROBLEM SOLVING

Extra Practice

See Extra Practice for more exercises.

13. **Life Science** Suppose a baby weighed 8 pounds at birth, and gained about 1.2 pounds each month during the first year of life. To the nearest pound, approximately what was the weight of the baby after the seventh month?

LINK Recreation

The volume of a typical hot air balloon is between 65,000 and 105,000 cubic feet. Most hot air balloons fly at altitudes of 1000 to 1500 feet.

14. **Economics** *Linear depreciation* means that the same amount is subtracted each year from the value of an item. Suppose a car valued at \$17,440 depreciates \$1375 each year for x years.
    a. Write a linear function for the car's value after x years.
    b. What will the car's value be in 7 years?

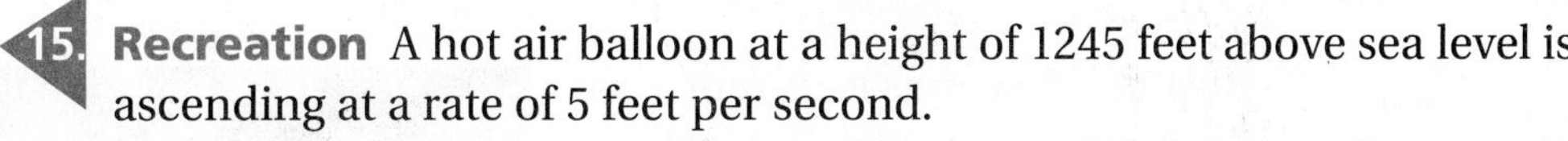

15. **Recreation** A hot air balloon at a height of 1245 feet above sea level is ascending at a rate of 5 feet per second.
    a. Write a linear function that describes the balloon's height after x seconds.
    b. What will the balloon's height be in 5 minutes? How high will it have climbed from its original starting point?

16. **Business** The table shows a carpenter's cost for wood and the price the carpenter charges the customer for the wood.

Carpenter Cost	\$45	\$52	\$60.50	\$80
Selling Price	\$54	\$62.40	\$72.60	\$96

    a. Write a linear function for the selling price of wood that costs the carpenter x dollars.
    b. If the cost to the carpenter is \$340, what is the customer's cost?

17. **What's the Question?** Consider the function $f(x) = -2x + 6$. If the answer is -4, what is the question?

18. **Write About It** Explain how you can determine whether a function is linear without graphing it or making a table of values.

19. **Challenge** What is the only kind of line on a coordinate plane that is not a linear function? Give an example of such a line.

Test Prep

20. **Multiple Choice** The function $f(x) = 12{,}800 - 1100x$ gives the value of a car x years after it was purchased. What will the car's value be in 8 years?

    Ⓐ \$4000　　Ⓑ \$5100　　Ⓒ \$6200　　Ⓓ \$7300

21. **Extended Response** A swimming pool contains 1800 gallons of water. It is being drained at a rate of 50 gallons per minute. Find a rule for the linear function that describes the amount of water in the pool. Use the rule to determine the amount of water in the pool after 30 minutes. After how many minutes will the pool be empty?

FABRICE COFFRINI/AFP/Getty Images

9-4 Comparing Multiple Representations

COMMON CORE

CC.8.F.2: Compare properties of two functions each represented in a different way (algebraically, graphically, numerically in tables, or by verbal descriptions). ***Also* *CC.8.EE.5, CC.8.F.4***

A spider descends a 20-foot drainpipe at a rate of 2.5 feet per minute. Another spider descends a drainpipe as shown in the table.

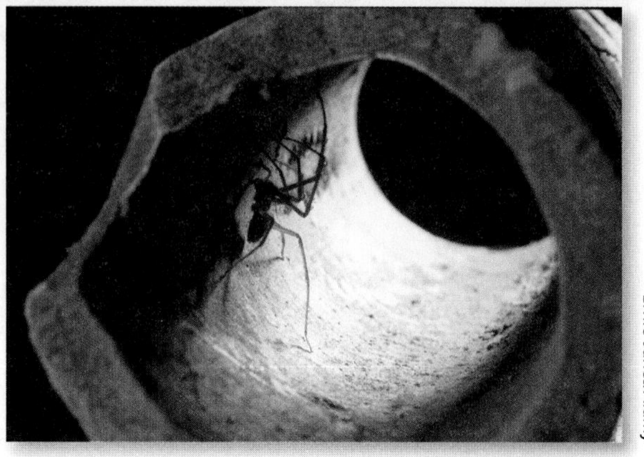
Ernie Janes/Alamy

Spider #1: $f(x) = -2.5x + 20$

Spider #2:

Time (min)	0	1	2
Height (ft)	32	29	26

These two spider situations are represented in different formats—a function rule and a function table.

A linear relationship can be represented as verbal descriptions, functions, graphs, and tables. In Example 1, you will compare slopes of linear functions that are represented in different ways.

EXAMPLE 1 Comparing Slopes

Helpful Hint

Remember that slope is rise (change in y) divided by run (change in x) or 'rise over run'.

Find and compare the slopes for the linear functions *f* and *g*.

$f(x) = 10x + 55$

x	0	1	2	3
$g(x)$	40	55	70	85

Find the slope of f.

Function f is written in slope-intercept form.

$f(x) = mx + b$

$f(x) = 10x + 55$

The slope of f is 10.

Find the slope of g.

$$m = \frac{y_2 - y_1}{x_2 - x_1}$$

$$= \frac{55 - 40}{1 - 0}$$

$$= \frac{15}{1}, \text{ or } 15$$

The slope of g is 15.

The slope of g is greater than the slope of f.

In Example 2, you will compare y-intercepts of linear functions that are represented in different ways.

EXAMPLE 2 Comparing Intercepts

Find and compare the y-intercepts for the linear functions f and g.

Find the y-intercept of f.

x	0	1	2	3
$f(x)$	3	1	−1	−3

When $x = 0$, $f(x) = 3$.

The y-intercept of f is 3.

Find the y-intercept of g.

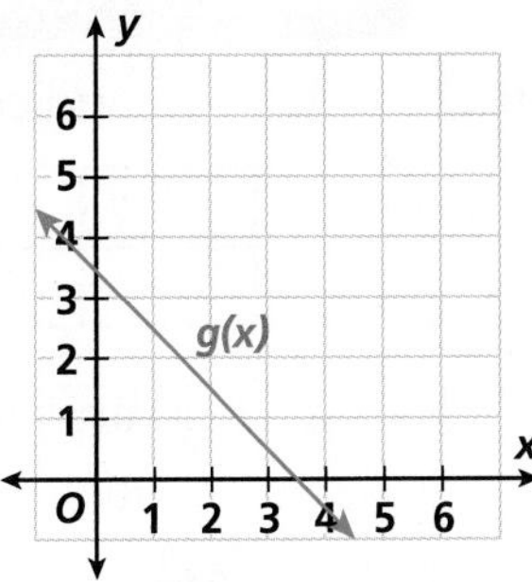

The graph of g crosses the y-axis at about 3.5.

The y-intercept of g is about 3.5.

The y-intercept of g is 0.5 greater than the y-intercept of f.

EXAMPLE 3 *Biology Application*

A spider descends a 20-foot drainpipe at a rate of 2.5 feet per minute. Another spider descends a drainpipe as shown in the table. Find and compare the rates of change and initial values of the linear functions in terms of the situations they model.

PhotoDisc/Getty Images

Rate of change is given by the slope and initial value is given by the y-intercept of a linear function.

Spider #1: $f(x) = -2.5x + 20$

Spider #2:

Time (min)	0	1	2
Height (ft)	32	29	26

Spider #1

$f(x) = mx + b$

$f(x) = -2.5x + 20$

The rate of change is −2.5.

The initial value is 20.

Spider #2

$m = \frac{y_2 - y_1}{x_2 - x_1} = \frac{29 - 32}{1 - 0} = \frac{-3}{1}$, or -3

The rate of change is −3.

The initial value is 32.

Spider #2 started at 32 feet, which is 12 feet higher than Spider #1. Spider #1 is descending at a rate of 2.5 feet per minute, which is 0.5 feet per minute slower than Spider #2.

Think and Discuss

1. **Give an example** of a linear function for a third spider with an initial height and rate of speed are between those of Spider #1 and Spider #2.

9-4 Exercises

GUIDED PRACTICE

See Example 1

1. Find and compare the slopes for the linear functions *f* and *g*.

x	0.00	0.50	1.00
f(x)	−2	−2.25	−2.50

and $g(x) = \frac{1}{2}x - 3$

See Example 2

2. Find and compare the *y*-intercepts for the linear functions *f* and *g*.

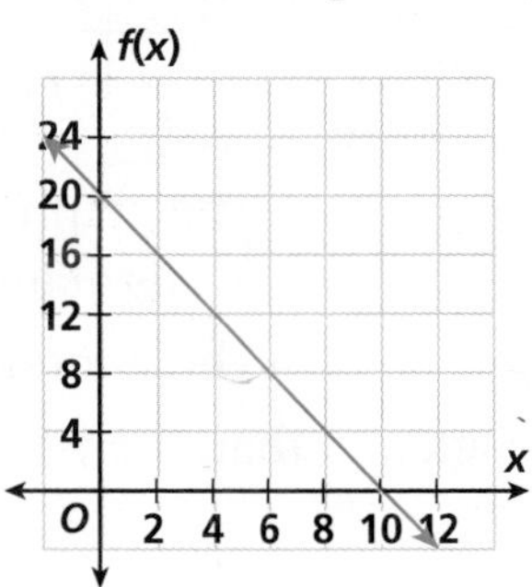

and

x	5	7	9
g(x)	−2.5	−11.5	−20.5

See Example 3

3. Interpret the rates of change and initial values of the linear functions in terms of the situations they model.

Distance traveled by two different snails

Snail #1: $f(x) = -2.5x + 8$

Snail #2:

Time (h)	0	1	2
Distance (in.)	4	7.5	11

INDEPENDENT PRACTICE

See Example 1

4. Find and compare the slopes for the linear functions *f* and *g*.

x	1	2	3
f(x)	8	6	4

and $g(x) = -x + 20$

See Example 2

5. Find and compare the *y*-intercepts for linear functions *f* and *g*.

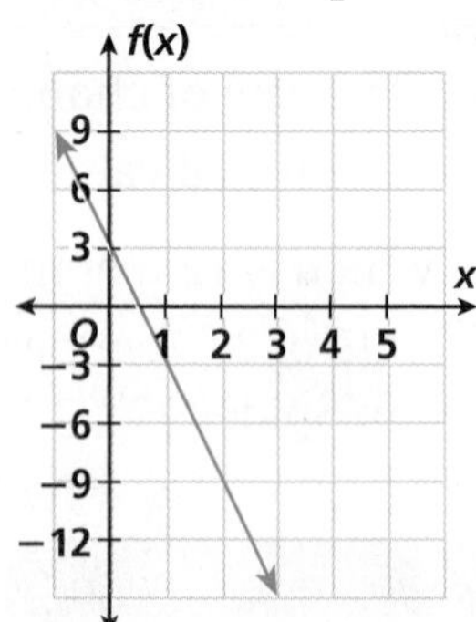

and

x	0.00	0.50	1.00
g(x)	−2	−2.25	−2.50

See Example 3

6. Interpret the rates of change and initial values of the linear functions in terms of the situations they model.

Region #1:

$f(x) = 50x + 12{,}000$

Region #2:

Floor Area (sq ft)	500	600	1000
Home price ($1000s)	40	48	80

PRACTICE AND PROBLEM SOLVING

Extra Practice

See Extra Practice for more exercises.

Find and compare the slopes and y-intercepts for the linear functions f and g.

7. $f(x) = -0.2x + 8$ and

x	0.0	1.0	4.0
$g(x)$	16.0	15.8	15.2

8. $f(x) = 1.5x + 2$ and

x	0.0	1.0	4.0
$g(x)$	8.0	6.5	5.0

9. **Science** Water pressure data is gathered from data to create a model. Find and compare the rates of change and initial values to determine whether the model is a good representation of the data.

$f(x) = 0.44x$ and

Vertical distance (ft)	200	220	300
Pressure (psi)	87.72	96.49	131.58

10. **Write About It** Write an exercise that requires the comparison of two relationships presented in different representations.

11. **Challenge** Create a believable context where a table and a function both have a positive linear relationship and one point of intersection.

LINK Science

Water pressure has a linear relationship with vertical distance. The greater the distance, the greater the water pressure.

PhotoDisc/Getty Images

Test Prep

12. **Multiple Choice** About how much less is the starting salary at Company #1 compared to Company #2?

Company #1

Experience (years) x	5	10	15
Salary ($1000s) y	25	33	41

Company #2

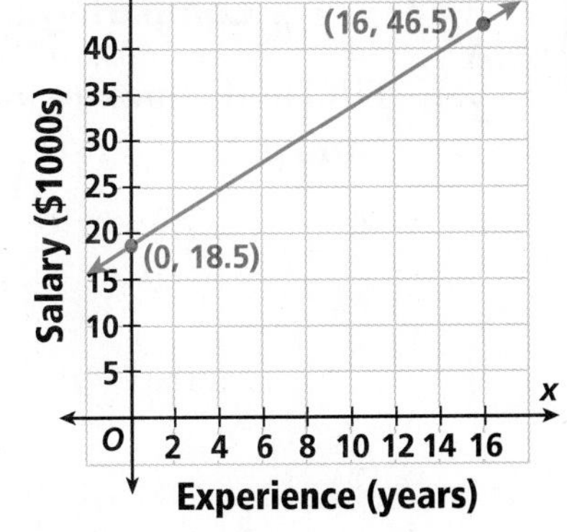

Ⓐ $500

Ⓑ $1,500

Ⓒ $7,500

Ⓓ $18,500

13. **Short Response** For the situation in Exercise 12, find and compare the rates of change and initial values of the linear functions in terms of the situations they model.

Quiz for Lessons 3 and 4

3 Linear Functions

Determine whether each function is linear. If so, give the slope and y-intercept of the function's graph.

1. $f(x) = 2x^3$
2. $f(x) = 6x - 3x + 1$
3. $f(x) = 2\left(\frac{1}{3}x - 1\right)$
4. Write a rule for the linear function shown in the graph.

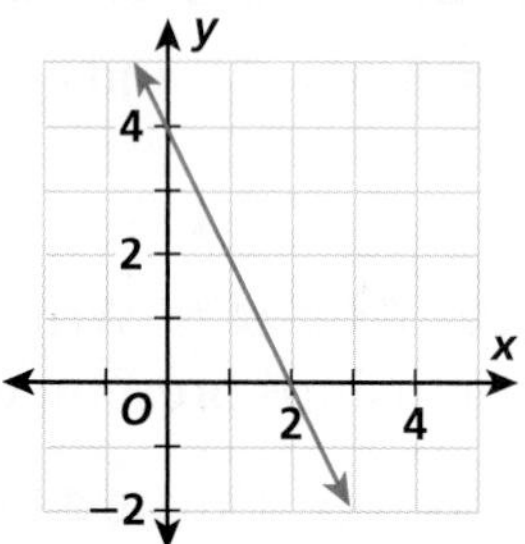

5. Kayo earns \$560 per week for 40 hours of work. If she works overtime, she makes \$21 per overtime hour. Find a rule for the linear function that describes her weekly salary if she works x hours of overtime. Use the rule to find how much Kayo earns if she works 8 hours of overtime.

Ready to Go On?

4 Comparing Multiple Representations

Find and compare a) the slopes and b) the y-intercepts of the linear functions f and g.

6. $f(x) = 6x - 2$ and

x	2	3	4
$g(x)$	6	10	14

7. 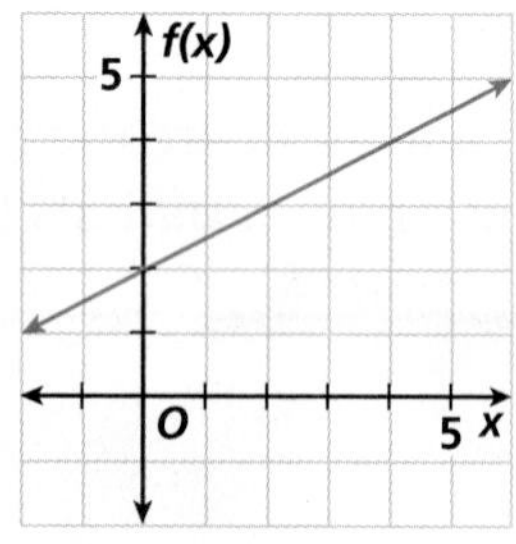

and $g(x) = -0.5x + 2$

Real-World CONNECTIONS

MATHEMATICAL PRACTICES Reason abstractly and quantitatively.

Black-Footed Ferrets The black-footed ferret is one of the rarest mammals in the United States. By the mid-1980s, the population of black-footed ferrets in the wild had declined to about 20 individuals. Since then, captive breeding programs have helped rescue these animals from extinction. Black-footed ferrets have been reintroduced to several states. The largest population is in the Conata Basin of South Dakota, home to about 300 black-footed ferrets.

SOUTH DAKOTA

Two researchers predicted the black-footed ferret population in Conata Basin for future years. Their predictions are shown in the table.

Black-Footed Ferret Population Predictions for Conata Basin

Year	Greg's Predictions	Maria's Predictions
1	300	325
2	340	360
3	380	395

1. Write a linear function based on Greg's predictions that gives the population in year n. Then use the rule to find the population in year 8.
2. According to Greg's predictions, in what year will the population of black-footed ferrets in the Conata Basin first reach 900? Explain.
3. Write a linear function based on Maria's predictions that gives the population in year n. Then use the rule to find the population in year 8.
4. A third researcher, Amir, makes his predictions using the function $f(x) = 45x + 250$, where x is the year and the population f is given in thousands. Use the function to find the population that Amir predicts in year 8.
5. Which of the three researchers predicts the greatest black-footed ferret population in the Conata Basin in year 12? What is this population?

Real-World Connections

Game Time

Squared Away

How many squares can you find in the figure at right?

Did you find 30 squares?

There are four different-sized squares in the figure.

Size of Square	Number of Squares
4 × 4	1
3 × 3	4
2 × 2	9
1 × 1	16
	Total 30

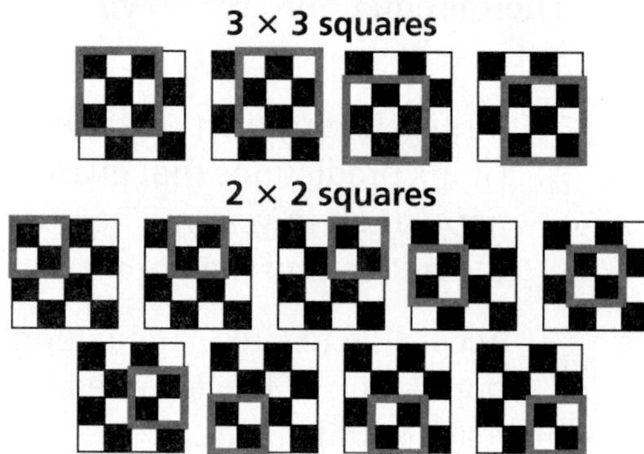

The total number of squares is $1 + 4 + 9 + 16 = 1^2 + 2^2 + 3^2 + 4^2$.

Draw a 5 × 5 grid and count the number of squares of each size. Can you see a pattern?

What is the total number of squares on a 6 × 6 grid? a 7 × 7 grid? Can you come up with a general formula for the sum of squares on an $n \times n$ grid?

What's Your Function?

One member from the first of two teams draws a function card from the deck, and the other team tries to guess the rule of the function. The guessing team gives a function input, and the card holder must give the corresponding output. Points are awarded based on the type of function and number of inputs required.

Complete rules and function cards are available online.

Learn It Online
Game Time Extra

Randall Hyman/HMH

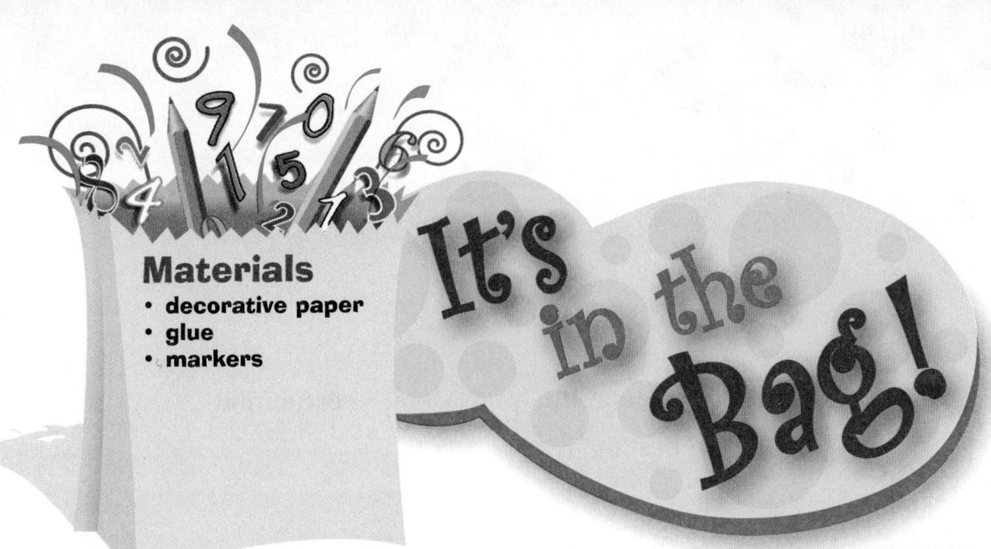

PROJECT Springboard to Functions

Make this springy organizer to record notes on data and functions.

Directions

1. Cut out four squares of decorative paper that are 6 inches by 6 inches.

2. Fold one of the squares of paper in half vertically and then horizontally. Unfold the paper. Then fold the square diagonally and unfold the paper. **Figure A**

3. Fold the diagonal crease back and forth so that it is easy to work with. Then bring the two ends of the diagonal together as shown. **Figure B**

4. Fold the other squares of paper in the same way.

5. Insert one folded square into another—one facing up, the next facing down—so that a pair of inner faces match up. Glue the matching faces together. **Figure C**

6. Do the same with the remaining squares to complete the springboard.

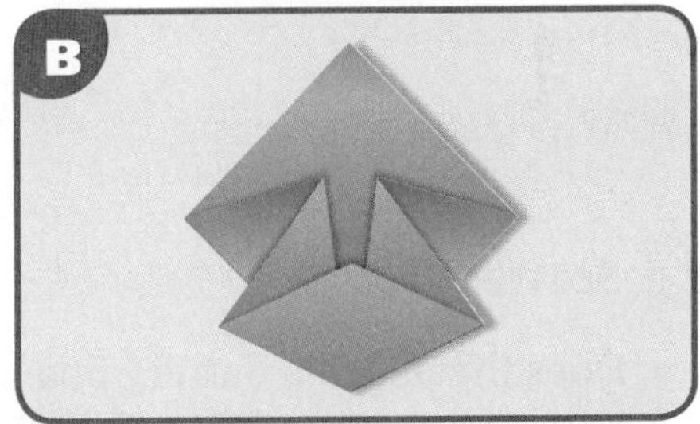

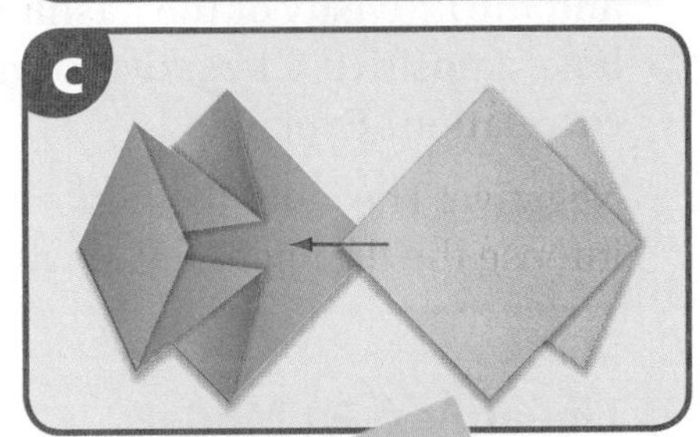

Taking Note of the Math

Write notes about data and functions on the various sections of the springboard.

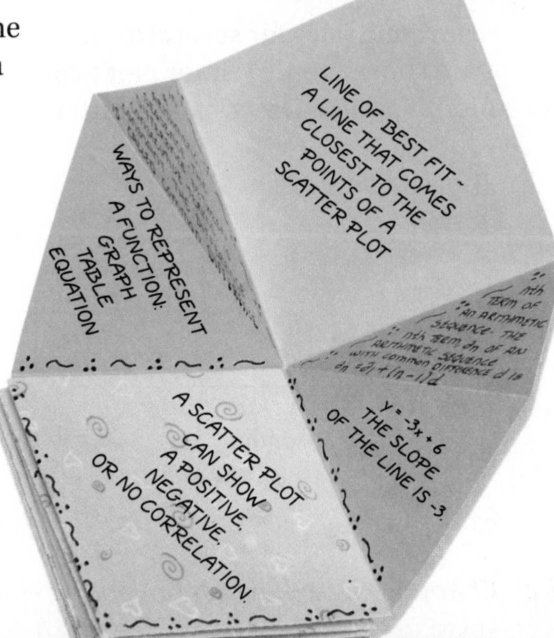

Sam Dudgeon/HMH

CHAPTER 9

Study Guide: Review

Vocabulary

correlation
clustering
function notation
line of best fit
scatter plot

Complete the sentences below with vocabulary words from the list above. Words may be used more than once.

1. When data points in a scatter plot are grouped more in one part of the graph than another, it is called ___?___.
2. ___?___ describes the relationship between two sets of data.
3. Rewriting $y = x - 3$ as $f(x) = x - 3$ is an example of ___?___.

EXAMPLES

EXERCISES

1 Scatter Plots

■ **Does the age of a battery in a flashlight and the intensity of the flashlight beam have a positive, a negative, or no correlation? Explain.**

Negative: The older the battery is, the less intense the flashlight beam will be.

4. Use the given data to make a scatter plot, and describe the correlation.

Day	0	2	4	6	8	10
Height (cm)	9	12	19	20	26	28

2 Linear Best Fit Models

■ **Ice cream cone sales for several local shops are shown in the scatter plot over an 8 month period. Describe the pattern.**

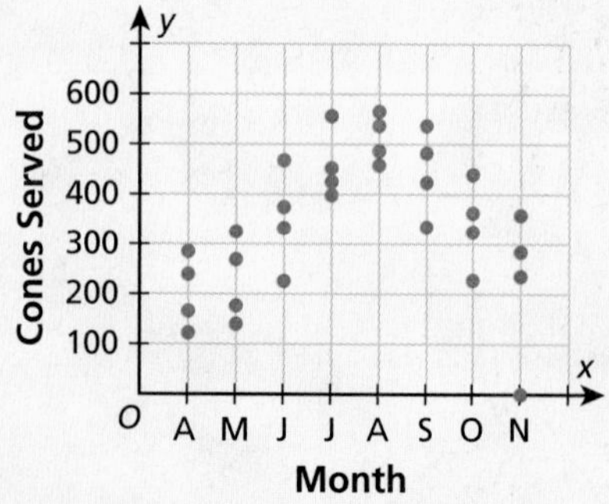

The points appear to follow a curved pattern.

For the scatter plot at left, answer the following questions.

5. Identify any clustering.
6. Identify any possible outliers in the data. What might explain the outlier?
7. How many shops are represented by the data? How do you know?

EXAMPLES

3 Linear Functions

■ **Write the rule for each linear function.**

x	y
−2	−10
−1	−3
0	4
1	11

The y-intercept b is $f(0) = 4$.

Use the point (1, 11) to solve for m.

$f(x) = mx + b$

$11 = m(1) + 4$

$7 = m$

The rule is $f(x) = 7x + 4$.

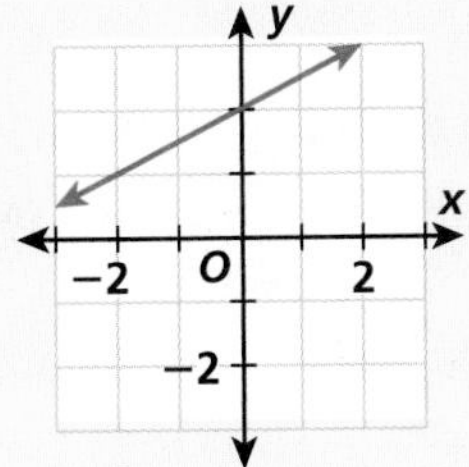

From the graph, the y-intercept b is 2.
Use the point (−2, 1) to solve for m.

$f(x) = mx + b$

$1 = m(-2) + 2$

$-1 = m(-2)$ *Subtract 2 from both sides.*

$\frac{1}{2} = m$ *Divide both sides by −2.*

The rule is $f(x) = \frac{1}{2}x + 2$.

EXERCISES

Write the equation for each linear function.

8.

x	y
−2	−3
−1	−2
0	−1
1	0

9.

x	y
−4	2
−2	3
0	4
2	5

10.

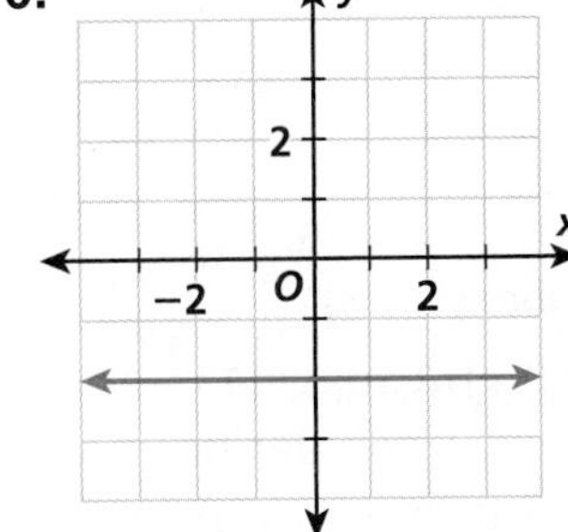

11.

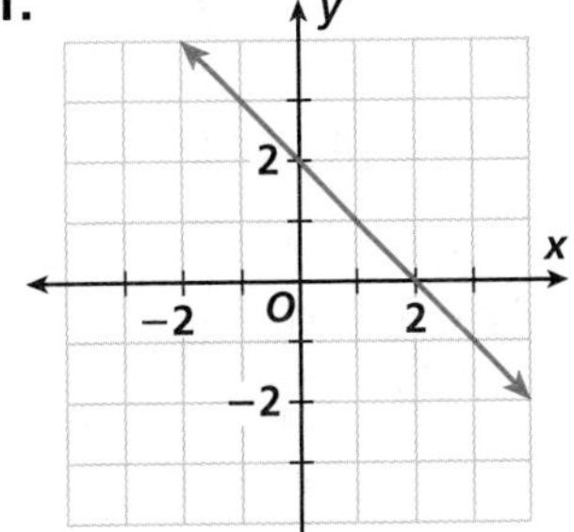

EXAMPLES

4 Comparing Multiple Representations

■ **Pete's Plumbing charges $120 per visit plus $50 per hour labor. House Depot charges as shown in the graph. Interpret and compare the cost of labor for each service.**

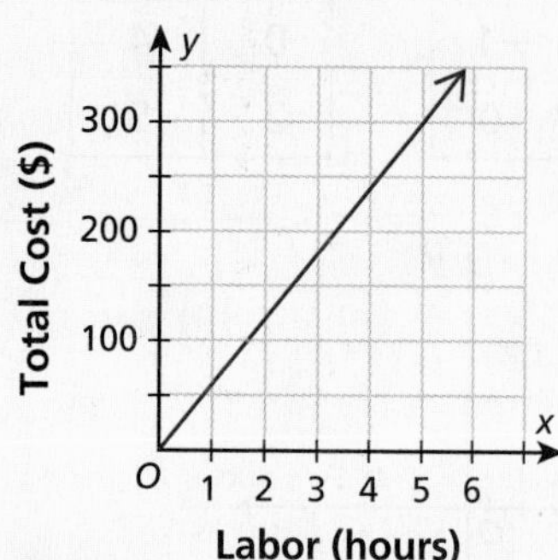

The slope of the graph suggests that House Depot charges $60 per hour for labor. This is $10 more per hour than Pete's Plumbing.

EXERCISES

Use the information at left for Exercises 12 and 13.

12. Compare and interpret the initial values of the services.

13. Compare the total cost for each service if a total of 10 hours of labor are needed.

14. Compare the slopes and y-intercepts of the linear functions f and g.

x	12	20	25
$f(x)$	44	60	70

and $g(x) = 2x + 30$

Study Guide: Review

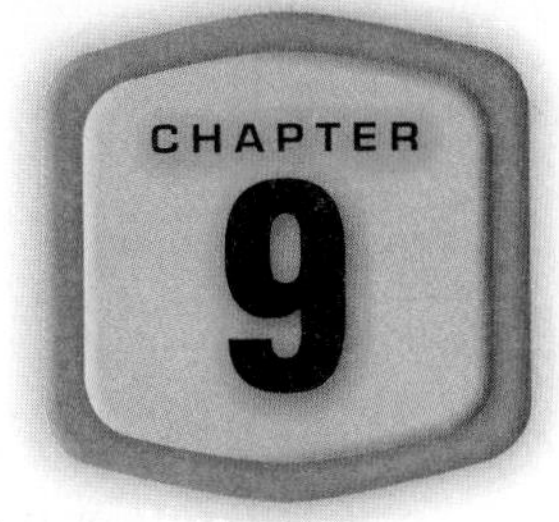

1. Use the given data to make a scatter plot, and describe the correlation.

Food	Pizza	Hamburger	Taco	Hot Dog	Caesar Salad	Taco Salad
Fat (g)	11	13	14	12	4	21
Calories	374	310	220	270	90	410

Write a rule for each linear function.

2.

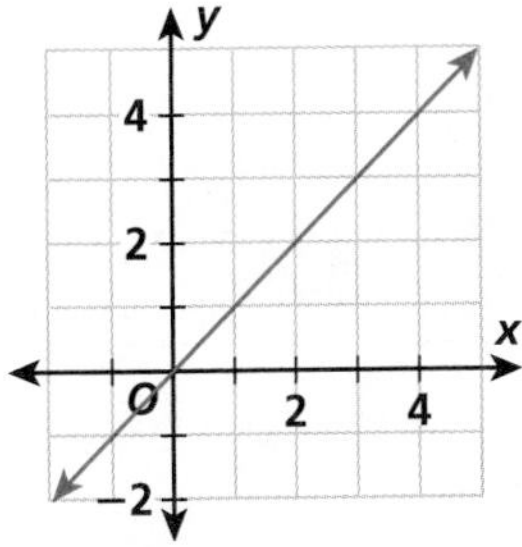

3.

x	y
−8	−7
−4	−4
0	−1
4	2

4. A small pool contains 1200 gallons of water. The pool is being drained at a rate of 45 gallons per minute. Find a rule for the linear function that describes the amount of water in the pool, and use the rule to determine how much water will be in the pool after 15 minutes.

5. Compare the scatter plots in Graph A and Graph B and their lines of best fit. Which model better fits the data? Explain your answer.

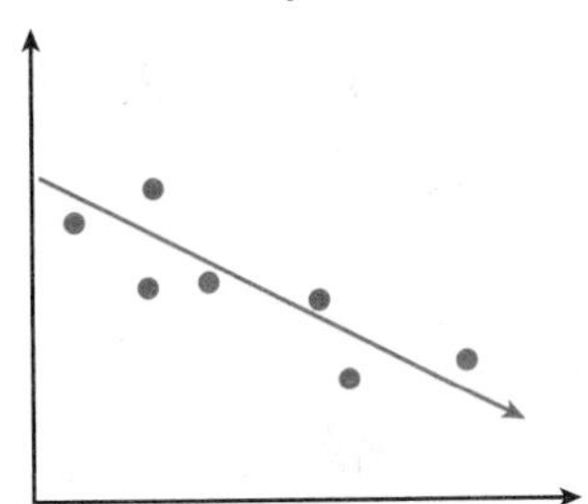

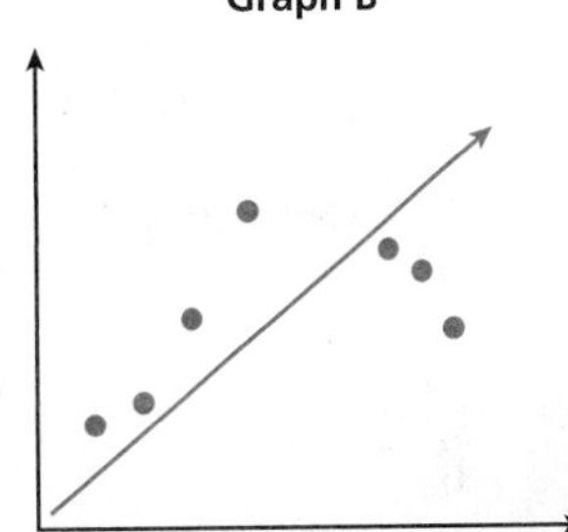

6. Find an equation for the line of best fit. What do the slope and vertical intercept represent in terms of the data it models?

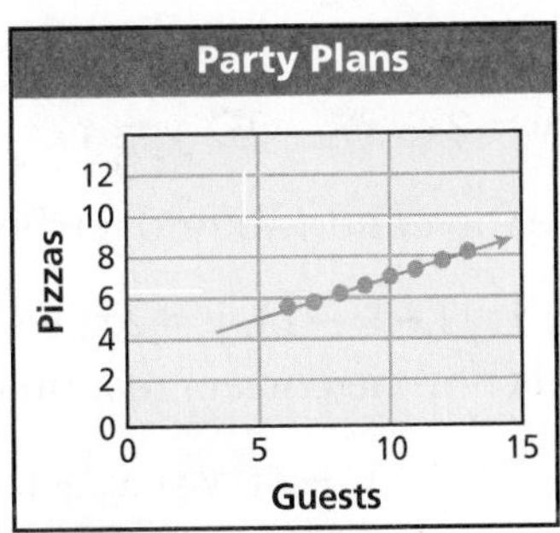

7. Compare the slopes and y-intercepts of the linear functions f and g.

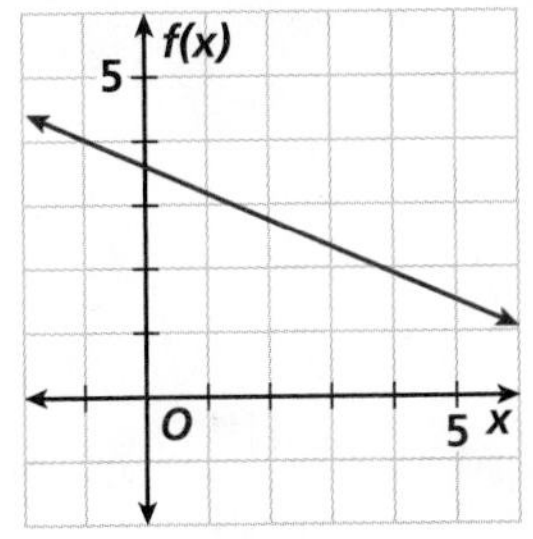

and

X	8	−2	−6
$g(X)$	−4	0	1.6

CHAPTER 9

Test Tackler

STANDARDIZED TEST STRATEGIES

Multiple Choice: Work Backward

When you do not know how to solve a multiple-choice test item, use the answer choices and work backward to make a guess. Try each option in the test item to see if it is correct and reasonable.

EXAMPLE 1

What is the solution to the system?

$y = 2x + 3$

$y = 3x - 2$

Ⓐ (1, 5) Ⓑ (−1, −5) Ⓒ (5, 13) Ⓓ (3, 2)

Use the answer choices to work backward to find the ordered pair that makes both equations true.

Option A: If $x = 1$, then $2(1) + 3 = 5$, so the solution checks in the first equation. However, $3(1) - 2 = 1 \neq 5$, so A is not the solution.

Option B: If $x = -1$, then $2(-1) + 3 = 1 \neq -5$, so B is not the solution.

Option C: If $x = 5$, then $2(5) + 3 = 13$. Also $3(5) - 2 = 13$, so both equations check.

Option C is the correct response.

EXAMPLE 2

What is the equation of the line that passes through the points (−1, −1) and (1, 3)?

Ⓕ $y = 2x$ Ⓖ $y = x$ Ⓗ $y = x + 1$ Ⓙ $y = 2x + 1$

Substitute for x and y to find a true equation.

Option F: Try $(-1, -1)$. $y = 2x$; $-1 \stackrel{?}{=} 2(-1)$; $-1 \neq -2$
Option F is not the correct response.

Option G: Try $(-1, -1)$. $y = x$; $-1 = -1$; the first point is true.
Now try $(1, 3)$: $1 \neq 3$. Option G is not the correct response.

Option H: Try $(-1, -1)$. $y = x + 1$; $-1 \stackrel{?}{=} -1 + 1$; $-1 \neq 0$
Option H is not the correct response.

Option J: Try $(-1, -1)$. $y = 2x + 1$; $-1 \stackrel{?}{=} 2(-1) + 1$; $-1 = -1$
Try $(1, 3)$. $y = 2x + 1$; $3 \stackrel{?}{=} 2(1) + 1$; $3 = 3$

Option J is the correct response.

Before answering a test item, check if you can eliminate any of the options immediately.

Read each test item and answer the questions that follow.

Item A

Solve: $\frac{3}{x} = \frac{1}{5}$

Ⓐ 2 Ⓒ 15

Ⓑ 10 Ⓓ 21

1. Explain which option you can eliminate because it is not reasonable.
2. Explain how to work backward to find the correct response.

Item B

Divide. Write the result in scientific notation.

$(6.4 \times 10^8) \div (8.0 \times 10^2)$

Ⓕ 8.0×10^5 Ⓗ 8.0×10^6

Ⓖ 0.8×10^6 Ⓙ 8×10^4

3. Describe how to use mental math to eliminate at least one option.
4. Describe how you know by working backward that options H and J are incorrect.

Item C

A line has the equation $3x - y = 8$. What is the slope of the line?

Ⓐ $\frac{1}{3}$ Ⓒ 3

Ⓑ -3 Ⓓ 8

5. Options B and D are distracters. Explain how these options were generated.
6. Explain how to work backward to find the correct response.

Item D

Which equation best describes the graph of the linear equation?

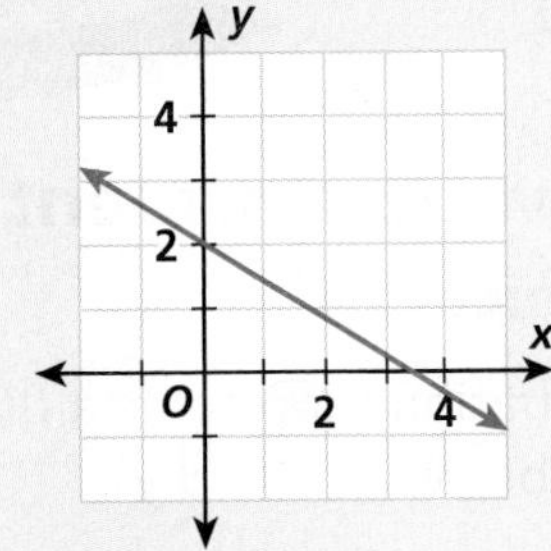

Ⓕ $f(x) = 2x + 2$

Ⓖ $f(x) = -0.6x + 2$

Ⓗ $f(x) = 0.6x + 2$

Ⓙ $f(x) = 4x + 2$

7. Can any of the options be eliminated immediately? Explain.
8. Explain how to work backward to find the correct response.

Item E

Which graph represents the equation $y = 3x$?

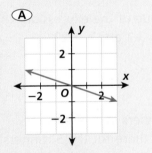

Ⓐ Ⓒ

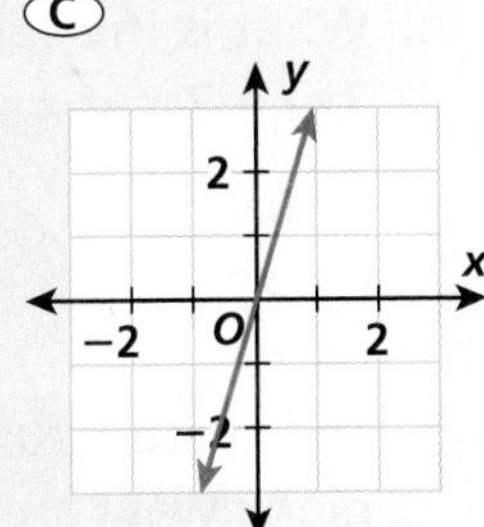

Ⓑ Ⓓ

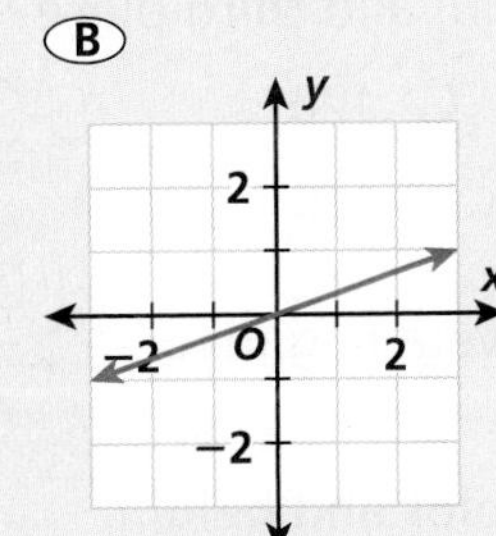

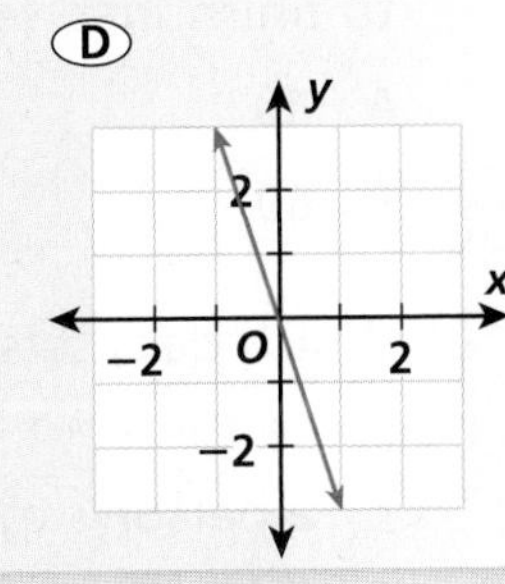

9. Explain which options you can eliminate because they are not reasonable.
10. Describe how to work backward to find the correct response.

CHAPTER 9

Standardized Test Prep

Cumulative Assessment

Multiple Choice

1. Which equation represents a direct variation between x and y?

   Ⓐ $y = x + 2$ Ⓒ $y = 2x$

   Ⓑ $y = \frac{2}{x}$ Ⓓ $y = 2 - x$

2. The sum of two numbers is 304 and their difference is 112. What is the greater of the two numbers?

   Ⓕ 96 Ⓗ 208

   Ⓖ 192 Ⓙ 416

3. Find the volume of a square pyramid with height 18 cm and a base edge length of 4 cm.

   Ⓐ 72 cm^3 Ⓒ 112 cm^3

   Ⓑ 96 cm^3 Ⓓ 114 cm^3

4. What is the value of the expression $3xy - 2y^2$ if $x = -1$ and $y = 2$?

   Ⓕ 14 Ⓗ -2

   Ⓖ 2 Ⓙ -14

5. There are 5 runners in a race. How many ways are there for the 5 runners to finish first, second, and third place?

   Ⓐ 30 Ⓒ 120

   Ⓑ 60 Ⓓ 180

6. Which data sets have a negative correlation?

   Ⓕ a person's eye color and height

   Ⓖ a person's height and weight

   Ⓗ the distance traveled and the time it takes to travel

   Ⓙ the outdoor temperature and the number of hours a heater is used

7. Which expression represents the perimeter of the figure?

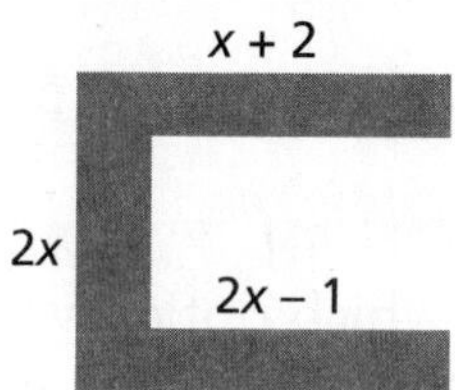

   Ⓐ $10x$ Ⓒ $6x + 1$

   Ⓑ $10x + 2$ Ⓓ $10x^2 + 4$

8. The sum of two numbers is 83. The difference of the numbers is 29. Which is the greater of the two numbers?

   Ⓕ 27 Ⓗ 56

   Ⓖ 54 Ⓙ 63

9. A triangle has two angles whose measures are 70° each. Which description fits this triangle?

   Ⓐ acute Ⓒ scalene

   Ⓑ obtuse Ⓓ equilateral

10. The rotational speed of a gear varies inversely as the number of teeth on the gear. A gear with 15 teeth has a rotational speed of 48 rpm. How many teeth are on a gear that has a rotational speed of 40 rpm?

   Ⓕ 13 teeth Ⓗ 58 teeth

   Ⓖ 18 teeth Ⓙ 128 teeth

11. An animal shelter needs to find homes for 40 dogs and 60 cats. If 15% of the dogs are female and 25% of the cats are female, what percent of the animals are female?

   Ⓐ 21% Ⓒ 40%

   Ⓑ 22% Ⓓ 42%

When trying to determine the slope of a line from a graph, first locate two points on the line. Then divide the change in the *y*-values by the change in the *x*-values.

Gridded Response

Use the graph for items 12 and 13.

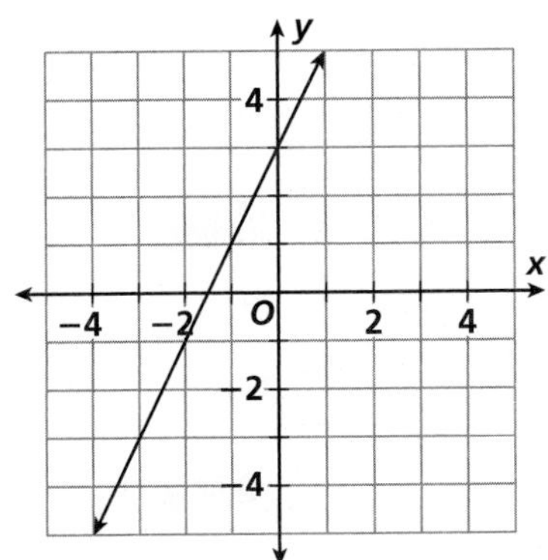

12. What is the slope of a line parallel to the line graphed?

13. What is the *y*-intercept of the graphed line?

14. If $3^{3x-2} = 81$, what is the value of *x*?

15. If *y* varies inversely with *x* and $y = \frac{2}{9}$ when $x = \frac{1}{3}$, what is the constant of variation?

16. What is the *x*-intercept of the function $f(x) = 2x - 5$?

17. The width of a rectangle is one-third the length. If the perimeter of the rectangle is 56 units, what is the area in square units?

Short Response

S1. Shane scored 20 points in a basketball game. He made twice as many field goals, worth 2 points each, as free throws, worth 1 point each. Determine the number of field goals and free throws Shane made.

S2. Quadrilateral $ABCD \cong$ quadrilateral $EFGH$. Find the values of the variables.

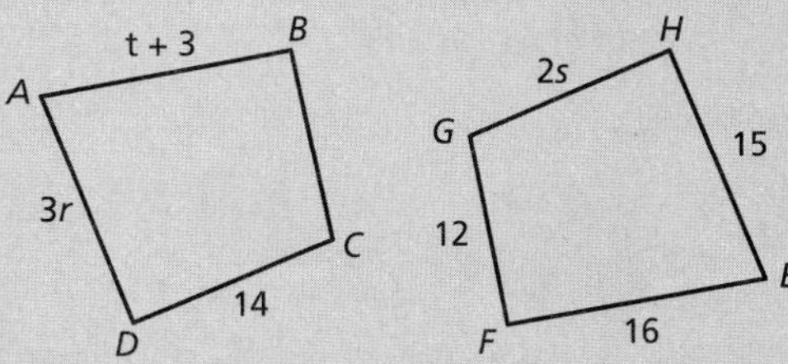

S3. The table shows some data points for a linear function.

x	17	22	40
y	11	18.5	45.5

a. Find the slope of the function.

b. Find the *y*-intercept of the function.

Extended Response

E1. A flea market charges $8 for admission, and sells packs of CDs for $5. There is no sales tax. A local store sells the same packs of CDs for $7, plus 5% sales tax.

a. Write linear functions *f*(*c*) and *s*(*c*) for the cost of *c* packs of CDs at the flea market and at the store.

b. Describe what the slopes and vertical intercepts of the functions represent.

c. Calculate *f*(3) and *s*(3). What do these values represent?

Student Handbook

Sam Dudgeon/HMH

Extra Practice ■■■ Chapter 1

LESSON 

Simplify.

1. $\frac{12}{96}$ 2. $\frac{6}{16}$ 3. $\frac{-10}{15}$ 4. $\frac{14}{42}$

Write each decimal as a fraction in simplest form.

5. 0.4 6. 0.05 7. 0.12 8. 0.625

Write each fraction as a decimal.

9. $\frac{3}{8}$ 10. $\frac{1}{4}$ 11. $\frac{9}{4}$ 12. $\frac{3}{5}$

LESSON 

Multiply. Write each answer in simplest form.

13. $\frac{3}{4}\left(-\frac{5}{9}\right)$ 14. $\frac{7}{12}\left(-\frac{3}{5}\right)$ 15. $-\frac{4}{5}\left(-\frac{9}{10}\right)$ 16. $-\frac{3}{7}\left(\frac{13}{14}\right)$

17. $-4.7(-8)$ 18. $-4.1(8.6)$ 19. $-0.06(5.2)$ 20. $-0.003(-2.6)$

21. Rosie ate $2\frac{1}{2}$ bananas on Saturday. On Sunday she ate $\frac{1}{2}$ as many bananas as she ate on Saturday. How many bananas did Rosie eat over the weekend?

LESSON 

Divide. Write each answer in simplest form.

22. $2\frac{3}{4} \div \frac{1}{3}$ 23. $5\frac{1}{5} \div \frac{7}{8}$ 24. $3\frac{5}{9} \div \frac{3}{4}$ 25. $3\frac{1}{8} \div \frac{2}{5}$

26. $5.68 \div 0.2$ 27. $7.65 \div 0.05$ 28. $1.76 \div 0.8$ 29. $0.744 \div 8$

Evaluate each expression for the given value of the variable.

30. $\frac{7.4}{x}$ for $x = 0.5$ 31. $\frac{11.88}{x}$ for $x = 0.08$ 32. $\frac{15.3}{x}$ for $x = -1.2$

33. Yolanda is making bows that take $21\frac{1}{2}$ inches of ribbon to make. She has 344 inches of ribbon. How many bows can she make?

LESSON 

Add or subtract.

34. $\frac{8}{9} + \frac{2}{7}$ 35. $\frac{3}{8} - \frac{2}{3}$ 36. $\frac{2}{3} + \frac{1}{7}$ 37. $\frac{5}{6} - \frac{4}{9}$

38. $4\frac{1}{5} + \left(-2\frac{1}{7}\right)$ 39. $3\frac{2}{3} + \left(-1\frac{7}{8}\right)$ 40. $4\frac{1}{8} + \left(-1\frac{3}{5}\right)$ 41. $8\frac{1}{7} + \left(-4\frac{1}{10}\right)$

Extra Practice ... Chapter 1

Evaluate each expression for the given value of the variable.

42. $8\frac{1}{2} + x$ for $x = 4\frac{2}{9}$ **43.** $n - \frac{1}{9}$ for $n = -1\frac{7}{8}$ **44.** $1\frac{1}{8} + y$ for $y = -\frac{4}{7}$

45. A container has $10\frac{1}{2}$ gallons of milk. If the children at a preschool drink $7\frac{3}{4}$ gallons of milk, how many gallons of milk are left in the container?

LESSON 

Solve.

46. $x - 3.2 = 5.1$ **47.** $-3.1p = 15.5$ **48.** $\frac{a}{-2.3} = 7.9$ **49.** $-4.3x = 34.4$

50. $m - \frac{1}{3} = \frac{5}{8}$ **51.** $x - \frac{3}{7} = \frac{1}{9}$ **52.** $\frac{4}{5}w = \frac{2}{3}$ **53.** $\frac{9}{10}z = \frac{5}{8}$

54. It is estimated that it will take Peter $9\frac{3}{4}$ hours to paint a room. If he gets two of his friends to help him and they work at the same rate as he does, how long should it take them to paint the room?

LESSON 

55. A bill from the plumber was \$383. The plumber charged \$175 for parts and \$52 per hour for labor. How long did the plumber work at this job?

56. Alicia bought \$116 worth of flowers and some bushes to plant around her house. The bushes cost \$28 each, and the bill totaled \$340. How many bushes did she buy?

Solve.

57. $\frac{a}{2} - 3 = 8$ **58.** $2.4 = -0.8x + 3.2$ **59.** $\frac{6 + z}{3} = 4$ **60.** $\frac{c}{6} + 2 = 5$

61. $0.9m - 1.6 = -5.2$ **62.** $\frac{x - 4}{3} = 7$ **63.** $\frac{b}{5} + 2 = -3$ **64.** $2.1d + 0.7 = 7$

65. $\frac{p + 5}{3} = 6$ **66.** $\frac{c}{6} - 8 = 3$ **67.** $\frac{r - 6}{9} = 5$ **68.** $-8.6 = 3.4k - 1.8$

Extra Practice

Extra Practice ... Chapter 2

LESSON 1

Determine whether each ordered pair is a solution of $2x + 3y = 16$.

1. (1, 5) **2.** (5, 2) **3.** (2, 4) **4.** (3, 3)

Use the given values to make a table of solutions.

5. $y = x - 3$ for $x = -2, -1, 0, 1, 2$

6. $y = 3x + 2$ for $x = -2, -1, 0, 1, 2$

7. The cost of mailing a first-class letter to Canada is \$0.31 per ounce plus \$0.38. The equation that gives the total cost c of mailing a letter is $c = 0.31w + 0.38$, where w is the weight in ounces. What is the cost of mailing a 5-ounce letter to Canada?

LESSON  2

Graph each point on a coordinate plane.

8. (4, 3) **9.** (3, 0) **10.** (−1, 3)

11. (0, −5) **12.** (−2, −4) **13.** (4, −2)

Find the distance between each pair of points.

14. A and B **15.** B and C

16. C and D **17.** D and E

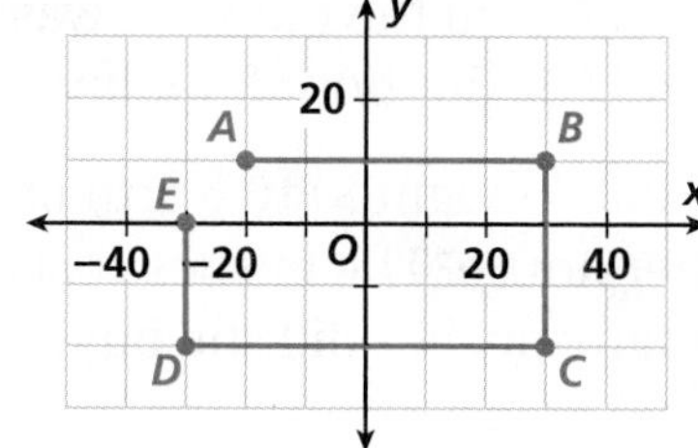

LESSON 3

Tell which graph corresponds to each situation described below.

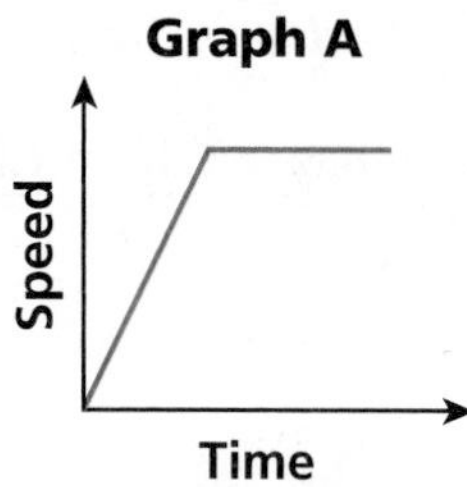

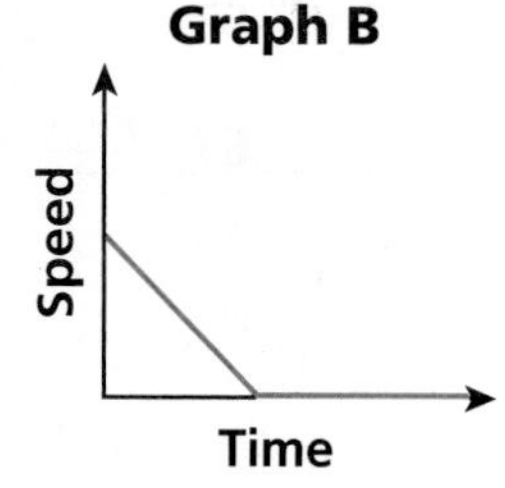

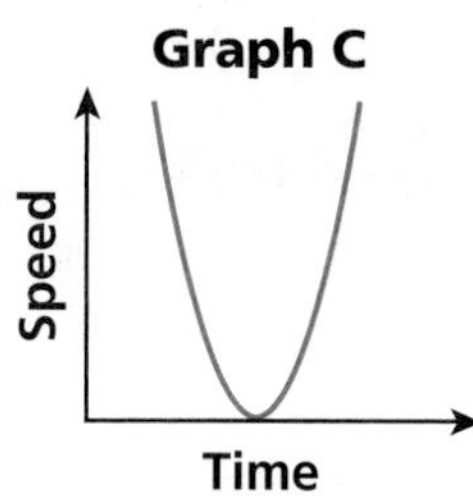

18. A person riding a bike increases speed and then maintains a high speed.

19. A person riding a bike goes up a hill and then accelerates going down the other side of the hill.

20. A person riding a bike in a race slows down after he reaches the finish line and then comes to a stop.

21. Micah has \$50 in his savings account. Each week he plans to add \$10. Create a graph for this situation. Tell whether the graph is continuous or discrete.

Extra Practice ... Chapter 2

LESSON 4

Make a table and graph of each function.

22. $y = x + 1$ **23.** $y = -x - 2$ **24.** $y = 3x + 1$ **25.** $y = 4(x - 1)$

Determine if each relationship represents a function.

26.

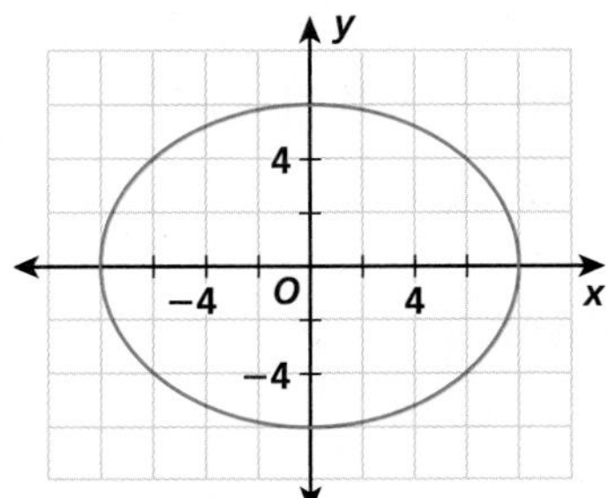

27.

x	y
−3	1
−1	−1
0	−2
2	0
4	2

28.

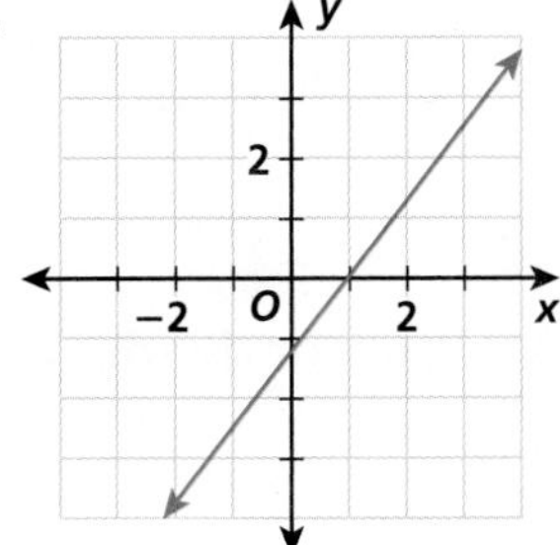

29. The table shows the cost of renting a clubhouse.

Hours rented	2	3	4	5	8
Cost ($)	50	60	75	90	100

a. Graph the data in the table.

b. Does the relation in the table represent a function? Explain how you know.

c. What is the domain of the relation in the table? What is the range?

LESSON 

30. The cost a caterer charges for a party is represented by the equation $c = \$13p$, where c is the amount paid to the caterer and p is the number of guests. Make a table and sketch a graph of the equation.

31. The equation $a = 50h + 50$ represents the amount a that an air-conditioning repair company charges for h hours of labor. Make a table and sketch a graph of the equation.

Use each table to make a graph and to write an equation.

32.

x	0	3	6	9	12
y	2	4	6	8	10

33.

x	−2	−1	0	1	2
y	4	3	2	1	0

Use each graph to make a table and to write an equation.

34.

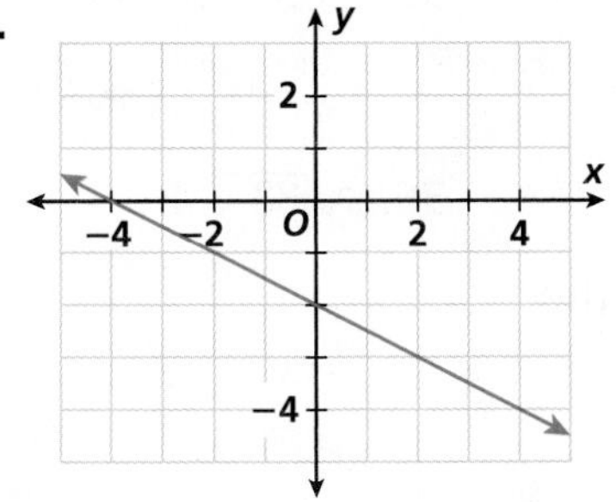

35.

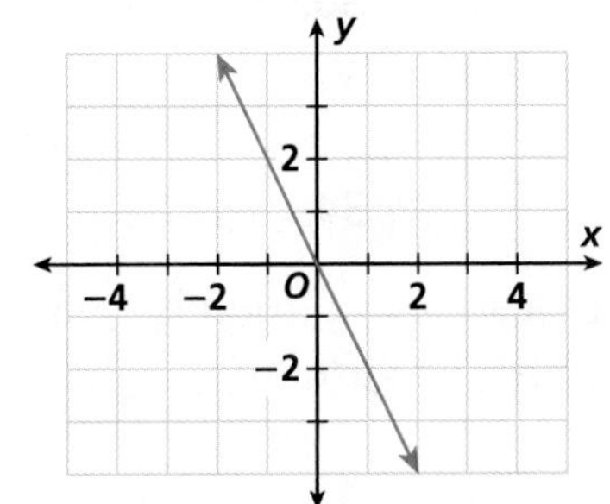

Extra Practice ▪▪▪ Chapter 3

LESSON 1

Simplify. Write in decimal form.

1. 10^{-1}　　**2.** 10^{-2}　　**3.** 10^{-3}　　**4.** 10^{-4}

Simplify.

5. $(-4)^{-2}$　　**6.** 3^{-3}　　**7.** $(-5)^{-4}$

8. $\frac{3^2}{3^4} + (9 + 3)^0$　　**9.** $13 - (-3) + 19(1 + 2)^2$　　**10.** $4^5 \cdot 3^2 \cdot (-3)^{-3}$

LESSON 2

Multiply or divide. Write the product or the quotient as one power.

11. $2^4 \cdot 2^5$　　**12.** $w^7 \cdot w^7$　　**13.** $\frac{4^9}{4^9}$　　**14.** $\frac{c^6}{c^2}$

15. $\frac{x^3}{y^3}$　　**16.** $(3^0)^4$　　**17.** $(3^{-2})^3$　　**18.** $(-a^3)^4$

LESSON 3

Write each number in standard notation.

19. 2.4×10^3　　**20.** 3.62×10^5　　**21.** 5.036×10^{-4}　　**22.** 8.93×10^{-2}

Write each number in scientific notation.

23. 0.00384　　**24.** 1,450,000,000　　**25.** 0.654

26. The distance from Earth to the Sun is about 93 million miles. The diameter of Earth is about 8,000 miles. About how many Earths would fit between Earth and the Sun? Write your answer in scientific notation.

LESSON 

27. In 1930, the U.S. gross debt was about 1.62×10^8 dollars. By 2009, it had grown to about 1.23×10^{13} dollars. About how many times greater was the debt in 2009 as in 1930?

28. A 6-letter computer password has about 3.1×10^8 possible passwords. When numbers are also allowed, this increases to about 2.2×10^9 possible passwords. How many more passwords is this?

LESSON 5

Find the two square roots of each number.

29. 25　　**30.** 49　　**31.** 289　　**32.** 169

Simplify.

33. $2\sqrt{4}$　　**34.** $3\sqrt{49}$　　**35.** $\sqrt{99 + 45}$　　**36.** $\sqrt{33 - 8}$

37. The area of a square garden is 1,681 square feet. What are the dimensions of the garden?

Extra Practice ... Chapter 3

LESSON 6

Each square root is between two integers. Name the integers. Explain your answer.

38. $\sqrt{30}$ **39.** $\sqrt{61}$ **40.** $\sqrt{93}$ **41.** $-\sqrt{124}$

Approximate each square root to the nearest hundredth.

42. $\sqrt{202}$ **43.** $\sqrt{184}$ **44.** $\sqrt{462}$ **45.** $\sqrt{319}$

46. Each tile on Michelle's patio is 18 square inches. If her patio is square shaped and consists of 81 tiles, about how big is her patio?

LESSON 7

Write all names that apply to each number.

47. $\sqrt{5}$ **48.** -61.2 **49.** $\frac{\sqrt{16}}{2}$ **50.** -6

State if the number is rational, irrational, or not a real number.

51. $\sqrt{\frac{4}{25}}$ **52.** $\sqrt{-9}$ **53.** $\sqrt{17}$ **54.** $\frac{13}{0}$

Find a real number between each pair of numbers.

55. $5\frac{1}{8}$ and $5\frac{2}{8}$ **56.** $4\frac{1}{3}$ and $4\frac{2}{3}$ **57.** $3\frac{5}{7}$ and $3\frac{6}{7}$

LESSON 8

Solve for the unknown side in each right triangle to the nearest tenth.

58.

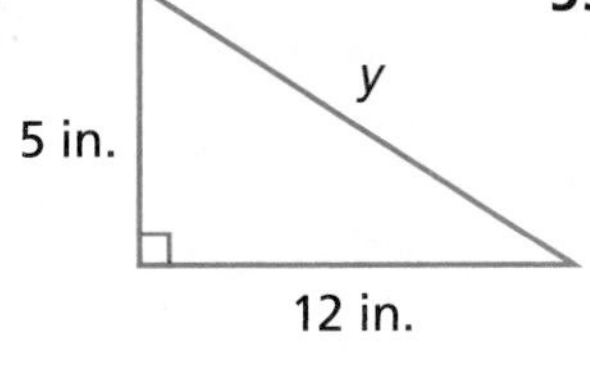

59.

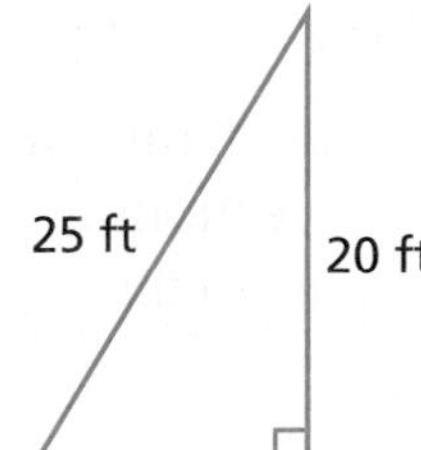

60.

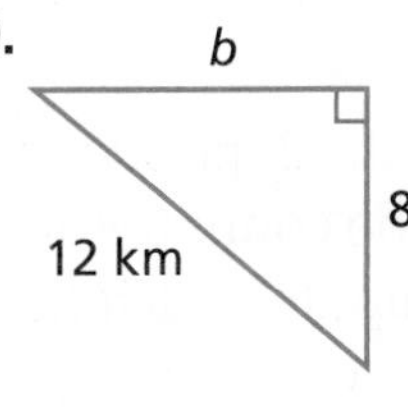

61.

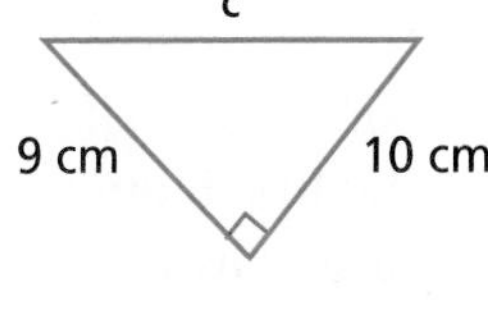

62. An 8-foot-long board rests against a wall at a height of 5 feet. To the nearest tenth, how far from the base of the wall is the end of the board?

63. A professional tournament pool table typically measures 4.5 ft by 9 ft. How far is it from one corner pocket to the opposite corner pocket? Round to the nearest hundredth of a foot.

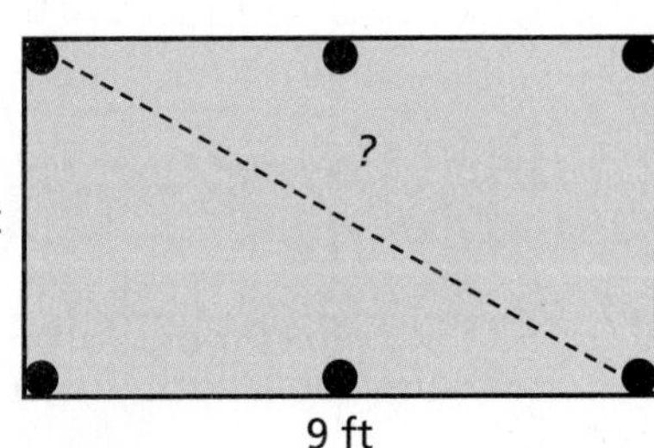

LESSON 9

Find the distance between the two points, to the nearest tenth.

64. (1, 9) and (6, 3) **65.** (0, 5) and (–4, 2) **66.** (–6, 4) and (2, –6)

Tell whether the given side lengths form a right triangle.

67. 6, 8, 10 **68.** 8, 11, 13 **69.** 30, 40, 45 **70.** 0.8, 1.5, 1.7

Extra Practice

Extra Practice ... Chapter 4

Extra Practice

LESSON 1

1. A penny has a mass of 2.5 g and a volume of approximately 0.442 cm^3. What is the approximate density of a penny?

2. Nikko jogs the first 3 miles of a 10-mile training run in 30 minutes.

a. What is Nikko's average speed in miles per hour?

b. Nikko estimates that at this speed, she will finish the entire run in less than 2 hours. Is Nikko's estimate reasonable? Explain.

3. Find the unit rate for each brand of detergent, and determine which brand is the best buy.

Product	Size	Price
Pizzazz detergent	128 oz	$3.08
Spring Clean detergent	64 oz	$1.60
Bubbling detergent	196 oz	$4.51

LESSON 2

Tell whether the ratios are proportional.

4. $\frac{7}{8}$ and $\frac{3}{4}$ **5.** $\frac{3}{4}$ and $\frac{24}{32}$ **6.** $\frac{32}{48}$ and $\frac{18}{27}$ **7.** $\frac{12}{20}$ and $\frac{6}{12}$

Solve each proportion.

8. $\frac{186 \text{ miles}}{3 \text{ hours}} = \frac{m \text{ miles}}{5 \text{ hours}}$ **9.** $\frac{10 \text{ invitations}}{12 \text{ envelopes}} = \frac{15 \text{ invitations}}{e \text{ envelopes}}$

10. $\frac{3}{8} = \frac{n}{12}$ **11.** $\frac{c}{15} = \frac{3}{45}$ **12.** $\frac{7}{18} = \frac{3}{m}$ **13.** $\frac{5}{f} = \frac{8}{12}$

14. Ricki jogged 4 miles in 36 minutes. At this rate, how long would it take Ricki to jog 12 miles?

15. Nicole is taking a test with 42 questions. It takes her 8 minutes to answer the first 6 questions. If she continues to answer questions at the same rate, how many more minutes will it take her to finish the test?

LESSON 3

16. Which triangles are similar?

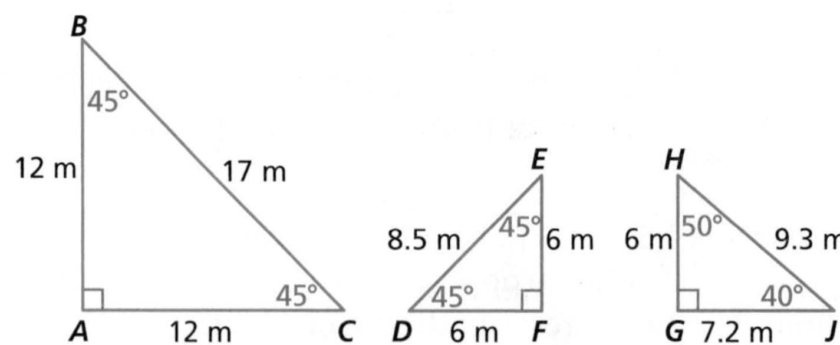

17. Khaled scans a photo that is 5 in. wide by 7 in. long into his computer. If he scales the length down to 3.5 in., how wide should the similar photo be?

18. Mutsuko drew an 8.5-inch-wide by 11-inch-tall picture that will be turned into a 34-inch-wide poster. How tall will the poster be?

Extra Practice ... Chapter 4

LESSON 

Tell whether each transformation is a dilation. Explain.

19.

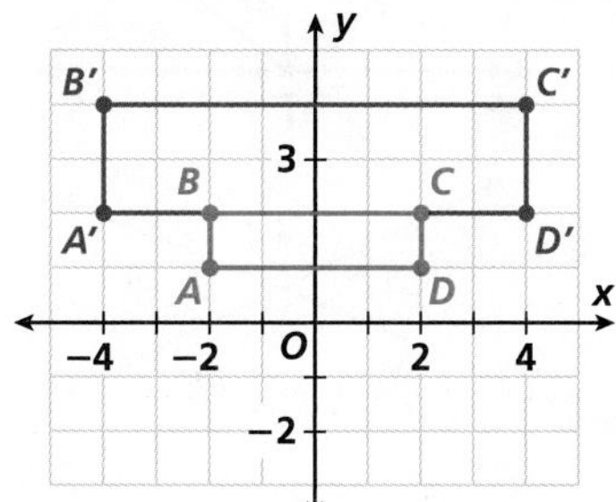

20.

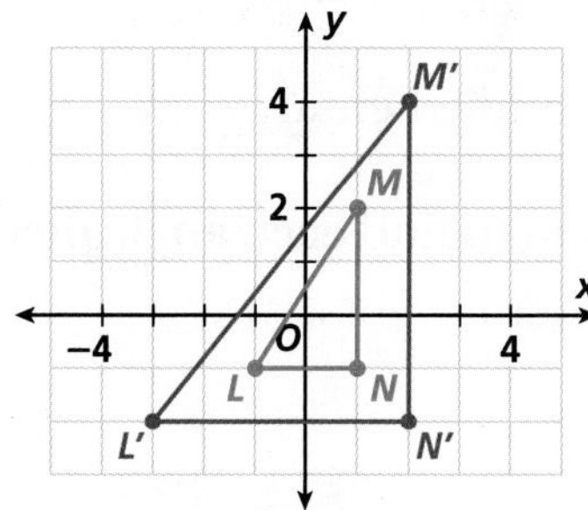

21. A figure has vertices at (2, 3), (3, 6), (6, 7), and (7, 2). The figure is dilated by a scale factor of 1.5 with the origin as the center of dilation. What are the vertices of the image?

Extra Practice

Extra Practice ... Chapter 5

LESSON 1

Use the diagram to name each figure.

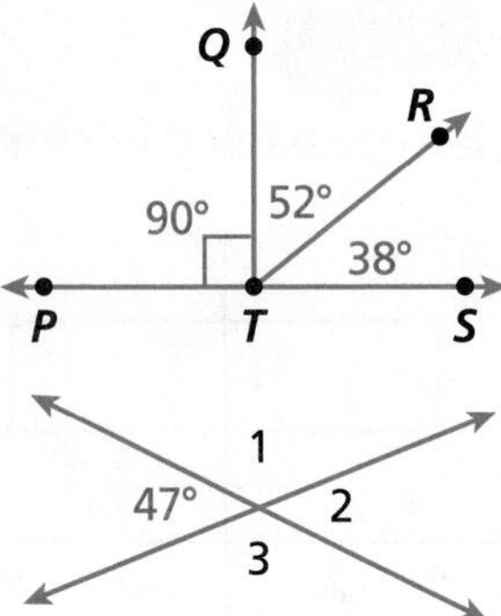

1. an obtuse angle
2. a pair of complementary angles

Use the diagram to find each angle measure.

3. m∠1 4. m∠2 5. m∠3

LESSON 2

In the figure, line *d* || line *f*. Find the measure of each angle. Justify your answer.

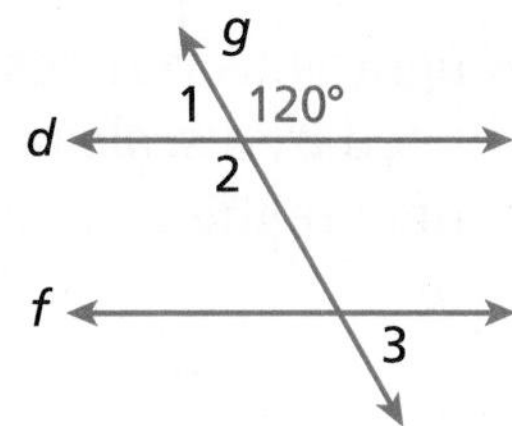

6. ∠1 7. ∠2 8. ∠3

LESSON 3

Find the missing angle measure in each triangle.

9.

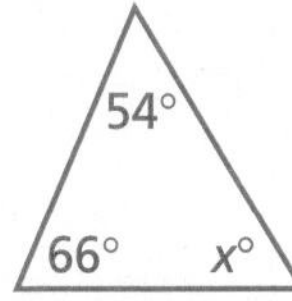

10.

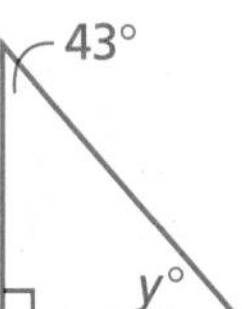

11.

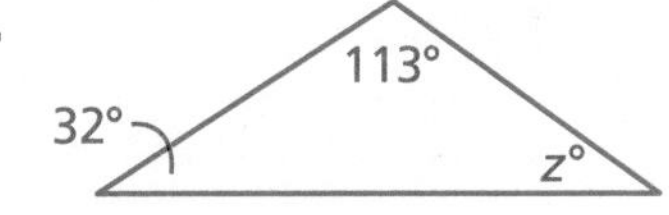

12. Tell whether a triangle can have sides measuring 8 cm, 9 cm, and 15 cm. Explain.

LESSON 4

13. Graph the polygon with the vertices *Q*(–2, 1), *R*(2, 1), *S*(1, –1), *T*(–1, –1). Give the most specific name for the polygon.

Find the coordinates of each missing vertex.

14. square *JKLM* with *J*(1, 1), *K*(4, 1), and *L*(4, −2)
15. rectangle *ABCD* with *A*(−4, 3), *B*(−1, 3), and *D*(−4, −1)

LESSON 5

In the figure, quadrilateral *ABCD* ≅ quadrilateral *KLMN*.

16. Find *x*.
17. Find *y*.
18. Find *z*.

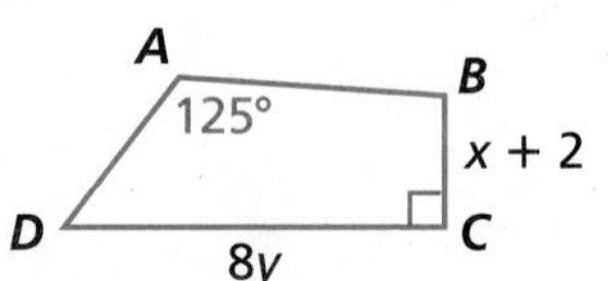

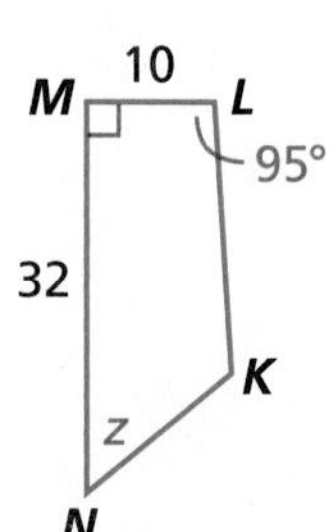

Extra Practice ... Chapter 5

LESSON 

Graph each translation.

19. 5 units left and 3 units down

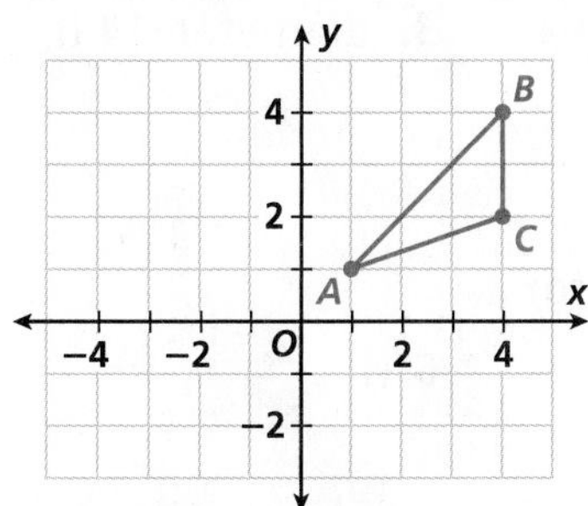

20. 3 units right and 4 units up

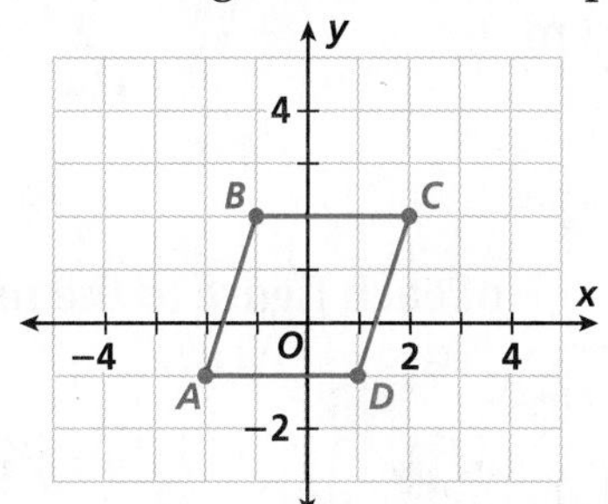

Graph each transformation.

21. reflection across the x-axis

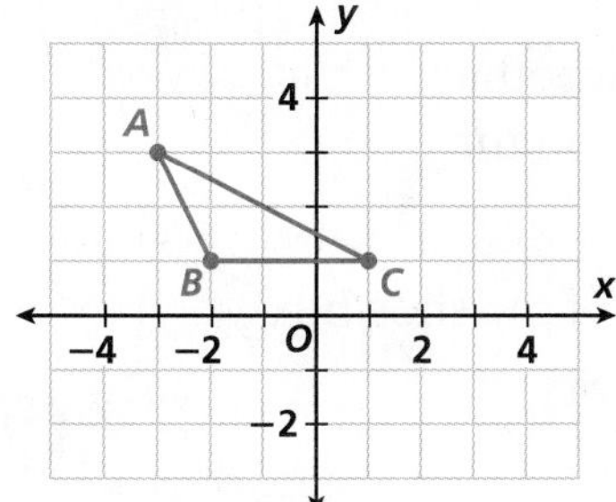

22. rotation 180° around the origin

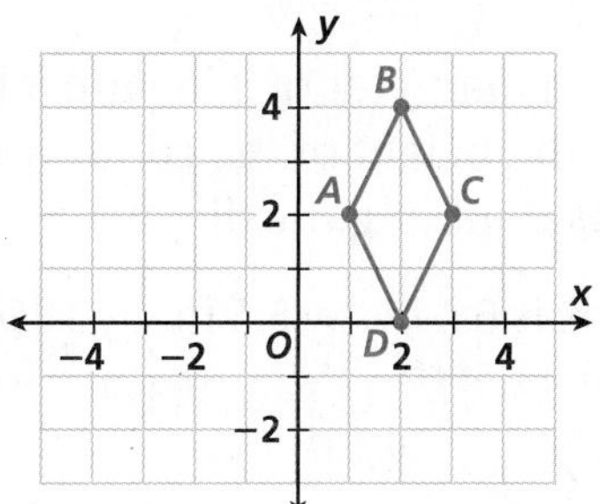

LESSON 

Identify each transformation from the original to the image, and tell whether the two figures are similar or congruent.

23. Original: $D(2, 3)$, $E(-1, 4)$, $F(2, 4)$
Image: $D'(1, 4)$, $E'(-2, 5)$, $F'(1, 5)$
Original: $A(7, 0)$, $B(-4, -6)$, $C(-5, 8)$, $D(1, 11)$
Image: $A'(3.5, 0)$, $B'(-2, -3)$, $C'(-2.5, 4)$, $D'(0.5, 5.5)$

LESSON 

24. Identify the combined transformations from the original to the final image, and tell whether the two images are similar or congruent.

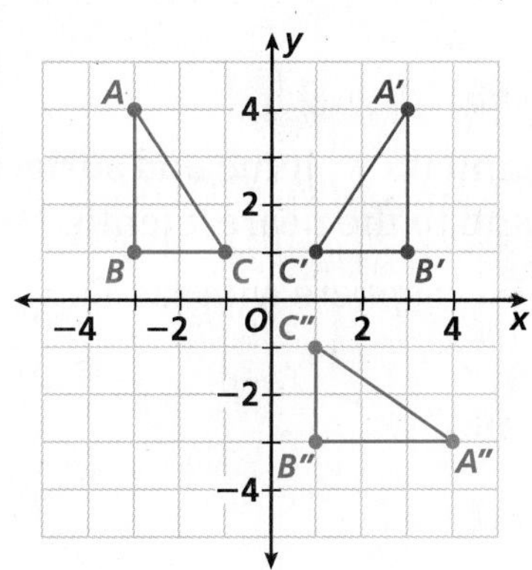

Extra Practice ... Chapter 6

LESSON 

Find the circumference and area of each circle, both in terms of π and to the nearest tenth. Use 3.14 for π.

1. radius 4 cm

2. radius 14 in.

3. diameter 14 ft

LESSON 

Find the volume of each figure to the nearest tenth. Use 3.14 for π.

4.

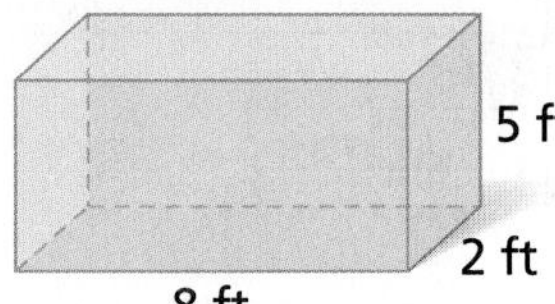

5.

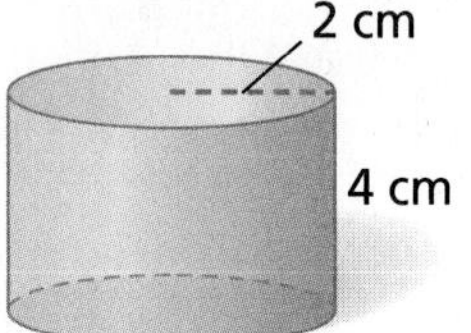

6.

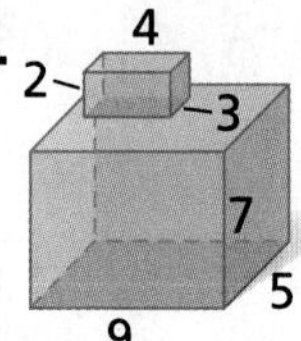

7. A can has a diameter of 3 in. and a height of 5 in. Explain whether doubling the height of the can would have the same effect on the volume as doubling the diameter.

8. A shoe box is 6.5 in. by 5.5 in. by 16 in. Estimate the volume of the shoe box.

LESSON 

Find the volume of each figure to the nearest tenth. Use 3.14 for π.

9.

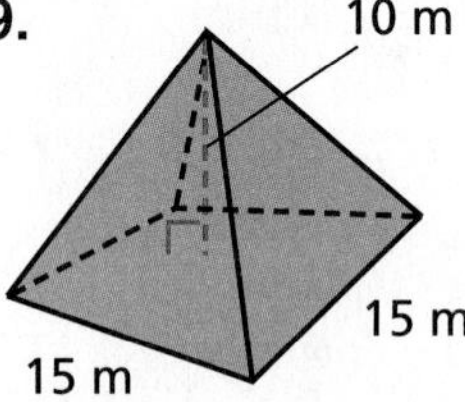

10.

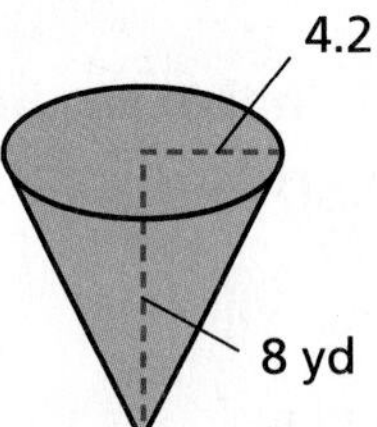

11.

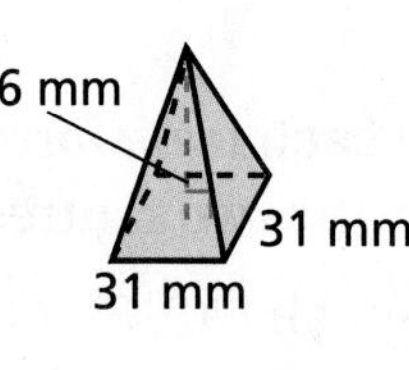

12. A rectangular pyramid has a height of 15 ft and a base that measures 5 ft by 7.5 ft. Explain whether doubling the height would double the volume of the pyramid.

LESSON 

Find the volume and surface area of each sphere, both in terms of π and to the nearest tenth. Use 3.14 for π.

13. a sphere with radius 5 ft

14. a sphere with diameter 40 cm

Extra Practice ... Chapter 7

Extra Practice

LESSON 1

Combine like terms.

1. $5x + 4x + 7x$ **2.** $6x^2 - 4x + 9 + 5x^2 + 7$ **3.** $2x + 3 - 2x + 5$

4. $7a - 2b + 6 + 4b - 5a$ **5.** $4s + 9t - 9$ **6.** $6m + 4n^3 - 6m + n^3$

Simplify.

7. $6(y + 4) - y$ **8.** $3(3b - 3) + 3b$ **9.** $4(x + 2) + 3x - 8$

Solve.

10. $8x - 4x = 80$ **11.** $5a - 3a = 44$ **12.** $3b + 6b = 63$ **13.** $5h + h = 90$

14. $5y + 3y = 24$ **15.** $8d - 3d = 40$ **16.** $2m + m = 42$ **17.** $9x - x = 48$

18. $a + 6a = 49$ **19.** $2p + 8p = 100$ **20.** $12y - 8y = 44$ **21.** $5f + 7f + 3f = 30$

LESSON 2

Solve.

22. $4a - 5 + 2a + 9 = 28$ **23.** $5 - 8b + 6 - 2b = 61$ **24.** $4x - 6 - 8x - 9 = 21$

25. $g - 9 + 4g + 6 = 12$ **26.** $2 - 3f - 5 + 5f = 6$ **27.** $4r - 8 + 7 - 6r = -9$

28. $4(a - 1) + 3 = 7$ **29.** $2(b - 2) + 6 = -10$ **30.** $8(z + 5) - 34 = -2$

31. $6(f - 3) + 12 = 18$ **32.** $20(c + 3) - 4 = 56$ **33.** $-9(x + 5) + 6 = -12$

34. $\frac{8}{9} - \frac{5m}{9} = \frac{23}{9}$ **35.** $\frac{9}{11} - \frac{3s}{11} = \frac{3}{11}$ **36.** $\frac{4p}{3} - \frac{2}{3} = 6$

37. $\frac{42y}{6} - \frac{9}{3} + \frac{16y}{8} = \frac{396}{12}$ **38.** $\frac{27a}{9} + \frac{15}{3} - \frac{8a}{2} = \frac{36}{6}$ **39.** $\frac{4b}{4} + \frac{b}{2} - \frac{6}{2} = \frac{12}{8}$

40. A round-trip car ride took 12 hours. The first half of the trip took 7 hours at a rate of 45 miles per hour. What was the average rate of speed on the return trip?

Extra Practice ... Chapter 7

LESSON 3

Solve.

41. $5x - 6 = 2x$

42. $4w + 5 = 20 - w$

43. $3y + 12 = -3y$

44. $2b + 6 = -b + 3$

45. $4z - 2 = z + 1$

46. $-4a - 4 = a + 11$

47. $4p - 6 = 3 + 4p$

48. $6 + 5c = 3c - 4$

49. $7d - 3 + 2d = 5d - 8 + 1$

50. $3f - 4 - 5f = f + 4 + f$

51. $5k - 4 - k = 3k - 6 + 2k$

52. $2w + 5 - 8w = 7 - 4w$

53. A cafeteria charges a fixed price per ounce for the salad bar. A sandwich costs \$3.10, and a drink costs \$1.75. If a 7-ounce salad and a drink cost the same as a 4-ounce salad and a sandwich, how much does the salad cost per ounce?

LESSON  4

Solve each system of equations.

54. $x - 2y = -10$
$5x + 2y = -2$

55. $y = 2x$
$y = x + 6$

56. $3x + 4y = 17$
$-2x + 4y = 2$

57. $y + 2x = 5$
$y = x - 4$

58. $y + 2x = -2$
$2y - 2x = 14$

59. $y = x + 4$
$y = 2x + 6$

60. $y = 3x - 1$
$y = 2x + 2$

61. $-y = x + 1$
$y = -2x - 4$

62. $2x + y = 0$
$2x + 3y = 8$

63. $x + y = -5$
$x - 2y = 7$

64. $y = x - 1$
$-3x + 3y = 4$

65. $-x - y = 0$
$y = x + 8$

66. $y = x - 5$
$x - y - 5 = 0$

67. $2y - x = 6$
$4y + 2x = -4$

68. $3y - 2x = -2$
$y + 2x = -6$

69. $y = -2x + 1$
$2x + y = 4$

70. Jacob bought a dozen breakfast tacos for a total of \$16. Bacon tacos cost \$1.25 each, and sausage tacos cost \$1.50 each. Solve the system of equations to find how many bacon tacos b and how many sausage tacos s Jacob bought.

$$b + s = 12$$
$$1.25b + 1.50s = 16$$

Extra Practice ... Chapter 8

LESSON 1

Graph each equation and tell whether it is linear.

1. $y = 4x - 2$
2. $y = -2x + 1$
3. $y = x^2 - 4$
4. $y = -x - 3$

5. A home improvement store charges a base fee of $150, plus $25 for each hour of machinery rental. The cost C for h hours is given by $C = 25h + 150$. Find the cost for 1, 2, 3, 4, and 5 hours. Graph the relationship between the cost and the number of hours of rental. Tell whether it is linear.

LESSON 2

Find the slope of each line.

6. 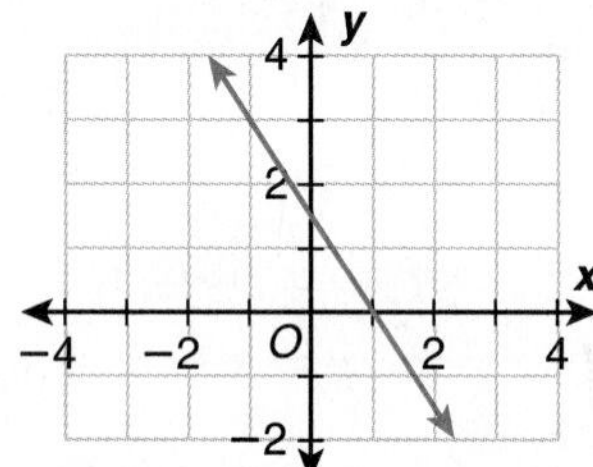

7. 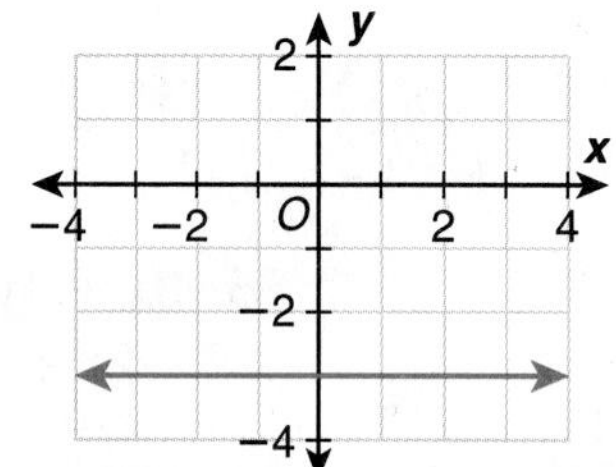

8. 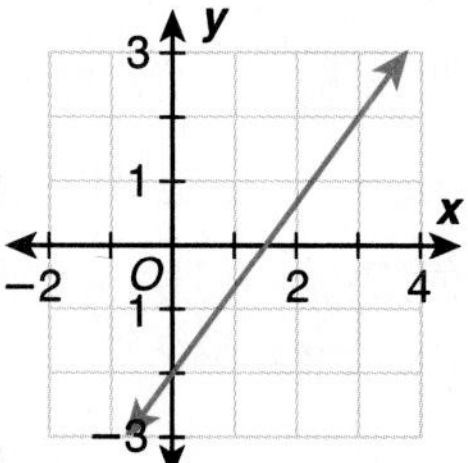

Find the slope of the line that passes through each pair of given points.

9. (3, 4) and (−2, 2)
10. (6, 2) and (−2, −6)
11. (3, 3) and (1, −4)
12. (−2, 4) and (1, 1)

13. The table shows how much money Andy and Margie made working at the concession stand at a baseball game one weekend. Use the data to make a graph. Find the slope of the line and explain what the slope means.

Time (h)	Money Earned($)
2	15
4	30
6	45
8	60

LESSON 3

Find the x-intercept and y-intercept of each line. Use the intercepts to graph the equation.

14. $5x - 3y = 8$
15. $3y - x = 9$
16. $7x + 1 = 4y$
17. $3y + x = 5$

Write each equation in slope-intercept form, and then find the slope and y-intercept.

18. $3x = y$
19. $3y = 5x$
20. $5x - y = 8$
21. $6y + 7 = 2x$

Write the equation of the line that passes through each pair of points in slope-intercept form.

22. (5, −1) and (−7, −4)
23. (5, 1) and (−1, −5)
24. (4, 9) and (−5, 3)

Extra Practice ... Chapter 8

LESSON 

Use the point-slope form of each equation to identify a point the line passes through and the slope of the line.

25. $y - 2 = \frac{1}{3}(x + 1)$ **26.** $y + 3 = -3(x - 2)$ **27.** $y - 4 = -\frac{1}{3}(x - 5)$

28. $y + 5 = 2(x - 1)$ **29.** $y - 2 = \frac{4}{7}(x + 5)$ **30.** $y = -\frac{3}{4}(x - 4)$

Write the point-slope form of the equation with the given slope that passes through the indicated point.

31. the line with slope 2 passing through (1, 4)

32. the line with slope $\frac{1}{4}$ passing through (−3, 2)

LESSON 5

Determine whether the data sets show direct variation.

33.

Weight (lb)	60	70	80	90
Dose (mg)	30	35	40	45

34.

Cards	200	300	400	500
Shipping ($)	5	6	7	8

Find each equation of direct variation, given that *y* varies directly with *x*.

35. *y* is 24 when *x* is 8. **36.** *y* is 18 when *x* is 12. **37.** *y* is 96 when *x* is 3.

38. *y* is 8 when *x* is 4. **39.** *y* is 102 when *x* is 17. **40.** *y* is 17 when *x* is 6.

41. Instructions for a swimming pool cleaner state that 2 ounces of concentrate should be added to every $1\frac{1}{2}$ gallons of water used. How much concentrate should be added to 18 gallons of water?

LESSON 

Solve each linear system by graphing. Check your answer algebraically.

42. $y = -x$
$y = 3 - 2x$

43. $2y - 3 = x$
$1 - x = -2y$

44. $6y + 12 = -2x$
$x + 3y = -6$

45. At 10 a.m., Emma begins walking on a path at a rate of 3 miles per hour. One hour later her friend Sara starts at the same point and begins walking on the path at 4 miles per hour. How long will it take Sara to catch up to Emma on the path?

Extra Practice

Extra Practice ■■■ Chapter 9

Extra Practice

LESSON 1

1. Make a scatter plot of the data, and draw a line of best fit. Then use the data to predict the salary of a person with 7 years of post-high school education.

Number of years of post High School Education and Salary												
Years	1	1	3	4	4	4	5	5	6	6	8	8
Salary ($1,000's)	18	20.5	28	35	51	43	58	52	64	58	75	73.5

LESSON 2

The scatter plot shows data for television screen sizes from 2001 to 2010.

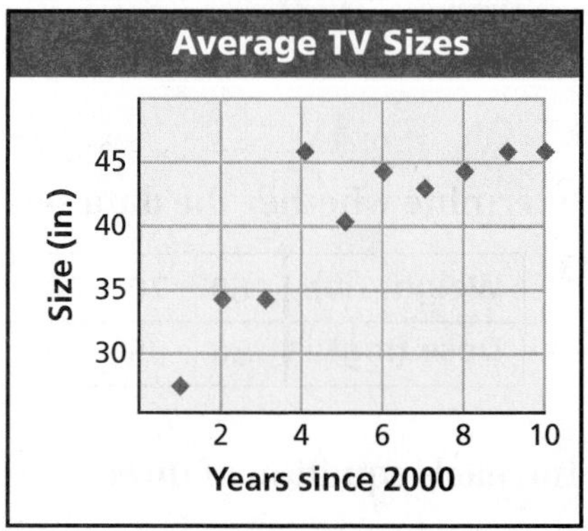

2. Find a line of best fit for the data.

3. Use your answer from Exercise 2 to predict the average television screen size in 2015.

4. How might your answers for Exercises 1 and 2 change if you only considered data from 2004 to 2010? Explain.

LESSON 3

Determine whether each function is linear. If so, give the slope and *y*-intercept of the function's graph.

5. $f(x) = -\frac{1}{x} + 4$

6. $f(x) = 6^x + 2$

7. $f(x) = \frac{2}{3}x$

8. $f(x) = 3x^{-5}$

9. $f(x) = 0.5x + 8$

10. $f(x) = 9$

Write a rule for each linear function.

11.

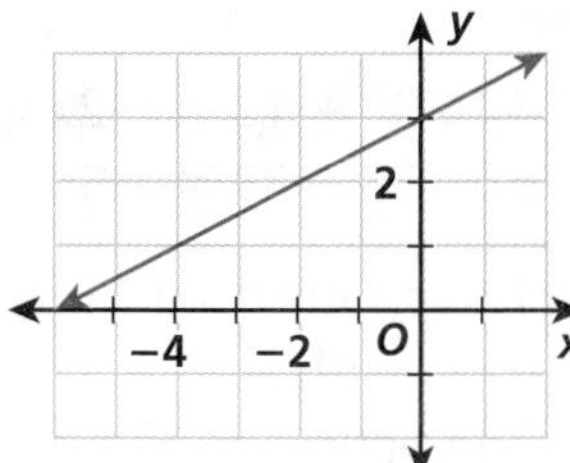

12.

x	y
−2	−5
−1	−3
0	−1
1	1
2	3

13.

x	y
−2	4
−1	3
0	2
1	1
2	0

14. Reo's cell phone company charges a monthly fee of $12, plus $0.10 each minute that he talks on the phone. Find a rule for the linear function that describes the monthly phone charges if Reo uses his phone *x* minutes in a month, and use it to find how much he pays if he talks 72 minutes in a month.

Extra Practice ... Chapter 9

LESSON 4

Find and compare the slopes of the two linear functions f and g.

15. $f(x) = \frac{5}{2}x - 8$ and

x	−0.3	0.5	0.9
$g(x)$	4	6	7

Find and compare the y-intercepts of the two linear functions f and g.

16.

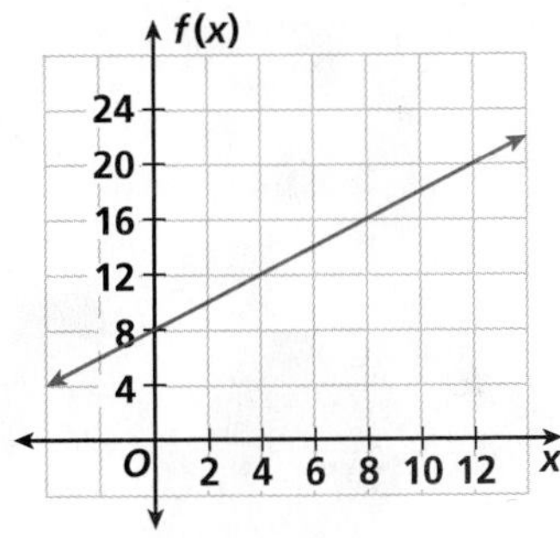

and

x	−2	4	7
$g(x)$	3	0	−1.5

Extra Practice

Draw a Diagram

When problems involve objects, distances, or places, drawing a diagram can make the problem clearer. You can **draw a diagram** to help understand the problem and to solve the problem.

Problem Solving Strategies

Draw a Diagram	Make a Table
Make a Model	Solve a Simpler Problem
Guess and Test	Use Logical Reasoning
Work Backward	Use a Venn Diagram
Find a Pattern	Make an Organized List

June is moving her cat, dog, and goldfish to her new apartment. She can only take 1 pet with her on each trip. She cannot leave the cat and the dog or the cat and the goldfish alone together. How can she get all of her pets safely to her new apartment?

Understand the Problem The answer will be the description of the trips to her new apartment. At no time can the cat be alone with the dog or the goldfish.

Make a Plan **Draw a diagram** to represent each trip to and from the apartment.

Solve In the beginning, the cat, dog, and goldfish are all at her old apartment.

Old Apartment		New Apartment	
June, Cat, Dog, Fish	June, Cat →	June, Cat	*Trip 1: She takes the cat and returns alone.*
June, Dog, Fish	← June	Cat	
June, Dog, Fish	June, Dog →	June, Dog, Cat	*Trip 2: She takes the dog and returns with the cat.*
June, Cat, Fish	← June, Cat	Dog	
June, Cat, Fish	June, Fish →	June, Dog, Fish	*Trip 3: She takes the fish and returns alone.*
June, Cat	← June	Dog, Fish	
June, Cat	June, Cat →	June, Cat, Dog, Fish	*Trip 4: She takes the cat.*

Look Back Check to make sure that the cat is never alone with either the fish or the dog.

PRACTICE

1. There are 8 flags evenly spaced around a circular track. It takes Ling 15 seconds to run from the first flag to the third flag. At this pace, how long will it take Ling to run around the track twice?

2. A frog is climbing a 22-foot tree. Every 5 minutes, it climbs up 3 feet, but slips back down 1 foot. How long will it take the frog to climb the tree?

Make a Model

A problem that involves objects may be solved by making a model out of similar items. **Make a model** to help you understand the problem and find the solution.

Problem Solving Strategies

Draw a Diagram	Make a Table
Make a Model	Solve a Simpler Problem
Guess and Test	Use Logical Reasoning
Work Backward	Use a Venn Diagram
Find a Pattern	Make an Organized List

The volume of a rectangular prism can be found by using the formula $V = \ell wh$, where ℓ is the length, w is the width, and h is the height of the prism. Find all possible rectangular prisms with a volume of 16 cubic units and dimensions that are all whole numbers.

Understand the Problem You need to find the different possible prisms. The length, width, and height will be whole numbers whose product is 16.

Make a Plan You can use unit cubes to make a model of every possible rectangular prism. Work in a systematic way to find all possible answers.

Solve Begin with a $16 \times 1 \times 1$ prism.

16 × 1 × 1

Keeping the height of the prism the same, explore what happens to the length as you change the width. Then try a height of 2. Notice that an $8 \times 2 \times 1$ prism is the same as an $8 \times 1 \times 2$ prism turned on its side.

8 × 2 × 1

Not a rectangular prism

4 × 4 × 1

4 × 2 × 2

The possible dimensions are $16 \times 1 \times 1$, $8 \times 2 \times 1$, $4 \times 4 \times 1$, and $4 \times 2 \times 2$.

Look Back The product of the length, width, and height must be 16. Look at the prime factorization of the volume: $16 = 2 \cdot 2 \cdot 2 \cdot 2$. Possible dimensions:

$1 \cdot 1 \cdot (2 \cdot 2 \cdot 2 \cdot 2) = 1 \cdot 1 \cdot 16$

$1 \cdot 2 \cdot (2 \cdot 2 \cdot 2) = 1 \cdot 2 \cdot 8$

$1 \cdot (2 \cdot 2) \cdot (2 \cdot 2) = 1 \cdot 4 \cdot 4$

$2 \cdot 2 \cdot (2 \cdot 2) = 2 \cdot 2 \cdot 4$

PRACTICE

1. Four unit squares are arranged so that each square shares a side with another square. How many different arrangements are possible?

2. Four triangles are formed by cutting a rectangle along its diagonals. What possible shapes can be formed by arranging these triangles?

Guess and Test

When you think that guessing may help you solve a problem, you can use **guess and test.** Using clues to make guesses can narrow your choices for the solution. Test whether your guess solves the problem, and continue guessing until you find the solution.

Problem Solving Strategies

Draw a Diagram	Make a Table
Make a Model	Solve a Simpler Problem
Guess and Test	Use Logical Reasoning
Work Backward	Use a Venn Diagram
Find a Pattern	Make an Organized List

North Middle School is planning to raise \$1200 by sponsoring a car wash. They are going to charge \$4 for each car and \$8 for each minivan. How many vehicles would have to be washed to raise \$1200 if they plan to wash twice as many cars as minivans?

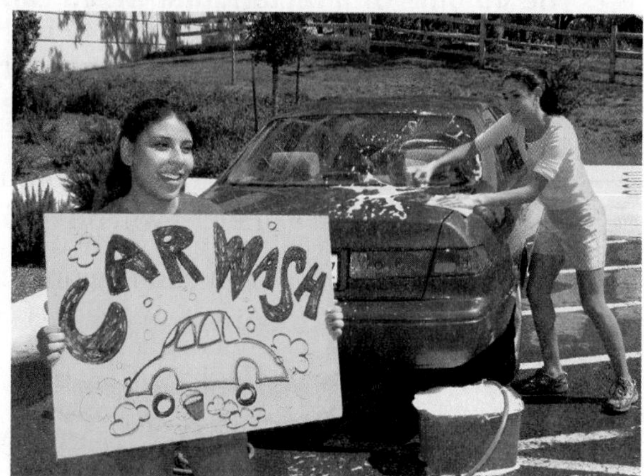

Understand the Problem You must determine the number of cars and the number of minivans that need to be washed to make \$1200. You know the charge for each vehicle.

Make a Plan You can **guess and test** to find the number of cars and minivans. Guess the number of cars, and then divide it by 2 to find the number of minivans.

Solve You can organize your guesses in a table.

	Cars	Minivans	Money Raised	
First guess	200	100	\$4(200) + \$8(100) = \$1600	*Too high*
Second guess	100	50	\$4(100) + \$8(50) = \$800	*Too low*
Third guess	150	75	\$4(150) + \$8(75) = \$1200	

They should wash 150 cars and 75 minivans, or 225 vehicles.

Look Back The total raised is \$4(150) + \$8(75) = \$1200, and the number of cars is twice the number of minivans. The answer is reasonable.

PRACTICE

1. At a baseball game, adult tickets cost \$15 and children's tickets cost \$8. Twice as many children attended as adults, and the total ticket sales were \$2480. How many people attended the game?

2. Angie is making friendship bracelets and pins. It takes her 6 minutes to make a bracelet and 4 minutes to make a pin. If she wants to make three times as many pins as bracelets, how many pins and bracelets can she make in 3 hours?

Work Backward

To solve a problem that asks for an initial value that precedes a series of steps, you may want to **work backward**.

Problem Solving Strategies

Draw a Diagram	Make a Table
Make a Model	Solve a Simpler Problem
Guess and Test	Use Logical Reasoning
Work Backward	Use a Venn Diagram
Find a Pattern	Make an Organized List

Tyrone has two clocks and a watch. If the power goes off during the day, the following happens:

- **Clock A stops and then continues when the power comes back on.**
- **Clock B stops and then resets to 12:00 A.M. when the power comes back on.**

When Tyrone gets home, his watch reads 4:27 P.M., clock B reads 5:21 A.M., and clock A reads 3:39 P.M. What time did the power go off, and for how long was it off?

Understand the Problem You need to find the time that the power went off and how long it was off. You know how each clock works.

Make a Plan **Work backward** to the time that the power went off. Subtract from the correct time of 4:27 P.M., the time on Tyrone's watch.

Solve The difference between the correct time and the time on clock A is the length of time the power was off.

4:27 P.M. − 3:39 P.M. = 48 min *The power was off for 48 min.*

Clock B reset to 12:00 A.M. when the power went on.

Clock B reads 5:21 A.M. *The power came on 5 h 21 min ago.*

Subtract 5 h 21 min from the correct time to find when the power came on.

4:27 P.M. − 5 h 21 min = 11:06 A.M. *The power came on at 11:06 A.M.*

Subtract 48 min from 11:06 A.M. to find when the power went off.

11:06 A.M. − 48 min = 10:18 A.M.

The power went off at 10:18 A.M. and was off for 48 minutes.

Look Back If the power went off at about 10 A.M. for about an hour, it would come on at about 11 A.M., and each clock would run for about $5\frac{1}{2}$ hours.

PRACTICE

1. Jackie is 4 years younger than Roger. Roger is $2\frac{1}{2}$ years older than Jade. Jade is 14 years old. How old is Jackie?

2. Becca is directing a play that starts at 8:15 P.M. She wants the cast ready 10 minutes before the play starts. The cast needs 45 minutes to put on make-up, 15 minutes for a director's meeting, and then 35 minutes to get in costume. What time should the cast arrive?

Problem Solving Handbook

Find a Pattern

If a problem involves numbers, shapes, or even codes, noticing a pattern can often help you solve it. To solve a problem that involves patterns, you need to use small steps that will help you **find a pattern**.

Problem Solving Strategies

Draw a Diagram	Make a Table
Make a Model	Solve a Simpler Problem
Guess and Test	Use Logical Reasoning
Work Backward	Use a Venn Diagram
Find a Pattern	Make an Organized List

Gil is trying to decode the following sentence, which may have been encoded using a pattern. What does the coded sentence say?

QEB NRFZH YOLTK CLU GRJMP LSBO QEB IXWV ALD.

Understand the Problem You need to find whether there was a pattern used to encode the sentence and then extend the pattern to decode the sentence.

Make a Plan **Find a pattern.** Try to decode one of the words first. Notice that *QEB* appears twice in the sentence.

Solve Gil thinks that *QEB* is probably the word *THE*. If *QEB* stands for *THE*, a pattern emerges with respect to the letters and their position in the alphabet.

Q: 17th letter	*T*: 20th letter	*+ 3 letters*
E: 5th letter	*H*: 8th letter	*+ 3 letters*
B: 2nd letter	*E*: 5th letter	*+ 3 letters*

Continue the pattern. Although there is no 27th, 28th, or 29th letter of the alphabet, the remaining letters should be obvious (27 = 1 = *A*, 28 = 2 = *B*, and 29 = 3 = *C*).

QEB NRFZH YOLTK CLU GRJMP LSBO QEB IXWV ALD.
THE QUICK BROWN FOX JUMPS OVER THE LAZY DOG.

Look Back The sentence makes sense, so the pattern fits.

PRACTICE

Decode each sentence.

1. RFC DGTC ZMVGLE UGXYPBQ HSKN OSGAIJW.
(*RFC* = *THE*)

2. U PYLS VUX KOUWE GCABN DCHR TCJJS ZIQFM.
(*U* = *A*)

Make a Table

To solve a problem that involves a relationship between two sets of numbers, you can **make a table.** A table can be used to organize data so that you can look at relationships and find the solution.

Problem Solving Strategies

Draw a Diagram	**Make a Table**
Make a Model	Solve a Simpler Problem
Guess and Test	Use Logical Reasoning
Work Backward	Use a Venn Diagram
Find a Pattern	Make an Organized List

Jill has 12 pieces of 2 ft long decorative edging. She wants to use the edging to enclose a garden with the greatest possible area against the back of her house. What is the largest garden she can make?

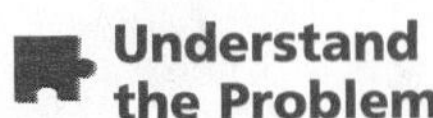

Understand the Problem

You must determine the length and width of the edging.

Make a Plan

Make a table of the possible widths and lengths. Begin with the least possible width and increase by multiples of 2 ft. Remember that the width is the same on two sides.

Solve

Use the table to solve.

Width (ft)	Length (ft)	Garden Area (ft^2)
2	20	40
4	16	64
6	12	72
8	8	64
10	4	40

The maximum area that the garden can be is 72 ft^2, with a width of 6 ft and a length of 12 ft.

Look Back

She can use 3 pieces of edging for the first side, 6 pieces for the second side, and another 3 pieces for the third side.

$3 + 6 + 3 = 12$ pieces
6 ft + 12 ft + 6 ft = 24 ft

PRACTICE

1. Suppose Jill decided not to use the house as one side of the garden. What is the greatest area that she could enclose?
2. A store sells batteries in packs of 3 for \$3.99 and 2 for \$2.99. Barry got 14 batteries for \$18.95. How many of each package did he buy?

Solve a Simpler Problem

If a problem contains large numbers or requires many steps, try to **solve a simpler problem** first. Look for similarities between the problems, and use them to solve the original problem.

Problem Solving Strategies

Draw a Diagram	Make a Table
Make a Model	**Solve a Simpler Problem**
Guess and Test	Use Logical Reasoning
Work Backward	Use a Venn Diagram
Find a Pattern	Make an Organized List

Noemi heard that 10 computers in her school would be connected to each other. She thought that there would be a cable connecting each computer to every other computer. How many cables would be needed if this were true?

Understand the Problem

You know that there are 10 computers and that each computer would require a separate cable to connect to every other computer. You need to find the total number of cables.

Make a Plan

Start by **solving a simpler problem** with fewer computers.

Solve

The simplest problem starts with 2 computers.

2 computers
1 connection

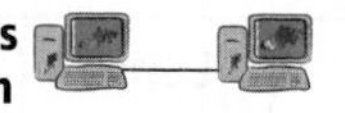

3 computers
3 connections

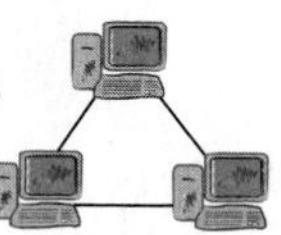

4 computers
6 connections

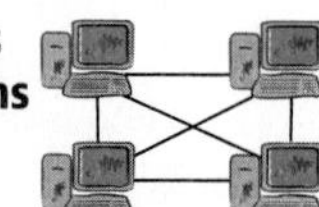

Organize the data in a table to help you find a pattern.

Number of Computers	Number of Connections
2	1
3	$1 + 2 = 3$
4	$1 + 2 + 3 = 6$
5	$1 + 2 + 3 + 4 = 10$
10	$1 + 2 + 3 + 4 + 5 + 6 + 7 + 8 + 9 = 45$

So if a separate cable were needed to connect each of 10 computers to every other one, 45 cables would be required.

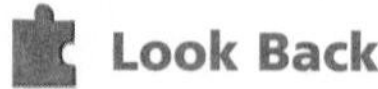

Look Back

Extend the number of computers to check that the pattern continues.

PRACTICE

1. A banquet table seats 2 people on each side and 1 at each end. If 6 tables are placed end to end, how many seats can there be?

2. How many diagonals are there in a dodecagon (a 12-sided polygon)?

Use Logical Reasoning

Sometimes a problem may provide clues and facts to help you find a solution. You can **use logical reasoning** to help solve this kind of problem.

Problem Solving Strategies

Draw a Diagram	Make a Table
Make a Model	Solve a Simpler Problem
Guess and Test	**Use Logical Reasoning**
Work Backward	Use a Venn Diagram
Find a Pattern	Make an Organized List

Kim, Lily, and Suki take ballet, tap, and jazz classes (but not in that order). Kim is the sister of the person who takes ballet. Lily takes tap. Match each girl with the class she takes.

Understand the Problem You want to determine which person is in which dance class. You know that there are three people and that each person takes only one dance class.

Make a Plan **Use logical reasoning** to make a table of the facts from the problem.

Solve List the types of dance and the people's names. Write *Yes* or *No* when you are sure of an answer. Lily takes tap.

	Ballet	Tap	Jazz
Kim		No	
Lily	No	Yes	No
Suki		No	

The person taking ballet is Kim's sister, so Kim does not take ballet. Suki must be the one taking ballet.

	Ballet	Tap	Jazz
Kim	No	No	
Lily	No	Yes	No
Suki	Yes	No	No

Kim must be the one taking jazz.

Kim takes jazz, Lily takes tap, and Suki takes ballet.

Look Back Make sure none of your conclusions conflict with the clues.

PRACTICE

1. Patrick, John, and Vanessa have a snake, a cat and a rabbit. Patrick's pet does not have fur. Vanessa does not have a cat. Match the owners with their pets.
2. Isabella, Keifer, Dylan, and Chrissy are in the sixth, seventh, eighth, and ninth grades. Isabella is not in seventh grade. The sixth-grader has band with Dylan and lunch with Isabella. Chrissy is in the ninth grade. Match the students with their grades.

Use a Venn Diagram

You can **use a Venn diagram** to display relationships among sets in a problem. Use ovals, circles, or other shapes to represent individual sets.

Problem Solving Strategies

Draw a Diagram	Make a Table
Make a Model	Solve a Simpler Problem
Guess and Test	Use Logical Reasoning
Work Backward	**Use a Venn Diagram**
Find a Pattern	Make an Organized List

Patricia took a poll of 100 students. She wrote down that 32 play basketball and 45 run track. Of those students, 19 do both. Mrs. Thornton wants to know how many of the students polled only play basketball.

Understand the Problem

You know that 100 students were polled, 32 play basketball, 45 run track, and 19 play basketball *and* run track.

The answer is the number of students who only play basketball.

Make a Plan

Use a Venn diagram to show the sets of students who play basketball, students who run track, and students who do both.

Solve

Draw and label two overlapping circles in a rectangle. Work from the inside out. Write 19 in the area where the two circles overlap. This represents the number of students who play basketball and run track.

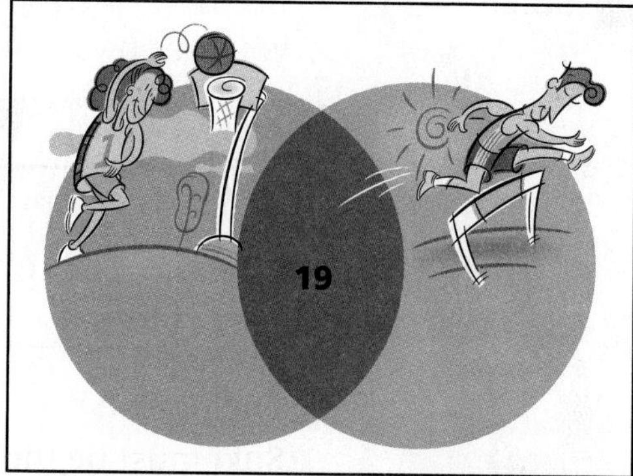

Use the information in the problem to complete the diagram. You know that 32 students play basketball, and 19 of those students run track.

So 13 students only play basketball.

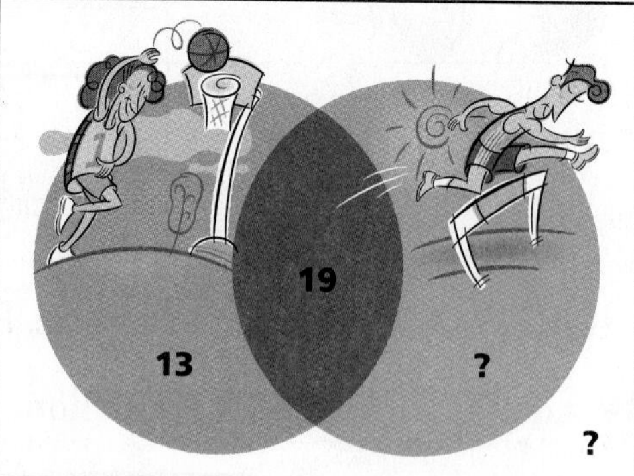

Look Back

When your Venn diagram is complete, check it carefully against the information in the problem to make sure it agrees with the facts given.

PRACTICE

1. How many of the students only run track?

2. How many of the students do not play basketball or run track?

Make an Organized List

In some problems, you will need to find out exactly how many different ways an event can happen. When solving this kind of problem, it is often helpful to **make an organized list**. This will help you count all the possible outcomes.

Problem Solving Strategies

Draw a Diagram	Make a Table
Make a Model	Solve a Simpler Problem
Guess and Test	Use Logical Reasoning
Work Backward	Use a Venn Diagram
Find a Pattern	**Make an Organized List**

What is the greatest amount of money you can have in coins (quarters, dimes, nickels, and pennies) without being able to make change for a dollar?

Understand the Problem

You are looking for an amount of money. You cannot have any combinations of coins that make a dollar, such as 4 quarters or 3 quarters, 2 dimes, and a nickel.

Make a Plan

Make an organized list, starting with the maximum possible number of each type of coin. Consider all the ways you can add other types of coins without making exactly one dollar.

Solve

List the maximum number of each kind of coin you can have.

3 quarters = 75¢ 9 dimes = 90¢ 19 nickels = 95¢ 99 pennies = 99¢

Next, list all the possible combinations of two kinds of coins.

3 quarters and 4 dimes = 115¢
3 quarters and 4 nickels = 95¢
3 quarters and 24 pennies = 99¢

9 dimes and 1 quarter = 115¢
9 dimes and 1 nickel = 95¢
9 dimes and 9 pennies = 99¢

19 nickels and 4 pennies = 99¢

Look for any combinations from this list that you could add another kind of coin to without making exactly one dollar.

3 quarters, 4 dimes, and 4 pennies = 119¢
3 quarters, 4 nickels, and 4 pennies = 99¢
9 dimes, 1 quarter, and 4 pennies = 119¢
9 dimes, 1 nickel, and 4 pennies = 99¢

The largest amount you can have is 119¢, or $1.19.

Look Back

Try adding one of any type of coin to either combination that makes $1.19, and then see if you could make change for a dollar.

PRACTICE

1. How can you arrange the numbers 2, 6, 7, and 12 with the symbols +, ×, and ÷ to create the expression with the greatest value?
2. How many ways are there to arrange 24 desks in 3 or more equal rows if each row must have at least 2 desks?

Skills Bank

Place Value

A place-value chart can help you read and write numbers. The number 345,012,678,912.5784 (three hundred forty-five billion, twelve million, six hundred seventy-eight thousand, nine hundred twelve and five thousand seven hundred eighty-four ten-thousandths) is shown.

Billions	Millions	Thousands	Ones		Tenths	Hundredths	Thousandths	Ten-Thousandths
345,	012,	678,	912	.	5	7	8	4

EXAMPLE

Name the place value of the digit.

A the 7 in the thousands column
7 ⟶ *ten thousands place*

B the 0 in the millions column
0 ⟶ *hundred millions place*

C the 5 in the billions column
5 ⟶ *one billion, or billions, place*

D the 8 to the right of the decimal point
8 ⟶ *thousandths*

PRACTICE

Name the place value of the underlined digit.

1. 123,<u>4</u>56,789,123.0594 **2.** 1<u>2</u>3,456,789,123.0594 **3.** 123,456,789,123.05<u>9</u>4

4. 123,456,789,12<u>3</u>.0594 **5.** 123,456,789,123.<u>0</u>594 **6.** 123,45<u>6</u>,789,123.0594

Rounding

To round to a certain place, follow these steps.

1. Locate the digit in that place, and consider the next digit to the right.
2. If the digit to the right is 5 or greater, round up. Otherwise, round down.
3. Change each digit to the right of the rounding place to zero.

EXAMPLE

A **Round 125,439.378 to the nearest thousand.**
125,439.378 *Locate digit.*
The digit to the right is less than 5, so round down.
125,000.000 = 125,000

B **Round 125,439.378 to the nearest tenth.**
125,439.378 *Locate digit.*
The digit to the right is greater than 5, so round up.
125,439.400 = 125,539.4

PRACTICE

Round 259,345.278 to the place indicated.

1. hundred thousand **2.** ten thousand **3.** thousand **4.** hundred

Factors and Multiples

When two whole numbers are multiplied to get a third, the two numbers are said to be **factors** of the third number. **Multiples** of a number can be found by multiplying the number by 1, 2, 3, 4, and so on.

EXAMPLE

A **List all the factors of 48.**

$1 \cdot 48 = 48$, $2 \cdot 24 = 48$, $3 \cdot 16 = 48$,
$4 \cdot 12 = 48$, and $6 \cdot 8 = 48$

So the factors of 48 are
1, 2, 3, 4, 6, 8, 12, 16, 24, and 48.

B **Find the first five multiples of 3.**

$3 \cdot 1 = 3$, $3 \cdot 2 = 6$, $3 \cdot 3 = 9$,
$3 \cdot 4 = 12$, and $3 \cdot 5 = 15$

So the first five multiples of 3 are
3, 6, 9, 12, and 15.

PRACTICE

List all the factors of each number.

1. 8 **2.** 20 **3.** 9 **4.** 51 **5.** 16 **6.** 27

Write the first five multiples of each number.

7. 9 **8.** 10 **9.** 20 **10.** 15 **11.** 7 **12.** 18

Divisibility Rules

A number is divisible by another number if the division results in a remainder of 0. Some divisibility rules are shown below.

A number is divisible by . . .	Divisible	Not Divisible
2 if the last digit is an even number.	11,994	2,175
3 if the sum of the digits is divisible by 3.	216	79
4 if the last two digits form a number divisible by 4.	1,028	621
5 if the last digit is 0 or 5.	15,195	10,007
6 if the number is even and divisible by 3.	1,332	44
8 if the last three digits form a number divisible by 8.	25,016	14,100
9 if the sum of the digits is divisible by 9.	144	33
10 if the last digit is 0.	2,790	9,325

PRACTICE

Determine which of these numbers each number is divisible by: 2, 3, 4, 5, 6, 8, 9, 10.

1. 56 **2.** 200 **3.** 75 **4.** 324 **5.** 42 **6.** 812

7. 784 **8.** 501 **9.** 2345 **10.** 555,555 **11.** 3009 **12.** 2001

Skills Bank

Prime and Composite Numbers

A **prime number** is a whole number greater than 1 that has exactly two factors, 1 and the number itself.

2	Factors: 1 and 2; prime
11	Factors: 1 and 11; prime
47	Factors: 1 and 47; prime

A **composite number** is a whole number greater than 1 that has more than two factors.

4	Factors: 1, 2, and 4; composite
12	Factors: 1, 2, 3, 4, 6, and 12; composite
63	Factors: 1, 3, 7, 9, 21, and 63; composite

EXAMPLE

Determine whether each number is prime or composite.

A 17

Factors
1, 17 ⟶ prime

B 16

Factors
1, 2, 4, 8, 16 ⟶ composite

C 51

Factors
1, 3, 17, 51 ⟶ composite

PRACTICE

Determine whether each number is prime or composite.

1. 5 **2.** 14 **3.** 18 **4.** 2 **5.** 23 **6.** 27

7. 13 **8.** 39 **9.** 72 **10.** 49 **11.** 9 **12.** 89

Prime Factorization

A composite number can be expressed as a product of prime numbers. This is the **prime factorization** of the number. To find the prime factorization of a number, you can use a factor tree.

EXAMPLE

Find the prime factorization of 24.

24 2 · 12 2 · 3 · 4 2 · 3 · 2 · 2	24 3 · 8 3 · 2 · 4 3 · 2 · 2 · 2	24 4 · 6 2 · 2 · 2 · 3

The prime factorization of 24 is 2 · 2 · 2 · 3, or $2^3 \cdot 3$.

PRACTICE

Find the prime factorization of each number.

1. 25 **2.** 16 **3.** 56 **4.** 18 **5.** 72 **6.** 40

Greatest Common Factor (GCF)

The **greatest common factor (GCF)** of two whole numbers is the greatest factor the numbers have in common.

EXAMPLE

Find the GCF of 24 and 60.

Method 1: List all the factors of both numbers.

Find all the common factors.

24: 1, 2, 3, 4, 6, 8, 12, 24
60: 1, 2, 3, 4, 5, 6, 10, 12, 15, 20, 30, 60

The common factors are 1, 2, 3, 4, 6, and 12.
So the GCF is 12.

Method 2: Find the prime factorizations.

24: $2^3 \cdot 3$
60: $2^2 \cdot 3 \cdot 5$

Find the least power of each common prime factor: 2^2 and 3. The product of these is the GCF.
So the GCF is $2^2 \cdot 3 = 12$.

PRACTICE

Find the GCF of each pair of numbers by either method.

1. 9, 15 **2.** 25, 75 **3.** 18, 30 **4.** 4, 10 **5.** 12, 17 **6.** 30, 96
7. 54, 72 **8.** 15, 20 **9.** 40, 60 **10.** 40, 50 **11.** 14, 21 **12.** 14, 28

Least Common Multiple (LCM)

The **least common multiple (LCM)** of two whole numbers is the least multiple the numbers share.

EXAMPLE

Find the least common multiple of 8 and 10.

Method 1: List multiples of both numbers.

8: 8, 16, 24, 32, 40, 48, 56, 64, 72, 80
10: 10, 20, 30, 40, 50, 60, 70, 80, 90

The smallest common multiple is 40.

So the LCM is 40.

Method 2: Find the prime factorizations.

8: 2^3
10: $2 \cdot 5$

Find the greatest power of each prime factor: 2^3 and 5. The product of these is the LCM.

So the LCM is $2^3 \cdot 5 = 40$.

PRACTICE

Find the LCM of each pair of numbers by either method.

1. 2, 4 **2.** 3, 15 **3.** 10, 25 **4.** 10, 15 **5.** 3, 7 **6.** 18, 27
7. 12, 21 **8.** 9, 21 **9.** 24, 30 **10.** 9, 18 **11.** 16, 24 **12.** 8, 36

Estimating by Rounding

To estimate a sum or difference, find the least number and identify its first nonzero digit (from the left). Round all the numbers to this place value. Then add or subtract the rounded numbers.

To estimate a product, round each number to its greatest place value. Then multiply the rounded numbers.

EXAMPLE

Use rounding to estimate.

A **128 + 52 + 86**

128 + 52 + 86
130 + 50 + 90
270

52 is least. Round each number to the nearest 10.

B **185 × 52**

185 × 52
200 × 50
10,000

Round each number to its greatest place value.

PRACTICE

Use rounding to estimate.

1. 218 + 42 + 77
2. 328 − 136
3. 64 × 57
4. 112 × 86
5. 45 + 623
6. 517 − 32
7. 1523 − 349
8. 322 × 58
9. 346 + 79 + 52
10. 1273 + 485
11. 2233 − 935
12. 863 × 433

Compatible Numbers

Compatible numbers are numbers that you can calculate with mentally and that are close to the numbers in a problem. You can use compatible numbers to estimate quotients.

EXAMPLE

Use compatible numbers to estimate each quotient.

A **6134 ÷ 32**

6134 ÷ 32
6000 ÷ 30 = 200 *Think: 6 ÷ 3 = 2*

Compatible numbers (6000, 30); *Estimate* (200)

B **647 ÷ 7**

647 ÷ 7
630 ÷ 7 = 90 *Think: 63 ÷ 7 = 9*

Compatible numbers (630, 7); *Estimate* (90)

PRACTICE

Estimate the quotient by using compatible numbers.

1. 345 ÷ 5
2. 5474 ÷ 88
3. 46,170 ÷ 59
4. 749 ÷ 7
5. 861 ÷ 41
6. 1225 ÷ 2
7. 968 ÷ 47
8. 3456 ÷ 432
9. 5765 ÷ 26
10. 25,012 ÷ 64
11. 99,170 ÷ 105
12. 868 ÷ 8

Estimating by Clustering

Sometimes all the numbers in an addition problem are close to the same number. When this happens, you can estimate the sum by *clustering*. To use clustering, round the numbers to the same value.

EXAMPLE

Estimate $44 + 38 + 36 + 42 + 41$ by clustering.

$40 + 40 + 40 + 40 + 40$ — *The addends cluster around 40, so round each to 40.*

$40(5) = 200$ — *Use multiplication instead of repeated addition.*

PRACTICE

Estimate by clustering.

1. $18 + 22 + 19$
2. $32 + 28 + 29 + 33 + 31$
3. $152 + 148 + 154 + 147$
4. $327 + 331 + 333$
5. $87 + 93 + 94 + 89$
6. $62 + 58 + 59$

Overestimates and Underestimates

An **overestimate** is an estimate that is greater than the actual answer.
An **underestimate** is an estimate that is less than the actual answer.

EXAMPLE

Gina has \$43.42. Her brother repays her \$28.50, and her mother loans her \$45.50. Gina wants to know if she can buy a portable music player that costs \$100. Find an overestimate and an underestimate of the total amount Gina has. Then determine which is more appropriate for the situation.

\$43.42 + \$28.50 + \$45.50

\$50 + \$30 + \$50 = \$130 — *To overestimate, round each number up.*

\$40 + \$20 + \$40 = \$100 — *To underestimate, round each number down.*

Gina should use the underestimate. Her actual amount of money will be greater than her underestimate. Her underestimate shows that she has more than \$100, so she has more than enough money for the music player.

PRACTICE

Find an overestimate and an underestimate for each situation. Then determine which is more appropriate.

1. Rasheed has \$25 to buy art supplies. He wants a tube of paint for \$5.45, a brush for \$8.95, and a sketch pad for \$9.75. He needs to determine if he has enough money.
2. Lionel received a paycheck for \$156.42 and earned \$39.50 in tips. He also has \$246.50 in his savings account. He wants to buy a new game system for \$420. He needs to determine if he has enough money.

Mental Math

You can use *decomposition* and *compensation* to solve problems mentally.

When adding and subtracting numbers, you can rewrite one of the numbers as a sum to make the computations easier. This method is called **decomposition**.

EXAMPLE 1

Use decomposition to add or subtract mentally.

A **37 + 19**

37 + 19	*Since 1 is easy to add to 19, rewrite 37 as 36 + 1.*
36 + 1 + 19	
36 + (1 + 19)	*Associative Property*
36 + 20	*Add mentally.*
56	

B **53 − 16**

53 − 16	*Since 13 is easy to subtract from 53, rewrite 16 as 13 + 3.*
53 − (13 + 3)	
53 − 13 − 3	*Distribute the minus sign.*
40 − 3	*Subtract mentally.*
37	

In the method of **compensation**, one number in a sum is adjusted up or down to make it easier to add, while the other number is adjusted in the opposite way to keep the sum the same.

EXAMPLE 2

Use compensation to add mentally.

A **198 + 46**

198 + 46	*Adjust 198 to 200 to make it easier to add.*
(198 + 2) + (46 − 2)	*Since you add 2 to 198, subtract 2 from 46.*
200 + 44	*Simplify mentally.*
244	

B **37 + 24**

37 + 24	*Adjust 37 to 40 to make it easier to add.*
(37 + 3) + (24 − 3)	*Since you add 3 to 37, subtract 3 from 24.*
40 + 21	*Simplify mentally.*
61	

PRACTICE

Use decomposition to add or subtract mentally.

1. 38 + 14　**2.** 19 + 24　**3.** 56 + 78　**4.** 195 + 134

5. 46 − 19　**6.** 52 − 24　**7.** 93 − 47　**8.** 125 − 98

Use compensation to add mentally.

9. 34 + 18　**10.** 48 + 39　**11.** 76 + 58　**12.** 89 + 75

13. 67 + 66　**14.** 83 + 29　**15.** 197 + 45　**16.** 294 + 56

Multiply and Divide Decimals by Powers of 10

Notice the pattern below.

$0.24 \cdot 10 = 2.4$
$0.24 \cdot 100 = 24$
$0.24 \cdot 1000 = 240$
$0.24 \cdot 10{,}000 = 2400$

$10 = 10^1$
$100 = 10^2$
$1000 = 10^3$
$10{,}000 = 10^4$

*Think: When multiplying decimals by powers of 10, move the decimal point one place to the **right** for each power of 10, or for each zero.*

Notice the pattern below.

$0.24 \div 10 = 0.024$
$0.24 \div 100 = 0.0024$
$0.24 \div 1000 = 0.00024$
$0.24 \div 10{,}000 = 0.000024$

*Think: When dividing decimals by powers of 10, move the decimal point one place to the **left** for each power of 10, or for each zero.*

PRACTICE

Find each product or quotient.

1. $10 \cdot 9.26$ **2.** $0.642 \cdot 100$ **3.** $10^3 \cdot 84.2$ **4.** $0.44 \cdot 10^4$

5. $69.7 \cdot 1000$ **6.** $11.32 \div 10$ **7.** $678 \cdot 10^8$ **8.** $1.276 \div 1000$

9. $536.5 \div 10^2$ **10.** $5.92 \div 10^3$ **11.** $25 \div 10{,}000$ **12.** $6.519 \cdot 10^2$

Order of Operations

When simplifying expressions, follow the order of operations.

1. Simplify within parentheses.
2. Evaluate exponents and roots.
3. Multiply and divide from left to right.
4. Add and subtract from left to right.

EXAMPLE

Simplify the expression $3^2 \cdot (11 - 4)$.

$3^2 \cdot (11 - 4)$

$3^2 \cdot 7$ *Simplify within parentheses.*

$9 \cdot 7$ *Evaluate the exponent.*

63 *Multiply.*

PRACTICE

Simplify each expression.

1. $45 - 15 \div 3$ **2.** $51 + 48 \div 8$ **3.** $35 \div (15 - 8)$

4. $\sqrt{9} \cdot 5 - 15$ **5.** $24 \div 3 - 6 + 12$ **6.** $(6 \cdot 8) \div 2^2$

7. $20 - 3 \cdot 4 + 30 \div 6$ **8.** $3^2 - 10 \div 2 + 4 \cdot 2$ **9.** $27 \div (3 + 6) + 6^2$

10. $4 \div 2 + 8 \cdot 2^3 - 4$ **11.** $33 - \sqrt{64} \cdot 3 - 5$ **12.** $(8^2 \cdot 4) - 12 \cdot 13 + 5$

Choose Appropriate Units

Use the following benchmarks to help you choose appropriate units of measurement and to estimate measurements.

	Customary Unit	Benchmark
Length	Inch (in.)	Length of a small paper clip
	Foot (ft)	Length of a standard sheet of paper
	Yard (yd)	Width of a doorway
Weight	Ounce (oz)	Weight of a slice of bread
	Pound (lb)	Weight of 3 apples
Capacity	Fluid ounce (fl oz)	Amount of water in two tablespoons
	Cup (c)	Capacity of a standard measuring cup
	Gallon (gal)	Capacity of a large milk jug

	Metric Unit	Benchmark
Length	Millimeter (mm)	Thickness of a dime
	Centimeter (cm)	Width of a large paper clip
	Meter (m)	Width of a doorway
Mass	Gram (g)	Mass of a small paper clip
	Kilogram (kg)	Mass of a textbook
Capacity	Milliliter (mL)	Amount of water in an eyedropper
	Liter (L)	Amount of water in a large water bottle

EXAMPLE

A **Choose the most appropriate customary unit to measure the length of a city bus. Justify your answer.**

Yards; the length of a city bus is similar to the width of several doorways.

B **Choose the most reasonable estimate of the mass of a rocking chair.**

A 2 g **B** 12 g **C** 2 kg **D** 12 kg

The most reasonable estimate is 12 kg (a mass of about 12 textbooks).

PRACTICE

Choose the most appropriate unit for each measurement. Justify your answer.

1. capacity of a soup bowl (customary)
2. weight of a box of tissue (customary)
3. mass of a carrot stick (metric)
4. length of pencil (metric)
5. width of a butterfly (customary)
6. capacity of a bathtub (metric)

Choose the most reasonable estimate.

7. capacity of a shampoo bottle
   A 5 mL **B** 0.5 L **C** 5 L
8. width of a cell phone
   A 2 in. **B** 2 ft **C** 2 yd

Skills Bank

Convert Measurements

You can use the information in the following tables to convert one measurement unit to another.

Customary System		
Length	**Capacity**	**Weight**
1 ft = 12 in. 1 yd = 3 ft 1 mi = 5280 ft	1 c = 8 fl oz 1 pt = 2 c 1 qt = 2 pt 1 gal = 4 qt	1 lb = 16 oz 1 ton = 2000 lb

Metric System		
Length	**Capacity**	**Weight**
1 cm = 10 mm 1 m = 100 cm 1 km = 1000 m	1 L = 1000 mL	1 g = 1000 mg 1 kg = 1000 g

EXAMPLE 1

A **Convert 3 cups to fluid ounces.**

$3\,\cancel{c} \cdot \left(\frac{8 \text{ fl oz}}{1\,\cancel{c}}\right) = 24 \text{ fl oz}$ *Multiply by the conversion factor.*

B **Convert 65,000 grams to kilograms.**

$65{,}000\,\cancel{g} \cdot \left(\frac{1 \text{ kg}}{1000\,\cancel{g}}\right) = 65 \text{ kg}$ *Multiply by the conversion factor.*

Convert measurements to the same unit to compare them.

EXAMPLE 2

Write <, >, or = to complete the statement. **35 in. ☐ 1 yd**

$1 \text{ yd} = 3 \text{ ft} = 3\,\cancel{\text{ft}} \cdot \left(\frac{12 \text{ in.}}{1\,\cancel{\text{ft}}}\right) = 36 \text{ in.}$ *Convert 1 yard to inches.*

Since 35 in. < 36 in., the correct statement is 35 in. < 1 yd.

PRACTICE

Convert each measurement.

1. 3 mi to feet **2.** 560 cm to meters **3.** 64 fl oz to cups

4. 340 mg to grams **5.** 3.5 L to milliliters **6.** 136 oz to pounds

Write <, >, or = to complete each statement.

7. 2 mi ☐ 3600 yd **8.** 4000 mm ☐ 4 m **9.** 5 lb ☐ 72 oz

10. 1 gal ☐ 10 pt **11.** 2 L ☐ 250 mL **12.** 0.5 kg ☐ 5000 g

Accuracy and Precision

Accuracy is the closeness of a measured value to the actual value. Since it is generally impossible to measure an object with complete accuracy, nearly all measurements are approximations.

Precision is the level of detail an instrument can measure. The smaller the unit an instrument can measure, the more precise its measurements will be.

EXAMPLE 1

Measure the segment to each level of precision.

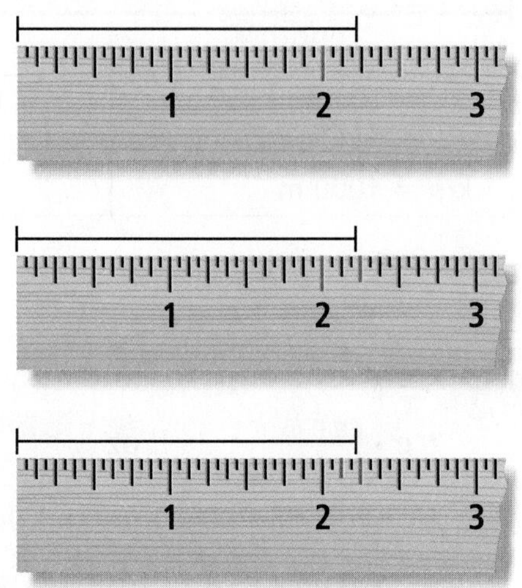

A The nearest $\frac{1}{2}$ inch

The length is slightly closer to 2 in. than $2\frac{1}{2}$ in.

2 inches

B The nearest $\frac{1}{4}$ inch

The length is closer to $2\frac{1}{4}$ in. than 2 in.

$2\frac{1}{4}$ inches

C The nearest $\frac{1}{8}$ inch

The length is slightly closer to $2\frac{1}{4}$ in. than $2\frac{1}{8}$ in.

$2\frac{1}{4}$ inches

EXAMPLE 2

Esteban measured the weight of a lamp as 2 pounds. Linda measured its weight as 34 ounces. The manufacturer lists the weight of the lamp as 32.5 ounces. Which student's measurement is more accurate? more precise?

Esteban's is more accurate. — *2 lb = 32 oz, and 32 oz is closer to the accepted weight of the lamp.*

Linda's is more precise. — *Ounces are smaller units than pounds.*

PRACTICE

Measure each segment to the nearest $\frac{1}{2}$ inch, $\frac{1}{4}$ inch, and $\frac{1}{8}$ inch.

1. ⊢————————————— **2.** ⊢—————————

Measure each segment to the nearest centimeter and nearest millimeter.

3. ⊢————————————— **4.** ⊢—————————

5. Kit measured the length of a skateboard as 156 cm. Lynn measured the length of the skateboard as 1.5 m. The manufacturer lists the length as 158 cm. Which student's measurement is more accurate? more precise?

Significant Digits

In a measurement, all digits that are known with certainty are called **significant digits**. The more precise a measurement is, the more significant digits there are in the measurement. The table shows some rules for identifying significant digits.

Rule	Example	Number of Significant Digits
All nonzero digits	15.32	All 4
Zeros beween significant digits	43,001	All 5
Zeros after the last nonzero digit that are to the right of the decimal point	0.0070	2; 0.0070

Zeros at the end of a whole number are assumed to be nonsignificant. (Example: 500)

EXAMPLE

A **Which is a more precise measurement, 14 ft or 14.2 ft?**

Because 14.2 ft has three significant digits and 14 ft has only two, 14.2 ft is more precise.

B **Determine the number of significant digits in 20.04 m, 200 m, and 200.0 m.**

20.04 All 4 digits are significant.
200 There is 1 significant digit.
200.0 All 4 digits are significant.

When calculating with measurements, the answer should be written using the precision of the least precise measurement.

C **Multiply 16.3 m by 2.5 m. Use the correct number of significant digits in your answer.**

When muliplying or dividing, use the least number of significant digits of the numbers.

16.3 m · 2.5 m = 40.75

Round to 2 significant digits. ⟶ **41** m^2

D **Add 4500 in. and 70 in. Use the correct number of significant digits in your answer.**

When adding or subtracting, line up the numbers. Round the answer to the last significant digit that is farthest to the left.

4500 in. *5 is farthest left. Round to hundreds.*
+ 70 in.
4570 Round to the hundreds. ⟶ **4600** in.

PRACTICE

Tell which is more precise.

1. 31.8 g or 32 g **2.** 496.5 mi or 496.50 mi **3.** 3.0 ft or 3.001 ft

Determine the number of significant digits in each measurement.

4. 12 lb **5.** 14.00 mm **6.** 1.009 yd **7.** 20.87 s

Perform the indicated operation. Use the correct number of significant digits in your answer.

8. 210 m + 43 m **9.** 4.7 ft · 1.04 ft **10.** 6.7 s − 0.08 s

Points, Lines, and Planes

Points, lines, and planes are the building blocks of geometry. Segments, rays, and angles are defined in terms of these basic figures.

Definition	Figure	Name
A **point** names a location.	• A	point *A*
A **line** is perfectly straight and extends forever in both directions.	ℓ, B, C	line ℓ, or $\overleftrightarrow{BC}$
A **plane** is a perfectly flat surface that extends forever in all directions.	$\mathcal{P}$, D, E, F	plane $\mathcal{P}$, or plane *DEF*
A **segment**, or line segment, is the part of a line between two points.	G, H	$\overline{GH}$
A **ray** is a part of a line that starts at one point and extends forever in one direction.	J, K	$\overrightarrow{KJ}$

EXAMPLE

Use the diagram to name each figure.

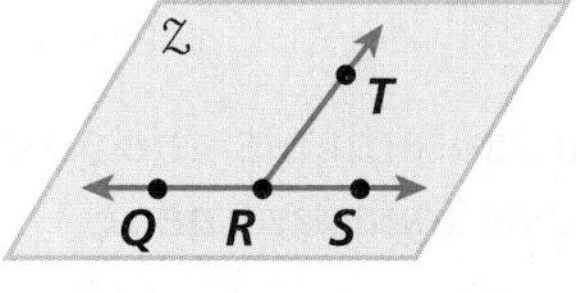

A **four points**

Q, R, S, T

B **a line**

Possible answers: $\overleftrightarrow{QR}$, $\overleftrightarrow{QS}$, or $\overleftrightarrow{RS}$

Use any two points on the line.

C **a plane**

Possible answers: plane $\mathcal{Z}$ or plane *QRT*

Use any three points in a plane that form a triangle to name the plane.

D **four segments**

Possible answers: $\overline{QR}$, $\overline{RS}$, $\overline{RT}$, $\overline{QS}$

Write the two endpoints in any order.

E **five rays**

$\overrightarrow{RQ}$, $\overrightarrow{RS}$, $\overrightarrow{RT}$, $\overrightarrow{SQ}$, $\overrightarrow{QS}$

Write the endpoint first.

PRACTICE

Use the diagram to name each figure.

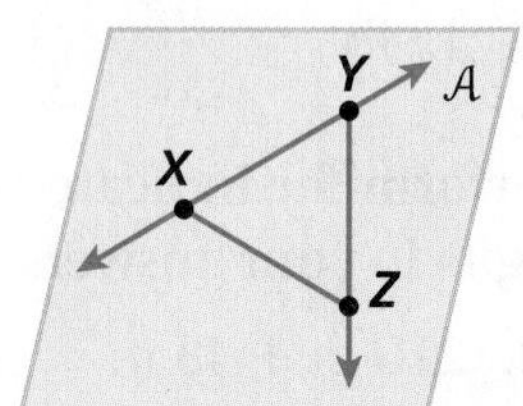

1. three points

2. a line

3. a plane

4. three segments

5. three rays

Measure Angles

You can use a protractor to measure angles. To measure an angle, place the base of the protractor on one of the rays of the angle and center the base on the vertex. Look at the protractor scale that has zero on the first ray. Read the scale where the second ray crosses it. Extend the rays, if necessary.

EXAMPLE

Use a protractor to measure the angles of quadrilateral *ABCD*.

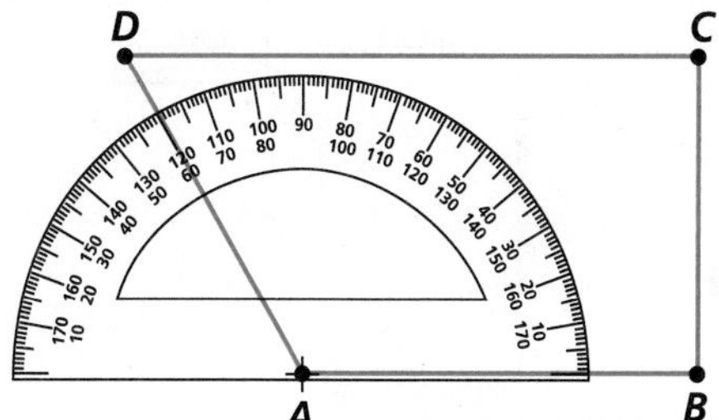

The measure of ∠*A*, or m∠*A*, equals 120°.

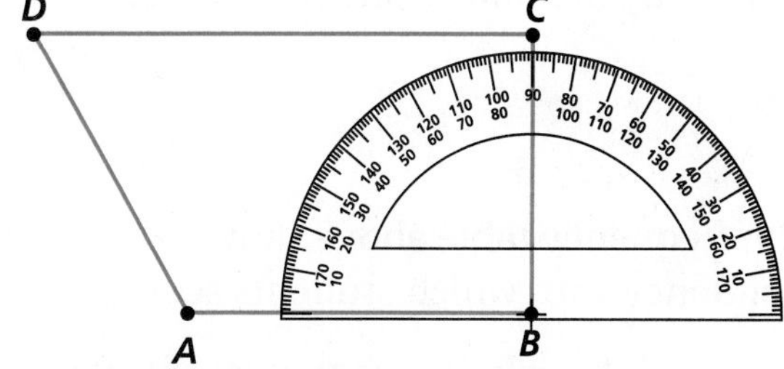

The measure of ∠*B*, or m∠*B*, equals 90°.

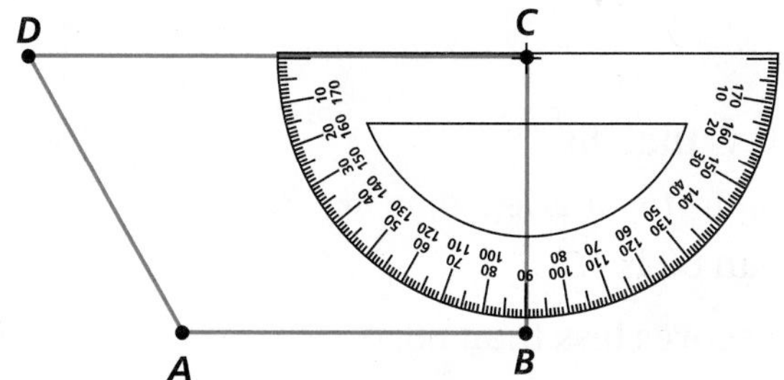

The measure of ∠*C*, or m∠*C*, equals 90°.

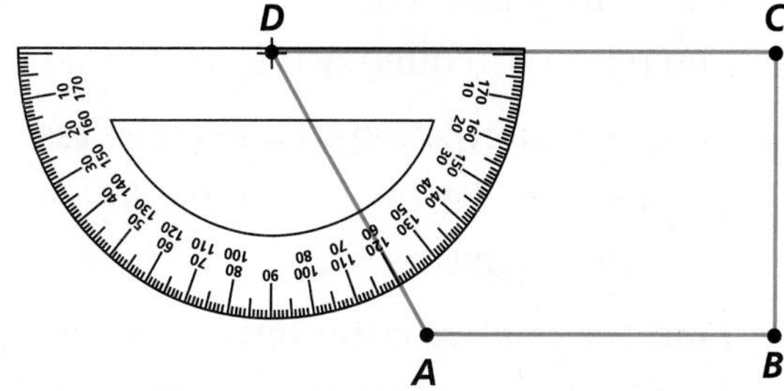

The measure of ∠*D*, or m∠*D*, equals 60°.

PRACTICE

Use a protractor to measure the angles of each polygon.

1. 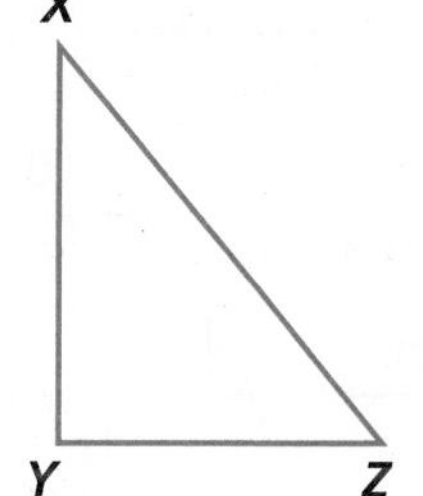

2. 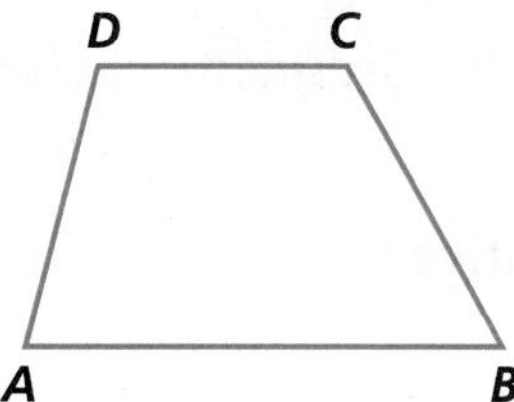

3. 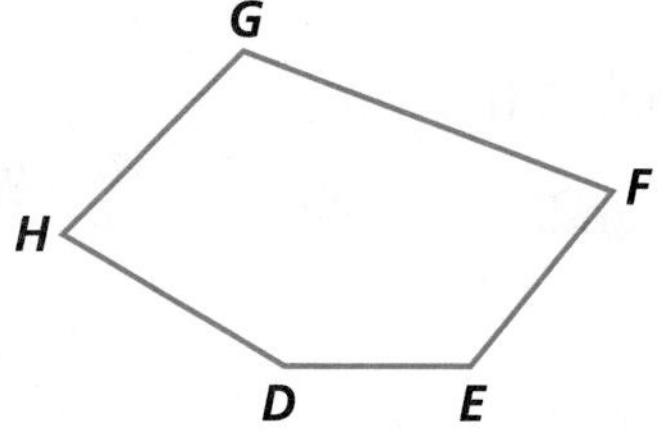

4. 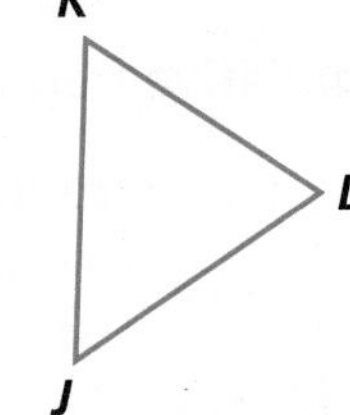

Relative and Cumulative Frequency

A **frequency table** lists each value or range of values of the data set followed by its **frequency**, or number of times it occurs.

Relative frequency is the frequency of a value or range of values divided by the total number of data values.

Cumulative frequency is the frequency of all data values that are less than a given value.

Relative cumulative frequency is the cumulative frequency divided by the total number of values.

Test Score	Frequency
66–70	3
71–75	1
76–80	4
81–85	7
86–90	5
91–95	6
96–100	2

EXAMPLE

The frequency table above shows ranges of test scores and the frequency with which students scored in each range.

A **Find the relative frequency of test scores in the range 76–80.**

$3 + 1 + 4 + 7 + 5 + 6 + 2 = 28$ *Find the total number of test scores.*

There are 4 test scores in the range 76–80.

The relative frequency is $\frac{4}{28} = \frac{1}{7} \approx 0.14$.

B **Find the cumulative frequency of test scores less than 86.**

$7 + 4 + 1 + 3 = 15$ *Add the frequencies of all test scores less than 86.*

The cumulative frequency of test scores less than 86 is 15.

C **Find the relative cumulative frequency of test scores less than 86.**

$\frac{15}{28} \approx 0.54$ *Divide the cumulative frequency by the total number of values.*

The relative cumulative frequency of test scores less than 86 is about 0.54.

PRACTICE

The frequency table shows the frequency of each range of heights among Mrs. Dawkin's students.

Height	Frequency
4 ft–4 ft 5 in.	2
4 ft 6 in.–4 ft 11 in.	8
5 ft–5 ft 5 in.	10
5 ft 6 in.–5 ft 11 in.	6
6 ft–6 ft 5 in.	1

1. What is the relative frequency of heights in the range 5 ft–5 ft 5 in.?
2. What is the relative frequency of heights in the range 4 ft–4 ft 5 in.?
3. What is the cumulative frequency of heights less than 6 ft?
4. What is the cumulative frequency of heights less than 5 ft?
5. What is the relative cumulative frequency of heights less than 5 ft 6 in.?
6. What is the relative cumulative frequency of heights less than 5 ft?

Inductive and Deductive Reasoning

Inductive reasoning involves examining a set of data to determine a pattern and then making a conjecture about the data. In **deductive reasoning**, you reach a conclusion by using logical reasoning based on given statements or premises that you assume to be true.

EXAMPLE

A **Use inductive reasoning to determine the 30th number of the sequence.**

3, 5, 7, 9, 11, . . .

Examine the pattern to determine a possible relationship between each term in the sequence and its value.

Term	1st	2nd	3rd	4th	5th
Value	3	5	7	9	11

$1 \cdot 2 + 1 = 2 + 1 = 3$

$2 \cdot 2 + 1 = 4 + 1 = 5$

$3 \cdot 2 + 1 = 6 + 1 = 7$

$4 \cdot 2 + 1 = 8 + 1 = 9$

$5 \cdot 2 + 1 = 10 + 1 = 11$

To obtain each value, multiply the term number by 2 and add 1. So the 30th term is $30 \cdot 2 + 1 = 60 + 1 = 61$.

B **Use deductive reasoning to make a conclusion from the given premises.**

Premise: Makayla needs at least an 89 on her exam to get a B for the quarter in math class.

Premise: Makayla got a B for the quarter in math class.

Conclusion: Makayla got at least an 89 on her exam.

PRACTICE

Use inductive reasoning to determine the 100th number in each pattern.

1. $\frac{1}{2}, 1, 1\frac{1}{2}, 2, 2\frac{1}{2}, \ldots$

2. 1, 4, 9, 16, 25, . . .

3. 4, 6, 8, 10, 12, . . .

4. 0, 3, 6, 9, 12, 15, . . .

Use deductive reasoning to make a conclusion from the given premises.

5. Premise: If it is raining, then there must be a cloud in the sky.

Premise: It is raining.

6. Premise: A quadrilateral with four congruent sides and four right angles is a square.

Premise: Quadrilateral *ABCD* has four right angles.

Premise: Quadrilateral *ABCD* has four congruent sides.

7. Premise: Darnell is 3 years younger than half his father's age.

Premise: Darnell's father is 40 years old.

Sets

A **set** is a collection of objects. Each object is called an **element** of the set. *Roster notation* can be used to list the elements in a set. For example, if set A is the set of factors of 8, then the set can be written in roster notation as $A = \{1, 2, 4, 8\}$.

A set that contains no elements is called the **null set** or **empty set**. The null set is symbolized by $\varnothing$ or $\{\ \}$.

Set A is a **subset** of set B if each element of A is also in B.

The **intersection** of A and B is the set of all elements that are in both A and B.

The **union** of A and B is the set of all elements that are in A or B.

EXAMPLE

Let A be the set of factors of 12, and let B be the set of factors of 20.

A **Find the intersection of A and B.**

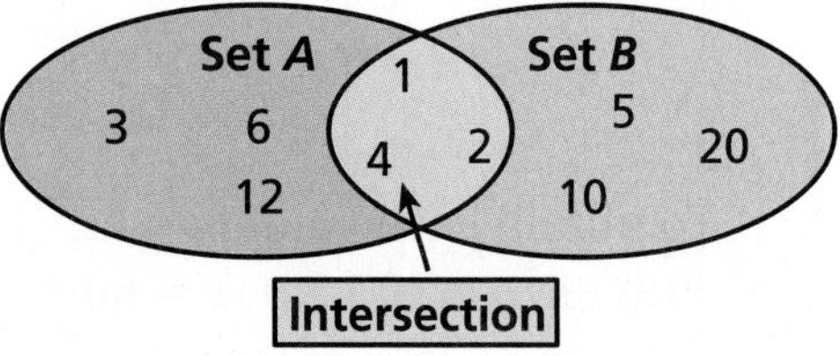

Write each set in roster notation.

$A = \{1, 2, 3, 4, 6, 12\}$ *Factors of 12*

$B = \{1, 2, 4, 5, 10, 20\}$ *Factors of 20*

The elements 1, 2, and 4 are in both sets.

The intersection of A and B is the set $\{1, 2, 4\}$.

B **Find the union of A and B.**

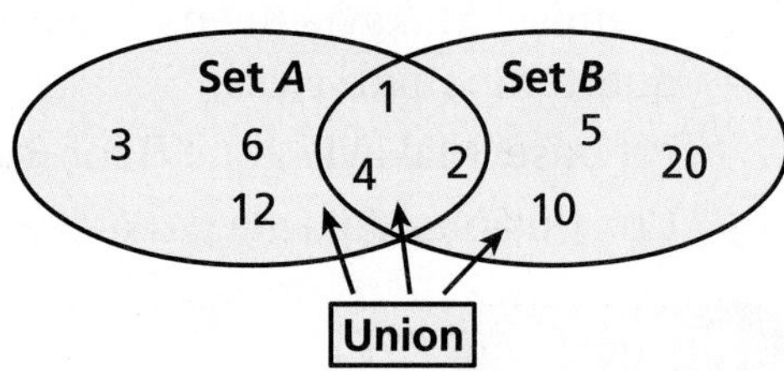

The elements 1, 2, 3, 4, 5, 6, 10, 12, and 20 are in either set A or set B.

The union of A and B is the set $\{1, 2, 3, 4, 5, 6, 10, 12, 20\}$.

PRACTICE

Find the intersection and the union of A and B.

1. $A = \{1, 3, 6, 9, 12, 15, 18\}$; $B = \{1, 6, 12, 18\}$
2. $A = \{2, 3, 4, 5, 6\}$; $B = \{4, 5, 6, 7, 8, 9\}$
3. $A = \{16, 24, 30, 60, 72\}$; $B = \{5, 10, 32, 48\}$
4. $A = \{\text{blue, red, green}\}$; $B = \{\text{orange, red, green, purple}\}$
5. A is the set of factors of 24; B is the set of factors of 18.
6. A is the set of factors of 10; B is the set of factors of 30.
7. A is the set of even whole numbers; B is the set of odd whole numbers.
8. A is the set of whole numbers greater than 12; B is the set of whole numbers less than 20.

Conditional Statements

If–then statements are called **conditional statements**. The phrase that follows *if* is the **hypothesis**, and the phrase that follows *then* is the **conclusion**. If the hypothesis is true, then the conclusion is also true. If the conclusion is true, then the hypothesis *may or may not* be true.

EXAMPLE

A **If a number is divisible by 4, then the number is divisible by 2. A number n is divisible by 4. What can you conclude? Explain.**

The number n is divisible by 2. The hypothesis is true, so the conclusion is also true.

B **If a polygon is a square, then it is a quadrilateral. Polygon *ABCD* is a quadrilateral. What can you conclude? Explain.**

Polygon *ABCD* may or may not be a square. The conclusion is true, so the hypothesis may or may not be true.

PRACTICE

1. If a number is a multiple of 6, then it is a multiple of 3. The number m is a multiple of 3. What can you conclude? Explain.
2. If a polygon is a rectangle, then it is a parallelogram. Polygon *JKLM* is a rectangle. What can you conclude? Explain.

Solve Absolute-Value Equations

Recall that the absolute value of a number is its distance from 0 on a number line. The equation $|x| = 5$ asks for values of x with an absolute value of 5. Since 5 and –5 are both 5 units from 0, the solutions of the equation are 5 and –5.

EXAMPLES

Solve each absolute-value equation.

A $|x| = 6$

$x = 6$ or $x = -6$ *6 and –6 are both 6 units from 0.*

B $|x| = -4$

The absolute value of a number cannot be negative. There is no solution.

PRACTICE

Solve each absolute-value equation.

1. $|x| = 8$	**2.** $|x| = -2$	**3.** $|x| = 3$	**4.** $|x| = 0$
5. $|x| = 20$	**6.** $|x| = -14$	**7.** $|x| = 10$	**8.** $|x| = 17$

Skills Bank

Compound Inequalities

A **compound inequality** is the result of combining two inequalities. The words *or* and *and* are used to describe how the two parts are related.

$x \geq 2$ or $x < -1$	x is either greater than or equal to 2 *or* less than -1.
$x > -2$ and $x < 1$	x is both greater than -2 *and* less than 1.

The compound inequality $x > -2$ and $x < 1$ can also be written as $-2 < x < 1$.

EXAMPLE 1

Write a compound inequality for each statement.

A **A number x is either less than -4 or greater than or equal to 3.**
$x < -4$ or $x \geq 3$

B **A number x is both greater than or equal to -7 and less than -2.**
$x \geq -7$ and $x < -2$

EXAMPLE 2

Graph each compound inequality.

A $x \geq 0$ or $x < -2$

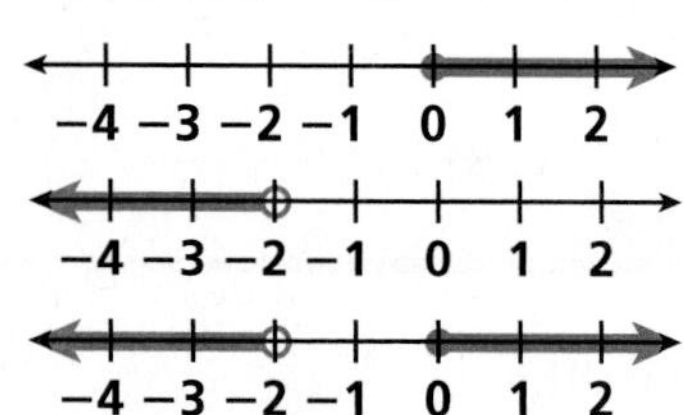

Graph $x \geq 0$.

Graph $x < -2$.

Combine the graphs.

B $-1 \leq x < 3$

Graph $-1 \leq x$.

Graph $x < 3$.

Graph the common solutions.

PRACTICE

Write a compound inequality for each statement.

1. A number x is either less than or equal to -3 or greater than 5.
2. A number x is both greater than 1 and less than or equal to 11.

Graph each compound inequality.

3. $x \leq -2$ or $x > 4$
4. $x \geq 3$ or $x < -4$
5. $x < 0$ or $x > 5$
6. $-3 \leq x < 1$
7. $-2 \leq x \leq 6$
8. $0 < x \leq 5$

Circles

A circle can be named by its center, using the ⊙ symbol. A circle with a center labeled C would be named $\odot C$. An unbroken part of a circle is called an **arc**. There are major arcs and minor arcs.

A **minor arc** of a circle is an arc that is less than half the circle and named by its endpoints. A **major arc** of a circle is an arc that is greater than half the circle and named by its endpoints and one other point on the arc.

$\widehat{BC}$ is a minor arc.

$\widehat{BAC}$ is a major arc.

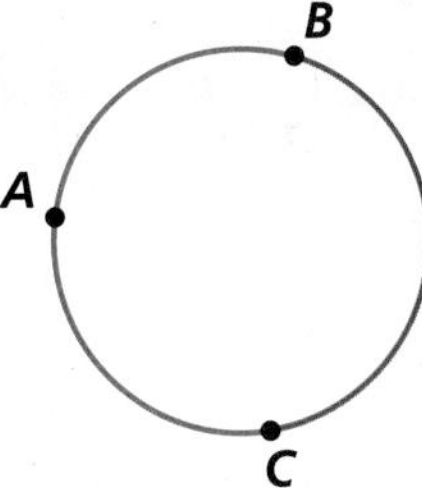

A **radius** connects the center with a point on a circle.

radius $\overline{CD}$

A **chord** connects two points on a circle. A **diameter** is a chord that passes through the center of a circle. A **semicircle** is an arc whose endpoints lie on a diameter.

chord $\overline{AB}$

diameter $\overline{CD}$

semicircle $\widehat{CAD}$

A **secant** is a line that intersects a circle at two points.

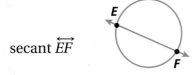

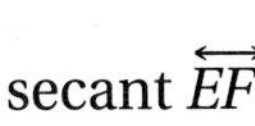

secant $\overleftrightarrow{EF}$

A **tangent** is a line that intersects a circle at one point.

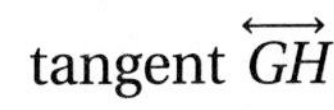

tangent $\overleftrightarrow{GH}$

A **central angle** has its vertex at the center of the circle.

central angle $\angle JKL$

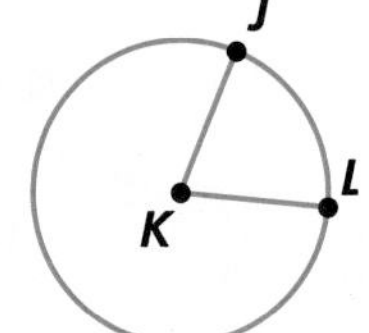

An **inscribed angle** has its vertex on the circle.

inscribed angle $\angle MNP$

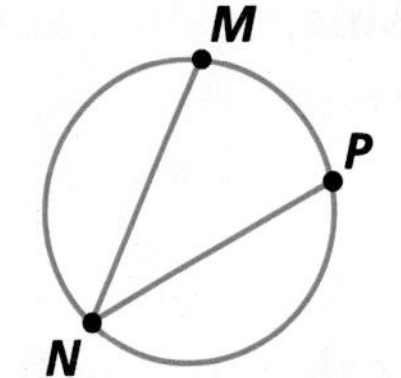

PRACTICE

Use the given diagram of $\odot A$ for exercises 1–6.

1. Name a radius.
2. What two chords make up the inscribed angle?
3. Name a secant.
4. Give the tangent line.
5. Name the central angle.
6. Name the inscribed angle.

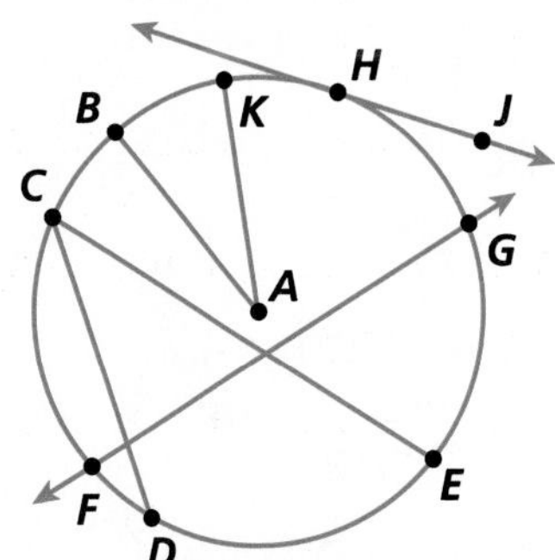

Trigonometric Ratios

A **trigonometric ratio** is a ratio of the lengths of two sides in a right triangle. Three of the ratios are named *sine* (abbreviated *sin*), *cosine* (abbreviated *cos*), and *tangent* (abbreviated *tan*).

The **sine** of $\angle 1 = \sin\angle 1 = \dfrac{\text{length of leg opposite } \angle 1}{\text{length of hypotenuse}} = \dfrac{a}{c}$.

The **cosine** of $\angle 1 = \cos\angle 1 = \dfrac{\text{length of leg adjacent to } \angle 1}{\text{length of hypotenuse}} = \dfrac{b}{c}$.

The **tangent** of $\angle 1 = \tan\angle 1 = \dfrac{\text{length of leg opposite } \angle 1}{\text{length of leg adjacent to } \angle 1} = \dfrac{a}{b}$.

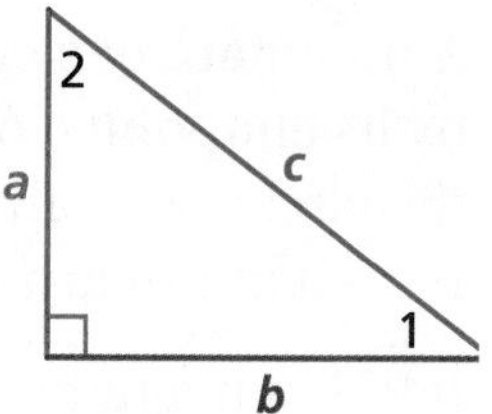

EXAMPLE

A **Find the sine, cosine, and tangent of $\angle R$.**

$\sin\angle R = \dfrac{\text{length of leg opposite } \angle R}{\text{length of hypotenuse}} = \dfrac{4}{5}$

$\cos\angle R = \dfrac{\text{length of leg adjacent to } \angle R}{\text{length of hypotenuse}} = \dfrac{3}{5}$

$\tan\angle R = \dfrac{\text{length of leg opposite } \angle R}{\text{length of leg adjacent to } \angle R} = \dfrac{4}{3}$

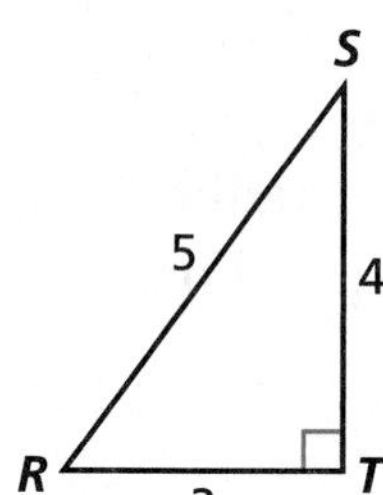

B **Use your calculator to find the length of $\overline{JL}$ to the nearest tenth.**

$\cos\angle J = \dfrac{JL}{JK}$ — *Use the cosine ratio.*

$\cos(40^\circ) = \dfrac{JL}{10}$ — *Substitute 40° for m∠J and 10 for JK.*

$10 \cdot \cos(40^\circ) = JL$ — *Multiply both sides by 10.*

10 [×] [COS] 40 [ENTER] — *Use your calculator.*

$JL \approx 7.7$

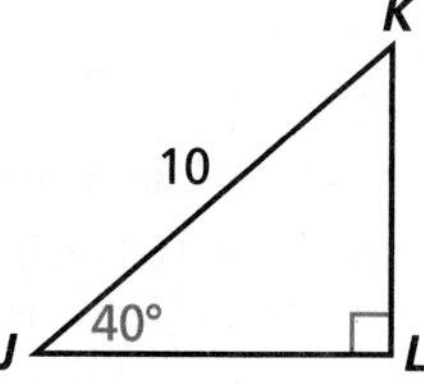

PRACTICE

Find the sine, cosine, and tangent of each angle.

1. $\angle P$
2. $\angle Q$

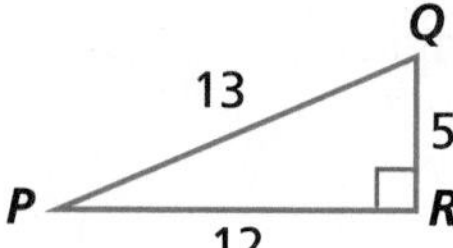

Use your calculator to find the length of each side to the nearest tenth.

3. $\overline{AB}$
4. $\overline{BC}$

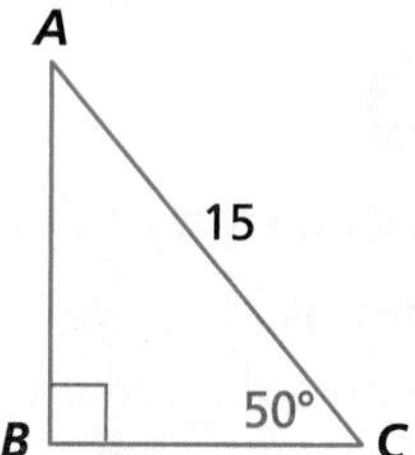

Cross Sections

When a solid and a plane intersect, the intersection is called a **cross section**.

EXAMPLE

Identify and draw each cross section.

A

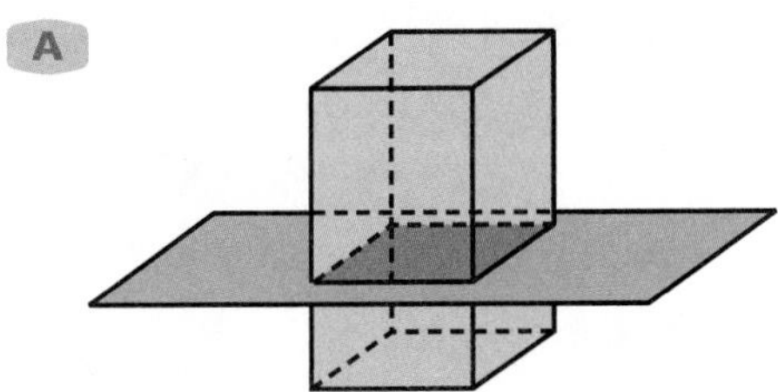

The figure shows the intersection of a square prism and a plane. The cross section is a square. The square has the same side length as the prism's base.

B

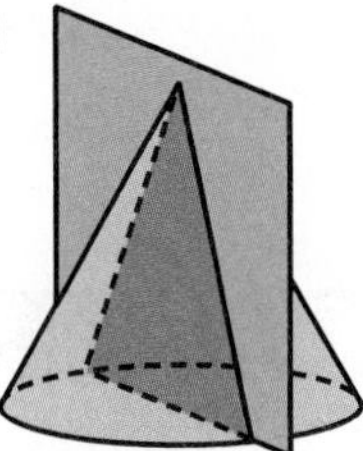

The figure shows the intersection of a cone and a plane. The cross section is an isosceles triangle. The base of the triangle corresponds to the diameter of the cone. The congruent sides of the triangle correspond to the slant height of the cone.

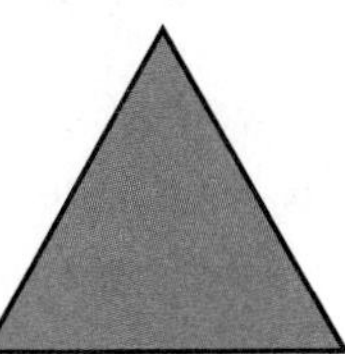

PRACTICE

Identify and draw each cross section.

1. 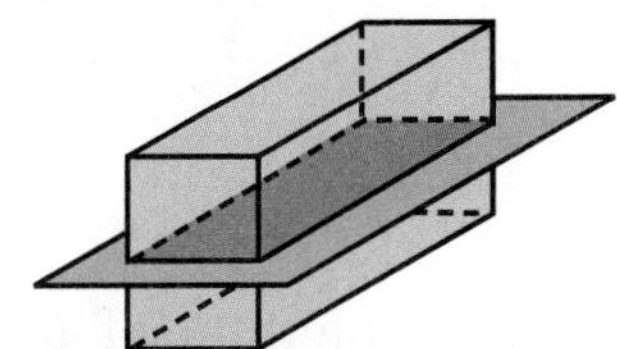

2. 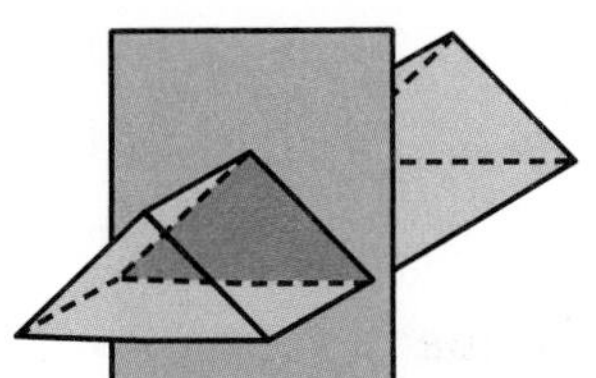

3. 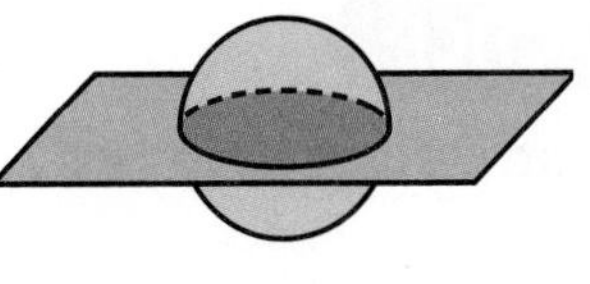

4. 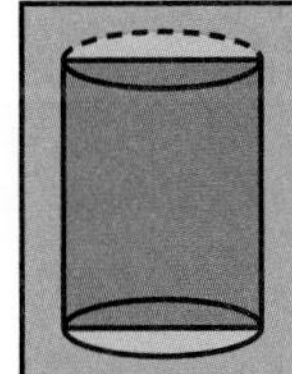

5. 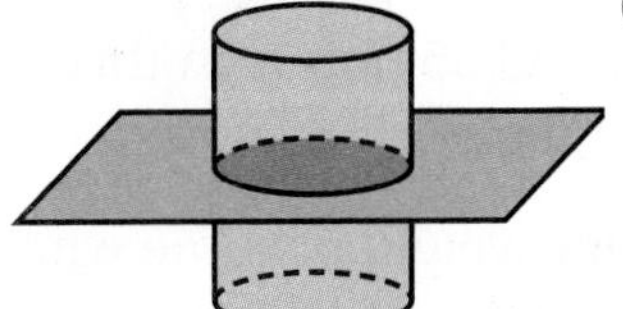

6. 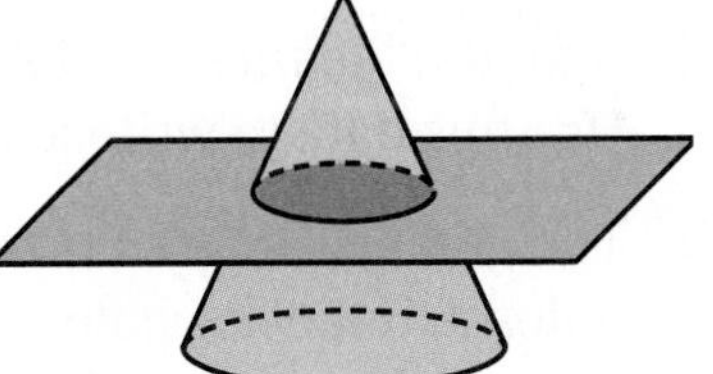

Matrices

A **matrix** is a rectangular arrangement of data enclosed in brackets. Matrices are used to list, organize, and sort data.

The **dimensions** of a matrix are given by the number of horizontal rows and vertical columns in the matrix. For example, matrix A below is an example of a 3×2 ("3-by-2") matrix because it has 3 rows and 2 columns, for a total of 6 **entries**. The number of rows is always given first. So a 3×2 matrix is not the same as a 2×3 matrix.

$$A = \begin{bmatrix} 86 & 137 \\ 103 & 0 \\ 115 & 78 \end{bmatrix} \begin{matrix} \leftarrow \text{Row 1} \\ \leftarrow \text{Row 2} \\ \leftarrow \text{Row 3} \end{matrix}$$

↑ Column 1 ↑ Column 2

Each matrix entry is identified by its row and column. The entry in row 2 column 1 is 103. You can use the notation $a_{21} = 103$ to express this.

EXAMPLE

Use the data shown in the bar graph to create a matrix.

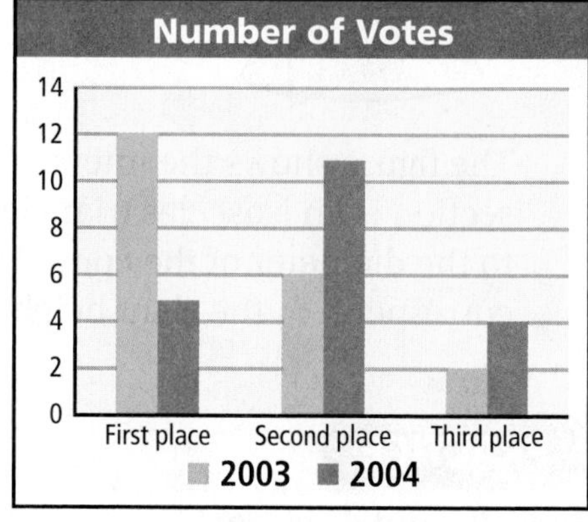

The matrix can be organized with the votes in each year as the columns:

$$\begin{bmatrix} 12 & 5 \\ 6 & 11 \\ 2 & 4 \end{bmatrix}$$

or with the votes in each year as the rows:

$$\begin{bmatrix} 12 & 6 & 2 \\ 5 & 11 & 4 \end{bmatrix}$$

PRACTICE

Use matrix B for Exercises 1–3.

$$B = \begin{bmatrix} 1 & 0 & 7 & 4 \\ 0 & 1 & 3 & 8 \\ 6 & 5 & 2 & 9 \end{bmatrix}$$

1. B is a ▒ × ▒ matrix.

2. Name the entry with a value of 5.

3. What is the value of b_{13}?

4. A football team scored 24, 13, and 35 points in three playoff games. Use this data to write a 3×1 matrix.

5. The greatest length and average weight of some whale species are as follows: finback whale—50 ft, 82 tons; humpback whale—33 ft, 49 tons; bowhead whale—50 ft, 59 tons; blue whale—84 ft, 98 tons; right whale—50 ft, 56 tons. Organize this data in a matrix.

6. The second matrix in the example is called the *transpose* of the first matrix. Write the transpose of matrix B above. What are its dimensions?

Networks

A **network** is a set of points and line segments or arcs that connect the points. Networks are useful in many real-world situations. The network at right at represents the flight routes of a small airline.

M Minneapolis
Denver
D
Kansas
K City
Pittsburgh
P
Houston H

The points of a network are called **vertices**.
The line segments or arcs connecting the vertices are called **edges**.
The **degree** of a vertex is the number of edges touching the vertex.
For example, vertex D has degree 3.

A **circuit** is a path along the edges that begins and ends at the same vertex and does not go through any edge more than once. An Euler circuit is a circuit that goes through every edge. An **Euler circuit** exists only when every vertex of a network has an even degree.

EXAMPLE

The map shows the highways that connect the cities on a florist's delivery route.

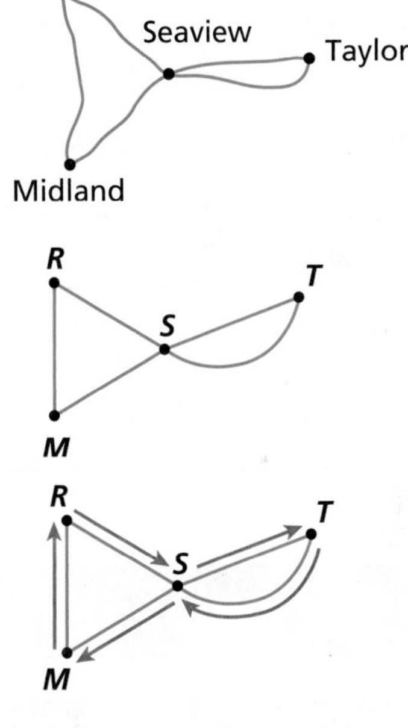

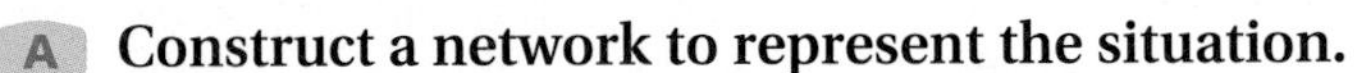

A Construct a network to represent the situation.

Use vertices to represent the cities and edges to represent the highways.

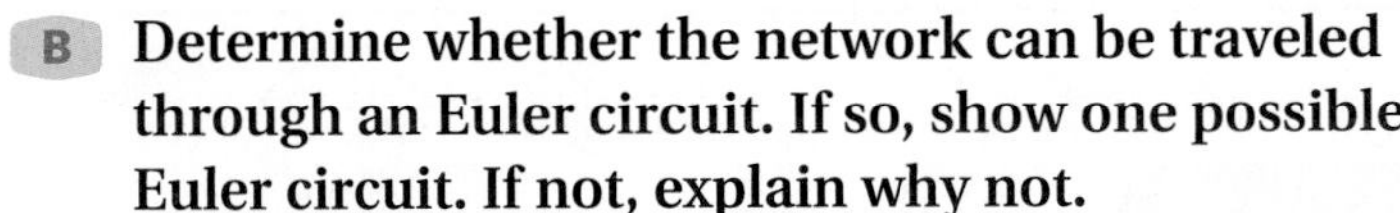

B Determine whether the network can be traveled through an Euler circuit. If so, show one possible Euler circuit. If not, explain why not.

First find the degree of each vertex.

Vertex	M	R	S	T
Degree	2	2	4	2

Every vertex has an even degree, so the network can be traveled by an Euler circuit, as shown.

PRACTICE

The map shows the roads and the houses of five families on Jake's newspaper route.

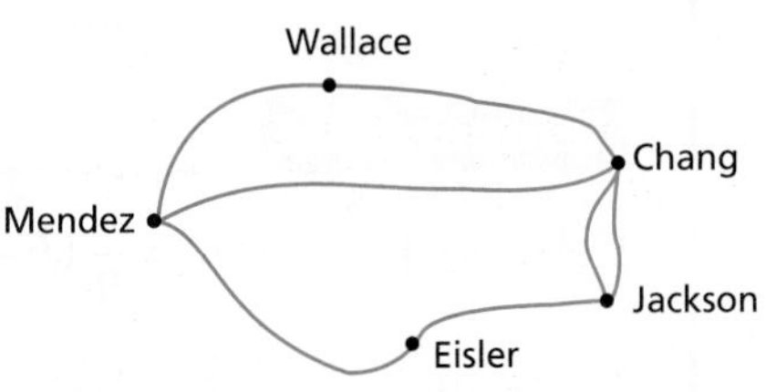

1. Construct a network to represent the situation.
2. Determine whether the network you drew in Exercise 1 can be traveled through an Euler circuit. If so, show one possible Euler circuit. If not, explain why not.

Skills Bank

Table of Measures

METRIC

Length

1 kilometer (km) = 1,000 meters (m)
1 meter = 100 centimeters (cm)
1 centimeter = 10 millimeters (mm)

Capacity

1 liter (L) = 1,000 milliliters (mL)

Mass

1 kilogram (kg) = 1,000 grams (g)
1 gram = 1,000 milligrams (mg)

CUSTOMARY

Length

1 mile (mi) = 5,280 feet (ft)
1 yard (yd) = 3 feet
1 foot = 12 inches (in.)

Capacity

1 gallon (gal) = 4 quarts (qt)
1 quart = 2 pints (pt)
1 pint = 2 cups (c)
1 cup = 8 fluid ounces (fl oz)

Weight

1 ton (T) = 2,000 pounds (lb)
1 pound = 16 ounces (oz)

TIME

1 year (yr) = 365 days
1 year = 12 months (mo)
1 year = 52 weeks (wk)
1 week = 7 days
1 day = 24 hours (h)
1 hour = 60 minutes (min)
1 minute = 60 seconds (s)

Formulas

Perimeter and Circumference

Square	$P = 4s$
Rectangle	$P = 2\ell + 2w$ or $P = 2(\ell + w)$
Polygon	$P =$ sum of the lengths of the sides
Circle	$C = 2\pi r$ or $C = \pi d$

Temperature

Celsius (°C)	$C = \frac{5}{9}(F - 32)$
Fahrenheit (°F)	$F = \frac{9}{5}C + 32$

Area

Square	$A = s^2$
Rectangle	$A = \ell w$ or $A = bh$
Parallelogram	$A = bh$
Triangle	$A = \frac{1}{2}bh$ or $A = \frac{bh}{2}$
Trapezoid	$A = \frac{1}{2}(b_1 + b_2)h$ or $A = \frac{(b_1 + b_2)h}{2}$
Circle	$A = \pi r^2$

Formulas

Volume*

Prism	$V = Bh$
Rectangular Prism	$V = Bh$ or $V = \ell wh$
Cylinder	$V = Bh$ or $V = \pi r^2 h$
Pyramid	$V = \frac{1}{3}Bh$
Cone	$V = \frac{1}{3}Bh$ or $V = \frac{1}{3}\pi r^2 h$

Surface Area*

Prism	$S = 2B + L$ or $S = 2B + Ph$
Cylinder	$S = 2B + L$ or $S = 2\pi r^2 + 2\pi rh$
Regular Pyramid	$S = B + L$ or $S = B + \frac{1}{2}P\ell$
Cone	$S = B + L$ or $S = \pi r^2 + \pi r\ell$
Sphere	$S = 4\pi r^2$

*B represents the area of the base of a solid figure.

Other

Simple Interest	$I = Prt$
Distance Traveled	$d = rt$
Slope of a Line	$m = \frac{y_2 - y_1}{x_2 - x_1}$
Slope-intercept Form	$y = mx + b$
Point-slope Form	$y - y_1 = m(x - x_1)$
Standard Form	$Ax + By = C$
Pythagorean Theorem	$a^2 + b^2 = c^2$
Distance (coordinate)	$d = \sqrt{(x_2 - x_1)^2 + (y_2 - y_1)^2}$
Midpoint	$M = \left(\frac{x_1 + x_2}{2}, \frac{y_1 + y_2}{2}\right)$
Arithmetic Sequence	$a_n = a_1 + (n - 1)d$
Geometric Sequence	$a_n = a_1 r^{n-1}$

Symbols

$<$	is less than
$>$	is greater than
$\leq$	is less than or equal to
$\geq$	is greater than or equal to
$\neq$	is not equal to
$\approx$	is approximately equal to
10^2	ten squared
10^3	ten cubed
2^6	two to the sixth power
2^{-5}	two to the negative fifth power
$2.\overline{6}$	repeating decimal 2.66666...
$\pm$	plus or minus
$\lvert -4 \rvert$	the absolute value of negative 4
$\sqrt{}$	square root
\$5/h	the rate \$5 per hour
1:2	ratio of 1 to 2
%	percent
(x, y)	ordered pair
$f(x)$	function notation: f of x
$\cong$	is congruent to
$\sim$	is similar to
$\perp$	is perpendicular to
$\parallel$	is parallel to
$\overleftrightarrow{AB}$	line AB
$\overrightarrow{AB}$	ray AB
$\overline{AB}$	line segment AB
$\angle ABC$	angle ABC
$m\angle A$	measure of $\angle A$
$\triangle ABC$	triangle ABC
$^\circ$	degree
π	pi; $\pi \approx 3.14$ or $\pi \approx \frac{22}{7}$
A'	A prime
P(event)	the probability of an event
$n!$	n factorial
$_nP_r$	r permutations of n items
$_nC_r$	r combinations of n items

Selected Answers ■ ■ ■ Chapter 1

1 Exercises

1. $\frac{1}{2}$ **3.** $-\frac{2}{3}$ **5.** $\frac{1}{3}$ **7.** $-\frac{3}{4}$ **9.** $\frac{7}{16}$ **11.** $\frac{3}{4}$ **13.** $\frac{2}{5}$ **15.** $-2\frac{1}{5}$ **17.** $3\frac{21}{100}$ **19.** 0.625 **21.** $0.41\overline{6}$ **23.** $0.\overline{1}$ **25.** 0.375 **27.** 1.25 **29.** $\frac{3}{4}$ **31.** $-\frac{1}{2}$ **33.** $\frac{5}{6}$ **35.** $\frac{22}{35}$ **37.** $-\frac{13}{21}$ **39.** $\frac{3}{5}$ **41.** $\frac{18}{25}$ **43.** $1\frac{377}{1000}$ **45.** $-1\frac{2}{5}$ **47.** -0.375 **49.** -1.8 **51.** 1.6 **53.** -4.6 **55.** 1.12 **59.** $3\frac{3}{8}$ **61a.** $\frac{4}{9}, \frac{1}{6}, \frac{1}{4}, \frac{7}{15}, \frac{9}{16}, \frac{12}{25}, \frac{5}{8}, \frac{3}{8}$ **63.** GCF = 2; $\frac{21}{34}$; No **69.** 29.7

2 Exercises

1. $2\frac{1}{2}$ **3.** $1\frac{7}{8}$ **5.** $\frac{5}{32}$ **7.** $5\frac{5}{8}$ **9.** 14.7 **11.** 9.6 **13.** $4\frac{1}{2}$ mi **15.** $-5\frac{1}{2}$ **17.** $-11\frac{2}{3}$ **19.** $-20\frac{1}{3}$ **21.** $-22\frac{2}{5}$ **23.** $-\frac{7}{36}$ **25.** $\frac{7}{24}$ **27.** $1\frac{1}{2}$ **29.** $\frac{21}{40}$ **31.** -0.235 **33.** -4.125 **35.** -0.469 **37.** -0.368 **39.** $\frac{3}{8}$ **41.** $-8\frac{7}{11}$ **43.** $15\frac{5}{9}$ **45.** $2\frac{53}{54}$ **47.** $-\frac{55}{192}$ **49.** -5 **51.** -2 **53a.** $1\frac{1}{4}$ tsp **b.** $1\frac{1}{2}$ tsp **c.** 2 tsp **57.** A **59.** C

3 Exercises

1. $\frac{2}{3}$ **3.** $-\frac{2}{7}$ **5.** $1\frac{11}{80}$ **7.** $1\frac{2}{5}$ **9.** 12.4 **11.** 15.3 **13.** $4.2\overline{3}$ **15.** 490 **17.** -19.4 **19.** 45 **21.** -18 **23.** $\frac{1}{6}$ serving **25.** $1\frac{9}{35}$ **27.** $1\frac{3}{5}$ **29.** $-\frac{8}{21}$ **31.** $2\frac{1}{28}$ **33.** 83 **35.** 9.7 **37.** 40.55 **39.** 13.6 **41.** 12 **43.** -11 **45.** 370 **47.** 11 glasses **49.** $3\frac{31}{48}$ in. **55.** G

4 Exercises

1. $\frac{19}{21}$ **3.** $-4\frac{3}{10}$ **5.** $1\frac{11}{72}$ **7.** $\frac{13}{14}$ **9.** $\frac{75}{91}$ **11.** $\frac{7}{60}$ **13.** $2\frac{18}{35}$ **15.** $-2\frac{5}{28}$ **17.** $-\frac{11}{12}$ **19.** $-\frac{1}{20}$ **21.** $-\frac{7}{39}$ **23.** $55\frac{1}{24}$ L **25.** $\frac{5}{8}$ in. **27.** 2 **29.** $\frac{1}{2}$ **31.** $\frac{73}{100}$ meter **33.** $19\frac{19}{100}$ meters

5 Exercises

1. $y = -82.3$ **3.** $m = -19.2$ **5.** $s = 97.146$ **7.** $x = -\frac{5}{9}$ **9.** $w = -\frac{7}{15}$ **11.** $y = -8$ **13.** 8 days **15.** $m = -7$ **17.** $k = -3.6$ **19.** $c = 3.12$ **21.** $d = \frac{6}{25}$ **23.** $x = -\frac{1}{24}$ **25.** $r = -\frac{5}{7}$ **27.** $d = 1\frac{1}{21}$ **29.** $2258\frac{4}{15}$ carats **31.** Cullinan III **33.** $z = \frac{1}{3}$ **35.** $j = -21.6$ **37.** $t = 7$ **39.** $d = -\frac{1}{2}$ **41.** $v = -30.25$ **43.** $y = -4.2$ **45.** $c = -\frac{1}{20}$ **51.** D

6 Exercises

1. 7 h **3.** $t = 56$ **5.** $x = 114$ **7.** $q = 126$ **9.** $y = 125$ **11.** $m = -18$ **13.** $g = -90$ **15.** $h = 19$ **17.** $z = 94$ **19.** $w = 2.02$ **21.** $m = 15$ **23.** $x = \frac{1}{15}$ **25.** $z = 0.5$ or $\frac{1}{2}$ **27.** $k = 10$ **29.** $n = 21$ **31.** $y = 1.3$ **33.** $b = -2\frac{1}{5}$ **35.** $\frac{n-7}{5} = 13$; 72 **39.** 110,000 **41.** 25 in. **43.** B

Chapter Study Guide: Review

1. rational number **2.** relatively prime **3.** reciprocal **4.** $\frac{3}{5}$ **5.** $\frac{1}{4}$ **6.** $\frac{21}{40}$ **7.** 1.75 **8.** $0.2\overline{6}$ **9.** $0.\overline{7}$ **10.** $\frac{2}{3}$ **11.** $\frac{2}{3}$ **12.** $\frac{3}{4}$ **13.** $-1\frac{1}{5}$ **14.** $7\frac{3}{5}$ **15.** $\frac{8}{15}$ **16.** -4 **17.** $2\frac{1}{4}$ **18.** $3\frac{1}{4}$ **19.** 13 **20.** 7 **21.** $37\frac{1}{8}$ Gb **22.** 17 **23.** -0.00125 **24.** 6 **25.** $\frac{3}{8}$ **26.** $\frac{2}{9}$ **27.** -16 **28.** $\frac{5}{4}$ **29.** 2 **30.** $1\frac{1}{6}$ **31.** $\frac{5}{18}$ **32.** $11\frac{3}{10}$ **33.** $4\frac{7}{20}$ **34.** $3\frac{17}{60}$ **35.** $-9\frac{11}{36}$ **36.** -21.8 **37.** -18 **38.** $-\frac{5}{8}$ **39.** 2 **40.** $\frac{95}{99}$ **41.** -2 **42.** 44.6 **43.** -6 **44.** \$108 **45.** $m = 10$ **46.** $y = -8$ **47.** $c = -16$ **48.** $r = -3$ **49.** $t = 16$ **50.** $w = 64$ **51.** $r = -42$ **52.** $h = -50$ **53.** $x = 52$ **54.** $d = -33$ **55.** $a = 67$ **56.** $c = 90$ **57.** 2.9 lb **58.** 158 songs

Selected Answers ... Chapter 2

1 Exercises

1. yes **3.** yes **7.** $2.95 **9.** no **11.** no **17.** yes **19.** yes **21.** no **23.** yes **25.** $c = 39.99 + 0.49m$; (29, 54.20) **31a.** (1980, 74) **b.** (2020, 81) **37.** J

2 Exercises

1. (−2, 3); Quadrant II **3.** (2, −3); Quadrant IV **5.** (5, 5); Quadrant I **15.** 30 units **17.** 40 units **19.** (0, 3); no quadrant **21.** (2, −4); Quadrant IV **23.** (−2, 5); Quadrant II **33.** 12 units **35.** 16 units **37.** 14 units **39.** 14 units

41a.

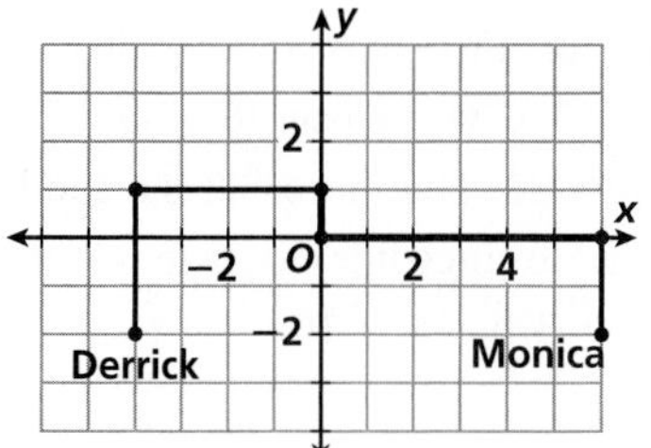

b. 10 km **45.** G

3 Exercises

1. Graph 2 **3.** Graph 1 **5.** discrete

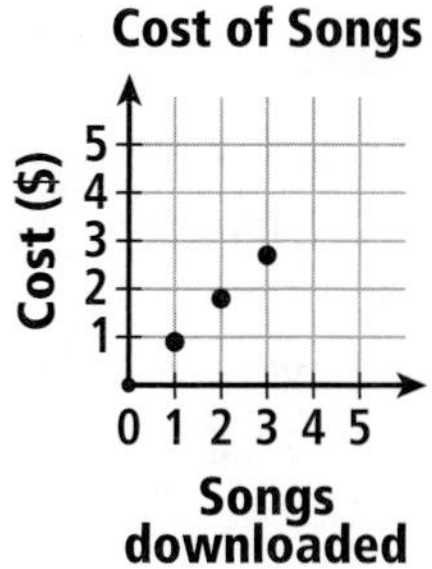

7. Graph 1 **9.** discrete

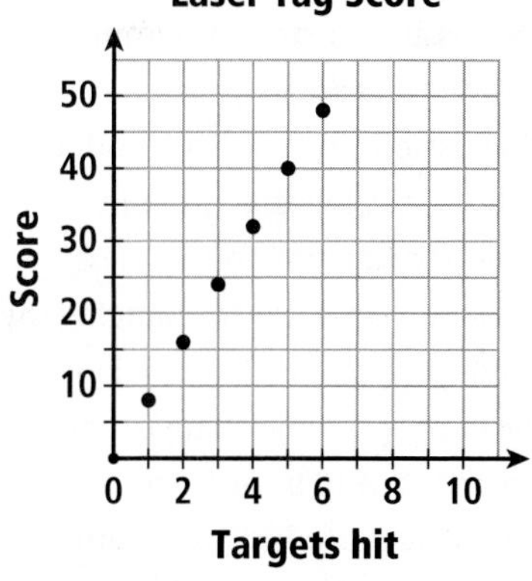

13. discrete **15.** discrete **17.** Possible answer: The rocket ascends rapidly, stays at nearly the same height for 4 seconds, and then quickly descends to the ground.

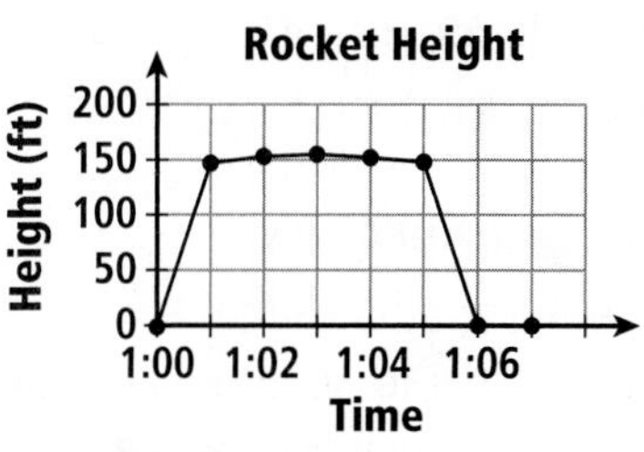

19a. Old Faithful **b.** Riverside **21.** D

4 Exercises

5. The relationship is a function. **7.** The relationship is a function. **13.** The relationship is not a function. **15.** $D = 1, 4, 8, 14$; $R = 27, 39, 56, 62$ **17.** $D = 30, 40, 50, 60$; $R = 60, 50, 40, 30$ **21a.** $0.20 **b.** any nonnegative number of hours ($x \geq 0$) **c.** The independent variable represents the number of hours the bulb is lit. The dependent variable represents the cost in dollars of using the bulb. Possible answer: For each extra hour the bulb is lit, the cost of using the bulb increases by $0.0036. **d.** 550 hours **25.** D

5 Exercises

3. $y = 3x$ **5.** $y = 12 - x$ **7.** Possible answer:

g	0	1	2	3	4	5
d	0	20	40	60	80	100

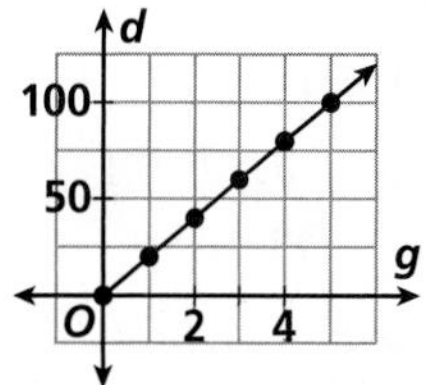

9. Possible answer:

x	0	1	2	3	4	5
y	0	2.5	5	7.5	10	12.5

$y = 2.5x$

Chapter Study Guide: Review

1. range **2.** function **3.** origin **4.** vertical line test **5.** x-axis; y-axis **6.** yes **7.** no **8.** yes **9.** no **22.** 15 units **23.** 12 units **24.** 18 units **25.** 24 units **26.** Graph 1 **27.** Graph 2 **32.** yes **33.** no **34.** $y = 2.3x$ **35.** $y = \frac{1}{2}x$ **36.** $y = x$ **37.** $y = 0.5x$ **38.** $y = -2$

Selected Answers ... Chapter 3

1 Exercises

1. 0.01 **3.** 0.000001 **5.** $\frac{1}{64}$ **7.** $\frac{1}{27}$ **9.** $13\frac{1}{125}$ **11.** $\frac{1}{8}$ **13.** 0.1 **15.** 0.00000001 **17.** $-\frac{1}{4}$ **19.** $\frac{1}{10,000}$, or 0.0001 **21.** $-1\frac{3}{4}$ **23.** $11\frac{4}{81}$ **25.** $\frac{1}{32}$ **27.** $\frac{1}{729}$ **29.** $\frac{4}{9}$ **31.** 28 **33.** 13.02 **35.** $\frac{3}{4}$ **37.** $\frac{1}{11 \times 11 \times 11 \times 11} = \frac{1}{14,641}$ **39.** $-\frac{1}{6 \times 6 \times 6} = -\frac{1}{216}$ **45.** 38,340 lb **49.** C

2 Exercises

1. 5^{15} **3.** m^4 **5.** 6^2 **7.** $12^0 = 1$ **9.** 3^{20} **11.** 4^{-6} or $\frac{1}{4^6}$ **13.** 10^{17} **15.** r **17.** 5^4 **19.** t^{13} **21.** $5^0 = 1$ **23.** 3^{-4} **25.** 4^4 **27.** a^7 **29.** x^{10} **31.** 7^{12} **33.** cannot combine **35.** $y^0 = 1$ **37.** 26^2, or 676 **39.** 12^2, 12^1 **41.** 4 **43.** 0 **45a.** 10^{100} **b.** 10^{200} **49.** B

3 Exercises

1. 4170 **3.** 62,000,000 **5.** 5.7×10^{-5} **7.** 6.98×10^6 **9.** 9.6×10^7 **11.** 9,200,000 **13.** 0.036 **15.** 7×10^{-5} **17.** 1×10^8 **19.** 9×10^9 kg **21.** 140,000 **23.** 78 **25.** 0.000000053 **27.** 559,000 **29.** 7,113,000 **31.** 0.00029 **33a.** 1.5×10^{-4} g **b.** 1.5×10^{26} g **35a.** $2(6.02 \times 10^{23}) = 1.505 \times 10^{24}$ atoms **b.** $10 \div 2.5 = 4$ g **c.** $4 \div (6.02 \times 10^{23}) \approx 6.64 \times 10^{-24}$ g **37.** 8.58×10^{-3} **39.** 5.9×10^6 **41.** 7.6×10^{-3} **49.** C

4 Exercises

1. 2.5×10^2 pp/sq mi **3.** 1.538×10^8 pets **5.** 7.65×10^6 g **7.** 5.5×10^6 **9.** 5.04×10^{15} **11.** 4.6×10^{33} **13.** 8.5×10^5 **15.** 2.205×10^{45} **17.** 2.95×10^{17} **19.** 2.1077×10^{27} atoms **21.** 1.4×10^{10} krill **23.** 5.6448×10^6 insects **25.** Possible answer: Assumption is that all stars are in a galaxy. **27.** Possible answer: The product is 40×10^{15}, but that is not in scientific notation format. The student's error was in changing the product 40 to 4 without making the corresponding change to the exponent of 10 from 15 to 16. The correct product in scientific notation is 40×10^{16} **29.** B

5 Exercises

1. ± 2 **3.** ± 8 **5.** ± 1 **7.** ± 3 **9.** 16 ft **11.** 3 **13.** -1 **15.** ± 12 **17.** ± 13 **19.** ± 20 **21.** ± 15 **23.** -1 **25.** -18 **27.** ± 23 **29.** ± 24 **35.** 26 ft **39.** $\pm\frac{1}{11}$ **41.** $\pm\frac{9}{4}$ **43.** ± 2 **45.** $\pm\frac{1}{2}$ **51.** C

6 Exercises

1. 6 and 7 **3.** 12 and 13 **5.** 15 and 16 **7.** 6.46 **9.** 12.48 **11.** 16.58 **13.** 5.8 **15.** 13.8 **17.** 7 and 8 **19.** 24 and 25 **21.** 20 and 21 **23.** 4.33 **25.** 11.09 **27.** 17.03 **29.** 9.6 **31.** 12.2 **33.** B **35.** E **37.** F **39.** 89.6 in. **41.** 40 ft **43.** $\frac{8}{9}, \frac{1}{3}\sqrt{9}, 1.1, \sqrt{2}$ **45.** 72 mi **51.** 62.83

7 Exercises

1. irrational, real **3.** rational, real **5.** rational **7.** irrational **9.** rational **11.** not real **13.** $3\frac{3}{16}$ **15.** $\frac{3}{16}$ **17.** rational, real **19.** integer, rational, real **21.** rational **23.** irrational **25.** irrational **27.** not real **31.** natural, whole, integer, rational, real **33.** irrational, real **35.** rational, real **37.** rational, real **39.** rational, real **41.** integer, rational, real **55.** $x \geq 0$ **57.** $x \geq 2$ **59.** $x \leq 5$ **63.** H

7 Extension

1. Irrational because its decimal form is nonterminating and nonrepeating. **3.** Rational because its decimal form is terminating. **5.** Rational because its decimal form is nonterminating and repeating. **7.** Rational because its decimal form is terminating **9.** Irrational because its decimal form is nonterminating and nonrepeating. **11.** Rational because its decimal form is nonterminating and repeating.

13.

17. 5, 6; Since 34 is closer to 36 than 25, $\sqrt{34}$ is closer to $\sqrt{36}$ than $\sqrt{25}$. Therefore, 5.8 is a good estimate since it is closer to 6 than 5. **19.** 3, 4 **21.** 9, 10 **23.** 8, 9

8 Exercises

1. 15 **3.** 8.49 **5.** 8 **7.** 16 **9.** 5.39 **11.** 26.93 **13.** 12 **15.** 10.2 **17.** 8.1 **19.** 78 **21.** 37.3 **23.** 22.6 ft **25.** $\approx$ 1.5 in. **31.** C

9 Exercises

1. 127.3 ft **3.** 5 **5.** yes **7.** yes **9.** $\approx$ 12.1 ft **11.** 4.2 **13.** yes **15.** no **17.** $\approx$ 6.4 **19.** 26 **21.** no **23.** yes **25.** yes **27.** no **29.** 8 units **37.** C

Chapter Study Guide: Review

1. perfect square **2.** irrational number **3.** scientific notation **4.** Pythagorean theorem; legs; hypotenuse **5.** real numbers **6.** $\frac{1}{125}$ **7.** $-\frac{1}{64}$ **8.** $\frac{1}{11}$ **9.** $\frac{1}{10,000}$ **10.** 1 **11.** $-\frac{1}{36}$ **12.** $\frac{1}{8}$ **13.** $-\frac{1}{27}$ **14.** 1 **15.** $\frac{1}{2}$ **16.** $\frac{1}{72}$ **17.** 0 **18.** 4^7 **19.** 9^6 **20.** p^4 **21.** 15^3 **22.** cannot combine **23.** x^{10} **24.** 8^3 **25.** 9^2 **26.** m^5 **27.** 3^7 **28.** 4^0 or 1 **29.** y^9 **30.** 5^3 **31.** y^5 **32.** k^0, or 1 **33.** 1620 **34.** 0.00162 **35.** 910,000 **36.** 0.000091 **37.** 3.85×10^2 **38.** 4×10^{-2} **39.** 8×10^{-9} **40.** 7.3×10^7 **41.** 9.6×10^{-6} **42.** 5.64×10^{10} **43.** 7.1×10^{-1} **44.** 1.92×10^{14} **45.** 5×10^{-2} **46.** 4.45×10^8 **47.** 4.749×10^{10} **48.** 4 and -4 **49.** 30 and -30 **50.** 26 and -26 **51.** 5 **52.** $\frac{1}{2}$ **53.** 9 **54.** 89.4 in. **55.** 167.3 cm **56.** 9 and 20 **57.** rational **58.** irrational **59.** not a real number **60.** irrational **61.** rational **62.** not a real number **63.** Possible answer: 3.5 **64.** 10 **65.** 10 **66.** 14.1 inches **67.** 3.2 **68.** 11.3 **69.** 10 **70.** 15 **71.** no **72.** yes **73.** yes **74.** yes

Selected Answers ... Chapter 4

1 Exercises

1. 75 times **3a.** 40 km/h **b.** The estimate is reasonable. At an average speed of 40 km/h, the bicyclist will finish the race in 5.5 hours. **5.** \$8 **7a.** 8.2 mi/h **b.** The estimate is not reasonable. At an average speed of 8.2 mi/h, it would take a rider slightly more than 9 hours to travel 75 miles. **9.** 16 oz package **11.** 14 points per game **13.** 16 beats per measure **15.** approximately 50 beats per minute **17.** approximately 50 words per minute **19.** 30.9 lb **23.** width: 20 in.; height: 15 in. **25.** The better buy is the bunch of 4 for \$2.48.

2 Exercises

1. yes **3.** no **5.** no **7.** 130 min, or 2 h 10 min **9.** no **11.** no **13.** yes **15.** 28 mi **17.** $\frac{8}{4}, \frac{24}{12}$ **19.** $\frac{81}{39}, \frac{27}{13}$ **21.** $\frac{0.5}{6}, \frac{1}{12}$ **23.** \$144 **25.** 64 minutes **27.** 12 computers **29.** 14 molecules **31.** 92 shirts **33.** Yes; the ratio is less than 2.82:1 **35.** B

3 Exercises

1. $\triangle ABC \sim \triangle FDE$ **3.** 16.5 cm **5.** $\approx$ 2.98 in. **7.** similar **9.** similar **11.** yes **13.** 18 in. **19.** 25

4 Exercises

1. no **3.** $A'(2, -1)$; $B'(1, -2)$; $C'(4, -3\frac{1}{3})$; $D'(3, -1)$ **5.** yes **7.** $A'(-9, 6)$; $B'(15, 12)$; $C'(-6, -9)$ **9.** $A'(3, 6)$; $B'(10.5, 6)$; $C'(10.5, 0)$; $D'(3, 0)$ **13.** 3 **17.** 19.2 ft; 76.8 ft; 368.64 ft^2

Chapter Study Guide: Review

1. unit price **2.** rate; unit rate **3.** dilation **4.** \$0.30 per CD; \$0.29 per CD; 75 CDs **5.** \$3.75 per box; \$3.75 per box; unit prices are the same. **6.** \$2.89 per divider; \$4.00 per divider; 8-pack **7.** $x = 15$ **8.** $h = 6$ **9.** $w = 21$ **10.** $y = 29\frac{1}{3}$ **11.** $m = 24$ **12.** $b = 13.75$ **13.** 180 min, or 3 h **14.** \$24.95 **15.** 12.5 in. **16.** 3.125 in. **17.** yes **18.** no

19.
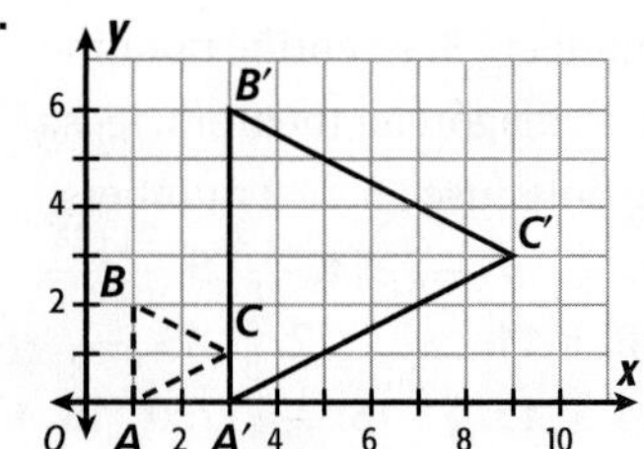

20.
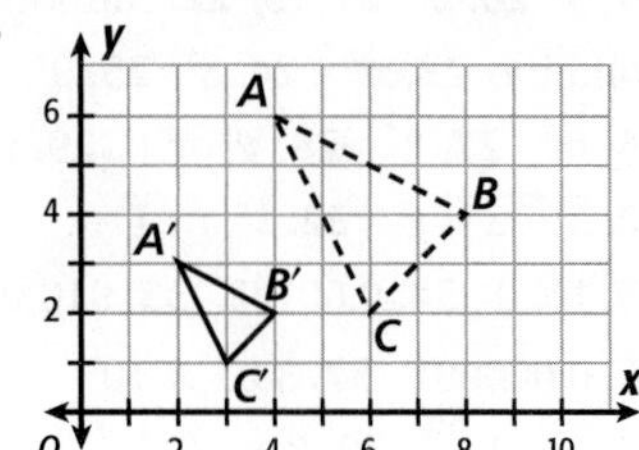

21.
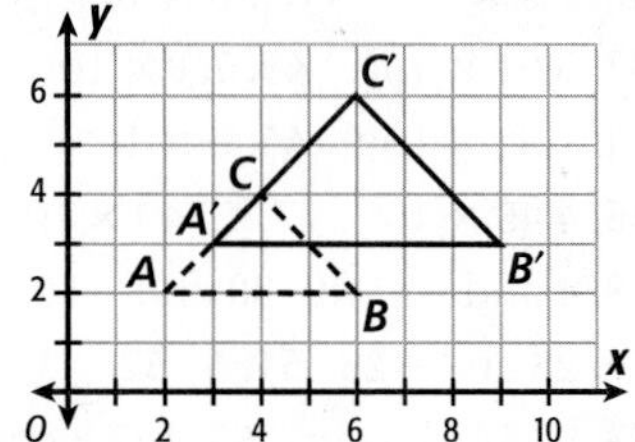

Selected Answers ... Chapter 5

1 Exercises

1. $\angle AEB$ or $\angle DEB$ **3.** $\angle AEC$ **5.** $\angle AEB$ and $\angle BED$, $\angle AEC$ and $\angle CED$ **7.** 114° **9.** $\angle YWZ$ **11.** $\angle VWY$, $\angle ZWX$ **13.** $\angle VWZ$ and $\angle ZWX$, $\angle VWY$ and $\angle YWX$ **15.** 126° **17.** False **19.** False **21.** False **23.** False **25.** 30°, 60° **27.** 140° **31.** 117°

2 Exercises

1. $\angle 1 \cong \angle 4 \cong \angle 5 \cong \angle 8$ (45°); $\angle 2 \cong \angle 3 \cong \angle 6 \cong \angle 7$ (135°) **3.** 62° **5.** 62° **7.** 70° **9.** 110° **11.** $\angle 4$, $\angle 5$, and $\angle 8$ **13.** Possible answers: $\angle 1$ and $\angle 2$, $\angle 1$ and $\angle 3$, $\angle 3$ and $\angle 4$ **15.** 129° **17.** 89° **25.** D

3 Exercises

1. $q° = 77°$ **3.** $a° = 60°$ **5.** $d° = 18°$, $4d° = 72°$, $5d° = 90°$ **7.** No; $4 + 7 \not> 14$ **9.** Yes; $10 + 15 > 20$, $10 + 20 > 15$, $20 + 15 > 10$ **11.** $t° = 115°$ **13.** $m° = 72°$ **15.** 27°, 135°, 18° **17.** No; $1 + 4 \not> 5$ **19.** $x° = 57°$ **21.** $w° = 30°$ **23.** not possible **25.** not possible **29.** 64° **31.** The bars that measure 6 ft, 4 ft, and 3 ft **33.** C **37.** 105°, obtuse

4 Exercises

1. acute isosceles triangle

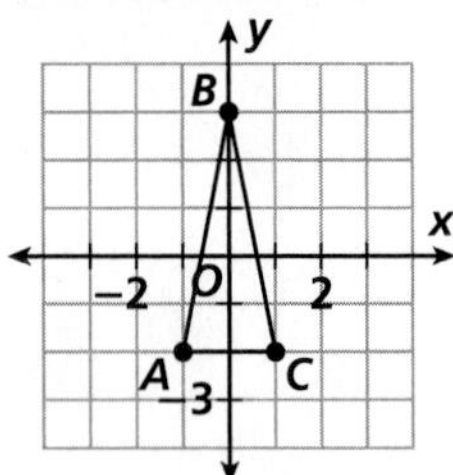

3. $T(4, 2)$ or $T(-2, 2)$ **5.** $\left(\frac{1}{2}, 2\right)$

7. obtuse scalene triangle

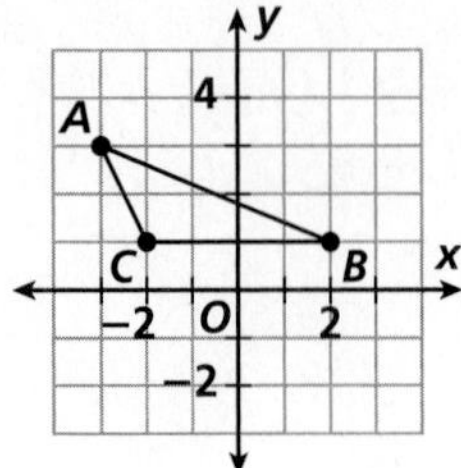

9. Possible answer: $D(-1, 1)$ **11.** $\left(-2\frac{1}{2}, 1\right)$ **13.** Possible answer: (0, −1) **15.** (10, 6) **17.** (1, 5) **19.** Either (5, 2) and (5, −2) or (−3, 2) and (−3, −2) **21.** (0, 0), (0, 3), (3, 0) **25.** D **27.** 1

5 Exercises

1. triangle $ABC \cong$ triangle FED **3.** $q = 5$ **5.** $s = 7$ **7.** quadrilateral $PQRS \cong$ quadrilateral $ZYXW$ **9.** $n = 7$ **11.** $x = 19$, $y = 27$, $z = 18.1$ **13.** $r = 24$, $s = 120$, $t = 48$ **19.** C **21.** 3

6 Exercises

1.

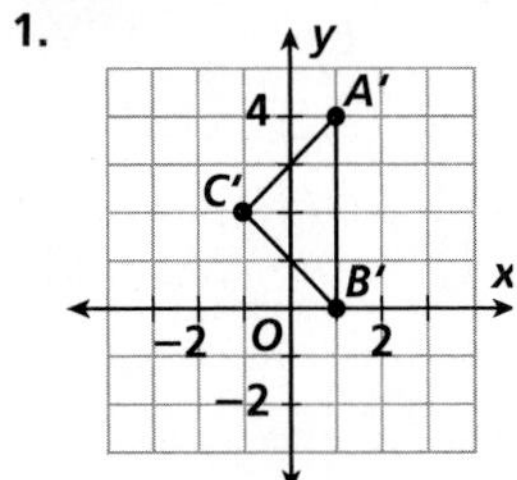

3.

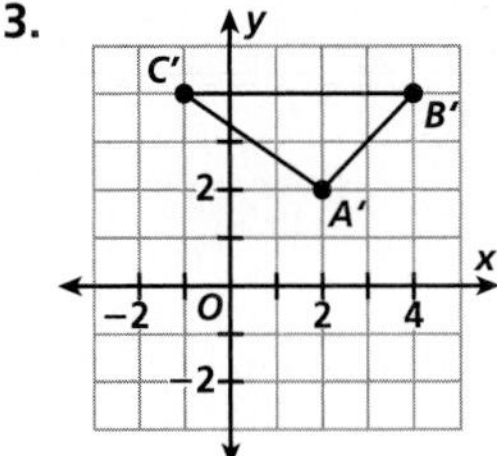

5.

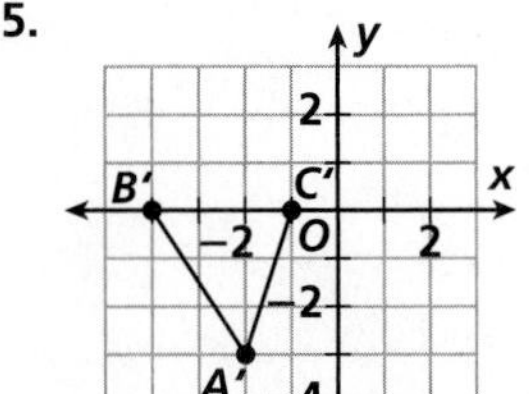

7.

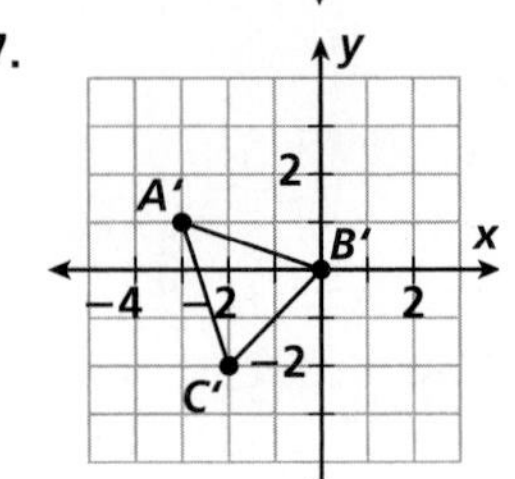

9.

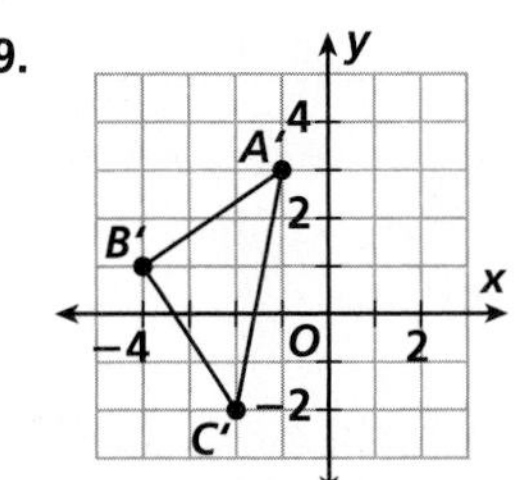

11.

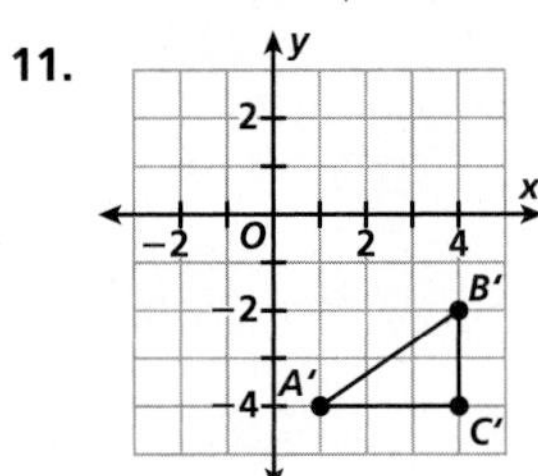

13a. (4, 1), (2, 1), (3, 4) **19.** (−3, −2) **21.** (−5, −2) **23.** $(-m, n)$ **31.** The vertices of the image are (1, 4), (5, 5), and (3, −1).

7 Exercises

1. Dilation; similar
3. Rotation 90° counter-clockwise around the origin; congruent
5. Dilation; similar
7. Reflection across the x-axis; congruent

11. Translation 3 units right and 5 units up; congruent
13. Rotation of 180° around the origin; congruent
15. Reflection over the y-axis; congruent
17. Translation 3 units left and 2 units down; congruent
19. Dilation by a scale factor of 0.2; similar
21. Reflection
23. Rotation, Translation
25. Possible answer: A different multiplier was used on B than on A and C. To fix, use the same multiplier on the coordinates of all points.
27. Rotation; possible answer: a reflection would have $\overline{A'D'}$ at the bottom of the rectangle.
29. A

8 Exercises

1. $(x, y) \rightarrow (-x, -y)$; $(x, y) \rightarrow (x, y + 5)$; congruent
3. $(x, y) \rightarrow (x, -y)$; $(x, y) \rightarrow (2x, 2y)$; similar
5. $(x, y) \rightarrow (-x, y)$; $(x, y) \rightarrow (-y, x)$; congruent
7. $(x, y) \rightarrow (x, -y)$; $(x, y) \rightarrow (x - 7, y - 1)$; congruent
9. No; possible answer: not all points of $ABCD$ are rotated.
11. $A''(-6, 3)$, $B''(6, 0)$, $C''(-3, -3)$; similar
13. $A''(4, 2)$, $B''(3, -2)$, $C''(5, -4)$; congruent
15. $A''(0, -5)$, $B''(-4, -5)$, $C''(0, -9)$; congruent
17. $(x, y) \rightarrow (x, y + 2)$; $(x, y) \rightarrow (-x, -y)$; congruent
19. Dilations involving multiplicative inverses. For example, $(x, y) \rightarrow (2x, 2y)$ followed by $(x, y) \rightarrow (0.5x, 0.5y)$ results in an image that is congruent to the original.
23. −6

Chapter Study Guide: Review

1. parallel lines; perpendicular lines 2. complementary; supplementary
3. 112° 4. 68° 5. 112° 6. 66°
7. 114° 8. 66° 9. 66° 10. 114°
11. $m° = 26°$ 12. $p° = 55°$ 13. yes
14. no
15. obtuse scalene triangle

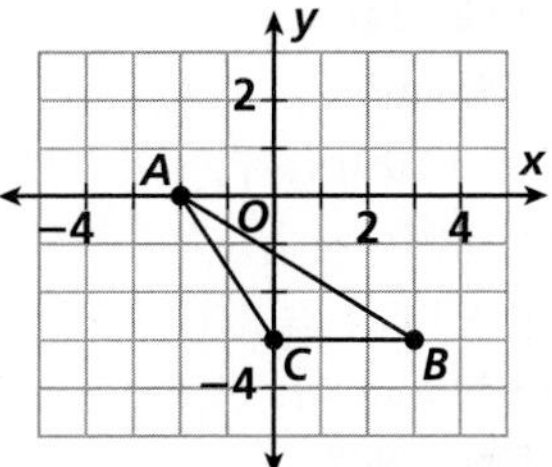

16. trapezoid

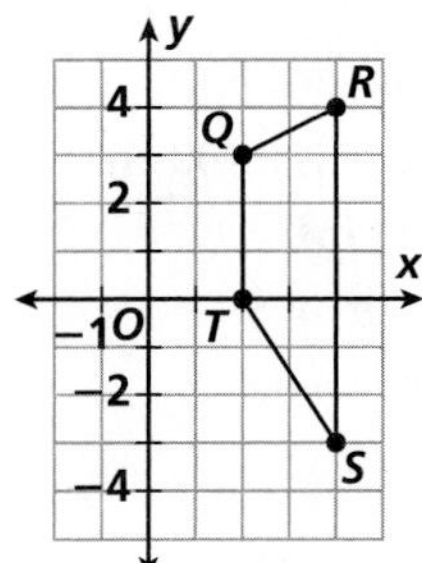

17. rhombus

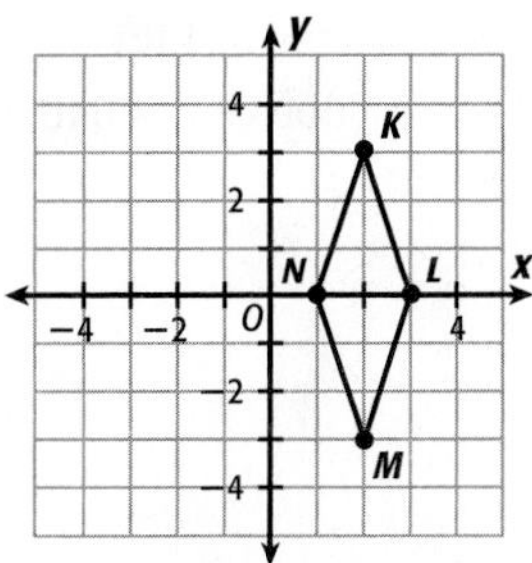

18. parallelogram

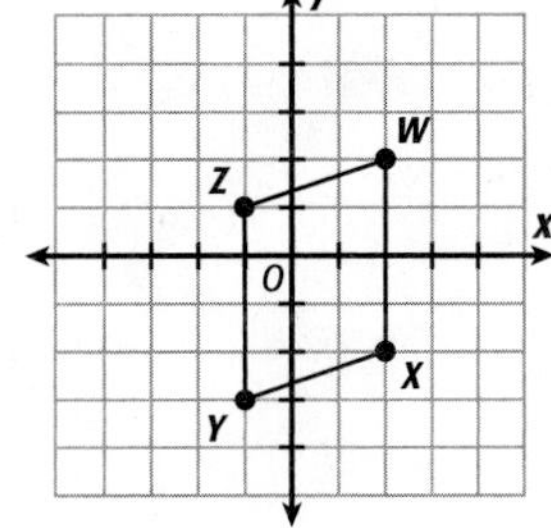

19. $x = 25$ 20. $t = 2.4$ 21. $q = 7$
22.

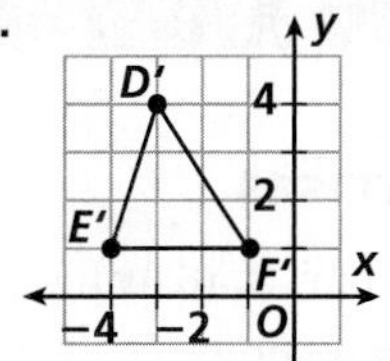

23.

24.

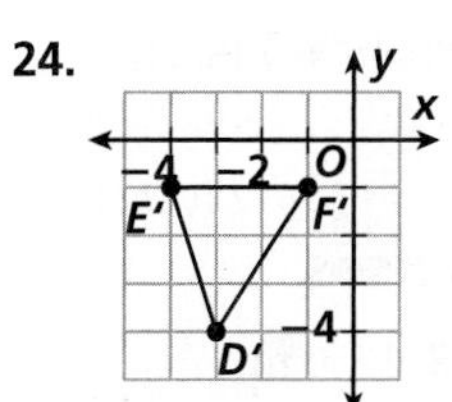

25.

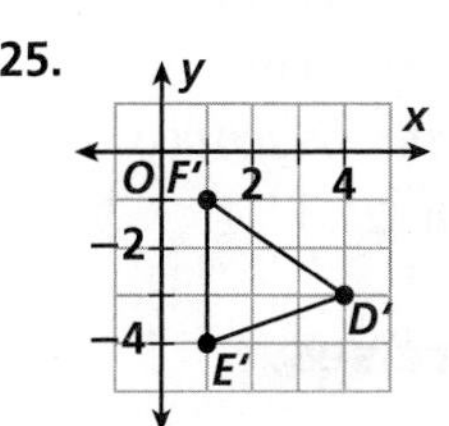

26. $(x, y) \rightarrow (2x, 2y)$; a dilation
27. $(x, y) \rightarrow (y, -x)$, a rotation of 90° clockwise about the origin; $(x, y) \rightarrow (-x, y)$, a reflection over the y-axis; congruent

Selected Answers ... Chapter 6

1 Exercises

1. 6π cm; 18.8 cm **3.** 16.8π ft^2; 52.8 ft^2 **5.** $A = 4\pi$ units^2; 12.6 units^2; $C = 4\pi$ units; 12.6 units **7.** 18π in.; 56.5 in. **9.** 256π cm^2 803.8 cm^2 **11.** $A = 16\pi$ units^2; 50.2 units^2; $C = 8\pi$ units; 25.1 units **13.** $C \approx 10.7$ m; $A \approx 9.1$ m^2 **15.** $C \approx 56.5$ in.; $A \approx 254.3$ in^2 **17.** 6.4 cm **19.** 6 cm **21.** 11.7 m **23.** 248.1 m^2 **25.** $C = 30\pi$ ft $\approx$ 94.2 ft; $A = 225\pi$ ft$^2 \approx 706.5$ ft^2 **31.** 785

2 Exercises

1. 463.1 cm^3 **3.** 1256 m^3 **5.** $\approx$ 1500 ft^3 **7.** 100 in^3 **9.** 351 m^3 **11.** $\approx$ 60 cm^3 **13a.** 800 in^3 **15a.** 46,200,000 in^3 **b.** about 18.8 ft **21.** J

3 Exercises

1. 20 cm^3 **3.** 99.7 ft^3 **5.** 9.1 cm^3 **7.** Yes **9.** 160.22 in^3 **11.** 35.0 m^3 **13.** 66.2 ft^3 **15.** 5494.5 units^3 **17.** 13,083.33 m^3 **19.** 6 in. **21.** 11 ft **23.** 600 in^3 **25.** 301,056 ft^3 **29.** A **31.** 4 cm

4 Exercises

1. 36π cm^3; 113.0 cm^3 **3.** 6.6π m^3; 207 m^3 **5.** 4π in^2; 12.6 in^2 **7.** 256π cm^2; 803.8 cm^2 **9.** The volume of the sphere and the cube are about equal. **11.** 246.9π cm^3 **13.** 1.3π in^3 **15.** 207.4π m^2 **17.** 49π cm^2 **19.** 366.17π in^3 **21.** $V = 52.41\pi$ yd^3; $S = 46.24\pi$ yd^2 **25.** $\approx$ 1767.15 cm^3 **29.** 113.04

Chapter Study Guide: Review

1. great circle **2.** diameter **3.** $A = 144\pi \approx 452.2$ in^2; $C = 24\pi \approx 75.4$ in. **4.** $A = 17.6\pi \approx 55.3$ cm^2; $C = 8.4\pi \approx 26.4$ cm **5.** $A = 9\pi \approx 28.3$ m^2; $C = 6\pi \approx 18.8$ m **6.** $A = 0.4\pi \approx 1.1$ ft^2; $C = 1.2\pi \approx 3.8$ ft **7.** $A = 49\pi \approx 153.9$ in^2; $C = 14\pi \approx 44$ in. **8.** $A = 625\pi \approx 1962.5$ ft^2; $C = 50\pi \approx 157$ ft **9.** 15.3 in. **10.** 415.4 mm^3 **11.** 364 cm^3 **12.** yes; the volume is 2,400 cm^3 **13.** 60 in^3 **14.** 314 in^3 **15.** $288\pi \approx 904.3$ in^3 **16.** $7776\pi \approx 24{,}416.6$ m^3 **17.** $\frac{5324\pi}{3}$ in^3, $\frac{5572}{5}$ in^3 **18.** $\frac{125\pi}{48}$ ft^3; 8.2 ft^3 **19.** sphere: S.A. = $\pi \approx 3.14$ ft^2, $V = \frac{\pi}{6} \approx 0.52$ ft^3; cube: S.A. = 6 ft^2, $V = 1$ ft^3

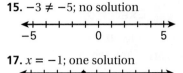

Selected Answers ··· Chapter 7

1 Exercises

1. $5x$ **3.** $16f^2 - 4f + 8$ **5.** $6p - 9$ **7.** $5x + 8y$ **9.** $9x^2 + y$ **11.** $7g + 5h - 12$ **13.** $r + 12$ **15.** $2t + 56$ **17.** $y = 15$ **19.** $13y$ **21.** $a^2 + 5a + 15$ **23.** $5x + 3$ **25.** $9p$ **27.** $13x^2 + 5$ **29.** $6a + z$ **31.** $9x + 6q + 2$ **33.** $9a + 7c^2 + c + 5$ **35.** $12y - 14$ **37.** $12y + 23$ **39.** $19x - 16$ **41.** $p = 6$ **43.** $y = 8$ **45.** $x = 12$ **47.** $12x$ **49.** $7d + 1$ **51.** $x = 15$ **53.** $25g + 19s + 19b$ **59.** 16

2 Exercises

1. $d = 3$ **3.** $e = 6$ **5.** $h = 7$ **7.** $x = -1$ **9.** $p = -1$ **11.** 6 hours **13.** $k = -10$ **15.** $w = 3$ **17.** $y = 5$ **19.** $h = 6$ **21.** $m = 2$ **23.** $x = -12$ **25.** $n = 2$ **27.** $b = -13$ **29.** $x = 17$ **31.** \$11.80 per hour **35.** 212 °F **39.** C

3 Exercises

1. $x = 1$ **3.** $x = -20$ **5.** $x = 1$ **7.** 250 min **9.** $h = \frac{2A}{b}$ **11.** $x = 1$ **13.** infinite number of solutions **15.** $n = 5$ **17.** 6 figures **19.** $y = 2$ **21.** $n = 5$ **23.** $x = 5$ **25.** 350 units **27.** $t = \frac{A - P}{Pr}$ **29.** \$25,000 **33.** C

3 Extension

1. $x = -\frac{1}{11}$; one solution
3. $-4 \neq 12$; no solution
5. $0 = 0$; infinitely many solutions
7. $0 = 0$; infinitely many solutions
9. $0 = 0$; infinitely many solutions
11. $-8 \neq 2$; no solution
13. $x = -1$; one solution
15. $-3 \neq -5$; no solution

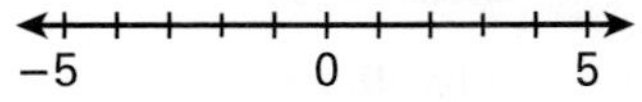

17. $x = -1$; one solution

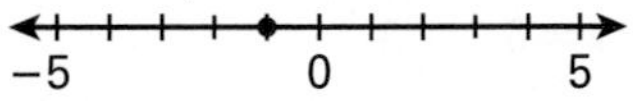

19. $2x - 1 = 2x - 2$; no solution
21. $4x = x - 4$; $x = -\frac{4}{3}$; one solution

4 Exercises

1. (2, 3) **3.** (−4, −17) **5.** (0, 7) **7.** (5, 3) **9.** (1, 10) **11.** (−9, 3) **13.** (−1, 1) **15.** (2, 7) **17.** (2, 5) **19.** (2, 3) **21.** (1, 3) **23.** (7, −3) **25.** 4 bookmarks and 3 wall hangings **27.** (2, −17) **29.** (2, 1) **31.** (−1.3, 5.8) **33.** no solution **35.** 25 dimes and 10 quarters **37.** $x = 11$ and $y = 6$ **41.** C

Chapter Study Guide: Review

1. system of equations **2.** like terms **3.** solution of a system of equations **4.** terms **5.** $19m - 10$ **6.** $14w + 6$ **7.** $2x + 3y$ **8.** $2t^2 - 4t + 3t^3$ **9.** $y = 6$ **10.** $z = 7$ **11.** $y = 5$ **12.** $z = 8$ **13.** Possible answer: $2(x + 0.6x)$; $3.2x$ **14.** $y = -1$ **15.** $h = 2$ **16.** $t = -1$ **17.** $r = 3$ **18.** $z = 2$ **19.** $a = 12$ **20.** \$5.00; \$10.00 **21.** $s = 7$ **22.** $c = 24$ **23.** $x = \frac{1}{6}$ **24.** $y = \frac{2}{3}$ **25.** no solution **26.** $z = 5$ **27.** $x = 8$ **28.** (−2, 1) **29.** (2, 6) **30.** (3, 5) **31.** (3, −2) **32.** no solution **33.** infinite solutions **34a.** $x + y = 32$; $2x = 6y$ **b.** $x = 24$; $y = 8$ **c.** $24 + 8 = 32$; $2(24) = 6(8)$ or $48 = 48$

Selected Answers ... Chapter 8

1 Exercises

1. linear **3.** not linear **5.** variable **7.** linear **9.** not linear **11.** not linear **13.** variable **15.** \$550, \$975, \$1400, \$1825, \$2250; linear **17.** 509.6 N **19.** (−1, −2), (0, 0), (1, 2) **21.** (−1, −6), (0, −1), (1, 4) **23.** (−1, −5), (0, −3), (1, −1) **25.** (−1, −6), (0, −4), (1, −2) **27.** (−1, 1.5), (0, 3.5), (1, 5.5) **29.** $C = 2.25b + 3$ **35.** −8, −5, −2; linear

2 Exercises

1. $\frac{1}{3}$ **3.** 1 **5.** $\frac{1}{4}$ **7.** 0 **9.** $-\frac{3}{2}$ **11.** −5 **13.** $1\frac{3}{4}$ **15.** The slope of the line is 4. **17.** a **19.** d **21.** $1\frac{1}{4}$ **23.** $y = -\frac{4}{5}x + 350$ **27.** 840/h; 12h **31.** C

3 Exercises

1. (4, 0), (0, −4) **3.** (−6, 0), (0, −4) **5.** $y = \frac{1}{3}x$; $\frac{1}{3}$, 0 **7.** $y = \frac{1}{4}x - 4$; $\frac{1}{4}$, −4 **9.** $m = 4.5$; $b = 25$ **11.** $y = -4x + 3$ **13.** (2, 0), (0, 6) **15.** (3, 0), (0, −12) **17.** $y = -3x$; −3, 0 **19.** $y = -2x - 2$; −2, −2 **21.** $m = 12$; $b = 250$ **23.** $y = -x$ **25.** $-2x + y = -10$ or $2x - y = 10$ **27.** $-5x + y = -1.5$ or $5x - y = 1.5$ **33.** D

4 Exercises

7. $y - 6 = 5x$ **9.** $y - 840 = -10.5(x - 40)$; 120 m **17.** $y = 6(x + 3)$ **19.** $y - 3 = 4(x + 2)$; $y = 4x + 11$ **21.** $y + 7 = -1(x + 5)$; $y = -x - 12$ **29.** C

5 Exercises

1. yes **3.** $y = 3x$ **5.** $y = \frac{1}{2}x$ **7.** $y = \frac{1}{9}x$ **9.** no **11.** $y = \frac{1}{3}x$ **13.** $y = \frac{2}{13}x$ **15.** $y = \frac{1}{10}x$ **17.** yes **19.** no **21.** no **27.** 28

6 Exercises

1. 3.5 min; 525 m **3.** (2, 2) **5.** (3, 6) **7.** (0, −3) **9.** (−5, 4) **11.** (1, 3) **13.** no solution **15.** (−3, 1) **17.** 25 **19.** no **25.** 0.5

Chapter Study Guide: Review

1. x-intercept; y-intercept **2.** slope intercept form; point-slope form **3.** direct variation **4.** linear **5.** linear **6.** not linear **7.** not linear **8.** not linear **9.** linear **10.** not linear **11.** not linear **12.** $\frac{3}{4}$ **13.** −4 **14.** $\frac{6}{5}$ **15.** −1 **16.** −1 **17.** $\frac{3}{2}$ **18.** $-\frac{9}{4}$ **19.** decrease in value after each smoothie purchased; initial card value **20.** $y = \frac{4}{3}x + 5$ **21.** $y = \frac{6}{5}x - 2$ **22.** $y = -\frac{2}{3}x + 4$ **23.** $y = \frac{7}{4}x + 3$ **24.** $y = 3x + 4$ **25.** $y = -3x + 2$ **26.** $y = -\frac{1}{3}x + 7$ **27.** $y = \frac{1}{2}x - \frac{5}{2}$ **28.** $y - 4 = 2(x - 3)$ **29.** $y - 3 = -4(x + 2)$ **30.** $y + 3 = -\frac{5}{6}x$ **31.** $y = \frac{2}{7}x$ **32.** $y = 6x$ **33.** $y = 13x$ **34.** $y = \frac{1}{7}x$ **35.** (−2, −4) **36.** (1, 1) **37.** no solution **38.** infinitely many solutions

Selected Answers ■■■ Chapter 9

1 Exercises

1.

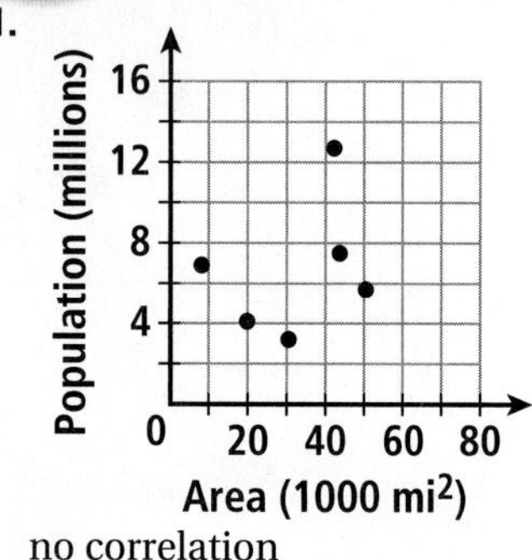

no correlation

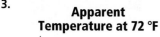

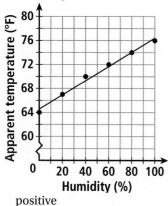

3. **Apparent Temperature at 72 °F**

Apparent temperature (°F)

80 76 72 68 64 60 0

20 40 60 80 100

Humidity (%)

positive

5a.

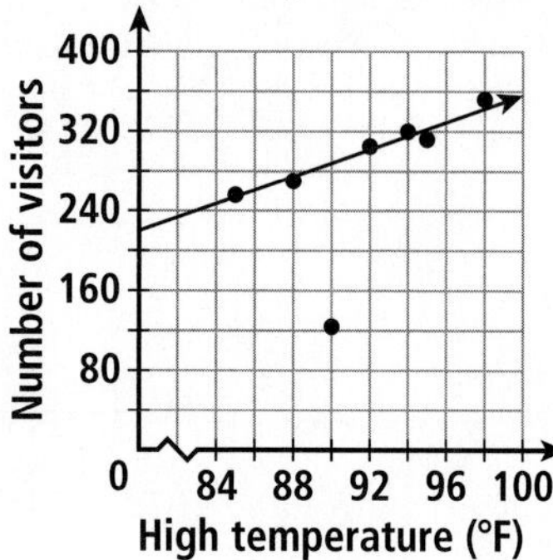

b. (90, 124); this data point lies far away from the rest of the data points. **c.** 360 **9.** positive **11.** A

2 Exercises

1. linear

3. No outliers

5. $y = \frac{8}{5}x + 39$; 39 in. at 0 years of age; rate of growth of 1.6 inches per year

7. No clustering

9. Possible answer: Graph A shows data points closer than Graph B to the line of best fit.

11. at $x = 60$

13. none

15. Positive

19. A

2 Extension

1.

	Dry food	Wet food	
Cats	10 (25%)	30 (75%)	40 (50%)
Dogs	20 (50%)	20 (50%)	40 (50%)
	30 (37.5%)	50 (62.5%)	80 (100%)

3. The student only looked at the numbers in the table, not the percentages. The greater number only shows that more 8th graders were asked. Once the percentages are inserted, it is clear that neither grade shows any preference.

	Soccer	Bask.	
7th Graders	15 (50%)	15 (50%)	30 (25%)
8th Graders	45 (50%)	45 (50%)	90 (75%)
	60 (50%)	60 (50%)	120 (100%)

3 Exercises

1. linear; $m = 6$; $b = -3$

3. linear; $m = 1$; $b = 3$

5. $f(x) = -2x + 4$

7. linear; $m = -4$; $b = 8$

9. not linear **11.** $f(x) = 6x - 5$

13. 16 lb **15a.** $f(x) = 5x + 1245$

b. 2745 ft; 1500 ft **21.** $f(t) = -50t + 1800$; 300 gal; 36 min

4 Exercises

1. Slope for f is -0.50; slope for g is 0.50; the slope for g is greater than the slope for f.

3. Snail #1 is descending at 2.5 in./h beginning at 8 in. Snail #2 is ascending at 3.5 in./h beginning at 4 in. Snail #2 is going 1 in./h faster than snail #1 and begins 4 in. below snail #1.

5. y-int. of f is 3; y-int. of g is -2; y-int. of f is greater.

7. Slope of f is -0.2; slope of g is -0.2; slopes are equal. y-int. of f is 8; y-int. of g is 16. y-int of g is twice as large as y-int. of f.

9. The table of data gives a slope of about 0.4386 and a y-intercept of 0. The function model has a slope of 0.44 and a y-intercept of 0; the function is a good model of the data in the table.

11. Possible answer: Kayak rental places; Place 1: \$15 fee + \$5/h; Place 2: \$25 flat fee. Intersect at $x = 2$

13. Company #1 increases annual salary by \$1600/year of experience; company #2 increases annual salary by \$1750/year of experience.

Chapter Study Guide: Review

1. clustering **2.** correlation
3. function notation
4. positive

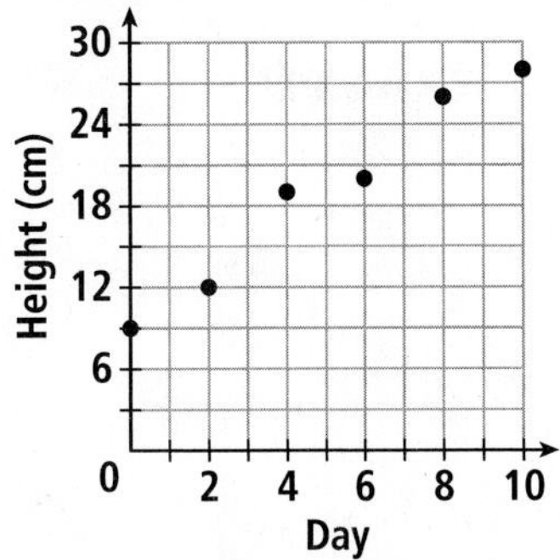

5. July and August have some clustering. **6.** November; the shop was likely closed. **7.** 4; every month has 4 data points.
8. $f(x) = x - 1$ **9.** $f(x) = \frac{1}{2}x + 4$
10. $f(x) = -2$ **11.** $f(x) = -x + 2$
12. Pete's Plumbing: \$120; House Depot: \$0 **13.** Pete's Plumbing: \$720; House Depot: \$600
14. slope of f = slope of $g = 2$; y-intercept of $f = 20$, y-intercept of $g = 30$

Glossary/Glosario

ENGLISH	SPANISH	EXAMPLES
absolute value The distance of a number from zero on a number line; shown by | |.	**valor absoluto** Distancia a la que está un número de 0 en una recta numérica. El símbolo del valor absoluto es | |.	$\|-5\| = 5$
accuracy The closeness of a given measurement or value to the actual measurement or value.	**exactitud** Cercanía de una medida o un valor a la medida o el valor real.	
acute angle An angle that measures greater than 0° and less than 90°.	**ángulo agudo** Ángulo que mide mas de 0° y menos de 90°.	
acute triangle A triangle with all angles measuring less than 90°.	**triángulo acutángulo** Triángulo en el que todos los ángulos miden menos de 90°.	
Addition Property of Equality The property that states that if you add the same number to both sides of an equation, the new equation will have the same solution.	**Propiedad de igualdad de la suma** Propiedad que establece que puedes sumar el mismo número a ambos lados de una ecuación y la nueva ecuación tendrá la misma solución.	$14 - 6 = 8$ $+6 \quad +6$ $14 = 14$
Addition Property of Opposites The property that states that the sum of a number and its opposite equals zero.	**Propiedad de la suma de los opuestos** Propiedad que establece que la suma de un número y su opuesto es cero.	$12 + (-12) = 0$
additive inverse The opposite of a number. 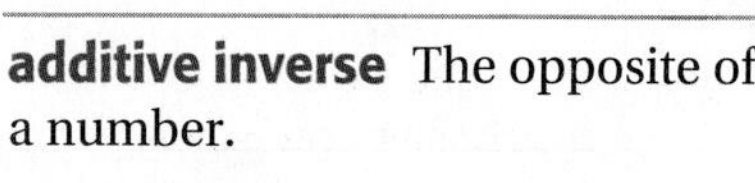	**inverso aditivo** El opuesto de un número.	The additive inverse of 5 is -5.
adjacent angles Angles in the same plane that have a common vertex and a common side.	**ángulos adyacentes** Ángulos en el mismo plano que comparten un vértice y un lado.	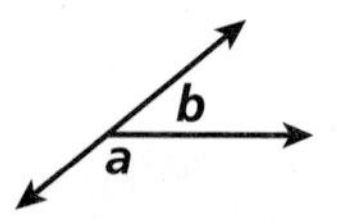
algebraic expression An expression that contains at least one variable.	**expresión algebraica** Expresión que contiene al menos una variable.	$x + 8$ $4(m - b)$
algebraic inequality An inequality that contains at least one variable.	**desigualdad algebraica** Desigualdad que contiene al menos una variable.	$x + 3 > 10$ $5a > b + 3$

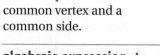

ENGLISH	SPANISH	EXAMPLES
alternate exterior angles For two lines intersected by a transversal, a pair of angles that lie on opposite sides of the transversal and outside the other two lines.	**ángulos alternos externos** Dadas dos rectas cortadas por una transversal, par de ángulos no adyacentes ubicados en los lados opuestos de la transversal y fuera de las otras dos rectas.	$\angle 4$ and $\angle 5$ are alternate exterior angles.
alternate interior angles For two lines intersected by a transversal, a pair of nonadjacent angles that lie on opposite sides of the transversal and between the other two lines.	**ángulos alternos internos** Dadas dos rectas cortadas por una transversal, par de ángulos no adyacentes ubicados en los lados opuestos de la transversal y entre de las otras dos rectas.	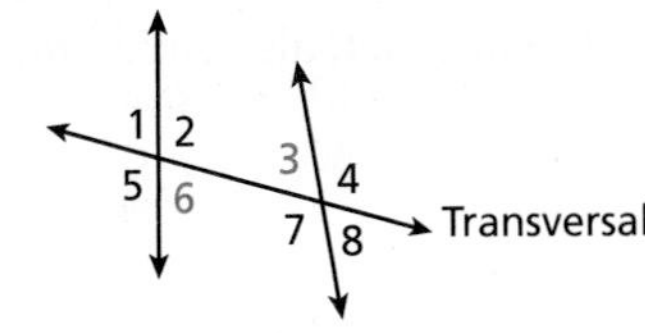 $\angle 3$ and $\angle 6$ are alternate interior angles.
angle A figure formed by two rays with a common endpoint called the vertex.	**ángulo** Figura formada por dos rayos con un extremo común llamado vértice.	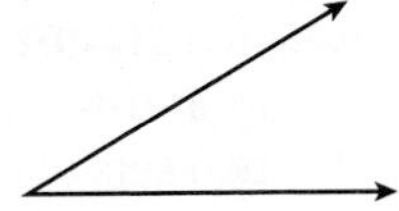
angle bisector A line, segment, or ray that divides an angle into two congruent angles.	**bisectriz de un ángulo** Línea, segmento o rayo que divide un ángulo en dos ángulos congruentes.	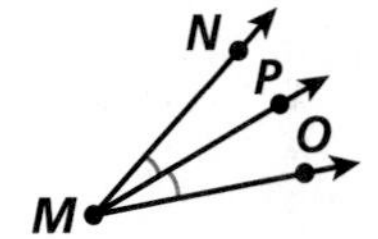
arc An unbroken part of a circle.	**arco** Parte continua de un círculo.	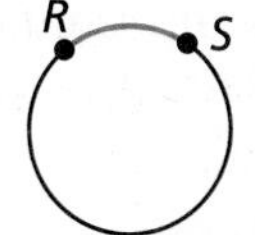
area The number of square units needed to cover a given surface.	**área** El número de unidades cuadradas que se necesitan para cubrir una superficie dada.	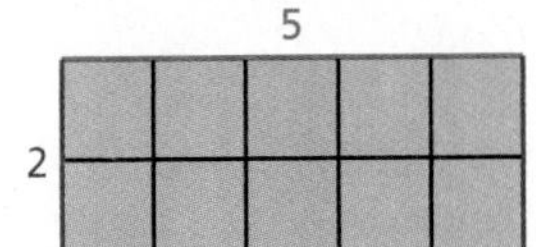 The area is 10 square units.
arithmetic sequence An ordered list of numbers in which the difference between consecutive terms is always the same.	**sucesión aritmética** Lista ordenada de números en la que la diferencia entre términos consecutivos es siempre la misma.	The sequence 2, 5, 8, 11, 14... is an arithmetic sequence.
Associative Property (of Addition) The property that states that for all real numbers *a, b,* and *c,* the sum is always the same, regardless of their grouping.	**Propiedad asociativa (de la suma)** Propiedad que establece que para todos los números reales *a, b* y *c,* la suma siempre es la misma sin importar cómo se agrupen.	$a + b + c = (a + b) + c = a + (b + c)$

ENGLISH	SPANISH	EXAMPLES
Associative Property (of Multiplication) The property that states that for all real numbers *a*, *b*, and *c*, their product is always the same, regardless of their grouping.	**Propiedad asociativa (de la multiplicación)** Propiedad que establece que para todos los números reales *a*, *b* y *c*, el producto siempre es el mismo, sin importar cómo se agrupen.	$a \cdot b \cdot c = (a \cdot b) \cdot c = a \cdot (b \cdot c)$
average The sum of a set of data divided by the number of items in the data set; also called *mean*.	**promedio** La suma de los elementos de un conjunto de datos dividida entre el número de elementos del conjunto. También se llama media.	Data set: 4, 6, 7, 8, 10 Average: $\frac{4+6+7+8+10}{5}$ $= \frac{35}{5} = 7$

B

ENGLISH	SPANISH	EXAMPLES
back-to-back stem-and-leaf plot A stem-and-leaf plot that compares two sets of data by displaying one set of data to the left of the stem and the other to the right.	**diagrama doble de tallo y hojas** Diagrama de tallo y hojas que compara dos conjuntos de datos presentando uno de ellos a la izquierda del tallo y el otro a la derecha.	Data set A: 9, 12, 14, 16, 23, 27 Data set B: 6, 8, 10, 13, 15, 16, 21 Set A | | Set B 9 | 0 | 6 8 6 4 2 | 1 | 0 3 5 6 3 7 | 2 | 1 *Key:* |2| 1 means 21 7 |2| means 27
bar graph A graph that uses vertical or horizontal bars to display data.	**gráfica de barras** Gráfica en la que se usan barras verticales u horizontales para presentar datos.	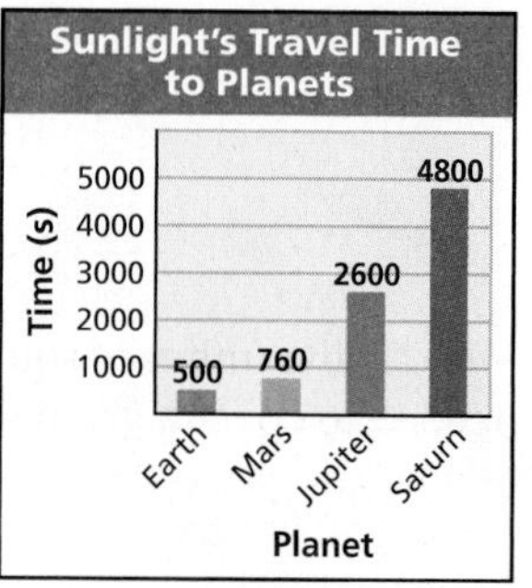
base When a number is raised to a power, the number that is used as a factor is the base.	**base** Cuando un número es elevado a una potencia, el número que se usa como factor es la base.	$3^5 = 3 \cdot 3 \cdot 3 \cdot 3 \cdot 3$; 3 is the base.
base (of a polygon or three-dimensional figure) A side of a polygon; a face of a three-dimensional figure by which the figure is measured or classified.	**base (de un polígono o figura tridimensional)** Lado de un polígono; cara de una figura tridimensional según la cual se mide o se clasifica la figura.	 Bases of a cylinder 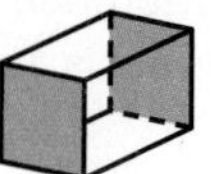 Bases of a prism  Base of a cone 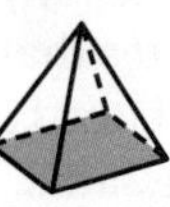 Base of a pyramid

ENGLISH | **SPANISH** | **EXAMPLES**

biased question A question that leads people to give a certain answer.

pregunta tendenciosa pregunta que lleva a las personas a dar una respuesta determinada

---

biased sample A sample that does not fairly represent the population.

muestra no representativa Muestra que no representa adecuadamente la población.

---

binomial A polynomial with two terms.

binomio Polinomio con dos términos.

$x + y$

$2a^2 - 3$

$4m^3n^2 + 6mn^4$

---

bisect To divide into two congruent parts.

trazar una bisectriz Dividir en dos partes congruentes.

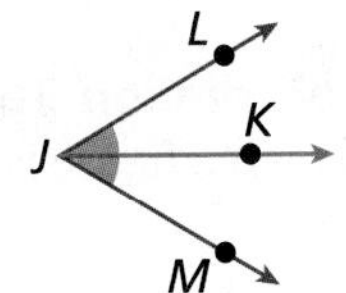

$\overrightarrow{JK}$ bisects $\angle LJM$

---

boundary line The set of points where the two sides of a two-variable linear inequality are equal.

línea de límite Conjunto de puntos donde los dos lados de una desigualdad lineal con dos variables son iguales.

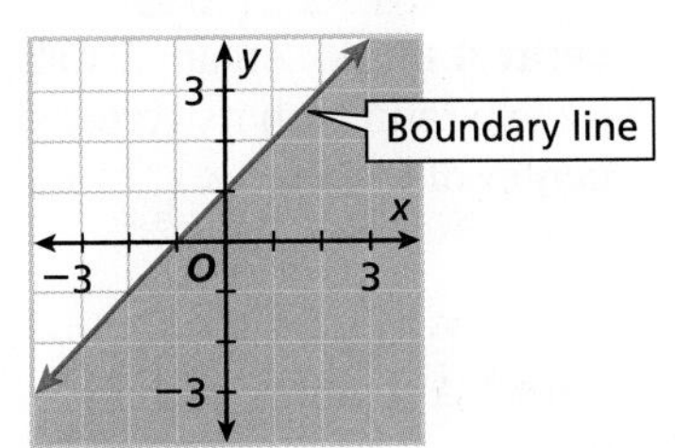

---

box-and-whisker plot A graph that shows how data are distributed by using the median, quartiles, least value, and greatest value; also called a *box plot.*

gráfica de mediana y rango Gráfica para demostrar la distribución de datos utilizando la mediana, los cuartiles y los valores menos y más grande; también llamado gráfica de caja.

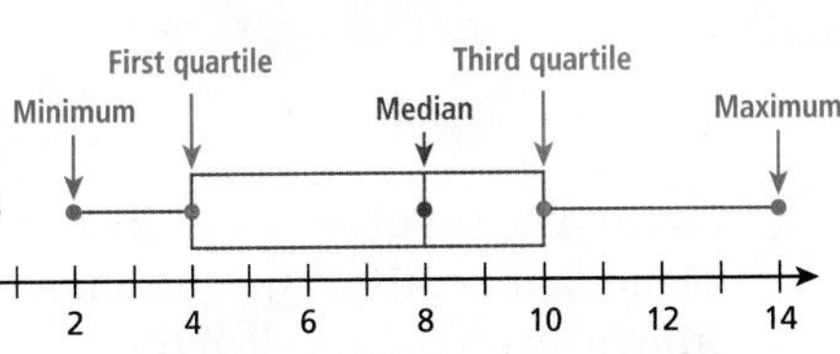

---

break (graph) A zigzag on a horizontal or vertical scale of a graph that indicates that some of the numbers on the scale have been omitted.

discontinuidad (gráfica) Zig-zag en la escala horizontal o vertical de una gráfica que indica la omisión de algunos de los números de la escala.

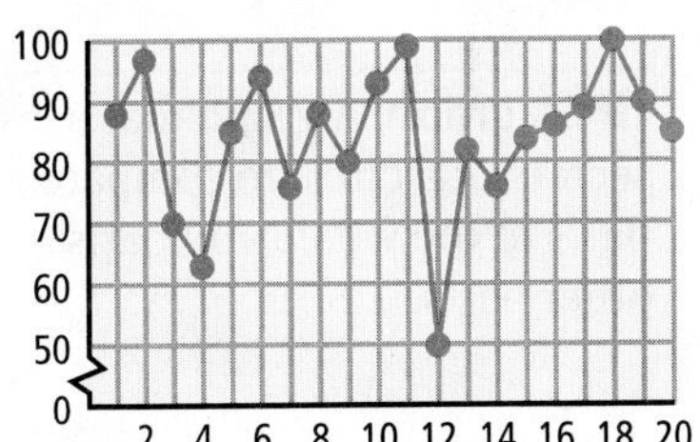

C

capacity The amount a container can hold when filled.

capacidad Cantidad que cabe en un recipiente cuando se llena.

A large milk container has a capacity of 1 gallon.

Celsius A metric scale for measuring temperature in which 0 °C is the freezing point of water and 100 °C is the boiling point of water; also called *centigrade.*

Celsius Escala métrica para medir la temperatura, en la que 0 °C es el punto de congelación del agua y 100 °C es el punto de ebullición. También se llama *centígrado.*

ENGLISH	SPANISH	EXAMPLES
center (of a circle) The point inside a circle that is the same distance from all the points on the circle.	**centro (de un círculo)** Punto interior de un círculo que se encuentra a la misma distancia de todos los puntos de la circunferencia.	A
center of dilation The point of intersection of lines through each pair of corresponding vertices in a dilation.	**centro de una dilatación** Punto de intersección de las líneas que pasan a través de cada par de vértices correspondientes en una dilatación.	center
center of rotation The point about which a figure is rotated.	**centro de una rotación** Punto alrededor del cual se hace girar una figura.	90° 90° Center 90° 90°
central angle An angle formed by two radii with its vertex at the center of a circle.	**ángulo central de un círculo** Ángulo formado por dos radios cuyo vértice se encuentra en el centro de un círculo.	
chord A segment with its endpoints on a circle.	**cuerda** Segmento de recta cuyos extremos forman parte de un círculo.	A Chord B
circle The set of all points in a plane that are the same distance from a given point called the center.	**círculo** Conjunto de todos los puntos en un plano que se encuentran a la misma distancia de un punto dado llamado centro.	
circle graph A graph that uses sectors of a circle to compare parts to the whole and parts to other parts.	**gráfica circular** Gráfica que usa secciones de un círculo para comparar partes con el todo y con otras partes.	Residents of Mesa, AZ 65+ 13% Under 18 27% 45–64 19% 18–24 11% 25–44 30%
circuit A path in a graph that begins and ends at the same vertex.	**circuito** Una trayectoria en una gráfica que empieza y termina en el mismo vértice.	
circumference The distance around a circle.	**circunferencia** Distancia alrededor de un círculo.	Circumference

ENGLISH	SPANISH	EXAMPLES
clockwise A circular movement to the right in the direction shown.	**en el sentido de las manecillas del reloj** Movimiento circular en la dirección que se indica.	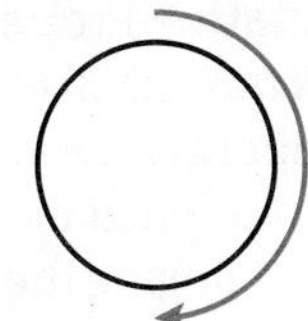
clustering A condition that occurs when data points in a scatter plot are grouped more in one part of the graph than another.	**arracimando** Una condición que ocurre cuando los datos están apiñando en una parte de una diagrama de dispersión mas que en otras partes.	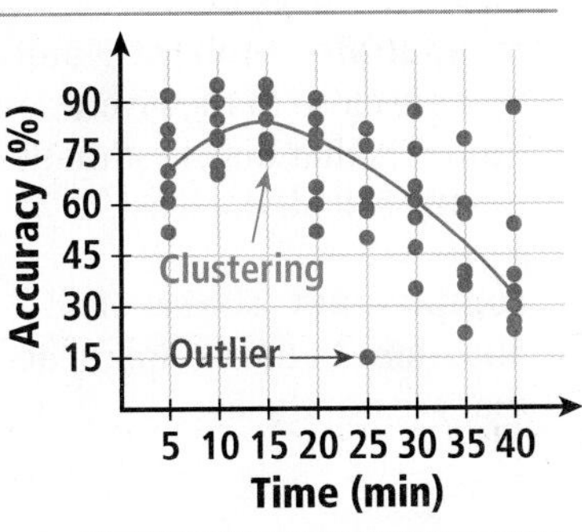
coefficient The number that is multiplied by the variable in an algebraic expression.	**coeficiente** Número que se multiplica por la variable en una expresión algebraica.	5 is the coefficient in $5b$.
combination An arrangement of items or events in which order does not matter.	**combinación** Agrupación de objetos o sucesos en la que el orden no es importante.	For objects *A, B, C,* and *D,* there are 6 different combinations of 2 objects: *AB, AC, AD, BC, BD, CD.*
commission A fee paid to a person for making a sale.	**comisión** Pago que recibe una persona por realizar una venta.	
commission rate The fee paid to a person who makes a sale expressed as a percent of the selling price.	**tasa de comisión** Pago que recibe una persona por hacer una venta, expresado como un porcentaje del precio de venta.	A commission rate of 5% and a sale of $10,000 results in a commission of $500.
common denominator A denominator that is the same in two or more fractions.	**común denominador** Denominador que es común a dos o más fracciones.	The common denominator of $\frac{5}{8}$ and $\frac{2}{8}$ is 8.
common factor A number that is a factor of two or more numbers.	**factor común** Número que es factor de dos o más números.	8 is a common factor of 16 and 40.
common multiple A number that is a multiple of each of two or more numbers.	**común múltiplo** Número que es múltiplo de dos o más números.	15 is a common multiple of 3 and 5.
common ratio The ratio each term is multiplied by to produce the next term in a geometric sequence.	**razón común** Razón por la que se multiplica cada término para obtener el siguiente término de una sucesión geométrica.	In the geometric sequence 32, 16, 8, 4, 2, ..., the common ratio is $\frac{1}{2}$.
Commutative Property (of Addition) The property that states that two or more numbers can be added in any order without changing the sum.	**Propiedad conmutativa (de la suma)** Propiedad que establece que sumar dos o más números en cualquier orden no altera la suma.	$8 + 20 = 20 + 8$; $a + b = b + a$

ENGLISH	SPANISH	EXAMPLES
Commutative Property (of Multiplication) The property that states that two or more numbers can be multiplied in any order without changing the product.	**Propiedad conmutativa (de la multiplicación)** Propiedad que establece que multiplicar dos o más números en cualquier orden no altera el producto.	$6 \cdot 12 = 12 \cdot 6$; $a \cdot b = b \cdot a$
compatible numbers Numbers that are close to the given numbers that make estimation or mental calculation easier.	**números compatibles** Números que están cerca de los números dados y hacen más fácil la estimación o el cálculo mental.	To estimate 7,957 + 5,009, use the compatible numbers 8,000 and 5,000: 8,000 + 5,000 = 13,000.
complement The set of all outcomes in the sample space that are not the event.	**complemento** La serie de resultados que no están en el suceso.	Experiment: Rolling a number cube Sample space: {1, 2, 3, 4, 5, 6} Event: rolling a 1, 3, 4, or 6 Complement: rolling a 2 or 5
complementary angles Two angles whose measures add to 90°.	**ángulos complementarios** Dos ángulos cuyas medidas suman 90°.	37° B; 53° A The complement of a 53°angle is a 37° angle.
composite figure A figure made up of simple geometric shapes.	**figura compuesta** Figura formada por figuras geométricas simples.	2 cm, 5 cm, 4 cm, 4 cm, 4 cm, 3 cm, 5 cm
composite number A number greater than 1 that has more than two whole-number factors.	**número compuesto** Número mayor que 1 que tiene más de dos factores que son números cabales.	4, 6, 8, and 9 are composite numbers.
compound interest Interest earned or paid on principal and previously earned or paid interest.	**interés compuesto** Interés que se gana o se paga sobre el capital y los intereses previamente ganados o pagados.	If \$100 is put into an account with an interest rate of 5% compounded monthly, then after 2 years, the account will have $100\left(1 + \frac{0.05}{12}\right)^{12 \cdot 2} = \$110.49$
cone A three-dimensional figure with one vertex and one circular base.	**cono** Figura tridimensional con un vértice y una base circular.	
congruence transformation A transformation that results in an image that is the same shape and the same size as the original figure.	**transformación de congruencia** Una transformación que resulta en una imagen que tiene la misma forma y el mismo tamaño como la figura original.	J M K L; J′ M′ K′ L′
congruent Having the same size and shape; the symbol for congruent is ≅.	**congruentes** Que tienen la misma forma y el mismo tamaño expresado por ≅.	P Q S R; Z W Y X *PQRS* ≅ *WXYZ*

ENGLISH	SPANISH	EXAMPLES
congruent angles Angles that have the same measure.	**ángulos congruentes** Ángulos que tienen la misma medida.	$\angle ABC = \angle DEF$
congruent figures See *congruent.*	**figures congruentes** Vea *congruente.*	
congruent segments Segments that have the same length.	**segmentos congruentes** Segmentos que tienen la misma longitud.	$\overline{PQ} \cong \overline{SR}$
conjecture A statement believed to be true.	**conjetura** Enunciado que se supone verdadero.	
constant A value that does not change.	**constante** Valor que no cambia.	3, 0, π
constant of variation The constant k in direct and inverse variation equations.	**constante de variación** La constante k en ecuaciones de variación directa e inversa.	$y = 5x$ ↑ constant of variation
continuous graph a graph made up of connected lines or curves.	**gráfica continua** Gráfica compuesta por líneas rectas *o* curvas conectadas.	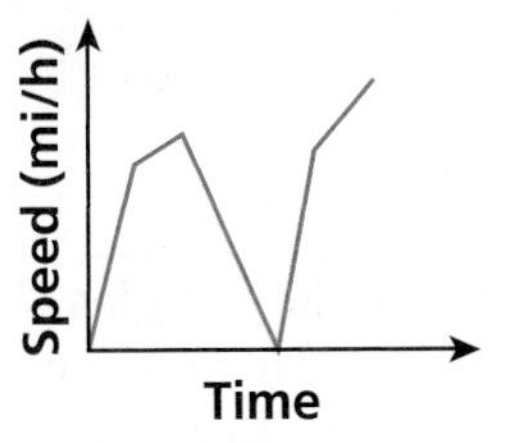
convenience sample A sample based on members of the population that are readily available.	**muestra de conveniencia** Una muestra basada en miembros de la población que están fácilmente disponibles.	
conversion factor A fraction whose numerator and denominator represent the same quantity but use different units; the fraction is equal to 1 because the numerator and denominator are equal.	**factor de conversión** Fracción cuyo numerador y denominador representan la misma cantidad pero con unidades distintas; la fracción es igual a 1 porque el numerador y el denominador son iguales.	$\frac{24\text{ hours}}{1\text{ day}}$ and $\frac{1\text{ day}}{24\text{ hours}}$
coordinate One of the numbers of an ordered pair that locate a point on a coordinate graph.	**coordenada** Uno de los números de un par ordenado que ubica un punto en una gráfica de coordenadas.	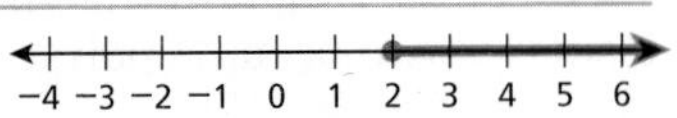 The coordinate of A is 2. The coordinates of B are $(-2, 3)$

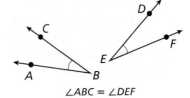

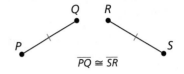

ENGLISH	SPANISH	EXAMPLES
coordinate plane A plane formed by the intersection of a horizontal number line called the *x*-axis and a vertical number line called the *y*-axis.	**plano cartesiano** Plano formado por la intersección de una recta numérica horizontal llamada eje *x* y otra vertical llamada eje *y*.	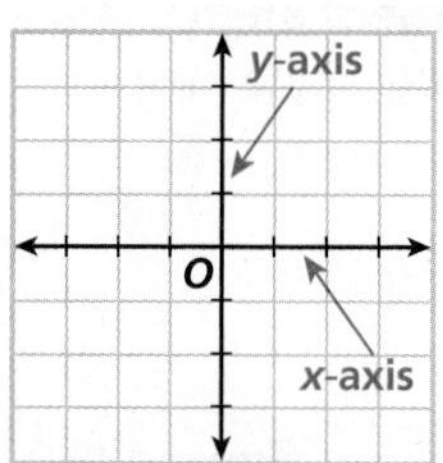
correlation The description of the relationship between two data sets.	**correlación** Descripción de la relación entre dos conjuntos de datos.	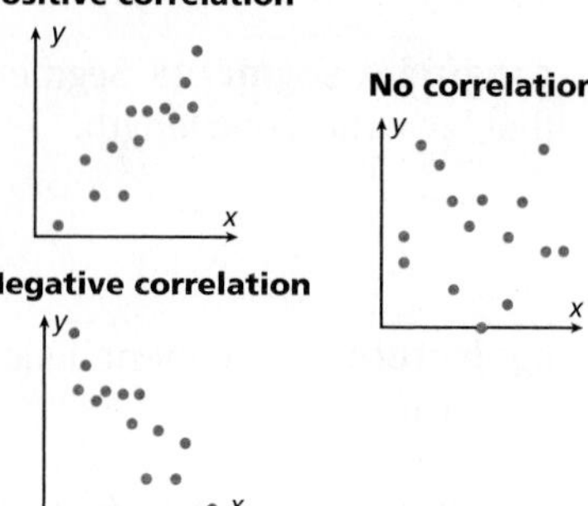
correspondence The relationship between two or more objects that are matched.	**correspondencia** La relación entre dos o más objetos que coinciden.	$\angle A$ and $\angle D$ are corresponding angles. 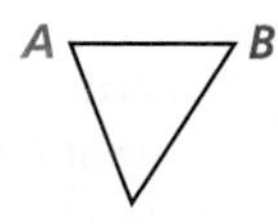 $\overline{AB}$ and $\overline{DE}$ are corresponding sides. 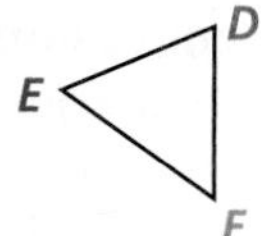
corresponding angles (for lines) For two lines intersected by a transversal, a pair of angles that lie on the same side of the transversal and on the same sides of the other two lines.	**ángulos correspondientes (en líneas)** Dadas dos rectas cortadas por una transversal, el par de ángulos ubicados en el mismo lado de la transversal y en los mismos lados de las otras dos rectas.	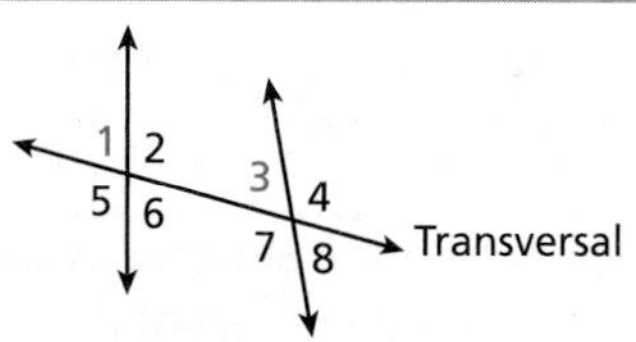 $\angle 1$ and $\angle 3$ are corresponding angles.
corresponding angles (of polygons) Angles in the same relative position in polygons with an equal number of sides.	**ángulos correspondientes (en polígonos)** Ángulos en la misma posición formaron cuando una tercera línea interseca dos líneas.	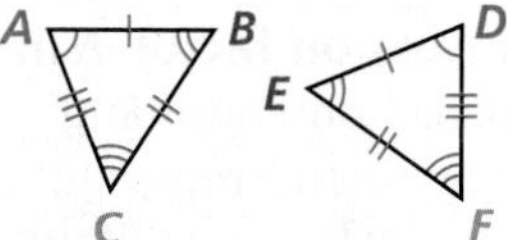 $\angle A$ and $\angle D$ are corresponding angles.
corresponding sides Matching sides of two or more polygons.	**lados correspondientes** Lados que se ubican en la misma posición relativa en dos o más polígonos.	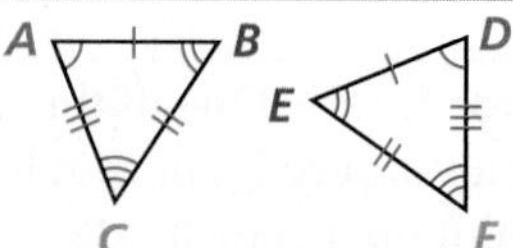 $\overline{AB}$ and $\overline{DE}$ are corresponding sides.
counterclockwise A circular movement to the left in the direction shown.	**en sentido contrario a las manecillas del reloj** Movimiento circular en la dirección que se indica.	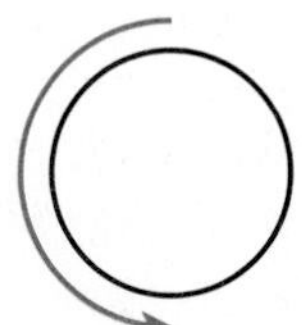

Glossary/Glosario

ENGLISH	SPANISH	EXAMPLES
cross product The product of numbers on the diagonal when comparing two ratios.	**producto cruzado** El producto de los números multiplicados en diagonal cuando se comparan dos razones.	 For the proportion $\frac{2}{3} = \frac{4}{6}$, the cross products are $2 \cdot 6 = 12$ and $3 \cdot 4 = 12$
counterexample An example that proves that a conjecture or statement is false.	**contraejemplo** Ejemplo que demuestra que una conjetura o enunciado es falso.	
cube (geometric figure) A rectangular prism with six congruent square faces.	**cubo (figura geométrica)** Prisma rectangular con seis caras cuadradas congruentes.	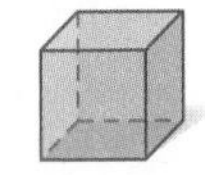
cube (in numeration) A number raised to the third power.	**cubo (en numeración)** Número elevado a la tercera potencia.	$2^3 = 2 \cdot 2 \cdot 2 = 8$ 8 is the cube of 2.
cumulative frequency The sum of successive data items.	**frecuencia acumulativa** La suma de datos sucesivos.	
customary system of measurement The measurement system often used in the United States.	**sistema usual de medidas** El sistema de medidas que se usa comúnmente en Estados Unidos.	inches, feet, miles, ounces, pounds, tons, cups, quarts, gallons
cylinder A three-dimensional figure with two parallel, congruent circular bases connected by a curved lateral surface.	**cilindro** Figura tridimensional con dos bases circulares paralelas y congruentes, unidas por una superficie lateral curva.	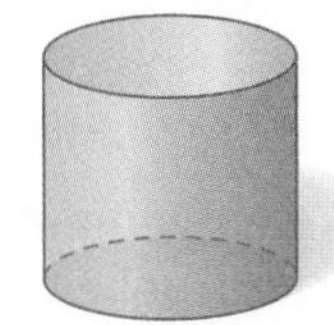

D

ENGLISH	SPANISH	EXAMPLES
decagon A polygon with ten sides.	**decágono** Polígono de diez lados.	
degree The unit of measure for angles or temperature.	**grado** Unidad de medida para ángulos y temperaturas.	
degree of a polynomial The highest power of the variable in a polynomial.	**grado de un polinomio** La potencia más alta de la variable en un polinomio.	The polynomial $4x^5 - 6x^2 + 7$ has degree 5
denominator The bottom number of a fraction that tells how many equal parts are in the whole.	**denominador** Número que está abajo en una fracción y que indica en cuántas partes iguales se divide el entero.	In the fraction $\frac{2}{5}$, 5 is the denominator.
Density Property The property that states that between any two real numbers, there is always another real number.	**Propiedad de densidad** Propiedad según la cual entre dos números reales cualesquiera siempre hay otro número real.	

ENGLISH	SPANISH	EXAMPLES
dependent events Events for which the outcome of one event affects the probability of the other.	**sucesos dependientes** Dos sucesos son dependientes si el resultado de uno afecta la probabilidad del otro.	A bag contains 3 red marbles and 2 blue marbles. Drawing a red marble and then drawing a blue marble without replacing the first marble is an example of dependent events.
dependent variable The output of a function; a variable whose value depends on the value of the input, or independent variable.	**variable dependiente** Salida de una función; variable cuyo valor depende del valor de la entrada, o variable independiente.	For $y = 2x + 1$, y is the dependent variable. input: x output: y
diagonal A line segment that connect two non-adjacent vertices of a polygon.	**diagonal** Segmento de recta que une dos vértices no adyacentes de un polígono.	
diameter A line segment that passes through the center of a circle and has endpoints on the circle, or the length of that segment.	**diámetro** Segmento de recta que pasa por el centro de un círculo y tiene sus extremos en la circunferencia, o bien la longitud de ese segmento.	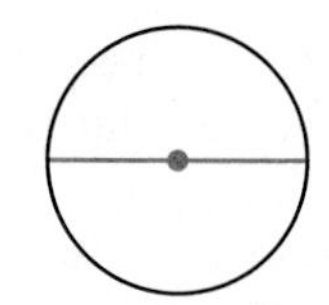
dilation A transformation that enlarges or reduces a figure.	**dilatación** Transformación que agranda o reduce una figura.	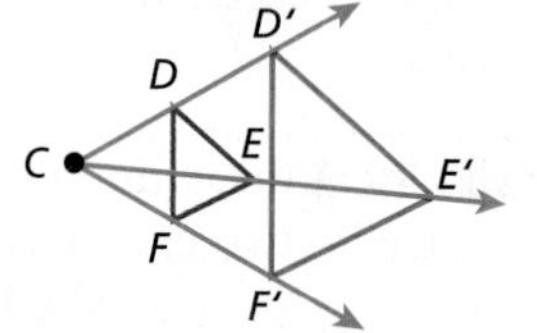
dimensions (geometry) The length, width, or height of a figure.	**dimensiones (geometría)** Longitud, ancho o altura de una figura.	
dimensions (of a matrix) The number of horizontal rows and vertical columns in a matrix.	**dimensiones (de una matriz)** Número de filas y columnas que hay en una matriz.	
direct variation A linear relationship between two variables, x and y, that can be written in the form $y = kx$, where k is a nonzero constant.	**variación directa** Relación lineal entre dos variables, x e y, que puede expresarse en la forma $y = kx$, donde k es una constante distinta de cero.	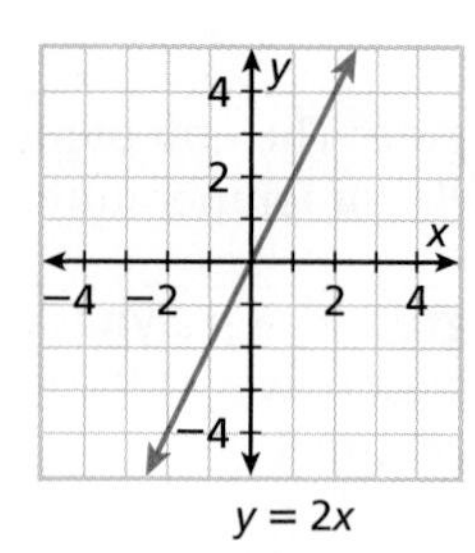 $y = 2x$
discount The amount by which the original price is reduced.	**descuento** Cantidad que se resta del precio original de un artículo.	

ENGLISH	SPANISH	EXAMPLES
discrete graph a graph made up of unconnected points.	**gráfica discreta** Gráfica compuesta de puntos no conectados.	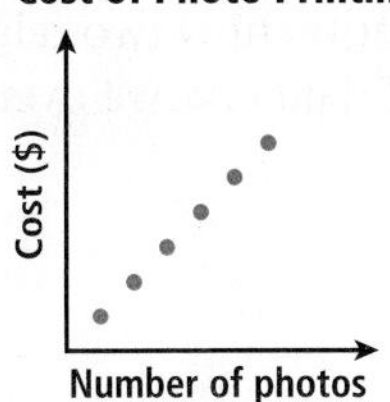
disjoint events See *mutually exclusive.*	**sucesos disjuntos** Vea *mutuamente excluyentes.*	
Distributive Property For all real numbers a, b, and c, $a(b + c) = ab + ac$, and $a(b - c)\ a = ab - ac$.	**Propiedad distributiva** Dados los números reales a, b, y c, $a(b + c) = ab + ac$, y $a(b - c)\ a = ab - ac$.	$5 \cdot 21 = 5(20 + 1) = (5 \cdot 20) + (5 \cdot 1)$
dividend The number to be divided in a division problem.	**dividendo** Número que se divide en un problema de división.	In $8 \div 4 = 2$, 8 is the dividend.
divisible Can be divided by a number without leaving a remainder.	**divisible** Que se puede dividir entre un número sin dejar residuo.	18 is divisible by 3.
Division Property of Equality The property that states that if you divide both sides of an equation by the same nonzero number, the new equation will have the same solution.	**Propiedad de igualdad de la división** Propiedad que establece que puedes dividir ambos lados de una ecuación entre el mismo número distinto de cero, y la nueva ecuación tendrá la misma solución.	
divisor The number you are dividing by in a division problem.	**divisor** El número entre el que se divide en un problema de división.	In $8 \div 4 = 2$, 4 is the divisor.
dodecahedron A polyhedron with 12 faces.	**dodecaedro** Poliedro de 12 caras.	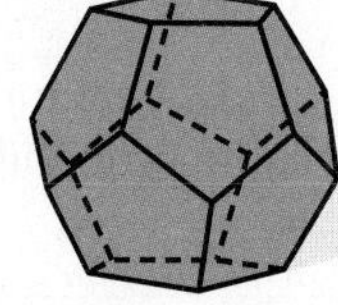
domain The set of all possible input values of a function.	**dominio** Conjunto de todos los posibles valores de entrada de una función.	The domain of the function $y = x^2 + 1$ is all real numbers.
double-bar graph A bar graph that compares two related sets of data.	**gráfica de doble barra** Gráfica de barras que compara dos conjuntos de datos relacionados.	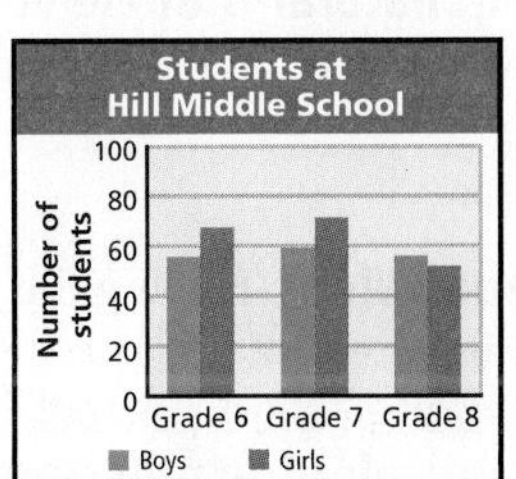

ENGLISH	SPANISH	EXAMPLES
double-line graph A line graph that shows how two related sets of data change over time.	**gráfica de doble línea** Gráfica lineal que muestra cómo cambian con el tiempo dos conjuntos de datos relacionados.	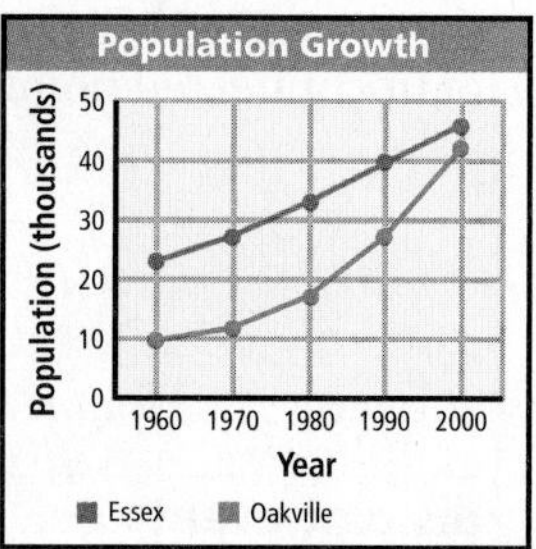

E

ENGLISH	SPANISH	EXAMPLES
edge The line segment along which two faces of a polyhedron intersect.	**arista** Segmento de recta donde se intersecan dos caras de un poliedro.	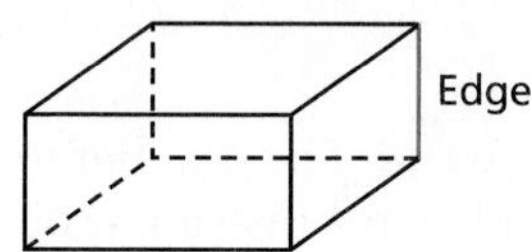
endpoint A point at the end of a line segment or ray.	**extremo** Un punto ubicado al final de un segmento de recta o rayo.	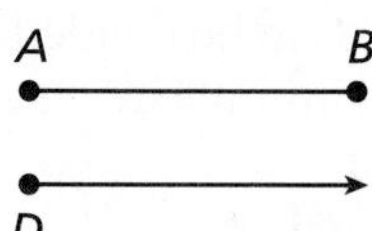
enlargement An increase in size of all dimensions in the same proportions.	**agrandamiento** Aumento de tamaño de todas las dimensiones en las mismas proporciones.	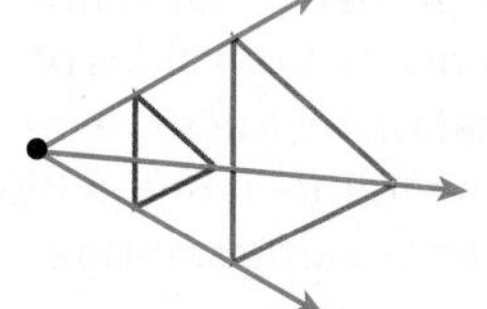
entries (of a matrix) Individual entries in a matrix.	**elementos (de una matriz)** Entradas individuales de una matriz.	
equally likely Outcomes that have the same probability.	**resultados igualmente probables** Resultados que tienen la misma probabilidad de ocurrir.	When tossing a coin, the outcomes "heads" and "tails" are equally likely.
equation A mathematical sentence that shows that two expressions are equivalent.	**ecuación** Enunciado matemático que indica que dos expresiones son equivalentes.	$x + 4 = 7$ $6 + 1 = 10 - 3$
equilateral triangle A triangle with three congruent sides.	**triángulo equilátero** Triángulo con tres lados congruentes.	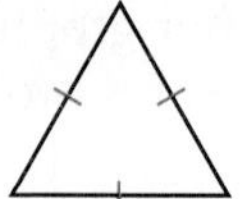
equivalent Having the same value.	**equivalentes** Que tienen el mismo valor. (pág. 28)	
equivalent expression Equivalent expressions have the same value for all values of the variables.	**expresión equivalente** Las expresiones equivalentes tienen el mismo valor para todos los valores de las variables.	$4x + 5x$ and $9x$ are equivalent expressions.
equivalent fractions Fractions that name the same amount or part.	**fracciones equivalentes** Fracciones que representan la misma cantidad o parte.	$\frac{1}{2}$ and $\frac{2}{4}$ are equivalent fractions.

ENGLISH	SPANISH	EXAMPLES
equivalent ratios Ratios that name the same comparison.	**razones equivalentes** Razones que representan la misma comparación.	$\frac{1}{2}$ and $\frac{2}{4}$ are equivalent ratios.
estimate (n) An answer that is close to the exact answer and is found by rounding or other methods. **(v)** To find such an answer.	**estimación (s)** Una solución aproximada a la respuesta exacta que se halla mediante el redondeo u otros métodos. **estimar (v)** Hallar una solución aproximada a la respuesta exacta.	500 is an estimate for the sum $98 + 287 + 104$.
evaluate To find the value of a numerical or algebraic expression.	**evaluar** Hallar el valor de una expresión numérica o algebraica.	Evaluate $2x + 7$ for $x = 3$ $2x + 7$ $2(3) + 7$ $6 + 7$ 13.
event An outcome or set of outcomes of an experiment or situation.	**suceso** Un resultado o una serie de resultados de un experimento o una situación.	When rolling a number cube, the event "an odd number" consists of the outcomes 1, 3, and 5.
expanded form A number written as the sum of the values of its digits.	**forma desarrollada** Número escrito como suma de los valores de sus dígitos.	236,536 written in expanded form is 200,000 + 30,000 + 6,000 + 500 + 30 + 6.
experiment (probability) In probability, any activity based on chance (such as tossing a coin).	**experimento (probabilidad)** En probabilidad, cualquier actividad basada en la posibilidad, como lanzar una moneda.	Tossing a coin 10 times and noting the number of "heads".
experimental probability The ratio of the number of times an event occurs to the total number of trials, or times that the activity is performed.	**probabilidad experimental** Razón del número de veces que ocurre un suceso al número total de pruebas o al número de que se realiza el experimento.	Kendra attempted 27 free throws and made 16 of them. Her experimental probability of making a free throw is $\frac{\text{number made}}{\text{number attempted}} = \frac{16}{27} \approx 0.59$.
exponent The number that indicates how many times the base is used as a factor.	**exponente** Número que indica cuántas veces se usa la base como factor.	$2^3 = 2 \times 2 \times 2 = 8$; 3 is the exponent.
exponential decay An exponential function of the form $f(x) = a \cdot r^x$ in which $0 < r < 1$.	**decremento exponencial** Función exponencial del tipo $f(x) = a \cdot r^x$ en la cual $0 < r < 1$.	
exponential form A number is in exponential form when it is written with a base and an exponent.	**forma exponencial** Se dice que un número está en forma exponencial cuando se escribe con una base y un exponente.	4^2 is the exponential form for $4 \cdot 4$.
exponential function A nonlinear function in which the variable is in the exponent.	**función exponencial** Función no lineal en la que la variable está en el exponente.	$f(x) = 4^x$

ENGLISH	SPANISH	EXAMPLES
exponential growth An exponential function of the form $f(x) = a \cdot r^x$ in which $r > 1$.	**crecimiento exponencial** Función exponencial del tipo $f(x) = a \cdot r^x$ en la cual $r > 1$.	
expression A mathematical phrase that contains operations, numbers, and/or variables.	**expresión** Enunciado matemático que contiene operaciones, números y/o variables.	$6x + 1$

F

ENGLISH	SPANISH	EXAMPLES
face A flat surface of a polyhedron.	**cara** Superficie plana de un poliedro.	Face
factor A number that is multiplied by another number to get a product.	**factor** Número que se multiplica por otro para hallar un producto.	7 is a factor of 21 since $7 \cdot 3 = 21$.
factorial The product of all whole numbers except zero that are less than or equal to a number.	**factorial** El producto de todos los números cabales, excepto cero, que son menores que o iguales a un número.	4 factorial $= 4! = 4 \cdot 3 \cdot 2 \cdot 1$
Fahrenheit A temperature scale in which 32 °F is the freezing point of water and 212 °F is the boiling point of water.	**Fahrenheit** Escala de temperatura en la que 32° F es el punto de congelación del agua y 212° F es el punto de ebullición.	
fair When all outcomes of an experiment are equally likely, the experiment is said to be fair.	**justo** Se dice de un experimento donde todos los resultados posibles son igualmente probables.	When tossing a coin, heads and tails are equally likely, so it is a fair experiment.
Fibonacci sequence The infinite sequence of numbers (1, 1, 2, 3, 5, 8, 13,...); starting with the third term, each number is the sum of the two previous numbers; it is named after the thirteenth century mathematician Leonardo Fibonacci.	**sucesión de Fibonacci** La sucesión infinita de números (1, 1, 2, 3, 5, 8, 13...); a partir del tercer término, cada número es la suma de los dos anteriores. Esta sucesión lleva el nombre de Leonardo Fibonacci, un matemático del siglo XIII.	1, 1, 2, 3, 5, 8, 13, . . .
first differences A sequence formed by subtracting each term of a sequence from the next term.	**primeras diferencias** Sucesión que se forma al restar cada término de una sucesión del término siguiente.	For the sequence 4, 7, 10, 13, 16, . . . , the first differences are all 3.
first quartile The median of the lower half of a set of data; also called *lower quartile.*	**primer cuartil** La mediana de la mitad inferior de un conjunto de datos. También se llama *cuartil inferior.*	First quartile, Third quartile, Minimum, Median, Maximum; 0 2 4 6 8 10 12 14

ENGLISH	SPANISH	EXAMPLES

FOIL An acronym for the terms used when multiplying two binomials: the First, Inner, Outer, and Last terms.

FOIL Sigla en inglés de los términos que se usan al multiplicar dos binomios: los primeros, los externos, los internos, y los últimos (First, Outer, Inner, Last).

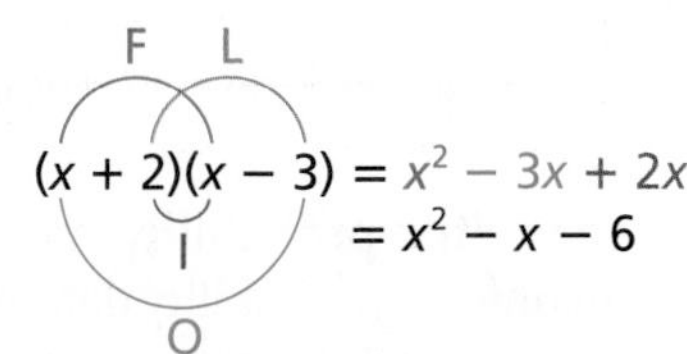

---

formula A rule showing relationships among quantities.

fórmula Regla que muestra relaciones entre cantidades.

$A = \ell w$ is the formula for the area of a rectangle.

---

fractal A structure with repeating patterns containing shapes that are like the whole but are of different sizes throughout.

fractal Estructura con patrones repetidos que contiene figuras similares al patrón general pero de diferente tamaño.

---

fraction A number in the form $\frac{a}{b}$, where $b \neq 0$.

fracción Número escrito en la forma $\frac{a}{b}$, donde $b \neq 0$.

$\frac{2}{3}$

---

frequency The number of times the value appears in the data set.

frecuencia Cantidad de veces que aparece el valor en un conjunto de datos.

Data set: 5, 6, 6, 7, 8, 9
The data value 6 has a frequency of 2.

---

frequency table A table that lists items together according to the number of times, or frequency, that the items occur.

tabla de frecuencia Una tabla en la que se organizan los datos de acuerdo con el número de veces que aparece cada valor (o la frecuencia).

Data set: 1, 1, 2, 2, 3, 5, 5, 5
Frequency table:

Data	Frequency
1	2
2	2
3	1

---

function An input-output relationship that has exactly one output for each input.

función Regla que relaciona dos candidates de forma que a cada valor de entrada corresponde exactamente un valor de salida.

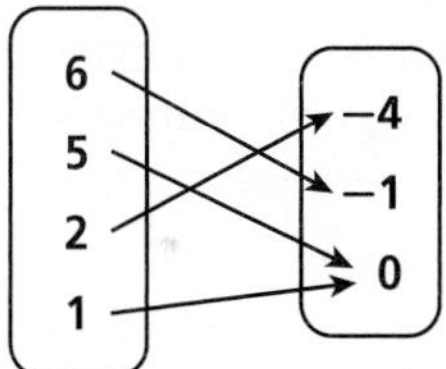

---

function notation The notation used to describe a function.

notación de función Notación que se usa para describir una función.

Equation: $y = 2x$
Function notation: $f(x) = 2x$

---

function table A table of ordered pairs that represent solutions of a function.

tabla de función Tabla de pares ordenados que representan soluciones de una función.

x	3	4	5	6
y	7	9	11	13

Fundamental Counting Principle If one event has m possible outcomes and a second event has n possible outcomes after the first event has occurred, then there are $m \cdot n$ total possible outcomes for the two events.

Principio fundamental de conteo Si un suceso tiene m resultados posibles y otro suceso tiene n resultados posibles después de ocurrido el primer suceso, entonces hay $m \cdot n$ resultados posibles en total para los dos sucesos.

There are 4 colors of shirts and 3 colors of pants. There are $4 \cdot 3 = 12$ possible outfits.

ENGLISH	SPANISH	EXAMPLES

geometric probability A form of theoretical probability determined by a ratio of geometric measures such as lengths, areas, or volumes.

probabilidad geométrica Método para calcular probabilidades basado en una medida geométrica como la longitud o el área.

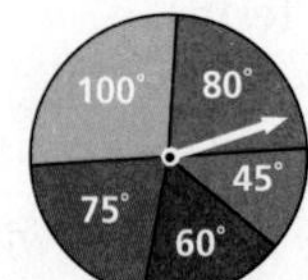

The probability of the pointer landing on red is $\frac{80}{360}$, or $\frac{2}{9}$

geometric sequence An ordered list of numbers that has a common ratio between consecutive terms.

sucesión geométrica Lista ordenada de números que tiene una razón común entre términos consecutivos.

The sequence 2, 4, 8, 16. . . is a geometric sequence.

graph of an equation A graph of the set of ordered pairs that are solutions of the equation.

gráfica de una ecuación Gráfica del conjunto de pares ordenados que son soluciones de la ecuación.

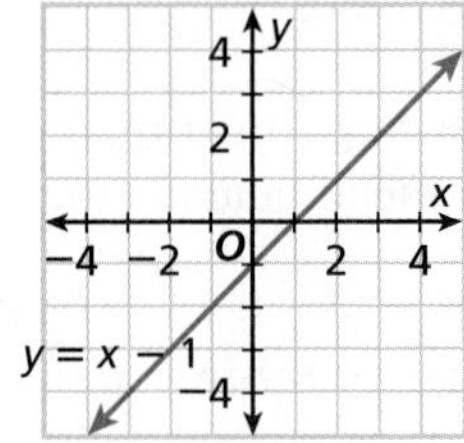

great circle A circle on a sphere such that the plane containing the circle passes through the center of the sphere.

círculo máximo Círculo de una esfera tal que el plano que contiene el círculo pasa por el centro de la esfera.

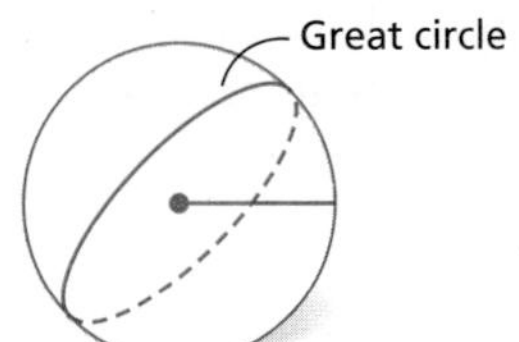

greatest common factor (GCF) The largest common factor of two or more given numbers.

máximo común divisor (MCD) El mayor de los factores comunes compartidos por dos o más números dados.

The GCF of 27 and 45 is 9.

height In a pyramid or cone, the perpendicular distance from the base to the opposite vertex.

altura En una pirámide o cono, la distancia perpendicular desde la base al vértice opuesto.

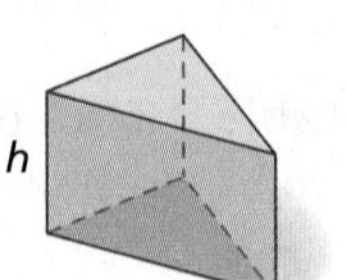

In a triangle or quadrilateral, the perpendicular distance from the base to the opposite vertex or side.

En un triángulo o cuadrilátero, la distancia perpendicular desde la base de la figura al vértice o lado opuesto.

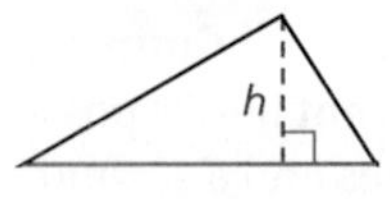

In a prism or cylinder, the perpendicular distance between the bases.

En un prisma o cilindro, la distancia perpendicular entre las bases.

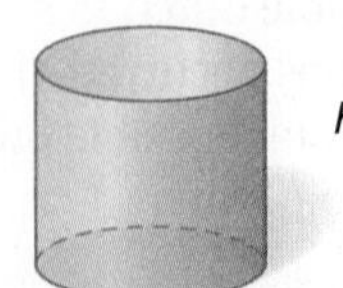

hemisphere A half of a sphere.

hemisferio La mitad de una esfera.

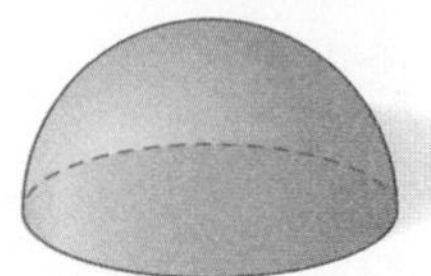

ENGLISH	SPANISH	EXAMPLES

heptagon A seven-sided polygon.

heptágono Polígono de siete lados.

hexagon A six-sided polygon.

hexágono Polígono de seis lados.

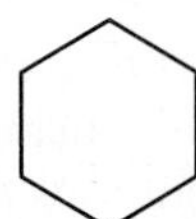

histogram A bar graph that shows the frequency of data within equal intervals.

histograma Gráfica de barras que muestra la frecuencia de los datos en intervalos iguales.

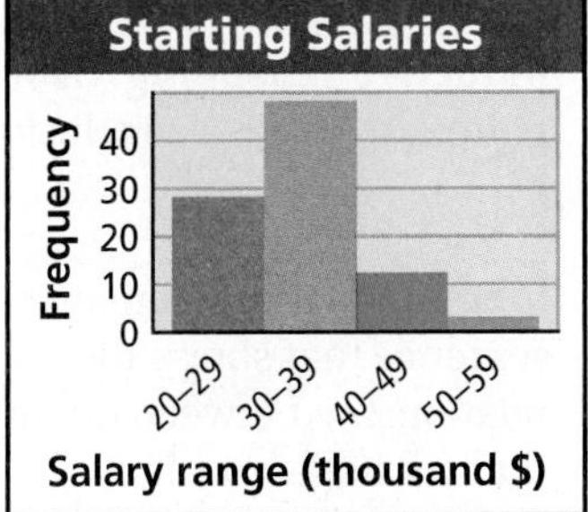

hypotenuse In a right triangle, the side opposite the right angle.

hipotenusa En un triángulo rectángulo, el lado opuesto al ángulo recto.

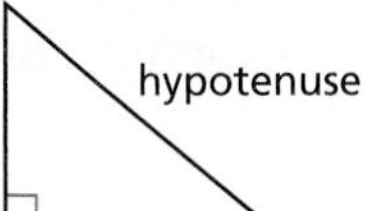

I

Identity Property (of One) The property that states that the product of 1 and any number is that number.

Propiedad de identidad (del uno) Propiedad que establece que el producto de 1 y cualquier número es ese número.

$4 \cdot 1 = 4$
$-3 \cdot 1 = -3$

Identity Property (of Zero) The property that states the sum of zero and any number is that number.

Propiedad de identidad (del cero) Propiedad que establece que la suma de cero y cualquier número es ese número.

$4 + 0 = 4$
$-3 + 0 = -3$

image A figure resulting from a transformation.

imagen Figura que resulta de una transformación.

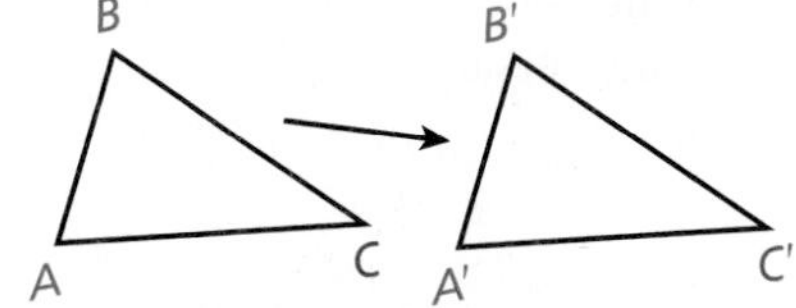

improper fraction A fraction in which the numerator is greater than or equal to the denominator.

fracción impropia Fracción cuyo numerador es mayor que o igual al denominador.

$\frac{17}{5}, \frac{3}{3}$

independent events Events for which the outcome of one event does not affect the probability of the other.

sucesos independientes Dos sucesos son independientes si el resultado de uno no afecta la probabilidad del otro.

A bag contains 3 red marbles and 2 blue marbles. Drawing a red marble, replacing it, and then drawing a blue marble is an example of independent events.

ENGLISH	SPANISH	EXAMPLES
independent variable The input of a function; a variable whose value determines the value of the output, or dependent variable.	**variable independiente** Entrada de una función; variable cuyo valor determina el valor de la salida, o variable dependiente.	For $y = 2x + 1$, x is the dependent variable. input: x output: y
indirect measurement The technique of using similar figures and proportions to find a measure.	**medición indirecta** La técnica de usar figuras semejantes y proporciones para hallar una medida.	
inductive reasoning Using a pattern to make a conclusion.	**razonamiento inductivo** Uso de un patrón para sacar una conclusión.	
inequality A mathematical sentence that shows the relationship between quantities that are not equivalent.	**desigualdad** Enunciado matemático que muestra una relación entre cantidades que no son equivalentes.	$5 < 8$ $5x + 2 \geq 12$
input The value substituted into an expression or function.	**valor de entrada** Valor que se usa para sustituir una variable en una expresión o función.	For the function $y = 6x$, the input 4 produces an output of 24.
inscribed angle An angle formed by two chords with its vertex on a circle.	**ángulo inscrito** Ángulo formado por dos cuerdas cuyo vértice está en un círculo.	D E F
integers The set of whole numbers and their opposites.	**enteros** Conjunto de todos los números cabales y sus opuestos.	$\ldots -3, -2, -1, 0, 1, 2, 3, \ldots$
interest The amount of money charged for borrowing or using money.	**interés** Cantidad de dinero que se cobra por el préstamo o uso del dinero.	
interior angles Angles on the inner sides of two lines cut by a transversal.	**ángulos internos** Ángulos en los lados internos de dos líneas intersecadas por una transversal.	1 $\angle 1$ is an interior angle.
interquartile range (IQR) The difference of the third (upper) and first (lower) quartiles in a data set, representing the middle half of the data.	**rango intercuartil (RIC)** Diferencia entre el tercer cuartil (superior) y el primer cuartil (inferior) de un conjunto de datos, que representa la mitad central de los datos.	Lower half Upper half 18, 23, 28, 29, 36, 42 First quartile Third quartile Interquartile range: $36 - 23 = 13$
intersecting lines Lines that cross at exactly one point.	**líneas secantes** Líneas que se cruzan en un solo punto.	m n
interval The space between marked values on a number line or the scale of a graph.	**intervalo** El espacio entre los valores marcados en una recta numérica o en la escala de una gráfica.	

ENGLISH	SPANISH	EXAMPLES
inverse operations Operations that undo each other: addition and subtraction, or multiplication and division.	**operaciones inversas** Operaciones que se cancelan mutuamente: suma y resta, o multiplicación y división.	Addition and subtraction are inverse operations: $5 + 3 + 8; 8 - 3 = 5$ Multiplication and division are inverse operations: $2 \cdot 3 = 6; 6 \div 3 = 2$
inverse variation A relationship in which one variable quantity increases as another variable quantity decreases; the product of the variables is a constant.	**variación inversa** Relación en la que una cantidad variable aumenta a medida que otra cantidad variable disminuye; el producto de las variables es una constante.	$xy = 7, y = \frac{7}{x}$
irrational number A number that cannot be expressed as a ratio of two integers or as a repeating or terminating decimal.	**número irracional** Número que no se puede expresar como una razón de dos enteros ni como un decimal periódico o finito.	$\sqrt{2}, \pi$
isolate the variable To get a variable alone on one side of an equation or inequality in order to solve the equation or inequality.	**despejar la variable** Dejar sola la variable en un lado de una ecuación o desigualdad para resolverla.	$x + 7 = 22$ $\underline{\;\;-7\;\;\;-7}$ $x \qquad = 15$ $\frac{12}{3} = \frac{3x}{3}$ $4 = x$
isometric drawing A representation of a three-dimensional figure that is drawn on a grid of equilateral triangles.	**dibujo isométrico** Representación de una figura tridimensional que se dibuja sobre una cuadrícula de triángulos equiláteros.	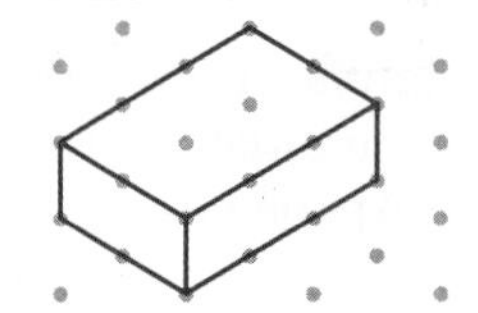
isosceles triangle A triangle with at least two congruent sides.	**triángulo isósceles** Triángulo que tiene al menos dos lados congruentes.	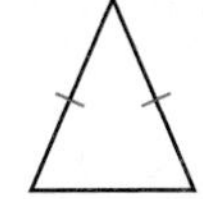

ENGLISH	SPANISH	EXAMPLES
lateral area The sum of the areas of the lateral faces of a prism or pyramid, or the area of the lateral surface of a cylinder or cone.	**rango intercuartil (RIC)** área lateral Suma de las áreas de las caras laterales de un prisma o pirámide, o área de la superficie lateral de un cilindro o cono.	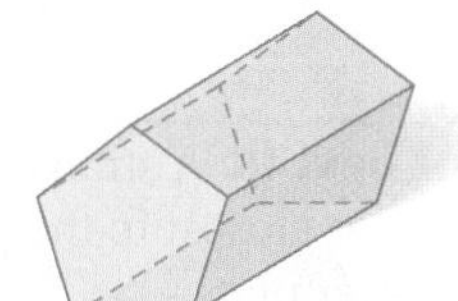 Lateral area = area of the 5 rectangular faces
lateral face In a prism or a pyramid, a face that is not a base.	**cara lateral** En un prisma o pirámide, una cara que no es la base.	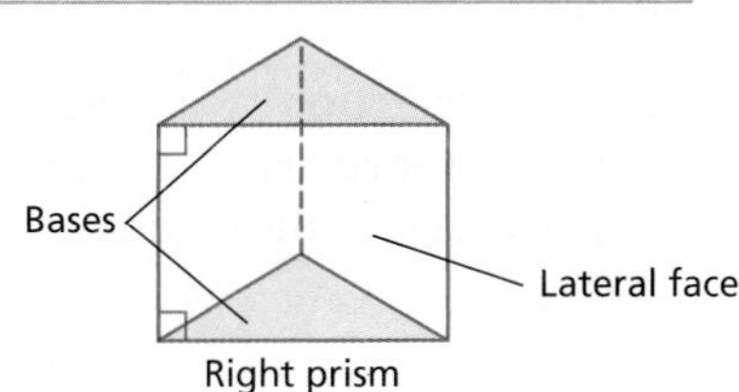

ENGLISH	SPANISH	EXAMPLES
lateral surface In a cylinder, the curved surface connecting the circular bases; in a cone, the curved surface that is not a base.	**superficie lateral** En un cilindro, superficie curva que une las bases circulares; en un cono, la superficie curva que no es la base.	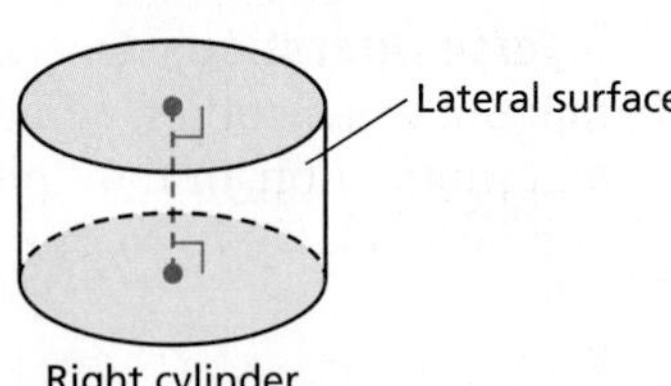 Right cylinder
least common denominator (LCD) The least common multiple of two or more denominators.	**mínimo común denominador (mcd)** El mínimo común múltiplo más pequeño de dos o más denominadores.	The LCD of $\frac{3}{4}$ and $\frac{5}{6}$ is 12.
least common multiple (LCM) The smallest whole number, other than zero, that is a multiple of two or more given numbers.	**mínimo común múltiplo (mcm)** El menor de los números cabales, distinto de cero, que es múltiplo de dos o más números dados.	The LCM of 6 and 10 is 30.
legs In a right triangle, the sides that include the right angle; in an isosceles triangle, the pair of congruent sides.	**catetos** En un triángulo rectángulo, los lados adyacentes al ángulo recto. En un triángulo isósceles, el par de lados congruentes.	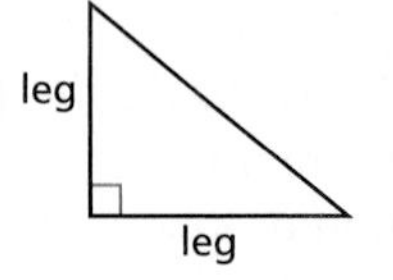
like fractions Fractions that have the same denominator.	**fracciones semejantes** Fracciones que tienen el mismo denominador.	$\frac{5}{12}$ and $\frac{7}{12}$ are like fractions.
like terms Terms with that have the same variable raised to the same exponentes.	**términos semejantes** Términos que contienen las mismas variables elevada a las mismas exponentes.	In the expression $3a^2 + 5b + 12a^2$, $3a^2$ and $12a^2$ are like terms.
line A straight path that has no thickness and extends forever.	**línea** Un trazo recto que no tiene grosor y se extiende infinitamente.	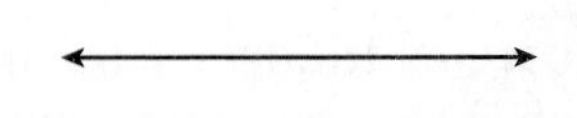
line graph A graph that uses line segments to show how data changes.	**gráfica lineal** Gráfica que muestra cómo cambian los datos mediante segmentos de recta.	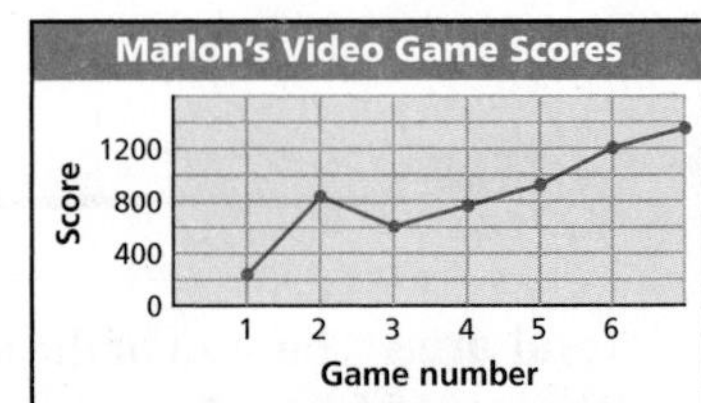
line of best fit A straight line that comes closest to the points on a scatter plot.	**línea de mejor ajuste** La línea recta que más se aproxima a los puntos de un diagrama de dispersión.	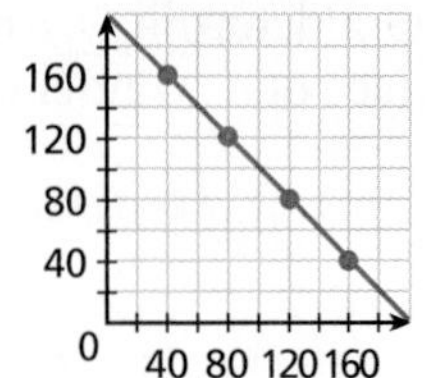
line of reflection A line that a figure is flipped across to create a mirror image of the original figure.	**línea de reflexión** Línea sobre la cual se invierte una figura para crear una imagen reflejada de la figura original.	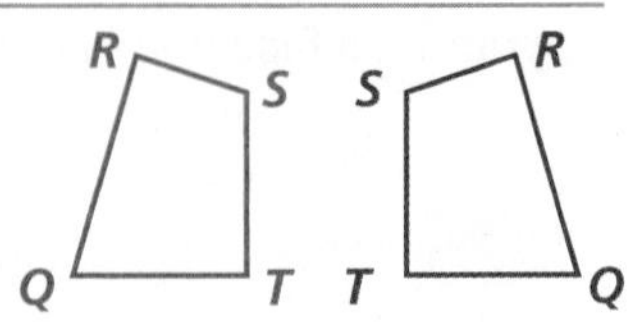
line of symmetry A line that divides a figure into two congruent reflected halves.	**eje de simetría** Línea que divide una figura en dos mitades reflejas.	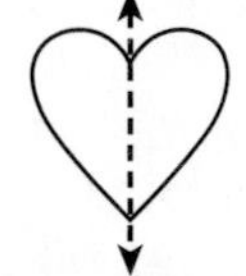

ENGLISH	SPANISH	EXAMPLES
line plot A number line with marks or dots that show frequency.	**diagrama de acumulación** Recta numérica con marcas o puntos que indican la frecuencia.	X X X X X X X X X 0 1 2 3 4 Number of pets
line segment A part of a line consisting of two endpoints and all points between them.	**segmento de recta** Parte de una línea que consiste en dos extremos y todos los puntos entre éstos.	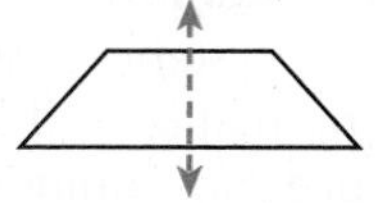
line symmetry A figure has line symmetry if one half is a mirror-image of the other half.	**simetría axial** Una figura tiene simetría axial si una de sus mitades es la imagen reflejada de la otra.	
linear equation An equation whose solutions form a straight line on a coordinate plane.	**ecuación lineal** Ecuación cuyas soluciones forman una línea recta en un plano cartesiano.	$y = 2x + 1$
linear function A function whose graph is a straight line.	**función lineal** Función cuya gráfica es una línea recta.	$y = x - 1$ 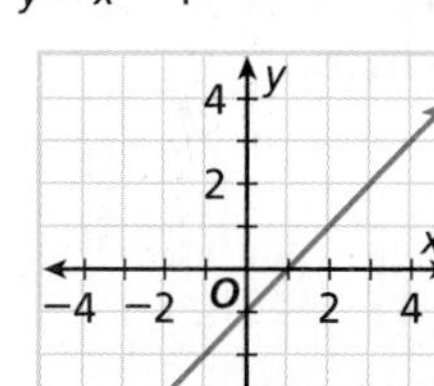
linear inequality A mathematical sentence using <, >, ≤, or ≥ whose graph is a region with a straight-line boundary.	**desigualdad lineal** Enunciado matemático en que se usan los símbolos <, >, ≤, o ≥ y cuya gráfica es una región con una línea de límite recta.	
literal equation An equation that contains two or more variables.	**ecuación literal** Ecuación que contiene dos o más variables.	$d = rt$ $A = bh$

M

ENGLISH	SPANISH	EXAMPLES
major arc An arc that is more than half of a circle.	**arco mayor** Arco que es más de la mitad de un círculo.	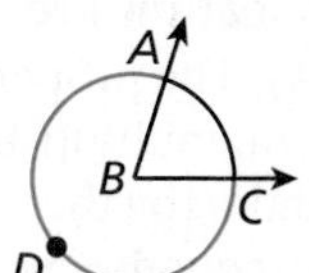$\overset{\frown}{ADC}$ is a major arc of the circle.
matrix A rectangular arrangement of data enclosed in brackets.	**matriz** Arreglo rectangular de datos encerrado entre corchetes.	$\begin{bmatrix} 1 & 0 & 3 \\ -2 & 2 & -5 \\ 7 & -6 & 3 \end{bmatrix}$
mean The sum of a set of data divided by the number of items in the data set; also called *average*.	**media** La suma de todos los elementos de un conjunto de datos dividida entre el número de elementos del conjunto. También se llama promedio.	Data set: 4, 6, 7, 8, 10 Mean: $\frac{4+6+7+8+10}{5} = \frac{35}{5} = 7$

ENGLISH	SPANISH	EXAMPLES
measure of central tendency A measure used to describe the middle of a data set; the mean, median, and mode are measures of central tendency.	**medida de tendencia dominante** Medida que describe la parte media de un conjunto de datos; la media, la mediana y la moda son medidas de tendencia dominante.	
median The middle number, or the mean (average) of the two middle numbers, in an ordered set of data.	**mediana** El número intermedio o la media (el promedio) de los dos números intermedios en un conjunto ordenado de datos.	Data set: 4, 6, 7, 8, 10 Median: 7
metric system of measurement A decimal system of weights and measures that is used universally in science and commonly throughout the world.	**sistema métrico de medición** Sistema decimal de pesos y medidas empleado universalmente en las ciencias y de uso común en todo el mundo.	centimeters, meters, kilometers, gram, kilograms, milliliters, liters
midpoint The point that divides a line segment into two congruent line segments.	**punto medio** El punto que divide un segmento de recta en dos segmentos de recta congruentes.	A B C B is the midpoint of $\overline{AC}$.
minor arc An arc that is less than half of a circle.	**arco menor** Arco que es menor que la mitad de un círculo.	A B C $\overset{\frown}{AC}$ is the minor arc of the circle.
mixed number A number made up of a whole number that is not zero and a fraction.	**número mixto** Número compuesto por un número cabal distinto de cero y una fracción.	$4\frac{1}{8}$
mode The number or numbers that occur most frequently in a set of data; when all numbers occur with the same frequency, we say there is no mode.	**moda** Número o números más frecuentes en un conjunto de datos; si todos los números aparecen con la misma frecuencia, no hay moda.	Data set: 3, 5, 8, 8, 10 Mode: 8
monomial A number or a product of numbers and variables with exponents that are whole numbers.	**monomio** Un número o un producto de números y variables con exponentes que son números cabales.	$3x^2y^4$
Multiplication Property of Equality The property that states that if you multiply both sides of an equation by the same number, the new equation will have the same solution.	**Propiedad de igualdad de la multiplicación** Propiedad que establece que puedes multiplicar ambos lados de una ecuación por el mismo número y la nueva ecuación tendrá la misma solución.	$3 \cdot 4 = 12$ $3 \cdot 4 \cdot 2 = 12 \cdot 2$ $24 = 24$
Multiplication Property of Zero The property that states that for all real numbers a, $a \cdot 0 = 0$ and $0 \cdot a = 0$.	**Propiedad de multiplicación del cero** Propiedad que establece que para todos los números reales a, $a \cdot 0 = 0$ y $0 \cdot a = 0$.	
multiplicative inverse A number times its multiplicative inverse is equal to 1; also called *reciprocal.*	**inverso multiplicativo** Un número multiplicado por su inverso multiplicativo es igual a 1. También se llama *recíproco.*	The multiplicative inverse of $\frac{4}{5}$ is $\frac{5}{4}$.

ENGLISH	SPANISH	EXAMPLES
multiple The product of any number and a non-zero whole number is a multiple of that number.	**múltiplo** El producto de cualquier número y un número cabal distinto de cero es un múltiplo de ese número.	
mutually exclusive Two events are mutually exclusive if they cannot occur in the same trial of an experiment.	**mutuamente excluyentes** Dos sucesos son mutuamente excluyentes cuando no pueden ocurrir en la misma prueba de un experimento.	When rolling a number cube, rolling a 3 and rolling an even number are mutually exclusive events.

N

ENGLISH	SPANISH	EXAMPLES
negative correlation Two data sets have a negative correlation if one set of data values increases while the other decreases.	**correlación negativa** Dos conjuntos de datos tienen correlación negativa si los valores de un conjunto aumentan a medida que los valores del otro conjunto disminuyen.	
negative integer An integer less than zero.	**entero negativo** Entero menor que cero.	−2 is a negative integer. −4 −3 −2 −1 0 1 2 3 4
net An arrangement of two-dimensional figures that can be folded to form a polyhedron.	**plantilla** Arreglo de figuras bidimensionales que se doblan para formar un poliedro.	10 m 6 m 10 m 6 m
network A set of points and the line segments or arcs that connect the points.	**red** Conjunto de puntos y los segmentos de recta o arcos que los conectan.	
no correlation Two data sets have no correlation when there is no relationship between their data values.	**sin correlación** Caso en que los valores de dos conjuntos no muestran ninguna relación.	
nonlinear function A function whose graph is not a straight line.	**función no lineal** Función cuya gráfica no es una línea recta.	$y = x^2 - 3$
nonterminating decimal A decimal that never ends.	**decimal infinito** Decimal que nunca termina.	
numerator The top number of a fraction that tells how many parts of a whole are being considered.	**numerador** El número de arriba de una fracción; indica cuántas partes de un entero se consideran.	$\frac{4}{5}$ ← numerator
numerical expression An expression that contains only numbers and operations.	**expresión numérica** Expresión que incluye sólo números y operaciones.	$(2 \cdot 3) + 1$

ENGLISH	SPANISH	EXAMPLES

obtuse angle An angle whose measure is greater than 90° but less than 180°.	**ángulo obtuso** Ángulo que mide más de 90° y menos de 180°.	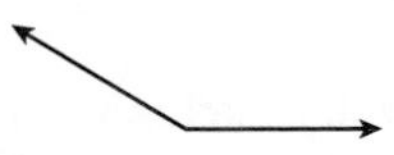
obtuse triangle A triangle containing one obtuse angle.	**triángulo obtusángulo** Triángulo que tiene un ángulo obtuso.	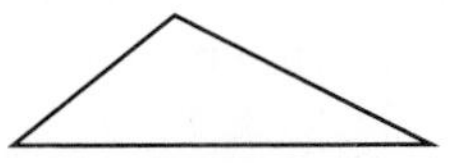
octagon An eight-sided polygon.	**octágono** Polígono de ocho lados.	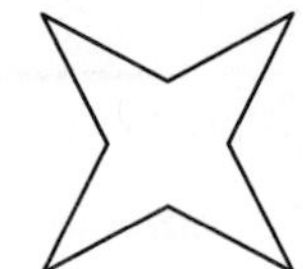
odds A comparison of the number of ways an event can occur and the number of ways an event can *not* occur.	**probabilidades** Comparación del numero de las maneras que puede ocurrir un suceso y el numero de maneras que no puede ocurrir el suceso.	
odds against The ratio of the number of unfavorable outcomes to the number of favorable outcomes.	**probabilidades en contra** Razón del número de resultados no favorables al número de resultados favorables.	The odds against rolling a 3 on a number cube are 5:1.
odds in favor The ratio of the number of favorable outcomes to the number of unfavorable outcomes.	**probabilidades a favor** Razón del número de resultados favorables al número de resultados no favorables.	The odds in favor of rolling a 3 on a number cube are 1:5.
opposites Two numbers that are an equal distance from zero on a number line; also called *additive inverse.*	**opuestos** Dos números que están a la misma distancia de cero en una recta numérica. También se llaman *inversos aditivos.*	5 and −5 are opposites. 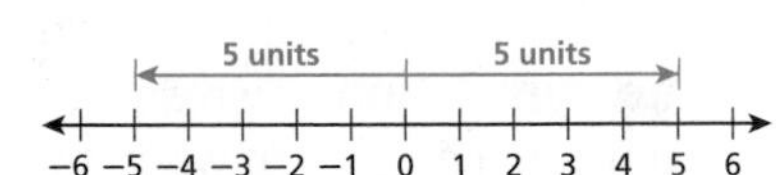
order of operations A rule for evaluating expressions: First perform the operations in parentheses, then compute powers and roots, then perform all multiplication and division from left to right, and then perform all addition and subtraction from left to right.	**orden de las operaciones** Regla para evaluar expresiones: primero se hacen las operaciones entre paréntesis, luego se hallan las potencias y raíces, después todas las multiplicaciones y divisiones de izquierda a derecha, y por último, todas las sumas y restas de izquierda a derecha.	$4^2 + 8 \div 2$ Evaluate the power. $16 + 8 \div 2$ Divide. $16 + 4$ Add. 20
ordered pair A pair of numbers that can be used to locate a point on a coordinate plane.	**par ordenado** Par de números que sirven para ubicar un punto en un plano cartesiano.	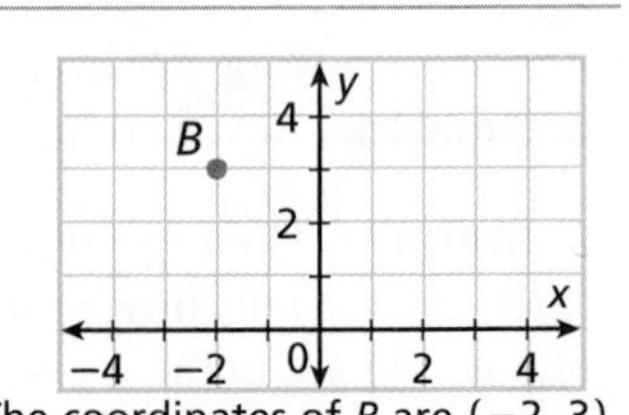 The coordinates of *B* are (−2, 3).

ENGLISH	SPANISH	EXAMPLES
origin The point where the *x*-axis and *y*-axis intersect on the coordinate plane; (0, 0).	**origen** Punto de intersección entre el eje *x* y el eje *y* en un plano cartesiano: (0, 0).	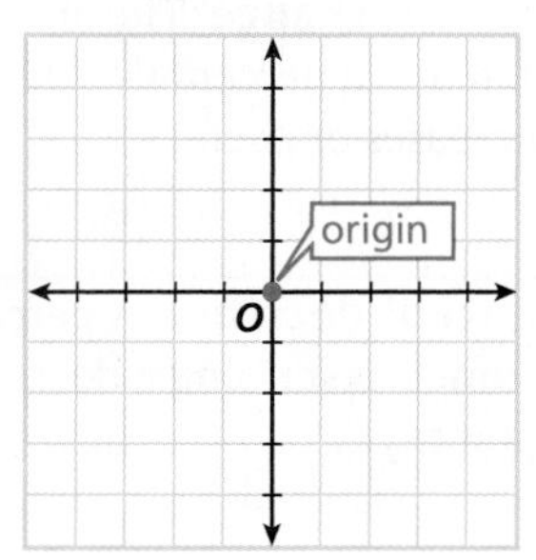
orthogonal views A drawing that shows the top, bottom, front, back, and side views of a three-dimensional object.	**vista ortogonal** Un dibujo que muestra la vista superior, inferior, frontal, posterior y lateral de un objecto de tres dimensiones.	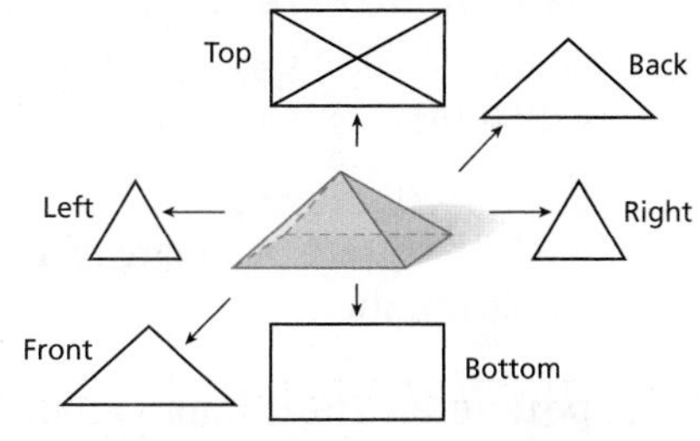
outcome (probability) A possible result of a probability experiment.	**resultado (en probabilidad)** Posible resultado de un experimento de probabilidad.	When rolling a number cube, the possible outcomes are 1, 2, 3, 4, 5, and 6.
outlier A value much greater or much less than the others in a data set.	**valor extremo** Un valor mucho mayor o menor que los demás valores de un conjunto de datos.	Most of data Mean Outlier
output The value that results from the substitution of a given input into an expression or function.	**valor de salida** Valor que resulta después de sustituir una variable por un valor de entrada determinado en una expresión o función.	For the function $y = 6x$, the input 4 produces an output of 24.

ENGLISH	SPANISH	EXAMPLES
parabola The graph of a quadratic function.	**parábola** Gráfica de una función cuadrática.	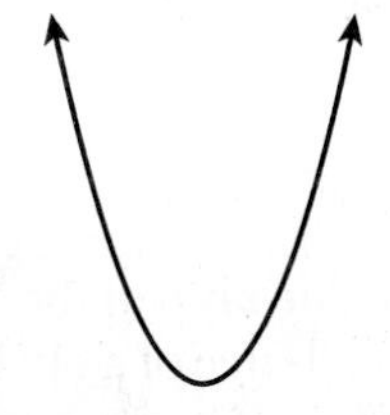
parallel lines Lines in a plane that do not intersect.	**líneas paralelas** Líneas que se encuentran en el mismo plano pero que nunca se intersecan.	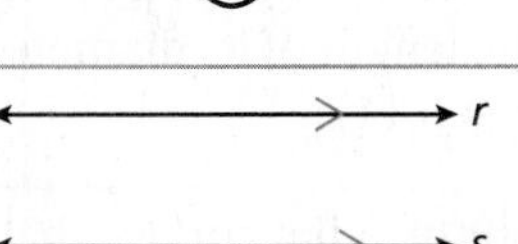
parallelogram A quadrilateral with two pairs of parallel sides.	**paralelogramo** Cuadrilátero con dos pares de lados paralelos.	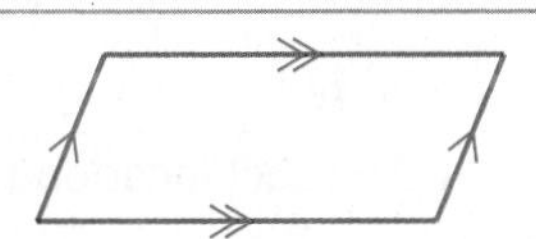
pentagon A five-sided polygon.	**pentágono** Polígono de cinco lados.	
percent A ratio comparing a number to 100.	**porcentaje** Razón que compara un número con el número 100.	$45\% = \frac{45}{100}$

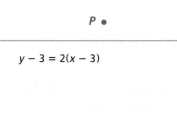

ENGLISH	SPANISH	EXAMPLES
percent change The amount stated as a percent that a number increases or decreases.	**porcentaje de cambio** Cantidad en que un número aumenta o disminuye, expresada como un porcentaje.	
percent decrease A percent change describing a decrease in a quantity.	**porcentaje de disminución** Porcentaje de cambio en que una cantidad disminuye.	An item that costs \$8 is marked down to \$6. The amount of the decrease is \$2 and the percent of decrease is $\frac{2}{8} = 0.25 = 25\%$.
percent increase A percent change describing an increase in a quantity.	**porcentaje de incremento** Porcentaje de cambio en que una cantidad aumenta.	The price of an item increases from \$8 to \$12. The amount of the increase is \$4 and the percent of increase is $\frac{4}{8} = 0.5 = 50\%$
perfect square A square of a whole number.	**cuadrado perfecto** El cuadrado de un número cabal.	$5^2 = 25$, so 25 is a perfect square.
perimeter The distance around a polygon.	**perímetro** Distancia alrededor de un polígono.	18 ft 6 ft perimeter = $18 + 6 + 18 + 6 = 48$ ft
permutation An arrangement of items or events in which order is important.	**permutación** Arreglo de objetos o sucesos en el que el orden es importante.	For objects *A*, *B*, and *C*, there are 6 different permutations: *ABC*, *ACB*, *BAC*, *BCA*, *CAB*, *CBA*.
perpendicular bisector A line that intersects a segment at its midpoint and is perpendicular to the segment.	**mediatriz** Línea que cruza un segmento en su punto medio y es perpendicular al segmento.	ℓ *A* *B*
perpendicular lines Lines that intersect to form right angles.	**líneas perpendiculares** Líneas que al intersecarse forman ángulos rectos.	*n* *m*
pi (π) The ratio of the circumference of a circle to the length of its diameter; $\pi \approx 3.14$ or $\frac{22}{7}$.	**pi (π)** Razón de la circunferencia de un círculo a la longitud de su diámetro; $\pi \approx 3.14$ ó $\frac{22}{7}$.	
plane A flat surface that has no thickness and extends forever.	**plano** Superficie plana que no tiene ningún grueso y que se extiende por siempre.	*A* • *C* • $\mathcal{R}$ *B* •
point An exact location that has no size.	**punto** Ubicación exacta que no tiene ningún tamaño.	*P* •
point-slope form The equation of a line in the form of $y - y_1 = m(x - x_1)$, where m is the slope and (x_1, y_1) is a specific point on the line.	**forma de punto y pendiente** Ecuación lineal del tipo $y - y_1 = m(x - x_1)$, donde m es la pendiente y (x_1, y_1) es un punto específico de la línea.	$y - 3 = 2(x - 3)$

ENGLISH	SPANISH	EXAMPLES
polygon A closed plane figure formed by three or more line segments that intersect only at their endpoints (vertices).	**polígono** Figura plana cerrada, formada por tres o más segmentos de recta que se intersecan sólo en sus extremos (vértices).	
polyhedron A three-dimensional figure in which all the surfaces or faces are polygons.	**poliedro** Figura tridimensional cuyas superficies o caras tiene forma de polígonos.	
polynomial One monomial or the sum or difference of monomials.	**polinomio** Un monomio o la suma o la diferencia de monomios.	$2x^2 + 3xy - 7y^2$
population The entire group of objects or individuals considered for a survey.	**población** Grupo completo de objetos o individuos que se desea estudiar.	In a survey about study habits of middle school students, the population is all middle school students.
positive correlation Two data sets have a positive correlation when their data values increase or decrease together.	**correlación positiva** Dos conjuntos de datos tienen una correlación positiva cuando los valores de ambos conjuntos aumentan o disminuyen al mismo tiempo.	y x
positive integer An integer greater than zero.	**entero positivo** Entero mayor que cero.	−4 −3 −2 −1 0 1 2 3 4 2 is a positive integer.
power A number produced by raising a base to an exponent.	**potencia** Número que resulta al elevar una base a un exponente.	$2^3 = 8$, so 2 to the 3rd power is 8.
prime factorization A number written as the product of its prime factors.	**factorización prima** Un número escrito como el producto de sus factores primos.	$10 = 2 \cdot 5$, $24 = 2^3 \cdot 3$
prime number A whole number greater than 1 that has exactly two factors, itself and 1.	**número primo** Número cabal mayor que 1 que sólo es divisible entre 1 y él mismo.	5 is prime because its only factors are 5 and 1.
principal The initial amount of money borrowed or saved.	**capital** Cantidad inicial de dinero depositada o recibida en préstamo.	
principal square root The nonnegative square root of a number.	**raíz cuadrada principal** Raíz cuadrada no negativa de un número.	$\sqrt{25} = 5$; the principal square root of 25 is 5.

ENGLISH	SPANISH	EXAMPLES
prism A polyhedron that has two congruent, polygon-shaped bases and other faces that are all parallelograms.	**prisma** Poliedro con dos bases congruentes con forma de polígono y caras con forma de paralelogramo.	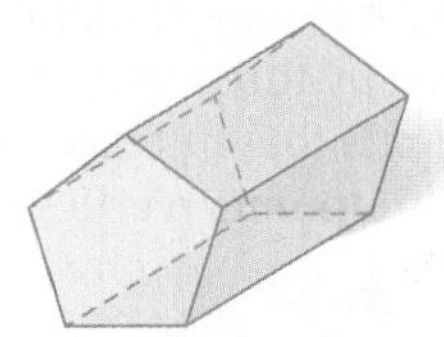
probability A number from 0 to 1 (or 0% to 100%) that describes how likely an event is to occur.	**probabilidad** Un número entre 0 y 1 (ó 0% y 100%) que describe qué tan probable es un suceso.	A bag contains 3 red marbles and 4 blue marbles. The probability of randomly choosing a red marble is $\frac{3}{7}$.
proper fraction A fraction in which the numerator is less than the denominator.	**fracción propia** Fracción en la que el numerador es menor que el denominador.	$\frac{3}{4}, \frac{1}{12}, \frac{7}{8}$
proportion An equation that states that two ratios are equivalent.	**proporción** Ecuación que establece que dos razones son equivalentes.	$\frac{2}{3} = \frac{4}{6}$
protractor A tool for measuring angles.	**transportador** Instrumento para medir ángulos.	
pyramid A polyhedron with a polygon base and triangular sides that all meet at a common vertex.	**pirámide** Poliedro cuya base es un polígono; tiene caras triangulares que se juntan en un vértice común.	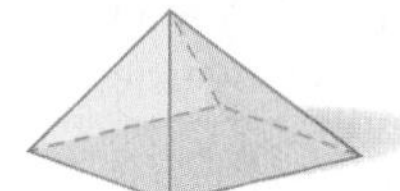
Pythagorean Theorem In a right triangle, the square of the length of the hypotenuse is equal to the sum of the squares of the lengths of the legs.	**Teorema de Pitágoras** En un triángulo rectángulo, la suma de los cuadrados de los catetos es igual al cuadrado de la hipotenusa.	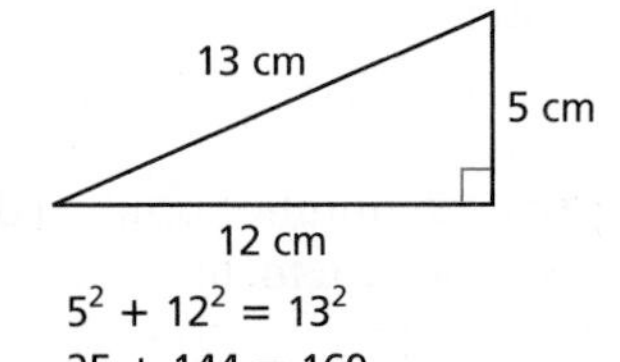 $5^2 + 12^2 = 13^2$ $25 + 144 = 169$
Pythagorean triple A set of three positive integers a, b, and c such that $a^2 + b^2 = c^2$.	**Tripleta de Pitágoras** Conjunto de tres números enteros positivos de cero a, b y c tal que $a^2 + b^2 = c^2$.	3, 4, 5 because $3^2 + 4^2 = 5^2$

Q

ENGLISH	SPANISH	EXAMPLES
quadrant The x- and y-axes divide the coordinate plane into four regions. Each region is called a quadrant.	**cuadrante** El eje x y el eje y dividen el plano cartesiano en cuatro regiones. Cada región recibe el nombre de cuadrante.	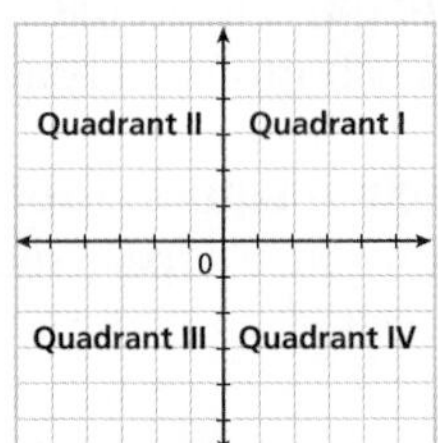
quadratic function A function of the form $y = ax^2 + bx + c$, where $a \neq 0$.	**función cuadrática** Función del tipo $y = ax^2 + bx + c$, donde $a \neq 0$.	$y = x^2 - 6x + 8$
quadrilateral A four-sided polygon.	**cuadrilátero** Polígono de cuatro lados.	

ENGLISH	SPANISH	EXAMPLES
quarterly Four times a year.	**trimestral** Cuatro veces al año.	
quartile Three values, one of which is the median, that divide a data set into fourths.	**cuartil** Cada uno de tres valores, uno de los cuales es la mediana, que dividen en cuartos un conjunto de datos.	First quartile; Third quartile; Minimum; Median; Maximum; 0 2 4 6 8 10 12 14
quotient The result when one number is divided by another.	**cociente** Resultado de dividir un número entre otro.	In 8 ÷ 4 = 2, 2 is the quotient.

R

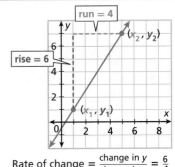

ENGLISH	SPANISH	EXAMPLES
radical symbol The symbol $\sqrt{}$ used to represent the nonnegative square root of a number.	**símbolo de radical** El símbolo $\sqrt{}$ con que se representa la raíz cuadrada no negativa de un número.	
radius A line segment with one endpoint at the center of the circle and the other endpoint on the circle, or the length of that segment.	**radio** Segmento de recta con un extremo en el centro de un círculo y el otro en la circunferencia, o bien se llama radio a la longitud de ese segmento.	Radius
random numbers In a set of random numbers, each number has an equal chance of appearing.	**muestra aleatoria** Muestra en la que cada individuo u objeto de la población tiene la misma posibilidad de ser elegido.	
random sample A sample in which each individual or object in the entire population has an equal chance of being selected.	**números aleatorios** En un conjunto de números aleatorios, todos los números tienen la misma probabilidad de ser seleccionados.	
range (in statistics) The difference between the greatest and least values in a data set.	**rango (en estadística)** Diferencia entre los valores máximo y mínimo de un conjunto de datos.	Data set: 3, 5, 7, 7, 12 Range: 12 − 3 = 9
range (of a function) The set of all possible output values of a function.	**rango (en una función)** El conjunto de todos los valores posibles de una función.	The range of $y = \|x\|$ is $y \geq 0$.
rate A ratio that compares two quantities measured in different units.	**tasa** Una razón que compara dos cantidades medidas en diferentes unidades.	The speed limit is 55 miles per hour or 55 mi/h.
rate of change A ratio that compares the amount of change in a dependent variable to the amount of change in an independent variable.	**tasa de cambio** Razón que compara la cantidad de cambio de la variable dependiente con la cantidad de cambio de la variable independiente.	run = 4; rise = 6; (x_1, y_1); (x_2, y_2) Rate of change = $\frac{\text{change in } y}{\text{change in } x} = \frac{6}{4} = \frac{3}{2}$

ENGLISH	SPANISH	EXAMPLES
rate of interest The percent charged or earned on an amount of money; see *simple interest.*	**tasa de interés** Porcentaje que se cobra por una cantidad de dinero prestada o que se gana por una cantidad de dinero ahorrada; ver *interés simple.*	
ratio A comparison of two quantities by division.	**razón** Comparación de dos cantidades mediante una división.	12 to 25, 12:25, $\frac{12}{25}$
rational number Any number that can be expressed as a ratio of two integers.	**número racional** Número que se puede escribir como una razón de dos enteros.	6 can be expressed as $\frac{6}{1}$. 0.5 can be expressed $\frac{1}{2}$.
ray A part of a line that starts at one endpoint and extends forever in one direction.	**rayo** Parte de una línea que comienza en un extremo y se extiende de manera infinitamente en una dirección.	D
real number A rational or irrational number.	**número real** Número racional o irracional.	
reciprocal One of two numbers whose product is 1; also called *multiplicative inverse.*	**recíproco** Uno de dos números cuyo producto es igual a 1. También se llama *inverso multiplicativo.*	The reciprocal of $\frac{2}{3}$ is $\frac{3}{2}$.
rectangle A parallelogram with four right angles.	**rectángulo** Paralelogramo con cuatro ángulos rectos.	
rectangular prism A polyhedron whose bases are rectangles and whose other faces are parallelograms.	**prisma rectangular** Poliedro cuyas bases son rectángulos y cuyas caras tienen forma de paralelogramo.	
reduction A decrease in the size of all dimensions.	**reducción** Disminución de tamaño en todas las dimensiones de una figura.	
reflection A transformation of a figure that flips the figure across a line.	**reflexión** Transformación que ocurre cuando se invierte una figura sobre una línea.	B, B′, A, C, C′, A′
regular polygon A polygon with congruent sides and angles.	**polígono regular** Polígono con lados y ángulos congruentes.	
regular pyramid A pyramid whose base is a regular polygon and whose lateral faces are all congruent.	**pirámide regular** Pirámide que tiene un polígono regular como base y caras laterales congruentes.	

ENGLISH	SPANISH	EXAMPLES
relation A set of ordered pairs.	**relación** Conjunto de pares ordenados.	(0, 5), (0, 4), (2, 3), (4, 0)
relative frequency The frequency of a data value of range of data values divided by the total number of data values in the set.	**frecuencia relativa** La frecuencia de un valor o un rango de valores dividido por el número total de los valores en el conjunto.	
relatively prime Two numbers are relatively prime if their greatest common factor (GCF) is 1.	**primo relativo** Dos números son primos relativos si su máximo común divisor (MCD) es 1.	8 and 15 are relatively prime.
repeating decimal A decimal in which one or more digits repeat infinitely.	**decimal periódico** Decimal en el que uno o más dígitos se repiten infinitamente.	$0.757575\ldots = 0.\overline{75}$
rhombus A parallelogram with all sides congruent.	**rombo** Paralelogramo en el que todos los lados son congruentes.	
right angle An angle that measures 90°.	**ángulo recto** Ángulo que mide exactamente 90°.	
right cone A cone in which a perpendicular line drawn from the base to the tip (vertex) passes through the center of the base.	**cono regular** Cono en el que una línea perpendicular trazada de la base a la punta (vértice) pasa por el centro de la base.	Axis Right cone
right triangle A triangle containing a right angle.	**triángulo rectángulo** Triángulo que tiene un ángulo recto.	
rise The vertical change when the slope of a line is expressed as the ratio $\frac{\text{rise}}{\text{run}}$, or "rise over run."	**distancia vertical** El cambio vertical cuando la pendiente de una línea se expresa como la razón $\frac{\text{distancia vertical}}{\text{distancia horizontal}}$, o "distancia vertical sobre distancia horizontal".	For the points (3, −1) and (6, 5) the rise is $5 - (-1) = 6$.
rotation A transformation in which a figure is turned around a point.	**rotación** Transformación que ocurre cuando una figura gira alrededor de un punto.	
rotational symmetry A figure has rotational symmetry if it can be rotated less than 360° around a central point and coincide with the original figure.	**simetría de rotación** Ocurre cuando una figura gira menos de 360° alrededor de un punto central sin dejar de ser congruente con la figura original.	90° 90° 90° 90°

ENGLISH	SPANISH	EXAMPLES
run The horizontal change when the slope of a line is expressed as the ratio $\frac{\text{rise}}{\text{run}}$, or "rise over run."	**distancia horizontal** El cambio horizontal cuando la pendiente de una línea se expresa como la razón $\frac{\text{distancia vertical}}{\text{distancia horizontal}}$, o "distancia vertical sobre distancia horizontal".	For the points (3, −1) and (6, 5) the run is 6 − 3 = 3.

sales tax A percent of the cost of an item, which is charged by governments to raise money.

impuesto sobre la venta Porcentaje del costo de un artículo que los gobiernos cobran para recaudar fondos.

---

sample A part of the population.

muestra Una parte de la población.

---

sample space All possible outcomes of an experiment.

espacio muestral Conjunto de todos los resultados posibles de un experimento.

When rolling a number cube, the sample space is 1, 2, 3, 4, 5, 6.

---

scale The ratio between two sets of measurements.

escala La razón entre dos conjuntos de medidas.

1 cm: 5 mi

---

scale drawing A drawing that uses a scale to make an object smaller than (a reduction) or larger than (an enlargement) the real object.

dibujo a escala Dibujo en el que se usa una escala para que un objeto se vea menor (reducción) o mayor (agrandamiento) que el objeto real al que representa.

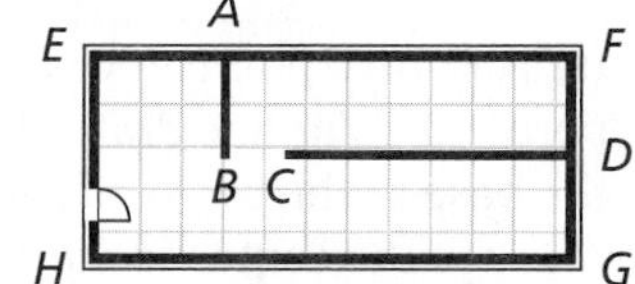

A blueprint is an example of a scale drawing.

---

scale factor The ratio used to enlarge or reduce similar figures.

factor de escala Razón empleada para agrandar o reducir figuras semejantes.

---

scale model A proportional model of a three-dimensional object.

modelo a escala Modelo proporcional de un objeto tridimensional.

---

scalene triangle A triangle with no congruent sides.

triángulo escaleno Triángulo que no tiene lados congruentes.

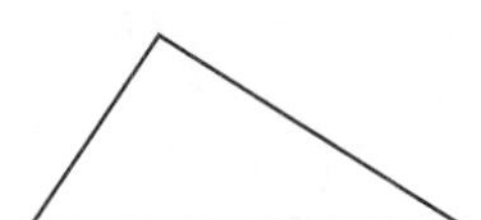

---

scatter plot A graph with points plotted to show a possible relationship between two sets of data.

diagrama de dispersión Gráfica de puntos que muestra una posible relación entre dos conjuntos de datos.

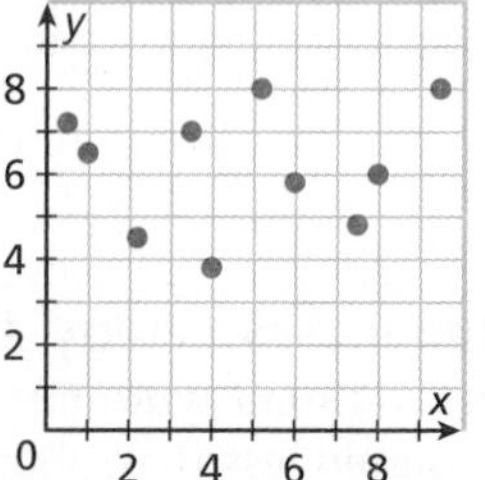

ENGLISH	SPANISH	EXAMPLES
scientific notation A method of writing very large or very small numbers by using powers of 10.	**notación científica** Método que se usa para escribir números muy grandes o muy pequeños mediante potencias de 10.	$12{,}560{,}000{,}000{,}000 = 1.256 \times 10^{13}$
second quartile The median of a set of data.	**segundo cuartil** Mediana de un conjunto de datos.	Data set: 4, 6, 7, 8, 10 Second quartile: 7
segment A part of a line between two endpoints.	**segmento** Parte de una línea entre dos extremos.	G H $\overline{GH}$
sequence An ordered list of numbers.	**sucesión** Lista ordenada de números.	2, 4, 6, 8, 10, . . .
self-selected sample A sample in which members choose to be in the sample.	**muestra auto-seleccionada** Una muestra en la que los miembros eligen participar.	A store provides survey cards for customers who choose to fill them out.
side A line bounding a geometric figure; one of the faces forming the outside of an object.	**lado** Línea que delimita las figuras geométricas; una de las caras que forman la parte exterior de un objeto.	A B C D E Side
similar Figures with the same shape but not necessarily the same size are similar.	**semejantes** Figuras que tienen la misma forma, pero no necesariamente el mismo tamaño.	
similarity transformation A transformation that results in an image that is the same shape, but not necessarily the same size as the original figure.	**transformación de semejanza** Una transformación que resulta en una imagen que tiene la misma forma, pero no necesariamente el mismo tamaño como la figura original.	C D E F D′ E′ F′
simple interest A fixed percent of the principal. It is found using the formula $I = Prt$, where P represents the principal, r the rate of interest, and t the time.	**interés simple** Un porcentaje fijo del capital. Se calcula con la fórmula $I = Cit$, donde C representa el capital, i, la tasa de interés y t, el tiempo.	\$100 is put into an account with a simple interest rate of 5%. After 2 years, the account will have earned $I = 100 \cdot 0.05 \cdot 2 = \$10$.
simplest form A fraction is in simplest form when the numerator and denominator have no common factors other than 1.	**mínima expresión** Una fracción está en su mínima expresión cuando el numerador y el denominador no tienen más factor común que 1.	Fraction: $\frac{8}{12}$ Simplest form: $\frac{2}{3}$
simplify To write a fraction or expression in simplest form.	**simplificar** Escribir una fracción o expresión numérica en su mínima expresión.	
simulation A model of an experiment, often one that would be too difficult or too time-consuming to actually perform.	**simulación** Representación de un experimento, por lo general, de uno cuya realización sería demasiado difícil o llevaría mucho tiempo.	

ENGLISH	SPANISH	EXAMPLES
slant height (of a right cone) The distance from the vertex of a right cone to a point on the edge of the base.	**altura inclinada (de un cono recto)** Distancia desde el vértice de un cono recto hasta un punto en el borde de la base.	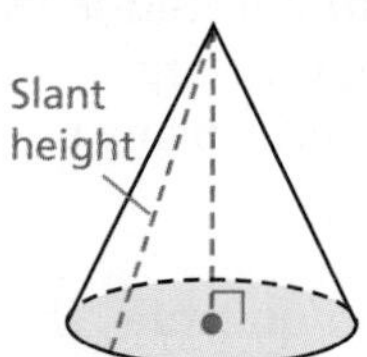
slant height (of a regular pyramid) The distance from the vertex of a regular pyramid to the midpoint of an edge of the base.	**altura inclinada (de una pirámide)** Distancia desde el vértice de una pirámide hasta el punto medio de una arista de la base.	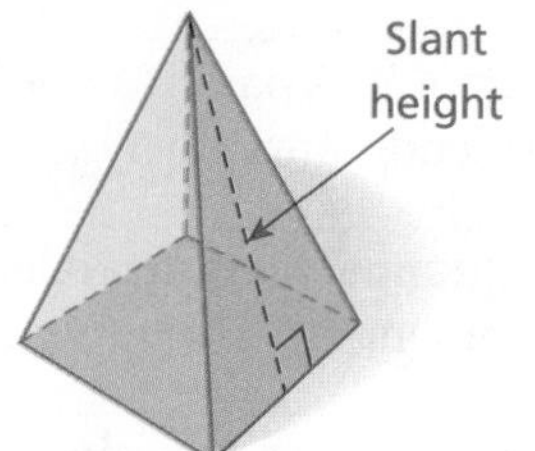 Regular pyramid
slope A measure of the steepness of a line on a graph; the rise divided by the run.	**pendiente** Medida de la inclinación de una línea en una gráfica. Razón de la distancia vertical a la distancia horizontal.	Slope $= \frac{\text{rise}}{\text{run}} = \frac{3}{4}$ 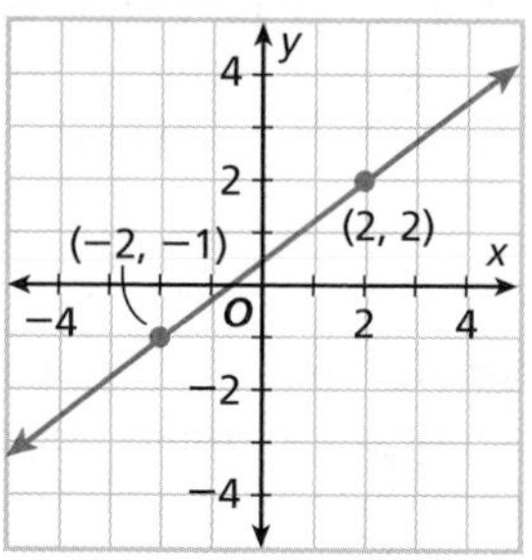
slope-intercept form A linear equation written in the form $y = mx + b$, where m represents slope and b represents the y-intercept.	**forma de pendiente-intersección** Ecuación lineal escrita en la forma $y = mx + b$, donde m es la pendiente y b es la intersección con el eje y.	$y = 6x - 3$
solution of an equation A value or values that make an equation true.	**solución de una ecuación** Valor o valores que hacen verdadera una ecuación.	Equation: $x + 2 = 6$ Solution: $x = 4$
solution of an inequality A value or values that make an inequality true.	**solución de una desigualdad** Valor o valores que hacen verdadera una desigualdad.	Inequality: $x + 3 \geq 10$ Solution: $x \geq 7$
solution of a system of equations A set of values that make all equations in a system true.	**solución de un sistema de ecuaciones** Conjunto de valores que hacen verdaderas todas las ecuaciones de un sistema.	System: $\begin{cases} x + y = -1 \\ -x + y = -3 \end{cases}$ Solution: $(1, -2)$
solution set The set of values that make a statement true.	**conjunto solución** Conjunto de valores que hacen verdadero un enunciado.	Inequality: $x + 3 \geq 5$ Solution set: $x \geq 2$ −4 −3 −2 −1 0 1 2 3 4 5 6
solve To find an answer or a solution.	**resolver** Hallar una respuesta o solución.	
sphere A three-dimensional figure with all points the same distance from the center.	**esfera** Figura tridimensional en la que todos los puntos están a la misma distancia del centro.	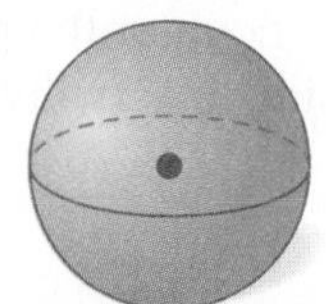

ENGLISH	SPANISH	EXAMPLES
square A rectangle with four congruent sides.	**cuadrado** Rectángulo con cuatro lados congruentes.	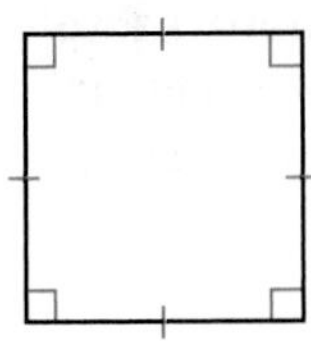
square (numeration) A number raised to the second power.	**cuadrado (en numeración)** Número elevado a la segunda potencia.	In 5^2, the number 5 is squared.
square root A number that is multiplied by itself to form a product is called a square root of that product.	**raíz quadrada** El número que se multiplica por sí mismo para formar un producto se denomina la raíz cuadrada de ese producto.	A square root of 16 is 4, because $4^2 = 4 \cdot 4 = 16$. Another square root of 16 is –4 because $(-4)^2 = (-4)(-4) = 16$.
stem-and-leaf plot A graph used to organize and display data so that the frequencies can be compared.	**diagrama de tallo y hojas** Gráfica que muestra y ordena los datos, y que sirve para comparar las frecuencias.	Stem | Leaves 3 | 2 3 4 4 7 9 4 | 0 1 5 7 7 7 8 5 | 1 2 2 3 *Key: 3|2 means 3.2*
straight angle An angle that measures 180°.	**ángulo llano** Ángulo que mide exactamente 180°.	
substitute To replace a variable with a number or another expression in an algebraic expression.	**sustituir** Reemplazar una variable por un número u otra expresión en una expresión algebraica.	Substituting 3 for m in the expression $5m - 2$ gives $5(3) - 2 = 15 - 2 = 13$.
Subtraction Property of Equality The property that states that if you subtract the same number from both sides of an equation, the new equation will have the same solution.	**Propiedad de igualdad de la resta** Propiedad que establece que puedes restar el mismo número de ambos lados de una ecuación y la nueva ecuación tendrá la misma solución.	$14 - 6 = 8$ $\underline{\quad - 6 = -6}$ $14 - 12 = 2$
supplementary angles Two angles whose measures have a sum of 180°.	**ángulos suplementarios** Dos ángulos cuyas medidas suman 180°.	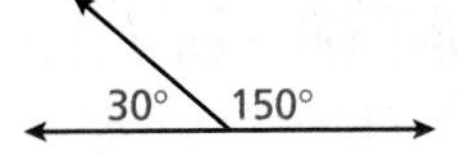
surface area The sum of the areas of the faces, or surfaces, of a three-dimensional figure.	**área total** Suma de las áreas de las caras, o superficies, de una figura tridimensional.	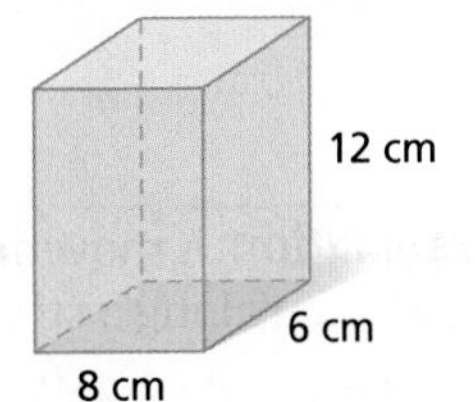 Surface area = $2(8)(12) + 2(8)(6) + 2(12)(6) = 432 \text{ cm}^2$
system of equations A set of two or more equations that contain two or more variables.	**sistema de ecuaciones** Conjunto de dos o más ecuaciones que contienen dos o más variables.	$\begin{cases} x + y = -1 \\ -x + y = -3 \end{cases}$

ENGLISH	SPANISH	EXAMPLES
systematic sample A sample of a population that has been selected using a pattern.	**muestra sistemática** Muestra de una población, que ha sido elegida mediante un patrón.	To conduct a phone survey, every tenth name is chosen from the phone book.

term (in an expression) The parts of an expression that are added or subtracted.

término (en una expresión) Las partes de una expresión que se suman o se restan.

$3x^2 + \; 6x - \; 8$ (each part labeled: Term, Term, Term)

---

term (in a sequence) An element or number in a sequence.

término (en una sucesión) Elemento o número de una sucesión.

5 is the third term in the sequence 1, 3, 5, 7, 9, ...

---

terminating decimal A decimal number that ends, or terminates.

decimal finito Decimal con un número determinado de posiciones decimales.

6.75

---

tessellation A repeating pattern of plane figures that completely cover a plane with no gaps or overlaps.

teselado Patrón repetido de figuras planas que cubren totalmente un plano sin superponerse ni dejar huecos.

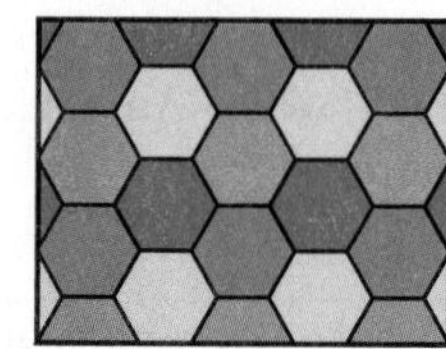

---

theoretical probability The ratio of the number of ways an event can occur to the number of equally likely outcomes.

probabilidad teórica Razón del número de las maneras que puede ocurrir un suceso al numero total de resultados igualmente probables.

When rolling a number cube, the theoretical probability of rolling a 4 is $\frac{1}{6}$.

---

third quartile The median of the upper half of a set of data; also called *upper quartile.*

tercer cuartil La mediana de la mitad superior de un conjunto de datos. También se llama *cuartil superior.*

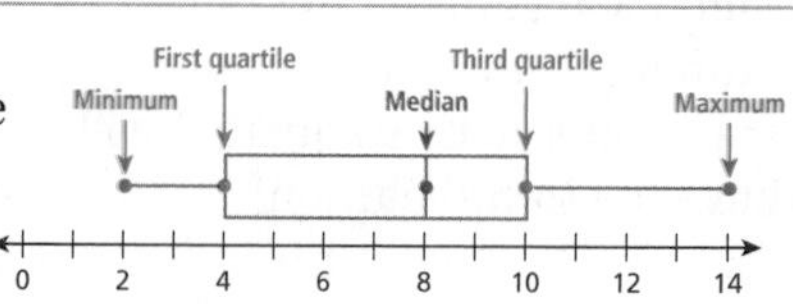

---

transformation A change in the size or position of a figure.

transformación Cambio en el tamaño o la posición de una figura.

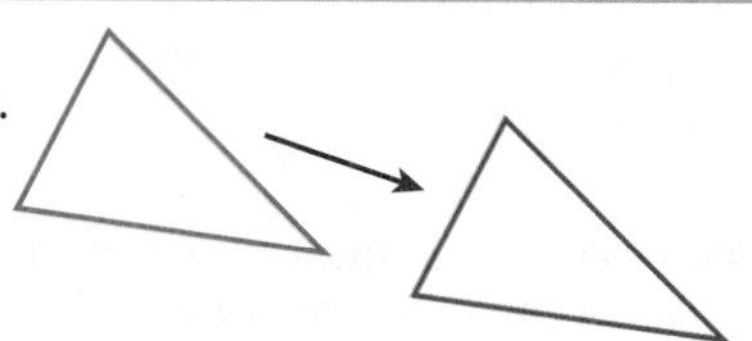

---

translation A movement (slide) of a figure along a straight line.

traslación Desplazamiento de una figura a lo largo de una línea recta.

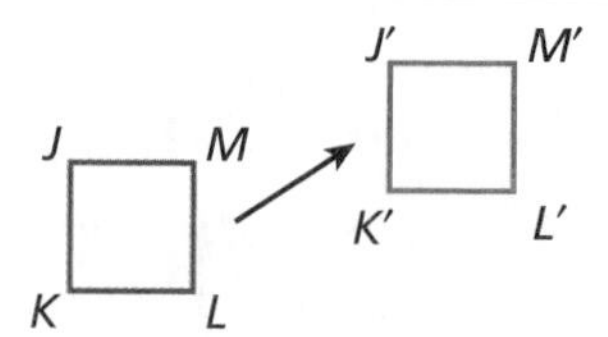

---

transversal A line that intersects two or more lines.

transversal Línea que cruza dos o más líneas.

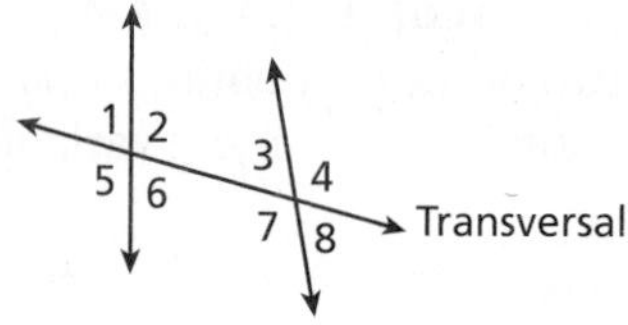

ENGLISH	SPANISH	EXAMPLES

trapezoid A quadrilateral with exactly one pair of parallel sides.

trapecio Cuadrilátero con un par de lados paralelos.

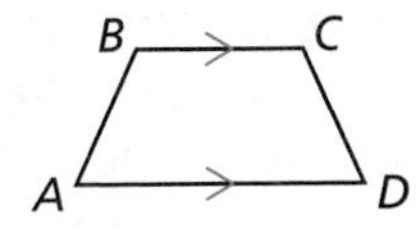

tree diagram A branching diagram that shows all possible combinations or outcomes of an event.

diagrama de árbol Diagrama ramificado que muestra todas las posibles combinaciones o resultados de un suceso.

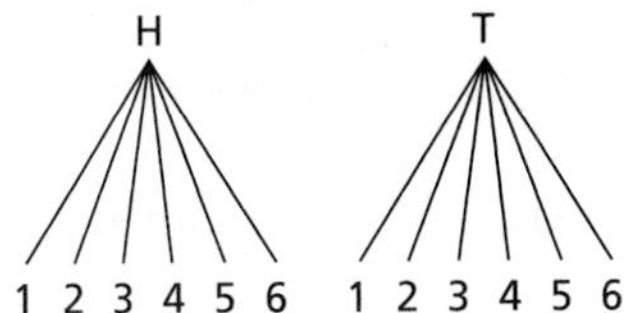

trial Each repetition or observation of an experiment.

prueba Una sola repetición u observación de un experimento.

When rolling a number cube, each roll is one trial.

Triangle Inequality Theorem The theorem that states that the sum of the lengths of any two sides of a triangle is greater than the length of the third side.

Teorema de Desigualdad de Triángulos El teorema dice que la suma de cualquier dos lados de un triangulo es mayor que la longitud del lado tercero.

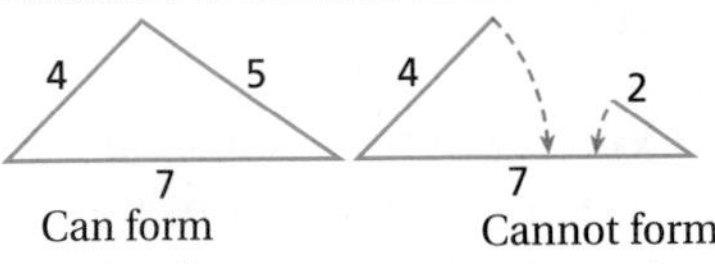

Can form a triangle

Cannot form a triangle

Triangle Sum Theorem The theorem that states that the measures of the angles in a triangle add up to 180°.

Teorema de la suma del triángulo Teorema que establece que las medidas de los ángulos de un triángulo suman 180°.

triangular prism A polyhedron whose bases are triangles and whose other faces are parallelograms.

prisma triangular Poliedro cuyas bases son triángulos y cuyas demás caras tienen forma de paralelogramo.

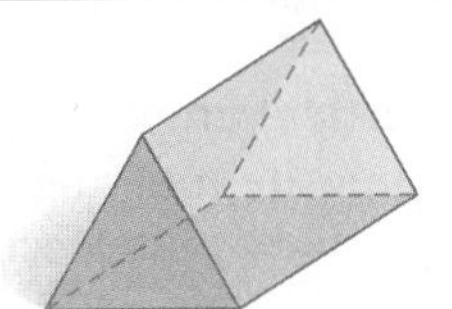

trinomial A polynomial with three terms.

trinomio Polinomio con tres términos.

$4x^2 + 3xy - 5y^2$

two-way table A table that displays two-variable data by organizing it into rows and columns.

tabla de doble entrada Una tabla que muestran los datos de dos variables por organizándolos en columnas y filas.

Pet	Preference: Inside	Outside	*Total*
Cats	35	15	50
Dogs	20	30	50
Total	55	45	100

unit conversion The process of changing one unit of measure to another.

conversión de unidades Proceso que consiste en cambiar una unidad de medida por otra.

unit conversion factor A fraction used in unit conversion in which the numerator and denominator represent the same amount but are in different units.

factor de conversión de unidades Fracción que se usa para la conversión de unidades, donde el numerador y el denominador representan la misma cantidad pero están en unidades distintas.

$\frac{60 \text{ min}}{1 \text{ h}}$ or $\frac{1 \text{ h}}{60 \text{ min}}$

unit price A unit rate used to compare prices.

precio unitario Tasa unitaria que sirve para comparar precios.

Cereal costs $0.23 per ounce.

ENGLISH	SPANISH	EXAMPLES
unit rate A rate in which the second quantity in the comparison is one unit.	**tasa unitaria** Una tasa en la que la segunda cantidad de la comparación es la unidad.	10 cm per minute

ENGLISH	SPANISH	EXAMPLES
variability The spread of values in a set of data.	**variabilidad** Amplitud de los valores de un conjunto de datos.	The data set {1, 5, 7, 10, 25} has greater variability than the data set {8, 8, 9, 9, 9}.
variable A symbol used to represent a quantity that can change.	**variable** Símbolo que representa una cantidad que puede cambiar.	In the expression $2x + 3$, x is the variable.
Venn diagram A diagram that is used to show relationships between sets.	**diagrama de Venn** Diagrama que muestra las relaciones entre conjuntos.	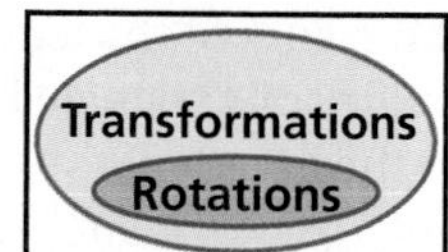
vertex On an angle or polygon, the point where two sides intersect; on a polyhedron, the intersection of three or more faces; on a cone or pyramid, the top point.	**vértice** En un ángulo o polígono, el punto de intersección de dos lados; en un poliedro, el punto de intersección de tres o más caras; en un cono o pirámide, la punta.	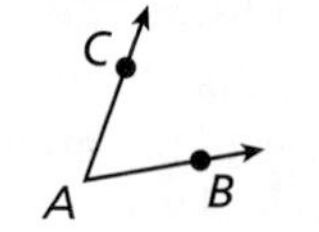 A is the vertex of $\angle CAB$.
vertical angles A pair of opposite congruent angles formed by intersecting lines.	**ángulos opuestos por el vértice** Par de ángulos opuestos congruentes formados por líneas secantes.	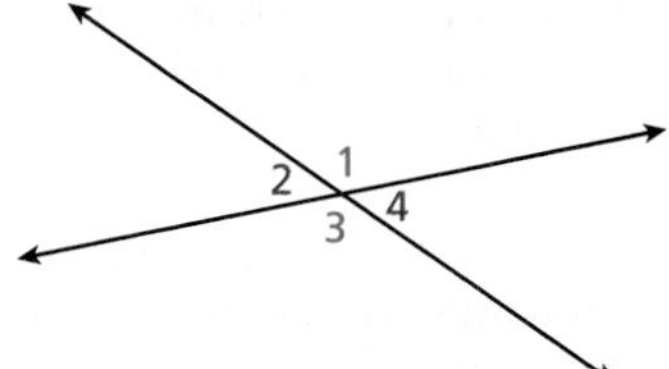 $\angle 1$ and $\angle 3$ are vertical angles.
vertical line test A test used to determine whether a relation is a function. If any vertical line crosses the graph of a relation more than once, the relation is not a function.	**prueba de la línea vertical** Prueba utilizada para determinar si una relación es una función. Si una línea vertical corta la gráfica de una relación más de una vez, la relación no es una función.	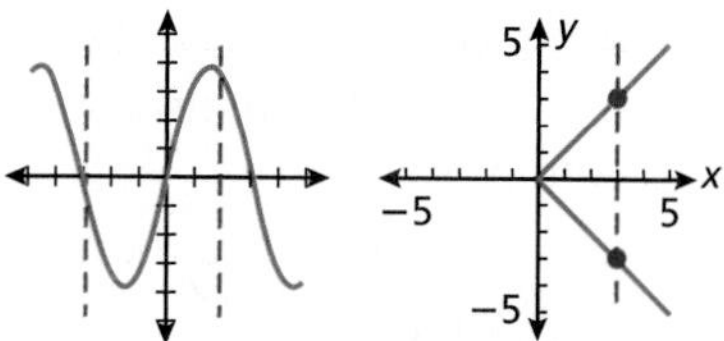 Function Not a function
volume The number of cubic units needed to fill a given space.	**volumen** Número de unidades cúbicas que se necesitan para llenar un espacio.	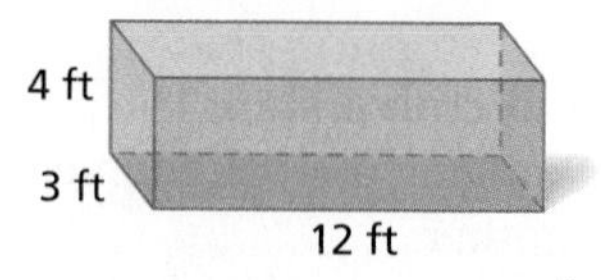 Volume $= 3 \cdot 4 \cdot 12 = 144$ ft^3

ENGLISH	SPANISH	EXAMPLES
weighted average A mean that is calculated by multiplying each data value by a weight, and dividing the sum of these products by the sum of the weights.	**promedio ponderado** Promedio que se calcula por multiplicando cada valor de datos por un peso, y dividiendo la suma de estos productos por la suma de los pesos.	If the data values 0, 5, and 10 are assigned the weights 0.1, 0.2, and 0.7, respectively, the weighted average is: $\frac{0(0.1) + 5(0.2) + 10(0.7)}{0.1 + 0.2 + 0.7} = \frac{8}{1}$

x-axis The horizontal axis on a coordinate plane.

eje x El eje horizontal del plano cartesiano.

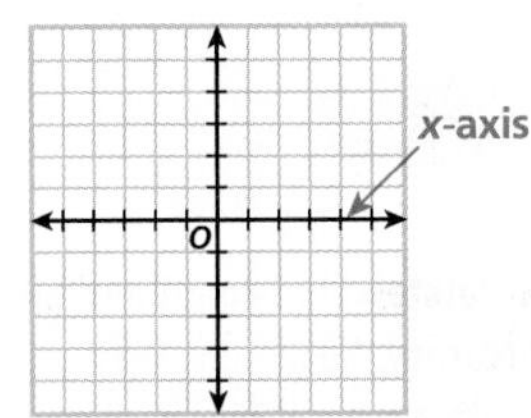

x-coordinate The first number in an ordered pair; it tells the distance to move right or left from the origin (0, 0).

coordenada x El primer número de un par ordenado; indica la distancia que debes moverte hacia la izquierda o la derecha desde el origen, (0, 0).

5 is the x-coordinate in (5, 3).

x-intercept The x-coordinate of the point where the graph of a line crosses the x-axis.

intersección con el eje x Coordenada x del punto donde la gráfica de una línea cruza el eje x.

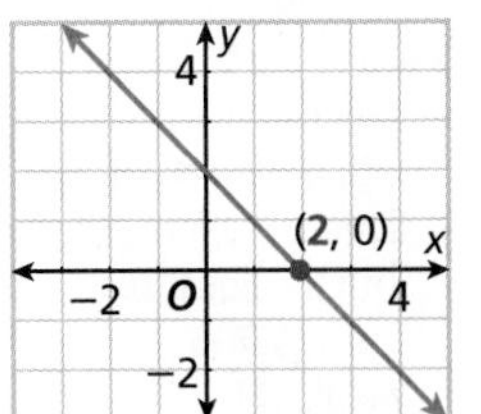

The x-intercept is 2.

y-axis The vertical axis on a coordinate plane.

eje y El eje vertical del plano cartesiano.

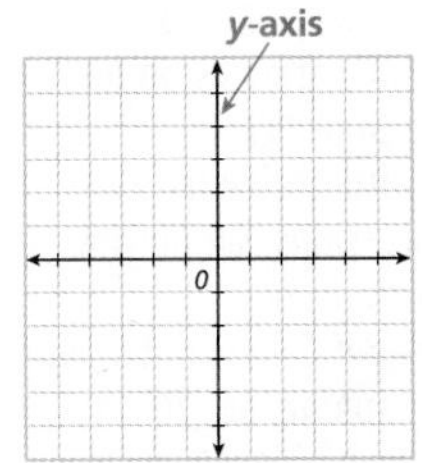

y-coordinate The second number in an ordered pair; it tells the distance to move up or down from the origin (0, 0).

coordenada y El segundo número de un par ordenado; indica la distancia que debes avanzar hacia arriba o hacia abajo desde el origen, (0, 0).

3 is the y-coordinate in (5, 3).

y-intercept The y-coordinate of the point where the graph of a line crosses the y-axis.

intersección con el eje y Coordenada y del punto donde la gráfica de una línea cruza el eje y.

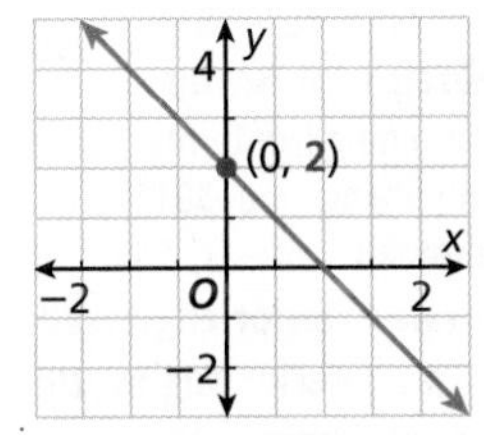

The y-intercept is 2.

Z

zero pair A number and its opposite, which add to 0.

par nulo Un número y su opuesto, cuya suma es 0.

18 and −18

Index

Index

Index

D

E

F

Index

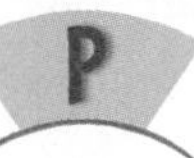

T

U

V